Rise of the American Nation
LIBERTY EDITION

LEWIS PAUL TODD   **MERLE CURTI**

EDITORIAL CONSULTANTS

PHYLLIS A. BAILEY Coordinator of Social Studies,
Baltimore County Public Schools, Towson, Maryland

MARV ELBERT Social Studies Chairperson, Streamwood High School,
Streamwood, Illinois

VIVIAN GLUCK Assistant Principal, Supervision Social Studies,
Stuyvesant High School, New York, New York

STANLEY HOLLIDAY Supervisor of Social Studies,
Indianapolis Public Schools, Indianapolis, Indiana

SARA KATZ Teacher, East High School,
Denver, Colorado

NORMA JEAN PETERS Supervisor of Secondary Social Studies,
Roanoke County Public Schools, Salem, Virginia

GARY SMUTS Department Head of Social Studies, Cerritos High School,
Cerritos, California

VERN WOLTHOFF Teacher, Medford High School,
Medford, Oregon

Rise of the American Nation

LIBERTY EDITION

LEWIS PAUL TODD

MERLE CURTI

HBJ **Harcourt Brace Jovanovich, Publishers**

New York   Chicago   San Francisco   Atlanta   Dallas   *and*   London

LEWIS PAUL TODD has acquired national distinction as a teacher and writer on American history and related subjects. He taught American history for many years and was head of the Department of Social Studies at Bound Brook High School, Bound Brook, New Jersey. He also has taught American history, historical geography of the United States, American government, and related courses at Queens College, New York, at Western Connecticut State College, Danbury, Connecticut, and at New York University.

Dr. Todd is widely known among social studies teachers for his textbook writing and for his many articles and editorials in social studies journals. He has contributed to the Yearbooks and other publications of the National Council for the Social Studies (NCSS). For many years he was editor of *Social Education,* the official journal of the NCSS. Dr. Todd also has served as editorial writer for *Civic Leader.* In addition to his collaboration on *Rise of the American Nation,* he co-authored two series of social studies textbooks for elementary schools.

MERLE CURTI is Frederick Jackson Turner Professor of American History, Emeritus, at the University of Wisconsin (Madison) and has been Visiting Professor of History at the University of Tokyo. He has lectured at many American colleges and at Cambridge University. He also has served as honorary consultant in American cultural history, Library of Congress. Dr. Curti was formerly Professor of American History at Teachers College, Columbia University, where he and Dr. Todd began their collaboration on instructional materials for American history classrooms.

Professor Curti has been president of the American Historical Association, the highest honor a historian in the United States can receive. He also received the award of the American Council of Learned Societies for particularly distinguished scholarship. His long list of distinguished historical writings includes *Human Nature in American Thought: A History, The Social Ideas of American Educators, The Making of an American Community, The American Paradox: The Conflict of Thought and Action,* and *The Growth of American Thought,* for which he won the Pulitzer prize for history.

Requests for permission to make copies of any part of the work should be mailed to: Permissions, Harcourt Brace Jovanovich, Publishers, 757 Third Avenue, New York, NY 10017

ACKNOWLEDGMENTS: For permission to reprint copyrighted material, grateful acknowledgment is made to Joan Daves Literary Agency for an excerpt from "I Have a Dream," an address by Martin Luther King, Jr., © 1963 by Martin Luther King, Jr., and to Harper & Row, Publishers, Inc. for an excerpt from *The Big Change* by Frederick Lewis Allen.

Printed in the United States of America
ISBN 0-15-376030-3

Contents

Sources

Changing Ways with Technology

Special Features

Charts

Text Maps

Historical Atlas
of the United States

Unit One

Building the Colonies

Beginnings to 1763

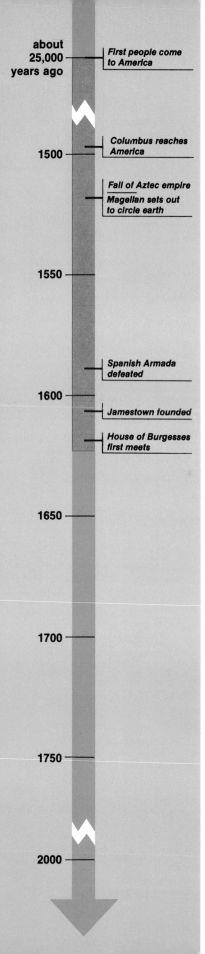

about 25,000 years ago — First people come to America

1500 — Columbus reaches America

— Fall of Aztec empire
— Magellan sets out to circle earth

1550 —

— Spanish Armada defeated

1600 —

— Jamestown founded

— House of Burgesses first meets

1650 —

1700 —

1750 —

2000 —

Chapter 1

Discovering and Settling the Americas

Beginnings to 1624

Five hundred years ago, the forbidding expanse of the Atlantic Ocean formed a mighty barrier. This barrier separated the peoples of Europe and Africa from the peoples of the Americas. Neither group knew or even dreamed that the other existed.

At this time the native peoples of the Americas had developed many varied ways of life, some of them highly advanced. The same was true of the peoples of Africa. The peoples of Europe were just entering a period of rapid development and were building new, powerful nations. They were also beginning to push beyond barriers like the Atlantic and to discover what were, to them, new lands.

During the period covered by the 1400's and 1500's, the isolation of the Native Americans from the Europeans and Africans came to an end. There on the American continents, the peoples of Europe, the Americas, and Africa were joined—willingly and unwillingly—for the first time.

These two centuries were a time of conflict and change. They marked one of the major turning points in human history. One age was dying; another age was being born.

THE CHAPTER IN OUTLINE

1. The first Americans discover and settle a new world.
2. Portugal and Spain lead the way to the Americas.
3. Portuguese and Spaniards explore and conquer.
4. Portugal and Spain plant their civilizations in the Americas.
5. England challenges Spain and gains a foothold in North America.

2

1 The first Americans discover and settle a new world

American Indians built prosperous cities while Europe was in its Dark Ages. These ruins ring the central plaza of Chichén Itzá, once a city of the Mayan Indians in what is now Mexico.

There was a time when the American continents lay empty of all human life. From the frozen wastes of the Arctic to the southern tip of South America, no human voice had ever echoed through the wilderness. No human foot had ever left its print upon the soil. The land belonged to the wildlife that roamed the forests and plains, soared through the air, and swam in the rivers and lakes.

The first Americans. Many historians believe that the first people to discover this immense wilderness came from Asia. The date on which those first people entered America is lost forever in the mists of history. Estimates place the date somewhere from 10,000 to more than 25,000 years ago. The widely accepted theory is that they traveled from Siberia, in Asia, to Alaska across land that now lies beneath the waters of the Bering Strait (see map, pages 10–11). At the time a glacier, a huge sheet of ice, covered much of what is now Canada and the northern United States. The ice locked up so much water that the level of the oceans dropped by several hundred feet. This drop in sea level exposed the land that then connected Asia and Alaska.

Through the centuries wave after wave of people wandered into Alaska from many parts of Asia. When the glacial ice melted and the sea rose again, the wanderers probably crossed the Bering Strait in small boats or, during the winter months, on foot over the ice.

These people of the dawn of American history brought little with them from Asia. They knew—or soon discovered—how to make fire. They may have brought dogs. For weapons they depended upon clubs and stone-tipped spears. The wild animals, or game, they killed provided them with food and with skins and furs for clothing.

In their never-ending search for better hunting grounds, they moved across the great central plain of Alaska and southward along the eastern foothills of the Rocky Mountains. Over many thousands of years, these people spread out across North, Central, and South America.

Settling the land. In these new lands, the early peoples gradually increased in number. No one knows the exact size of the native population by the time Europeans first reached these shores. Estimates range from as low as 16 million to as high as 112 million. Recent estimates give a total population of 90 to 100 million, of which 10 to 12 million lived in the area that is now the United States and Canada. Today we call all of these people and their descendants Native Americans, or Indians.

The Native Americans were divided into many hundreds of different tribes speaking more than 1,000 different languages and dialects. As time passed, they invented new weapons and tools and learned to grow crops.

The Native Americans developed rich and varied **cultures,°** or ways of life. Some lived by hunting, fishing, and gathering roots, nuts, and berries. Others depended mainly on farming. Still others hunted and fished to supplement the crops they grew in garden patches around their villages. Some Native Americans wandered across the land in small groups. Others settled down and lived in towns and

°A **culture** includes the whole way of life of a people—their habits and customs, their religion and education, their government, and their arts.

villages. Some created **civilizations,** or highly advanced cultures, which flourished long before Europeans came to America.

The Mayas.   One of the great early Indian civilizations was that of the Mayas of Yucatán and Central America (see map, pages 10–11). It rivaled in richness and complexity the civilizations of Europe, Africa, and Asia. Great cities—used mainly as religious centers—contained broad plazas, massive public buildings, and magnificent temples that rose above the rain forest. Mayan artisans and artists decorated the buildings with colorful murals and striking stone carvings and sculptures. Mayan scholars developed a method of writing. Mathematicians created an accurate numbering system that included the use of the zero. Scientists worked out a calendar more precise than the one then used in Europe. Mayan astronomers made such careful observations of the stars and planets that they could predict the dates of solar eclipses.

The Mayan civilization reached its peak of brilliance more than 500 years before Columbus sailed to America. Then it began to decline, possibly because the Mayan population increased too rapidly for the available food supply. The Mayas abandoned their cities, and lush jungle growth quickly covered the Mayan ruins. Some groups of Mayas were absorbed into other tribes, while others survived until the 1540's. Their descendants still live in the same area today.

The Incas.   Far to the south of the Mayas, another civilization arose, centered in what is now Peru, in South America (see map, pages 10–11). Here the Incas conquered neighboring states and organized a rich and powerful empire. From their capital city of Cuzco, high in the Andes Mountains, ran a network of roads and bridges uniting the empire. Their fortified cities, their highway system, and their terraced fields and irrigation works on the mountain slopes were marvels of engineering.

Like the Mayas, the Incas depended upon farming for their livelihood. Two domesticated animals, the llama and the alpaca, served as beasts of burden and sources of food. Wool from these animals and from the wild vicuña provided not only everyday clothing but also material from which weavers created beautiful fabrics with intricate and colorful designs. Artisans fashioned gold and silver from the Incan mines into jewelry and rich ornaments for the temples and palaces.

The Incas rigidly organized their empire in a pyramid-like structure. Every member of the society had an assigned place and task. At the base were the farmers, laborers, and artisans. Next came the noble class, composed of priests, military leaders, and government officials. At the top was the supreme ruler—The Inca, who was called the "Sun God." All power and all authority flowed from The Inca down through the nobles to the workers. As you will see, when the ruler was destroyed, the entire social structure collapsed.

The Aztecs.   In Mexico, far to the north of the Incas (see map, pages 10–11), the Aztecs once lived as hunters. As they wandered, they quickly learned new ways of life from other tribes they met. They developed well-trained armies that conquered the peoples around them. In three or four hundred years, they created a mighty empire that by 1500 ruled much of Central America. Though they depended mainly on farming, the Aztecs also carried on a busy trade with distant communities. Aztec merchants traveled far and wide, dealing in precious stones, cacao beans, and gold and silver.

The Aztecs collected great wealth from the people they conquered. Part of it went toward building a beautiful capital city, called Tenochtitlán (tay·noch·tee·TLAN), on the site where Mexico City now stands. There the Aztecs raised great temples, palaces, and other public buildings.

The Aztecs who constructed this marvel were harsh rulers. The people they had conquered would need little urging to rise in rebellion against them.

The Indians of North America.   The Native Americans of what are now the United States and Canada did not live as subject people in empires like those of the Incas and the Aztecs. In a few instances, several tribes did join together for mutual support or protection. Sometimes tribes traded with neighbors and staged raids against nearby enemies. As a rule, however, each of the numerous North American tribes lived a largely independent life in its own territory.

Each tribe adapted its way of life to its own environment. Usually tribes that lived near each other had similar ways of life. A region in

A TIME OF FEARFUL WAITING

In ages past, according to legends told by the Aztecs, the Valley of Mexico where they lived had been a place of wonders. The earth gave forth all kinds of fruits and vegetables without being farmed. Cotton took on beautiful colors while still on the stalk. The air was sweet with delicate perfumes. People had enjoyed this golden age during the reign of Quetzalcoatl (ket·sal·KOAT·ul), the god of the air and of learning.

Quetzalcoatl (whose name means "feathered serpent") was tall and white-skinned, with a flowing dark beard. A kindly god, he had taught his people how to farm, make metal, and govern themselves. Then, for some reason never known, he had angered one of the greater gods and had been exiled from the land of the Aztecs. Before he sailed away, he promised that some day he and his descendants would come back from the east.

During the reign of the emperor Moctezuma, the Aztecs felt that the time for Quetzalcoatl's return was approaching. Would he bring good or evil? There were ominous signs. Lake Texcoco overflowed its banks for no apparent reason, destroying many buildings in Tenochtitlán. The city's great temple mysteriously caught fire. Comets flashed across the sky. The voice of a woman was heard wailing night after night, "My children, we must flee far away from this city! My children, where shall I take you?"

Added to the legends and the omens were rumors. Tall, bearded men had been seen in regions near Mexico, men with white skins who carried thunder and lightning in their hands. These years, the early 1500's by European calendars, were a time of uncertainty. The Aztecs were fearfully awaiting the return of a god. When the Spanish explorer Cortés landed on their shores, they thought Quetzalcoatl had arrived. The Aztecs would quickly learn just how wrong they were.

which most of the tribes had the same sort of culture is described as a **culture area.** The different culture areas produced a rich variety of ways of life on the North American continent.

In the next few pages, we will look briefly at a few of the principal tribes in different culture areas as they were before the Europeans arrived (see map, page 6). In later chapters, as we follow the advancing line of settlement across the country, we will see how these same tribes dealt with the invasion of their lands by white settlers.

Indians of the Southwest. Three major Indian groups lived in the hot, dry, semi-desert area of what is now the southwestern United States. These were the Pueblos, the Navajos, and the Apaches.

"Pueblo" is the Spanish name for "town." It is an appropriate name for a tribe that built and lived in the first "apartment houses" in America. A thousand years ago, ancestors of the Pueblos carved apartment-like dwellings out of the walls of canyons. They built other "apartments," one with 800 rooms, of stone and **adobe,** or sun-dried brick.

The Pueblos were peaceful people. In irrigated fields they grew corn, beans, squash, and cotton. They wove textiles and created beautiful pottery. In colorful ceremonies enriched with songs, the sound of drums, and dances, they worshiped the gods and the animals, earth, and sky that the gods had created. Specially chosen and trained storytellers passed on from generation to generation the history of creation and of the human place in it.

The Navajos and the Apaches were two of the Pueblos' closest neighbors. The Navajos learned how to farm from the Pueblos. They also became skilled weavers who created wonderful designs for rugs and blankets. Unlike the Pueblos, who lived in compact towns made

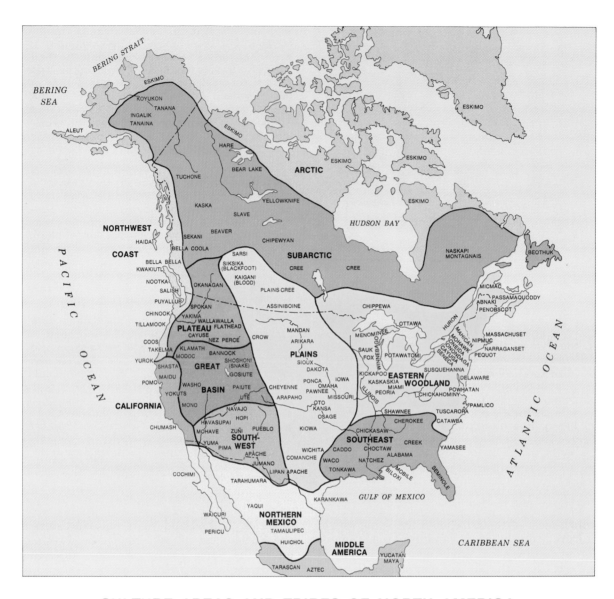

CULTURE AREAS AND TRIBES OF NORTH AMERICA

up of dwellings that were shared by several families, each Navajo family instead lived in its own **hogan**. This was a lodge built of adobe and logs.

The Apaches were wandering hunters who depended upon deer and buffalo for food, shelter, and clothing. They lived in **wickiups**, circular huts of brush that could be constructed in a few minutes. Neighboring tribes respected their fierceness and endurance. One of these tribes, the Pueblos, gave them the name "Apache," which means "enemy."

The Plains Indians. The Plains Indians—among them the Sioux, Pawnees, Kiowas, Dakotas, Osages, and Comanches—combined hunting and farming. For much of the year the Plains Indians lived in villages along the banks of the Missouri and the other rivers that drained into the Mississippi. There the women cultivated corn and other crops in fields around the villages.

During the summer, however, small bands of closely related families moved out onto the Great Plains to hunt buffalo. They slept in

6

tepees—cone-shaped tents of buffalo skins stretched over a frame of lodge poles. The buffalo provided the Indians with almost all of their basic needs. From the skins they made clothing, tents, ropes, and wool. With the sinews they made threads with which to sew their clothes and tents. From the bones they made tools. On the treeless plains, dried buffalo droppings served as the chief fuel for cooking and for campfires.

The Plains Indians lived under a democratic form of government. Chiefs were chosen for specific purposes—to lead a hunting party or a raiding expedition. No single chief had total control for any extended length of time. Leading members of a band or of a tribe gathered in council meetings to make important decisions. Like so many other tribes of North America, the Plains Indians prized their freedom and independence.

Other Western tribes. The Shoshone, Pima, and Nez Percé (NAY per·SAY) Indians were among the tribes inhabiting the lands west of the Great Plains. This is a region of dramatic contrasts. It includes towering mountains, high rocky plateaus, deep mountain valleys, and the coastal lands of California. Much of the region is very dry, and life for the Indians there was hard. They have been called "Seed Gatherers" because they depended for food upon seeds, nuts, berries, and roots, although they also hunted small game. They were skilled in the art of basket-making. Some of their baskets were so tightly woven that they could hold water.

The Northwest Coast offered a more generous environment. From the sea and the forest, the Northwest Coast tribes secured a never-failing supply of food and materials for clothing and shelter. With the essentials of life so plentiful, they were able to enjoy community life in large villages along the seacoast.

Indians of the Eastern Woodlands. The Eastern Woodland area reached from what is now Canada to the Gulf of Mexico and from the Atlantic seaboard to west of the Mississippi River. The people who lived in much of this area long ago were called "Mound Builders" after the huge ceremonial mounds that they built in the form of birds, bears, wolves, and other animals.

The people living in the Eastern Woodland region when the Europeans arrived were de-

Hopi Indians of the southwestern United States made these jars and tiles in the early 1900's, following an ancient style. This style was then revived by Nampeyo, a famous Hopi potter, after she watched an archeologist uncover such pieces.

scended from the Mound Builders. Like their ancestors, the numerous tribes shared a land of plenty. Many lakes sparkled in the forest. Clear streams and rivers flowed down to the sea. The people lived in villages surrounded by the fields that they had cleared and in which they raised corn, beans, squash, tobacco, and other crops. Their hunting grounds provided them with additional food as well as skins that could be used for moccasins and furs for blankets and robes.

From the Algonquins and Iroquois in the north to the Creeks and Cherokees in the south, the Indians prized their independence. In Chapter 3 you will get a closer look at the way they lived and how they organized their tribal life. You will also see how the coming of the white settlers disrupted these age-old patterns of Indian living and, in some cases, even destroyed them.

Shared beliefs of the Indians. Despite their variety, Indians in different culture areas shared certain ways of seeing the world. They felt it was necessary to live in harmony with the natural world. This belief in a harmony with nature was at the heart of the social, eco-

7

nomic, and religious practices of the Indians. They worshiped the gods who had created the world, and they viewed the land as a sacred trust that they were privileged to use but were obligated to pass on unspoiled to future generations.

The Indians also shared a strong sense of pride. They were proud of their tribes and communities and of themselves as individuals. They prized their self-reliance, their individual initiative, and their independence.

The understanding that enabled the Indians to develop methods for living in harmony with the land did not prepare them for an invasion by people of another culture. This understanding was no match for the guns and other technological developments that the Europeans would bring to the Americas.

SECTION SURVEY

IDENTIFY: Native Americans, culture, civilization, Mayas, Incas, Aztecs, Pueblos, Navajos, Apaches, Plains Indians, Mound Builders, Eastern Woodland Indians.

1. (a) On what did the Mayas and the Incas depend for their livelihood? (b) In what way did Aztec society differ from Mayan and Incan society?

2. How did the cultures of each of the following groups of Native Americans reflect their environment: (a) the Pueblos, (b) the Plains Indians, (c) the Seed Gatherers, (d) the Northwest Coast Indians?

3. Map Study: Look at the map on page 6. (a) In what culture area is your community located? (b) What Indian tribes lived in this area? (c) Are there any traces of these Indians (place names, reservations, or artifacts, for example) in your community today?

2 Portugal and Spain lead the way to the Americas

During the 1300's and 1400's, far from the Americas, Europe was stirring with new ideas. Many Europeans were filled with burning curiosity and intense energy. They were living in a period called the **Renaissance** (ren·eh·ZAHNS), meaning a time of "new birth."

A time of energy and change. Through much of the preceding Middle Ages, Europeans had been concerned primarily with scratching out a bare living and preparing through religion for life beyond the grave. Now their interest increasingly shifted to the everyday world around them. Some turned to the sea to search for new trade routes and to explore distant lands. Others turned to art, architecture, and writing.

What started Europeans thinking new thoughts and dreaming new dreams? A series of wars called the Crusades were partly responsible. Starting in 1096 and continuing for nearly 200 years, army after army of Christians set forth from Europe on what they considered a holy mission. Their objective was to battle with Muslims for control of the Holy Land in the Middle East. Many Crusaders died in battle, while others settled down to live in the Middle East. Those who did return to Europe brought back new ideas and new products. The ideas spread, creating new ways of living and stimulating the Renaissance. The use of the new products also spread, creating new demands and stimulating more trade between Europe and Asia.

The importance of trade. Europeans wanted the products they got from Asia. They wanted the tough Damascus steel for their swords and armor. They wanted Persian rugs, Chinese porcelain, and glass to make their cold, damp castles and manor houses more livable. More than anything else, perhaps, they wanted spices. They wanted cloves, cinnamon, and nutmeg from the Spice Islands of the East Indies and, most important, pepper, or "black gold," from India. These spices gave variety and flavor to their coarse food, particularly to their meat. Spices also were used to preserve food. To pay for these products, Europeans sent woolen goods, tin, gold, and silver back along the trade routes.

The difficulty of trade. The old trade routes (see map, pages 10–11) had always been very difficult, dangerous, and expensive. Months, sometimes years, passed before a box of spices reached Europe from Asia.

Camel caravans carrying products overland from China and central Asia crossed vast wastelands and high mountain passes. Goods moving from the East Indies along the sea-land route made a long sea voyage westward across

On his voyages Christopher Columbus sailed in ships like these Portuguese trading vessels called carracks. However, the ships in which he crossed the Atlantic were much smaller. The *Niña* and the *Pinta* were only 50 feet (15 meters) long.

the Indian Ocean. Then the goods were carried over the burning Arabian Desert by camel caravans. Next came another sea voyage, this time across the Mediterranean Sea on ships bound for the Italian cities of Genoa or Venice. The Italian merchants of Genoa and Venice had a **monopoly**—that is, exclusive control over the supply of a product or service—on trade between the eastern Mediterranean and Europe. Finally, Asia's much-wanted products reached Europe's markets.

Many European merchants wanted to get Asian goods more cheaply and to end the control of east-west trade by the Venetians and Genoans. The Portuguese and Spaniards, and later the French, English, and Dutch, began to search for new ocean routes to Asia.

Before the search ended, European explorers had pushed back the frontiers of the world they knew. This expansion of European trade, which was linked with new forms of business and the rise of banking, has become known as the **Commercial Revolution.**

Portugal's sea route to Asia. Portuguese sailors led the search for an all-water route to Asia. They were financed by Prince Henry of Portugal, also known as Prince Henry the Navigator.

Fascinated by exploration, Prince Henry built a shipyard and a school for navigators on the coast of Portugal. There he and his followers built new types of sailing ships seaworthy enough to brave the Atlantic Ocean. They experimented with new methods of navigation and better maps. They began to use instruments, such as the compass and the astrolabe, for determining distances and direction.

Prince Henry did more than experiment. He sent many expeditions south along the unexplored coast of Africa (see map, pages 10–11). After his death in 1460, Portuguese sailors continued to explore the African coast.

At small harbor settlements where they anchored their ships, the Portuguese may have learned of African kingdoms inland. They had little interest in exploring these kingdoms at that time. After trading such European goods as brass bowls, bracelets, beads, and textiles for fresh water and food, the Portuguese sailed on. Besides supplies, however, the Portuguese also took aboard African servants and slaves, carrying them back to Portugal and Spain on

Text continues on page 12.

9

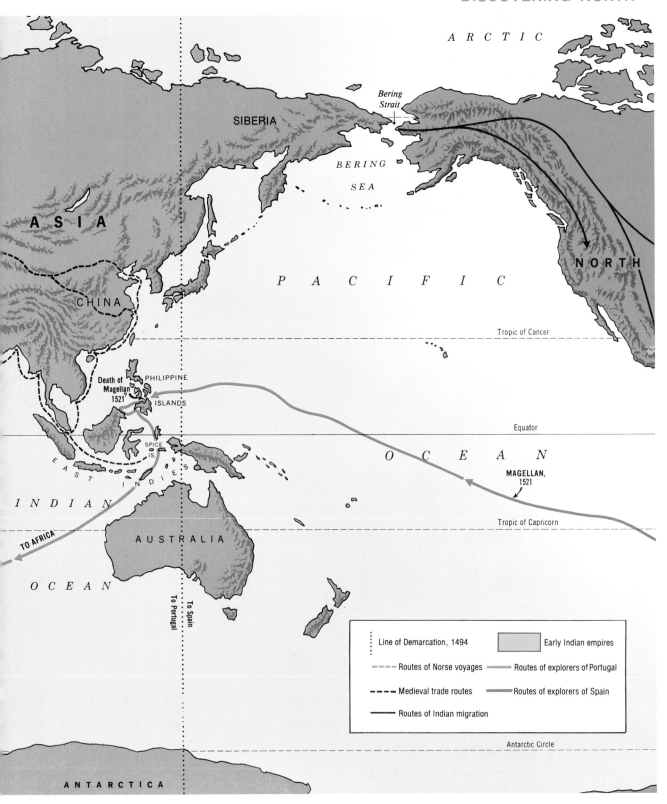

A R C T I C

SIBERIA

Bering
Strait

BERING

SEA

ASIA

NORTH

CHINA

P A C I F I C

Tropic of Cancer

Death of
Magellan
1521

PHILIPPINE

ISLANDS

Equator

SPICE
IS.

O C E A N

MAGELLAN,
1521

E A S T   I N D I E S

I N D I A N

Tropic of Capricorn

TO AFRICA

AUSTRALIA

O C E A N

To Portugal
To Spain

⋮ Line of Demarcation, 1494	▨ Early Indian empires
– – – Routes of Norse voyages	—— Routes of explorers of Portugal
- - - Medieval trade routes	—— Routes of explorers of Spain
—— Routes of Indian migration	

Antarctic Circle

ANTARCTICA

OCEAN

GREENLAND

Arctic Circle

ICELAND

NORWAY

SWEDEN

NORSE VOYAGES,
ABOUT 1000

ENGLAND

NETH.

EUROPE

ASIA

FRANCE

Genoa

Venice

ITALY

PORTUGAL

SPAIN

Mediterranean

Sea

Damascus

PERSIA

Baghdad

ARABIA

"WINELAND"?

NEWFOUNDLAND

AMERICA

A T L A N T I C

COLUMBUS,
1492

BAHAMA

AZTEC

IS.

MAYA

BALBOA,
1513

PANAMA

CABRAL,
1500

AFRICA

DA GAMA,
1498

Calicut

INDIAN

SOUTH

OCEAN

DA GAMA,
1497

DIAS,
1486-88

INDIAN

INCA

BRAZIL

AMERICA

VESPUCCI,
1501

OCEAN

To Portugal

To Spain

Cape of
Good Hope

MAGELLAN,
1520

MAGELLAN'S SHIP
"VICTORIA," 1522

TIERRA
DEL FUEGO

Strait of
Magellan

ANTARCTICA

11

the return voyages. In later years some of these Africans or their descendants took part in the explorations of the Americas.

With every expedition Portuguese sailors pushed farther and farther south. In 1487 Bartholomeu Dias (DEE·ahs) and his crew rounded the southern tip of Africa. Eleven years later, in 1498, Vasco da Gama, also from Portugal, followed Dias's route around the Cape of Good Hope. He continued across the Indian Ocean, reaching Calicut in far-off India.

The voyages of Dias and da Gama were enormously important to the little kingdom of Portugal and to the world. Within a few years, Portuguese vessels were sailing back and forth along the new, all-water route to India and the Spice Islands of the East Indies.

Columbus's fateful voyage. While Portuguese sailors were exploring the African coast, an Italian named Christopher Columbus set out in 1492 under the flag of Spain on the first of four great voyages. Convinced that the earth was round, a knowledge shared by many informed people of the day, Columbus believed that if he sailed far enough to the west he would reach Asia. In trying to prove his point, Columbus made a key contribution to what has been called the **Geographic Revolution,** the rapid growth of European knowledge of the earth's surface.

The expedition led by Columbus included three small ships, the *Niña,* the *Pinta,* and the *Santa María.* The able crews of these ships were mainly Spaniards, but one member described as a "man of color" may have been one of the Africans brought back to Europe by the Portuguese explorers.

Finding a world unknown to Europe. Instead of reaching Asia, Columbus came upon a small island in the Bahamas (see map, pages 10–11). On the morning of October 12, 1492, Columbus and his crews went ashore and thanked God for leading them safely across the sea. Thinking that he had reached the East Indies, Columbus called the dark-skinned people on the island "Indians." Neither Columbus nor anyone in his party realized that they had, in fact, arrived at an island near the coast of North America, a continent unknown at this time to Europeans.

Columbus tried three more times to find an all-water route to the East Indies and the riches of Asia. He failed in this, but his voyages

established Spain's claims in the Americas. Columbus returned from his fourth voyage a poor, lonely, broken-hearted man. He died in 1506 without knowing that his explorations would, in time, have more influence on Europe than all the riches of Asia.

An earlier European voyage. In reality, Columbus was not the first European to reach America. The Norse, or Vikings, were probably the first Europeans to land there. In the late 900's, Eric the Red and his followers built a settlement in Greenland. In the year 1000, Eric's son Leif and his crew were blown off course and landed on the northeast coast of North America. They called the country Vinland or "Wineland the Good," after the wild grapes that grew there. Other Norse followed Leif to Vinland and established settlements there, but the settlements did not last and Norse voyages to Vinland stopped suddenly. Historians still do not know why the voyages ended so abruptly.

Other Europeans may also have reached America before Columbus. If so, they left no written record.

English and French claims. Other nations also established claims to large areas of North America soon after Columbus. In 1497 John Cabot, an Italian sea captain in the pay of King Henry VII of England, sailed to North America out of the harbor of Bristol. Little is known about Cabot and even less about his famous voyage. Historians believe that on this voyage and another made the following year, he sailed along the coasts of what are now Newfoundland, Nova Scotia, and New England (see map, page 13), claiming these lands for England in the name of King Henry. For this work the thrifty king presented Cabot with a gift of ten pounds and an annual pension of twenty pounds. This was a small reward indeed for the explorer who gave England its first claim to the North American continent.

French claims to a share of North America were based on the voyages of Giovanni da Verrazano (vayr·rah·TSAH·noh) and Jacques Cartier (kar·TYAY). Verrazano, an Italian sailing under the French flag, set out in 1524 to find a water route through America to Asia. He failed, but his explorations (see map, page 13) gave the French their first claim to new lands overseas.

Ten years later, in 1534, Cartier made the

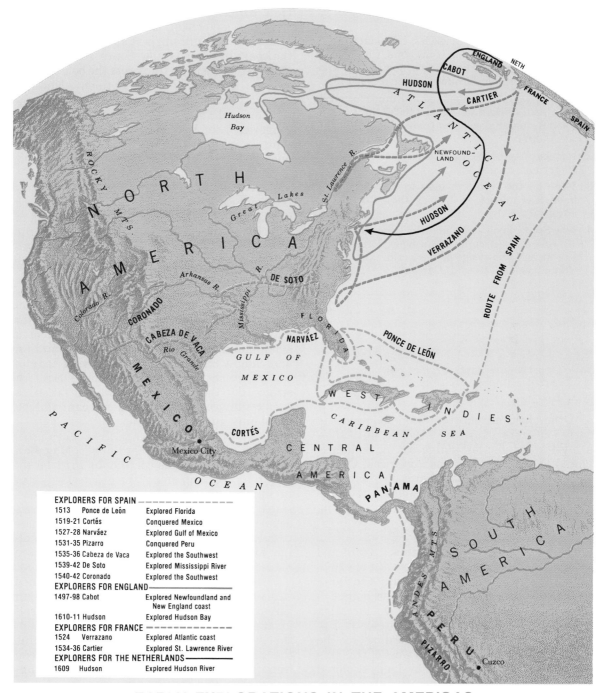

EXPLORERS FOR SPAIN ------------------
1513   Ponce de León   Explored Florida
1519-21 Cortés   Conquered Mexico
1527-28 Narváez   Explored Gulf of Mexico
1531-35 Pizarro   Conquered Peru
1535-36 Cabeza de Vaca   Explored the Southwest
1539-42 De Soto   Explored Mississippi River
1540-42 Coronado   Explored the Southwest
EXPLORERS FOR ENGLAND------------
1497-98 Cabot   Explored Newfoundland and
                          New England coast
1610-11 Hudson   Explored Hudson Bay
EXPLORERS FOR FRANCE ---------------
1524   Verrazano   Explored Atlantic coast
1534-36 Cartier   Explored St. Lawrence River
EXPLORERS FOR THE NETHERLANDS-----------
1609   Hudson   Explored Hudson River

EARLY EXPLORATIONS IN THE AMERICAS

first of three voyages to the lands across the Atlantic. On the first voyage, he explored the Gulf of St. Lawrence, and on his second and third voyages, he explored the St. Lawrence River as far as the present site of Montreal. He also tried to start a settlement on a spot not far away from where Quebec now stands. The settlement was not a success, but Cartier's efforts helped to strengthen French claims to what is now Canada.

13

1. (a) Why was there a demand in Europe for goods from Asia in the 1300's and 1400's? (b) Why did some Europeans seek new trade routes to Asia in the 1400's?

2. List four improvements in navigation that Prince Henry encouraged.

3. Why did the Norse voyages to North America have less impact on history than Columbus's voyages?

4. Map Study: Look at the maps on pages 10–11 and 13. How did each of the following explorers add to Europeans' knowledge of the world: (a) Dias, (b) Columbus, (c) Cabot, (d) Cartier?

3 Portuguese and Spaniards explore and conquer

Other bold adventurers soon followed the early explorers across the Atlantic, until then a mysterious and forbidding ocean. Some explored the coastline of the Americas. Others pushed into the interior. Close on their footsteps came the Spanish soldiers known as **conquistadors** (kohn·KEES·tah·dorz), that is, the conquerors.

Spanish and Portuguese claims. Spain and Portugal, both leaders in the new age of exploration and discovery, did not hesitate to claim all of the Americas. In 1494 they signed a treaty establishing a Line of Demarcation about 1,100 miles (1,760 kilometers) west of the Cape Verde Islands. According to the treaty, all new lands explored west of this line were to belong to Spain. All new lands explored to the east were to belong to Portugal (see map, pages 10–11).

A few years later a Portuguese explorer, Pedro Álvares Cabral (cah·BRAHL), was sailing around Africa to India. His ship was blown off course, and in 1500 he landed on the shore of what is now Brazil (see map, pages 10–11). Cabral then claimed this territory for Portugal.

How America got its name. Amerigo Vespucci (ves·POO·chee), an Italian, sailed on at least one expedition, perhaps several, along the coast of what is now South America. His observations led him to express the bold opinion that he had seen a new continent. News of Vespucci's conclusion reached a famous geographer, who proposed calling these lands "America" in honor of Amerigo Vespucci. Thus, ironically, Columbus missed even the honor of having the lands named after him.

Discovering a "new" ocean. In 1513 a Spanish explorer, Balboa (bal·BOH·ah), started on an expedition across the Isthmus of Panama in search of gold. His expedition, like many of the expeditions that pushed into the endless wilderness of the Americas, included Africans as well as Europeans. Thirty Africans, in fact, traveled in Balboa's party.

Indian guides led Balboa's expedition through a hot, steaming rain forest. After many hardships they reached the foot of a small mountain. Balboa climbed the mountain and caught his first glimpse of a vast body of water, which he called the "South Sea." It stretched to the south and the west as far as his eyes could see. Was it another ocean? Balboa could only guess that it was.

Circling the earth. Ferdinand Magellan proved Balboa's guess correct. In 1519 he set sail from Spain on one of the greatest voyages in human history. Magellan, a Portuguese, sailed under the flag of Spain. A year after his departure, he led his small fleet through a narrow waterway, now called the Strait of Magellan, at the southern tip of South America (see map, pages 10–11).

For more than a month, Magellan sailed westward through the strait. At last, passing through the strait, Magellan found himself upon an immense sea—a sea so vast and calm that he named it the Pacific Ocean. Was this the mighty "South Sea" that Balboa had seen from the mountain in Panama? Magellan sailed on to find the answer.

Two years later, in September 1522, a small vessel named the *Victoria* sailed into a Spanish harbor. The 18 sailors aboard were the only survivors of the 237 who had sailed with Magellan from Spain three years earlier. These 18 men had done what no one had ever done before. They had crossed Balboa's "South Sea" and had sailed around the world. Magel-

According to Aztec legend, the god Quetzalcoatl was supposed to return from across the sea. For a time, the Aztecs believed Cortés to be Quetzalcoatl's descendant. This painting shows the Aztec ruler Moctezuma welcoming Cortés into the great city of Tenochtitlán as a returning god.

lan, their leader, was not among them. Killed in a battle, he lay buried in the Philippine Islands, half a world away.

Magellan's expedition proved that the lands Columbus had discovered were indeed part of a new world—continents not known to the Europeans of that day. The expedition also gave Spain its claim to the Philippine Islands. In the years that followed, Spain sent soldiers to conquer the Filipinos, missionaries to convert them to Christianity, and merchants to open up trade.

Conquest of the Aztecs and Incas. Meanwhile, other Spaniards came to the New World looking for gold. "The Spaniards are troubled with a disease of the heart for which gold is the remedy," said Hernando Cortés (kor·TAYS), a conquistador. In their search for riches, Cortés and the other conquistadors destroyed the great civilizations of the Aztecs and the Incas.

Cortés landed on the coast of Mexico in the year 1519 as leader of a small army of about 550, among them some Africans. The Spanish ships seemed like "towers on the sea" to the Indians, and the guns, horses, and iron-clad men were strange and fearful sights. The Indians thought that Cortés might be the god Quetzalcoatl (ket·sal·KOAT·ul), returning as he had promised (see feature, page 5). They quickly learned he was not and began to fight back

fiercely. Cortés might have perished if he had not persuaded enemies of the Aztecs to join his army. With the aid of these Indians, who greatly outnumbered his own soldiers, Cortés laid seige to Tenochtitlán, the Aztec capital. Moctezuma, the Aztec emperor, was murdered, and Cortés conquered the wealthy empire. The conquest brought glory and fortune to Cortés and enormous treasures of gold and silver to Spain.

Several years later, in 1531–35, another Spaniard, Francisco Pizarro (pee·ZAHR·oh), led an even smaller army against the Incas. The Incas, frightened and divided, did not resist, and Pizarro advanced to the very heart of the Incan empire high in the Andes. There, through treachery, he kidnapped The Inca, collected a huge ransom of gold and silver, and then ruthlessly murdered his captive. The death of The Inca, their "Sun God," left the Incas without a leader, and control of the empire quickly passed into the hands of the Spaniards.

The search for gold. Other conquistadors pushed north and west in search of fame and fortune. In 1513 Juan Ponce de León (POHN·say day lay·OHN) first explored the land he named Florida. He was killed on a later expedition by the natives after looting their villages and capturing some as slaves.

Gold was a powerful lure for Spanish conquistadors. They found such treasures as this gold breastplate made by the Mixtec Indians of Central America.

In 1527 and 1528, Pánfilo de Narváez (nahr·VAH·ez) led another army into Florida. Years later, after wandering more than half-way across North America, only four survivors, Narváez not among them, reached Mexico City and safety. One survivor, Cabeza de Vaca (cah·BAY·sah day VAH·kuh), returned to Spain and wrote a book about the journey. Another survivor, a black named Estevanico (es·tay·vah·NEE·koh), led a later search for treasure on which he was killed.

In 1539 an expedition led by Hernando De Soto pushed into what is now the southeastern United States. De Soto, too, searched for riches and found none. Before he died in 1542, he reached the Mississippi River, the "Father of Waters." He was buried in the river he discovered.

Another conquistador, Francisco Vásquez de Coronado (kor·oh·NAH·doh), led a group northward from Mexico into what is now the southwestern United States. Lured by Indian tales of seven cities with streets of gold and buildings studded with precious gems, his expedition searched for two years. Looting villages, enslaving the Indians, and killing those who fought back, Coronado and his followers reached what is now Kansas. They discovered the Grand Canyon but found no golden cities. Coronado returned to Mexico City without treasure.

These conquistadors failed to discover the great riches that Cortés and Pizarro had found, but they did succeed in giving Spain control of vital parts of North and Central America.

New settlements for Spain. During the second half of the 1500's, the Spaniards devoted serious attention to the borderlands east and north of Mexico (see map, page 19). Disturbed by reports of French and English activities, the Spaniards built a fort at St. Augustine, Florida, in 1565. In the next few years, they established missions and **presidios** (pray· SID·ee·ohs), or forts, up the coast as far as South Carolina.

It seemed more realistic, however, to secure firm control of the land in the northern part of Mexico. In 1598 Don Juan de Oñate (oh·NYAH·tay), son of one of the richest mine owners in Mexico, set out to conquer and settle the area known as New Mexico. A large and well-equipped military force and a number of Roman Catholic missionaries supported his expedition. After overcoming strong resistance by the Indians of the Acoma pueblo, Oñate claimed the land for Spain and started a settlement at San Juan. In 1609 Santa Fe became the permanent capital of this region.

Nearly a hundred years later, in 1680, the Pueblo Indians joined in a revolt and drove out the Spaniards, but the Spaniards soon reconquered the area. During the following years, the area was widely explored by Roman Catholic missionaries, including the famed Father Eusébio Francisco Kino (KEE·noh). In journals he kept of his travels, Father Kino provided an invaluable record of the land and people. These explorations and the establishment later of missions, towns, and presidios gave the Spaniards firm control of the area.

Expansion into California. During all these years, the Spaniards paid little attention to California. Even after Sebastián Vizcaíno (beth·kah·EE·noh) explored the coast in 1602, they remained indifferent. However, when both the English and the Russians began to show an interest in the Pacific coast, the Spaniards decided to expand their borders to include California. In the mid-1700's Spaniards led by Gaspar de Portolá (por·toh·LAH) and Father Junípero Serra established a chain of missions and presidios up the coast as far as San Francisco Bay (see map, page 19). You will return to the story of these missions in Chapter 15.

SECTION SURVEY

IDENTIFY: Amerigo Vespucci, Balboa, Moctezuma, Francisco Pizarro, Juan Ponce de León, Hernando De Soto, Francisco Vásquez de Coronado, Juan de Oñate, Father Kino.

1. How did Spain and Portugal settle the problem of conflicting claims in lands they wished to explore?
2. Why was Magellan's expedition important?
3. What was the chief motive for Cortés's and Pizarro's conquests of the Aztecs and Incas?
4. How did the Spanish try to protect their settlements in Florida and Mexico?

In 1667 Juana Inés de la Cruz entered a convent in New Mexico, and later she became a great poet. She is also famous for her protest against the exclusion of women from university study.

 # Portugal and Spain plant their civilizations in the Americas

Many of the soldiers who fought to conquer the Americas remained there to seek their fortunes. They, together with the Native Americans and the Africans, created a new culture in the Americas.

The colonial population. Both Portugal and Spain started colonies in the Americas. A **colony** is a land settled by people from another country that remains under the control of that country. New settlers came to these colonies in growing numbers—the Portuguese to the northeast coast of Brazil, the Spaniards to the Caribbean islands and to Mexico and Central and South America. Here in the New World, they reproduced a system of privileged classes resembling the social system they had left behind in Europe.

Spaniards born in Spain claimed the most privileged position in the colonies. Within a hundred years after Columbus's voyages, some 15,000 Spaniards were living in the Americas. Occupying a class just below them were the **creoles,** Spaniards born in the New World. Still lower in the class structure and even more numerous were the **mestizos,** men and women born of mixed Spanish and Indian marriages. By far the most numerous of all were the Indians, most of whom continued to live in villages apart from their conquerors. There was also an increasing population of Africans, including those transported as slaves as well as many

who came as free people. Finally, there were **mulattoes,** people of black and Spanish ancestry, and **zambos,** those who were of Indian and black ancestry.

Old World ways in the New World. To their American colonies the Portuguese and Spaniards brought domestic animals, plants, and seeds never before seen in the New World. In pens and crates on the decks of their ships, they transported horses, donkeys, cattle, pigs, sheep, goats, and poultry. Using barrels cut in half and filled with earth, they carried fruit and nut trees—olive, lemon, orange, lime, apple, apricot, cherry, pear, fig, almond, and walnut. In bags they brought seeds of wheat, barley, rye, rice, peas, lentils, and flax. They also transplanted sugar cane and many kinds of flowers.

In addition to these products, the Spaniards and Portuguese brought their languages and their political, economic, and social systems to the Americas. They brought their tools and their technology, as well as their religious beliefs and institutions.

The colonizers did not simply recreate European culture in the Americas. New conditions in the New World changed European ways of life. For example, the Europeans began to grow crops native to the Americas, such as corn, potatoes, pumpkins, tomatoes, tobacco, avocados, and peanuts.

17

After defeating the Aztecs, the Spaniards tore down Tenochtitlán and built Mexico City on the ruins. By the 1700's Mexico City was the largest Spanish city in the world. The beautiful central plaza of the city is shown in this painting.

The colonists prosper. By 1580, before the English or the French had won even a foothold in the Americas, Portugal and Spain had firmly established their New World colonies. The Portuguese, unlike the Spaniards, found no huge treasures of gold and silver. They had, however, developed flourishing sugar plantations in the lowlands along the northeast coast of Brazil.

The Spaniards were even more successful. In less than a hundred years after the first settlers arrived, they had built prosperous farms, ranches, and cities in the New World. They continued to secure immense fortunes in gold and silver from the old Indian mines in Mexico and in Central and South America. They operated seaports that served as centers of vigorous trade between the Old World and the New. They printed books in the New World and educated at least some of their youth in newly built colleges and universities. Mexico City and Lima in Peru compared favorably with many cities in the Old World.

Slavery in the colonies. The Europeans needed a large labor force to work the colonial mines and plantations. At first, they enslaved the Indians for these jobs, although many Indians escaped or rebelled. The systems of Indian slavery sometimes produced disastrous results. In the Caribbean islands and coastal lowlands, European cruelty and the spread of European diseases wiped out almost all of the Indian population. Faced with a severe labor shortage, the Portuguese and the Spaniards began to transport black slaves from Africa. Their numbers grew rapidly, and some historians estimate that by the mid-1500's more Africans than Europeans were living in the New World.

In the mining regions and farming lands of the interior, the Indians, many of them slaves, continued to provide the main labor source. After the Spanish government abolished Indian slavery in the 1540's, the Spaniards still used forced labor but under a different system.

Forced labor. Before the Europeans arrived, the Indians of the Aztec and Incan empires had lived as subject peoples. The Spanish conquest simply substituted European for Indian rulers. It was easy for the new rulers to introduce a system of Indian labor that was only a step away from outright slavery. This system included both the **encomienda** (en·coh·mee·EN·dah) and the **repartimiento** (ray·par·tee·mee·EN·toh).

The encomienda was a grant of those Indians who lived on a specific piece of land. A new Spanish settler might receive a grant of land and the accompanying encomienda. The settler who received the grant owned neither the land nor the Indians but served as a trustee for both. In return for the use of the land and the Indians, the settler paid taxes to the Spanish Crown—to the king and queen—and, in some cases, to the Church.

A repartimiento was another system of forced Indian labor. It gave the receiver a

18

specified number of Indians to work as forced laborers on a ranch or in a factory, mine, or monastery. From their meager wages, the Indians, including women and children, had to pay taxes to the Crown and to the Church.

The Church and the Indians. From the beginning of colonization, the Spanish king and queen, the ruling class, and the officials of the Roman Catholic Church had proclaimed that their major aim was to Christianize the Indians. A few hundred years earlier, European Crusaders had fought the Muslims to rescue the Holy Land for Christianity. Now the Spanish clergy determined to free the Indians from what the Europeans saw as false gods.

Priests and missionaries came to the colonies in large numbers. They worked tirelessly to convert the Indians. In the towns and cities, they built churches and cathedrals. In the countryside they set up missions around which they gathered the Indians. There the priests taught them the ways of European agriculture, carpentry, masonry, and other skills.

The mission system had faults. It imposed a European way of life on the natives and, in doing so, weakened or destroyed their native cultures. Nevertheless, the kindness and dedication of many of the missionaries stood in sharp contrast to the harsh exploitation practiced by other colonizers.

The most famous of the missionaries was Friar Bartolomé de Las Casas. Throughout his life he fought for freedom and justice for the Indians. He urged the Spanish Crown to forbid people from entering the New World who could not show that they were moved by love and believed in freedom. He and those who shared his faith and his convictions fought a losing battle.

Governing the Spanish colonies. At the peak of its power, Spain ruled the largest empire in the world since the time of ancient Rome. In the New World, it reached from the Atlantic to the Pacific and from California southward to the Strait of Magellan.

In law and in theory, all authority centered in the Spanish king. He ruled in the name of God and with the assistance of advisers.

In the New World, the king was represented by two **viceroys** — officials who ruled in the king's name. The viceroy located in Mexico City ruled New Spain — the Caribbean, Central America, Spanish North America, and part of South America. The viceroy located in Lima, Peru, ruled the rest of the Spanish colonies in South America. Lesser officials in descending order of rank served the viceroys. The smallest political unit in the empire was the town or village.

The system sometimes worked better in theory than in practice. Orders issued by the Crown and by the Church in Spain had to

SPANISH SETTLEMENTS AND MISSIONS

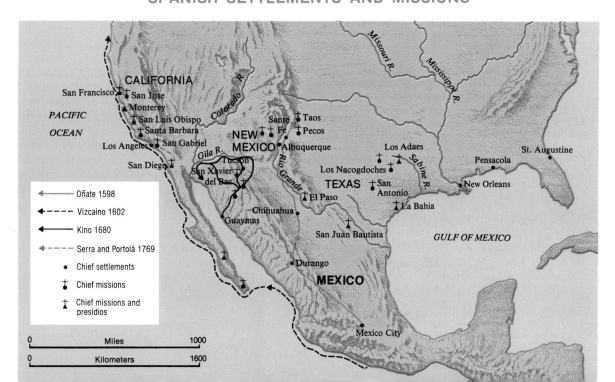

travel thousands of miles by sailing ship and then by horseback or by foot to reach the outposts of the empire. Officials at every level of the Church or government sometimes ignored the orders and laws they disliked. The system was also strained by conflicts between the high colonial officials born in Spain and the creoles, who held the lower offices. In spite of these weaknesses, the system succeeded in holding the vast empire together until well into the 1800's.

The crest of Spanish power. The gold and silver of the New World were carried to Spain in great treasure fleets. These fleets included treasure-laden galleons—huge vessels for their day, slow and clumsy, but heavily armed. Surrounding them in a great circle was a protecting convoy of smaller, swifter warships. Year after year these fleets moved the wealth of the New World to the Old.

Then, in 1580, Spain had another stroke of good fortune. King Philip II of Spain became ruler of Portugal. The two kingdoms of Spain and Portugal were united. For 60 years, until Portugal once again became an independent country, its thriving colonies were joined to those of Spain. Portugal's rich trade with India and the Spice Islands of the East Indies brought still greater wealth to Spain. Spanish power seemed unbeatable, yet that power would soon diminish.

The new wealth helped to ruin Spain. Instead of building industries to produce goods at home, the Spaniards used gold and silver from America to buy needed products from other countries. As a result, when the flow of gold and silver decreased, Spaniards could neither pay for the goods they needed nor produce such goods themselves.

Spain paid another price for its success. It became involved in wars and rebellions all over Europe. Enemies rose up, jealous of Spain's wealth and power and eager to destroy its supremacy.

SECTION SURVEY

IDENTIFY: colony, creoles, mestizos, mulattoes, encomienda, repartimiento, Bartolomé de Las Casas, viceroys, Philip II.

1. How was life in Spain's American colonies influenced by local conditions?
2. (a) Describe the system of Indian labor in the Spanish colonies before 1540. (b) How and why did this system change after 1540?
3. (a) Why did Spanish missionaries try to convert the Indians to Christianity? (b) How did the Indians both benefit and suffer from these attempts?
4. How were Spain's American colonies governed?
5. Map Study: Compare the map of Spanish settlements on page 19 with a map of the United States today (see pages 840–41). What states once held Spanish settlements, missions, or presidios?

5 England challenges Spain and gains a foothold in North America

English and Dutch sailors called "sea dogs" hastened Spain's decline by attacking the Spanish treasure ships and seizing their cargoes.

The sea dogs. John Hawkins was the first famous English sea dog. Today he would be called a pirate—which is just what the Spaniards called him—but the English people and Queen Elizabeth I looked upon him as a hero.

Hawkins began his career in the 1560's by transporting African slaves to the Spanish islands in the Caribbean. However, he soon discovered an easier—though riskier—way to make a fortune. He began to raid Spanish seaports and attack Spanish treasure ships.

The fame and fortune enjoyed by Hawkins inspired other daring adventurers to follow his example. Among the boldest was Francis Drake. In 1577 he left England with a fleet of swift, heavily armed vessels. He headed southward, sailed through the Strait of Magellan, and then turned to the north. Along the western coast of South America, he attacked the unsuspecting and unprotected Spanish ships carrying gold and silver from the mines of Peru. Then, his own vessels loaded with the riches stolen from Spain, he wintered on the coast of California. The following year he returned to England by way of the Pacific and Indian oceans. Like Magellan's expedition, Drake had circumnavigated the globe. On his return to England, Queen Elizabeth I welcomed Drake as a hero and knighted him on the deck of his ship.

A GREAT FLEET MEETS DISASTER

The lookouts stared uneasily into the darkness from the decks and rigging of the Spanish ships. The Armada was riding at anchor in the harbor at Calais, on the French coast. Not far up the coast lay Dunkirk, where the Armada was to meet a Spanish army and join it for the invasion of England. On this night, though, the rumor of a terrible English weapon swept through the Spanish ships. The weapon was the "hellburner," a huge floating bomb that could smash an entire fleet in a single blast.

All the preceding week, the 130 ships of the Armada had fought their way up the English Channel. The swifter, better-equipped English ships had hovered around the edges of the Spanish fleet, swooping down on stragglers and stinging the Spanish ships with broadsides from their longer-range cannon. Both sides lost a few hundred men and the Spanish lost several ships. Nevertheless, the Armada sailed on, always trying to draw the English ships into close combat, where the Spanish ships would have the advantage.

Now, at midnight near Calais, the English tried one more time to break the Spanish formation. Eight ships, their guns loaded, their holds stuffed with anything that would burn, were set afire. Picked crews stayed with the ships long enough to be sure they were headed toward the heart of the Spanish fleet.

As the flaming ships bore down on the Armada, their cannons exploding, the Spaniards panicked. These must be the "hellburners"! The Spanish ships cut their anchor cables and scattered into the English Channel. There the English fleet battered the Spanish ships. One by one, the Spanish ships began to sink or run aground. Sudden, fierce storms drove the disorganized fleet into the North Sea, ending the Spanish threat. When the last of the Armada limped home to Spain in the fall, half of the fleet was gone—and England was safe.

England and the Armada. Queen Elizabeth's honoring of Drake was a direct challenge to the Spaniards. King Philip II was quick to meet the challenge. He assembled a mighty fleet and army to invade and conquer England.

The Spanish Armada, the most powerful invasion force ever seen up to that time, sailed against England in the year 1588. The boldness and skill of English sailors, combined with a disastrous storm, broke the back of the Armada. Most of the ships never returned to Spain.

The year 1588 was, therefore, a turning point in history. With its powerful fleet destroyed and weakened by troubles at home, Spain began to decline in power. To be sure, for many years Spain remained strong in both the Old World and the New, but it was no longer the most feared nation in Europe.

While Spain weakened, England, France, and the Netherlands grew stronger. In time, the English Royal Navy won for England the proud title of "Mistress of the Seas." By the end of the 1500's, no nation could prevent England from building colonies in the New World. By this time many people in England were eager to do just that.

The failure of early colonies. Even before the defeat of the Spanish Armada, two English adventurers had tried to build colonies in America, but both had failed. In 1583 Sir Humphrey Gilbert sailed to plant a colony in Newfoundland, but he and his companions were lost in a storm. The following year Queen Elizabeth gave Sir Walter Raleigh permission to build colonies in an area that he named Virginia.

In 1587, after one expedition had ended in failure, Raleigh sent a second group of settlers. They landed on Roanoke Island off the coast of what is now North Carolina (see map, page 24). Unfortunately, the Spanish attempt to invade England in 1588 prevented Raleigh from sending supplies for three years. In 1591, when a relief expedition finally reached Roanoke, the settlers were gone. The fate of this "Lost Colony" remains a mystery to this day.

The defeat of the "Invincible Armada" is seen behind Queen Elizabeth in her *Armada Portrait*. England would most likely have been defeated by Spain without a shipbuilding program that was ordered by Elizabeth.

The famous charter of 1606. Nearly ten years passed before anyone in England attempted to build another colony in America. Then in 1606 King James I gave a single **charter**—an official grant of certain rights, powers, or privileges—to two groups. One group, based in Plymouth, England, was known as the Plymouth Company. The other, based in London, was known as the London Company.

Both of these business ventures were organized as **joint-stock companies.** Joint-stock companies were forerunners of modern corporations. A number of people bought shares of stock in the company. The money they invested would pay the expenses of the venture—for example, the founding of a colony. Any profit the company made from trade and development of the colony would be shared by the investors. In the back of many of the investors' minds was the tantalizing picture of the vast treasures that Spain had discovered in its New World colonies!

The charter granted to the Plymouth and London companies included a very important promise by King James. All people who served either company in the English colonies would retain their rights and privileges as English subjects. Among these rights were those set forth long ago in the *Magna Carta,* the Great Charter, written in 1215. In the words of the charter of 1606, the colonists would "have and enjoy all liberties, franchises, and immunities . . . as if they had been abiding and born within this our realm of England, or any other of our said dominions."

A poor start for Jamestown. It was Christmas time, 1606, when three small ships of the London Company left England and sailed out on the wintry sea. The London Company was sending more than 100 men to start a colony in America. From the beginning almost everything seemed to go wrong. The ships took a roundabout way to America, following Columbus's route. Many of the men died on the long voyage. When the colonists finally reached Virginia in the spring of 1607, they began to build a settlement named Jamestown in honor of the king (see map, page 24). They picked the poorest possible location—a low, wooded island in a river, which they called the James, near a marsh filled with malaria-carrying mosquitoes. The men did not take time to dig wells but instead drank the river water. Because they built only the flimsiest of shelters, they were drenched by rain in summer and half-frozen by cold when winter came.

The directors of the London Company back in England also made mistakes. Remembering Spain's rich discoveries, they insisted that the settlers hunt for gold. The settlers did so in vain, wasting valuable time that could have been spent in building houses and cultivating crops. To make matters worse, the settlers were not allowed to own anything, and they received, if they were fortunate, only as much food and clothing as they needed.

The worst mistake of all, perhaps, was the failure of the directors to send enough real workers to develop the resources of the settlement. The original group of settlers that sailed for Jamestown included only 12 laborers and skilled workers. The rest were "gentlemen"—in those days defined as men who had never done a day's work with their hands. Not a single settler was a farmer.

Difficult times at Jamestown. Not surprisingly, by the end of the first year, fewer than half of the settlers were still alive. They, too, might have perished had it not been for John Smith. Smith set himself up as the leader of the colony. He ordered the men to dig wells, build better shelters, clear the land, and plant corn and other crops.

John Smith was a harsh ruler. Every morning he marched the men into the fields to cultivate the crops or into the forest to cut wood. They grumbled and complained, but the rule was "No work, no food." The men worked. Thanks to John Smith and to the Indians, the colony survived. In Smith's own words, "The Indians brought us great store both of Corne and of bread ready made." Smith also raided Indian villages to get needed food for Jamestown.

When Smith returned to England, however, matters went from bad to worse. The winter of 1609–10 was terrible beyond belief. In later years the survivors called it "the starving time." When spring came, the half-starved colonists were prepared to abandon Jamestown. Fortunately, just at this time ships arrived from England bringing more settlers and fresh supplies, giving the colonists new hope.

In 1609 the king granted a new charter, which gave more land to the Virginia colony (see map, page 24).

Better times at Jamestown. Slowly, after 1610, the conditions began to improve. Much to everyone's surprise, tobacco saved the colony.

Europeans first learned about smoking tobacco from the Indians. By the early 1600's, the habit of smoking was spreading throughout England and the rest of Europe.

Until Jamestown was settled, the Caribbean islands supplied all the tobacco smoked by the English and other Europeans. Then around 1612 John Rolfe (who later married the Indian princess Pocahontas) learned how to grow and cure tobacco in Virginia. Within a few years, the colonists were shipping large quantities of this valuable product to England. By 1619 there were more than 1,000 colonists in Virginia, and most of them were making a living by raising tobacco.

Jamestown grew for other reasons, too. Among the new settlers were many skilled workers—carpenters, masons, blacksmiths, and farmers. Starting in 1618, each man who paid his own way to Jamestown was given 50 acres (20.2 hectares) of land. The colonists now were able to own their fields and sell their own products.

The start of self-government. In 1619 the London Company took another big step forward by giving the colonists the right to share in their own government.

July 30, 1619, is a memorable date in American history. On that date 22 **burgesses,** or representatives, two from each of the settled districts along the James River, met in Jamestown. Each of the burgesses had been elected by the land-owning voters of the district in which he lived. The **House of Burgesses,** as this law-making body was called, marked the first step toward representative government in the New World.

The growth of Virginia. The date 1619 is memorable for other reasons. In that year 20 Africans arrived in the colony. These newcomers were the first of countless thousands of men and women from Africa who would work with people from many other lands in building the English colonies.

In the early years many, if not all, of the Africans were regarded as servants, bound for a period of years to the master who paid a ship captain for transporting them to America. At the end of a term of service, some of the Africans acquired land and worked it for themselves. By the 1640's, however, Africans were also being brought to the English colonies as slaves.

SOURCES

MAGNA CARTA (1215)

No freeman shall be seized, imprisoned, dispossessed, outlawed, or exiled, or in any way destroyed, nor will we proceed against or prosecute him, except by the lawful judgment of his peers or by the law of the land.

To none will we sell, to none will we deny, to none will we delay, right or justice. . . .

Wherefore our will is, and we firmly command, that the Church of England be free, and that the men in our kingdom have and hold the aforesaid liberties, rights, and concessions well and in peace, freely and quietly, fully and entirely, to them and their heirs, of us and our heirs, in all things and places forever, as is aforesaid. . . .

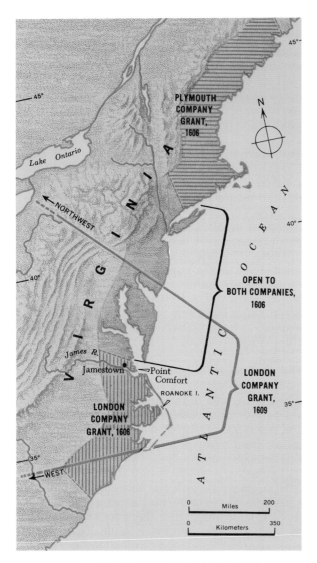

VIRGINIA LAND GRANTS

colony. On March 22, 1622, Indians attacked the outlying farmhouses, killed 347 settlers, including John Rolfe, and burned most of the buildings. The survivors struck back at the Indians. In one episode 250 Indians who had come seeking peace died after drinking poisoned wine at a toast-drinking ceremony. Earlier efforts by the Virginians and Indians to understand and tolerate each other were largely abandoned.

Virginia becomes a royal colony. In spite of the colony's growth, King James I decided that it had been badly managed. In 1624 he withdrew the charter from the London Company and took over the management of the colony. From then on, Virginia was a **royal colony**, ruled by the king of England and his ministers. The king now appointed the governor and gave the governor power to veto, or reject, any laws. He also appointed a council, consisting of 12 members, to assist the governor.

The government of Virginia was not as restrictive as that of the Spanish colonies to the south and west, where the king of Spain and his viceroys still held absolute power. King James I did not attempt to end the House of Burgesses. The House of Burgesses continued to make the laws, subject to the approval of the governor and of the king, and the settlers continued to elect the members of the House of Burgesses.

SECTION SURVEY

IDENTIFY: John Hawkins, Francis Drake, Elizabeth I, 1588, Roanoke Island, charter, Plymouth Company, London Company, John Smith, House of Burgesses, royal colony.

1. (a) How did England interfere with Spain's American colonies? (b) How did Spain act to stop English interference? (c) What was the result of Spain's action?

2. (a) What problems threatened to defeat the settlement at Jamestown? (b) How were these problems solved?

3. Name two important events that took place in Virginia in 1619. Why were these events important?

4. How did the government of Virginia change in 1624?

5. Source Study: Read the section of the Magna Carta on page 23. Who in the Virginia colony of the 1640's would not be protected by these guarantees?

In the early years, also, there were few women in Virginia. In 1619 the directors of the London Company sent 60 unmarried women to the colony. These women quickly married Jamestown settlers.

The directors of the London Company, encouraged by Virginia's growing prosperity, sent out hundreds of new settlers. Some of them started an ironworks on the James River. Others planted olive trees and laid out vineyards, but most of the newcomers cleared a piece of land and began to grow tobacco.

Then disaster struck. Nearby Indians had become alarmed at the rapid growth of the

Chapter Survey

Summary: Tracing the Main Ideas

The first Americans entered the New World by way of the Bering Strait so long ago that the date of their arrival is lost forever in the mists of history. Over a period of many thousands of years, they spread throughout the American continents. Long before the Europeans reached these shores, the Native Americans were firmly settled on the land. Some were farmers. Others were hunters or fishers. Some lived in tiny groups. Others, like the Aztecs, built great cities. In North, Central, and South America, these Native Americans developed many colorful and complex ways of life.

In the meantime, during the 1300's and 1400's, Europe was being swept into a new age by developments so far-reaching in their consequences that they were truly revolutionary. There was the revolution called the Renaissance, in which Europeans became increasingly curious about the world around them. There was the Commercial Revolution, in which traders from Spain, Portugal, England, and other nations facing the Atlantic discovered new all-water routes to Asia. There was the Geographic Revolution, in which European explorers traced the coastlines of Africa and discovered what to them was a new world across the Atlantic.

Portugal and Spain led the way in exploring and conquering the American continents. Soon England and the other European nations joined them. These nations also began to build colonies in the Americas.

Thus the door to a new age in human history was opened. Here in the Americas, the peoples of three different continents were brought together for the first time. Here, in what was truly a new world for all of them, they had to learn to share the land and build a common future.

This chapter has traced some of the beginnings of that experiment. The experiment itself is still unfinished.

Inquiring into History

1. The years between 1450 and 1624 can be termed a revolutionary period. (a) What is meant by this statement? (b) Why did revolutionary changes take place in Europe at that time? (c) Did these changes benefit all the people in Europe? Explain.
2. Compare Native Americans and Europeans in 1450 in terms of their (a) cultures, (b) attitudes toward the land, and (c) ways of making a living. How might these similarities and differences have affected Native Americans' and Europeans' attitudes toward one another?
3. Do you think that most people in London in 1600 realized that they were living in a revolutionary age? Why or why not?
4. In what ways are a colonist and an explorer alike? How are they different?
5. Explain each of the following terms in relation to European exploration and settlement of the New World: (a) freedom, (b) riches, (c) political rivalry between nations, (d) Christianity.
6. The seeds of troubled race relations in America were planted early in the history of European exploration and settlement of the New World. Comment. What evidence have you found in this chapter that would support this statement?

Relating Past to Present

1. Do nations today desire power for the same reasons that nations desired power in the 1500's? Explain.
2. Do you think the present is as revolutionary as the period of history discussed in this chapter? Explain.
3. The Renaissance resulted in part from increased contact between previously isolated cultures. What developments in modern times have led to greater contact between cultures? What have been some of the effects of such contacts?

Developing Social Science Skills

1. Using the map on pages 10–11, answer the following: (a) If you had been a trader in the Middle Ages, which of the medieval trade routes would you have used? Why? (b) Which parts of the world were known to Europeans in 1500? Which parts were still unexplored?
2. Prepare a timeline covering the period 1450 to 1624 for classroom display. Using drawings or pictures, show important events in Europe's exploration and settlement of the Americas.

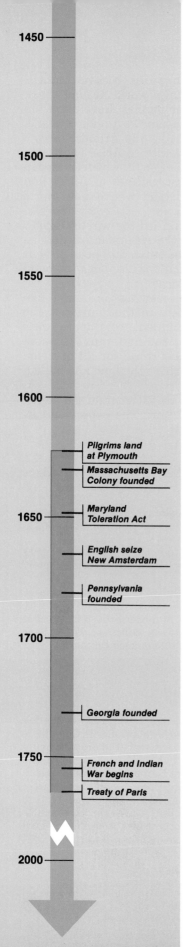

1450 —

1500 —

1550 —

1600 —

Pilgrims land
at Plymouth

Massachusetts Bay
Colony founded

1650 —
Maryland
Toleration Act

English seize
New Amsterdam

Pennsylvania
founded

1700 —

Georgia founded

1750 —
French and Indian
War begins

Treaty of Paris

2000 —

Chapter 2

The Growth of British Territory and Power

1620-1763

If Europe had been a happier place in the 1600's, the attractions of the New World would not have been so compelling. However, Europe was not a happy place for many people. For this reason, the lands across the sea became doubly attractive.

Men and women with little hope of ever making a better living in Europe looked to America with new hope. Those who thought about America pictured it as a rich yet thinly populated land waiting for the ax and the plow of new settlers. Ignoring the fact that the land was already occupied by the Indians, most Europeans regarded America as theirs for the taking. Here in the New World was opportunity, almost limitless, for men and women bold enough to seize it.

So they came — to Mexico, to Quebec, to Jamestown, to New England. They came in the greatest numbers from England to settle along the Atlantic seaboard. By 1733, when Georgia was founded, British settlers had planted colonies in the West Indies and had established thirteen colonies on the mainland. The boldest of the pioneers were pushing westward through the forest, clearing land, and building homes in the New World.

During these years, however, Great Britain's bitter rival France had grown stronger, not only in Europe but in all its far-flung colonies. In four different wars from 1689 to 1763, the two European powers battled for supremacy on the high seas and in Europe, Asia, and North America. Out of the final struggle, the British emerged victorious. One of their grand prizes was the huge French territory in North America.

THE CHAPTER IN OUTLINE

1. Pilgrims and Puritans search for a better life in North America.

2. English settlers build more colonies in New England.

3. People from several nations settle the Middle Colonies.

4. A distinctive way of life develops in the Southern Colonies.

5. New France grows and threatens the British colonies.

6. Great Britain smashes French power in North America.

1 Pilgrims and Puritans search for a better life in North America

Opportunity! That was the great attraction. Like a magnet, opportunity drew men and women from Europe to the New World. Even so, people would not have come in such great numbers if conditions in Europe had been better than they were.

Conflict over religion. During the 1500's and 1600's, Europe was torn by religious strife that broke out shortly after Columbus's voyages. At that time nearly everyone in Western Europe belonged to the Roman Catholic Church. The conflict began when some people began to question certain Church practices and beliefs. Martin Luther in Germany and John Calvin in Switzerland were two such people.

These religious leaders and people who shared their feelings broke away from the Roman Catholic Church and established Protestant, or "protesting," religious organizations. Roman Catholics called this movement the **Protestant Revolt.** Protestants called the same movement the **Reformation.** By whatever name, this religious conflict was not just a battle of words and ideas. Armies marched, wars were fought, and thousands of people died in battle or were burned at the stake in the name of religion.

England broke with the Roman Catholic Church in 1534. At that time King Henry VIII established the Church of England, sometimes called the **Anglican Church.** The king of England became the head of this Church. According to English law, all English citizens, regardless of religious beliefs, had to belong to the Anglican Church and contribute to its support.

The search for religious freedom. In spite of the law, many people in England objected to the Anglican Church. Roman Catholics insisted upon their right to worship as they always had. Among those who accepted the Protestant Reformation, some felt that the Anglican Church was too much like the Roman Catholic Church. They wanted to carry the Reformation further and to simplify or "purify" the Anglican Church. These people were known as **Puritans** or **Dissenters.**

One group defied the law by refusing to attend the Anglican Church or to pay taxes for its support. These people, who broke away and formed their own organizations, were called **Separatists.**

Life in England was grim for all of the protesting groups, Catholic and Protestant alike. They were persecuted by their neighbors, fined by the government, and sometimes sent to jail. Thousands left England, hoping to find greater religious freedom in the New World. As the years passed, other religious refugees—Catholics, Protestants, and Jews—also fled to America from many of the other European countries.

The Pilgrims, a group of English Separatists, settled for a time in the Netherlands in their search for religious freedom. Finally they decided to form their own colony in North America and in 1620 they set sail.

The search for political freedom. The desire to be free from political persecution also drove many English men and women—as well as other Europeans—to the New World. Political problems in England came to a head during the reign of James I, who ruled from 1603 to 1625. King James believed in the **divine right of kings.** That is, he insisted that a king was responsible for his actions only to God, not to any earthly power. This belief brought him into conflict with the **Parliament,** the law-making body of England.

The quarrel between king and Parliament became even more intense when Charles I became king. For eleven years, from 1629 to 1640, Charles I ruled without Parliament. Then in 1642 the country plunged into a civil war called the Puritan Revolution that lasted until 1649 when Charles I was beheaded. For the next eleven years, the country was ruled by a group of Puritans led by Oliver Cromwell until his death in 1658.

During this long period of political unrest, many people fled to the New World to escape persecution by an unsympathetic government.

Economic changes. Sweeping economic and social changes also contributed to the movement of people overseas and the development of the colonies.

During the 1500's and early 1600's, Europeans faced the problem of rising prices—a situation that today we call **inflation.** One reason for rising prices was the gold and silver that poured into Spain from its American colonies. Spain's increased wealth enabled it to buy more products from other countries. The growing Spanish demand for goods whose supply was limited enabled farmers and manufacturers in England and other countries to raise their prices. Then they in turn had more money to spend. Prices rose higher and higher.

Unhappily, inflation created hardships for many thousands of English families. When the price of wool, a raw material for cloth, rose, landowners realized that they could make more money raising sheep than renting their lands to tenant farmers. Many landowners evicted these farmers from their lands.

Some of the displaced tenants found work in the towns and cities. Others remained unemployed—homeless, hungry, and desperate. Still others were willing to risk anything to get a fresh start in life. America seemed to offer just such an opportunity. Many unemployed men

and women signed contracts called **indentures.** In these contracts they promised, in return for transportation to America, to work without wages for a period ranging from two to seven years. People who signed such contracts were called **indentured servants.**

Not all English people were hurt by the economic changes that were transforming the country. Certain groups prospered, among them merchants, landowners, traders, and manufacturers. As their fortunes grew, these people began to look for profitable ways to invest their money. Many bought shares in the new joint-stock companies. The more daring financed colonies in the New World. One such group of investors, a company of London merchants, financed the first permanent settlement in New England.

The Pilgrims arrive in New England. On November 11, 1620, after two months at sea, a small, storm-battered English vessel rounded the tip of Cape Cod and dropped its anchor in the quiet harbor of what is now Provincetown, Massachusetts. Why had those on board come to the New World? Not one of the 102 passengers on the *Mayflower* could have answered for all the others.

Many were Separatists who refused to follow the practices of the Church of England. Some of the Separatists had been living in the Netherlands, where the Dutch had allowed them to worship in their own way. However, they did not want their children to grow up speaking Dutch instead of English, living more like Dutch than English subjects. These Separatists were known as the **Pilgrims.**

Others came for personal reasons. John Alden, a young cooper, or barrelmaker, had helped to outfit the *Mayflower* for its long voyage. He decided to make the journey largely out of a spirit of adventure.

Whatever their reasons for coming, most passengers on board the *Mayflower* firmly intended to build new homes and a new way of life for themselves and their children in the New World.

The Mayflower Compact. The London Company had given the Pilgrims a grant of land south of the Hudson River, in what was then part of Virginia, but storms blew the *Mayflower* off course. As a result, the Pilgrims found themselves on the New England coast where they had no legal right to land or to set-

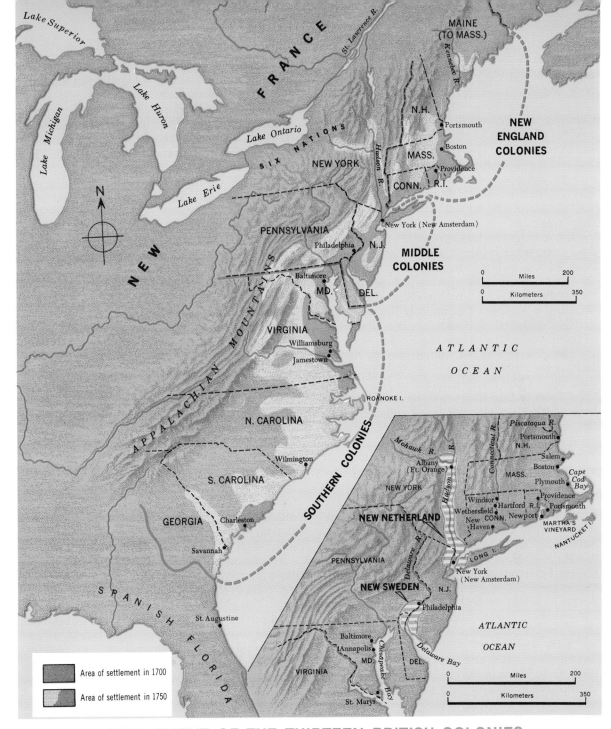

SETTLEMENT OF THE THIRTEEN BRITISH COLONIES

tle. Nor did the Pilgrims have any plans for governing the colony once they landed.

While the crew furled the sails, the Pilgrim leaders gathered in the cabin. There they wrote and signed the document that is now called the **Mayflower Compact.** In this compact, or agreement, they promised "all due sub-

mission and obedience" to the laws that they themselves would adopt.

The Mayflower Compact was intended to meet an emergency. It was not a plan of government. It did not pledge the Pilgrims to establish a democratic way of life. Nevertheless, this short document represented an important step along the road to self-government in the New World.

Landing at Plymouth. For more than a month, while the *Mayflower* swung at anchor in Provincetown harbor, a landing party looked for a place to settle. They finally chose a site on the southwestern shore of Cape Cod Bay. In earlier years English explorers had visited this place and named it Plymouth (see map, page 29).

If the Pilgrims had arrived at Plymouth a few years earlier, they would have found a busy Indian village surrounded by farmland. As it was, an epidemic had wiped out most of the Indians. Those who survived had abandoned the village. Fortunately for the Pilgrims, the cleared fields remained, and a brook of fresh water flowed into the harbor.

The Pilgrims sailed into Plymouth harbor late in December 1620 and as William Bradford, one of the leaders, noted in his journal, "The Twenty-fifth day began to erect the first house." Those who could work toiled through the cold, cheerless winter months. Many sickened and died. Before spring arrived, half the Pilgrims had perished, but not one settler left the colony in April when the *Mayflower* returned to England.

Those who were still alive might not have survived much longer had it not been for the friendship of the Indians. One in particular, named Squanto, taught the Pilgrims how to use the resources of forest, sea, and soil effectively. Perhaps most important, he brought them seeds of native plants—Indian corn, beans, squash, pumpkins, and others—and showed them how to plant, fertilize, and grow these crops in the cleared fields.

In the autumn of 1621, the Pilgrims celebrated their first year in the New World by setting aside several days for recreation and thanksgiving. Nearly 100 Indians and more than 30 settlers newly arrived from England joined them in the celebration.

Like the Indians who had settled the land before them, the Pilgrims lived mainly by farming, although fish and game remained for many years an important source of food. They also traded with the Indians and in turn with England. With money earned from the sale of furs and lumber, they settled their debt with the London Company. However, the colony never attracted many new settlers. Finally, under a charter that was granted in 1691, Plymouth became a part of its much larger neighbor to the north, the Massachusetts Bay Colony.

The roots of Massachusetts. The Puritans of Massachusetts Bay Colony also moved to the New World largely for religious reasons. Unlike the Pilgrims, however, the Massachusetts Bay settlers did not insist on a formal separation from the Church of England. However, they did want to change some of its practices, including Catholic-like ritual in worship and church rule by bishops. Charles I, who became king of England in 1625, refused to accept the Puritan proposals.

Finally, some prominent Puritan leaders, including John Winthrop and Sir Richard Saltonstall, decided to form a company and start a colony in America. In 1629 they secured a charter from the king and organized the Massachusetts Bay Company.

Fortunately for the Puritans, the charter did not name the place where the directors of the company would hold their annual meetings. The shrewd Puritan directors made the most of this oversight. They voted to take the charter and move to the New World, where they could run the company as they pleased. Thus Massachusetts became a **self-governing colony**, almost independent of the king and Parliament.

SOURCES

THE
MAYFLOWER
COMPACT
(1620)

We whose names are underwritten, ... having undertaken ... a voyage to plant the first colony in the northern parts of Virginia, do ... solemnly and mutually in the presence of God, and one of another, covenant and combine ourselves together into a civil body politic ... to enact, constitute, and frame such just and equal laws, ordinances, acts, constitutions, and offices from time to time, as shall be thought most meet and convenient for the general good of the colony unto which we promise all due submission and obedience....

This royal charter gave the power to rule to a few shareholders in the Massachusetts Bay Company. Once the settlers arrived, however, they too demanded a say in how the colony would be governed. Soon all male church members in good standing were given the right to vote.

The arrival of the Puritans. The Puritans began to arrive in Massachusetts during the summer of 1630 — nearly 1,000 men, women, and children aboard 17 ships. Unlike the Pilgrims, the Puritan settlers had ample supplies of food, clothing, and tools. Among the colonists were skilled carpenters, masons, blacksmiths, shipbuilders, and workers trained in other trades. Several colonists were graduates of Cambridge and Oxford, England's leading universities.

One by one the ships unloaded their cargoes, and the Puritans began to build villages along the coast north of Plymouth. Like the Pilgrims, they found many cleared fields abandoned by the Indians. Some Puritans settled at Shawmut, later called Boston (see map, page 29). Others settled in small villages near Boston. A few settled at Naumkeag (NOM-keg), later called Salem, which had been a fishing and trading village since 1626.

During the next few years, shipload after shipload of passengers from England arrived to join the early settlers. By the year 1640, more than 20,000 English men, women, and children were living in Massachusetts Bay Colony.

Government in Massachusetts. Religion and government were closely tied in Massachusetts Bay Colony. The Puritan leaders wanted to establish a "Bible Commonwealth," in which the Scriptures guided every aspect of life. To make sure the settlers remained true to Puritan beliefs, the leaders required everyone to attend the Puritan version of the Church of England. Local churches were formed by mutual agreement or "covenant," and the members of each church formed a congregation. In these churches the "saints," or true believers, chose the minister. This form of congregational church organization came to be known as "the New England way."

The Puritan leaders also kept all governmental power in the General Court, which was the lawmaking body of the Massachusetts Bay Company. Only owners of stock or shares in the company — a minority of the settlers — could belong to the General Court.

From the start some settlers rebelled against the rule of the leaders. They demanded the right to share in the government. John Winthrop — the first governor — and the other leaders were soon forced to loosen their control. They granted the right to vote to all Puritan men who were good church members. They also granted each town the right to send representatives to the General Court. Thus very early in its history, Massachusetts Bay Colony, like Jamestown, possessed a representative form of government.

SECTION SURVEY

IDENTIFY: Protestant Reformation, Puritans, Separatists, divine right of kings, indentured servants, 1620, 1630, self-governing colony, John Winthrop.

1. List three reasons why people from Europe came to America in the 1500's and 1600's.

2. Compare the conditions facing the Pilgrims, who arrived in New England in 1620, with those facing the Puritans, who arrived between 1630 and 1640. Which group was better prepared for life in the New World? Why?

3. What steps did the Puritans take to establish self-government in the Massachusetts Bay Colony?

4. Source Study: Read the Source on page 30. According to the Mayflower Compact, why were the Pilgrims entering into an agreement?

31

2 English settlers build more colonies in New England

Though political and economic concerns moved many Puritans to settle in the Massachusetts Bay Colony, the Puritans hoped above all to find greater religious freedom in the New World. Yet once settled in America, the Puritans dealt harshly with people who did not worship as they did. Such people were forced to leave Massachusetts.

Other colonists left Massachusetts to search for new and better farmland and greater opportunities. In this way, exiles and pioneers set up new colonies throughout New England.

The founding of Rhode Island. In 1631 a deeply religious young man named Roger Wil-

Anne Hutchinson had weekly discussion meetings in her Massachusetts home at which she expressed her religious views. Finally she and her family were forced to move and settled in neighboring Rhode Island.

liams arrived in Massachusetts Bay Colony. Before long he became pastor of a church in Salem.

The young pastor's ideas soon aroused the opposition of the leaders of the colony. Williams taught that the colonists had no right to their land unless they first bought it from the Indians. He also preached that political leaders could have no authority over religious matters. Political control or even influence over the church could only weaken or corrupt it. He also insisted that individuals had the right to worship God as their conscience directed them.

The Puritan leaders saw Williams and his ideas as threats to the Massachusetts Bay Colony. They decided to send him back to England. Williams escaped, however, fleeing for safety through the wilderness to his friends the Narragansett Indians. He lived with them for several months. Then, in 1636, with old friends from Massachusetts, he founded the village of Providence (see map, page 29) at the head of Narragansett Bay.

Another exile from Massachusetts was Anne Hutchinson, a forceful and courageous member of a prominent family and a devout student of the Bible. When she, too, challenged accepted Puritan beliefs, she was condemned as a heretic and exiled from Massachusetts. With her husband and some followers, she founded a settlement on Narragansett Bay. Other communities were also settled by men and women dissatisfied with the established order in Massachusetts Bay.

In 1644 Roger Williams secured a charter for the colony of Rhode Island. Under this charter the government of Rhode Island rested upon the **consent of the governed**. In this case, it rested upon the right of all adult males to vote and have a say in their government. The settlers were also guaranteed the right to worship as they wished.

A later charter, granted in 1663, deprived more than half of the adult males of their right to vote by requiring that a man had to own a certain amount of property before he could vote. This property qualification caused much discontent. Even with this restriction on the right to vote, however, Rhode Island offered more freedom to more settlers than any other colony in New England.

Westward to Connecticut. Connecticut, like Rhode Island, sprang from the older colony of Massachusetts, but the men and women who

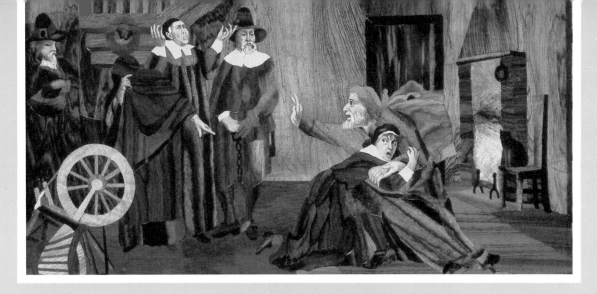

HYSTERIA IN SALEM

Sometimes the two girls moaned or cried out that they were being pierced with pins. Sometimes they stared blankly into space. The local doctor could find no physical cause. He said that the girls had been touched by "the evil hand." Everyone in the town of Salem, Massachusetts, knew what he meant: the devil was working evil powers through witches. In 1692 just about everyone in America and Europe believed in witchcraft.

Other teen-aged girls also began to suffer from the mysterious fits. Prayers did no good. As winter melted into spring, the girls named three "tormentors." One was a slave. The others were village women of shady reputation. Although the accused women firmly denied the charges, they were put in prison to await trial.

Throughout the spring, the girls accused more witches and wizards (male witches). Now their targets were respected figures in the community, including a former minister. Some of the accused broke under the strain and named others as witches. Some refused to be frightened. An old man named George Jacobs spoke up sharply: "I am as innocent as the child born tonight. You accuse me of being a wizard. You may as well accuse me of being a buzzard!" The individual responses made no difference. Terror walked the streets of Salem, and the jail filled.

The trials began in June. During the tense summer, 19 of the accused—Jacobs among them—were found guilty and hanged. One man, who refused to plead either guilty or innocent, was pressed to death with weights.

Then, in the fall of 1692, people came to their senses. The girls had begun accusing people who were obviously innocent, like the governor's wife. A terrible mistake had been made. The trials were stopped and those still in prison were released. One of the judges publicly confessed his errors, and the jurymen asked forgiveness. The hysteria was over, and nothing like it ever happened again in England's New World colonies.

---

settled Connecticut were not exiles. They were sturdy pioneers who moved out to the **frontier**, the territory just beyond the line of white settlements. They moved to this territory in search of greater opportunities for themselves and their families.

In 1635 the Reverend Thomas Hooker and nearly all the members of his church in Newtown (later Cambridge), Massachusetts, decided to move farther out. In the spring of 1636, they traveled southwest through the wilderness and settled finally at Hartford, Connecticut (see inset map, page 29).

Other pioneers started neighboring settlements. In 1639 the settlements of Windsor and Wethersfield joined with Hartford and adopted a plan of government. This plan was called the **Fundamental Orders of Connecticut.**

More than 20 years later, in 1662, after 15 towns had been settled, Connecticut secured a charter from King Charles II. This charter extended the Connecticut boundaries to include settlements along Long Island Sound, the most important of which was New Haven. The charter also gave the settlers the right to govern themselves, thus making legal a practice followed from the first days at Hartford. The charter of 1662 proved so satisfactory that the citizens of Connecticut kept it as their plan of government after winning their independence in the Revolutionary War.

New Hampshire and Maine. While Connecticut was growing into a self-governing colony, pioneers were pushing northward from Massachusetts into the area that later became the states of New Hampshire and Maine.

As early as 1622, John Mason and Sir Ferdinando Gorges (GOR·jez) had been granted the right to settle this territory. In 1629 the two men divided the land between them, ignoring the Abenaki and other Indian tribes living there. Gorges took the northern territory and Mason the southern. Both men tried to build colonies, but for a number of years, their settlements remained small trading posts.

By the late 1630's, growing numbers of settlers were moving northward from Massachusetts, building settlements on the land

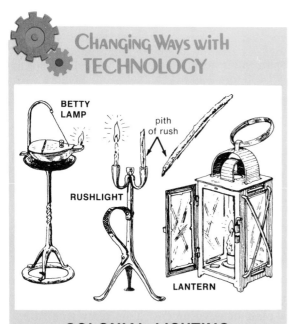

CHANGING WAYS WITH TECHNOLOGY

BETTY LAMP

RUSHLIGHT

pith of rush

LANTERN

COLONIAL LIGHTING

The betty lamp gave light from a burning wick floating in animal fat. A rushlight was made by soaking the pith of a dried rush in grease. Candles, often used in lanterns, were produced either by repeatedly dipping a wick into hot tallow or by pouring tallow into a mold containing a wick.

claimed by Mason and Gorges. The Puritan authorities watched this development with keen interest and decided to claim the territory for Massachusetts. By the 1650's Massachusetts had gained control over both New Hampshire and Maine. It held control over Maine until 1820, when Maine entered the Union as a separate state. New Hampshire broke away from Massachusetts in 1679, when it received a charter from Charles II and became a royal colony.

Indian resistance. By 1635 the most powerful Indians in southern New England, the Pequots (PEE·kwots), realized that the rapid expansion of white settlements threatened their way of life and even their survival. Mounting tension between the two races led to the Pequot War of 1635–37. The Puritans and the Pequots led a series of raids on each other's settlements. Then, in 1637, the Puritans set out to destroy the Pequots. They surrounded a fortified Pequot village and set fire to it. Nearly 400 Pequots—mostly women, children, and old men—burned to death or were shot as they tried to escape. Others were hunted down and killed or sold into slavery. Only a few Pequots survived the war. Smoldering hatred among the remaining Indian tribes toward the white settlers of New England was fanned by the contempt shown by most whites toward Indians.

The growing hatred led in 1675 to King Philip's War. Metacomet, a proud Wampanoag chief whom the Puritans called King Philip, made an alliance with the Narragansetts and other tribes. When Metacomet decided on war, the Indians at first outmaneuvered the settlers, burning or partly destroying several villages, but the tide soon turned. The Indians, outnumbered four to one, faced starvation. The final blow came when a Christianized, or "praying," Indian murdered Metacomet. The New England authorities executed other leaders of King Philip's War and sent scores of Indian warriors into slavery in the West Indies. The Indians who survived or evaded capture were bitter. In later wars between English and French settlers, these Indians allied themselves with the French and raided New England's frontier villages.

New England in the 1750's. Although the New England Colonies had their own governments and were completely independent of one another, they all developed along much the

The Indians houses

Their Streets

This picture is a detail from a drawing made in 1638 of the Puritan attack on a fortified Pequot Indian village. The Puritans and their Indian allies surrounded the walled village and set it on fire.

same lines. Most of the New England settlers shared similar origins, since the vast majority came from England and Scotland. However, black slaves could be found in all the New England Colonies.

By the 1750's towns and cities had been built around all the good harbors along the New England coast. Boston had a population of about 15,000. All of the seaport towns were busy, thriving places.

Inland the colonies were dotted with small villages. From the beginning New England farmers had settled together in small communities rather than on remote farmsteads. Religion, the Indians, and geography influenced the development of small communities in New England.

Many New England communities had been started by friends and neighbors who belonged to the same local church. Hartford, Connecticut, you will recall, began this way. These communities were carefully planned. The plan usually included a "common," or central area; land adjoining the common for houses; land for the church, or "meetinghouse"; and nearby farmland for each settler. Surplus land was held by the original settlers of a community for sale to newcomers.

Frontier communities in New England were also compact because of the need to be close to a fort or blockhouse, which the first settlers built as quickly as possible in case of conflicts with nearby Indians.

Geography also influenced the spread of small farming communities in New England. In many places the soil was shallow and filled with rocks and boulders, the land hilly and covered with forests. On such land settlers could rarely clear a large area or build a big farm. Thus New England communities remained small and compact.

SECTION SURVEY

IDENTIFY: New England Colonies, Roger Williams, consent of the governed, Anne Hutchinson, Fundamental Orders of Connecticut, Pequot War, Metacomet.

1. (a) For what reason did Roger Williams, Anne Hutchinson, and Thomas Hooker each leave Massachusetts Bay Colony to found neighboring colonies? (b) How do these reasons compare with the original reasons for settling Massachusetts Bay Colony?

2. The New England Colonies relied on England to make their laws; they practiced little self-government. Do you agree or disagree? Give evidence from the text.

3. Explain how religion, the Indians, and geography influenced the colonists in New England to form compact villages rather than scattered settlements.

4. Map Study:Locate the chief towns of New England on the maps on page 29. How did the location of these towns make them good places for settlement?

35

3 People from several nations settle the Middle Colonies

People from the Netherlands and Sweden established the first settlements in the Middle Colonies. In 1609 Henry Hudson, an English subject sailing in the service of the Dutch East India Company of the Netherlands, explored the river that ever since has carried his name.

During the next few years, Dutch traders made voyages to the Middle Atlantic coast. As a result of their favorable reports, Dutch investors secured a charter from the government of the Netherlands and organized the Dutch West India Company. The charter gave the company control over all trade and colonies in the New World. This charter conflicted with the charter granted by James I to the London Company, which founded Jamestown.

The rise of New Netherland. The Dutch West India Company acted promptly to secure the trade of the entire Middle Atlantic coast. The Dutch called the land they claimed New Netherland (see inset map, page 29). Around a fort that they built on the lower tip of Manhattan Island, they started the settlement of New Amsterdam, now New York City. They also established forts and trading posts on the Hudson River at the present site of Albany, on the Connecticut River near the present site of Hartford, and on the Delaware River below the present site of Philadelphia.

To attract settlers to New Netherland, the Dutch West India Company in 1629 offered huge land grants to all members who would settle at least 50 tenant farmers on their estates within four years. Some members who accepted the offer became **patroons,** or owners of large tracts of land.

Most Dutch citizens, who were free men and women, refused to go to America to live on a patroon's estate. As a result, the Dutch West India Company introduced slavery into the colony at an early date. Some of the patroons used African slaves to cultivate their estates.

In spite of attempts to attract settlers, New Netherland grew very slowly. Under the company's control, it never had more than 10,000 inhabitants. Most settlers lived in the trading center of New Amsterdam. These men and women came from many European nations as well as from Africa.

Another community outside New Amsterdam was founded and led by Lady Deborah Moody, a well-to-do landowner from Salem, Massachusetts. When she was warned in 1643 that her religious views did not agree with accepted Puritan beliefs, she and some followers received from Dutch officials a patent for a self-governing community on Long Island. She was an enlightened leader who paid the Indians for land, planned her community well, and maintained religious freedom.

At New Amsterdam in 1651, the crane and gallows near the wharf were used to weigh and display goods. Inside the fort were the city's largest buildings: the director's house and a stone church.

The Dutch threat to the English. From the beginning New Netherland posed a threat to the English colonies. From their base at New Amsterdam, Dutch warships could strike at English ships bound to and from New England and the Southern Colonies. From New Amsterdam the Dutch also controlled the trade of three vital river valleys—the Hudson, the Connecticut, and the Delaware (see inset map, page 29). The Dutch strengthened their control even further when, in 1655, they seized Fort Christina and other Swedish settlements on the banks of the Delaware River, an area known as New Sweden.

Especially valuable to the Dutch was their control of the Hudson River. From a point north of Fort Orange (now Albany), the Mohawk Valley provided a route through the mountains into the Great Lakes region and the interior of the continent. The powerful league of Iroquois Indians known as the Five Nations (later the Six Nations) dominated this route. These Indians were friendly with the Dutch. They brought furs from the Great Lakes region to the Dutch posts on the Hudson River. New England settlers also wanted to share in this rich fur trade, and they were angered by Dutch control of the Hudson River.

Conflict between English and Dutch. Dutch expansion eastward into Long Island and northward in the Connecticut Valley finally brought matters to a head. This expansion plunged the Dutch into conflict with traders and settlers who were pushing southward from New England. In 1643, fearing Dutch expansion and possible Indian raids, the colonies of Massachusetts, Plymouth, Connecticut, and New Haven united their military forces in the New England Confederation. A **confederation** is a political league in which members retain most of the power of government, while a central government body takes care of common problems, such as defense.

Not only New England was threatened. Dutch expansion also threatened Maryland and Virginia to the south. The showdown between the English and the Dutch came in 1664 when an English fleet sailed into the Hudson River. Overwhelmed by superior English strength, Peter Stuyvesant, the Dutch governor, hauled down his nation's flag at New Amsterdam. Without firing a shot, the English thus ended the rival colonial power of the Dutch in North America.

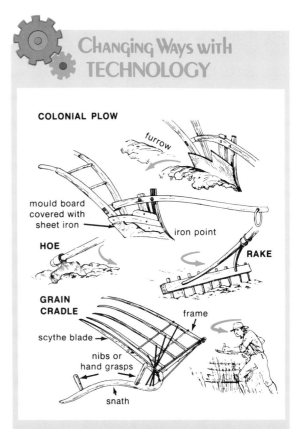

COLONIAL PLOW

furrow

mould board covered with sheet iron

iron point

HOE

RAKE

GRAIN CRADLE

frame

scythe blade

nibs or hand grasps

snath

COLONIAL FARM IMPLEMENTS

Before planting seed, farmers used a horse-drawn plow with an iron point to break the soil, and hoes and rakes to pulverize it. They harvested grain by swinging a grain cradle, which cut the grain stalks and collected them neatly on the frame. The stalks were then taken to the barn to be threshed.

New York and New Jersey. Charles II, then king of England, presented all the territory that had once been New Netherland to his younger brother James, the Duke of York. The gift included not only the land between the Connecticut and the Delaware rivers but also Long Island, the islands of Nantucket and Martha's Vineyard, and all of Maine east of the Kennebec River. This vast territory became the property of the 30-year-old Duke of York.

James gave the name New York to part of the former Dutch colony. Then he began to hand out generous gifts of land to his friends. The largest gift, New Jersey (see inset map, page 29), went to Lord John Berkeley and Sir George Carteret.

37

SOURCES _____

In 1664 New Jersey was almost all Indian land, with only a few hundred white settlers. Dutch and Swedish colonists had earlier built several small settlements along the Delaware River. Colonists from New England had settled a few villages in the north. Berkeley and Carteret tried to attract more settlers, but they had limited success. Finally, in 1702, after these lands had changed hands many times, the king of England claimed New Jersey as a royal colony.

New York under English rule. The colony of New York had a much different history from that of New Jersey. The young Duke of York took a keen interest in the former Dutch colony. As one of his first and wisest acts, he ordered his colonial officials to treat the Dutch with "humanity and gentleness." He allowed the Dutch to speak their own language and worship in their own churches.

However, in the long run the duke was a harsh ruler. He levied heavy taxes without the consent of the people, and, except for a brief two years (1683–85), he allowed them no voice in the government. Under his rule, also, many more Africans were brought as slaves to the colony. English interest in the slave trade continued to grow.

The Dominion of New England. In 1685 the Duke of York became King James II of England. A year later, in 1686, he combined New Jersey, New York, and the New England colonies under a form of government called the Dominion of New England. He then abolished representative government in these colonies and appointed Sir Edmund Andros as governor of the Dominion.

The Dominion lasted only about two years. Citizens in England resented the harsh rule of King James as much as the colonists resented his governor, Andros. English Protestants were also disturbed by James's conversion to Catholicism. In 1688 a revolt in England called the Glorious Revolution drove James II from the throne. In 1689 England adopted a **Bill of Rights.** This was a list of certain rights and liberties guaranteed to every citizen by the government (see Source, this page). Included in the Bill was the right to representative government. The new king and queen, William and Mary of Orange, restored the colonial charters, and the representative assemblies in the colonies regained their power.

Pennsylvania and Delaware. One of the most remarkable of the English founders of colonies in the New World was William Penn. Penn, the son of an admiral in the Royal Navy, seemed destined for the fashionable life of the English court. Then one day in 1667, at age 22, young Penn heard a Quaker sermon on the text "There is a faith that overcometh the world." The sermon converted Penn. He became a member of the Society of Friends, often called Quakers.

Penn's father was shocked and angered by his son's conversion. The Quakers at this time were one of the most disliked religious groups in England. Penn held firm to his new faith, and his father finally forgave him and left him a large inheritance.

Part of Penn's inheritance was a debt that Charles II had owed his father. In place of the money, the king in 1681 gave Penn a charter making him **proprietor,** or full owner, of a huge grant of land in the New World. On this land Penn founded a colony, which the king named Pennsylvania. Penn's power over this **proprietary colony** was almost as great as the king's power over a royal colony.

Pennsylvania had no coastline. Penn solved this problem in 1682 by obtaining another grant of land to the south on the west bank of

Delaware Bay. This new grant, long called "the lower counties," was later named Delaware (see map, page 29).

Pennsylvania, which Penn liked to call the "Holy Experiment," attracted many settlers. Penn wrote and published a pamphlet in English, French, Dutch, and German describing the colony he proposed to build. He invited honest, hardworking settlers to come, promising them religious toleration, representative government, and cheap land. Penn offered large amounts of free land, with the right to buy additional land, to settlers who established their homes in the colony.

Settlers poured in—Quakers from England, Wales, and Ireland; Scotch-Irish Presbyterians; Swiss and German Protestants; Catholics and Jews from many countries of Europe. Africans were also brought to the Pennsylvania colony, but the black population was never large. However, in 1700 slavery in Pennsylvania was legally recognized.

Penn kept his promises to the settlers. As for the Indians, chiefly the Delaware-Lenape, Penn treated them fairly and paid them for their land. When Penn returned to England, discontent developed. During his later years and after his death in 1718, Penn's wife Hannah helped to keep the colony intact and its people contented.

The Middle Colonies in the 1750's. By the 1750's the Middle Colonies—Pennsylvania, Delaware, New Jersey, and New York—were very prosperous. Philadelphia, on the Delaware River, was the largest, busiest seaport in America, and New York was almost as large.

From the beginning most people made their living by farming, but they did not settle in small farming villages, as in New England. Because of generally peaceful relations with the Indians, except on the western frontier, the newcomers scattered freely over the countryside. Since the soil was fertile and the land gently rolling, settlers cultivated fairly large farms. On these farms families produced not only food for their own needs but also a surplus for sale. Indeed, the Middle Colonies soon became known as the "breadbasket" of the New World. The harbors of Philadelphia and New York were always filled with ships loading flour, meat, and other foodstuffs for sale in England and the West Indies.

People in the Middle Colonies worked at a great variety of occupations. Although most

Edward Hicks was a Quaker preacher and a self-trained artist. He painted William Penn, proprietor of Pennsylvania, buying land from Indians. Penn's belief in fair dealing led to peaceful relations with the native tribes.

were farmers, these colonists were also famous for their iron mines, their shipyards, and their manufacture of glass, paper, and textiles. From the beginning these colonies were the home of people from many different nations with many different backgrounds—much more so than any of the other colonies.

SECTION SURVEY

IDENTIFY: Middle Colonies, 1609, Henry Hudson, patroons, Lady Deborah Moody, New England Confederation, Duke of York, 1664, proprietary colony, William Penn.

1. (a) Give two reasons for the conflict between the Dutch and English settlers in America. (b) How was the conflict resolved?

2. What guarantee in the English Bill of Rights was especially important to the English colonists?

3. Why was Pennsylvania colony a success?

4. How were the Middle Colonies different from the New England Colonies geographically and economically?

5. Map Study: Look at the maps on page 29. What geographic features seem to have influenced the settlement of New Sweden and New Netherland? How would these features have affected settlement?

4 A distinctive way of life develops in the Southern Colonies

Virginia, the first Southern Colony, started with the struggling settlement at Jamestown in 1607. By 1632, when Maryland was chartered, Virginia was firmly established.

The founding of Maryland. Sir George Calvert, the first Lord Baltimore, wanted to build a colony in the New World as a refuge for persecuted Catholics but with religious freedom for Protestants as well. After an unsuccessful effort in Newfoundland, he applied for a charter to more favorable land north of Virginia. He died just after the king granted a charter for Maryland. However, his son, the second Lord Baltimore, became proprietor and carried on the work dreamed of by his father. He remained in England but appointed able deputy governors to act for him.

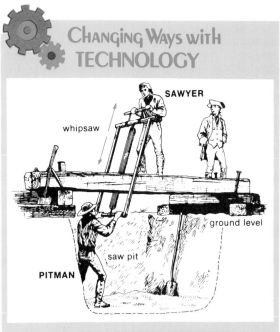

CHANGING WAYS WITH TECHNOLOGY

SAWYER

whipsaw

ground level

saw pit

PITMAN

SAWING SHIPS' TIMBER

Timber to be cut was squared and secured above the saw pit. The pitman pulled to produce the cutting stroke. The sawyer returned the blade and guided it along a chalk line while he walked across the board.

The first 200 Maryland settlers, including many Catholics, sailed up Chesapeake Bay in the late winter of 1634 and settled at St. Mary's (see inset map, page 29). Large plantations soon spread up and down the banks of Maryland's **tidewater rivers.**°

The deputy governor, Leonard Calvert, died in 1647. Margaret Brent, his business manager, demanded the right to vote and as a landowner to be seated in the colonial assembly. She was permitted to vote but was denied a seat in the assembly.

As more and more Protestants arrived, some of them threatened to take over the government by force from the Calverts. Soldiers from Virginia were brought in as protection. When these soldiers threatened to mutiny because they had not been paid, Brent took bold action to solve this crisis by selling some of the proprietor's cattle to pay the troops.

To help prevent another crisis of this sort, Lord Baltimore persuaded the legislative assembly to pass the Toleration Act of 1649. This act guaranteed freedom of worship to anyone who believed in Jesus Christ. This was not complete religious freedom, since only Christians could settle in Maryland. Nevertheless, the Toleration Act marked another important step in the continuing struggle for religious freedom.

Creation of the Carolinas. In 1663 Charles II gave a charter for Carolina to eight English nobles, who were to be the proprietors of the new colony. The grant included all the territory between Virginia and Spanish Florida and westward to the "south seas."

With the aid of John Locke, a young English philosopher, the proprietors drew up a plan of government for the new colony. The plan provided a rigid system of social classes from nobles at the top to ordinary colonists at the bottom. Slaves were not even included in this system, for Locke had written that "every freeman of Carolina shall have absolute power and authority over his Negro slaves, of whatever opinion or religion soever."

The proprietor's plan was doomed to failure, since it ignored actual conditions in the New World. From the first days, the colony began to divide into two parts (see map, page 29), as determined by geography and the desire of the settlers.

°**tidewater rivers:** rivers into which, at high tide, the ocean pushes salt water some distance upstream.

Because of its excellent harbor, Baltimore, named for the Maryland colony's founder, soon became a major colonial shipping center for tobacco and grain. What means of making a living can be seen in this painting from 1752?

Settling the Carolinas. The northern section, North Carolina, was settled mostly by pioneers from Virginia. They built cabins, cleared the land, grew their own food, and raised tobacco to sell in England. Many also earned their living from the pine forests, which supplied lumber and naval stores (tar, pitch, resin, turpentine)—products that were needed by England's Royal Navy and by its merchant ships.

The southern section, South Carolina, proved more attractive to settlers from overseas. Through the seaport of Charles Town (later shortened to Charleston), settlers of many different religious faiths from many different nations passed to new homes in the New World. There were Anglicans and other religious groups from England; Scots in considerable numbers; French Huguenots (HYOO·guh·nahts), who were Protestants fleeing persecution in France; Germans; Jews from various parts of Europe; emigrants from the West Indies; and, as the years passed, growing numbers of African slaves. Many settlers built large, prosperous rice plantations on the rich coastal lowlands. Others earned their living from the production of naval stores from the pine forests and from the fur trade on the frontier. After indigo (a plant used to make dye) was grown successfully by Eliza Lucas, it became another important crop.

The early colonists of North and South Carolina waged a continuing struggle for a larger voice in the government. Finally, in 1729 the proprietors sold their rights to the king. Both North Carolina and South Carolina then became royal colonies with their own representative assemblies.

The founding of Georgia. In 1732, three years after North and South Carolina became royal colonies, the king granted a charter for Georgia (see map, page 29), home of the Creek, Cherokee, and Choctaw Indians. The British° government hoped that Georgia would serve as a "buffer" against attacks from Spanish Florida, but the compelling motive for starting Georgia had little to do with politics or business. The colony was started in order to provide a place where debtors released from English prisons could start a new life.

James Oglethorpe, the leader of Georgia's founders, arrived in the colony in 1733 with the first debtors. They settled at Savannah, each person receiving 50 free acres (20.2 hectares) of land. Slavery and the sale of rum were not allowed in the colony.

Oglethorpe and the other founders tried to recruit settlers, offering liberal grants of land to all who came. Only a small number of immigrants arrived, among them New Englanders, Germans, and Scots. Some settlers de-

°**British:** In 1707 the separate countries of England and Scotland were united into a single country called Great Britain. Throughout the colonial period, however, the words "England" and "English" are often used to mean "Great Britain" and "British."

On southern plantations, such as this one in South Carolina, the slave quarters were called the "street." The "street" was set up like a small village.

manded that slavery be allowed in the colony. Finally, in 1750 the founders reluctantly agreed to make slavery legal in Georgia. In 1752 the founders turned Georgia over to the king as a royal colony.

The Southern Colonies in the 1750's. By the 1750's the Southern Colonies — Maryland, Virginia, North and South Carolina, and Georgia — had all developed their own special ways of life. The great tobacco plantations in Maryland, Virginia, and North Carolina covered the rich lands along the tidewater rivers near the coast and extended inland on the Atlantic coastal plains. Farther south the luxurious homes of wealthy rice planters were scattered over the coastal lowlands. The only large towns in the Southern Colonies at this time were Charleston, with a population of 10,000, and Baltimore, with 5,000.

A distinguishing feature of the Southern Colonies was slavery. The tobacco and rice plantations required large numbers of workers. With plenty of land available on the frontier, few settlers were willing to work for wages on the plantations. As a result, the planters relied more and more upon black slave labor. By the 1750's the slavery system was firmly fixed in all the Southern Colonies.

If slaves could have been used profitably on the farms of the Middle Colonies or on the smaller farms of New England, slavery might have become more widespread in those colonies as well. In colonial times only a very small minority of people objected to slavery as such. Slavery was either profitable or unprofitable. In the Southern Colonies, it was profitable, and slaves were used in ever-increasing numbers.

Although the planters set the pattern of southern life, most southern people lived in the back country — the inland areas that lay "back" from the seacoast. These men and women — pioneers and small farmers — lived much like the people in rural New England and the Middle Colonies.

SECTION SURVEY

IDENTIFY: Southern Colonies, Lord Baltimore, Margaret Brent, Toleration Act of 1649, James Oglethorpe, 1732.

1. For what purpose did Lord Baltimore want to start the colony of Maryland?

2. Name three differences in the way that North Carolina and South Carolina were settled.

3. What were the two motives for establishing the colony of Georgia?

4. What were the two chief crops grown in the Southern Colonies? In what regions were they grown?

5. What was the most important difference between the labor force in the South and in the North? What created this difference?

5 New France grows and threatens the British colonies

The vast colonial territories claimed by Great Britain, France, Portugal, Spain, and the Netherlands spread slowly across the map of the world. These colonial areas were prizes for which each of the contending nations was ready to sacrifice blood and effort. Thus, during most of the 1600's and 1700's, the people of European nations were engaged in almost constant warfare.

Colonial rivalry in the New World. In the New World, the British flag waved proudly over islands in the Caribbean and over thirteen colonies along the Atlantic seaboard. Warships of the Royal Navy stood guard over the nearly 1,500,000 men, women, and children who lived in the seaboard colonies. The warships were needed, for Great Britain had powerful enemies.

To the south were the Spaniards. They had built a series of forts and missions that stretched from Florida to California along what is now the southern border of the United States. During the 1600's and the 1700's, however, Spain's power had been declining. By the mid-1700's the British did not think of Spain as a major threat.

To the north and west was New France, the vast territory claimed by France. This was a different story. The French had been strengthening their naval and military power in North America, and their armed forces presented a growing threat to the British colonies.

French claims in North America. French claims in North America were based on the early voyages of Verrazano and Cartier (see page 12). The French, like other colonizing nations, simply ignored the claims of Indians to lands on which they and their ancestors had long lived.

The first French explorer to establish settlements in the New World was Samuel de Champlain, who made his first voyage there in 1603. Before he died in 1635, he had built a settlement at Quebec, won for France the friendship of the powerful Algonquin Indians, and explored most of the St. Lawrence Valley (see map, page 44).

Other French explorers pushed up the St. Lawrence River into the Great Lakes and the heart of the vast North American wilderness. Among these daring explorers were Marquette (mar·KET), Joliet (joh·lee·ET), and La Salle.

In 1673 Father Marquette, a Jesuit missionary, and Joliet, a fur trader, crossed the Great Lakes and paddled down the Mississippi River as far as the mouth of the Arkansas River. Eight years later, in 1681–82, La Salle followed the same route to the Gulf of Mexico (see map, page 44). He claimed the entire Mississippi Valley for France, calling it Louisiana in honor of King Louis XIV. Later, in 1718, the French built New Orleans near the mouth of the Mississippi River.

By the early 1700's, then, the French controlled the two major gateways into the heart of North America. New Orleans gave them control of the southern entrance to the entire Mississippi Valley. Quebec and Montreal gave them control of the St. Lawrence River.

Combined with the Great Lakes, the St. Lawrence River provided a natural water route. By paddling and by carrying their canoes short distances overland, French explorers and traders could bring their canoes to the Mississippi or one of the rivers flowing into it. From there they could travel to the entire region between the Appalachians and the Rockies.

French settlements. The settled area of New France consisted largely of farmhouses stretching along the banks of the St. Lawrence from Quebec to Montreal and up the Richelieu (RISH·eh·loo) River. Most of the settlers came from France, but some slaves were brought from Africa to work on the farms and to provide a labor force for New Orleans. Africans also came to New France as members of the French expeditions that explored the Great Lakes and the Mississippi Valley.

The fur trade. Beyond the settled areas of New France lay an immense wilderness inhabited by Indians with well-established patterns of hunting and farming. In this vast area, the most easily exploited resource was furs. Furs drew adventurous French pioneers into the forests. Courageous *coureurs de bois* (koo·RUR deh BWAH), or runners-of-the-woods, paddled their canoes into the interior and wintered

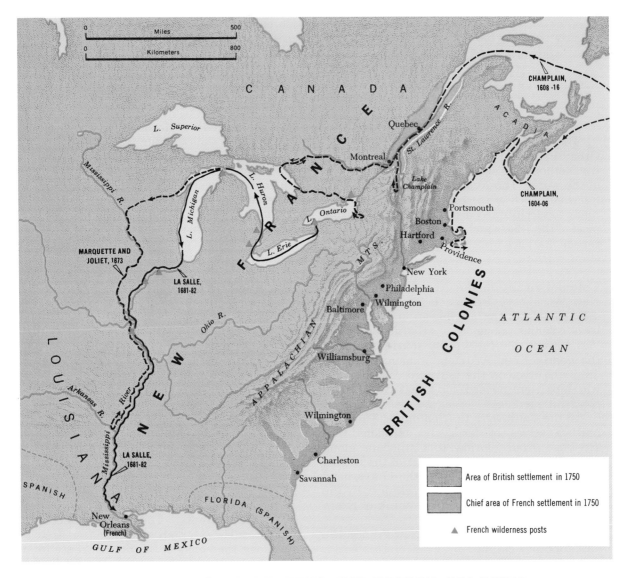

NEW FRANCE THREATENS THE BRITISH COLONIES

with friendly Indian tribes. Then they returned in the spring with their Indian allies to the trading center at Montreal.

For several weeks active trading took place on the river below the city. Indians exchanged their furs for European goods—blankets, cloaks, cloth, spoons, knives, hatchets, guns, powder, and liquor. When the trading finally came to an end, the Indians and the *coureurs de bois* loaded their canoes and returned to the wilderness. The French ships then began their long voyage back to Europe with the cargoes of precious furs.

The profits of the fur trade were far greater for the French than for the Indians. The fur trade also disrupted age-old patterns of Indian life. Able-bodied Indians left their villages for long periods of time to hunt, to trap, and to trade. As the years passed, the Indians depended more and more upon the fur trade for their livelihood and less upon hunting and farming. Since the different tribes also became dependent upon one or another of the rival colonial powers, they were frequently drawn into Europe's colonial wars. Moreover, competition among the Indians for the best hunting and

44

trapping grounds became a source of growing friction and often led to war among the Indians themselves.

The weakness of New France. On the map New France covered an immense area, including Canada and the entire Mississippi Valley (see map, page 44), but the map was misleading. Except for Quebec and Montreal, the settled areas of Canada consisted largely of farmhouses strung along the St. Lawrence like beads on a string. Beyond the settled areas, a chain of small forts and trading posts stretched in a long arc through the Great Lakes and the upper Mississippi Valley. Only the Indians and the *coureurs de bois* inhabited the vast forests of New France.

The fur trade proved to be both a strength and a weakness for New France. The fur trade provided a living for thousands—for manufacturers and workers back in France, for shipowners and merchants, and for the *coureurs de bois* and their Indian allies. However, the carefree life of the *coureur de bois* attracted the young and strong into the forests rather than to the settled areas. As a result, the French never strengthened the settled areas along the St. Lawrence River.

French and British power. By 1750 the British had certain advantages over their French rivals to the north. The British colonies were well established. British colonists outnumbered French colonists by 23 to 1. Most of the British settlements were confined to a fairly narrow belt of land along the Atlantic coast, whereas the settlements, forts, and trading posts of the French were scattered over half the continent.

However, the French also enjoyed advantages. New France, united under a single government, could act quickly when action was necessary. In contrast, the separate governments of the British colonies seldom acted together even when danger threatened.

The French also had the support of a great many more Indians than did the British. French fur traders did not destroy forests and drive away game as did British settlers, who cleared the land for farming. However, members of the powerful Six Nations refused to ally themselves with the French.

Finally, France in the early 1750's was the most powerful nation in Europe. French armies were second to none. French naval forces competed with the British for control of the seas.

In New France, the owners of huge estates along the St. Lawrence River rented their lands to settlers who were called *habitants*. These *habitants* were considered part of the estate. This is a typical *habitant* farm.

Between 1689 and 1748, a fierce rivalry kept France and Great Britain at war with each other off and on for a total of nearly 25 years. The two nations fought for control of the seas and possession of distant colonies. In each war North America was only one of several prizes the British and French hoped to win. Armed forces of the two powers clashed on the seas and in Europe and Asia as well as North America, but none of the wars proved decisive.

In 1754 war clouds gathered once again. The two European nations began still another test of strength. The outcome of this struggle was to determine the destiny of the North American continent.

SECTION SURVEY

IDENTIFY: Samuel de Champlain, Marquette, Joliet, La Salle, *coureurs de bois.*

1. What was the chief reason that the French settled in the New World?
2. The fur trade proved to be both a strength and a weakness for New France. Explain.
3. Compare French and British power in America in 1750. What advantages did the British colonies have? What advantages did New France have?
4. Map Study: Locate New Orleans, Quebec, and Montreal on the map on page 44. Why can these French settlements be called "gateways" to North America?

6 Great Britain smashes French power in North America

The decisive worldwide struggle between the British and the French broke out in 1754. The British colonies in North America were involved when the expanding empires of France and Great Britain clashed in the land beyond the Appalachian Mountains. The conflict was called the French and Indian War in America, or the Seven Years' War in Europe.

The first clash in America. Wealthy Virginians caused the first of a series of events that led to the French and Indian War. These colonists formed a company and secured from the British king a huge grant of land in the upper Ohio Valley. They intended to make a profit by dividing the land into small farms and selling the farms to settlers.

The French were alarmed by the Virginians' real estate activities on territory which the French claimed as their own. In 1753 the French started constructing a chain of forts connecting Lake Erie with the Ohio River (see map, page 47).

The governor of Virginia sent George Washington, a 21-year-old surveyor from Virginia, to the Ohio Valley to warn the French that the land belonged to the British. (The land had been originally granted to Virginia by the charter of 1609. See map, page 24.) The French ignored Washington's warning.

The following year Washington, now a major, returned to the Ohio Valley. Leading a company of **militia,** civilians who trained as soldiers to fight in times of emergency, he built Fort Necessity a few miles south of the French Fort Duquesne (doo·KAYN). Fort Duquesne itself was situated at the strategic point where the Monongahela and Allegheny rivers join to form the Ohio River—the present site of Pittsburgh (see map, page 47). A small force of French and Indians defeated Washington and his troops in a battle fought at Fort Necessity on July 4, 1754.

Failure of the colonies to unite. The French were now entrenched along a line of scattered points from the Great Lakes south to the Ohio River, with outposts in the Allegheny Mountains. The entire northern frontier of the British colonies was open to attack from the Indian allies of the French. Moreover, the western country was closed to British traders and British settlers.

At this critical moment, delegates from seven British colonies met at Albany, New York, to discuss united action against the French and their Indian allies. They were joined by Indian representatives from the Six Nations. The Six Nations, also known as the Iroquois Confederation, occupied most of what is now central New York. Armed first by the Dutch and then by the English, they were the most powerful Indians in the eastern part of North America. They were also longstanding enemies of the French and of the Indians friendly to the French. The British colonists welcomed the Iroquois representatives to the Albany Congress.

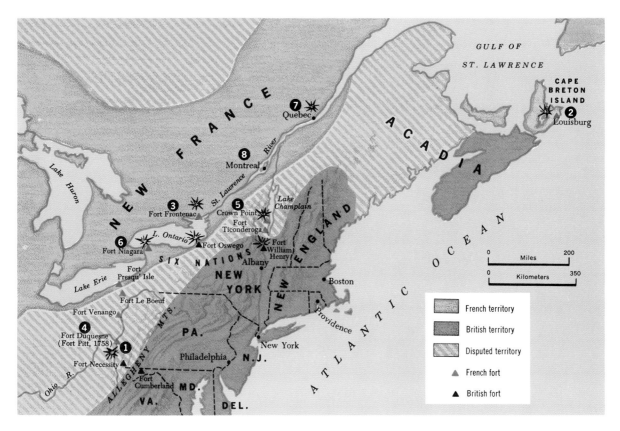

FRENCH AND INDIAN WAR

The example of the Iroquois Confederation had an influence on Benjamin Franklin and his efforts to promote an intercolonial union. At the Albany Congress of 1754, he proposed that the British colonies in America unite in a permanent union for defense. Franklin's Albany Plan of Union was rejected by the colonists because each colony did not want to give up its right to act independently. The colonists also turned down a somewhat similar proposal by the British government. Although rejected, these proposals forced many colonists to think about the advantages of united action.

British disasters. Only a few months after the failure of the Albany Congress, General Edward Braddock arrived from England with regiments of British regulars, or "redcoats." British redcoats and Virginia militia then advanced through the wilderness toward the French at Fort Duquesne. They were ambushed when they had almost reached their goal (see number 1 on map, this page).

Braddock and most of his officers were killed. More than half his soldiers were killed, wounded, or captured. The disaster would have been even greater if George Washington and the Virginia militia had not fought back, in ways common to Indian warfare, from the cover of rocks and trees.

Braddock's disaster left the long frontier of Pennsylvania, Maryland, and Virginia open to Indian attack. Matters got even worse when British expeditions against the French forts at Niagara and Crown Point also failed and the French captured Fort Oswego and Fort William Henry (see map, this page).

British success under Pitt. Fortunately for Great Britain, William Pitt became the leader of the British government in the autumn of 1756. Pitt was determined to win complete victory for British arms. He was a strong leader, a man of enormous energy and supreme self-confidence. "I know that I can save England and that nobody else can," he reportedly said.

On September 8, 1755, the French and their Indian allies attacked an English and Mohawk camp on the shores of Lake George in upstate New York. The English force beat back the French force in fierce fighting.

Under Pitt's leadership the British empire rallied. Pitt fired incompetent officials and replaced them with able leaders. He gave colonial officers rank equal to those in the king's own troops. He also strengthened the British navy and moved additional troops to America. Everywhere throughout the British empire, Pitt took the offensive, and his efforts soon met with success.

British victories. In 1758 a British naval and land force under General Jeffrey Amherst captured Louisburg, a powerfully armed French fort on Cape Breton Island (see number 2 on map, page 47). The fall of Louisburg doomed New France. The victory gave the British navy a base for cutting off French reinforcements and supplies to America. During the same year, the British also captured Fort Frontenac on Lake Ontario (see number 3 on map, page 47). This victory weakened French lines of communication to Fort Duquesne. The French promptly abandoned Fort Duquesne, and the British then occupied it without a struggle (see number 4 on map, page 47). They renamed it Fort Pitt, in honor of their great leader.

In 1759 the British won even more sweeping victories. Amherst forced the French to retreat from their forts at Crown Point and Ticonderoga (see number 5 on map, page 47). Some of Amherst's forces seized Fort Niagara (see number 6 on map, page 47). This latter victory forced the French to abandon their forts in the upper Ohio Valley. In September 1759 the British captured Quebec (see number 7 on map, page 47). The battle of Quebec was a magnificent victory for the British. In the same year, Great Britain also won significant victories in Europe, in the Mediterranean, and in India.

The following year, 1760, after only slight resistance, the French surrendered Montreal to General Amherst (see number 8 on map, page 47). In 1762 Spain, fearful of British victory, entered the worldwide conflict on the side of France, but Spanish aid was too little and too late. The British kept winning all over the world. They completed their string of victories by seizing the Philippine Islands and Cuba from Spain, the West Indies sugar islands of Martinique (mar·tih·NEEK) and Guadeloupe (gwah·duh·LOOP) from France, and French territory in India.

The spoils of war. Out of this worldwide struggle, the British emerged victorious. Meeting in Paris, representatives of Great Britain, France, and Spain drew up the Treaty of Paris in 1763. Disregarding the claims and interests of native peoples of these lands, Great Britain secured most of India and all of North America to the east of the Mississippi River, except for New Orleans.

France, on the other hand, lost nearly all of its possessions in India and in America. The British allowed France to keep only four small islands in the New World. Two of these were the sugar islands of Guadeloupe and Martinique in the Caribbean.

As an ally of France, Spain was forced to give Florida to Great Britain. To make up for this loss, however, the French gave the Spaniards New Orleans and the vast territory of Louisiana west of the Mississippi River (see map, page 49). The British returned Cuba and the Philippine Islands to Spain.

How war influenced the colonies. The American colonists as well as Great Britain profited from the long struggle. The colonial militias gained valuable new experience in methods of warfare. Their experience in fighting Indians was broadened by joint combat with the British against powerful French forces.

Although the colonial militias welcomed all able-bodied men, they were at first reluctant to accept black men. Most colonists did not like the idea of supplying blacks with guns, but shortages of troops finally forced them to accept black men into the militia.

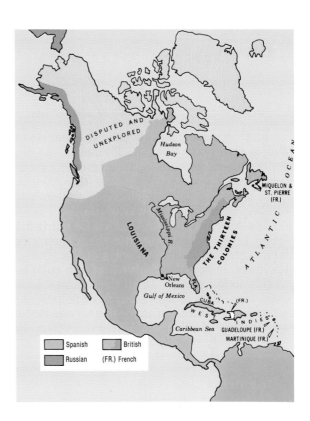

NORTH AMERICA IN 1763

The long struggle also taught the colonists that only by cooperating with one another could they hope to defend themselves. Yet colonial Americans in 1763 were still far from united.

SECTION SURVEY

IDENTIFY: 1754, militia, Six Nations, Albany Plan of Union, William Pitt, Jeffrey Amherst, Treaty of Paris of 1763.

1. Summarize the chain of events that led to the French and Indian War.

2. Why did the British colonies in America reject the Albany Plan of Union?

3. (a) In what year did success in the French and Indian War begin to shift from the French to the British side? (b) What event in Great Britain helped bring about this shift?

4. (a) Summarize the terms of the Treaty of Paris of 1763. (b) What was the significance of this treaty?

5. Map Study: Locate Louisburg on the map on page 47. Why was this fort important to both sides in the French and Indian War?

Chapter Survey

Summary: Tracing the Main Ideas

English settlement began at Jamestown and, a few years later, at Plymouth. As the years passed, settlers came in growing numbers. Every good harbor along the Atlantic coast became a landing place for settlers and the beginning of a new way of life.

The settlers came to America for many different reasons, bringing with them their own languages and their own ways of life. One of the most impressive features of the colonial world was its variety. In all the colonies, however, regardless of backgrounds or beliefs, the settlers shared a burning desire to win larger opportunities in the New World than could be found in the countries they had left behind. These were the colonial roots of the American nation—and of "the American way of life."

Unhappily, there were also disturbing chapters in the story of colonial development. The blacks, most of them slaves, helped to build America but were denied their share of its opportunities. The Indians, the original settlers, were ruthlessly driven from their homelands and pushed steadily westward. Even the British colonists themselves lived in the ever-present fear of New France, their colonial rival to the north and west. During more than half a century, the French threatened to conquer the British colonies and win for France control of the entire North American continent. The victory of Great Britain in the Seven Years' War finally shattered the French dream of an empire in North America and finally ended the threat to the British colonies along the Atlantic seaboard.

Inquiring into History

1. How did most colonists regard the Indians? What were some consequences of this attitude? How did Indians who had encountered colonists regard them? What were some consequences of this attitude?
2. How did geography influence these aspects of life in the New England, Middle, and Southern Colonies: (a) patterns of land use and settlement, (b) economic development?
3. Why is agriculture considered an essential occupation for any new settlement of people?
4. The four statements below follow each other in cause and effect. Explain the cause-and-effect relationship in each statement.
   (a) Nations desiring power (cause) needed to possess colonies (effect).
   (b) Nations possessing colonies (cause) needed large armies and navies (effect).
   (c) Large armies and navies (cause) required large military budgets (effect).
   (d) Large military budgets (cause) led to. . . .
   What effects can you name here?
5. By 1750 there were fewer blacks in New France and the New England and Middle Colonies than in the Southern Colonies. Why?
6. Relate the conflicts among the powerful European nations for supremacy in Europe with their conflicts on the North American continent.

Relating Past to Present

1. Explain how life in the colonies was characterized by undemocratic as well as democratic elements. Is this true of American society today? Explain.
2. Power struggles between nations today are different from those between nations in the 1600's and 1700's. How? Why?

Developing Social Science Skills

1. Using the maps in Chapters 1 and 2, answer the following questions: (a) What natural features formed protective barriers for the colonial settlers? (b) How did these natural barriers eventually promote a feeling of unity among the colonists? (c) How did inland waterways and oceans influence the location of early settlements?
2. Read the excerpt from the Mayflower Compact on page 30. (a) Why can this document be considered an important step toward self-government? (b) Compare this excerpt from the actual document (a primary source) with your textbook's description of it (a secondary source). How can each source be helpful to you in understanding the Mayflower Compact? What disadvantages might a primary source have? a secondary source?
3. Prepare a chart with the headings "New England Colonies," "Middle Colonies," and "Southern Colonies." In each column, fill in information about (a) religious beliefs, (b) attitudes toward slavery, (c) type of government, and (d) reasons for settlement. Based on the chart you have prepared, do you think the colonies were basically similar or different? Explain.

Chapter 3

The Start of an American Way of Life

Changing Ways of American Life

1607–1763

Benjamin Franklin became Postmaster General of the British colonies in North America in 1753. Franklin required careful accounts from everyone handling the mails. He started new postal routes, some using horse-drawn stagecoaches instead of postriders. His ideas and suggestions provided better mail service and helped unite the colonies.

In 1763 Franklin made a trip of more than 1,600 miles (more than 2,500 kilometers), traveling over nearly every post road. On his travels Franklin saw many colonists and learned how they were living and what they were thinking. He visited southern planters, lived with frontier townspeople, stopped overnight with farmers, and talked with frontier settlers. Franklin also saw two groups who lived in colonial America but were excluded from it—Africans, most of whom were slaves, and Indians.

In this chapter you are going to look at each of these groups of people. You will see, as Franklin saw, that they were sharply divided on many matters. You will also see, as Franklin saw, that by the 1760's, from one end of the British colonies to the other, many people were beginning to think of themselves as Americans.

THE CHAPTER IN OUTLINE

1. The southern planters seem more English than American.

2. The townspeople mix English with American ideas.

3. The pioneers gradually become the new Americans.

4. The Africans are denied a share in colonial life.

5. The Indians play a major role in colonial history.

The southern planters seem more English than American

On Franklin's travels through the Southern Colonies in 1763, he saw few towns or cities. Baltimore, Maryland, founded in 1729, contained only a few thousand people. Charleston, South Carolina, the largest and wealthiest southern port, had only about 10,000 people.

Southern population. By the 1760's more than 2 million people lived in the British colonies of North America. Although most of these people came from Great Britain, thousands came from other lands, including Africa. About half of the total colonial population lived in the five Southern Colonies—Maryland, Virginia, North Carolina, South Carolina, and Georgia.

Throughout the colonies the majority of people lived in the country. In the South the proportion of country dwellers was especially high. Most southerners lived on small farms similar to those in New England and the Middle Colonies. Some lived on the frontier in small clearings cut from the forest. The wealthy planter families lived on the fertile coastal plains. A few owned plantations several thousand acres in size. These planter families lived much like wealthy English landowners.

The plantation. The wealth of southern plantation owners came from agriculture. Food used on the plantation was grown there, but the riches of the plantation usually came from a single **cash crop,** that is, a crop raised to be sold at a profit. In Georgia and the Carolinas, especially South Carolina, rice was the most important product. In the colonies of Maryland, Virginia, and North Carolina, the chief cash crop was tobacco.

The large plantation was a complete economic unit. In the center stood a large house that was usually built in the Georgian style of architecture then popular among the wealthy country landowners of England. Around the mansion were the simpler homes of the overseer, or supervisor, and the artisans, or skilled workers, many of whom were slaves. George Washington's estate at Mount Vernon, Virginia, for example, had cabins for carpenters, bricklayers, masons, blacksmiths, millers, and weavers.

Each plantation was almost self-sufficient, that is, it supplied almost all of its own needs. Meat was butchered from herds of cattle

Many large southern plantations were elegant, hospitable homes, but they were also big businesses. To be successful, a plantation had to be run by people with a thorough understanding of production and marketing.

ELIZA LUCAS, PLANTER

"I was very early fond of the vegetable world," wrote Eliza Lucas about her interest in plants. It was no idle hobby, for this colonial woman was given the responsibility of running three plantations when she was only seventeen. Her father, an army officer in the West Indies, settled Eliza and her two sisters, together with their ailing mother, in South Carolina in 1738. The next year, when he returned to the islands, Eliza took over.

Eliza was not content merely to manage the plantations. She decided to experiment. One crop she chose was indigo, a major source of blue dye. At that time most indigo came from French colonies. England would have preferred to import the dye from its own colonies, but earlier experiments in South Carolina had been unsuccessful.

First Eliza had her father send her seeds from the West Indies. Frost killed the first crop.

Her next crop was supervised—and ruined—by an experienced indigo grower whom her father had sent up from the Caribbean. Jealous of competition from Eliza, he "threw in so large a quantity of lime water as to spoil the color."

Eliza kept trying and in 1744 was able to send six pounds (2.7 kilograms) of dye to England. She gave away seeds from this crop "in small quantities to a great number of people." As a result, in 1746 Carolina planters shipped 40,000 pounds (18,000 kilograms) of dye to England and the next year more than doubled this amount.

Indigo remained a major cash crop in South Carolina until the 1770's, when the Revolution cut off trade. Meanwhile, Eliza had married Charles Pinckney, borne four children, and tried raising silkworms in her spare time. When she died in 1793, George Washington was one of her pallbearers.

and hogs, and other foods and raw materials for clothing came from the land. The planter's wife supervised indentured servants and slaves in the spinning and weaving of cloth and other tasks. Often she took part in the work herself. The planter family needed good business ability to run a plantation.

English economic ties. Every year on the tobacco plantations, slaves rolled the large barrels of tobacco to the wharves and loaded them on vessels often owned by northern merchants. With these shipments planters often sent lists of goods that they wanted their agents in London to purchase for them. The agents sold the tobacco, rice, or indigo, bought the articles requested by the planters, and shipped these articles to them.

In this way well-to-do planter families filled their homes with Old World luxuries—fine furniture, table silver, clothes, tapestries, wines, and books. Few luxuries were bought in the

colonies, because even as late as the 1750's, American colonists produced few manufactured goods.

Social life. Since the plantations were more or less isolated, visits between plantation families became great social events. During two months in 1768, George and Martha Washington entertained guests at dinner 29 times and were invited out 7 times. These dinners were splendid affairs, followed by evenings of conversation or card playing. The gracious tradition of southern hospitality, which has continued to this day, grew out of the colonial custom of social visiting.

Many of the richer planter families also owned town houses where they spent several months each year. During these months they enjoyed dancing, music, art, dramatics, and lectures. The men also spent time playing cards, watching cockfights, racing horses, and hunting foxes.

This scene of leisure activities in the 1700's is done in needlepoint. The design of this scene is made by working wool, silk, metallic yarns, beads, and spangles into linen. What activities can you identify?

English influence. The plantations of the South reminded visitors of country estates in England. They were, in a sense, part of England carried to the New World. Wealthy planter families dressed, talked, and acted much like rich English landowners. Indeed, in some ways they had more in common with well-to-do English people than with the small farmers and frontier people who lived nearby.

Yet, as you will see, when the break with England finally came, some southern planters were among the first to fight for independence. A southern planter, Thomas Jefferson, wrote most of the Declaration of Independence. Another southern planter, George Washington, led the American armies to victory.

It is also true that when the Revolution began, some wealthy southern families remained loyal to England, as did some wealthy people in the New England and Middle Colonies. Their ties with Great Britain were too strong to break.

SECTION SURVEY

IDENTIFY: plantation, cash crop, overseer, artisan.

1. Describe the different social groups that lived in the Southern Colonies.

2. (a) Plantation owners generally relied upon a single cash crop for their profit. Explain this statement. (b) Name the main cash crops grown in the Southern Colonies. (c) How might this plantation system be an advantage to the plantation owners? How might it be a disadvantage?

3. How were plantations organized to be self-sufficient? List the goods and services that plantations could provide for themselves.

4. How did the well-to-do planter families entertain themselves in the country? How did they entertain themselves in the towns?

5. (a) What were the economic ties that bound the southern planters to England? (b) In what ways might these ties have had an influence on their feelings in a controversy between England and the other American colonies?

2 The townspeople mix English with American ideas

Like southern plantation families, wealthy townspeople in all the colonies dressed and acted like people in England. This is not surprising. Most colonial cities and towns were seaports with strong commercial ties to England. All travel and trade between the Old World and the British colonies flowed through these seaports.

By the 1750's Philadelphia, with a population of 20,000, was the largest colonial city. In one year, 1754, a total of 471 trading vessels entered and left its busy harbor. New York and Boston were a close second and third in importance. Charleston, South Carolina, and Baltimore, Maryland, were the only towns of considerable size south of Pennsylvania.

Social divisions. By the 1760's merchants were the most influential citizens in all large northern towns. This was true even in New England, where ministers had once been the leaders. The merchants together with lawyers and the families of the royal governors set the fashions for the wealthier people. The merchants drew their wealth from trade and from buying and selling land. Some owned country estates worked by tenant farmers.

Below the merchants on the social ladder were the majority of the townspeople. This group included laborers and artisans, shopkeepers, bakers, pharmacists, and printers. Women followed many of these occupations, either as partners of their husbands or as widows who carried on the enterprises. Below all these were female and male indentured servants. Far below them were male and female slaves.

Most of these classes of people resembled similar classes in England, but class distinctions in the colonies were not as rigid as in England. Through hard work and ability, artisans or even white servants could improve their positions in life. In some cases they could even join the society of the influential townspeople and southern planters. A black slave, however, could not.

Influence of the Old World. European influence could be seen in many features of town life. Some wealthy families built houses similar to those seen on their visits to the Old World. Like the wealthy southern planters, wealthy town families imported furniture and household luxuries from England. The interiors of their houses as well as the exteriors reminded visitors of the Old World.

Like well-to-do people in England, wealthy town families led an active social life, with elaborate dinners and parties. Many well-to-do townspeople also enjoyed card playing, horse racing, cockfighting, and the theater. In Boston, however, strict Puritan ideas still prevailed, and such recreation was frowned upon.

Only the wealthier townspeople enjoyed this lively social life. Household servants usually lived in simply furnished rooms over the family quarters. Artisans often lived be-

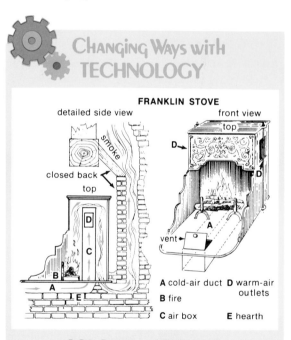

Changing Ways with TECHNOLOGY

FRANKLIN STOVE

detailed side view — front view

A cold-air duct D warm-air outlets
B fire
C air box E hearth

COLONIAL HEATING

The colonial fireplace was inefficient, allowing much of its heat to escape up the chimney. The Franklin stove, made of cast iron, was an improvement. The stove was placed in a former fireplace opening, part of whose chimney had been shut off. Cold air entered a duct (A) beneath the stove through a vent in the front. When a fire was built in the stove (B), this air was heated in the air box (C) and entered the room through warm-air outlets (D). Smoke was drawn above and behind the air box and out through the chimney.

hind their small shops that fronted on the streets.

A visit to Philadelphia. Imagine that you are in colonial America, strolling through the seaport of Philadelphia in, say, 1754. In other colonial towns, the streets wind this way and that, following the early cowpaths and farm lanes. Philadelphia is different. Here William Penn's careful planning has proved worthwhile. The streets run neatly north and south, east and west. Some are paved with cobblestones; others are merely hard-pressed earth. As you walk, you pass the homes of the wealthy — red brick and white stone houses surrounded by gardens and lawns. You also pass the small shops of the artisans.

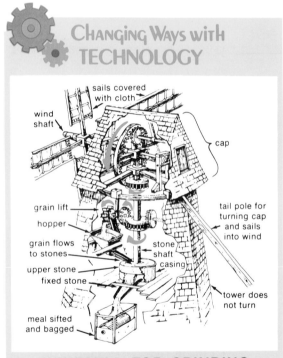

CHANGING WAYS WITH TECHNOLOGY

WINDMILL FOR GRINDING GRAIN

Power from the turning wind shaft was transferred by wooden gears to the wooden stone shaft, which turned, the heavy upper stone against the fixed stone. Grain rose in the grain lift, powered by the stone shaft through another set of gears. Grain flowed through a hole in the upper stone and was ground between the stones, which were grooved. It was then ejected into a device where the meal was sifted and bagged. Similar mills elsewhere in the country were driven by water power.

Hearing the sound of a bell, you pause to listen to the town crier. Introducing the news with "Hear ye, hear ye," he announces a sale of indentured servants who have just arrived from England.

On your way to the waterfront, you pass the market house. Throngs of housewives and servants with baskets on their arms crowd around the stalls. Farm men and women from the surrounding countryside are displaying produce for sale — butter, cheese, poultry, beef, mutton, and vegetables.

Along the waterfront. Reaching the water, you continue along Dock Street, which parallels the Delaware River. The noise of hammers and saws attracts your attention, and you see a shipyard where a small vessel is being built. Next to it fishing boats are heaving the day's catch onto the planks of the wharf. Beyond lies an English ship at anchor.

Approaching the ship, you find yourself in the midst of bustle and confusion. Men carrying boxes and bales on their shoulders push their way toward the nearby warehouse. At one side colonists, eager for the latest news from the Old World, surround a sailor and ask him many questions. On the deck of the ship are the indentured servants, waiting to be bought, some looking extremely bewildered and unhappy.

English ways of life. Walking back into town, you pass the open door of a merchant's counting house. Inside, clerks on tall stools record business transactions in their account books. Across the street is a tavern. A row of hitching posts stands in front of the tavern, and a hollow log serves as a watering trough for horses.

You have not seen the town hall or the jail or the several churches that are important parts of the city. You have seen enough to learn that life in the colonial towns is similar in many ways to life in English towns. The people dress and talk like people in England. The houses and public buildings are English in style. You see the same social divisions that exist in English towns.

A mixture of peoples. In some ways, though, the colonial towns are different from the towns of England. For one thing, people from many different nations are learning to live together in colonial America. The colonial towns as well

William Penn, Philadelphia's designer, had the city streets made twice as wide as usual. By the 1700's, the time of this painting, many of the lawns and orchards that Penn had planned were gone and solid walls had been built.

as the frontier and the farming areas contain settlers from many nations. German settlers fill the section of Philadelphia known as Germantown. On the streets you pass men and women from Ireland and Scotland, many on their way to western frontier lands. Listening carefully, you hear the accents of people from France, Switzerland, Sweden, and many other European countries.

This mixture of people in colonial America is producing a new American vocabulary. English visitors to the colonies hear many new, unfamiliar words. The colonists are speaking what Samuel Johnson, the famous English dictionary maker, in 1756 called the "American dialect." The new American vocabulary has borrowed many words from other languages. From the Indians it has borrowed skunk, hickory, squash, raccoon, canoe, toboggan, moccasin, tomahawk, and wigwam. From the Dutch it has borrowed cruller, stoop, waffle, scow, boss, and cookie. From the French it has borrowed bureau, gopher, chowder, bogus, portage, and prairie. The colonists themselves have invented many new words—bullfrog, eggplant, snowplow, cold snap, trail, popcorn, shingle, and backlog.

Building the towns. The colonists are also trying to find new solutions to the many problems faced by all townspeople. Working together, they are trying to solve problems of water supply, sewage, sanitation, health, and police and fire protection. In Philadelphia, Benjamin Franklin's newspaper, the *Pennsylvania Gazette,* publishes a steady stream of articles dealing with solutions to these problems. Largely because of Franklin's efforts, Philadelphia is one of the first cities in the world to have paved streets, street lights, police and fire departments, and a public library.

A land of opportunity. The greatest difference between English and American towns can be summed up in the word "opportunity." There is plenty of work for everyone in Philadelphia, New York, Boston, and every other colonial town. Except for slaves, who usually remain slaves for life, no one need remain a servant for very long. If the town itself does not offer enough opportunity, the more venturesome of the colonists can always move west. Some stay in town only long enough to save a little money. Then they are off over the roads that lead them to a new way of life.

IDENTIFY: "American dialect."

1. The social ladder in America was similar to that in England but different in one important way. Explain.

2. In what ways did Philadelphia in 1754 resemble an English town? In what ways was it different?

3. List three ways in which European styles of living influenced those of well-to-do townspeople in the colonies.

4. How did the American variety of spoken English reflect conditions in the New World?

5. What improvements in the quality of life in Philadelphia was Benjamin Franklin responsible for?

3. The pioneers gradually become the new Americans

The area of America most different from the Old World lay back from the seacoast. Here in the country lived more than 90 percent of all the colonists.

Farming villages. Not far from the coast, particularly in New England, New Jersey, and Pennsylvania, were many small farming villages of 50 to 100 families. Each had its own church or meetinghouse, a school, and several shops. Many villages had a cobbler to make shoes, a blacksmith to shoe horses and fix wagons, and a doctor to give medical attention. There usually was a general store to sell sugar, spices, and English cloth for dresses. Traveling barbers also came to the villages to cut hair and pull teeth.

To pay for these services, the farm families of the village and the surrounding territory hauled their surplus tobacco, grain, cattle, and hogs to the nearest seaboard or river-port town. There they sold their products.

Before returning home, farm families often stopped to make purchases in the shops displaying English luxury goods—tableware, silver and pewter vessels, and fine cloth. Thus settlers living in areas where they could market their surplus products were able to live better than more isolated colonists.

Moving inland. Many people married young in colonial America. Some newly married couples settled on land near their parents. Many more became pioneers who moved farther inland to unsettled areas, where land was cheaper. It was a common sight to see a couple pass through a village on their way to a new home. Behind them an ox or a horse might pull a small cart containing a few boxes with all

Scutching flax, which means beating the raw flax in order to separate the woody fiber, was a tedious task. It was pleasanter, even fun, when pioneers gathered to do it together, as in this painting, "The Scutching Bee," by Linton Park.

their belongings. Bringing up the rear, tied to the cart by a rope, might be a scrawny cow.

Pioneer shelters. At first many pioneers lived in caves along the riverbanks or in shallow pits roofed with branches and covered with sod to keep out the rain. Frequently newcomers put up three-sided log shelters with the open side facing away from prevailing winds. Sooner or later those who stayed to farm the land built a full log cabin. This practical structure for forested country was introduced into the colonies by Swedish settlers.

The log cabins were usually crude, drafty, one-room affairs with a dirt floor, no windows, and a door hung on leather hinges. The most important feature of most cabins was a huge fireplace where the settlers huddled for warmth and where they cooked their food. Later, if the pioneers prospered, they improved the cabin. They might buy one of the stoves invented by Benjamin Franklin to improve the heating (see page 55). They might lay a wooden floor, cut windows in the walls, and cover the openings with waxed paper or glass. They often built lofts for the children to sleep in and added new rooms. If all went well, they finally nailed clapboards on the outside walls of the cabin over the rough logs.

Pioneer families rose at dawn and went to bed at dusk. There were few books, even for those who could read, and the pioneers felt little need to light the cabins at night. Usually the glow from the fireplace furnished the cabin's only light. When more light was needed, people put large splinters of pine wood into cracks in the walls, where they burned with a bright, smoky flame. Pioneer families used candles only on special occasions, for tallow was hard to get. Only wealthy townspeople used candles and oil lamps to any extent.

Household equipment. Pioneer families did all their cooking in the fireplace. They boiled vegetables, soups, and stews in large copper or iron kettles—which hung from a pole in the chimney. They baked in Dutch ovens beside the fireplace or in ovens in a side wall of the fireplace itself.

Early pioneer furniture and utensils were homemade and crude. Beds were little more than wooden bunks placed along the wall. Logs, hewn smooth with an ax, became chairs and benches. Smooth boards placed on trestles served as tables. Dishes were slabs of wood with a hollow place in the center to hold food. The pioneers carved spoons out of wood. They drank from gourds or from tankards that they made from wood, leather, or the horns of cattle.

Food and clothing. Once colonial Americans learned to use the abundant resources of the New World, they rarely lacked food and drink. The rivers and lakes were alive with fish, and the forests were filled with game. In the early days, settlers near the forts often saw herds of deer numbering several hundred. Turkeys were seen in all the colonies, although the settlers rapidly wiped them out. Pigeons were so plentiful from Virginia northward that they sometimes darkened the sky and broke limbs of trees in which they roosted. Wild rabbits and squirrels destroyed so many crops that payments were offered for their pelts. Pioneer women and girls tended the gardens, raised poultry, helped with the milking and butchering, and, especially in German and Dutch families, sometimes worked in the fields.

Pioneer women and girls also made the family's clothing, using spinning and weaving skills brought from the Old World. They made thread from the wool of their sheep and from the flax they grew in their fields. They spun this thread, wove it into cloth, and cut and sewed it into garments. They also tanned deerskin for moccasins, shoes, and jackets.

Life on the frontier. Some pioneers, mainly young men, chose not to settle down. They preferred to roam the frontier. Every year, in all the colonies, hundreds of adventurous youths left home to find excitement in the western forests.

Living in the wilderness, they shed many traces of European civilization. All that they owned they carried in their hands or on their backs—a hunting knife, a long rifle (see page 130), powder, and shot. Yet with this meager equipment, they managed to survive. They shed their European clothing for coonskin caps, buckskin shirts and trousers, and moccasins of deerskin. Game, fish, nuts, and berries furnished much of their food. They slept beneath the stars, in caves, or in crude log shelters.

Most of these frontiersmen, as they were known, preferred the lonely life of the forest to the ties of a family. Now and then they appeared at a trading post to exchange a few furs for new supplies of powder, shot, and perhaps a

stoneboat

STONE FENCE

Before planting crops, many New England farmers collected stones from their fields and built fences or walls. Early fences were low and wide; later ones, as here, were higher and narrower. Some of these later fences can still be seen in New England.

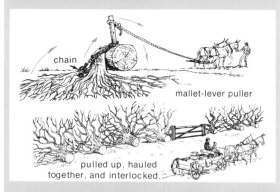

chain

mallet-lever puller

pulled up, hauled together, and interlocked.

STUMP FENCE

Some colonial farmers made effective fences by pulling up tree stumps, hauling them to the edge of a field, and interlocking the roots.

RAIL FENCE

Where timber was plentiful, farmers built wooden rail fences to surround their fields. A common type was this snake fence, in which trees were split into rails and interlaced in a zigzag pattern. Two diagonal rails supported each intersection.

little corn. Many frontiersmen never returned from their travels in the woods. Theirs was a wild and dangerous life, in which they constantly matched wits and skills against Indians and nature.

Social life and recreation. The hard life of the pioneers and frontiersmen left little time or energy for recreation. Nevertheless, they did occasionally combine work and play.

Now and then frontiersmen for miles around gathered for companionship and sport. Shooting matches were common. So were games of physical strength—foot races, wrestling matches, jumping contests, and the hurling of heavy fence rails. In the evening, before a crackling log fire, they swapped colorful tales of forest adventure and told jokes about newcomers to the wilderness.

When a pioneer family was ready to build a cabin or had cut the trees and was ready to drag them from the land to clear a field, all the neighbors came to help. House-raisings sometimes lasted several days. In the morning the men lifted the logs into place to form the cabin walls. Meanwhile, the women prepared dinner, baking great piles of cornbread and barbecuing an entire beef or deer over an open fire. After dinner there were sports, such as wrestling, foot racing, and shooting contests. In the early evening, the settlers danced.

People who lived in areas that had been settled for some years had more opportunity to be neighborly. In these areas the farms were closer together and small villages had been built. On Sundays most settlers went to church. During the week, in appropriate seasons, they helped one another with the corn-husking, sheepshearing, sewing, and quilting. Weddings were always times of celebration. Most work also ceased on election days and on training days, when the local militia drilled in an open field in the morning and then spent the afternoon in sports and conversation.

Self-sufficiency. With a gun, an ax, a knife, a hoe, a sickle, and a kettle or two, a pioneer family could clear the land, build a house, and grow the crops. However, most pioneers lived a harsh life. They were self-sufficient not from choice but because they had to be. The great majority had no doctors, no schools, and few churches. They usually had a roof over their heads, enough to eat, and freedom from oppressive laws and heavy taxes. They paid for these advantages with lives of back-breaking labor.

New ideas among pioneers. Among these self-reliant pioneers, certain ideas began to take root and grow. The pioneers were free women and men who had created new lives in the wilderness. They were individualists, for their success depended on their own strength and skill, but they also believed in cooperation, for only by helping one another could they clear land and build houses. Even the independent frontiersmen were aware that an additional pair of strong arms and an extra rifle could sometimes mean the difference between life and death.

The pioneers considered themselves the equals of other men and women, for they saw most of their neighbors living similar lives. Finally, they were optimists, for they saw the forests yielding to their axes and homes and villages springing up in what had been wilderness land. They saw neighbors who had started with nothing raising their families in security and increasing comfort.

Along the whole length of the colonies, from New France to Spanish Florida, the pioneers lived much the same sort of life. The Germans, Scotch-Irish, and English settling the Virginia frontier had more in common with those settling the Massachusetts frontier than they had with the rich planters of their own colony or with the townspeople of the colonial seaports. Gradually their ties with European ways of life weakened, and many began to think of themselves as Americans.

SECTION SURVEY

IDENTIFY: log cabin, pioneers, frontiersmen.

1. To survive in a new environment, a person must adapt. Explain how pioneer families adapted in terms of (a) shelter, (b) household equipment, (c) food, (d) clothing, and (e) social life.

2. (a) In what ways were pioneer families self-reliant? (b) In what ways did they benefit from the help of their neighbors?

3. (a) Why would self-reliant people tend to value freedom and equality? (b) Why would self-reliant people tend to be optimistic?

4. How did the life of frontiersmen differ from the life of pioneer farm families in terms of (a) personal possessions, (b) clothing, (c) food, (d) shelter, and (e) social life?

---

4 The Africans are denied a share in colonial life

In the 1760's, of the 2 million people living in the British colonies, an estimated 300,000 to 400,000 were of African birth or background. These black colonists lived in and helped build all of the colonies, yet they were denied the opportunities that other colonial groups took for granted.

A class apart. For European settlers America meant freedom and an opportunity to build a better life. For black men and women it meant nothing of the kind. Unlike the vast majority of Europeans, the Africans did not come to America freely. The Africans were brought against their will, by force, literally in chains.

In the very early colonial years, the Africans were generally treated as indentured servants. However, white colonists soon came to regard the black Africans as property—a valuable kind of property, but property nonetheless. Denied their humanity, Africans became slaves, and most remained slaves for life, as did their children. Every other group in colonial society regarded black people as inferior. Even the few black people who gained their freedom were often looked down upon and denied the rights other colonists enjoyed.

Slaveowners usually taught the Africans only as much as was necessary to do their work. Thus most slaves learned the simpler skills involved in colonial farming, building, and manufacturing and enough English to obey orders.

The white colonists ignored the skills already possessed by the black arrivals. Few white colonists knew or cared that the Africans came from civilizations hundreds or even thousands of years old.

The Middle Passage. As colonial demands for slaves increased, the brutal African slave trade grew and flourished. From central and western Africa, long lines of Africans, captured by enemy tribes, were marched to west African seaports. To prevent their escape, the captives were forced to wear iron collars and were linked together by chains. The survivors of these long, cruel marches were sold to European or American sea captains. Such buyers

PROUD TRADITIONS OF AFRICA

"The town seems to be very great. When you enter it, you go into a broad street seven or eight times wider than Warmoes Street in Amsterdam. It goes straight out and never bends." So wrote a Dutchman, impressed by the African city of Benin, which he visited in the early 1600's. Here, as they had for centuries in West Africa, people maintained prosperous, well-organized communities where art and learning flourished.

Along the western Niger River, three kingdoms—each larger than the one before it—had risen and fallen long before the first English ships arrived at Jamestown. All of them carried on extensive trade north across the Sahara, dealing chiefly in gold, copper, and salt. The first, the kingdom of Ghana, reached its peak in the 900's. It was gradually absorbed by Mali, which flourished in the 1300's. Mali in turn was taken over by Songhay, a great empire some 2,000 miles (over 3,000 kilometers) across. A major city of both Mali and Songhay was Timbuktu, a center of Muslim learning.

After Songhay's decline in the 1500's, the focus shifted to Guinea, the area around the Niger delta. Here arose several small trading states noted especially for their beautiful sculptures in wood, terra cotta, ivory, and bronze. The best known of these states were Benin (with its capital city of the same name), Oyo, Ashanti, and Dahomey. Unfortunately, the slave trade had disastrous effects on these kingdoms, and only Dahomey was able to survive into the late 1800's.

would select only the strongest and healthiest young Africans.

Once the slaves were selected, they were branded and packed into the slave ships. Chained together two by two, they were packed together between decks where there was not room enough for them to stand.

The weeks-long voyage to the New World, called the **Middle Passage,** was a nightmare. Some slaves killed themselves by jumping overboard or choking themselves with their chains. Many died from spoiled food. Disease, fostered by overcrowding and filthy conditions, took many more lives. Sharks trailed the slave ships and fed on the bodies of the dead that were thrown overboard. Some slaves revolted against these inhuman conditions, but these revolts seldom succeeded. Scholars estimate that from 13 to 33 percent of the slaves did not survive the horrors of the Middle Passage. This heavy loss of life did not discourage the slave traders, who made enormous profits.

Traders from several countries, including England and its colonies, usually sold the surviving Africans to planters in the West Indies. Here, before they were sent to the colonies along the Atlantic seaboard, the African newcomers were "seasoned," or broken in, by overseers. It is very likely that fewer than half the slaves survived this harsh "seasoning" period on the sugar plantations of the West Indies.

Slavery in New England. By the 1770's a relatively small number of black slaves, perhaps about 12,000, lived in New England. The small New England farms did not require the labor of large numbers of slaves. New England slaves worked as household servants for wealthy families and as farm laborers, lumberjacks, carpenters, barrelmakers, blacksmiths, millers, fishers, and shipbuilders.

Slaves in New England had some legal rights. They could buy property and had the right to trial by jury in the courts. Slaves could attend church as long as they sat in "African pews," but they could not become church members. In early New England, church membership conferred political rights, such as the right to vote and to hold office. Such political rights were denied to slaves.

Most New Englanders looked upon their slaves as wards, or adopted children, of the family. Yet these "adopted children," even in rare instances when their owners taught them to read and write, were property to be bought and sold as their owners wished.

Although slaves in New England had some rights, New England slavery still was harsh. New England slaves, like slaves everywhere, would not accept the central idea of slavery — the total and permanent ownership of human beings by other human beings. Many New England slaves fled from their masters, no matter how kind their masters might be.

Slavery in the Middle Colonies. Slaves in the Middle Colonies contributed their labor and skills to commerce, industry, and farming. As in New England, however, the number of slaves was relatively small — perhaps about 35,000.

In New Netherland, Dutch patroons and merchants, like New Englanders, often regarded their slaves as adopted children. When the British seized the area, this attitude changed. Under British rule all black slaves in

TO BE SOLD on board the Ship *Bance-Iſland*, on tueſday the 6th of *May* next, at *Aſhley-Ferry*; a choice cargo of about 250 fine healthy NEGROES, juſt arrived from the Windward & Rice Coaſt. —The utmoſt care has already been taken, and ſhall be continued, to keep them free from the leaſt danger of being infected with the SMALL-POX, no boat having been on board, and all other communication with people from *Charles-Town* prevented. *Auſtin, Laurens, & Appleby.*

N. B. Full one Half of the above Negroes have had the SMALL-POX in their own Country.

Henry Laurens of Charleston, is the slave trader named in this notice. Laurens went on to become president of the Continental Congress, the first government of the independent colonies.

New York except household servants were strictly separated from white colonists. Severe rules of discipline governed the slaves. Violence between white colonists and black slaves became fairly common in New York.

Attitudes toward slavery in Pennsylvania and much of New Jersey differed somewhat from those in New York. From the earliest days, at least some Quaker and German settlers in Pennsylvania and New Jersey doubted the morality of slave labor as well as its usefulness. A few of them began to speak out against the evils of slavery.

Slavery in the Southern Colonies. Of the 300,000 to 400,000 blacks in colonial America in 1765, the vast majority, or nearly seven out of eight, lived in the Southern Colonies. Almost all of these black men, women, and children were slaves.

Most southern slaves labored on tobacco, rice, and indigo plantations, but southern slaves also did many other kinds of work. Between 1732 and 1736, the *South Carolina Gazette* mentioned 28 trades that made use of slave labor. Black slaves thus made an enormous contribution to the development of the Southern Colonies.

Tobacco became one of the South's biggest cash crops. In this English advertisement for tobacco, slaves are shown packing the dried leaves in barrels and rolling them down to the docks for shipment.

In the Carolinas slavery grew rapidly, as it did in Georgia once it was allowed. The early colonists of Virginia and Maryland, however, came to depend upon black slave labor only gradually. First they tried without success to enslave the Indians. Then they tried to rely on white indentured servants, but indentured servants were hard to get and harder to keep. Black slaves provided a more dependable labor force — and a permanent one.

The status of Africans in Virginia was for some time uncertain. The first African arrivals were regarded more or less as indentured servants, but their contracts did not always insure their freedom after their term of service was completed. After 1661 the institution of slavery was clearly established in Virginia.

Throughout the late 1600's and the 1700's, slavery grew rapidly in the Southern Colonies. Planters developed new and larger plantations, requiring the labor of more and more slaves. Slave traders rushed to fill the demand.

The slave codes. As the proportion of slaves to white people increased in the Southern Colonies, white southerners became alarmed. If plantation agriculture was to expand and be profitable, the southerners needed slaves. White southerners feared that large numbers of black people would threaten white supremacy, that is, control of the blacks by whites.

Slaves concentrated in large numbers might successfully revolt against their masters. Reports of occasional slave revolts in the West Indies, where black slaves far outnumbered white settlers, added to these fears.

Beginning in the 1680's, southern slaveowners tried to solve this problem by passing slave codes. These laws had a double purpose. First, they safeguarded slaveowners' investments in their slave property by setting up detailed regulations to prevent the theft or escape of slaves. Second, they protected slaveowners against slave violence by setting up strict rules for slave behavior.

To prevent slave revolts, the codes forbade slaves to meet together, leave the plantation, or own weapons. By law, slaves could not learn to read or write. Special guards circulated among the slaves to insure that these slave codes were obeyed.

Black resistance to slavery. In the 1600's and 1700's, punishments for all crimes were extremely cruel. Under the slave codes, however, punishments for slaves were more severe than punishments for white colonists who committed similar crimes.

For minor crimes slaves could be beaten or even have their noses split or their ears cut off. For major crimes, such as rape or murder, a slave could be hanged or burned to death.

Not all slaves submitted meekly to the slaveowners' attempts to own and control them. Slaves found many ways to harass their masters. Often they purposely slowed down their work or did it poorly. Sometimes they struck back or even killed their white masters.

Slaves sometimes succeeded in running away from their owners, but because of their skin color, they did not automatically win their freedom. In all colonies an unknown black person was immediately suspected of being a runaway slave.

Slaves could and did plot uprisings to secure their freedom. Slaveowners lived in terror of such revolts. The vaguest rumor of a slave uprising could cause panic in a white community. Whether the revolt was real or imagined, the punishment for the slaves was severe.

Vague rumors appear to have been the only evidence used against more than 100 slaves convicted of plotting a revolt in New York in 1741. Eighteen slaves were hanged, 13 burned to death, and 78 "transported," probably to the British West Indies, where the slave codes were extremely severe.

White opposition to slavery. A few white colonists condemned slavery. In 1700 Samuel Sewall of Boston, an influential judge, published a famous antislavery pamphlet called *The Selling of Joseph.* A devout Puritan, Judge Sewall gathered examples from the Bible to show that slavery was evil.

In 1688, twelve years before Judge Sewall's pamphlet appeared, the Quakers of Germantown, Pennsylvania, spoke out against slavery. These Quakers denounced the evils of owning and selling human beings as property and of separating husbands from their wives and children, which happened often when slaves were sold.

Not until the mid-1700's, however, did Quakers generally begin to oppose the brutal slave trade and, gradually, slavery itself. John Woolman, a conscientious and thoughtful Quaker tailor, journeyed through the colonies trying to persuade Quakers to free their slaves and educate them. His journal is still read and admired today.

Free blacks. A few freed slaves lived in every colony. They gained their freedom in several ways. Descendants of the early indentured Africans in Virginia inherited their freedom. Children of a white mother, regardless of the father's race, were regarded as free persons. Occasionally masters freed some or all of their slaves as a reward for faithful service or to avoid supporting them in their old age. A few slaves bought their freedom, using savings their owners allowed them to earn and keep.

Most free blacks earned their living as skilled workers. A few owned small farms or businesses. Free black men could not serve in colonial militias in peacetime, though both free black colonists and slaves were recruited into the militia in times of war. In the 1700's free blacks were not allowed to vote in any of the Southern Colonies except, for a time, in North Carolina.

White colonists seldom associated openly with free blacks except in casual, unimportant ways. A few free blacks won a respected place in their communities, but most had to endure discrimination from the white colonists.

Separate and unequal. White colonists, especially the English, regarded blacks, whether free or slave, as a class apart—and an inferior class at that. Most were forced to live apart from white colonists and obey special laws enforced by white colonists. Even so, black men and women contributed enormously to the growth of the colonies. White colonists not only expected hard labor from blacks, they demanded it. Yet in a new land abounding with opportunity, few black men and women were permitted to work, to save, or to build better ways of life for themselves or for their families.

SECTION SURVEY

IDENTIFY: Middle Passage, white supremacy, slave codes, Samuel Sewall, John Woolman.

1. For each of the three groups of colonies, answer the following: (a) How great was the need for slave labor? (b) What legal and social rights did slaves have? (c) What jobs did slaves perform?

2. How did slaves resist slavery?

3. On what grounds did some white colonists base their opposition to slavery?

4. How did some slaves gain freedom? What legal and social rights did free blacks have?

5. How might slavery affect a slave's feelings toward white people? How might slavery affect a slaveowner's feelings toward black people?

6. Picture Study: Look at the slave sale notice on page 63. What do you think that buyers of slaves would worry about? Why would this worry them?

5 The Indians play a major role in colonial history

From the days of the first settlements, the Indians played an important role in the development of the English colonies.

Indians of the Eastern Woodlands. Many Indian tribes were living in the region between the Atlantic coast and the Appalachian Mountains when the first European settlers reached these shores (see map, page 00). Almost all of these Indians depended upon agriculture for their food. Among the exceptions were the Algonquin (al·GAWN·kwin) tribes of Canada. In much of their territory, the summers were too short for raising most crops, and the northern Indians, therefore, relied upon hunting for food as well as for clothing and shelter.

Tribes in the lands from Canada south to Florida used hunting only to supplement the crops they grew. Each of these tribes had its own hunting ground with clearly defined boundaries. Indians who entered a neighboring tribe's hunting ground without permission did so at their own risk.

Farming methods. The Eastern Woodland Indians had no plows, and their only domestic animal was the dog. Nevertheless, they had an effective method of farming. In the spring the men broke the sod with hoe-like tools, and the women then planted the seeds. One woman led the way down a row, using a digging stick to open shallow holes in the soil at regular intervals. Other women, following in her footsteps, dropped seed for corn, squash, or beans in the holes. Sometimes a small fish was first placed in each of the holes as fertilizer.

The care the Indians took to keep their fields free of weeds impressed the colonists. On one occasion the settlers in a New England village became alarmed when they noticed weeds springing up in the fields belonging to neighboring Indians. The villagers took this sign of neglect to mean that the Indians were preparing for war!

Indian fields yielded ample harvests, and surplus grain was stored for winter use. Often the Indians were able to give or to sell corn and beans from their surplus to the English settlers.

Social and political life. Most Eastern Woodland Indians lived in permanent villages. These communities were made up of families and groups of related families, or clans. Each village was a close-knit social unit, and all of the members participated in work, recreation, and religious ceremonies. The tribe itself included many villages spread over the tribal territory.

The Eastern Woodland Indians—and most other North American tribes—shared a more or less democratic form of government. A **sachem** (SAY·chum), or chief, seldom held absolute power. Usually there were several sachems. One might lead a hunting party; another might lead a raid against an enemy tribe; and another might lead in peacetime. Moreover, the chiefs were usually advised by a council of older men. Decisions were reached in council meetings by unanimous vote.

The Iroquois Confederation. In general, the tribes were independent of one another. There were, however, several confederations, the most powerful of which was formed during the 1500's. At that time the Seneca, Cayuga, Onondaga, Oneida, and Mohawk tribes in the land between the Hudson River and Lake Erie joined in the Iroquois Confederation.

An Indian prophet named Deganawidah (dee·gan·ah·WEE·dah) supposedly first dreamed of the Confederation. He saw a day when the Confederation would include all Indians, war would be abolished, and peace would prevail throughout the world. His vision was passed by word of mouth from generation to generation (see Source, page 68). Some historians believe that the first appearance of white explorers may have been another reason that the five tribes united. In the 1700's, as you have read, the Confederation accepted the Tuscaroras as members and became the Six Nations.

Iroquois organization. Each tribe made its own decisions in daily life. For larger issues, such as going to war or making a treaty, the Confederation as a whole made the decisions. The governing body of the Confederation was made up of a number of sachems from each of the six tribes. Each tribe's sachems had to agree on a decision before it could take effect.

Although all the sachems were men, women had great influence in the tribes. They chose the sachems and could remove them. Women controlled the distribution of food and

The Algonquins are shown here in a village near Quebec. They were bitter enemies of the Iroquois, another Eastern Woodlands tribe, who finally succeeded in pushing them off their lands and to the west.

owned most of the property, including the **longhouses**. These were large, rectangular structures in which several families lived together, each with its own quarters.

The Iroquois Confederation grew out of a vision of peace, but the Iroquois soon became the most feared and respected Indian fighting force in North America. Iroquois warriors subdued one after another of the surrounding tribes. At the peak of its power, the Iroquois Confederation controlled tribes from the Atlantic coast to as far west as Lake Michigan and from Canada south to what is now Tennessee. In the colonial wars between the French and British, and later during the American Revolution, the opposing sides tried to outbid each other for the support of the Iroquois.

Spiritual beliefs and practices. The Eastern Woodland Indians shared with other Native Americans deeply held religious and spiritual beliefs. At the heart of their beliefs was the vision of a force that lived in every part of the universe. This spiritual force existed in the sun, moon, and stars. It existed in the wind, the rain, the running water, the forests, the growing plants, and the earth, the mother of all life.

It was present in the objects that men and women made for daily use. It was present in all living creatures—in the wildlife of the forest and the sea and in the humans who shared the earth with all other forms of life.

Among the tribes were **shamans** (SHAY· munz), or medicine men, and prophets. The shamans and prophets claimed the ability to communicate with this spiritual force. Those who possessed this ability called upon the spirit world to bring rain to thirsty crops, to grant victory in warfare, and to heal the wounded and the sick. In songs, dances, and elaborate ceremonies, the Indians worshiped this spiritual force.

The legacy from the Indians. The first British settlers along the Atlantic seaboard owed a great deal—in some cases, even life itself—to the Indians who received them with friendliness mixed with curiosity. Indian food, given freely or traded for English products, saved many of the early settlers from starvation. Many of the settlements—among them Jamestown, Plymouth, Boston, and Philadelphia —were built on the sites of former Indian villages.

Indian knowledge and skills were invaluable to the colonists. The Indians provided seeds and taught the whites how to plant and cultivate the fields. From the Indians the colonists learned how to live off the game, fish, and plants of the forest lands. Along Indian trails the whites, in time, advanced into the heart of the continent. Many of today's highways follow the routes of the old Indian trails. Hundreds of Indian words survive in our language and in place names across the land.

The whole world owes much to the Indians and their cultures. In agriculture alone the Indians' contributions have been priceless. Nearly 500 years have passed since men and women from Europe began to settle the American continents. During all that time, none of the settlers or their descendants has discovered and developed a single major agricultural product from the wild trees and plants of the New World. Yet long before the first Europeans arrived, the Indians had developed more than 50 valuable products. In addition, they had learned to use many other products of the forests and the grasslands, including a large number of medicinal plants still in use today. More than half of all the agricultural goods produced in the world today come from plants originally discovered and cultivated by American Indians.

How different our eating habits would be if we did not have corn, tomatoes, white and sweet potatoes, and the many varieties of beans! If we did not have peanuts, chestnuts, pumpkins, strawberries, blackberries, blueberries, cranberries, and crab apples! If we did not have chocolate and maple syrup! If we did not have turkeys!

Clash of cultures. These were and are impressive contributions, and the colonists gladly accepted them. Yet the colonists ignored other important lessons that the Indians could have taught them. The colonists had beliefs and values that differed from those of the Indians. Each group found it difficult to understand and accept many of the other group's ideas.

The Native Americans had learned to live in harmony with their environment. They lived on and with the land without polluting it and without exhausting its resources. They had, as John Collier expressed it in his book *Indians of the Americas,* a "reverence and passion for the earth and its web of life."

The colonists did not understand these ideas. To them success and progress depended upon changing the natural environment. The resources of the New World appeared to have no end. They were there to be used. This was especially true in the British colonies. The French relied heavily on the fur trade, which disturbed the environment less than farming did. The French also had fewer and smaller settlements. In the British colonies, though, farming was highly important. So, heedless of the future, the colonists slashed and burned the trees, dug and planted the fields, and raised towns and cities on the former hunting grounds of the Indians.

The colonists and the Indians also had different ideas about land and property. The colonists acquired Indian lands by purchase, by treaty, and, at times, by fraud and by force. The colonists believed that property could be bought and sold by individuals. The colonists did not understand that Indian property was held collectively by the tribe. An Indian chief was actually a trustee for the tribe and had no right to give away or sell any part of the tribal lands.

Two such different ways of life could not long exist peaceably side by side. Conflict was inevitable. As the colonists pushed westward, driving the Indians from their homelands, the fighting on both sides became increasingly fierce. Finally, most colonists decided that the only solution was to exterminate the Indians.

Efforts at conversion. Not all colonists thought of the Indians as cruel, inferior beings.

SOURCES

DEGANAWIDAH'S VISION

I, Deganawidah, and the Confederated Chiefs now uproot the tallest pine tree, and into the cavity thereby made we cast all weapons of war. Into the depths of the earth, deep down into the underearth currents of water flowing to unknown regions, we cast all weapons of strife. We bury them from sight and plant again the tree. Thus shall the Great Peace be established.

Such colonists believed that it was important to draw them away from their own religious beliefs and convert them to Christianity. Roger Williams, John Eliot, Jonathan Edwards, and others tried to teach Christianity to the Indians and to deal fairly with them. Judge Samuel Sewall, who argued against slavery for black people, also criticized New Englanders for regarding the Indians as little better than animals.

Other religious groups also tried to convert the Indians to Christianity. The Quakers and Moravians especially tried to understand the Indians, to deal fairly with them, and to prove that love could overcome all barriers.

Efforts at education. A few attempts to educate the Indians in European ways of living met with little success. Eleazar Wheelock raised funds to start a college in New Hampshire where Indians could be educated and converted to Christianity, but the experiment had little success. In Virginia, at the College of William and Mary, a few Indian boys were taught in separate classes. When the boys returned to their tribes, the chiefs complained that they had been made unfit for Indian life.

Benjamin Franklin offered to supervise the education of some Indian boys. He was courteously told that Indian methods of education were better suited to the boys' development. The Indians offered instead to take some white boys and teach them Indian arts and skills. The colonists declined the offer.

Attempts at understanding. A few thoughtful colonists took genuine interest in Indian life. Roger Williams in the 1600's learned one of the Indian languages and wrote an Indian dictionary. In the 1700's Benjamin Franklin, Thomas Jefferson, and a few other scholarly colonists became interested in the customs as well as the languages of the Indians. Jefferson admired the eloquence of Indian chiefs at treaty-making ceremonies. He also appreciated the dignity and nobility they showed when facing hardship.

On the whole, however, genuine concern for the Native Americans was extremely rare in colonial America. Most colonists made no effort to understand them, distrusting and despising them instead. For their part, the Indians found little to value in the whites' way of life. Nor were the Indians able to understand why the colonists feared and hated them so intensely.

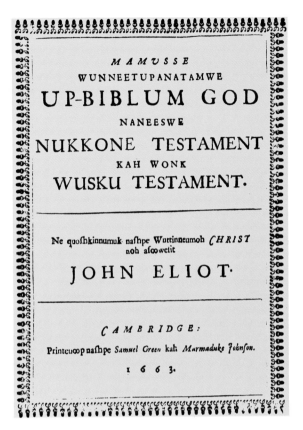

This title page comes from a Mamusse Bible translated by John Eliot, who was known as the "Apostle to the Indians." It was the first Bible printed in this country.

With such deep misunderstanding on both sides, a long-lasting pattern of conflict between the Indians and the settlers was planted and nourished in colonial America.

SECTION SURVEY

IDENTIFY: sachem, Deganawidah, longhouse, shaman, Eleazar Wheelock.

1. What methods of plowing and planting did the Indians of the Eastern Woodlands use?

2. Describe the political organization of the Iroquois Confederation.

3. Indian knowledge and skills were invaluable to the colonists. Explain.

4. (a) How did the colonists' and the Indians' views of the environment and land ownership differ? (b) Why might such differing views lead to conflict?

5. Picture Study: Look at the Indian village shown on page 67. How do you think the Indians pictured there might have made their living?

Chapter Survey

Summary: Tracing the Main Ideas

The settlers who arrived in the British colonies along the Atlantic seaboard were European in language, dress, customs, and ways of thinking and acting. They naturally tried to reproduce the everyday ways of life with which they had been familiar in the Old World. This, of course, proved to be impossible. Plunged, as they were, into a new and strange environment, they soon changed the material aspects of their lives—including houses, clothing, tools, and weapons. More slowly they began to change the ideas and practices that they had brought with them from the Old World.

The southern planters and the wealthy townspeople changed more slowly than the other colonial groups. Because their ties with England were so close, they continued in some ways to be more English than they were American. The pioneer farmers and frontiersmen changed much more rapidly. Because they had so few ties with England, they became much more American than they were English.

Two other groups, the Native Americans and the blacks, played key roles in shaping colonial life. The contributions of the Indians, especially during the early years of settlement, are beyond calculation. The forced labor of the blacks built the prosperous southern plantations. But both these groups were kept out of the mainstream of American life. Blacks were enslaved, and the Indians were treated as enemies. Thus in their treatment of the blacks and the Indians, the colonists planted the seeds of future conflicts.

With only a few exceptions, though, the colonists were unaware of the problems they were creating for future generations. In the next chapter, you will see how the emerging ideas and ideals of the colonists influenced the development of colonial schools, churches, and government. You will see the beginnings of what in time was to become the American nation.

Inquiring into History

1. (a) Many of the colonial planters and merchants were able to reproduce some of the familiar ways of life they had known in the Old World. Why? (b) Why were pioneer farmers and frontiersmen unable to continue as many Old World ways?
2. The pioneer's individualism was cooperative as well as competitive. Does this statement contradict itself? Explain.
3. From what you have learned in Chapters 1–3, why do you think colonial cities grew up where they did—along the coast of the more northern colonies—instead of elsewhere? Use evidence from the chapters to support your answer.
4. Compare the experiences of black Americans and Indians in colonial America. How were their experiences similar? How were they different?

Relating Past to Present

1. Do Americans today face the same problems that the colonists faced in learning to adapt to a new and changing environment? Explain.
2. In what ways is the white settlers' treatment of blacks and Indians during the colonial period a dramatic example of the fact that America's past shaped America's present?
3. Many people today are interested in restoring and preserving the natural environment. In what ways would these people benefit from studying the attitudes toward nature held by the Indians?

Developing Social Science Skills

1. The pictures in this chapter provide evidence about life in the colonies. Study the pictures and then make some hypotheses, or tentative statements, about the differences in the lives of southern planters, townspeople, and pioneer farmers.
2. Investigate and prepare a report on an early African civilization, such as Ghana, Mali, Songhai, or Benin. Try to find out (a) when the civilization reached its height, (b) where it was located, (c) what its accomplishments were, and (d) why it declined.
3. Much of Indian culture was passed on orally from one generation to the next. Research in the library for examples of Eastern Woodlands tales and legends. Read one or more of them before the class.

Agriculture

Agriculture has played an important part in building both a strong American economy and an enterprising, independent American character. Agriculture in America goes back centuries before settlers arrived from Europe. While some Native Americans had hunting and gathering economies, others had developed methods of growing maize (corn), pumpkins, squashes, and other crops. Certain Indian tribes of the Southwest had also developed methods of irrigating their crops. European settlers soon learned to grow the native crops. These settlers also introduced many plants from Europe such as wheat, alfalfa, oats, and barley.

The first European illustration of maize appeared in 1535.

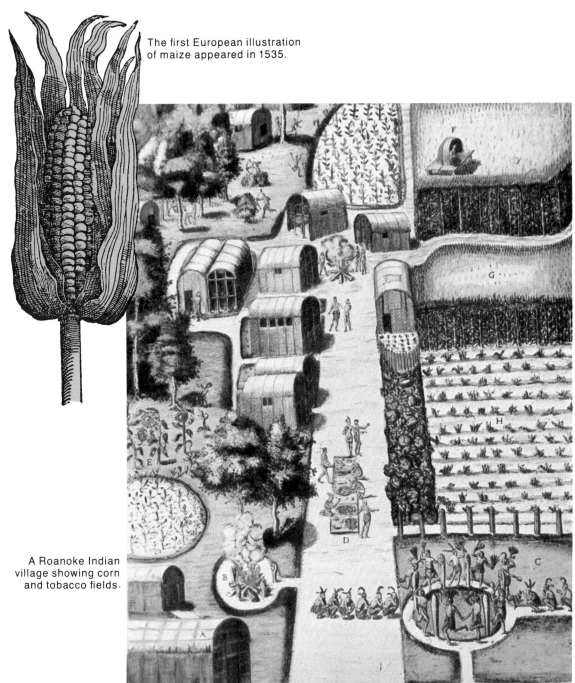

A Roanoke Indian village showing corn and tobacco fields.

Wooden plows were soon replaced by more efficient cast iron and steel plows.

Settlers pushed west beyond the Appalachians, chopping and burning to clear the land for farms.

Early inventors made many attempts to improve agricultural tools.

American farmers quickly moved beyond raising food for their own needs. In the fertile valleys of Pennsylvania and New Jersey, some farmers grew surplus grains that could be sold in towns and cities or they used the surplus to raise livestock that could be sold. In the South agriculture tended to be more specialized. There farmers planted crops such as tobacco, rice, or indigo, most of which were intended for export.

Pioneer farmers, meanwhile, continued to push west. They cleared new land for plowing and planting and produced the food the growing nation needed.

Swedish immigrants sowing grain on an Illinois farm about 1850.

The cattle business began on Spanish *ranchos* in lands that would one day be the southwestern United States.

A prosperous Pennsylvania farm as it looked in the mid-1800's.

73

A McCormick reaper and
binder.

Whitney's cotton gin helped
turn plantations like this
one in Mississippi into
profitable businesses. The
plantation economy also
relied on the labor of the
slaves.

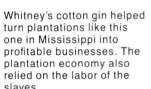

Grant Wood painted this idealized picture of an American farm.

Advances in technology during the 1800's led to increased agricultural output. Eli Whitney's cotton gin helped turn the South into the Cotton Kingdom. Cyrus McCormick's reaper and binder speeded the harvesting of wheat. The railroads opened new lands for farming and also provided a means of shipping the products of the farms to the cities. The early self-propelled tractors were yet another step in improving the efficiency of the nation's farms. All these advances helped to transform farming into big business.

The transcontinental railroad companies received vast grants of land. Selling this land to farmers helped to create business for the railroad.

A gasoline tractor and plow.

75

America's farms produce an abundance of products such as the grain and cattle shown here.

Modern farm machinery can perform many complex tasks.

Today's farms are more productive than ever. New machines plow, plant, tend, and harvest crops. Scientists study and develop new ways to increase the yields of livestock and land.

Fewer people than ever now work on the nation's farms, yet the output of those farms has never been higher. In 1900 the labor of one farm worker fed about seven people. Today one farm worker feeds about 68 people.

This growth in productivity means that a surplus of some crops is available for export to other countries. Thus American farmers feed not only this nation but also many of the world's people.

Chapter 4

Democratic Ideas in Colonial America

Roger Williams, Puritan leader, fleeing for safety through the snow-covered forests of New England to live with his friends, the Narragansett Indians . . .

Anne Hutchinson, devout student of the Bible, founding a new settlement because she refused to submit to the authorities of Massachusetts Bay Colony . . .

Lord Baltimore, wealthy Catholic proprietor of Maryland, arguing vigorously for the passage of his famous Toleration Act . . .

John Peter Zenger, editor of the *New York Weekly Journal,* a lonely figure in a cold and cheerless prison cell, writing articles for his newspaper . . .

They form a proud company, these and other leaders who battled for the colonists' right to be free. And there were others— many others whose names we do not know. From the earliest days of settlement, and despite the blot of slavery, a great number of colonists struggled for freedom. They fought for the right to worship as they pleased, to secure an education, to speak their minds freely, to take part in government. When people have these rights and freedoms, they are said to live in a "democratic society," or simply in a "democracy."

In Chapter 2 you saw how the colonists built their settlements along the Atlantic seaboard. In this chapter you will see how they began to carry the idea of freedom into their churches, schools, and government. This idea of freedom lies at the root of what is often called "the American way of life."

THE CHAPTER IN OUTLINE

1. Religious tolerance spreads through the colonies.

2. Freedom to learn and freedom to think strike fertile soil.

3. The colonists gain valuable experience in self-government.

4. Colonial legislative assemblies gain power in America.

Changing Ways of American Life

1607–1763

1 Religious tolerance spreads through the colonies

When settlers first left Europe to build colonies in the New World, little or no religious freedom existed in the Old World. Each European nation had an **established church,** or official church. In each nation the government collected taxes to support the established church. Everyone was required to be a member of the church and contribute to its support.

European religious practices. Naturally enough, the first settlers who came to the New World brought the idea of an established church with them. In the French, Spanish, and Portuguese colonies of the Americas, the Roman Catholic Church was the established church. In part of New York and in all of the Southern Colonies, including Maryland after 1692, the Anglican Church became the established church. The official church in the New England Colonies of Massachusetts, Connecticut, and New Hampshire was the Con-gregational Church. The Middle Colonies, on the other hand, had so many different religious groups that no single church was established, except for the Anglican Church in part of New York.

The early settlers also brought to the New World the bitter religious conflicts and rivalries of the Old World. Border warfare often broke out between the Protestant British colonists of New England and the Roman Catholic French colonists of New France. Although these clashes were mainly caused by economic and political differences, they were made worse by religious differences.

Even within the colonies, the various religious groups often persecuted one another. Many colonists came to the New World searching for religious freedom. However, they were thinking of freedom only for themselves. Plymouth was for Separatists. Massachusetts Bay Colony was for Puritans who had not at first completely rejected the Anglican Church. Colonists who refused to accept the official religious beliefs were often thrown into jail or driven from the colony. Once exiled, they might be put to death if they returned. Such was the fate of

The Pilgrims set up the colony at Plymouth for "the advancement of the Christian faith." However, they understood this to mean the "advancement" of their sect only and at times harshly repressed those with different beliefs.

Mary Dyer, a Quaker, who was hanged in Boston in 1660 when she returned to protest the persecution of other Quakers.

Roger Williams and a new idea. Roger Williams, as you have read, was one colonist who dared to fight against intolerance. The colony of Rhode Island, of which he was the leading founder, became a symbol of religious freedom for America and the whole world. In Rhode Island there was no established church. Church and state—that is, the government—were separate. No one could be taxed for the support of a church. No one could be forced to attend church. No one had to belong to a church in order to vote. People could worship as they pleased and speak their minds freely.

Lord Baltimore and William Penn. In the struggle for greater religious tolerance, Lord Baltimore and William Penn also won notable victories. In both Maryland and Pennsylvania, the principle of religious toleration became part of the basic law.

In Maryland, as you have read, Lord Baltimore secured passage of the Toleration Act of 1649. The Toleration Act provided that all those "professing to believe in Jesus Christ" were free to practice their religion. They could not be persecuted because of their religious beliefs. The Maryland law, however, gave no protection to Jews and others who did not profess belief in Jesus Christ. Thus it did not establish the complete religious freedom that existed in Rhode Island.

In Pennsylvania religious toleration was broader than in Maryland but not as broad as in Rhode Island. Any person could settle in Pennsylvania if he or she believed that "one Almighty and Eternal God" was the "Creator, Upholder, and Ruler of the World." Only Christians, however, could take part in the government.

The growth of toleration. With Rhode Island, Maryland, and Pennsylvania leading the way, all of the colonies eventually grew more tolerant in matters of religion. As time passed, religious groups found it increasingly difficult to control the lives of all the settlers.

For practical reasons, the leaders of each colony wanted as many people as possible to settle in their colony. Increased population was likely to bring wealth to the king, the propri-

SOURCES

THE RHODE ISLAND CHARTER (1663)

No person within the said colony, at any time hereafter, shall be any wise molested, punished, disquieted, or called in question for any differences in opinion in matters of religion . . . . All and every person and persons may, from time to time, and at all times hereafter, freely and fully have and enjoy his and their own judgments and consciences in matters of religious concernments. . . .

THE MARYLAND TOLERATION ACT (1649)

Be it . . . enacted . . . that no person or persons . . . professing to believe in Jesus Christ shall . . . henceforth be any ways troubled, molested, or discountenanced . . . in respect of his or her religion nor in the free exercise thereof within this province. . . .

THE PENNSYLVANIA CHARTER OF PRIVILEGES (1701)

I [William Penn] do hereby grant and declare that no person or persons inhabiting . . . this province or territories who shall confess and acknowledge *One* Almighty God . . . shall be in any case molested or prejudiced in his or their person or estate because of his or their conscientious persuasion or practice. . . . .

etors, business owners, and the people in general. Thus the colonial leaders found it almost impossible to keep people out simply because they held different religious beliefs. As people of many different religions began to settle side by side in the British colonies, religious toleration began to increase.

Restrictions upon blacks. White colonists did little to spread Christianity among black colonists, slave or free. The white colonists knew that Christianity taught the importance and dignity of each person. Slaveowners, especially in the 1600's, feared that if black people

This needlepoint of people going to church was made in the Middle Colonies in the mid-1700's. The Middle Colonies were more tolerant of religious differences than were the New England Colonies.

learned this Christian teaching, they might rebel against slavery. Though many blacks did merge some aspects of Christianity with African religious traditions, during much of the colonial period the majority of black people in the colonies were in effect excluded from Christianity.

There were exceptions. Some masters taught their slaves lessons about Christianity and included them in sessions of family worship. In the early 1700's, Anglican missionary groups urged slaveowners to give Christian instruction to their slaves. The Anglicans also set up schools in various colonial towns where black people could learn Christian teachings.

The Quakers did more than any other religious group to teach Christianity to black colonists. At Philadelphia in 1700, the Quakers established a yearly religious meeting for blacks. In later colonial times, a few smaller religious groups made some efforts to include black members. In 1758, for example, a Baptist congregation in Virginia accepted black members.

Even blacks who were allowed to join Christian churches, however, were almost always kept separate, or **segregated,** from white church members. Anglicans in the Southern Colonies sometimes built separate chapels on

their plantations where slaves could worship. Puritans reserved an "African pew" for their few black members. As late as 1787, a Methodist congregation in Philadelphia forced black members to sit in the back row of the gallery. Angered by this discrimination, the black members withdrew and founded their own church—the African Methodist Episcopal Church.

Separation of church and state. Among the white colonists, the growing spirit of religious toleration weakened the foundations of the established churches. The state found it harder to collect taxes for the support of a church to which many taxpayers did not belong.

As the years passed, the established churches in the British colonies lost more and more power. Established churches continued to exist in the New England Colonies, except Rhode Island, and in the Southern Colonies until after the Revolutionary War. However, the movement that was to destroy their privileged position gathered strength in colonial America.

The Great Awakening. One major force that weakened the position of the established churches was a movement known as the Great

80

Awakening. In the 1730's and 1740's, a wave of religious revivals swept through the colonies. The religious awakening was led by visiting ministers from England, notably George White-field (WHIT·feeld) and John Wesley. They were joined by local preachers, of whom Jonathan Edwards of Northampton, Massachusetts, was most outstanding. Their message was clear and direct: Belonging to an established church was not enough to assure being saved. Salvation was freely available to all—men, women, or children—who of their own free will repented of their sins, believed in Christ as saviour, and experienced the Holy Spirit.

The Great Awakening gave many people the experience of freedom of choice in their religious lives. This in turn helped strengthen the democratic forces in colonial life.

SECTION SURVEY

IDENTIFY: religious freedom, religious toleration, segregation, separation of church and state, Great Awakening, Jonathan Edwards.

1. (a) What is an established church? (b) Which British colonies had established churches? (c) Why did some colonies not have them?
2. How did Roger Williams, Lord Baltimore, and William Penn contribute to the growth of religious toleration in colonial America?
3. (a) Why were most blacks in the colonies excluded from Christianity? (b) In what other ways were blacks discriminated against by colonial churches?
4. Source Study: According to the Sources on page 79, who was entitled to religious freedom in Rhode Island, Maryland, and Pennsylvania?

---

2 Freedom to learn and freedom to think strike fertile soil

In addition to religious freedom, freedom to learn, to think, to speak, and to publish are among the essentials of a democratic way of life. People who do not have these freedoms cannot vote intelligently or solve the problems, public and personal, that they face from day to day.

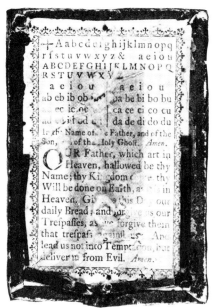

At a time when paper was scarce, New England school children learned from hornbooks. One costly sheet of paper was pasted onto a board and then covered with clear horn to protect it.

In the 1600's and 1700's, freedom to learn, to think, to speak, and to publish was severely limited throughout most of Europe.

Ideas about education. Europeans in general believed that only the sons of wealthy families needed a formal education. Of course, every now and then, an able boy from a middle- or lower-income home got an education and rose to prominence. A few daughters of wealthy families received some formal education from tutors. Girls in middle- and lower-income families, though, had even fewer educational opportunities than their brothers. In some Protestant families, especially Puritan families, the stress on personal knowledge of the Bible resulted in girls as well as boys learning to read.

The European settlers brought these ideas about education to the colonies. The wealthy colonial families in the towns and on large plantations hired tutors for their sons. They could also afford to buy books, pamphlets, and newspapers. Some wealthy colonists sent their sons to private schools and universities in England. Others sent their sons to one of the colonial colleges. Daughters in such families usually learned some music and literature from tutors and, in rare cases, subjects taught to

Phillis Wheatley, a Massachusetts slave, was unusual for her poetic talent as well as for having had the chance to learn. This picture appeared in the British edition of her poems.

their brothers. Thus, for example, Jane Colden, daughter of the lieutenant-governor of New York, became known for her work in botany.

Nine colonial colleges for male students— among them Harvard, William and Mary, Queen's College (later named Rutgers), and King's College (later named Columbia)—were started before the Revolutionary War to train ministers. They offered about the same subjects as English colleges on which they were modeled. Latin and Greek were required.

Changing ideas in education. Before long, however, the well-to-do colonists began to feel that their children needed a different kind of education. In the first place, the planters, who made their money by exporting goods to England, took an active part in business. Some of these planters became prosperous merchants who wanted their sons to know more about practical business affairs. Some colonial schools began to offer courses in navigation, geography, modern languages, accounting, and commercial law.

In the second place, the well-to-do colonists realized that they lived in a rural, isolated society. Their children could easily grow up in ignorance, no better educated than the children of poorer people were.

Finally, the scarcity of books in the colonies led many merchants to organize library societies. Members of these societies paid small fees to borrow books. In a few communities, some small public and commercial libraries were also established.

Thus conditions in the New World changed the traditional ideas about education that the wealthy colonists brought with them from England.

Limitations on schooling. Most colonists— the small farmers living near the villages, the pioneers, and the shopkeepers and artisans of the towns—did not have money to buy books. Nor could they afford to hire tutors or to send their children to private schools and colleges. Most of their energy went into the hard job of earning a living. Yet many men and women in the colonies knew how to read, write, and do simple arithmetic. Even on the frontier, where neither schools nor churches existed, some children were taught to read by their parents. In the towns some children, while learning a trade as apprentices, also learned to read and write and do simple arithmetic through the kindness of their masters. In all of the colonies, there were a few elementary schools that children of poorer families could attend.

In the Middle and Southern Colonies, some schools were maintained by the churches, but these schools were few and far between. South of Delaware the children of farmers and other workers had only limited opportunities to go to school.

Few children of black parents, whether slave or free, could get an education in any of the colonies. Anglican missionary societies and the Quakers offered simple schooling to a few black people. One Quaker, Anthony Benezet, opened a school for blacks in Philadelphia in 1750. Very rarely, a master or mistress taught a household slave to read and write. Phillis Wheatley, a slave child who learned in this way, studied English and Latin as well as geography, history, and astronomy. As a teenager Phillis began to write lyric poems that were later published and highly praised.

The first public schools. New England colonists could get an education more easily than people in any of the other colonies. The Puritan leaders believed that people were more likely to become God-fearing and law-abiding citizens if they could read the Bible.

For hundreds of years in Europe, the Bible had been copied mostly in Latin. During the Protestant Reformation, however, the Bible was translated and printed in German, French, English, and other European languages. The New England leaders were determined that the ability to read the English Bible should not die out in the New World.

To insure that this ability would be fostered, the Massachusetts government passed a law in 1647. This law ordered that every town having 50 householders or more should appoint a teacher of reading and writing to be paid out of town funds. The law also provided that every town having 100 householders or more must either provide a school to prepare young men for college or else pay a penalty. Families able to pay rates, or tuition, to the towns for the schooling of their children were required to do so. Tuition money for children from the poorest families, however, was paid directly out of town funds.

This law was the first of its kind in the English-speaking world. It was not popular everywhere in Massachusetts. Towns sometimes neglected to provide the education ordered by the law. Nevertheless, the law was a landmark in the history of education. It expressed a new and daring idea—that education of all the people was a public responsibility.

The town schools of colonial New England, then, were one of America's greatest contributions to modern civilization. Free public education, paid for with public funds, remains one of the strongest roots of democracy.

The quality of schooling. The quality of education in colonial schools was not always high. Many teachers were not much better educated than the children they taught. Often, especially in New England, the teacher of the very youngest pupils was one of the mothers. She heard the children recite their lessons while she did her washing and baking. Sometimes the village preacher conducted the classes.

In many schools indentured male servants did the teaching. Although some of them were able scholars of excellent character, others were inferior in every way.

Classes were often held in a church, a town hall, or a private home. Children of all ages generally sat in the same room and were taught by the same teacher. School terms were short. Attendance was irregular, for at any time a child might have to stay at home to help plant or harvest crops or to cut wood.

Chalkboards, paper, and crayons were seldom available, and textbooks were rare. The one exception was the *New England Primer.* This little book first appeared about 1690, and more than 3 million copies were sold during the 1700's. The primer was more than a reader. It taught school children to be obedient, to be law-abiding citizens, and to worship God.

Education on farms and frontier. The education of the ordinary people in the colonies was not limited to what they could learn from their parents, in the classroom, or as apprentices. Much of the education of the frontier settlers and pioneer farmers came from experience. Faced with problems for which they had nothing to guide them, people learned to think for themselves and to work out their own solutions. On the farm and frontier, people had to be practical, inventive, self-sufficient, and flexible in their thinking. This was a new kind of education, and it would have great influence upon the development of American democracy.

Few books reached the frontier, but many pioneer farm families owned copies of the Bible and much-thumbed **almanacs.** The almanacs were books containing a wide variety of information. They offered advice on medicine, recipes, planting, and harvesting. They contained discussions of politics and religion and selec-

SOURCES _____

POOR RICHARD'S
ALMANAC
(1758)

But dost thou love Life, then do not squander Time; for that's the stuff Life is made of.

Early to Bed, and early to rise, makes a Man healthy, wealthy, and wise.

At the working Man's House Hunger looks in, but dares not enter.

A Ploughman on his Legs is higher than a Gentleman on his Knees.

'Tis easier to build two Chimnies, than to keep one in Fuel.

This household, like most in colonial times, was an extended family. All the generations as well as the unmarried members of the family lived together. This meant more people were available to share the daily household tasks.

tions from great European writers. In many simple proverbs, they urged farmers to be content with their lives, obedient, respectful, thrifty, and industrious. The farmers also received some intellectual stimulation from public meetings and from Sunday church sermons.

Education in towns. The ordinary townspeople—owners of small shops, artisans, dock workers, and the like—had more opportunities than the farmers or pioneers for formal education. By the 1700's, in addition to the regular schools, an increasing number of private evening schools taught young men mathematics, accounting, modern languages, and other subjects useful in business.

Townspeople could also obtain reading material more easily than farmers or frontier settlers. Townspeople had Bibles, almanacs, a few books, pamphlets, and, by the 1700's, a growing number of newspapers. People who could not afford to buy the newspapers could read them or hear them read at a nearby tavern.

The papers contained news, sermons, and articles contributed by readers. People in the towns also picked up news and ideas from public meetings, gatherings at taverns, and debating societies. In these ways many colonial townspeople learned to think for themselves and to express their opinions.

Changing roles of women. The new conditions in the colonies changed the way people thought and learned. They also helped change attitudes toward women and their roles. Women played a special part in creating colonial America. Their contributions were noteworthy in the lives of colonial families and in colonial society alike.

During the 1600's and 1700's, women in the colonies, like women everywhere, were not considered equal to men. In all of the colonies, law, religion, and custom recognized men as the heads of their families. By law, men were given full authority and control over their children. Women could not vote or, if married, own property. Any wages that women earned outside the home belonged to their husbands or, if they were unmarried, to their fathers. Most girls did not attend school beyond the elementary level unless their families were rich and hired private teachers. Thus, in America, as in Europe, women lacked the higher education needed to become ministers, lawyers, or doctors.

Despite such disadvantages, women in America had greater opportunities than women in Europe. For one thing, far more young men than women immigrated to the American colonies. Also, during these years many women died during childbirth. As a result, women were a smaller part of the population than men. This fact, in many ways, favored a wider range of opportunities and greater influence for colonial women. Moreover, there was a great shortage of labor throughout the colonies. Thus some women ran shops and small businesses, printed newspapers, took up blacksmithing, and followed many other trades. As a result, women enjoyed higher status and a greater degree of economic independence in the American colonies than they did in Europe.

In the colonies girls and women made many of the furnishings for their homes. In farming areas they also raised poultry, milked the cows, and at times helped in the fields during the harvest. On plantations the ability of women to organize and manage contributed to economic success. Those women who went to the frontier with their husbands shared the dangers of frontier life and did many of the customary tasks of men.

Women also took an active part in settling many new communities. They helped to establish churches in these new settlements and also taught the children and cared for the sick. By such contributions colonial women achieved a sense of importance despite limitations on their political rights, property rights, choice of careers, and authority within the family.

Victory for a free press. From the earliest days, many colonial leaders disliked anything that threatened the respect that they felt the ordinary people owed them. These leaders believed that it was dangerous to educate men and women or allow them to read freely. This point of view was expressed by William Berkeley, governor of Virginia, who once boasted that while he was governor, Virginia had neither free schools nor printing presses.

Many colonists held a directly opposite point of view. They believed that people should be free to learn, to think, and to express their opinions. They also believed that printers should be free to print and distribute their own thoughts and the thoughts of others. Many colonists believed that a newspaper should be allowed to print the truth even if the truth offended the governing authorities.

One colonial printer, John Peter Zenger, was arrested in 1734 for publishing newspaper articles that criticized the royal governor of New York. Under British law, this made him guilty of criminal libel, even if his criticisms were true.

Zenger was defended by Andrew Hamilton, an able lawyer. In deciding Zenger's case, Hamilton told the jury, they would be deciding the fate of every free person in the colonies. "Truth," Hamilton argued, "ought to govern the whole affair of libels." Hamilton's plea succeeded, and the jury found Zenger innocent.

The Zenger case did not change the British law on libel, nor did it insure freedom of the press. Still, it marked a long step toward freedom of the press. From their beginnings in colonial times, freedom of speech and of the press have developed into two of the stronger roots of democratic society.

SECTION SURVEY

IDENTIFY: Phillis Wheatley, Anthony Benezet, public schools, *New England Primer*, almanacs, freedom of the press.

1. (a) What Old World ideas about education did the colonists bring with them to the New World? (b) In what ways did conditions in the New World help to change these ideas?

2. Free public education is one of the strongest roots of democracy. Do you agree or disagree? Explain your answer.

3. Why was the education law that the government of Massachusetts passed in 1647 a landmark in the history of education?

4. What disadvantages did women in the colonies suffer? What opportunities did they have?

5. Why was the trial of John Peter Zenger a step forward toward freedom of the press?

6. Picture Study: Identify the tasks performed by women in the picture on page 84.

3 The colonists gain valuable experience in self-government

In their colonial governments as well as in religion and education, the colonists fought for more freedom. During their struggle for freedom, they gained experience in politics and firmly planted the roots of representative government.

Virginia led the way in 1619, as you have read, by creating the House of Burgesses. The House of Burgesses gave Virginia the first representative government in America. It also provided an example for the other colonies.

Types of colonial governments. England established three types of colonies in America: (1) royal colonies administered by the English government, (2) proprietary colonies belonging to proprietors, and (3) self-governing colonies largely independent of English control. Each colony had a governor, a council, and a representative assembly.

In a royal colony—and by the 1760's eight of the thirteen colonies were royal colonies—the king appointed the governor and councilors. These men administered the laws, sat as a high court of justice, and acted as the upper house of the **legislature,** or law-making body. The lower house, or assembly, was elected by the qualified voters. Although the lower house helped to make the laws, the king or his representative could veto its actions.

In proprietary colonies—including, by the 1760's, Maryland, Pennsylvania, and Delaware—the proprietor was granted a large amount of power by the king of England. The proprietor, who usually lived in England, appointed the governor and, in the case of Maryland, the councilors who formed the upper house of the legislature. The lower house was elected by the voters, just as in the eight royal colonies. Pennsylvania's legislature had only one house—the assembly.

The two remaining colonies, Rhode Island and Connecticut, were self-governing. Each was in large part independent of England. The voters elected the governor and the representatives in both the upper and lower houses of the legislature.

The Fundamental Orders. Connecticut was the first colony to adopt a **written constitution,** or written plan of government. This constitution was known as the Fundamental Orders of Connecticut. As you have read, the Orders were adopted in 1639, only three years after Thomas Hooker and his party of settlers arrived on the banks of the Connecticut River.

The Fundamental Orders may be regarded as a written constitution even though they could be revoked or amended by a simple majority of the legislature. The "eleven orders" were a detailed guide for organizing the government and electing government officials. When disputes arose, the written law, not the opinions of the lawmakers, was to be the guide for deciding issues. This principle of government under a written constitution became a cornerstone of American government.

It is important to remember, however, that none of the colonists, including the colonists of Connecticut, were thinking of what today is called democracy. The idea of a representative assembly had already been established in England with the House of Commons, the lower house of Parliament. In organizing their representative assemblies, the colonists were simply following the British example. Thomas Hooker and his followers wrote the Fundamental Orders because this seemed the best way to solve the problem of how to govern themselves in a new community.

SOURCES

FUNDAMENTAL ORDERS OF CONNECTICUT (1639)

It is ordered ... that there shall be yearly two general assemblies or courts: ... The first shall be called the Court of Election....

It is ordered ... that no person be chosen governor above once in two years....

It is ordered ... that to the aforesaid Court of Election the several towns shall send their deputies....

The Founding of the American Colonies

Colonies	Date founded – reasons for founding	Types of government before 1776
NEW ENGLAND COLONIES		
Massachusetts	1620—religious freedom	Plymouth—joint-stock company from 1620 until united with Massachusetts Bay Colony in 1691. Massachusetts Bay Colony joint-stock company 1620–84; royal 1684–1776
New Hampshire	1623—agriculture, trade, and fishing	Proprietary 1623–41; joint-stock company 1641–79; royal 1679–1776
Connecticut	1635—agriculture, trade	Self-governing 1635–62; joint-stock company 1662–87, 1689–1776; royal 1686–89
Rhode Island	1636—religious freedom	Self-governing 1636–44; royal 1686–89; joint-stock company 1644–86, 1689–1776
MIDDLE COLONIES		
New York	1624—agriculture, trade	Dutch colony 1624–64; proprietary 1664–85; royal 1685–1776
New Jersey	1629—agriculture, trade	Dutch, Swedish colonies 1629–64; proprietary 1664–1702; royal 1702–1776
Delaware	1638—agriculture, trade	Swedish colony 1638–55; Dutch colony 1655–64; proprietary 1664–1776
Pennsylvania	1682—religious freedom, agriculture, and trade	Proprietary 1682–1776
SOUTHERN COLONIES		
Virginia	1607—agriculture, trade	Joint-stock company 1607–24; royal 1624–1776
Maryland	1634—religious freedom, agriculture, and trade	Proprietary 1634–91, 1715–76; royal 1691–1715
North Carolina	1653—agriculture, trade	Self-governing 1653–63; proprietary 1663–1729; royal 1729–76
South Carolina	1670—agriculture, trade	Proprietary 1670–1721; royal 1721–76
Georgia	1733—refuge for debtors, buffer against Spanish Florida, agriculture, and trade	Proprietary 1733–52; royal 1752–76

Limitations on self-government. Regardless of the reason, the fact remains that many colonists had a voice in the government of the British colonies in North America. However, in the colonies, as in England at that time, the voice was still a limited one.

The right to vote, or **suffrage,** was limited in several ways. In the first place, only adult males who owned a specified amount of property could vote. To vote, a man had to prove that he owned a farm or town lot of a certain size or that he had an income and paid taxes of a certain amount. These property qualifications existed even in the self-governing colonies of Connecticut and Rhode Island.

In the second place, religious qualifications kept many people from voting. In many colonies, particularly during the 1600's, men who did not belong to the established church could not vote. Slaves were not permitted to vote in any of the colonies. Neither were women.

In addition to the people who were not permitted to vote, many who might have voted did not bother to do so. Some of these people had never enjoyed political rights in Europe. When they came to the colonies, they did not concern themselves with political matters. They were content to leave them to men of greater wealth and education. Finally, the isolation of frontier life kept many pioneers from voting and participating in the government.

To be elected to the colonial assemblies, a man had to meet even higher qualifications than he did to vote. These qualifications varied from colony to colony. In South Carolina, for example, an assemblyman had to own 500 acres (202.4 hectares) of land and ten slaves, or own land, houses, and other property worth a substantial sum of money. Because of these qualifications, the representatives who were elected to the colonial assemblies generally were men of wealth and influence.

The struggle over the assemblies. Many ordinary people in the colonies resented the amount of political power in the hands of the well-to-do. Their resentment sometimes led to outbreaks of violence.

Patrick Henry of Virginia first gained fame as a lawyer in 1763 in what was known as the case of the Parson's Cause. In this case Henry argued that a ruler who governs badly by so doing gives up the right to be obeyed.

This conflict between the well-to-do and the ordinary people, most of whom were farmers, is sometimes called the conflict between the seaboard and the frontier. The wealthy people on the seaboard—planters, rich town merchants, and influential lawyers—controlled the assemblies. They tended to vote for laws that protected their own interests. The ordinary people—wage earners, farmers, and frontier settlers—had only a limited voice in the assemblies. They had few legal ways to pass laws that they wanted or to protect themselves from laws that harmed their interests.

Bacon's Rebellion. In Virginia in 1676, the conflict between the well-to-do and the ordinary people finally erupted into a clash of violence. This became known as Bacon's Rebellion, after its leader Nathaniel Bacon.

For many years the frontier settlers and small farmers of Virginia had been dissatisfied with the rule of Governor Berkeley. These groups claimed that they, the ordinary people, were not fairly represented in the colonial legislature. They were in debt, taxes were high, and the price of tobacco was low. They further claimed that Governor Berkeley and the wealthy planters had deliberately refused to crush an Indian uprising, not wishing to anger the Indians. Many of the planters had a profitable fur trade with these Indians.

Settlers who had moved into Indian lands in the outlying regions of Virginia were eager to open up the country to white settlers. When the Susquehanna Indians resisted, the settlers demanded military action. After an Indian attack in which many colonists were killed, a wealthy young settler, Nathaniel Bacon, gathered a force of several hundred men. They marched to the frontier and wiped out the Occaneechees (awk·uh·NEE·cheez), a friendly tribe. Bacon's followers then seized Jamestown, gained control of the legislature, and passed laws favoring the ordinary people.

Bacon's Rebellion was short-lived. When Nathaniel Bacon died a few months later, Berkeley and the large planters recovered power and crushed what was left of the resistance.

The need for local government. Out of their long struggle for control of the colonial legislatures, the colonists acquired practical experience in politics. It was in local government, however, especially in New England, that the colonists enjoyed the greatest opportunity to practice self-government.

From the very beginning, every colonial community, large or small, had to make rules or laws to carry on the everyday affairs of community life. In many early communities, conflicts with the Indians required defense against attack and organized force for counterattack. All communities also faced problems of fire and police protection, sanitation, and schooling. They also had to settle disputes between citizens and solve many other everyday problems.

No one questioned the need for local government. However, all the colonists had to answer one big question. Who would make and enforce the local laws?

Local government in New England. The Pilgrims thought about this question even before they set foot in New England. As you have read, in writing the Mayflower Compact, the Pilgrims drew up an agreement under which they were to live.

After they settled at Plymouth, using the Mayflower Compact as their guide, the Pilgrims established a form of local government that was later adopted by other New England communities. This new form of local government came to be called the **town meeting.**

On town-meeting days most citizens gathered in the town hall to discuss town problems, levy taxes on themselves, and elect town officers. The discussions sometimes became heated, for all citizens had the right to say what they thought.

The principal town officers were the **selectmen,** usually three in number. The selectmen administered the laws that the voters adopted in the town meeting. Only the men voted and, in the early days, the right to vote was also limited by religious and property qualifications. Nevertheless, the New England town meetings provided larger opportunities to take part in government than citizens enjoyed in either the Middle or the Southern Colonies.

Local government in other colonies. The town meeting type of government met the needs of people living in the small farming villages and towns of New England. In the Southern Colonies, most people lived on large plantations or on more or less isolated farms. Local government there had to cover a much larger area than a town. In the Southern Colonies, therefore, the people established the county as the unit of local government. Some southern counties covered several hundred square miles.

The chief officers of the county included the **justices of the peace.** These officers carried out the laws, acted as judges in legal disputes, and levied and collected taxes. They also provided for roads and distributed county funds to widows, orphans, and other people who could not support themselves. A county lieutenant was in charge of defending the county against Indian attacks and against serious disturbances by the colonists. These officers were usually appointed by the governor, but they were chosen from people living in the county itself.

The Middle Colonies adopted a mixture of both the town and the county type of local government. In New York the town was generally the unit of local government. In Pennsylvania the county type of local government was more important.

SECTION SURVEY

IDENTIFY: written constitution, suffrage, Bacon's Rebellion, town meeting, selectmen, county, justice of the peace.

1. Describe the differences in the three types of colonial governments. What features did they have in common?
2. What kinds of restrictions on voting and office holding existed in the colonies? List three examples.
3. What were the causes of Bacon's Rebellion?
4. (a) What was the usual form of local government in the New England Colonies? in the Middle and Southern Colonies? (b) Why did this difference arise?

4 Colonial legislative assemblies gain power in America

The struggle for a larger voice in the colonial governments was only one continuing conflict of the colonial period. Except in the self-governing colonies of Rhode Island and Connecticut, the colonial governments were really split into two parts. In general, the governor and the councilors usually served the interests of the British empire as a whole. The assemblies, on the other hand, represented the interests of the colonists.

89

Punishment for crime in colonial times was harsh. The convicted forger in this drawing was put on public display in the pillory for one hour. Then he had an ear cut off and received 20 lashes.

Attitude of British officials. Because of this division, political controversy in the colonies often centered on the royal governors. Most governors were selected from the ruling group in Great Britain—politicians, lawyers, and soldiers. At times, though, the Crown appointed a favored or privileged colonist as governor.

In making appointments to the royal colonies, the Crown did not necessarily look for those with ability. Sometimes the king awarded the positions to his friends and favorites. Some royal governors were excellent administrators who tried to balance British and colonial interests. A few were narrow-minded, shortsighted, and without training or experience for the offices they held.

Whether good, bad, or indifferent, most of the governors used their positions to increase their own fortunes. Many were willing to pay handsomely to secure the jobs.

The military officers and clerks who served the royal governors were, as a rule, no better than their superiors. They were often appointed merely because they were friends of the governor. Such practices were common in Great Britain as well as in the colonies.

Even so, many able people held positions of authority in the colonies. As a result, the colonies, which enjoyed the advantage of being part of a growing British empire, owed a great deal to the mother country.

Growing power of the assemblies. As representatives of the British government, the royal officials naturally stressed the Crown's point of view. Most colonists, speaking through their representatives in the assemblies, held the opposite point of view. Why, they asked, should they pay taxes to provide high salaries to countless outsiders from Great Britain, many of whom were lazy and incompetent? What right had anybody to say that the interests of the colonists were less important than the interests of the people in Great Britain?

Fortunately for the colonists, they had one extremely powerful weapon that helped curb the authority of the royal governors. The colonists controlled the purse strings. That is, the colonial assemblies had the power to vote all grants of money to be spent by the colonial governments.

Suppose the governor asked for money to pay the salaries of nine new clerks he wanted to appoint. The assembly could say, "Yes, we'll grant you the money—provided you allow us to name the men you appoint." Or suppose the governor requested money to pay his official expenses. The assembly could say, "Yes, we'll grant the money—provided you first submit a statement explaining in detail how you will spend the money."

Sometimes the assemblies refused to grant funds to pay the governors' salaries until the end of each year. In this way the colonists let the governors know that they would do well to rule wisely.

The governors hated these limits on their power, but they could not do much about them. They needed money to carry on the everyday business of the colonies and they wanted good salaries for themselves. This money could come only from the assemblies. Even before the Revolutionary War, the colonial assemblies were practically their own masters. They had, to a great degree, already won their freedom from British control.

SECTION SURVEY

1. Due to a conflict of interests, colonial governments were split into two parts. Explain.

2. (a) How were royal governors chosen? (b) What effect did this process have on the quality of their leadership?

3. (a) What power did the colonial assemblies have over the royal governors? (b) How did the assemblies use this power?

Chapter Survey

Summary: Tracing the Main Ideas

The first small roots of democracy struck fertile soil in the British seaboard colonies. The colonists brought with them European ideas of restrictions on individual freedoms in religion, education, and the right to vote and hold public office.

However, discontent with these European ideas began to grow. The discontent grew slowly during the early years of colonization. It was growing more rapidly by the mid-1700's.

Stimulated by the growth of freedom in England itself and even more by the environment of the colonies, the settlers began to demand larger freedom for themselves. During the course of their struggles, they gained practical experience in politics and self-government. These colonists laid the groundwork for the principles of religious toleration, free public education, and representative government.

As you will see in Chapter 5, in the process of developing their own way of life, the colonists had in some ways grown much further away from Great Britain by 1763 than the British realized. This growth and the lack of understanding that accompanied it led to controversies between Great Britain and the colonies. Finally, in 1775, armed conflict broke out.

Inquiring into History

1. The environment of the colonies gradually caused changes in the ideas and ways of life brought from the Old World. Compare and discuss Old World and New World ideas concerning religion, education, representative government, and the role of women.
2. Compare education on the colonial frontier with education in colonial towns.
3. During the colonial period, many slaves were excluded from Christianity. How did this religious discrimination help to maintain slavery?
4. From 1607 to 1763, the colonists developed a spirit of independence that weakened their ties with England. Explain how each of the following contributed to this growing spirit of independence: (a) opportunities in America, (b) geography, including distance from England, and (c) growth of colonial democracy.

Relating Past to Present

1. Which of America's current democratic practices can be traced to ideas and institutions from its colonial past?
2. Are Americans still engaged in the process of furthering the democratic ideas and practices that were first developed during the colonial period? Give evidence to support your views.

Developing Social Science Skills

1. Suppose that it is 1740 and Great Britain has decided to draft American men into the British army to help fight a war against France. (a) Write the speech that the royal governor of New Jersey might give in response to the British draft plan. (b) Write a speech that a member of New Jersey's colonial assembly might give in reaction to the plan. (c) In what ways are the speeches different? Why are they different?
2. Read one or more poems by Anne Bradstreet, who lived in Massachusetts Bay Colony. (a) What do the poems reveal about life in the colonies for the people generally? for women? (b) Do you think her attitudes were typical of the attitudes of colonial women? Why or why not?
3. Works in needlepoint, like the one shown on page 80, are a part of America's folk-art heritage. Such works offer glimpses into daily life at the time they were made. Make a collection of pictures of needlepoint works for the bulletin board. Your local library, historical society, or art museum can be a good starting point.

Unit Survey

For Further Inquiry

1. (a) What aspects of culture did most Indian groups have in common? (b) In what aspects of life did Indian groups differ?
2. Do you think that, if Columbus had not "rediscovered" America, another explorer certainly would have? Why or why not?
3. (a) Name several reasons why people came to America. (b) Give examples of groups who came for each of those reasons.
4. Compare and contrast the colonial governments in (a) New Spain and (b) the English colonies.
5. Compare the relations between Indians and Europeans in (a) New Spain, (b) the English colonies, and (c) New France. How do you account for the similarities? the differences?

Projects and Activities

1. Study the maps on pages 6 and 29. (a) In what ways are the maps similar in terms of content or emphasis? How are they different? (b) Name two Indian tribes that might be particularly disturbed by European settlement.
2. Report on and demonstrate the musical contributions made to American culture by the American Indians, Africans, or some other group.
3. Imagine that you are a colonist in New Spain, New France, or an English colony. Write a letter to a friend "back home" about your life in America. Be sure to identify your age and where you live, as well as to describe the details of your daily life.
4. On a blank map of the world, illustrate the fact that people from many parts of the world settled the Americas before 1775. (You might do this with arrows showing routes of migration or by using colors to show how people's places of origin affected their area of settlement.)
5. Study the timeline on this page. (a) What general theme do all of the entries focus on? Explain how you can tell. (b) If this timeline were going to appear in a Mexican textbook, which entries would be most likely to be included? Why? (c) Make a timeline of your own covering the same years, but focusing on a different theme. (d) Will any of your entries be the same as those in the timeline above? Why or why not?

Exploring Your Region

1. Using a map of your state, locate cities, rivers, lakes, and other natural features that have names that are French, Spanish, Dutch, or Indian. You might also try to find translations of these names.
2. Prepare a bulletin-board display on the Indian tribes that lived in your region before the European settlers arrived.

Suggested Reading

1. *History of the Thirteen Colonies,* American Heritage. A lavishly illustrated account of life in America from the years before the Europeans arrived until 1776.
2. *Americans Before Columbus,* Elizabeth Baity. The story of America's earliest Indian civilizations.
3. *The Scarlet Letter,* Nathaniel Hawthorne. The classic psychological novel, set in colonial New England.
4. *White Falcon,* Elliot Arnold. A novel based on the real-life experiences of a white boy who lived with the Ottawa Indians.

Unit Two

Winning Independence

1763-1789

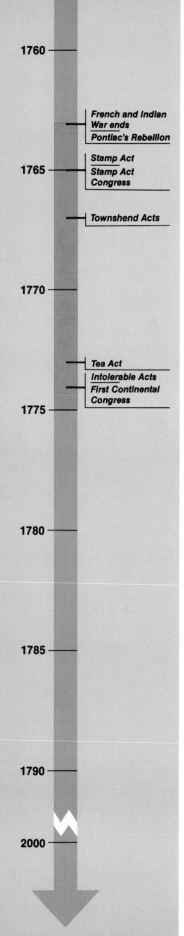

1760 —

French and Indian
War ends
Pontiac's Rebellion

Stamp Act
1765 — Stamp Act
Congress

Townshend Acts

1770 —

Tea Act
Intolerable Acts
First Continental
Congress
1775 —

1780 —

1785 —

1790 —

2000 —

Chapter 5

Moving Toward Independence

1763–1775

In the year 1763, the British people shared a deep sense of pride. Victorious over all its rivals, Great Britain had established claims to an empire that circled the globe. British harbors were jammed with shipping. Battered ships of the British navy and weatherworn transports rode on the incoming tides, bringing the fighting men of Great Britain back to their homes and families. Other British vessels weighed anchor and sailed out of the harbors, carrying government and military officials to the far-flung outposts of the empire.

To the average Britisher, the future appeared brighter than it had for many years. But thoughtful people in Great Britain and in other countries realized that the British empire faced many new and troublesome problems, particularly in the American colonies of the New World. One of these thoughtful observers of the colonies was a French government official named Count Vergennes (vair·ZHEN).

Vergennes, mindful that France had been driven from the North American continent, predicted a similar speedy end to Great Britain's moment of glory. "The American colonies stand no longer in need of England's protection," he said. England, he continued, "will call on them to help contribute toward supporting the burden they have helped to bring on her, and they will answer by striking off all dependence."

Vergennes proved to be an accurate prophet. Just 13 years after his prediction, the British colonies along the Atlantic seaboard declared their independence from Great Britain.

THE CHAPTER IN OUTLINE

1. Great Britain regulates colonial industry and trade.

2. The British face new problems in governing their empire.

3. The colonists oppose taxation without representation.

4. Tensions increase between Great Britain and the colonies.

5. The gap between Great Britain and the colonies grows wider.

1 Great Britain regulates colonial industry and trade

In 1763 Great Britain's steadily growing empire included 33 different colonies. Only 13 of these were located along the Atlantic seaboard. The other colonies were scattered throughout the world.

The mercantile system of trade. Why were British as well as other European leaders so eager to win colonies and build a colonial empire? To answer this question, you must understand what historians and economists have called **mercantilism.**

Briefly, mercantilism is an economic and political policy whereby a nation tries to gain greater wealth and power than its rivals. The mercantilism of the 1600's and 1700's aimed at building a powerful, self-sufficient empire in a world divided by religious wars and bitter commercial rivalry. Under mercantilism a nation's government tried to gain greater power than its rivals by building a larger army and navy. To build greater military power, a nation needed money. To get money, a nation tried to sell to other nations more goods than it bought from them. It tried, in other words, to build a **favorable balance of trade.** A nation gains a favorable balance of trade when it **exports,** or sells abroad, more products than it **imports,** or buys from other nations.

With a highly favorable balance of trade, a nation could (1) be self-sufficient, (2) become wealthy, and (3) build a powerful army and navy. Colonies were an essential part of the plan. The British, for example, thought that colonies would strengthen Great Britain in four ways.

First, colonies would provide the raw materials essential to a small island kingdom with a growing population. Second, colonies would provide markets for goods produced in Great Britain, particularly manufactured goods. Third, colonies would encourage the growth of a strong merchant fleet, which would serve as a training school for the Royal Navy. Fourth, colonies would also provide bases from which the Royal Navy could operate.

Restrictions on manufacturing. To apply the policy of mercantilism, the British Parliament passed many laws. One series of laws re-

In spite of Great Britain's policy of mercantilism, New York City thrived. Financiers and shippers met at Water and Wall streets in the Tontine Coffee House, on the left. It was the city's first stock exchange.

stricted nearly all the manufacturing of the British empire to England. A 1699 law, for example, forbade the colonists to export any wool or woolen cloth—even to a neighboring colony. Later laws forbade the colonists to manufacture beaver hats or iron products for export. The British government also tried to prevent skilled workers from leaving Great Britain, fearing that they would help the colonists start their own manufacturing plants.

At first, the American colonists did not find these restrictions a burden, since they had neither the money nor the skilled labor to establish industries.

Restrictions on shipping. Beginning in 1651, another series of laws, the Navigation Acts, restricted all trade within the empire to British, including colonial, ships. Only such ships could carry goods imported from Africa, Asia, and the American colonies of Great Britain's rivals into any port of the British empire.

Encouraged by the Navigation Acts, a powerful British merchant fleet was soon sailing the seas between the colonies and Great Britain. The American colonists, as British citizens, could build and sail their own ships and thus benefited greatly from the Navigation Acts. By the early 1770's, colonial shipyards were building one third of all merchant ships sailing under the British flag. Many American colonial merchants were becoming wealthy.

Restrictions on selling and buying. The Navigation Act of 1660 listed, or "enumerated," specific colonial products that could be shipped only to England. These **enumerated goods** included such important products as tobacco, cotton, and sugar. The colonists could not sell these products to other European countries, where they might have gotten higher prices.

By the 1700's the British government was paying **bounties** on some enumerated goods. Bounties are payments made to stimulate production of certain goods. The British paid bounties on tar, resin, turpentine, and hemp to stimulate colonial production of these naval stores, needed by the merchant fleet and the Royal Navy.

In 1663 Parliament passed a new Navigation Act. This act required the colonists to buy most of their manufactured goods from England. Further, all European goods headed for the colonies had to be sent first to England,

where the British unloaded the goods and collected an import **duty**—or tax—on them. Then they reloaded the products on a British vessel and sent them across the Atlantic. These requirements protected British manufacturers from the competition of their European rivals.

Friction under mercantilism. Other European nations with overseas colonies followed policies similar to Great Britain's. Thus mercantilism deepened rivalries between nations. This competition was a basic cause of the long years of war between Great Britain and France.

The mercantile policies also created friction within the British empire itself. They aroused jealousies even between colonial merchants. Colonial merchants with close family ties or other sources of influence in Great Britain received favors denied to other merchants.

Mercantile policies also created friction between Great Britain and some of its colonies in North America. At first, mercantilism seemed to threaten the prosperity of New England and the Middle Colonies. These colonies produced

MAJOR COLONIAL TRADE ROUTES

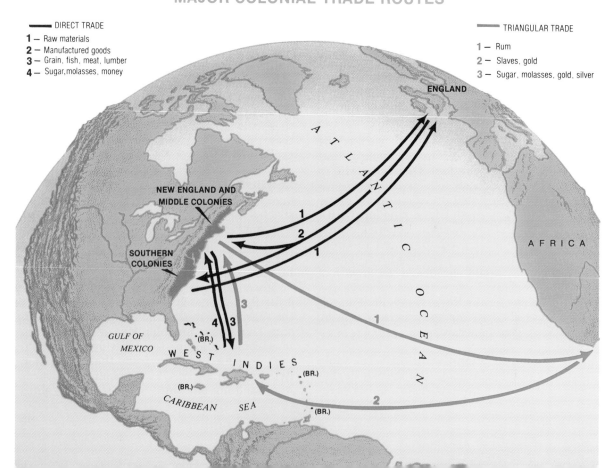

DIRECT TRADE

1 — Raw materials
2 — Manufactured goods
3 — Grain, fish, meat, lumber
4 — Sugar, molasses, money

TRIANGULAR TRADE

1 — Rum
2 — Slaves, gold
3 — Sugar, molasses, gold, silver

Slaves were shipped and traded as if they were cargo. This watercolor of the hold of the slave ship *Albatross* was painted in 1846 by a British naval officer. It is the only picture drawn from life of conditions on board a slave ship.

goods similar to those produced in Great Britain — grain, lumber, fish, cloth, iron, and other products. Great Britain did not want or need these colonial products. Parliament actually passed laws barring them from Great Britain.

Fortunately, the New England and Middle Colonies soon established new markets for their goods. As a result, the mercantile laws did not seriously disturb them.

Colonial trade routes.   A major source of income for the colonial merchants was what has been called a **triangular trade** involving Africa, the West Indies, and the colonies (see map, page 96).

Vessels from colonial ports set sail for Africa on the first leg of the triangle, carrying kegs of rum produced in colonial distilleries. On the west coast of Africa, the rum was exchanged for slaves or gold. From Africa the vessels set sail on the second leg of the voyage. They took the human cargoes crowded in the holds to the West Indies, where they exchanged them for molasses, sugar, or money. The final leg of the triangle brought the ships home to the colonies loaded with sugar or molasses, for making more rum, and a balance of gold and silver. Ships did not always follow this triangular trade route exactly. As often as not, their routes were dictated by the weather, by market conditions, by chance, or by the whim of the captain.

Another busy trade route directly con-

nected the colonies with the islands in the Caribbean Sea (see map, page 96). Ships from New England and the Middle Colonies sailed southward with grain, fish, meat, cloth, soap, lumber, shingles, knocked-down shacks for the slaves, and casks for molasses and sugar. On the return voyage, the ships carried sugar, molasses, and money.

Evading the mercantile laws.   Most of this trade was perfectly legal, but some of it directly violated British mercantile laws. One of the laws most violated was the Molasses Act of 1733.

Planters in the British West Indies had pushed the Molasses Act through Parliament. They hoped it would force the American colonists to buy all their sugar and molasses from the British West Indies. The Molasses Act stated that the colonists could buy similar supplies from French, Dutch, or Spanish islands only by paying a very high duty. Unfortunately, the British West Indies could supply only about one eighth of the molasses needed by the colonists. The colonial merchants thus felt compelled to evade the law.

A policy of salutary neglect.   If the British government had enforced the Molasses Act, many colonial merchants and businesses would have been ruined. Most rum distilleries would have been closed, and many workers would have lost their jobs.

However, for a long time Great Britain did not seriously attempt to enforce the Molasses Act. Indeed, the British government did not seriously attempt to enforce most of its mercantile laws. Instead, the British followed a policy of **salutary neglect**. This means that they deliberately failed to enforce the mercantile laws.

SECTION SURVEY

IDENTIFY: balance of trade, Navigation Acts, enumerated goods, bounty, import duty, triangular trade, Molasses Act of 1733.

1. Explain the mercantile system of trade as an economic and political policy.
2. (a) Under mercantilism, how did colonies benefit the colonizing nation? (b) How did the colonizing nation benefit its colonies?
3. Explain why it was important for a nation operating under mercantilism to place restrictions on the (a) manufacturing of goods, (b) shipping of goods, and (c) buying and selling of goods.
4. (a) In the 1600's and early 1700's, why were mercantile laws a potential source of tension between the New England and Middle Colonies and England? (b) In what ways did the colonists and the British avoid this tension?
5. Map Study: A nation's imports are sometimes directly useful in producing goods for export. Look at the map on page 96 and find three examples to support this statement.

2 **The British face new problems in governing their empire**

In 1763 Great Britain faced new problems in governing its empire. Candles and lamps in government offices burned late into the nights as British leaders wrestled with ways of dealing with its rapid growth.

The need for new taxes. One problem was the need for more money. Between 1689 and 1763 the British had fought four wars, which had left their nation heavily in debt. To make matters worse, the British government now needed even more money to maintain the defenses of its expanding worldwide empire.

British leaders quite naturally expected the American colonists to help pay the war debts. After all, the British reasoned, the colonists were subjects of the king. They ought to help pay for the cost of defense, especially their own defense.

Florida and Canada. Another troublesome problem was what to do with Florida and Canada — lands acquired by the British at the end of the French and Indian War. The governments of Florida and Canada had to be completely reorganized. The Spaniards and French in these areas, long-time enemies of Great Britain, were now British subjects, but subjects in name only. How could they be made loyal subjects? What kind of government would work best in these new regions?

The western lands. Particularly confusing for the British government was the problem of the former French territory west of the Appalachian Mountains. The British themselves could not agree on what policy to apply to these lands.

One group, led by the Hudson's Bay Company, was interested solely in the fur trade. This group wanted to prohibit settlers from moving west of the mountains. A much larger group, including most of the colonists, urged the government to open the western lands to pioneer farmers and **land speculators**. Land speculators were people who bought land hoping for a quick profit from its resale. To add to the complications, several different colonies claimed that their charters had given them grants of land in this region (see map, page 99).

Pontiac's Rebellion. In back of all the proposals and claims by the whites was the simple fact that this was Indian land. For more than 150 years, from the time the English first built settlements along the Atlantic coast, the Indians had been pushed steadily westward. In 1763 they had every reason to fear that colonial farmers would begin to pour over the mountains and drive them once again from their villages and hunting grounds.

Under the able leadership of Pontiac, an Ottawa chief, the Indians joined forces to prevent any further invasion of their lands. For nearly a year, the Indians and whites were locked in a desperate struggle. The Indians destroyed most of the British forts west of Niagara. Death and destruction raged along the length of the western frontier.

CONFLICTING CLAIMS TO WESTERN LANDS

Finally, British and colonial troops recaptured the forts. The Indians accepted generous peace terms. Pontiac declared, "We shall reject everything that tends to evil, and strive with each other to see who shall be of the most service in keeping up that friendship that is so happily established between us."

Pontiac's Rebellion, as the British and colonists called the struggle, was over. However, the problem of how to govern the western lands remained unsolved.

Weakness of British leaders. War debts and defense costs, the government of Florida and Canada, and the ownership of the western lands—these were only a few of the serious problems facing the British government in 1763.

To solve its many problems, Great Britain needed government leaders with ideals and wisdom, leaders who could satisfy both the needs of the colonies and the needs of Great Britain. But such officials were not in power at the time. George III, who was king from 1760 to 1820, was ineffective and stubborn. He viewed the colonies as mere overseas territories owned by Great Britain. When he became king, he surrounded himself with ministers whose first thought was always to please their ruler.

99

The stage set for trouble. In 1763, then, serious differences of opinion separated British officials and American colonists. The British pointed out that they had saved the colonists from the French and Indian menace. They also pointed out that the colonists were still being protected by the British army and navy. The British believed, therefore, that the colonists should help pay the cost of protecting the empire and themselves.

To this argument many colonists replied that the war was over and now they wanted to be left alone. Colonial farmers, frontier settlers, merchants, and manufacturers wanted to pursue their own interests. They felt that the problems faced by the British in keeping an empire together were no concern of theirs. Settlers in all the colonies, although many were British, had begun to look upon their problems as being quite different from those of Great Britain.

SECTION SURVEY

IDENTIFY: land speculators, Pontiac's Rebellion, 1763, George III.

1. What new problems did the British government face in governing its colonies after 1763?
2. What factors led to Pontiac's Rebellion? How might this conflict have been avoided?
3. (a) What arguments did the British use in trying to persuade the colonists that they should help pay the cost of protecting the empire and themselves? (b) How did the colonists answer these arguments?
4. Map Study: Look at the map on page 99. Which colonies claimed land west of the Proclamation Line of 1763?

3 The colonists oppose taxation without representation

In 1763 the British began to adopt measures to put the empire on a sound footing. The person responsible for these measures was George Grenville, who became Prime Minister, or leader of the British government, in 1763. To the surprise of Grenville and other British officials, their efforts to reform colonial administration met with strong opposition from the colonists. The colonists were especially angered by laws passed by a Parliament in which they were not represented. Step by step, the gap between the mother country and the American colonies grew wider.

The Proclamation of 1763. Pontiac's uprising prompted George III and his ministers to initiate the new colonial program. This program was intended to reduce conflict between the settlers and the Indians in the western lands formerly claimed by France that now belonged to the British. The Proclamation of

Changing Ways with TECHNOLOGY

IRON FURNACE

DETAIL OF IRON FURNACE

iron ore, charcoal, and limestone

bellows   slag   molten iron

IRON FURNACE

To produce molten iron, iron ore was poured into the top of the furnace along with charcoal to feed the fire and limestone to free the ore of impurities. At the bottom of the furnace, impurities called slag were collected and removed. The molten iron was drained out and poured into molds. The extreme heat was produced by a water-powered bellows, which forced a blast of air through the burning charcoal.

1763 ordered the settlers to withdraw temporarily from all lands west of the Appalachian Mountains. The Proclamation also reserved certain lands for the Indians, thus recognizing limited Indian rights to some of their hunting grounds. The fur trade in the western lands was brought under royal control. No trader was permitted to cross the mountains without the consent of British officials.

To the average Britisher, the measure appeared reasonable. At last, Great Britain was trying to establish a uniform policy for the Indians, the fur trade, and the disposal of western lands. This temporary stop to settlement and trade in the western lands would give the British government the time to form a policy for the colonies without the distraction of conflicts between settlers and Indians.

However, American fur traders and colonists who wanted to settle the western lands resented the Proclamation. Colonial merchants who outfitted the traders opposed it, as did land speculators.

The Sugar Act of 1764. While the colonists were still angered by the Proclamation of 1763, Parliament landed another stinging blow by passing the Sugar Act of 1764. By this measure Parliament hoped to raise money to help pay the expenses of "protecting and securing" the colonies against attack. The Sugar Act placed a duty on molasses, sugar, and other products imported from places outside the British empire. A similar law, the Molasses Act, had been enacted in 1733, but the duty set by the act of 1733 was so high that the colonists had openly broken the law by smuggling. British officials had made little effort to enforce the law and thus to prevent this smuggling. As a result, the British were spending far more to maintain the customs officials than the officials themselves were collecting under the Molasses Act.

Parliament was determined to enforce the Sugar Act of 1764 and collect the **revenue°** the government needed. To make smuggling less profitable, Parliament set the new duty on molasses at only half—and in 1766 at only one sixth—of what it had been in 1733. Then British officials began to enforce the new law. British naval patrols inspected ships entering colonial harbors. Royal inspectors searched warehouses and even private homes, looking

°**revenue:** the money collected by a government from taxes, duties, and the like.

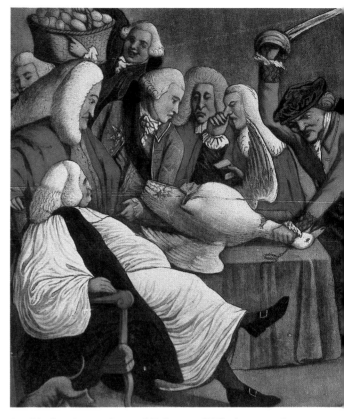

As this London cartoon of February 1776 shows, not everyone in England wanted harsh colonial laws. In what ways were England's policies toward the colonies like killing the goose that laid golden eggs?

for smuggled goods. The revenue collectors also tried to enlist the aid of the colonists themselves by offering rewards to citizens who reported that their neighbors were smuggling. Special courts, having no juries and presided over by navy officers, tried the cases and passed sentence.

Parliament hoped that the Sugar Act of 1764 would reduce taxes for citizens in Great Britain. Until now they had borne almost all the defense costs of the entire empire, including the colonies in North America. Parliament also hoped that the act would help the sugar planters of the British West Indies by preventing the smuggling of sugar from other areas.

Despite the lower duty on molasses, the Sugar Act cut sharply into the business of colonial merchants, shipowners, and rum distillers. These colonists had been earning profits on duty-free molasses and other goods smuggled in from French, Dutch, and Spanish islands in the Caribbean. Angry colonial merchants began to organize committees to discuss means of resistance.

The Currency Act of 1764. Soon after the Sugar Act, Parliament passed another law forbidding the colonies to issue paper money. Parliament also required that in the future the colonists must pay all taxes in gold or silver coin rather than in paper money.

This regulation, called the Currency Act of 1764, antagonized many colonists, particularly colonial merchants. Money had been scarce in the colonies even before Parliament passed the new law. Since 1750 the balance of trade between Great Britain and the colonies had shifted in favor of Great Britain. To restore the balance, colonial merchants had to send large amounts of currency, in addition to trade goods, to Great Britain. These currency shipments were draining away the supply of currency in the colonies. Where, then, could the colonists find the money to carry on their business activities and pay their taxes?

The Quartering Act of 1765. While colonial tempers were still running high, Parliament passed another unpopular law—the Quartering Act of 1765. This law required the colonial authorities to provide barracks and supplies for British troops stationed in America.

The Stamp Act of 1765. In the midst of the growing colonial agitation, Parliament adopted the Stamp Act of 1765. The Stamp Act, like the Sugar Act, attempted to raise revenue to pay for the defense of the colonies, but the Stamp Act was far more sweeping. It levied taxes on licenses of all kinds, on college diplomas, playing cards, newspapers, advertisements, and legal documents such as deeds to land and mortgages on property. All such documents and materials had to bear a stamp showing that the tax had been paid.

Prime Minister Grenville had announced in 1764 that he wanted Parliament to impose a stamp tax. Parliament, however, did not pass the act until 1765. Thus the colonists had a full year to propose a more acceptable form of taxation. They failed to suggest an alternative. For this reason the British government was astonished when many colonists greeted the Stamp Act with angry protests. Several colonies had used such a tax themselves, and the British people had long been accustomed to it.

Also, the colonists had always paid taxes to support the empire.

The colonists, however, said that the earlier taxes had been **indirect taxes**—duties, for example, collected on goods entering colonial ports. These duties were finally paid only by those colonists who actually bought the products. Colonists often did not know that they were paying these duties because they were hidden in the price of the product. The earlier duties, the colonists insisted, had been levied to help regulate trade. The colonists argued that the stamp tax was different. It was a **direct tax.** Unlike an indirect tax, hidden in the price of the product, a direct tax had to be paid directly to the government.

The colonists were used to paying direct taxes levied by their own colonial assemblies. They regarded this power to levy their own taxes as the key to the large measure of self-government they had come to take for granted. The stamp tax, however, was a direct tax levied not by a colonial assembly but by Parliament. The American colonists had no representatives in Parliament.

The Stamp Act, then, threatened to take money directly from the colonists without their consent. Settlers buying land on the frontier would have to pay a special tax on the deed to their property. Small farmers would have to pay taxes on warehouse receipts for tobacco or grain. Artisans in the towns would be required to pay taxes for playing cards and newspapers. Planters, merchants, lawyers, and editors would be paying taxes every time they turned around. This "vicious" tax, the colonists insisted, violated their right to tax themselves. It was levied without the consent of their own representatives. Here, indeed, was "taxation without representation." Thus it violated the great British tradition, which had been won only after centuries of struggle between kings and Parliaments.

Many colonists refused to listen to the British argument that Parliament represented all British subjects, including the colonists. True, British officials admitted, colonial representatives did not sit in Parliament, but other large groups of Britishers also were not directly represented in Parliament. For example, many thousands of people living in the new, rapidly growing English cities of Manchester and Birmingham did not have the right to vote. Therefore they were not directly represented in Parliament. British officials argued that repre-

Philadelphia was a major shipping center with a lively shipbuilding trade. Many people in the city were willing to obey the Stamp Act rather than risk upsetting their profitable business. However, protesters forced the stamp distributors to leave the city, thereby making it impossible for people to pay the tax.

sentation of the American colonies in Parliament was similar to that of these British cities. It was, they said, "virtual representation." Parliament, they insisted, represented not only the citizens of Great Britain but all the people of the empire. What did the colonists mean by "no taxation without representation"? To these arguments the colonists turned deaf ears.

Opposition to the Stamp Act. After the Stamp Act of 1765 was passed, resolutions condemning the measure poured into England from the colonies. Colonial lawyers, merchants, and publishers met in protest. Colonial assemblies declared that all taxes were illegal except those levied by representatives of the people in their own legislatures.

In October 1765, delegates from nine colonies met in New York to hold a meeting known as the Stamp Act Congress. They first asserted their loyalty to the king and promised "all due subordination" to Parliament. Then the delegates vowed to resist all taxes levied without the consent of their own colonial legislatures.

Many colonial merchants, joined by other leading citizens, went a step further. They signed **nonimportation agreements,** promising not to buy or import British goods. Within a few months, products made in Great Britain almost vanished from colonial stores and warehouses.

Some colonial townspeople took even more direct action. Organized in societies called Sons of Liberty, they rioted in large towns and destroyed the offices of stamp tax collectors. They burned stamps in the streets, destroyed the houses of royal officials, and tarred and feathered citizens sympathetic to Great Britain. They justified their violent actions by claiming that they were battling for their rights as English subjects.

Repeal of the Stamp Act. The British accepted the news of colonial resistance to the Stamp Act with mixed feelings. George III exclaimed, "It is undoubtedly the most serious matter that ever came before Parliament."

British merchants were shocked. The colonial nonimportation agreements had brought British-American trade almost to a standstill. Many British merchants faced financial ruin. To prevent this, they demanded that Parliament repeal the Stamp Act. Powerful Britishers who sympathized with the colonists joined

103

in the demand for repeal. Edmund Burke, a British leader and writer, expressed his pride in those who fought such "illegal" measures. William Pitt, who had led Great Britain to victory in the Seven Years' War, declared, "I rejoice that America has resisted."

Under such heavy pressure, Parliament repealed the Stamp Act in March 1766. News of the repeal brought wild rejoicing in the colonies and sighs of relief from British merchants and friends of the colonists. In New York City, Sons of Liberty erected a huge flagpole, called a "liberty pole." Colonists gathered around the liberty pole to celebrate the repeal. There they pledged their devotion to the cause of liberty.

The Declaratory Act of 1766. In the excitement most colonists paid little attention to another law passed by Parliament — the Declaratory Act of 1766. In the Declaratory Act, Parliament asserted that it had the "full power and authority to make laws to bind the colonies and people of America . . . in all cases whatsoever."

Thus, despite rejoicing in the colonies, the basic issue dividing the colonies from Great Britain remained unsettled. Did the British Parliament have the right to make laws for the American colonists and to tax them when the colonists had no elected representatives in Parliament? This was the basic question.

SECTION SURVEY

IDENTIFY: George Grenville, Sugar Act of 1764, Quartering Act of 1765, indirect tax, "taxation without representation," "virtual representation," nonimportation agreements, Sons of Liberty, Declaratory Act of 1766.

1. Why did the Crown and Parliament approve the following measures and why did the colonists object to them: (a) the Proclamation of 1763, (b) the Sugar Act of 1764, (c) the Currency Act of 1764, (d) the Quartering Act of 1765?
2. Why did many colonists consider the stamp tax different from all previous taxes and duties?
3. (a) What steps did the colonists take to oppose the Stamp Act of 1765? (b) Why was the Stamp Act repealed?
4. (a) How did the Declaratory Act symbolize the British government's position on representation of the colonies in Parliament? (b) How did the British government and the colonists differ on this issue?

4 Tensions increase between Great Britain and the colonies

In 1767, under the leadership of Charles Townshend, Parliament decided once again to try to raise revenue in America. However, the members of Parliament still had painful memories of the Stamp Act. They knew how deeply the colonists resented direct taxes.

The Townshend Acts. Parliament decided, therefore, to return to the long-accepted method of collecting duties on goods entering the seaports. Since the colonists had always paid such indirect taxes, Parliament hoped the new duties would not cause any trouble.

The Townshend Acts levied import duties on articles of everyday use in America — tea, lead, glass, and colors for paint. Had Parliament stopped at this point, the colonists might not have objected, but Parliament did not stop.

Writs of assistance. In an effort to insure that the new law would be enforced, Parliament legalized **writs of assistance,** or search warrants. "Writ" is an old word meaning "written." Writs of assistance, then, were written statements giving government officials the legal right to search the colonists' businesses, their ships, and even their homes for smuggled goods.

The writs of assistance used in colonial times were quite different from present-day search warrants. Today a search warrant must state the exact article sought and the specific places to be searched. In colonial times, however, a British customs official, armed with a general search warrant, could enter any vessel or warehouse or home in America at any time. And the official could ransack the place in the mere hope of finding smuggled goods.

For many years American colonial merchants had been arguing that the writs of assistance were illegal and an invasion of their rights as English subjects. Now, in 1767, Parliament had legalized the hated writs. The colonists could not change this fact, but they could and did protest.

Arguments and resolutions. Many colonists openly expressed their resentment of the

Townshend Acts and the writs of assistance. Many colonial courts, for example, refused to issue the writs; by 1772 almost none would.

New Yorkers refused to provide living quarters for British soldiers sent to enforce the law. Parliament promptly punished the colony by suspending its assembly, thus depriving New Yorkers of their right to representative government.

Other colonists poured out their anger in a flood of pamphlets, resolutions, and petitions. Led by Samuel Adams, the legislature of Massachusetts drafted a letter to the other colonies urging them to unite for resistance. The assemblies of Maryland, South Carolina, and Georgia promptly endorsed the letter. Parliament replied by forbidding the legislatures of these four colonies to meet.

The Virginia House of Burgesses adopted a set of resolutions summarizing the American case. The resolutions began with a statement by George Washington referring to "our lordly masters in Great Britain." The resolutions then repeated the American claim that only colonial legislatures had the right to levy taxes on the colonists.

Direct action – and violence. While many colonial leaders protested in writing, other colonists decided to act. They signed new nonimportation agreements, promising not to import or buy British goods. The earlier agreements at the time of the Stamp Act of 1765 had almost ruined British merchants and had forced Parliament to repeal the measure. Many colonists reasoned that such nonimportation agreements would work again.

Some Americans were not content with these agreements. Once again mobs poured into the streets. They boarded and smashed British ships, attacked British customs officials, and tarred and feathered anyone who informed on smugglers. British soldiers sent to protect customs officials and to keep order were sometimes attacked.

In Boston crowds taunted the soldiers, calling them "lobsters," "redcoats," and "bloody backs." Now and then a crowd hurled stones and snowballs at the soldiers. Every month friction between the citizens and the soldiers became more intense. Thoughtful colonial leaders and British commanders alike did everything possible to avoid more serious trouble, but an incident such as they dreaded finally occurred.

Samuel Adams, leader of the most extreme Patriots, was feared as a mob leader by those in power. Adams knew how to move people to action with his stirring speeches and writings.

The Boston Massacre. On March 5, 1770, a large crowd gathered in Boston around soldiers of the 29th British Regiment. The crowd yelled insults and threw snowballs. Such outbursts had occurred many times before. This time matters got out of hand. As the mob pressed closer against the soldiers, someone gave an order to fire. Three civilians were killed and two others were mortally wounded.

One of those killed was Crispus Attucks, a former slave, who had escaped 20 years earlier from his master. As a fugitive slave, he did not share the same degree of freedom as other citizens of Boston. Yet Crispus Attucks was among the first to die in the struggle over colonial freedom between Great Britain and the American colonies.

As news of the shooting spread, the people of Boston went wild with anger. A "massacre" they called the affair. They also demanded that the British withdraw all troops from their city.

Later, when passions had cooled somewhat, the British soldiers were tried for murder.

Crispus Attucks is the man grasping at the musket of a British redcoat in this rather inaccurate drawing of the Boston Massacre. Actually there were only ten soldiers and about sixty protesters who clashed on that March day in 1770.

They were defended by Josiah Quincy, Jr., and John Adams, who later became the second President of the United States. Neither of these men had any sympathy for the British, but they insisted that every person was entitled to a fair trial. All except two of the soldiers were acquitted. These two were convicted of manslaughter but were released soon after.

Repeal—and continued unrest. When Lord Frederick North became Prime Minister of Great Britain in 1770, the gap between Great Britain and the American colonies was wide indeed. The new Prime Minister urged Parliament to repeal the Townshend Acts. As Lord North pointed out, the nonimportation agreements were once again ruining the business of many British merchants. Besides, the cost of enforcing the law was proving much too heavy for Great Britain.

In 1770 Parliament repealed the Townshend Acts. Parliament also allowed the Quar-

tering Act to expire. But in a new law, the British government was careful to retain a small import duty on tea as a symbol that Parliament had the power to tax the colonists. As George III put it, there must "always be one tax to keep up the right."

The repeal of the Townshend Acts brought a temporary end to much colonial unrest. Only an occasional act of violence reminded the British that the basic issue remained unsettled.

One such outbreak occurred in June 1772 when colonists attacked and burned the British revenue ship *Gaspee* a few miles south of Providence, Rhode Island. For the colonists the most alarming thing about the *Gaspee* affair was the British announcement that the accused colonists would be sent to England for trial. This British decision threatened to weaken the practice of self-government in Rhode Island.

No less alarming was an announcement made at this time by the royal governor of Massachusetts. From now on, Governor Thomas

Hutchinson declared, the British Crown, not the colonial assemblies, would pay the salaries of the governor and the Massachusetts judges. This action freed the governor and the judges from all dependence upon the Massachusetts legislature.

Committees of Correspondence. These new threats to colonial freedom did not go unchallenged. Led by Samuel Adams, citizens of Boston met in a special town meeting with James Otis presiding. They created a Committee of Correspondence consisting of 21 members to keep other colonies—and "the World"—informed about what was happening in Massachusetts. The idea worked so well that, during the next few months, other colonies organized similar committees. Many of the most prominent colonial leaders served on these committees. In Virginia, for example, the committee included Thomas Jefferson, Patrick Henry, and Richard Henry Lee.

Because the colonies had no central government where leaders of the various colonies could meet, the Committees of Correspondence performed an important service. They kept each colony informed of events and opinions in the other colonies. As it turned out, the colonists organized this new method of communication none too soon, for in 1773 Parliament adopted another measure that really started tempers boiling.

SECTION SURVEY

IDENTIFY: writs of assistance, Samuel Adams, "redcoat," Boston Massacre, Crispus Attucks, John Adams, Committees of Correspondence, Lord Frederick North.

1. (a) How did the British justify the Townshend Acts of 1767? (b) Why did the colonists object to them?
2. (a) How did writs of assistance differ from present-day search warrants? (b) Why did the colonists object to them?
3. (a) List five actions that the colonists took to protest the Townshend Acts. (b) How did the British respond to these actions?
4. Why did the British choose to retain the tax on tea when they repealed the Townshend Acts in 1770?
5. What new threat to the rights of the American colonists did the British response to the burning of the *Gaspee* present?

5 The gap between Great Britain and the colonies grows wider

The series of events that brought the American colonies to the edge of rebellion started in 1773 with the passage of the Tea Act. Parliament passed this law to help the British East India Company, a trading company with headquarters in England.

The Tea Act of 1773. The East India Company was in serious trouble. Part of its problem was the fact that many American colonists refused to buy English tea. When the Townshend Acts were repealed, the British government, you recall, insisted on retaining a duty on tea as a symbol of its power to tax the colonies. The tax was a small one, but many colonists refused to pay it. In fact, they refused to buy tea imported from England. As a result, large amounts of unsold tea were piling up in the company's warehouses in London.

Faced with possible bankruptcy, the East India Company turned to Parliament for help.

In colonial days tea was shipped in beautifully decorated wooden chests. This chest may be one of those thrown into Boston harbor during the Tea Party.

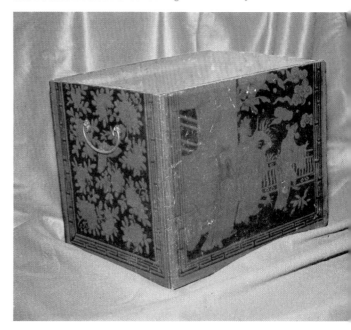

The members of Parliament, many of whom owned stock in the company, quickly responded. They immediately lent the company a large sum of money. Then they passed a law that, in effect, gave the East India Company a monopoly of the sale of tea in America.

The new law, known as the Tea Act, permitted the company to bypass British wholesalers and sell the tea directly to the colonists through company agents. Although the Americans would still have to pay the Townshend duty, or tax, the tea itself would cost less than ever before.

Violent colonial reaction. Why, given lower prices for tea, did the colonists protest? For one thing, by now many colonists opposed all taxes levied by Parliament. A more immediate issue, however, was the impact of the Tea Act upon colonial tea merchants. These merchants could no longer compete with the low prices offered by the East India Company. As a result, they would be driven out of business. True, the act affected only the sale of tea, but if a monopoly were granted to one British company, what was to prevent Parliament from granting monopolies to other British companies?

Faced with this threat to their businesses, the colonists reacted swiftly. Crowds rioted in the streets. The British East India Company could not sell any of its tea. In Charleston colonists stored tea in damp cellars so it would rot. In Annapolis a ship and its cargo of tea were burned. Philadelphians and New Yorkers refused to allow British ships carrying tea to enter their harbors.

In Boston, late in 1773, colonists disguised as Indians boarded ships and heaved their cargoes into the water. In one wild night, they destroyed 342 chests of tea valued at what today would be many thousands of dollars. The Boston Tea Party, as it was called, drew widespread attention. Many colonists approved; others were shocked at the violence.

The Intolerable Acts of 1774. British officials and merchants were furious. It had been bad enough for the colonists to refuse to pay taxes. It was far worse for them to destroy property.

By overwhelming majorities Parliament passed four laws to discourage further violence and to strengthen British control over the colonists. The British called these the Coercive Acts. The colonists called them the Intolerable Acts—that is, acts they could not endure.

One law closed the port of Boston to all shipping until the colonists paid for the tea they had destroyed there. A second law revoked the Massachusetts charter of 1691 and forbade Massachusetts colonists to hold town meetings. A third law, a new Quartering Act, required the colonists to provide food and housing for British soldiers sent to America to enforce the laws. A fourth law provided that British officials in Massachusetts charged with crimes committed while enforcing British laws could have their cases tried not in that colony but in England.

Great Britain was determined to enforce the Coercive Acts. General Thomas Gage, commander in chief of the British armed forces

SOURCES

DECLARATION
AND RESOLVES
OF THE FIRST
CONTINENTAL
CONGRESS
(1774)

The good people of the several colonies . . . declare . . . that the inhabitants of the English colonies in North America, by the immutable laws of nature, the principles of the English constitution, and the several charters or compacts, have the following rights:

Resolved,

That they are entitled to life, liberty, and property, and they have never ceded to any sovereign power whatever a right to dispose of either without their consent.

That our ancestors, who first settled these colonies, were at the time of their emigration from the mother country entitled to all the rights, liberties, and immunities of free and natural-born subjects within the realm of England. . . .

That the foundation of English liberty and of all free government is a right in the people to participate in their legislative council. . . .

Currier and Ives were artists who made many very popular prints of American scenes during the 1800's. In this one the Boston Tea Party looks like quite a public event. Actually the raiders sneaked on board the ship at night.

in America, was named governor of Massachusetts. He was then given more troops to help him maintain order.

The Quebec Act of 1774. While passing what the colonists called the Intolerable Acts, Parliament also passed a fifth law, the Quebec Act. The Quebec Act was intended to establish order in Canada, which, as you recall, the British had won by treaty from the French in 1763.

The Quebec Act greatly enlarged the province of Quebec. It established the southern boundary of Canada at the Ohio River and the western boundary at the Mississippi River. It permitted French laws to continue in Canada. It also guaranteed religious freedom to French Canadians, most of whom were Roman Catholics.

Parliament had no thought of punishing the colonists when it passed the Quebec Act. Indeed, the act was a sound piece of legislation, but it came at the same time as the hated Coercive Acts. The colonists regarded it as another attempt to punish them by destroying the claims of Massachusetts, Connecticut, and Virginia to the western lands and by strengthening the Catholicism that they disliked.

Reaction to the Intolerable Acts. In spite of British actions, many colonists remained completely loyal to Great Britain. They believed that the colonists, as British citizens, should obey the laws passed by Parliament without protesting. Other colonists tried to persuade the British to work out a compromise.

By and large, however, the colonists strongly opposed the Intolerable Acts. In some cases the reaction came close to rebellion. At mass meetings colonists condemned the actions of Parliament. The colonists also began to experiment with new political organizations that would avoid or replace the royal governments. In this way they formed committees that took over many functions of government.

Many of these committees worked at the local level. In some colonies new "congresses"

TEMPESTS, TEAPOTS, AND HOMESPUN

No more shall my teapot so generous
be
In filling the cups with this pernicious
tea,
For I'll fill it with water and drink out
the same,
Before I'll lose Liberty, that dearest
name,
Before she shall part I will die in the
cause,
For I'll never be governed by tyranny's
laws.

One way ordinary citizens can affect a country's policies is through a boycott—a refusal to buy certain goods or to cooperate with those seen as wrongdoers. A boycott of British goods was the aim of the colonial nonimportation agreements following the Townshend Acts and the Tea Act.

Ordinary citizens, though, sometimes had to be nudged into carrying out these boycotts. That was the purpose of the poem about tea and the song below about homespun clothing. Verses like these were printed in newspapers or handbills and sometimes sung at public gatherings. They helped to remind the colonists of their own virtue in refusing to use products from Great Britain.

Young ladies in town and those that
live round,
Wear none but your own country linen.
Of economy boast, let your pride be the
most
To wear clothes of your own make and
spinning.
And as one all agree that you'll not
married be
To such as will wear London factory.
But at first sight refuse, and tell 'em
you'll choose
As encourage our own manufactory.

took on some of the tasks of the colonial assemblies. The most important step came late in the summer of 1774, when a general congress of the colonies was held.

The First Continental Congress. On September 5, 1774, delegates from all the colonies except Georgia assembled in Philadelphia at a meeting called the First Continental Congress. The Congress, pushed by delegates from Massachusetts and Virginia, adopted a number of resolutions. Denying any thought of independence, the delegates nevertheless demanded an immediate change in British policies. They solemnly asserted their rights to "life, liberty, and property"; to "all the rights, liberties, and immunities" of English subjects; to the "free and exclusive power of legislation in their own several legislatures." They pledged each other mutual support. They revived the nonimportation agreements against British products. They further agreed not to sell goods to Great Britain or the British West Indies if, by January 1775, the British had not made compromises. Finally they resolved to create local "committees of safety and inspection" that would provide firm and uniform action against the British government.

Finally, the First Continental Congress ended. The delegates agreed, however, to meet again in the spring of 1775 to take further steps if the Intolerable Acts had not been withdrawn by then.

SECTION SURVEY

IDENTIFY: British East India Company, Boston Tea Party, General Thomas Gage, Quebec Act of 1774, First Continental Congress.

1. (a) Why did the colonists object to the Tea Act of 1773? (b) How did they express their objections?

2. (a) Describe the provisions of the Intolerable Acts. (b) What was the purpose of the Intolerable Acts?

3. Why did the colonists oppose the Quebec Act?

4. (a) List three actions that the First Continental Congress took in response to the Intolerable Acts. (b) Why do you suppose that the delegates at this First Continental Congress did not talk of independence?

5. Source Study: Read the Source on page 108. (a) What rights do the delegates to the Congress claim? (b) On what grounds do they claim these rights?

Chapter Survey

Summary: Tracing the Main Ideas

British victory in the Seven Years' War, called in America the French and Indian War, made Great Britain the leading colonial power in the world. British citizens had paid in blood and treasure to win their great empire. By 1763 the struggle was finally settled. France had been defeated, and peace had come at long last.

Peace brought new problems. During the long years of colonial warfare, the American seaboard colonies had in many ways become less dependent upon the mother country. The people who settled in each colony had learned to think of their colony—and, in a sense, of America itself—as *their* land, as a place apart from England.

The American colonists had learned to love the new land that had brought most of them better lives than they or their parents had known in the Old World. By the 1760's many were beginning to think of themselves as Americans. However, nearly all of them continued to consider themselves loyal citizens of the British empire.

A new way of life was developing in America. It was now about 150 years since the first English settlers had come to America, and the peoples of the Old World and the New were finding it increasingly difficult to understand each other.

By 1763 the American seaboard colonies were beginning to think of themselves as junior partners in the expanding British empire. The British government, on the other hand, continued to regard the colonies as subordinate children.

Step by step, between 1763 and 1775, the mother country and its colonies moved further apart, yet even by 1775 it was perhaps not too late to reconcile the differences. As you will see in Chapter 6, however, the reconciliation never came.

Inquiring into History

1. Explain how Great Britain applied the principles of mercantilism by means of (a) the Navigation Acts, (b) restrictions on colonial manufacturing, and (c) the Currency Act of 1764.
2. Wise leaders could have resolved the differences between Great Britain and the colonies in 1775. Do you agree? Why or why not?
3. Do you think the protests of American colonists after 1763 were based more on economic or political considerations? Use historical evidence to support your opinion.
4. Trace the events from 1754 to 1775 that illustrate the increased unity of the colonists. Why did the colonists become more unified as time went on? In what ways did the colonists still lack unity?

Relating Past to Present

1. Do nations still consider a favorable balance of trade to be an important factor in their economic relations? Why or why not?
2. Does the use of violence breed more violence? In answering this question, cite examples of violence during the 1770's and examples from American society today.
3. In recent years people in many cities have started neighborhood block associations and community school boards to work toward goals they consider important. Why might people feel that they need such organizations when city government usually has official responsibility for providing community services?

Developing Social Science Skills

1. Using the map on page 96, (a) explain how the trade routes were an outgrowth of Great Britain's mercantile policies, and (b) describe the triangular trade routes and explain who profited from the trade.
2. Write a brief account of the Boston Massacre or the Boston Tea Party as the event might have been described in (a) an American newspaper article and (b) a British newspaper article.
3. Create a chart of the major events leading to the Revolution. Include on the chart the dates of the events and a brief sentence explaining the importance of each event.

1760

1765

1770

1775 — Battle of
Lexington

Declaration of
Independence

British defeat at
Saratoga

France agrees to
help U.S.

1780 —

British surrender
at Yorktown

Treaty of Paris

1785

1790

2000

Chapter 6

Winning a War for Independence

1775-1783

John Howe, a private in the army of King George III, was a spy. Fortunately for him, he did not look like a spy. The people he met as he walked along the Massachusetts roads took him for an honest Yankee artisan. He even sounded like a Yankee. His regiment had been stationed in Boston long enough for him to learn how Yankees talked—and, sometimes, what they were thinking about.

General Gage, British commander in Boston, had heard that the New Englanders were collecting arms and ammunition. He sent Private Howe and other spies out into the surrounding countryside to learn the truth. John Howe learned fast. He learned where powder and rifles were stored. He also learned that the Yankees were ready to fight. At a farmhouse near Lexington, he stopped to talk to an old man who was cleaning a gun. Howe asked him what he intended to shoot. "A flock of redcoats at Boston," the man replied.

Howe heard the same story everywhere he went. He saw rebellious colonists—by now called Patriots—cleaning their guns and drilling openly on village greens. In taverns and public buildings, he saw lists posted bearing the names of Loyalists, or people who remained loyal to the king. He heard of Loyalists who had been tarred and feathered. He heard of Loyalists whose homes had been burned because they dared to defend the British point of view.

This was the report John Howe carried back to General Gage in Boston. General Gage, who had heard the same story from other British spies, decided the time had come to act.

THE CHAPTER IN OUTLINE

1. British-American differences break out in open war.

2. The colonists decide to fight for their independence.

3. British plans for an early victory end in disaster.

4. American Patriots defeat the British army.

5. Events off the battlefield lead to an American victory.

112

1 British-American differences break out in open war

General Gage decided to move swiftly and nip rebellion in the bud. He planned to surprise the colonists and seize supplies of ammunition at Concord and several other towns. He chose April 18, 1775, to make his move. Under cover of darkness, British troops left their quarters in the sleeping city of Boston, moved through the quiet streets, and began to row across the Charles River.

Lexington and Concord. The Patriots were not caught napping. Watchers on the west bank of the Charles River sprang to attention at the sight of two lanterns flickering in the window of the Old North Church in Boston. This was the signal that the redcoats were planning to march through the night down the road to Lexington.

Three Patriots—Paul Revere, William Dawes, Jr., and Dr. Samuel Prescott—leaped into the saddles of their waiting horses and galloped off into the night—and into the pages of history. They rode through that fateful night, pounding on farmhouse doors, shouting their cries of alarm. Behind them, as the hoofbeats of their horses faded into the distance, lamps winked on in kitchens. Women, their eyes filled with worry, hastily prepared food while the men in the family hurriedly pulled on clothes and lifted their muskets and powder horns from pegs on the wall. Then the men marched off across the fields to join their friends and neighbors at the appointed meeting place.

British troops, meanwhile, had assembled on the west bank of the river and were marching through the night (see map 1, page 115). They reached Lexington at dawn on April 19, 1775. The **minutemen**—militia members who had promised to be ready for action at a minute's notice—were there before them, gathered in ranks on the village green. The commander of the British patrol ordered the colonists to drop their guns and leave the green. The colonists started to leave, but held on to their guns. Then someone fired a shot—in years to come it would be known as "the shot heard round the world." Immediately, without waiting for orders, the British troops fired several volleys into the group of minutemen. When the smoke cleared, eight colonists lay dead, and ten others were wounded.

The British troops went on to Concord, where they cut down a liberty pole, set fire to the courthouse, and destroyed several gun carriages. After clashing with armed Patriot forces at Concord's North Bridge, the British started back toward Boston. By now, the coun-

This painting of the British troops at Concord is by Ralph Earl, who was an eyewitness to the events there. Known for his solemn, direct style, Earl studied under Benjamin West, a renowned American historical painter.

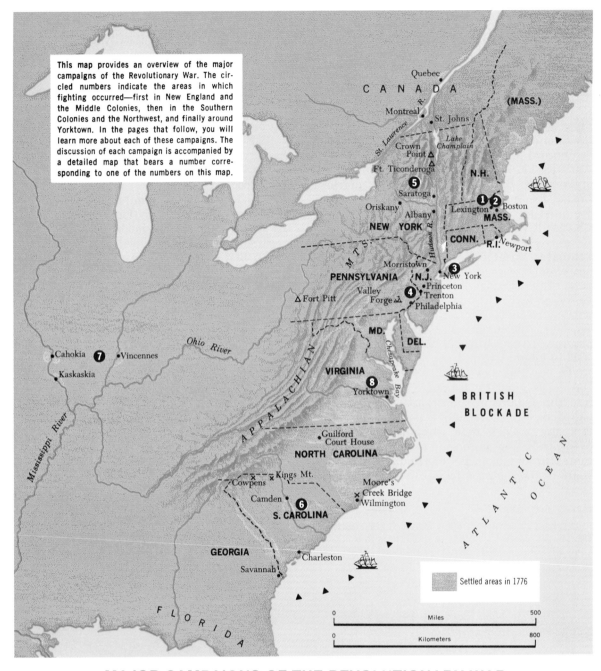

This map provides an overview of the major campaigns of the Revolutionary War. The circled numbers indicate the areas in which fighting occurred—first in New England and the Middle Colonies, then in the Southern Colonies and the Northwest, and finally around Yorktown. In the pages that follow, you will learn more about each of these campaigns. The discussion of each campaign is accompanied by a detailed map that bears a number corresponding to one of the numbers on this map.

MAJOR CAMPAIGNS OF THE REVOLUTIONARY WAR

As you read the text and examine each numbered map in the pages that follow, look frequently at the map above so that you will understand the progress of the war and the relationships among the various campaigns. On all the detailed maps, colored symbols stand for American forces, black symbols for British. These symbols are used on the detailed maps:

American advance   American retreat   American victory

British advance   British retreat   British victory

tryside was swarming with angry colonists. From behind stone walls and the shelter of buildings, the colonists fired steadily as the redcoats retreated to Boston. British casualties amounted to 73 killed, 174 wounded, and 26 missing.

The redcoats reached Boston late in the day. Curious townspeople saw weary faces, bloody bandages, and men in tattered uniforms carrying their wounded comrades. When night fell, the lights of campfires rimmed the city. These were the fires of rebellion, fed by many of the 16,000 minutemen from the surrounding countryside.

Ticonderoga and Crown Point. The days slipped by. In May came news that the "Green Mountain Boys," a small colonial force from what is now Vermont, led by Ethan Allen, had seized the British forts at Ticonderoga and Crown Point on Lake Champlain (see map, page 114). Most welcome of all was news that powder, shot, and cannons from the captured forts were on their way to Boston.

The Second Continental Congress. Delegates to the First Continental Congress had agreed the previous year to assemble again if the British government did not meet their demands. On May 10, 1775, then, the delegates to a Second Continental Congress met. The site once again was Philadelphia.

Some of these delegates, among them Samuel Adams of Massachusetts and Patrick Henry of Virginia, were **radical** in their outlook and called for extreme action. They were ready to declare independence, seize British officials, and ask France and Spain for help.

Most delegates were more **conservative,** urging more moderate action. Led by John Dickinson of Pennsylvania, they assured the king that they had "not raised armies with ambitious designs of separating from Great Britain." They made it clear, however, that they

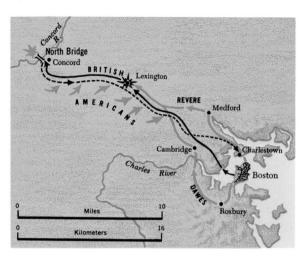

❶ War Breaks Out, April 19, 1775

would resist tyranny with force if necessary. To show that they meant business, they appointed George Washington of Virginia as commander in chief of the Continental Army.

The Battle of Breed's (Bunker) Hill. Before Washington arrived to take command of the minutemen in the Boston area, blood had again been shed. General Gage, the British commander, ordered a frontal attack on the armed New Englanders at Charlestown, overlooking Boston harbor. On June 17, 1775, in three bold assaults, the British redcoats attacked the Americans on Breed's Hill, mistakenly called Bunker Hill (see map 2, page 116). Both sides lost heavily. Finally, the Patriots, their ammunition exhausted, retreated with a loss of almost 450 men. However, the British left more than 1,000 men killed or wounded upon the battlefield.

Shocked at news of this disaster, George III proclaimed the colonists rebels. He ordered the Royal Navy to begin a tight naval blockade to close off all shipping to the colonies. He also hired 10,000 soldiers from the German state of

SOURCES

PATRICK HENRY'S SPEECH BEFORE THE VIRGINIA CONVENTION (1775)

Gentlemen may cry peace, peace. But there is no peace. The war is actually begun! The next gale that sweeps from the north will bring to our ears the clash of resounding arms! Our brethren are already in the field! Why stand we here idle? What is it that gentlemen wish? What would they have? Is life so dear, or peace so sweet, as to be purchased at the price of chains and slavery? Forbid it, Almighty God! I know not what course others may take; but as for me, give me liberty or give me death!

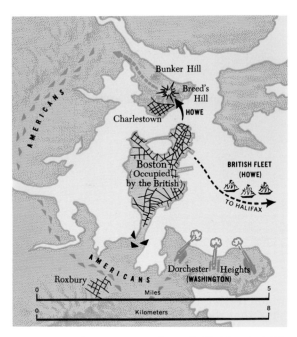

Ⓞ Fighting Near Boston: June 1775–March 1776

Hesse, called Hessians (HESH·unz), to help fight and subdue the Americans.

British evacuation of Boston. The Second Continental Congress promptly took further steps to strengthen the colonial position. The Congress sent diplomatic agents to request aid from several European countries, including France, Spain, and the Netherlands. Late in 1775 the Congress also sent a military expedition to Canada, hoping to encourage the French Canadians to rise against the British. However, the French Canadians did not show much sympathy, and the expedition failed.

Early in 1776, the colonists were cheered by other news. In a surprise move one night, Washington occupied Dorchester Heights, overlooking Boston and the British fleet anchored in the harbor (see map, this page).

The British general, Sir William Howe, who had replaced General Gage as the commanding officer, decided that it was useless to try to hold Boston. The British fleet sailed out of the harbor on March 17, 1776. With the fleet went the entire garrison of British soldiers and about 1,000 civilian Loyalists.

Moore's Creek Bridge. Meanwhile, another important military engagement had been fought in North Carolina. This was the Battle of Moore's Creek Bridge (see map, page 114), sometimes called the "Lexington and Concord of the South," a battle that ended in a decisive victory for the Patriot cause.

During 1775 Governor Martin of North Carolina had recruited nearly 2,000 Loyalists, mostly Scottish Highlanders who had come to North Carolina since 1770. These Loyalist troops were to march on the seaports of Wilmington and Brunswick. There they were to be joined by regiments of British troops and by a powerful British fleet. Operating from these bases, this combined Loyalist and British force would then control the colony.

The Patriots were fully aware of the plan, and James Moore, a Patriot leader, stationed a force of about 1,100 Patriots at Moore's Creek Bridge. This force ripped up the planking from the bridge and greased the log supports with soap and tallow. Then they hid and waited.

The sun was just rising on February 27, 1776, when the Loyalists reached the bridge, exhausted from marching all night. Attempting to cross on the slippery logs, they were met by withering fire from the opposite bank. In a short but fierce fight, the Patriots, with only one killed and one wounded, won the battle. They took 850 prisoners, many weapons and wagons, and a large supply of gold.

When the British forces arrived in May, they found no Loyalist troops waiting to welcome them, and they sailed away. The Battle of Moore's Creek Bridge had shattered the British plan to hold North Carolina loyal to Great Britain.

SECTION SURVEY

IDENTIFY: Patriots, Loyalists, Paul Revere, minutemen, Ethan Allen, Patrick Henry, John Dickinson, George Washington, Hessians, William Howe, James Moore, April 19, 1775.

1. By early 1775, what preparations had some colonists made to defend themselves from attack by the British?

2. How did General Gage's decision to "nip rebellion in the bud" lead to open war?

3. Most delegates to the Second Continental Congress had a conservative, rather than a radical, view of colonial relations with Great Britain. Explain your answer.

4. Map Study: Look at the map on this page. Why were Breed's Hill and Dorchester Heights important to the British defense of Boston?

2 The colonists decide to fight for their independence

Until the spring of 1776, most colonists refused to admit that they were fighting a war. In their opinion, they were merely resisting unjust acts of Parliament.

Reasons for caution. A few Patriots, as you know, had already urged the colonists to declare their independence. Most colonists, however, were reluctant to make the final break. For one thing, the British government maintained law, order, and stability in the colonies. Some colonists feared that, without British control, they would become victims of mob rule and lawlessness. Local colonial leaders had seen mobs in action against tax collectors, British revenue officers, and Loyalists. They did not want to exchange the tyranny of Great Britain for the greater tyranny of colonial mobs.

The colonists hesitated to declare their independence for other reasons, too. First, if they revolted and failed to win, they could be executed for treason. Second, as long as the colonists were merely resisting specific acts of Parliament, they could count upon powerful support from friends in Great Britain. Such prominent Britishers as Edmund Burke, William Pitt, John Wilkes, and Isaac Barré (bah·RAY) had joined British merchants in demanding that Parliament repeal objectionable laws. However, the colonists knew that the moment they began to talk of separation from Great Britain, their British friends would turn against them and fight to preserve the British empire. Indeed many, perhaps most, men and women in the colonies remained loyal to the British empire at this time.

Reasons for independence. Two bitter facts offset these arguments against a break with Great Britain. First, the British government had committed acts that many colonists believed violated their rights as English subjects. Second, colonial blood had already been shed defending these rights.

In this explosive atmosphere, Thomas Paine's pamphlet *Common Sense* was like a spark dropped in a keg of gunpowder. Paine was a former British political writer who had come to America in 1774. His widely read pamphlet appeared in January 1776.

"I offer nothing more than simple facts, plain arguments, and common sense," Paine wrote. In ringing words he pointed out that America had grown into a new and different nation with interests of its own. "The period of debate is closed. Arms, as the last resource, must decide the contest. . . . Everything that is right or reasonable pleads for separation. The blood of the slain, the weeping voice of nature cries, 'Tis Time to Part!'" Paine's stirring words helped to kindle the spirit of independence.

By declaring their independence, Paine pointed out, the colonists could gain practical advantages. First, as citizens of an indepen-

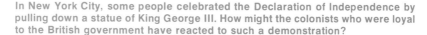

In New York City, some people celebrated the Declaration of Independence by pulling down a statue of King George III. How might the colonists who were loyal to the British government have reacted to such a demonstration?

dent nation, captured Patriot soldiers could demand to be treated as prisoners of war and avoid being shot as rebels. Second, the Patriot governments could seize the property of all Americans who remained loyal to the Crown. Third, the Patriots would have a better chance of winning foreign aid. France and Spain, for example, would probably favor and support a war that threatened to weaken the power of the British empire.

Independence declared. Under the pressure of these arguments, colonial sentiment began to shift in favor of independence. On June 7, 1776, Richard Henry Lee of Virginia introduced a resolution in the Second Continental Congress declaring that "these United Colonies are, and of right ought to be, free and independent states." On June 11, before voting on Lee's resolution, the Congress appointed a committee of five to write a formal Declaration of Independence. These five were Thomas Jefferson, Benjamin Franklin, John Adams, Robert R. Livingston, and Roger Sherman. Jefferson was asked by the others on the committee to do the actual writing.

On June 28 the committee presented Jefferson's Declaration—with a few changes by Franklin and Adams—to the Congress. Congress did not at once discuss the Declaration itself. Instead, it debated Lee's resolution and, by adopting it on July 2, officially declared the new United States of America to be independent of Great Britain. Then the delegates turned to Jefferson's statement, which they continued to discuss on July 3.

Finally, after making some changes, Congress adopted the Declaration of Independence on July 4. In bold strokes John Hancock of Massachusetts, president of the Congress, signed the document. Then copies were rushed to the legislatures of the newly created states. On July 8, the Declaration was read and officially proclaimed in Philadelphia.

Reactions to the Declaration. Many Americans, especially the Patriots (also known as **Whigs°**), greeted the news of independence with wild rejoicing. Bells rang. People sang and danced around bonfires and held banquets to celebrate. The long period of indecision had finally ended.

° **Whigs:** American Patriots were given this name after a political party in Great Britain that opposed taxing the colonies.

Other Americans greeted the news with indifference. These people—and there were many in every colony—were not much concerned one way or the other.

A third group, the Loyalists (also known as **Tories°**), refused to join in the celebrations. Some sat in silence behind closed doors and barricaded windows. For them the bonfires were omens of terror. They had seen violence during the past ten years. They knew what to expect—beatings, tar and feathers, burning houses, flights for safety to Canada or the British West Indies or England. These Tories, regarded by the Patriots as traitors in their own land, included many people of wealth and influence—merchants, lawyers, landowners, former officers of the king, church leaders.

The Declaration of Independence. The document that declared the nation's independence has become one of history's most cherished statements. For 200 years its noble ideas and remarkable eloquence have inspired freedom-seeking people all over the world. Admiration for the Declaration, however, should not obscure the fact that it was a practical document with three major purposes.

1. Preamble and reasons for separation.

In the first place, the Declaration was an attempt to win public support for independence. This appeal to people in Europe and America was contained in the preamble, or introduction, and in the 27 "reasons for separation" from Great Britain (see text, pages 120–21). The king was pictured as an evil ruler who intended to establish an absolute tyranny over the colonies. Each grievance pictured George III as a harsh tyrant. "He has forbidden . . . he has plundered . . . he has refused . . . he has constrained . . ." In contrast, the colonists were pictured as patient, submissive, long-suffering citizens. "We have petitioned . . . we have warned . . . we have reminded . . . we have appealed . . ."

2. A theory of government.

The second major purpose of the Declaration of Independence was to outline a theory of government. This inspiring theory explains why the Declaration remains today one of the most influential documents ever written.

In the opening lines of the second paragraph, Thomas Jefferson clearly and simply

° **Tories:** Americans who supported the king were called Tories, after the political party in Great Britain that opposed the Whigs.

This painting depicts the signing of the Declaration of Independence. It is one of four works by John Trumbull, an American historical painter, that can be found in the Capitol building in Washington, D.C.

stated the basic principles of democracy. "All men are created equal," Jefferson wrote. ". . . They are endowed by their Creator with certain unalienable rights; . . . among these are life, liberty, and the pursuit of happiness." "Unalienable rights" are rights that cannot be taken away from the people—not by any government, not even by the people themselves.

What is the purpose of government? Jefferson replied that governments exist "to secure these rights." Where do governments obtain this authority? They derive "their just powers from the consent of the governed." What happens when a government begins to act like a tyrant? "It is the right of the people to alter or to abolish it, and to institute new government."

The Declaration of Independence, in this passage, clearly stated the right of the American colonists to revolt against their British rulers. It stated this idea in terms familiar to many people in both Europe and America.

Thomas Jefferson was not expressing merely his own beliefs about government when he wrote the Declaration. His ideas came from two major sources. First, they came from scholars in Europe, among them John Locke, who during the 1600's and 1700's had been thinking about and developing new theories of government. Second, Jefferson's ideas came from the American colonists' practical experience in self-government.

The Declaration was an invitation to all peoples, in all times, to assume the right to rule themselves and to rid themselves forever of the tyranny of unwanted rulers.

3. A formal declaration of war.

The third major purpose of the Declaration, contained in the final paragraph, was to announce formally that war existed. If the Patriots failed to win independence, the leaders of the revolution could be judged guilty of treason against the British Crown and executed.

The delegates' pledge of "our lives, our fortunes, and our sacred honor" was not an idle oath. The delegates who signed the document must have done so with a deep sense of anxiety. They were pledging everything to the cause. Failure would mean ruin; it might mean death.

SECTION SURVEY

IDENTIFY: Thomas Paine, *Common Sense,* Richard Henry Lee, Thomas Jefferson, John Hancock, Whigs, Tories, "unalienable rights," "consent of the governed," John Locke, July 4, 1776.

1. State the main arguments for and against the final break with Great Britain in 1776.
2. The colonists were not unanimous in their reaction to the Declaration of Independence. Why not?
3. (a) What were the three major purposes of the Declaration of Independence? (b) Why can it be called a practical document?
4. What was the theory of government presented in the Declaration? Why was it significant?

119

The Declaration of Independence

PREAMBLE

When, in the course of human events, it becomes necessary for one people to dissolve the political bands which have connected them with another, and to assume, among the powers of the earth, the separate and equal station to which the laws of nature and of nature's God entitle them, a decent respect to the opinions of mankind requires that they should declare the causes which impel them to the separation.

A NEW THEORY OF GOVERNMENT

We hold these truths to be self-evident: that all men are created equal, that they are endowed by their Creator with certain unalienable rights, that among these are life, liberty, and the pursuit of happiness.

That, to secure these rights, governments are instituted among men, deriving their just powers from the consent of the governed;

That whenever any form of government becomes destructive of these ends, it is the right of the people to alter or to abolish it, and to institute new government, laying its foundation on such principles, and organizing its powers in such form, as to them shall seem most likely to effect their safety and happiness. Prudence, indeed, will dictate that governments long established should not be changed for light and transient causes; and accordingly all experience hath shown that mankind are more disposed to suffer while evils are sufferable, than to right themselves by abolishing the forms to which they are accustomed. But when a long train of abuses and usurpations, pursuing invariably the same object, evinces a design to reduce them under absolute despotism, it is their right, it is their duty, to throw off such government, and to provide new guards for their future security.

REASONS FOR SEPARATION

Such has been the patient sufferance of these colonies; and such is now the necessity which constrains them to alter their former systems of government. The history of the present king of Great Britain is a history of repeated injuries and usurpations, all having in direct object the establishment of an absolute tyranny over these states. To prove this, let facts be submitted to a candid world.

He has refused his assent to laws the most wholesome and necessary for the public good.

He has forbidden his governors to pass laws of immediate and pressing importance unless suspended in their operation till his assent should be obtained; and when so suspended, he has utterly neglected to attend to them.

He has refused to pass other laws for the accommodation of large districts of people, unless those people would relinquish the right of representation in the legislature, a right inestimable to them, and formidable to tyrants only.

He has called together legislative bodies at places unusual, uncomfortable, and distant from the depository of their public records, for the sole purpose of fatiguing them into compliance with his measures.

He has dissolved representative houses repeatedly, for opposing, with manly firmness, his invasions on the rights of the people.

He has refused, for a long time after such dissolutions, to cause others to be elected; whereby the legislative powers, incapable of annihilation, have returned to the people at large for their exercise; the state remaining, in the mean time, exposed to all the dangers of invasion from without and convulsions within.

He has endeavored to prevent the population of these states; for that purpose obstructing the laws of naturalization of foreigners, refusing to pass others to encourage their migration hither, and raising the conditions of new appropriations of lands.

He has obstructed the administration of justice, by refusing his assent to laws for establishing judiciary powers.

He has made judges dependent on his will alone for the tenure of their offices, and the amount and payment of their salaries.

He has erected a multitude of new offices, and sent hither swarms of officers to harass our people and eat out their substance.

He has kept among us, in times of peace, standing armies, without the consent of our legislature.

He has affected to render the military independent of, and superior to, the civil power.

He has combined with others to subject us to a jurisdiction foreign to our constitution and unacknowledged by our laws, giving his assent to their acts of pretended legislation:

For quartering large bodies of armed troops among us;

For protecting them, by a mock trial, from punishment for any murders which they should commit on the inhabitants of these states;

For cutting off our trade with all parts of the world;

For imposing taxes on us without our consent;

For depriving us, in many cases, of the benefits of trial by jury;

For transporting us beyond seas, to be tried for pretended offenses;

For abolishing the free system of English laws in a neighboring province, establishing therein an arbitrary government, and enlarging its boundaries, so as to render it at once an example and fit instrument for introducing the same absolute rule into these colonies;

For taking away our charters, abolishing our most valuable laws, and altering, fundamentally, the forms of our governments;

For suspending our own legislature, and declaring themselves invested with power to legislate for us in all cases whatsoever.

He has abdicated government here, by declaring us out of his protection and waging war against us.

He has plundered our seas, ravaged our coasts, burned our towns, and destroyed the lives of our people.

He is at this time transporting large armies of foreign mercenaries to complete the works of death, desolation, and tyranny already begun with circumstances of cruelty and perfidy scarcely paralleled in the most barbarous ages, and totally unworthy the head of a civilized nation.

He has constrained our fellow-citizens, taken captive on the high seas, to bear arms against their country, to become the executioners of their friends and brethren, or to fall themselves by their hands.

He has excited domestic insurrections among us, and has endeavored to bring on the inhabitants of our frontiers the merciless Indian savages, whose known rule of warfare is an undistinguished destruction of all ages, sexes, and conditions.

In every stage of these oppressions we have petitioned for redress in the most humble terms; our repeated petitions have been answered only by repeated injury. A prince whose character is thus marked by every act which may define a tyrant is unfit to be the ruler of a free people.

Nor have we been wanting in attention to our British brethren. We have warned them, from time to time, of attempts by their legislature to extend an unwarrantable jurisdiction over us. We have reminded them of the circumstances of our emigration and settlement here. We have appealed to their native justice and magnanimity; and we have conjured them, by the ties of our common kindred, to disavow these usurpations, which would inevitably interrupt our connections and correspondence. They, too, have been deaf to the voice of justice and of consanguinity. We must, therefore, acquiesce in the necessity which denounces our separation, and hold them, as we hold the rest of mankind, enemies in war, in peace, friends.

A FORMAL DECLARATION OF WAR

We, therefore, the representatives of the United States of America, in General Congress assembled, appealing to the Supreme Judge of the world for the rectitude of our intentions, do, in the name and by authority of the good people of these colonies, solemnly publish and declare, that these united colonies are, and of right ought to be, free and independent states; that they are absolved from all allegiance to the British crown, and that all political connection between them and the state of Great Britain is, and ought to be, totally dissolved; and that, as free and independent states, they have full power to levy war, conclude peace, contract alliances, establish commerce, and to do all other acts and things which independent states may of right do. And, for the support of this declaration, with a firm reliance on the protection of Divine Providence, we mutually pledge to each other our lives, our fortunes, and our sacred honor.

3 British plans for an early victory end in disaster

In the spring of 1776, while the colonists were debating the question of independence, General Washington moved the Continental Army from Boston to New York. Washington was sure that the British would try to seize New York City and use it as a base of operations for their land and naval forces. By July Washington had nearly 30,000 troops guarding the city.

Fighting around New York City. On July 2, the same day that the Second Continental Congress voted to declare independence, General Sir William Howe sailed into New York harbor and landed British and Hessian troops on Staten Island (see map 2, page 123). A few days later Howe's brother, Admiral Lord Richard Howe, arrived with powerful naval reinforcements. By the end of August, British forces in the New York area exceeded 30,000, more than 8,000 of them Hessian soldiers.

Late in August General Howe landed about 20,000 troops on Long Island, where General Washington had stationed the bulk of the Continental Army. Howe's troops forced the Americans back to Brooklyn Heights.

The Americans were now caught in a trap. The British army was in front of them. The British fleet was behind them, ready to sail into the East River to cut off their only avenue of escape.

Fortunately for Washington, General Howe did not attack immediately. Under cover of fog and darkness, the Americans crossed the East River in small boats and reached the temporary safety of Manhattan Island.

With the British fleet controlling the water around Manhattan Island, Washington was unable to hold the city. After several sharp engagements, he withdrew northward to White Plains, leaving the British in command of New York City and its splendid harbor.

Retreat across New Jersey. By late October 1776, Washington's position was becoming desperate. Winter was approaching, and the Americans had suffered heavy losses in soldiers and supplies. The army was rapidly

The American General Hugh Mercer was killed in the Battle of Princeton in 1777. Ten years later the general's son, William Mercer, did this painting of the battle.

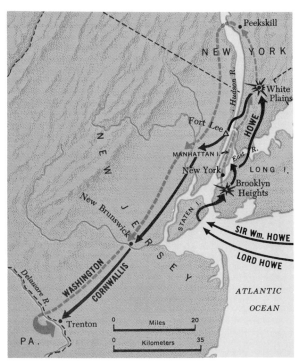

③ Fighting Near New York: July–December 1776

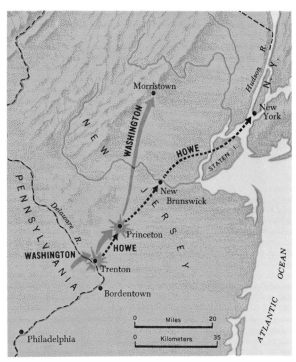

④ New Jersey Campaigns: Winter 1776–77

melting away as its members, faced with what seemed like certain defeat, picked up their guns and returned to their homes.

In this difficult situation, General Washington decided to retreat across New Jersey into Pennsylvania. Once in Pennsylvania, the Delaware River would separate him from the British. There he would gain time to regroup his battered forces.

During the retreat across New Jersey, soldiers continued to slip away from the army. By the time Washington reached the Delaware River, only about 3,000 troops remained. Weary and discouraged, the soldiers combed the river for small boats, which they then rowed across to the Pennsylvania side (see map 3, this page).

Trenton and Princeton. Confident that the war was almost won, General Howe prepared to celebrate Christmas in New York. To keep a watch on the Americans, General Charles Cornwallis, commanding the British forces in the field, stationed 1,300 Hessians at Trenton and a second force nearby, farther south.

Howe's Christmas celebration was rudely interrupted Opening a brilliant military cam-

paign, Washington and his troops crossed the ice-choked Delaware on Christmas night. Early the next morning, they surprised the Hessians and took more than 1,000 prisoners.

British reinforcements under Cornwallis rushed to the Trenton area, arriving on January 2, 1777. Cornwallis, certain that he had Washington in a trap, prepared to attack in the morning. During the night the American troops slipped quietly away, leaving their campfires burning brightly to deceive the British into thinking that they were still there.

Instead of retiring to the safety of the west bank of the Delaware River, Washington struck inland. His troops badly cut up three British regiments at Princeton, then withdrew swiftly to the hills around Morristown in northern New Jersey (see map 4, this page). From here he could raid the British lines of communication and supply to New Brunswick and Trenton. Since these cities were no longer of any particular value to the British, Howe pulled his troops out of New Jersey and back to New York.

Washington's victories at Trenton and Princeton ruined British plans for ending the war in the winter of 1776–77. In contrast,

George Washington reviews his exhausted, nearly starving army at Valley Forge in the winter of 1777–78. The army had trouble getting supplies because few farmers or merchants would accept the Continental money.

American spirits began to revive. The Americans now believed they could win battles against British regulars. During the next few months, volunteers began to swell the ranks of the Continental Army. Washington had taken great chances, but he had won the gamble.

British disaster at Saratoga. Aroused to greater efforts by their defeats at Trenton and Princeton, the British now determined to end the war in 1777. They decided upon a plan that would separate New England from the rest of the states.

Lieutenant Colonel Barry St. Leger (SAYNT LEJ·er) was to lead an expedition, with some Indian allies, from Fort Oswego (os·WEE·goh) on Lake Ontario, through the Mohawk Valley to the Hudson River (see map 5, page 125). General John Burgoyne was to lead a second expedition from Canada down the Richelieu River–Lake Champlain route. General Howe was to lead a third expedition from New York up the Hudson River. These three forces were to meet at Albany and crush the American forces.

The plan looked beautifully simple to officials drawing lines on a map in the warmth and comfort of the London War Office. What they did not know, or ignored, was that these lines crossed lakes, swamps, mountains, and trackless forests swarming with militia ready to defend their homes, villages, and farms.

St. Leger reached the Mohawk Valley on schedule and laid siege to Fort Stanwix, where American forces were stationed. If the fort fell, St. Leger would have a clear road open before him to Albany. General Nicholas Herkimer of New York and a force of German-American militia tried to reach Fort Stanwix and rein-

SOURCES

THOMAS PAINE'S "THE CRISIS" (1776)

These are the times that try men's souls. The summer soldier and the sunshine patriot will, in this crisis, shrink from the service of their country; but he that stands by it now deserves the love and thanks of man and woman. Tyranny, like hell, is not easily conquered; yet we have this consolation with us, that the harder the conflict, the more glorious the triumph. What we obtain too cheap, we esteem too lightly; it is dearness only that gives everything its value. Heaven knows how to put a proper price upon its goods; and it would be strange indeed if so celestial an article as FREEDOM should not be highly rated. . . .

force it, but a party of Tories and Indians ambushed them near the town of Oriskany (oh·RIS·kah·nee). The situation for the Americans in Fort Stanwix was desperate. Then suddenly word spread through St. Leger's forces that Benedict Arnold was approaching with a large American army. St. Leger's Indians deserted, and the British retreated to Canada.

Meanwhile, a second British force was moving southward from Canada down the difficult Richelieu River–Lake Champlain route. General Burgoyne, its leader, knew as little about the American wilderness as his superiors in London. He reached and occupied Fort Ticonderoga without serious opposition. Then his troubles began. Trying to obtain additional supplies, he sent a raiding party into what is now Vermont. There they were destroyed at Bennington by General John Stark and a force of New England militia.

Burgoyne's position was now difficult, if not impossible. His provisions were almost gone. His lines of supply were stretched to a dangerous length from Canada through the forests. The militia of New England and New York were swarming around him like angry bees.

At Bemis Heights, near Saratoga on the Hudson River, Burgoyne met the main body of the American forces in the area. Outnumbered by more than two to one and outmaneuvered by the American leaders—Philip Schuyler of New York, Horatio Gates of Virginia, Benjamin Lincoln of Massachusetts, Daniel Morgan of Virginia, and Benedict Arnold of Connecticut—Burgoyne surrendered his entire force of nearly 6,000 troops at Saratoga on October 17, 1777.

An unexplained blunder. Burgoyne might have been saved if the planned British expedition up the Hudson River had appeared in time, but it never did. Instead of marching northward from New York City, Howe embarked his troops and sailed southward. American scouts followed his progress down the coast. Much to their surprise, he passed the mouth of the Delaware River, sailed to the head of Chesapeake Bay, and disembarked. Then he marched to Philadelphia, overcoming the Patriots in the battles of Brandywine Creek on September 11 and Germantown on October 4 (see map 5, this page). Once he was in Philadelphia, Howe settled down for the winter of 1777–78. Washington, meanwhile, went into winter quarters at Valley Forge.

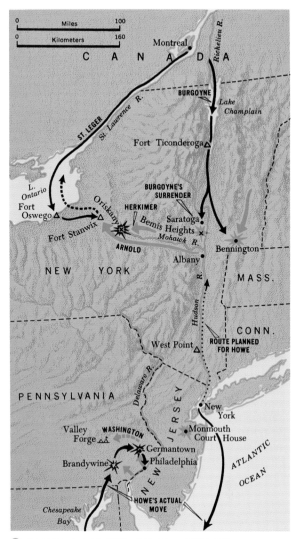

⑤ Saratoga and Philadelphia: 1777–78

Why Howe failed to carry through his part of the plan to split the colonies remains uncertain. Perhaps the British War Office blundered and neglected to send the orders in time. Perhaps Howe decided that Burgoyne could handle the situation without help. For whatever reason, Howe's failure to proceed up the Hudson River contributed to the British disaster at Saratoga.

The British Parliament, sobered by the news of Burgoyne's defeat, sent commissioners to the Continental Congress. They offered to suspend the Coercive Acts and pardon the Patriots. Unfortunately for the British, their concessions came nearly two years too late.

1. Why was the capture of New York City an important part of British war plans?
2. Why were Washington's victories at Trenton and Princeton so important?
3. Map Study: Look at the map on page 125. (a) What routes did St. Leger, Burgoyne, and Howe plan to follow? (b) What would the result have been if the British plan had succeeded?

4 American Patriots defeat the British army

Americans went wild with joy at the news of Burgoyne's defeat. The French, who sympathized with the American cause, celebrated as though they, too, had won a victory.

Aid from France. From the beginning France had been secretly providing the Americans with desperately needed arms and supplies. Benjamin Franklin, one of the American commissioners in France, began some shrewd bargaining. His negotiations were crowned with success.

On February 6, 1778, France and the United States of America signed two treaties. In the first, a commercial treaty, the two nations agreed to give each other favored treatment in matters of trade. In the other, a treaty of alliance, France agreed to recognize the independence of the United States and to wage war upon Great Britain until America was free. America promised to defend the French West Indies. Both countries promised not to make a separate peace with Great Britain.

The treaty with France came at a crucial time. Despite the victory at Saratoga, the Americans were in bad shape. Washington's army at Valley Forge was reduced to a poorly equipped, sick, hungry handful. The glad news that they now had a powerful ally filled the Patriots with new hope. Recruits began again to fill the thinned ranks of the army.

Help from abroad. France sent important aid to America in the form of gold, powder, shot, equipment, a fleet, and a considerable number of troops. Spain and the Netherlands, too, gave some support to the American cause. In addition, volunteers from a number of European countries came to America. From Prussia came Baron von Steuben, who took charge of organizing and drilling the Continental Army. From Poland came Casimir Pulaski (poo·LAS·kee) and Thaddeus Kosciusko (koz·ih·US·koh), who planned the American defenses of West Point on the Hudson River

At Cowpens, Daniel Morgan used a mock retreat and this well-timed cavalry charge to destroy nearly a third of the British army in the South. Cornwallis called the defeat by the Americans a "very unexpected and severe blow."

and Bemis Heights near Saratoga. From France came the German-born officer Baron de Kalb and the young Marquis de Lafayette (lah·fah·YET), who arrived in America with 12 other officers just before the Battle of Brandywine.

Changing British plans. French intervention forced the British to revise their plans for conquering their former colonies. As a first step, they replaced General Howe with Sir Henry Clinton.

Clinton had orders to strike the next blow at the southern states. Before doing this, however, he withdrew the British troops from Philadelphia and set out across New Jersey toward New York City. Washington pursued the British and overtook them at Monmouth Court House (see map 4, page 125). The battle was indecisive, with about 350 casualties on each side. After the battle the British continued their withdrawal to New York.

From then on, there were no major military activities in the North. At times, though, British raiding parties swept down on towns near New York City.

War in the South. In shifting the attack to the South, Great Britain hoped to profit from the aid of the Tories, who were reported to be especially numerous in the southern states.

As in the North, the British had no great trouble occupying seaports. In December 1778 they seized Savannah, Georgia. In May 1780 they forced General Benjamin Lincoln to surrender Charleston, South Carolina, and 5,000 troops. This was almost the entire American army south of the Potomac River. From these bases General Cornwallis, who now commanded the British armies in the southern states, was able to move where and when he pleased. British forces raided the countryside. They plundered and burned, trying to terrorize the Patriots and force them into submission.

But for every Tory who rallied to the British, a Patriot sprang up to oppose the British war effort. In South Carolina such southerners as Francis Marion (called "the Swamp Fox"), Andrew Pickens, and Thomas Sumter led **guerrilla** bands against the British forces. The guerrillas were hunters and farmers, not part of the regular army, who stung the British with sabotage and surprise raids. To aid these guerrilla bands, Congress sent a small army under the command of General Horatio Gates.

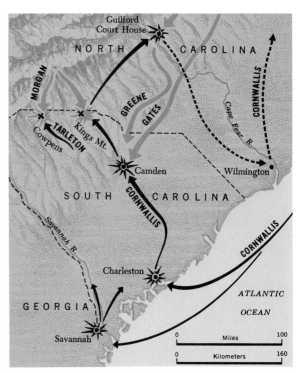

Ⓖ Fighting in the South: 1778–81

Gates, however, was badly defeated at Camden, South Carolina, in August 1780 (see map 6, this page).

The South seemed lost to the Patriot cause. Then in October 1780, a frontier militia led by Isaac Shelby, John Sevier, and others defeated a party of Tories at Kings Mountain, near the boundary between the Carolinas. At the same time, Nathanael Greene of Rhode Island replaced Gates as commander of the American forces in the South.

Although General Greene won no major battles, he and General Daniel Morgan of Virginia, supported by the guerrillas, made the British occupation of inland regions extremely costly. In January 1781 Morgan defeated a British force at Cowpens in South Carolina. Two months later, in March, the Americans struck a serious blow against Cornwallis's forces at Guilford Court House, North Carolina (see map 6, page 127). Although Cornwallis won, his losses were so great that he abandoned the entire campaign. He withdrew to the security of the coast, where the Royal Navy could support him. Thus, by 1781, the British were back where they had been in 1778, holding only New York City and a few southern ports.

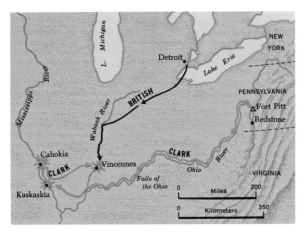

⓻ Fighting in the Northwest: 1778–79

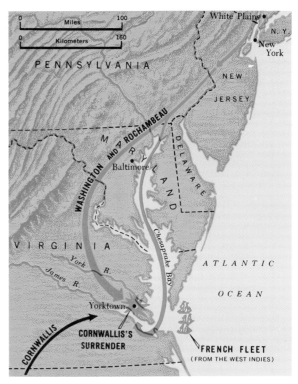

⓼ Fighting at Yorktown: August–October 1781

Campaign in the Northwest. Meanwhile, Lieutenant Colonel George Rogers Clark of Virginia had been clearing the western lands of British troops. From Virginia, whose claim to this territory went back to the charter of 1609, Clark secured money and supplies for the expedition. With a small group of frontier fighters, he made his way down the Ohio River and up the Mississippi in the summer of 1778. He won Indian aid and surprised the British forts at Kaskaskia, Cahokia, and Vincennes (see map 7, this page). In December, however, Clark suffered a setback when the British recaptured Vincennes. In February 1779, in the dead of winter, Clark marched 170 miles (275 kilometers) eastward through the wilderness to overwhelm the British at Fort Vincennes. This bold blow cleared the entire western lands of British forces.

The British surrender. During the summer of 1781. the war proceeded swiftly to an end. Cornwallis moved northward into Virginia. There he based his army at Yorktown, on the peninsula between the York and James rivers (see map 8, this page). He was supplied by the British fleet operating out of New York harbor. A small American army under Generals Lafayette, Von Steuben, and Anthony Wayne of Pennsylvania watched the British closely, but the American forces were too weak to attack. Washington and a number of American and French soldiers remained at White Plains, New York. From there they kept an eye on the British under Clinton in New York City.

Then a messenger from Admiral de Grasse, commander of the French fleet in the West In-

dies, arrived at Washington's headquarters. De Grasse reported that the fleet could be spared for a few months. Where, he asked, could General Washington use it most effectively?

With skill and speed, Washington formed a brilliant plan. Following Washington's instructions, de Grasse placed his fleet across the mouth of Chesapeake Bay, cutting off Cornwallis from supplies and reinforcements. The American army in White Plains then moved toward New York, leading General Clinton to expect an attack upon the city. Instead of striking at New York, however, Washington and his army joined the French and American forces in front of Yorktown in Virginia (see map 8, this page).

Cornwallis was hopelessly trapped. Behind him was the French fleet. Before him was a greatly superior force of American troops, reinforced by 6,000 French troops. After a British squadron failed to break the French blockade, Cornwallis was ready to admit defeat. He surrendered his entire army of 7,000 soldiers on October 19, 1781. Although the formal treaty of peace was not signed until 1783, all serious fighting on the American continent ceased with the American victory at Yorktown.

SECTION SURVEY

IDENTIFY: Valley Forge, Casimir Pulaski, Marquis de Lafayette, Henry Clinton, Nathanael Greene, Yorktown.

1. (a) List three ways in which the French aided the Americans in the Revolutionary War. (b) What did the French hope to gain by such aid? (c) Did any other European nations also support the Americans?
2. Why did the British campaign in the South fail?
3. Why was George Rogers Clark's campaign important to the Americans?
4. Map Study: Look at the map on page 128. How did the Patriots use geography in defeating the British at Yorktown?

---

5 Events off the battlefield lead to an American victory

Both sides—the United States of America and Great Britain—faced serious problems during the eight long years of the war.

Shortage of troops and supplies. One major American weakness was the relatively small number of colonists who were willing to fight in the war. Many Americans were indifferent to the outcome of the conflict. A good number of these devoted their efforts to making the war as profitable for themselves as possible. Some merchants charged high prices for shoddy goods that they sold to the American armies. Some farmers sold their produce for the greatest profit, not caring whether it reached American or British hands. Because of this indifference and selfishness, Washington's troops starved and froze at Morristown in the winter of 1776–77 and at Valley Forge in the winter of 1777–78 while the British soldiers lived in comfort in New York and in Philadelphia.

Despite the shortage of troops, Washington at first ordered that no black soldiers, slave or free, could be recruited. Some colonial leaders feared that slaves would revolt if given arms. Some of Washington's officers believed that blacks did not make good soldiers.

Washington and other leaders changed their thinking late in 1775 when Lord Dunmore, royal governor of Virginia, offered freedom to all slaves who joined the British forces.

Washington now consented to enlist free black men in the Continental armies. State militias, except in South Carolina and Georgia, enlisted slaves as well. Slaves were promised their freedom when the war ended. In most cases, however, the promise was not carried out despite the fact that black colonists had fought at Lexington, Concord, Ticonderoga, and Breed's Hill. At Breed's Hill, in fact, two black Americans, Peter Salem and Salem Poor, had been singled out for outstanding heroism.

Of some 300,000 Americans who fought in the war, about 5,000 were black. They served with courage and skill in the Continental navy and armies and in the navies and militias of the states. A French officer at Yorktown wrote: ". . . three quarters of the Rhode Island regiment consists of Negroes, and that regiment is the most neatly dressed, the best under arms, and the most precise in its maneuvers."

Weak central government. Troop shortages were not the only American problem. Another major weakness was the lack of an effective central government. The Second Continental Congress, which governed the country until 1781, had no real authority. It could only *ask* the states for troops, supplies, and money. If a state refused, the matter ended Congress could and did borrow money from foreign coun-

James Armistead, a slave, worked for Lafayette as a spy and received this certificate for his work. The government of Virginia later granted Armistead his freedom.

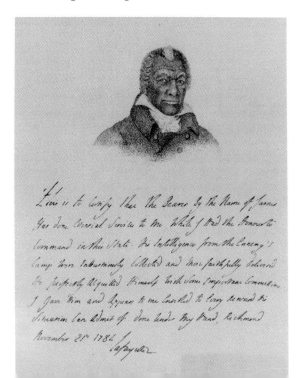

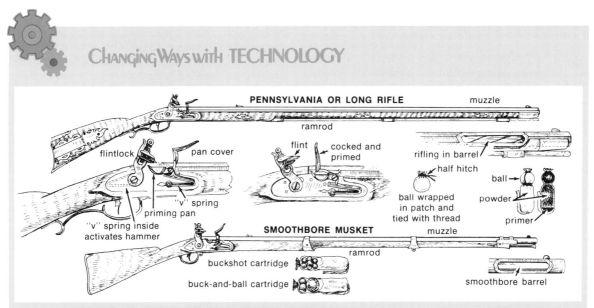

PENNSYLVANIA OR LONG RIFLE — muzzle — ramrod — flintlock — pan cover — flint — cocked and primed — rifling in barrel — half hitch — ball wrapped in patch and tied with thread — ball — powder — primer — "v" spring — priming pan — "v" spring inside activates hammer — **SMOOTHBORE MUSKET** — muzzle — ramrod — buckshot cartridge — buck-and-ball cartridge — smoothbore barrel

THE PENNSYLVANIA RIFLE

For early frontier settlers, a good gun could be as useful as a good ax. Yet the settlers often found that the best available guns were not right for their purposes—small-game hunting and protection. The German Jaeger rifle was accurate but heavy and required a mallet to pound the tight-fitting bullets into the barrel. The smoothbore musket was light and easy to load, but inaccurate.

Around 1727, German gunsmiths who had settled near Lancaster, Pennsylvania, developed the Pennsylvania rifle, sometimes called the long rifle or the Kentucky rifle. It was light enough to be used readily to hunt small game. The spiral rifling inside its barrel gave a rapid spin to the rifle ball. This enabled the ball to travel farther and truer than with a smoothbore gun. Accuracy was also improved by the lengthened barrel (the entire gun measured nearly five feet, or 1.5 meters) and the smaller

bore. Up to a range of about 100 yards (about 90 meters) the Pennsylvania rifles were about as accurate as ordinary rifles are today.

Loading took about a minute. The charge was pushed through the muzzle into position with a ramrod slung under the barrel. The charge might be a manufactured paper cartridge. Or the operator might pour loose powder down the barrel and ram in after it a lead ball wrapped and tied in a greased linen patch. These patches were stored in a hollow section of the stock. For firing, a pinch of powder in the priming pan was ignited by a piece of flint locked in the hammer.

The Pennsylvania rifle played an important role in the American Revolution. In reports sent back to England, the British generals spoke of the "terrible guns of the rebels." The smooth-bore muskets used by the British proved no match for these long rifles.

---

tries and from American citizens. However, it financed most of the war costs by issuing paper money known as "Continental currency."

These problems kept the American military effort weak and disorganized. Except for the first few weeks of the war, Washington never had more than 16,000 troops under his command at any one time. At no time was he sure how many of these he could rely on. After each victory volunteers poured in. After each defeat the army melted away. "What we need is a good army, not a large one," Washington once remarked bitterly, yet his faith and courage

never faltered. It was this faith combined with the unselfish devotion of many soldiers and citizens that finally brought victory.

Women in the Revolution. This faith and devotion was shared by many women Patriots. Even before 1776 women played an important part in boycotting British goods. In the struggle for independence, women found many ways to support the Revolution. Mercy Otis Warren published plays that satirized the British and Loyalists, and she started writing her *History of the American Revolution.* Many women collected lead and helped manufacture bullets. Others made uniforms for the soldiers or collected and distributed medical and hospital supplies. Still others accompanied the troops, helping as cooks, doing laundry, and serving as nurses. A few performed dangerous missions as spies and messengers.

There are many legends about women who fought in the ranks, but it seems well established that Margaret Corbin and Molly Pitcher took the places of their wounded husbands. Deborah Sampson, a young Massachusetts girl, disguised herself in soldier's clothing and took part in several battles.

British problems. Fortunately for the Americans, the British, too, faced difficult problems during the Revolutionary War. One of these was the problem created by geography.

When the war started, the Americans occupied the enormous territory from Canada to Florida. The only British foothold was the seaport of Boston. To win the war, the Americans needed only to hold on to what they had. The British, on the other hand, had to regain control of this enormous territory. To regain control, they had to send troops and supplies across the Atlantic in slow sailing ships. Handicapped by the problem of supply, the British were never able to conquer and hold any sizable inland area.

British blunders. The British were also guilty of many blunders and much mismanagement. They made no great effort to concentrate an overwhelming force against the Americans.

Great Britain's major asset was its professional army. Well organized, well trained, well equipped, and well fed, the British regulars were more than a match for the Patriot troops on open, unforested land. But the British regulars were often used badly. Their superiors in England often revealed a hopeless ignorance of the land and the people of America.

One of Great Britain's major mistakes was its reliance upon the Hessian soldiers hired by George III. Many of these unfortunate Germans had been seized forcibly by their rulers, who received payment for them from George III and shipped them to America. Bewildered and homesick, they knew nothing about the war and cared less. As a result, they made poor soldiers.

The Loyalists, or Tories, who served under British colors, estimated at from 50,000 to

Disguised as a man, Deborah Sampson served well in the Continental army. She was wounded twice in battle. Upon discovery she was dismissed, but she later received a soldier's pension.

60,000, fought bitterly and even savagely against their former neighbors, as is common in civil war. However, they too were untrained and unorganized. Often the presence of the Loyalist troops in the British ranks aroused the fighting spirit of the American Patriots opposing them.

Leaks in the blockade. The Royal Navy expected to sweep all enemy ships from the sea and by a tight blockade to cut off resources that the Americans needed to fight the war. However, America was a self-sufficient agricultural region, and the blockade was an inconvenience rather than a disaster for the Americans.

Then, too, the Americans did have a navy. During the war more than 50 ships were built and commissioned by the Continental Congress. They were commanded by such men as John Paul Jones.

Jones's most memorable victory—and perhaps the greatest naval victory of the war—took place in 1779. Jones's ship, the *Bon Homme Richard,* engaged the British ship *Serapis* in battle. With his own warship about to sink, Jones lashed the two ships together and in desperate fighting won the victory. At the height of this battle, when asked to surrender, Jones boldly declared, "I have not yet begun to fight."

THOSE WHO DISAGREED: THE LOYALISTS

American physician John Jeffries is known in aviation history for his pioneer balloon flight across the English Channel in 1785. When he died in 1819, a wealthy and respected citizen of Boston, not much was said about his record during the Revolutionary War. For Jeffries—like many other Americans—had been a Loyalist and had fought on the side of Great Britain.

During the Revolution, about a third of the American colonists opposed independence. (Roughly a third were Patriots, while the rest were neutral or simply indifferent.) Loyalists, or Tories, lived in all sections of the country, often with Patriots as next-door neighbors. Loyalists also came from all social classes, although wealthy landowners, rich merchants, and professional people were especially numerous.

Altogether, about 60,000 colonists fought on the Loyalist side. Relatively few Loyalists were exiled, but several thousand left voluntarily, most to go to Canada. According to one estimate, the colonies had lost some 200,000 Tory citizens by war's end. Their property was taken over and few were ever repaid.

All things considered, however, the Loyalists were not badly treated. Many thousands remained in the thirteen American colonies unharmed or returned after the war. Even those who had fought with the British, like Jeffries, usually went unpunished. Another well-known Tory was Philip B. Key, whose nephew years later wrote "The Star-Spangled Banner." After serving in a Loyalist regiment, he was elected a federal judge—while still receiving his British army pension!

All the states except Delaware and New Jersey also built and manned their own naval vessels. Although these ships were small, the British had to spend much time in tracking them down and destroying them.

More difficult for the British to cope with were the American **privateers**. Privateers were privately owned ships whose owners were authorized by the Continental Congress or the state governments to attack enemy shipping. Slipping through the British blockade in fog or darkness, the privateers struck at naval vessels and defenseless British merchant ships. The money from the sale of captured ships and cargoes was divided among owners, captains, and crews. Since fortunes could quickly be made, this risky business attracted thousands of adventurous colonists.

Opposition to British naval policy. The British fleet interfered with the shipping of neutral nations. Angered by the interference, several nations formed the League of Armed Neutrality. Before the war ended, this league included Russia, Sweden, Denmark, Prussia, Portugal, Naples, and several other European states. In addition, France, Spain, and the Netherlands were openly at war with Great Britain. Throughout the later years of conflict, the warships of these European nations, combined with the American navy and privateers, put a drain upon Great Britain's resources.

British opposition to the war. As a result, the war became increasingly unpopular in Great Britain. In fact, many leaders in Great Britain opposed the war effort. The situation was so bad that some British politicians and officers rejoiced at the news of an American victory. Some officers actually refused to serve in America. British merchants, shipowners, and business people were losing heavily.

Great Britain could have continued to fight after Cornwallis's defeat at Yorktown in 1781. The British might have concentrated overwhelming forces against the Americans. They might have finally worn them down with a strict and long-continued blockade to the point where they would have asked for peace. But the price of continuing the war was heavier than most British people were willing to pay.

The peace treaty of 1783. Negotiations to end the war began soon after the surrender of Cornwallis in October 1781. The final treaty, called the Treaty of Paris, was not completed until September 3, 1783.

The four American commissioners—Benjamin Franklin, John Jay, John Adams, and Henry Laurens—could hardly have won better terms. By the terms of the treaty, the Americans gained (1) independence, (2) all the land between the Appalachian Mountains and the Mississippi River from the Great Lakes south to Florida, and (3) the right to fish in the Gulf of St. Lawrence and off the coast of Newfoundland.

A very difficult problem arose when Great Britain demanded that all property and land taken from the Tories be returned to them and that all debts owed by Americans to Britishers be paid in full. Franklin and the other American commissioners insisted that this was impossible. The Tory property had been seized by the different states and had long since been sold. Large estates had been divided into many smaller pieces. The Continental Congress had no money for purchasing these properties and returning them to their former Tory owners.

Finally, after a long deadlock, the peace commissioners agreed to recommend that the new states allow persons with claims to use the American courts to recover their property.

The commissioners also agreed to recommend that private debts be handled in the same way. Actually, these recommendations were meaningless, since Congress could not force the states to open their courts to Tory claims. The British made the best of the situation and signed a preliminary treaty. Astonished at the liberal terms, the French foreign minister Vergennes declared, "The English do not make peace; they buy it."

The French were not represented in the peace talks until these decisions had been reached. They were angry as well as surprised that the United States and Great Britain had agreed upon peace terms. Franklin had to use all his arts of persuasion to smooth the ruffled feelings of the French leaders. His success in negotiating the final Treaty of Paris in 1783 proved his great skill as a diplomat.

The Americans were fortunate to be represented so ably. They were even more fortunate that the peace commissioners decided to negotiate directly with Great Britain. Spain wanted to confine the United States of America to the land between the Atlantic and the Appalachians. If the American commissioners had been forced to sit around a peace table with

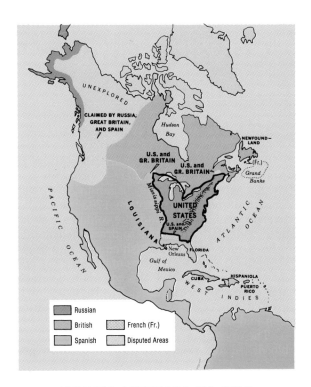

NORTH AMERICA IN 1783

representatives from Spain, France, and Great Britain, the thirteen colonies would have won only their independence—nothing more. As it was, by making the most of Great Britain's desire for a quick end to the war, American peace commissioners won for their country a number of liberal concessions and a vast expanse of land west of the Appalachians.

SECTION SURVEY

IDENTIFY: Continental currency, John Paul Jones, privateers, League of Armed Neutrality, Treaty of Paris of 1783.

1. What role did black soldiers play in America's struggle for independence?

2. What contributions did women make to the Patriot cause?

3. (a) Make a chart of the weaknesses and strengths of each side in the Revolution. (b) What was the most important strength and the most important weakness on each side? Explain.

4. Map Study: Look at the map on this page. (a) What nations had claims in North America in 1783? (b) What was the western boundary of the United States after the Treaty of Paris?

133

Chapter Survey

Summary: Tracing the Main Ideas

From the day the first British settlers in America began to adapt themselves to life in a strange environment, they began to grow away from their mother country. By 1763 the gap between Great Britain and the colonies was indeed wide. British efforts to draw the colonies more firmly into the British empire and to get them to help pay for the cost of running the empire only antagonized the colonists. Protests and even violence against the British slowly grew in the colonies. By early 1775 the situation had become exceedingly tense.

The uncertainty ended in gunfire. With the bloodshed at Lexington and Concord on April 19, 1775, and later at Bunker Hill, hope of compromise vanished.

In their Declaration of Independence, the American colonists broke their ties with Great Britain and proclaimed their message of freedom to the entire world. On the battlefields of America, aided by French troops and by French naval forces in the Atlantic, the Americans finally succeeded in wearing down the British. When Cornwallis surrendered his army at Yorktown, America had, in effect, won independence.

With the Treaty of Paris in 1783, the world recognized that a new nation had been born. It was the first nation in the modern world to break the ties that bound it to another nation and to launch out as an independent country.

As you will see in the next chapter, however, the people of the new nation faced many more problems. The most important of these was how to organize an effective government around which Americans could rally with confidence and pride.

Inquiring into History

1. If, after 1763, Great Britain had maintained the same policy toward the colonies that it had followed before 1763, the Revolution might not have occurred. Comment.
2. British subjects in America fought not to obtain freedom but to confirm the freedoms they already had. Do you agree or disagree with this statement? Why?
3. Some British textbooks blame the American Revolution on a small group of radical agitators in America who were impatient with British leaders. (a) Do you agree or disagree with this interpretation? Explain. (b) Why do you think that British textbooks might present this interpretation of the Revolution?
4. Why can the Battle of Saratoga be called the turning point of the Revolutionary War? Why can it be called one of the turning points of world history?
5. Select one battle or campaign of the Revolutionary War. How did this battle or campaign illustrate the strengths and weaknesses of the Americans? the strengths and weaknesses of the British? Use specific examples to support your answer.
6. Many historians believe that French aid was the key factor in the American victory in the Revolutionary War. Use historical evidence to support or refute this statement.

Relating Past to Present

1. To what extent do the ideals of equality and human rights expressed in the Declaration of Independence affect American policies within the country today? American relations with other nations?
2. In what ways was the American Revolution fought as wars are fought today? In what ways was it fought differently?

Developing Social Science Skills

1. (a) What does the word "propaganda" mean? (b) Would you describe the writings of Thomas Paine as propaganda? Why or why not? (c) How is the Declaration of Independence an example of propaganda? Quote specific words and phrases to support your answer.
2. Conduct research and prepare a written or pictorial report on one of these people and the role he or she played in the Revolution: (a) Molly Pitcher, (b) Salem Poor, (c) Mercy Otis Warren, (d) Francis Marion, (e) Thaddeus Kosciusko, (f) Haym Salomon.
3. The American Revolution has served as a model for other countries in their struggles for independence and democracy. Prepare brief reports on two countries that you believe have been influenced by the American Revolution.

Chapter 7

Creating a Confederation of States

1775-1787

"The American war is over," one of America's leaders declared in 1783, "but this is far from being the case with the American Revolution." The speaker was Dr. Benjamin Rush, a prominent Philadelphia doctor and one of the signers of the Declaration of Independence. Dr. Rush knew—as did Thomas Jefferson and many other Americans—that it was easier to outline a theory of government than it was to build a government that really worked.

Many problems faced the now independent American people. One of the most serious was whether the thirteen states, which for seven years had joined together in rebellion against British rule, would remain united now that the crisis was over. "A long time, and much prudence, will be necessary to reproduce a spirit of union and . . . reverence for government," David Ramsay of South Carolina declared.

Actually, as it turned out, the American people developed a "spirit of union" and "reverence for government" in an amazingly short time. Long before the Revolution was over, the states had organized new governments. In 1781, the year the fighting ended, all thirteen states finally agreed to enter a union. Despite these steps, as you will see, there were moments when the future of the states indeed looked dark.

THE CHAPTER IN OUTLINE

1. The former colonies create new state governments.
2. The states unite under the Articles of Confederation.
3. The Confederation lacks the power to solve important problems.

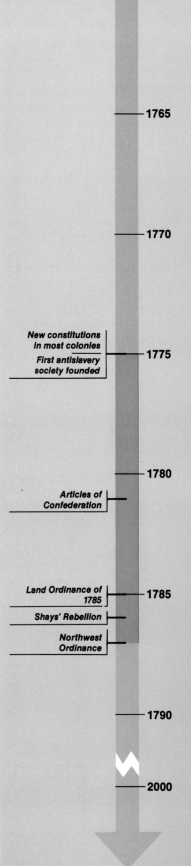

1760

1765

1770

New constitutions in most colonies

First antislavery society founded

1775

1780

Articles of Confederation

Land Ordinance of 1785

1785

Shays' Rebellion

Northwest Ordinance

1790

2000

1 The former colonies create new state governments

In 1775, even before the start of actual fighting, the long-established governments of the colonies began to crumble. After the fighting at Lexington and at Breed's Hill, several royal governors returned to England. The more conservative members of the colonial legislatures also returned to their homes. By 1776 nearly all colonial government had disappeared. Only the local governments, most of them now in the hands of the Patriots, continued to meet and carry on business.

From old governments to new. The members of the Second Continental Congress were alarmed at this situation. They had no power to act as a government for the colonies. On the other hand, they knew that someone had to do something to prevent lawlessness and disorder from ripping the colonies apart. Thus, on May 10, 1775, the Second Continental Congress adopted a resolution urging the colonies to organize new governments to replace the colonial governments.

The legislatures of New Hampshire and South Carolina, both controlled by Patriots, had already written new state constitutions. During the next few months, all the colonies except Connecticut, Rhode Island, and Massachusetts adopted new state constitutions.

Connecticut and Rhode Island had always been self-governing colonies. They continued to use their colonial charters as state constitutions until well into the 1800's. However, Massachusetts operated under a temporary government for most of the war.

Although the American people were fighting for the right to govern themselves, most of them had little or nothing to do with the writing of the new constitutions. In most states the legislatures prepared the constitutions without consulting the people themselves.

This method of organizing the new governments did not suit Massachusetts and New Hampshire. Both these states held constitutional conventions at which specially elected delegates drafted the constitutions. When the delegates finished their work, the voters themselves then had the chance to accept or reject the proposed constitutions.

Governments under law. The democratic ideas expressed in the Declaration of Independence helped to shape the new state constitutions. Those who wrote the constitutions wanted especially to provide ironclad guarantees of each person's natural rights. They wanted to protect the "unalienable rights" of "life, liberty, and the pursuit of happiness." As a result, the new state constitutions began with a bill of rights. These bills of rights contained guarantees of religious freedom, the right to free speech and a free press, the right to assemble, the right to a fair trial by jury, and equality of all citizens before the law.

It was significant that the framers of the new state constitutions put the guarantees into written constitutions. Under these written state constitutions, the new American states were adopting "government of laws, and not of men."

To establish a government of laws, the new constitutions provided for a **separation of powers.** This meant that the powers of government were divided among the executive, legislative, and judicial departments. The constitu-

Abigail Adams, wife of John Adams, wrote concerning the nation's future: "We shall be daily making new advances and vie in some future date with the most celebrated European nation."

tion of Massachusetts provided that "in the government of this commonwealth, the legislative department shall never exercise the executive and judicial powers or either of them: the executive shall never exercise the legislative and judicial powers or either of them: the judicial shall never exercise the legislative and executive powers or either of them: to the end it may be a government of laws, and not of men." Although other state constitutions did not provide as clear a separation of powers as that of Massachusetts, all the states did limit the power of the executive department.

Separating church and state. The states also strengthened the principle of separation of church and government. When the Revolutionary War broke out, people in nine of the thirteen colonies were required by law to pay taxes to support an established church. The people had to pay these taxes even if they belonged to another church or to no church at all. By 1787, however, official churches had been abolished in all but three states—New Hampshire, Massachusetts, and Connecticut. In time, these three states also abolished their official churches.

Concern over slavery. The contradiction between the principles of the Declaration of Independence and the fact of slavery also troubled a growing number of Americans. Leading preachers, educators, lawyers, and public figures condemned slavery. In 1773 Patrick Henry said that slavery was "as repugnant to humanity as it is inconsistent with the Bible and destructive of liberty." This antislavery feeling led many slaveowners to free their slaves. Some did so because they were moved by the contradictions between slavery and the ideals of the Revolution. Other owners freed their slaves because they found slavery an expensive and inefficient system.

Thomas Jefferson was well aware that slavery contradicted the ideals set forth in the Declaration of Independence. In his writings he deplored the effects that slavery had of making slaveowners arrogant and of robbing slaves of human dignity.

Like most Americans of the time, however, Jefferson was not certain about what the exact role of blacks in American life should be. Jefferson did not want the full **abolition,** or ending, of slavery. He feared that white people and black people could not live peacefully side by side, especially in the southern states, where slaves were so numerous. Jefferson also accepted the false, but common, thinking of his time that black people lacked the capacity for self-government. He suggested, but did not advocate, the idea that slaves might be freed and established in an area of their own on the western lands.

Some of the new state governments were moved to action by the clash between slavery and the ideals of the war they were fighting. The Continental Congress and several states for a time prohibited the importation of slaves. During the war many of the states enlisted slaves in their armed forces and granted them their freedom. Several states adopted laws providing for the gradual freeing of slaves and the eventual abolition of slavery. In Massachusetts the Superior Court ruled that every slave within the state's borders had been freed by its constitution of 1780, which declared that "all men are born free and equal."

Antislavery sentiment stemming from the Revolutionary War also led to the formation of **abolition societies,** or groups working to end slavery. The first such society was founded by Philadelphia Quakers in 1775. By 1792 active

SOURCES

VIRGINIA STATUTE FOR RELIGIOUS FREEDOM (1786)

Well aware that Almighty God has created the mind free; that all attempts to influence it by temporal punishments ... tend only to ... [produce] habits of hypocrisy and meanness; ... that to compel a man to furnish contributions of money for the propagation of opinions which he disbelieves is sinful and tyrannical; ... that truth is great and will prevail if left to herself ...

Be it enacted by the General Assembly that no man shall be compelled to frequent or support any religious worship ... whatsoever; ... all men shall be free to profess ... their opinion in matters of religion; ... the same shall in no wise diminish, enlarge, or affect their civil capacities....

In 1780 Pennsylvania passed a law calling for a gradual end to slavery there. Nevertheless, free blacks, like these woodcutters in Philadelphia, still faced discrimination and economic disadvantages.

to vote continued to be limited by religious and property qualifications.

The democratic forces set in motion by the Revolutionary War did little at the time to advance the role of women. They were not permitted to vote. Married women were limited in the control of their property and in important decisions about their children. Such restrictions troubled Abigail Adams, who was successfully managing the farm and business affairs of her husband, John Adams. In a letter she urged that he and other members of the Continental Congress "remember the ladies and be more generous to them than your ancestors. Do not put such unlimited power in the hands of husbands. Remember all men would be tyrants if they could. If particular care and attention is not paid to the ladies, we are determined to foment rebellion, and will not be bound by any laws in which we have no voice or representation." Her advice was not heeded, however.

Because of these restrictions on the freedom of many Americans, the ideals set forth in the Declaration of Independence were only partially realized in the 1780's. Nevertheless, the men and women who fought the Revolutionary War had taken a long step toward the democratic way of life, and in 1783 they were about to take other steps. This is what Dr. Benjamin Rush had in mind when he wrote, "The American war is over, but this is far from being the case with the American Revolution."

abolition societies existed in all the states from Massachusetts southward to Virginia.

Moving toward democracy. During the Revolutionary War, then, Americans continued to strengthen the roots of democracy that had already been planted during the colonial period. For example, the gulf between the very rich and the ordinary narrowed somewhat due to the sale of confiscated Loyalist land. Much of this land was sold by the states to finance the military struggle, and a good deal of it sooner or later found its way into the hands of small landowners. However, the democratic way of life did not emerge full blown from the Revolutionary War. Economic differences still separated the well-to-do from the ordinary citizens. In spite of rising anti-slavery feeling, slavery still existed in much of the country. The right

SECTION SURVEY

IDENTIFY: written constitution, "government of laws, and not of men," abolition.

1. (a) Why was it necessary for the individual colonies to organize new governments during the Revolutionary War? (b) How did they go about doing it?

2. Why did the new state constitutions provide for (a) a bill of rights, (b) separation of powers, (c) separation of church and state?

3. (a) What effects did the American Revolution have on the position of slaves in American society? (b) on the position of women? (c) What evidence is there that the contradictions between the ideals of the Declaration and the actual conditions of blacks and women troubled some people?

4. Source Study: According to the Source on page 137, what happens when a state tries to force someone to follow a religion or support it financially?

138

2 The states unite under the Articles of Confederation

By the summer of 1776, when independence was declared, the thirteen former British colonies had become thirteen states. Each of these states was separate and independent.

The problem of unity. The delegates to the Continental Congress agreed that the thirteen states had to unite. But in what kind of union? What kind of government should they form?

Some delegates, Benjamin Franklin among them, wanted a strong central government, stronger than any of the state governments. Most delegates, however, objected to a strong central government. They pointed out that the states were fighting a war to win their independence. Why, then, should the states deliberately create an American government that might turn out to be as tyrannical as British rule had been?

A plan for Confederation. After long debate the Continental Congress agreed that some kind of unity was needed to fight the war. Congress then appointed a committee to propose a workable plan of union.

On July 12, 1776, the committee, headed by John Dickinson of Pennsylvania, presented a report to the Continental Congress bearing the title "Articles of Confederation and Perpetual Union." After debating these Articles for more than a year, the delegates finally, on November 15, 1777, voted to adopt the Articles of Confederation.

The Articles of Confederation created a confederation, or league, of free and independent states known as "The United States of America." The central government of the league was to consist of a Congress having from two to seven delegates from each state. Each state delegation was to have only one vote in the Congress.

This was only the first step in forming a union. Before the Articles of Confederation could become effective, each of the thirteen states had to **ratify**, or accept, the proposal.

Adoption of the Confederation. Not until 1781 did all the states agree to enter the Confederation. Maryland was the last.

During the discussion over the Confederation, the delegates from Maryland insisted that all the states with claims to land lying between the Appalachian Mountains and the Mississippi River (see map, page 142) had to surrender their claims to the Confederation.

The Maryland delegates felt that if all the states helped to free the western lands from the British, then all the states should share the fruits of victory. They also pointed out that when the war was over, the states owning this immense western territory would have an unfair advantage over their smaller neighbors.

Maryland's stand provoked heated debates. Finally, the states with claims to western lands agreed to surrender their claims, and in 1781 Maryland ratified the Articles of Confederation. Thus the new league of states came into existence.

Land—the first problem. Control of the land west of the Appalachian Mountains gave the Confederation its first real power and a heavy

SOURCES

ARTICLES OF CONFEDERATION (1781)

Article 1. The style of this confederacy shall be "The United States of America."

Article 2. Each state retains its sovereignty, freedom, and independence, and every power, jurisdiction, and right which is not by this confederation expressly delegated to the United States in Congress assembled.

Article 3. The said states hereby severally enter into a firm league of friendship with each other for their common defense, the security of their liberties, and their mutual and general welfare, binding themselves to assist each other against all force offered to or attacks made upon them or any of them on account of religion, sovereignty, trade, or any other pretense whatever. . . .

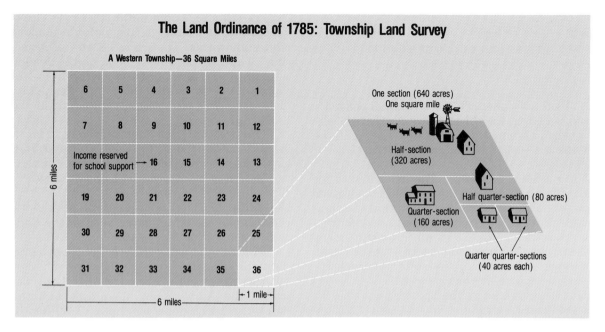

The Land Ordinance of 1785: Township Land Survey

A Western Township—36 Square Miles

6	5	4	3	2	1
7	8	9	10	11	12
Income reserved for school support → 16		15	14	13	
19	20	21	22	23	24
30	29	28	27	26	25
31	32	33	34	35	36

6 miles

6 miles ←1 mile→

One section (640 acres)
One square mile

Half-section (320 acres)

Half quarter-section (80 acres)

Quarter-section (160 acres)

Quarter quarter-sections (40 acres each)

Viewed from an airplane, many parts of the United States show a neat pattern of farms and roads. This orderliness goes back to the township system of land survey first adopted in 1785. The income secured from the sale of Section 16 was to be used for school support, although the school might be built elsewhere. Four other sections in the township were reserved for government use.

responsibility. Now, in 1781, the Confederation faced many of the same problems that Great Britain and other colonial powers had faced when they first established colonies in the New World.

Settlers were already moving into the lands between the Appalachians and the Mississippi River. Nothing was more certain than that the tide of settlers would increase.

What, if anything, would be done about Indian claims to the lands on which they had lived long before Europeans arrived in America? How were the new lands to be distributed among those who "colonized" America's frontier? Who would profit from the sale of the land—a few land speculators or the settlers? Who would make laws for the towns and cities and states that would appear—the Confederation or the settlers?

Nature of the land problem. Great Britain had never developed a satisfactory land policy for the American colonies. As a result, the methods that new settlers used to secure land varied from colony to colony.

In colonial New England, a fairly orderly system had been worked out. There men and

women wishing to move west secured from the colonial assembly a grant of land that was carefully surveyed, or measured.

In other colonies, especially in Virginia, people moved to the frontier, selected whatever land appealed to them, and settled on it. This method of settlement led to frequent boundary disputes among settlers and conflict with the Indians.

The Land Ordinance of 1785. The government of the Confederation decided to work out a system by which settlers could get **titles,** or guarantees of ownership, to land beyond the Appalachian Mountains.

The Confederation's system of land settlement was written down in the Land Ordinance of 1785. It remained in effect with some changes until 1862, when it was replaced by the Homestead Act.

The Land Ordinance of 1785 provided for government survey of squares of land 6 miles long and 6 miles wide (9.7 kilometers by 9.7 kilometers), to be known as **townships.** Each township was further surveyed and divided into 36 smaller squares of 640 acres (259 hectares), or 1 square mile (2.6 square kilometers),

140

to be known as **sections.** One section in every township, section number 16, was to be set aside for the support of public schools. Four other sections were reserved for the United States. The remaining 31 sections were to be sold by the government at a price of not less than one dollar an acre (.4 hectare). (See chart, page 140.)

This plan had several advantages. Since settlements would be close together, they would be easier to defend if Indian conflicts arose. Also, disputes over boundaries and titles would be largely eliminated. Now government surveyors would determine the exact location of every section before settlers arrived. Finally, the sale of lands would provide the Confederation with desperately needed funds to meet current expenses and to pay off part of the Revolutionary War debt.

Government of new lands. After adopting a plan for western settlement, the Confederation turned to another problem. How should the western lands be governed?

If the Americans had followed the British example, they would have regarded the whole western area as a colony. But Americans could hardly forget their recent war. They had fought, in part, against the mercantile theory of trade, which put Great Britain's interests above the interests of the colonies. With this in mind, the Continental Congress had already adopted, in 1780, a resolution promising that new western states could come into the Confederation equal in all respects to the older states.

This decision had been hastened by other developments. Before the Revolutionary War, daring pioneers such as Daniel Boone had crossed the mountain passes and settled in what are now Kentucky and Tennessee (see map, page 142). This westward movement had been checked by the British in the Proclamation of 1763 and the Quebec Act of 1774. Both of these measures closed the western lands to settlers. Once the Revolution began, however, more and more people crossed the mountains to enter the forbidden land. For these people the problem of government had to be solved as quickly as possible.

Land speculators also were eager for the Confederation to adopt a plan for governing the western lands. These speculators stood a better chance of selling the land if settlers knew that a program for orderly land development and self-government existed.

SOURCES _____

THE NORTHWEST ORDINANCE (1787)

Article 1. No person . . . shall ever be molested on account of his mode of worship or religious sentiments. . . .

Article 2. The inhabitants of the said territory shall always be entitled to the benefits of the writ of habeas corpus and of the trial by jury. . . .

Article 3. Religion, morality, and knowledge being necessary to good government and the happiness of mankind, schools and the means of education shall forever be encouraged. The utmost good faith shall always be observed toward the Indians; their lands and property shall never be taken from them without their consent; and, in their property, rights, and liberty, they shall never be invaded or disturbed, unless in just and lawful wars authorized by Congress; but laws founded in justice and humanity shall from time to time be made for preventing wrongs being done to them, and for preserving peace and friendship with them. . . .

Article 6. There shall be neither slavery nor involuntary servitude in the said territory, otherwise than in punishment of crimes. . . .

The Northwest Ordinance of 1787. In 1787 the Confederation partly fulfilled its earlier promise by passing the Northwest Ordinance. This ordinance provided for the governing of the Northwest Territory (see map, page 142).

In the beginning the Northwest Territory was to be ruled by a governor and three judges appointed by the Congress of the Confederation in Philadelphia. Later on, when the population included 5,000 free males of voting age, the settlers might elect a legislature to pass laws for themselves. They might also appoint a delegate to speak for them, but not to vote, in the Congress at Philadelphia. Still later, when the population of any part of the Northwest Territory reached 60,000 free inhabitants, the people could draft a constitution. Once this constitution had been approved by Congress, that part of the Northwest Territory would become a state. It would be equal in every respect to the older states. Not less than three

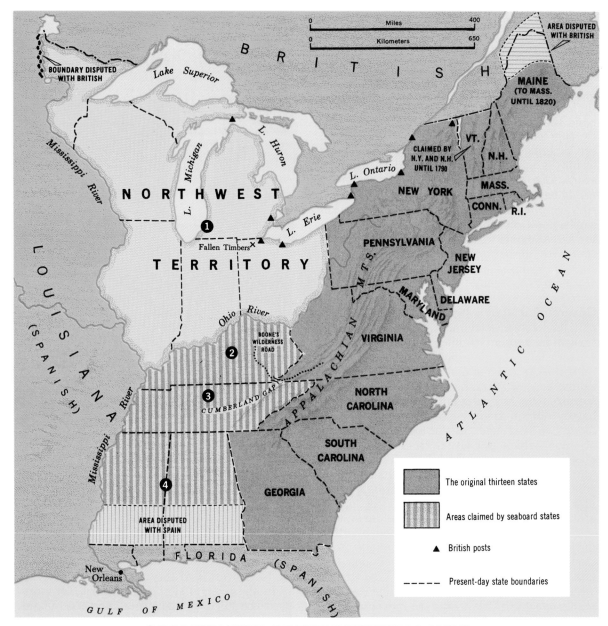

ORGANIZATION OF THE WESTERN LANDS

Notice the regions numbered 1 to 4 on the map above. As people moved into the unsettled lands in these numbered regions west of the Appalachian Mountains, new states were created and admitted to the Union. The following states were created out of the four regions north and south of the Ohio River:

❶ These states were carved out of the Northwest Territory: Ohio (1803), Indiana (1816), Illinois (1818), Michigan (1837), Wisconsin (1848), and part of Minnesota (1858).

❷ Originally claimed by Virginia; admitted as state of Kentucky in 1792.

❸ North Carolina and South Carolina claims ceded to federal government in 1792; admitted as state of Tennessee in 1796.

❹ Georgia claims relinquished by 1802; became part of Mississippi Territory; admitted as states of Mississippi (1817) and Alabama (1819).

142

Daniel Boone (center), one of the best known pioneers, blazed trails west across the Appalachians. He is shown here leading settlers through Cumberland Gap into Kentucky, which is a Cherokee word for "dark and bloody ground."

nor more than five states were to be carved out of the Northwest Territory.

Democratic achievements. Two other provisions in the Northwest Ordinance of 1787 encouraged the growth of democracy. One barred slavery from the Northwest Territory. A second encouraged public education.

The Confederation Congress believed that public education was necessary for the successful working of representative government. As a result, the Northwest Ordinance declared that "religion, morality, and knowledge being necessary to good government and the happiness of mankind, schools and the means of education shall forever be encouraged." This provision stimulated public support of schools and colleges in the territory.

The ordinance also promised that the Indians living in the territory would be treated with the "utmost good faith." This policy toward Indians was rarely followed.

Still, the overall policy developed in the ordinance was the most democratic colonial policy the modern world had known. It provided the machinery by which newer, less settled areas could eventually become equal members with parent communities. Under this general plan, almost all the new lands acquired by the United States in its march to the Pacific shores and beyond were admitted to the Union—first as territories, later as states.

The inhabitants of the western territories sometimes had complaints against the na-

tional government. With one or two exceptions, however, no territory ever seriously considered leaving the Union, for the people knew that, sooner or later, they would be admitted as equal members. They also knew that as their population grew, their influence on government policy would become greater.

SECTION SURVEY

IDENTIFY: Confederation, ratify, Land Ordinance of 1785, townships, sections, Northwest Ordinance of 1787.

1. (a) What issue delayed ratification of the Articles of Confederation? (b) How was this issue successfully resolved?

2. How did the Land Ordinance of 1785 deal with the following problems: (a) property rights in the western lands, (b) security in the western lands, (c) American war debts?

3. (a) How did the Northwest Ordinance of 1787 provide for the admission of new states to the Confederation? (b) Explain two ways that the ordinance promoted democracy in the Northwest Territory.

4. Source Study: According to the Source on page 139, for what purpose did the states enter into a confederation?

5. Map Study: Look at the map on page 142. (a) What geographic feature that the original thirteen states share is missing from the Northwest Territory? (b) How might this difference have affected the rate of settlement of the Northwest Territory?

143

3 The Confederation lacks the power to solve important problems

The government created by the Articles of Confederation was able to solve some of the important problems facing the new nation. Other serious problems remained that the leaders of the new government could not solve.

The problem of weakness. Many Americans insisted that the central government was too weak. On paper the Confederation appeared to have certain powers. It could regulate weights and measures. It could create post offices. It could borrow money and coin money. It could direct foreign affairs and declare war and make peace. It could build and equip a navy. It could ask the states to provide recruits and money for an army.

These powers looked sufficient on paper, but each state, jealous of its own rights, care-fully guarded the use of these powers. The delegates who sat in Congress had no real authority. They were paid by the states and voted as their state legislatures directed them to vote. Each state delegation was entitled to only one vote in Congress. Rhode Island, smallest of the states, had as much influence in deciding national issues as the larger states of Virginia, New York, and Massachusetts.

No matter of importance could be settled without the consent of at least nine states. Any changes in the Articles themselves required the unanimous votes of the thirteen states. The Confederation also lacked an executive, such as a President, with power to enforce measures adopted by Congress. Finally, it had no central national court, like the Supreme Court, to protect the rights of citizens.

Lack of power to regulate finances. Money would have been a serious postwar problem even if the Articles of Confederation had created a stronger central government. As it was, the weakness of the Confederation made the money problem more difficult to solve.

In 1790 Detroit was still in British hands. The fort was vital to the British fur trade, and not until 1796 did the Americans finally gain control of it.

To illustrate the problem, imagine a scene in a colonial store in 1783. A customer has just chosen some goods. As she counts out the money to pay the bill, she must sort through a pile of coins and paper money. There are French, Spanish, English, Dutch, German, and Portuguese coins. There are pennies coined in Vermont, Massachusetts, Connecticut, New Jersey, and Pennsylvania. There is paper money issued by the Continental Congress during the opening years of the Revolutionary War. There is also paper money issued by several of the states.

Some of the coins have been "clipped." That is, someone has stolen part of their value by scraping gold or silver from their edges. Some of the money may be counterfeit. The paper money is almost worthless—"not worth a Continental," many people grumble. Both the storekeeper and the customer would willingly exchange $1,000 worth of paper money issued by the Continental Congress for $1 worth of silver.

Obviously, only a government with power to regulate finances in all thirteen states could bring order out of such chaos. Nevertheless, the states, each fearful of losing some of its newly won authority, had not given this power to the Confederation. The Confederation could coin its own money, but it had no way of obtaining gold and silver to be coined. The Confederation had no power to force the states to contribute money for the support of the general government. Less than one fourth of the money requested by Congress was ever raised.

No wonder the Confederation could not pay even the interest on the war debts. No wonder Europeans made bets as to how long the United States could survive.

Lack of power over trade. Europeans had other reasons for regarding the new nation with scorn. The colonists had rebelled against Great Britain partly because they wanted to regulate their own trade. Now, with independence won, each state proceeded to make trade regulations to benefit its own citizens. The resulting confusion led many Americans to think that perhaps the British had been right in insisting that only a central authority could best regulate trade.

Trade with foreign countries as well as trade between the states suffered from the Confederation's lack of power to impose any regulations. The trade advantages that colonial

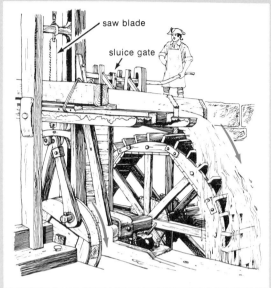

WATER-POWERED SAW

The sawyer started the saw by opening the sluice gate. This allowed back-up water to fall into the buckets of the water wheel and turn it. A shaft from the wheel turned another wheel, which propelled a rod connected to the saw in an up-and-down motion.

merchants had formerly enjoyed with the British West Indies and Great Britain were now denied to them. The British, regarding the Americans as a foreign people, no longer gave them bounties and favored treatment in British ports.

Manufacturers and the workers in manufacturing industries also suffered from the lack of controls over trade. During the Revolutionary War, when the British naval blockade made it difficult for Americans to import goods, Americans developed their own industries. As soon as the war ended, though, British merchants flooded American markets with cheaper British manufactured goods.

American manufacturers began to talk about a central government with power to levy import duties on manufactured goods from Great Britain and other countries. Such duties, added to the costs of imported goods, would

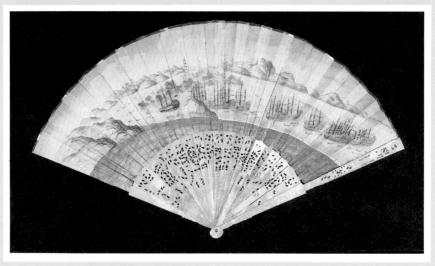

THIRTY TONS OF IMMORTALITY

On February 22, 1784—George Washington's fifty-second birthday—a ship called the *Empress of China* sailed out of New York harbor. It carried forty-four crew members, two merchants, and thirty tons of ginseng. This medicinal herb, which grew wild in America, was thought by the Chinese to have almost miraculous healing powers. Americans knew that Chinese merchants would pay well for what they termed the "dose of immortality." Thus it was the main cargo on this first American voyage ever made to China.

American merchants needed new trade outlets at this time, since they could no longer exchange goods with British colonies or carry on the profitable triangular trade. Chinese tea was much in demand in the United States, as were silks and porcelain. So a group of investors decided to take a chance and sponsor a voyage "to encourage others."

The *Empress of China* docked at Canton, China, in August. "All Chinamen very much love your country," declared a local Chinese merchant. This may have been true, but they regarded Americans, like other Westerners, as barbarians and restricted them to a tiny area of the city. After four months of gawking at strange oriental ships, harbor houseboats, and the Chinese who came to gawk at *them,* the Americans were happy to set sail back to the United States. They had sold all their cargo and had loaded over 200 tons of tea, several crates of porcelain, and bolts of gorgeous silk into the hold of the *Empress.*

When the *Empress* arrived back in New York in May 1785, it was greeted by a thirteen-gun salute and its investors, who made a handsome profit of 25 percent. Thus began a new era for the commerce of the young United States.

make the prices of foreign goods and of American goods more nearly equal.

Lack of power to enforce treaties. To add to the confusion, the Confederation did not have the power to enforce its own treaties. When John Adams tried to negotiate a commercial treaty with Great Britain in 1785, the British only smiled. Of what value was a treaty, they politely asked Adams, when any one of the thirteen states could ignore it? No, the British said, under the American system of government, not one but thirteen treaties would be needed.

The British were right, of course. American leaders like John Jay admitted that the peace treaty of 1783 was constantly being "violated . . . by one or other of the states." Britishers found it impossible to collect the debts owed them by Americans. Tories found it impossible to secure compensation for the property seized from them during the Revolution.

Britishers grew increasingly angry at the failure of the Americans to pay the Tories. Using this failure as an excuse, the British refused to withdraw from the forts and trading posts in the Northwest Territory, as they had agreed to do in the Treaty of Paris in 1783.

Lack of military power. The refusal of the British to leave the western forts, which protected their fur trade, aroused the anger of the Americans living west of the Appalachians. The westerners wanted a display of military power, but the Confederation was unable to meet their demands.

Also as a result of its lack of military strength, the Confederation was powerless to solve the problems between the settlers and the Indians. The Indians continued to resist the advance of the settlers, who continued to cut down forests and farm the land on which the Indians depended for their livelihood.

To make matters worse, reckless Spanish and British officers in North America sometimes urged the Indians to attack western settlers. From their forts in the Northwest Territory, the British supplied the Indians with guns and ammunition. The Spaniards, who controlled Florida and Louisiana, including all of the land west of the Mississippi River, also supplied the Indians with weapons and encouraged their use against the settlers.

John Adams negotiated with the British to get them to give up their forts in the Northwest Territory. Meanwhile, other Americans tried to get the Spaniards to make concessions. Both efforts failed.

Americans also failed to get the Spaniards to give them the right to use the port of New Orleans (see map, page 142). This port was important to settlers living in the Ohio Valley and in the land east of the Mississippi River. These settlers had no roads over which they could carry their products across the mountains to the eastern markets and seaports. The only way they could sell their products was to float them down the Mississippi River to New Orleans. There they could load them on seagoing vessels and ship them to the Atlantic ports or to Europe. Unfortunately for the western settlers, the Spaniards who controlled New Orleans refused to guarantee Americans the right to use this seaport. The American government was not strong enough to force Spain to grant this right.

The threat of civil war. Following the Revolution, the country went into an economic **depression**—a sharp decline in business activity and jobs.

The farmers of Massachusetts were especially hard hit. Before the Revolutionary War, much of their cash income had come from the sale of their farm produce and forest products to the British West Indies. After the break with Great Britain, this market was closed to them. Thus they found it increasingly difficult to get money to pay their taxes and the interest on their mortgages. To make matters worse, merchants and owners of businesses, mostly from Boston, controlled the Massachusetts legislature. This group passed new laws that shifted the burden of taxation onto the farmers. Among these taxes was a heavy tax on land.

During the summer of 1786, farmers gathered in hastily assembled meetings to demand relief, but the Massachusetts legislature refused to act. Farm after farm was **foreclosed,** or seized for nonpayment of taxes or interest on the mortgage. Finally, some Massachusetts farmers banded together and took matters into their own hands.

Shays' Rebellion. Led by Daniel Shays, the Massachusetts farmers demanded that the state legislature end the foreclosure of farms and give farmers a larger representation in the legislature. A group under Shays also tried unsuccessfully to seize the arsenal at Springfield in an effort to secure guns.

Frightened by this defiance of the law, citizens of Boston raised funds to equip a militia to put down Shays' Rebellion. The troops hunted Shays and his men through the snowy woods. They killed many and drove some across the state boundary into what is now Vermont. Some of the rebels were caught and put on trial. A few were hanged. Shays himself was later pardoned. His rebellion was thoroughly crushed.

Nevertheless, many Americans were deeply alarmed by Shays' Rebellion. These people thought that the armed revolt would undermine law and order and might even destroy the new nation. George Washington said of the troubles, "Good God! who but a tory could have foreseen or a Briton predicted them!"

Signs of returning prosperity. Not all of the problems facing the country in the 1780's could be blamed on the weaknesses of the Articles of Confederation. Hard times would have followed the war even if the government had been stronger. After all, property had been destroyed, trade connections had been broken, and commerce and business had been seriously disturbed.

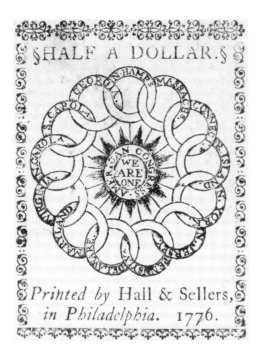
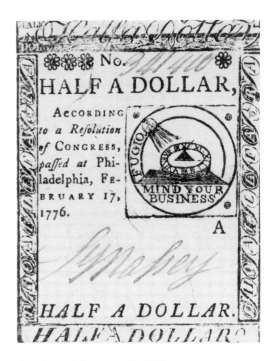

Bills like these "Continentals," issued by the Continental Congress in 1776, were still in circulation at the time the Articles of Confederation were in effect.

Even as early as 1785, only two years after the war ended, there were signs of better times ahead. By then American ships were once again busily trading with countries outside the British empire. Sailors, shipowners, merchants, farmers, and manufacturers were sharing in the profits of this growing trade. Many of the trade barriers between states were not enforced. As a result, American products continued to cross state lines in considerable quantities.

By 1785 some Americans were satisfied with the system of government under the Articles of Confederation. They were pleased with the signs of returning prosperity. They were satisfied with the wise policy that the Confederation was developing for the western lands.

A need for change. Despite these improvements, the central government still was too weak to solve many of the problems facing the new country. It was not strong enough to establish a sound financial system, to regulate trade, to enforce treaties, or to use military force when force was needed.

These government weaknesses disturbed groups of Americans—merchants and manufacturers, workers in the cities, and western-ers, who needed a strong central government to protect them from the Indians, the Spaniards, and the British.

A meeting to discuss the Articles of Confederation had been planned for Philadelphia in the spring of 1787. News of Shays' Rebellion spread rapidly and helped convince delegates to the meeting that major changes were needed in the Articles.

SECTION SURVEY

IDENTIFY: "not worth a Continental," import duties, depression, foreclose.

1. (a) What powers did the Articles of Confederation give to the central government? (b) What were three major weaknesses of the central government under the Articles of Confederation?

2. What would have been your chief problems in the 1780's if you had been (a) a merchant or (b) a farmer?

3. (a) What were the causes of Shays' Rebellion? (b) Why did this rebellion alarm many Americans?

4. Map Study: On the map on page 142, locate the posts that the British continued to occupy in the 1780's. How did these British posts affect American security?

Chapter Survey

Summary: Tracing the Main Ideas

Early in 1775, more than a year before the colonists declared their independence, the old colonial governments began to crumble. British officials left the colonies. Tories, loyal to the British king and Parliament, fled to Canada, the British West Indies, and Great Britain. By 1776 the Americans faced the problem of creating new state governments and a new central government.

The state constitutions that Americans wrote during the Revolutionary War reflected the people's deep-seated desire for a voice in their own government. All of the new governments were based upon written constitutions. All of the new constitutions contained bills of rights guaranteeing freedom to every citizen.

During the Revolutionary War, Americans also tackled the problem of building a central government. In their first effort to govern themselves at the national level, the leaders of the thirteen free states wrote the Articles of Confederation. However, this experiment with a league of more or less independent states was only partly successful.

There were two basic problems. First, there was the problem of dividing powers between the states and the central government. The Confederation had given no answer to this problem. Second, the Confederation could not establish laws binding upon all the states and the people of the states.

Even before 1787 a number of leaders in America had become convinced that only a stronger central government could secure order in the new nation. Once this conclusion had been reached, many of America's leaders then took steps to change the existing form of government. As you will see in Chapter 8, these steps led to the drafting of the Constitution of the United States of America.

Inquiring into History

1. (a) During the Revolutionary War, in what ways did democracy increase in America? (b) Why do you think America became more democratic during this period? (c) What undemocratic practices still existed?
2. Benjamin Rush, a signer of the Declaration of Independence from Pennsylvania, once said, "The American war is over, but this is far from being the case with the American Revolution." Explain what he meant.
3. What attitude was generally held by each of the following groups toward the Articles of Confederation: (a) merchants, (b) artisans, (c) farmers?
4. Do you think the government under the Articles of Confederation was a success or a failure? Use historical evidence to support your opinion.
5. Explain how the Northwest Ordinance of 1787 produced lasting benefits to the United States.

Relating Past to Present

1. Do the arguments presented in 1785 against a strong central government apply today? Why or why not?
2. Starting with the Articles of Confederation, American government has been faced with the problems of finding (a) a balance between the power of the states and the power of the central government and (b) a balance between liberty and authority. Explain.

Developing Social Science Skills

1. Suppose you lived in Connecticut in 1786 and decided to move with your family to the region west of North Carolina near the Mississippi River. Using the map on page 142, (a) describe two routes that you might follow to reach your new home, (b) calculate about how many miles (or kilometers) you would travel on each route, and (c) explain why you would probably favor friendly relations between the United States and Spain.
2. In 1790, 66.3 percent of the American population was English or Welsh. Black slaves made up 17.5 percent of the population, while free blacks made up 1.8 percent. At the same time, 5.6 percent of Americans were Scottish, 4.5 percent were German, 2.0 percent were Dutch (from the Netherlands), and 1.6 percent were Irish. Make a chart or graph presenting this information on national origins. Then answer this question: Why do you think English is the official language in the United States today?

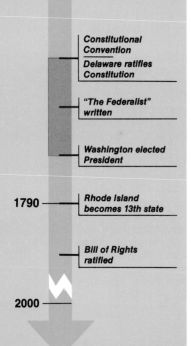

1775

1780

1785

Constitutional
Convention

Delaware ratifies
Constitution

"The Federalist"
written

Washington elected
President

1790 — Rhode Island
becomes 13th state

Bill of Rights
ratified

2000

Chapter **8**

Creating a Federal Union

1787–1789

In the spring of 1787, a number of the most distinguished men in America traveled toward Philadelphia. They came from all the states except Rhode Island, some on sailing vessels, some in carriages, some on horseback with their extra clothing packed in saddlebags. These men were official delegates from the states to a meeting called the Constitutional Convention.

The Congress of the Confederation decided to hold this convention because of a meeting at Annapolis, Maryland, in 1786. The Annapolis meeting had been called to discuss a uniform system of trade regulations for all of the states.

Only five states, however, were represented at Annapolis. The delegates decided that they could accomplish nothing with such a slim representation. Instead, they petitioned Congress to call another meeting of all the states. This meeting would not only discuss commercial problems but also study the weaknesses of the Confederation. Congress was slow to act on this proposal. Finally, it called the meeting for "the sole and express purpose of revising the Articles of Confederation."

The delegates to the Convention soon decided to do more than merely strengthen the Articles of Confederation. They decided to write a wholly new Constitution. Between May and September of 1787, they drafted a Constitution that remains the foundation of government in the United States. It has also become a model for representative government throughout the world.

THE CHAPTER IN OUTLINE

1. A spirit of compromise prevails at the Constitutional Convention.
2. The states ratify the Constitution only after heated debate.
3. The Constitution establishes a workable form of government.
4. The Constitution separates and balances the powers of government.
5. The Constitution seeks to safeguard individual liberty.
6. The Constitution is a flexible, living document.

A spirit of compromise prevails at the Constitutional Convention

On the morning of May 14, 1787, the date set for the start of the Constitutional Convention, Philadelphia's State House (later known as Independence Hall) was open and waiting for the delegates. Only the delegations from Pennsylvania and Virginia appeared. By May 25, however, delegates from seven states—a majority—were present, and the most famous convention in American history began.

The delegates. The 55 delegates to the Constitutional Convention were a remarkable cross section of American leadership. Most of them had played active parts in their state governments. Many were learned in history and political philosophy. More than half had been members of the Second Continental Congress or the Congress of the Confederation. Eight had signed the Declaration of Independence. Nearly all had taken part in the American Revolution. Several had been diplomatic representatives from the United States to the governments of Europe. These men understood the problems their country faced.

Benjamin Franklin, now 81 years old, was the oldest member of the Convention. Deeply respected by the other delegates, Franklin often helped to calm rising tempers. Most of the delegates, however, were relatively young. George Washington, unanimously chosen presiding officer, was one of the older members at 55. James Madison of Virginia was 36, James Wilson of Pennsylvania was 45, and Alexander Hamilton of New York was only 32.

Several important leaders who had helped win the struggle for independence were not present at the Convention. Patrick Henry of Virginia refused to attend, saying that he "smelled a rat." He feared that the Convention would take away too much of the power that he believed should belong to the states. Samuel Adams of Massachusetts had not been chosen as a delegate. Thomas Jefferson, John Adams, and Thomas Paine were in Europe.

Meeting in secrecy. The Convention was held in secret. Guards stood watch at every

James Madison of Virginia (left) had already helped to draft that state's constitution. Benjamin Franklin (right) had helped draw up both the Declaration of Independence and the treaty that ended the war.

Edmund Randolph of Virginia (left) refused to sign the Constitution, although he later supported its adoption. Alexander Hamilton (right) was one of the most persuasive backers of a strong federal government.

door. Each delegate agreed not to discuss Convention business with outsiders.

Why all this secrecy? The delegates feared that news of what they were doing would plunge the country into argument. They also knew that it would be easier to iron out differences in a private conference room than in a public debate. They felt that they must first agree among themselves before presenting proposals to the public.

Official notes of the proceedings were kept, but they were not released until 1818. James Madison kept an unofficial record. He jotted down notes during the meetings and then labored far into the night writing them out with a quill pen. Madison's notes, which were far more complete than the official record, were kept secret until after his death in 1836.

Areas of agreement. The delegates to the Constitutional Convention represented different sections of the country with different interests. Yet from the beginning, they agreed on a number of important matters.

Most of the delegates agreed that the country needed a strong central government. They recognized that the new government would be respected only if it had the power to tax, to raise an army, and to regulate commerce. They had learned this from their experience with the Articles of Confederation.

However, none of the delegates favored a government with unlimited power. They agreed that they must build a **republican** form of government. In such a government, the supreme power would rest in the voters, who would elect representative officials to run the government for them. The delegates also agreed that they wanted a government in which no single section of the country or group of people could dominate the rest.

There were many other issues on which the delegates did not agree. Sectional issues and economic problems divided them. If the delegates had refused to compromise, the writing of the Constitution would have been impossible. Fortunately for later generations, most of the delegates at Philadelphia arrived at compromises time and again.

The Great Compromise. One of the most serious conflicts of the Convention was a struggle between the large and small states over representation in Congress. Governor Edmund Randolph of Virginia, a large state, presented one plan. It provided that the population of each state would determine the number of representatives that it could send to Congress. William Paterson of New Jersey, speaking for the small states, proposed that each state would have equal representation in Congress. Paterson firmly opposed Randolph's Virginia Plan. "New Jersey will never confederate on the plan before the committee," he declared. "She would be swallowed up."

Speaking for the larger states, James Wilson of Pennsylvania threw back a challenging question: "Are not the citizens of Pennsylvania equal to those of New Jersey? Does it require 150 of the former to balance 50 of the latter? No," Wilson warned, "if the small states will not confederate on this plan, Pennsylvania . . . would not confederate on any other."

After a month of debate, the delegates finally adopted what is known as the Great Compromise. It was first proposed by Roger Sherman of Connecticut. By a narrow margin, the Convention voted for a Congress of two houses—a Senate and a House of Representatives. Each state, large or small, would be represented by two Senators, thereby giving each state equal power in the Senate. In the House, however, representatives would be based upon population.

The three-fifths compromise. Equally complicated differences arose between delegates from the northern and the southern states. These differences arose from a conflict between the economic interests of northern merchants and southern planters.

One dispute arose over the counting of slaves. Southerners wanted slaves to be counted when figuring the number of representatives to be elected to the House of Representatives. However, they did not want slaves to be counted when determining the amount of taxes to be paid. Northerners, on the other hand, thought that slaves should be counted when figuring taxes, but not when figuring representatives.

As a compromise northerners and southerners agreed to count three fifths of the slaves for purposes of establishing both represen-

Pennsylvania's State House was not only where the Constitution was written, but also where the Declaration of Independence was signed. From here, too, the famed Liberty Bell rang out to announce that signing.

AN INVENTOR AHEAD OF HIS TIME

For the people of Philadelphia, the summer of 1787 was remarkable for two reasons. One was the Constitutional Convention, which met there from May to September. The other was the presence on the Delaware River of a strange-looking boat built by a cantankerous inventor named John Fitch. From June until late fall, Fitch's vessel—one of America's first steamboats—made trial runs up and down the river.

Curious onlookers watched the trials, and some even ventured out for short trips. The painter Rembrandt Peale wrote that when he first heard about the boat, he "eagerly ran to the spot." After the furnace was fired up to heat the boiler, "the boat to my great delight moved against the tide, without wind or hand." Among the many convention delegates who took a ride on the strange invention was William Samuel Johnson. He wrote Fitch thanking him and noting that "the exhibition yesterday gave the gentlemen present much satisfaction."

Encouraged by his success, Fitch soon constructed a bigger boat to carry passengers regularly up and down the Delaware. One happy rider praised Fitch as an "ingenious creature" and predicted that he would "certainly make his fortune." Unfortunately this prophecy failed to come true. Fitch could never gain adequate financial backing. In 1798, poor and embittered, he took his own life.

Fitch was just a little ahead of his time. Less than ten years after his death, another inventor, Robert Fulton, demonstrated his steamboat the *Clermont* on the Hudson River. Fulton had better luck commercially, and travel by steamboat soon changed American transportation history.

tatives and taxes. For example, if a state's population included 100,000 free persons and 100,000 slaves, the state would be assigned a population figure of 160,000 for determining the amount of taxes to be paid and the number of representatives to be elected.

The commerce compromises. Other clashes between the economic interests of the South and the North arose over the control of commerce and the regulation of the slave trade.

Northern merchants wanted the central government to regulate commerce with foreign nations as well as among the states. Southern planters opposed this proposal. They feared that the government might pass laws unfavorable to southern interests. For example, southern planters earned much of their income by exporting tobacco to Europe and the northern states. In turn, they imported either from

Europe or the northern states many finished goods, such as household furnishings and farm equipment. If Congress imposed **tariffs,** or duties, on exports, overseas buyers would have to pay a higher price for southern tobacco. The planters feared that this rise in price would make them lose customers. Tariffs on imported goods, on the other hand, would raise the prices of products purchased by the planters. Under the circumstances, the southern delegates were opposed to all tariffs. They therefore opposed giving Congress unlimited power to regulate trade.

The delegates finally reached a compromise acceptable to both the North and the South. This compromise gave Congress the power "to regulate commerce with foreign nations, and among the several states," including the power to levy tariffs on imports. However, Congress was denied the power to levy tariffs on exports of any kind.

The southern planters were troubled by still another problem. Since Congress now had the power to regulate commerce and to tax imports, would it not be possible for Congress to outlaw the slave trade or to levy taxes on slaves imported into the country?

After a vigorous discussion, the Convention agreed that until 1808 the states could continue to import slaves. But after 1808 Congress would have the right to decide whether to regulate or prohibit the further importation of slaves.

The slave trade compromise was probably necessary for the Constitution to gain needed support in the South, but it was a setback for the antislavery forces. At the time the Constitution was written, many Americans believed that slavery was gradually dying out in the United States. They felt it would no longer be a problem in 1808. That was a fateful mistake. More than half a century would pass before a tragic war would bring an end to slavery in the United States.

Completing the Constitution. Finally, as the summer months of 1787 passed and as agreements were reached, the Constitution was completed. Time and again the Convention seemed near failure. Time and again angry members threatened to leave unless they got what they wanted. In the end, wise judgment prevailed. The delegates always found a way to compromise the differences that threatened to divide the country.

SECTION SURVEY

IDENTIFY: James Madison, Edmund Randolph, William Paterson, Great Compromise, Roger Sherman, three-fifths compromise, tariffs.

1. How do you think the presence of Benjamin Franklin and George Washington helped the proceedings of the Constitutional Convention?

2. Why do you think the delegates to the Constitutional Convention felt that it was important to meet in secret?

3. On what ideas for a central government did the delegates agree at the beginning of the Constitutional Convention?

4. The delegates reached compromises to settle their differences on four important issues. (a) Describe each of the issues. (b) Present the different points of view on each issue. (c) What compromises did the delegates finally arrive at?

5. (a) What assumption did many antislavery Americans make when they agreed to the provisions on the slave trade that were written into the Constitution? (b) Why was this assumption incorrect?

The states ratify the Constitution only after heated debate

On September 17, 1787, after 39 delegates had signed the document prepared over the long, hot summer, the members of the Constitutional Convention met for a farewell dinner. The next day they began to leave Philadelphia. Each delegation was in a hurry to return to its state, for the decisive struggle was yet to be waged. The decision to ratify, or approve, the Constitution would be made in special conventions to be held in each of the states. The Constitution would not become "the supreme law of the land" until conventions in nine of the thirteen states had ratified it.

Differing opinions. Most of the delegates who left Philadelphia in September were prepared to lead the struggle for ratification. A few who had refused to sign the Constitution hurried home to lead the fight against it.

In general, the American people divided into two groups in their thinking about the

Pulled by ten horses, this "federal ship," complete with full sail and thirty-two guns, honored Alexander Hamilton. It led a parade of tradespeople who celebrated New York's ratification of the Constitution.

Constitution. One group, the Federalists, wanted a strong **federal government.°** The other group, the Anti-Federalists, just as strongly opposed strengthening the powers of the central government. The Anti-Federalists preferred to protect the rights and the powers of the individual states.

Objections to the Constitution. Concern over surrendering too much power to the federal government was only one of the issues troubling those who opposed the Constitution. Many opponents believed that the new Constitution did not give the voters enough control over the officials who would run the new federal government. The Constitution permitted the states to retain the right to decide who could vote and who could not vote. As you know, most states had property restrictions on voting, and several states still had religious restrictions. These restrictions prevented many men from voting. Neither the Constitution nor the states granted suffrage to women. Slaves, most free blacks, and even Indians living in settled areas surrounded by white settlements

°**federal government:** This term is used in the United States to refer to the national government as opposed to the separate governments of the individual states.

were not included in discussions regarding the right to vote. In brief, the **franchise,** or the right to vote, was limited to a minority of the population.

To be sure, the Constitution did create a republican, or representative, form of government. However, the Constitution sharply limited the influence of even that select group of male citizens who were allowed to vote. The President and the Vice-President were to be chosen by **electors.** The electors were to be selected not by the voters but "in such manner" as each state legislature should direct. Senators were to be chosen not by the voters but by the state legislatures. Only the members of the House of Representatives were to be elected directly by the voters.

Another serious objection to the Constitution was the lack of a bill of rights. Without a bill of rights, many Americans feared that the new federal government could take away their hard-won rights.

Struggles for ratification. In December 1787 Delaware became the first state to ratify the Constitution. Before the year's end, New Jersey and Pennsylvania followed Delaware's example. Georgia and Connecticut ratified early in 1788.

In February 1788 Massachusetts, one of the larger, crucial states, ratified the Constitution by the margin of 19 votes. Next came Maryland, South Carolina, and finally New Hampshire. Now the count stood at nine states, the number needed.

Meantime, however, Americans directed their attention to the ratification struggles going on in Virginia and New York. The new government could hardly hope to succeed without these large and important states.

The battles in Virginia and New York were fought with much feeling on both sides. The final victory in favor of the Constitution was very close. A change of only eleven votes in Virginia and of three votes in New York would have defeated ratification in these states. The victory in Virginia was largely due to the enormous influence of George Washington. The victory in New York was to some extent a personal triumph for Alexander Hamilton, James Madison, and John Jay. These three men defended the Constitution in a series of brilliant essays that were printed in the newspapers and widely read. Later the essays were published as a famous volume, *The Federalist.*

Time for celebration. When Virginia and New York ratified the Constitution, eleven states made up the Union. The new government could be started with some degree of confidence. Now only two states remained outside the Union. North Carolina did not enter until November 1789, and Rhode Island delayed ratifying the Constitution until the spring of 1790.

The fight over ratification had been a bitter one, and the margin of victory was close. Nevertheless, it was a victory, and during the summer and fall of 1788 the country celebrated it. The old government was ended. The new government was ready to start.

The first election. When all the states except North Carolina and Rhode Island had accepted the Constitution, elections were held. George Washington was unanimously elected President, and John Adams Vice-President. Elections for the new Congress of the United States did not arouse much enthusiasm. In general, those elected to Congress had favored the Constitution either in the Convention or during the struggle for ratification, or both.

Traveling over the bad roads, the new Senators and Representatives slowly gathered in New York, the temporary capital of the nation. They awaited the coming of President-elect Washington and the inauguration of the new government.

SECTION SURVEY

IDENTIFY: federal government, Federalists, anti-Federalists, franchise, electors.

1. How was the Constitution to be ratified?
2. What were the differing opinions of the Constitution held by the American people?
3. What roles did Washington, Hamilton, Jay, and Madison play in the Constitution's ratification?
4. Why do you think that Washington was unanimously elected the first President of the United States?

3 The Constitution establishes a workable form of government

The form of government created under the Constitution is based upon four fundamental principles. One is the principle of **federalism,** or the division of powers between the national, or federal, government and the state governments.

Creating a federal union. Under the Articles of Confederation, the relations between the central government and the state governments had been a thorny problem. The Confederation left most power in the hands of thirteen free and equal states. The central government held no real authority over the states or over the people themselves. The delegates to the Constitutional Convention wanted to correct the weaknesses of this form of government.

Most delegates agreed that only a **federal union** would be strong enough to establish an orderly society. In a federal union, each state delegates some of its power to the national government. The framers of the Constitution corrected most of the weaknesses of the Articles of Confederation by creating such a union.

Individuals and the law. Having agreed to organize a federal union, the delegates faced

The delegates to the Constitutional Convention met here, in the East Room of the Pennsylvania State House during the hot summer of 1787. The raised table between the fireplaces is where the Convention's president, George Washington, sat throughout the four months of debate over the new Constitution.

another troublesome problem. How could the federal, or national, government enforce its laws? Suppose, for example, that a citizen of New Jersey refused to obey a federal law. Should the federal government ask New Jersey to punish the offender? Suppose New Jersey refused to comply. Would not the federal government need to have the power to maintain its authority?

The longer the delegates debated this matter, the more convinced they became of the answer. To avoid trouble between the states and the federal government, all laws passed by the federal government had to apply equally to every individual within the union. To insure obedience to these laws, the delegates decided that the federal government had to have the power to reach into the states themselves to punish violators.

Because of this decision, Americans have always lived under two governments and two systems of law—federal and state. They have two citizenships. That is, they are citizens both of the United States and of the state in which they live.

Delegated powers. The decision to give the federal government power to enforce its laws led to another difficult problem. What laws should the federal government be allowed to pass? In other words, what powers should the states delegate, or surrender, to the federal government?

After long debate the delegates decided to give certain specific powers to the Congress of the United States. All of these powers, known as **delegated powers,** are listed in the Constitution. They include the powers "to lay and collect taxes . . . to borrow money . . . to coin money . . . to regulate commerce with foreign nations, and among the several states . . . to raise and support armies . . . to provide and maintain a navy."

From this listing it is clear that the delegates gave the federal government authority only over matters of common concern to the people of all the states. It is also clear that in selecting these delegated powers, the framers of the Constitution tried to correct major weaknesses of the Articles of Confederation—lack of financial power, lack of power to regulate commerce, and lack of military power.

Reserved powers. In a federal union, the member states still retain freedom to act on matters not delegated to the federal government or expressly forbidden to the states. To guarantee the states' independence of action, the delegates listed several powers that could not be exercised by the federal authorities. For example, the federal government is forbidden to levy any "tax or duty . . . on articles exported from any state."

By implication all powers not specifically granted to the federal government, nor denied to the states, were kept by the states. But to avoid any misunderstanding, the Ninth and Tenth Amendments were adopted in 1791. The Tenth Amendment leaves no room for doubt: "The powers not delegated to the United States by the Constitution, nor prohibited by it to the states, are reserved to the states respectively, or to the people." Those powers retained by the states are known as **reserved powers.** They include control over transportation within the state, marriage, divorce, and public education.°

Shared powers. Every government must possess certain powers simply to exist and function effectively. All governments, for example, must have the power to raise money and to enforce law and order. Both the federal government and state governments use the same methods to raise money—taxation and borrowing. Both levels of government also have police forces to maintain order. In addition, both governments have court systems for trying people who violate laws.

Powers shared by the federal government and the states are called **concurrent powers.** They exist concurrently with, or at the same time as, powers delegated to the federal government on the one hand and powers reserved for the states on the other.

The supreme law of the land. The framers of the Constitution realized that conflicts might arise between federal and state laws. To settle such conflicts, they inserted this clear statement in the Constitution: "This Constitution, and the laws of the United States which shall be made in pursuance thereof, and all treaties made, or which shall be made, under the authority of the United States, shall be the supreme law of the land." By including this statement, they proclaimed that in cases of conflict the Constitution and the laws of the federal government should rank higher than state constitutions and state laws.

°In recent years the federal government has secured a great deal of control over public education by means of financial support, Supreme Court decisions, and the creation of a Department of Education.

SECTION SURVEY

IDENTIFY: federalism, federal union, delegated powers, reserved powers, concurrent powers.

1. In what ways does a federal union differ from a confederation?
2. What principles did the delegates to the Constitutional Convention follow in choosing delegated powers? Name four of these powers.
3. How was independence of action for the states protected in the Constitution by (a) the reserved powers and (b) the Tenth Amendment?
4. Name two concurrent powers of the federal and state governments.
5. How does the Constitution resolve conflicts between the federal and state governments?

4 The Constitution separates and balances the powers of government

The second fundamental principle of American government is the **separation of powers** within the federal government. This separation of powers includes a system of checks and balances on these powers.

Protection against tyranny. The framers of the Constitution firmly believed in government under law. They wanted to protect the country from tyranny in any form. They believed that a misguided majority might be as dangerous to good government under law as a privileged minority or a power-mad dictator.

When they wrote the Constitution, therefore, the framers tried to guard against what one of them called an "excess of democracy." At no time did they seriously consider including a guarantee of the right to vote in the Constitution. Instead, they left it to the states to decide who could vote and who could not.

The framers were equally careful to guard against seizure of the government by a military dictator. They had not forgotten the troubled years before the Revolutionary War. Even closer to them were recent attempts to establish a military dictatorship over the thirteen states. In 1782, for example, army officers had offered the title of king to General Washington. If Washington had wanted to be a dictator, the history of the United States might have been different.

159

Separation of powers. To help guard against tyranny in any form and to keep any one branch of the government from becoming too strong, the delegates agreed that the legislative, executive, and judicial powers of the government must be kept separate.

With this idea in mind, the delegates set up three separate branches of the government, each having certain powers. To Congress they gave the legislative, or law-making, power (Article 1). To the Chief Executive, or President, they granted the power to execute, or carry out, the laws (Article 2). To the judiciary—that is, the federal courts—they gave the power to interpret the laws (Article 3).

In addition to separating the powers of the federal government, the delegates wrote a system of **checks and balances** into the Constitution. Each branch was given certain powers that could restrain or balance the powers of the other branches if either of the other branches tried to abuse or exceed its powers.

Checks on the President. A President who is thought to be guilty of "treason, bribery, or other high crimes and misdemeanors" can be **impeached.** That is, the President can be accused by the House of Representatives of acting unlawfully or misusing power and then be tried by the Senate. If found guilty, the President can be removed from office. A President can make a treaty, but a two-thirds vote of the Senate is necessary to ratify it. A President can appoint important officers, but the Senate must confirm these appointments by a majority vote. Since Congress has control over taxes and spending, it can interfere with any Presidential policy that requires the spending of money. Finally, a two-thirds vote of Congress can overrule the President's **veto,** or rejection, of laws proposed by Congress.

Checks on Congress. The President, in turn, can check and balance the powers of Congress. Perhaps the President's most important check is the power to veto Congressional legislation. Congress needs a two-thirds majority to override a veto, and this is difficult to obtain. The President can also influence the thinking of Congress through annual State of the Union messages and special messages to Congress. The Chief Executive can also bring pressure on Congress by calling a special session and asking for the passage of specific laws.

The President also can exert influence by directing public attention to specific issues. As the office of the Chief Executive developed, press conferences and speeches directly to the people became more important. If a press conference or a public address results in a barrage of letters and telegrams to Congress, it may be more willing to accept the President's point of view.

Checks by and on the judiciary. The federal judiciary—the Supreme Court and the lower federal courts—interprets the laws. As you will read, the federal judiciary has the power to declare that a law passed by Congress and approved by the President is unconstitutional.

However, the powers of the Supreme Court and of other federal courts can be checked in several ways. Congress can impeach federal judges. Congress also determines by law the number of justices on the Supreme Court. At different times laws have set the number of justices at as few as five and as many as ten.

The President, in turn, appoints all federal judges, with the consent of the Senate. The President's desire for a certain interpretation of the Constitution may sometimes conflict either with Congress or the Supreme Court. If the President appoints justices to the Supreme Court who are friendly to the administration's viewpoint, and if the Senate approves these appointments, the President is checking or balancing the power of Congress, of the judiciary, or of both. A further check on the judiciary is the President's power to pardon or reprieve persons who have been convicted of crimes in the federal courts.

Pros and cons of checks and balances. The separation of powers with checks and balances in the federal government has sometimes been criticized for slowing down the workings of government. Important laws may be needed, but a President belonging to one party and a Congress dominated by another party may not be able to agree on a law. As a general rule, however, the system has worked well.

In time of war or other crisis, Congress usually declares a national emergency and grants all the special powers the President may need in order to act quickly. When the emergency is over, the special powers can be withdrawn.

The principle of the separation of powers with checks and balances was written into the Constitution as a safeguard for the future. It was meant to protect the liberties of the people.

1. Why did the framers of the Constitution fear "an excess of democracy"?

2. (a) What is the purpose of the separation of powers in government? (b) What are some disadvantages of this separation of powers?

3. What are the chief responsibilities of the three branches of the federal government?

4. List the principal checks on the power of (a) the President, (b) the Congress, and (c) the federal judiciary. (d) What is the purpose of these checks?

5 The Constitution seeks to safeguard individual liberty

A third fundamental principle of American government under the Constitution is protection of the liberties of individuals.

For a long time, American colonists had insisted upon protection of their rights as individuals against the powers of government—that is, protection of their **civil liberties.** The separation of powers with checks and balances is one way that the Constitution protects the rights of individuals. There are many other safeguards. Some appear in the Constitution itself. Others were written into the first ten amendments—the Bill of Rights. Still others have been added in later amendments.

Guarantees in the Constitution. The Constitution itself provides important guarantees of civil liberties. For example, it prohibits both *ex post facto* laws and **bills of attainder.**

An *ex post facto* law is a law passed "after the deed." Such a law sets a penalty for an act that was not illegal when it was committed.

A bill of attainder is a law that punishes a person by fine, imprisonment, or seizure of property without a court trial. If Congress had the power to adopt bills of attainder, the lawmakers could punish any American, and that person could do nothing to appeal the sentence. Instead, the Constitution provides that only the courts can impose punishment for unlawful

acts, and then only by following the duly established law. To prevent arbitrary convictions by judges, the Constitution also provides that "the trial of all crimes . . . shall be by jury."

The Constitution also protects the citizen's right to the **writ of *habeas corpus.*** The writ of *habeas corpus* is a legal document that forces a jailer to release a person from prison unless the person has been formally charged with, or convicted of, a crime. The Constitution states that "the privilege of the writ of *habeas corpus* shall not be suspended, unless when in cases of rebellion or invasion the public safety may require it."

The Constitution also gives special protection to people accused of **treason.** The framers of the Constitution knew that the charge of treason was an old device used by tyrants to get rid of persons they did not like. Such rulers might bring the charge of treason against persons who merely criticized the government, not just against those involved in an armed uprising against the government. To prevent such use of this charge, the Constitution carefully defines treason: "Treason against the United States shall consist only in levying war against them, or in adhering to their enemies, giving them aid and comfort. No person shall be convicted of treason unless on the testimony of two witnesses to the same overt act, or on confession in open court."

The Constitution also protects the innocent relatives of a person accused of treason. Only the convicted person can be punished. No penalty can be imposed upon that person's family.

These are only a few of the guarantees of personal rights that were written into the Constitution. They are important examples of the way that the Constitution establishes a common standard of law for every American citizen, old and young, rich and poor alike.

The Bill of Rights. Despite the safeguards written into the Constitution, some states at first refused to ratify it because it did not offer greater protection to the rights of individuals. They finally agreed to ratification after they had been promised that a bill of rights would be added to the Constitution by amendment when Congress met.

In 1789–90 the first Congress of the United States wrote the ideals of the Declaration of Independence into the Bill of Rights, the first ten amendments to the Constitution. The Bill of Rights protects individuals against any ac-

Here the Convention delegates assemble in Independence Hall. Benjamin Franklin said of the product of their labors, "It astonishes me . . . to find this system approaching so near perfection as it does. . . ."

tion by the federal government that may deprive them of life, liberty, or property without "due process of law."

Among the guarantees of liberty in the Bill of Rights, several are especially important. The First Amendment guarantees freedom of religion, speech, press, assembly, and petition. The Fourth Amendment forbids unreasonable searches and seizures of any person's home. The Fifth, Sixth, and Eighth Amendments protect individuals from arbitrary arrest and punishment by the federal government.

The Bill of Rights was ratified by the states in 1791. It has remained one of the best-known features of the Constitution. The American people have turned to it for support whenever their rights as individuals have seemed to be in danger. No document in American history, except, perhaps, the Declaration of Independence, has been cherished more deeply.

Interpreting individual rights. Although the Constitution, Bill of Rights, and later amendments guarantee certain rights equally to all Americans, individual rights are not absolute. The rights of an individual exist in relation to

the rights of others. In guaranteeing freedom of speech and of the press, for example, the Bill of Rights does not grant individuals the right to say or print anything they like at any time. For example, laws forbid individuals to say or print anything that may defame an innocent person's character. Freedom of speech and of the press as well as all the other rights guaranteed by the first ten amendments must be interpreted by the courts if they are to have any real meaning.

SECTION SURVEY

IDENTIFY: civil liberties, Bill of Rights, *ex post facto* law, bill of attainder, writ of *habeas corpus,* treason.

1. Why were the framers of the Constitution especially interested in protecting civil liberties?

2. How do the civil liberties guaranteed to Americans in the Constitution and the Bill of Rights help to prevent abuses of power?

3. (a) Which branch of the federal government makes decisions on the limits to an individual's rights? (b) Why is it that the rights of individuals are not unlimited?

162

6 The Constitution is a flexible, living document

The fourth fundamental principle of American government is the **adaptability** of the Constitution to changing times and changing circumstances.

The Constitution has successfully survived the years for two main reasons. First, it lays down rules of procedure that must be followed even in critical times. Second, it is a "living" document, flexible enough to meet the changing needs of a growing nation. Americans have been able to adapt the Constitution to changing ways and changing times. In general, the Constitution works as well today for an industrialized nation of fifty states and a population of over 226 million people as it once worked for an agricultural nation of thirteen states and 4 million people.

Provision for amendment. The framers of the Constitution were as wise in what they did *not* write as in what they did write. They wrote down only the fundamental laws for the nation. They left it to Congress to pass additional laws as they might be needed. Each time Congress meets, it passes such laws.

Even so, the framers knew that changes in the fundamental law might have to be made from time to time. Accordingly, they wrote Article 5, which carefully specifies the procedure by which the Constitution may be amended (see chart, page 185).

Because the amending process is slow and difficult, it is seldom used unless the need for change appears great. Some people think the process is too slow and difficult. Others think it wise that no changes can be made in the "supreme law of the land" until the pros and cons have been thoroughly debated. In any event, only 26 amendments have been adopted since 1789, including the first ten amendments—the Bill of Rights.

The elastic clause. The framers provided still greater flexibility to the Constitution by inserting what is known as the **elastic clause.** To the specific powers granted to Congress, this clause adds the power "to make all laws which shall be necessary and proper for carrying into execution the foregoing powers.

When the Convention had agreed on the basic content of the Constitution, a style committee wrote the document into its final form. Much of the actual wording of the Constitution was the work of Gouverneur Morris, a delegate from Pennsylvania. The opening passages of the original document are shown here.

We the People of the United States, in Order to form a more perfect Union, establish Justice, insure domestic Tranquility, provide for the common defence, promote the general Welfare, and secure the Blessings of Liberty to ourselves and our Posterity, do ordain and establish this Constitution for the United States of America.

Article. I.

Section. 1. All legislative Powers herein granted shall be vested in a Congress of the United States, which shall consist of a Senate and House of Representatives.

Section. 2. The House of Representatives shall be composed of Members chosen every second Year by the People of the several States, and the Electors in each State shall have the Qualifications requisite for Electors of the most numerous Branch of the State Legislature.

No Person shall be a Representative who shall not have attained to the Age of twenty five Years, and been seven Years a Citizen of the United States, and who shall not, when elected, be an Inhabitant of that State in which he shall be chosen.

Representatives and direct Taxes shall be apportioned among the several States which may be included within this Union, according to their respective Numbers, which shall be determined by adding to the whole Number of free Persons, including those bound to Service for a Term of Years, and excluding Indians not taxed, three fifths of all other Persons. The actual Enumeration shall be made within three Years after the first Meeting of the Congress of the United States, and within every subsequent Term of ten Years, in such Manner as they shall by Law direct. The Number of Representatives shall not exceed one for every thirty Thousand, but each State shall have at Least one Representative; and until such enumeration shall be made, the State of New Hampshire shall be entitled to chuse three, Massachusetts eight, Rhode Island and Providence Plantations one, Connecticut five, New York six, New Jersey four, Pennsylvania eight, Delaware one, Maryland six, Virginia ten, North Carolina five, South Carolina five, and Georgia three.

When vacancies happen in the Representation from any State, the Executive Authority thereof shall issue Writs of Election to fill such Vacancies.

The House of Representatives shall chuse their Speaker and other Officers; and shall have the sole Power of Impeachment.

Section. 3. The Senate of the United States shall be composed of two Senators from each State, chosen by the Legislature thereof for six Years; and each Senator shall have one Vote.

Immediately after they shall be assembled in Consequence of the first Election, they shall be divided as equally as may be into three Classes. The Seats of the Senators of the first Class shall be vacated at the Expiration of the second Year, of the second Class at the Expiration of the fourth Year, and of the third Class at the Expiration of the sixth Year, so that one third may be chosen every second Year; and if Vacancies happen by Resignation, or otherwise, during the Recess of the Legislature of any State, the Executive thereof may make temporary Appointments until the next Meeting of the Legislature, which shall then fill such Vacancies.

No Person shall be a Senator who shall not have attained to the Age of thirty Years, and been nine Years a Citizen of the United States, and who shall not, when elected, be an Inhabitant of that State for which he shall be chosen.

The Vice President of the United States shall be President of the Senate, but shall have no Vote, unless they be equally divided.

The Senate shall chuse their other Officers, and also a President pro tempore, in the Absence of the Vice President, or when he shall exercise the Office of President of the United States.

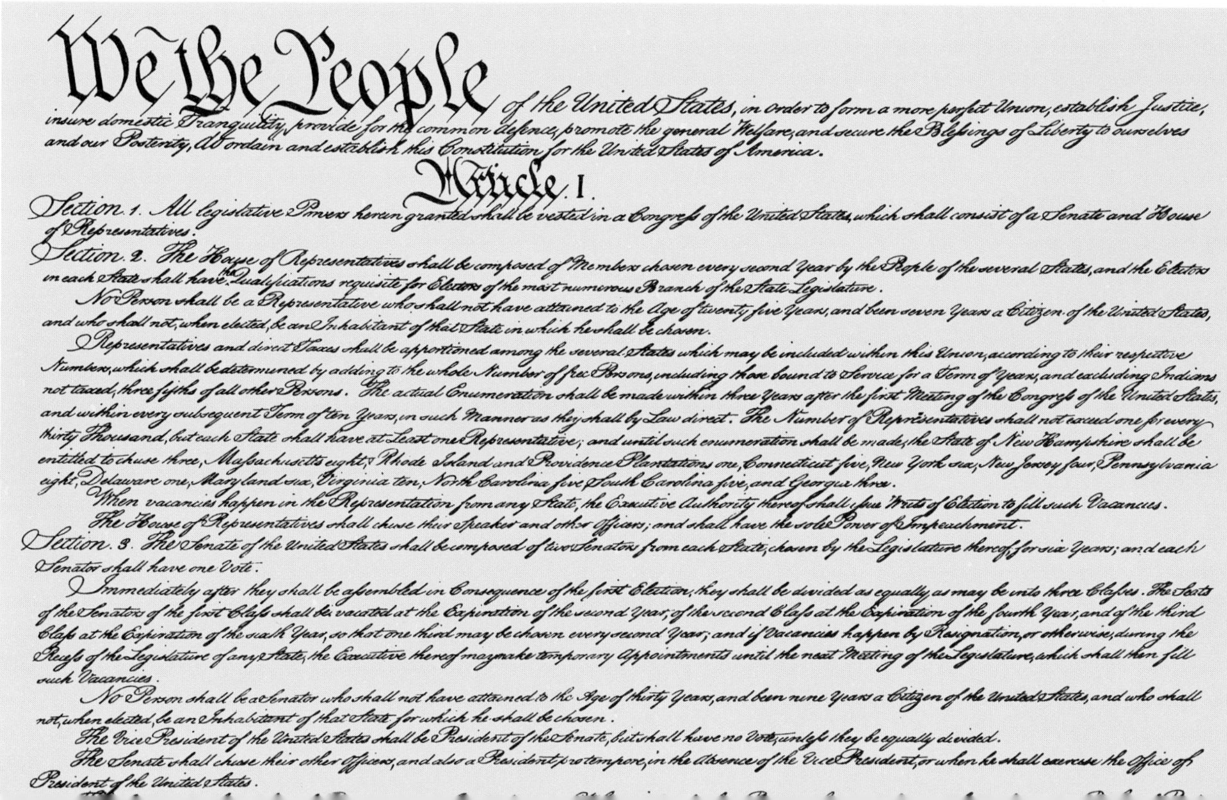

The elastic clause allows Congress to stretch its powers and to pass laws not specifically authorized in the Constitution. Congress, for example, has the delegated power to regulate commerce. It has stretched this power to improve rivers and harbors and to require the payment of minimum wages to workers employed by industries engaged in interstate commerce.

Whenever Congress has stretched its powers in this way, a question has arisen over whether such actions are "necessary and proper." The Constitution does not clearly state how this question should be answered. In 1803, however, Chief Justice John Marshall established the tradition that the power to answer such questions rests in the Supreme Court.

The Supreme Court as referee. The power of the Supreme Court to decide whether or not a law or a treaty violates the Constitution is known as the power of **judicial review**. This means that the Supreme Court has the power to review, or examine, an act of Congress and to determine whether or not the Constitution permits such an act. When the Supreme Court exercises this power, it acts as a referee.

When the Supreme Court acts, its word is final, but the Supreme Court can — and sometimes does — reverse an earlier decision. Also, the people of the United States can, by the process of amendment, alter the Constitution.

The "unwritten Constitution." The Constitution, then, has proved to be a flexible, enduring plan of government. Amendments have altered certain provisions of the Constitution and added others. Court decisions and acts of Congress, especially under the elastic clause, have given new meanings to certain provisions of the Constitution.

Other changes in American government have come about through custom. For example, the Constitution says nothing about political parties, which Washington and others distrusted as likely to cause quarrels. Neither does the Constitution provide for regular meetings of the heads of the executive departments concerned with defense, foreign affairs, finances, and other matters. Such meetings, nevertheless, take place and have become an important part of the executive system.

Custom has established other important practices in the operation of the federal government. For example, before a federal official is appointed to work in a state, the President usually seeks the advice of the Senators of that state, provided that they belong to the same political party. This custom is called **senatorial courtesy.** Custom and the pressure of work have also led Congress to use an elaborate system of committees in making laws.

Practices such as these, growing out of custom and tradition, are sometimes called the **unwritten Constitution.** The Constitution does not refer to them, but they are so firmly established that they can be thought of as unwritten laws.

Admitting new states. The delegates, as you have seen, had drawn up a Constitution in which power was distributed between the states and the federal government. By making it possible for new states to enter the Union with minimum difficulty, they added more flexibility and strength to the government.

Since it was clear that the population of the western lands would grow rapidly, it was important to provide in advance for the admission of new states. So long as a western area remained a territory, Congress was responsible for its government. When the population grew large enough, the territory could apply for admission as a state. In general, the laws Congress passed to govern the admission of new states followed the Northwest Ordinance (see pages 141–142).

SECTION SURVEY

IDENTIFY: elastic clause, judicial review, senatorial courtesy.

1. (a) Why did the framers of the Constitution provide for an amendment process? (b) Why did they choose to make this amendment process a difficult one?

2. (a) How does the elastic clause of the Constitution broaden the powers specifically granted to Congress? (b) How are these powers limited by the federal judiciary?

3. (a) What is the "unwritten Constitution"? (b) Give three examples of this "unwritten Constitution" and explain why each arose.

4. Why was it important for the framers of the Constitution to write into that document provisions for new states to enter the Union?

5. The Constitution's success results from its combination of fixed procedure and adaptability. Do you agree or disagree with this statement? Explain your answer.

Chapter Survey

Summary: Tracing the Main Ideas

By the mid-1780's increasing numbers of Americans believed that the Articles of Confederation were not providing an effective government. Difficulties with trade and difficulties with foreign nations were two major problems that the Confederation government could not seem to handle. Shays' Rebellion in 1786 convinced other Americans that serious changes would have to be made.

The delegates who met in the spring of 1787 to revise the Articles of Confederation included many of the ablest leaders in America. Convinced that the Confederation was not strong enough to bring order and prosperity to their country, they abandoned all thought of revision and proceeded to draw up a completely new Constitution. Patrick Henry called this action "a revolution as radical as that which separated us from Great Britain." Out of their long political experience, their keen intelligence, and their great learning, the framers of the Constitution fashioned a blueprint for the United States of America.

An observer once referred to the Constitution as "the most wonderful work ever struck off at a given time by the brain and purpose of man." Revised, modified, and amended, it has served the American people for nearly two hundred years. It stands as a lasting tribute to the wisdom and foresight of its creators.

The Constitution created a republican form of government. It did not, however, create the nation. In Chapter 9 you will see how men and women from many walks of life began to work at the task of unifying their country and of establishing it as a respected member of the family of nations.

Inquiring into History

1. How did the new Constitution reflect the political experiences of the colonies before 1775?
2. Describe the connections between the Preamble to the Constitution and the theory of government that is described in the Declaration of Independence.
3. The Constitution is fundamentally a document of compromises. Explain this statement, using specific examples.
4. Benjamin Franklin was once asked what sort of government was set up in the Constitution. He answered, "A republic, if you can keep it." (a) What is a republic? (b) What did Franklin mean by his statement? (c) What provisions in the Constitution were intended to help us keep our republic?

Relating Past to Present

1. This chapter describes four fundamental principles that form the basis of the government set up under the Constitution. Are these principles still important today? Support your answers with examples from recent American history.
2. Name five ways in which government touches your life directly. (a) Which of these areas is specifically provided for in the Constitution? (b) Which has arisen as a result of the flexibility of the Constitution? Explain.

Developing Social Science Skills

1. Study the chart on page 172. (a) In your opinion, which step in the passage of a bill is the most important? Why? (b) How does the Rules Committee play a key role in the passage of a bill? (c) What is the purpose of the Conference Committee? (d) Name the three courses of action that a President can follow when he receives a bill.
2. Look at the chart on page 167. (a) In your opinion, which is the most important delegated power? the most important reserved power? the most important concurrent power? Why? (b) Explain why certain powers are denied to both the federal government and the state governments.
3. Look at the Constitution on page 166 and the map on pages 840–41. (a) In the first session of Congress, which state had the most Representatives? (b) Which state had the fewest? (c) Members of Congress from which state had to travel farthest to attend the session?
4. Make a bulletin board display showing the Bill of Rights in action today. Use illustrations from newspapers and magazines or make your own drawings or cartoons.
5. Look at the chart on page 167. (a) Which standing committees of the House and Senate do you think consider policies for each executive department? (b) Read about the proceedings of one committee in a newspaper or magazine. What changes in the operation of an executive department has the committee been considering?

Constitution of the United States

PREAMBLE

We the people of the United States, in order to form a more perfect Union, establish justice, insure domestic tranquillity, provide for the common defense, promote the general welfare, and secure the blessings of liberty to ourselves and our posterity, do ordain and establish this CONSTITUTION for the United States of America.

¶ In addition to stating the purposes of the Constitution, the Preamble makes it clear that the government is established by consent of the governed. "We the people, . . . ordain and establish" the government. We, the people, have supreme power in establishing the government of the United States of America.

ARTICLE 1. LEGISLATIVE DEPARTMENT

SECTION 1. CONGRESS

All legislative powers herein granted shall be vested in a Congress of the United States, which shall consist of a Senate and House of Representatives.

¶ By separating the functions of government among branches concerned with lawmaking (Article 1), law executing (Article 2), and law interpreting (Article 3), the framers of the Constitution were applying the principle of separation of powers and developing a system of checks and balances as a defense against tyranny.

¶ Practice has modified the provision that all lawmaking powers granted in the Constitution are vested in Congress. For example, such administrative agencies as the Interstate Commerce Commission can issue regulations that in some ways have the force of laws.

SECTION 2. HOUSE OF REPRESENTATIVES

1. Election and term of members. The House of Representatives shall be composed of members chosen every second year by the people of the several states, and the electors in each state shall have the qualifications requisite for electors of the most numerous branch of the state legislature.

¶ *Clause 1.* The members of the House of Representatives are elected every two years by the "electors" (voters) of the states. Except for the provisions of Amendments 15, 19, 24, and 26, the individual states decide who may or may not vote.

2. Qualifications. No person shall be a Representative who shall not have attained to the age of twenty-five years, and been seven years a citizen of the United States, and who shall not, when elected, be an inhabitant of that state in which he shall be chosen.

¶ *Clause 2.* This clause specifies that a member of the House of Representatives must be (1) at least 25 years of age, (2) a United States citizen for at least 7 years, and (3) a resident of the state in which elected. (Custom has added the requirement of residence in the Congressional district from which a Representative is elected.) Each state is divided into Congressional districts for the purpose of electing Representatives; each district elects one. ¶ TERM OF OFFICE: 2 years.

THE THREE BRANCHES OF THE FEDERAL GOVERNMENT

LEGISLATIVE BRANCH

HOUSE OF REPRESENTATIVES

Each state is represented in the House of Representatives based on population.

SENATE

Each state is represented in the Senate equally by two Senators.

Standing Committees of the House

Agriculture
Appropriations
Armed Services
Banking, Finance, and
  Urban Affairs
Budget
District of Columbia
Education and Labor
Foreign Affairs
Government Operations
House Administration
Interior and Insular
  Affairs
Interstate and Foreign
  Commerce

Judiciary
Merchant Marine and
  Fisheries
Post Office and Civil
  Service
Public Works and
  Transportation
Rules
Science and Technology
Small Business
Standards of Official
  Conduct
Veterans' Affairs
Ways and Means

Standing Committees of the Senate

Agriculture, Nutrition,
  and Forestry
Appropriations
Armed Services
Banking, Housing, and
  Urban Affairs
Budget
Commerce, Science, and
  Transportation
Energy and Natural
  Resources
Environment and Public
  Works

Finance
Foreign Relations
Governmental Affairs
Judiciary
Labor and Human
  Resources
Rules and Administration
Veterans' Affairs

EXECUTIVE BRANCH

Executive Departments

Department of State
Department of the Treasury
Department of Defense
Department of Justice
Department of the Interior
Department of Agriculture
Department of Commerce
Department of Labor
Department of Health and Human
  Services
Department of Education
Department of Housing and Urban
  Development
Department of Transportation
Department of Energy

The Executive Office

The White House
Office of Management and Budget
Council of Economic Advisers
Council on Environmental Quality
Domestic Policy Staff
National Security Council
Central Intelligence Agency
Office of Administration
Office of Science and Technology
  Policy
Office of the Special Representative
  for Trade

Independent Federal Agencies (Partial Listing)

ACTION
American Red Cross
Board of Governors of
  the Federal Reserve
  System
Environmental Protec-
  tion Agency
Equal Employment
  Opportunity Commis-
  sion
Farm Credit Administra-
  tion
Federal Communications
  Commission

Federal Deposit Insur-
  ance Corporation
Federal Election Com-
  mission
Federal Mediation and
  Conciliation Service
Federal Trade Commis-
  sion
General Services Admini-
  stration
Interstate Commerce
  Commission

National Academy of
  Sciences
National Aeronautics and
  Space Administration
National Foundation on
  the Arts and
  Humanities
National Labor Relations
  Board
National Science Foun-
  dation
National Transportation
  Safety Board

Nuclear Regulatory Com-
  mission
Securities and Exchange
  Commission
Small Business Admini-
  stration
Smithsonian Institution
Tennessee Valley
  Authority
United States Postal
  Service
Veterans Administration

JUDICIAL BRANCH

SUPREME COURT

Courts of Appeals

District Courts

Courts of the District of Columbia

Special Courts

Court of Claims
Court of Customs and Patent Appeals
Customs Court
Tax Court
Court of Military Appeals
Territorial Courts

¶ *Clause 3.* The bracketed portion of this clause beginning on line 5 forms what came to be called the "three-fifths compromise." Amendment 13 and Section 2 of Amendment 14 overruled this provision in the case of black Americans but not for Indians. However, since 1940 Indians have been included in the population census. ¶ Originally each state was entitled to one Representative for every 30,000 people. Later, membership was limited by law to a total of 435. ¶ A population census of the United States is taken every ten years to determine the number of Representatives to which each state is entitled. Regardless of its population, however, each state is entitled to at least one Representative in Congress.

¶ *Clause 4.* The "executive authority" refers to the governor of the state; a "writ of election" is an order for a special election to fill the vacant seat.

¶ *Clause 5.* In actual practice it is the majority party—the political party having the largest number of members in the House—that chooses the Speaker of the House and other House officials (clerk, doorkeeper, sergeant-at-arms, postmaster, and chaplain). The Speaker is the only official chosen from among the members of the House. ¶ The House, by a majority vote, can impeach (accuse) an Executive Department officer or a federal judge. The trial of the impeached official takes place in the Senate. (See Section 3, Clause 6.)

¶ *Clause 1.* Under the provisions of Amendment 17, the 100 Senators are now elected directly by the voters of the states in the same manner as the Representatives. The method of electing Senators provided here, by which the state legislatures chose Senators, came to be considered undemocratic and was therefore changed.

¶ *Clause 2.* One third of the Senate comes up for election every two years. This procedure was established in the first Senate, whose Senators were divided into three groups. One group was to serve for two years, the second for four years, and the third for six years. As a result, the terms of Senators today overlap, making the Senate a "continuing" body, in which two thirds of the members are "carried over" through every election. In contrast, the total membership of the House of Representatives is elected every two years. ¶ Under Amendment 17, if a Senator resigns or dies, the state governor can call a special election to fill the vacancy. The state legislature, however, may empower the governor to name a temporary Senator.

3. Apportionment of Representatives and direct taxes. Representatives [and direct taxes] shall be apportioned among the several states which may be included within this Union, according to their respective numbers [which shall be determined by adding to the whole number of free persons, including those bound to service for a term of years, and excluding Indians not taxed, three fifths of all other persons]. The actual enumeration shall be made within three years after the first meeting of the Congress of the United States, and within every subsequent term of ten years, in such manner as they shall by law direct. The number of Representatives shall not exceed 1 for every 30,000, but each state shall have at least 1 Representative; [and until such enumeration shall be made, the state of New Hampshire shall be entitled to choose 3; Massachusetts, 8; Rhode Island and Providence Plantations, 1; Connecticut, 5; New York, 6; New Jersey, 4; Pennsylvania, 8; Delaware, 1; Maryland, 6; Virginia, 10; North Carolina, 5; South Carolina, 5; and Georgia, 3.]

4. Filling vacancies. When vacancies happen in the representation from any state, the executive authority thereof shall issue writs of election to fill such vacancies.

5. Officers; impeachment. The House of Representatives shall choose their Speaker and other officers; and shall have the sole power of impeachment.

SECTION 3. SENATE

1. Number of members and terms of office. The Senate of the United States shall be composed of two Senators from each state [chosen by the legislature thereof], for six years, and each Senator shall have one vote.

2. Classification; filling vacancies. [Immediately after they shall be assembled in consequence of the first election, they shall be divided as equally as may be into three classes. The seats of the Senators of the first class shall be vacated at the expiration of the second year, of the second class at the expiration of the fourth year, and of the third class at the expiration of the sixth year, so that one third may be chosen every second year; and if vacancies happen by resignation, or otherwise, during the recess of the legislature of any state, the executive thereof may make temporary appointments until the next meeting of the legislature, which shall then fill such vacancies.]

3. Qualifications.
No person shall be a Senator who shall not have attained to the age of thirty years, and been nine years a citizen of the United States, and who shall not, when elected, be an inhabitant of that state for which he shall be chosen.

¶ *Clause 3.* This clause specifies that a Senator must be (1) at least 30 years of age, (2) a United States citizen for at least 9 years, and (3) a resident of the state in which elected. ¶ TERM OF OFFICE: 6 years.

4. President of the Senate.
The Vice-President of the United States shall be president of the Senate, but shall have no vote, unless they be equally divided.

Clause 4. To serve as president of the Senate and vote only in case of a tie is the sole duty the Constitution assigns to the Vice-President. In recent years the Vice-President has assumed additional duties at the President's request, such as attending cabinet meetings, traveling abroad on good-will tours, and carrying out such ceremonial duties as entertaining leading officials from abroad and representing the government at important events.

5. Other officers.
The Senate shall choose their other officers, and also a president *pro tempore,* in the absence of the Vice-President, or when he shall exercise the office of the President of the United States.

¶ *Clause 5.* "Other officers" include a secretary, chaplain, and sergeant-at-arms. These officers are not members of the Senate. *Pro tempore* is a Latin expression meaning "for the time being," or "temporarily." Thus, the president *pro tempore* acts as a temporary president of the Senate.

6. Trial of impeachments.
The Senate shall have the sole power to try all impeachments. When sitting for that purpose, they shall be on oath or affirmation. When the President of the United States is tried, the Chief Justice shall preside; and no person shall be convicted without the concurrence of two thirds of the members present.

¶ *Clause 6.* Only the President, Vice-President, cabinet officials, and federal judges are subject to impeachment and removal from office. Members of the House and Senate cannot be impeached, but they can be censured and even removed from office by the members of their respective houses. ¶ Officials may be impeached only for committing "treason, bribery, or other high crimes and misdemeanors" (see Article 2, Section 4). The Chief Justice of the Supreme Court presides at the impeachment trial of a President. The Vice-President presides over all other impeachment trials. The Senate can find an impeached official guilty only if two thirds of the Senators present agree on the verdict. The only President ever impeached was Andrew Johnson, in 1867; he was saved from conviction by one vote. In 1974 Richard M. Nixon resigned as President after the Judiciary Committee of the House of Representatives recommended to the House that he be impeached.

7. Penalty for conviction.
Judgment in cases of impeachment shall not extend further than to removal from office, and disqualification to hold and enjoy any office of honor, trust, or profit under the United States; but the party convicted shall nevertheless be liable and subject to indictment, trial, judgment, and punishment, according to law.

¶ *Clause 7.* The punishment for conviction in impeachment cases can consist only of removal from office and disqualification from holding any other federal office. However, the convicted person may also be tried in a regular court of law for this same offense. Although not impeached, President Nixon was granted a Presidential pardon, which spared him a possible criminal court trial.

¶ *Clause 1.* Under this provision Congress has passed a law stating that, unless the constitution of a state provides otherwise, Congressional elections must be held on the Tuesday following the first Monday in November of even-numbered years. (Until 1960 Maine held elections in September.) Congress has also ruled that Representatives must be elected by districts, rather than by the state as a whole, and that secret ballots (or voting machines, where required by state law) must be used.

¶ *Clause 2.* Under Amendment 20 Congress now meets on January 3, unless it sets another day by law.

¶ *Clause 1.* Until 1969 Congress used this clause to disqualify elected candidates and prevent them from taking office on the grounds of public policy. On one occasion the House refused to admit to membership an elected candidate who had violated the criminal laws. On another occasion the Senate refused to seat a victorious candidate whose election campaign had been characterized by "fraud and corruption." When the House refused to seat Adam Clayton Powell in 1967 on grounds of "gross misconduct," he sued. Two years later, the Supreme Court ruled that Congress had to seat all Senators and Representatives who met the requirements of Article 1, Section 2, Clause 2. ¶ A *quorum* is the minimum number of persons required to be present to transact business; a majority of the House or Senate constitutes a quorum. In practice, business is often transacted with less than a quorum present, and may go on as long as no member objects to the lack of a quorum.

¶ *Clause 2.* Each house has extensive rules of procedure. Each house can censure, punish, or expel a member. Expulsion requires a two-thirds vote.

¶ *Clause 3.* Each house is required to keep a journal of its activities. These journals, called the *House Journal* and the *Senate Journal,* are published at the end of each session of Congress. A third journal, called the *Congressional Record,* is published every day that Congress is in session, and furnishes a daily account of what Representatives and Senators do and say. ¶ If one fifth of those present insist on a roll call of the members' votes, each member's vote must be recorded in the proper house journal.

¶ *Clause 4.* Both houses must remain in session for the same period of time and in the same place.

SECTION 4. ELECTIONS AND MEETINGS

1. Holding elections. The times, places, and manner of holding elections for Senators and Representatives shall be prescribed in each state by the legislature thereof; but the Congress may at any time by law make or alter such regulations, except as to the places of choosing Senators.

2. Meetings. The Congress shall assemble at least once in every year, [and such meeting shall be on the first Monday in December,] unless they shall by law appoint a different day.

SECTION 5. RULES OF PROCEDURE

1. Organization. Each house shall be the judge of the elections, returns, and qualifications of its own members, and a majority of each shall constitute a quorum to do business; but a smaller number may adjourn from day to day, and may be authorized to compel the attendance of absent members, in such manner, and under such penalties, as each house may provide.

2. Proceedings. Each house may determine the rules of its proceedings, punish its members for disorderly behavior, and with the concurrence of two thirds, expel a member.

3. Journal. Each house shall keep a journal of its proceedings, and from time to time publish the same, excepting such parts as may in their judgment require secrecy; and the yeas and nays of the members of either house on any question shall, at the desire of one fifth of those present, be entered on the journal.

4. Adjournment. Neither house, during the session of Congress, shall, without the consent of the other, adjourn for more than three days, nor to any other place than that in which the two houses shall be sitting.

SECTION 6. PRIVILEGES AND RESTRICTIONS

1. Pay and privileges. The Senators and Representatives shall receive a compensation for their services, to be ascertained by law and paid out of the Treasury of the United States. They shall in all cases, except treason, felony, and breach of the peace, be privileged from arrest during their attendance at the session of their respective houses, and in going to and returning from the same; and for any speech or debate in either house, they shall not be questioned in any other place.

¶ *Clause 1.* In 1981 the salary of a member of Congress was $60,662.50 a year. ¶ The provision concerning privilege from arrest establishes the principle of "Congressional immunity." According to this principle, members cannot be arrested or brought into court for what they say in speeches and debates in Congress. The aim of this provision is to enable members of Congress to speak freely. They are subject to arrest, however, if they commit a crime, and, under the laws governing slander and libel, are liable for any false or defamatory statements they may make outside Congress.

2. Restrictions. No Senator or Representative shall, during the time for which he was elected, be appointed to any civil office under the authority of the United States, which shall have been created, or the emoluments whereof shall have been increased, during such time; and no person holding any office under the United States shall be a member of either house during his continuance in office.

¶ *Clause 2.* This clause emphasizes the separation of powers in the federal government. Legislators cannot, while they are members of Congress, hold positions also in the executive or judicial departments. Nor can legislators resign and then accept positions that were created during their term of office. Thus members of Congress cannot set up jobs for themselves in the executive or judicial branches of the government. Furthermore, if a member resigns and is appointed to an existing executive or judicial position, he or she cannot profit from any increase in pay in this position that was voted during the member's term in Congress.

SECTION 7. METHOD OF PASSING LAWS

1. Revenue bills. All bills for raising revenue shall originate in the House of Representatives; but the Senate may propose or concur with amendments as on other bills.

¶ *Clause 1.* All revenue, or money-raising, bills must be introduced in the House of Representatives. This provision grew out of a demand that the popularly elected branch of the legislature should have the "power of the purse." (Until Amendment 17 was ratified, the House was the only popularly elected branch.) It was also felt that the voters had more control over Representatives, who are elected for two-year terms, than over Senators, who are elected for six-year terms. Thus Representatives would be more careful than Senators in considering revenue bills. Since the Senate has the power to amend any bill, however, it can amend a revenue bill in such a way as actually to introduce a revenue bill of its own.

2. How a bill becomes a law. Every bill which shall have passed the House of Representatives and the Senate shall, before it become a law, be presented to the President of the United States; if he approve, he shall sign it, but if not, he shall return it, with his objections, to that house in which it shall have originated, who shall enter the objections at large on their journal, and proceed to reconsider it. If after such reconsideration two-thirds of that house shall agree to pass the bill, it shall be sent, together with the objections, to the other house, by which it shall likewise be reconsidered, and, if approved by two-thirds of that house, it shall become a law. But in all such cases the votes of

¶ *Clause 2.* When both houses of Congress pass a law, it is then sent to the President. ¶ If the President does not approve of a bill, one of several things may occur. The President may (1) veto, or refuse to sign, the bill; (2) permit the bill to become a law without signing it by holding it for ten days (not counting Sundays) while Congress is in session; (3) hold the bill near the end of a session in the hope that Congress will adjourn within ten days. In that case, the bill fails to become a law, just as though the President had formally vetoed it. This type of veto is called a "pocket veto." ¶ A bill vetoed by the President can become a law, however, if two thirds or more of both houses vote for the bill a second time. When this happens, Congress is said to have "overridden the Presidential veto."

HOW A BILL BECOMES A LAW

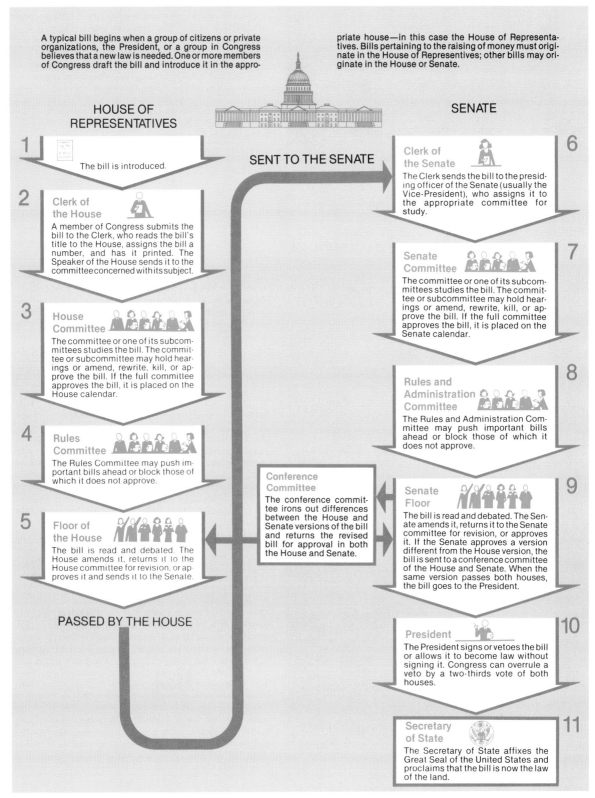

A typical bill begins when a group of citizens or private organizations, the President, or a group in Congress believes that a new law is needed. One or more members of Congress draft the bill and introduce it in the appro-priate house—in this case the House of Representatives. Bills pertaining to the raising of money must originate in the House of Representives; other bills may originate in the House or Senate.

HOUSE OF REPRESENTATIVES

SENATE

1 The bill is introduced.

SENT TO THE SENATE

2 Clerk of the House
A member of Congress submits the bill to the Clerk, who reads the bill's title to the House, assigns the bill a number, and has it printed. The Speaker of the House sends it to the committee concerned with its subject.

3 House Committee
The committee or one of its subcommittees studies the bill. The committee or subcommittee may hold hearings or amend, rewrite, kill, or approve the bill. If the full committee approves the bill, it is placed on the House calendar.

4 Rules Committee
The Rules Committee may push important bills ahead or block those of which it does not approve.

5 Floor of the House
The bill is read and debated. The House amends it, returns it to the House committee for revision, or approves it and sends it to the Senate.

PASSED BY THE HOUSE

6 Clerk of the Senate
The Clerk sends the bill to the presiding officer of the Senate (usually the Vice-President), who assigns it to the appropriate committee for study.

7 Senate Committee
The committee or one of its subcommittees studies the bill. The committee or subcommittee may hold hearings or amend, rewrite, kill, or approve the bill. If the full committee approves the bill, it is placed on the Senate calendar.

8 Rules and Administration Committee
The Rules and Administration Committee may push important bills ahead or block those of which it does not approve.

Conference Committee
The conference committee irons out differences between the House and Senate versions of the bill and returns the revised bill for approval in both the House and Senate.

9 Senate Floor
The bill is read and debated. The Senate amends it, returns it to the Senate committee for revision, or approves it. If the Senate approves a version different from the House version, the bill is sent to a conference committee of the House and Senate. When the same version passes both houses, the bill goes to the President.

10 President
The President signs or vetoes the bill or allows it to become law without signing it. Congress can overrule a veto by a two-thirds vote of both houses.

11 Secretary of State
The Secretary of State affixes the Great Seal of the United States and proclaims that the bill is now the law of the land.

both houses shall be determined by yeas and nays, and the names of the persons voting for and against the bill shall be entered on the journal of each house respectively. If any bill shall not be returned by the President within ten days (Sundays excepted) after it shall have been presented to him, the same bill shall be a law, in like manner as if he had signed it, unless the Congress by their adjournment prevent its return, in which case it shall not be a law.

3. Presidential approval or veto. Every order, resolution, or vote to which the concurrence of the Senate and House of Representatives may be necessary (except on a question of adjournment) shall be presented to the President of the United States; and before the same shall take effect, shall be approved by him, or being disapproved by him, shall be repassed by two thirds of the Senate and House of Representatives, according to the rules and limitations prescribed in the case of a bill.

SECTION 8. POWERS DELEGATED TO CONGRESS

The Congress shall have power

1. To lay and collect taxes, duties, imposts, and excises, to pay the debts and provide for the common defense and general welfare of the United States; but all duties, imposts, and excises shall be uniform throughout the United States;

2. To borrow money on the credit of the United States;

3. To regulate commerce with foreign nations, and among the several states, [and with the Indian tribes];

¶ *Clause 3.* A *joint resolution* results from declarations passed by both houses of Congress on the same subject. It becomes a law in the same manner as a bill. A Congressional declaration of war takes the form of a joint resolution. A *concurrent resolution* represents only an expression of opinion on the part of either house of Congress. It does not have the force of law and, therefore, does not require Presidential approval. The process of amending the Constitution may start this way. A vote censuring a Representative or Senator, or an expression of sympathy, takes the form of a concurrent resolution.

¶ Section 8 places important powers in the hands of Congress, indicating that the framers of the Constitution were aware of the weaknesses of the Congress under the Articles of Confederation. This section lists 18 powers granted to Congress—the *delegated* or *enumerated powers.* The first 17 are expressed powers because they clearly designate specific areas in which Congress may exercise its authority. The eighteenth power is contained in the famous elastic clause, from which has come the doctrine of implied powers. The elastic clause permits the stretching of the other 17 powers.

¶ *Clause 1.* This clause gives Congress the power to levy and collect taxes, duties, or tariffs (taxes on imported goods collected at customhouses), and excises (taxes on goods produced, sold, or consumed within the country). The term "imposts" includes duties and excise taxes. Notice that these taxes must be uniform throughout the United States. According to this clause, the power to tax may be used only (1) to pay the government's debts and (2) to provide for the common defense and general welfare. The Social Security tax on payrolls is a present-day use of the power to tax.

¶ *Clause 2.* The power granted in Clause 2 enables the government to borrow money by issuing bonds for sale, on which the government pays interest. This clause, extended by Clause 18, has also given Congress the power to establish national banks and the Federal Reserve System.

¶ *Clause 3.* Congress is given direct control over interstate and foreign commerce. This provision has been extended, by the use of Clause 18, to give Congress control over transportation, communication, and navigation. In order to exercise this broad power, Congress has set up administrative agencies, such as the Interstate Commerce Commission and the Federal Communications Commission.

¶ *Clause 4.* This clause provides the power to regulate the methods by which aliens become citizens of the United States and to form rules regarding bankruptcy.

¶ *Clause 5.* Congress is permitted to coin money, to determine the gold and silver content of money, and to order the printing of paper money. It also permits Congress to set up uniform standards for measuring weights and distances.

¶ *Clause 6.* Under this clause Congress authorizes the Treasury Department to investigate counterfeiting of money or of government bonds.

¶ *Clause 7.* In 1970 Congress transferred authority over the postal system to the executive branch in the Postal Reorganization Act. The Post Office Department was replaced by an independent agency, the United States Postal Service.

¶ *Clause 8.* This clause shows that the framers of the Constitution were eager to promote the progress of science and the arts. Under this power Congress has passed laws providing that inventors be granted *patents* (exclusive rights to manufacture and sell their inventions for 17 years) and that authors and composers be granted *copyrights* (exclusive rights to control the publication or performance of their works for their lifetimes plus 50 years).

¶ *Clause 9.* Congress is granted the power to establish the federal district courts, the Courts of Appeals, and special courts.

¶ *Clause 10.* Congress protects and controls citizens and ships of the United States when they are out of the country. It may also punish counterfeiting in the United States of bonds and notes of a foreign government.

¶ *Clause 11.* Congress is given the power to declare war. Although Congress alone has this power, several Presidents have taken military action without prior consent of Congress. In 1846 President Polk sent troops into an area claimed by both the United States and Mexico. In 1950 President Truman ordered American troops into Korea. And in the mid-1960's, through executive order, American troops became involved in the conflict in South Vietnam without a formal declaration of war. The War Powers Act of 1973 requires the President to report to Congress within 48 hours any new commitment of American troops to a foreign war. Unless Congress declares war, the President must end hostilities within 60 days and withdraw the troops within 90 days. Congress can require earlier withdrawal by passing a joint resolution, which the President cannot veto. ¶ Letters of marque and reprisal were licenses issued by the government to privateers (armed ships, privately owned), allowing them to attack enemy ships during wartime. In the War of 1812, the government of the United States issued many of these licenses to American privateers, who did extensive damage to British trade. Today, the issuing of such licenses is outlawed by international agreement.

4. To establish a uniform rule of naturalization, and uniform laws on the subject of bankruptcies throughout the United States;

5. To coin money, regulate the value thereof, and of foreign coin, and fix the standard of weights and measures;

6. To provide for the punishment of counterfeiting the securities and current coin of the United States;

7. To establish post offices and post roads;

8. To promote the progress of science and useful arts by securing for limited times to authors and inventors the exclusive right to their respective writings and discoveries;

9. To constitute tribunals inferior to the Supreme Court;

10. To define and punish piracies and felonies committed on the high seas and offenses against the law of nations;

11. To declare war, [grant letters of marque and reprisal,] and make rules concerning captures on land and water;

12. To raise and support armies, but no appropriation of money to that use shall be for a longer term than two years;

13. To provide and maintain a navy;

14. To make rules for the government and regulation of the land and naval forces;

15. To provide for calling forth the militia to execute the laws of the Union, suppress insurrections, and repel invasions;

16. To provide for organizing, arming, and disciplining the militia, and for governing such part of them as may be employed in the service of the United States, reserving to the states, respectively, the appointment of the officers, and the authority of training the militia according to the discipline prescribed by Congress;

17. To exercise exclusive legislation in all cases whatsoever, over such district (not exceeding ten miles square) as may, by cession of particular states, and the acceptance of Congress, become the seat of government of the United States, and to exercise like authority over all places purchased by the consent of the legislature of the state in which the same shall be, for the erection of forts, magazines, arsenals, dock-yards, and other needful buildings;—and

18. To make all laws which shall be necessary and proper for carrying into execution the foregoing powers, and all other powers vested by this Constitution in the government of the United States, or in any department or officer thereof.

SECTION 9. POWERS DENIED TO THE FEDERAL GOVERNMENT

1. [The migration or importation of such persons as any of the states now existing shall think proper to admit shall not be prohibited by the Congress prior to the year 1808; but a tax or duty may be imposed on such importation, not exceeding $10 for each person.]

¶ *Clause 12.* The two-year limit in Clause 12 on money appropriations for the army was included to keep the major military power under strict civilian control.

¶ *Clause 13.* Notice that appropriations for the navy were not limited. An air force, of course, was not dreamed of when the Constitution was written.

¶ *Clause 14.* Under the power granted in this clause, Congress has established rules and regulations governing military discipline and the procedure of courts-martial.

¶ *Clause 15.* The term "militia" now refers to the National Guard units of the states. These units may now be called up by the President to keep law and order. They can become part of the United States Army in emergencies.

¶ *Clause 16.* Congress is authorized to help states support their militia.

¶ *Clause 17.* This clause enables Congress to exercise exclusive control over the government of the District of Columbia. In 1973 Congress relinquished some of this control by allowing the District to choose local officials. By this clause Congress also controls all installations owned and operated by the federal government in the various states.

¶ *Clause 18.* "Necessary and proper" are the key words in the so-called *elastic clause*. Only by combining the power granted in this clause with one of the other 17 powers can Congress use the implied powers granted to it in the Constitution. Laws based on this clause are, of course, subject to review by the judicial branch.

¶ Section 9 limits the powers of Congress.

¶ *Clause 1.* "Such persons" refers to slaves. This provision grew out of the commerce compromise at the Constitutional Convention held in Philadelphia in 1787. It was agreed that Congress would not prohibit the importation of slaves prior to 1808, and that it would not impose an import tax of more than $10 per slave. The importation of slaves into the United States became illegal in 1808.

¶ *Clause 2.* The guarantee of the *writ of habeas corpus* (meaning "you may have the body, or person") has been called the most important single safeguard of personal liberty under Anglo-American law. It protects a person against being held in jail on insufficient evidence or no evidence at all. The lawyer of a person arrested can obtain a writ, or court order, that requires the arrested person to be brought before a judge who must determine whether there are sufficient grounds to hold the person in jail. If there are no such grounds, the person must be freed.

¶ *Clause 3.* A "bill of attainder" is a legislative measure that condemns and punishes a person without a jury trial. Such measures were used in England, where Parliament could, by law, declare persons guilty of treason and punish them by death and confiscation of property. Under the Constitution Congress cannot by law single out certain persons and inflict punishment on them. The power to punish belongs to the judiciary. ¶ An *ex post facto law* is a law that punishes a person for doing something that was legal before the law was passed, or that increases the penalty for earlier actions. Because of this clause, the Lindbergh kidnaping law of 1932, for example, could not be applied to persons who committed the crime of kidnaping before that year.

¶ *Clause 4.* A capitation tax is a direct tax imposed on each person, such as the poll tax on persons voting. This provision was inserted to prevent Congress from taxing slaves per poll, or per person, for the purpose of abolishing slavery. Amendment 16 overrules this clause. Amendment 24 outlaws federal poll taxes.

¶ *Clause 5.* This clause also resulted from the commerce compromise. The southern states wanted to make sure that Congress could not use its taxing power to impose taxes on southern exports, such as cotton and tobacco.

¶ *Clause 6.* This clause declares that the United States is an open market in which all states have equal trading and commercial opportunities.

¶ *Clause 7.* This clause concerns the all-important power of the purse. Since Congress controls expenditures, it can limit the powers of the President by limiting the amount of money the Chief Executive may spend to run the government. This clause is perhaps the single most important curb on Presidential power in the Constitution. Furthermore, the requirement to account for money spent and received helps to protect against misuse of funds.

¶ *Clause 8.* This clause prohibits the establishment of a nobility. It also discourages bribery of American officials by foreign governments.

2. The privilege of the writ of *habeas corpus* shall not be suspended, unless when in cases of rebellion or invasion the public safety may require it.

3. No bill of attainder or *ex post facto* law shall be passed.

4. [No capitation or other direct tax shall be laid, unless in proportion to the census herein before directed to be taken.]

5. No tax or duty shall be laid on articles exported from any state.

6. No preference shall be given any regulation of commerce or revenue to the ports of one state over those of another; nor shall vessels bound to, or from, one state, be obliged to enter, clear, or pay duties in another.

7. No money shall be drawn from the Treasury, but in consequence of appropriations made by law; and a regular statement and account of the receipts and expenditures of all public money shall be published from time to time.

8. No title of nobility shall be granted by the United States; and no person holding any office of profit or trust under them, shall, without the consent of the Congress, accept of any present, emolument, office, or title, of any kind whatever, from any king, prince, or foreign state.

SECTION 10.
POWERS DENIED TO THE STATES

1. No state shall enter into any treaty, alliance, or confederation; grant letters of marque and reprisal; coin money; emit bills of credit; make anything but gold and silver coin a tender in payment of debts; pass any bill of attainder, *ex post facto* law, or law impairing the obligation of contracts, or grant any title of nobility.

2. No state shall, without the consent of the Congress, lay any imposts or duties on imports or exports, except what may be absolutely necessary for executing its inspection laws; and the net produce of all duties and imposts, laid by any state on imports or exports, shall be for the use of the Treasury of the United States; and all such laws shall be subject to the revision and control of the Congress.

3. No state shall, without the consent of Congress, lay any duty of tonnage, keep troops, or ships of war in time of peace, enter into any agreement or compact with another state, or with a foreign power, or engage in war, unless actually invaded, or in such imminent danger as will not admit of delay.

ARTICLE 2.
EXECUTIVE DEPARTMENT

SECTION 1. PRESIDENT AND VICE-PRESIDENT

1. Term of office. The executive power shall be vested in a President of the United States of America. He shall hold his office during the term of four years, and together with the Vice-President, chosen for the same term, be elected as follows:

¶ According to Section 10, states cannot (1) make treaties, (2) coin money, (3) pass either bills of attainder or *ex post facto* laws, (4) impair obligations of contract, (5) grant titles of nobility, (6) tax imports or exports without the consent of Congress, (7) keep troops or warships in time of peace, (8) deal with another state or foreign power without the consent of Congress, and (9) engage in war unless invaded.

¶ *Clause 1.* Because Shays' Rebellion was still fresh in the minds of the delegates to the Constitutional Convention, and since several of the states at that time were being urged to pass legislation relieving debtors from the payment of their debts, the delegates decided to protect creditors once and for all by denying states the right to pass laws that would impair obligations of contract. During the Great Depression, which began in 1929, and the New Deal period (1933–45), the Supreme Court upheld state laws relieving debtors or mortgagees from paying their debts on the due dates, but payments were simply postponed, not canceled.

¶ *Clause 2.* The powers forbidden to the states in this clause are to vote for taxes on goods sent in or out of a state, unless Congress agrees.

¶ *Clause 3.* This clause forbids the states to keep troops or warships in peacetime or to deal with another state or a foreign nation, unless Congress agrees.

¶ *Clause 1.* This provision gives the executive power to the President. The President may use all of the means available to carry out the laws or refrain from using some of these means. Of course, the power and prestige of the Presidency depend to some extent on the personality of the person who holds the office.

THE FEDERAL SYSTEM

DIVISION OF POWERS

FEDERAL GOVERNMENT	FEDERAL AND STATE GOVERNMENTS	STATE GOVERNMENTS
Enumerated powers delegated to the Congress:	**Concurrent powers shared by the federal and state governments:**	**Reserved powers retained by the state governments:**
• to regulate interstate and foreign commerce	• to tax	• to regulate suffrage for state elections
• to establish laws governing citizenship	• to borrow money	• to maintain a system of public education
• to coin money	• to establish penal laws	• to establish marriage and divorce laws
• to control the postal system	• to charter banks	• to establish laws governing corporations
• to regulate patents and copyrights	• to take property for public purposes by eminent domain	• to establish traffic laws
• to establish federal courts lower than the Supreme Court		• to regulate intrastate commerce
• to declare war		• Amendment 10 of the Constitution reserves to the state governments all powers not delegated to the federal government or prohibited by the Constitution.
• to establish and support the armed forces		
• to pass all laws necessary and proper for carrying out the preceding powers		

PROHIBITED POWERS

Powers denied the federal government:	Powers denied the federal and state governments:	Powers denied the state governments:
• to suspend the writ of *habeas corpus* except in cases of rebellion or invasion	• to pass bills of attainder	• to enter into treaties with other nations or with other states without the consent of Congress
• to levy taxes on exports	• to pass *ex post facto* laws	• to coin money
• to give preferential treatment in commerce or revenue to the ports of any state	• to grant titles of nobility	• to impair obligations of contract
• to draw money from the Treasury except by appropriation under a specific law		• to place a tax on imports or exports except to carry out their inspection laws
• to permit persons holding federal office to accept gifts from a foreign country without consent of Congress		• to keep troops or ships in time of peace without consent of Congress

2. Electoral system. Each state shall appoint, in such manner as the legislature thereof may direct, a number of electors, equal to the whole number of Senators and Representatives to which the state may be entitled in the Congress; but no Senator or Representative, or person holding an office of trust or profit under the United States, shall be appointed an elector.

3. Former method of using the electoral system. [The electors shall meet in their respective states, and vote by ballot for two persons, of whom one at least shall not be an inhabitant of the same state with themselves. And they shall make a list of all the persons voted for, and of the number of votes for each; which list they shall sign and certify, and transmit sealed to the seat of the government of the United States, directed to the president of the Senate. The president of the Senate shall, in the presence of the Senate and House of Representatives, open all the certificates, and the votes shall then be counted. The person having the greatest number of votes shall be the President, if such number be a majority of the whole number of electors appointed; and if there be more than one who have such majority, and have an equal number of votes, then the House of Representatives shall immediately choose by ballot one of them for President; and if no person have a majority, then from the five highest on the list the said House shall in like manner choose the President. But in choosing the President the votes shall be taken by states, the representation from each state having one vote. A quorum for this purpose shall consist of a member or members from two thirds of the states, and a majority of all the states shall be necessary to a choice. In every case, after the choice of the President, the person having the greatest number of votes of the electors shall be the Vice-President. But if there should remain two or more who have equal votes, the Senate shall choose from them by ballot the Vice-President.]

4. Time of elections. The Congress may determine the time of choosing the electors, and the day on which they shall give their votes; which day shall be the same throughout the United States.

¶ *Clauses 2, 3.* These clauses established the electoral system, but very little that the framers decided about electing a President has survived in the form they intended. The delegates to the Constitutional Convention, still fearful of popular rule, decided that the President and Vice-President ought to be elected by a small group of persons called "electors" chosen according to a method determined by each state legislature. Until Andrew Jackson's Presidency, electors were chosen by state legislatures. Since then the people have voted directly for the electors. Some changes in the method of electing a President have been made by formal amendment, as in Amendment 12; other changes have resulted from political practice.

¶ *Clause 4.* Today Presidential elections are held on the Tuesday after the first Monday in November. Electoral votes are cast on the Monday after the second Wednesday in December.

179

¶ *Clause 5.* This clause specifies that the President must be (1) a native-born citizen of the United States, (2) at least 35 years of age, and (3) a resident of the United States for at least 14 years. ¶ TERM OF OFFICE: 4 years.

¶ *Clause 6.* If a President dies or is removed from office, the Vice-President succeeds to the office. John Tyler, in 1841, was the first Vice-President to succeed to the Presidency. By assuming the office of President, not simply serving as an acting President, Tyler established a precedent that has since been followed. ¶ Under the Presidential Succession Act of 1947, if both the President and the Vice-President die or are removed from office, the order of succession is as follows: (1) Speaker of the House, (2) President *pro tempore* of the Senate, and (3) the cabinet members in the order in which their offices were created. ¶ Amendment 25, adopted in 1967, clarifies the procedure to be followed in case the President or Vice-President is unable to serve or resigns.

¶ *Clause 7.* In 1981 the President's salary was $200,000 a year, plus a $50,000 expense account and a nontaxable fund for travel and official entertainment limited to $112,000. The Vice-President's salary was $79,125 a year plus a $10,000 expense allowance.

¶ *Clause 8.* The President assumes office officially only after taking the oath of office, which is administered by the Chief Justice of the United States.

¶ *Clause 1.* The important point in this provision is that it places the armed forces under civilian control. The President is a civilian but is superior in military power to any military officer. ¶ The words "principal officer in each of the executive departments" are the basis for the creation of the President's cabinet. Each cabinet member is the head of one of the executive departments. The President chooses the cabinet members, with the consent of the Senate, and can remove any cabinet official without asking Senate approval.

¶ *Clause 2.* The President makes treaties with the advice and consent of two thirds of the Senate. A treaty ratified by the Senate becomes the supreme law of the land. The Pres-

5. Qualifications for President. No person except a natural-born citizen [or a citizen of the United States, at the time of the adoption of this Constitution], shall be eligible to the office of the President; neither shall any person be eligible to that office who shall not have attained to the age of thirty-five years, and been fourteen years a resident within the United States.

6. Filling vacancies. In case of the removal of the President from office, or of his death, resignation, or inability to discharge the powers and duties of the said office, the same shall devolve on the Vice-President, and the Congress may by law provide for the case of removal, death, resignation, or inability, both of the President and Vice-President, declaring what officer shall then act as President, and such officer shall act accordingly, until the disability be removed, or a President shall be elected.

7. Salary. The President shall, at stated times, receive for his services, a compensation, which shall neither be increased nor diminished during the period for which he shall have been elected, and he shall not receive within that period any other emolument from the United States, or any of them.

8. Oath of office. Before he enter on the execution of his office, he shall take the following oath or affirmation: — "I do solemnly swear (or affirm) that I will faithfully execute the office of President of the United States, and will to the best of my ability, preserve, protect, and defend the Constitution of the United States."

SECTION 2. POWERS OF THE PRESIDENT

1. Military powers. The President shall be Commander in Chief of the Army and Navy of the United States, and of the militia of the several states, when called into the actual service of the United States; he may require the option, in writing, of the principal officer in each of the executive departments, upon any subject relating to the duties of their respective offices, and he shall have power to grant reprieves and pardons for offenses against the United States, except in cases of impeachment.

2. Treaties and appointments. He shall have power, by and with the advice and consent of the Senate, to make treaties, provided two thirds of the

Senators present concur; and he shall nominate, and by and with the advice and consent of the Senate, shall appoint ambassadors, other public ministers and consuls, judges of the Supreme Court, and all other officers of the United States, whose appointments are not herein otherwise provided for, and which shall be established by law; but the Congress may by law vest the appointment of such inferior officers, as they think proper, in the President alone, in the courts of law, or in the heads of departments.

3. Filling vacancies. The President shall have power to fill up all vacancies that may happen during the recess of the Senate, by granting commissions which shall expire at the end of their next session.

ident can also enter into executive agreements with foreign governments that have the same force as treaties but do not require Senate approval. ¶ With the consent of the Senate, the President can appoint ambassadors, public ministers, consuls, and other diplomatic officials, as well as federal judges, military officers, and members of administrative agencies. "Inferior officers" are those subordinate to the cabinet members or to federal judges. ¶ At the present time, a majority of federal government positions are filled by men and women who have passed examinations given by the United States Civil Service Commission.

¶ *Clause 3.* If a vacancy in an important position occurs when Congress is not in session, the President has the power to fill such a vacancy with an interim appointment. When Congress meets again, this appointment or a new appointment must be submitted to the Senate so that it may be approved.

SEPARATION OF FEDERAL POWERS: Examples of Checks and Balances

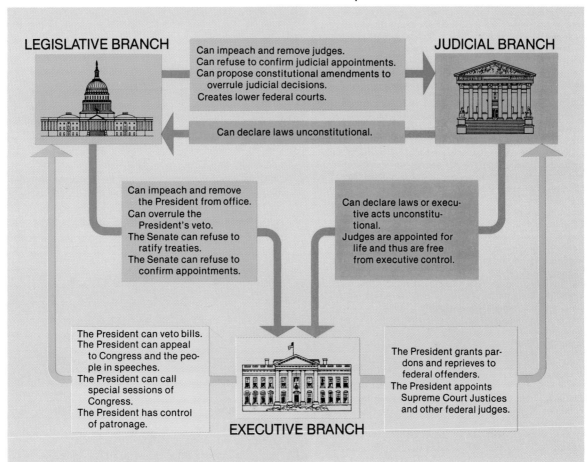

LEGISLATIVE BRANCH

Can impeach and remove judges.
Can refuse to confirm judicial appointments.
Can propose constitutional amendments to overrule judicial decisions.
Creates lower federal courts.

JUDICIAL BRANCH

Can declare laws unconstitutional.

Can impeach and remove the President from office.
Can overrule the President's veto.
The Senate can refuse to ratify treaties.
The Senate can refuse to confirm appointments.

Can declare laws or executive acts unconstitutional.
Judges are appointed for life and thus are free from executive control.

The President can veto bills.
The President can appeal to Congress and the people in speeches.
The President can call special sessions of Congress.
The President has control of patronage.

The President grants pardons and reprieves to federal offenders.
The President appoints Supreme Court Justices and other federal judges.

EXECUTIVE BRANCH

¶ The President's duties include the following: (1) *Legislative duties:* delivering annual and special messages to Congress; calling special sessions of Congress; approving or vetoing bills (see Article 1, Section 7). (2) *Diplomatic duties:* receiving (or refusing to receive) ambassadors or ministers of foreign countries to indicate that the United States recognizes (or refuses to recognize) the government of these countries. The President can also send home the ambassador of a foreign country as a sign that the United States is breaking off diplomatic relations with that country. (3) *Executive duties:* executing all the laws. In actual fact the administration and enforcement of the laws are in the hands of the various government departments, commissions, and administrative agencies; but the President is responsible for seeing that they are carried out. (4) *Military duties:* commissioning of United States armed forces officers.

¶ (See annotation of Article 1, Section 3, Clauses 6–7.)

¶ By authorizing the establishment of a system of federal courts, Article 3 creates the judicial power—the power to hear and decide cases. Under the judicial powers granted by the Constitution or developed through Supreme Court decisions, the courts have declared unconstitutional certain laws of Congress, acts of the President, laws of the state legislatures, and decisions of the state courts.

¶ Only the Supreme Court is established by the Constitution itself, but the Constitution gives Congress the authority to establish the lower courts that exist today. Since the Constitution does not state the number of justices to be appointed to the Supreme Court, Congress decides the number by law. Today the Supreme Court has nine justices. ¶ Congress has created two types of lower courts. One type includes federal district courts and Courts of Appeals, which review cases sent up by the district courts. District courts and Courts of Appeals are called "constitutional courts" because they are general courts deriving their power directly from the Constitution. The second type of court deals with cases of a specialized nature. The Court of Claims, the Tax Court, and the Court of Customs and Patent Appeals are included in this second group. ¶ The framers of the Constitution wanted to make sure that federal judges would be independent of political influence. Accordingly federal judges are appointed for life, subject to good behavior, and their pay cannot be reduced by law during their term of office.

¶ *Clause 1.* Here the words "law" and "equity" have special meanings. "Law" means the common law—the laws that originated in England and that have been based on centuries of judicial decisions. "Equity" refers to principles of justice also developed in England to remedy wrongs in situations in which the common law was inadequate. Today, in the United States, law and equity are applied by the same judges in the same courts. ¶ The power of the federal courts extends to two types of cases: (1) those involv-

SECTION 3. DUTIES OF THE PRESIDENT

He shall from time to time give to the Congress information of the state of the Union, and recommend to their consideration such measures as he shall judge necessary and expedient; he may, on extraordinary occasions, convene both houses, or either of them, and in case of disagreement between them, with respect to the time of adjournment, he may adjourn them to such time as he shall think proper; he shall receive ambassadors and other public ministers; he shall take care that the laws be faithfully executed, and shall commission all the officers of the United States.

SECTION 4. IMPEACHMENT

The President, Vice-President, and all civil officers of the United States, shall be removed from office on impeachment for, and conviction of, treason, bribery, or other high crimes and misdemeanors.

ARTICLE 3.
JUDICIAL DEPARTMENT

SECTION 1. FEDERAL COURTS

The judicial power of the United States shall be vested in one Supreme Court, and in such inferior courts as the Congress may from time to time ordain and establish. The judges, both of the Supreme and inferior courts, shall hold their offices during good behavior, and shall, at stated times, receive for their services a compensation, which shall not be diminished during their continuance in office.

SECTION 2. JURISDICTION OF FEDERAL COURTS

1. General jurisdiction. The judicial power shall extend to all cases, in law and equity, arising under this Constitution, the laws of the United States, and treaties made or which shall be made, under their authority; to all cases affecting ambassadors, other public ministers and consuls; to all cases of admiralty and maritime jurisdiction; to controversies to which the United States shall be a party; to controversies between two or more states; [between a state and citizens of another state;] between citizens of the same state claiming lands under grants of different states, and between a state or the citizens thereof, and foreign states, citizens, or subjects.

2. Supreme Court. In all cases affecting ambassadors, other public ministers and consuls, and those in which a state shall be a party, the Supreme Court shall have original jurisdiction. In all the other cases before mentioned, the Supreme Court shall have appellate jurisdiction, both as to law and fact, with such exceptions, and under such regulations as the Congress shall make.

3. Conduct of trials. The trial of all crimes, except in cases of impeachment, shall be by jury; and such trial shall be held in the state where the said crimes shall have been commited; but when not committed within any state, the trial shall be at such place or places as the Congress may by law have directed.

SECTION 3. TREASON

1. Definition. Treason against the United States shall consist only in levying war against them, or in adhering to their enemies, giving them aid and comfort. No person shall be convicted of treason unless on the testimony of two witnesses to the same overt act, or on confession in open court.

2. Punishment. The Congress shall have power to declare the punishment of treason, but no attainder of treason shall work corruption of blood or forfeiture except during the life of the person attainted.

ARTICLE 4.
RELATIONS AMONG THE STATES

SECTION 1. OFFICIAL ACTS

Full faith and credit shall be given in each state to the public acts, records, and judicial proceedings of every other state. And the Congress may by general laws prescribe the manner in which such acts, records, and proceedings shall be proved, and the effect thereof.

ing the interpretation of the Constitution, federal laws, treaties, and laws relating to ships on the high seas and navigable waters; and (2) those involving the United States government itself, foreign diplomatic officials, two or more state governments, citizens of different states when the sum involved is more than $10,000, and a state or its citizens versus foreign countries or citizens of foreign countries.

¶ *Clause 2.* "Original jurisdiction" means the right to try a case before any other court may hear it. "Appellate jurisdiction" means the right of a court to try cases appealed from lower courts. Most of the cases tried by the Supreme Court are cases appealed from lower federal and state courts. Cases involving foreign diplomats and any state of the United States may be started directly in the Supreme Court.

¶ *Clause 3.* Every person accused of a federal crime is guaranteed a jury trial near the scene of the crime. But accused persons may give up this privilege, if they wish. ¶ Amendments 5, 6, and 7 expand the provisions of this clause.

¶ *Clause 1.* Treason is the only crime specifically defined in the Constitution. To be found guilty of treason, a person must be shown to have helped wage war against the United States, or to have given aid and comfort to its enemies. A person cannot be convicted without the testimony of two witnesses to the same act unless the person confesses in open court.

¶ *Clause 2.* The punishment for treason, as determined by Congress, is death or a fine of $10,000 and imprisonment for not less than five years. This clause further states that the punishment for treason cannot be extended to the children of a traitor. They cannot be deprived of their rights and their property — as had been done in England.

¶ The purpose of this provision is to make sure that the official records of one state are respected in all the other states. Official records of this kind include birth certificates, marriage licenses, death certificates, corporation charters, wills, and court decisions. This provision also protects a citizen's right to collect money that has been awarded by a court decision in one state, even if the person who owes the money moves to another state.

¶ *Clause 1.* The terms "privileges" and "immunities" simply mean the rights of citizens. Thus a state cannot discriminate against citizens of other states in favor of its own citizens, except in certain very special areas—such as voting, for example. A state can impose residence requirements for voting, so that citizens of another state must reside in the state for a specified period before they can vote as citizens of their new state.

¶ *Clause 2.* This provision prevents a prisoner or a person charged with a crime from escaping justice by fleeing across a state line. It provides that a criminal be returned by the state where captured to the state where the crime was committed—a process known as extradition. A governor of a state cannot be forced to extradite, or return, a prisoner, however, if the governor feels that such action will result in injustice to the accused person.

¶ *Clause 3.* Since the ratification of Amendment 13 in 1865 brought an end to slavery in this country, the clause is now of historical interest only.

¶ *Clause 1.* The Northwest Ordinance of 1787 provided that new states be admitted to the Union on completely equal footing with the original thirteen states. Although the Constitution declares here that new states may not be created within the territory of any other state without its consent, an exception did occur in 1863, when West Virginia was formed from the western part of the state of Virginia. This exception occurred during the Civil War, and West Virginia received permission from the loyal, rather than the secessionist, government of Virginia.

¶ *Clause 2.* Under this provision Congress has the power to control all property belonging to the federal government. It can set up governments for territories and colonies of the United States. It can grant independence to a colony, as it did to the Philippines in 1946. It can set aside land for national parks and build dams for flood control.

¶ If public property is being destroyed and public safety endangered in a state, the President may decide to send troops into that state without having been requested to do so by local authorities. The President may even proclaim martial law in a state. This section also guarantees that states can govern only by consent of the governed.

SECTION 2. PRIVILEGES OF CITIZENS

1. Privileges. The citizens of each state shall be entitled to all privileges and immunities of citizens in the several states.

2. Extradition. A person charged in any state with treason, felony, or other crime, who shall flee from justice, and be found in another state, shall on demand of the executive authority of the state from which he fled, be delivered up, to be removed to the state having jurisdiction of the crime.

3. Fugitive slaves. [No person held in service or labor in one state, under the laws thereof, escaping into another, shall in consequence of any law or regulation therein, be discharged from such service or labor, but shall be delivered up on claim of the party to whom such service or labor may be due.]

SECTION 3. NEW STATES AND TERRITORIES

1. Admission of new states. New states may be admitted by the Congress into this Union; but no new state shall be formed or erected within the jurisdiction of any other state; nor any state be formed by the junction of two or more states, or parts of states, without the consent of the legislatures of the states concerned as well as of the Congress.

2. Powers of Congress over territories and other property. The Congress shall have power to dispose of and make all needful rules and regulations respecting the territory or other property belonging to the United States; and nothing in this Constitution shall be so construed as to prejudice any claims of the United States, or of any particular state.

SECTION 4. GUARANTEES TO THE STATES

The United States shall guarantee to every state in this Union a republican form of government, and shall protect each of them against invasion; and on application of the legislature, or of the executive (when the legislature cannot be convened) against domestic violence.

HOW THE CONSTITUTION MAY BE AMENDED

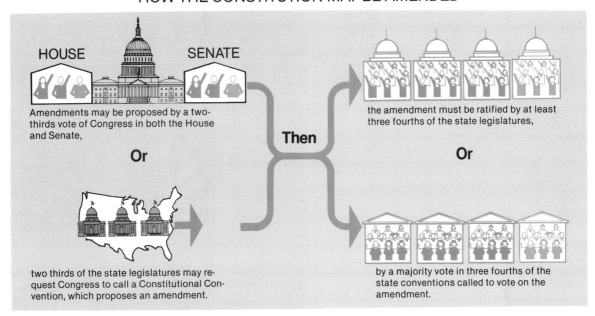

HOUSE **SENATE**

Amendments may be proposed by a two-thirds vote of Congress in both the House and Senate,

Or

two thirds of the state legislatures may request Congress to call a Constitutional Convention, which proposes an amendment.

Then

the amendment must be ratified by at least three fourths of the state legislatures,

Or

by a majority vote in three fourths of the state conventions called to vote on the amendment.

ARTICLE 5.
METHODS OF AMENDMENT

The Congress, whenever two thirds of both houses shall deem it necessary, shall propose amendments to this Constitution, or, on the application of the legislatures of two thirds of the several states, shall call a convention for proposing amendments, which, in either case, shall be valid to all intents and purposes, as part of this Constitution, when ratified by the legislatures of three fourths of the several states, or by conventions in three fourths thereof, as the one or the other mode of ratification may be proposed by the Congress; provided that [no amendments which may be made prior to the year 1808 shall in any manner affect the first and fourth clauses in the Ninth Section of the First Article; and that] no state, without its consent, shall be deprived of its equal suffrage in the Senate.

ARTICLE 6.
GENERAL PROVISIONS

1. Public debts. All debts contracted and engagements entered into, before the adoption of this Constitution, shall be as valid against the United States under this Constitution, as under the Confederation.

¶ One of the most important features of the Constitution is that it can be amended, or changed. This adaptability is one of the four main principles of the Constitution. ¶ An amendment must first be *proposed* and then *ratified*. There are four methods of amending the Constitution. So far, all amendments have been proposed by Congress and ratified by state legislatures except Amendment 21, which was ratified by the convention method. ¶ The fact that only 26 amendments have been adopted since 1789—and only 16 since 1791—indicates that it is not easy to change the Constitution, and that changing it is a serious matter, requiring much thought and discussion in Congress, in the state legislatures, and among the people. ¶ Notice that there are two areas in which the Constitution cannot be amended under any circumstances. The first exception is obsolete because it is a reference to the period that preceded 1808. The second exception is still very important because it guarantees that every state shall have equal representation in the Senate.

¶ *Clause 1.* This provision was important because it announced to all that the new government would assume and pay back all debts of the government under the Articles of Confederation. It was one of several actions favored by Alexander Hamilton and undertaken by Congress in order to establish the credit of the new government.

185

¶ *Clause 2.* This is the famous "supremacy clause" of the Constitution. It declares that the "supreme law of the land" is (1) the Constitution, (2) the laws of the United States passed under this Constitution, and (3) the treaties made under the authority of the United States. ¶ According to the supremacy clause, the power of the national government is superior to the power of the state governments, provided that its actions are in accordance with the Constitution. The Supreme Court determines whether the actions of the President and Congress are constitutional.

¶ *Clause 3.* No religious qualification shall ever be required as a condition for holding public office. This provision results from the fact that in the United States there is separation of church and state. This means that a person's religion is supposed to remain a private matter, with no bearing on consideration for public office.

¶ The Constitutional Convention was summoned by the Congress of the Confederation to amend the Articles of Confederation. Under the Articles amendments had to be approved by all thirteen states. Instead of amending the Articles, however, the delegates to the Constitutional Convention drafted an entirely new plan of government. Realizing that it would be difficult to get the approval of all the states—Rhode Island, for example, had not even sent delegates to Philadelphia—the framers provided that the Constitution would go into effect after ratification by only nine states, not thirteen. As a result opponents of the Constitution said it had been adopted by revolutionary means.

2. The supreme law. This Constitution, and the laws of the United States which shall be made in pursuance thereof, and all treaties made, or which shall be made, under the authority of the United States, shall be the supreme law of the land; and the judges in every state shall be bound thereby, anything in the constitution or laws of any state to the contrary notwithstanding.

3. Oaths of office. The Senators and Representatives before mentioned, and the members of the several state legislatures, and all executive and judicial officers, both of the United States and of the several states, shall be bound by oath or affirmation, to support this Constitution; but no religious test shall ever be required as a qualification to any office or public trust under the United States.

ARTICLE 7. RATIFICATION

The ratification of the convention of nine states shall be sufficient for the establishment of the Constitution between the states so ratifying the same.

DONE in Convention by the unanimous consent of the States present the seventeenth day of September in the year of our Lord one thousand seven hundred and eighty-seven and of the independence of the United States of America the twelfth. In witness whereof we have hereunto subscribed our names.

G Washington —*President and deputy from Virginia*

NEW HAMPSHIRE

John Langdon
Nicholas Gilman

MASSACHUSETTS

Nathaniel Gorman
Rufus King

CONNECTICUT

William Samuel Johnson
Roger Sherman

NEW YORK

Alexander Hamilton

NEW JERSEY

William Livingston
David Brearley
William Paterson
Jonathan Dayton

PENNSYLVANIA

Benjamin Franklin
Thomas Mifflin
Robert Morris
George Clymer
Thomas FitzSimons
Jared Ingersoll
James Wilson
Gouverneur Morris

DELAWARE

George Read
Gunning Bedford
John Dickinson
Richard Bassett
Jacob Broom

MARYLAND

James McHenry
Daniel of St. Thomas Jenifer
Daniel Carroll

VIRGINIA

John Blair
James Madison

NORTH CAROLINA

William Blount
Richard Dobbs Spaight
Hugh Williamson

SOUTH CAROLINA

John Rutledge
Charles Cotesworth Pinckney
Charles Pinckney
Pierce Butler

GEORGIA

William Few
Abraham Baldwin

Amendments to the Constitution

(The first ten amendments to the Constitution are called the Bill of Rights. The Bill of Rights limits the powers of the federal government but not the powers of the states. The Supreme Court has ruled, however, that the "due process" clause of Amendment 14 protects individuals against denial by the states of certain rights included in the Bill of Rights. For example, the Supreme Court has decided that neither the federal government nor the states can deprive any individual of freedom of religion, speech, press, petition, assembly, or of several other rights that pertain to the fair treatment of an accused person.)

AMENDMENT 1.
FREEDOM OF RELIGION, SPEECH, PRESS, ASSEMBLY, AND PETITION (1791)

Congress shall make no law respecting an establishment of religion, or prohibiting the free exercise thereof; or abridging the freedom of speech, or of the press; or the right of the people peaceably to assemble, and to petition the government for a redress of grievances.

¶ Amendment 1 protects five great civil liberties: (1) Freedom of religion means that Congress cannot interfere with the right to worship as one sees fit. The Supreme Court, however, has ruled that Congress can require "conscientious objectors" to bear arms during wartime. Congress has, however, made special provisions to permit conscientious objectors to participate in war work without bearing arms. In interpreting the phrase "establishment of religion," the Supreme Court has decided that this phrase erects a wall of separation between church and state. The Supreme Court has prohibited state and local school authorities from requiring prayers or devotional reading of the Bible in public schools. (2) Freedom of speech means the right to speak out privately and publicly. However, this right does not permit anyone to slander people (make false and malicious remarks about them). Furthermore, the Supreme Court has declared that freedom of speech can be limited by the federal government if there is a "clear and present" danger that what is said may injure the general welfare. (3) Freedom of the press gives newspapers, television, and magazines the right to express ideas and opinions provided they do not libel people (publish false and malicious remarks about them) or incite the violent overthrow of the government. Also, the use of the United States mails may be denied to those publications that spread obscenity and fraudulent ideas. (4) Freedom to assemble is the right to attend meetings and join clubs. (5) The right to petition for redress of grievances means the opportunity to express complaints to any official of the federal government.

AMENDMENT 2.
RIGHT TO KEEP ARMS (1791)

A well-regulated militia, being necessary to the security of a free state, the right of the people to keep and bear arms shall not be infringed.

¶ The purpose of this amendment was to prevent Congress from denying states the right to have a militia (or National Guard) of armed citizens. It also protected Americans' right to keep weapons in order to resist a tyrannical government. In the public interest, however, Congress and many states have regulated the ownership and use of weapons by citizens through gun control legislation.

AMENDMENT 3.
QUARTERING OF TROOPS (1791)

No soldier shall, in time of peace, be quartered in any house, without the consent of the owner; nor in time of war, but in a manner to be prescribed by law.

¶ Amendments 3 and 4 guarantee all citizens the right to privacy and security in their own homes. ¶ Amendment 3 was designed to prevent the national government from requiring citizens to house and feed military personnel in their homes. The quartering of troops in the colonists' homes by the British government had been a source of friction between the American colonists and the British before the American Revolution.

¶ With the hated writs of assistance still fresh in their minds, the supporters of this amendment aimed to limit issuance of search warrants to the following conditions: (1) The warrant must be issued by a judge. (2) There must be a good reason for its use. (3) The officer who asks for a search warrant must take an oath affirming reasons for demanding the warrant. (4) The warrant must describe the place to be searched and the persons or things to be seized. ¶ The Supreme Court has decided that evidence illegally seized cannot be used in either federal or state courts. Under this amendment the federal government prohibits wiretapping unless a court permit is obtained showing a reasonable certainty that one of a certain list of crimes is being committed. ¶ In 1967 the Supreme Court held that eavesdropping and bugging by electronic means are permissible but only within certain limits; for example, police may use electronic eavesdropping devices if they secure a warrant in advance by showing probable cause. ¶ In 1968 the Supreme Court forbade the use of criminal evidence obtained by police listening in on a party line, but evidence derived from wiretapping is permitted in federal courts in some crimes.

¶ This amendment lists the rights of an accused person: (1) A person accused of a capital crime or any other serious crime must first be accused by a grand jury (a jury of 12 to 23 persons) before being brought to trial. An indictment or presentment by a grand jury is merely a formal accusation. (2) A person cannot be tried twice for the same crime. (3) A person cannot be required to give incriminating testimony in a courtroom or before a grand jury or Congressional committee. However, under the Immunity Act of 1954, a witness can be required to testify in certain cases if the evidence he or she may provide cannot be used in any trial of that person. (4) A person cannot be deprived of life, liberty, or property without due process of law – or according to the law of the land. (5) Congress cannot take private property for public use without paying a fair price for it. This provision, an important protection of property rights, establishes the principle of eminent domain. ¶ Members of the armed forces are tried by military courts and commissions and are not subject to the provision calling for indictment by a grand jury.

¶ This amendment continues the rights of an accused person. Notice that all witnesses against an accused person must appear on the witness stand, and that the government must help the accused to produce favorable witnesses. If an accused person cannot afford to hire a lawyer, the judge will assign one, and the government will pay the lawyer's fee. These provisions under Amendment 6 apply to federal courts. However, under the "due process" clause of Amendment 14, the Supreme Court has decided that state courts must also assign a lawyer to defend an accused person who cannot afford one.

AMENDMENT 4.
SEARCH AND SEIZURE; WARRANTS (1791)

The right of the people to be secure in their persons, houses, papers, and effects, against unreasonable searches and seizures, shall not be violated; and no warrants shall issue but upon probable cause, supported by oath or affirmation, and particularly describing the place to be searched, and the person or things to be seized.

AMENDMENT 5.
RIGHTS OF ACCUSED PERSONS (1791)

No person shall be held to answer for a capital, or otherwise infamous, crime, unless on a presentment or indictment of a grand jury, except in cases arising in the land or naval forces, or in the militia, when in actual service in time of war or public danger; nor shall any person be subject for the same offense to be twice put in jeopardy of life and limb; nor shall be compelled, in any criminal case, to be a witness against himself; nor be deprived of life, liberty, or property, without due process of law; nor shall private property be taken for public use, without just compensation.

AMENDMENT 6.
RIGHT TO SPEEDY TRIAL (1791)

In all criminal prosecutions, the accused shall enjoy the right to a speedy and public trial, by an impartial jury of the state and district wherein the crime shall have been committed, which district shall have been previously ascertained by law, and to be informed of the nature and cause of the accusation; to be confronted with the witnesses against him; to have compulsory process for obtaining witnesses in his favor, and to have the assistance of counsel for his defense.

AMENDMENT 7.
JURY TRIAL IN CIVIL CASES
(1791)

In suits at common law, where the value in controversy shall exceed $20, the right of trial by jury shall be preserved, and no fact tried by a jury shall be otherwise re-examined in any court of the United States than according to the rules of the common law.

¶ This amendment provides for a jury trial in federal civil cases (trials where one person sues another) in which more than $20 is involved. By custom, however, civil cases are not tried before federal courts unless they involve much larger sums of money.

AMENDMENT 8.
BAILS, FINES, PUNISHMENTS
(1791)

Excessive bail shall not be required, nor excessive fines imposed, nor cruel and unusual punishments inflicted.

¶ Persons accused of a crime and awaiting trial may be permitted to leave jail if they or someone else posts bail—a sum of money serving as a guarantee that the accused will appear for trial. The courts determine the amount of bail asked for. Cruel and unusual punishments, such as torture and beheading, are prohibited. ¶ In a series of rulings, the Supreme Court declared invalid convictions of accused persons based on confessions secured by torture or other "third degree" methods.

AMENDMENT 9.
POWERS RESERVED
TO THE PEOPLE (1791)

The enumeration in the Constitution, of certain rights, shall not be construed to deny or disparage others retained by the people.

¶ The Constitution does not describe specifically all the rights to be retained by the people. This amendment was added in order to guarantee that those fundamental rights not enumerated must be respected by the national government at all times.

AMENDMENT 10.
POWERS RESERVED
TO THE STATES (1791)

The powers not delegated to the United States by the Constitution, nor prohibited by it to the states, are reserved to the states respectively, or to the people.

¶ This is known as the reserved power amendment. Powers delegated to the national government are listed in Article 1, Section 8. Powers prohibited to the states are found in Article 1, Section 10. Amendment 10 makes it clear that all other powers—the so-called reserved powers—are left to the states or to the people.

AMENDMENT 11.
SUITS AGAINST STATES (1798)

The judicial power of the United States shall not be construed to extend to any suit in law or equity, commenced or prosecuted against one of the United States, by citizens of another state, or by citizens or subjects of any foreign state.

¶ This is the first amendment to the Constitution that was designed to overrule a Supreme Court decision. In the case of *Chisholm v. Georgia* (1793), the Supreme Court ruled that two citizens of South Carolina could sue Georgia in a federal court for property that Georgia had confiscated. The states objected, arguing that since the states were sovereign, it was undignified to permit a state to be sued by a citizen of another state in a federal court. As a result of this amendment, a citizen of the United States or of a foreign nation who wishes to bring suit against any state is required to introduce the case in the courts of the state that is being sued.

¶ This amendment alters Article 2, Section 1, Clause 3. Before this amendment the electors voted for two persons, without designating which was to be President and which Vice-President. As a result in 1796 the people elected a Federalist President (John Adams) and a Republican Vice-President (Jefferson). In 1800 the electors of the victorious Republican Party each cast one vote for Jefferson, whom they wanted to be President, and one vote for Burr, whom they wanted to be Vice-President. The result, of course, was a tie. Amendment 12, which instructs electors to cast separate ballots for President and Vice-President, prevents such situations. (See also Amendment 23, which makes provision for choosing electors of President and Vice-President by the District of Columbia.)

AMENDMENT 12. ELECTION OF PRESIDENT AND VICE-PRESIDENT (1804)

The electors shall meet in their respective states, and vote by ballot for President and Vice-President, one of whom, at least, shall not be an inhabitant of the same state with themselves; they shall name in their ballots the person voted for as President, and in distinct ballots the person voted for as Vice-President, and they shall make distinct lists of all persons voted for as President, and of all persons voted for as Vice-President, and of the number of votes for each, which lists they shall sign and certify, and transmit, sealed, to the seat of government of the United States, directed to the President of the Senate; the President of the Senate shall, in the presence of the Senate and House of Representatives, open all the certificates and the votes shall then be counted; the person having the greatest number of votes for President shall be the President, if such number be a majority of the whole number of electors appointed; and if no person have such majority, then from the persons having the highest numbers not exceeding three on the list of those voted for as President, the House of Representatives shall choose immediately, by ballot, the President. But in choosing the President, the votes shall be taken by states, the representation from each state having one vote; a quorum for this purpose shall consist of a member or members from two thirds of the states, and a majority of all the states shall be necessary to a choice. [And if the House of Representatives shall not choose a President whenever the right of choice shall devolve upon them, before the fourth day of March next following, then the Vice-President shall act as President, as in the case of the death or other constitutional disability of the President.] The person having the greatest number of votes as Vice-President, shall be the Vice-President, if such number be a majority of the whole number of electors appointed, and if no person have a majority, then, from the two highest numbers on the list, the Senate shall choose the Vice-President; a quorum for the purpose shall consist of two thirds of the whole number of Senators, and a majority of the whole number shall be necessary to a choice. But no person constitutionally ineligible to the office of President shall be eligible to that of Vice-President of the United States.

HOW A PRESIDENT IS ELECTED

TIME SEQUENCE			

STATE PRIMARIES   **STATE CAUCUSES**   **STATE PARTY LEADERS**

WINTER AND SPRING OF ELECTION YEAR

In some states political parties hold primaries and caucuses to choose delegates to their national conventions. In other states party leaders choose these delegates.

SUMMER OF ELECTION YEAR

REPUBLICAN NATIONAL CONVENTION

The delegates to the Republican National Convention nominate candidates for President and Vice-President and adopt a platform on which they run.

DEMOCRATIC NATIONAL CONVENTION

The delegates to the Democratic National Convention nominate candidates for President and Vice-President and adopt a platform on which they run.

BEFORE ELECTION

STATE REPUBLICAN HEADQUARTERS

The Republican Party in each state chooses electors who promise to vote for the party's candidates for President and Vice-President. The number of electors chosen is equal to the number of the state's Senators and Representatives.

STATE DEMOCRATIC HEADQUARTERS

The Democratic Party in each state chooses electors who promise to vote for the party's candidates for President and Vice-President. The number of electors chosen is equal to the number of the state's Senators and Representatives.

ELECTION DAY (NOVEMBER)

In voting for a Presidential nominee, the voters actually vote for the electors of the nominee's party. This is the popular vote.

IF PARTY WINS...   **IF PARTY WINS...**

DECEMBER

In each state the electors of the party with the greatest popular vote assemble at the state capital. There they vote separately for Presidential and Vice-Presidential candidates, usually those of their own party. This is the electoral vote. Certified copies of the vote are sent to the President of the United States Senate.

JANUARY

The President of the Senate counts the electoral votes in the presence of both houses of Congress.

To be elected, a candidate must receive a majority of the electoral vote.

¶ Amendments 13, 14, and 15 resulted from the Civil War. Amendment 13 freed the slaves, Amendment 14 made blacks citizens, and Amendment 15 forbade the states to deny black Americans the right to vote. ¶ Amendment 13 forbids slavery, and under Section 2, Congress has the power to enforce this order.

¶ This section contains a number of important provisions. By the definition of citizenship given here, black Americans were granted citizenship. The second sentence, forbidding states to abridge the privileges and immunities—the rights—of citizens, meant that the states could not interfere with the right of black Americans and other citizens to live a peaceful, useful life or to travel. ¶ This amendment, like Amendment 5, contains a "due process of law" clause. Amendment 5 denies to Congress and Amendment 14 denies to the states the power to deprive any person of life, liberty, or property without due process of law. This amendment, originally intended to protect black citizenship, has been broadly interpreted by the courts as a protection for corporations. Corporations, under this interpretation, are considered as persons. Their property cannot be taken away except by fair, legal methods. Thus, for example, the Interstate Commerce Commission can fix railroad rates only after giving railroad corporations an opportunity to present their side of the case. ¶ The "due process" clause also protects individuals from unfair actions by their state governments. It protects their rights of freedom of religion, speech, press, petition, and peaceful assembly and the rights of persons accused of crimes against state abuses. It prevents a state, in the exercise of its police power (the power to protect its people), from depriving anyone of civil liberties, except during a national emergency. ¶ The last provision of Section 1 prevents a state from denying equal protection of the laws. In 1954, in the case of *Brown v. Board of Education of Topeka,* the Supreme Court interpreted this provision to mean that segregation in public schools is unconstitutional. Also, in *Baker v. Carr* (1962) the Supreme Court ruled that unfair apportionment of representation in state legislatures violates the "equal protection" clause of this amendment.

¶ This section was never implemented, but later civil rights laws and Amendment 24 guaranteed the vote to black Americans. Amendment 19 gave women the right to vote. The Dawes Act and the 1924 citizenship law enfranchised Indians. And Amendment 26 changed the voting age from 21 to 18. This section dealing with apportionment of Representatives is sometimes called the "dead letter clause" of Amendment 14 since its provisions were never carried out.

AMENDMENT 13.
SLAVERY ABOLISHED (1865)

SECTION 1. Neither slavery nor involuntary servitude, except as a punishment for crime whereof the party shall have been duly convicted, shall exist within the United States, or any place subject to their jurisdiction.

SECTION 2. Congress shall have power to enforce this article by appropriate legislation.

AMENDMENT 14.
RIGHTS OF CITIZENS (1868)

SECTION 1. Citizenship defined. All persons born or naturalized in the United States and subject to the jurisdiction thereof, are citizens of the United States and of the state wherein they reside. No state shall make or enforce any law which shall abridge the privileges or immunities of citizens of the United States; nor shall any state deprive any person of life, liberty, or property, without due process of law; nor deny to any person within its jurisdiction the equal protection of the laws.

SECTION 2. Apportionment of Representatives. Representatives shall be apportioned among the several states according to their respective numbers, counting the whole number of persons in each state [excluding Indians not taxed]. But when the right to vote at any election for the choice of electors for President and Vice-President of the United States, Representatives in Congress, the executive and judicial officers of a state, or the members of the legislature thereof, is denied to any of the [male] inhabitants of such state, [being twenty-one years of age] and citizens of the United States, or in any way abridged, except for participation in rebellion, or other crime, the basis of representation therein shall be reduced in the proportion which the number of such [male] citizens shall bear to the whole number of male citizens [twenty-one years of age] in such state.

SECTION 3. Disability for engaging in insurrection. No person shall be a Senator or Representative in Congress, or elector of President and Vice-President, or hold any office, civil or military, under the United States, or under any state, who, having previously taken an oath, as a member of Congress, or as an officer of the United States, or as a member of any state legislature, or as an executive or judicial officer of any state, to support the Constitution of the United States, shall have engaged in insurrection or rebellion against the same, or given aid or comfort to the enemies thereof. But Congress may, by vote of two thirds of each house, remove such disability.

¶ This section aimed to punish the leaders of the Confederacy for having broken their oath to support the Constitution of the United States. All officials who had taken this oath and who later joined the Confederacy in the Civil War were disqualified from holding federal or state offices. Although many southern leaders were excluded under this section from holding office after the war, by 1872 most of them were permitted to return to political life. In 1898 all of the others were pardoned.

SECTION 4. Public debt. The validity of the public debt of the United States, authorized by law, including debts incurred for payment of pensions and bounties for services in suppressing insurrection or rebellion, shall not be questioned. But neither the United States nor any state shall assume or pay any debt or obligation incurred in aid of insurrection or rebellion against the United States [or any claim for the loss or emancipation of any slave]; but all such debts, obligations, and claims shall be held illegal and void.

¶ This section makes three important points: (1) The public debt of the United States incurred in fighting the Civil War was valid and could never be questioned by southerners. (2) The Confederate debt was void. It was illegal for the federal government or the states to pay any money on Confederate debts. This provision was meant to serve as a harsh lesson to all who had invested money in Confederate bonds. (3) No payment was to be made for the loss of former slaves.

SECTION 5. Enforcement. The Congress shall have power to enforce, by appropriate legislation, the provisions of this article.

AMENDMENT 15.
RIGHT OF SUFFRAGE (1870)

¶ The purpose of this amendment was to extend the *franchise,* or the right to vote, to blacks. Thus, according to this amendment, any person who can meet all of the qualifications for suffrage in a particular state cannot be deprived of the right to vote simply because of race or color.

SECTION 1. The right of citizens of the United States to vote shall not be denied or abridged by the United States or any state on account of race, color, or previous condition of servitude.

SECTION 2. The Congress shall have power to enforce this article by appropriate legislation.

¶ In 1894 Congress passed an income tax law. The following year the Supreme Court declared this tax law unconstitutional. The Court stated that the income tax was a direct tax and, therefore, according to the Constitution (Article 1, Section 2, Clause 3; Article 1, Section 9, Clause 4) should have been apportioned among the states according to their population. This decision was unpopular because it prevented the government from taxing people on the basis of their incomes in order to pay for government expenses, which were already large and growing larger. Amendment 16 overruled the Supreme Court decision and gave Congress the power to tax incomes from any source and without apportionment among the states according to population. Today income taxes are the federal government's major source of income.

¶ Before the passage of this amendment, Senators were chosen by the state legislatures (see Article 1, Section 3, Clause 1). There was a great deal of dissatisfaction with this method because it gave the voters little control over the Senate. Amendment 17 provides for the direct election of Senators by the voters of each state, thus making Senators more responsive to the will of the voters who put them in office.

¶ This amendment outlawed the making, sale, or transportation of alcoholic beverages in the United States except for special purposes. This amendment was later repealed by Amendment 21.

AMENDMENT 16.
INCOME TAX (1913)

The Congress shall have power to lay and collect taxes on incomes, from whatever source derived, without apportionment among the several states, and without regard to any census or enumeration.

AMENDMENT 17.
ELECTION OF SENATORS (1913)

SECTION 1. Method of election. The Senate of the United States shall be composed of two Senators from each state, elected by the people thereof, for six years; and each Senator shall have one vote. The electors in each state shall have the qualifications requisite for electors of the most numerous branch of the state legislatures.

SECTION 2. Filling vacancies. When vacancies happen in the representation of any state in the Senate, the executive authority of such state shall issue writs of election to fill such vacancies: *Provided* that the legislature of any state may empower the executive thereof to make temporary appointments until the people fill the vacancies by election as the legislature may direct.

[**SECTION 3. Not retroactive.** This amendment shall not be so construed as to affect the election or term of any Senator chosen before it becomes valid as part of the Constitution.]

AMENDMENT 18.
NATIONAL PROHIBITION (1919)

[**SECTION 1.** After one year from the ratification of this article the manufacture, sale, or transportation of intoxicating liquors within, the importation thereof into, or the exportation thereof from, the United States and all territory subject to the jurisdiction thereof for beverage purposes is hereby prohibited.

SECTION 2. The Congress and the several states shall have concurrent power to enforce this article by appropriate legislation.

SECTION 3. This article shall be inoperative unless it shall have been ratified as an amendment to the Constitution by the legislatures of the several states, as provided in the Constitution, within seven years from the date of the submission hereof to the states by the Congress.]

AMENDMENT 19.
WOMAN SUFFRAGE (1920)

SECTION 1. The right of citizens of the United States to vote shall not be denied or abridged by the United States or by any state on account of sex.

SECTION 2. Congress shall have power to enforce this article by appropriate legislation.

¶ This amendment, extending the right to vote to all qualified women, marked the greatest single step in extending the suffrage in the United States. Women's struggle to win this basic right began many years before Amendment 19 was finally ratified.

AMENDMENT 20.
"LAME DUCK" AMENDMENT (1933)

SECTION 1. Beginning of terms. The terms of the President and Vice-President shall end at noon on the 20th day of January, and the terms of Senators and Representatives at noon on the 3rd day of January, of the years in which such terms would have ended if this article had not been ratified; and the terms of their successors shall then begin.

SECTION 2. Beginning of Congressional sessions. The Congress shall assemble at least once in every year, and such meeting shall begin at noon on the 3d day of January, unless they shall by law appoint a different day.

SECTION 3. Presidential succession. If at the time fixed for the beginning of the term of the President, the President-elect shall have died, the Vice-President-elect shall become President. If a President shall not have been chosen before the time fixed for the beginning of his term, or if the President-elect shall have failed to qualify, then the Vice-President-elect shall act as President until a President shall have qualified; and the Congress may by law provide for the case wherein neither a President-elect nor a Vice-President-elect shall have qualified, declaring who shall then act as President, or the manner in which one who is to act shall be selected, and such person shall act accordingly until a President or Vice-President shall have qualified.

¶ When the Constitution was written, transportation and communication were so slow that a new President and new members of Congress elected in November could not reach the capital to take office until March 4. However, since sessions of Congress began in December, a session including newly elected members could not be held until 13 months after their election. Thus, even if a member running for reelection were defeated in November, he or she would serve in the session of Congress that began the month after this election and continue to serve several more months. Since defeated candidates had been rejected by the voters, they were called "lame ducks," suggesting that their political wings had been clipped. One purpose of Amendment 20 was to limit the term and power of lame duck members.

SECTION 4. Filling Presidential vacancy. The Congress may by law provide for the case of the death of any of the persons from whom the House of Representatives may choose a President whenever the right of choice shall have devolved upon them, and for the case of the death of any of the persons from whom the Senate may choose a Vice-President whenever the right of choice shall have devolved upon them.

[**SECTION 5. Effective date.** Sections 1 and 2 shall take effect on the 15th day of October following the ratification of this article.

SECTION 6. Time limit for ratification. This article shall be inoperative unless it shall have been ratified as an amendment to the Constitution by the legislatures of three fourths of the several states within seven years from the date of its submission.]

AMENDMENT 21.
REPEAL OF PROHIBITION (1933)

SECTION 1. The eighteenth article of amendment to the Constitution of the United States is hereby repealed.

SECTION 2. The transportation or importation into any state, territory, or possession of the United States for delivery or use therein of intoxicating liquors, in violation of the laws thereof, is hereby prohibited.

[**SECTION 3.** This article shall be inoperative unless it shall have been ratified as an amendment to the Constitution by conventions in the several states, as provided in the Constitution, within seven years from the date of the submission hereof to the states by the Congress.]

AMENDMENT 22.
TWO-TERM LIMIT FOR PRESIDENTS (1951)

SECTION 1. No person shall be elected to the office of the President more than twice, and no person who has held the office of President, or acted as President, for more than two years of a term to which some other person was elected President shall be elected to the office of the President more than once. [But this Article shall not apply to any

¶ This amendment, which repealed Amendment 18, was the only amendment ratified by special state conventions instead of state legislatures. Congress felt that a popular referendum (vote) would give the people a better chance to voice their opinions on prohibition. As in Amendments 18 and 20, Congress included a provision that the amendment, to become law, have a seven-year limit for ratification by the states.

¶ The original Constitution placed no limit on the number of terms a President could be elected to office. Washington and Jefferson, however, set a two-term precedent. In 1940 this tradition was broken when Franklin D. Roosevelt was elected for a third term, and in 1944, when he won a fourth term. The purpose of this amendment was to write the two-term precedent into law. The bracket portion was included so that the amendment would not apply to President Truman, who was in office at the time the amendment was ratified. Note that anyone who succeeds to the Presidency and completes less than two years of another person's term may be elected for two more terms.

196

person holding the office of President when this Article was proposed by the Congress, and shall not prevent any person who may be holding the office of President, or acting as President, during the term within which this Article becomes operative from holding the office of President or acting as President during the remainder of such term.]

[**SECTION 2.** This Article shall be inoperative unless it shall have been ratified as an amendment to the Constitution by the legislatures of three fourths of the several states within seven years from the date of its submission to the states by the Congress.]

AMENDMENT 23.
PRESIDENTIAL ELECTORS FOR DISTRICT OF COLUMBIA (1961)

SECTION 1. The District constituting the seat of Government of the United States shall appoint in such manner as the Congress may direct:

A number of electors of President and Vice-President equal to the whole number of Senators and Representatives in Congress to which the District would be entitled if it were a State, but in no event more than the least populous State; they shall be in addition to those appointed by the States, but they shall be considered, for the purposes of the election of President and Vice-President, to be electors appointed by a State; and they shall meet in the District and perform such duties as provided by the twelfth article of amendment.

SECTION 2. The Congress shall have power to enforce this article by appropriate legislation.

AMENDMENT 24.
POLL TAX BANNED IN NATIONAL ELECTIONS (1964)

SECTION 1. The right of citizens of the United States to vote in any primary or other election for President or Vice-President, for electors of President or Vice-President, or for Senator or Representative in Congress, shall not be denied or abridged by the United States or any state by reason of failure to pay any poll tax or other tax.

SECTION 2. The Congress shall have the power to enforce this article by appropriate legislation.

¶ Amendment 23 enabled residents of the District of Columbia to vote for President and Vice-President. In effect, it gave the capital city three members in the Electoral College, the same number elected by each of the six least populous states.

¶ This amendment forbade the collection of poll taxes—taxes persons had to pay before they were able to vote—as a requirement for voting in federal elections. (In 1964 five southern states still had poll taxes.) In 1966 the Supreme Court ruled that poll taxes were illegal as a requirement for voting in state and local elections as well.

197

¶ This amendment was intended to clarify Article 2, Section 1, Clause 6, particularly in the case of the temporary disability of a President. The problem of disability in office existed during the last part of President Wilson's term and occurred again when President Eisenhower was disabled by a heart attack. This amendment provided two ways (see sections 3 and 4) the Vice-President could assume the duties of the office of the President, as well as a procedure by which the President could again perform the duties of office when the disability ended.

¶ However, the first use of this amendment did not involve Presidential disability. It involved a Presidential resignation. In 1974 Richard M. Nixon became the first President in American history to resign from office. And Vice-President Gerald R. Ford, who succeeded as President, became the first person to become President without being first elected to that office or to the Vice-Presidency. ¶ This unique situation occurred in the following way. In 1973 Vice-President Spiro T. Agnew had resigned, and President Nixon had filled the vacancy according to the provisions of Section 2 of this amendment. Gerald R. Ford, a member of the House of Representatives, had been named Vice-President with the approval of Congress. Therefore when Nixon resigned as President during the Watergate scandal, Ford took over the Presidency. A vacancy then existed in the Vice-Presidency (see Section 2). President Ford named Nelson A. Rockefeller as Vice-President, and this nomination was also approved by a majority vote of both houses of Congress.

AMENDMENT 25.
PRESIDENTAL DISABILITY AND SUCCESSION (1967)

1. In case of the removal of the President from office or his death or resignation, the Vice-President shall become President.

2. Whenever there is a vacancy in the office of the Vice-President, the President shall nominate a Vice-President who shall take the office upon confirmation by a majority vote of both houses of Congress.

3. Whenever the President transmits to the President *pro tempore* of the Senate and the Speaker of the House of Representatives his written declaration that he is unable to discharge the powers and duties of his office, and until he transmits to them a written declaration to the contrary, such powers and duties shall be discharged by the Vice-President as Acting President.

4. Whenever the Vice-President and a majority of either the principal officers of the executive departments or of such other body as Congress may by law provide, transmit to the President *pro tempore* of the Senate and the Speaker of the House of Representatives their written declaration that the President is unable to discharge the powers and duties of his office, the Vice-President shall immediately assume the powers and duties of the office as Acting President.

Thereafter, when the President transmits to the President *pro tempore* of the Senate and the Speaker of the House of Representatives his written declaration that no inability exists, he shall resume the powers and duties of his office unless the Vice-President and a majority of either the principal officers of the executive department or of such other body as Congress may by law provide, transmit within four days to the President *pro tempore* of the Senate and the Speaker of the House of Representatives their written declaration that the President is unable to discharge the powers and duties of his office. Thereupon Congress shall decide the issue, assembling within 48 hours for that purpose if not in session. If the Congress, within 21 days after receipt of the latter written declaration, or, if Congress is not in session, within 21 days after Congress is required to assemble, determines by two-thirds vote of both houses that the President is unable to discharge the powers and duties of his office, the Vice-President shall continue to discharge the same as Acting President; otherwise, the President shall assume the powers and duties of his office.

AMENDMENT 26.
VOTING AGE LOWERED TO 18
(1971)

SECTION 1. The right of citizens of the United States, who are 18 years of age or older, to vote shall not be denied or abridged by the United States or any State on account of age.

SECTION 2. The Congress shall have the power to enforce this article by appropriate legislation.

¶ Congress, in the Voting Rights Act of 1970, had lowered the minimum voting age from 21 to 18, but the Supreme Court ruled that this law applied only to federal elections. Amendment 26 specified that 18 was the legal voting age in state, local, and federal elections.

PROPOSED AMENDMENT.
THE WOMEN'S RIGHTS
AMENDMENT

SECTION 1. Equality of rights under the law shall not be denied or abridged by the United States or by any State on account of sex.

SECTION 2. Congress shall have the power to enforce, by appropriate legislation, the provisions of this article.

¶ This amendment, submitted to the states for ratification in 1972, would prohibit discrimination based on a person's sex.

PROPOSED AMENDMENT.
REPRESENTATION FOR THE
DISTRICT OF COLUMBIA

1. For purposes of representation in the Congress, election of the President and Vice-President, and article 5 of this Constitution, the District constituting the seat of government of the United States shall be treated as though it were a State.

2. The exercise of the rights and powers conferred under this article shall be by the people of the District constituting the seat of government, and as shall be provided by the Congress.

3. The twenty-third article of amendment to the Constitution of the United States is hereby repealed.

¶ This amendment, proposed in 1978, would give the District of Columbia two Senators and one or two Representatives. The number of Presidential electors—three, at present—would be changed to the total number of Senators and Representatives. The District would also acquire the power of a state in amending the Constitution.

Unit Survey

For Further Inquiry

1. Why did the American Revolution occur? Give specific evidence to support your answer.
2. (a) Why were the Americans able to win the Revolution? (b) What handicaps did they face in their effort to win the war?
3. (a) Why did American leaders decide to write the Constitution? (b) How did the Constitution solve the problems that arose during the Confederation period?
4. In what ways does the Constitution reflect the reasons that Americans fought the Revolutionary War?
5. Alexander Hamilton told the Constitutional Convention, "Take mankind in general, they are vicious." How did Hamilton's view of the average person's basic nature influence his political beliefs?

Projects and Activities

1. Make a series of army recruiting posters that might have been used during the Revolution to encourage Americans to join the army.
2. Prepare a bulletin board display on the role of black Americans during the Revolution.
3. Write a skit dramatizing the meeting of the Stamp Act Congress. Be sure to present all of the points of view that would have been expressed at the Congress. You might want to act out the skit with some of your classmates.
4. Suppose you were a European political cartoonist in the 1780's. Create a series of a cartoons to illustrate your attitude toward the newly formed United States.
5. Conduct research and write a report on the legal and social status of women during the 1700's. (a) Did their status change during those years? (b) Did women's status vary according to location? (That is, was their status different in the North than in the South? Was it different in the cities than on the frontier?)
6. Timelines are often useful in illustrating cause-and-effect relationships. (a) Identify one example of a cause-and-effect relationship between two events listed on the timeline on this page. (b) Select five other events listed on the timeline. For each event, name another event (not necessarily on the timeline) that either helped to cause it or in part was caused by it.

Exploring Your Region

1. Read your state constitution. (a) In what ways is it similar to the United States Constitution? How is it different? (b) Find examples of powers that your state government shares with the federal government. (c) Find examples of powers that your state government has that the federal government does not. (d) Does your state government have a system of dividing powers between the state and local governments?
2. Investigate the early history of your state and prepare an oral report that explains (a) how it was first organized—as a colony or a territory of the United States, (b) under what circumstances it became a state, and (c) who were some of the important people who helped in the early development of the state.

Suggested Reading

1. *Autobiography*, Benjamin Franklin. The life story of this outstanding American.
2. *Book of the Revolution*, American Heritage. A general account of the Revolution, with lavish illustrations.
3. *The Great Rights of Mankind, a History of the American Bill of Rights*, Bernard Schwartz. A history of the origins of the Bill of Rights.
4. *Celia Garth*, Gwen Bristow. An exciting novel about a young seamstress in Charleston who serves the war effort by becoming a spy for the Continental army.
5. *Oliver Wiswell*, Kenneth Roberts. A novel of the Revolution from the Loyalist point of view.

Unit Three

Building the Nation

1789-1845

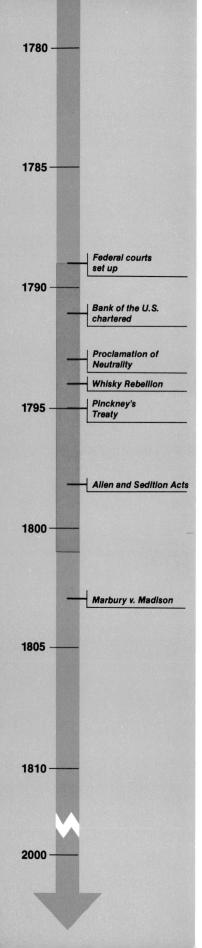

Federal courts set up

Bank of the U.S. chartered

Proclamation of Neutrality

Whisky Rebellion

Pinckney's Treaty

Allen and Sedition Acts

Marbury v. Madison

Chapter 9

A Strong Start for the Nation

1789–1801

It is April 30, 1789. At New York City, the temporary capital of the nation, a crowd has gathered in Wall Street to watch the inauguration of the first President of the United States. Above the crowd, on the balcony of Federal Hall, stands George Washington. Robert R. Livingston, Chancellor of the State of New York, administers the oath of office to him. For a moment there is silence, then a burst of cheers and applause breaks from the crowd below.

What thoughts may have passed through Washington's mind as he gazed down on the sea of faces and as the waves of sound rose around him?

Perhaps Washington weighed in his mind the chances for the new government's success. He knew that most people still thought of themselves as citizens of individual states—of New York, or Delaware, or Virginia—rather than as citizens of the United States. The people might now hail him as President of the United States, but Washington was fully aware that the United States was not yet a nation.

Indeed, many of Washington's close associates worried about the future of the new nation. John Adams, newly elected Vice-President, feared that the Republic might not last beyond his own lifetime. Alexander Hamilton had on one occasion felt that the Constitution was "frail and worthless." Washington himself was deeply concerned. The new President thought of the United States as an "experiment entrusted to the hands of the American people."

For better or worse, however, this great American experiment was now under way.

THE CHAPTER IN OUTLINE

1. The new federal government is organized.

2. Congress deals with the nation's money problems.

3. The national government adopts a foreign policy.

4. Political parties develop an active role.

5. The Federalist Party struggles to stay in power.

6. Federalist ideas and methods persist under the Republicans.

202

1 The new federal government is organized

Washington's trip from Mount Vernon, his home in Virginia, to New York City had been a triumph. All along his route crowds gathered to watch him pass, to cheer him, to scatter flowers in his path. His welcome in New York had been overwhelming.

Now the celebrations were over. President Washington and the other elected officials— Vice-President John Adams; the Senators, two from each state; and the 59 Representatives—had taken the oath to uphold the Constitution. Now they had to face the tasks of organizing the new government and of making it work.

Basic problems. To guide them, the newly elected federal officials had only the Constitution and their experience in the various colonial governments and in the Confederation. They had, as yet, no federal laws, no courts, no law-enforcement officers. They had to build everything from the ground up. Each act they took would establish a **precedent,** or model, for future action.

The new leaders also faced serious financial problems, but there was no federal treasury and no method for collecting taxes. Worse still, there was little money in the country with which the people could pay the taxes that the new government would have to levy. Finally, the new government owed a large debt from the Revolutionary War and from the government under the Confederation.

Difficult problems also lay ahead for the new nation in its relations with other nations. The President had to work out a foreign policy acceptable to Congress. He had to appoint diplomatic officials and instruct them in their duties. If trouble should arise, the President had little military strength to call upon. The navy built by the Continental Congress had been disbanded, and the army now included only some 600 officers and enlisted soldiers.

The Constitution gave the new government the power to deal with these and other problems. Dealing with them successfully would call for hard work and strong leadership by the President and Congress.

Congress goes to work. One of the first and most important measures Congress adopted was the Judiciary Act of 1789. The act established the basic structure of the federal court system. It provided for a Chief Justice

Americans cheered George Washington as he was rowed across the Hudson River to New York City on the last lap of the journey to his inauguration. His satin-trimmed barge had a crew of 13, one member for each state in the Union.

and five Associate Justices of the Supreme Court. The first Chief Justice appointed by the President and approved by the Senate was John Jay. The Judiciary Act also established thirteen district courts and three circuit courts.

The Judiciary Act gave the Supreme Court the power to declare void, or without force, state laws and decisions of state courts that violated the federal Constitution or laws and treaties made under it. If this power—the power of judicial review—had not been granted to the Supreme Court, each state would have been free to interpret federal laws in its own way. The United States would have been a league of **sovereign,** or independent, states, not a federal union. For this reason, the Judiciary Act was essential to building the federal system. Important though it was, the Judiciary Act did not definitely settle the question of state or federal sovereignty. As you will see, the issue remained to trouble the nation until it was finally decided by the tragedy of the Civil War.

The first Congress also took other important steps. It sent the Bill of Rights to the states to be ratified. It re-enacted, or passed for a second time, the Northwest Ordinance providing a government for the Northwest Territory. Mainly to raise revenue, it levied a small tariff on imports.

Creating a cabinet. Congress also created three executive departments to help President Washington with his work. The Department of State was created to help the President handle foreign and other affairs. The Department of the Treasury was set up to deal with financial problems, and the Department of War to manage military matters.

The heads of these departments came to be known as the President's **cabinet,** or advisers. However, the cabinet as it exists today was not officially recognized in law until 1907. The heads of these departments, called Secretaries, met with the President in informal meetings. The Secretaries, however, could only advise the President. Then, as now, the responsibility for making final decisions in the Executive Department rested with the President alone.

President Washington's first cabinet included Thomas Jefferson as Secretary of State, Alexander Hamilton as Secretary of the Treasury, and Henry Knox as Secretary of War. Washington also appointed Edmund Randolph as Attorney General. Randolph's responsibility

was to advise the President on matters of law. This was at first a part-time job. The Department of Justice was not created until 1870. Samuel Osgood received the appointment of Postmaster General.

SECTION SURVEY

IDENTIFY: Judiciary Act of 1789, Department of State, Department of the Treasury, Department of War, cabinet.

1. List the basic problems faced by the young republic in 1789 in (a) maintaining order, (b) regulating finances, and (c) developing a foreign policy.
2. What guidelines did the newly elected officials have for organizing the new government?
3. Describe the measures adopted by the first Congress in its efforts to solve the republic's problems.
4. How did the Judiciary Act help to prevent conflicts between federal and state governments?
5. Name the members of Washington's first cabinet and the positions they held.

2 Congress deals with the nation's money problems

Among the many problems faced by the new federal government, the most urgent was that of raising money. During the first year or two, the problem was exceptionally difficult.

The problem of finances. As one of its first acts, Congress adopted a small tariff on articles imported into the United States. Congress realized that the revenue from this tariff would not even begin to pay the expenses of running the new government. More money, much more, would have to come from other taxes. But what kind of taxes?

There was another big question. Where would the American people get the gold and silver coin or the paper money to pay their taxes? In 1789 there was very little currency in the United States. The Constitution gave Congress the power "to coin money," but where were the gold and silver to come from?

To find solutions to these and other financial problems, Congress turned to the new Secretary of the Treasury, Alexander Hamilton, for help. In turning to the Secretary of the Treasury, the first Congress set an important precedent. While Congress is responsible for passing laws, it has always relied heavily on the Executive Department both for advice and for guidance.

Repaying the war debt. Hamilton devised a program that would put the nation's finances on a sound basis. First, he asked Congress to establish the nation's credit by paying its debts. Hamilton knew that a nation, like an individual, must pay its debts or lose the trust of its neighbors and find it impossible to borrow in the future.

The United States and the separate states owed a combined war debt of over $80 million —a staggering sum for those days. Hamilton proposed to repay all of this debt.

Everybody agreed that the United States should pay $12 million owed to France, the Netherlands, and Spain. The United States therefore arranged to repay with interest, over a fixed period, the money that these countries had lent.

The domestic debt was another matter. Many members of Congress objected to Hamilton's proposal to repay $44 million borrowed from Americans during the course of the Revolutionary War.

The Continental Congress had borrowed this money by issuing paper money and selling **government bonds.** Government bonds are certificates issued by a government in exchange for a loan of money. Each certificate is a promise that the loan, plus interest, will in time be repaid. But, as you know, the government's credit during and after the war was so low that its paper money was "not worth a Continental." Government bonds were equally low in value. Many people who had originally held the bonds and paper money had sold them to speculators for a fraction of their original, or face, value.

Hamilton now proposed that the bonds and paper money be paid off at their original value. Hamilton's opponents objected. Why should the entire country pay out its hard-earned money to benefit a few speculators? However, Hamilton convinced Congress that if the nation's credit was to be established all debts must be paid.

The remainder of the total debt, about $25 million, was owed by several states to Ameri-

One of the earliest United States coins was called the Brasher doubloon (top). It was named for the goldsmith who made the first one in 1787. Later came other coins bearing a profile symbolizing Liberty.

205

The Washington, D.C., of the early 1800's was a rustic place. Here is a view of the Senate section of the Capitol. It would be several years before the great central dome would be built, joining it to the House of Representatives.

can citizens. Hamilton wanted the federal government to take over, or assume, this debt and pay back every penny the states owed. This proposal started a violent argument. States with small debts and states that had paid their war debts argued that it was unfair to force them to assume their neighbors' burdens. Southerners protested that most state bonds, too, were in the hands of speculators, who would profit at the expense of the people.

Defeat seemed certain, but at the last moment a compromise was arranged. In the Assumption Bill, southerners, led by Jefferson, agreed that the national government should assume the state debts. Northerners, led by Hamilton, agreed to vote for a bill to locate the new national capital on the banks of the Potomac River on land donated by Virginia and Maryland. The government was moved to the new capital, Washington, D.C., in 1800.

Hamilton's bank proposal. The second part of Hamilton's program called for Congress to pass a bill creating a **national bank,** to be called the Bank of the United States. By a national bank Hamilton did not mean just one bank, but a banking system. The system would consist of a large central bank with branch banks in major American cities.

Hamilton carefully pointed out the advantages of a national banking system. The branch banks would provide safe places for tax officials to deposit money collected from the people. When the government wanted to transfer money from one place to another, the branch banks could do this by sending checks. This would avoid the risk of actually shipping gold and silver. Moreover, when the central bank did not have as much money to lend as the government wanted to borrow, it could always turn to its branch banks for help.

Finally, the Bank of the United States would provide what Hamilton called "a sound, uniform currency." Currency would have the same value all over the country. People would have faith in paper money, or **bank notes,** bearing the name of the Bank of the United States. People would prefer these bank notes to the paper money printed by small local or state banks. As a result, Hamilton predicted, small, shaky banks would close down. Other banks would work hard to win the public's confidence. All this would be good for business—and for the country as a whole.

Adoption of the bank proposal. Hamilton's arguments in favor of a Bank of the United States were sound. His opponents, led by Jefferson, also had sound arguments.

First, according to Hamilton's proposal, the Bank of the United States would sell 25,000 shares of stock at $400 each. This amounted to a total **capital stock,** or money value, of $10 million. The government would buy one fifth of all the shares. The other four fifths would be bought by private investors, who would, of course, be wealthy Americans. Jefferson argued that this would give wealthy people control over the country's money power.

Jefferson also argued that a national bank would have an unfair advantage over local or state banks. Again he was right. All government funds would be deposited in the Bank of the United States and its branches. These funds could be loaned to individuals and businesses at a profit to the national bank. Private banks would thus have no opportunity to earn profits on the deposit and loan of government funds.

Finally, Jefferson claimed that the bank would be unconstitutional. The Constitution did not give the federal government power to create a bank. In reply, Hamilton pointed to the elastic clause of the Constitution. This clause gave Congress the right "to make all laws which shall be necessary and proper for carrying into execution the foregoing powers," including the power "to lay and collect taxes" and "to borrow money on the credit of the United States." Hamilton said that it was "necessary and proper" to create a bank that would help Congress collect taxes and borrow money.

Thus the arguments ran for and against Hamilton's proposal. In spite of heated debate in the cabinet, Washington leaned toward Hamilton's side. In 1791 Congress passed a bill granting a charter to the Bank of the United States despite strong opposition.

Hamilton's tariff proposal. The third part of Hamilton's financial program called on Congress to pass another tariff law. Congress earlier had levied a small tariff on imported goods, mainly to raise revenue. Now Hamilton proposed a new kind of tariff—what is now called a "protective" tariff.

The difference between a tariff to raise revenue and a protective tariff is one of purpose and therefore of rates. For example, Congress might place a low tariff, or duty, on a blanket manufactured in Great Britain. British manufacturers could pay the duty and still compete with American manufacturers for American trade. This would be a **revenue tariff.** Now imagine that Congress placed a very high tariff on each British-made blanket, perhaps as high as 100 percent of its value. Then the British-made blanket would have to be sold in the United States for at least twice what it cost the British manufacturer to make it. The British manufacturer could not sell blankets in America that would compete with those of American manufacturers. A tariff of this kind would not raise revenue for the government, since the British manufacturer would have to abandon the American market. However, it would protect American manufacturers from competition and thus be a **protective tariff.**

Congress did not even consider Hamilton's proposal for a protective tariff. Nevertheless, the proposal shows how Hamilton wanted to bind wealthy Americans—in this case, manufacturers—to the government by ties of self-interest. This proposal also reveals how well Hamilton understood the young nation's needs. He saw that the United States could not become truly independent until it could produce most of the goods that it needed.

The Whisky Rebellion. In a fourth proposal, Hamilton urged Congress to levy an **excise tax** on distilled liquors. All distillers would have to pay this tax on every gallon (3.8 liters) of liquor they produced and sold.

Congress passed the tax. For reasons that become clear when you picture the country as it was in the 1790's, the tax fell most heavily on the people living on the frontier.

In the 1790's the frontier was almost totally isolated from the settled areas along the Atlantic coast. Only the roughest of trails—for the most part the old Indian trails—connected the frontier with the eastern seaboard. As a result, frontier farmers could not transport their corn to markets in the settled areas. This was a major problem, for corn was the most impor-

George Caleb Bingham of Missouri was one of the great American painters of the West. Here he shows the crew of a flatboat, which may have been bound for New Orleans, taking time out for relaxation as they float downriver. A country fiddler, like the one on the right, was the mainstay of such frontier entertainment.

tant crop of the frontier farmers. Fortunately, there was an easy solution to the problem. The farmers built stills and converted the corn into whisky. Then they loaded the jugs and kegs of whisky on the backs of mules and drove the mules eastward to the markets. Whisky was the major source of cash for the frontier farmers, and it was whisky that was now being taxed by the federal government.

The freedom-loving frontier settlers refused to pay the tax. Federal marshalls tried to enforce the law, but armed groups of farmers drove them away. The governor of Pennsylvania at first refused to call out the militia to crush the uprising. In this so-called "Whisky Rebellion," frontier farmers challenged the power of the new federal government.

At Hamilton's urging, President Washington called out the militia from neighboring states. The rebellion melted away when 15,000 militiamen were sent to the scene. No lives were lost, but the federal government had demonstrated its strength.

Success for Hamilton's program. Hamilton's financial program proved a great success. By paying off its debts, the new government showed that it was powerful enough to meet its obligations. The national banking system provided a sound, uniform currency. The excise

tax brought a small amount of much-needed revenue. More important, it extended the influence of the government to the frontier.

To be sure, Hamilton's financial program put money into the pockets of the well-to-do. Americans who owned government bonds, who invested in the Bank of the United States, and who needed a sound, uniform currency were delighted. They became supporters of the new government.

Hamilton's financial program benefited not just the wealthy, but all Americans. It gave the United States a workable money system and a credit reputation that few of the older nations of Europe enjoyed.

SECTION SURVEY

IDENTIFY: government bonds, Assumption Bill, revenue tariff, protective tariff, Whisky Rebellion, excise tax.

1. (a) What precedent did the first Congress set when it asked Hamilton for advice on its financial problems? (b) What policies did Hamilton propose to solve these problems?

2. (a) Why did some Americans object to having Congress repay both national and state war debts to American citizens? (b) How were these issues resolved?

208

3. (a) What were Hamilton's arguments for a national bank? (b) Why did Jefferson oppose the national bank? (c) How did Hamilton justify the constitutionality of the bank?

4. (a) What were the causes of the Whisky Rebellion? (b) Of what significance was the role taken by the federal government in dealing with the rebellion?

5. Why was Hamilton's financial program a success?

3 The national government adopts a foreign policy

The United States was born in a world torn by revolution and warfare. The world situation greatly complicated the problems of the new government.

The French Revolution. Even while the first American Congress was gathering in the spring of 1789, a revolution broke out in France. The revolutionists were inspired by, and shared, some of the ideas expressed in the American Declaration of Independence. They expressed their goals in the ringing cry "liberty, equality, fraternity."

Unhappily, the revolution soon became a bloodbath. The revolutionists mobbed and beheaded thousands of people in the upper classes and nobility, including King Louis XVI and Queen Marie Antoinette. Thousands of other upper-class French men and women escaped to England and other neighboring countries. There, safe from the sharp blade of the guillotine, they laid their plans to regain control of France.

It was impossible for people in neighboring countries to remain indifferent. Many, particularly the ruling classes, were filled with horror. They feared that the example set by the French revolutionists might spread to their own countries. As a result, they were eager to see the revolution crushed. By 1793, in response to this widely expressed concern, the governments of Great Britain and other European countries were at war with what was now the Republic of France.

American reactions. American citizens did not remain untouched by the fires of revolution and warfare raging in Europe and on the seas. The French seized American ships carrying goods to Great Britain and its possessions. The British seized American ships carrying goods to France or its colonies. They also **impressed,** or kidnaped, American sailors to serve in the British navy.

American citizens took sides. Hamilton and his followers favored Great Britain, while Jefferson and his followers favored France.

What policy should the United States adopt? According to a treaty made with France in 1778, the United States was obliged to defend the French West Indies, but if the United States aided France, it would soon find itself at war with Great Britain. Such a war would be suicidal. The new nation was not prepared for armed conflict on either land or sea.

It was a grave situation that President Washington faced in April 1793 when the minister from France, Edmond Genêt (zheh·NAY), arrived in the United States. Genêt reminded Americans of the Treaty of 1778. He did not insist that America defend the French West Indies. He did, however, demand that the United States open its seaports to French naval vessels and privateers.

If the United States agreed to do as Genêt demanded, the American nation would be at war with Great Britain. Nevertheless, many Americans welcomed Genêt with enthusiasm. They urged President Washington to honor America's obligations to France. Other Americans, friendly to Great Britain, urged Washington to break all relations with France—an act that would invite war with our former ally.

President Washington ignored the pressures from both groups. Choosing a wiser course and backed unanimously by his cabinet, on April 22, 1793, he issued a Proclamation of Neutrality. The proclamation forbade American citizens to give active support on land or sea to any of the warring nations. Congress supported President Washington by passing a neutrality act.

War with Great Britain avoided. In spite of the neutrality act, the United States remained on the brink of war. Indeed, in 1793, conflict with Great Britain seemed certain.

To save its West Indian colonies from starvation, France for the first time permitted Americans to trade with the French West Indies. The British then seized American ships, claiming that trade not permitted in peacetime could not be carried on in wartime.

As American ships were seized and American sailors were impressed into the British navy, many Americans became increasingly angry. They began to drill on village greens, to fortify harbor entrances, and to build warships. In the midst of these war preparations, Congress closed all American ports and talked of forbidding Americans to buy British products.

In an effort to prevent war, President Washington sent Chief Justice of the Supreme Court John Jay to try to settle the outstanding differences between Great Britain and the United States. Jay was only partly successful. "Jay's Treaty," as the settlement was called, greatly disappointed many Americans.

In the treaty the British won the right to trade freely in all American ports. In return, they promised to withdraw their troops by 1796 from certain forts they continued to occupy on the northwestern frontier. They continued to insist upon the right of British fur traders to carry on their business in American territory. The important issue of impressment remained unsettled.

The more hot-headed Americans claimed that Jay had sold out to the British. Mobs burned Jay in effigy, but Jay had accomplished his major purpose. The treaty had prevented war with Great Britain. At the same time, it had prodded the Spaniards into actions that proved extremely helpful to the United States.

The end of differences with Spain. News of Jay's Treaty came as a blow to Spain. The Spaniards had just signed an agreement with the French Republic. Because of this agreement, the Spaniards faced a probable war with Great Britain. When the United States and

Great Britain settled their differences, Spain acted to insure American neutrality in the war that Spain and France were now waging against Great Britain.

In 1795, in a treaty negotiated by Thomas Pinckney, the Spaniards granted everything that Americans had been demanding since 1783. The treaty settled the dispute between the United States and Spain over boundaries between Florida and Georgia. Spain also agreed to curb Indian attacks upon settlements in Georgia and in the western lands. Even more important, Spain gave Americans the right to navigate the Mississippi River freely. This right allowed Americans to transfer goods at the port city of New Orleans from river boats to oceangoing ships without paying duties to Spain.

This right—the **right of deposit**—was especially important to western farmers. They floated their heavy products on rafts down the Ohio and the Mississippi to New Orleans. There they sold the products to ships bound for Europe or the Atlantic coast ports. After completing the sale, they broke up their rafts and sold the lumber.

Although this was a clumsy method of carrying on trade, it was cheaper than sending bulky goods by pack train directly to eastern markets. Pinckney's Treaty seemed to assure westerners that Spain would no longer threaten to close their vital trade route, the Mississippi River.

Washington's Farewell Address. In 1796 President Washington, refusing to serve a third term, prepared to return to Mount Vernon. During his two terms, he had helped to set the new nation on a solid foundation. His ad-

SOURCES

WASHINGTON'S
FAREWELL
ADDRESS
(1796)

The great rule of conduct for us in regard to foreign nations is in extending our commercial relations to have with them as little political connection as possible. So far as we have already formed engagements, let them be fulfilled with perfect good faith. . . .

Europe has a set of primary interests which to us have none or a very remote relation. Hence she must be engaged in frequent controversies, the causes of which are essentially foreign to our concerns. . . .

It is our true policy to steer clear of permanent alliances with any portion of the foreign world, so far, I mean, as we are now at liberty to do it. . . .

THE BATTLE OF FALLEN TIMBERS

Little Turtle, Black Wolf, Blue Jacket, Tecumseh, Turkey Foot, and many other Indian chiefs, with about 1,000 warriors at their sides, were confident of victory. Twice before they had defeated American armies in the Northwest Territory. Now, in the summer of 1794, they were well supplied with British guns and powder and shot, and the position they held was a natural fortress. Some years earlier, a tornado had roared along the crest of a hill, leaving behind it a long path of torn and twisted trees. In this wild tangle, the Indians took shelter and waited for the attack.

General "Mad Anthony" Wayne (so called because of his hot temper) was also confident of victory. Among the 2,000 troops he had trained and now commanded were several hundred mounted Kentucky riflemen, tough frontiersmen with long experience in Indian warfare. On August 20 the Americans struck swiftly. They first fired a volley and then charged with their bayonets. In less than an hour the battle was over, and the Indians had been scattered.

The Battle of Fallen Timbers, as it has since been called, brought an end to almost twenty years of Indian warfare. For the first time since the Revolutionary War, peace came to the frontier. When the British finally withdrew from the forts they had been holding in American territory, the vast region beyond the Appalachians was open to settlement.

ministration had organized the machinery of government. It had avoided war with Great Britain and France and had settled the long-standing argument with Spain. These were solid accomplishments.

Nevertheless, Washington was troubled. Disliking political factions, he was troubled by the sharp, often bitter arguments between Hamilton and his followers and Jefferson and his followers. Washington was also troubled about the relations of the United States with other countries.

In his Farewell Address to Congress, Washington urged the American people to avoid the formation of political parties. He also warned them to avoid "permanent alliances" with "any portion of the foreign world." Washington feared that such foreign alliances might prevent the United States government from acting in its own best interests.

SECTION SURVEY

IDENTIFY: impressment, neutrality, Jay's Treaty, Thomas Pinckney, right of deposit.

1. (a) How did the French Revolution affect the political situation in Europe in the early 1790's? (b) How did this situation in turn affect the policies of Great Britain and France toward America?

2. What positions did Jefferson and Hamilton advocate in America's relations toward France and Great Britain?

3. How were America's relations toward France and Great Britain redefined by (a) the Treaty of Neutrality and (b) Jay's Treaty?

4. (a) Summarize the provisions of Pinckney's Treaty. (b) Why was the treaty important?

5. Source Study: According to the Source on page 210, what economic and political policy did Washington urge in America's dealings with foreign nations?

211

Political parties develop an active role

The Constitution said nothing about the political parties that Washington had warned against. As early as the Presidential election of 1792, however, something resembling two major parties appeared in American politics. These parties centered around Alexander Hamilton and Thomas Jefferson.

Rise of the two-party system. In the election of 1792, Washington was re-elected by unanimous vote. Vice-President John Adams was also re-elected but against strong opposition. He was opposed by George Clinton of New York, a candidate backed by Thomas Jefferson and his followers.

Hamilton's followers came to be called Federalists. The Federalist Party was strongest in New England and along the Atlantic seaboard. It included many wealthy merchants, manufacturers, lawyers, and church leaders. John Adams, himself a Federalist, said that Federalists represented "the rich, the well-born, and the able."

The opposition party was led by Thomas Jefferson. Its members called themselves Republicans. Although some wealthy people were Republicans, most of Jefferson's supporters were the owners of small farms or wage earners in the growing towns.

Party differences. Jefferson's beliefs were quite different from Hamilton's. Hamilton had little faith in the ability of average people to govern themselves. Jefferson, on the other hand, had great faith in the average person's ability to play an effective part in government. Jefferson had expressed this faith in the Declaration of Independence when he wrote that all governments should secure their power from "the consent of the governed."

Hamilton, distrusting average people, wanted to give power to wealthy people. He wanted to create a strong federal government under their control. He knew that a **strict,** or literal, **interpretation** of the Constitution would not permit a sufficiently strong federal government. Thus Hamilton chose to read his own meaning into the Constitution by a **loose,** or elastic, **interpretation.**

Jefferson wanted the people, particularly the small farmers who made up 90 percent of the total population, to have controlling power in the country. He favored a limited federal government, strong state governments, and ironclad guarantees of individual liberties. He believed that the Constitution *as written* gave sufficient power to the government. When a question arose as to the meaning of the Consti-

In this cartoon the spirit of George Washington looks down upon two men who symbolize opposing political views. They are pulling at the pillars that support the nation. "Should you remove one," he warns, "you destroy the whole."

tution, Jefferson chose a strict interpretation. For example, as you have read, Jefferson argued against a national bank on the ground that the Constitution did not mention a bank or banking. Hamilton, interpreting the Constitution loosely, argued that the Constitution gave the government power to regulate money. Since a bank was needed to carry out this regulation, Congress could create such a bank.

By 1794 most voters had chosen the political party they preferred. From that day to this, American political life has revolved around the **two-party system.** In 1794, however, political parties were not like political parties today. They were loosely grouped alliances centering around leaders of different political beliefs. Later, third parties also developed from time to time to press for policies they felt the two major parties were neglecting.

Nominating candidates. On March 4, 1797, President John Adams, a Federalist, took the oath of office. A few minutes later, Thomas Jefferson, a Republican, was sworn in as Vice-President.

A Federalist President, a Republican Vice-President. How did such a curious situation develop? The answer lies in the election of 1796. This election also provides an example of how custom helped to shape American political institutions.

Both the Federalists and the Republicans entered the election year determined to win. President Washington had announced that he intended to retire. The Presidency and the Vice-Presidency now were wide open.

The Constitution gave no directions for nominating candidates for the Presidency and Vice-Presidency. The leaders of the two parties decided to keep political power in their own hands by holding Congressional conferences, later called **caucuses.** In these caucuses the leaders would choose the candidates. The voters at large would have no part in choosing those who were nominated.

Months before election day, the Federalists in Congress held their caucus. They chose John Adams and Thomas Pinckney as the Federalist candidates for President and Vice-President. Republican members of Congress, in a similar party meeting, chose as their candidates Thomas Jefferson and Aaron Burr. Thus the leaders of the political parties selected the candidates that they, the leaders, wanted to run.

The artist John Lewis Krimmel captured the excitement and holiday spirit of an early election day in the city of Philadelphia. The voters lined up in front of the building in the center (later known as Independence Hall) to meet, to argue, and to cast their votes.

Role of the electors. On election day voters all over the country traveled to polling places and voted for officials in local, state, and federal governments. The voters did *not,* however, vote directly for the President and Vice-President. Instead, they voted for **electors** who had already been chosen. Each state selected its electors in any way it chose—by popular vote, by the choice of the state legislature, or by a combination of both methods.

These chosen electors in each state then voted, as the Constitution provided, "by ballot for two persons." That is, they cast electoral votes for President and Vice-President. The candidate receiving the largest vote, provided it was a majority, was declared President. The candidate with the second largest vote was declared Vice-President.

According to the Constitution, the electors could vote for anyone they wished. This small, select group was supposed to be better informed, and therefore able to choose more wisely, than the American voters at large.

213

The framers of the Constitution had not known that the country would divide into two political parties. They had not foreseen that the electors might choose a President from one political party and a Vice-President from another. In 1796, however, this happened.

The election of 1796. When the electors gathered to vote for the President and the Vice-President, they had before them four names—the Federalist candidates, John Adams and Thomas Pinckney, and the Republican candidates, Thomas Jefferson and Aaron Burr. It was expected that the electors would choose either *both* Federalist candidates or *both* Republican candidates.

Some leading Federalists did not like John Adams, however, and they worked out a plan to make Pinckney President and Adams Vice-President. Their plan backfired. John Adams received the largest number of votes, Thomas Jefferson the next largest. As a result, the United States had a Federalist President and a Republican Vice-President.

Custom and the Constitution. Custom, rather than law, prevented a similar situation from happening again. After 1796, electors began to understand that they were expected to vote only for the previously nominated candidates. The Federalist electors, for example, understood that they should vote for the Federalist candidates. Likewise, the Republican electors understood that they were to cast their votes for the Republican candidates. This custom became a part of the "unwritten Constitution."

SECTION SURVEY

IDENTIFY: two-party system, caucus, electors.

1. How did Presidential politics in 1792 indicate the rise of political parties?
2. (a) Why were the Federalist Party and the Republican Party formed? (b) Who belonged to each?
3. (a) What did Jefferson and Hamilton believe about the average person? (b) What did they believe about the proper interpretation of the Constitution? (c) How did these beliefs reflect the kind of government each wanted for the nation?
4. In the election of 1796, the elected President and Vice-President belonged to different political parties. (a) How did this happen? (b) Why is it unlikely to happen again?

5 The Federalist Party struggles to stay in power

President John Adams was not pleased at having a Republican Vice-President, but he had little time to worry about it. By the time he took office, the United States was threatened by war with France.

On the verge of war. American relations with France had grown steadily worse since 1793. The French resented America's refusal to aid France as it was obliged to do by the Treaty of 1778. The French also resented Jay's Treaty, which France regarded as pro-British.

As a result, France had become increasingly hostile during Washington's second administration. The French navy had seized American ships and had kept them from reaching British ports. The French government had refused to receive the diplomatic representative sent by President Washington to Paris. Nevertheless, President Adams decided to make one more effort toward maintaining peace with France.

The XYZ affair. Early in 1797 President Adams sent three prominent Americans to Paris to try to reach an agreement with France. The Americans were visited privately by three French officials. The French officials, later identified only as "X, Y, and Z," made three insulting demands.

First, the American government must apologize publicly to France for remarks made by President Adams in a speech to Congress. Second, the United States must grant a loan to France. Third, the American envoys must pay a bribe of $250,000.

When news of this insult reached America, many Americans demanded war. Rallying around the slogan "Millions for defense, but not one cent for tribute," Americans began war preparations. In 1798 the government created the Navy Department, built warships, fortified harbors, and strengthened the army. The United States was actually at war, although no formal declaration had been made. Within a few months, American warships captured more than 80 vessels flying the French flag.

War avoided. President Adams then performed one of the most courageous acts of his

This 1799 cartoon concerns the XYZ affair. It shows three American commissioners being threatened by a five-headed monster, representing the French government. "Money, Money, Money," the monster demands.

career. Although many members of his own party were demanding war, Adams tried once again to secure peace. In 1799 he sent another group of commissioners to Paris.

By the time the Americans arrived, Napoleon had overthrown the government and made himself dictator of France. Napoleon wanted to begin his rule free from conflicts with foreign nations. Thus he was eager to reach a settlement with the United States.

The Americans and the French agreed to abandon the old treaty of 1778. The United States agreed to drop its claims against France for illegally seizing American ships. Nevertheless, the French continued to seize American ships that attempted to trade with the British.

In spite of the agreement's shortcomings, President Adams had avoided full-scale war with France. Like Washington before him, Adams believed that the infant nation could survive only if it avoided European conflicts. In avoiding war, President Adams sacrificed any popularity that he might have enjoyed with his own party.

The Alien and Sedition Acts. In 1798, while anti-French feeling was running high, the Fed-

eralist majority in Congress passed a series of laws designed, they said, to unite the country. It was generally understood, however, that the laws would also weaken the Republican Party.

These measures, often called the Alien and Sedition Acts, included four different laws. Congress passed these laws against the advice of President Adams and other leaders of the Federalist Party.

The Naturalization Act stated that aliens, or foreigners, must reside in the United States for 14 years before they could become naturalized citizens. Up to that time, only 5 years of United States residence had been required. Congress said that this act would help protect the country from enemy aliens in wartime. However, since most newcomers joined the Republican Party as soon as they became citizens, the real reason for the law was clear. The Federalist Party wanted to remain in office.

The Alien Act authorized the President to expel "all such aliens as he shall judge dangerous to the peace and safety of the United States" or those involved in plots against the government. The Alien Enemies Act authorized the President, in time of war or invasion, to imprison or banish any foreigners the Pres-

215

Gilbert Stuart painted this portrait of John Adams in 1815. Both Adams and his sometime political rival Thomas Jefferson would die on July 4, 1826—the fiftieth anniversary of the republic.

ident considered a danger to public security. The Federalists said that these two laws were necessary war precautions. It was clear, though, that they could also be used to silence anti-Federalist opinion. After all, a Federalist President would be able to decide which aliens were "dangerous" to American security.

The Sedition Act was intended to silence American citizens themselves. **Sedition** means, among other things, the use of language to stir up discontent or rebellion against a government. Under the Sedition Act, fines and imprisonment could silence anybody who wrote, said, or printed anything "false, scandalous, and malicious" against the government, the Congress, or the President "with intent to defame."

If these laws had been fully enforced, they would have ended all opposition to the Federalist Party. The Naturalization Act went into ef-

fect at once. The Alien Act and the Alien Enemies Act were not enforced, but the mere threat of them drove many French aliens from the country. Likewise, fear of punishment under the Sedition Act undoubtedly kept many Americans silent.

Twenty-five persons were prosecuted under the Sedition Act. Ten—all Republicans and most of them newspaper publishers—were fined and jailed. The Sedition Act thus interfered with freedom of the press and freedom of speech, two principles protected by the First Amendment and deeply cherished by Americans then and now. Many Americans believed that the Alien and Sedition Acts were unjust attempts by the government to interfere with the rights of individuals—aliens and citizens alike.

Virginia and Kentucky Resolutions. The Republicans were furious. They claimed that these measures destroyed free speech and greatly increased the power of the federal government, particularly the power of the President. They voiced their protest in the Kentucky and Virginia Resolutions.

The Kentucky Resolutions, prepared by Thomas Jefferson, were adopted by the legislature of the new state of Kentucky in 1798 and 1799. The Virginia Resolutions, prepared by James Madison, were adopted by the legislature of Virginia in 1798. Together, these resolutions outlined the **states' rights,** or **compact, theory** of the Constitution. This theory included the following ideas: (1) The federal government had been created by the states. (2) The federal government was merely an agent for the states, operating under a compact, or agreement, that had delegated to the federal government certain specific powers and no more. (3) The federal government, or its agent, could be criticized by its creators, the states, if it committed unauthorized acts. Who would determine when an act was unauthorized, or unconstitutional? Why, the states, of course.

Carried to an extreme, the states' rights, or compact, theory would give the states the power to declare **null and void,** or not lawful and binding, any act of Congress that the states felt was unconstitutional. The theory could lead to **secession,** or withdrawal, of one or more states from the Union. Of course, Hamilton and the Federalists completely opposed this interpretation of the Constitution.

The Federalists claimed that the government had been created by the people, not by the states. They also said that the Supreme Court was the sole judge of whether or not an act of Congress was unconstitutional.

The Kentucky and Virginia Resolutions were sent to the other state legislatures. To the disappointment of Jefferson and Madison, the Resolutions did not receive favorable action. The Federalists controlled most of the state governments, and they opposed the Resolutions. Nevertheless, the Resolutions proved to be effective political weapons. They offered the voters a choice between a strong federal government and a weaker union in which the power of the states would be greater than the power of the federal union.

SECTION SURVEY

IDENTIFY: naturalized citizen, alien, sedition, compact theory, null and void, secession.

1. Why were relations between France and the United States strained between 1793 and 1797?

2. (a) How did President Adams attempt to repair relations with France in 1797? (b) Why did his attempt fail?

3. (a) Describe the agreement that France and the United States reached in 1799. (b) What was the main goal of each country in reaching an agreement?

4. (a) List the main provisions of the Alien and Sedition Acts. (b) How did they violate the Bill of Rights?

5. (a) In what way were the Kentucky and Virginia Resolutions an answer to the Alien and Sedition Acts? (b) How would nationwide adoption of the Resolutions have changed American government?

6 Federalist ideas and methods persist under the Republicans

By the end of President Adams's administration, the Federalists had lost much of their earlier influence. Many Americans, including many Federalists, disliked the high taxes levied to prepare for war. Most damaging to the Federalists, however, was the public's anger at the Alien and Sedition Acts.

The courts of early rural America generally were informal and friendly places. In this scene the jury hears a lawyer plead his case in the barn that serves as a court while small boys play in the hayloft.

The election of 1800. In the election year 1800, members of both parties in Congress met in caucuses to select candidates, as they had done in 1796. The Federalists chose President John Adams to run for a second term, with Charles C. Pinckney as his running mate for Vice-President. The Republicans again chose Thomas Jefferson for President and Aaron Burr for Vice-President. Burr was a brilliant New York lawyer and a top-ranking leader of the Republican Party.

The Republicans won the election, gaining control of the Presidency and of both houses of Congress. Despite their victory, however, the Republicans and the country faced an extremely serious situation. There were even rumors of civil war.

The problem was that Jefferson and Burr had both received the same number of electoral

217

votes. The candidate with the largest number of electoral votes was to be President. The candidate with the second largest number was to be Vice-President. Now there was a tie.

At first glance, this problem seemed easy to solve. The Constitution clearly stated that in case of a tie, the House of Representatives would make the final decision, with the total representation from each state having a single vote. Ordinarily, the House would have given the Presidency to Jefferson since the Republican caucus had nominated him for this position. Some Federalists in the House, however, preferred Aaron Burr. Burr was a Republican but was not as strong a supporter of Republican principles as Jefferson. Hamilton distrusted Burr and supported Jefferson as the lesser of two evils.

The Federalists did not have enough voting strength to win the office for Burr. They could and did prevent Jefferson from winning a majority of the votes on 35 successive ballots. Finally with Inaugural Day little more than two weeks away, the deadlock broke. Jefferson won on the thirty-sixth ballot, and Burr became Vice-President.

Because of the confusion in the election of 1800, Congress drew up the Twelfth Amendment. Ratified in 1804, the amendment stated that electors must vote on separate ballots for President and for Vice-President.

The midnight appointments. Having lost control of the executive and legislative branches, the Federalists strengthened their hold on the judicial branch. During the four months between Election Day and Jefferson's inauguration on March 4, 1801, the Federalist majority in the old Congress passed a new Judiciary Act. This act of 1801 increased the number of judges in the federal courts by 16.

President Adams appointed Federalists to these positions, working until late in the evening of his last day in office signing the commissions of the new judges. These last appointees were given the scornful name of "midnight judges."

Chief Justice John Marshall. The most significant appointment made by Adams—though not one of his midnight appointments—was that of John Marshall of Virginia as Chief Justice of the Supreme Court. Probably no single act of President Adams's administration had more far-reaching results.

John Marshall remains one of the most highly regarded of America's Chief Justices. A firm Federalist, he largely dominated the other justices on the Supreme Court during the 34 years he served, from 1801 to 1835. In more than 500 opinions, Chief Justice Marshall helped to mold the political and economic structure of the new nation.

Basic principles under Marshall. During his long term as Chief Justice, John Marshall established three basic principles of American law. These principles became foundation stones of the federal union.

Marshall stated (1) that the Supreme Court had the power to determine when a law of Congress was unconstitutional. This principle —the power of judicial review—had been included in the Judiciary Act of 1789. However, it was not made clear until John Marshall handed down in 1803 a famous decision in the case of *Marbury v. Madison.* In this decision Marshall declared that part of the Judiciary Act passed by Congress in 1789 was unconstitutional. "It is emphatically the province and duty of the judicial department to say what the law is," Marshall stated. Jefferson and others were shocked at this interpretation of the Constitution. As Jefferson expressed it, Marshall had turned the Constitution into "a mere thing of wax in the hands of the judiciary, which . . .

SOURCES

MARBURY v.
MADISON
(1803)

The powers of the legislature are defined and limited; and that those limits may not be mistaken, or forgotten, the Constitution is written. To what purpose are powers limited, and to what purpose is that limitation committed to writing, if these limits may, at any time, be passed by those intended to be restrained? . . . It is a proposition too plain to be contested that the Constitution controls any legislative act repugnant to it. . . . A legislative act contrary to the Constitution is not law. . . . It is emphatically the province and duty of the judicial department to say what the law is. . . .

Samuel F. B. Morse, an artist and the inventor of the telegraph, painted this picture entitled "The Old House of Representatives." In the painting the members of the Supreme Court, including Chief Justice John Marshall (second from the right, top row), meet with the members of Congress.

[they] may twist and shape into any form they please."

In later decisions Marshall established two other basic principles. He declared (2) that the Supreme Court had the power to set aside laws of state legislatures when these laws were contrary to the federal Constitution. He also stated (3) that the Supreme Court had the power to reverse the decision of a state court.

Significance of Marshall's work. Marshall strengthened the federal government at the expense of the states by weakening the legal basis for the states' rights, or compact, theory of government. He helped to shape the loose collection of states into a *national* union.

As the years passed and as the Supreme Court handed down its decisions, Jefferson's alarm increased. From his home at Monticello, Virginia, the former President wrote, "The great object of my fear is the federal judiciary. That body . . . ever acting, with noiseless foot . . . gaining ground step by step, and holding what it gains, is engulfing insidiously the special [state] governments."

Despite his fears, Jefferson could not alter the course of events. In decision after decision, the Supreme Court broadened the meaning of the Constitution. Owing largely to John Marshall's efforts, the federal government became increasingly powerful. When he later became President, Jefferson himself would help to strengthen the federal government.

SECTION SURVEY

IDENTIFY: Judiciary Act of 1801, "midnight judges," John Marshall, *Marbury v. Madison.*

1. Why had the Federalist cause become unpopular by 1800?
2. (a) How did the election of 1800 become deadlocked? (b) How were similar difficulties prevented in the future?
3. Discuss how each of three decisions by Chief Justice John Marshall established basic principles that strengthened the federal government.
4. Source Study: According to the Source on page 218, how are limits on the powers of Congress established?

Chapter Survey

Summary: Tracing the Main Ideas

Between 1789 and 1800, the nation's leaders breathed life into the Constitution. During these years they organized a new government and welded the more or less independent states into a union.

Under President Washington and President John Adams, the Federalists made important strides. They set the machinery of government into motion and successfully launched the United States into the hazardous current of world affairs.

These early years of life under the Constitution were full of peril for the young nation. More than once a false step would have torn the "frail fabric" of the new republic into shreds. Despite this danger, by the time President Adams and most of the Federalist Congressmen left office, they could look with pride upon a growing nation. They could see that the people of that nation were slowly being knit together.

Americans were still a divided people, not yet sure of themselves and of their future. The division increasingly expressed itself through national political parties. State boundaries were gradually becoming less and less important, while the national government was steadily gaining in strength. The American nation was taking form.

In the next chapter, you will see how the new nation acquired a vast new territory beyond the Mississippi River, survived the strain of war, and grew in strength and unity of purpose.

Inquiring into History

1. How would each of these people have felt about Hamilton's economic program: (a) a farmer from Kentucky, (b) a shipowner from Boston, (c) a plantation owner from South Carolina?
2. Compare Shays' Rebellion with the Whisky Rebellion in terms of (a) their causes, (b) the reactions of the federal government, and (c) their outcomes.
3. Describe President Washington's policy toward foreign nations. Why did he favor this policy?
4. Refute or defend the claim that the Sedition Act violated the First Amendment.
5. Find historical evidence to support or refute this statement: A belief in a strong central government was the basis of many actions taken by the Federalists while in office.
6. (a) What issue do the Kentucky and Virginia Resolutions have in common with Justice Marshall's decision in *Marbury v. Madison?* (b) What opinion do the Resolutions and the court decision express about this issue? (c) With which document would Alexander Hamilton have agreed? Why?

Relating Past to Present

1. What purpose did political parties serve in the 1790's? What do you think might have happened if there had been no political parties? Do political parties serve the same purpose today? Explain.
2. Can the foreign-policy advice in Washington's Farewell Address be applied to the United States today? Why or why not?
3. Compare the President's cabinet today to the cabinet in the 1790's in terms of (a) their size, (b) the types of departments, (c) the types of people appointed as Secretaries, and (d) their decision-making powers.

Developing Social Science Skills

1. Prepare a chart comparing the views of the Federalists and Republicans on these issues: (a) federal-state relations, (b) economic affairs, (c) interpretation of the Constitution, (d) foreign policy. Now use your chart to decide how each party would have acted in this situation: The President receives an offer from another nation to buy an enormous area of land. Buying the land would greatly increase the size of the United States.
2. Using the chart on page 845 and 838, (a) determine the approximate population of the United States in 1790. (b) What state had the largest population? What state had the smallest?
3. Look at the map on page 846. Locate the area showing the extent of settlement in the United States in 1790. (a) Which of the states, according to the map, were settled? (b) Which of the states still had unsettled territory? Of these, which state had the most? The least?

Chapter **10**

The Nation's Growing Size and Power

1801–1817

On March 4, 1801, John Adams, the outgoing President, left the "President's House" a worried, troubled man. He did not attend the inaugural ceremony for his successor, Thomas Jefferson. A firm Federalist, Adams feared that the victory of Jefferson and the Republican Party might mean the end of the new nation. Another Federalist politician felt that Jefferson's election showed the way "to anarchy and ruin."

While Adams's carriage was jolting over the rough road leading out of Washington, D.C., Jefferson was reading his Inaugural Address. Jefferson himself referred to the election as "the Revolution of 1800." Nevertheless, in his address Jefferson tried to quiet the fears of many Federalists who believed that such a revolution was about to sweep across the country.

Jefferson pledged himself to "the honest payment of our debts" and promised to preserve "the general government in its whole constitutional vigor." His speech was a moderate one designed to reassure the Federalists.

Jefferson's speech succeeded. Alexander Hamilton accepted it as "a pledge . . . that the new President will not lend himself to dangerous innovations, but in essential points will tread in the steps of his predecessors."

The inauguration of Thomas Jefferson marked the beginning of a long period of Republican control in the United States. During these years the United States more than doubled in territorial size. It also fought a war to protect its rights and emerged from the war stronger than it had ever been.

THE CHAPTER IN OUTLINE

1. The nation doubles in size under President Jefferson.

2. The nation grows stronger during Jefferson's administration.

3. The war in Europe creates serious problems for the United States.

4. Americans again fight the British in the War of 1812.

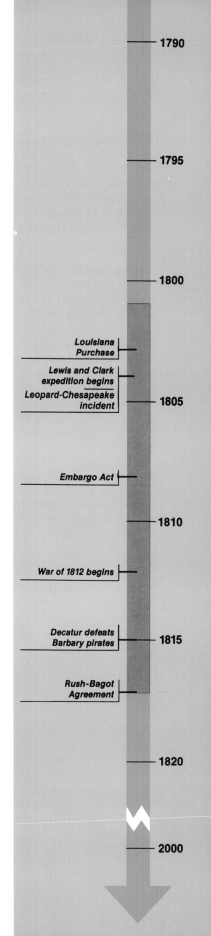

1790

1795

1800

Louisiana Purchase

Lewis and Clark expedition begins

Leopard-Chesapeake incident

1805

Embargo Act

1810

War of 1812 begins

Decatur defeats Barbary pirates

1815

Rush-Bagot Agreement

1820

2000

1 The nation doubles in size under President Jefferson

Thomas Jefferson's pledge that Republicans would act with moderation did not prevent him from taking vigorous leadership as President. When the opportunity came to double the territorial size of the United States, Jefferson acted quickly, even though he was not at all sure the Constitution gave him the power to act as he did.

A rising threat. In 1800 Napoleon, then the ruler of France, secured from Spain the territory of Louisiana. This was the same territory that France had ceded to Spain in 1762.

In the early 1800's, Louisiana covered an enormous but vaguely defined area stretching westward from the Mississippi River to the Rocky Mountains and northward to Canada (see map, page 224). Some people believed that it included Texas. Although Spain and France attempted to keep the news a secret, rumors of this huge deal soon reached the United States government.

The rumors alarmed Jefferson and other American leaders. Even when the weak Spanish nation had held the mouth of the Mississippi River, the United States had been concerned. France, a mighty nation with a steadily growing empire, was a still greater threat. French control of the Gulf of Mexico and the mouth of the Mississippi could deprive westerners of the right of deposit at New Orleans and severely limit their trade. French possession of Louisiana would check American expansion into the interior of the continent. It would also place France, a powerful and aggressive nation, upon the western border of the United States.

President Jefferson had a strong interest in the western country. Unlike many Federalists, who were concerned with eastern shipping and finance, the Republican Jefferson believed that strengthening western lands was necessary. He believed that the westerners would remain loyal citizens only if the federal government insured a free outlet for their goods into the Gulf of Mexico. "The day that France takes New Orleans," Jefferson warned Americans, "we must marry ourselves to the British fleet and nation."

Jefferson did not assume that war with France was inevitable. He urged the American minister to Paris, Robert R. Livingston, to offer Napoleon as much as $10 million for New Orleans and for West Florida—an area east of New Orleans. This would guarantee American control of the Mississippi River and an outlet for western farm products. To aid Livingston, Jefferson sent James Monroe to Paris.

The sale of Louisiana. When the American commissioners made their offer to Napoleon's

New Orleans was almost a hundred years old when it became a part of the United States in 1803 as a result of the Louisiana Purchase. Its people were proud of its international importance as a prosperous port city.

UNDER MY WINGS EVERY THING PROSPERS

representative, there was a moment of silence. Then the representative smiled. How much would they pay for *all* of Louisiana, he asked. The Americans tried to conceal their astonishment. After some discussion they agreed that the United States would pay the equivalent of about $15 million for the entire area. This land sale, probably the largest in history, was negotiated early in 1803.

Why did Napoleon sell this valuable French territory? The answer lay in the Caribbean Sea. Before France could control Louisiana, it had to have a strong naval base in the West Indies. One possible base was the island of Santo Domingo, site of the former French colony of Haiti.

In 1791, during the French Revolution, the black people of Haiti, most of them slaves, had risen in revolt against the French. Under the leadership of Toussaint L'Ouverture (too·SAN loo·vair·TYUR), they had won independence. In 1800 Napoleon had tried to reconquer the entire island of Santo Domingo but had failed.

Without control of Santo Domingo, France had little use for Louisiana. Moreover, by 1802 Napoleon was planning to conquer all of Europe, which would mean a renewal of war with Great Britain. Napoleon knew that the British navy could easily seize his overseas possessions, including those in America. Therefore he decided to save what he could, and $15 million was better than nothing.

Purchase despite questions. Napoleon's offer to sell Louisiana pleased Jefferson but also troubled him. Jefferson, as you know, had always opposed giving the federal government any powers not specifically granted by the Constitution. The Constitution said nothing about the government's right to buy territory from a

President Thomas Jefferson wanted Americans to inform themselves about their government. "If a nation expects to be ignorant and free," Jefferson said, "it expects what never was and never will be."

foreign nation. Jefferson felt that an amendment to the Constitution would be necessary before the purchase could be made. However, his advisers warned him that Napoleon might change his mind while the amendment was being adopted. Jefferson therefore sent the treaty of purchase to the Senate for approval. He later admitted that he had "done an act beyond the Constitution."

In the Senate, Jefferson's political enemies, including some Federalists, strongly objected to the treaty. They declared that $15 million was too high a price for a wilderness. They frankly expressed their fear that when farmers filled this vast western territory, the eastern commercial interests in Congress would be outvoted.

Most Federalists insisted that the Constitu-

SOURCES

JEFFERSON'S
FIRST INAUGURAL
ADDRESS
(1801)

It is proper you should understand what I deem the essential principles of our government: . . . equal and exact justice to all men, of whatever state or persuasion, religious or political; peace, commerce, and honest friendship with all nations, entangling alliances with none; the support of the state governments in all their rights, as the most competent administrations for our domestic concerns and the surest bulwarks against anti-republican tendencies; the preservation of the general government in its whole constitutional vigor, as the sheet anchor of our peace at home and safety abroad; a jealous care of the right of election by the people. . . .

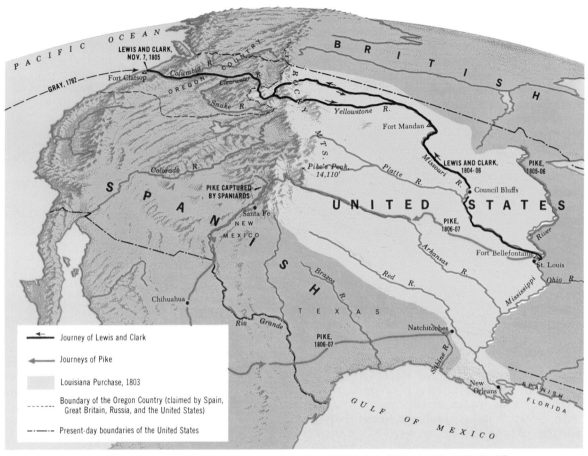

LOUISIANA PURCHASE AND WESTERN EXPLORATIONS

Map legend:

— Journey of Lewis and Clark

← Journeys of Pike

▨ Louisiana Purchase, 1803

- - - - Boundary of the Oregon Country (claimed by Spain, Great Britain, Russia, and the United States)

–·–·– Present-day boundaries of the United States

tion did not give the federal government power to buy territory. The Federalists' position was as inconsistent as Jefferson's. The Federalists had long claimed that the Constitution should be broadly interpreted and that it gave the federal government all powers not specifically denied to it.

The stands taken by Jefferson and the Federalists on this issue illustrate how ideas change as interests and situations change. Despite Federalist objections, the treaty of purchase was approved. In 1803 Louisiana, or the Louisiana Purchase, became part of the United States.

During the transfer of ownership, apparently no one considered the claims of Indian tribes to the lands across the Mississippi River that they and their ancestors had regarded as their own. Jefferson had once hoped to see the eastern tribes adopt an agricultural way of life and the white settlers' culture. Now he favored the removal of these Indians to lands across the Mississippi already occupied by western tribes.

The Lewis and Clark expedition. Nobody knew the boundaries of Louisiana, although a few white trappers and many Indian tribes had some idea of what lay within the territory. Jefferson decided to explore the vast region that the nation had bought. He assigned the task to a United States army expedition led by Meriwether Lewis and William Clark (see map, this page).

The expedition of about 45 men left the Mississippi at St. Louis on May 14, 1804, and traveled up the Missouri River to its headwaters. There they hired Indian guides and horses and journeyed over perilous mountain trails to the headwaters of the Clearwater River. Then they built canoes and made their way down the Clearwater and the Columbia Rivers to the Pacific Ocean.

In this mural in Oregon's capitol building, Lewis and Clark (center) are shown at Celilo Falls on their journey toward the Pacific. They reached this point in 1805 with the help of their Indian guide, Sacajawea (right).

The expedition enjoyed good luck, good planning, and the friendliness of several Indian tribes, notably the Mandans and the Shoshones. During the first winter, Lewis and Clark hired a French-Canadian fur trader and his Indian wife, Sacajawea (sak·uh·juh·WEE· uh), to serve as guides and interpreters. Their aid in understanding Indian ways of life was vital.

The expedition's relations with the Indians were further aided by York, Clark's black slave, whom Clark freed at the end of the expedition. His dark skin made York seem less strange to the Indians than the whites did.

On September 23, 1806, the Lewis and Clark expedition returned to St. Louis. They brought back maps, journals, specimens of plants and insects, the bones and pelts of animals, and boxes of soil and stones.

Meanwhile, other bold explorers, including Zebulon Pike, were pushing into Spanish lands to the west. These early expeditions gave Americans their first real knowledge of the lands beyond the Mississippi.

The purchase of Louisiana, with its immense area and rich resources, was an outstanding event in American history. As Robert R. Livingston observed when the treaty of purchase was signed, "From this day the United States take their place among the powers of the first rank."

SECTION SURVEY

IDENTIFY: Toussaint L'Ouverture, Louisiana Purchase, Lewis and Clark, Sacajawea, Zebulon Pike.

1. Why were Americans uneasy about France's takeover of Louisiana from Spain in 1800?

2. (a) What objections were made to the Louisiana Purchase? (b) How was the Constitution involved in these objections?

3. Map Study: Trace the expeditions of Lewis and Clark and of Pike on the map on page 224. (a) What areas within the Louisiana Purchase, and beyond it, did these expeditions visit? (b) What evidence can you find on the map that might foreshadow disagreements with other nations as a result of the Louisiana Purchase?

2 The nation grows stronger during Jefferson's administration

Thomas Jefferson's prompt action in the purchase of Louisiana was only one of several vigorous steps he took as President. He urged Congress to repeal a number of Federalist laws that he felt were harmful to the nation's best interests. He also did not hesitate to use military force to protect American rights.

Federalist laws repealed. The Alien and Sedition Acts of 1798, which Jefferson strongly opposed, had expired before he became President. The Naturalization Act, also passed in 1798, was still in effect, and at Jefferson's urging Congress promptly repealed it. Congress also repealed the excise tax on whisky, which Jefferson regarded as unconstitutional. Congress likewise repealed the Judiciary Act of 1801. Thus the "midnight judges" appointed by President Adams on the eve of Jefferson's inauguration could not assume office.

Jefferson then turned his attention to the army and the navy. He persuaded Congress to cut funds for them and reduce them in size. Jefferson opposed a strong military establishment because it would greatly strengthen the federal government. Moreover, by reducing the armed forces, Jefferson could operate the government more economically.

Federalist programs continued. The Republicans, however, did not wipe out all the work of the Federalists. Jefferson acted with moderation. During his administration he continued many Federalist programs and kept many Federalists in office.

Hoping to end the bitterness between the Federalists and the Republicans, Jefferson said in his Inaugural Address, "We are all Republicans; we are all Federalists." Then Jefferson proceeded to show through actions that he meant what he said about bringing unity to the nation.

Although Jefferson had argued that the Bank of the United States was unconstitutional, he could do nothing to disturb it, for its charter ran until 1811. Jefferson had also opposed Hamilton's plan to have the federal government assume the state debts. Nevertheless,

Secretary of the Treasury Albert Gallatin paid off installments on the public debt as rapidly as he could.

Defending American rights. In a war with the pirates of North Africa, Jefferson actually pushed forward the Federalist ideal of a strong federal government.

The Muslim rulers of the Barbary States of North Africa—Morocco, Algiers, Tunis, and Tripoli—had long been seizing the ships of Christian nations and holding their crews for ransom. Instead of declaring war on the pirates, the European governments had decided that it was cheaper to make the yearly payments of tribute, or bribes. Since 1783 the United States, whose merchants traded with the Mediterranean countries, had also been paying this tribute. However, when the rulers of Tripoli made exorbitant demands upon the United States, Jefferson met the challenge. He sent a squadron of naval ships to attack the harbor of Tripoli in the Mediterranean (see map, this page).

This did not end the trouble, however. In 1805 the ruler of Tripoli finally signed a peace treaty, but the piracy of other Barbary States continued until 1815. In that year an American fleet under Captain Stephen Decatur, reinforced by European warships, finally ended all payment of American tribute to the pirates along the Barbary coast.

American ships could now sail the Mediterranean freely. Europeans regarded the United States with new respect and admiration. More-

BARBARY STATES

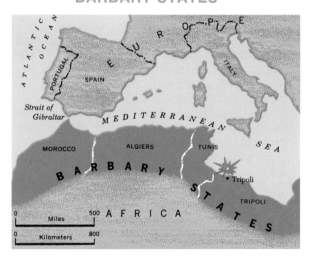

Here the American ship *Intrepid* explodes in the harbor of Tripoli in 1804. Over a hundred Tripoli pirates had boarded the ship and surrounded its crew. Rather than surrender their ship and be captured, the Americans blew up the *Intrepid*.

over, American naval forces gained valuable experience during the war. The American people took great pride in the heroic exploits of Decatur and other naval commanders. These new heroes, honored by people in every section of the United States, stimulated pride in the growing nation.

The election of 1804. The Republicans entered the Presidential election of 1804 confident of victory. For their Presidential candidate they turned again to Thomas Jefferson. Instead of Aaron Burr, who had served as Vice-President during Jefferson's first term, they chose George Clinton of New York as Jefferson's running mate. Jefferson and Clinton won a sweeping victory, carrying all the states except Delaware and Connecticut.

Hamilton and Burr. In the meantime, Burr had accepted Federalist support in his campaign for governor of New York in the spring of 1804. Alexander Hamilton, who did not trust Burr, urged the Federalists to vote against him. Burr lost the election. Blaming Hamilton for his defeat, Burr demanded an apology for an uncomplimentary remark that Hamilton had supposedly made during the election campaign. When Hamilton refused to apologize, Burr challenged him to a duel.

The two men met in the early morning of July 11. At the signal to fire, Burr raised his pistol, took careful aim, and shot. Hamilton, who had not tried to fire, fell mortally wounded and died shortly afterward.

Aaron Burr's next adventure puzzled Americans at the time and has puzzled historians ever since. In 1805 and 1806, he involved several prominent Americans in vague schemes. He might have wanted to persuade westerners to leave the Union and set up a separate republic or wanted to conquer Mexico and set up an independent empire. Whatever the facts were, Burr was arrested and charged with treason.

Chief Justice John Marshall, who presided at the trial, followed the strict definition of treason given in the Constitution. Burr was acquitted and chose to live in Europe in exile. Later he returned to New York, where he lived and died under the shadow of disapproval.

227

IDENTIFY: tribute, Barbary States, Stephen Decatur, Aaron Burr.

1. (a) What important changes did the Jefferson administration make in the Federalist program? (b) Which Federalist policies did the administration continue and why?

2. How did the country respond to Jefferson's blend of Federalism and Republicanism in the election of 1804?

3. May Study: Look at the map on page 226. (a) How did the location of the Barbary States enable them to interfere with American trade in the Mediterranean? (b) How did the war with the Barbary pirates strengthen the federal government?

3 The war in Europe creates serious problems for the United States

In 1803 Napoleon began his conquest of Europe. By 1807, after a series of brilliant victories, Napoleon had almost attained his goal, but he still faced major obstacles. To the east stood Russia. To the west, across the English Channel, stood Great Britain. British troops had been driven from the European mainland, but the British navy was powerful at sea. Napoleon also knew that Great Britain might soon put its troops back on European soil.

Wartime profits. One of Napoleon's desperate problems was that of supply. The British navy controlled the seas across which France had to bring needed products.

America was an important source of supply for both France and Great Britain, but especially France. Great Britain could send its merchant fleet to any part of the world to obtain imports. France had few ships and therefore relied upon American merchant vessels. American merchants made handsome profits from the European war. From 1789 to 1805 the tonnage, or carrying capacity, of the American merchant marine increased enormously.

Interference with America's trade. Great Britain was determined to destroy America's trade with France. In 1807 the British adopted a series of measures called Orders in Council.

These Orders forbade American vessels to enter any ports under Napoleon's control in Europe, the West Indies, or India.

While Great Britain was trying to shut off all trade with France, Napoleon attempted to **blockade,** or seal off, the British Isles. In a series of Orders, he forbade all nations, including the United States, to trade with the British. He further warned that he would seize every ship that entered French ports after stopping at Great Britain or any British colony. Moreover, he threatened to seize every ship that submitted to inspection by British cruisers or that paid duties to the British government.

The British Orders in Council and Napoleon's Orders both violated the principle of **freedom of the seas.** This principle soon became, and has remained, an important pillar of American foreign policy.

For many months American merchants matched wits with the French and British navies by engaging in the dangerous but highly profitable practice of blockade running. The profits attracted so many merchants and shippers that in 1807 United States foreign trade soared to the highest level in the nation's history. This risky trade involved the United States in constant conflict with both the British and the French.

Another source of conflict between the United States and Great Britain was continuing British **impressment,** or seizure, of American sailors.

In the summer of 1807, the British ship *Leopard* demanded the right to search the American frigate *Chesapeake* for deserters from the British navy. The commander of the *Chesapeake* refused, whereupon the *Leopard* opened fire. Three Americans were killed and 18 wounded. Four *Chesapeake* sailors were seized and taken aboard the *Leopard.* Many outraged Americans demanded war.

The Embargo Act of 1807. Jefferson did not want war. However, he did want to end the continuing American conflict with Great Britain and France. He decided that the only answer short of war was to remove American ships from the high seas.

With this in mind and with his cabinet's approval, Jefferson urged Congress to pass an **embargo.** This was a law forbidding Americans to trade with any foreign nation, including, of course, Great Britain and France. Late in December 1807, Congress passed the Embargo Act, which forbade American vessels to leave for foreign ports. With the Embargo Act the United States temporarily abandoned the principle of freedom of the seas in the hope of avoiding war.

From the outset the Embargo Act could not be fully enforced. Americans smuggled goods across the border to Canada. Some merchants kept their vessels abroad. There, sailing under British or French licenses, they continued to earn large profits. Nevertheless, American trade suffered badly.

New England merchants were the first to feel the pinch. They angrily demanded repeal of the Embargo Act, claiming that Jefferson was deliberately trying to ruin them. Farmers, unable to sell their crops to foreign buyers, and unemployed sailors joined the merchants in demanding repeal.

Reluctantly Jefferson gave in to the growing pressure. On March 1, 1809, three days before he left office, Congress, with his support, repealed the Embargo Act.

Drifting toward war. Following the precedent started by George Washington, Jefferson refused to run for a third term. In the Presidential election of 1808, James Madison of Virginia, a Republican, won the office by a substantial vote.

Madison was a quiet, scholarly man. For eight years before becoming President, he had served as Jefferson's Secretary of State. Madison shared Jefferson's views. He was determined to gain respect for American rights on the high seas, but by peaceful means. However, during his first administration, the country moved toward war.

Madison's diplomacy. In place of the Embargo Act, Congress in 1809 passed the Non-Intercourse Act. This law forbade American merchants to do business with Great Britain or France, although trade with other nations was allowed. Yet trade with Great Britain and France was precisely what Americans were demanding. Because of continued pressure from merchants, Congress in 1810 allowed the Non-Intercourse Act to expire. American shipowners and captains once again turned to the dangerous business of running the blockade.

Still searching for a way to avoid war, President Madison on May 1, 1810, signed a new

According to this cartoon, in order to maintain peace, President Jefferson (center) and the United States had to suffer the insults of both King George III of Great Britain (left) and Napoleon, Emperor of France (right).

law. This law urged Great Britain and France to remove their restrictions on American shipping. It also promised that when either nation did this, the United States would refuse to trade with the other nation.

Failure of Madison's policy. The keen-witted Napoleon quickly seized the chance to force the United States to take sides against Great Britain. In August 1810 he announced that France would no longer interfere with American shipping. As the United States later learned, Napoleon had no intention of keeping his word. Nevertheless, President Madison had no choice but to forbid all trade with Great Britain. From the British point of view, the United States had chosen to become an enemy. Madison's policy had failed.

Declaration of war. Instead of declaring war on the United States, however, the British decided to remove *their* restrictions on American shipping. On June 16, 1812, Parliament suspended the Orders in Council that had

SMUGGLING IN NEW ENGLAND

They call it Smuggler's Notch for good reason. This gap through Vermont's Green Mountains, at the foot of rugged Mount Mansfield, is full of hiding places. In the early 1800's, Vermonters carried on an illegal trade with their Canadian neighbors. They used the caves and crevices of Smuggler's Notch to hide cattle, sheep, and other products from their farms. On dark nights they would smuggle them across the border.

It was the Embargo Act of 1807 that pushed Vermonters and other New Englanders into this illegal trade. They depended for a living on the sale of their farm products and they needed manufactured goods that they could not make themselves. The British in Canada needed food for their troops, and they had manufactured products to exchange for it. So when the embargo cut off trade with foreign ports, the fiercely independent people of New England took matters into their own hands.

Smuggler's Notch was just one hiding place on one route. There were many others. Some smugglers used rafts to carry goods across Lake Champlain. Other clever traders stored goods in specially constructed shacks, built to straddle the boundary line between the United States and Canada. When loose stones were knocked out from under the foundation of one of these shacks, it tilted. Then the goods simply rolled across the border from one country to the other!

interfered with American trade. Unhappily, there was no trans-Atlantic cable, telephone, or radio to carry this news to the American people. So, unaware of the British action, only two days later, on June 18, Congress declared war on Great Britain. Why?

Most historians agree that the War of 1812 was fought mainly over freedom of the seas and the impressment of American sailors, but there were other reasons as well. Members of Congress from eastern states with a strong interest in trade were divided in their feelings about the war. However, the great majority of members from the agricultural southern and western states favored the war. How can this be explained?

Land hunger. Western land hunger was an old story. Pioneer farmers quickly exhausted the fertility of their soil. Then they moved westward to new land, which they cleared, planted—and eventually wore out. By 1812 the pioneers had almost reached the end of the forested areas.

The northwestern farmers did not want to move onto the treeless prairies of the United States, where there was no timber to build houses and fences. Some farmers mistakenly believed that the prairie soil was poor. To them the rich wooded land of southern Canada lying just across the border looked much more attractive.

Farmers living in Tennessee, western Georgia, and what is now northern Alabama longed for the lands of Spanish Florida bordering the Gulf of Mexico (see map, page 234). They wanted this land not only for farming, but also because it served as a safe hiding place for runaway slaves and as a base for Indians who kept attacking American frontier settlements. People from this section of the country clamored for the conquest of Florida. War with Great Britain would provide an excuse for conquest, because Spain had been Britain's ally ever since Napoleon had invaded Spain.

National pride. The rising spirit of pride in the new nation also led to the War of 1812. Americans resented impressment of American sailors and insults to the flag. Many Americans now believed that the United States was destined to expand until the American flag flew over the Western Hemisphere from the North Pole to the Strait of Magellan. At the very least, they said, Canada, Mexico, and the land as far as the Pacific Ocean should belong to the United States.

Indian relations. Troubled relations with the Indians also led westerners to demand war.

Many Indians in the northwestern areas had been reluctantly persuaded, bribed, or forced to give up more and more of their land to the advancing white settlers. Time after time, they had been promised that this was the last land they would be forced to give up. Every time the promise had been broken.

A great leader of the Shawnee tribe, Tecumseh, decided to make a final stand against expansion by whites. Encouraged by Canadian officials and fur traders, he formed a defensive confederation of Indian tribes in the Ohio country.

In the early 1800's Tecumseh and his brother, the Prophet, kindled a religious revival among the Indians of the Northwest. Indian warrior and Indian priest, they traveled far and wide among the scattered tribes, urging them to preserve their traditions and not to sell any more land to white settlers. "Sell a country!" Tecumseh cried. "Why not sell the air, the clouds, and the great sea? . . . Did not the Great Spirit make them all for the use of his children?"

Tecumseh had no wish to start a war. He asked only that white settlers leave the Indians alone and stop taking their lands. Although Tecumseh opposed war, he gathered warriors at Tippecanoe on the Wabash River. Even this show of readiness to resist by the Indian tribes could not stop the westward movement of white settlers.

Demands of the "War Hawks." As the influence of Tecumseh and his brother spread along the frontier, westerners became alarmed. Most of them believed that British fur traders in Canada were supplying the Indians with arms. Why not seize Canada, the westerners asked, and put an end, once and for all, to the dangers of an alliance between the British and the Indians?

In the Congressional elections of 1810, the citizens of the frontier regions elected several young men to Congress. Among them were Henry Clay of Kentucky, John C. Calhoun of South Carolina, Felix Grundy of Tennessee, and Peter B. Porter of western New York. Known as "War Hawks," these youthful members helped to whip up a war spirit in Congress. "We shall drive the British from our continent," declared Felix Grundy. "They will no longer have an opportunity of intriguing with our Indian neighbors. . . . That nation [Britain] will lose her Canadian trade, and by

"These lands are ours," Tecumseh pleaded in 1810. "No one has a right to remove us, because we were the first owners." The great Shawnee chief would die in battle against American troops for this belief.

having no resting place in this country, her means of annoying us will be diminished."

Because of western demands, in the late fall of 1811, General William Henry Harrison led American troops into what is now Indiana. The Indians had gathered at the point where the Tippecanoe River flows into the Wabash River (see map, page 234). Tecumseh, at the time, was away seeking the support of southern Indians—the Creeks, Choctaws, and Cherokees. The Prophet sprang a surprise attack against the American troops, but the Indians were forced back. They fought bravely, and Harrison lost many soldiers. When Harrison left the battlefield, he was not sure of the outcome, but the Indians, who had also suffered badly, fled northward. Although the Battle of Tippecanoe was not a decisive victory for Harrison, it helped make him a frontier military hero.

In 1813 Harrison defeated the British and their Indian allies at the Battle of the Thames in Canada. Tecumseh was killed, and the confederation that he and his brother had organized fell apart. British hopes of regaining power in the area were destroyed.

IDENTIFY: blockade, freedom of the seas, *Leopard*, *Chesapeake*, Embargo Act of 1807, James Madison, Tecumseh, "War Hawks," 1812.

1. How did American merchants profit from the Napoleonic Wars in Europe?

2. (a) How did France and Great Britain attempt to hinder each other's trade with America? (b) What action did President Jefferson take in response to these attempts? (b) How did the country respond to Jefferson's action?

3. Describe two measures that President Madison took to try to prevent European interference with American trade.

4. Explain how each of the following led to the War of 1812: (a) land hunger, (b) national pride, (c) settler-Indian conflict, (d) fur trade, (e) desire for freedom of the seas, (f) impressment of American sailors.

4 Americans again fight the British in the War of 1812

When Congress declared war against Great Britain on June 18, 1812, many Americans expected a swift victory. Henry Clay, among others, believed that the Kentucky militia could conquer Canada in three weeks. As it turned out, the war dragged on for more than two years.

The election of 1812. In May, only a few weeks before war was declared, Republican leaders nominated Madison for a second term. The Federalists, most of whom opposed the war, supported De Witt Clinton of New York, whom anti-war Republicans had nominated. Although Madison won the election by a comfortable margin, Clinton carried all the New England and Middle Atlantic states except Vermont and Pennsylvania. Moreover, the Federalists made heavy gains in Congress. The election clearly revealed that many Americans, especially New Englanders, strongly opposed the war.

A divided country. Even after the conflict started, many Federalists continued to feel that it was unnecessary. Merchants realized that war would ruin what was left of their ship-

ping. Furthermore, they objected to proposals to annex Canada and Florida to the United States. They saw clearly that additional land would greatly increase the power of the farmers. Why, the Federalist merchants asked, should they fight a war that would weaken their influence in the federal government?

Even some Republicans had misgivings about the war. John Randolph of Virginia raised an issue that would haunt the halls of Congress for many years. He declared that annexing Canada would increase the strength of that part of the United States that did not have slavery and weaken the power of the southern states. Randolph also feared that a war would so increase the powers of the federal government that the traditional rights of the states would be endangered.

Handicaps to the war effort. The opposition of most Federalists and some Republicans weakened the war effort in other ways as well. Governors of New England states would not permit their state militias to invade Canada. When Congress debated a compulsory draft law to raise troops for the army, the New England Federalists denounced the measure.

Daniel Webster, a gifted young orator from Massachusetts, declared that compulsory military service was unconstitutional. "Where is it written in the Constitution?" Webster cried. "In what article is it contained that you may take children from their parents and parents from their children and compel them to fight the battles of any war in which the folly or the wickedness of the government may engage it?" New Englanders in general and Federalists in particular referred to the War of 1812 with contempt as "Mr. Madison's War."

When the war dragged on without success and American ships were swept from the seas, New England Federalists became increasingly bitter. Finally, on December 15, 1814, a group met in secret session at Hartford, Connecticut, in what was known as the Hartford Convention. The delegates proposed several amendments to the Constitution increasing the influence and power of the commercial sections of the country. A desperate minority even threatened to declare null and void any federal laws they believed to be unconstitutional. However, the Hartford Convention met too late to have any effect upon the war.

Although most southerners and westerners favored the war, they too were divided. South-

In August 1814, British troops sailed up Chesapeake Bay and marched on Washington, D.C. They easily captured the poorly defended city and set fire to most of its public buildings before a storm forced them to retreat. Both the Capitol and the White House suffered extensive fire damage.

erners wanted to conquer Florida. Westerners were just as eager to conquer Canada. As a result, the American military leaders found it difficult to make plans that would please even those who supported the war.

Lack of preparation. The country was not prepared for war. The navy's fleet of a dozen ships was helpless before the more than 800 warships of the British Royal Navy. The army had fewer than 7,000 troops at the outbreak of the war. Many of its commanders were well-meaning but elderly Revolutionary War veterans. They proved no match for superior British commanders.

Another weakness was the American failure to appoint a single commander to direct the entire war effort. Moreover, the militia on which the Americans chiefly depended was poorly equipped and trained.

Black soldiers and sailors. Little effort was made to recruit blacks, except in New York. There the legislature passed a special act for raising two regiments of black troops. Yet many black men, slave and free, took part in the war. Fugitive slaves, hoping to win their freedom, fought both on the American side and on the British side.

Black soldiers fighting on the American side made many contributions. After British forces seized Washington, D.C., American leaders in Philadelphia, also fearing seizure, appealed to local blacks to help secure the city's defenses. About 2,500 responded.

In Louisiana, General Andrew Jackson ignored the fear of many white officers that it would be dangerous to arm black troops. Instead, he called on "the free men of color" to fight the British. He promised them the same pay as white soldiers and the same bonuses in cash and land that white soldiers would receive after the war. When the war was over, Jackson addressed his black troops: "I expected much from you, but you have surpassed my hopes."

Naval officers also testified to the bravery of black sailors under fire. Captain Oliver H. Perry had at first been disturbed when he was sent "blacks, soldiers, and boys" as naval reinforcements. He later wrote that the blacks in his crew "seemed absolutely insensible to danger."

Despite their contributions and bravery, not many of the slaves who fought in the war were granted their freedom.

Ending in stalemate. The chief military goal of the Americans in the War of 1812 was the conquest of Canada. Despite several attempts, the Americans failed to achieve this goal.

On the other hand, by gaining control of Lake Erie, the Americans succeeded in keeping a Canadian force from occupying American

Text continues on page 235.

233

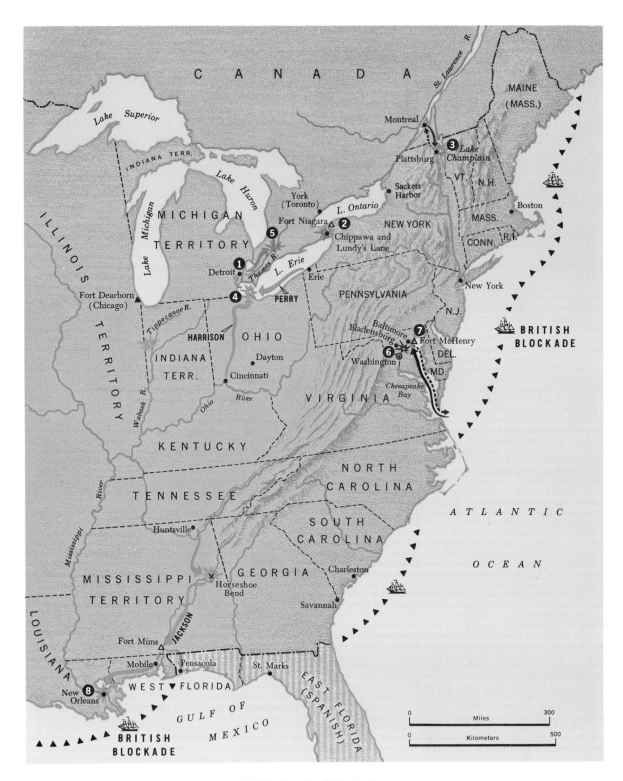

THE WAR OF 1812

The United States entered the War of 1812 with a plan for a three-pronged drive into Canada. The three attacking forces, composed mainly of poorly trained militia, were to start their drives from De-troit ❶, the Niagara area ❷, and Plattsburg ❸.

1812 — The year 1812 brought a series of disas-ters for the American side. In July General William Hull crossed the Detroit River into Canada ❶.

Then, fearing that his lines of communication would be cut by a strong force of British and Indians, General Hull withdrew from Canada and surrendered Detroit without firing a shot. Farther west the American garrison at Fort Dearborn, where Chicago now stands, was wiped out. Later in the year, the British repulsed two feeble attacks across the Niagara River ❷. And in November a drive launched from Plattsburg ❸ against Montreal ended on the Canadian border when the American militia refused to leave United States territory.

1813 — The situation improved somewhat in 1813. In April a combined naval and military expedition sailed from Sackett's Harbor, raided York (now Toronto), and, contrary to orders, burned the public buildings of that city before withdrawing. Some months later Captain Perry's naval victory on Lake Erie ❹ forced the British to abandon Detroit. General William Henry Harrison pursued the retreating troops and their Indian allies, overtook them at Moravian Town on the north bank of the Thames River ❺, and on October 5 won a decisive victory. With the death of their leader Tecumseh, who was killed in this battle, the Indians who had been helping the British deserted the British cause.

1814–1815 — In 1814, with the defeat of Napoleon in Europe, the British were able to send strong forces to America. Before the reinforcements arrived, however, an American army under General Jacob Brown had crossed the Niagara River and on July 5 had defeated the British troops in the Battle of Chippawa ❷. A second battle, fought on July 25, near the Canadian village of Lundy's Lane, ended in a draw.

The British, in 1814, launched three campaigns. A powerful British invading force of more than 10,000 regular troops was stopped by Captain Macdonough's victory on Lake Champlain ❸. A second invading force landed on the Potomac below Washington, marched into the city against only token resistance, and burned the public buildings before retiring ❻. This same force was prevented from landing at Baltimore by the fierce resistance put up by the troops manning Fort McHenry — when Francis Scott Key wrote "The Star-Spangled Banner" ❼. The third invading force, which landed near New Orleans ❽, was decisively defeated by American troops commanded by Major General Andrew Jackson, in a battle fought two weeks after a peace treaty had been signed.

territory for any length of time. Lake Erie was secured in 1813 through the victory of Captain Oliver H. Perry and his small naval force. His report of the victory — "We have met the enemy and they are ours" — is still an honored part of American naval tradition. Equally important was the victory of Captain Thomas Macdonough on Lake Champlain, near Plattsburg, New York, in 1814. Macdonough's victory prevented a British invasion of the United States from Canada.

The one outstanding American military victory of the War of 1812 was that of General Andrew Jackson at New Orleans. Jackson, born near the border between North and South Carolina, had already won fame as an Indian fighter in Tennessee. When he heard of British operations near New Orleans, he rushed to Louisiana. In a large-scale encounter with British forces, Jackson won. This victory helped promote the future political fortunes of General Jackson. It also gave the people of the United States the impression that they had won the War of 1812.

Actually, the victory at New Orleans had no effect upon the war's outcome. Negotiations for a peace treaty between the Americans and the British at Ghent in Belgium had been under way for some time. The Americans and the British had reached an agreement before the battle of New Orleans was fought. Lack of modern means of communication kept this news from reaching New Orleans in time to stop the battle.

The Treaty of Ghent. The Treaty of Ghent, signed on Christmas Eve, 1814, had limited direct results. It said nothing about the impressment of American sailors or about neutral rights on the high seas. The treaty did arrange for the release of all prisoners of war and for the restoration of all occupied territory. It also provided for a commission to settle boundary disputes between the United States and Canada. Most important, it restored peace and led eventually to greatly improved relations between the United States and Great Britain.

Settling disputes peaceably. Shortly after the war ended, the United States and Great Britain created a number of other commissions. These tackled the long-standing problems of trade, furs, and fishing rights along the North Atlantic coast.

These commissions produced worthwhile

Land surveying was a popular occupation for the adventuresome in the growing nation. Here a group of surveyors seek to determine where the border between Maine and Canada actually lay.

results. One commission did away with trade discriminations and allowed American ships to sail to all British ports except those in the West Indies. Another commission gave Americans the right to fish along the Canadian coast and to dry their fish on Canadian shores.

The Rush-Bagot Agreement. While the commissions were at work, the United States and Great Britain signed another treaty of even greater importance.

Immediately after the war, both the United States and Canada had begun to build warships on the Great Lakes to defend their frontiers. American, Canadian, and British leaders agreed that this was a needless expense and an invitation to future trouble. The Rush-Bagot Agreement, signed in Washington in 1817, provided that the United States and Canada would maintain only a few small vessels for police purposes on Lake Champlain and the Great Lakes. Years later the agree-

ment was extended to include land fortifications as well. Thus the agreement was one of the lasting outcomes of the War of 1812.

In 1818 another commission established the boundary between the United States and Canada extending from Lake of the Woods, west of Lake Superior, to the Rocky Mountains. The northeastern boundary from the Atlantic Ocean to Lake of the Woods was later settled by the Webster-Ashburton Treaty of 1842. The boundary from the Rocky Mountains to the Pacific Ocean was fixed by treaty in 1846 (see map, pages 836-37).

The war as a turning point. The War of 1812 also marked a turning point in American history. From 1789 to 1815, events in Europe had helped to shape United States policies, especially foreign policies. After the Treaty of Ghent, the United States became much more independent of Europe. Equally important, the nations of Europe treated with growing respect the young country that had not hesitated to go to war with the greatest naval power in the world.

During the next 100 years, moreover, the United States was not directly involved in European wars. Americans concentrated upon the job of developing their own country. After 1815 the American people as a whole turned their backs on Europe and began the exciting task of occupying the western lands.

SECTION SURVEY

IDENTIFY: compulsory military service, Daniel Webster, "Mr. Madison's War," Hartford Convention.

1. (a) How did the election of 1812 reflect popular feelings about the approaching war with Britain? (b) Why did some Americans oppose the war?

2. In what ways was the United States militarily unprepared for war in 1812?

3. How did the Treaty of Ghent and the Rush-Bagot Agreement settle the main differences between the United States and Great Britain?

4. In what way was the War of 1812 a turning point in American history?

5. Map Study: Look at the map on page 234. (a) What was the United States' principal military aim in the war? (b) Why did it fail to achieve this aim? (c) How did Oliver H. Perry, Thomas Macdonough, and Andrew Jackson contribute to the American cause?

Chapter Survey

Summary: Tracing the Main Ideas

Between 1801 and 1815 the young, struggling United States doubled in size, adding the vast territory of Louisiana to its domain. The Louisiana Purchase was one of Thomas Jefferson's outstanding accomplishments as President. By 1815 the Indians had been driven from the new state of Ohio and the territory of Michigan, both of which had been carved out of the Northwest Territory. The way was now open for the advance of pioneers into the Mississippi Valley.

During this time the United States became involved in the Napoleonic Wars, which plunged Europe and the rest of the Western world into turmoil between 1796 and 1815. The United States failed to maintain for itself freedom of the seas, and it failed to stay out of war. Nevertheless, it emerged from the conflict without the loss of territory or of national strength. The War of 1812 marked a turning point in the relations between Canada and the United States. Despite bitterness between the two nations stirred up by the war, the way was paved for the peaceable settlement of disputes in the future.

Finally, the troubles that Americans faced in this period of turmoil helped to draw them together into a united nation. The American people emerged from the War of 1812 with a strong feeling of unity.

In the next chapter, you will see how the rapidly growing United States undertook to become economically as well as politically independent of Europe and to stand on its own as a nation.

Inquiring into History

1. In his Inaugural Address, Jefferson said, "We are all Republicans, we are all Federalists." (a) What did he mean by this statement? (b) Were his actions as President consistent with this statement? Give specific examples.
2. In the early 1800's, Americans feared an alliance between the Indians and the British. How would such an alliance have benefited the Indians? the British?
3. The delegates to the Hartford Convention of 1814 were accused of treason by some of their opponents. (a) What did they do that might be considered an act of treason? (b) Do you think they were guilty of treason? (c) Does the fact that the nation was at war at the time affect your answer?
4. Some historians believe that the War of 1812 was really the Second War of Independence. Do you agree or disagree? Why?
5. Why do you think that, despite their intentions, the first four Presidents of the United States were unable to avoid involvement in European affairs?

Relating Past to Present

1. What parallels do you see between the purchase and exploration of the Louisiana Territory and the United States space program?
2. Thomas Jefferson made this statement: "Were it left to me to decide whether we should have a government without newspapers or newspapers without a government, I should not hesitate a moment to prefer the latter." (a) What did he mean? (b) Do you think his statement applies today? Why or why not?
3. What did a person have to do to become a naturalized citizen at the time Jefferson was President? How do these requirements differ from those in force today?

Developing Social Science Skills

1. Write a newspaper editorial on America's participation in the War of 1812 from the point of view of a newspaper in (a) the New England states, (b) the Middle Atlantic states, (c) the Southern states, or (d) the West.
2. Conduct research and prepare a written or oral report on one of these topics: (a) the writing of "The Star Spangled Banner," (b) the burning of Washington, D.C., during the War of 1812, (c) the career of the U.S.S. *Constitution.*
3. Look at the maps on pages 224 and 836–37, which show the Louisiana Purchase. (a) What features are shown on both maps? (b) What features appear only on the map on page 224? only on the map on pages 836–37? (c) If you wanted to know when the boundary between the United States and Canada was agreed upon, which map would you use? Why? (d) If you wanted to locate the best route west through the Rocky Mountains, which map would you use? Why?

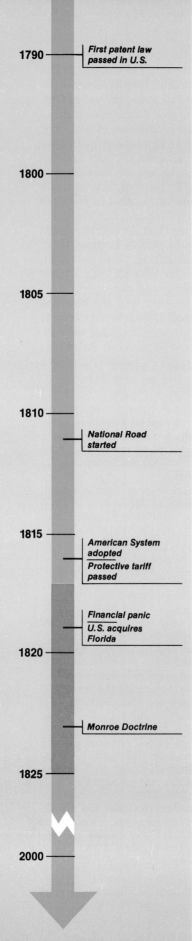

1790 — First patent law passed in U.S.

1800 —

1805 —

1810 —
National Road started

1815 —
American System adopted
Protective tariff passed

Financial panic
U.S. acquires Florida

1820 —

Monroe Doctrine

1825 —

2000 —

Chapter 11

Prosperity and Respect for the Unified Nation

1817-1825

The War of 1812 marked a turning point in American affairs. Freed at last from involvement in the affairs of Europe, Americans in 1815 now turned their full attention to developing their own nation.

The war itself had greatly stimulated a feeling of national pride. It had also helped unite Americans in their determination to strengthen the growing nation. So strong was this feeling during the years from about 1817 to 1825 that this period came to be known as the "Era of Good Feelings."

However, the term "Era of Good Feelings" was not entirely accurate. The spirit of sectionalism was also gaining strength as the different sections of the country continued to develop in their different ways.

The Northeast, particularly New England, was being reshaped by the Industrial Revolution. The South, mainly an agricultural region, was devoting more and more of its effort to the growing of cotton. The West, which most Americans still thought of as the land between the Appalachian Mountains and the Mississippi River, was attracting growing numbers of pioneer settlers.

Members of Congress naturally looked out for the special interests of their states and their own sections of the country. Congress and the President also had to weld the three sections of the rapidly growing country — the Northeast, the South, and the West — into a unified whole. They solved this problem, at least temporarily, by means of a program that was called the "American System."

THE CHAPTER IN OUTLINE

1. The Industrial Revolution reaches the United States.

2. New leaders develop the "American System."

3. The growing nation struggles with new and complex problems.

4. The United States warns Europe to stay out of the Western Hemisphere.

5. American education and arts reveal pride in the growing nation.

238

1 The Industrial Revolution reaches the United States

In the 1700's the invention and development of power-driven machines changed the way many products were made. More and more manufacturing was done in factories and less and less in the homes and small shops of workers.

The arrival of Samuel Slater. The shift to factories and machines has become known as the **Industrial Revolution.** Samuel Slater, who landed in New York in 1789, was one of many inventors and skilled workers who became pioneers of this revolution.

Although only 21 years old when he left England, Slater was already a highly skilled mechanic. He had worked in a cotton textile mill and knew a great deal about the new spinning and weaving machines built by British inventors. What is more, he knew that British industrialists wanted to keep the secrets of these new machines from other countries. For this reason, the British government had forbidden the machines to be sold. It had also passed laws forbidding textile workers to leave the country.

Slater nevertheless slipped away. He arrived in New York with empty hands and almost empty pockets, but in his head were plans for power-driven machines to spin and weave cloth.

Samuel Slater went to Rhode Island. There, with the financial aid of Moses Brown, a Quaker merchant, Slater reproduced from memory the machines he had used in England. Indeed, he even improved them. Soon Slater was operating a successful cotton factory, or mill, using water-powered machinery.

The growth of the factory system. Soon other Americans began to operate mills at water-power sites in New England and the Middle Atlantic states. At first the new mills did nothing more than spin thread with power-driven machines. The mill owners then distributed the thread to homes scattered over the surrounding countryside. Working at hand looms in their own homes, women wove the thread into cloth, which they then returned to the mill owners. Within a few years, however, mills began to weave the cloth as well as spin the yarn. This development came to be known as the **factory system.** During the early 1800's,

Slater's Mill, still standing in Pawtucket, Rhode Island, looked like this to an unknown artist in the early 1800's. The power in such mills came from water. The water flowed through a canal that ran beside or under the mill building.

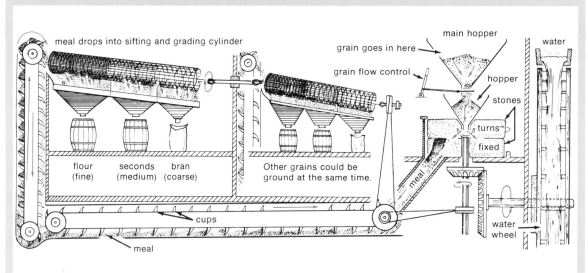

meal drops into sifting and grading cylinder

grain goes in here

main hopper

water

grain flow control

hopper

stones

turns

fixed

flour (fine)

seconds (medium)

bran (coarse)

Other grains could be ground at the same time.

cups

meal

water wheel

MECHANICAL GRISTMILL

Two grinding, sifting, and grading systems could be operated by one person using one water-power source. The operator fed grain into the main hoppers, where flow-control devices provided a steady supply for the grind-stones (only one grinding system shown). Conveyors and cups then carried the meal to revolving cylinders for sifting and grading. The operator replaced containers for the meal as they filled up.

more and more work was done by this factory system.

The power-driven machines and the buildings to house them were very expensive to build and maintain. Individual workers could not afford them. Thus **capitalists°** like Moses Brown built the factories, installed the machinery, purchased raw materials, hired workers, and distributed the finished products. After starting in the textile industry, the Industrial Revolution spread rapidly to the manufacturing of many other products, among them firearms, clocks, and watches.

The Industrial Revolution would have come to America in time even without Samuel Slater. As it turned out, however, Slater pioneered in developing America's factory system.

° The property, equipment, and money used to produce goods or provide services are known as **capital**. A **capitalist** is a person who invests capital in a business with the hope of earning profits.

The search for labor-saving machines. From the earliest days of settlement, the colonial towns and villages never had enough workers to develop America's seemingly limitless natural resources. Slowly but steadily, pioneer men and women pushed westward. With so much land available, they preferred to own their own farms rather than work as hired hands. Faced with this labor shortage, American farmers put their numerous sons and daughters to work at an early age.

The growing towns also had more work to be done than they had people to do it. This shortage of labor stimulated colonial manufacturers to invent labor-saving machines for factories and farms and to provide better working conditions and higher wages than were common in Europe.

Encouraging inventors. Because of these conditions, the American government took steps

240

to encourage inventors. In 1790 Congress enacted a law granting inventors as well as authors exclusive rights for 14 years to all profits made from their ideas. This law meant that the new tools or the new books belonged to their inventors or authors and could be produced and sold only with their permission for a period of 14 years.

New sources of power. Another important part of the Industrial Revolution was the discovery and use of new sources of power to run machinery. The textile machinery first used in Great Britain was driven by water power. In 1769, however, James Watt, a Scottish inventor, took out an English patent for a steam engine. By the 1790's steam power was rapidly replacing water power in British mills.

Although Americans in the 1790's knew about steam engines and were even building some of their own, steam power did not come quickly to the United States. By 1812 there were only ten steam-powered mills in the new nation. Americans were not uninterested in steam as a power source, but their rivers and streams, especially in New England, provided an ample supply of water to power the nation's first factories.

Interchangeable parts. Meanwhile Eli Whitney, a Connecticut resident, hit upon a new idea for building machines, an idea that French inventors also developed. Whitney's idea grew out of his work with guns. Before the early 1800's, all guns were manufactured by gunsmiths, who hammered out each part separately and assembled the parts by hand. When any gun part was damaged, a new part had to be made by hand to replace it.

In 1798 Eli Whitney decided that he could manufacture guns using a new principle of production. He wrote to the Secretary of the Treasury requesting a contract. "I should like," he wrote, "to undertake the manufacture of 10,000 or 15,000 stand of arms. I am persuaded that machinery moved by water, adapted to this business, would greatly diminish the labor and facilitate the manufacture of this article. Machines for forging, rolling, floating, boring, grinding, polishing, etc., may all be made use of to advantage."

Although Whitney's request was unusual, he got his contract from the government. When more than two years had passed, though, people began to think Whitney's project had failed.

Then the young inventor made a trip to Washington. Before a group of skeptical officials, he unpacked a box containing the parts of ten identical guns. At Whitney's request an official selected one part from each of the piles scattered about the table. The first gun was then assembled. This process was repeated until all ten guns had been assembled from these **interchangeable parts** and fired. Those present witnessed what was actually the beginning of **mass production** in America.

A look ahead. Not even the most far-sighted Americans ever dreamed that the developments taking place around them were destined to change life everywhere.

In years to come, the Industrial Revolution would help to unite the American people. It would help solve problems of transportation by binding the nation together with a web of steel rails. It would provide Americans with unheard-of labor-saving devices. It would profoundly affect the roles and status of both women and men in American life. It would help Americans conquer the wilderness and make use of what were then considered the inexhaustible resources of forest and sea and soil. It would in time transform the United States into the wealthiest nation on earth.

SECTION SURVEY

IDENTIFY: Industrial Revolution, factory system, capitalist, interchangeable parts, mass production.

1. (a) What technological advance helped to bring about the Industrial Revolution? (b) How did the Industrial Revolution change the system of manufacturing in Great Britain and the United States?

2. What role did Samuel Slater play in the development of the American factory system?

3. How was the American factory system aided by (a) the investment of capitalists, (b) the shortage of labor in American towns, and (c) laws governing inventions?

4. (a) How did Eli Whitney and James Watt contribute to the Industrial Revolution? (b) Why were their contributions significant?

5. Picture Study: How many people might it take to do by hand the work done mechanically by the gristmill on page 240? What conveniences might this type of gristmill bring to society? What inconveniences might it cause?

Three brilliant political figures defended the interests of the nation's major sections. Daniel Webster (top) used moving oratory to gain legislation that favored the industrial Northeast. John C. Calhoun (middle) strove equally hard to protect the very different interests of the agricultural South. Henry Clay (bottom) worked tirelessly to balance these sections' conflicting needs and to further the interests of the West.

2 New leaders develop the "American System"

Most of those who tackled the job of running the new nation after the War of 1812 were new on the national scene. The older leaders of the Revolutionary War period and the opening years of the nation's history were passing from the scene.

The famous three. Three of the new leaders were particularly outstanding. They were destined to play prominent roles in the nation's history for the next 35 years. Each came from a different section of the country.

Henry Clay, a Republican from Kentucky, entered Congress in 1811. Clay, as you know, was one of the "War Hawks" who had clamored for war with Great Britain in 1812. Trained in the law and striking in appearance, Henry Clay was an impressive orator. He became the acknowledged representative of the western parts of the country.

John C. Calhoun of South Carolina also entered Congress in 1811. He, too, was a lawyer, a persuasive speaker, and a Republican. Like Clay, he had also favored the War of 1812. With his keen mind and his devotion to politics, Calhoun soon became the major representative of the southern states and of the doctrine of states' rights.

Daniel Webster, a Federalist from Massachusetts, entered Congress in 1813. He was born on a farm in New Hampshire. Like Clay and Calhoun, Webster became a lawyer, practicing first in New Hampshire and later in Boston, Massachusetts. Like Clay and Calhoun, Webster was a powerful speaker. In Congress he quickly became the outstanding representative of the northeastern part of the country. At first Webster favored low tariffs. Then, as industrial interests in the Northeast replaced shipping interests, he became a defender of high protective tariffs.

The elections of 1816 and 1820. It was an older leader, however, who won the Presidential election of 1816. James Monroe, a Republican who had served as Secretary of State under President Madison, easily defeated the Federalist candidate, Rufus King. King, a brilliant and able Senator from New York, represented a dying party. By 1816 the Federalists were so weakened that they won only three states.

In 1817 even a Boston publication that had opposed Monroe in the election said that the times ahead would prove to be an "Era of Good Feelings." This phrase pleased the new President, and as the years passed it did seem to describe national life. The different groups in the country began to work together on common problems. The Federalist Party as such disappeared. For more than ten years, the Republican Party, originally founded by Thomas Jefferson, was the only political party in the United States.

By 1820 political harmony was so widespread, at least on the surface, that President Monroe ran for re-election without opposition. He won all of the electoral votes but one and was re-elected President.

The American System. In 1816, even before President Monroe was elected for the first time, the Republicans took steps to strengthen the growing nation. In so doing, they increased the powers of the federal government at the expense of states' rights. To justify their actions, they used a loose interpretation of the Constitution, like the one favored earlier by Alexander Hamilton and the Federalists. This was one reason that the Federalist Party disappeared. By 1816 the Republicans were doing many things the Federalists had favored doing for years.

National-minded leaders like Henry Clay of Kentucky insisted that the nation needed a sound economic program that would enable the United States to become independent of the rest of the world. The economic program that the Republicans adopted in 1816 came to be called the **American System**, a term later used by Henry Clay in a speech in Congress.

The American System developed by the Republicans rested on three major foundations. (1) A national bank would provide a sound, uniform financial system. (2) A protective tariff would provide a wall behind which American factories could grow and prosper. (3) A transportation system would ease trade between the northeastern manufacturers and the western and southern farmers.

The second Bank of the United States. In 1816 a national bank was badly needed. Five years earlier, in 1811, the charter of the first Bank of the United States had expired. When

this happened, a number of state legislatures, especially in the West, promptly began to grant bank charters to private individuals. These state charters permitted individual investors to organize and operate their own banks.

Between 1811 and 1816, the number of state banks nearly tripled. Many of the new banks were poorly regulated. As a result, some of them began to issue more and more of their own paper money. Much of the new paper money declined in value, and some of it soon became worthless.

This unhealthy financial situation could not be tolerated. It was clear that a national bank was essential to the nation's well-being. Thus in 1816, Congress granted a charter creating the second Bank of the United States.

The protective tariff of 1816. In 1816 the Republicans enacted a protective tariff. In doing so, they adopted another of Hamilton's basic ideas and made it part of the American System. During the early 1800's and especially during the war years from 1812 to 1815, Americans had found it difficult to get manufactured goods from Europe. As a result, new factories had sprung up on American soil. When the War of 1812 ended, British manufacturers naturally wanted to drive their American competitors out of business.

The ink was hardly dry on the Treaty of Ghent in 1815 before British ships began to deliver factory-made goods to American ports. The British manufacturers were dumping goods. That is, they were selling large quantities of their goods below cost to drive rival manufacturers out of business. Once American factories closed, the British manufacturers would raise the prices of their products. They could then recover their earlier losses, knowing that they faced little competition from the ruined Americans.

American factory owners had no intention of being driven out of business. They demanded government protection against their British rivals. Thus Congress adopted the Tariff Act of 1816, which levied what seemed to be high duties on manufactured goods shipped into the United States.

In 1816 most Americans favored the protective tariff. Even Thomas Jefferson, who had earlier opposed the protective tariff recommended by Hamilton, now approved the Tariff Act of 1816. John C. Calhoun of South Carolina, who later became a strong foe of tariffs, supported the Tariff Act of 1816, assuming that the South would develop industries of its own. In protecting its infant industries, the young nation was looking forward to becoming self-sufficient and economically independent of Great Britain.

SECTION SURVEY

IDENTIFY: Henry Clay, John C. Calhoun, Daniel Webster, James Monroe, American System, Tariff Act of 1816.

1. (a) Why was the period from about 1817 to 1825 known as the "Era of Good Feelings"? (b) How did the Republican Party of this period differ from the earlier Republican Party?
2. (a) What were the three major foundations of the American System? (b) How did each of these promote national unity?
3. Why had a second national bank become necessary by 1816?
4. (a) How did the War of 1812 affect American and British manufacturing? (b) What action did British manufacturers take after the war? (c) How did the American government respond?

3 The growing nation struggles with new and complex problems

The new nation grew by leaps and bounds. Soon after the Constitution went into effect, four new states were added to the original thirteen—Vermont (1791), Kentucky (1792), Tennessee (1796), and Ohio (1803). Between 1810 and 1820, the population west of the mountains more than doubled, from about 1 million to more than 2 million. Five new states entered the Union—Louisiana (1812), Indiana (1816), Mississippi (1817), Illinois (1818), and Alabama (1819).

Demand for better transportation. Until shortly after the War of 1812, the western settlers depended almost entirely upon the rivers or upon very poor roads for transportation. Flatboats and rafts could float products downriver, but westerners could not use them to transport manufactured goods upriver. Keelboats, invented for this purpose, were la-

borious and slow. As a result, most manufactured products from the eastern areas reached the western lands by means of rough roads across the mountains. Transporting goods by wagon over these roads was costly and time-consuming.

A good transportation system was as essential to the new nation as a good Constitution and a strong federal government. Farmers in the new western states needed roads and canals to carry their products to eastern markets. Northeastern manufacturers needed roads and canals to move their manufactured goods into the sparsely settled areas of the country. Southerners were also interested in improving transportation. As John C. Calhoun of South Carolina put it, "We are greatly and rapidly—I was about to say fearfully—growing. This is our pride and our danger, our weakness and our strength. . . . Let us, then, bind the republic together with a perfect system of roads and canals."

First steps by private enterprise. The need for better transportation had long been clear. During the 1790's and early 1800's, owners of businesses throughout the country organized private companies to build roads and canals. By 1811, private companies had built more than 1,400 miles (2,250 kilometers) of improved **toll roads** in New York State alone. These were private roads that charged a fee, or toll, to those who used them.

Nearly all of the new roads and canals built by the early 1800's reached out from the coastal cities—Boston, New York, Philadelphia, Baltimore, Charleston—into the surrounding country. These roads and canals did not run into sparsely settled regions or through the Appalachian Mountains. No private investors wanted to spend money to build a transportation system in thinly populated areas. The risks were too great and the profits were too small.

Improvements at public expense. A growing number of citizens demanded that the federal government finance and build the needed highways and canals. During President Jefferson's administration, Albert Gallatin, Secretary of the Treasury, proposed that the federal government build a network of highways covering the entire United States. Congress did not adopt Gallatin's ambitious proposal. It did, however, vote money in 1806 for building a

The Fairview Inn, near Baltimore, was obviously a popular stopping place for people and wagons traveling the Cumberland Road that led to Ohio and Illinois. In a single year, 12,000 wagons passed here on the trip westward.

road from Cumberland, Maryland, across the mountains into what is now West Virginia.

Construction began in 1811. Within a few years this road, called the Cumberland Road or the National Road, was pushed westward from Cumberland as far as Ohio. Between 1822 and 1838, with additional grants of money from Congress, the National Road was extended across Ohio and Indiana to Vandalia, Illinois (see map, page 276). As each section was finished, the federal government turned it over to the states through which it ran. Thousands of settlers poured into the western country over the National Road, particularly after the War of 1812.

In 1816, with the National Road progressing westward, Congress approved a bill calling for "internal improvements" at government expense. President Madison vetoed the bill because he felt that the Constitution did not give Congress the power to spend money in this way. President Monroe shared Madison's convictions. Then Congress abandoned its plans for further internal improvements at the public expense.

Even so, the economic program adopted by Congress during Madison's administration had accomplished a great deal. It had set up a na-tional bank that provided Americans with a reasonably sound currency. It had given the manufacturers a protective tariff. It had helped to open up the western areas by pushing the National Road farther westward. In general, it had strengthened the different sections and had drawn them closer together.

The Panic of 1819. By 1818 all sections of the United States were enjoying prosperity. Conditions were so prosperous, in fact, that various groups had begun to indulge in **overspeculation.** This was excessive, risky investment in land, stock, or commodities in the hope of making large profits. Southerners, tempted by rising prices for cotton, bought land at inflated prices. Western settlers, tempted by rising prices for grain and meat, also scrambled to buy land. Manufacturers in the Northeast, eager to take advantage of the general prosperity, bought land and built new mills and factories.

All of these groups borrowed money to finance their enterprises. Many banks encouraged the frenzy of speculation by lending money too freely on the flimsiest security.

Then came the crash. Late in 1818 the directors of the Bank of the United States or-

245

dered all their branch banks not to renew any personal mortgages. The directors also ordered the branch banks to present all state bank notes to the state banks for immediate payment in gold or silver or in national bank notes. State banks could not make their payments and closed their doors. Farmers and manufacturers could not renew their mortgages, and many lost their property.

By mid-1819, because of numerous foreclosures, the Bank of the United States had acquired huge areas of land in the South and Middle West and many businesses in the East. People ruined by foreclosure blamed the bank for their troubles and called it "the Monster."

Increased federal power. In the midst of the financial panic, Chief Justice Marshall of the Supreme Court handed down one of his most important decisions in the case of *McCulloch v. Maryland.* The Maryland state legislature had attempted to tax the Baltimore branch of the Bank of the United States. When the bank refused to pay the tax to Maryland, the case went first to the state Court of Appeals and finally to the Supreme Court.

Three major issues were involved. (1) Who has sovereign power — the federal government or the state governments? (2) Does the Constitution give Congress power to create a national bank? (3) If Congress does have this power, do the states then have the right to tax the bank?

In 1819 Marshall decided all these issues in favor of the federal government. Referring to the first point, he declared that "the government of the Union, then, . . . is emphatically and truly a government of the people." Thus,

concluded Marshall, since the federal government was created by the people, not by the states, the power of the federal government was supreme.

Referring to the second point, Marshall admitted that the Constitution did not specifically give Congress the power to create a bank. He went on to say that the Constitution *did* give Congress the right to do whatever was "necessary and proper" to carry out any of its specific powers. Thus, reasoned Marshall, since Congress had the power to levy and collect taxes and to borrow money, it also had the right to create a national bank to carry out these financial powers.

Referring to the third point, Marshall declared that "the power to tax involves the power to destroy." If a state had the power to tax a national institution such as the Bank of the United States, it could severely weaken or destroy federal power. Therefore, Marshall stated, neither Maryland nor any other state had the right or the power to tax the Bank of the United States.

Marshall's continuing influence. In 1819 Marshall wrote another far-reaching decision. In the case of *Trustees of Dartmouth College v. Woodward,* Marshall set aside a law passed by the state legislature of New Hampshire. This law changed the charter of Dartmouth College, a private institution. The college's trustees claimed that the new law was unconstitutional. When the case came before the Supreme Court, John Marshall supported the trustees. Marshall pointed out that a charter was a valid contract guaranteed by the Constitution. Thus

SOURCES

McCULLOCH v.
MARYLAND
(1819)

The power to tax involves the power to destroy. . . . If the states may tax one instrument, employed by the [federal] government in the execution of its powers, they may tax any and every other instrument. They may tax the mail; they may tax the mint; they may tax patent rights; they may tax the papers of the customhouse; they may tax judicial process; they may tax all the means employed by the government, to an excess which would defeat all the ends of government. This was not intended by the American people. They did not design to make their government dependent on the states. . . .

The question is, in truth, a question of supremacy; and if the right of the states to tax the means employed by the general government be conceded, the declaration that the Constitution, and the laws made in pursuance thereof, shall be the supreme law of the land, is empty and unmeaning declamation. . . .

The Mississippi River was another pathway for Americans on the move. In 1832 artist Leon Pomarede captured this "View of St. Louis." The early steamboats shown would soon be replaced by giant "paddle wheelers."

no state had the power to interfere with such a contract.

This decision was important for two reasons. First, it asserted the right of the Supreme Court to set aside state laws when such laws were unconstitutional. Second, it guaranteed that corporations operating under state charters would not be subject to the whims of state legislators.

Five years later, in 1824, in *Gibbons v. Ogden,* Marshall declared another state law unconstitutional. The New York legislature had attempted to give Robert Fulton and his business associates a monopoly on steamboat traffic on the Hudson River. Marshall argued that the Constitution had given the federal government the power to regulate interstate commerce. Since navigation on the Hudson River involved interstate commerce, the state had no right to grant a monopoly. The monopoly granted by the state legislature was therefore unconstitutional.

Marshall's argument greatly broadened the definition of interstate commerce. His decision thus paved the way for later federal control of such interstate commerce as telegraph, telephone, radio, and television, as well as kidnaping and car theft if the criminals were to cross state lines.

John Marshall's decisions did much to strengthen the powers of the federal government. While Congress, through the American System, was seeking to build a stronger, more unified nation, Marshall on the Supreme Court bench was moving toward the same goal.

SECTION SURVEY

IDENTIFY: toll roads, National Road, overspeculation, interstate commerce.

1. Why did each section of the country want to develop a good transportation system?

2. (a) Where and by whom were the first American canals and roads built? (b) What action did the federal government take to improve transportation?

3. (a) What caused the Panic of 1819? (b) Why did many people blame the Bank of the United States for their troubles?

4. What principles concerning the power of federal and state governments were decided in the following Supreme Court cases: (a) *McCulloch v. Maryland,* (b) *Trustees of Dartmouth College v. Woodward,* (c) *Gibbons v. Ogden?*

4 The United States warns Europe to stay out of the Western Hemisphere

The growing spirit of national pride and the increase in federal power strongly influenced developments within the United States. These new feelings of pride and strength also influenced American foreign policy.

At this time the people of Latin America were struggling to win their independence from Spain and Portugal. Americans were deeply interested in the revolutions that were taking place in the lands south of the United States.

Revolutions in Latin America. In the early 1800's, as you know, Napoleon was trying to control all of Europe. In 1808 he conquered Spain. This was the signal for Latin Americans to rise in revolt.

The enormous South American continent is broken by mighty mountain barriers, such as the Andes, and by dense rain forests, such as those of the Amazon River Valley. As a result, the Latin-American struggle for independence took place in a number of separate revolutions (see map, page 249). These separate struggles were fought for essentially the same objectives: freedom and independence.

By 1822 the American continents were not yet free of foreign control. Russia still claimed the vast unexplored territory of Alaska. Great Britain still ruled Canada, British Honduras, British Guiana (gee·AHN·ah), and a number of West Indian islands. Spain still ruled Cuba and Puerto Rico. France and the Netherlands still ruled French and Dutch Guiana and several of the islands in the Caribbean. However, Europeans were on their way out. The growing forces of democracy and the drive toward national independence were remaking the map. These independence movements also struck a massive blow at slavery throughout Latin America. Soon slavery persisted only in Cuba and Brazil.

American control of Florida. The revolutions in Mexico and other Latin-American countries greatly affected the United States. Many Americans viewed the struggle for independence of their Latin-American neighbors

as a continuation of their own earlier struggle for independence.

The American government was officially neutral in the conflicts between Spain and Portugal on the one hand and their colonies on the other. However, between 1810 and 1813, the United States annexed the territory known as West Florida. Spain protested but was powerless to act.

Spanish authorities in East Florida at about this time were unable or unwilling to return growing numbers of fugitive slaves to their American owners or to those who claimed to own them. Nor did the Spanish authorities restrain the Seminole Indians of East Florida from launching raids into southern Georgia and Alabama.

In 1816 the United States government ordered Andrew Jackson to move troops up to the Spanish forts in East Florida. He proposed instead to his superiors in Washington that American troops conquer all of East Florida within 60 days. Receiving no reply, Jackson seized two Spanish forts and executed two British fur traders accused of giving arms to Indians. Once again the Spaniards, deeply involved with troubles in Latin America, could only protest. Jackson's invasion of East Florida, called the First Seminole War, convinced Spain that the United States would not rest until the Stars and Stripes flew over all of Florida. Thus Spain decided to sell Florida while it still held claim to the area.

In 1819 the two countries signed the Adams-Onís Treaty. It gave the United States all the land east of the Mississippi River, together with any claims that Spain might have to the Oregon country. In return, the United States agreed to assume claims totaling $5 million that American citizens held against Spain for damages to American shipping during the Napoleonic Wars. More important in the long run, the United States agreed to abandon its claim to Texas as part of the Louisiana Purchase.

British interest in Latin America. As a colonial power, Great Britain did not sympathize with the revolutions in Latin America. Nevertheless, like many United States citizens, the British looked forward to an increasingly profitable trade with the former colonies of Spain and Portugal. The British wanted to retain the trade of Latin America, which, since the start of the revolutions, had been carried largely in

British ships. If the Spanish colonies were restored to Spain, British merchants would lose the profitable trade.

European interference. Until 1815 and Napoleon's final defeat, the European nations were too busy with their own problems to take an active part in Latin-American affairs. After the fall of Napoleon, however, a number of European nations joined in an alliance to put down revolutions. Americans became alarmed at rumors that France, encouraged by the European alliance, might help Spain recover its New World colonies.

To add to American alarm, in 1821 the tsar of Russia warned the ships of other nations to avoid the Pacific coast from Alaska southward to the 51st parallel. This order barred American vessels from the Oregon coast, which the United States claimed jointly with Great Britain. The Oregon country had already become a useful port of call for Yankee traders, who traded cloth and other manufactured goods to the Indians in exchange for furs. Russia was

INDEPENDENCE IN THE AMERICAS

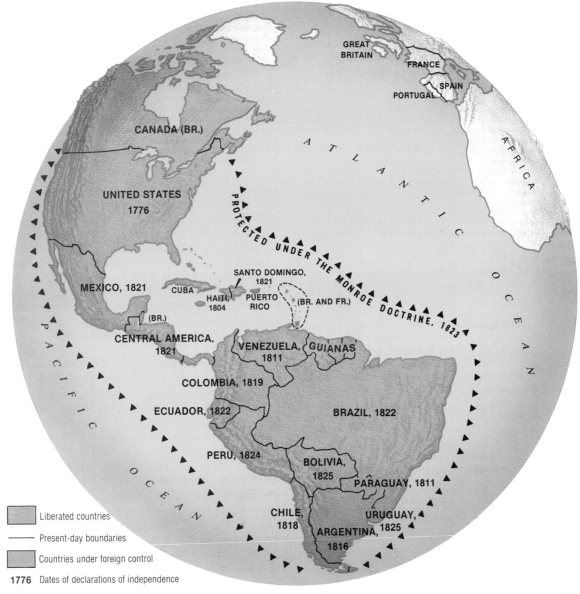

GREAT BRITAIN
FRANCE
SPAIN
PORTUGAL
AFRICA

CANADA (BR.)

ATLANTIC OCEAN

UNITED STATES 1776

PROTECTED UNDER THE MONROE DOCTRINE, 1823

MEXICO, 1821
CUBA
HAITI, 1804
SANTO DOMINGO, 1821
PUERTO RICO
(BR. AND FR.)

(BR.)

CENTRAL AMERICA, 1821

VENEZUELA 1811
GUIANAS

COLOMBIA, 1819

PACIFIC OCEAN

ECUADOR, 1822

BRAZIL, 1822

PERU, 1824

BOLIVIA, 1825

PARAGUAY, 1811

CHILE, 1818

URUGUAY, 1825

ARGENTINA, 1816

Liberated countries
Present-day boundaries
Countries under foreign control
1776 Dates of declarations of independence

249

also establishing trading posts along the coast of northern California. For these reasons, the American government did not permit the tsar's order to go unchallenged.

The Monroe Doctrine. The United States met the Russian threat and possible European intervention in Latin America with three specific actions. (1) Secretary of State John Quincy Adams sent a strong note of protest to Russia, bluntly asserting American rights to sail the Pacific waters. (2) The United States recognized the independence of the revolutionary governments of Latin America. (3) President Monroe, in his annual message to Congress on December 2, 1823, announced an American foreign policy that later came to be known as the Monroe Doctrine. The Monroe Doctrine actually extended the policy that Washington had stated in his Farewell Address and that Jefferson had added to in his statements on foreign policy.

SOURCES

THE MONROE DOCTRINE
(1823)

The American continents . . . are henceforth not to be considered as subjects for future colonization by any European powers. . . . We owe it, therefore, to candor and to the amicable relations existing between the United States and those powers [Quadruple Alliance] to declare that we should consider any attempt on their part to extend their system to any portion of this hemisphere as dangerous to our peace and safety. With the existing colonies or dependencies of any European power, we have not interfered and shall not interfere. But with the governments who have declared their independence and maintained it, and whose independence we have . . . acknowledged, we could not view any interposition for the purpose of oppressing them, or controlling in any other manner their destiny, by any European power in any other light than as the manifestation of an unfriendly disposition toward the United States. . . .

Our policy in regard to Europe, which was adopted at an early stage of the wars which have so long agitated that quarter of the globe, nevertheless remains the same, which is, not to interfere in the internal concerns of any of its powers. . . .

In this famous message, President Monroe made four clear declarations. (1) The Western Hemisphere was no longer open to colonization by European powers. (2) Any attempt by any European country to establish colonies in the New World or to gain political control of any American country would be viewed as an unfriendly act toward the United States. (3) The United States would not interfere in the affairs of European nations or in the affairs of their colonies already established in the Americas. (4) In return, Europe must not in any way disturb the political status of any free country in the Western Hemisphere.

Enforcing the Doctrine. With the Monroe Doctrine, the United States proclaimed a policy of "America for Americans." The important question, of course, was whether the United States could enforce the Monroe Doctrine.

Fortunately for the United States, Latin Americans resisted European intervention, as did Great Britain. Although Latin Americans knew that the United States was acting in its own self-interest, they welcomed its commitment to the independence of all the Americas from Europe.

Great Britain gave the Doctrine its real strength. In 1823 and, in fact, until well into the 1900's, the British navy controlled the Atlantic sea lanes. Only with British consent could ships of any nation, including the United States, move between Europe and the Americas. Americans were fortunate that British merchants were keenly interested in preserving the independence of the countries of Central and South America. At the first hint of interference from any European power, Great Britain sided with the Americas.

Significance of the Doctrine. The Monroe Doctrine was a direct warning to the European powers that the United States was vitally concerned in the affairs of all the nations in North, Central, and South America. The Doctrine was to become a major principle of United States foreign policy.

The Monroe Doctrine also revealed the growing spirit of American strength and unity. President Monroe spoke for a united people of more than 10 million citizens. He spoke for a nation that was becoming increasingly conscious of its own strength and that was determined to retain its independence from Europe and to decide its own policies.

IDENTIFY: First Seminole War, Monroe Doctrine, 1823.

1. What effect did Napoleon's conquest of Spain in 1808 have on Spain's colonies in North and South America?

2. (a) Describe how the United States acquired East and West Florida. (b) Summarize the terms of the Adams-Onís Treaty.

3. (a) Why were Americans fearful of European intervention in the Western Hemisphere after 1815? (b) What actions did President Monroe take to prevent intervention?

4. Source Study: (a) According to the Source on page 250, what were three main provisions of the Monroe Doctrine? (b) How did the Doctrine reflect growing feelings of American pride and strength?

5 American education and arts reveal pride in the growing nation

Benjamin Banneker surveyed the site of Washington, D.C., and made the first wooden clock in America. He learned to read and write from his grandmother, who had been an indentured servant.

With the American System, Americans revealed their intention of becoming *economically* independent of Europe. With the Monroe Doctrine, the United States declared its complete *political* independence from Europe.

A third step in the nation's growth was the development of truly American religion, education, art, and literature. With this new development, the United States began to become less dependent on Europe *culturally.*

After the American Revolution, American Protestant churches cut their close ties with church authorities in Europe. Many, though not all, educators, artists, and writers of this period revealed in their work the growing spirit of **nationalism,** or national pride. They helped to unite the nation perhaps as much as the business and political leaders who were at the same time working for economic and political independence.

A national university proposed. Pride in their new nation prompted some Americans to favor a national university to train people for public service and provide the nation with educated citizens. George Washington had wanted such an institution. So had John

Quincy Adams, who became President in 1826. Other patriotic Americans favored the idea of a national university. In spite of this strong support, the proposal never became a reality.

Noah Webster — author and educator. An illustration of the growing spirit of independence was Noah Webster's project for molding an American language, distinct from English. "America," Webster had declared in 1783, "must be as independent in *literature* as she is in *politics,* as famous for *arts* as for *arms.*" With this in mind, Webster labored at the tremendous task of publishing a dictionary — *An American Dictionary of the English Language.* In it the British spelling of many words was simplified. When his dictionary was finally published in 1828, Webster hoped that it would help Americans to achieve a uniform language.

Webster also prepared a spelling book. Published as early as 1783, it was used in nearly every elementary school in America. By the time Webster died in 1843, more than 15 million copies had been sold, and nearly 100 million copies were sold before the book went out of general use. Like Webster's dictionary, his spelling book helped Americans develop a uniform national language.

American history and geography. In addition to his work on the dictionary and the spelling book, Webster edited a famous school reader, *An American Selection of Lessons in Reading and Speaking.* Hoping to arouse a spirit of national pride as well as a reverence for American heroes, Webster devoted more than half of his school reader to material from American history. He later wrote complete books about American history.

Meanwhile Jedidiah Morse, a minister and scholar, was introducing American youth to the geography of their country. His geographies were also largely devoted to the story of American life.

A number of other authors wrote American history books. Among them was Hannah Adams of Massachusetts, probably the first American woman to support herself by writing. Before the Era of Good Feelings ended, American history had become an accepted part of the course of study in many American elementary schools. One indication of growing national pride was legislation passed in 1827 by Massachusetts and Vermont. This legislation required all the larger schools in these states to teach American history.

The arts. During the early years of the nation's growth, the spirit of nationalism also influenced a number of artists.

There were, for instance, the architects who first designed the nation's capital, Washington, D.C., among them the French engineer, Pierre L'Enfant (lon·FON). There was Benjamin Banneker, a free black from Maryland, who helped to survey the site of the city. Many others also played a large part in the design and construction of the city. Thomas Jefferson, for example, proposed the locations of the Capitol building and the White House. As the city of Washington grew, it helped give American citizens a feeling of permanence, a conviction that the new nation was destined to endure.

During this same period, such painters as Charles Willson Peale, Gilbert Stuart, and John Trumbull painted many portraits of the

Samuel F. B. Morse captured the new spirit of American art early in his life. He was just 19 when he painted this watercolor of his family. He is at the left of his father, who was a minister and the author of schoolbooks about geography.

NEEDED: A HERO

"You have a great deal of money lying in the bones of old George if you will but exert yourself to extract it." So wrote Mason Locke Weems (Parson Weems) to his publisher, Matthew Carey. "Old George" was none other than George Washington, the subject of a best-selling biography by the clergyman-author. Eager customers bought over 50,000 copies in the ten years after it was first published in 1800.

Parson Weems did much to make a near-mythical figure out of our first President. As a traveling bookseller, he realized that Americans were hungry for heroes. The young United States was anxious to take its place among far older countries with legendary pasts. Who could be a better symbol of national pride than George Washington?

At the time of his death in 1799, Washington was certainly admired, but as a human being with human flaws. For example, he was not a brilliant general or a spellbinding orator, and he was known to have lost his temper now and then. But Weems made him almost godlike, creating incidents to serve his purpose. It was Weems who created the cherry-tree story, in which Washington's honesty more than made up for his carelessness with his hatchet.

Weems's hero worship set the tone for decades. Scholarly biographies depicted Washington as a perfect leader. His correspondence was edited to remove its saltier phrases. Flowery speeches were made every year on his birthday. Dignified pictures of him hung everywhere. The capital of the new nation bore his name. Many years were to pass before Americans allowed Washington to come out from under his halo and be admired as a man rather than revered as a saint.

nation's leaders. Although these painters lacked the originality and skill of the greatest artists, their portraits helped make the nation's founders known to many Americans.

Writers. During the early 1800's, some writers began to draw upon the American scene for the material in their stories. Mason Locke Weems (better known as Parson Weems) published a biography of George Washington, written in glowing terms. Washington Irving turned chiefly to the Dutch society of the Hudson Valley for his material. He produced such works as "The Legend of Sleepy Hollow," "Rip Van Winkle," and the *Knickerbocker History of New York.* James Fenimore Cooper's *Leatherstocking Tales,* a series of novels, had as its hero a white frontier scout skilled in forest crafts and versed in Indian lore. The tales stereotyped Indians as either "fine" and "noble" or "treacherous" and "savage."

A new feeling of unity. Nationalism was one of the forces that helped to shape American life during the first 30 or more years of the nation's history. This national pride influenced rich and poor alike in all sections of the country. It influenced the lives of pioneers clearing the forests, the owners of businesses in the growing cities, and the political leaders in Washington. It stimulated educators, artists, and writers as well as the men, women, and children who listened to their ideas and read their books and looked at their paintings. Thus the new nation became stronger and more unified as the years went by.

SECTION SURVEY

IDENTIFY: nationalism, Hannah Adams, Benjamin Banneker, John Trumbull, Washington Irving.

1. What does the term "cultural independence" mean?
2. What contributions did Noah Webster make to American education?
3. How did Americans in the early 1800's express their spirit of nationalism in the following areas: (a) history, (b) geography, (c) painting, (d) literature?

Chapter Survey

Summary: Tracing the Main Ideas

The desire for independence and for national unity reached a peak in the United States during the decade following the War of 1812. Because the people were so united in their efforts to strengthen the new nation, the period from about 1817 to 1825 was called the "Era of Good Feelings."

During the Era of Good Feelings, Americans from all walks of life worked at the task of making their nation strong and independent of the rest of the world. Congress, supported by many in business and farming, adopted the American System to make the United States economically independent and self-sufficient. The system consisted of a national bank to provide a sound financial base, a high tariff to protect American industry, and a national transportation system to connect the East and the West.

Meanwhile, President Monroe and his advisers took steps to keep the nation politically independent of Europe. The means they used for this purpose was the Monroe Doctrine.

During these same years, educators, artists, and writers devoted their efforts to American themes and heroes, thus helping to make the United States culturally independent of Europe as well.

Beneath the surface of the Era of Good Feelings, divisive forces were at work. As a result, the new nation was soon split by the sectional controversy that in time plunged the country into four terrible years of warfare.

Before turning to this controversy, however, let us look at how the American people, while building a new nation, also strengthened the spirit and practices of democracy. This is the story told in the next chapter.

Inquiring into History

1. Explain the role that each of the following contributed to the growth of industry in the young nation: (a) the War of 1812, (b) the shortage of labor in the United States, (c) the policies of the government.
2. Why was the growth of the nation's transportation system so important to the development of the nation?
3. The program of road building and other internal improvements begun after the War of 1812 ignored the Indians who lived in the area. (a) Suggest two possible policies that the federal government might have adopted concerning the Indian population of these lands. (b) What arguments might have been made in support of each policy?
4. Thomas Jefferson said that John Marshall made the Constitution "a mere thing of wax . . . which . . . [the justices of the Supreme Court] may twist and shape into any form they please." Do you agree or disagree with Jefferson's feelings about Marshall's decisions? Give evidence to support your opinion.
5. Explain how each of the following revealed the growing spirit of nationalism: (a) the American System, (b) the decisions of the Supreme Court, (c) Webster's *American Dictionary of the English Language*.

Relating Past to Present

1. Study the excerpt from the Monroe Doctrine on page 250. Which of the ideas it contains are still important today? Name some recent world events that have caused the United States to apply ideas expressed in the Monroe Doctrine.
2. Can isolationism—a nation's separating itself from the affairs of other nations—help bring about peace in today's world? Why or why not?
3. Make a list of key inventions, developments, and improvements that revolutionized American industry and transportation during the early 1800's. (a) Explain why each was important. (b) Name one lasting result of each.

Developing Social Science Skills

1. Study the map on page 249. (a) What color shows countries that were not yet independent? (b) Name four countries that became independent during the 1820's. (c) Why might the Monroe Doctrine have been difficult to enforce?
2. Read a short story or novel by Washington Irving or James Fenimore Cooper. (a) What evidence do you find of nationalism in the story? (b) Do you think the story is uniquely American? That is, could a European have written essentially the same story? Explain.

Chapter **12**

The Nation's Growing Democratic Strength

1825–1845

What is democracy? Abraham Lincoln partly defined it when he referred to "government of the people, by the people, for the people." The right of all qualified persons to vote and hold office—that is, to take part in their own government—is sometimes called *political* democracy.

There is more than this to democracy. You often hear of an *economic* and *social* democracy. That is a society in which all people have an equal opportunity to gain an education, to choose the careers they want, to achieve individual economic independence, and to live from day to day in freedom, equal in the eyes of the law to all their neighbors.

This larger idea of democracy began to develop roots in the early years of America's history. For most Americans, however, democracy remained sharply limited. The noble ideal of the Declaration of Independence that all persons are created equal by no means applied to all people. It did not yet apply to blacks, to Indians, to other minorities, or to women.

Political democracy was limited in the early years. When the Constitution was adopted, the right to vote and to hold public office was restricted in varying degrees in the states. Many states required that voters own a certain amount of real estate or property.

During the early years of the nation's history, however, political democracy made increasing gains. The constitutions of the new western states allowed all white male taxpayers the right to vote. Gradually the eastern states relaxed their requirements. By the late 1820's many of the earlier voting restrictions on white male adults were gone. Political democracy also scored a major victory in 1828 with the election of Andrew Jackson as President.

THE CHAPTER IN OUTLINE

1. Andrew Jackson emerges as "the people's choice."
2. The people take a more active part in government.
3. Andrew Jackson exercises his Presidential powers.
4. The Jacksonian era ends in an economic depression.

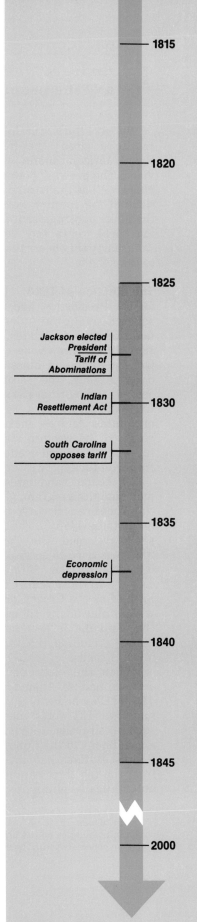

1815

1820

1825

Jackson elected President

Tariff of Abominations

Indian Resettlement Act — 1830

South Carolina opposes tariff

1835

Economic depression

1840

1845

2000

1 Andrew Jackson emerges as "the people's choice"

By 1824 the Era of Good Feelings was drawing to a close. The Republican Party and the American public were increasingly divided. The growing power of the ordinary people as well as the rivalry among the major sections of the country were clearly revealed in the political struggles from 1824 to 1828. During these years the Democratic Party – the same party that bears that name today – began to take shape.

The election of 1824. In 1824 four men ran for the Presidency, and all four called themselves Republicans. At least three of them were **favorite son°** candidates, nominated to represent different sections of the country. John Quincy Adams of Massachusetts – the son of John Adams, the second President – represented the northeastern states. William H. Crawford of Georgia represented the southern states. Andrew Jackson of Tennessee represented the western states. Henry Clay saw himself a national leader, although he came from Kentucky, a western state.

Of the four candidates, Henry Clay had the most definite program. Clay urged support for the American System that he had done so much to develop. In the American System, as you have read, Clay and other leaders in Congress tried to serve as well as balance the interests of the different sections of the country. In these years Clay began to establish himself as the Great Compromiser – a role he was to play many times in the years ahead. Crawford and Jackson hedged on most specific issues, including the tariff and the development of roads.

When the electoral votes were counted, Jackson had 99, Adams had 84, Crawford had 41, and Clay had only 37. No candidate had the majority (131 votes) needed for election. In such a situation, according to the Twelfth Amendment to the Constitution, the House of Representatives had to choose the President from the top three candidates. Clay, who was automatically eliminated as the fourth candidate, persuaded his followers in the House to vote for Adams. With Clay's support, Adams won. John C. Calhoun of South Carolina became Vice-President.

Jackson against Adams. The new President, John Quincy Adams, appointed Henry Clay as his Secretary of State. Jackson and his followers claimed that this was part of a "corrupt bargain." They maintained that Clay had supported Adams in exchange for the top post in the cabinet.

The charge of a "corrupt bargain" was false. Both Clay and Adams had done what they thought was best for the country. Jackson, however, believed that the charge was true. He was especially bitter because he had won the largest number of electoral votes.

Jackson was so angry that he resigned from the Senate in 1825 and launched a vigorous campaign to become President in 1828. During this three-year battle, both Adams and Jackson called themselves Republicans. Adams, however, referred to himself as a National-Republican, while Jackson called himself a Democratic-Republican.

By the 1830's, however, Jackson's party was officially calling itself the Democratic Party. Jackson's opponents organized the Whig Party in 1834, taking their name from the old Whig Party in England, which had opposed the tyranny of George III. For the next 20 years, the Democrats and Whigs were the two major political parties in the country.

The election of 1828. By 1828 most white adult male citizens had won the right to vote. Many of these new voters considered Jackson to be their leader. They were proud that he had been born in a log cabin and had achieved success by his own efforts.

In the election of 1828, Jackson won a sweeping victory over Adams. Jackson won every state west of the Appalachian Mountains and south of the Potomac River and also won in Pennsylvania and New York. John C. Calhoun was re-elected as Vice-President.

Jackson's first inauguration. On March 4, 1829, political democracy celebrated its greatest victory up to that time. Everywhere ordinary Americans rejoiced at Jackson's election. The nation's tiny capital on the banks of the Potomac was jammed with 10,000 visitors. "A monstrous crowd of people is in the city," Dan-

---

°**favorite son:** The term usually refers to a candidate placed in nomination on the first ballot by a state delegation as an honor – but with little hope of being nominated.

iel Webster wrote. "I never saw anything like it before. Persons have come five hundred miles to see General Jackson, and they really seem to think that the country is rescued from some dreadful danger."

The inaugural celebration was itself a symbol of a new era. After his Inaugural Address, the new President held open house in the Executive Mansion—the White House. Jackson's followers jammed in to greet him. Men with muddy boots climbed on chairs and tables to get a better view. Furniture was broken, trays of food were knocked over, and fights broke out.

The President himself narrowly escaped injury from the excited crowd and had to flee from the mansion. Dignified citizens watching the scene with horror feared that "King Mob" had replaced law and order in America.

Jackson, the man. What was he like, this man who aroused such conflicting emotions?

Born on the Carolina frontier in 1767, Jackson was the son of immigrant parents from northern Ireland. He grew up without formal schooling. Like many other Americans, he moved westward with the advancing line of settlement.

Jackson's opponents made fun of him. They claimed that he could not spell, that he told rough stories, chewed tobacco, and wore strange-looking "backwoods" clothes. Whether or not these claims were ever true, they certainly did not apply to Jackson's later life. When he became a wealthy planter and a famous American hero, Jackson took on the manners of a gentleman. Tall and slender with thick, white hair, he looked very distinguished. His followers called him "Old Hickory."

Jackson's outlook and attitudes seem to have been the same as those of many white Americans. This was especially true of his attitude toward blacks. Although his attitude was often contradictory, Jackson apparently was not aware of the contradictions. During the War of 1812, as you recall, he praised "free men of color" for their courage, patriotism, and valor. Yet later, as a slaveowner and national leader, he wrote letters expressing different, very unfavorable opinions about slaves. However, on at least one occasion he instructed that "my Negroes shall be treated humanely."

Jackson's attitude toward the Indians was also contradictory. Before becoming President, he had won a reputation as an Indian fighter. In ruthless, hard fighting, Jackson had de-

By the time Andrew Jackson became President at the age of 62 (top), he had been through enough occupations to fill several lifetimes. Lawyer, cotton planter, land speculator, frontier fighter, army officer (top), Congressman, Senator, and judge—Jackson had been all of them. Following his two terms as President, he retired as an old and sick man (bottom) to his beloved home, the Hermitage, near Nashville, Tennessee. This photo, taken in 1845, was the first ever of an American President.

Washington, D.C., had never seen anything quite like Jackson's inaugural celebration. His happy supporters overran the White House, tracking mud and
damaging furniture. After several hours, tubs of punch were placed on the lawn to
draw them out and get them on their way.

feated the Creek Indians in Mississippi and
Alabama and the Seminoles in Florida. Jackson respected the Indian military leaders and
honored them in defeat. Still, like most white
Americans, he regarded the Indians as primitive people who were inefficient and incapable
of "improvement."

Significance of the 1828 election. Jackson's
triumph in the election of 1828 was largely the
result of advancing democratic forces in
America. Great changes had clearly taken
place since the days of President Washington
and the Federalists. For one thing, political
power was now more evenly divided between
well-to-do people and average people. The
average people no longer stood in awe of leaders who, it had been supposed, were especially
qualified by birth and education to lead the
nation. Before the inauguration of 1829, all
the Presidents were men from wealthy backgrounds. Andrew Jackson, in contrast, had
been born into poverty and had risen through
his own efforts.

Jackson's election also indicated that the
western section of the country was a new force
to be reckoned with in national politics. Andrew Jackson was from Tennessee. He was the
first President from a state that did not border
on the Atlantic.

Not all of Jackson's followers were westerners. Of course, many western settlers had voted
for him because they felt that he would under-

stand their problems, but many small farmers
everywhere voted for him for the same reason.
Many southern planters voted for him because,
as a planter and slaveowner himself, he would
understand their point of view. Some city
workers as well as owners of small businesses
voted for him because they believed he would
help them to get the laws they wanted. Many
owners of small businesses, fearful of the
growth of big business, wanted the opportunity
to expand their own enterprises. They believed
that Andrew Jackson, a self-made man, would
help them. Thus with the support of a majority
of ordinary white Americans, Andrew Jackson
became President.

SECTION SURVEY

IDENTIFY: political democracy, "favorite son" candidate, John Quincy Adams, "King Mob."

1. (a) What was unusual about the election of 1824?
(b) Why did Jackson think a "corrupt bargain"
had been made?

2. Jackson was a representative of "the people." (a)
Who were "the people"? (b) In what ways did
Jackson represent their interests? (c) In what
ways was he one of them?

3. Explain the widely different reactions to Jackson's election in 1828.

4. (a) Why was the election of 1828 significant? (b)
Why can it be called the "Revolution of 1828"?

The people take a more active part in government

Andrew Jackson, the new President, had no carefully developed political program. Despite this lack of a clear-cut program, Jackson held three firm convictions.

First, he believed in greater political democracy. He believed that the government belonged to all of the people who could vote, and he was determined that the majority must rule. Second, although Jackson believed that the federal government's powers should be limited, he also believed in the Union — that is, the United States as a whole. Thus he believed the young nation had to be preserved at any cost. Third, Jackson believed in the power of the Presidency.

Extending the spoils system. As one of his first steps, the President removed many of his political opponents from public (government) office and replaced them with his supporters. Under the **spoils system,** as it came to be called, a victorious political party could fill public offices with party supporters. It often did so without regard for their abilities or qualifications. The name "spoils system" came from the popular expression "to the victor belong the spoils." The spoils system had already become common in some northern and western states. It had also been used to some extent in the federal government. Jackson applied it more vigorously then ever.

In general, Jackson removed those officeholders he suspected of having supported his political opponents. All these officeholders were men. Women were denied government jobs as well as the vote. Although Jackson replaced only about one fifth of all federal officeholders, he set a precedent that later Presidents often followed with drastic results.

Defending the spoils system. Jackson maintained that the spoils system actually improved the government. He claimed that any person was as good an any other. "The duties of all public officers are, or at least admit of being made, so plain and simple that men of intelligence may readily qualify themselves for their performance," Jackson stated.

Jackson also believed that it was sound policy to keep changing officeholders. He felt that government workers who remained too long in office became indifferent to the public welfare and forgot that they were, in fact, servants of the people.

Above all, Jackson believed that as many Americans as possible should learn by experience how the government worked. He felt it was good democratic practice to rotate the offices among as many people as possible. He believed that the more people who held office, the more able the government would be to meet the changing needs of the people.

Jackson's policies brought politics into the range of the ordinary white male citizen. Even a poor man could risk devoting his time to political activities if he could hope for a job as a reward for faithful service.

Defects of the spoils system. Because of Jackson's policies, however, political parties came to be led and supported by officeholders who were paid by the government. These officeholders also contributed a certain percentage of their salaries to their political organizations. The spoils system also encouraged many people to use the public payroll for their own gain, enriching themselves at the taxpayers' expense. Jackson was not entirely responsible for these political abuses, but extending the spoils system helped such abuses to spread through national politics.

Nominating conventions. During Jackson's administration, the use of nominating conventions to choose candidates for federal office increased. Until this time candidates for federal office had been selected by legislators gathered in closed meetings, or caucuses. The voters at large had little if any voice in the nominating process. In the meantime, however, a different practice had been developing at the local level. Groups of voters, meeting in their own communities, chose delegates for county conventions. These conventions in turn nominated officials for county offices.

This practice gradually spread upward into state politics and eventually into national politics. By 1832 the present practice of nominating the President and Vice-President in nominating conventions had been established.

The "kitchen cabinet." Hoping to bring the government and the people closer together, Andrew Jackson surrounded himself with a

THE MAN WHO LEFT A TRAIL OF TREES

He would walk into a wilderness clearing, usually barefoot, wearing ragged trousers and a flour sack for a shirt. The isolated farm family, always eager for news and companionship, would offer him a meal and a place to sleep. In return, he would entertain them with stories of his wilderness adventures. Sooner or later, he would pull a pamphlet from his shirt and speak earnestly of God, for he was a kind of preacher. When offered a bed for the night, he would refuse, sleeping instead on the floor. He expected no beds in "the world to come," he said, so he preferred not to get used to them here.

His real name was John Chapman, but everyone called him Johnny Appleseed. He was known far and wide for the apple trees he planted as he moved westward with America, for apples were a mainstay of the frontier diet, and orchards were much needed.

Like many other pioneers, Johnny Appleseed was born in New England. About 1800, when he was twenty-five or so, he began his wandering life. His travels took him across Pennsylvania, through Ohio, and finally to Indiana, where he died in 1845. Here and there he bought land, but he never stayed in one place long.

Johnny Appleseed's ramblings inspired hundreds of tall tales. Gnarled old trees from Virginia to Wisconsin (neither of which he ever visited) are said to be "Johnny Appleseed trees." All sorts of heroic deeds are credited to him. Most accounts do agree that he was a kindly man who got along well with Indians and tried to live in harmony with nature. His generosity and simplicity are summed up in the single sentence on one of the many memorials to him: "He lived for others."

---

group of unofficial advisers. Jackson's political enemies called these advisers the "kitchen cabinet." The term implied that these advisers entered the White House by a back door and met with the President in secret.

Some of the members of the "kitchen cabinet" were newspaper editors. Recognizing the importance of friendly relations with the press, President Jackson placed a number of well-known editors in public office. In return, they helped Jackson to mold public opinion, to gain good publicity, and to win support for the policies he favored.

Speaking for "the people." On most issues, Jackson believed that only the President could speak for the nation as a whole. He felt that members of Congress and state officials spoke for their own section of the country. Of course, not all the people in each section of the country shared the same interests or agreed on all issues. Still, by 1830 the views of the three sections of the nation were becoming more defined.

Each section had its outstanding champion. Daniel Webster of Massachusetts represented the most powerful interests of the Northeast—the merchants, manufacturers, bankers, and property owners in general. John C. Calhoun of South Carolina represented the planters of the South. Thomas Hart Benton of Missouri became the advocate of the West, especially of western farmers and land speculators, who wanted cheap, or free, public land. Henry Clay of Kentucky, the Great Compromiser, tried to balance the interests of the sections and, in the process, to become President.

Andrew Jackson claimed to speak for most ordinary white Americans everywhere. He placed himself, as he said, at the head of "the humbler members of society—the farmers, mechanics, and laborers" who had "neither the time nor the means" to secure the things that they wanted from government.

Jackson's Indian policy. As an old Indian fighter and frontiersman, Jackson shared with other westerners a belief that Indians were primitive people who were blocking the westward movement of "civilization." Thus it was easy for Jackson to conclude, along with Jefferson, Monroe, and other national leaders, that Indians would be happier and better off in lands west of the Mississippi River, far from white neighbors. In these areas, Jackson felt, the Indians might keep their own ways of life or gradually accept the practices of the whites.

The process of uprooting the Indians had been going on for a long time. Many tribes had been persuaded, often by bribery or trickery, to give up their claims to ancestral lands and move into lands set aside for them by Congress. Indian resettlement was often marked by dishonesty and brutality on the part of government officials. Sometimes Indian removal took place at gunpoint.

With President Jackson's encouragement, Congress passed the Indian Resettlement Act of 1830. This act provided for the removal of Indian tribes to lands west of the Mississippi in the area of the Red River and the Arkansas River. Four years later Congress established this area as a special Indian territory. During Jackson's two terms, 94 treaties were negotiated with Indian tribes. These treaties ended Indian titles to lands in the existing states and provided for removals to Indian territory.

Many Indians resisted these policies and practices. The Sauk and Fox Indians of southern Wisconsin and northern Illinois had been forced to move into Iowa Territory across the Mississippi River. Discontented, they reoccupied the homelands they had given up. White forces moved against them in 1832 in what was called the Black Hawk War. The Indian leader Black Hawk and his followers fought bravely and skillfully, but the Sauks and Foxes were overwhelmed.

In Georgia, Florida, Alabama, and Mississippi, the once powerful Creeks, Choctaws, Chickasaws, Cherokees, and Seminoles had adopted many of the white settlers' ways of life. They came to be known as the Five Civilized Tribes. By the end of 1833, the Creeks, Choctaws, and Chickasaws had signed removal

In 1800 a Cherokee silversmith named Sequoyah created a written language for his people. Combining English, Hebrew, and Greek letters with other symbols, he developed a Cherokee alphabet. By 1828 his people could publish their own newspaper, *The Cherokee Phoenix*.

This painting captures the emotions and conditions of Cherokees being forced to leave their native land in Georgia and move west. Thousands died on the journey, which the Cherokees came to call the "Trail of Tears."

treaties. The Seminoles refused to sign, bringing on the costly Second Seminole War, which lasted until 1842. Finally defeated, most of the Seminoles moved westward. A few hid in the Florida Everglades, where their descendants remain today.

The fate of the Cherokees. Most of the Cherokees, too, refused to sign a removal treaty. With the aid of missionary teachers, the Cherokees had developed a written language. They published a widely read newspaper in their own language and supported schools for their children. Some owned plantations and slaves. The Cherokees governed themselves under a written constitution that provided for a legislature, a judicial system, and a law-enforcing militia. They were proud of their advanced agriculture, arts, and crafts.

White settlers and land speculators in Georgia were determined to crush the Cherokees, especially after gold was discovered. Using legal and illegal means, they gained control of rich Cherokee lands. They also tried to force the Cherokees to sign a removal treaty. The Georgia legislature passed a law stating that Cherokee laws and treaty rights were null and void—that is, of no effect. The United States Supreme Court, with Chief Justice John Marshall presiding, declared the Georgia law unconstitutional. The Court held that forcible removal of the Cherokees from their lands violated their treaties with the federal government. President Jackson is reported to have said, "John Marshall has made his decision; now let him enforce it."

The removal of Indians, including the Cherokees, went forward. Little or no preparation was made for their resettlement. Tragic stories are told of how Indians, especially the Cherokees, were driven from their homes during the bitter cold of winter to follow what became known as the "Trail of Tears." Thinly dressed, without moccasins, sometimes in chains, often without food, the Indians were forced by federal troops into what was for them a strange and barren wilderness to the west of the Mississippi River.

Although Jackson showed some personal concern for the plight of the Indians, in his role as President he was responsible for the removal of a great many. His official position remained one of uncompromising support for Indian resettlement. He refused to listen to missionary groups who wanted to help the Indians achieve orderly, settled lives. He ignored not only the Supreme Court but also political critics, including Henry Clay, who opposed his Indian policy. When Jackson left the White House, the first major Indian removals had been largely carried out.

A product of his times. In the 1820's and 1830's, most white Americans shared Andrew Jackson's attitudes toward Indians. Although American ideas of equality and justice had been stated, they were not yet widely practiced. They did not apply to Indians or to black Americans, either slave or free. They did not apply to women, who more than 50 years after the Declaration of Independence were still treated as inferiors both in law and by custom. Moreover, criminals and mentally ill persons had few rights and were badly mistreated; few Americans saw anything wrong with this. Employers, too, often treated their workers harshly and unjustly.

Andrew Jackson, by the standards of the times, took important strides toward fuller political democracy for average white male Americans. Important as these steps were, the democratic ideal of equal opportunity for each citizen remained a distant goal.

SECTION SURVEY

IDENTIFY: spoils system, nominating convention, "kitchen cabinet," Indian resettlement.

1. What three convictions underlay Jackson's actions as President?
2. Describe the arguments for and against the spoils system.
3. How did nominating conventions bring the government and the people closer together?
4. (a) What was Jackson's attitude toward American Indians? (b) How do his actions before and during his Presidency reflect these attitudes?
5. (a) In what ways was democracy strengthened during Jackson's term as President? (b) In what ways was the nation still undemocratic?

3 Andrew Jackson exercises his Presidential powers

President Jackson, in his first message to Congress early in 1829, opened his attack against the second Bank of the United States.

Opposing the Bank. Jackson's attack came partly because he disliked banks and failed to understand banking. He saw the Bank of the United States as a "money power"—a monopoly that "the rich and powerful" used to their own advantage. He pointed out that a majority of the shares of Bank stock were owned by wealthy investors in seaboard states. The handful of investors living west of the Appalachians owned only a small fraction of the stock.

Why, the President asked, should the government continue to grant control of the Bank to a few wealthy people, most of them easterners? "Many of our rich men," he declared, ". . . have besought us to make them richer by acts of Congress. By attempting to gratify their desires, we have in the results of our legislation arrayed section against section, interest against interest, and man against man, in a fearful commotion which threatens to shake the foundations of our Union."

To his charge that the Bank was a tool of rich easterners Jackson added the serious charge that it engaged in questionable political activities. He charged, for example, that by granting loans to members of Congress, the Bank was able to influence legislation. There is little doubt that it did, at least after Jackson made his accusation—an accusation that many people considered unfair. Once its directors were convinced that the President intended to destroy their Bank, they fought back with every weapon at their command.

Jackson also claimed that the mere existence of the Bank was unconstitutional. In so doing, he expressed his belief in the limited powers of the federal government. He also ignored the Supreme Court decision of 1819 in *McCulloch v. Maryland* that the Bank was acceptable under the Constitution. Jackson, however, indicated that he did not intend to be bound by verdicts of the Supreme Court.

Many Americans joined Jackson in opposing the Bank. Farmers and wage earners who wanted easy credit opposed the Bank's lending policies. They were angry because the Bank refused to lend them money without adequate security in land or goods as a pledge of repayment. From a banker's point of view, this was sound practice.

Some business owners also resented the sound banking policies of the second Bank of the United States. Being refused easy credit by the national Bank, they turned to private and state banks. Powerful banking interests centering in New York City also resented the special privileges enjoyed by the Bank of the United States. Popular slogans of the day denounced the Bank as a monstrous monopoly.

The Bank as an election issue. Angered at the opposition, the supporters of the Bank, including Henry Clay, decided to force a showdown. They persuaded Bank president Nicholas Biddle to apply for a renewal of the Bank's charter. The bill passed both houses of Congress in the summer of 1832, four years before the charter was due to expire.

Henry Clay and the National-Republicans deliberately raised the issue at this time. They hoped that Jackson would veto the bill. If he did, the National-Republicans could make the Bank a major issue in the election of 1832. President Jackson did as they wished. In forceful terms he vetoed the bill to recharter the Bank of the United States.

Late in 1832 the National-Republicans nominated Henry Clay for the Presidency. Clay and his followers campaigned in favor of rechartering the Bank. Andrew Jackson, running for re-election as the Democratic candidate, continued his vigorous opposition. The Bank became the major campaign issue.

Jackson won the election, with Martin Van Buren of New York as his Vice-President. Clay and the National-Republicans suffered a crushing defeat. Under these circumstances, everyone understood that the Bank charter would not be renewed in 1836.

Destroying the Bank. Not content to wait for the Bank to die a natural death in 1836, Jackson set out to destroy it by gradually withdrawing all federal deposits. Federal funds were now deposited in certain state banks. These so-called "pet banks" were selected, Jackson's enemies claimed, on the basis of their loyalty to President Jackson and to his party. The Bank of the United States, now deprived of federal deposits, was badly crippled. Nevertheless, it survived until its charter expired in 1836.

Andrew Jackson and his supporters felt that they had won a great victory over a government-approved monopoly of the money power by wealthy easterners. In their opinion, this was another triumph for democracy. It was also a reflection of Jackson's concern with the need for easy credit for the people in the rising middle class.

Jackson's support of the Union. In his fight with the Bank of the United States, Andrew Jackson flatly stated that he, as President, did not intend to be restricted by the Supreme Court. This statement did not indicate any lack of respect for the federal Union set up by the Constitution. Indeed, beginning in 1830, Jackson fought so strongly in support of the Union that southern champions of states' rights, who had supported Jackson, were completely con-

SOURCES

JACKSON VETOES
THE BANK BILL
(1832)

Distinctions in society will always exist under every just government. Equality of talents, of education, or of wealth cannot be produced by human institutions. In the full enjoyment of the gifts of Heaven and the fruits of superior industry, economy, and virtue, every man is equally entitled to protection by law; but when the laws undertake to add to these natural and just advantages artificial distinctions, to grant titles, gratuities, and exclusive privileges, to make the rich richer and the potent powerful, the humble members of society—the farmers, mechanics, and laborers—who have neither the time nor the means of securing like favors to themselves, have a right to complain of the injustice of their government. There are no necessary evils in government. Its evils exist only in its abuses. . . .

In this newspaper cartoon, "The Downfall of Mother Bank," Andrew Jackson is shown triumphing over the downfall of the second Bank of the United States. The fleeing figure with horns is Nicholas Biddle, the president of the Bank. What do you suppose the newspaper's opinion of the event was?

fused. The issue that forced Jackson into his firm position was a revolt of South Carolina planters against a high protective tariff.

Southern reaction to rising tariffs. As you have read (page 243), Congress passed the tariff of 1816 to protect America's new and growing manufacturing industries from foreign competition. The tariff rates were raised in 1824 and again in 1828.

Because of its high rates, the Tariff Act of 1828 was called the "Tariff of Abominations" by its enemies. The tariff was passed by such a large majority in Congress that southern planters became alarmed. Reflecting their alarm, Vice-President John C. Calhoun wrote — but did not sign — a statement expressing his views about the tariff and the larger issue of states' rights. Calhoun argued that each state had the right to **nullify,** or refuse to obey, any act of Congress that it considered unconstitutional. This was a restatement of the compact theory of government earlier set forth in the Kentucky and Virginia Resolutions.

The legislature of South Carolina adopted Calhoun's statement, which came to be known as the "South Carolina Exposition and Protest." It also passed a set of resolutions calling the tariff unconstitutional and unjust. Georgia, Mississippi, and Virginia adopted their own similar resolutions.

Webster's defense of the Union. Calhoun's doctrine of states' rights set off bitter debate in Congress. A widely held southern view was clearly expressed by Senator Robert Y. Hayne of South Carolina. Hayne argued that in opposing the tariff, southerners were simply resisting "unauthorized taxation." Hayne also restated Calhoun's views that the states could nullify unconstitutional acts of Congress.

A different viewpoint was widely held in the North. Daniel Webster of Massachusetts eloquently expressed it in one of the most famous speeches ever given in the Senate. Webster declared that the United States was not a mere league, or compact, of states. He argued that it was "the people's government,

265

made for the people, made by the people, and answerable to the people." No state had the power to declare an act of Congress unconstitutional, Webster insisted. If each state could obey only those laws it chose to accept, Webster declared, the Union would become a "mere rope of sand."

Webster maintained that only one agency had the power to decide whether acts of Congress were unconstitutional. That agency, he said, was the Supreme Court. In thunderous words he flung out his challenge to Calhoun and Hayne and all who accepted the doctrine of states' rights and nullification: "Liberty *and* Union, now and forever, one and inseparable!"

Jackson's defense of the Union. Which side would the President support? The answer was not long in coming.

At a dinner in April 1830, President Jackson rose from his chair, fixed his eyes upon Vice-President Calhoun, held his glass in the air, and proposed a toast: "Our Federal Union — it must and shall be preserved."

A long moment of silence followed. Then the fiery Calhoun, voice of the southern planters, rose and threw back a defiant challenge: "The Union — next to our liberty, the most dear! May we always remember that it can only be preserved by respecting the rights of the states."

The battle was on. The leaders of both sides were able fighters who were reluctant to compromise when principles were at stake.

The conflict smoldered for two years. Then, in 1832, Congress adopted a new tariff measure with somewhat lower rates than the "Tariff of Abominations." The new act was still a protective tariff, and southerners therefore felt that it was no better than the old tariff. Convinced that the supporters of a protective tariff controlled Congress, South Carolina decided to take action.

South Carolina's threat to secede. In November 1832 South Carolina adopted the Ordinance of Nullification. It declared the tariff acts of 1828 and 1832 "null, void, and no law," and not "binding upon this state, its officers, or citizens." The ordinance was a clear defiance of the United States government. It closed with a solemn warning. If the federal authorities tried to enforce the tariff law after February 1, 1833, South Carolina would secede from the Union.

The President's reaction. President Jackson now moved into the spotlight. As Chief Executive of the United States, he was charged with enforcing the laws. He acted promptly. In off-the-record statements he lived up to his reputation as a fighting man. He warned that he was prepared to "hang every leader . . . irrespective of his name or political or social position. . . . Tell them," he said to a member of Congress, "that they can talk and write resolutions and print threats to their hearts' content. But if one drop of blood be shed there in defiance of the laws of the United States, I will hang the first man of them I can get my hands on to the first tree I can find."

For the public record, Jackson was more moderate. A carefully worded statement repeated his belief in the Union and his determination to uphold it. Nevertheless, he left the way open for a peaceable solution.

Calhoun was out on a limb. The other southern states had refused to follow South Carolina along the road to secession. Calhoun and his followers stood alone against the full might of the United States. With possible violence facing the country, political leaders proposed to end the crisis by compromise.

SOURCES

WEBSTER'S REPLY TO HAYNE (1830)

When my eyes shall be turned to behold, for the last time, the sun in heaven, may I not see him shining on the broken and dishonored fragments of a once glorious Union; . . . Let their last feeble and lingering glance, rather, behold the gorgeous ensign of the republic . . . bearing for its motto no such miserable interrogatory as, *What is all this worth?* Nor those other words of delusion and folly, *Liberty first, and Union afterwards:* but everywhere, spread all over the land, and in every wind under the whole heavens, that other sentiment, dear to every true American heart — Liberty *and* Union, now and forever, one and inseparable!

Jackson's destruction of the Bank and establishment of "pet banks" brought him ridicule in many forms, including this joke currency. What devices does this "humbug money" use to make fun of Jackson?

A compromise tariff. Under the leadership of Henry Clay, the Great Compromiser, Congress adopted a compromise measure, the Tariff Act of 1833. Under this act, tariff rates were to be reduced gradually to the level of 1816, which Calhoun had once supported. This reduction was part of what many southern leaders demanded, but the reductions in the rates were to take place over ten years. In this way manufacturers would be better able to adjust to the lack of high-tariff protection.

Along with the compromise tariff act, Congress in 1833 also adopted the Force Act. This act gave the President the power to enforce federal tariff laws, by military force if necessary.

Secession had been avoided. "Old Hickory" became a symbol of a strong, united nation.

SECTION SURVEY

IDENTIFY: Nicholas Biddle, "pet banks," "Tariff of Abominations," nullify, doctrine of states' rights, secede, Force Act.

1. (a) Why did Jackson oppose the Bank of the United States? (b) What evidence is there that many Americans agreed with him?

2. Contrast the views of Webster and Calhoun in regard to states' rights.

3. Describe the disagreement over tariffs that reached its peak in 1828.

4. How did Clay's compromise tariff of 1833 satisfy (a) the South, (b) the North, and (c) Jackson?

5. Jackson believed in a strong Presidency. Give examples from his own Presidency to support this statement.

4 The Jacksonian era ends in an economic depression

In March 1835 Andrew Jackson passed the midpoint of his second term as President and paused to consider his accomplishments. From Jackson's point of view, his administration had been a great success. He had won every major battle with his political opponents. His supporters were devoted to him. One of them expressed a widely held opinion that "General Jackson may be President for life if he wishes." Despite such support Jackson made it clear that he was ready to retire.

The election of 1836. In 1835, after Jackson announced that he would not run for a third term, the Democratic Party held a nominating convention in Baltimore. The convention chose Martin Van Buren of New York as its Presidential candidate.

Martin Van Buren had served in Jackson's first administration as Secretary of State and in his second as Vice-President. Van Buren was a shrewd politician, sometimes called the "Little Magician" or even the "Sly Fox." He entered the race with Jackson's strong support.

The Whig Party, organized in 1834, was made up of various groups united chiefly by their dislike of "King Andrew" Jackson and the policies of the Democratic Party. The Whigs did not nominate one candidate. They chose instead to use a "favorite son" strategy. In each section of the country, the Whigs selected a "favorite son" to run for President. They thus hoped to divide the total vote and prevent Van Buren from getting a majority, throwing the election into the House of Representatives. There the Whigs hoped to have enough strength to be able to choose one of their own candidates.

The Whig strategy failed. Van Buren won a majority of the electoral votes. In his Inaugural Address on March 4, 1837, Van Buren announced that he would follow in Jackson's footsteps. He soon discovered that this was impossible. He was hardly in office before the nation plunged into an economic depression.

The roots of the depression. The depression of 1837 had its roots in events that occurred largely during Jackson's administration. After his election in 1832, Jackson had gradually withdrawn federal funds from the Bank of the United States. He then deposited this money in "pet banks," many in western states. With the federal money as security, the "pet banks" printed large amounts of their own bank notes.

Many "pet banks" were also "wildcat banks," which issued bank notes far in excess of the federal funds on deposit. Because they

The panic of 1837 left workers idle and forced some women and children to beg. The signs on the buildings in this cartoon illustrate the problem. The federal government demanded to be paid in specie. However, people could not obtain specie because banks were no longer redeeming bank notes with it.

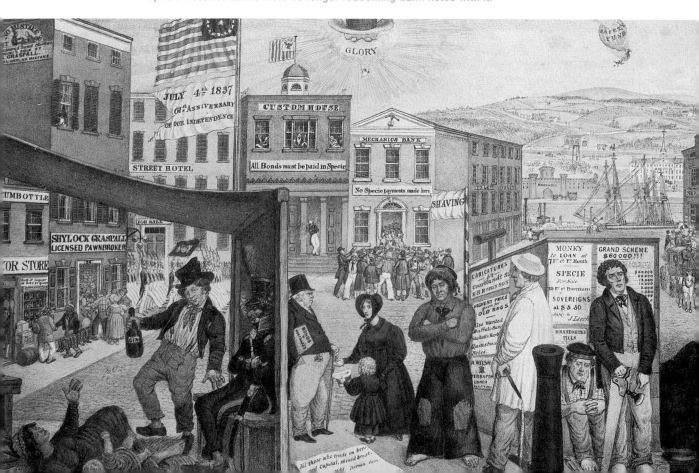

were so plentiful and had so little real value, these bank notes were easy to borrow. People borrowed this "easy money," often with a minimum of security, to buy land and to invest in the nation's growing transportation system. For a time it seemed as though almost everyone was speculating with borrowed money.

Land speculators were especially active. Between 1830 and 1836, yearly federal income from the sale of public land rose from about $2 million to about $24 million. Much of this money was in the form of "wildcat" bank notes. The United States Treasury was flooded with this unsound currency.

In July 1836 President Jackson acted to check the wave of speculation sweeping across the country by issuing the Specie Circular. This Executive Order forbade the Treasury to accept as payment for public land anything except gold and silver, known as **specie,** or bank notes backed by specie.

The panic of 1837. Shortly after Jackson issued his order, the trouble began. The sale of public land dropped off sharply because few people had gold or silver coins to pay for the land. Persons holding bank notes began to ask the banks to exchange the bank notes for the gold or silver itself. Many banks could not redeem their own bank notes. As a result, banks began to fail. By the end of May 1837, soon after President Van Buren took office, every bank in the United States had suspended specie payment. Before the panic ended, hundreds of banks had gone out of business.

As the banks failed and sound money disappeared from circulation, business suffered. Factories closed. Construction work ended on buildings and roads. Thousands of workers lost their jobs. Hungry people rioted in the streets of New York and Philadelphia.

President Van Buren and other leaders of the time did not think that the government could or should do anything to try to stop the depression. Van Buren declared that "the less government interferes with private pursuits, the better for the general prosperity." Thus he could only sit back and wait for the depression to run its course.

The depression was only one problem President Van Buren faced. More than anything else, though, it cost him re-election.

The election of 1840. In December 1839 the Whig Party held a nominating convention

In the rowdy campaign of 1840, hard cider became a symbol of Benjamin Harrison's homeyness. Here he uses cider to entertain his supporters while his opponent, Martin Van Buren, attempts to cut off the supply.

at Harrisburg, Pennsylvania. The delegates sniffed victory in the air. They did not attempt to publish a **platform,** or statement of the party's political policies. Instead, they chose to fight the campaign entirely on the issue of the depression, which they of course blamed on Van Buren and the Democrats. To lead the fight, they nominated a hero of the War of 1812, General William Henry Harrison of Ohio, with John Tyler of Virginia as his running mate.

The campaign of 1840 was one of the most boisterous in American history. Although Harrison owned a large, prosperous farm, he was pictured as a poor but honest man who lived in a log cabin and earned his daily bread by hard labor. The Whigs built log cabins for headquarters. They entertained the crowds at political rallies with barrels of hard cider. Recalling General Harrison's battle with the Indians at the Tippecanoe River in 1811, the

Harrison supporters also used the log cabin to present their candidate as a simple man of the people, as this hand-sewn emblem shows. Actually, Harrison's home was a stately white mansion, containing 22 rooms.

Whigs aroused enthusiasm for their candidates by shouting, "Tippecanoe, and Tyler, too." To ridicule their opposition, the Whigs shouted, "Van, Van is a used-up man."

The Whigs won an overwhelming victory, but General Harrison did not live to enjoy his triumph for long. He died shortly after he took office. Vice-President John Tyler, a states' rights Democrat who intensely opposed Jackson, succeeded to the Presidency.

A look ahead. During President Tyler's administration and that of his Democratic successor, James K. Polk, who was inaugurated in 1845, the boundaries of the nation were extended to the Pacific Ocean. During these same years, the differences between the North and South became increasingly serious. As you will see in Unit Four, these differences produced severe tensions that finally ended in the outbreak of a tragic war.

SECTION SURVEY

IDENTIFY: "wildcat banks," specie, Specie Circular, Martin Van Buren, party platform, William Henry Harrison, John Tyler.

1. What strategy did the Whig Party follow in the election of 1836?
2. How did each of the following help cause the depression of 1837: (a) "pet banks" and "wildcat banks," (b) the rise in land speculation, (c) the Specie Circular?
3. What did Van Buren think the federal government should do during the 1837 depression?
4. (a) Who were the candidates in the election of 1840? (b) What were the campaign issues? (c) Why and how was Harrison pictured as a "common man"?
5. Cartoon Study: Look at the political cartoon on page 268. (a) What aspects of a depression are pictured? (b) What point of view do you think is expressed?

Chapter Survey

Summary: Tracing the Main Ideas

The Jacksonian era ended with the triumph of the Whigs in the inauguration of General Harrison on March 4, 1841. During most of the years between 1824 and 1841, Andrew Jackson occupied the center of the national stage. During these years Jackson stood as a symbol of democracy and national unity.

Jackson was far more than a symbol. He firmly believed that the President should assume an active role as the nation's leader and that the people should share in the task of government. He firmly believed that the Union established by the Constitution was a national Union. In the eight years of his administration, he did much to make the government more democratic. He brought the people into closer touch with the government. During the tariff controversy, he fought the battle to maintain national unity.

The depression that started in 1837 and continued through the administration of Jackson's successor, the Democrat Martin Van Buren, gave the Whigs a chance to win control of the government. They made the most of their opportunity. In the campaign of 1840, they sent General Harrison to the White House. With the Whig victory, a colorful era came to an end.

The democratic impulse remained strong. Democracy is more than the right to vote and to hold public office. It is, in a larger sense, a way of life that offers to every citizen an equal opportunity to live and work as a free individual. The continuing democratic impulse helped to send Andrew Jackson to the Presidency in 1829. It also helped to set in motion a wave of reforms that affected many phases of American life.

As you will see in Unit Four, these reforms were taking place side by side with the division of the nation into three distinct sections—the North, the South, and the West.

Inquiring into History

1. (a) Explain the connection between the Kentucky and Virginia Resolutions, the Hartford Convention, and the "South Carolina Exposition and Protest." (b) What was the effect of each in national affairs?
2. Describe the circumstances under which the following statements were made: (a) "Liberty *and* Union, now and forever, one and inseparable!" (Webster) (b) "Our Federal Union—it must and shall be preserved." (Jackson) (c) "The Union—next to our liberty, the most dear!" (Calhoun)
3. Jackson's enemies called him "King Andrew" while his friends called him "a man of the people." How could Jackson's policies produce such opposite reactions?
4. Look again at the three convictions Jackson held when he became President (page 259). (a) Do his actions indicate that he held these convictions throughout his Presidency? If so, give specific examples. (b) Did he ever seem to waver in these convictions? If so, describe the circumstances.
5. Trace the increase in sectionalism during the first half of the 1800's. Give specific examples of events indicating that sectional disagreement was growing.

Relating Past to Present

1. Would today's federal government respond to a depression or recession in the same way that the federal government responded to the business panics of 1819 and 1837? Explain.
2. During the 1820's and 1830's, a man from an average family who had risen by his own efforts and who had done military service was regarded as an attractive political candidate. (a) Why? (b) Is this still true today? Explain.
3. Does the federal government today retain any aspects of the spoils system? Give examples to support your answer.

Developing Social Science Skills

1. Draw a political cartoon about an issue discussed in this chapter.
2. Write a newspaper editorial protesting or defending Jackson's treatment of the Indians.
3. Begin a graph charting the tariff history of the United States. It should include tariffs from 1789 to 1845. (a) Did the rates generally go up or down? (b) Why did the rates change? (c) What sections of the nation benefited the most?

Unit Survey

For Further Inquiry

1. (a) How would you decide whether a person had been a good President or not? (b) Use those standards to decide who you think was the best President between 1789 and 1841. (c) Defend your choice.
2. By 1830, what principles of American foreign policy had been established by (a) Presidential proclamations, (b) the War of 1812, and (c) the Monroe Doctrine?
3. (a) What was Jackson's concept of the Presidency? of the function of the federal government? (b) Compare his views to Jefferson's.
4. The character of George Washington strengthened the new government and the brilliance of Hamilton enabled it to function successfully. Comment.
5. (a) Trace the growth of democracy from 1787 to 1840. Be sure to define democracy as you give examples of its growth. (b) Why was democracy growing in this period?
6. How do you explain the difference between what was said and what was done concerning minority groups in America between 1789 and 1845?

Projects and Activities

1. Study the timeline on this page. (a) Divide the entries into categories, such as transportation, agriculture, and government actions. (b) Write one sentence summarizing each category and its entries. (c) Use the sentences you wrote in *b* as a basis for a short essay on technology during the years 1790 to 1845.
2. Make a chart showing the advantages and disadvantages of Great Britain and the United States at the beginning of the War of 1812.
3. Make a map of the United States as it appeared in 1841. The map should show important land features, such as rivers and mountains, as well as the chief transportation routes, such as the National Road and the Erie Canal.
4. Write an article about Jefferson that might have appeared after his inauguration in the *National Intelligencer and Washington Advertizer,* a newspaper friendly to him.
5. Write a skit dramatizing an argument over the tariff question between a South Carolina planter and a northern cotton cloth manufacturer.

Exploring Your Region

1. Find out about the history of voting rights in your state. (a) Were there property requirements for voting at one time? religious requirements? (b) When did women first get the right to vote in your state? (c) Did the growing political democracy in your state parallel the growth of democracy in the nation, as discussed in this chapter?
2. Many early highways, such as the National Road, were designed to take advantage of natural terrain—to follow river valleys or to cross mountains through mountain gaps. With the use of road map and topographical map of your community or state, find examples of roads that were built with these features in mind.

Suggested Reading

1. *Abigail Adams,* Dorothie Bobbe. Biography of one of America's "founding mothers."
2. *The Nation Takes Shape: 1789-1837,* Marcus Cunliffe. A standard history of this formative period in American history.
3. *The Age of Jackson,* Arthur M. Schlesinger, Jr. A prize-winning history of the rise of industrialism and its effects.
4. *Of Courage Undaunted,* James Daugherty. An adventure story based on the journals of Lewis and Clark.
5. *A Man Without a Country,* Edward Everett Hale. The classic novel of a young officer involved in the Burr conspiracy.

Unit Four

The Rise of Sectionalism

1820's - 1860's

Chapter 13
Building New Industries in the Northern States

1. Improved transportation unites the nation and stimulates business.
2. Wage earners help create the early industrial system.
3. Immigration swells the nation's rapidly growing population.

Chapter 14
Creating a Cotton Economy in the Southern States

1. The southern states develop into the Cotton Kingdom.
2. The planters control the positions of power.
3. The slaves play leading roles in the development of the South.

Chapter 15
Expanding the Nation's Boundaries to the Pacific

1. Fur traders and settlers expand into the Oregon country.
2. American settlers create the Lone Star Republic of Texas.
3. War with Mexico adds the entire Southwest to the nation.
4. A surge of migration brings California into the Union.

Chapter 16
Stirring the American People with Ideas of Reform

1. Reformers struggle to improve American life.
2. Free public education makes a promising start.
3. A strong movement develops to abolish slavery.
4. The antislavery movement begins to divide the nation.
5. Writers preach faith in democracy and the individual.

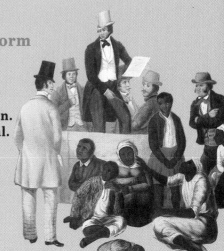

Chapter 13

Building New Industries in the Northern States

By the 1840's the Industrial Revolution was moving steadily ahead in the United States. "I visited the . . . factory . . . at Waltham, within a few miles of Boston," Harriet Martineau, an English traveler, wrote of a trip she made in 1834–35. "Five hundred persons were employed at the time of my visit."

The Waltham textile plant was one of the largest in the country, but there were many others, most of them only a few years old. The mills and factories were simple structures of wood or stone or brick. They stood on the banks of swift-flowing rivers and streams, which provided their power. Nearby were the small houses of the workers and the larger houses of the owners.

Factories and the towns springing up around them were becoming an increasingly important part of American life by the 1840's, particularly in the northeastern states. They were clear evidence of the changes that were beginning to alter life in the Northeast. These changes would, in time, affect the entire nation.

In her travels the English visitor also saw other signs of change. She saw new roads, new canals, and new railroads connecting the growing towns with one another and with the surrounding countryside. This transportation system reached across the Appalachians to the farms and towns in the growing western regions. The rapidly developing transportation system and the new mills and factories were part of the Industrial Revolution that was beginning to transform the United States from an agricultural to an industrial nation.

THE CHAPTER IN OUTLINE

1. Improved transportation unites the nation and stimulates business.
2. Wage earners help create the early industrial system.
3. Immigration swells the nation's rapidly growing population.

1 Improved transportation unites the nation and stimulates business

Without a good system of transportation, the United States could never have expanded westward to the Pacific coast. Just as the Constitution gave the American people a strong federal union of states, so roads, canals, railways, and steamboats enabled Americans to exchange products and ideas and to work together to build their nation.

Roads and highways. The development of better roads and highways was well under way by the 1820's. Especially in the East, private companies had built hundreds of miles of good roads and turnpikes. To open up the western region, several state legislatures had financed the building of state-owned roads leading into the interior.

The most important road project was the National Road, started in 1811. Financed by the federal government, the National Road cut across state boundaries and progressed slowly westward. By 1853 it had reached almost to the Mississippi River (see map, page 276), and the federal government then turned the road over to the states.

By 1860, Americans could look with pride at the roads and highways that crisscrossed the eastern half of the nation. In 1790, according to estimates of the Bureau of the Census, there had not been a single important stretch of hard-surfaced road in the entire United States. By 1860 more than 88,000 miles (141,000 kilometers) of surfaced roads had been completed in the nation.

Effects of the roads. The developing network of roads changed the lives of many thousands of Americans. Farmers in the outlying parts of the eastern states and in the lands west of the Appalachian Mountains could at last buy and sell products in the city markets of the East. The roads were usually crowded with freight wagons and other traffic.

Although moving produce by wagon cost less than carrying it on the backs of horses or mules, wagon transportation still was quite expensive. In 1817, for instance, it cost $13 to transport a barrel of flour some 275 miles (440 kilometers) from Pittsburgh to Philadelphia, and this was over what was one of the nation's best highways.

The Erie Canal. Canals were one answer to the demand for cheaper transportation. As early as the 1780's, leaders of New York State had urged that a canal be built between Albany and Buffalo. Such a canal would provide

As American industry and trade expanded, fairs like this one became popular. They provided a central showcase where hopeful sellers could display their new products and potential buyers could come to inspect them.

inexpensive water transportation from New York City to the Great Lakes.

Demand for the canal grew stronger when the National Road was started. New Yorkers saw that Baltimore would be connected to areas to the west by the only highway through the mountains. Baltimore might thus become the leading Atlantic port. Thoroughly alarmed, the New York legislature, acting under the leadership of Governor De Witt Clinton, authorized the building of the Erie Canal.

In 1817 the dirt began to fly in one of the major engineering feats in American history. When the canal was finished in 1825, a new waterway, 42 feet (12.8 meters) wide and at least 4 feet (1.2 meters) deep, stretched all the way westward from the Hudson River at Troy to Lake Erie at Buffalo (see map, this page).

EARLY ROADS, CANALS, AND WATERWAYS (1785–1860)

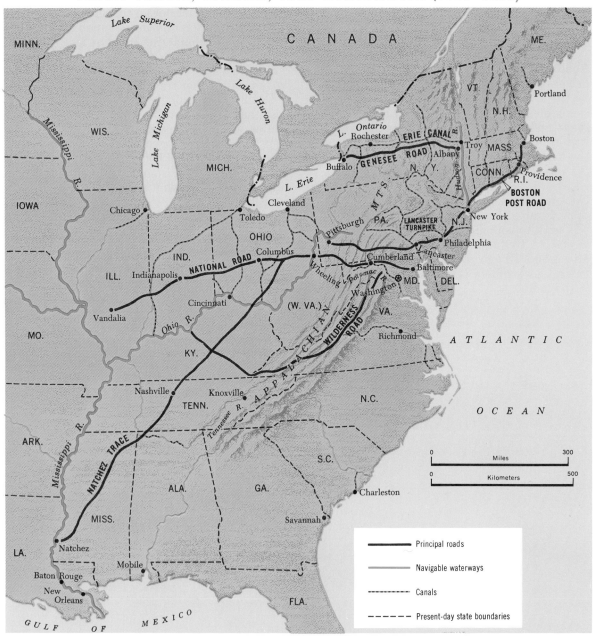

By the 1850's railroad stations like this one at Stratford, Connecticut, were bustling with freight loading and passengers. Watching the trains come and go was an exciting pastime, especially for children (left).

The Erie Canal was an immediate success. Heavy barges were drawn through the water by ropes tied to horses and mules plodding along a towpath bordering the canal. Passengers rode in luxury barges with gaily colored curtains at the windows.

Cities began to grow along the canal route, among them Utica, Syracuse, and Rochester. New York City became the "gateway to the West" and the nation's leading commercial port. Its population doubled within ten years after the canal's opening. Cheap water transportation had done all this. Before the canal was built, transporting a ton of goods by road from Buffalo to New York cost more than $100. Now the same ton of goods could be carried through the canal and down the Hudson River for $5 to $10.

The canal-building era. As New York City investors made huge profits, business people in other commercial cities, such as Philadelphia and Baltimore, also began to build canals. By the 1830's canals were being dug throughout the country. When the depression of 1837 hit, more than 3,000 miles (4,800 kilometers) of canals had been built, most of them in the northern states. With the depression, however, the enthusiasm for canal building ended abruptly. This was partly because railroads were becoming important and partly because the states now were unable or unwilling to invest in canals. Several states failed to repay money that people had invested in canal bonds. Some states sold the state-owned canals to private companies. Others continued to operate the canals they had built, but for some

time, state development of transportation facilities ended.

River steamboats. Another essential link in the new transportation system was the steamboat, or steamer. Before 1800, inventors in both Europe and America had built steam-driven boats. In 1787, for example, a steamboat invented and built by John Fitch had made a successful trial run on the Delaware River. However, it was Robert Fulton's demonstration of the *Clermont* on the Hudson River in 1807 that first drew widespread attention.

Fulton and his business partners realized that huge profits could be earned in the western areas. Up to this time, as you know, riverboats could not navigate economically upstream. In 1811 Fulton and his partners built a steamboat at Pittsburgh and took it down the Ohio River to the Mississippi. Called the *New Orleans,* it ran successfully up and down the Mississippi until July 1814, when it ripped its hull on a snag near Baton Rouge, Louisiana, and sank. By this time, other enterprising people were building and operating steamboats. During the next 50 years, river steamers handled most of the traffic in the Mississippi Valley. Steamers threaded their way east and west to the growing villages and towns on the rivers flowing into the Mississippi. Other steamboats appeared on the Great Lakes.

Building railroads. Like the early roads and canals, the railroads grew out of commercial rivalry among the eastern cities. Baltimore led the way. Construction of the first section of the Baltimore and Ohio Railroad began on July 4,

GROWTH OF THE RAILROADS TO 1860

1828, but there were few signs of the railroads' future success at that time.

The first locomotive on the Baltimore and Ohio—the *Tom Thumb*, built by Peter Cooper of New York—was a crude, undependable contraption. The rails on which the engine ran were wooden timbers with thin strips of metal along the top. With much clanging of metal, fearsome showers of sparks, and loud hissing of steam, the *Tom Thumb* could reach a top speed of about 10 miles (16 kilometers) an hour.

From this feeble beginning, railroads soon made rapid progress despite violent opposition from the stagecoach lines. Rival seaports built rail lines into the interior. By 1833, merchants of Charleston, South Carolina, had financed a 136-mile (219-kilometer) railroad into the interior of the state (see map, this page). At the time it was the longest railway line in the world under a single management. Boston, New York, and Philadelphia followed suit.

The railroads developed rapidly. By 1840,

iron rails had replaced the early wooden rails, and greatly improved locomotives were operating over a network of nearly 3,000 miles (4,800 kilometers) of track. By 1860 some 30,000 miles (48,000 kilometers) of track linked the older eastern seaboard states with the western region as far as the Mississippi River (see map, page 278).

Effects of improved transportation. As each new stage of the transportation system was completed, new western areas were linked with the eastern seaboard. Eastern products moved west in ever-growing volume, stimulating the development of eastern industries.

The new means of transportation also spurred the development of the western regions. Pioneer settlers could now travel to these lands more easily than ever. Once settled, the pioneers could send their surplus crops to the eastern cities. The improved system of transportation brought the western farms and eastern factories closer together.

At the same time, western villages began growing into large towns and even cities. At first these communities served mainly as centers of trade between western farms and eastern factories. By 1860 the towns and cities in what is now called the Middle West were developing thriving industries of their own.

As the Industrial Revolution gained momentum, Americans built more and more mills and factories. Some were built in the South, and growing numbers sprang up in the Middle West, but most were located in New England and the Middle Atlantic states.

A growing nation. A protective tariff shielded the developing industries from foreign competition. They also benefited from an ever-expanding market area and from a rapidly growing population.

In 1790 the nation consisted of only 13 states, all located along the Atlantic seaboard. By 1860 the nation consisted of 33 states, eight of them west of the Mississippi River, including California and Oregon on the Pacific coast.

Over this same 70-year period, the population had grown from about 4 million to more than 31 million. The overwhelming majority of these people, like their parents and grandparents before them, earned their livelihood by farming. In 1840 nearly nine out of every ten Americans lived in rural areas.

The towns, however, were growing in number and in size. In 1790 there had been 24 towns and cities with more than 2,500 people. By 1860 there were 392 such towns and cities.

Investment of capital. Where did the money, or capital, invested in the new mills and factories come from?

Some of the necessary capital came from European investors, but much came from well-to-do Americans—especially merchants. During the years of the Embargo Act (1807–09) and the War of 1812, many Americans had money to invest. By 1820 about $50 million had been invested in manufacturing in the United States. The amount had risen by 1850 to $500 million. By 1860 it totaled more than $1 billion.

This money was used mainly to build small, **individually owned** factories or mills. The owner was often the manager, who hired and directed the workers and worked side by side with them. Sometimes larger businesses were organized as **partnerships.** In these, two or more persons shared ownership and operation of the business.

The merchant marine. While industry was growing, American ships were carrying American goods to all parts of the world. Even before 1800, Yankee sailing vessels had been familiar sights in the ports of China, Java, Sumatra, Siam (now Thailand), India, and the Philippines. The ships left their home ports with cargoes of beads, knives, gunpowder, cotton goods, pottery, and rum. Stopping at harbors in the Pacific Northwest, the captains traded these goods with the Indians for furs. The furs were then carried to China and sold. The returning vessels brought tea and other luxuries to the United States.

From the 1820's to the 1860's, ever larger and faster sailing ships were added to the American **merchant marine,** or commercial fleet. Americans carried on a flourishing trade with China and other Asian countries. By 1860, Americans had secured more than half of all the commerce to and from the great Chinese port of Shanghai and were trading along the Yangtze (YANG·tsee) River in China. American whalers were likely to appear for water and provisions in almost any port of the world (see map, pages 280–81).

Yankee traders were equally successful on the Atlantic. As early as 1824, they carried most of the traffic in passengers and freight be-

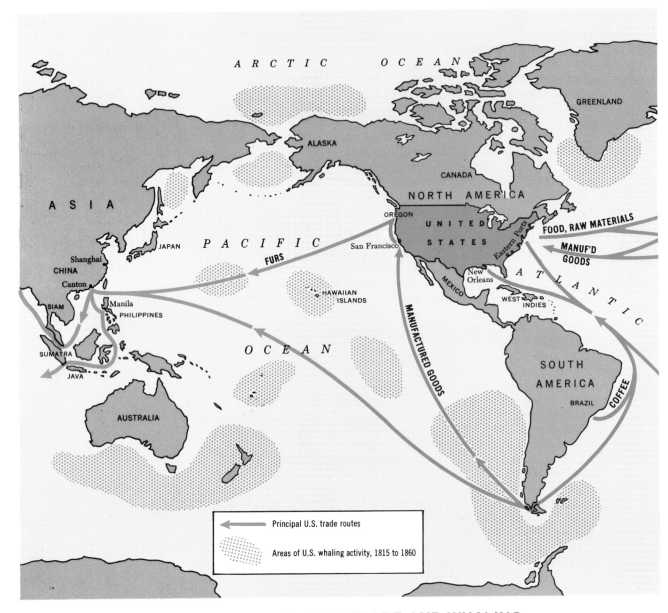

UNITED STATES FOREIGN TRADE AND WHALING

tween Liverpool, England, and the ports of Boston and New York.

Clipper ships. During the 1840's and 1850's, the sailing ships of American merchants became world-famous. The celebrated clipper ships were the pride and glory of the seas, outdistancing every other ship afloat. The clippers made the run from China to New York in as little as 75 days. They captured the rich trade of the Orient from slower vessels that required

nearly a year to make the same journey. The activities of the merchant fleet kept American shipyards busy. The fortunes made from commerce helped to pay for America's growing factories and railroads.

At this same time, the British, who had been outdistanced by the Yankee sailors and shipbuilders for 50 years, were busily building ocean-going steamships. By 1860, steamships had shown their superiority over sailing vessels. During the Civil War, American ship-

280

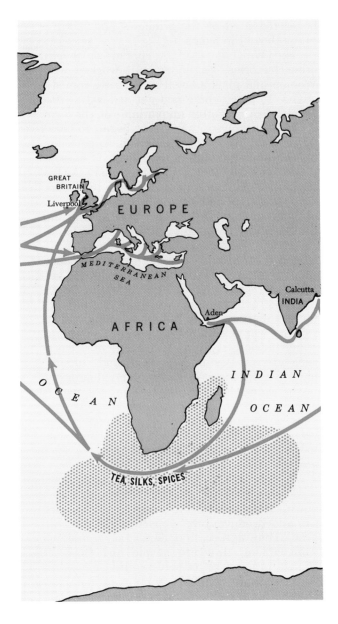

GREAT BRITAIN

Liverpool

EUROPE

MEDITERRANEAN SEA

AFRICA

Aden

Calcutta

INDIA

INDIAN

OCEAN

OCEAN

TEA, SILKS, SPICES

owners lost much of their already dwindling business. Thereafter, the United States merchant marine declined until the 1900's.

SECTION SURVEY

IDENTIFY: National Road, Erie Canal, *Clermont*, *Tom Thumb*, partnership, clipper ship.

1. How did improved transportation affect the various regions of the nation?

2. Which section of the country do you think benefited the most from improvements in transportation?

3. (a) What factors helped make the American merchant marine so successful between 1820 and 1860? (b) Why did it decline after 1860?

4. Map Study: Look at the map on page 276. (a) In what general direction did most of the roads go? Why do you think this was so? (b) Name two cities that were linked by the National Road. (c) Trace two different routes from New York City to New Orleans.

2 Wage earners help create the early industrial system

Manufacturers had to find workers to run the machines and do other work in the growing number of new factories. Where did they find these workers?

Early labor supply. Until about 1830 most wage earners were native-born American women and children. In 1816 there were 100,000 industrial workers; two out of three were women or girls. By 1822, women worked in over 100 industrial occupations. In 1831, children under 12 years of age made up about 40 percent of all the wage earners in the cotton textile mills of Rhode Island.

Why did so many women take jobs in industry? In New York and New England, one reason was the need of many farm families for greater income. Another reason was the desire of some women to escape the drudgery of farm work. As for the children, they did whatever their parents told them at a time when it was commonly believed that hard work, even hard industrial work, was good for children.

During the early 1800's, factory owners often contracted for the labor of an entire family. Advertisements like the following were frequently printed in the newspapers of the industrial towns: "Families Wanted—Ten or twelve good respectable families, consisting of four or five children each, from 9 to 16 years of age, are wanted to work in a cotton mill in the vicinity of Providence [Rhode Island]." Of course, employers also hired individual men and women.

Conditions of labor. The family system of labor seems harsh today, but it had certain advantages for the workers. The family was kept together instead of being split up to work in different towns. The work was not always difficult. Machinery ran much more slowly than it does today, and the children did the lighter tasks. In a textile mill, for example, children might mend broken threads or carry boxes containing bobbins, or spools. The hours were long — 12 to 14 hours a day six days a week. Even so, the workdays were no longer than those on the farms during the seasons of planting and harvesting.

Conditions in Great Britain. Conditions in the factories of America at this time were generally better than in those of Great Britain, where the Industrial Revolution had advanced further. During the early 1800's, young children in Great Britain were taken from orphanages and poorhouses to do hard work in factories, mills, and mines. As late as 1830, a Parliamentary investigating committee reported that children only 8 and 9 years old were working from dawn to dusk under harsh, unhealthy conditions.

This report led Parliament in 1833 to pass a factory act, placing limits on the working hours of children. Over the years other laws helped to eliminate the worst evils of the British factory system.

One reason that conditions were better for American workers was that labor was more scarce in the United States than it was in Great Britain. Thus a ruthless employer would have difficulty hiring and keeping workers. Also, American workers could be lured from the factories by the vision of cheap, abundant land to the west. As a result, some employers honestly tried to provide good working conditions and decent treatment for their workers in order to keep them.

The Waltham system. A notable but short-lived experiment was begun at Waltham, Massachusetts, in 1813. Only persons of good character were employed in the Waltham textile plant. The women and girls lived in company-owned boarding houses, with matrons in charge to see that certain rules were observed. Employees were fired for lying, profanity, and laziness. All employees were required to attend church. Educational programs, lectures, debates, and social gatherings were organized for and by the workers. The factories at Waltham were clean and cheerful. There were flower boxes mounted at the windows and pictures hung above the looms.

The Waltham system spread to several other factories. For a while it worked well. Women and girls as well as men welcomed a chance to leave home and get at least a little "book learning," often unavailable on the farm. By 1840, however, the system began to break down. Many workers resented the supervision of almost every detail of their lives. Others objected to unduly long hours for low pay. As factories grew in size, employers began to hire immigrants, who had begun to stream into the country during the 1830's. The immigrants could usually be hired for lower wages.

Rising discontent. Although working conditions in American factories were generally better than those in Great Britain, by the 1830's and 1840's many American workers labored under extremely harsh conditions. Some workers were forced to toil as many as 16 hours a day in the dirty, crowded tenement areas of such cities as Boston, New York, and Philadelphia. Conditions were particularly depressing in the clothing industries. Its workers, mostly women and children, labored in lofts — the dark, dirty upper stories of buildings. Other women and children did sewing in their slum lodgings, receiving a tiny payment for each garment that they completed.

As time passed, the argument that hard work was good for children began to break down. More people, including some workers, demanded educational opportunities for children. They agreed that democracy could not work among illiterate people and that the chance to improve oneself required schooling. To meet these demands, some manufacturers opened Sunday schools and evening schools for the boys and girls, but such efforts were unsuccessful. Children who had worked long hours six days a week were in no condition to attend classes in their few hours of free time.

Early labor organizations. The wage earners felt a rising discontent with many features of the new industrial economy. Some skilled workers, especially bootmakers and printers, reacted by forming local workers' organizations. These organizations — the earliest American labor unions — tried to get higher wages and better working conditions for their members. Thus the growth of the labor movement accompanied the growth of industry.

LOWELL'S "MILL GIRLS"

Most of them were young farm women. They came from all over New England to work in the textile mills at Lowell, Massachusetts. Their work was monotonous and their hours long—at least 66 a week. In the crowded company boardinghouses where these "operatives" lived, every hour was supervised and they had to sleep two and sometimes three to a bed. A good weekly wage for the women mill hands was $3.00. (The Lowell managers knew what they were doing by employing mainly women. The managers would have had to pay men mill hands twice as much.)

There were always plenty of recruits. After all, for young American women in the 1830's and 1840's, opportunities were very limited. At Lowell they enjoyed social contacts unavailable in the bleak rural countryside. They were used to hard work for no pay at all. Said one mill girl in a letter to her sister, "The thought that I am living on no one is a happy one indeed for me."

Another advantage was the possibility of self-improvement—a goal dear to the hearts of New Englanders. For at Lowell there were evening classes and lectures on many subjects, from drawing and music to German and philosophy. Lending libraries could hardly keep up with the demand for books. The young women even had their own publication, the *Lowell Offering*. Its poems, stories, and essays were praised by the British writer Charles Dickens, who liked the fact that the women wrote about the mills, not about "fine clothes, fine marriages, fine houses, or fine life." Yes, the work was "toilsome," wrote one of America's first blue-collar women, but few would give it up. "Yankee girls have too much *independence* for *that!*"

The labor movement was especially active during the late 1820's and the early 1830's. By 1834, when representatives of labor met in their first national convention, there may have been as many as 300,000 organized workers in the United States. Also in 1834 a group of workers organized the National Trades Union. The National Trades Union never became powerful. Nevertheless it did represent a significant beginning for labor organizations and for labor philosophy.

The workers' demands. The workers' organizations made a number of demands, including higher wages and a ten-hour workday. The workers won partial success in 1840 when President Martin Van Buren established the ten-hour day for all government workers.

Most wage earners had other important goals in addition to shorter hours. Many workers wanted equality of educational opportunity. They also demanded an end to the common practice of putting persons who were not able to pay their debts into prison. By the early 1840's, nearly all of the states had ended this practice.

By the 1830's and 1840's, organized labor had become a new force in American life. Workers had begun to develop the idea of unions and of **collective bargaining.** This is bargaining between union representatives and employers over wages, hours, and working conditions. Unions had begun to develop other methods of trying to win their points as well. They used the **strike,** or the union members' refusal to work until their employers met their demands. They also used the **picket line,** or a group of union members marching outside a factory during a strike to persuade other workers not to take their jobs.

Problems of women workers. In 1824 more than 100 women mill workers joined in a strike of men workers in Rhode Island. Ten years later some of the young women in the mills at Lowell, Massachusetts, left their jobs to protest what they regarded as unfair treatment. In 1844 Sarah Bagley, a Lowell mill worker, organized the Lowell Female Labor Reform Organization. This group gathered signatures for a petition to the state legislature demanding a ten-hour day. The group also published a paper and organized branches in other mill towns.

The fact that Lowell, Massachusetts, was located where two rivers, the Merrimack and the Concord, met made it a prime location for textile mills. Following the building of the first mill there, Lowell became one of the great textile centers in the country. This view shows several factories along the Merrimack.

Such efforts met with little success. When large-scale Irish immigration got under way in the 1840's, penniless Irish men and women had to take whatever wages they could get. Often factory owners paid barely enough for workers to survive on. Both immigrants and native-born women, whether working in mills and factories or doing piecework at home for the clothing industry, received lower wages than men. Often the wages they were paid were just above starvation levels.

Problems of black workers. The aims of the early labor unions did not include better working conditions for black workers. Since competition for jobs was often fierce, white workers resented the fact that blacks, to get jobs at all, often accepted lower wages.

White workers refused to work in the same shops and factories with blacks. Black workers were barred from membership in the trade unions. Excluded from the unions, black workers often served as strikebreakers. On rare occasions when white workers and black workers did agree to organize, the white workers insisted on separate unions.

Things were no better for black workers in the unskilled trades. During hard times blacks working at unskilled jobs in canal construction and railroad building were often fired and replaced by white workers.

Because of these conditions, resentment and bitterness on both sides led to labor riots in Philadelphia, New York, and other cities. In 1855, for example, violence erupted when black wage earners took the jobs of white dock workers on the New York City waterfront.

Weakness of organized labor. In these early years, the American labor movement was not yet strong enough to win many of the workers' demands. There were several reasons for this weakness.

In the first place, many wage earners did not realize that they formed a new and important group in the nation's economy and that they had interests in common. This was partly the result of tradition. Most Americans had been farmers, and the early factories and mills drew most of their labor supply from the farms. The Americans' strong spirit of independence and individualism made it hard to draw workers into labor unions. Wage earners continued to think of themselves as individuals who could look after their own interests.

In the second place, cheap land was always available. This cheap land did not actually attract many dissatisfied workers. Nevertheless, cheap land did draw westward thousands of farmers who might otherwise have turned to the cities for jobs.

In the third place, until 1842 labor unions

were not recognized by law. In that year the supreme court of Massachusetts decided in one case that labor unions had a legal right to exist in Massachusetts. This decision set a precedent, though not a strong one. Wage earners had to struggle in one state after another for the right to organize.

In the fourth place, the depression of 1837 threw thousands of men and women out of work. These unemployed workers could not afford to pay union dues. They usually had to accept any job they could get, regardless of what the job paid.

Finally, during the 1830's immigrants began to come to the United States in large numbers. Many of them were willing to work for low wages. Immigration, therefore, forced down the wages of many native-born American workers and almost brought the labor movement to a halt.

SECTION SURVEY

IDENTIFY: Waltham system, collective bargaining, strike, picket line, Sarah Bagley, strikebreaker.

1. What groups of people made up most of the factory labor force during the early 1800's?

2. (a) Why did workers begin organizing labor unions during the 1820's and 1830's? (b) What did these unions want?

3. Why were early attempts to organize unions only partially successful?

4. (a) In what ways was the situation of women workers different from that of men workers? (b) In what ways was it similar?

5. (a) How were black workers discriminated against in jobs and unions? (b) How were they used by employers to weaken the labor movement?

3 Immigration swells the nation's rapidly growing population

Between 1790 and 1830, the population of the United States more than tripled. It increased from about 4 million to nearly 13 million. Nearly all of this growth resulted from births in the United States itself. During these years fewer than 400,000 immigrants entered the country.

In the 1830's, however, the small stream of immigration swelled to a great flood. From 1830 to 1840, more than half a million immigrants poured into the United States. Forty-four percent came from Ireland, 30 percent from Germany, 15 percent from Great Britain, and the remainder from other European countries. Between 1840 and 1850, a million and a half immigrants arrived in the United States, 49 percent of them from Ireland.

Irish immigrants. The Irish came to escape terrible conditions in their homeland. In Ireland during those years, many people worked as tenant farmers on the estates of landowners who lived in England. The landowners did little or nothing to improve the conditions of their tenants, who barely managed to make a living. Then, in 1846, a terrible famine struck Ireland. Thousands died during the "Potato Famine," as it was called. Other thousands fled across the Atlantic to America.

The people who left Ireland were attracted to the United States for several reasons. They liked what they had heard about American democracy. They were thrilled at the reports of plenty in the United States. Moreover, American contractors encouraged them to come and work on the roads, canals, and railroads. American manufacturers attracted them into the new mills and factories.

Hardships of immigration. The immigrants endured terrible hardships in reaching the United States. The following news item from the *Edinburgh Review* of July 1854 gives an idea of their sufferings: "Liverpool was crowded with emigrants. . . . The poor creatures were packed in dense masses in ill-ventilated and unseaworthy vessels, under charge of improper masters, and the natural result followed. Pestilence [disease] chased the fugitive to complete the work of famine. Fifteen thousand out of ninety thousand emigrants . . . in British bottoms [ships] in 1847 died on the passage or soon after arrival. The American vessels, owing to a stringent [strict] passenger law, were better managed; but the hospitals of New York and Boston were nevertheless crowded with patients from Irish estates."

Poor, unable to move to the western lands, many Irish immigrants found homes in the slums of such growing cities as New York, Boston, Albany, Baltimore, St. Louis, Cincinnati,

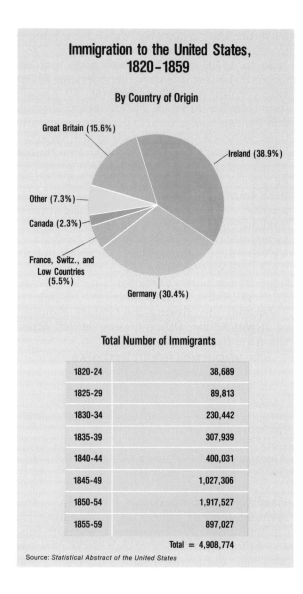

Immigration to the United States, 1820–1859

By Country of Origin

Great Britain (15.6%)

Ireland (38.9%)

Other (7.3%)

Canada (2.3%)

France, Switz., and Low Countries (5.5%)

Germany (30.4%)

Total Number of Immigrants

1820-24	38,689
1825-29	89,813
1830-34	230,442
1835-39	307,939
1840-44	400,031
1845-49	1,027,306
1850-54	1,917,527
1855-59	897,027
	Total = 4,908,774

Source: *Statistical Abstract of the United States*

and New Orleans. Many Irish men went to work as unskilled laborers on roads, canals, and railroads. Many Irish women took jobs in factories, where they displaced native-born American wage earners.

German immigrants. Germans formed the second largest group of immigrants. Between 1845 and 1860, more than 1.3 million Germans landed in the United States.

Many Germans came because, after 1815, Europe (and the German states in particular) was controlled by rulers who opposed democracy. Thousands of Germans who rebelled against political oppression fled when their revolutions failed. Other Germans came to escape military service. Above all, they came to earn a better living.

Most German immigrants settled in the middle western states—Ohio, Indiana, Illinois, Wisconsin, Iowa, and Missouri. Able, thrifty farmers, they built prosperous farms. Many also settled in the cities. By the 1860's they formed large communities in such cities as Buffalo, Detroit, Cleveland, Cincinnati, Chicago, and St. Louis.

Immigrants resented. Most immigrants quickly became American citizens. Because many had come to the United States in search of political freedom, they helped to strengthen political democracy. Because they were eager to work, they contributed to the wealth of the growing nation. Despite these contributions, many native-born Americans resented the immigrants. They feared that large numbers of "foreigners" would change the older ways of living in America.

Some Germans, for instance, aroused suspicion because they organized their own clubs, gathered in social halls to talk and sing, established their own churches and schools, published their own newspapers, and continued to speak German. Many native-born Americans viewed these activities with misgivings.

The Irish became the chief targets of American resentment. Like many newcomers to a strange land, they tried to settle near their friends from the Old Country. As a result, growing numbers of Irish people settled in the cities. Many dressed as they had in Ireland. Their accent sounded strange to other Americans. Many native-born Protestants disliked the Irish immigrants simply because most of them were Roman Catholics. Because the Irish were "different" in these and other ways, some Americans at first looked upon the newcomers with suspicion. Suspicion of this kind unfortunately has been the fate of every large immigrant group.

Resentment against the immigrants often led to friction and violence. Riots broke out in several cities. As more immigrants arrived, resentment against them increased. In 1845 a national organization of native-born Americans was started. A year later, this society was reorganized as a secret order called the Supreme Order of the Star-Spangled Banner or the Sons of the Sires of '76. Members solemnly promised to oppose foreigners and to support

In this picture, painted in 1855, the artist captures the excitement and hopeful spirit of Irish immigrants as they land in New York City. Nearly 400,000 immigrants like them had arrived in the United States in the previous year alone.

only American-born Protestants for public office. When asked about the society, members would answer, "I know nothing." Because of such answers, the organization came to be known as the Know-Nothing Party.

During the early 1850's, the Know-Nothing Party, by now officially called the American Party, was very strong in American political life. In the election of 1854, it polled one fourth of the total vote of New York and two fifths of Pennsylvania's vote. In Massachusetts it elected every state officer and nearly the entire legislature. However, the election of 1854 was the high tide of the movement. In the national convention of the Know-Nothing Party in 1855, southern members and northern members split over the question of slavery. As a result of this split, the Know-Nothing Party gradually lost its strength.

Changing ways of life. From the 1830's to the 1860's, familiar, traditional ways of American life were replaced by new and unfamiliar ways. Most older Americans did not realize that machines, factories, and an **urban,** or city,

way of life were causing the revolution taking place around them. Immigrants were only one of many new elements in the changing pattern of American society. However, many native-born Americans blamed all their troubles, both real and imaginary, on the flood of new immigrants.

SECTION SURVEY

IDENTIFY: Potato Famine, Know-Nothing Party, urban.

1. (a) What conditions led the Irish to emigrate to the United States? (b) Where did they settle? Why?

2. Why did some native-born Americans resent the immigrants?

3. (a) What was the major aim of the Know-Nothing Party? (b) How successful was it in achieving this aim?

4. Graph Study: Look at the graph on page 286. According to it, from what countries did the largest number of immigrants come?

287

Chapter Survey

Summary: Tracing the Main Ideas

The Industrial Revolution gained momentum in the United States during the early 1800's. As the years passed, every region of the nation was influenced by the development of industry. Even in the South, textile mills, iron-making plants, and other industrial establishments appeared, but the major industrial development took place in New England, New York, Pennsylvania, and the growing cities of the Middle West. It was in the North and the Middle West that immigrants mainly settled. There they sought jobs in railroad building, industry, and farming.

Industrial towns and cities with their factories, their whirring machines, and their manufacturers, financiers, and wage earners were becoming a major influence in America. Industrialism strengthened democracy by making it possible for the people to buy goods never before available to them and by raising their standards of living. It strengthened national unity by binding the nation together with a network of roads, canals, and railroads.

Industrialism also created new problems. Wage earners, more and more dependent for their pay upon forces beyond their individual control, began to join together in labor unions. Conflict between workers and owners became increasingly common. Finally, industrialism transformed the North into a new and distinct section of the country. In the process serious differences between the North and the South were created.

Inquiring into History

1. The development of better methods of transportation was as important in uniting the country as the Constitution itself. Do you agree or disagree with this statement? Explain your answer.
2. The growth of labor unions paralleled the growth of industry. Explain this statement.
3. Explain the connection between immigration and industrialization during the period from the 1820's to the 1860's.
4. (a) Compare the reasons for immigration during colonial times with the reasons for immigration during the period 1830–50. (b) Why did native-born Americans blame immigrants for many of their troubles?
5. (a) Why would immigrants tend at first to keep their old ways of life? (b) Why would this lead to resentment against them? (c) Would the children and grandchildren of immigrants be as likely to follow the old ways? Why or why not?
6. (a) In what ways did industrialization strengthen democracy and unite the nation? (b) In what ways did it promote sectionalism?

Relating Past to Present

1. How is the federal government today continuing the effort to improve transportation begun in the early 1800s? In what ways are America's transportation needs similar to and different from those of the earlier period?

2. Compare the extent of American whaling now and in the early 1800's. How can you account for the difference?
3. Do groups similar to the Know-Nothing Party have the right to exist in the United States today? Explain.
4. For each of the following, compare current conditions in America with conditions during the mid-1800's: (a) strength of labor unions, (b) child labor, (c) working conditions.

Developing Social Science Skills

1. Study the pictures in Chapter 13. (a) What information do the pictures provide about the changes taking place in the nation between 1820 and 1860? (b) What sort of information can probably *not* be gained through a study of pictures?
2. Look closely at the map on pages 280–81. (a) Locate three areas where American sailors hunted for whales during the 1800's. (b) What products did the United States buy from China in exchange for furs? (c) Using the colonial trade map on page 96, explain ways in which American trade had changed since colonial times. Why had it changed?
3. Research primary or secondary sources about women workers in the 1800's and answer the following: (a) Why did women take jobs in the 1800's? (b) What problems did women workers face? (c) Were these problems similar to those women face today?

A colonial couple on horseback bumping down a forest path. A Conestoga wagon creaking its way to California. A locomotive chugging across an arched stone bridge. All these are stages in the development of American transportation.

The social, economic, political, and military history of any nation is closely tied to the development of transportation. Good transportation aids trade and spurs development. It promotes communication and unity. In thousands of ways it binds people together just as surely as do customs, language, and government. The America we know owes much to the growth of its transportation network.

First built in the mid-1700's, Conestoga wagons moved America west until the completion of the transcontinental railroad in 1869.

For those who traveled light, the horse was an important means of transportation during the early days of the nation.

The nation's first boats were windpowered or moved by human muscle.

Steamboats made travel up and down the nation's rivers and lakes easier and more dependable.

On May 10, 1869, the last spike was driven in the world's first transcontinental railroad.

Canals expanded the nation's waterways and were alternatives to roads.

One of the most modern rail passenger systems is Washington, D.C.'s Metro.

In the 1930's streamlined diesel-powered passenger trains were streaking across the country.

By 1843 all major Eastern cities were connected by rail.

1843. RAIL-ROAD ROUTE 1843.
BETWEEN
Albany & Buffalo.

FARE REDUCED—ARRANGEMENT TO COMMENCE JULY 10. 1843.

Those who pay *through* between Albany and Buffalo, - $10. in the best cars,
do.   do.   do.   8. in accomodation cars,
which have been re-arranged, cushioned and lighted.
Those who pay *through* between Albany & Rochester, $8. in the best cars.
do.   do.   do.   6.50 in accomodation cars.

THREE DAILY LINES.
Through in 25 hours.

| GOING WEST. | | | GOING EAST. | | |

Passengers will procure tickets at the offices at Albany, Buffalo or Rochester *through*, to be entitled to seats at the reduced rates.
Fare will be received at each of the above places to any other places named on the route.

EMIGRANTS WILL BE CARRIED ONLY BY SPECIAL CONTRACT.

The transportation needs of the early colonists were fairly simple. The colonists who settled on the Atlantic seacoast or along major rivers used these natural waterways as means of transportation. There was little interaction between settlements, and what overland travel there was often followed ancient Indian footpaths. Only as the colonies grew, pushed westward, and became interdependent did the need for better means of transportation develop.

As the need arose, the colonists built roads connecting towns and settlements. No longer relying simply on nature's waterways, Americans built a network of canals. Eventually, they built a railroad to cross the continent. The distant parts of the land were linked together in one great nation.

Behind every major advance in transportation have been people of vision—inventors and innovators with dreams and people who saw the value of these dreams. Thomas Jefferson, Henry Clay, John C. Calhoun, and others of their day recognized the need for a national road and argued for the money to build one. John A. Roebling saw the need for a bridge to span great distances and worked to perfect one. Henry Ford dreamed of making automobiles affordable for everyone.

All these dreams came true because of the efforts of people of vision. Today the nation is bound together by its vast network of roads, highways, and bridges. The passenger cars, as well as the trucks, buses, and motorcycles that travel these roads, have greatly affected the character of modern America.

Animals remained a major source of power for transportation in America for hundreds of years.

Automobiles transformed American life. They affected not only how people traveled but also how they worked, where they lived, and how they amused themselves.

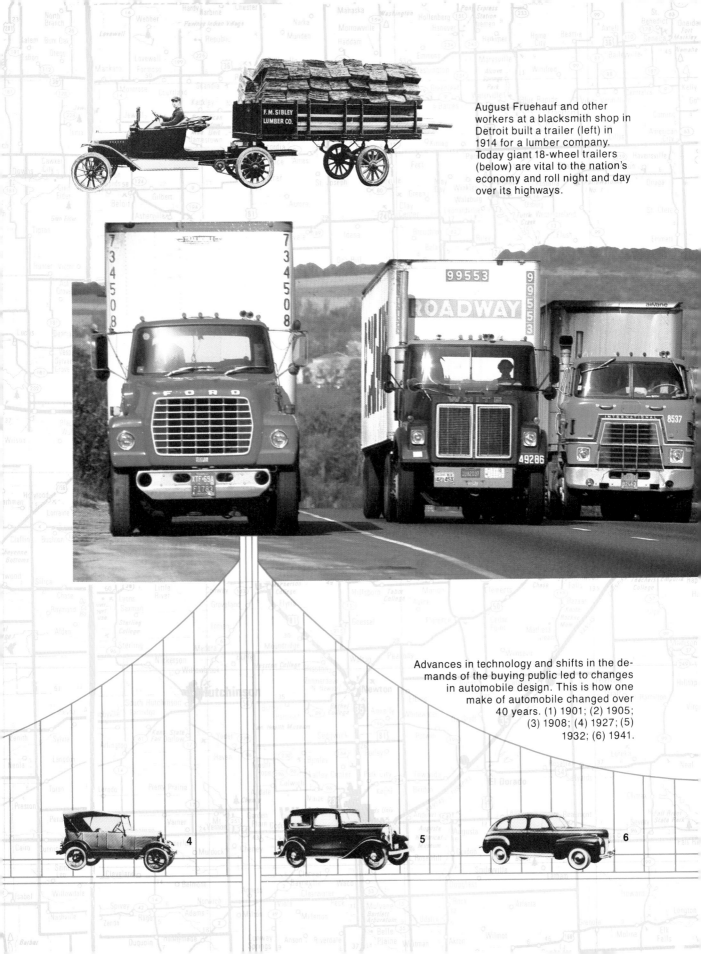

August Fruehauf and other workers at a blacksmith shop in Detroit built a trailer (left) in 1914 for a lumber company. Today giant 18-wheel trailers (below) are vital to the nation's economy and roll night and day over its highways.

Advances in technology and shifts in the demands of the buying public led to changes in automobile design. This is how one make of automobile changed over 40 years. (1) 1901; (2) 1905; (3) 1908; (4) 1927; (5) 1932; (6) 1941.

4

5

6

The success of the Wright brothers sent the nation's dreams "a-flyin."

When the Wright brothers achieved their dream of powered flight, they dramatically changed the lives of generations to come. Airplanes quickened the pace of life around the world, binding the people within a nation more tightly together and creating closer links among nations.

Today's Americans of vision are looking into space. Astronauts have orbited the earth and landed on the moon. The dream of living and working in space on a regular basis remains to be realized.

With the launch of the space shuttle *Columbia*, Americans renewed their dreams of future travel in space.

Today, air travel is a way of life for many people.

Chapter 14

Creating a Cotton Economy in the Southern States

Changing Ways of American Life

1820's–1860's

"Cotton is king" was an expression heard often in the South during the 1840's and 1850's. Cotton was indeed important to a great majority of the people living in the southern states. By the 1850's the cotton grown, shipped, and sold by southerners was worth more than all the rest of America's exports put together.

In talking about the importance of "King Cotton," southerners were not thinking of themselves alone. They knew that countless other people—in the northern states, in Europe, and around the world—depended upon southern cotton for their living. There were merchants who traded and shipped cotton and sailors who manned the ships. There were owners of cotton textile factories and the workers in them. There were also storekeepers and traders who sold cotton goods in the United States, in Europe, in Africa, in India—wherever, in fact, they could find buyers.

Southerners could ask in the 1840's and 1850's, "What other product grown on the land and fashioned into finished articles affects so many people in so many different parts of the world?" The answer was "None."

Great changes had taken place in the southern states since the 1790's. When the Constitution was adopted, tobacco, not cotton, had been the most important southern crop. At that time, also, many people in the South as well as in the North had thought that slavery would soon disappear in the United States.

Now, in the 1850's, cotton was "king," and nearly 4 million black slaves lived and worked in the South. The Cotton Kingdom, with its system of slave labor, was becoming increasingly different from the North with its growing cities, its growing population, and its free labor.

THE CHAPTER IN OUTLINE

1. The southern states develop into the Cotton Kingdom.
2. The planters control the positions of power.
3. The slaves play leading roles in the development of the South.

1 The southern states develop into the Cotton Kingdom

The southern states, by the 1840's and 1850's, covered a vast area stretching southward from Maryland and the Ohio River to the Gulf of Mexico. Louisiana, Arkansas, and Texas were also part of this great cotton-growing region.

The farm lands. Travelers in the South at this time were most impressed by the endless cotton fields, but they also saw many other staple crops, including tobacco, rice, and sugar cane. In Virginia, North Carolina, Kentucky, Tennessee, and Missouri, where the climate

After a visit to New Orleans, the famous French artist Edgar Degas painted this picture of the activity in a cotton buyer's office there. The cotton buyer was the link between the farmers who grew the cotton and the manufacturers who turned it into cloth.

and soil were most favorable for tobacco growing, the fields were green with broad, flat tobacco leaves. Rice fields flourished in the swampy coastal areas of South Carolina and Georgia. To the west, in the delta of the Mississippi River, sugar cane ripened in the warm winds that swept in from the Gulf of Mexico. Travelers in Virginia might see large fields of wheat and corn. In Texas they could see herds of long-horned cattle.

Southerners received much of their cash income from their staple crops—mainly cotton, tobacco, rice, and sugar cane. Most, though not all, of these staple crops were grown on large plantations. However, travelers in the South in the 1850's also saw many small subsistence farms, much like those in the Northeast and Middle West. On these farms families raised corn and other food crops and livestock largely for their own use.

Towns and industries. Since the southern economy depended mainly on agriculture, industries and towns grew more slowly in the South than in the North. But the southern states had many towns and a few important cities, among them Richmond, Virginia; Charleston, South Carolina; and New Orleans, Louisiana.

The southern towns and cities had their shopkeepers, skilled workers, and professional people—doctors, lawyers, ministers, and teachers. Along the wharves and on the streets, visitors could see sawmills, paper mills, brickyards, leather tanneries, foundries, turpentine and whisky distilleries, and a few cotton mills.

By 1860 about 10,000 miles (16,000 kilometers) of railroad tracks had been laid throughout the southern states. Along the rivers and coastlines, hundreds of steamboats carried the South's staple crops to northern and European markets. On return trips they brought manufactured goods to the South.

By the 1850's some leading southerners were urging further development of southern industry and commerce. The southern economy, in short, was varied and complex, but southerners never lost sight of the reality that "cotton is king."

The growing cotton economy. In the late 1700's, as you know, British investors developed power-driven machinery for spinning thread and weaving cloth. Before long, textile

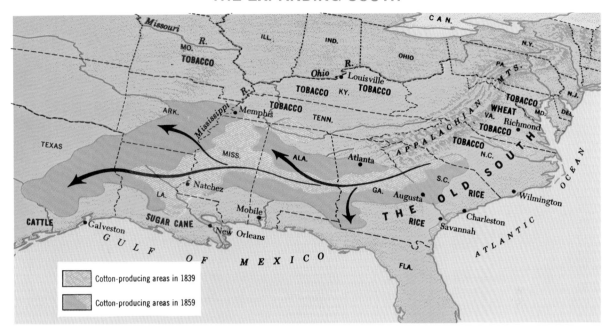

Cotton-producing areas in 1839

Cotton-producing areas in 1859

mills were operating in the New England and the Middle Atlantic states. The new mills consumed ever larger amounts of raw cotton fiber. To meet the growing demand, Southern farmers and plantation owners raised more cotton. This brought them face to face with a problem that threatened to slow the further development of the cotton economy.

The problem centered in the cotton plant itself. The heart of the plant, called the boll, is a tangle of fibers and seeds. These had to be separated before the cotton could be used. When done by hand, this was a slow and therefore expensive process, even with slave labor.

Eli Whitney, who also invented interchangeable gun parts, solved the problem. In 1793 he invented the cotton gin, a machine that separated the seeds from the cotton fiber. Before this invention, a man or woman working a full day could at best separate by hand only a few pounds of fiber. Whitney's cotton gin, when operated by power, could separate more than 1,000 pounds (450 kilograms) a day!

More and more southern farmers now began to raise and sell cotton, first in Georgia and South Carolina and later in the rich soils of the Gulf Coast states and the Mississippi Valley (see map, this page). Big 500-pound (226.8-kilogram) bales of raw cotton fiber were shipped in ever greater quantities to the textile

mills of New England, the Middle Atlantic states, and Great Britain.

The cloth woven on the looms of the American and British mills went to clothing manufacturers. Soon ready-made dresses, shirts, and trousers were being sold in worldwide markets.

In 1791 total American production of cotton fiber had been only 4,000 bales. By 1830 it had jumped to 732,000 bales. In 1860 the figure stood at more than 4 million bales, two thirds of the world's total production of cotton. Cotton alone represented about two thirds of the value of the entire nation's exports in the year 1860.

The cotton-growing area expands. From 1800 to 1860, southern prosperity increasingly depended on cotton. Textile manufacturers paid higher and higher prices for the supply that was often too small to meet their needs. Rising prices tempted southern planters to clear more land and grow more cotton.

As the demand for cotton increased, the rich soils of the Gulf Coast states and the Mississippi Valley attracted cotton growers. Many southerners saw a chance to get ahead by moving west, clearing the soil, and starting cotton plantations. Thus, by 1845, the states of Louisiana, Mississippi, Alabama, Arkansas, Florida, and Texas were added to the original southern states.

297

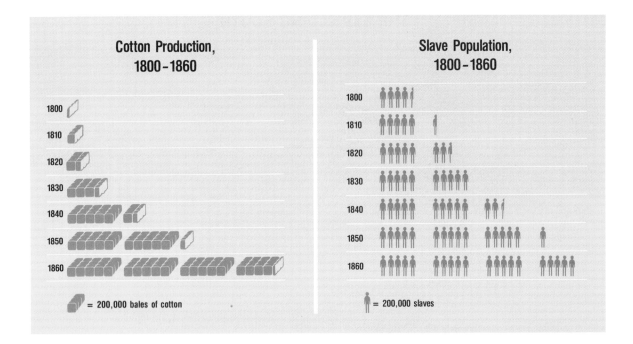

Cotton Production, 1800–1860

1800
1810
1820
1830
1840
1850
1860

= 200,000 bales of cotton

Slave Population, 1800–1860

1800
1810
1820
1830
1840
1850
1860

= 200,000 slaves

By the late 1850's, the cotton economy had reached the height of its power. The cotton lands, or cotton belt, stretched in a long crescent from North Carolina in the east to Texas in the west (see map, page 297). Travelers journeying in the fall along the dusty roads throughout the region saw the major wealth of the South in every field. Ripe cotton bolls shone white in the hot sunlight, ready to be picked, cleaned of seed, packed in bales, and shipped to mills in New England and Great Britain.

Growth of population. During the first half of the 1800's, the Cotton Kingdom grew in population as well as in area. By 1860 the population of the South had risen to approximately 12 million. About 4 million were black slaves. The rest were, for the most part, descendants of pre-Revolutionary settlers. They were mostly of English and Scotch-Irish ancestry, although many people of French origin lived in the coastal plains of the Carolinas and around New Orleans. Also, groups of Germans had started settlements in Texas.

On the whole, though, European immigrants were not attracted to the South. Up to this time, most of the immigrants to the United States had come from countries of northern Europe, like Ireland and Germany. The climate and ways of living in the northern states were more familiar to them than were the warmer climate and ways of living in the South. Of the more than 4 million immigrants living in the United States by 1860, only 13.5 percent lived in the southern states.

Southern social groups. In the South, as in other parts of the country, the population was divided into a number of social and economic groups. Except for the slaves, who had no opportunity to better their lot, energetic and ambitious people continually moved from lower to higher economic groups. In the words of one southern historian, a family could mount "from log cabin to plantation mansion on a stairway of cotton bales."

Who were the men and women who built the Cotton Kingdom? What were the major social and economic groups to be found in the South in 1860?

The slaves. From the day they first arrived in the New World, the slaves were at the bottom of the social and economic ladder. In 1790, when the new nation was in its first year under the Constitution, there were about 700,000 slaves and 60,000 free blacks in the original thirteen states. Their numbers increased rapidly. By 1820 the slave population had more than doubled. By 1840 more than half of the men, women, and children in Mississippi were slaves. In that year the proportion of slaves to free people was almost as high in Alabama and Louisiana.

By 1860 the total slave population had reached roughly 4 million. Of this total population, about 500,000 lived and worked in towns and cities. The rest, about 3.5 million, worked on farms and plantations.

As white planters moved from the older southern states into the rich new cotton areas of the Gulf Coast states, some of them took their slaves with them. Others sold their slaves before leaving and bought new ones on arrival. The increasing demand for slaves in the Gulf Coast states led to a flourishing interstate slave trade. Professional slave traders bought slaves in the border states and transported them to slave auction centers in New Orleans and Natchez, Mississippi. There the slaves were driven to auction blocks and sold to the highest bidders.

Free blacks. Not all the blacks in the South were slaves. By 1860 about 250,000 free blacks lived in the South, most of them in towns and cities. Some of them had been freed by their owners. However, as slavery became more firmly established, masters became more and more reluctant to free their slaves. To do so meant large financial loss and the disapproval of neighbors.

Free blacks in the South enjoyed less and less freedom in the early 1800's. After 1830 the legislatures of all the southern states passed laws severely restricting the movements of free black people. Free blacks had to register with town authorities and carry a pass to show that they were not runaway slaves. Often they had to post **bonds**—money or a pledge of property—to guarantee their good behavior. Their property was taxed, but they could not vote. Nor could they testify in court against white citizens or slaves, although slaves as well as white citizens could testify against them.

There were many other discriminations. Free black southerners could not assemble freely for any purpose. In many places they were forbidden to attend churches, even all-black churches, unless a white person was present. Laws in some areas forbade them to learn how to read and write.

Although these severe laws and regulations were not always enforced, free black southerners lived under the constant threat that they might be. In addition, free blacks never knew when some new law or discrimination might be

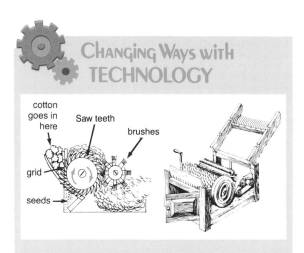

CHANGING WAYS WITH TECHNOLOGY

cotton goes in here

Saw teeth

brushes

grid

seeds

COTTON GIN

In the late 1700's, the invention of efficient spinning machines expanded the market for southern cotton. However, producing pure cotton fiber was difficult because it involved removing seeds by hand. Eli Whitney's cotton gin, invented in 1793, performed this job so successfully that cotton became almost the only crop in much of the South.

Sets of wire teeth on a cylinder were turned by human, animal, or water power. These teeth pulled raw fiber through a grid. The seeds were too large to pass through the grid and fell below. Brushes removed the pure fiber from the teeth so it could be collected.

imposed. They never knew when they might be punished or even sold into slavery for some minor violation.

The poor whites. Poor whites, about 10 or 12 percent of the southern white population, formed another distinct social and economic group in the South. Other white southerners looked down on the poor whites, calling them "hillbillies," "crackers," or "piney woods folks."

Most poor whites were frontier families, many of whom lived in rough log cabins. They lived on the poorer soils, called "pine barrens," or along the rugged Appalachian mountainsides and other hilly areas that were hard to farm. Partly for this reason, their standard of living was low. These people often suffered from poor health, but they had pride and a fierce independence.

Laborers and tenants. White farm laborers and tenant farmers formed another large southern group. The farm laborers were hired to work for wages during the harvest season or to do work regarded as too dangerous for slaves, who were expensive to buy and keep. The tenant farmers rented and tilled fields that were usually worn out from overuse. These tenant farmers generally lived hard lives and were in debt to the landowners.

Small farmers. Many independent farmers in the South owned small plots of productive land and lived much like small farmers in other parts of the country. They built simple but reasonably comfortable frame houses, considerably better than the log cabins of the poor whites. Each year the small farmers sold a bale or two of cotton as a cash crop. Their food came largely from the corn, potato, and vegetable patches around their houses. They were almost self-sufficient and also had a small cash income of about $100 a year.

The slaveowners. None of the white groups mentioned so far owned slaves. These groups made up about three fourths of the white southern families. The remaining fourth, fewer than 305,000 families, owned the roughly 4 million slaves in the South. These slaveowners can be divided into two groups—the small slaveowners and the planters.

Some small southern farmers who prospered bought a slave or two, or perhaps a slave family. A prosperous small farmer might have eight or ten slaves.

When small farmers acquired a few slaves, their scale of living usually did not change. They often continued to work in the fields, alongside their newly purchased slaves. Although the farmers' cash income might increase to perhaps several hundred dollars a year, they remained separated from the rich planters on the one hand and the poor whites on the other. Some small farmers lived in the cotton belt, with only a fence separating them from the plantations. However, most of them lived to the north of the cotton belt and in the fertile valleys of the Appalachian Mountains.

The most influential people in the South—the planters—were also the fewest in number. According to the Bureau of the Census, a planter was a person engaged in agriculture who owned 20 slaves or more. In 1860 the Bureau of the Census reported that there were only about 50,000 planters in the South.

SECTION SURVEY

IDENTIFY: "King Cotton," staple crop, cotton gin, subsistence farm, interstate slave trade, tenant farmer, planter.

1. The southern economy before 1860 was varied and complex. Explain.
2. Why was the South able to become the world's greatest cotton-producing area by 1860?
3. In what ways were free blacks discriminated against in the South after 1830?
4. Map Study: Look at the map on page 297. (a) Locate the cotton belt. (b) Where is the Old South? (c) What do the arrows represent? (d) In what directions did cotton production expand between 1839 and 1859?

2 The planters control the positions of power

As a general rule, the planters held most of the important political positions in the South. They were usually chosen by the voters in the southern states as their Senators and Representatives in the Congress of the United States.

Who were the planters? Many southern planters were descendants of the wealthy colonial planters of the eastern seaboard states. Others worked their way up the economic and social ladder. For example, Joseph Emory Davis, a brother of Jefferson Davis, produced 3,000 bales of cotton each year on Mississippi land he had carved out of frontier wilderness. Southerners who started life as small farmers and rose to high positions included John C. Calhoun of South Carolina and Andrew Jackson of Tennessee.

Educational leadership. For the most part, the wealthy planters and their families received excellent educations. This in itself helps to explain their strong influence. Believing firmly in the importance of education, they hired private tutors for their children or sent the boys to private schools. While few girls were sent to college, a high proportion of boys went to college. Most young southern men attended William and Mary College, the University of Virginia, or some other southern col-

This Louisiana sugar plantation, like many southern plantations, was both elegant and functional. Columns and verandas grace the front of the plantation house at the left. The red building at the right is the sugar refinery.

lege. Many others went north to Yale, Harvard, Princeton, West Point, and Annapolis. Hundreds of these young graduates of southern and northern colleges became leaders in the South.

Political leadership. The county form of local government found throughout the South had been introduced into Virginia by the first English settlers. It later spread throughout the southern states. This form of local government enabled the planters to control the machinery of southern government and to hold most of the leading political offices in the South.

The county was the most important southern political unit, and the most important county officers were the justices of the peace. These officers — varying in numbers up to 35 for each county — were appointed by the governor of each state, who was usually a wealthy planter. The justices had broad powers. They levied taxes. They provided for the building of roads, bridges, and schoolhouses. They appointed sheriffs to enforce the law.

Once a month the justices of each county met as a judicial body to try cases. The justices also met informally and unofficially to choose candidates for election to their state legislature and to Congress. Without their approval it

was difficult if not impossible for any southerner to win an election for county, state, or national office.

The plantation home. Travelers who journeyed through the counties of the South in the 1850's occasionally passed imposing mansions set well back from the road, with close-clipped lawns sweeping down to the fields or a river. The houses were shaded by tall trees and surrounded by formal gardens. They looked cool and inviting with wide verandas and white Grecian pillars supporting the roof.

Many of these mansions, often having 12 or 15 luxuriously furnished rooms, were places of great beauty. These were the homes of the wealthy planter families who owned 100 to 500 slaves or more. However, even as late as 1860, fewer than 2,500 planters could afford such luxury.

The planter family that owned from 20 to 100 slaves lived well, but more modestly. Their home might have as many as eight or ten rooms, with wide halls and deep verandas, or porches, surrounded by spacious, shaded grounds. The furnishings inside the house were usually comfortable but not luxurious, for most of the family's wealth was tied up in land and slaves. They could not afford expensive

HEWLETT & BRIGHT.

SALE OF

VALUABLE SLAVES,

(On account of departure)

The Owner of the following named and valuable Slaves, being on the eve of departure for Europe, will cause the same to be offered for sale, at the NEW EXCHANGE, corner of St. Louis and Chartres streets, on *Saturday*, May 16, at Twelve o'Clock, *viz.*

1. SARAH, a mulatress, aged 45 years, a good cook and accustomed to house work in general, is an excellent and faithful nurse for sick persons, and is in every respect a first rate character.

2. DENNIS, her son, a mulatto, aged 24 years, a first rate cook and steward for a vessel, having been in that capacity for many years on board one of the Mobile packets; is strictly honest, temperate, and a first rate subject.

3. CHOLE, a mulatress, aged 36 years, she is, without exception, one of the most competent servants in the country, a first rate washer and ironer, does up lace, a good cook, and for a bachelor who wishes a house-keeper she would be invaluable; she is also a good ladies' maid, having travelled to the North in that capacity.

4. FANNY, her daughter, a mulatress, aged 16 years, speaks French and English, is a superior hair-dresser, (pupil of Guillac,) a good seamstress and ladies' maid, is smart, intelligent, and a first rate character.

5. DANDRIDGE, a mulatto, aged 26 years, a first rate dining-room servant, a good painter and rough carpenter, and has but few equals for honesty and sobriety.

6. NANCY, his wife, aged about 24 years, a confidential house servant, good seamstress, mantuamaker and tailoress, a good cook, washer and ironer, etc.

7. MARY ANN, her child, a creole, aged 7 years, speaks French and English, is smart, active and intelligent.

8. FANNY or FRANCES, a mulatress, aged 22 years, is a first rate washer and ironer, good cook and house servant, and has an excellent character.

9. EMMA, an orphan, aged 10 or 11 years, speaks French and English, has been in the country 7 years, has been accustomed to waiting on table, sewing etc.; is intelligent and active.

10. FRANK, a mulatto, aged about 32 years speaks French and English, is a first rate hostler and coachman, understands perfectly well the management of horses, and is, in every respect, a first rate character, with the exception that he will occasionally drink, though not an habitual drunkard.

☞ All the above named Slaves are acclimated and excellent subjects; they were purchased by their present vendor many years ago, and will, therefore, be severally warranted against all vices and maladies prescribed by law, save and except FRANK, who is fully guaranteed in every other respect but the one above mentioned.

TERMS:—One-half Cash, and the other half in notes at Six months, drawn and endorsed to the satisfaction of the Vendor, with special mortgage on the Slaves until final payment. The Acts of Sale to be passed before WILLIAM BOSWELL, Notary Public, at the expense of the Purchaser.

The firm of Hewlett and Bright, a slave-auctioning firm in New Orleans, circulated this poster advertising a sale in 1835. The firm offers to the public a variety of slaves — cooks, housekeepers, coachmen — aged 7 to 45.

household goods or lavish entertainment. In fact, such planter families often lived lonely, isolated lives.

The planter's duties. The owner, or master, of a plantation, regardless of its size, had to attend to an endless number of details. In addition to supervising the work on the plantation itself, the planter had to keep records of his business transactions. Letters and orders had to be written to shipowners and bankers and to the agents who sold the cotton to the textile mills.

The day-by-day management of the plantation was very time-consuming. Each morning the planter or an overseer assigned jobs to the slaves, such as tending the cotton, hoeing corn, cultivating other food crops, cutting wood, carrying water, feeding livestock, and doing household jobs. There was always much work to be done, for a cotton grower also raised most of the food eaten by the family and the slaves.

In terms of money in the bank, the planter was not usually rich. The planter shipped cotton through an agent in the North Atlantic states or in Great Britain. The agent sold the cotton and shipped back whatever agricultural tools, clothing, books, and household furnishings the planter wanted. Frequently, after the cotton was sold and the purchases were made, the planter ended up in debt to the agent who handled the business.

The mistress of the plantation has often been romanticized as a frail and lovely person of leisure. In fact, she usually had her hands full as the supervisor of a large household. The many activities for which she was responsible might include spinning and weaving as well as preparing and storing food. The mistress also looked after the health of everyone who lived and worked on the plantation. Often she taught the younger children when it was hard to find a tutor.

Economics of slavery. It is impossible to say whether or not slave labor was really profitable for the southern planters. Many planters and most small farmers did not keep accurate accounts. Thus they did not know from one year to the next just how much they had earned or lost.

Before 1840 some southerners believed that slave labor was becoming less profitable than hired labor. In 1837 George Tucker, a professor at the University of Virginia, argued in a book entitled *The Law of Wages, Profits, and Rents* that slavery was an inefficient system of labor. To support this argument, Tucker and others pointed to the high cost of buying slaves; to the fact that unwilling workers were usually poor workers; to the expensive supervision that was required to keep slaves at work; to the cost of food, clothing, and shelter; and to the economic losses caused by a slave's illness or death.

After 1840 such arguments were heard less often. Many southerners had come to feel that slavery was not only necessary for the South, but that it was also profitable. Thus southerners were angered when, in 1857, a farmer from North Carolina published a book that tried to prove that the South was economically inferior to the North because of the inefficiency of slavery. The author, Hinton Rowan Helper, called his book *The Impending Crisis.* Feeling in the South ran so high against Helper that he found it wise to move to the North.

Actually, most historians today would not agree with Helper. There is evidence that the large rice, sugar, and cotton plantations were often profitable to their owners, depending partly upon weather conditions and market prices and depending especially on managerial skill. On the other hand, some planters were regularly in debt, and many were barely able to break even.

The proslavery argument. Whether or not slavery was a profitable labor system, by 1860 it had become firmly established on all southern plantations and many small southern farms. As slavery grew and spread, it became the subject of increasingly bitter controversy between southerners and northerners. In defending their way of life, southerners developed what has come to be called "the proslavery argument."

The proslavery argument declared, in part, that slavery was necessary because without it southern planters would not have an adequate labor supply. The argument held further that the institution of slavery was not only necessary but was of positive value to the slaves themselves. It gave them shelter, clothing, and food. It took care of them in sickness and old age. In short, it provided them with a secure and stable existence.

The champions of slavery often contrasted the secure life of the slave with the uncertain lot of wage earners in the mills, factories, and mines of the North and of Europe. These white workers, it was argued, were exploited mercilessly by employers who had no concern for their well-being. Their employers paid them barely enough to live on, fired them when there was no work to do, and discarded them when they were too ill or too old to work.

The proslavery arguments were popularized throughout the South by leaders at rallies, by newspaper editors, by novelists and short-story writers, and by preachers. The arguments were mainly advanced by, or on behalf of, the large plantation owners. The small planters, who often wanted to become large planters, also accepted the argument, as did small farmers who owned no slaves but who hoped in time to buy some. Even the poor whites accepted the proslavery argument. It added to their sense of solidarity and pride in being members of the white society of the South.

Most white southerners, then, accepted the arguments in defense of slavery and opposed the arguments against slavery. White southerners largely accepted the leadership of the great plantation owners and the institution of slavery itself. They identified slavery with the southern way of life. They saw any criticism of slavery, or any efforts to restrict it, as a threat to their homes, their land, and their way of life.

SECTION SURVEY

IDENTIFY: county, justice of the peace, Hinton R. Helper.

1. Why did large planters hold most of the leading political positions in the South?
2. The life of a large plantation owner was comfortable, but not easy. Support or refute this statement using specific examples.
3. Summarize the main points of the proslavery argument.
4. Why did the average non-slave-holding white southerner accept the institution of slavery?

3 The slaves play leading roles in the development of the South

No American today can fully imagine what it was like to be a slave. Historians have had to use a variety of sources and methods in attempting to picture slave life in the southern states in the years before 1860.

The study of slavery. On the basis of documents and records alone, no historian can accurately reconstruct what it was like to be a slave. There are many records, but most of them were written by white southerners or by white travelers from the North or from Europe.

A few slaves who could write left short accounts of their lives. A larger number who escaped to the North or to Canada wrote more detailed autobiographies. Long after slavery ended, scholars interviewed former slaves and recorded their memories.

In addition to written records, historians have examined the surviving work songs and religious songs in which the slaves expressed some of their feelings. Historians have also used some of the scholarly methods of sociology, anthropology, and psychology. What, then, are some things that can be said about slavery as the slaves actually lived it?

Posters like that on page 302 drew buyers to scenes like this one, in St. Louis. The slave auctioneer (center) announces the strengths and skills of the slaves to the audience. At such a sale, a child might be bought for only $200 or $300. However, a strong field hand in the group might sell for $1,500.

The work the slaves did. By 1860 the nearly 4 million slaves in the South performed a wide variety of jobs. Many worked in the homes of the planters, merchants, lawyers, and doctors, cooking the meals, doing the housekeeping, and tending the children.

Some of the slaves became skilled workers. Women learned to spin, weave, and sew. Some became cooks, maids, and nursemaids. Men became blacksmiths, painters, shoemakers, jewelers, and silversmiths. Others learned carpentry, bricklaying, and other tasks required to build a house. Some could not only build the house but also could make necessary plans, draw up contracts, and complete the entire structure.

Some slaves were hired out by their owners to work in tobacco factories, in sugar and flour mills, and in iron works. A great many did hard, unskilled work in building canals, roads, and railroads and in draining swamps. Large numbers were used as dock workers, lifting and carrying heavy loads on and off ships.

The great majority of the slaves on the cotton, rice, and sugar-cane plantations did the hard work of the fields. These men and women planted the crops in the spring and cultivated them through the summer. In the fall they picked cotton, cut sugar cane, harvested rice and grain, and slaughtered livestock. In the winter the slaves mended fences and cleared new land.

How slave labor was organized. On farms and small plantations, the slaves were usually supervised by their owners. On small farms owners sometimes worked alongside their slaves.

On large plantations work was organized either by the task system or by the gang system. Under the task system, each slave was given a particular job to do each day and could stop working when the job was finished. At such times some slaves earned wages by working for someone else. Under the more widely used gang system, an overseer assigned groups of slaves to work under drivers. A white overseer often was used, but black overseers were common. The drivers usually were slaves. The gang worked as long and as hard as the overseer or driver saw fit. The purpose of the gang system was to get as much work as possible out of the slave labor force.

How slaves were treated. On some plantations, especially those with overseers, slaves were often treated harshly, if not brutally. However, many slaveowners treated their slaves reasonably well because the slaves were valuable property. For example, suppose a planter owned 50 slaves. At a cost of from $1,000 to $1,500 for each slave (an average price in the 1850's), the planter's investment in slaves was from $50,000 to $75,000. The death of a single slave meant a serious financial loss. Even the illness of a slave meant a setback. Any illness or injury resulting from ill-treatment was against the planters' interests. To protect their investment, therefore, they were apt to keep their slaves adequately fed, clothed, and housed.

Much of the proslavery argument was based on these grounds. Advocates of slavery argued that the living conditions of the slaves —their workday, food, clothing, and shelter— were better and more secure than those of workers in the mills and factories of the North.

That argument left out much. Industrial workers of the North could quit their jobs and look for other work. If they had some cash, they could move to the relatively cheap farmland of the western regions. Most important, they were free persons. Slaves, by contrast, were property. They had no voice in deciding the conditions of their work or even of their own lives. Free workers, to be sure, had to submit to the discipline and rules of the mill or factory where they worked, but that discipline differed sharply from slave discipline.

Slave discipline. Slaveowners had to teach their slaves to be slaves—that is, to be obedient and accept their lot. Slaveowners did this partly by persuasion. They taught their slaves that it was their religious duty to obey their master, mistress, or overseer. Slaves were taught to believe that any white person was superior by nature to any black person.

These efforts were conscious and deliberate. Plantation owners bought handbooks on how to manage slaves. Some handbooks contained question-and-answer lessons, which the slaves had to memorize. These lessons were meant to teach them always to obey and respect white people, never to argue with them, and to accept their own condition as slaves.

Under these psychological pressures and dependent as they were upon their masters for food, clothing, and shelter, some slaves came to regard themselves as children. Many masters encouraged this attitude by giving small gifts or special privileges to obedient slaves, as is often done with children.

When persuasion failed, masters and overseers could and often did resort to brutal-

ity. If slaves showed signs of disobedience, stubbornness, or independence, they might be flogged or whipped. If this did not work, slaves might suffer even more painful and degrading punishments. They might be branded or have their noses slit. The worst threat that the slaves faced was that they might be sold and thus deprived of the few cherished family ties they had developed.

This discipline did encourage many slaves to be outwardly childlike and obedient toward white people. However, it also forced them to be deceitful. Many slaves showed outward respect and obedience to escape penalties or win rewards. Such outward behavior sometimes concealed bitter resentment and hatred toward white people.

How slaves resisted. Despite all the efforts to control them, many slaves found ways of resisting slavery. No one knows how many slaves escaped from the plantations. Some fled to join relatives from whom they had been separated while others sought freedom in the North or in Canada. The number of fugitives probably ran into thousands each year. Many, however, were captured by professional slave catchers, who used bloodhounds to hunt down runaways.

Beginning in colonial times, slaves had plotted uprisings to gain their freedom. These rebellions continued into the 1800's.

In 1791 the slaves of Haiti carried out a successful revolt against their French masters. In Henrico County, Virginia, a slave named Gabriel Prosser heard of this revolt and was inspired by it. He secretly organized a group of slaves, forged weapons, and set a date for an uprising in 1800. Gabriel Prosser's plot was betrayed by two fellow slaves. Pursued by a Virginia militia, the group disbanded but was caught and punished.

An uprising was said to have been organized in Charleston, South Carolina, in 1822 by Denmark Vesey, a former slave. Reports of this plot may have rested largely on unfounded fears among white southerners, since no actual act of rebellion took place. Whatever the facts may have been, 37 blacks were put to death and others were severely punished.

In 1831 a slave named Nat Turner led a slave uprising in Southampton County, Virginia. Outwardly obedient, Nat Turner had learned to read the Bible and was deeply religious. Believing that God had chosen him to

Nat Turner (center) was convinced that God meant him to lead the slaves to freedom. Turner persuaded 60 others to join him in his rebellion. After his capture, he freely admitted what he had done but pleaded "not guilty" to the charges. When asked why, he replied, "Because I don't feel guilty."

slaughter white people and free the slaves, Nat Turner began his rebellion. Before troops suppressed it, 60 white people and more than 100 slaves were killed. Turner was captured, brought to trial, and hanged. After this rebellion all southern states tightened their control over black people, free as well as slave.

Most slaves, of course, took no part in rebellions. Most never tried to run away. Yet despite the discipline and restrictions of slavery, black men and women were not wholly robbed of their personality. They found ways of expressing their thoughts and feelings within the family and in the distinctive life of the slave quarters. These expressions combined survivals of their African heritage with some traits of white southern culture.

Slaves often expressed joy in songs and dances, and humor in folk tales and jokes. They also found outlets for their unhappiness and misery under bondage in haunting religious songs called **spirituals**. These hymns, rich in Biblical lore, were modeled in part on the "gospel hymns" sung by white Christians, but they were also strongly influenced by traditional African musical forms. Nearly all these spirituals movingly expressed the slaves' deep longing for freedom.

The heritage of slavery. The slaves made enormously valuable contributions to the wealth of their owners, of the southern economy, and of the nation. They also made valuable contributions to the culture of the South. However, these contributions were made at enormous costs to the slaves. While slavery existed in the United States, black people were deprived of the opportunities and freedoms enjoyed by most other Americans.

SECTION SURVEY

IDENTIFY: task system, gang system, Gabriel Prosser, Denmark Vesey, Nat Turner, spirituals.

1. (a) What resources have historians used to develop an understanding of southern slave life in the years before 1860? (b) Can their understanding ever be complete? Why or why not?

2. (a) What work did slaves do? (b) How was their work organized? (c) How were they treated? (d) What was the basic difference between southern slaves and northern white workers?

3. (a) Why was it necessary to teach slaves how to be slaves? (b) How did the methods of disciplining slaves affect the way slaves behaved?

4. How did slaves attempt to resist slavery?

Chapter Survey

Summary: Tracing the Main Ideas

The South, like the Northeast, was greatly influenced by the Industrial Revolution. The invention of power-driven machines for spinning and weaving yarn created a growing demand for cotton fiber. The invention of the cotton gin gave planters an effective machine for cleaning the seeds from cotton. Inventions like the railroad and the steamboat and the development of an improved system of canals and roads also helped the South's booming economy. Such advances made it possible for planters to ship their cotton to the new factories in the Northeast and in Great Britain.

Except for the cotton gin, however, machines were not much used on farmland in the South. It was the slaves who cleared the land, plowed the fields, planted the seeds, and harvested the highly profitable crop of cotton. As the years passed and larger areas of the South were planted in cotton, slaves became more and more numerous and increasingly valuable to the planters.

To be sure, only a small percentage of the southerners owned slaves, but the slaveowners were, in general, the wealthiest, the best educated, and the most influential people in the South. They were the political leaders who ran the governments in the southern states and who represented the South in the Congress of the United States. These southern leaders—and their families—helped to create a way of living different from that in any other section of the country.

You have now seen how distinctive ways of living and working developed in the North and the South. We turn now to the third section of the country—that vast and rapidly expanding region known as the West. As you will see, it too was being transformed during the first half of the 1800's.

Inquiring into History

1. Explain the relationship (a) between cotton production and westward expansion and (b) between cotton production and slavery.
2. Imagine that southern society could be described as a pyramid, with the lowest economic groups at the bottom and the highest at the top. (a) Which group would form the base of the pyramid? (b) Which group would be at the top? (c) Was it possible for people in southern society to move up to a higher level on the pyramid? Explain.
3. Most white southerners saw slavery as an essential part of the distinctive southern way of life. Comment.
4. It has been said that both blacks and whites suffered from the institution of slavery. Do you agree or disagree? Why?

Relating Past to Present

1. Do you think that effects of slavery can still be found in American society today? Explain.
2. Does today's South still have its own distinctive way of life? Explain.
3. Research the value of the South's cotton crop in a recent year. Compare it to the value of other crops in the South, such as soybeans and tobacco. Compare it to the value of manufactured goods produced in the South. Is cotton still "king" in the South? Why or why not?

Developing Social Science Skills

1. Write a newspaper editorial in which you disagree with the proslavery argument. In your editorial include details of the conditions under which slaves lived.
2. Study the illustrations in this chapter. (a) What conclusions can you draw about life in the South before the Civil War? (b) Do you think that these illustrations present a realistic picture of life at that time? Why or why not?
3. Read an account of slavery written by a former slave, such as *Up from Slavery* by Booker T. Washington or *A Narrative of the Life of Frederick Douglass*. Prepare an oral or pictorial report to present to the class.
4. Find a record or songbook that includes such spirituals as "Go Down, Moses," "Didn't My Lord Deliver Daniel," and "All God's Chillun Got Wings." Then answer these questions: (a) What is the general mood of the songs? (b) What attitudes and values are reflected in the songs? (c) How useful are songs as a source of information about slavery? Explain.

Chapter 15

Expanding the Nation's Boundaries to the Pacific

Changing Ways of American Life

1820's–1860's

From the early 1800's to the 1860's, while the Indians were being persuaded, bribed, or forced to move across the Mississippi River, restless white settlers also were moving across the river and casting eager eyes even farther westward. In 1821 Missouri, west of the Mississippi, was admitted to the Union. Pioneers also crossed the river farther north, subdued the Iowas and other tribes, and formed Iowa Territory in 1838.

Immediately to the west of Missouri and Iowa lay the Great Plains, known to the pioneers as the Great American Desert and an area that did not attract them until later. This vast region of grasslands provided food for huge herds of buffalo and hunting grounds for such tribes as the Dakotas, Sioux, Omahas, Cheyennes, Crows, Arapahos, Osages, Kansa, and Poncas. Just west of the plains, in the Rocky Mountain area, were the homelands of the Shoshones, Flatheads, Coeur d'Alenes, Nez Percés, Utes, and other tribes. Still farther west and north, the Oregon country beckoned to the pioneers. Its forests, its fertile valleys, and some of its dry stretches were the homelands of the Cayuses, Modocs, Yakimas, Chinooks, and other tribes.

South and southwest of the northern Great Plains lay Texas, New Mexico, and Arizona, settled by Spaniards, Mexicans, Wichitas, Kiowas, Apaches, Comanches, Hopis, Zuñis, Pueblos, Papagos, Yumas, and Mohaves. Still farther west, in California, were other small groups of Indians.

From the 1820's to the 1860's, as you have read, the Industrial Revolution was creating a distinctive way of life in the North, while cotton cultivation was creating a different way of life in the South. In this chapter you will learn how the third great section of the United States—the "West," as it is known today—was added to the nation.

THE CHAPTER IN OUTLINE

1. Fur traders and settlers expand into the Oregon country.

2. American settlers create the Lone Star Republic of Texas.

3. War with Mexico adds the entire Southwest to the nation.

4. A surge of migration brings California into the Union.

1 Fur traders and settlers expand into the Oregon country

Far to the northwest of Missouri, beyond the Rocky Mountains, lay an enormous area of towering mountains, magnificent forests, and fertile valleys drained by rivers teeming with fish. This area is now called the Pacific Northwest. In the 1800's it was known as the Oregon country or simply as Oregon. It stretched northward from the 42nd parallel, the northern border of California, to the parallel of 54°40′, the southern boundary of Alaska (see map, this page). Until the early 1820's, the Oregon country was simultaneously claimed by four nations—Spain, Russia, Great Britain, and the United States. All of these claims ignored the historic roots and presence of the Native Americans.

Conflicting claims. The Spanish claim to the Oregon country dated back to an agreement between Spain and Portugal in 1494. Spain gave up its claim in 1819 under the same treaty in which it ceded Florida to the United States (page 248).

Russia based its claims to the Oregon country on the explorations of Vitus Bering, a Dane who had explored the area for Russia in

EARLY ROUTES TO THE FAR WEST

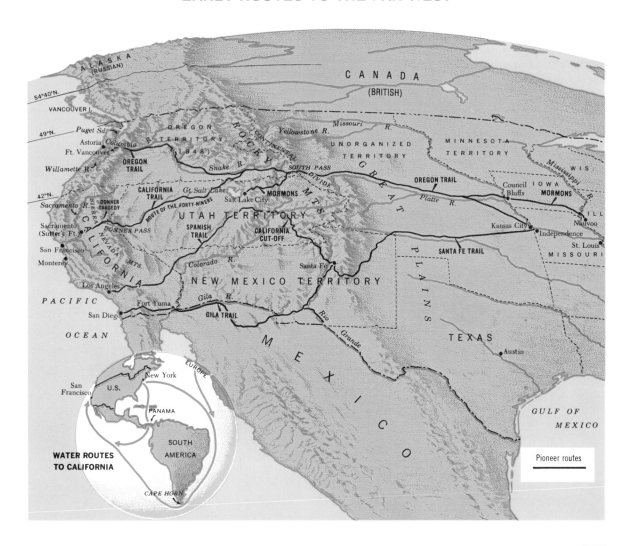

309

1741. After Bering's explorations, the Russians had established missions and trading posts in Alaska and in the Pacific Northwest.

Increasing Russian pressure along the Pacific coast after 1815, you recall, was one reason why in 1823 President Monroe had warned Russia and other European nations not to colonize the Western Hemisphere. The Russian tsar decided not to force the issue. In 1824 the Russians withdrew their claims to all land south of the 54th parallel.

Great Britain based its claim to the Oregon country on voyages made to the Pacific by Francis Drake in 1577–80 and by Captain James Cook in 1776–78. The government of Great Britain encouraged a profitable British fur trade with the Indians of the Pacific Northwest.

The United States had established its first claim to the Oregon country in 1792. In that year Captain Robert Gray, a merchant sea captain from Boston, discovered the Columbia River. Gray promptly began trading for furs with the Indians there. The claim was strengthened when American fur traders began traveling overland to the Oregon country in the early 1800's.

In 1818 Great Britain and the United States agreed to occupy the Oregon country jointly for ten years. Ten years later, after Spain and Russia had given up their claims, Great Britain and the United States renewed their agreement.

American fur traders. The American interest in the far western fur trade began in earnest after the Lewis and Clark expedition of 1804–06 (page 224). Centering in St. Louis, the western trade was gradually organized by enterprising business concerns such as the Rocky Mountain Fur Company. This company outfitted rugged "Mountain Men" who roamed the West searching for animal skins, or pelts. Mountain Men like Jedediah Smith and James Beckwourth were as rough-and-ready a group as one could find in America at this time.

In their explorations of the Far West, the Mountain Men followed Indian trails across the Rockies and through passes that were later used by settlers moving west. One of these, South Pass in what is now Wyoming, led to a trail that crossed the Continental Divide and cut through the Snake and Columbia river valleys to the Pacific Ocean. This route came,

Following the 2,000-mile (3,200-kilometer) Oregon Trail usually took a wagon train about six months. Albert Bierstadt, who had gone on an expedition to map a wagon route to the Pacific, recreated this breathtaking scene along the way.

KING OF THE MOUNTAIN MEN

That was what they called Jim Bridger, and small wonder. His life was like a legend, full of improbable adventures and narrow escapes. Some of them actually happened—enough to make him a genuine hero of the West.

Born in Richmond, Virginia, Bridger moved to St. Louis as a boy. In 1822, at the age of eighteen, he went to work as a fur trapper. For the next twenty years, he lived in and near the Rockies, following the beaver and selling his catch once a year at the "trappers' rendezvous." His knowledge of the area and the Indians who lived there was unequaled. He may have been the first white man to visit Great Salt Lake and was one of the first to see the wonders of what is now Yellowstone National Park.

Like most mountain men, Jim Bridger loved tall tales, and many were told by and about him. There was the Eight-Hour-Echo Canyon he discovered. If he shouted, "Time to get up!" and went to sleep, he would be awakened when the echo returned next morning. At the "peetrified" forest he stumbled upon, he could leap a wide chasm without falling, since the law of gravity had "peetrified" too.

Bridger quit the fur business in the early 1840's and built a fort in southwestern Wyoming on the Oregon Trail. He became known for his hospitality and, later, for his scouting services to army and private expeditions exploring the West. Bridger outlived his three wives, all of them Indians, and retired "back east" near Kansas City.

Bridger never learned to read or write, but he left his name on passes, lakes, and trails throughout the Rocky Mountains. Perhaps his best memorial is the Bridger National Forest in Wyoming, where he used to camp and tell his tall tales.

in time, to be known as the Oregon Trail (see map, page 309).

Rivalry for furs. Another successful western business venture was the American Fur Company. It was formed in 1808 in New York by John Jacob Astor, a German immigrant. By the 1820's it controlled most of the American trade in the Upper Mississippi Valley, in the Rockies, and in the Oregon country. Astor soon had sales offices in St. Louis, New York, England, France, Austria, and China. In 1832 the company sold 25,000 beaver skins, nearly 50,000 buffalo hides, about 30,000 deerskins, and many other pelts.

Rivalry among the fur trade companies and greed for profits often led to dishonest and unfair trading with the Indians. The federal government tried for a while to solve these problems by setting fixed prices for animal pelts. Largely because of pressure from the private trading companies, the government gave up its effort in 1823.

Missionaries in Oregon. The fur trade led in the 1830's and 1840's to the settlement of the Oregon country south of the Columbia River. The surge of settlement was set off mainly by missionaries and by New England business groups interested in trade and fishing.

The first missionaries traveled to the Oregon country with fur traders. Jason Lee, a Methodist, built a mission and a school for Indian children in the fertile Willamette Valley in 1834. Samuel Parker, a Presbyterian minister, followed a year later. In 1836 four Presbyterian missionaries—Dr. Marcus Whitman, Narcissa Prentice Whitman, Henry Spalding, and Elizabeth Hart Spalding—made the long, hard trip across the Rocky Mountains. In 1840 Father Pierre De Smet, a Jesuit priest, arrived in the Oregon country.

By the 1840's pioneers were entering the Oregon country at the rate of a thousand a year. At first the Indians were generally friendly. However, they soon became alarmed at the threat to their own ways of life from the arrival of so many settlers. Friction and misunderstanding often arose. One example was a tragic event in 1847. The new settlers of that year brought with them an epidemic of measles. Dr. Marcus Whitman's medication kept white children alive but failed to save Indian children, who had never been exposed to this disease. The Cayuses (ki·oos·ez), suspecting that their children had been poisoned, killed Dr. Whitman, his wife, and twelve other persons. Settlers struck back in what was called the Cayuse War.

Some years later a Yakima chief, Kamaiakan (kah·mi·ah·kahn), became troubled by the changes he saw in Indians who were in close contact with white settlers. He also opposed a treaty calling for tribal removal. Kamaiakan, a great orator, called on the northwestern tribes to resist. Finally, he and his men were defeated in major battles in 1856 and 1858.

The early settlers. During these same years, some white settlers brought black slaves with them. However, most of the settlers opposed slavery, and in 1845 it was prohibited by law in the Oregon country. The same law set up severe discriminations against free black settlers, ordering them to leave the country within two years.

From the beginning the settlers in the Oregon country felt a need for government. In 1843 nine settlers drew up a resolution, which said in part, "We the people of Oregon territory, for the purposes of mutual protection and to secure peace and prosperity among ourselves, agree to adopt . . . laws and regulations, until such time as the United States of America extend their jurisdiction over us."

Settling British-American claims. According to the agreement reached in 1818 and later renewed, Great Britain and the United States were to occupy the Oregon country jointly. By 1840 a new solution was needed to settle rival British-American claims.

Many Americans were demanding that the British withdraw all claims to the land south of the line 54° 40'. This demand became a major issue in the Presidential election of 1844. The Democrats, led by James K. Polk of Tennessee, made western expansion the main issue of their campaign.

Although some Americans spoke with bitter and even warlike words about this issue, calmer minds won out. Great Britain agreed in the Treaty of 1846 to give up its claims to the Oregon country south of the 49th parallel (see map, page 309). Thus by 1846 a boundary existed between the United States and Canada from the Atlantic to the Pacific Ocean. At first this boundary was marked by a few small fortifications. Since then it has been completely unfortified.

In 1848 that part of the Oregon country that now clearly belonged to the United States was organized as Oregon Territory.

SECTION SURVEY

IDENTIFY: Mountain Men, Oregon Trail, John Jacob Astor, the Whitmans, Kamaiakan, Treaty of 1846 (with Great Britain).

1. (a) Which countries in addition to the United States claimed the Oregon country? (b) What was the basis of their claims?

2. How did each of the following help to lay the basis for American claims to the Oregon country: (a) Captain Gray, (b) Lewis and Clark, (c) Mountain Men, (d) Astor, (e) missionaries, (f) settlers?

3. How did the United States finally acquire the Oregon country?

4. Map Study: Look at the map on page 309. (a) Locate the boundaries of the Russian claims. (b) Locate the United States–Canada boundary established in 1846. (c) Which route to the West Coast might have been the easiest to follow? Why?

2 American settlers create the Lone Star Republic of Texas

In the early 1820's, when Americans first began showing interest in the Oregon country, other American traders and settlers were already drifting southwestward into Indian and Mexican lands. Their arrival began a chain of events that led the United States to acquire the vast area that is now Texas, New Mexico, Arizona, California, Nevada, and Utah as well as parts of Colorado and Wyoming.

Early Spanish settlement. As you have read (pages 5–6), many Indian tribes lived in this immense area long before the Spaniards arrived in the Americas. The Spaniards ignored the Indians and immediately claimed the land for the Spanish Crown and called it New Spain. The Spaniards based their claim on the early explorations of Coronado and others and on later Spanish settlements throughout the area.

During the 1600's and 1700's, the Spaniards spread northward from Mexico City—the heart of their New World empire. As early as 1609, they established Santa Fe in what is now New Mexico. From Santa Fe, their chief northern outpost, the Spaniards kept a firm hold on the region for many years, with only a temporary setback in a Pueblo revolt that broke out in 1680. In the 1700's, fearing French and British expansion, the Spaniards strengthened their colonizing efforts. They established presidios (or forts), missions, villages, towns, and large ranches throughout the present states of Texas, New Mexico, Arizona, and California.

The missions. The center of each mission was the church, often a beautiful structure built of stone or adobe. Surrounding the church were living quarters for the priests and workshops in which the Indians learned weaving, silver working, blacksmithing, and other crafts. Generally the main buildings were enclosed within an adobe or stone wall. Around the mission buildings were farming areas where the priests and Indians grew grain, grapes, and other crops and at times raised cattle. Indians who had won the confidence of the priests sometimes had farms of their own near the missions.

Most of the missions were set up by Franciscan priests. The priests tried to win the Indians to Christianity, to teach them some of the Spanish ways of life, and to make them loyal Spanish subjects. The priests, however, were only partly successful. In their zeal they tried to suppress Indian religions and customs, thinking that this was in the best interests of the Indians. They often treated the Indians as children and punished them for breaking mission rules. Indians often resented the labor that was forced on them and were unhappy with the suppression of their own culture. Many of them fled from the missions.

The Spaniards hoped strong communities would develop around the missions, with each mission as the center of community life. Although this goal was only partly realized, the missions did play a major role in shaping the life of the northern areas of New Spain.

Ways of life in New Spain. The Spanish ranches also played a key role. These huge estates, some with thousands of sheep or cattle, were widely scattered over the vast northern part of New Spain. Usually far from missions and presidios, the ranches were complete communities in themselves. Here lived a few Spaniards, a larger number of creoles, and a much larger number of mestizos and Indians. The owners often lived in town houses in Mexico City or in Spain. They visited their estates only occasionally. Thus many of the workers became very capable in the management and supervision of the estates. Other workers developed great skills as riders. They became models for the American cowboys, who would later work on the plains.

From California to Texas, the ruling groups shared certain values and beliefs. They were Roman Catholics. They had a deep pride in Spanish culture. They were also fiercely independent—a trait encouraged by their remoteness from the centers of government in Santa Fe and Mexico City. Coupled with this spirit of independence was a suspicion of outsiders—whether explorers, military scouts, or traders. The Spaniards tried to protect themselves from intruders by forbidding all trade with Americans. At times, they seized and imprisoned American explorers and traders who entered their lands.

Throughout the region, as indeed throughout Latin America, attitudes toward the lower classes, especially the Indians, varied greatly. On the one hand, mission priests often treated the lower classes as children. On the other hand, the owners of mines, ranches, and businesses often mistreated and abused the workers. In time, the smoldering unrest and resentment of the lower classes burst into revolution.

The Mexican Revolution. The Spanish and Portuguese colonies in the Americas could not remain untouched by the revolutions and wars that swept across Europe in the early 1800's. In 1810 a Mexican priest, Father Miguel Hidalgo y Costilla (ee·DAHL·goh ee koh·STEE·yah), led an uprising of the oppressed people of New Spain. He was joined by another priest, Father José Maria Morelos y Pavón (moh·RAY·lohs ee

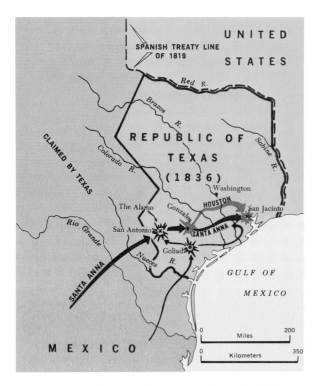

TEXAS WINS INDEPENDENCE

thriving trade developed over what came to be called the Santa Fe Trail (see map, page 309). Wagons loaded with household goods, tools, and other products lumbered west from St. Louis, Missouri. They followed the rugged trail to Santa Fe, the distributing center for much of northern Mexico. On their return trip, the wagons carried valuable loads of silver, gold, and hides. The journey was always dangerous. The traders were often attacked by Indians—especially the Comanches—whose lands they crossed. The traders sometimes attacked, or counterattacked, the Indians. Bitterness and resentment on both sides deepened.

Settlers in Texas. The new Mexican government was divided over the question of opening the Texas region to American settlers. Some Mexican leaders were opposed to American settlement. Others thought that a relatively small number of American settlers would soon become Mexican citizens. As such, they would serve as a buffer against a rush of Americans into Texas and the seizure of the region by the United States. At the time, the Mexican population of Texas, largely concentrated in four small towns, numbered between 4,000 and 8,000.

The pro-settlement side won the debate. In 1821 the Mexican government gave Stephen F. Austin a renewal of the grant of land that his father Moses had received. That same year Stephen Austin and the "Old Three Hundred," his hand-picked settlers, began to build a vigorous American colony in Texas.

Other settlers soon followed. By 1830 more than 20,000 Americans, many of them southerners, had entered Texas. By that time, slavery had been outlawed in Mexico. Thus it was technically illegal for southerners to bring slaves into Texas. However, since the Mexican authorities did little to enforce this law, many southerners brought their slaves anyway.

The Mexican leaders soon saw that their liberal policies were encouraging the growth of an American community, or even an American state, within Mexico itself. Convinced that too many independence-minded Americans were entering, the Mexican government began to shut off further settlement. In 1830 it passed a law to restrict further settlement in the Mexican states bordering the United States. Land grants not already taken up were canceled. The Mexicans also restated that slavery on Mexican lands was forbidden. To enforce their

pah·VOHN). The revolution at first had some success. Soon, however, control passed into the hands of ambitious military leaders. Their chief interest was in winning independence from Spain. In this they were successful. In 1821 the former colony of New Spain became the independent Republic of Mexico. In the meantime, Fathers Hidalgo and Morelos, who had been largely responsible for starting the revolution, suffered the fate of martyrs. The oppression of the Indians and the workers remained largely untouched by the struggle for national independence.

A change in policy. Even before Mexico won its independence, the Spanish authorities began to relax their attitude toward outsiders. In 1820, Moses Austin, a Connecticut-born pioneer, received permission to start a colony of a few hundred families in what is now the state of Texas. In return, he promised that the settlers would become loyal Spanish subjects.

Moses Austin died in 1821 before he could establish his colony. By then, however, the new government of Mexico had adopted a more liberal attitude toward American traders. Soon a

314

laws, the Mexicans strengthened their army posts throughout Texas.

The fight for independence. The American settlers in Texas protested vigorously against what they said were restrictions on their rights. The Mexican leaders would not reconsider, because in their eyes the settlers had broken their promises to obey Mexican laws. After several clashes with Mexican officials, fighting broke out.

An event sometimes called "the Lexington of Texas" took place on October 2, 1835. The commander of Mexican troops at San Antonio tried to seize a cannon that had been given to the settlers at Gonzales (gohn·ZAH·lais) for defense against the Indians (see map, page 314). A group of settlers blocked his efforts.

Later a band of volunteers led by Ben Milam defeated a large Mexican force in desperate house-to-house fighting in San Antonio. Prisoners taken in the battle were permitted to return to Mexico.

Infuriated by this defeat, General Santa Anna, the dictator President of Mexico, promptly led a large army back into Texas. The Mexican army besieged a force of almost 200 settlers in the Alamo, a fortified former mission at San Antonio (see map, page 314). Among the defenders were James Bowie and William B. Travis, the joint commanders, and newcomer Davy Crockett. They refused to surrender despite overwhelming odds. When Santa Anna stormed the fort on March 6, 1836, the defenders all were killed. On March 27 another force was put to death by the Mexicans at Goliad (goh·lee·AHD) after it had surrendered and laid down its arms.

Rallying under the cry "Remember the Alamo! Remember Goliad!" the Texans led by Sam Houston destroyed Santa Anna's advance guard at San Jacinto (SAN yah·SIN·toh) on April 21, 1836, and captured Santa Anna. After a secret treaty was signed, Santa Anna was released with the understanding that he would use his influence to make Mexico recognize the independence of Texas, with its southern boundary at the Rio Grande. However, the Mexican government refused to accept the treaty.

Independence for Texas. Back in March, while the defenders of the Alamo were still holding off the Mexicans, a group of delegates assembled at Washington-on-the-Brazos

When Davy Crockett and his band of volunteers arrived at the Alamo, Crockett announced, "We heard you were having trouble. . .and we allowed as how we might help you since we like a good fight."

(BRAZ·us), then just a small village. There, in a cold, drafty gun shop, the Texans declared their independence on March 2, 1836. The group, made up mostly of American settlers, also drafted a constitution for a new Republic of Texas, often called the Lone Star Republic. Sam Houston, a former governor of Tennessee, became the first elected president of the Republic of Texas, and Lorenzo de Zavala (day sah·VAH·lah) the first vice-president.

During the struggle for independence, many American colonizers had come to regard the Mexican inhabitants of Texas—the Tejanos (TAY·hah·nos), who were of mixed Spanish and Indian ancestry—as inferior people even though some Tejanos had also fought for independence. They failed to understand the Tejanos' traditions or way of life. Thus seeds of prejudice and hostility were planted. In time, this prejudice and hostility forced many Tejanos to flee from their homeland.

Annexation delayed. During the revolution American sympathy was with the Texans. American volunteers crossed into Texas and fought against Santa Anna. When the new republic petitioned to join the United States, strong opposition developed. Since Texas wanted to permit slavery, northerners in

315

Congress feared that its admission would increase southern influence in Congress. Others feared that to admit Texas would be to invite war with Mexico, which had not recognized Texas' independence. Thus the admission of Texas was delayed until 1845.

Free blacks and Indians in Texas. Texas wanted to allow slavery, but it did not want free black settlers within its borders. In 1840 the new Lone Star Republic ordered them to leave Texas or be sold into slavery. The free black settlers, many of whom had fought for Texas' independence, protested. The Texans then decided that they could remain – but only if they made a special appeal to the Congress of the Lone Star Republic.

In some southeastern counties of Texas, free blacks formed a sizable minority. The Ashworth family, for example, had come to Texas in the early 1830's to take up land granted to them by the Mexican government. The Ashworths as well as other free black settlers in Texas owned land, cattle, and even slaves. For a time the free blacks got along fairly well with their white neighbors, but as the war between North and South approached, tensions and even feuds arose.

The American newcomers found various Indian tribes in possession of great stretches of the plains and highlands. Raids by the Comanches of west Texas and New Mexico cost the Americans cattle, horses, and some lives. As time passed, the Americans sought to push many of these tribes northward into Indian Territory, into Mexico, or onto reservations.

SECTION SURVEY

IDENTIFY: Father Hidalgo, Father Morelos, Moses Austin, Santa Fe Trail, Stephen Austin, Santa Anna, Alamo, Sam Houston, Lone Star Republic, Tejanos, Ashworth family.

1. Describe the importance of missions and ranches to the development of New Spain.

2. Why did the Texans fight to gain their independence from Mexico?

3. (a) Explain the historical importance of the slogan "Remember the Alamo! Remember Goliad!" (b) What is the purpose of such slogans?

4. Why did the United States delay the annexation of Texas?

5. What was the Texas policy toward Tejanos, Indians, and free blacks?

3 War with Mexico adds the entire Southwest to the nation

The annexation of Texas in 1845 moved the United States one step closer to war with Mexico. Other factors also led to the Mexican War, which broke out in 1846.

Sources of friction. A major factor in the conflict was the difference in the two ways of life that met and clashed in the vast region west of Texas. This region included the Mexican area known as Upper California, now the state of California. Mexico inherited this entire area from the Spaniards, who claimed it as early as 1494. This was more than a hundred years before the first English settlement on the Atlantic coast. Spanish language, law, architecture, and customs prevailed except in those areas where the original Indian cultures had been untouched by the missions.

Against this frontier of Spanish culture pressed a tide of energetic, land-hungry Americans. These Americans believed firmly that it was the **manifest destiny** – the historic duty – of their nation to expand to the Pacific Ocean.

In the 1830's and early 1840's, ill feeling between Mexico and the United States steadily mounted. During most of these years, the Republic of Mexico was torn by revolutions. Its government was often powerless to control local affairs. The Mexican government tried, but failed, to keep Americans from settling on Mexican soil.

Americans often violated Mexican laws and were thrown into jail. Frequently they were mistreated. In one incident 22 Americans suspected of plotting a revolution were executed by the Mexicans in 1835.

Debts owed by the impoverished Mexican government to United States citizens also contributed to the ill feeling. During Mexico's revolutions, the property of many Americans living in Mexico had been damaged or destroyed. In 1839 an international commission examined American claims and awarded United States citizens about $2 million. By 1845 Mexico had paid only three installments on this debt. The Americans chose to ignore the fact that at this time they themselves were far behind in payments of some $200 million to Great Britain.

The Mexicans also had many grievances against the United States. They were bitter about American expansion into Texas and the violations of Mexican laws by American settlers. They were bitter, too, about the Texas revolution of 1836, which they blamed on the United States. They feared that events in Texas were only the beginning of an American attempt to win control of the entire Southwest.

Rising war fever. American naval and military commanders in the Pacific area had orders to seize Upper California if war broke out. In 1842 Commodore Thomas A. C. Jones, hearing a false rumor that war had been declared, sailed swiftly to Upper California and seized the capital at Monterey. He hauled down the Mexican flag and raised the Stars and Stripes. The next day, learning that he had made a mistake, Jones apologized profusely and withdrew in haste.

In the Presidential election of 1844, the Democrats demanded that Texas as well as Oregon be annexed to the nation. When the Democrats won by a very narrow popular majority, the government took steps to admit Texas to the Union without delay. To the Mexicans, who had never officially recognized the Republic of Texas, this was the final blow. The Mexican government broke off diplomatic relations with the United States.

Texas was finally admitted to the Union in December 1845. Meanwhile, the new President, James K. Polk, had more ambitious plans. He wanted the United States to acquire the whole vast area stretching from Texas to the Pacific Ocean, but he hoped to do so by peaceful means. In November 1845 he sent Ambassador John Slidell to the Mexican government with an offer to buy Upper California and New Mexico. The Mexican government refused to receive Slidell, and he returned empty-handed.

Outbreak of war. President Polk was now sure that Mexico would never give up New Mexico and Upper California or its claim to Texas. However, he still wanted this area to belong to the United States and was ready to declare war to get it. Several members of his cabinet urged him to delay, saying that Mexico would probably soon commit some act that would justify war.

In January 1846, however, Polk ordered troops under General Zachary Taylor to move

Chapultepec Castle, built by the Spaniards just outside Mexico City, became the traditional home of Mexican rulers. It was the scene of heavy fighting during the Mexican War.

southward from the Nueces (noo·AY·ses) River to the north bank of the Rio Grande (see map, page 319). Ever since Texas had declared its independence from Mexico, the Texans had claimed that their territory reached southward to the Rio Grande. The Mexicans, for their part, rightly insisted that it ended farther north at the Nueces River.

Both American and European maps had accepted the Nueces River as the southern boundary of Texas. This was the boundary Spain had fixed in 1816, three years before the United States gave up all claims to Texas in the treaty by which Florida was purchased from Spain. Now, however, when he sent troops into this area, Polk claimed that he was acting defensively. The Mexicans insisted that the United States was acting aggressively.

Months passed, and President Polk's impatience grew daily. Finally, on May 9, the President notified his cabinet that he intended to recommend war with Mexico within a few days. That very night he received the news he had long been wanting. Mexican troops had crossed the Rio Grande and had fought with American forces.

317

Convinced that the American people would approve his action, Polk sent his war message to Congress on May 11. He declared, "Mexico has passed the boundary of the United States, has invaded our territory and shed American blood upon American soil. . . . War exists, and notwithstanding all our efforts to avoid it, exists by the act of Mexico herself." On May 13, Congress declared war.

Opposition to the war. Although Congress declared war, many of its members questioned American actions. One of these was Abraham Lincoln, a young Illinois lawyer then serving his only term in Congress. In 1847 he introduced in Congress his famous Spot Resolutions. In them he questioned whether the "spot" on the north bank of the Rio Grande where American blood had been shed was really United States soil. As you have just read, there was good reason to believe that the land between the Rio Grande and the Nueces River was not a part of Texas.

Others in Congress shared Lincoln's concern. In addition, many American citizens, especially in the North and East, voiced their opposition to the war. They felt that Polk had deliberately provoked the war, a view that most historians share today. They believed that the true cause of the war was Polk's determination to have New Mexico and California for the United States. Despite this opposition, however, the Congress and the American people generally supported the war once it began.

The war in the West. Armed forces of the United States operated in three different areas (see map, page 319). The American forces had the easiest time in California and New Mexico, which included present-day Arizona. For one thing, the Mexicans had not kept strong forces in the presidios in these regions. Equally important, in both California and New Mexico, many wealthy Spanish families had political, economic, and even marriage ties with the newly arrived American settlers. As a result, many Mexicans did not resist the invading American armies.

In the summer of 1846, an expedition under Brigadier General Kearny left Fort Leavenworth on the Missouri River, took Santa Fe, and won control of New Mexico. Kearny then went on to southern California. Despite stiff resistance near San Diego, with a Mexican victory at the Battle of San Pascual, Kearny managed to get the upper hand. Other Mexican victories at Los Angeles, Santa Barbara, and Chino Rancho failed to halt American advances.

Even before news of the war reached Upper California, a few dozen Americans led by William B. Ide had begun to plot against Mexican rule. They carried on their discussions in the camp of Captain John C. Frémont, a famous explorer who had arrived in California the previous autumn. At Sonoma on June 14, 1846, Ide and a band of American settlers proclaimed the Republic of California, or the Bear Flag Republic. They hoisted a flag with a bear and a star painted on it as a symbol of independence.

On July 7 Commodore J. D. Sloat of the United States Navy, hearing of the outbreak of war, landed naval forces at Monterey on the California coast. There he raised the American flag and proclaimed California a part of the United States. Frémont then organized most of the Americans, including the Bear Flaggers, into a "California battalion." With Commodore Robert F. Stockton, Frémont's forces moved south and captured Los Angeles.

The war in Mexico. Fighting was fierce in the region south of the Rio Grande. An expedition under General Zachary Taylor won victories at Palo Alto and Resaca de la Palma (ray·SAH·kah day lah PAHL·mah) on May 8 and 9, 1846, before war was actually declared. Taylor then went on to capture Monterrey, Mexico, in September 1846 and to check the Mexican forces under Santa Anna at Buena Vista (BWAY·nah VEES·tah) in February 1847.

Despite these defeats the Mexicans continued to fight. Polk ordered an expedition to advance against Mexico City, the capital of Mexico, over the route once traveled by Cortés. Led by General Winfield Scott, an expeditionary force including marines landed near Veracruz on the Gulf of Mexico. Nearly every step of the long, mountainous road to the "Halls of Montezuma" was bitterly contested. Hard battles were fought at several places, but on September 14, 1847, American troops entered Mexico City as victors.

End of the war. By 1848 Upper California, New Mexico, and all of northern Mexico were in American hands. General Taylor's troops held northern Mexico, and General Scott's forces walked the streets of the Mexican capital. The defeated Mexicans had to end the

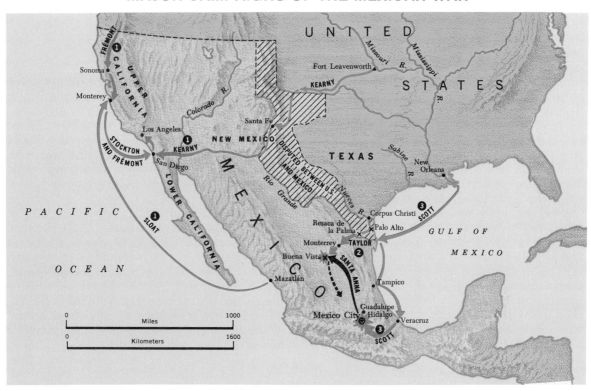

war on the Americans' terms. These were written down in the Treaty of Guadalupe Hidalgo (gwah·dah·LOO·pay ee·DAHL·goh) in 1848.

From the Mexican point of view, these terms are severe indeed. Mexico was forced to give up Texas, New Mexico, and Upper California — two fifths of Mexico's land. In return for this huge area, called the Mexican Cession (see map, page 322), the United States gave Mexico $15 million. The United States also agreed to pay debts totaling over $3 million that Mexicans owed to Americans. It further promised to respect the religious preferences and the civil and property rights of Mexicans in the newly acquired territory.

The dreams of Americans who had believed in their nation's "manifest destiny" had come true. The southwestern boundary of the United States reached to the Pacific.

Finally, in 1853, Congress approved a payment to Mexico of $10 million for the Gadsden Purchase (see map, page 322). This was an area of land south of the Gila River needed to construct a southern transcontinental railroad. It was named for James Gadsden of South Carolina, who, as minister to Mexico, negotiated the purchase.

Culture conflicts. Two fifths of Mexico's territory and about 75,000 Spanish-speaking people passed into United States hands as a result of the war. Differences in the cultures of the Americans and the new Spanish-speaking citizens created serious problems that were to continue for many years and that are still, in part, unresolved.

For the well-to-do Spanish families with ties to the Americans in New Mexico and California, adjustments to the new order were not usually too difficult. Other Spanish-speaking people did not fare so well. Some lost part or all of their property. At times, armed bands of Americans seized their lands. Also, Americans challenged land titles that had come down from Spanish or Mexican authorities by starting costly legal battles. Even when American courts upheld the original land titles, long-lasting bitterness remained.

Many of the new Spanish-speaking citizens were of mixed white, Indian, and, in a few

319

cases, black ancestry. Under the treaty of 1848, they were granted all the rights of American citizenship. All too often, these were only "paper" rights. Their culture blended Spanish, Mexican, and Indian ways of life. It was regarded by many English-speaking Americans as inferior to their own. This prejudice helped spark rebellions in Santa Barbara, Los Angeles, and Taos, New Mexico.

Poor Mexican-American workers, or peons, suffered even more. Most of them had worked on the ranches of well-to-do Spanish or Mexican landowners. They had shared mutual understanding and respect with these owners. After the American takeover, many of them worked for low wages on American ranches, mines, and railroads. Their new employers looked down on them as lazy, superstitious, and inefficient. They, in turn, saw the Americans as arrogant and domineering. They found their own traditions of family loyalty, personal honor, and devout Catholicism less respected than in the past. When the peons were permitted to vote, they were often bribed or otherwise used by English-speaking politicians or their Mexican-American allies.

Not all Mexican Americans accepted the new American regime passively. During the turbulent early years of the American Southwest, Mexican-American bandits and outlaws sometimes raided American settlements. These raids, in part, were protests against injustices suffered by the peons. In response, local American vigilante committees and Texas and New Mexico Rangers were organized to enforce law and order. Often, though, they resorted to beatings and lynchings.

SECTION SURVEY

IDENTIFY: manifest destiny, James K. Polk, Zachary Taylor, Spot Resolutions, Bear Flag Republic, Winfield Scott, Mexican Cession, peons.

1. (a) How would President Polk have described the events leading to the Mexican War? (b) How would a Mexican have described the same events?

2. (a) What were the terms of the Treaty of Guadalupe Hidalgo? (b) What was the significance of this treaty in American history? (c) Why did the Mexicans think the treaty terms were harsh?

3. Why was the Gadsden Purchase important?

4. Two cultures were in conflict in Texas and the region west of Texas. Explain.

4 A surge of migration brings California into the Union

As early as the 1820's and 1830's, even before the questions of Oregon and the Southwest had been settled, a stream of settlers had pushed west. They crossed the Great Plains and threaded their way through the Rocky Mountains and beyond. When the war with Mexico ended, this stream of settlers would become a flood.

The Mormons and Utah. One of the largest groups was the Mormons. The Mormon Church, or the Church of Jesus Christ of Latter-Day Saints, was founded in western New York in 1830 by young Joseph Smith. Smith announced that he had found golden plates on which sacred scriptures were engraved. When translated, these became known as the *Book of Mormon*. Thousands of converts joined the new religious faith.

In Kirkland, Ohio, in Independence, Missouri, and in Nauvoo, Illinois, Mormons attempted to build an ideal society where they could live and worship in their own way. In each place they were driven away by hostile neighbors. These neighbors did not understand them and disliked the Mormon idea that they were a chosen people with a special revelation of truth. Many people further disapproved of the Mormons because they openly accepted polygamy—the practice of a husband having more than one wife at the same time. In Missouri people who favored slavery disliked the Mormons simply because most Mormons came from the Northeast. They feared that these Mormons would oppose slavery. It made little difference to the proslavery Missourians that Joseph Smith opposed the abolition of slavery.

The Nauvoo community in Illinois prospered more than the other two. By 1844 it had become a thriving town of 15,000 persons, but trouble was brewing. Some Mormons opposed polygamy and disliked Smith. Finally people in nearby towns, fearing and resenting the prosperity of the Mormons, attacked Nauvoo. Joseph Smith and his brother Hiram were killed. Once again the Mormons were forced to move west.

Under the able leadership of Brigham Young, the Mormons moved out of Nauvoo.

In Missouri in the spring of 1847, nearly 5,000 Mormons assembled to begin their migration west. When they first set eyes on the valley of the Great Salt Lake, their leader Brigham Young proclaimed, "This is the place!"

Their loaded wagons moved westward across the plains and through the towering Rockies, finally stopping in 1847 on the eastern shore of Great Salt Lake (see map, page 309). There the Mormons plowed and irrigated the fields, learning many lessons about desert farming that they passed on to later western settlers. They laid out Salt Lake City on the Jordan River and erected a temple that would become famous throughout the world. The Mormons also sent missionaries to other parts of the world and brought converts to their new communities. Finally, in 1896, Utah entered the Union as the 45th state.

Spanish influence in California. Beyond the shore of Great Salt Lake, hidden by the towering Sierra Nevada mountains, lay Upper California. Neither Spain nor Mexico had ever been strong enough to develop this rich land into a thriving region. By the early 1800's, the Spaniards had completed the chain of missions begun by Gaspar de Portola and Father Junípero Serra. They had also built a few presidios and several small towns, among them San Diego, Los Angeles, Monterey, and Yerba Buena (YAIR·bah BWAY·nah), where San Francisco now stands (see map, page 19). Also, scattered over this immense territory were the estates, small communities in themselves, of powerful Spanish landowners. The Mexican

Revolution of 1821 caused few changes in this vast region.

Life in this land of rare beauty, vast distances, and unbelievable contrasts of climate and topography moved at an easy, leisurely pace. As late as 1846, when the Mexican War broke out, only about 4,000 Mexicans lived in California. Fewer than 500 of them were soldiers in a half dozen or so forts.

Although Spanish, and later Mexican, control was never strong, the influence of Spanish culture can be seen to the present day throughout California. Towns, rivers, and mountains bear Spanish names. Spanish laws, customs, and architecture continue to enrich life in California to this day.

American settlers in California. A region so rich and beautiful naturally attracted restless Americans pressing westward. In 1841 a party of men, women, and children led by John Bidwell, "the prince of California pioneers," set out from Missouri. Their trip across the plains and mountains, as revealed in the journal of their leader, is a tribute to human courage. "We knew only," Bidwell wrote, "that California lay to the west."

The Bidwell pioneers were followed by many others, and by 1848 several hundred Americans had settled in California. Among those who set out for California were members

321

THE NATION'S GROWTH TO 1853

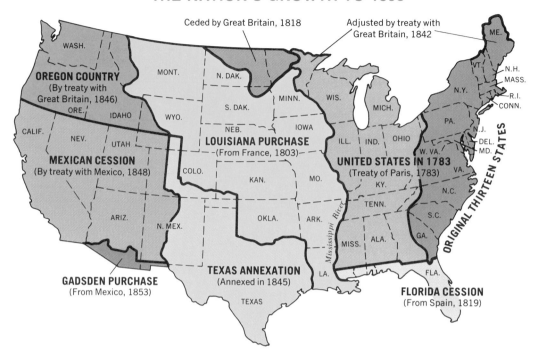

of the ill-fated Donner party. Caught in 1846 by the icy grip of an early winter in the Sierra Nevada, the Donner party built crude shelters and struggled to survive. Soup made of boiled leather and powdered bones became a luxury. Of the 79 persons who started out in the Donner party, 34 died before an expedition out of California rescued the survivors.

Gold in California. Among the early settlers in California was John A. Sutter from Switzerland. His sawmill and fort at Sacramento were the center of bustling activity. On the morning of January 24, 1848, one of his employees, James W. Marshall, detected flakes of yellow metal at the bottom of a stream where a new mill was being built. The shining metal was gold. Despite Sutter's desire to keep the discovery secret until the new mill was built, the news spread like wildfire.

Stories of huge fortunes made overnight spread throughout the nation. Some stories were true; most were false. True or false, the stories stirred everyone's imagination. In 1849, a year after the discovery of gold, thousands of adventurous Americans sold all they owned and joined the westward rush to the gold fields of California.

The gold rush. Adventurers from Europe and the eastern United States reached California by three routes (see map, page 309). The longest route was the safest and most comfortable, as comfort went in those days. This route was by ship around Cape Horn.

The quickest, most crowded, and most expensive route was by ship to Central America. From there travelers went by land across the Isthmus of Panama and by another ship from there to San Francisco. Every old ship that could float was pressed into service. Crowds of men in bright shirts and slouch hats, armed with bowie knives and pistols, raced to cross the isthmus and board one of the few ships sailing between Panama and California.

A third route was fit only for the rugged and the brave. It led across the Great Plains and through the mountain passes—the route of the Bidwell and Donner parties. Many of the wagon trains of the "Forty-Niners" took as long as five months to make the trip from the eastern seaboard. Many trails along the route were lined with household goods thrown away to lighten the load, with dead bodies of animals, and with the graves of those struck down by Indians, disease, hunger, thirst, cold, or heat.

322

The first wave of "Forty-Niners" jammed into lawless mining camps. Some found riches beyond their wildest dreams; most found only disappointment. As the months went by, two streams of travelers passed each other on the trails and roads leading from San Francisco to the mining regions. Going were newcomers eager for fortunes. On the way back were the disappointed gold seekers who had given up the search.

Included in the wave of "Forty-Niners" were black people, slave and free. Some worked as servants. Others searched for gold in crews under the direction of a slaveowner. A few became independent miners. Moses Rodgers, for example, born a slave in Missouri, became a mining authority whose advice was often sought by other gold seekers.

Statehood for California. Gradually the uproar subsided, and some newcomers began to build houses, hotels, stores, and shops in the rapidly growing towns and cities. Some settled on the land and began to farm. Settlers built schools and churches. A government that was partly military and partly civilian was formed.

Late in 1849 a convention met and drafted a state constitution, which was accepted by the people. The constitution outlawed slavery in California but included restrictions and discriminations against Indians. In 1850 Congress approved the constitution, and California entered the Union as a free state.

The fate of the Indians. The Indians of California suffered an unhappy fate under both Spanish and Mexican rule. In 1834 the Mexican government responded to complaints of ill treatment of the mission Indians. Eager to seize mission lands and wealth, it removed the missions from control of the Catholic Church. The mission Indians were not adequately prepared to get along on their own in the white settlers' society. Deprived of much of their own culture, they were easy prey for settlers. Some of the Indians became virtual slaves on the great ranches.

The Indians suffered even more cruelly when American settlers moved in and California became part of the United States. From 1848 to 1871, more than 50,000 California Indians died of disease, starvation, and violence. In northern California the Karok, Yurok, Shasta, and Hupa tribes, after bitter struggles, gave up their lands to white newcomers.

The Treaty of Fort Laramie. The Indians who lived on the western plains and in the mountains along the newly opened routes to the Far West also faced a grim future. An endless stream of covered wagons and herds of cattle moved westward across Indian territory. Ancient hunting grounds were disturbed and age-old traditions and ways of life were disrupted. Faced with this threat, the Indians resorted to attacking the wagon trains and their night encampments.

In an effort to solve the problem, the United States government invited the Indians to a great conference to be held at Fort Laramie in what is now the state of Wyoming. The conference opened in the autumn of 1851. Large delegations of Indians arrived and set up colorful camps around the fort. Led by their chiefs, they included the Sioux, Assiniboins, Arikaris, Crows, Gros Ventres, Shoshones, Arapahos, and Cheyennes. The American delegation included government officials and army detachments. Father de Smet arrived from Oregon. Jim Bridger, leader of the Mountain Men, acted as interpreter. For several days there were games, celebrations, and speeches.

Out of the meeting came the Treaty of Fort Laramie. In it the federal government agreed to pay $50,000 to the Indians each year for 50 years in return for the safety of the settlers moving west. The treaty also gave the government the right to build forts along the western trails. The Senate did not ratify the treaty, but the government made the annual payments for 15 years. The Indians generally kept the agreement until after the Civil War. Then they became increasingly disturbed by new waves of settlers.

SECTION SURVEY

IDENTIFY: Joseph Smith, Brigham Young, John Bidwell, Donner expedition, John Sutter, Treaty of Fort Laramie.

1. (a) Why were the Mormons persecuted? (b) How did they respond to persecution?

2. Why were the Americans able to seize California from Mexico without much difficulty?

3. (a) Who were the "Forty-Niners"? (b) Why did they go to California? (c) How did they get there?

4. (a) How were the Indians treated by the Spanish, Mexican, and United States governments? (b) Why do you suppose they received such treatment?

Chapter Survey

Summary: Tracing the Main Ideas

The westward movement began with the first settlers along the eastern seaboard of North America. As the movement progressed, the original settlers, the American Indians, were ruthlessly forced onto poorer lands or onto reservations.

By the early 1800's, the white frontier had advanced beyond the Mississippi River. By the 1840's bold pioneers had crossed the continent and were building new homes in the Oregon country. Other settlers were moving into Texas, California, and other Mexican territory.

The Mexican authorities failed to prevent or even to control the tide of American settlers moving into what was then Mexico's northwestern territory. Finally, the United States, eager to acquire territory all the way to the Pacific coast, declared war on Mexico. As a result of this struggle, the United States won what is now the American Southwest—including Texas, New Mexico, Arizona, Utah, Nevada, and California. Manifest destiny—the belief that the United States was fated to own the land from sea to sea—had been fulfilled.

The United States' newly acquired area had been settled by Spaniards and by Mexicans and other Spanish-speaking people of mixed blood. These people spoke languages, followed life styles, and held ideas different from those of the American newcomers. These differences produced the bitter fruit of prejudice and conflict. Even so, in the mid-1800's the differences seemed less important than the fact that the West was growing rapidly in population and in political strength.

As you will see in the next unit, both the North and the South struggled for control of the West. They struggled in the halls of Congress as well as on the western lands themselves. This struggle is one of the keys to an understanding of American history during the generation before the Civil War.

Before turning to this story, however, you will read in the next chapter about some of the developments that transformed American life between the 1820's and the 1860's.

Inquiring into History

1. Explain why the following ideas played an important part in the history of the United States: (a) the idea of the frontier and (b) the idea of manifest destiny.
2. Compare the motives of the Americans who pioneered in the Pacific Northwest with those who pioneered in Texas.
3. What motives led Americans to settle Utah and California?
4. How would you have felt about the American annexation of Texas if you had been (a) a Mexican living in Texas, (b) an American living in Texas, (c) a southern slave owner, (d) an opponent of slavery, or (e) a farmer living on the American frontier?
5. (a) What effect did the expansion of American boundaries after 1820 have on the Spanish-speaking people who lived in these areas? (b) What effect did this expansion have on the Indians who lived there?
6. What was the general strategy of American forces in the Mexican War? How did they carry out this strategy? Use the map on page 319 to help you.

Relating Past to Present

1. Look at a modern road map of the western United States and at the map on page 309. (a) Determine whether the modern highways follow the old western trails. (b) Which modern cities already existed by 1860?
2. In the period covered in this chapter, America's foreign policy was based on the idea of manifest destiny. What do you believe is the main goal of American foreign policy today?
3. Is a westward movement still going on in America? Compare population figures for an eastern state and a western state for 1960, 1970, and 1980.

Developing Social Science Skills

1. Make a timeline of the important events presented in this chapter. (a) Which events concern military history? economic history? political history? (b) Explain your answers fully.
2. Prepare a bulletin board display illustrating ways in which Spanish culture and language are still apparent in the United States today.

Chapter 16

Stirring the American People with Ideas of Reform

1820's–1860's

The term "to ferment" means "to be inwardly active, agitated, or excited; to seethe mentally or emotionally."

It would be difficult to find a more accurate term than "ferment" to describe the activities of the American people in the years from the 1820's to the 1860's.

During this period changes in the United States were taking place with bewildering speed. The very appearance of America was changing. Industrialism was transforming the North. Cotton growing was bringing prosperity to large areas of the South. Land-hungry pioneers were pushing across the Great Plains, through the Rocky Mountains, and into the fertile valleys of the Pacific Northwest and sunny California. In outward appearance the United States by the 1830's and 1840's was a much different country from the United States of the 1790's.

The ideas of the people were also changing. By the time Andrew Jackson became President in 1829, nearly all white male adults had won the right to vote. Political democracy brought new hope to the people. Those who had won the right to vote, and those who hoped to win it, expected to use their newly won power to make the ideals of democracy work more effectively in everyday affairs.

During the period from the 1820's to the 1860's, reformers were seeking to improve almost every aspect of society. "We are all a little wild here with numberless projects of social reform," Ralph Waldo Emerson, the New England writer and philosopher, wrote to a friend in England. The story of this period of reform, this age of change, is told in this chapter.

THE CHAPTER IN OUTLINE

1. Reformers struggle to improve American life.

2. Free public education makes a promising start.

3. A strong movement develops to abolish slavery.

4. The antislavery movement begins to divide the nation.

5. Writers preach faith in democracy and the individual.

1 Reformers struggle to improve American life

One of the many reforms Americans were working for in the period from the 1820's to the 1860's was a more important place for women in American life.

The status of women. From the earliest days, women worked together with men to build America. They shared the loneliness, the dangers, the desperately hard work. They helped transform the wilderness into a land of prosperous farms and thriving towns and expanding cities.

But women were regarded almost everywhere as inferior by nature to men, mentally as well as physically. Tradition, religious ideas, and the law contributed to this attitude. If a marriage was unhappy, divorce laws made it almost impossible for a woman to end the marriage. As late as the 1860's, married women in many states had no control over property they inherited or over wages they earned. Nor did they have legal control over

their children. In practice, however, men seldom used their full legal rights over their wives and children.

Some of the changes in the America of the early 1800's also affected women unfairly. For example, the increasing importance given to high school and college education and to specialized training—from which women were excluded—restricted some occupations to men. Among these were medicine and midwife service. In earlier years, American women had worked in such jobs.

The Industrial Revolution also undermined the economic self-sufficiency of most American families. In doing so, it reduced the very difficult and important economic role that women had played in earlier family life. Moreover, it created a new and exploited class of women workers. The Industrial Revolution also led to an expanding middle class. This middle class held an ideal of the "lady." "Ladies" practiced only "genteel" activities in the home, such as needlework and the entertainment of guests. It was considered "unladylike" for a woman to take any active part either in public meetings or in politics.

Declaring women's rights. In the 1820's and 1830's, a few women began to protest their exclusion from high school and college education, the professions, and participation in public affairs. A few leaders of the **women's rights movement** came from Europe, where a similar struggle was under way. For example, Ernestine L. Rose of Poland and Frances Wright of Scotland crossed the Atlantic to help American women in their struggle for equal rights.

American women bore the brunt of the struggle. One of the American leaders was Lucretia Mott, a Philadelphia Quaker. Another was Elizabeth Cady Stanton who, as a girl, had been troubled by legal discriminations against the women clients of her father, an upstate New York lawyer. These two were largely responsible for organizing the first women's rights convention. It was held at Seneca Falls, New York, in July 1848. The women delegates adopted a Declaration of Sentiments, which said, "All men and women are created equal," and went on to list demands for political, social, and economic equality with men. In spite of these early demands, decisive gains in these fields did not come until after 1850. Early victories came mainly in the field of education.

Although women made up much of the industrial labor force, they received very low wages. At times they resorted to strikes. This strike took place in Lowell, Massachusetts, in 1860.

Education for women. By the 1820's education for girls and women was getting under way. Emma Hart Willard opened the Troy Female Seminary at Troy, New York, in 1821 and began to teach mathematics, science, history, and other subjects. During the next few years, Catharine Esther Beecher, Mary Lyon, and other dedicated women opened schools for girls. In 1837 Mount Holyoke Female Seminary opened in Massachusetts. Later known as Mount Holyoke College, it was the first women's college in the United States.

The coeducation movement made some headway in the Middle West. The first male college to open its doors to women was Oberlin Collegiate Institute in Ohio. Against bitter protests, Oberlin admitted women four years after it was founded in 1833. A few colleges in the Middle West followed Oberlin's example. In 1856 the University of Iowa became the first state university to admit women.

Early achievements. Slowly and against strong opposition, women began to win places in what had been considered a "man's world." Dr. Elizabeth Blackwell became the first woman to win a medical diploma in the United States. She began to practice medicine in New York City in 1850 and later founded the first school of nursing in the United States. In 1875 Blackwell became a professor in the London School of Medicine for Women. Her sister-in-law, Antoinette Louisa Blackwell, became the first fully ordained female minister in the United States.

Other women won distinction as writers and editors. Louisa May Alcott wrote a number of children's books, among them *Little Women,* which was translated into several languages. Harriet Beecher Stowe wrote *Uncle Tom's Cabin* (page 336). Margaret Fuller's *Woman in the Nineteenth Century* is a classic in the history of feminism. It defied the customs that restricted women to conventional roles and urged the full development of women's potentials. Fuller's brilliant literary criticism was published in *The Dial* and in the *New York Tribune.* Jane Swisshelm edited several papers in which she advocated property rights and other rights for women and opposed slavery.

The most influential woman in journalism was Sarah Josepha Hale, editor of *Godey's Lady's Book.* In this widely read magazine, she supported many of the traditional ideals of the "lady." Hale opposed women's suffrage but

SOURCES

THE SENECA FALLS DECLARATION OF SENTIMENTS AND RESOLUTIONS (1848)

When, in the course of human events, it becomes necessary for one portion of the family of man to assume among the people of the earth a position different from that which they have hitherto occupied, but one to which the laws of nature and of nature's God entitle them, a decent respect to the opinions of mankind requires that they should declare the causes that impel them to such a course.

We hold these truths to be self-evident; that all men and women are created equal. . . . Now, in view of this entire disfranchisement of one half of the people of this country, their social and religious degradation . . . and because women do feel themselves aggrieved, oppressed, and fraudulently deprived of their most sacred rights, we insist that they have immediate admission to all the rights and privileges which belong to them as citizens of the United States.

was strongly in favor of educational opportunities for women.

Dorothea Lynde Dix. Another woman who exerted enormous influence was Dorothea Dix. In 1841 she was horrified by the cold, bare, filthy conditions of a jail she inspected near Boston. She laid the facts she discovered before the Massachusetts legislature, but the lawmakers did nothing.

Goaded to further action, Dorothea Dix visited every jail and poorhouse in Massachusetts and gathered overwhelming evidence. She packed notebook after notebook with horrors almost beyond belief. In all of the jails and poorhouses, she found old men, young girls, the poor, and the mentally ill thrown together in cold, dirty prisons. Some were chained to walls, beds, or floors. Some wore iron collars or straitjackets. Some had been kept in cages for years.

Finally, Dorothea Dix returned to the Massachusetts legislature with her evidence. This time the legislators listened. They began to pass laws to improve conditions in jails and poorhouses and to establish a public institution for the mentally ill. During the next few years, she repeated her reform work in other states. Moreover, her efforts helped to improve conditions in European jails and institutions for the poor and mentally ill.

By the 1850's, largely because of Dorothea Dix and others who shared her views, important reforms had been made in the United States. The death penalty for some crimes had been abolished. A growing number of people were demanding the abolition of capital punishment. Most states had outlawed the whipping of prisoners. Imprisonment for debt had been ended. Men and women were kept in separate sections of prisons. The mentally ill were separated from other prisoners. More attention was given to the individual criminal, and more effort was made to reform than to punish.

Dorothea Dix died in 1887 at the age of 85. A famous English doctor said of her, "Thus has died and been laid to rest . . . the most useful and distinguished woman that America has ever produced."

The crusade against alcohol. A struggle against the use of alcoholic beverages enlisted men and women who saw drunkenness as a threat both to religion and to family life. This battle was known as the "temperance movement." It got under way on a national scale in 1833 when advocates of temperance held a convention in Philadelphia. The delegates included not only religious leaders but also physicians and business people who believed that drinking was physically harmful. They also felt it decreased the efficiency of workers, caused accidents, and added to the tax bills for maintaining public order.

The temperance movement grew rapidly. In 1836 several groups united to form the American Temperance Union. Politicians, hoping to attract votes, took up the cause. Some reformers, insisting that any drinking was harmful and sinful, demanded state laws prohibiting both the manufacture and the sale of all alcoholic drinks.

The widespread agitation soon produced results. In 1834, only a year after the national movement got under way, Congress passed a law forbidding the sale of alcoholic beverages to Indians. Quakers, missionaries, and some Indian leaders had long been trying to stop the sale of rum and whisky to Indians. They believed that unscrupulous white traders defrauded the Indians of their treaty rights

The women shown here were among the most prominent reformers in the United States during the mid-1800's. They are (from left to right) Frances Wright, Dorothea Dix, Margaret Fuller, and Elizabeth Cady Stanton.

QUEEN OF THE PLATFORM

"I was a rebel at the age of five," Ernestine Rose once said. In her youth she used to argue with her father, the rabbi of a Polish-Russian town called Piotrkow. Having no son, he taught his daughter to read the Scriptures in Hebrew. Soon she was asking questions: How did evil begin? Why did God allow suffering? "Little girls must not ask questions," chided her father. Naturally enough, Ernestine's reply was, "Why must little girls not ask questions?"

By the age of sixteen, Ernestine had become a very independent young woman. When her father arranged for her marriage to a man his age, she went to court to break the contract legally. Then she left home forever, going first to Berlin, then to Paris and London. In England Ernestine became a disciple of the reformer Robert Owen. Through him she met a young jeweler named William Rose. They were married in 1836, when Ernestine was twenty-six, and soon afterward sailed for the United States.

In America Ernestine Rose continued to ask probing questions: Why couldn't women vote? Why were black people enslaved? Why were factory workers paid so little? Battling injustice as an eloquent speaker, she became widely known as "Queen of the Platform."

What Ernestine Rose wanted most to do was arouse people to the wrongs that needed righting. Once, after speaking at a meeting of farmers on Long Island, she commented that perhaps she had given her audience something to think and talk about "besides prayer meetings and potatoes." She added, "A little tempest is better than none at all, where all has been oppressive stagnation."

---

while the Indians were under the influence of liquor. These people welcomed the 1834 law, but as it turned out, the law banning the sale of liquor was generally ignored.

State laws prohibiting the use of alcoholic beverages were more effective. In 1846 Maine became the first state to pass a prohibition act. Other states soon followed.

Many people, especially brewers and distillers, opposed these laws. Other citizens protested that the states had no power to decide what anyone should or should not drink.

One unexpected by-product of the prohibition laws was a sharp rise in sales of patent medicines with a high alcohol content. However, the reformers did produce some results, and drinking among most classes decreased. In many communities a drunken man became an object of curiosity or even of contempt.

Efforts to end war. From about 1820 to 1860, many Americans as well as Europeans devoted their efforts to the peace movement. Quakers in the United States had always opposed the use of force, except when necessary for police purposes. However, an organized antiwar movement did not develop in America until after the War of 1812. In 1828 many local peace societies joined together to form the American Peace Society. The members of the society insisted that war was anti-Christian, inhumane, and uneconomical.

One leader of the peace movement was Elihu Burritt, a self-educated Connecticut blacksmith. He developed a pledge card against war that was signed by more than 40,000 persons in America and England. Influenced by William Ladd, a Maine sea captain and farmer known as "the apostle of peace," Burritt urged the nations of the world to form an international organization and a world court for the purpose of settling international disputes.

Efforts to build ideal communities. Not all the people who longed for a better world tried to change existing institutions of daily life. Some men and women chose to follow the example of religiously inspired groups. They chose to withdraw from the world around them to build **utopian** (yoo·TOH·pee·un), or ideal, communities.

Robert Owen, a wealthy British manufacturer, started a utopian community in 1825 at New Harmony in Indiana. It failed, but its failure did not discourage other utopian experiments. Two well-known but short-lived experiments were Brook Farm, near Boston, and the Oneida (oh·NI·dah) Community in central New York State.

SECTION SURVEY

IDENTIFY: reformer, women's rights movement, temperance movement, prohibition, American Peace Society, utopian communities.

1. (a) What were the goals of the women's rights movement during the 1840's and 1850's? (b) How did the movement's supporters try to reach these goals? (c) How successful were they?

2. Explain the importance of (a) Sarah Josepha Hale, (b) Dorothea Dix, (c) Elizabeth Blackwell.

3. (a) Describe the growth of the temperance movement. (b) What were its results? (c) Why did Congress forbid the sale of liquor to Indians?

4. In what way did utopian communities reflect the spirit of this period in American history?

5. (a) In your opinion, which of the reform movements had the most lasting effects on American society? (b) Which had the least? Explain.

2 Free public education makes a promising start

There were many reform programs in the period from the 1820's to the 1860's. None was more closely related to the growth of democracy than the movement for free public schools.

The problem of education. In colonial times New England towns were required by law to provide elementary schools. These New England schools were not entirely free. Parents who could afford to do so paid tuition fees for their children. The towns paid only for the children of poor parents.

By the early 1800's, however, these so-called "common" schools of New England had reached a very low level. Buildings were inadequate, and the quality of teaching was generally poor. Conditions were even worse in the Middle Atlantic and southern states, where people lived farther apart. Indeed, in many areas schools run by churches provided almost the only chance children had to get an elementary education.

By the 1820's and the 1830's, this situation was changing. Many people were demanding public, tax-supported schools. Reformers insisted that public education was necessary both to insure that voters were intelligently informed and to prevent the spread of crime and social disorder.

Leaders in the movement. Among the outstanding leaders of the struggle for free and improved public education were Horace Mann and Henry Barnard. Horace Mann turned from a brilliant legal and political career to become a crusader for public schools in Massachusetts. When the Massachusetts legislature created a state Board of Education in 1837, Mann became its first secretary. He used his growing power to establish normal schools for training teachers. He also began to organize the local school districts into a statewide system of education.

Henry Barnard did for Connecticut and Rhode Island what Horace Mann was doing for Massachusetts. His efforts won national recognition. In 1867 Barnard became the first United States Commissioner of Education.

The work of these and other leaders, among them Calvin E. Stowe of Ohio, Caleb Mills of

SOURCES

HORACE MANN
ON EDUCATION
(1848)

Education, then, beyond all other devices of human origin, is a great equalizer of the conditions of men—the balance-wheel of the social machinery. I do not here mean that it so elevates the moral nature as to make men disdain and abhor the oppression of their fellow men. ... But I mean that it gives each man the independence and the means by which he can resist the selfishness of other men. It does better than to disarm the poor of their hostility toward the rich: it prevents being poor. ...

By the 1860's, when E. L. Henry painted this picture of a country schoolroom, all the states had agreed that they should provide tax-supported elementary schools. However, state and local funds were often short and public schools often were roughly furnished and lacked adequate supplies.

Indiana, John Swett of California, and Emma Hart Willard of Connecticut and New York, was of great importance. It helped to set the pattern of free public education throughout the United States.

Objections to public education. The struggle for free, tax-supported elementary schools was not won easily. Churches that had already set up religious schools, or that hoped to do so, objected strongly. Private schools, both religious and secular, voiced their opposition. Many taxpayers, including some wage earners and farmers, objected to using tax money to pay for schools.

Many Americans also had strong prejudices against "book larnin'." A pioneer in Illinois said that he "didn't think folks was any better off for reading, an' books cost a heap and took a power of time. 'Twant so bad for men to read," he admitted, "for there was a heap of time when they couldn't work out and could jest set by the fire; and if a man had books and keered to read he mought; but women had no business to hurtle away their time."

Early victories. In spite of such opposition, the movement for tax-supported elementary schools gained strength. In 1832 New York City established a system of free public elementary schools. Four years later, in 1836,

Philadelphia followed suit. By the 1850's nearly all white children, at least in the northern cities, could obtain a free elementary school education.

Meanwhile, New England led the way in efforts to provide free high school education. The first public high school in America, the English High School of Boston, opened in 1821. In 1827, Massachusetts adopted the first state law requiring towns with 500 or more families to provide a high school education for town youths at public expense.

The movement grew slowly. By 1850 the nation had only 55 public high schools, although there were more than 6,000 private high schools, or **academies,** as they were called. A high school education was still beyond the reach of most American youths.

The educational ladder. The democratic system of free public education in the United States has been called "a great educational ladder." By the 1860's the "ladder" was beginning to be erected. Most white children could expect to receive an elementary school education. In some larger towns, those who did not have to go to work could attend free public high schools.

A growing number of states established public universities. North Carolina pioneered by providing in 1776 in its constitution for a state university. The University of North Carolina graduated its first class in 1798. Other states followed North Carolina's example. By the late 1850's, 16 states had universities supported in part by public funds.

Alongside this system of free public schools and universities was the older system of private elementary schools, academies, and more than 100 church-supported colleges. Most of these colleges were small, with 100 to 300 male students and 6 to 12 professors.

It was significant that the principle of the separation of church and state was being written into all of the state constitutions. By the 1830's no person could be compelled to pay taxes to support any church or any school that taught particular religious doctrines.

Black students in college. In the period from the 1820's to the 1860's, the doors of higher education began to be opened—but only slightly—to qualified black students. In 1823 Alexander Twilight received a degree from Middlebury College. A few years later, the first blacks graduated from Amherst, Bowdoin, and Ohio universities.

Three colleges for black students were established in this period—Avery College and Lincoln College in Pennsylvania and Wilberforce College in Ohio. However, the only truly co-racial as well as coeducational college was Oberlin in Ohio. Oberlin was founded in 1833 by people who believed in abolition. Out of 8,800 young men and women who attended Oberlin between 1833 and 1861, 245 were black. Some were fugitive slaves or the sons and daughters of fugitives.

Most of the black women at Oberlin were enrolled in a Preparatory Department or in a special Ladies' Course. Mary Jane Patterson became, in 1862, the first black American woman to receive a college degree. After graduation, she taught school in Philadelphia for several years. Then, in 1871, she became the first black principal of a newly established high school for blacks in Washington, D.C.

SECTION SURVEY

IDENTIFY: free public school, normal school, academy, Oberlin, Mary Jane Patterson.

1. Describe the contributions made to American education that were made by (a) Horace Mann and (b) Henry Barnard.

2. Why was there opposition to free public schools?
3. List four achievements accomplished by the supporters of free public schools.
4. Does political democracy depend on free public schools? Explain your answer.
5. Source Study: Read the Source on page 330. (a) What does Mann mean by calling education "a great equalizer"? (b) Do you agree or disagree with him? Explain your answer.

3 A strong movement develops to abolish slavery

The most vigorous reform movement between the 1820's and the 1860's was the antislavery, or abolition, crusade. No other single movement did as much to arouse controversy and to drive a wedge between the North and the South.

Background of abolition. A few Americans in colonial days objected to slavery, as you have read (page 65). After the Revolutionary War, this antislavery sentiment grew. By the 1780's and 1790's, several antislavery societies had been organized in the North.

In the nation's early years, some thoughtful southerners as well as northerners believed that slavery was morally wrong. These southerners found support among some planters who believed that slavery was no longer profitable. Tobacco growing used up the fertility of the soil and decreased the value of both land and crops. At the same time, the cost of feeding, clothing, and housing slaves either remained the same or increased.

A few planters, as you know, freed their slaves. But the problem was complex. Some southern slaveowners, even though they believed that slavery was wrong or unprofitable, hesitated to free their slaves. They worried that their slaves would be unable to take care of themselves in a difficult and even hostile society. They also worried about the effects of a freed black population on southern society. Their views were strengthened by the common belief that black people were inferior.

Slavery and cotton. The conflict in southerners' minds over whether or not to free their slaves was largely erased after Eli Whitney's invention of the cotton gin in 1793. Because of the cotton gin, the demand for slaves grew by leaps and bounds. Moral and political questions about slavery were raised less and less as the Cotton Kingdom became prosperous.

The renewed value of slaves to the economy did not wholly stop the antislavery movement, even in the South. As late as 1830, several Virginians publicly opposed slavery. Some also proposed measures for doing away with it gradually.

In the early 1820's, Benjamin Lundy, a mild-mannered but persistent Quaker, published a weekly antislavery newspaper, *The Genius of Universal Emancipation,* in Baltimore. Like most antislavery advocates in the 1820's, Lundy was moderate in his approach. He had hopes of bringing about the gradual **emancipation,** or freeing, of the slaves by appealing to the public's moral instincts.

Attempts at colonization. Lundy, like many others who opposed slavery, supported the American Colonization Society. This society was founded in 1817 to colonize free black people and to buy slaves to be returned to freedom in Africa. There they set up the West African country of Liberia. They modeled it after Sierra Leone, which was a nearby British refuge for freed slaves.

Lundy sincerely hoped to encourage emancipation by giving financial help to owners who wanted to free their slaves. However, the most influential members of the society — planters in Kentucky, Virginia, and Maryland — were not opposed to slavery. These planters wanted to rid the nation of free blacks. They believed that the presence of free blacks encouraged slaves in their desire to be free. The planters thought that colonization offered the best solution to the "race problem."

Faults in colonization. The colonization experiment was not very successful. By 1831 only 1,420 black Americans had been settled in Liberia. In part, the problem was lack of money. It was also true that most American blacks opposed the colonization movement. There were exceptions, of course. Paul Cuffe, a successful black merchant, had sent 38 black Americans to West Africa at his own expense even before the American Colonization Society was formed.

The growing opposition to colonization among blacks was strengthened by discourag-

At the time of the antislavery meetings advertised in this handbill, abolitionist groups were flooding the South with antislavery pamphlets and the House of Representatives with petitions to outlaw slavery.

ing reports of hardships in Liberia. To most black Americans, Africa was a strange, far-off place. Despite their grim lot, most black Americans had come to think of the United States as their home.

Early efforts by black people. In addition to condemning colonization, free blacks took steps early in the nation's history to improve their own lot, and, if possible, that of the slaves. They formed their own Afro-American churches. They organized societies for mutual aid and for improving opportunities in education and social life for black people.

Free blacks also took legal action to improve their circumstances. In 1794, free blacks asked Congress in a formal petition to take steps for "the relief of our people." In 1800, free black Americans of Philadelphia petitioned Congress to correct injustices in a law requiring fugitive slaves to be returned to their owners or to persons who might claim to be their owners. The same petition also asked Congress to provide for gradual emancipation of all slaves.

The first of a new, more vigorous series of

Because slaves were valuable property, their owners needed a system to hold onto them. Slaves were sometimes forced to wear tags like these. Such tags registered the slaves by location, number, and occupation.

conventions held by black Americans met in Philadelphia in 1830. The delegates suggested that some black Americans might like to move to Canada. Those who did not choose to emigrate were urged to use every legal means to improve their lives in the United States.

David Walker's *Appeal*. These moderate activities were overshadowed in 1829 by the publication of *Appeal,* an essay by David Walker. Walker, a black American, began his *Appeal* by describing black slaves as "the most degraded, wretched, and abject set of beings that ever lived since the world began."

Walker's essay was a powerful call for bold and vigorous action by black Americans. Southern blacks, slave and free, must strike for their freedom — violently, if necessary. If white Americans wanted to prevent racial war, insisted Walker, they had to recognize at once the rights and humanity of black Americans.

Northerners, including white antislavery forces, condemned Walker's book as inflammatory and dangerous. Southerners put a price on Walker's head and tried to halt circulation of his *Appeal.*

A new mood. David Walker's *Appeal* was one example of growing militancy, or aggressiveness, in the abolition movement. William Lloyd Garrison's newspaper, the *Liberator,* was another example of this mood.

In his very first issue of the *Liberator,* published in Boston in 1831, Garrison, a white abolitionist, wrote, "I shall strenuously contend for the immediate enfranchisement [freeing] of our slave population. . . . I am in earnest — I will not equivocate — I will not excuse — AND I WILL BE HEARD."

Slavery, Garrison insisted, contradicted the Bible and the Declaration of Independence. It was both a sin and a crime. It had to be abolished at once.

Garrison condemned southern slaveowners, but he also condemned northerners who apologized for slavery or kept silent about it. Equal rights for blacks in the North was a leading object of Garrison's crusade.

Garrison's outspoken language offended many moderate white Americans who were against slavery. However, his religious and moral fervor and that of his New England followers was shared by rising abolitionist leaders elsewhere. In New York, Arthur and Lewis Tappan, deeply religious men and wealthy merchants, fought for abolition, as did Isaac Hooper, a Quaker who aided runaway slaves. Many people became abolitionists at religious revivals led by Charles G. Finney. In fact, revivalism was an important factor in the development of the abolition movement.

The most important abolitionist leader outside the East was Theodore Weld. He trained 70 young men who carried abolitionism into hundreds of communities in Ohio, western Pennsylvania, and upstate New York.

The abolitionist movement was mainly confined to the Northeast and the West, where people had no investment in slaves. A few southerners did free their slaves and move north, where they worked for abolition. James G. Birney of Alabama was an example.

Angelina and Sarah Grimké, daughters of a prominent South Carolina slaveholder, left their home in Charleston in protest against slavery. As writers and speakers, the Grimké sisters were doubly impressive since they testified from firsthand experience with slavery. Barred from many lecture platforms because of the prejudice against women in public affairs, the sisters became champions of the rights of women as well as of slaves.

IDENTIFY: abolition movement, Benjamin Lundy, emancipation, American Colonization Society, David Walker's *Appeal,* William Lloyd Garrison, *Liberator,* Theodore Weld, Angelina and Sarah Grimké.

1. (a) What were the goals of the colonization movement? (b) Why did attempts at colonization fail?
2. How was the belief that blacks were inferior used to justify not setting them free?
3. (a) How did free blacks try to improve their own situation and that of the slaves? (b) What was Walker's position on how to achieve equality? (c) What do you suppose was the reaction to his *Appeal?*
4. In what ways did the abolition movement become more militant?
5. Why was the abolition movement confined mainly to the Northeast and the West?

4 The antislavery movement begins to divide the nation

Frederick Douglass, the black abolitionist, once said, "No man can put a chain about the ankle of his fellow man without at last finding the other end fastened about his own neck." What do you think Douglass meant?

In 1833 the abolition movement gained strength when the British Antislavery Society forced Parliament to end slavery in the British empire. Also in 1833 American abolitionists formed the American Anti-Slavery Society, modeled on the British society.

The American Anti-Slavery Society, a national organization, had many affiliated groups on the local and regional level. These groups quickly multiplied. By the mid-1830's there were more than 1,000 of them in the United States, with about 150,000 members.

The American Anti-Slavery Society tried to influence public opinion by appealing to the conscience of white America. It circulated pamphlets and poured petitions into Congress and into state legislatures. The society also supported many lecturers, including Theodore Weld and the young men he had trained.

Frederick Douglass. Probably the most effective lecturer of the American Anti-Slavery Society was Frederick Douglass, a self-educated former slave. Douglass told northern and midwestern audiences of his cruel treatment as a young slave in Maryland. He spoke of how his master had tried to prevent him from learning how to read. He told how a professional slave-breaker had overworked, beaten, and nearly starved him. He told how, finally, he had attacked and beaten the slave-breaker. Of this experience Douglass said, "I was a changed being from that night. I was nothing before, I was a man now . . . with a renewed determination to be a free man."

Douglass condemned slavery and demanded its immediate abolition. He also insisted that it was time for the American people to listen to his message. "The lesson which they must learn, or neglect to do so at their own peril, is that Equal Manhood means Equal Rights, and further, that the American people must stand each for all and all for each without respect to color or race."

Split in the movement. The American Anti-Slavery Society was soon split by differences among its members. In particular, the militant position of William Lloyd Garrison alienated more moderate members. Garrison insisted on the right of women to hold leading offices in the

American Anti-Slavery Society and to speak publicly to mixed audiences. He stood firm even when, in 1838, an angry mob tried to break up a meeting in Philadelphia at which Angelina Grimké and other women spoke. The mob burned the hall itself the next day. Garrison's abolitionist foes insisted that the struggle for women's rights should be kept separate from the antislavery movement.

Garrison antagonized members of the society in other ways. He denounced the churches and the federal government for compromising with slavery. Claiming that the Constitution itself protected slavery, he insisted that antislavery people should refuse to vote or to hold public office.

Other leaders of the American Anti-Slavery Society deplored Garrison's militant views and actions. Thus in 1840 the society split apart. Garrison controlled the original organization, while a new society promoted the more moderate program of his opponents.

Moderate programs. In their first major attempt at political action, moderates formed the Liberty Party. In 1840 they nominated James G. Birney, a former Alabama slaveowner, as their Presidential candidate. In the election of that year, Birney polled only 7,000 votes. In the election of 1844, the Liberty Party won more votes, but only 62,000 of the 2.5 million votes cast. Nevertheless, the political abolitionists were not discouraged. They kept working to influence politicians of the major parties.

Militant programs. Some abolitionists demanded more vigorous action. In their eyes the laws protecting slavery were immoral and should be defied. The most outspoken of these abolitionists was Henry Highland Garnet, a former slave from Maryland.

Garnet made a fiery speech before the National Convention of Colored Citizens in Buffalo in 1843. He proclaimed, "Brethren, arise, arise! Let every slave throughout the land do this, and the days of slavery are numbered. You cannot be more oppressed than you have been; you cannot suffer greater cruelties than you have already. Rather die like free men than live as slaves." By a majority of one, the convention voted to suppress Garnet's speech. Several years later, however, it was published.

The underground railroad. Some antislavery Americans took more direct action in the abolition movement by helping runaway slaves escape. They formed what came to be known as the "underground railroad." Slaves who learned about the railroad might hide until pursuit died down and then flee north across the Ohio River or the Mason-Dixon line into Pennsylvania.

Fleeing north, however, did not bring the slaves their freedom because of a Fugitive Slave Law passed by Congress in 1793. Owners of runaway slaves could recover the slaves simply by appearing before a magistrate and declaring that the captured slaves belonged to them. Thus fugitive slaves were not safe until they reached Canada.

Once across the Mason-Dixon line or the Ohio River, however, runaway slaves hoped to contact an agent on the underground railroad. The agent would arrange their escape. Hiding in attics and haylofts by day and taken to the next "station" by night, the slaves slowly made the long trip northward. In time, with good luck, they completed the dangerous journey and found freedom in Canada.

Black Americans as well as whites were active in the underground movement. Some of these black Americans were well-to-do, such as James Forten, a Philadelphia sailmaker, and Robert Purvis, a free black born in Charleston, South Carolina, and educated at Amherst College. Purvis's zeal in helping slaves to freedom won him the title of "president" of the underground railroad.

Other black Americans active in the underground movement were themselves escaped slaves. Frederick Douglass was one. Another was William Wells Brown, the first black American novelist. Harriet Tubman, a fugitive slave, returned to the South time and time again. At great personal risk, she led many slaves to freedom by way of the underground railroad. Tubman was often called "the Moses of her people."

Uncle Tom's Cabin. The perils of escaping from slavery were vividly portrayed in the famous novel, *Uncle Tom's Cabin,* written by Harriet Beecher Stowe, a northern white woman, and published in 1852.

In *Uncle Tom's Cabin,* Stowe described the inhumanity of the slave system and efforts to escape from slavery as she had heard about them from fugitives. The book was often moralistic in tone, as was common in the writing style of the times, but the characters came

Harriet Tubman is shown here at the left with a group of former slaves whom she led to freedom. Tubman said later, "I started with this idea in my head: 'There's two things I've got a right to . . . death or liberty.'"

alive in a way readers never forgot. *Uncle Tom's Cabin* was made into a play, which became one of the most popular in American theater history.

In the South *Uncle Tom's Cabin* was bitterly denounced for presenting a false and distorted picture of slavery. Southerners were angered in spite of the fact that the book gave examples of masters' kindnesses toward slaves and of loyalty and affection on the part of slaves toward masters. Southerners were especially furious because Stowe's book encouraged support for the activities of the underground railroad.

Northern resistance. The abolitionists aroused widespread opposition in the North as well as in the South. William Lloyd Garrison once remarked that he found "contempt more bitter, opposition more stubborn, and apathy more frozen" in the New England states than in the South.

Garrison's remark was an overstatement, but not by much. Abolitionist preachers in the North were sometimes forced to quit by their churches. Leading citizens such as Wendell Phillips of Boston, a gifted writer and speaker, were barred from clubs and social gatherings because of their antislavery activities. William Lloyd Garrison was once forced to flee for safety to a Boston jail. More than once Theodore Weld and his students were attacked by

angry audiences. Elijah P. Lovejoy, an abolitionist editor who lived in Alton, Illinois, was murdered as he tried to prevent a hostile mob from destroying his printing press.

Citizens at Canterbury, Connecticut, became angry when Prudence Crandall turned her boarding school into a teacher-training institution for black girls. They polluted her water supply, tried to burn her house, and otherwise harassed her. Only after a mob assault in 1834 did she end her courageous but losing struggle. Sojourner Truth, a former slave, was attacked by mobs that were determined to break up meetings in which she denounced both slavery and the unequal treatment of women.

Many wage earners and business people opposed the abolition movement. Northern wage earners feared the job competition of free black workers and often broke up antislavery meetings. Most northern trade union leaders were either indifferent to the antislavery movement or actively opposed to it. They feared that abolition of slavery would flood northern cities with low-paid, competitive black workers. Most northern business groups frowned upon the abolitionists. The groups believed that such activities would hamper trade between the North and South.

Some northerners feared that the abolitionists' activities might lead the South to leave the Union. In fact, this was exactly what Garrison and many of his militant followers hoped would happen.

Southern reactions. Southerners, understandably, were most embittered by the antislavery movement. Nat Turner's rebellion of 1831 (page 305) came at the very time that the new, militant abolition movement was beginning. Many southerners dreaded the thought of widespread slave revolts. They angrily blamed abolitionists in general and William Lloyd Garrison in particular.

As losses from runaway slaves grew, slaveowners became furious. Trying to prevent further rebellion and to stop the flight of slaves, southern legislatures tightened the slave codes. Free blacks as well as slaves were placed under strict supervision.

Even federal officials resisted the abolitionists. When southern postmasters refused to deliver abolitionist literature, the United States Post Office Department supported them. In 1836, southerners in the House of Representatives pushed through the so-called "gag rule." This forbade any member to read an antislavery petition in the House.

Such actions by federal officials violated freedom of speech and of the press — basic civil liberties guaranteed by the Constitution. The "gag rule" was finally repealed, mainly through the efforts of former President John Quincy Adams, who had been elected a Representative to Congress from Massachusetts. However, the struggle for civil liberties was just beginning, and the North and South drew further apart.

SECTION SURVEY

IDENTIFY: American Anti-Slavery Society, Frederick Douglass, Liberty Party, underground railroad, Harriet Tubman, *Uncle Tom's Cabin.*

1. How was the antislavery movement in step with the times (a) outside the United States and (b) inside the United States?

2. How did each of the following aid the abolition movement while increasing bitterness: (a) Garrison, (b) Douglass, (c) Stowe, (d) Garnet, (e) underground railroad, (f) "gag rule"?

3. What were the reasons for northern and southern opposition to the abolition movement?

4. (a) What methods did militant and moderate abolitionists use? (b) Which methods do you think were most effective? Why?

5 Writers preach faith in democracy and the individual

Michel Chevalier, a French visitor to the United States in the year 1834, was impressed by the young nation's vigor. "All is here . . . boiling agitation," he commented. "Experiment follows experiment. . . . Men change their houses, their climate, their trade, their condition, their sect; states change their laws, their officers, their constitutions." All of this activity — mental as well as physical — was reflected in the work of writers and scholars.

The "American Renaissance." The experiments in writing between the 1820's and 1860's produced a new American literature. Many earlier American writers had felt inferior to British writers. Some, like Washington Irving, imitated British styles, even when dealing with American subjects. Others, like Noah Webster, wanted an independent American literature. Such writers vigorously rejected British models.

By the 1840's the question of whether to follow or reject models of British literature seemed less important. American writers seemed surer of their nation and themselves. They felt freer to treat the subjects that concerned them.

The result was a flowering of American literature. Edgar Allan Poe broke new ground in writing criticism, poetry, and short stories. Nathaniel Hawthorne, in his novels *The Scarlet Letter* (1850) and *The House of the Seven Gables* (1851), dealt with themes of sin and guilt. Herman Melville explored the struggle between good and evil in *Moby-Dick* (1851), which has been called one of the world's great novels.

These writers and many others brought fresh voices and ideas to American literature. This fruitful period is sometimes referred to as the "American Renaissance." Three key figures in it were Henry David Thoreau, Ralph Waldo Emerson, and Walt Whitman.

Henry David Thoreau (1817–1862). Henry David Thoreau hated the industrial society that he saw rising in the United States. To Thoreau machines were unnecessary gadgets

The American artist Asher Durand painted this majestic picture, "Kindred Spirits." In it he shows members of the "American Renaissance"—the painter Thomas Cole and the writer William Cullen Bryant.

that complicated life. "Nature is sufficient," Thoreau declared. To prove his point, he lived alone for about two years in a cabin that he built on the banks of Walden Pond near Concord, Massachusetts. There, free from the machines and the institutions that he believed imprisoned the human spirit, he wrote the classic book *Walden* in 1854.

Thoreau distrusted the power of the national government as much as he feared the new industrial society. Thoreau objected strongly to a government that allowed slavery to exist. He wrote, "I cannot for an instant recognize that political organization as *my* government which is the *slave's* government also."

Thoreau did not limit his distrust to verbal or written criticism. In 1846, believing that war with Mexico was an unjust attack and an attempt to extend slavery, he refused to pay his poll tax to the government. Thoreau was jailed but released the next day when a member of his family paid the tax without his knowledge.

Thoreau argued that people had a duty to disobey unjust laws, even at the cost of imprisonment, if their consciences told them that the laws were unjust. He explained these ideas in an essay published in 1849, which has become famous as "Civil Disobedience." Its ideas later influenced Leo Tolstoy in Russia, Mohandas Gandhi in India, and Martin Luther King, Jr., in the United States.

Thoreau foresaw two grave dangers to human liberty. He feared industrialism, with its concern for the material things of life and its disregard for the individual. He also distrusted the national state, with its indifference to the individual and its glorification of power.

Ralph Waldo Emerson (1803–1882). Henry David Thoreau and Ralph Waldo Emerson were close friends. Both lived in Concord, Massachusetts. Both believed in the supreme importance of individual freedom.

Emerson started his career as a Unitarian minister. He left his church in 1832, at age 29, to become a "preacher to the world." For most of the next 50 years, Emerson wrote and lectured. He traveled widely, and wherever he went he urged people to stand on their own feet, to free themselves from ignorance and prejudice, to think for themselves, and to respect others. Democracy with its free institutions would not work, he said, if the individuals in a democratic society were not free.

Emerson had a deep faith in America, in democracy, and in the ability of men and women

339

SOURCES

WHITMAN'S PREFACE TO *LEAVES OF GRASS* (1855)

The Americans of all nations at any time upon the earth have probably the fullest poetical nature. The United States themselves are essentially the greatest poem. In the history of the earth hitherto the largest and most stirring appear tame and orderly to their ampler largeness and stir. Here at last is something in the doings of man that corresponds with the broadcast doings of the day and night. Here is not merely a nation but a teeming nation of nations. . . .

Other states indicate themselves in their deputies . . . but the genius of the United States is not best or most in its executives or legislatures, nor in its ambassadors or authors or colleges or churches or parlors, nor even in its newspapers or inventors . . . but always most in the common people. . . . It awaits the gigantic and generous treatment worthy of it.

---

to solve their problems and build a better world. Emerson was critical of the growing emphasis on material things and the growing power of the national government. However, Emerson did not share Thoreau's fear of industrialism.

Nor was Emerson troubled, as many Americans were, by the swelling tide of immigration. Welcome the immigrants, he urged, "The energy of Irish, Germans, Swedes, Poles, and Cossacks, and all the European tribes — and of the Africans, and of the Polynesians — will construct a new race, a new religion, a new state, a new literature, which will be as vigorous as the new Europe which came out of the smelting-pot of the Dark Ages."

Walt Whitman (1819–1892). One day in 1855, Emerson received a copy of a newly published volume of poems entitled *Leaves of Grass*. Emerson was greatly impressed by the originality of the book. He wrote the author, Walt Whitman, "I greet you at the beginning of a great career."

In *Leaves of Grass,* Whitman sang the praises of the growing nation. Even more than Emerson, he believed deeply in democracy. He believed in the ability of the American people

to build an ever better way of life for themselves and their children. "The old and moth-eaten systems of Europe have had their day," he wrote. "Here [in America], we have planted the standard of freedom, and here we will test the capacities of men for self-government."

Whitman, like Emerson, did not share Thoreau's fear of industrialism. On the contrary, he hailed science and industry as liberating forces that would end the age-old burdens of superstition and toil. In his "Carol of Occupations," he glorified workers and the machines they operated. In "Pioneers! O Pioneers!," he challenged Americans to share his faith in the future. "We must march" he wrote,

We the youthful sinewy races,
all the rest on us depend,
Pioneers! O Pioneers!

The larger meaning. Emerson, Thoreau, Whitman, and many others raised powerful voices in praise of freedom and democracy. This faith in the individual and in democracy lay at the roots of the reform movements you have read about in this chapter.

Years earlier, in 1776, Thomas Jefferson had expressed the same faith in the words "We hold these truths to be self-evident: that all men are created equal, that they are endowed by their Creator with certain unalienable rights, that among these are life, liberty, and the pursuit of happiness." Emerson, Thoreau, Whitman, the reformers you have been reading about, and many other people were trying to apply the principles of the Declaration of Independence to the everyday affairs of their lives.

SECTION SURVEY

IDENTIFY: "American Renaissance," *Walden,* "Civil Disobedience," *Leaves of Grass.*

1. (a) What two major developments did Henry David Thoreau fear as threats to human liberty? (b) Why is it significant that Thoreau went to jail for his beliefs?

2. (a) Why did Ralph Waldo Emerson think of himself as a "preacher to the world"? (b) Summarize the main ideas of his "message."

3. Explain Walt Whitman's idea that Americans are pioneers who must march forward.

4. Why could this period be called an "American Renaissance"?

Chapter Survey

Summary: Tracing the Main Ideas

From the 1820's to the 1860's, new developments transformed the United States with bewildering speed. Factories and factory towns sprang up in the northern states. Slavery became increasingly important in the cotton-growing areas of the South. New means of transportation stimulated trade and sped the westward movement of land-hungry pioneers. Immigrants in steadily mounting numbers poured into the nation's growing cities and out upon the farmland.

The American people plunged enthusiastically into the job of building the nation, spurred by new ideas and by the desire to make democracy work. This faith in democracy stimulated wave after wave of reform movements. Among them were the struggles for women's rights, for more humane treatment of criminals and the mentally ill, for ending the sale of alcoholic beverages, and for equality of educational opportunity.

One other reform movement played a leading role in the political events of this period—the movement for the abolition of slavery. Abolitionism quickly took on a militant and uncompromising tone. The gap widened between people disturbed by the evils of slavery and people whose way of life was built around an economy based on slavery.

These reform movements continued throughout the 1830's, 1840's, and 1850's. Democracy made large advances during these years. But as you will see in the next unit, the problem of slavery became increasingly severe, reaching a bitter climax in armed conflict between North and South.

Inquiring into History

1. Why do you think that the movement for women's rights failed to gain strength before the Civil War?
2. Which women reformers do you think made the most significant contribution to American life? Explain.
3. Why did a split develop in the abolition movement between the militants and moderates?
4. Thoreau, Emerson, and Whitman represented the American spirit at this time. Give reasons to support this statement.
5. In what ways did this reform era (a) seek humanitarian goals and (b) try to make the nation more democratic?
6. Reread the Preamble to the Constitution of the United States (page 166). What steps toward fulfilling the ideals stated in the Preamble were taken during the period covered in Chapter 16?
7. In general, do you agree with Horace Mann that education "prevents being poor"? Did any social conditions other than lack of education cause poverty in Mann's time?

Relating Past to Present

1. Has Burritt's dream of an international organization and a world court been realized? Explain.

2. (a) Which of the reform movements begun during the period from the 1820's to the 1860's are still going on? (b) Why does reform often take a great deal of time?
3. In your view, has Walt Whitman's faith in science and industry as liberating forces proved sound? Has Henry David Thoreau's fear that science and industry would complicate people's lives come true? Use specific examples to support your answers.

Developing Social Science Skills

1. Slogans and cartoons are ways of calling attention to a needed reform. Devise slogans and cartoons that might have been used in the 1800's in reform movements. (a) How does each slogan or cartoon try to persuade? (b) Which types of persuasion seem most effective?
2. Read the poem "The Slave Ships" by John Greenleaf Whittier, which was based on an actual event. (a) What feeling does the poem convey? (b) What details does Whittier emphasize? (c) What effect do you think this poem had when it was first published in the *Liberator?*
3. Conduct research and prepare a written report on one of the following: (a) Elizabeth Cady Stanton, (b) Susan B. Anthony, (c) Catharine Beecher, (d) Brook Farm, (e) Liberia, (f) Sojourner Truth.

Unit Survey

For Further Inquiry

1. (a) Why did the planters become the political leaders in the South? (b) Who do you suppose were the political leaders in the North? Why? (c) Who might have been the political leaders in the West? Explain.
2. (a) What is manifest destiny? (b) What evidence is there that many Americans believed in manifest destiny by the mid-1800's? (c) Is the idea of manifest destiny consistent with the reform impulse felt by many Americans during the same period?
3. How was improved transportation important to the development of the (a) North, (b) South, and (c) West?
4. Do you think the Mexican War was inevitable? Why or why not?
5. How did the various reform movements that arose in the early and mid-1800's reflect faith in democracy?
6. Compare the lives of Northern industrial workers with the lives of slaves on Southern plantations.

Projects and Activities

1. Study the timeline here. (a) Which entries fall into the area of political history? social history? economic history? Explain your answers fully. (b) Judging from this timeline, which area of reform was the most important during this period? How can you tell? Why do you suppose that was so?
2. (a) Make a drawing to illustrate Southern society before the Civil War, showing the various economic groups and their standing in the society. (b) How would your drawing be different if it represented Northern society? Western society?
3. Read some poems by Emerson, Longfellow, Thoreau, or Whitman. (a) How did the poet seem to feel about America? (b) Do his poems seem characteristic of the period in which they were written? Explain.
4. Write a speech that might have been given at a meeting in support of women's rights, temperance, or peace.
5. Conduct research on high school education in the mid-1800's. How did it compare with your education in terms of (a) subjects studied, (b) size of classes, and (c) extracurricular activities.

Exploring Your Region

1. How might people in your region in the 1800's have felt about (a) the Mexican War, (b) the abolition movement, and (c) increasing immigration? Explain.
2. Study the map on pages 836–37. (a) Locate your state. (b) When did your state first become part of the United States? Under what circumstances? (c) Was the territory on which your state is located ever disputed with another nation? If so, how was the dispute settled?
3. Suppose that you lived in 1849 where you live now and that you wanted to get to the gold fields in California. What would have been the best method of transportation and the best route for you to use? Make a map showing your route.

Suggested Reading

1. *Harriet Tubman: Conductor on the Underground Railroad*, Ann Petry. An exciting biography of this former slave, called the "Moses of her people."
2. *Freedom's Ferment*, Alice Felt Tyler. Excellent summary of the major reform movements of the 1820's–1850's.
3. *We Came to America*, Frances Cavannah. First-person accounts by immigrants.
4. *Stories*, Edgar Allan Poe. A collection of short stories and poems by this master of suspense.

Unit Five

The Nation
Torn Apart

1845-1865

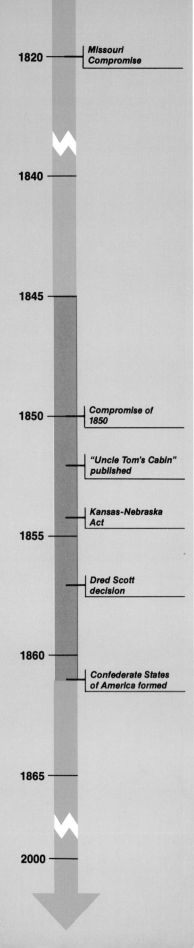

1820 — Missouri Compromise

1840 —

1845 —

1850 — Compromise of 1850

"Uncle Tom's Cabin" published

Kansas-Nebraska Act

1855 —

Dred Scott decision

1860 —

Confederate States of America formed

1865 —

2000 —

Chapter 17

A Time of Crisis and Compromise

1845-1861

The growing conflict among the three sections of the country—North, South, and West—forms the tragic theme of American history during the years preceding the Civil War, or the War Between the States, as this conflict is also sometimes called. The story that unfolds during this unhappy period is one of compromise, of breakdowns of compromise, of growing conflict, and of ever more desperate attempts to restore harmony.

The basic problem was that the North and South and West had developed along very different lines. To be sure, many people in all sections shared common institutions and beliefs. It is also true that there were many differences within each section. Yet each section had developed its own characteristic way of life.

The industrial North had its growing factories and towns. Large areas of the agricultural South were increasingly dependent upon the single crop of cotton. And the West was filled with growing towns and with restless pioneers pressing toward ever new frontiers.

It is not surprising, then, that people in each of the three sections held radically different views about such issues as internal improvements at federal expense, tariffs, banking and currency, public lands, and slavery.

To understand the tensions rising among the three sections of the country in this period, it is necessary to review events that had been taking place between the administrations of President Monroe and President Polk.

THE CHAPTER IN OUTLINE

1. The North and South maintain an uneasy political balance.

2. The Compromise of 1850 eases mounting tensions.

3. The long period of compromise finally comes to an end.

4. The North and South move steadily toward war.

5. Southern states withdraw from the Union and war begins.

344

1 The North and South maintain an uneasy political balance

The first serious clash between the North and the South over the issue of slavery had arisen in 1819–20, when President Monroe was in office. It involved the question of admitting Missouri to the Union. At times the controversy had become so heated that some politicians talked boldly of "disunion" and "civil war." Former President Thomas Jefferson followed the debates from his hilltop home. He wrote that "this momentous question, like a fire bell in the night, awakened and filled me with terror. I considered it at once as the knell of the Union."

Dispute over Missouri. To understand Jefferson's grave concern, you have to turn back to 1819, when the United States was composed of 11 free states and 10 slave states. At that time Alabama was about to be admitted to the Union as the eleventh slave state. With Alabama admitted to the Union, the North and the South would each then have 22 votes in the Senate.

Then the Territory of Missouri, in which slavery already existed, asked to be admitted to the Union. If Missouri entered as a slave state, the South would have 24 Senate votes and the North would have only 22.

Tallmadge's explosive proposal. On February 13, 1819, before Alabama was admitted, Representative James Tallmadge of New York offered an amendment to Missouri's application. Tallmadge proposed to outlaw the further introduction of slaves into Missouri. He also proposed to free, on their twenty-fifth birthday, all children born into slavery in Missouri after it became a state.

Tallmadge and his supporters argued that Congress had the power to prohibit slavery in any territory of the United States. He pointed out that Congress had already used this power when it created the Northwest Ordinance (see page 141).

The Missouri Compromise. The House of Representatives, where the North held a majority, adopted the Tallmadge Amendment, but the Senate rejected it.

This picture painted in 1851 shows the artist's idea of what Washington, D.C., would soon look like. The Capitol building in the foreground had not yet reached this size. Its great new dome had not yet been designed.

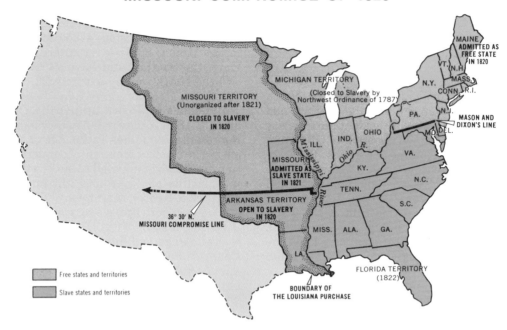

Why, with 11 free states and only 10 slave states represented in the Senate at this time, was the South able to win this victory? The answer is that certain northern Senators voted with the southern **bloc,** or solid group of legislators, to defeat the amendment.

Congress was now deadlocked. The House favored the amendment, while the Senate opposed it. The deadlock was broken, however, through mutual concessions known as the Missouri Compromise.

At this time, Maine was also petitioning Congress to enter the Union—as a free state. To keep an even balance of free and slave states, the Senate agreed to combine the admission of Maine with that of Missouri. Senator Jesse Thomas of Illinois introduced an amendment that received strong support from Henry Clay of Kentucky. This amendment proposed that Missouri be admitted as a slave state. It also proposed that slavery be prohibited in the rest of the Louisiana Purchase, north of latitude 36° 30′ (see map, this page). Southern members of Congress were willing to accept this restriction because cotton could not be grown profitably on the land to the north of the 36° 30′ line.

The crisis seemed to have passed, but in 1820 the antislavery forces in Congress threatened to exclude Missouri from the Union. They objected to Missouri's constitution, which discriminated against free blacks. Henry Clay then proposed the so-called second Missouri Compromise. Clay argued that the proposed constitution of Missouri could not deny citizens of Missouri the privileges and protections they were entitled to under the Constitution of the United States. When this proposal was accepted, Missouri was admitted as a slave state.

Thus the crisis of 1819–20 passed, but thoughtful Americans realized that danger lay ahead for the young nation. "This is a reprieve only, not a final sentence," Jefferson declared. John Quincy Adams wrote in his diary that the conflict over Missouri was a "mere preamble— a title page to a great, tragic volume."

Other divisive issues. As you have read (pages 265–67), during the years from 1828 to 1832 conflicting views over the tariff brought the United States perilously close to disunion. Indeed, South Carolina had threatened to secede. Although this crisis passed, the growing antislavery movement continued to inflame emotions and divide the nation (pages 332–38).

The deadlock over Texas. The slavery issue grew larger and more ominous. As it did, the struggle for control of the western areas became more intense. Every time a territory applied for admission to the Union as a state, northern and southern members of Congress came into conflict.

In 1836 and 1837, Congress admitted Arkansas and Michigan into the Union without dispute, for one was slave and the other free. Trouble arose when the newly organized Republic of Texas (pages 312–16) applied for admission. Since slavery already existed in Texas, Congress would have to admit Texas as a slave state. Doing so would upset the balance between the North and the South.

President Van Buren and many Congressional leaders were eager at this time to keep the slavery issue out of politics, but Texans could not afford to let the matter rest. Only 50,000 free people lived in the Lone Star Republic. If Mexico, with its population of 6 to 7 million, decided to reconquer its former territory, Texas would be in serious trouble. Texans needed a powerful ally to protect them against Mexico. Faced with this situation, Texas began to negotiate treaties of friendship and trade with France, Belgium, the Netherlands, and Great Britain.

For several years the issue of Texas hung in the balance. Mexico refused to recognize Texas' independence. Great Britain and France, on the other hand, continued to support an independent Texas. American opinion remained divided over whether or not to admit Texas to the Union.

The election of 1844. This was the situation in the United States in the election year of 1844. Henry Clay, the Whig candidate, tried to avoid the issue. James G. Birney, again the candidate of the antislavery Liberty Party, firmly opposed the admission of Texas. James K. Polk of Tennessee, the Democratic candidate, came out for "the re-annexation of Texas and re-occupation of Oregon!"

The Democratic Party's 1844 slogan was clever politics. It implied that the United States had always owned Texas and Oregon. This was not true, but the slogan shifted the focus from the troublesome issue of slavery to the popular issue of expansion. Northerners and southerners alike wanted their country to expand westward.

Polk won the election. In February 1845, shortly before he took office, Congress voted to admit Texas into the Union. The provisions for admission included the following points. (1) With the consent of Texas, a total of five states could be carved out of the territory. (2) If Texas did divide, any land north of the 36° 30′ line would be closed to slavery. (3) The United States would take over the boundary dispute with Mexico. (4) Texas would retain its lands and pay its debts.

Texas accepted these terms and entered the Union in December 1845. Thus the balance between North and South swung by two states in favor of the South. (It had already swung in favor of the South when Florida entered the Union in March 1845.) The balance was restored by the admission of Iowa in 1846 and Wisconsin in 1848, both free states.

Thus, for more than 25 years, from the Missouri Compromise of 1820 to the year 1846, Congress had walked a tightrope. By a series of compromises, the North and the South had managed to resolve the troublesome problems that had threatened to split them apart. This was the situation in 1846 when the United States went to war with Mexico.

SECTION SURVEY

IDENTIFY: Tallmadge Amendment, Henry Clay, "the re-annexation of Texas and re-occupation of Oregon!", James G. Birney.

1. (a) Why did Missouri's application for admission to the Union create a crisis? (b) How was the crisis settled?

2. (a) What did the North and South each gain by the Missouri Compromise? (b) Why did Jefferson call the Compromise "a reprieve only, not a final sentence"?

3. How did the election of 1844 reflect the issues of the time?

4. Map Study: Look at the map on page 346. (a) How many slave states were there at this time? How many free states? (b) By 1821, which states from the Louisiana Purchase had been admitted to the Union?

2 The Compromise of 1850 eases mounting tensions

In February 1848, the United States signed a treaty with Mexico, ending the war between the countries. In it, as you recall, Mexico ceded to the United States its northern territory, a huge area of land called the Mexican Cession.

Would slavery now be permitted or prohibited in the states that were to be carved out of this new area?

Division over the Mexican Cession. In general, Americans held four different views as to what should be done with this new area — land now regarded as the nation's Southwest.

First, President Polk and many citizens felt that the problem could best be solved by building upon the Missouri Compromise of 1820. The Missouri Compromise, you recall, outlawed slavery in all remaining areas of the Louisiana Purchase north of latitude 36° 30′ (see map, page 346). President Polk now proposed to extend this line to the Pacific, prohibiting slavery north of the line and allowing slavery south of the line.

Second, citizens strongly opposed to slavery accepted the Wilmot Proviso. In August 1846, shortly after the Mexican War started, David Wilmot, a Democratic representative from Pennsylvania, presented a resolution to Congress. The Wilmot Proviso flatly declared that "neither slavery nor involuntary servitude shall ever exist" in the lands acquired from Mexico. All but one of the northern states adopted resolutions that approved of the Wilmot Proviso.

Southerners took a third point of view. John C. Calhoun, probably the most influential southern voice, insisted that Congress had no right to prohibit slavery in the Southwest. Indeed, he insisted, Congress had a duty to protect the rights of slaveowners to their "property," the slaves, in *all* the territories. Calhoun based his argument on the Fifth Amendment to the Constitution. This amendment guarantees that no person shall "be deprived of life, liberty, or property, without due process of law."

A fourth group was led by Senator Lewis Cass of Michigan and Senator Stephen A. Douglas of Illinois. This group argued that the people of each territory should decide whether or not to permit slavery in their territory. The solution proposed by Cass and Douglas came to be known as "popular sovereignty" or "squatter sovereignty."

Straddling the issue. The problem of slavery in the territories was the burning issue in the Presidential election of 1848. However, both major parties, the Democrats and the Whigs, refused to take a stand on this issue. Both parties included southerners as well as northerners, and any strong stand would have split either party.

President Polk, exhausted by four years in office, refused in 1848 to run for reelection on the Democratic ticket. The Democrats then turned to Lewis Cass of Michigan, one of the authors of "popular sovereignty."

The Whigs nominated General Zachary Taylor, who had earned the title "Old Rough and Ready" as a fighter in the Mexican War. General Taylor was a southerner, but he had never been seriously involved in politics. His political views were not widely known.

Effects of a third party. The efforts of the Whigs and Democrats to straddle the slavery question drove many northerners to a newly formed third party — the Free-Soil Party. The Free-Soilers opposed any further extension of slavery into the territories. Using the slogan "Free Soil, Free Speech, Free Labor, and Free Men," they nominated former President Martin Van Buren of New York.

Van Buren and the Free-Soilers had great influence on the election, even though they failed to carry a single state. By capturing Democratic votes, especially in New York State, Van Buren unintentionally helped to throw the election to the Whig candidate, General Zachary Taylor. More important, the Free-Soilers won 12 seats in the House of Representatives. Otherwise, the House was almost evenly divided between Whigs and Democrats. The Free-Soil Party therefore held the balance of power in the lower house. It is important to note, however, that in many cases, especially in New York, religious and ethnic considerations were at least as influential as the slavery issue in determining how people voted.

Another crisis. The Congress that assembled in December 1849 was torn by dissension. In fact, tempers were so much on edge that members of the House of Representatives had to vote 63 times before electing a Speaker of the House and getting down to business.

One issue facing Congress was California's application to enter the Union as a free state. Southerners refused to consider the application. If California entered the Union as a free state, the existing balance of 15 slave and 15 free states would be upset in favor of the North.

Another issue before Congress was the controversy between the state of Texas and the newly acquired but as yet unorganized territory of New Mexico. Texas, where slavery was permitted, claimed that its boundary extended westward into country that the federal government had decided belonged to New Mexico. The antislavery members of Congress naturally tried to confine Texas to the smallest possible limits. Southerners just as naturally resented northern attempts to limit the area of Texas.

Arguments over other issues echoed through the halls of Congress. Southerners strongly resisted a proposal to abolish slavery in the District of Columbia. They also resisted a proposal to organize New Mexico and Utah into territories, since the proposal made no reference to slavery. Southerners wanted the proposal to state clearly their right to own slaves in New Mexico and Utah during the territorial period.

Many northerners, on the other hand, were just as strongly opposed to a southern proposal for a new and more effective fugitive slave law. The original Fugitive Slave Law of 1793 made state and local officials responsible for capturing runaway slaves and returning them to their owners. In 1842, however, the Supreme Court had ruled that state officials did not have to help federal officials in the capture and return of runaway slaves. Southerners now wanted a new law that would require state officials to assist in capturing runaway slaves.

All of these issues were loaded with political dynamite. Any one could lead to a break between the North and the South. In the opening months of 1850, many people felt that the United States stood on the brink of disunion, if not on the brink of war.

Clay's compromise. Henry Clay of Kentucky, whose earlier compromises had saved the Union from disasters, was known and respected as the "Great Compromiser." Now, in 1850, ill and weary from years of devoted effort to the Union, he stood before the Senate to plead once more for reason and moderation.

Clay's proposed compromise included several parts: (1) The admission of California as a free state. (2) The organization of the land acquired from Mexico (except California) into territories on the basis of "popular sovereignty." Thus the settlers might decide for themselves whether or not they wanted slavery in their territory. (3) A payment of $10 million to Texas by the United States, if Texas abandoned all claims to New Mexico east of the Rio Grande. (4) The abolition of the slave trade — that is, of the buying and selling of slaves — but not of slavery itself in the District of Columbia. (5) A more effective fugitive slave law, one that would compel state and local law enforcement officials to aid federal officials in the capture and return of runaway slaves.

The Great Debate. For more than six months, Clay's proposals provoked one of the most critical debates in American history.

The Great Debate of 1850 was the great effort of three political leaders. Clay (center) asks for compromise as Webster (head on hand at the left) and Calhoun (standing at far right) listen. Within two years, all three would be dead.

Daniel Webster—like Clay, a veteran Whig leader—supported Clay's compromise. He argued that slavery was not likely to prosper in the newly acquired lands. For this reason, Webster declared, it would be unnecessary and unwise for the North to insist on excluding slavery from this area. Many northerners opposed Webster and accused him of betraying the cause of freedom. Stephen A. Douglas of Illinois, who had argued for "popular sovereignty," supported Webster and Clay.

John C. Calhoun of South Carolina spoke for the South. He opposed "popular sovereignty" and all other compromises on the question of slavery. Calhoun was an old man. Like Webster and Clay, he had served his country in Congress for almost 40 years. He was so weak that he had to be carried into the Senate, where a colleague read his speech condemning the compromise. Calhoun insisted, as he had always done, that slaveowners had the right to take their property anywhere in any of the territories and that Congress had the duty to protect this right. Most southern Senators supported Calhoun.

Other Senators, Whigs and Democrats alike, strongly opposed Calhoun. Among this group were Thomas Hart Benton of Missouri, Salmon P. Chase of Ohio, and William H. Seward of New York. These men sternly denied that the Constitution protected slavery. They opposed the proposed fugitive slave law and urged Congress to exclude slavery from the territories. Many of them agreed with Seward that there is a "higher law than the Constitution." They felt that "all legislative compromises are radically wrong and essentially vicious."

Victory for compromise. As it turned out, most Americans in both the North and the South favored compromise at this time. In September 1850 both houses of Congress adopted all of Clay's compromise measures by large majorities.

John C. Calhoun did not live to see the outcome of the Great Debate. He died in March, leaving a great gap in the ranks of southern leaders. Nor did President Taylor live to see the outcome. He died in July, and his successor, President Millard Fillmore of New York, signed the compromise bills.

Thus compromise, sometimes called "the essence of politics," once again saved the day. Throughout the nation Americans hailed the work of Clay and his colleagues as a great triumph for national unity. Business groups supported it, expressing their fear that continued controversy between the North and the South would ruin business everywhere.

Would the compromise endure? This was the major question on the lips of many Americans in the fall of 1850.

SECTION SURVEY

IDENTIFY: Wilmot Proviso, "popular sovereignty," Stephen A. Douglas, Zachary Taylor, Free-Soil Party, Henry Clay, Daniel Webster, John C. Calhoun, Millard Fillmore.

1. How did American victory over Mexico in 1848 aggravate the slavery issue?
2. (a) Describe the four proposals for handling the slavery issue in the Mexican Cession. (b) What groups supported each proposal?
3. (a) State and evaluate the terms of Clay's compromise of 1850. (b) Which section of the country profited most from the compromise? (c) Who were the main figures involved in the Great Debate and what positions did each take?
4. Why is compromise sometimes called the "essence of politics"?

3 **The long period of compromise finally comes to an end**

The Compromise of 1850 lasted about four years. These four years proved to be the lull before the storm.

Prosperity and growth. Prosperity and growth—these were two of the striking characteristics of the United States during the early 1850's. The South prospered as the price of cotton rose and the annual production of cotton more than doubled. The Northeast prospered as new factories were built to meet a growing demand for manufactured products. The factories provided plenty of jobs for large numbers of people, including many European immigrants. The Middle West prospered and expanded as railroads opened up the fertile prairie lands. The railroads enabled the farmers to transport and sell their products, often at

A dramatized version of Harriet Beecher Stowe's *Uncle Tom's Cabin* played to packed houses both in the United States and abroad. This poster shows the heroine, Eliza, racing across an icy river as fierce bloodhounds pursue her.

greatly increased prices. The railroads also increased the price of farmland and encouraged the growth of new towns.

The railroads were becoming a vital part of the nation's growing economy. Between 1847 and 1861, railroad mileage in the United States increased from about 9,000 miles (14,500 kilometers) to more than 30,000 miles (48,300 kilometers). Most of the new railway lines reached from the Northeast into the Middle West, helping to bind these two areas together (see map, page 278). As a result, when war did come in 1861, the South faced a much more powerful combination than it would have faced had war broken out in 1850 or earlier.

The attention of most Americans in both the North and the South had for the moment shifted from the problem of slavery to prosperity and growth. As a result, the election of 1852 was uneventful. Both major parties condemned further argument over slavery and accepted the Compromise of 1850 as final. When the votes were counted, the Democratic candidate, Franklin Pierce of New Hampshire, had won 27 states. His rival, the Whig candidate, General Winfield Scott, a hero in the Mexico War, had won only 4 states.

Ominous undercurrents. In his Inaugural Address, President Pierce urged the American people to work for national harmony. However, that hoped-for harmony was being ruined by dissension.

The publication of Harriet Beecher Stowe's *Uncle Tom's Cabin* in 1852 infuriated southerners. They insisted that her picture of slavery was a vicious falsehood. Many northerners,

on the other hand, accepted the picture as absolute truth, and their attitudes against slavery hardened.

The Fugitive Slave Law of 1850, which was part of the Compromise of 1850, also helped to keep the issue of slavery before the people. The writer Ralph Waldo Emerson expressed the feelings of most militant abolitionists about the Fugitive Slave Law when he wrote, "This filthy enactment was made in the nineteenth century by people who could read and write. I will not obey it."

Several northern states responded to the pressure of abolitionists. These states openly defied the Fugitive Slave Law by passing "personal liberty laws." Such laws forbade local officials to help in the capture and return of fugitive slaves.

Many northerners defied the Fugitive Slave Law. Meanwhile, some southerners talked of increasing their power in Congress by acquiring new slave territory. The Spanish colony of Cuba seemed especially attractive. In fact, many advocates of manifest destiny, or expansionism, had long hoped to gain control over that island.

The Ostend Manifesto. In 1848 President Polk had tried to buy Cuba for $100 million. Spain had refused to consider the offer, but some southerners continued to cast longing eyes at Cuba. Finally, in 1854, the American ministers to Great Britain, France, and Spain met in Ostend, Belgium. They issued a statement now known as the "Ostend Manifesto."

The ministers declared that, if Spain refused to sell Cuba to the United States, the

351

United States would have the right to seize it by force. President Pierce disavowed this statement, but northern abolitionists were furious. They pointed out that southerners were ready to plunge the nation into war in order to add slave territory to the Union.

The Kansas-Nebraska Act. Thus, in 1854, undercurrents like these were eroding national unity. Senator Stephen A. Douglas of Illinois then increased the tensions without meaning to do so. Douglas wanted federal support for building a transcontinental railroad westward from Chicago. He felt that if the land west of the Missouri River were cleared of Indians and organized as a territory, it would be settled faster and its need for a railroad would be increased. To achieve these ends, Douglas sponsored and carried through Congress the Kansas-Nebraska Act. This act had the effect of repealing the Missouri Compromise.

The Missouri Compromise of 1820, as you know, had established the 36° 30′ parallel of latitude from the Mississippi River to the Rocky Mountains as the boundary between slave and free territory. Missouri was the only exception. The Kansas-Nebraska Act created two new organized territories in the West— Kansas and Nebraska (see map, this page). Both these territories were north of the old 36° 30′ line and, therefore, closed to slavery. However, the Kansas-Nebraska Act of 1854 abolished the Missouri Compromise dividing line. It stated that the territories were now "perfectly free to form and regulate their domestic institutions in their own way."

Northern reaction. Both major political parties were split by the Kansas-Nebraska Act. Most southern Democrats and southern Whigs voted for the bill. Many northern Democrats joined northern Whigs in opposing it. From 1854 until 1861, when war broke out, neither party was able to reunite its northern and southern wings.

Indeed, the Kansas-Nebraska Act plunged the entire nation into violent controversy over the slavery question. In Illinois an obscure lawyer, Abraham Lincoln, protested against opening the new territories to slavery. In Bos-

COMPROMISE OF 1850 AND KANSAS-NEBRASKA ACT OF 1854

Free states and territories

Slave states

Open to slavery by principle of popular sovereignty, Compromise of 1850

Open to slavery by principle of popular sovereignty, Kansas-Nebraska Act of 1854

ton, the day after the Kansas-Nebraska Act was passed, armed forces were needed to enforce the Fugitive Slave Law. A battalion of United States artillery, four platoons of marines, and a sheriff's posse were called out to escort a runaway slave from the courthouse to the ship that was waiting to carry him back to the South.

Everywhere throughout the North, people once again talked about slavery. The Fugitive Slave Law became increasingly difficult to enforce. "Anti-Nebraska" meetings were held, at which Douglas was denounced for reopening the slavery dispute.

The race for Kansas. Senator Charles Sumner of Massachusetts was one of many militant abolitionists who believed that the Kansas-Nebraska Act would plunge the country into serious trouble. "It puts freedom and slavery face to face and bids them grapple." And grapple they did on the plains of the new territory of Kansas.

The ink was hardly dry on the Kansas-Nebraska Act before eager pioneers and land speculators from both the North and the South rushed into the new territory. Competition over the choicest land and the most promising town sites quickly led to bitter disputes.

The confusion worsened when northern and southern extremists on the slavery issue began a race to control the new territory. Northerners formed an "Emigrant Aid Company" to encourage antislavery settlers to move into Kansas. The northern settlers founded Lawrence, Topeka, and other new settlements. Meanwhile, proslavery settlers from Missouri crossed over the border into Kansas and started the towns of Atchison, Leavenworth, and Lecompton (see map, page 352). In the mad scramble for land and for control of the territory, the land claims of the Indians were brushed aside or ignored.

The time soon came for the settlers in Kansas to draw up a constitution and organize a territorial government. This brought them face to face with the crucial question: Was slavery to be allowed in Kansas or not? The proslavery forces rushed voters into the territory and elected a proslavery legislature, which promptly passed laws favoring slaveowners. The antislavery forces then drafted a constitution forbidding slavery and elected an antislavery legislature. By the end of 1855, the territory of Kansas had two different constitutions and two different governments—one proslavery, one antislavery.

Dilemma in Washington. Back in Washington, members of Congress watched the struggle with dismay—and no one with greater dismay than the author of the Kansas-Nebraska Act, Stephen A. Douglas. When Douglas had argued for "popular sovereignty," he had hoped to remove the bitter issue of slavery from the heated politics of Congress and to allow the settlers in the territories themselves to decide the issue.

Obviously, Douglas's intentions had backfired. Congress was now forced to take sides and, hopelessly divided, it was not able to reach a decision.

Bleeding Kansas. While Congress argued, violence raged in what people called "Bleeding Kansas." Northerners and southerners alike rushed weapons into the territory. An armed proslavery group burned part of the town of Lawrence, a center of the antislavery settlers. In revenge, a fanatical white abolitionist, John Brown, gathered an armed group, including his own sons, and murdered five unarmed proslavery men. The fighting over slavery and over disputed land claims took the lives of more than 200 men and women before federal troops moved in to restore order.

The Republican Party. One immediate result of the struggle over Kansas was the formation of a new political party. Neither of the two major parties, the Whigs and the Democrats, dared take a stand on Kansas or any other issue involving slavery. Each party needed the support of its members in the Middle West, where the Kansas-Nebraska Act was popular. For this reason, antislavery members in both parties decided that the time had come to organize a new party pledging to prevent the further expansion of slavery in the territories.

Many towns and cities in the Middle West claim to be the birthplace of the Republican Party. However, it was at a convention in Jackson, Michigan, on July 6, 1854, that the delegates chose a name. They took the old label of Thomas Jefferson's party for their new organization and called themselves "Republicans."

The election of 1856. The election returns in the Presidential contest of 1856 showed that sectional lines were rapidly stiffening in the nation. The Whigs, who had tried to dodge the slavery issue, came in a poor third, with only 8 electoral votes. The Democrats nominated James Buchanan of Pennsylvania. They supported the Compromise of 1850 and the Kansas-Nebraska Act "as the only sound and safe solution of the slavery question." They came in first with 174 electoral votes (14 slave and 5 free states).

It was the Republican Party, however, that showed most clearly the danger facing the Union. The Republicans, who nominated John C. Frémont, the explorer of the Great West, came out squarely against any further expansion of slavery. Under the slogan "Free Soil, Free Speech, Free Men, and Frémont," the new Republican Party received 114 electoral votes — all of them from 11 free states. The Republican Party was plainly a purely sectional political organization, drawing all its support from the North. It seemed almost certain that the long period of compromise had come to an end.

SECTION SURVEY

IDENTIFY: Franklin Pierce, Fugitive Slave Law of 1850, Ostend Manifesto, "Bleeding Kansas," John Brown, John C. Frémont, James Buchanan.

1. Although the period from 1850 to 1854 was a prosperous one, the issue of slavery continued to cause trouble. Comment.
2. (a) What were the provisions of the Kansas-Nebraska Act? (b) Describe the consequences of the act's passage.
3. Explain the conditions that led to the formation of the Republican Party in 1854.

4 The North and South move steadily toward war

By 1857 the hope of compromise in the struggle between the North and the South seemed remote. From 1857 to 1861, the nation drifted toward disunion.

The Dred Scott decision. On March 6, 1857, two days after President Buchanan took the oath of office, the Supreme Court handed down an explosive decision. The decision involved a slave named Dred Scott.

Dred Scott's owner had taken him from Missouri, a slave state, into Illinois, a free state, and into Wisconsin Territory, which was free under the terms of the Missouri Compromise. His owner then took him back into Missouri. Befriended by members of a family that had once owned him, Dred Scott was eager to prove in court that he was a free man because he had lived in a free state and a free territory. One lower court decided for Scott, another Court against him. Finally the case reached the Supreme Court.

The Supreme Court ruled that residence in a free territory and free state had not given Dred Scott his right to freedom. It decided that Scott (and therefore all slaves) was not a citizen of the United States or of the state of Missouri. Therefore, he had no right to sue in either a state or a federal court.

Had the Supreme Court stopped at this point, the Dred Scott case might have gone almost unnoticed by the general public. However, the Supreme Court went on to rule that the Missouri Compromise was unconstitutional because Congress had no power to exclude slavery from the territories. The Court based this decision on the Fifth Amendment, which prohibited Congress from depriving any person of "property, without due process of law." The only other time that the Court had declared an act of Congress unconstitutional was in the case of *Marbury v. Madison* in 1803.

The abolitionist forces in the North were severely jolted by the Dred Scott decision. Now, because of the Supreme Court decision, only an amendment to the Constitution could keep slavery out of the territories. Such an amendment would have to be ratified by three fourths of all the states. In view of southern opposition, such a majority was out of the question. The antislavery forces now determined to gain strength and win the election of 1860.

A new leader. The contest for the office of United States Senator from Illinois in 1858 turned out to be a prelude to the general election of 1860. Stephen A. Douglas was running for reelection as a Democrat. He knew that if he won the Senate race in 1858, he had a good chance of winning the Democratic nomination for the Presidency in 1860.

To oppose Douglas, the Illinois Republicans put up Abraham Lincoln. Born in a log cabin in Kentucky, Lincoln was a self-made man. Gifted with a down-to-earth sense of humor and with much political shrewdness, Lincoln was a match for Douglas in wit, in logical argument, and in general ability.

Lincoln was not an abolitionist. However, he believed that slavery was morally wrong. He accepted the basic principle of the new Republican Party that slavery must not be extended any further. In accepting his nomination as Senator, he declared, "A house divided against itself cannot stand. I believe this government cannot endure permanently half slave and half free. I do not expect the Union to be dissolved — I do not expect the house to fall — but I do expect it will cease to be divided. Either the opponents of slavery will arrest the further spread of it, and place it where the public mind shall rest in the belief that it is in the course of ultimate extinction, or its advocates will push it forward till it shall become alike lawful in all the states, old as well as new, North as well as South."

The Lincoln-Douglas debates. Confident of his position and of his ability to defend it, Lincoln challenged Douglas to a series of debates. Throngs of people came to seven Illinois towns to hear Lincoln and Douglas vigorously debate the issues of the day. Newspapers in every section of the land reported the debates. Lincoln greatly impressed those who heard him and many who read what he said.

In the debates Lincoln asked Douglas how he could reconcile his principle of "popular sovereignty" with the Dred Scott decision. This put Douglas in a tight spot. In the Dred Scott decision, the Supreme Court had ruled that no one had the right to outlaw slavery in any territory. Douglas, on the other hand, had argued for "popular sovereignty," allowing the people in each territory to make their own decision about slavery. If Douglas replied that he believed in the Dred Scott decision, he would win the support of southerners but lose much northern support. If he continued to argue for "popular sovereignty," he would lose southern support but win many northern votes. With his eye on the Presidency in 1860, what could Douglas say to please both northerners and southerners?

Douglas was a skillful politician. His answer to Lincoln became known as the Freeport Doctrine, after the Illinois town where the debate took place. Douglas cleverly replied that the legislature of a territory could refuse to pass a law supporting slavery and in effect could exclude slavery from the territory.

Douglas's statement met with enough approval in Illinois to elect him Senator. Nevertheless, the Freeport Doctrine weakened Douglas in the South. By doing so, it also cost him the nomination for the Presidency in 1860 by a united Democratic Party. Southerners began to realize that Douglas's "popular sovereignty" did not mean that he favored the expansion of slavery.

John Brown's raid. In the fall of 1859, John Brown tried to start a slave rebellion in Virginia. With money obtained from abolitionists, he armed a party of about 18 men. On October 16 he seized the federal arsenal at the town of Harpers Ferry, in what is now West Virginia. He planned to seize the guns stored in the arsenal, give them to nearby slaves, and lead the slaves in what he hoped would be a widespread rebellion.

It was a bold idea, but almost certain to fail. Brown and his followers were captured by Colonel Robert E. Lee of the United States Army in command of a unit of marines. After a trial

SOURCES

DRED SCOTT v. SANFORD (1857)

The right of property in a slave is distinctly and expressly affirmed in the Constitution. The right to traffic in it, like an ordinary article of merchandise and property, was guaranteed to the citizens of the United States, in every state that might desire it, for twenty years. And the government in express terms is pledged to protect it in all future time, if the slave escapes from his owner. . . . And no word can be found in the Constitution which gives Congress a greater power over slave property, or which entitles property of that kind to less protection than property of any other description. The only power conferred is the power coupled with the duty of guarding and protecting the owner in his rights. . . .

that Brown admitted was more fair than he had reason to expect, he was hanged for "murder, criminal conspiracy, and treason against the Commonwealth of Virginia."

Many southerners believed that most northerners approved of Brown's action. In fact, many northerners were shocked at the news of John Brown's raid and quickly condemned it. But many northern abolitionists hailed Brown as a hero and a martyr. Emerson declared that Brown was a "new saint." Lydia Maria Child, a prominent writer and abolitionist, offered her help to Brown in prison. Frederick Douglass, who had refused to join Brown's scheme because he felt that it was doomed to fail, applauded Brown's courage. Southern newspapers quoted the opinions of such abolitionists as typical of what the whole North was thinking. To southerners, John Brown's raid was convincing evidence that the North was determined to abolish slavery.

SECTION SURVEY

IDENTIFY: Dred Scott decision, Abraham Lincoln, Freeport Doctrine, John Brown's raid.

1. (a) What was the decision of the Supreme Court in the Dred Scott case? (b) Why did this decision arouse widespread opposition in the North?
2. Explain the main issues in the Lincoln-Douglas debates.
3. (a) What was the purpose of John Brown's raid? (b) Describe the reaction of northerners and southerners to the raid.

5 Southern states withdraw from the Union and war begins

By 1860 the ties binding the North and the South had almost disappeared. The break between the two sections was reflected in the tensions dividing the political parties. The widening split became clear in 1860, when the national parties met to draw up platforms and to nominate candidates for the Presidency.

The parties take their stands. The Whig Party was greatly weakened by 1856, when many southern Whigs voted for the Democrats. In 1860 what was left of the old Whig Party

nominated John Bell of Tennessee for the Presidency and changed its name to the Constitutional Union Party. The party adopted a platform that called upon all citizens to recognize "no political principles other than the Constitution of the country, the Union of the states, and the enforcement of the law."

The Democratic Party split wide open in 1860. One group, consisting mostly of southerners, took a strong proslavery position. This group nominated John C. Breckinridge of Kentucky for the Presidency and demanded federal protection for slavery in the territories. The other group, mostly northern Democrats, nominated Stephen A. Douglas for the Presidency. It took the position that "popular sovereignty" should decide the slavery question in the territories.

The Republicans, meeting in Chicago, determined to make the most of the split in the Democratic Party. They abandoned one strongly antislavery candidate, Governor William H. Seward of New York, partly because he seemed to be identified with eastern "money interests." The Republicans also believed that a candidate from the Middle West was more likely to win the election. The convention then went on to name Abraham Lincoln as its candidate.

The Republican platform was a purely sectional platform. It was designed to win the support of northern industrialists and wage earners and of farmers, particularly in the Middle West. The platform opposed the extension of slavery into the new territories.

Thus four political parties entered the Presidential race in 1860. The Republicans, with Lincoln at their head, were supported by many northern industrialists and midwestern farmers who opposed any further extension of slavery. Aligned against the Republicans in the North were Democrats led by Douglas. The Douglas Democrats wanted to keep things much as they were. Douglas urged the people to vote for him on the ground that, if Lincoln were elected, the South would then secede from the Union.

In the South the contest was between the moderate Constitutional Unionists, led by Bell, and the southern Democrats, led by Breckinridge. The southern Democrats made it clear that they would regard the election of Lincoln as proof that the North was using its superior strength to encroach upon the rights and interests of the South.

Results of the election. Lincoln won the election, receiving 180 electoral votes, all from the northern free states. Breckinridge mustered 72 electoral votes, all from the southern slave states. Douglas drew 12 electoral votes, while Bell received 39.

The count of the popular vote showed that Lincoln had polled 40 percent, Douglas 29 percent, Breckinridge 18 percent, and Bell nearly 13 percent. Lincoln was elected President, but by a minority of the popular vote.

In both the North and the South, Lincoln and Breckinridge, who opposed any compromise on the issue of slavery in the territories, won more electoral votes than the moderates, Douglas and Bell. Thoughtful observers noted this development with alarm. Did it mean that the southern states would carry out their threat to secede?

Secession from the Union. The fateful answer came quickly. Shortly after the November election, the legislature of South Carolina called a special convention to consider secession. The delegates unanimously voted that

South Carolina was no longer a state of the Union. Other southern states, not without some opposition, followed South Carolina's example. Mississippi, Florida, Alabama, Georgia, Louisiana, and Texas soon passed acts of secession (see map, this page).

Early in 1861, delegates from six of the seven seceding states met at Montgomery, Alabama. There they drafted a constitution for the Confederate States of America. Although the Confederate Constitution resembled the Constitution of the United States, there were some major differences. The Confederate Constitution stressed "the sovereign and independent character" of each state. It also guaranteed the right to own slaves.

The Montgomery convention elected as President of the Confederacy Jefferson Davis, a Mississippi planter who had formerly served as United States Senator and Secretary of War. The delegates also elected Alexander H. Stephens of Georgia as Vice-President.

Buchanan's inaction. While southern states were seceding from the Union, what did Pres-

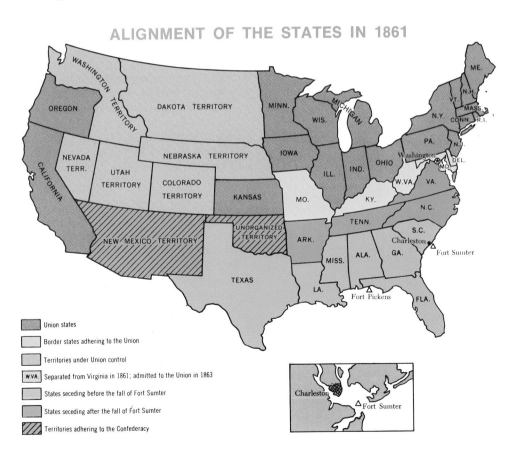

ALIGNMENT OF THE STATES IN 1861

Union states

Border states adhering to the Union

Territories under Union control

W.VA. Separated from Virginia in 1861; admitted to the Union in 1863

States seceding before the fall of Fort Sumter

States seceding after the fall of Fort Sumter

Territories adhering to the Confederacy

A tattered Confederate flag flew over wind-swept Fort Sumter after Union troops surrendered following 34 hours of shelling by southern cannons.

ident Buchanan do? The answer was, almost nothing. He did announce that no state in the Union had the right to secede, but he also stated that the federal government had no power to hold any state in the Union against its will. Thus, for four months, from Lincoln's election until the inauguration, the only efforts to meet the crisis were several half-hearted proposals for compromise. All these proposals were quickly rejected by leaders in both the North and the South.

In fairness to Buchanan, it should be said that his policy did prevent war for several months. It also gave compromise proposals a chance to be heard. Since he had only four months more in the White House, Buchanan may have concluded that the incoming President should be allowed to settle the problem in his own way.

Outbreak of war. During this time Confederate troops occupied—without resistance—all but two of the forts and navy yards in the states that had seceded. By the time Lincoln was inaugurated on March 4, 1861, only Fort Pickens at Pensacola, Florida, and Fort Sumter at Charleston, South Carolina (see map, page 357), remained in the hands of the federal government. Southerners—or at least those southerners who held the most extreme point of view—claimed that these forts belonged to the Confederate States of America, not to the United States of America. Confeder-

ate troops moved into strong positions against these two forts but did not attack.

In March, Major Robert Anderson, commanding Fort Sumter, notified the War Department in Washington that his supplies were almost gone. This situation presented President Lincoln with a major problem. If he sent new supplies to Fort Sumter, the Confederacy would consider this to be an act of war. If he failed to send supplies, the fort would pass into Confederate hands. Were this to happen, many people would conclude that the United States government had recognized the right of the southern states to secede.

Finally, toward the end of March, and against the advice of the majority of his cabinet, Lincoln sent a relief expedition to Fort Sumter. When the Confederate government heard this news, it notified General Pierre Beauregard (BOH·reh·gard), commander of the Charleston district. It ordered him to fire upon Fort Sumter if such action were necessary to prevent United States reinforcements from reaching it.

On April 12 at 4:30 in the morning, the Confederate guns around the harbor opened fire on Fort Sumter. Major Anderson, in command of the fort, promptly returned the fire. The relief expedition, unable to pass the Confederate batteries, lay helpless outside the harbor. Two days later, on April 14, Major Anderson led his troops out of the fort, which then passed into Confederate hands.

News of the fall of Fort Sumter ended all hopes of compromise. Men in the North and in the South rushed to join the armed forces. War had begun.

SECTION SURVEY

IDENTIFY: Constitutional Union Party, John C. Breckinridge, secede, Confederacy, Jefferson Davis, Fort Sumter.

1. In the election of 1860, those "who opposed any compromise on the issue of slavery . . . won more electoral votes than the moderates." Comment.

2. How did Lincoln's election in 1860 help bring on the Civil War?

3. Chart Study: Make a chart with four columns— each column headed by the name of a political party in 1860. In each column, fill in (a) the name of the Presidential candidate, (b) his position on the main issues, (c) the regions of the country supporting his party, and (d) the number of electoral votes he received.

Chapter Survey

Summary: Tracing the Main Ideas

Why did the North and South go to war in 1861? What was the immediate cause of the tragic conflict?

There is no easy way to answer these questions. Historians have studied the problem and recorded their conclusions in scholarly volumes that today fill row after row of library shelves.

Some historians stress basic differences in the economic and social systems of the North and South, differences that increased as the years passed. Other historians point to differences of opinion over the tariff, over internal improvements at public expense, over money and banking, and over the disposal of public lands. Others stress the conflict over slavery. Still other historians emphasize the issue of states' rights.

These are only a few of the ways in which historians explain the war. It seems at times as though there were as many explanations as there are historians. This does not mean that the scholars are wrong. Each has put a finger on one or more of the many factors that led to armed conflict.

Thoughtful historians do not attempt to give short and simple explanations of the war between the North and South. All they can safely do is try to explain why northern extremists and southern extremists, a minority in each section, felt and acted as they did. The historians can only point out that the great majority in the North held that the benefits of the Union were too important and the sentiment of patriotism was too precious to permit the Union to be destroyed. They can only indicate that many in the South who loved the Union and would have preferred to stay in it had equally compelling reasons for their actions. They supported the Confederacy out of loyalty to the principle of states' rights, out of determination to protect their homes, and out of consideration for the position taken by kinfolk, neighbors, and friends.

Inquiring into History

1. How did each of the following events and people increase sectional bitterness: (a) the Mexican War, (b) William Lloyd Garrison, (c) Harriet Beecher Stowe, (d) the Dred Scott decision, (e) John Brown's raid?
2. (a) Do you believe that white southerners were the only Americans who regarded blacks as inferior during the period before the Civil War? Give evidence to support your opinion. (b) Why would it be unfair to make the generalization that all southerners were proslavery and all northerners were antislavery?
3. Make a list of events leading to the Civil War. Then make a second list of the issues that caused the war. (a) Are the lists different? the same? (b) What can you conclude from your answers in part a? (c) Do you think the war could have been avoided if any of these events had not taken place? Why?

Relating Past to Present

1. When President Lincoln met Harriet Beecher Stowe, he said, "Well, so you're the little lady who started this great war!" (a) What did Lincoln mean by this remark? Was he justified? (b) Can you think of any writers today whose works have had as great an impact on the nation as Lincoln attributed to Stowe? Why or why not?
2. Between 1854 and 1860, the Republican Party replaced the Whig Party as the second major party. Would it be possible today for a new political party to replace one of the two major parties? If so, under what conditions? Would such a change be likely?

Developing Social Science Skills

1. Study the map on page 352. (a) When did Kansas become a territory? (b) Note the inset map. What does it show? (c) On the inset map, which towns were settled by people who opposed slavery? How can you tell? (d) On the inset map, note the location of Atchison. How might Atchison's location affect the way its citizens might vote about slavery?
2. Read the excerpt from the Dred Scott decision on page 355. (a) How did the Supreme Court justify its opinion that slaves were property? (b) According to the decision, should slaves have been treated differently from other types of property? Explain.

1850

1855

1860

First Battle of Bull Run

North sets up sea blockade

Homestead Act

Battle of Gettysburg

Emancipation Proclamation

Grant becomes Union commander

1865

Lee surrenders at Appomattox

2000

Chapter 18

A Nation Divided by War

1861–1865

On April 15, 1861, the day after Fort Sumter fell, President Abraham Lincoln declared that the government of the United States faced an armed revolt against its authority. He called for 75,000 volunteers for three months' service in the army.

In the northern states, recruits enthusiastically answered Lincoln's call to arms. From all walks of life, they rushed to join the army—Republicans and Democrats, native-born Americans and newly arrived immigrants. For the time being, the North was united as it had never been united before in its history.

The poet Walt Whitman remembered the opening weeks of the war and captured in verse the feeling of unity that gripped northerners in those trying days:

> Beat! beat! drums!—blow! bugles! blow!
> Through the windows—through the doors—
> burst like a ruthless force,
> Into the solemn church, and scatter the congregation;
> Into the school where the scholar is studying;
> Leave not the bridegroom quiet—no happiness must he
> have now with his bride;
> Nor the peaceful farmer any peace, ploughing his field
> or gathering his grain;
> So fierce you whirr and pound, you drums—
> so shrill you bugles blow.

In the South as well as in the North, the beat of drums and the shrill voice of the bugle summoned the people to war.

THE CHAPTER IN OUTLINE

1. The North and South develop their war strategies.
2. The North and South struggle through four years of conflict.
3. Freeing the slaves becomes a goal for the Union.
4. The war brings severe hardship and suffering to the South.
5. Life behind Union lines undergoes important changes.
6. The Union faces political problems at home and abroad.

1 The North and South develop their war strategies

When President Lincoln called for Union volunteers, there were only seven states in the Confederate States of America, or the Confederacy—South Carolina, Georgia, Florida, Alabama, Mississippi, Louisiana, and Texas. With Lincoln's call to arms, every state had to make its fateful choice.

Choosing sides. Virginia, on April 17, 1861, became the eighth state to join the Confederacy. When Virginia left the Union, the United States Army lost several of its ablest officers. The most famous Virginian to take up arms for the South was Robert E. Lee, to whom President Lincoln had offered command of the Union forces. Arkansas, Tennessee, and North Carolina soon followed Virginia into the Confederacy. By May 20, eleven states had seceded from the Union to join the Confederacy (see map, page 357).

The mountainous counties in northwestern Virginia did not follow the rest of the state into the Confederacy. In 1863 these counties were admitted to the Union as the state of West Virginia. Control of this area, part of which lay on the Ohio River, was important to the North. It helped to keep open the lines of communication between the states of the Northeast and the Mississippi River.

The border states—Delaware, Maryland, Kentucky, and Missouri—were also important to the Union. For a time, it remained uncertain which side some of them would join.

Maryland was especially important. If it joined the Confederacy, the Union capital at Washington, D.C., would be cut off from the northern states. Many Marylanders sympathized with the Confederacy, and for a time the state hung in the balance. On April 19 a mob of angry citizens attacked the Sixth Massachusetts Regiment as it passed through Baltimore. To prevent the passage of Union troops and to avoid further bloodshed, Maryland authorities burned the railroad bridges connecting Baltimore with Philadelphia and Harrisburg. Lincoln was determined to keep Maryland in the Union. He sent federal troops into the state and arrested the leading Confederate sympathizers. Pro-Union leaders soon

Recruiting posters such as this one called for northerners to rush into the fight. At first, enough volunteers joined up to get the army going, but as the war dragged on enlistments dropped and a draft became necessary.

won power, and Maryland then remained in the Union.

The other border states—Delaware, Kentucky, and Missouri—also decided in favor of the Union. Delaware never hesitated. Kentucky at first ignored Lincoln's call for volunteers and tried to remain neutral. However, when the Confederate army invaded Kentucky in September, the state declared for the Union. Missouri's government was controlled by southern sympathizers. After several battles had been fought, however, Missouri officially lined up with the North.

The "North" also included the Pacific coast states of California and Oregon. In 1863, after West Virginia joined the Union, a total of 24 states were fighting on the northern side.

In many states, especially in the border states, families were torn apart as some members enlisted with the Confederacy, others with the Union. Three of Mrs. Lincoln's brothers fought and died for the South. Robert E. Lee's nephew commanded Union naval forces on the James River in Virginia while his famous uncle was fighting Union army forces not many miles away. These divisions within families and the breakup of lifelong friendships were among the many tragic results of the war.

Northern advantages. The North had tremendous material advantages over the South. It was greatly superior in population, in manufacturing, in agricultural and natural resources, in finances, and in transportation facilities. The strength of the North had recently been increased by the admission of three new states to the Union—Minnesota (1858), Oregon (1859), and Kansas (1861).

The population of the 24 northern, western, and border states totaled 22 million, plus about 800,000 immigrants who entered during the war years. About 400,000 foreign-born men served in the Union armies.

Varied economic resources gave the North a huge advantage over the chiefly agricultural South. When the war began, the North had 92 percent of the nation's industries and almost all the known supplies of coal, iron, copper, and other metals. The North also owned most of the nation's gold. Confederate wealth was largely in land and slaves.

Northern transportation facilities were also far superior to those of the South. Most of the nation's railroad lines were located in the North and the Middle West. Thus the North could move troops and supplies almost at will. It could easily transport food from midwestern farms to workers in the eastern cities and to armies in the field. Moreover, with control of the navy and most of the merchant marine, the North could continue to carry on trade with nations overseas.

Southern advantages. The 11 states of the Confederacy had a combined population of only about 9 million. This figure included more than 3.5 million slaves. Northerners therefore outnumbered white southerners by more than four to one.

Nevertheless, southerners felt confident because to win, they had only to fight a defensive war. The South needed only to protect its territory until the North tired of the struggle. The North, on the other hand, had to conquer an area almost as large as Western Europe.

The Confederacy also had the advantage that many of its ablest officers were West Point graduates with long years of army experience. Also, southerners were used to outdoor living. They were generally more familiar with firearms and horses than many soldiers from the Northeast, who had been raised in cities.

Another reason for southern optimism was the belief that cotton was "king." Southerners believed that the textile mills of Great Britain and France were so dependent on raw cotton that these countries would have to come to the aid of the Confederacy.

War aims. Another advantage that southerners had over northerners was the fact that southerners were fighting for more clearly defined goals. The major aim of the Confederacy never varied. Southerners fought to win their independence—the right to govern themselves as they saw fit. Also, once northern armies invaded the Confederacy, southerners fought to defend the things that people cherish most—their homes and families. In addition, many southerners—both slaveholders and nonslaveholders alike—were fighting to preserve slavery. By this time, as you know, slavery had become firmly established in the South. Most white southerners had come to identify with its way of life.

In contrast, northerners who supported the war were fighting for less tangible goals, no matter how deeply felt. At the start of the war, most northerners believed with President Lincoln that they were fighting for one major aim—to preserve the Union. Only a few extreme abolitionists saw the war as a means to end slavery. As the war dragged on, more and more northerners came to believe that freeing the slaves was as important as restoring the Union—that the two aims, indeed, were inseparable.

War strategies. The overall strategy of the South was as clear and simple as its war aims. Southerners proposed to fight a defensive war. They would try to hold the North at arm's length until northerners grew war-weary and agreed to peace on southern terms. There was one exception to this defensive strategy. It was a plan to seize Washington, D.C., and strike northward through the Shenandoah Valley into Maryland and Pennsylvania. By this plan the South hoped to drive a wedge between the Northeast and the Middle West and disrupt Union communications. This would bring the war to a speedy end.

Overall northern strategy included three different plans of attack. (1) The North would try to strangle the South by blockading the Confederate coastline. (2) It would try to split the Confederacy in two by seizing control of the Mississippi River and interior railroad lines. (3) It would try to seize Richmond, Virginia,

MAJOR CAMPAIGNS OF THE CIVIL WAR

This map shows the main points of Union strategy and provides an overview of the major campaigns of the Civil War. The circled numbers indicate the areas in which fighting occurred. In the pages that follow, you will learn more about each of these campaigns. The discussion of each campaign is accompanied by a detailed map that bears a number corresponding to one of the numbers on this map. As you read the text that follows and examine each numbered map, look frequently at the map above so that you will understand the sequence of the war. On the map above and on the detailed maps, Union states and Confederate states appear in different colors. On all of the detailed maps, colored symbols stand for Union forces, black symbols for Confederate forces. The following symbols are used:

⟶ Union advance	----▶ Union retreat	✹ Union victory
⟶ Confederate advance	----▶ Confederate retreat	✸ Confederate victory

363

which had become the Confederate capital in May 1861, and then to drive southward and finally link up with Union forces driving eastward from the Mississippi Valley.

Such were the war aims and plans of the two opposing sides. In the spring of 1861, as the northern "Boys in Blue" and the southern "Boys in Gray" trudged to their first battlefield, no one knew that four long, cruel years of fighting lay ahead.

SECTION SURVEY

IDENTIFY: Robert E. Lee, border states, "Boys in Blue," "Boys in Gray."

1. (a) Name the states that joined the Confederacy. (b) Name the border states.
2. Compare the war aims and military strategy of the North and the South.
3. Chart Study: Make a chart comparing the North and the South with respect to (a) number of states, (b) population, (c) industrial development, (d) transportation facilities, (e) financial resources, and (f) naval power. Based on your chart, which side appears to have been the stronger? Why?

2 The North and South struggle through four years of conflict

The first important battle of the Civil War was fought on July 21, 1861, near a stream called Bull Run in northern Virginia (see map 1, page 365). In this engagement, the First Battle of Bull Run, the Confederates defeated the northern recruits, who fled in confusion to Washington, D.C.

Northerners were stunned. If the Confederate commanders had taken advantage of their victory, they could easily have captured Washington, D.C. However, the Confederate troops, elated by victory, scattered to celebrate instead of pursuing the Union army.

The Union blockade. Meanwhile, Union warships and other vessels hastily converted into naval service had begun to blockade the Confederate coastline (see map, page 363). As time passed, the blockade became increasingly effective. Daring Confederate sea captains kept trying to run the blockade, but as the years wore on fewer and fewer ships slipped through.

The blockade was a severe handicap to Confederate plans. The South had counted on exporting cotton, tobacco, sugar, and other products to Europe for sale there. The profits would then go to buy European military equipment and manufactured goods. As the blockade tightened, European products vanished from southern stores. Southern manufacturers could not make up the deficiencies.

As products became increasingly scarce, the prices of southern goods shot skyward. Patriotic southern women began to make substitutes. Using looms and spinning wheels brought down from dusty attics, they spun and wove fabrics for clothing and uniforms. Before the war ended, southerners were melting church bells to make cannons.

War at sea. Although the Confederacy failed to break the Union blockade, daring Confederate ships made the sea lanes dangerous for northern shipping. Between Lincoln's election and the fall of Fort Sumter, the South seized a number of United States vessels then in southern harbors. During the war southerners also purchased in England the *Alabama,* the *Florida,* and 17 other warships. Although these few vessels posed no serious threat to the United States Navy, they did sink more than 250 merchant ships before the war ended.

More important to the war's outcome was the ever-present possibility of Union naval actions. These could be attacks on southern harbors or the landing of a Union army behind Confederate lines. Fortunately for the South, all of its important harbors had been heavily fortified long before the war. Early in 1861 the Confederacy seized these fortifications and held them throughout the war. Nevertheless, Union forces managed to capture New Orleans and several forts on the Atlantic coast.

The Union on the offensive. The Appalachian Mountains divided land operations into two major theaters of war — the eastern theater and the western theater.

Shortly after the Union disaster at the First Battle of Bull Run, President Lincoln gave 34-year-old General George B. McClellan, a West Point graduate, command of the eastern theater of war. A superb organizer and popular with his troops, McClellan quickly turned a mob of untrained volunteers into the Army of the Potomac. In November 1861 Lincoln elevated McClellan to General-in-Chief of all the Union armies. But McClellan was overly cautious, refusing to attack until he was thoroughly prepared. The saying "All quiet along the Potomac" became a public joke. Lincoln finally commented, "If General McClellan does not want to use the army, I would like to *borrow* it."

While the Army of the Potomac marked time in the East, Union forces in the western theater fought small skirmishes in Missouri. The goal was to prevent that state from joining the Confederacy. By 1862 Missouri had been made secure, and General Henry W. Halleck, commander of the western theater, opened a drive into Tennessee.

War in the West. The Union drive began in western Kentucky where the Tennessee River empties into the Ohio River. From here an infantry unit commanded by General Ulysses S. Grant—one of General Halleck's subordinate officers—moved southward. On February 6, 1862, Grant captured Fort Henry on the upper Tennessee River. On February 16 he captured Fort Donelson on the Cumberland River (see map 2, this page). These victories opened the way for an invasion of the Deep South by way of the Tennessee and Cumberland rivers.

General Nathan Bedford Forrest, one of the South's best generals, managed to escape capture. Forrest would prove to be so dangerous that Union General William T. Sherman later ordered his troops to hunt Forrest down "if it costs ten thousand lives and bankrupts the federal treasury."

In the operations along the Tennessee, the Union infantry was assisted by gunboats. These small warships were capable of steaming along the shallow river waters. Indeed, in both this campaign and the Mississippi River campaign, gunboats proved extremely useful to both sides.

With Fort Donelson in Union hands, Grant continued southward along the Tennessee River to Pittsburg Landing, sometimes called Shiloh (SHY·loh), in Tennessee. Here General Albert S. Johnston of Texas, Confederate commander in the West, surprised and completely defeated him. However, Johnston died and his death coupled with the arrival of Union reinforcements allowed Grant to take the offensive. After desperate fighting, Grant finally drove the Confederate army from the field. At the

1 First Battle of Bull Run: July 21, 1861

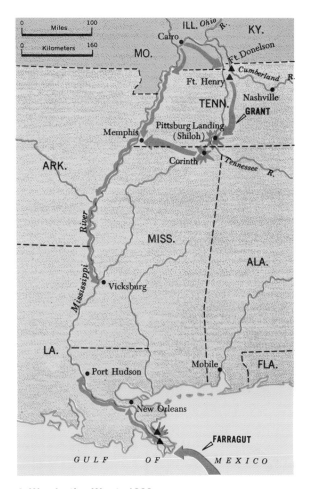

2 War in the West: 1862

365

end of May, Union forces occupied Corinth, in northern Mississippi.

At the same time, other Union forces were fighting to the south and north to gain control of the Mississippi River. On the night of April 23, Union Flag Officer (later Admiral) David G. Farragut of Tennessee ran his gunboats past the forts guarding New Orleans and captured the city. Meanwhile, a combined Union naval and land expedition under Commodore A. H. Foote and General John Pope was moving southward down the Mississippi. In June this expedition seized Memphis, Tennessee. It then continued as far south as Vicksburg, Mississippi (see map 2, page 365).

Thus, by the summer of 1862, Union forces in the western theater had almost split the Confederacy in two along the Mississippi. Casualties had been enormous on both sides. Confederate armies made the Union troops pay dearly for their gains. Nevertheless, Union armies had driven the Confederates out of Kentucky and western Tennessee. Only a short length of the Mississippi and Port Hudson, Louisiana, remained in Confederate hands.

War in the East. Union victories in the West during 1862 were more than balanced by major Confederate victories in the East.

❸ War in the East: 1862

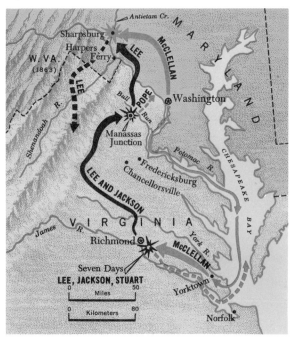

In April 1862 General McClellan finally started the long-awaited offensive against the Confederate capital at Richmond, Virginia. Leaving General Irving McDowell with 40,000 troops to guard Washington, D.C., McClellan transported more than 100,000 troops down the Potomac River. After he seized Yorktown, Virginia, McClellan began a slow, cautious advance up the peninsula between the York and the James rivers (see map 3, this page). By mid-May McClellan's troops were within a few miles of Richmond. Here McClellan paused to wait for reinforcements.

Because of the actions of the brilliant Confederate officer General Thomas J. ("Stonewall") Jackson, McClellan's reinforcements never arrived. In May and June, with only 18,000 soldiers, Jackson fought a series of engagements in the Shenandoah Valley where he defeated Union forces three times larger. Jackson presented a constant threat to Washington, D.C., and kept badly needed reinforcements from reaching McClellan.

In June Confederate troops defending Richmond launched furious counterattacks, known as the Seven Days' Battles, against McClellan's army. Led by General Robert E. Lee, General "Stonewall" Jackson, and the dashing cavalry officer General James E. B. ("Jeb") Stuart, the Confederate troops forced McClellan to drop back to the James River.

On August 29–30, the Confederates won another victory at the Second Battle of Bull Run (see map 3, this page). Union General John Pope, overconfident because of his victories in the western theater, launched a new drive toward Richmond, but Lee and Jackson caught Pope at Bull Run and defeated him.

Encouraged by these successes, the Confederacy decided to stage three powerful offensives. Their goals were (1) to regain control of the Mississippi, (2) to recover the ground lost in Tennessee and Kentucky, and (3) to invade Maryland and draw that state into the Confederacy. All three offensives failed.

On September 4 General Lee crossed the Potomac into Maryland with 40,000 picked troops, confident of victory. On September 17, at Sharpsburg near Antietam Creek (see map 3, this page), Lee engaged General McClellan's force of 70,000 troops and was stopped. The Battle of Antietam was the bloodiest single day of the war. Both sides were so exhausted that McClellan did not try to pursue the Confederates and win a decisive victory.

The Battle of Gettysburg. The year 1863 opened with both sides discouraged. The southern offensive in the fall of 1862 had failed, and the South had begun to despair of winning support from Great Britain and France. The North, although victorious in the western theater, had suffered defeats in the east. The capture of Richmond by the Union seemed extremely remote.

Such was the situation when in June 1863 General Lee again struck into the North. He still hoped to drive a wedge into the Union and deal a fatal blow to the northern war effort. By the end of the month, his army, 75,000 strong, was moving northward across Maryland into Pennsylvania. On June 30, advance patrols of the Confederate and Union armies met at Gettysburg, Pennsylvania (see map 4, this page). For two days the main armies fought desperately on the hills around the town.

On July 3 Lee staked the fate of his army and, as it turned out, of the Confederacy itself on a bid for victory. Led by General George E. Pickett, 15,000 of Lee's finest troops charged up Cemetery Ridge through the devastating fire of Union troops commanded by George G. Meade. For a brief moment, the Confederate battle flag floated on the crest of the ridge. However, the Union forces proved to be too strong, and the broken remnants of Pickett's force had to fall back.

④ Battle of Gettysburg, July 1–3, 1863

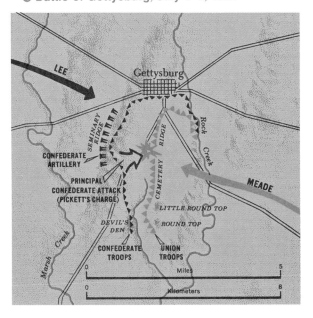

SOURCES

LINCOLN'S GETTYSBURG ADDRESS (1863)

Four score and seven years ago our fathers brought forth on this continent a new nation, conceived in liberty, and dedicated to the proposition that all men are created equal.

Now we are engaged in a great civil war, testing whether that nation, or any nation so conceived and so dedicated, can long endure. We are met on a great battlefield of that war. We have come to dedicate a portion of that field as a final resting place for those who here gave their lives that that nation might live. It is altogether fitting and proper that we should do this.

But, in a larger sense, we cannot dedicate—we cannot consecrate—we cannot hallow—this ground. The brave men, living and dead, who struggled here, have consecrated it far above our poor power to add or detract. The world will little note nor long remember what we say here, but it can never forget what they did here. It is for us, the living, rather, to be dedicated here to the unfinished work which they who fought here have thus far so nobly advanced. It is rather for us to be here dedicated to the great task remaining before us—that from these honored dead we take increased devotion to that cause for which they gave the last full measure of devotion; that we here highly resolve that these dead shall not have died in vain; that this nation, under God, shall have a new birth of freedom; and that government of the people, by the people, for the people, shall not perish from the earth.

The next day, July 4, Lee started his sorrowful but skillful retreat back to Virginia. To Lincoln's disappointment, the overcautious Meade did not pursue the Confederate forces. "Our army held the war in the hollow of their hand," Lincoln said, "and they would not close it. Still, I am very grateful to Meade for the great service he did at Gettysburg."

The battle for Vicksburg. On July 4, 1863, the Union won another victory with the fall of Vicksburg, Mississippi. Starting in March 1863, General Ulysses S. Grant marched his army southward from Memphis and rapidly overcame Confederate opposition in five bat-

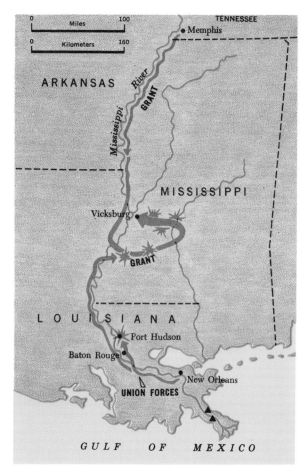

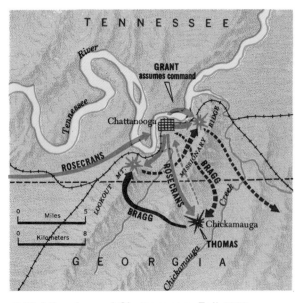

⑤ War in the West: March–July 1863

⑥ Fighting Around Chattanooga: Fall 1863

tles. On May 22 he laid siege to Vicksburg, the stronghold of Confederate forces on the Mississippi (see map 5, this page).

For six weeks Vicksburg held out, suffering terrible punishment from Grant's cannons and from Union gunboats in the river. Finally, on July 4, reduced to starvation, the Confederate defenders surrendered. Five days later Port Hudson, Louisiana, fell into Union hands. Within a week a Union steamboat from St. Louis arrived in New Orleans, which had been held by Union forces for more than a year.

With Union control of the Mississippi River, the Confederacy was finally split in two along the Mississippi. Another of the North's major objectives had been accomplished. The time was approaching for the final drive to end the war.

A Union breakthrough. On September 9, 1863, a Union army under General William S. Rosecrans occupied Chattanooga, Tennessee, a key railway center and gateway to the Deep South (see map 6, this page). Rosecrans then set out after the Confederates, commanded by General Braxton Bragg. Bragg turned on Rosecrans at Chickamauga Creek and defeated him, driving him back into Chattanooga. If troops under General George H. Thomas had not held back the Confederates long enough to allow Rosecrans to retreat, the battle would have ended in utter disaster for the North. For his part in the battle, General Thomas won the title "Rock of Chickamauga" and replaced Rosecrans as commander of the Union army at Chattanooga.

The Union army stayed in Chattanooga until late November. Then, reinforced with fresh troops, the army, under the command of General Grant himself, opened an offensive. In the bitter battles of Lookout Mountain and Missionary Ridge, the Union troops broke through Confederate defenses and opened the way into the Deep South.

Beginning of the end. On March 9, 1864, General Grant became supreme commander of all Union armies. Two months later, on Grant's orders, General William T. Sherman set out from Chattanooga with 100,000 troops to invade Georgia. The greatly outnumbered Confederate army under General Joseph E. Johnston fell back, fighting heroically and destroying railroads and bridges as it retreated. Sherman pushed on relentlessly, and on September 2 he entered Atlanta. Two months later, with some 60,000 troops, he left Atlanta and started toward Savannah, Georgia (see map 7, this page). On December 22 Sherman wired President Lincoln, "I beg to present you as a Christmas gift the city of Savannah."

Behind him on his "March to the Sea," Sherman left a path of destruction 300 miles (480 kilometers) long and 60 miles (96 kilometers) wide. Railroad tracks, heated red-hot in giant bonfires, were twisted around trees and telegraph poles. Bridges lay in tumbled ruins. Crops were uprooted, livestock slaughtered, and farmhouses burned to ashes. Sherman intended to weaken southern resistance, but he also left a legacy of southern bitterness.

By the spring of 1865, Sherman's army was moving northward through the Carolinas. General Joseph E. Johnston's weary army was trying to slow him down.

Meanwhile, in May 1864, General Grant had been hammering away at Richmond, Virginia, pushing through difficult terrain against fierce Confederate resistance (see map 8, this page). Despite enormous losses in this Wilderness Campaign, Grant fought on. "I propose to fight it out along this line if it takes all summer," he wrote.

Appomattox Court House. In the spring of 1865, Sherman's army continued to move northward, and Grant's troops were hammering at the doors of Richmond. On April 2 Lee withdrew from the city.

From Richmond, Lee moved swiftly westward toward Lynchburg, Virginia, with Grant close on his heels (see map 8, this page). Lee thought that he might escape with his army into North Carolina and there join forces with General Johnston, who was as yet undefeated. However, Lee's position was hopeless, and on April 9 he surrendered.

The two generals, Lee and Grant, met in a house in the small village of Appomattox Court House in Virginia. Lee was in full dress uniform with a jewel-studded sword at his side. Grant wore a private's shirt, unbuttoned at the neck. Aided by his military secretary, Lieutenant Colonel Ely Samuel Parker—a Seneca Indian and a civil engineer—Grant drafted the terms of surrender.

Grant offered Lee generous terms. He allowed the officers and soldiers to return to their homes after their promise that they would not again take up arms against the Union. The

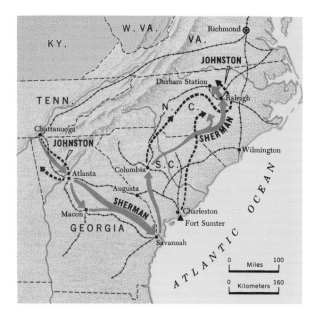

❼ Sherman's Drive to the East and North: May 1864–April 1865

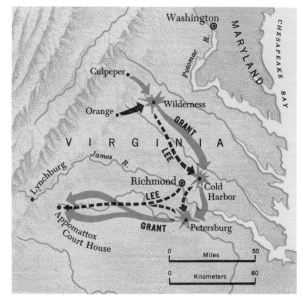

❽ Grant's Campaign Around Richmond: May 1864–April 9, 1865

troops had to surrender their weapons, but Grant permitted Lee's officers to keep their pistols and swords. When Lee mentioned the distressing condition of southern agriculture, Grant said, "Let all the men who claim to own a horse or mule take the animals home with them to work their little farms. This," he said, "will do much toward conciliating our people."

The meeting ended, Lee mounted his horse and rode off. Union troops started to cheer. Grant ordered them to be silent. "The war is over; the rebels are our countrymen again," he said.

Thus the long, bitter conflict ended.

SECTION SURVEY

IDENTIFY: Battles of Bull Run, George McClellan, Army of the Potomac, Henry Halleck, Nathan Forrest, Albert S. Johnston, David Farragut, "Stonewall" Jackson, "Jeb" Stuart, John Pope, George Pickett, George Meade, Joseph E. Johnston, Wilderness Campaign, April 9, 1865.

1. It has been said that the Union blockade was as effective in overpowering the South as were the armies of Grant and Sherman. Explain.

2. (a) What was the purpose of Sherman's "March to the Sea"? (b) What were its consequences?

3. Explain the significance of the battles at Gettysburg and Vicksburg.

4. What were the terms of surrender that Grant offered Lee?

5. Map Study: Select one of the battle or campaign maps appearing on pages 365–69. Study the map. Then describe the battle or campaign in a few paragraphs.

3 Freeing the slaves becomes a goal for the Union

The soldiers dying for the Confederacy and for the Union were not the only Americans willing to sacrifice everything for their beliefs. As the war dragged on, a small but growing number of northern abolitionists began to speak out more loudly. They were determined at all costs to link the freeing of the slaves to the saving of the Union.

Growing abolitionist activity. The war quickened abolitionist activities. Frederick Douglass expressed the view of all abolitionists when he declared that the Union could not be preserved unless the slaves were emancipated, or given their freedom.

The abolitionists added practical reasons to their moral and humane arguments for freeing the slaves. Emancipating the slaves, they said, would encourage slaves to flee the South. This would strike a heavy blow at the southern wartime economy, which depended on slave labor. Moreover, freeing the slaves would rally strong antislavery sentiment elsewhere in the world to the Union side. Soon after the war started, the abolitionists pressured the national government to issue an immediate declaration of emancipation.

Lincoln's early opposition. President Lincoln had long believed slavery to be wrong. However, he now insisted that the issue of slavery had to be subordinated to the main issue of saving the Union. Lincoln feared the emancipation of the slaves would force the border states—Missouri, Kentucky, and Maryland—to leave the Union.

As late as August 1862, Lincoln expressed his reluctance to turn the war into a crusade to free the slaves. "My paramount object in the struggle," he declared, "is to save the Union, and it is not either to save or to destroy slavery. If I could save the Union without freeing any slave, I would do it, and if I could save it by freeing all the slaves, I would do it. And if I could save it by freeing some and leaving others alone, I would do that. What I do about slavery and the colored race I do because I believe it helps to save this Union."

Abolitionist gains. Deeply disappointed, the antislavery forces in Congress challenged the President's position. In April 1862 Congress abolished slavery in the District of Columbia, paying owners for the loss of their slaves. In July of the same year, Congress confiscated the property, including slaves, of all persons who were in rebellion against the Union. A short time later, Congress abolished slavery in United States territories. Congress also supported a plan for giving financial aid to states that would adopt a program for setting slaves free over a period of years. To committed abolitionists, however, these moves by Congress were far from enough.

The Emancipation Proclamation. By September 1862 Lincoln had reluctantly decided that a war fought at least partly to free the slaves would win European support and lessen the danger of foreign intervention on the side of the Confederacy. It would also strike a blow at the Confederacy and win wholehearted sup-

Fleeing to what they hoped was freedom, slaves crossed the Rappahannock River in Virginia to Union lines in 1862. Earlier in the war, not knowing what to do with such slaves, the Union sometimes returned them to their masters.

port for the Union from growing numbers of American abolitionists.

Lincoln prepared an Emancipation Proclamation but kept it secret, waiting for news of a northern victory to add to its impact. On September 22, 1862, five days after Union forces stopped Lee's troops at the bloody Battle of Antietam, Lincoln issued a preliminary Proclamation of Emancipation. In it he declared that all slaves in states or parts of states still fighting against the United States on January 1, 1863, would from that time on be forever emancipated — free, that is, wherever Union armies could liberate them or they could escape to the North.

On January 1, 1863, Lincoln issued his final Emancipation Proclamation. Abolitionists, although pleased, were still skeptical of Lincoln's intentions. For one thing, the Emancipation Proclamation did not free slaves in the border states or in certain parts of Virginia and Louisiana that were under Union control. Lincoln made these exceptions because he was still worried about driving the border states out of the Union. He was also uncertain that the Constitution gave him the authority to free any slaves anywhere.

Despite these criticisms most people in the United States and overseas now concluded that Lincoln had at last clearly stated a second vital issue of the war.

The Thirteenth Amendment. When President Lincoln issued his Emancipation Procla-

mation, he based it upon his constitutional authority as commander in chief of United States military forces. Whether this authority gave him the right to free the slaves — whether, that is, his Proclamation had the force of law — was an unanswered question.

To settle the slavery question once and for all, Congress early in 1865 approved an amendment to the Constitution. This Thirteenth Amendment freed slaves everywhere in the United States and its territories. The amendment was finally ratified by the necessary three fourths of the states eight months after the end of the war.

Continuing discrimination. The Emancipation Proclamation had little effect on the pattern of racial discrimination in the North. Thus black and white abolitionists continued their campaign on federal, state, and local levels of government. As a result of these pressures, Congress repealed a law forbidding black Americans to be employed as mail carriers. Congress in 1865 also passed a law that required horse-drawn streetcars in Washington, D.C., to carry black passengers without discrimination. Sojourner Truth boldly defied conductors and passengers to test this law and was successful.

The Department of State and the Department of Justice ruled in individual cases that black men were citizens. The Supreme Court of the United States for the first time permitted a black lawyer to argue a case before the Court.

371

Because of these actions by branches of the federal government, the Dred Scott decision of 1857 was in effect overturned. That decision, you recall, had denied that a black person could be a citizen (page 354).

With the help of white abolitionists, blacks campaigned in several states for the right to vote and to receive legal equality in courts. In California, Illinois, and Indiana, laws forbidding black Americans to enter these states were challenged. Blacks vigorously attacked segregated public schools. Where they were not able to bring about school desegregation, they demanded improvements in the inferior all-black schools their children attended – when they were able to attend any school at all.

Not all of these campaigns for civil rights succeeded during the war or for a long time thereafter. However, they did start to break down barriers that had set black Americans apart as less than equal citizens.

Aid to fugitives. Northern blacks also took part in efforts to bring relief to fugitive slaves, or **contrabands,** as they were called. During the war years, these people were held in federal camps. Often they faced conditions of gross neglect in these camps.

Church groups and black and white abolitionists organized volunteer aid societies that sent clothing and medical supplies to the contrabands. These societies also prodded the federal government into organizing work and relief opportunities as well as schools for the contrabands. Teachers in these schools were dedicated young abolitionists from the North, black and white. Nevertheless, the efforts made on behalf of the contrabands were small compared with the need.

Black noncombatants in the war. While abolitionists kept up their pressure on the government, black Americans made important contributions to northern victory.

Early in the war, some runaway slaves who reached the Union lines in search of freedom were sent back to Confederate lines. In 1862 Congress finally forbade these practices. In so doing, Congress supported such Union officers as Benjamin Butler and John C. Frémont. These officers had welcomed the fugitives and put them to work at important noncombatant tasks. At that time, northern commanders were forbidden to use blacks, either slave or free, as fighters.

Before the war ended, about 200,000 blacks served the northern fighting forces as noncombatants. Among them were cooks, teamsters, nurses, scouts, spies, and steamboat pilots.

Exclusion from military service. There were several reasons why black Americans, slave and free, were at first forbidden to fight in the war. First, official northern policy stated that the war was being fought to suppress rebellion and restore the Union. Thus the issues of slavery and of black participation in the war were officially downgraded, although they could not be ignored. Second, President Lincoln and other northern officials feared that the use of black soldiers would antagonize the loyal border states. Third, many white northern recruits made it clear that they did not want to serve with black soldiers.

Abolitionists, white and black, denounced the policy of excluding blacks from the Union forces. They declared that it was unfair to prevent black men from fighting for the emancipation of their own people.

The heavy demands of war eventually caused the North to accept black soldiers in the Union army. When it proved harder and harder to recruit white northern soldiers, the rejection of black volunteers could no longer be justified. Several Union generals in the conquered areas of the South asked permission to use black troops and to test their fighting ability. In Louisiana, Union commanders wanted to use free blacks who had organized their own regiment and were eager to fight.

Blacks in military service. These increasing pressures led at last to a change in northern military policy. In the summer of 1862, the War Department authorized the raising of five regiments of black troops in the Sea Islands off the coast of South Carolina, occupied by Union forces. In Massachusetts and other northern states, free blacks were organized into regiments. Before the war ended, about 186,000 black Americans served in northern armed forces, including 29,000 in the navy.

The reluctant admission of blacks into the Union forces did not mean that they lived and fought on equal terms with white soldiers. Black soldiers were less well trained than white soldiers and received less adequate medical services. They frequently were assigned the menial, nonmilitary chores around camp. Although blacks served as noncommissioned

THE COURAGEOUS 54TH

On a hot July evening in 1863, the men of the 54th Massachusetts Regiment found themselves on Morris Island in the harbor of Charleston, South Carolina. In front of them rose the sloping walls of Fort Wagner. A day-long Union artillery bombardment had failed to do much damage, and their orders were to spearhead an assault on the fort.

This was no ordinary engagement. The 54th Massachusetts was composed of the first blacks to be recruited for the Union army. And this was the first time black soldiers had been assigned a key role in a major battle. Moreover, they faced a danger that white troops did not. If captured, according to Confederate law, they were to be treated as outlaws—shot, hanged, or sold into slavery.

The 54th's commanding officer, Colonel Robert Gould Shaw, gave the order "Forward!" and the men advanced. The quiet evening exploded into a storm of gunfire. It seemed impossible that anyone could survive the rain of bullets. But somehow Shaw and 90 of his men clawed their way to the top of the sloping walls. For a moment Shaw stood silhouetted against the sky. Then he was hit and fell, mortally wounded, inside the fort. Some 80 of his troops leaped in after him and fought hand-to-hand until every one of them was killed.

Fort Wagner did not fall that night. (Charleston, in fact, held out until the last year of the war.) The attack on the fort was repulsed with heavy losses. But the courage of the 54th won its men a special place in history.

officers, only a very small number actually received commissions.

Black soldiers were often badly treated, not only by white soldiers but also by northern white civilians. Through most of the war, black soldiers received less pay than white soldiers. Some black troops refused to accept any pay at all until this injustice was ended. Finally, Congress in 1864 provided that black soldiers were to receive the same pay as white soldiers.

Despite the discriminations against them, after 1862, black soldiers and sailors fought bravely in almost all battles of the war. Their courage and ability often astounded their officers and foes. For unusual valor in the Civil War, 21 black Americans received the Congressional Medal of Honor.

SECTION SURVEY

IDENTIFY: Emancipation Proclamation, Thirteenth Amendment, Sojourner Truth.

1. (a) How did the Civil War affect abolitionist activities? (b) How did abolitionist activities affect the war?

2. (a) Why did Lincoln at first oppose freeing the slaves? (b) Why did he change his mind and issue the Emancipation Proclamation?

3. Why was the Thirteenth Amendment passed?

4. (a) In what ways did blacks contribute to the war effort? (b) Why were blacks at first excluded from military service?

5. (a) How were black troops discriminated against? (b) How did abolitionists fight racial discrimination on the home front?

4 The war brings severe hardship and suffering to the South

The appearance of former slaves in the invading northern armies was dramatic proof that the War Between the States was completely transforming the lives of people in the Confederacy.

During the first few weeks of the war, there was excitement—and confidence—in the air. Southern men and boys left for the battlefields, filled with high-spirited notions of adventure. After a few months, casualty lists grew and food and supplies became scarce. The war then became a grim reality, relieved only occasionally by news of a Confederate victory. From 1861 to 1865, the South was a nation in arms.

General Robert E. Lee, commander of the Confederate armies, witnessed many grim scenes of war. After surveying one group of dying soldiers, he said, "It is well that war is so terrible, or we should grow too fond of it."

Raising an army. During the war, by volunteer enlistments and the draft, the Confederacy raised an army of about 400,000 soldiers. In the first year of the war, the Confederacy relied entirely on volunteer enlistments. In April 1862, however, it turned to **conscription,** or the draft. The draft made every white male citizen between 18 and 35 liable for military service.

The draft was unpopular, and many southerners claimed that it was unfair. The original conscription law exempted workers in many occupations. It also permitted a drafted man to hire a substitute. This "substitute" provision favored wealthy people, who could afford to hire substitutes. Poorer people grumbled that the conflict was "a rich man's war and a poor man's fight." Late in 1863 the Confederate government stopped the privilege of hiring substitutes. In 1864 it reduced exemptions and increased draft limits to include all white males between 17 and 50. In the last months of the war, the Confederacy's need for troops grew so desperate that it reluctantly decided to recruit slaves. It promised to set them free if they remained loyal to the end of the war.

States' rights. Many southerners insisted that conscription was contrary to the Confederate constitution. Believing strongly in states' rights, they therefore denied that the Confederate government had the authority to force the citizens of a state into military service. The state authorities in North Carolina refused to enforce the conscription law.

Southerners also objected to other policies of the central government at Richmond on the ground that states' rights were violated. When President Davis suspended the writ of *habeas corpus,* the state courts promptly denied his right to do so. Many southerners applauded the decision of the courts and South Carolinians even talked about seceding from the Confederacy itself.

Southern finances. Raising money was a far more difficult problem for the Confederacy than raising an army, for most southern wealth was in land and slaves. The Union blockade, which cut off most southern trade, also prevented the Confederacy from raising money from customs duties.

Early in the war, patriotic southerners lent $100 million to the Confederacy in return for war bonds, but this source of income was soon

The impact of war is clear in this photo, taken in Richmond, Virginia, the once proud capital of the Confederacy. During the war it was the target of Union attack, though it held out bravely until April 1865, when Lee evacuated the city.

exhausted. The government borrowed another $15 million from abroad and raised about $100 million from taxation. All this income was far from adequate, and the Confederacy had to rely mainly on paper money.

Before the war ended, the government had printed more than $1 billion in Confederate bank notes. The Confederate government promised to exchange these notes for gold or silver "after the ratification of a treaty of peace between the Confederate States and the United States of America." As southern victory became increasingly remote, the Confederate currency steadily declined in value while prices skyrocketed. By 1865 each dollar bill was worth only 1.6 cents in gold. With northern victory the Confederate war bonds and bank notes became worthless.

Southern industry. Paper money was only one reason for skyrocketing prices. Another was the shortage of goods. The Union blockade of southern ports cut off almost all luxuries, such as tea and coffee, as well as many essentials—clothing, hardware, medicines, and soap. As one historian put it, "The blockade was the real destroyer of the South."

Despite heroic efforts, mills and factories in the Confederacy could not supply the needs of either the army or the civilian population. Confederate soldiers often marched without shoes, slept without blankets, and lived in ragged clothing. Fortunately for the Confederates, they managed to capture large supplies of food, clothing, and munitions.

Agriculture and transportation. Civilians felt the pinch of hard times even more than the soldiers. City families especially suffered from the shortage of goods and the soaring prices. By 1863 many southerners were facing near-starvation.

This tragic situation was not caused by lack of food, for the South was an agricultural region. Despite the flight of slaves to the Union lines, there was still enough labor, slave and free, to work the farms and plantations. The serious problem was lack of transportation.

When the war started, the Confederacy had only about 9,000 miles (14,500 kilometers) of railroads out of a total of more than 30,000 miles (48,000 kilometers) for the entire country. Southern planters had depended largely on the rivers to send their cotton to the seaports. As the war continued, the Confederacy had difficulty keeping even its limited railroad mileage in operation. Southerners tore up branch lines and used branch line engines, cars, and rails to keep main lines in operation. The southern transportation problem grew increasingly severe. Before the war ended, people in Richmond rioted for food while barns in the Shenandoah Valley were filled with wheat.

During the last few months of the war, the food shortage became so desperate that many Confederate soldiers deserted to get back home and help feed their families. The war brought sorrow and suffering to rich and poor alike in the South.

SECTION SURVEY

IDENTIFY: conscription, writ of *habeas corpus.*

1. (a) Describe the changes in the way the South raised troops during the war. (b) Why did many southerners object to military conscription?
2. What methods did the Confederate government use to raise money for the war?
3. Why was issuing huge amounts of paper money harmful to the South?
4. How did each of the following help to defeat the South: (a) the Union blockade, (b) lack of industry, (c) lack of transportation?

5 Life behind Union lines undergoes important changes

Northerners, with their superiority in material resources, never experienced the hardship and suffering endured by southerners. Nevertheless, the war created problems and brought many changes in northern life.

Raising an army. During the war more than 2 million soldiers, including 186,000 blacks, served in the Union forces. The North, like the South, at first recruited its troops by volunteer enlistments. In March 1863, however, Congress passed a conscription law making all able-bodied male citizens between 20 and 45 liable for military service. As in the South, the law allowed a drafted man to hire a substitute.

The federal law also permitted a drafted man to buy exemption from military service by paying $300 to the government.

The Conscription Act aroused violent opposition, especially among recent immigrants from Ireland. The Irish newcomers did not want to be forced to fight a war that was likely to increase the number of free black workers, with whom they competed for unskilled jobs. Moreover, black workers, unable to get jobs, at times broke strikes organized by Irish dockworkers and other laborers. Racial tensions then reached the boiling point.

Riots, combining opposition to the draft with opposition to blacks, broke out in a number of cities. The most serious riot, beginning on July 13, 1863 in New York City, lasted for four terror-filled days. Mobs of whites burned an orphan asylum for black children. They demolished shops and houses of black Americans as well as those of white abolitionists. Seventy-six people were killed.

The bounty system. The draft provided only a small fraction of the Union troops. Much more effective as a means of raising troops was the bounty system. To attract volunteers, federal, state, and local governments each paid a bounty to all who volunteered for service. When the bounties were totaled, a man might receive as much as $1,000 for enlisting.

While the bounty system was an effective recruitment device, it did give rise to the dishonest practice of "bounty jumping." A volunteer would enlist in one locality and collect bounties. Then he would desert and re-enlist under another name in another locality and collect additional bounties. Some "bounty jumpers" enlisted and deserted as many as 20 or 30 times before they were caught.

Northern finances. To raise money for the war, the North relied on four sources of revenue: the tariff, war bonds, an income tax, and issuance of paper money.

From 1832 to 1861, southern planters and many western farmers had opposed high tariffs. In 1861, however, with several southern states out of the Union, the Republicans in Congress promptly passed the Morrill Tariff Act. This raised import duties to an average of 25 percent of the value of the imported goods. The Morrill Tariff Act protected American manufacturers from the competition of European rivals. After war broke out, Congress

The Union navy underwent a major buildup during the Civil War. It was especially important in cutting off shipping into and out of southern ports. This is the crew of the U.S.S. *Hunchback* during a brief lull in the action.

raised the rates until by 1864 they reached an average of 47 percent, the highest rates up to that time.

Southern planters and midwestern farmers had also favored a decentralized banking system. In such a system, state and local banks could issue their own bank notes and make loans with little if any federal control. After 1861, however, the Republican Congress adopted a law that did away with state bank notes and established a system of national banks.

In 1863 Congress passed the National Banking Act. The new law permitted five or more individuals with a capital of $50,000 to organize a national bank. The bank directors were required to invest at least one third of the bank's capital in United States bonds. When the bank had deposited these bonds with the Secretary of the Treasury, it was allowed to issue national bank notes up to 90 percent of the value of the bonds. This provision had two important effects. First, it encouraged banks to buy government bonds (that is, to lend the government money). Second, it provided a sound and uniform currency for the entire country.

Neither the tariff nor the sale of government bonds, however, provided enough money to pay northern war costs. Therefore, Congress passed an income tax. By the war's end, incomes between $600 and $5,000 were being taxed 5 percent. Incomes of $5,000 or more were being taxed 10 percent.

Congress also issued paper money, known as **greenbacks** because the back of the money was usually printed in green. The value of the greenbacks, like the value of the Confederate paper money, depended upon the government's ability to redeem them in gold or silver at some future date. Thus their value rose with every northern victory and fell with every northern defeat. At one point the greenback dollar was worth only 35 cents in gold, but by the war's end it was worth 78 cents. Paper money helped to drive prices upward, but inflation never got out of hand as it did in the South.

Booming northern industry. Inflation did not get out of hand in the North partly because northern industry could produce all the materials needed by the armed services and the civilian population. With the tariff to protect them from foreign competition and huge war orders to meet, manufacturers built new factories during the war years. Thus the war continued a development that was well under way before 1861.

The war also stimulated the development and use of laborsaving machines. Elias Howe's sewing machine, first patented in 1846, enabled clothing manufacturers to produce uniforms more rapidly for the Union armies. An

377

Industrial development in the North produced several new types of weapons. The North soon had a fleet of ironclad, steam-powered Union gunboats to patrol rivers and to enforce the blockade. This fleet, for example, bombarded Vicksburg, Mississippi, and carried troops across the Mississippi River for an attack.

improved version of a shoe-making machine patented by Gordon McKay in 1862 made it possible to mass-produce shoes.

There was a great deal of profiteering during the war as greedy businesses took unfair profits at a time of national crisis. Even worse, there were cases of outright fraud. Some manufacturers sold the government blankets and uniforms of such poor quality that they fell apart in the first heavy rains.

Agricultural expansion. Northeastern and midwestern agriculture also boomed during the war. It was stimulated by government aid, war orders, and the development of laborsaving machines.

The Republican Party, as you have read, represented a combination of midwestern farmers and northeastern business groups. It is not surprising, therefore, that the Republican Congress passed laws favorable to farmers.

The Homestead Act of 1862 gave 160 acres (64.8 hectares) of land to anyone who paid a small registration fee and lived on the land as a **homestead** for five years. Under this act, between 1862 and 1865 the United States government gave about 2.5 million acres (over 1 million hectares) of land in the **public domain** — government land — to some 15,000 settlers. Much of this land now available for homesteads had been owned by Indians who ceded their rights in Texas and Kansas and much of Nebraska to the government.

In 1862 the government also adopted two other measures to aid agriculture as well as industry. (1) It created the United States Department of Agriculture. (2) With the Morrill Act of 1862, it launched the United States upon a huge program of agricultural and industrial education. The Morrill Act gave each state 30,000 acres (12,140 hectares) of land for each Senator and Representative it had in Congress under the 1860 census. The income from the sale or rental of this land was to be used to support at least one college in which agriculture and the mechanic arts, such as engineering,

SOURCES

HOMESTEAD ACT (1862)

Any person who is the head of a family, or who has arrived at the age of twenty-one years, and is a citizen of the United States . . . shall . . . be entitled to one quarter-section or a less quantity of . . . public lands, upon which said person may have filed a . . . claim.

Northern industry also gave the Union army giant mortars like this one that could fire at cities and armies from great distances. Because of such weapons and because of other advances in transportation and communication used by the armies, the Civil War is sometimes considered to be the first modern war.

were to be emphasized. These colleges came to be called "land grant colleges."

Farmers of the northeastern and midwestern states prospered with rising prices and a ready market for all they could produce. With money in their pockets, thousands of farmers were able to buy such laborsaving machinery as mechanical reapers, which had been invented by Obed Hussey and Cyrus H. McCormick in the early 1830's. The reaper, improved plows, and other farm machinery helped to speed a revolution in agriculture.

Growth of the railroads. Railroads also prospered during the war. For example, the value of Erie Railroad stock increased sevenfold in three years. New lines were built, many with the help of government **subsidies,** or financial aids, and land grants. These railroad lines helped to unite the states of the Northeast and the Middle West.

During the war the Republican Congress decided to build a transcontinental railroad, which people had been talking about for a long time. In 1862 Congress granted a charter to the Union Pacific Railroad, and California granted one to the Central Pacific Railroad. The charter authorized them to build a railway between Omaha, in Nebraska Territory, and California. Congress also promised the railroads liberal cash subsidies and generous gifts of land along the right of way. The actual con-

struction did not begin until after the war had ended. However, the subsidies and land grants approved by Congress and the President showed how far the new Republican government was prepared to go in providing federal aid for business and industry.

The changes that took place behind the Union lines from 1861 to 1865 were of great importance to the nation's future. In particular, the growth of industry, stimulated by the war, gained momentum in the years following the war.

SECTION SURVEY

IDENTIFY: "bounty jumpers," National Banking Act, greenbacks, Elias Howe, profiteering, Homestead Act of 1862, land grant colleges, Cyrus McCormick, subsidies.

1. (a) What methods did the North use to raise an army? (b) What abuses developed in this process? (c) Why did some recent Irish immigrants object to the draft?

2. Describe the methods used by the North to finance the war.

3. Why was there an industrial boom in the North during the war? How did the war affect the growth of technology?

4. What conditions promoted agricultural prosperity during the war?

5. What steps did Congress take during the war to encourage the building of railroads?

6 The Union faces political problems at home and abroad

The war thrust an almost unbearable burden on President Lincoln. Even while he was occupied with the fighting itself, he had to deal with a host of other problems, including foreign affairs.

Great Britain and France. During the first two years of war, the governments of Great Britain and France were friendly to the Confederate States of America. There were reasons why many Europeans wanted the South to win. European manufacturers, particularly the British, looked forward to the creation of a new nation. They thought the Confederacy would provide them with cotton and other raw materials and, at the same time, place no tariffs on the importation of their manufactured goods. European shipowners looked forward to the weakening of their business competitors in New England and the Middle Atlantic states.

To be sure, millions of Europeans hoped for the end of slavery in the South. However, Lincoln at first discouraged these people when he made it clear that he was fighting the war not to free the slaves but to preserve the Union.

Strained relations. Only a few months after the war started, one incident nearly led to a disastrous break between the United States and Great Britain. A Union warship commanded by Captain Charles Wilkes stopped a British steamer, the *Trent*, and seized two Confederate commissioners to Great Britain and France— James M. Mason and John Slidell. The British, furious at this violation of their rights as a neutral, talked of war with the United States and actually sent troops to Canada. President Lincoln managed to avoid trouble by releasing the two Confederate agents and admitting that Wilkes had been wrong.

Even more serious was the problem of Confederate warships built in British shipyards. Some of these warships, among them the *Florida* and the *Alabama,* left Great Britain in the summer of 1862 and began to destroy Union merchant vessels. Great Britain stopped the construction of other such Confederate warships when the American minister to Great Britain warned the British foreign minister that "this is war."

Northern victories on the battlefield and the Emancipation Proclamation issued by President Lincoln finally ended the threat of foreign intervention in the war in favor of the Confederacy.

The Copperheads. Foreign intervention was not the only danger that the Union faced. In the North—as well as in the South—there was from the beginning active opposition to the war. Leaders of the opposition in the North were called "Copperheads" by Union sympathizers, after the poisonous snake of that name. The Copperheads argued that the war's costs in lives, money, and loss of personal liberty were too great to be justified. They also argued that the South could not be defeated and that the war was therefore useless. Finally, they insisted that even if the North should win, a Union based on compulsion was a denial of the Constitution and of democracy.

The strength of the Copperheads, most of whom were members of the Democratic Party, varied from place to place and from month to month. The more extreme Copperheads organized secret societies called the Knights of the Golden Circle and the Sons of Liberty. They discouraged enlistment and encouraged men to desert from the army. They also helped Confederate prisoners to escape and smuggled war materials into the Confederacy.

The most influential Copperhead leader was Clement L. Vallandigham, a member of Congress from Ohio. He was finally arrested in 1863 and convicted of opposing the war effort. Lincoln banished him to the Confederacy, but Vallandigham promptly moved to Canada.

The election of 1864. Dissatisfaction over the war split the Democratic Party. In the election of 1864, many Democrats joined the Republicans to form the Union Party. This party chose Lincoln for the Presidency and Andrew Johnson of Tennessee, a former Democratic member of Congress but an opponent of the Confederacy, for the Vice-Presidency. The Democratic Party responded by naming General George B. McClellan as its candidate for the Presidency.

Antiwar feeling was running so high in 1864 that President Lincoln fully expected to be defeated. "We are now on the brink of destruction," he wrote to a friend. "It appears to

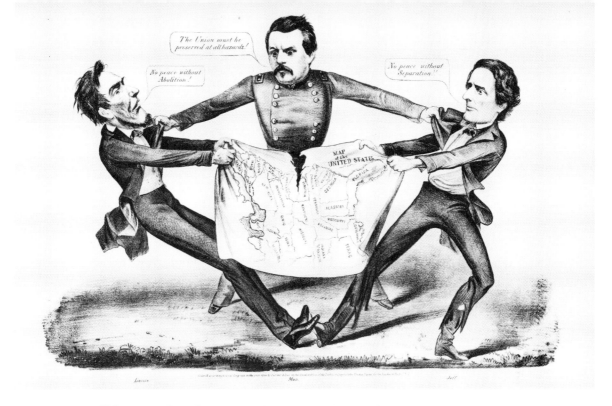

This cartoon from the 1864 election seems to favor McClellan, who tries to keep his opponent, Lincoln, and Jefferson Davis from pulling the Union apart. But the voters gave Lincoln 212 electoral votes to McClellan's 21.

me that the Almighty is against me, and I can hardly see a ray of hope."

The tide of the war turned in favor of the North shortly before the election. Sherman's capture of Atlanta convinced many voters that the end of the war was near. Moreover, Lincoln's opponent, General McClellan, refused to support the platform of his own Democratic Party, which declared that the war was a failure and ought to be stopped immediately. As a result, Lincoln won an overwhelming victory, receiving 212 electoral votes to 21 for the Democratic candidate. That a Presidential election was successfully held in wartime was in itself a victory for representative government.

Expanding roles for women. The continuing strength of representative government during the war did not bring any broadening of the suffrage to include women. In fact, leaders in the women's rights movement largely suspended their activities to work for other causes. Several, including a 20-year-old newcomer to the movement, Anna E. Dickinson, spoke publicly for the Union cause.

Elizabeth Cady Stanton (page 326) organized the National Woman's Loyal League. The League supported the abolitionist effort to convert the war into one for the emancipation of the slaves. Her friend and associate Susan B. Anthony provided leadership in the collection of 400,000 petitions in support of the Thirteenth Amendment. Lucy Stone, an Oberlin graduate and an effective speaker and worker, also supported the National Woman's Loyal League. After the war, she helped organize the American Equal Rights Association, which sought voting rights for blacks and women.

While the cause of women's rights made little progress during the war, other important developments were taking place. Women on both sides of the conflict demonstrated their organizational skill and the capacity for hard work in activities for which they had little or no experience. Their important contributions to the war effort in both North and South gave them greater self-confidence and opened new possibilities to them. On farms and plantations, they did the work of their husbands, fathers, and brothers. They taught in schools, replacing men who were now soldiers. As never before, their efforts were needed in mills, factories, munitions plants, shops, banks, and government offices.

Women had long been employed in textile factories, but the war sent them into other factories as well. These women are at work in a factory making bullets for northern guns.

At the start of the war, army medical services scarcely existed in the Confederacy and were woefully inadequate in the North. Before the war was over, at least 3,200 northern and southern women had served as full-time army nurses. Dorothea Dix (page 327) served as Superintendent of Nurses in the Union armies. She brought some order and efficiency into hastily improvised hospitals, despite army prejudice against the presence of women. Clara Barton, with no official position, collected medical supplies and food and managed, against great odds, to get them to battlefields where they were most needed. "Mother" Ann Brickerdyke—colorful, brusque, and completely devoted to her "soldier boys"—defied army red tape and introduced sanitation, proper food, and medical supplies into many Union army hospitals. In the Confederacy, Phoebe Pember, Ella Newsom, and Kate Cummings were outstanding among hundreds of women who cared for the sick and wounded in army hospitals.

At the outbreak of the Civil War, 20,000 women's relief societies were organized in the North and South. These societies staffed canteens, sewed uniforms, made bandages, and collected medicines. Lacking an overall organization, southern women in these societies nevertheless carried out desperately needed relief work. In the North, the women's societies raised about $15 million for war relief.

Policy toward the Indians. In the 1860's most American Indians had no interest in fighting what was, essentially, white America's civil war. Still, it is estimated that about 3,000 Indians fought on the northern side. Meanwhile, the southerners recruited four brigades from the Five Civilized Tribes, then living in Indian Territory, and with their help attempted to control the area that is now New Mexico and Arizona.

Some ominous events also took place. In the new state of Minnesota, the Eastern Sioux became angry when they failed to receive promised payments and grew resentful at injustices by government agents and settlers. They burned and looted Minnesota farms and towns and killed about 500 settlers and soldiers. Retaliation was swift and brutal. At Mankato 38 Indians were publicly hanged.

In the Colorado Territory, Arapahos and Cheyennes resented the intrusion of miners and ranchers on their lands. They raided stagecoach stations and ranches and murdered a white family. In reprisal, Colonel J. M. Chivington, a preacher commanding a unit of militia, surprised a larger group of Indians at Sand Creek and killed 500 of them, including women and children. Mutilation of the Indian bodies by the militia matched in brutality practices long condemned in Indian fighting. General Nelson A. Miles of the United States Army later called the Sand Creek massacre "the foulest and most unjustifiable crime in the annals of America."

The violence in Minnesota and Colorado were omens of the conflict between Indians and whites that was to break out when the Civil War ended.

SECTION SURVEY

IDENTIFY: *Trent* affair, Clement L. Vallandigham, suffrage, Elizabeth Cady Stanton, Lucy Stone, Clara Barton, Sand Creek massacre.

1. Why did some European governments sympathize with the Confederacy?
2. (a) Who were the Copperheads? (b) What were their opinions on the war?
3. (a) What were the issues in the election of 1864? (b) Why was this election a victory for representative government?
4. How did women contribute to the war effort in the North and the South?
5. Describe relations between Indians and the United States government during the Civil War.

Chapter Survey

Summary: Tracing the Main Ideas

In 1865 the terrible trial by fire and sword came to an end and the nation estimated its losses.

The war cost the southern states more than a billion dollars, the northern states several times that amount. After all pensions and other costs were paid, the war probably cost the American people a total of ten billion dollars — an equivalent in today's dollars of many, many times that amount.

The conflict was also terribly costly in life. Not counting those permanently injured and maimed, the North lost about 369,000 men. The South lost about 258,000 men. There were also the uncounted losses of women and children as well as men from hunger, starvation, and disease.

The war had many far-reaching results. It ended the institution of slavery. It settled once and for all the doctrine of secession. It strengthened the Union by increasing the power of the federal government at the expense of the states. It strengthened democracy by showing that a representative form of government could operate successfully in wartime. Not least important, the four-year ordeal helped to speed the development of American industry.

In the spring of 1865, the people of the United States stood on the threshold of a new era. New opportunities were opening before them. But of course they could not know this at the time. They could look only into the immediate future. And the big problem they faced, northerners and southerners alike, was "to bind the nation's wounds" and join hands as a reunited people.

Inquiring into History

1. Select one battle or campaign of the Civil War. Explain how the fighting and outcome of the battle or campaign illustrated the strengths and weaknesses of each side.
2. Explain the differences between the Emancipation Proclamation and the Thirteenth Amendment.
3. Discuss Lincoln's attitude toward black Americans. Explain how some of his beliefs changed over time.
4. It has been said that the Gettysburg Address contains one of the great definitions of democracy. (a) What important democratic ideals are explained in the speech? (b) Which ideas are held in common by the Declaration of Independence, the Preamble to the Constitution, and the Gettysburg Address?
5. The Civil War caused changes in the roles of women. (a) What kinds of situations and jobs did the war open up to them? (b) Do you think that wars have generally had an effect on the roles of women in American society? Why or why not?

Relating Past to Present

1. Lincoln suspended the writ of *habeas corpus* and suppressed freedom of speech and freedom of the press during the war. Does a national crisis justify suspension of civil liberties? Should the President have this power? Should Congress have this power? Explain your answers.
2. Lincoln's unpopularity in the North increased as the war continued. In America's more recent wars, has a similar thing ever happened to a President? Explain.

Developing Social Science Skills

1. Study the photographs in this chapter, such as the one of Richmond, Virginia, on page 375. (a) What impressions of the Civil War do you get from the photographs? (b) How valuable are such photographs as a source of information about the war? Explain.
2. Find a record or a songbook of Civil War songs, such as "Dixie" and "The Battle Cry of Freedom." (Make sure that you have songs from both the North and the South.) (a) How does each song reflect the northern or southern point of view? (b) What is the general mood or tone of the songs? (c) How does each song make you feel about the war?
3. Suppose you lived during the Civil War and had a brother fighting in the army. Write a letter to him describing life at home. Be sure to include experiences that show how your life is being affected by the war and how you view issues such as conscription.

Unit Survey

Projects and Activities

1. The timeline here lists political events before and during the Civil War. Of course, not every political event is listed. Study the five events named below. Explain whether or not it would be appropriate to list each event on the timeline. (a) 1820: Missouri Compromise, (b) 1848: Mexican War ends, (c) 1861: Civil War begins, (d) 1864: Sand Creek Massacre, (e) 1865: Freedmen's Bureau formed.
2. Write a newspaper account of (a) the Lincoln-Douglas debates, (b) "bleeding Kansas," or (c) the creation of the Confederate States of America.
3. Compare the maps on pages 346 and 352 in terms of (a) size of the United States, (b) extent of slave and free area, (c) number of states. Note specific changes that occurred between 1820 and 1854.
4. Draw two political cartoons about the Dred Scott decision—one favoring the opinion and one opposing it.
5. Prepare a bulletin board display on a phase of the Civil War, including such items as pictures, maps, newspaper articles, and songs.

Exploring Your Region

1. (a) To what extent was your local area involved in the Civil War? (For example, did local men fight in the war? Did local women help provide supplies for the army?) (b) How was your local area affected by the outcome of the war?
2. Turn to the map on page 354. (a) Locate your state. (b) In 1854, was it a state or a territory? (c) Was slavery permitted in the area? Explain how you can tell from the map.

For Further Inquiry

1. Why did the Civil War happen? Give evidence to support your answer.
2. Describe (a) the sequence of events that led to the secession of 11 states and (b) the disputes that arose in the border states.
3. (a) What were the war aims of the North? (b) Had the North accomplished those aims by the end of the war?
4. Why did the North win the Civil War? Explain fully.
5. One result of the Civil War was the strengthening of democracy. Do you agree or disagree? Why?
6. How did the Civil War affect the lives of (a) women, (b) blacks, (c) Indians? Why did it have those effects?
7. In what ways are the American Revolution and the Civil War similar? (b) How are they different?

Suggested Readings

1. *President of the Confederacy, Jefferson Davis,* Margaret Green. Life story of the man who served his country as soldier, Representative, Senator, but who will always be remembered as leader of the South during the Civil War.
2. *Cornelia, The Story of a Civil War Nurse,* Jane McConnell. A beautiful Quaker girl leaves her home to nurse Union soldiers during the Civil War.
3. *Glory Road, Stillness at Appomattox,* and others, Bruce Catton. This leading expert on the Civil War has written numerous excellent histories on various aspects of the war.
4. *Worth Fighting For,* Agnes McCarthy and Lawrence Reddick. The true story of black Americans during the Civil War.
5. *Red Badge of Courage,* Stephen Crane. A classic novel of the Civil War, told from the point of view of a young Union soldier.

Unit Six

Rebuilding
the Nation

1865-1900

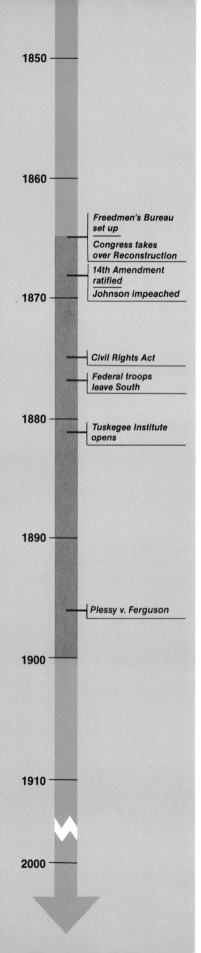

1850

1860

Freedmen's Bureau
set up

Congress takes
over Reconstruction

14th Amendment
ratified

Johnson impeached

1870

Civil Rights Act

Federal troops
leave South

1880

Tuskegee Institute
opens

1890

Plessy v. Ferguson

1900

1910

2000

Chapter 19

Restoring the South to the Union

1865-1900

After the Civil War came to an end, bitterness between the North and the South continued for many years. In part this was the inevitable result of a terrible conflict in which most people on each side believed that their cause was right and just.

However, equally important as a cause of resentment was the decade of rebuilding the Union that followed the war. During this period bitter feelings arose over the stubborn political and constitutional problems involved in bringing the southern states back into the Union. There were also the grave economic problems of rebuilding devastated southern industries and reopening normal trade relations among the states. Finally, there was the continuing social problem of bringing black Americans into the mainstream of national life.

As you will read in this and the next chapter, these problems had to be dealt with at a time when both the North and the South faced a breakdown of public morality. Corruption then reached into every level of government—local, state, and national. This breakdown was due not only to the war, which had dislocated life in every section of the country. It was brought about also by the changes taking place in the United States during the latter half of the 1800's—the rapid development of industry, a flood of immigration, and the growth of cities.

THE CHAPTER IN OUTLINE

1. President Lincoln strives for lenient reconstruction.

2. The nation struggles to restore order in the South.

3. The Radical Republicans enact a program of reconstruction.

4. White southerners regain control of their state governments.

5. The New South advances in agriculture, industry, and education.

6. Black southerners struggle for a place in the New South.

1 President Lincoln strives for lenient reconstruction

On March 4, 1865, when the war was rapidly drawing to an end, President Lincoln stated the policy of reconstruction he intended to follow in regard to the South. The sullen roar of the cannons massed in front of Richmond would soon be stilled, but the moving language of Abraham Lincoln's Second Inaugural Address was destined to live on as part of the nation's heritage.

"With malice toward none," he said, "with charity for all, with firmness in the right, as God gives us to see the right, let us strive on to finish the work we are in, to bind up the nation's wounds, to care for him who shall have borne the battle, and for his widow, and his orphan—to do all which may achieve and cherish a just and lasting peace among ourselves and with all nations."

Lincoln's program. Lincoln's were not idle words. He had already begun to develop a program of reconstruction based upon "charity for all," and he fully intended to carry out that program.

As early as December 8, 1863, Lincoln outlined his program for restoring the South to the Union in his Proclamation of Amnesty° and Reconstruction. The practical, flexible program rested on Lincoln's theory that the Confederate states had never succeeded in leaving the Union. They had for a time left the family circle, but they were still part of the family. The immediate problem was to get them back into the circle quickly.

First, he offered full pardon to all southerners who would take an oath of allegiance to the Union and promise to accept federal laws and proclamations dealing with slavery. The only southerners who were excluded from Lincoln's offer were those who had resigned positions in the federal government to serve in the Confederacy, members of the Confederate government, high-ranking Confederate army and naval officers, and Confederates who had mistreated prisoners of war.

Second, Lincoln declared that a state could draw up a new constitution, elect new officials,

°**amnesty:** a broad pardon for offenses committed against a government.

and return to the Union on a basis of full equality with all other states when it met certain conditions. A minimum number of persons (at least 10 percent of those who had voted in the election of 1860) must take the oath of allegiance. Each person taking the oath must have been a qualified voter in the state before its secession from the Union.

In 1863 this program applied only to areas conquered by Union armies. Lincoln intended to apply it to all other Confederate areas as soon as they were in Union hands. Lincoln did not insist that this proposal was the only acceptable one. He agreed that Congress must give final approval to admitting members of Congress from the reconstructed states. More-

Lincoln pledged that "when I come to lay down the reins of power, [even if] I lost every other friend on earth, I shall at least have one friend left, and that friend shall be down inside me."

over, as time passed, Lincoln revealed flexibility in his own thinking. For example, in a letter written in 1864, he stated that the restoration of the southern states to the Union "must rest upon the principle of civil and political equality of both races; and it must be sealed by a general amnesty." In his last public address, delivered on April 11, 1865, only four days before his death, he declared that he favored giving the vote to those blacks who had fought for the Union and to those with some educational qualifications.

Opposition to Lincoln's program. Not all Republican leaders agreed with Lincoln's ideas on reconstruction. Many opposed the idea of pardoning former Confederates and allowing them to vote and hold office. These Republican leaders doubted the loyalty of former Confederates. They also doubted whether, if given political power, the former Confederates would permit blacks to enjoy legal and political rights.

The Republicans who were most opposed to Lincoln's reconstruction policy were called Radicals. The Radical Republicans were by no means a well-defined group. Different Radicals took different positions on political and economic issues and on methods of readmitting the former Confederate states. The two most outspoken Radicals were Senator Charles Sumner of Massachusetts and Representative Thaddeus Stevens of Pennsylvania.

Senator Sumner insisted on measures to guarantee the political and legal equality of black Americans and to educate them for the responsibilities of freedom. Representative Stevens wanted to punish the South for all the injustices and discriminations that black southerners had suffered under white rule. Stevens also wanted to do everything possible to make sure that in the future the freed slaves would be treated justly. Stevens also believed that political and legal rights for former slaves would be meaningless if the blacks did not have economic independence. He urged that the estates of "rebel traitors" be divided up and given to the freed slaves. Few Radical Republicans accepted so extreme a policy.

During the war and in the months following Confederate surrender, a majority of Republican leaders, more moderate in their views, lined up with Lincoln's reconstruction policies. However, many moderates agreed with the Radicals that Lincoln, in exercising his war powers, had encroached upon the constitutional powers of the legislative branch. They all felt that Congress, not the President, should lay down the rules for restoring the southern states to the Union.

Some Republicans frankly admitted that their thinking about reconstruction was influenced by practical politics. They believed that, when the war ended, white southerners would reject the wartime Republican Party and flock to the Democratic Party. Southern Democrats returning to Congress would probably support northern Democrats, thus making the Republicans a minority party. Such a combination might endanger measures supported by many Republicans—a high tariff, national banks, free land, and federal aid to railroads.

The Republicans could keep the Democrats from gaining majority power in state as well as federal governments in two ways. First, they could give voting rights to the former slaves. These new voters would support the Republicans at the polls in gratitude for emancipation. Second, they could keep former Confederate leaders from voting and holding public office.

Such political considerations played some part in shaping the attitudes of many Republicans toward reconstruction. Historians disagree as to how large a part. However, many Republican members of Congress approached the difficult problems of reconstruction with a genuine desire to help the freed slaves and to guarantee them fair treatment in American life.

The Wade-Davis Bill. Opposition to President Lincoln's plan for reconstruction found expression in the Wade-Davis Bill. Some Radical Republican members of Congress thought the bill was too mild. However, enough moderate Republicans supported it to allow the bill to be passed by a slender majority in early July 1864.

The Wade-Davis Bill provided for readmitting the southern states into the Union under harsher conditions than those favored by Lincoln. The bill was intended to give political power to southerners who had remained loyal to the Union. It was also intended to insure that the new constitutions of the southern states would recognize the freedom of black southerners. Finally, the bill was intended to insure that Confederate war debts were **repudiated,** or not paid.

President Lincoln refused to sign the Wade-Davis Bill. He felt that its rigid provisions

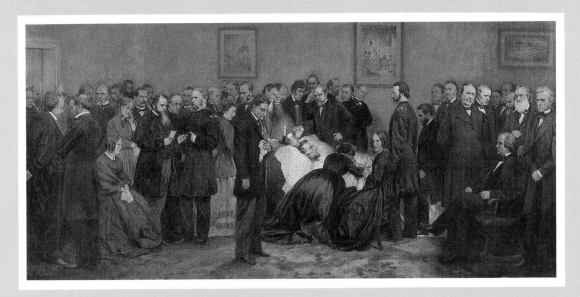

THE DEATH OF LINCOLN

It was Friday—Good Friday—April 14, 1865. The long war was finally over, and President and Mrs. Lincoln had arranged to go to the theater with friends. The play was a popular comedy called *Our American Cousin.*

At Ford's Theater the Lincoln party watched the performance from a special box that had been draped with flags. Shortly after ten o'clock, a former actor named John Wilkes Booth slipped quietly into the President's box. Resting his pistol on the back of Lincoln's chair, he shot the President in the head. Then Booth jumped to the stage, shouting "*Sic semper tyrannis!* [Thus always to tyrants!] The South is avenged!"

They carried Lincoln to a house across the street, for he was too badly wounded to be taken back to the White House. There he lay unconscious for hours. One eyewitness wrote that "the giant sufferer lay extended diagonally across the bed, which was not long enough for him." Physicians, cabinet officers, Mrs. Lincoln, their son Robert—all gathered in the small room.

What of Booth? He was a proslavery fanatic who apparently decided to kill Lincoln after the President's speech of April 11, in which he advocated limited suffrage for blacks. The assassin broke his left leg as he leaped to the stage but escaped on horseback. He ended up hiding in a Virginia barn, where he was found by Union soldiers. Whether Booth was shot or took his own life is unclear, but his end came on April 26.

Lincoln had lingered on through the night of April 14 and into the dark and gloomy morning of the next day. About seven o'clock he breathed his last. When told of Lincoln's death, Secretary of War Edwin Stanton said sadly, "Now he belongs to the ages."

would restrict him when the time came to rebuild the Union. He also believed that Congress did not have the constitutional authority to compel a state to abolish slavery. Abolition of slavery, he believed, would require an amendment to the Constitution.

Lincoln's assassination. Whether or not Lincoln could have won acceptance of his policy must remain unanswered. On April 14, 1865, he was assassinated in Washington, D.C., by John Wilkes Booth, an actor.

Sorrow and anger gripped the nation—South as well as North, black as well as white. White southerners had despised Lincoln during the war. Yet many had come to feel that he was a wise, compassionate leader who offered the best program of reconstruction. Flags flew at halfmast, bells tolled, and weeping crowds filed through the funeral train as it stopped in cities between Washington, D.C., and Lincoln's burial place in Springfield, Illinois. Meanwhile, Vice-President Andrew Johnson became President.

President Johnson. Andrew Johnson was a self-educated man. Without any formal schooling, he had spent his boyhood as a tailor's apprentice. Later his devoted wife had helped him to improve his meager writing ability. While still a young man, he was elected mayor of his community, a small mountain village in eastern Tennessee. This was the beginning of a political career in the Democratic Party that took him to the Senate of the United States in 1857. Although he owned a few slaves, Johnson disliked the large planters who were so influential in the South. He had resisted the secession of Tennessee in 1861.

Johnson's service for the Union during the war won him an appointment as military governor of Tennessee. He was responsible for controlling those areas of his state occupied by Union troops. When the Republicans, including Lincoln himself, feared that they might lose the Presidential election in 1864, Johnson, a Democrat, was placed on the "Union" ticket. The hope of the Republicans was that he would draw votes for Lincoln.

Andrew Johnson had many admirable qualities. He possessed a stubborn fighting spirit and the moral courage to act according to his convictions. Unfortunately, he was not a flexible man. Whereas Lincoln always tried to understand the positions of his political opponents, Johnson tended to insist upon the rightness of his own views. Johnson lacked sufficient patience, tact, and political skill to be the effective leader that the nation needed at this critical time in its history.

Johnson and reconstruction. One of Johnson's first decisions as President was to offer rewards for the arrest of Jefferson Davis and other former Confederate leaders. Most Radical Republicans were pleased with Johnson's action. The Radicals believed that he would help them carry out their harsher program of reconstruction.

President Johnson soon disappointed the Radicals. He adopted a more conciliatory attitude toward the South and claimed that he intended to follow Lincoln's program. For a time he seemed to be doing so. He officially recognized the reconstructed governments of Tennessee, Arkansas, Louisiana, and Virginia. Johnson also kept all of the members of Lincoln's cabinet.

In several ways, however, Johnson did not follow Lincoln's program, either in details or in general approach. Lincoln had kept an open mind about the best method of reconstructing the Union. Johnson refused to consider any plan but his own. His stubbornness antagonized the Radical Republicans, as did his policy of pardoning former Confederates. When the Radicals objected to his policies, Johnson answered their arguments with name-calling and personal abuse.

Johnson managed even to antagonize the moderate Republicans. Most moderates shared with the Radicals the belief that any program of reconstruction must provide civil and political equality for both races. Johnson opposed this viewpoint.

End of Presidential reconstruction. Nevertheless, the reconstruction program proceeded for a time along the lines laid down by Lincoln and modified by Johnson. Within a few months, all the former Confederate states except Texas had adopted new constitutions and organized new governments.

When Congress assembled on December 4, 1865, Senators and Representatives from the southern states, most of whom had been leaders in the Confederacy, were waiting outside the doors to take their seats in the national legislature. To many observers it looked as though the long and dreadful war was finally ended and the restored nation was about to start anew.

SECTION SURVEY

IDENTIFY: amnesty, reconstruction, Charles Sumner, Thaddeus Stevens, Wade-Davis Bill, John Wilkes Booth, Andrew Johnson.

1. (a) What did Lincoln mean when he said, "With malice toward none, with charity for all"? (b) What were the main terms of Lincoln's reconstruction plan. (c) Which terms show how he intended to put into practice the ideas expressed in his Second Inaugural Address?

2. (a) What were the main arguments against Lincoln's reconstruction plan? (b) Explain the reasoning of Lincoln's opponents.

3. (a) What were the provisions of the Wade-Davis Bill? Why did (b) Lincoln and (c) some Radical Republicans object to the bill?

4. To what extent was reconstruction policy (a) a struggle between the two major political parties and (b) a struggle between two branches of the federal government?

2 · The nation struggles to restore order in the South

A new chapter in American history opened when Congress assembled on December 4, 1865, but it was not the chapter outlined by either Lincoln or Johnson. It proved, instead, to be one of the most troubled chapters in the nation's history.

Economic chaos in the South.   The scene in the South at the end of the war was one of utter poverty. Crumbling chimneys rose from the ashes of once lovely mansions. Grass grew in the roads, bridges lay in ruins, and two thirds of the railroads were destroyed.

The devastation in the cities was especially grim. A visitor reported that Columbia, South Carolina, was "a wilderness of crumbling walls, naked chimneys, and trees killed by flames." Rubble covered the business section of Richmond, Virginia, one of the great southern manufacturing centers. The scene in Atlanta, Georgia, was one of devastation. City and countryside alike, wherever armies had fought, were largely in ruins.

Social chaos.   The southern economy as well as southern property had been torn apart by the war. A citizen of Mississippi wrote in April 1865 that "our fields everywhere lie untilled. Naked chimneys and charred ruins all over the land mark the spots where happy homes . . . once stood. Their former inhabitants wander in poverty and exile, wherever chance or charity affords them shelter or food. Childless, old age widows, and helpless orphans beggared and hopeless, are everywhere." Conditions were not as bad as this everywhere, but they were bad enough.

The plight of some 3.5 million freed slaves was far worse. The former slaves were at last free, at least in name, but free to do what? Most of them had never been given an opportunity to learn how to read and write. None had owned land. Few knew what it was like to work for their own wages. Nor could most of their former owners pay them wages, for Confederate money was worthless and United States currency was scarcely to be found in the South. The land itself remained, but seeds and farm tools had almost disappeared.

After the war many schools were set up throughout the South to educate the newly freed slaves, young as well as old. One observer noted the eagerness of the new learners: "I have seen three generations sitting on the same bench, spelling the same lesson."

Disease, always the companion of hunger and lack of sanitation, swept across the South. It was especially serious in the cities and their outskirts, where uprooted people struggled to survive in makeshift shelters. Thousands died during the summer and winter of 1865–66. In some crowded urban areas, as much as one quarter to one third of the black population died of disease. The death rate among the white population was almost as grim.

Relief efforts for freed slaves.   Even during the war, some abolitionists tried to aid the freed slaves who had fled into areas controlled by Union forces. When white planters abandoned their plantations on islands off the coast of South Carolina, black people there were left helpless and destitute. Idealistic men and women, white and black, helped the freed slaves to operate these plantations and to set up schools there. Outstanding among the volunteers was Laura Towne of Massachusetts. She looked after the health of former slaves, helped them with legal problems, and established the Penn School. This school later became a teacher-training institution with vocational as well as academic programs.

Elsewhere, relief societies financed by northern religious and charitable groups tried to fill the needs of freed slaves for food, shelter, jobs, and schooling. Josephine Griffing, an Ohio abolitionist and women's rights leader, set up one such program in Washington, D.C., that provided food, clothing, shelter, and job training for freed blacks. She also urged Congress to undertake a program to find places to live in the North and West for homeless black people and to help them become self-supporting citizens. She herself helped thousands find homes and jobs in many localities.

The Freedmen's Bureau. During the war, the United States Army provided food and clothing for impoverished southerners, black and white, in areas under its control. Once the war was over, it was clear that neither the army nor the voluntary relief societies could meet the pressing needs of southerners, especially the freed slaves. At the urging of Josephine Griffing and others, Congress in 1865 created the Freedmen's Bureau to look after "refugees, freedmen°, and abandoned lands." This was the first important example in the nation's history of federal support for needy and underprivileged people. The Freedmen's Bureau was headed by General Oliver Otis Howard of Maine. In 1867 General Howard also founded Howard University in Washington, D.C., which offered higher education to the freed slaves.

Northerners and southerners differed in their attitude toward the Freedmen's Bureau. Most northerners regarded it as an honest effort to help the South bring order out of chaos. Most white southerners, on the other hand, resented the bureau. They charged that many bureau agents encouraged the freed slaves to look upon their former owners as enemies and, by doing so, created racial friction.

White southerners also charged the bureau with raising false hopes among the freed slaves, thereby making readjustment increasingly difficult. One of these false hopes was the former slaves' belief that they would all receive farms. During the summer and fall of 1865, the rumor spread that every former slave would get "forty acres and a mule" as a Christmas gift from the federal government. This rumor was based on a statement in the

°**freedmen** was the term used in these years to refer to former slaves—women and children as well as men.

Freedmen's Bureau bill that abandoned land or land for which taxes had not been paid could be distributed among the former slaves. Many freed slaves accepted the rumor as truth. Overjoyed at the prospect of soon owning farms and understandably linking freedom with the right to choose where and how they worked, some freed slaves decided not to work for white southerners.

Restrictions on freed slaves. In this situation southern leaders began to take steps to restore life as they had known it. One step was the adoption of laws to regulate the conduct of the freed slaves.

Laws of this kind, known as "slave codes," had existed before the war. The new black codes, which varied from state to state, contained many of the same provisions as the old slave codes. As white southerners pointed out, however, they also included certain improvements in civil rights for the former slaves. Under the new codes, former slaves were permitted to own personal property, to sue and be sued in court, to act in court cases involving one or more black persons, and legally to marry members of their own race.

However, in general the codes denied blacks their basic civil rights. Mississippi, for example, using its old code, merely substituted the word "Negro" for "slave." Black southerners were forbidden to possess firearms unless licensed to do so. They were forbidden to assemble unless white southerners were present. Nor could blacks appear on the streets after sunset or travel without permits. Above all, the codes established white control over black labor. They prohibited black southerners from starting businesses. They provided for strict labor contracts, including severe apprenticeship regulations and stern punishments if contracts were broken. Some codes also restricted black southerners from renting or leasing farmland. The black codes indicated that white southerners had the intention of confining the freed slaves to a clearly defined, subordinate way of life.

Such was the situation in December 1865 when the newly elected Senators and Representatives from all the former Confederate states except Texas appeared in Washington to take their seats in Congress. The former Confederate states had taken some, but not all, of the steps required by both President Lincoln and President Johnson for readmission to the

Union. The new Senators and Representatives fully expected to take their seats in Congress and to share with northern members the task of rebuilding the Union.

Congress, however, refused to admit the southern Senators and Representatives. What motives prompted Congress to reject the South's newly elected representatives? Why did Congress refuse to accept Lincoln's and Johnson's programs for restoring the South to the Union?

Reasons behind rejection. From the time Lincoln's program began to take shape, Radical Republicans had argued that southern leaders could not be trusted. Now, in December 1865, the Radicals pointed to the black codes as evidence that white southerners were unwilling to recognize the complete freedom of black Americans.

The Radical Republicans also opposed the Lincoln and Johnson theory about the nature of the war. Both Lincoln and Johnson had argued that the conflict was a "rebellion of individuals." This being so, they believed that the President could use the pardoning power granted him by the Constitution to restore the South to the Union.

Senator Charles Sumner opposed Lincoln's theory with the "state suicide" argument. According to Sumner, the southern states, as complete political organizations, had committed "state suicide" when they seceded from the Union. Now, with the war over, they were like any other unorganized territory of the United States. This being the case, Congress alone had the constitutional right to establish the terms for admitting them to the Union.

Representative Thaddeus Stevens held an even more drastic point of view. According to Stevens, the former Confederate states did not exist even as territories. In Stevens's opinion they were "conquered provinces" and should be treated as such.

Historians cannot be sure of the motives that led Radical Republicans to take the positions they did. Some Radicals were influenced by economic and political considerations. However, a good many Radical and moderate Republicans had a sincere feeling of obligation to the freed slaves. They genuinely wanted to make sure that white southerners did not deprive black southerners of their freedom or take steps to reduce them to a permanently inferior way of life.

Many moderate Republicans shared Lincoln's attitude toward the South. If Johnson had been less insistent upon having his own way, if he had been willing to work with the moderate Republicans, they and the Democratic members of the House and Senate might have carried through a reconstruction program acceptable to white southern leaders. However, President Johnson would not change his views, and control of Congress passed into the hands of the Radicals.

SECTION SURVEY

IDENTIFY: Josephine Griffing, General Oliver Otis Howard, black codes, "rebellion of individuals" theory, "state suicide" theory, "conquered provinces" theory.

1. Describe the most pressing problems facing the South in 1865.
2. (a) Describe the work of the Freedmen's Bureau. (b) Contrast northern and southern opinions about the bureau.
3. (a) Name the main restrictions placed on black southerners by white southern leaders. (b) How did the new black codes differ from the old slave codes?
4. What reasons led Congress to reject the new southern members of Congress?
5. How did Andrew Johnson contribute to the problems of reconstruction?

3 The Radical Republicans enact a program of reconstruction

By refusing in December 1865 to seat the southern members of Congress, the Radical Republicans practically guaranteed their own control of both houses of Congress. Within a few months, they restored military rule in the South and sowed seeds of bitterness that were to live for many years.

The first steps. Congress immediately appointed a joint committee of six Senators and nine Representatives to study the entire question of reconstruction. While Congress waited for the committee's report, it passed a bill enlarging the powers of the Freedmen's Bureau. The new law gave the bureau power to prosecute in military courts, rather than in civil courts, any person accused of depriving freed slaves of their civil rights. President Johnson promptly vetoed the bill. He argued (1) that trial by military courts violated the Fifth Amendment of the Constitution and (2) that Congress had no power to pass *any* laws with 11 states unrepresented. Johnson's veto infuriated the Radical Republicans, who finally gathered enough votes to pass the bill over the President's veto.

In the meantime, Congress passed a civil rights bill. It was the first in a series of federal acts designed to give black Americans full citizenship and guarantee them complete equality of treatment. Johnson also vetoed this bill on the ground that it was an unconstitutional invasion of states' rights. Enough moderate Republicans joined the Radicals to pass the Civil Rights Act over Johnson's veto.

Johnson's vetoes cost him the support of moderate Republicans who, without any desire to punish white southerners, believed that Congress should protect the rights of former slaves. The vetoes also strengthened the influence of Thaddeus Stevens and the other Radical Republicans.

The Fourteenth Amendment. Congress feared that the Supreme Court might declare the Civil Rights Act unconstitutional. It decided to write the provisions of the act into the Constitution by amendment. This amendment, the Fourteenth, was the outcome of compromise between moderate and Radical Republicans. Some Radicals had hoped to outlaw all forms of racial segregation and discrimination. That objective does not seem to have been shared by the moderates, nor even by all Radicals who shaped the Amendment.

The Fourteenth Amendment (pages 192–93) made black Americans citizens of the United States and of the states in which they lived. It forbade states to deprive citizens of the rights of life, liberty, and property without due process of law or to deny any citizen "the equal protection of the laws." It went further and excluded former Confederate leaders from holding public office, state or federal. It provided for reduction of Congressional representation of states that deprived black Americans of their rights as citizens. The amendment also forbade southern states to repay Confederate war debts or to pay former slaveowners for the loss of their slaves.

Congressional elections of 1866. Tennessee ratified the Fourteenth Amendment in July 1866 and was immediately readmitted to the Union. On the advice of President Johnson, all of the other southern states rejected the amendment by overwhelming votes.

What would Congress do next? The answer depended in part on the Congressional elections in the fall of 1866. If the Democrats won control of Congress, they might return to Lincoln's and Johnson's programs or modify them. If the Republicans won, they might fight for further restrictions on the political role of the former Confederates and for stronger guarantees of the rights of blacks.

Several events helped to swing voters toward the Republicans. Violent race riots were especially influential in shaping public opinion. In Memphis, Tennessee, 46 blacks were killed and 12 black schools and 4 black churches were burned. In a riot at New Orleans, about 200 people, mostly black, were killed or wounded. Many northerners, shocked by such violence, began to feel that perhaps the Radical Republicans were right to demand further federal protection for the freed slaves.

In the late summer of 1866, President Johnson made a trip to Chicago, stopping along the way to make election speeches. When opponents heckled him, Johnson's answers often seemed to reflect a lack of understanding of the election issues, as well as bitter hatred of Radical Republicans. His language, often blunt and crude, antagonized many voters.

More important, however, as a reason for Republican strength was the memory of the war itself. During the terrible conflict, both sides had suffered immense casualties. Voters, fearful of losing the fruits of hard-won military victory, voted for Republican candidates.

In the election the Republicans increased their hold on both houses of Congress. With more than a two-thirds majority in both the Senate and the House, the Republicans, if they held together, could now override Johnson's Presidential vetoes.

Reconstructing the South. In March 1867 a combination of Radical and moderate Republicans passed, over Johnson's vetoes, a complete program for reconstruction. The new program contained five major provisions.

First, Congress divided the ten southern states that had rejected the Fourteenth Amendment into five military districts. Each

In February 1868 this House committee, led by an old, ill, and unforgiving Thaddeus Stevens (standing), drafted the articles of impeachment against President Johnson. Tickets for the trial that followed were in great demand.

district was under a military governor, with federal troops to maintain law and order while the states drafted new constitutions and organized new governments.

Second, Congress deprived most former Confederate leaders of the right to vote and hold office. The restrictions were the same as those that had already been written into the Fourteenth Amendment.

Third, Congress gave the freed slaves the right to vote and hold office.

Fourth, Congress authorized the states to write new constitutions that guaranteed freed slaves the right to vote.

Fifth, Congress required the states to ratify the Fourteenth Amendment.

The white southern governments that had been formed under the Presidential plan of reconstruction now had no choice but to accept the new program. One by one, the states held conventions and drafted new constitutions. They then organized their new governments and entered the Union under the terms that were laid down by Congress.

Johnson's impeachment and trial. By the summer of 1868, all but three southern states had returned to the Union on the terms laid down by Congress. (Mississippi, Texas, and Virginia finally accepted the terms and were readmitted in 1870.) Meanwhile, the Radical Republicans determined to remove their hated enemy, President Johnson, from office.

Several things led the Radical Republicans to this decision. They certainly were affected by the emotional hatreds and tensions of the times. More important, the Radicals knew that the success of their reconstruction program depended heavily on its enforcement. They were convinced that Johnson would not enforce Congressional policy. He confirmed their suspicions when, by executive order, he restricted the power of military commanders in the South and removed commanders known to be sympathetic to Radical programs.

To find grounds for impeachment and to reduce the President's power, Congress in 1867 adopted the Tenure of Office° Act over Johnson's veto. Under this law the President could not dismiss important civil officers without the Senate's consent. Believing the law unconsti-

°tenure of office: the period during which an individual has the right to continue in office.

395

"Let Us Have Peace" was Ulysses S. Grant's campaign slogan in the 1868 Presidential election. This campaign poster mentions peace, but it plays up Grant's war record, which was the source of his great popularity.

168, 169, and 182). Although the charges brought by the House against President Johnson were of doubtful legality, he was nevertheless impeached.

Johnson's trial before the Senate, presided over by Chief Justice Salmon P. Chase, lasted about two months. After prolonged debate it became clear that Johnson was not guilty of any offense for which he could legally be removed from office. Nevertheless, when the Senate vote was counted, it stood 35 to 19 against Johnson, just one vote short of the necessary two-thirds majority required for removal from office. Johnson continued to serve as President for almost a year, until his term expired, but his influence was at an end.

Decline of Radical power. It soon became apparent, however, that the Radical Republicans had overreached themselves. When they tried to remove the President from office, they lost the support of many moderate Republicans. Moreover, public opinion finally began to turn against them.

As the election of 1868 approached, the Republicans realized they were in trouble. In hopes of winning the election, they unanimously nominated Ulysses S. Grant for the Presidency. Grant had no political experience. He did not share the moral conviction of many Radical Republicans of the need to protect the freed slaves. Nevertheless, he was popular as a war hero.

The Democrats chose as their Presidential candidate Horatio Seymour, a wealthy New Yorker and former governor of his state. The Democratic platform denounced the Radical Republican program of reconstruction, declaring it unconstitutional. It also condemned the Radicals for their attempt to remove Johnson from office.

Economic issues were also important in the election of 1868. The platform of the Democratic Party, for example, favored a "cheap money" policy. During the war the federal government had issued $450 million in paper money known as "greenbacks." After the war, in 1866, the Republican Congress had provided for the gradual withdrawal of the greenbacks from circulation. By 1868 nearly $100 million had been withdrawn. In their 1868 platform the Democrats promised, if elected, to reverse this policy and reissue the paper money. The Democrats knew that this "cheap money" plank would antagonize wealthy bondholders.

tutional, Johnson decided to put it to a test. In February 1868 he demanded the resignation of Secretary of War Edwin M. Stanton. Stanton had consistently cooperated with Johnson's political enemies.

The House immediately adopted a resolution that "Andrew Johnson, President of the United States, be impeached of high crimes and misdemeanors in office." The Radicals also charged that Johnson "did attempt to bring into disgrace, ridicule, contempt, and reproach the Congress of the United States." The Radicals cited occasions when the President publicly made "with a loud voice certain intemperate, inflammatory, and scandalous harangues" against Congress "and did therein utter loud threats and bitter menaces."

Under the Constitution a President may be impeached on grounds of "treason, bribery, or other high crimes and misdemeanors" (pages

Those bondholders fully expected that the money they had lent the government would be repaid in gold. The Democrats also knew that the proposal would appeal to many less well-to-do voters, particularly those who owed money. With more currency in circulation, debtors could more easily pay off their debts.

Republican candidate Ulysses S. Grant barely squeaked through to victory. Although he won by an electoral vote of 214 to 80, capturing 24 of the 36 states, his popular majority was only 309,000 out of almost 6 million votes.

The Radical Republicans studied the election returns with growing concern. They realized that many voters had turned against the Republicans because of their "hard money" policy. They also realized that the black vote had made possible their thin majority of the popular vote.

The Fifteenth Amendment. With this disturbing conclusion in mind, the Radicals drew up the Fifteenth Amendment and submitted it to the states for ratification. The Fifteenth Amendment was short and to the point: "The right of citizens of the United States to vote shall not be denied or abridged by the United States or any state on account of race, color, or previous condition of servitude."

The Fifteenth Amendment was ratified by the necessary three fourths of the states and became part of the Constitution in 1870. Mississippi, Texas, and Virginia—the last three southern states to return to the Union—were required to ratify the amendment as a condition for readmission.

Women, you recall, made many contributions to Union victory in the Civil War. Leaders of the women's rights movement expected, in return, that women would now receive the same legal protections and voting rights as blacks. Despite their protests, women were included in neither the Fourteenth nor the Fifteenth Amendments.

SECTION SURVEY

IDENTIFY: Civil Rights Act, due process of law, equal protection of the laws, Tenure of Office Act, Ulysses S. Grant, "cheap money."

1. (a) Explain how the new Freedmen's Bureau law and the Civil Rights Act aimed at protecting the freed slaves. (b) Why did Johnson veto both laws? (c) What were the results of Johnson's vetoes?

2. Describe the five major provisions of the Congressional plan for reconstruction.

3. (a) Why was Johnson impeached? (b) What were the consequences of his impeachment?

4. Source Study: (a) Read the Fourteenth Amendment on pages 192–93 and summarize the main ideas in each section. (b) Why did Congress propose the Fourteenth Amendment?

5. Source Study: Read the Fifteenth Amendment on page 193. (a) What does it provide? (b) Why was it passed? (c) What did the amendment do for the status of women?

4 White southerners regain control of their state governments

The Radical Republican program of reconstruction brought far-reaching changes to the South, but only for a relatively short time. For varying periods—as long as ten years in only three states—Radical Republicans and their allies controlled the former Confederate states.

Help from the North. In the ten years after the surrender of the Confederacy, the main concern of the federal government was the restoration of the Union. Providing aid to the war-ravaged South and to needy southerners took second place. The Freedmen's Bureau was severely limited by lack of funds and by opposition from most southerners and many northerners. Its work was supplemented, however, by teachers and missionaries, black as well as white. Most of the northern volunteers were moved by humanitarian and democratic ideals. Many won the confidence of the men, women, and children whom they had come to help. Others, equally well-meaning but unfamiliar with southern ways of life and perhaps less tactful, antagonized the people with whom they tried to work.

Carpetbaggers and scalawags. White southerners especially resented the arrival in the South of northerners whom they jeeringly called "carpetbaggers." This nickname implied, wrongly, that the newcomers were all fly-by-night adventurers who carried everything they owned in suitcases made of carpeting material, which were common at the time.

In all, 22 blacks from former Confederate states were elected to serve in Congress after the Civil War. Shown here are Senator Hiram Revels of South Carolina (far left) and six members of the House of Representatives.

The carpetbaggers came for many different reasons. Some sincerely wanted to help the freed slaves exercise their newly acquired rights. Some hoped to get themselves elected to political office. Some came to make their fortunes by acquiring farmland or by starting new businesses. However, some came for reasons of pure greed or fraud. Horace Greeley, the editor of the *New York Tribune,* wrote that such carpetbaggers were "stealing and plundering, many of them with both arms around the Negroes, and their hands in their rear pockets, seeing if they cannot pick a paltry dollar out of them."

Most white southerners and some northerners scorned the northern carpetbaggers who moved into the South. Especially strong scorn and abuse were directed toward those native-born southerners who had chosen to cooperate with the northern authorities.

Some of these native-born southerners had the best of motives. Having opposed slavery and secession, they had sympathized with the Union during the war. Now they believed that the best way to restore peace and prosperity to the South and to the nation was to forgive and forget. However, others were selfish and ambitious individuals who seized any opportunity to advance their own fortunes at the expense of their neighbors.

Whatever the motives of these native-born southerners, most were held in contempt by other white southerners. They were often referred to as "scalawags," which was a word used to describe scoundrels.

Reconstruction governments. Such were the individuals who largely controlled southern state governments during part of the Radical reconstruction period. Northerners held most of the important political offices, at least during the early years. They were able to get themselves elected partly because they persuaded the freed slaves to vote for them. Also, many white southerners were deprived of the right to vote and others refused to take part in political activities.

The enormous influence of northerners in southern politics can be seen by examining the election results in the seven southern states readmitted to the Union by 1868. As a result of the first postwar elections held in these states, 4 of the 7 governors, 10 of the 14 United States Senators, and 20 of the 35 United States Representatives were carpetbaggers. In general, southern scalawags and freed slaves had to be content with the less important state and federal offices.

Black southerners in public life. Blacks were elected to the southern reconstruction governments, and they played an important role in some of them. However, the black's role in these governments has often been exaggerated. Only one black American served briefly as a southern governor. In only one southern state — South Carolina — did black members for a time hold a majority in the state legislature. Only Mississippi sent black Senators, two of them, to Washington. One was Hiram Revels, a native of North Carolina who, after studying at Knox College in Illinois, had been a teacher and minister. The other was Blanche K. Bruce, who had escaped from slavery in Virginia and who had also been a teacher.

Many other blacks in reconstruction politics showed independence and political skill. Among them were Robert Brown Elliott of South Carolina, a brilliant lawyer and scholar, and P. B. S. Pinchback of Louisiana, son of a Mississippi planter and a black mother.

The blacks in public life during reconstruction did not demand revenge upon white southerners. In fact, most black leaders favored returning the right to vote to their former white masters. The records of those elected to the United States Congress compared well with the records of many of their white colleagues.

Reconstruction governments at work. The southern reconstruction legislatures started many needed and long overdue public improvements. The new legislatures, for example, strengthened public education and, for the first time, made it available to large numbers of black children.

The reconstruction governments also pushed forward other constructive programs. They spread the tax burden more equitably. They introduced overdue reforms in local government and the judicial system. They abolished imprisonment for debt. They extended the legal rights of women. They passed laws to protect homes and farms against illegal foreclosures — that is, against unjustified seizure by dishonest officials. Most of the southern state constitutions drafted during the period of reconstruction continued in effect for many years.

Such programs greatly increased the debts of the southern states. In addition, the reconstruction governments misspent huge amounts of money.

White southerners who had once dominated public life deplored large expenditures for needless luxuries authorized by legislators, white and black, in some reconstruction governments. They also denounced some reconstruction legislators for outright corruption.

Some of the new legislators were all too willing to enrich themselves while granting favorable railroad and corporation charters to business groups, often northern, who wanted to develop southern enterprises. However, southern Democrats who briefly controlled southern legislatures in the first years after the war had followed some of the same corrupt practices. As you will read, public morality in all sections of the United States sank to an extremely low level during the years following the Civil War.

Secret societies. Whatever the merits and demerits of the reconstruction governments may have been, most white southerners resented them. Since many former Confederate leaders were denied the vote and since others chose to boycott politics, some white southerners expressed their opposition by defying the law through intimidation and violence. By 1867 some white southerners were attacking carpetbaggers, scalawags, and politically active black southerners through a number of secret societies. The best known were the Knights of the White Camellia and the Ku Klux Klan.

These secret organizations tried to frighten black southerners and their white sympathizers into staying out of politics. Bands of hooded members clad in ghostly white costumes rode through the countryside at night, stopping now and then at a house to issue warnings. When warnings failed, cabins and churches were burned and some freed slaves were beaten or killed. White sympathizers and friends of blacks sometimes received the same treatment. Moderate white southerners, disgusted with the brutality and fearful of northern reaction, disapproved of these actions. However, for a time they were unable to prevent them.

Congress tried to end the lawlessness by passing a series of Military Enforcement Acts, sometimes called the Force Acts (1870–71). These acts gave the President power to use federal military forces to control the secret societies, to call upon the state militias when neces-

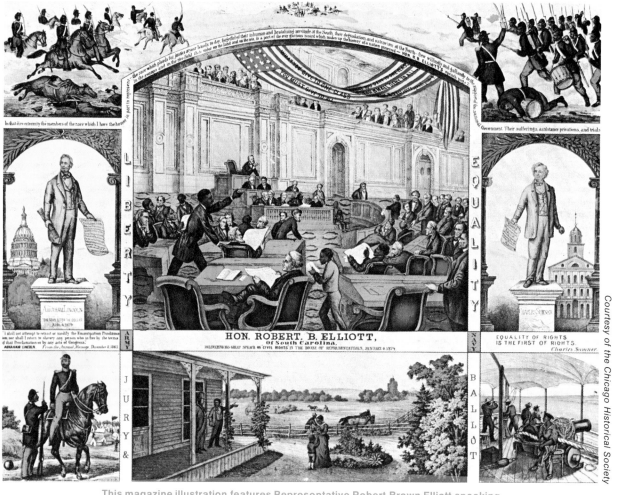

This magazine illustration features Representative Robert Brown Elliott speaking to Congress in 1874. The words at the top are his: "What you give to one class, you must give to all. What you deny to one class, you shall deny to all."

sary, and to suspend the writ of *habeas corpus.* They also provided for federal supervision of southern elections.

To many white southerners, the Force Acts seemed unduly harsh. Yet compared with the treatment of the losers in civil wars elsewhere, the former Confederates were not severely punished. There were never more than 25,000 federal troops in the occupied states after the war. No political leader was executed, few were imprisoned, and President Johnson made liberal use of his pardoning power. Jefferson Davis, for example, was released from prison within two years. Except for the loss of slaves, property was seldom seized by the federal government as punishment for what many northerners regarded as treason.

Further leniency prevailed in 1872, when Congress passed the Amnesty Act. This act restored political rights, including the right to vote, to about 160,000 former Confederates.

After 1872 only about 500 white southerners were still barred from political activity.

The Force Acts, the withdrawal of many southerners from the secret societies, and finally the Amnesty Act virtually ended the power of the Ku Klux Klan and other such groups at that time. Most white southerners began to vote again, and white southern leadership reemerged. The reconstruction governments in several states were thus replaced by governments representing traditional white southern rule.

The end of reconstruction. During the early 1870's, northerners began to lose interest in the problems of southern reconstruction. Radical Republican power and leadership was diminished by the death of Thaddeus Stevens in 1868 and of Charles Summer in 1874.

At first many northerners had championed the cause of the freed slaves. Now they became

was planting and harvesting one third of all the nation's cotton.

Improved farming methods led to greatly increased production of tobacco, rice, sugar, corn, and other traditional crops. However, the most important change in southern agricultural life was the development of truck farming and fruit growing. Because of the growth of railroads and the invention of the refrigerator car, fresh vegetables and fruit could be shipped to northern cities. The long growing season in the South and an abundance of cheap labor also stimulated truck farming. As early as 1900, thousands of refrigerator cars were rolling northward with welcome cargoes of vegetables, watermelons, strawberries, oranges, apples, and peaches.

Industrial progress. An even more remarkable development in the New South was the growth of industry. In industry as in agriculture, the South responded to forces that were transforming economic life in other regions of the United States and, for that matter, in most of Europe.

Southern industrial development actually started before the outbreak of the Civil War. By 1860 about 10 percent of the manufactured wealth of the United States came from southern textile mills, ironworks, lumber projects, and sugar refineries. The war and reconstruction ruined many southern industries, and for nearly 20 years the South made little industrial progress.

By the late 1870's, more and more southerners felt that southern progress depended upon industrialization. The development of industry would enable the South to make better use of its rich natural resources.

Money to build factories, mines, steel mills, railroads, and other industries came in part from northern investors and in still larger part from the South itself. Profits from expanding agriculture were poured into new industrial ventures. In community after community, the people themselves gathered in mass assemblies to plan a factory, often a textile mill, and to raise the necessary capital. By 1900 more than 400 cotton textile mills had been built. Throughout the South farming villages were transformed into mill towns within a few short years. Poor whites provided most of the labor for the new factories. Black laborers were almost entirely excluded from the new industrial development.

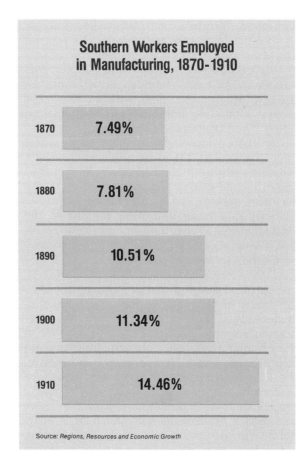

Southern Workers Employed in Manufacturing, 1870–1910

Year	Percent
1870	7.49%
1880	7.81%
1890	10.51%
1900	11.34%
1910	14.46%

Source: *Regions, Resources and Economic Growth*

Many early mills were controlled by a single family or a small group of persons. They owned the houses in which the workers lived, the stores where they bought their goods, and the other town buildings. The men and women who worked in these mills depended on the owners for their jobs and had to spend their wages to rent company-owned dwellings and to buy supplies from company-owned stores. As a result, the labor organizations that were rapidly growing in the North during these years made little headway in the South.

The growth of southern industry also depended on improvements and extensions of southern railroads. The war left southern railroads in terrible condition, but old railroads were quickly rebuilt, and new lines constructed. By 1890 the southern railroad system was twice as large as in 1860.

Industrial development in the New South led to the growth of cities. Between 1870 and 1890 Durham, North Carolina, developed from a small village to a flourishing tobacco center.

Richmond, Virginia, and Nashville, Tennessee, became leading urban centers. The population of Atlanta, Georgia, increased from 37,000 to 65,000 between 1880 and 1890. Birmingham, Alabama, founded in 1871 on the site of a former cotton field, within a few years became a bustling iron and steel center, often called "the Pittsburgh of the South."

By 1900, southern manufactured products were worth four times as much as in 1860. With its growing industrial cities, its factories and mills and mines, and its developing transportation system, the South was beginning to be more and more like other regions of the United States. Nevertheless, the New South had a long way to go to catch up industrially with other sections of the country.

Educational developments. During the closing years of the 1800's, able and far-seeing leaders urged southerners to improve their educational system and thus make better use of their human resources. Southern education did improve, but every forward step was taken in the face of tremendous handicaps. Southern leaders had to deal with widespread poverty despite improving economic conditions. There was also a traditional reluctance to support public education with tax money. Maintaining separate schools for white and black children added to the cost of education.

Among the outstanding contributions to southern education were the gifts of northern philanthropists. Especially noteworthy were the gifts of George Peabody and John F. Slater, both northern millionaires. The Peabody Fund was created in 1867, the Slater Fund in 1882. Money from these funds helped to provide educational opportunities for white and black southerners alike in the postwar years.

The money from private sources, however, was only a fraction of what was needed. Most of the burden of rebuilding schools and opening up educational opportunities for whites as well as blacks had to be shouldered by the southern states. Slowly, as the economic situation improved, the South provided more opportunities.

The "Solid South." Most southerners belonged to the Democratic Party. There were southern Republicans, to be sure, but they were completely outnumbered in local, state, and national elections. For example, when the Presidential elections rolled around, the former Confederate states cast all their electoral votes for the Democratic candidates. Thus people began to refer to the southern states as the "Solid South."

The "Solid South" was born during reconstruction days, when Radical Republican governments controlled the southern states. In their determination to rid themselves of Republican rule, white southerners poured into the Democratic Party. After 1877, when the last federal troops were withdrawn from the South, most white southerners continued to support the Democratic Party.

IDENTIFY: New South, one-crop agriculture, "the Pittsburgh of the South," philanthropist, George Peabody, John Slater, "Solid South."

1. (a) Define tenant farming and sharecropping. (b) Explain why they were common in the postwar South. (c) Why was it hard for a tenant farmer or sharecropper to become a farm owner?

2. (a) Give three reasons for southern industrial development. (b) What were some results of industrial growth?

3. What handicaps hindered the development of education in the South?

4. Why did the South generally support the Democratic Party after the Civil War?

5. Graph Study: Look at the graph on page 403. What does the graph tell you about the growth of industry in the South after the Civil War?

6 **Black southerners struggle for a place in the New South**

Black southerners had hoped to share in the agricultural, industrial, and educational progress of the New South and in the nation's ideals of freedom and equality. They did not for several reasons. First, the federal government suspended its program for helping black southerners make the transition from slavery to freedom. Second and equally important, whites in both the North and the South continued to think of blacks not as equals but as inferiors. Third, white southerners feared that the white southern way of life would be threatened if blacks were not firmly "kept in their place."

Cartoonist Thomas Nast depicted a black man casting his vote in an election shortly after the Civil War. Who do you think the figures on the left represent?

Preventing blacks from voting. For more than ten years after white southern Democrats regained control of southern governments in 1877, many blacks continued to vote. A few even held public office.

Early in the 1890's, however, the new Populist Party threatened the power of both the Democratic and Republican parties (Chapter 20). In the South, Populist organizers had their greatest success among poor white people, but some also worked hard to win the support of black voters. Southern Democrats, alarmed by this development, attempted to prevent blacks from voting.

Beginning with Mississippi in 1890, the southern states adopted laws and framed new constitutions that in effect kept most blacks from voting on grounds other than "race, color, or previous condition of servitude." By the early 1900's, the guarantees of civil rights in the Fourteenth and Fifteenth Amendments had become largely ineffective in the South. In most areas, few blacks voted and fewer still held public office, even in minor positions.

A number of states adopted a **poll tax**—a fixed tax imposed on every voter—and also a **literacy test**—and examination to determine whether a person can read or write. Since many black southerners had little money and

little, if any, education, these laws kept large numbers from voting.

The poll tax and the literacy test also deprived many poor whites of the vote. To remedy this situation, several states, starting with Louisiana in 1898, added a "grandfather clause" to their constitutions. This clause declared that even if a man could not pay the poll tax or pass the literacy test, he could still vote if he had been eligible to do so on January 1, 1867, or if he were the son or the grandson of a man who had been eligible to vote on January 1, 1867. The grandfather clause was declared unconstitutional by the Supreme Court in 1915. While it was in force, it kept many black southerners from voting.

Segregating the races. Meanwhile, a pattern of segregation, or separation, of white and black southerners was taking shape.

Except in a few instances, the Radical Republicans had not tried to bring white and black children together in southern public schools. However, black and white southerners used the same transportation facilities and other public services. The Civil Rights Act of 1875 had declared that "all persons within the jurisdiction of the United States shall be entitled to the full and equal enjoyment of the ac-

Tuskegee Institute was the scene for many breakthroughs in agricultural research. Booker T. Washington (center), founder of the Institute, directed his students in experiments that helped to strengthen the South's economy.

commodations, advantages, facilities, and privileges of inns, public conveyances on land or water, theaters and other places of public amusement; subject only to the conditions and limitations established by law and applicable alike to citizens of every race and color, regardless of any previous condition of servitude."

Even after white southern rule was restored in 1877, southerners of both races often used the same transportation facilities and other public services. Then in 1883 the Supreme Court ruled against the Civil Rights Act of 1875 on the ground that the Fourteenth Amendment forbade only states, not individuals or corporations (such as railroads), from discriminating against black citizens. In spite of their decision, black and white southerners in many places continued to use the same public accommodations.

In 1881 Tennessee passed the first of the so-called "Jim Crow" laws. Under this law, white southerners and black southerners were required to ride in separate railway cars. Other states followed Tennessee's example. By the 1890's all southern states required such separation, not only in schools but in streetcars, railroads, and railroad stations. Within a few years, this pattern of segregation spread to parks, playgrounds, and other public facilities.

In 1896 the Supreme Court added legal support to segregation. In the case of *Plessy v. Ferguson,* the Court ruled that it was not a violation of the Fourteenth Amendment to provide "separate but equal" facilities for blacks. This 1896 ruling by the Supreme Court was a serious blow to the efforts of black Americans to improve their lives.

Black southerners' reactions. Confronted by segregation and denied their political and civil rights, some black southerners migrated to other nearby states, such as Oklahoma and Kansas, or moved to the growing northern cities. Most, however, stayed in the South and worked to develop their own black communities. Black southerners strengthened their own churches, lodges, and mutual aid societies, developed their own businesses, and, against handicaps, tried to secure an education. Their efforts began to produce results. In 1865 only about 5 percent of all black adults could read and write. By 1900 more than 50 percent possessed these basic skills.

Southern black leaders also protested the growing pattern of segregation and discrimination and the denial of civil rights guaranteed by the Fourteenth Amendment. On the lecture platform, in churches, in the press, and in conventions, they demanded their constitutional rights. In 1889 the former black abolitionist Frederick Douglass, now an old man, asked whether "American justice, American liberty, American civilization, American law, and American Christianity could be made to include and protect alike and forever all American citizens in the rights which have been guaranteed to them by the organic and fundamental laws of the land."

In Baltimore, E. J. Waring, a black lawyer, urged blacks to fight discrimination by lawsuits against officials and citizens guilty of violating their rights. In Memphis, Ida Wells Barnett, teacher and publisher, was dismissed from teaching for denouncing the inferior segregated schools for black children. She then launched a single-handed crusade against black lynchings—that is, the murder of black people by white mobs. Even after a mob broke into her newspaper office and threatened her life, she persisted in exposing the evils of "lynch law."

Booker T. Washington. The leading black voice from 1890 to 1915 was that of Booker T. Washington. The son of a slave mother and a white father, Washington received a vocational education at Hampton Institute in Virginia. He then founded and built Tuskegee Institute in Alabama. Washington was convinced that vocational education, not classical or liberal arts education, was necessary to provide black people with the skills they needed to earn a living. He felt that such education would prepare blacks for jobs in the skilled trades, small businesses, farming, and household work.

Washington also spoke out against lynching and illegal discrimination, especially in the years just before his death in 1915. Generally, Washington remained convinced that black southerners would make greater progress by avoiding protests and emphasizing vocational training and by owning farms, homes, and small businesses.

W. E. B. Du Bois. Booker T. Washington's views met a strong challenge from a younger black, W. E. B. Du Bois (doo·BOYCE). Born and reared in western Massachusetts, Du Bois studied in German universities and earned his Ph.D. at Harvard. At first he felt that if white Americans came to understand past black achievements and present black conditions, their attitudes toward black Americans would in time improve.

Gradually, however, Du Bois came to believe that only vigorous and continuous protests against inequalities and injustices, and effective appeals to black pride, could change existing conditions. In *The Souls of Black Folk,* a book of eloquent essays, Du Bois criticized

Booker T. Washington's emphasis on vocational training. He urged broader educational opportunities, including liberal arts education, for blacks. Du Bois urged blacks to demand their rights to have whatever kind of education they needed to achieve full equality and opportunity in American life. Along with a few like-minded black leaders, he organized a meeting in 1905 at Niagara Falls that demanded an end to all unequal treatment based on race and color.

The appeals and demands of the Niagara Movement aroused many Americans, white as well as black. One outcome was the formation of the National Association for the Advancement of Colored People (NAACP). The NAACP worked through the courts to end restrictions on voting and other civil injustices. In time it succeeded in winning Supreme Court decisions that declared unconstitutional the grandfather clause in southern state constitutions, jury trials conducted under mob pressure, and segregation by local law of housing for black people. The Urban League, likewise organized by both blacks and whites, fought for equal job opportunities for black workers and against discrimination in urban housing.

The work of the NAACP and the Urban League brought some progress for black citizens in the North and West. These national organizations were also represented in the southern states, but they made less progress there. Most black southerners continued to experience discrimination, segregation, and denial of equal rights.

SECTION SURVEY

IDENTIFY: segregation, "Jim Crow" laws, *Plessy v. Ferguson,* "separate but equal," Ida Wells Barnett, Booker T. Washington, W. E. B. Du Bois, NAACP, Urban League.

1. Why did black southerners not share in the progress of the New South?

2. Explain how each of the following affected the right of black southerners to vote: (a) poll tax, (b) literacy test, (c) "grandfather clause."

3. (a) How was a new pattern of segregation established in the South? (b) How did the Supreme Court contribute to the separation of the races?

4. Describe the disagreement between Booker T. Washington and W. E. B. Du Bois over what blacks should do to improve their situation.

Chapter Survey

Summary: Tracing the Main Ideas

In 1865, just before his tragic death, President Lincoln urged the victorious North to act "with malice toward none; with charity for all." This was the way, he felt, to build "a just and lasting peace."

President Johnson's efforts to apply Lincoln's policy by quickly restoring the Union were effectively blocked by the Radical Republicans, who controlled Congress. For various reasons, the Radical Republicans wished to decide how the former Confederate states should be reconstructed. The more extreme members of the Radical group wanted to transfer political power from the white leaders to the blacks.

Southern blacks, meanwhile, were faced with the challenge of developing new ways of life for themselves after more than two hundred years of slavery. They eagerly looked forward to the prospects of working at jobs of their choosing, of owning farms, of receiving formal education, and of taking part in the political process.

White southerners were disturbed at the prospect of living in a position of political, economic, and social equality with former slaves. They used every means at their command to defeat the northern program of reconstruction. Unable to enforce their will upon the South, northerners gradually lost interest. In 1877 the last federal troops were withdrawn from the former Confederate states.

During the 1880's and 1890's, the outline of a New South began to appear. With the slow but steady development of more varied agriculture, truck farmers began to ship growing quantities of fruit and vegetables to markets in the North. Southern mines began to supply increasing amounts of ore to southern furnaces. Textile mills and other factories began to transform quiet southern villages into growing towns.

In 1900 the South was still basically an agricultural region. Southerners were still struggling to recover from the economic disaster of the war. With the tragic exception of the blacks, who were desperately struggling to find a place for themselves in the New South, the southern states were making great strides forward. Like people in the northern and the western states, southerners were being swept along into the future by the growing forces of industry.

Inquiring into History

1. How did the Supreme Court decision in *Plessy v. Ferguson* reflect the spirit of the times?
2. Did the black codes and "Jim Crow" laws reestablish slavery in the South? Explain.
3. (a) What problems that caused the Civil War were solved by the war and reconstruction? (b) What new problems were created by the war and reconstruction?
4. If Lincoln had lived to carry out his plan of reconstruction, do you think he would have encountered the same difficulties that President Johnson did? Explain.
5. Why might the period of reconstruction be called the "tragic era"?

Relating Past to Present

1. Compare the federal government's attitude toward minorities during reconstruction and today.
2. Compare the relationship between the President and Congress during reconstruction with their relationship today.
3. During reconstruction only the South was prejudiced against black Americans. Today there is little difference among the various sections of the nation regarding racial prejudice. Do you agree or disagree with these statements? Use examples to explain your answer.

Developing Social Science Skills

1. Read *Freedom Road* by Howard Fast, a novel about reconstruction. (a) Write an essay discussing how reconstruction changed the lives of the people portrayed. (b) How is the novel's presentation similar to the account in your textbook? How is it different? (c) How do you account for these similarities and differences?
2. Construct a chart showing the differing ideas of Lincoln, Johnson, and the Radical Republicans on reconstruction.

Chapter 20

Severe Trials for Democracy

1865-1897

Change is often disturbing, and in no period of American history was change more disturbing than in the generation following the Civil War. You have read how white and black southerners struggled to adjust to the drastic changes that took place during the reconstruction period. Equally striking changes were occuring in the Northeast, the Middle West, and the West during these years.

The major cause of these changes was the rapid growth of industry after the war. New power-driven machinery was invented and installed in large factories. Giant corporations were organized. New methods of mass production were adopted. These exciting developments made many new products and services available to more and more Americans and helped to raise their standard of living.

There were dark shadows in this bright picture. As American industries grew, American cities also grew and became overcrowded. Other problems arose with the growth of the cities — problems of sanitation, disease, fire, and transportation.

In order to see this dramatic and disturbing period of American history clearly, it is necessary to look at it from several different points of view. In later chapters you will see how the growth of big business created complex problems, not only for many business people, large and small, but also for farmers, miners, and wage earners. In this chapter you will see how graft and corruption plagued American political life during the postwar years. This graft and corruption posed a major threat to the workings of the American political system. In this chapter you will also learn how repeated efforts were made to root out this dishonesty in government.

THE CHAPTER IN OUTLINE

1. Graft and corruption spread in the postwar years.

2. A start is made toward restoring honesty to government.

3. Efforts at political reform move forward.

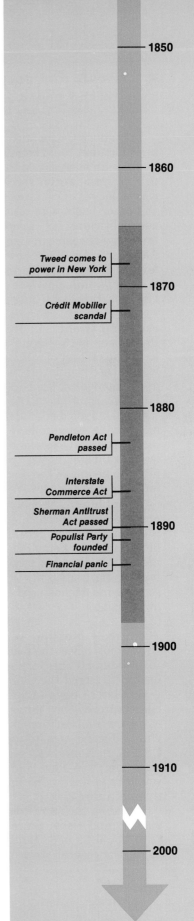

1850

1860

Tweed comes to power in New York

1870

Crédit Mobilier scandal

1880

Pendleton Act passed

Interstate Commerce Act

Sherman Antitrust Act passed

1890

Populist Party founded

Financial panic

1900

1910

2000

1 Graft and corruption spread in the postwar years

As industry expanded after the Civil War, huge fortunes could be and, in fact, were made by those in business. Many Americans seemed to approve financial success no matter how it was achieved. Operators of railroads, mines, and other businesses often did not hesitate to ask politicians for favors or to return such favors with cash payments or other rewards. As a result, graft and corruption infected every level of American government. It was Ulysses S. Grant's unhappy fate to occupy the White House at this disturbing time.

President Grant. In 1868, when he won the Presidency on the Republican ticket, Grant enjoyed the respect of millions of Americans. His well-earned reputation rested upon his success as commander of the Union armies during the latter years of the Civil War. Had he never served as President, Grant would have lived and died a popular hero. Unfortunately, his lack of political experience was a serious handicap. Grant's eight-year administration would prove to be one of the darker pages in the history of the Presidency.

Grant himself was honest and upright. His great weakness—which could have been a virtue if tempered by reason—was his total loyalty to friends. Being honest himself, he could not believe that his associates were any less honest. He stubbornly refused to admit that some of his friends used him to advance their own fortunes.

The Crédit Mobilier scandal. Even before Grant took office, the federal government was involved in an unsavory scandal. In 1861 California chartered the Central Pacific Railroad. A year later Congress chartered the Union Pacific Railroad. The Central Pacific was to build eastward from Sacramento, California, and the Union Pacific was to build westward from Omaha, in Nebraska Territory. When the two lines met, the East and West coasts at last would be joined by the nation's first transcontinental railroad.

Building such a railroad was extremely expensive and risky. Since the completed railroad would be important to national development, the federal government gave generous subsidies to the railroad companies. Among these subsidies were loans in the form of government bonds. The companies would receive $16,000 in bonds for every mile of track completed on the level plains, $32,000 for every mile through hilly country, and $48,000 for every mile in the mountains.

The small group of stockholders who controlled the Union Pacific Railroad looked greedily at these subsidies. They saw a chance to make enormous profits from the construction of the railroad itself. They organized a construction company called the Crédit Mobilier (kray·DEE moh·bee·LYAY). Their control of the Union Pacific enabled them to award construction contracts to their own construction company, the Crédit Mobilier. These contracts were paid for by other stockholders of the Union Pacific at several times what the job actually cost. As a result, much of the money invested by stockholders in the Union Pacific as well as a large share of the government subsidies flowed into the pockets of this small group of greedy men.

When Congressional committees finally investigated, they discovered that some members of Congress had owned stock in the Crédit Mobilier company. The company owners had given these members stock or had sold it to them at half price in an effort to bribe them and to block investigations.

The "salary grab" and tax scandals. In 1873, while the Crédit Mobilier scandal was occupying Congress, the Senators and Representatives voted themselves a 50 percent increase in salaries—from $5,000 to $7,500 per year. Moreover, each member of Congress would receive two years' back pay, or $5,000. The public was so outraged at this "salary grab" that Congress hastily repealed the act at the opening of its next session.

Public resentment had hardly died when another scandal made newspaper headlines. Secretary of the Treasury William A. Richardson signed a contract with a private citizen, John D. Sanborn. The contract gave Sanborn authority to collect overdue federal taxes, with the right to keep half of all he could collect. By various devious methods, Sanborn collected $427,000, keeping about half for himself.

When asked to explain the affair, Sanborn swore that he had kept only a small part of the "commission," having been forced to give $156,000 to his "assistants"! The "assistants" were politicians who had used their influence to swing the tax-collection contract to Sanborn. However, the contract was legal, and the "commission" was paid in full. A new law prevented the situation from recurring, however, and Richardson resigned.

The new Secretary of the Treasury, Benjamin H. Bristow, an honest official, discovered that taxes were not being collected on nearly 90 percent of the liquor distilled in the United States. Further investigation revealed that high public officials were guilty of blackmail and fraud.

According to the tax law, a distiller who failed to pay revenue taxes on distilled liquor had to pay a double tax if caught. Any informer who revealed to the government that a company had failed to pay its taxes received 10 percent of the tax penalty as a reward. Informers soon saw, however, that they could collect more by blackmailing the tax-evading company than by reporting the evasion. The Secretary of the Treasury discovered that a ring, or group, of whisky distillers and blackmailers had been defrauding the federal government of at least a million dollars a year.

Graft in the federal governments. Meanwhile, yet another scandal was unearthed. It was discovered that Secretary of War William W. Belknap had accepted $24,500 in bribes from a trader at Fort Sill in what is now Oklahoma. Belknap had decided to give the profitable trading rights with the Indians to a New York friend, but the trader who had the contract was making a huge profit from the Indians around Fort Sill. Therefore, the trader agreed to pay Belknap and his friend each $6,000 a year if he were allowed to keep his trading rights.

When evidence of this bribery was presented in 1876, the House of Representatives voted unanimously to impeach Belknap, who hastily resigned. Despite all the evidence, the Senate's impeachment trial failed to convict him. The Senators who voted "not guilty" claimed that because Belknap had resigned he was no longer subject to trial by the Senate.

There were still other evidences of graft in the federal government. The Secretary of the Navy "sold" business to builders and suppliers of ships. The Secretary of the Interior was involved with land speculators. President Grant himself had no part in these illegal activities. Nevertheless many people felt that Grant was at fault for allowing his friends to hide behind his good name.

Other scandals. Corruption was as bad, if not worse, in the state governments. In 1868 the Erie Railroad, which was controlled by Daniel Drew, James ("Jim") Fisk, Jr., and Jay Gould, wanted to sell $10 million worth of additional stock. Gould, to smooth the way, went to the New York State capital at Albany with a trunk full of money to bribe lawmakers to legalize the stock sale. Evidence suggested that the governor of New York sold his influence for $20,000 and that state senators got $15,000.

Perhaps worst of all was the corruption in municipal, or city, government. William M. Tweed, an uneducated chairmaker, rose in 15 years to be a multimillionaire "dictator" of New York City in the 1860's and 1870's. Working with Tammany Hall—as the city's Democratic **machine,** or political organization, was known—"Boss" Tweed largely controlled the city government.

Tweed gained control very simply. He or some of his followers met immigrant families when they landed, fed them, found them jobs and housing, and left them baskets of food at Thanksgiving and Christmas. After they secured the right to vote, the newcomers returned Tweed's "friendship" by voting for can-

According to one magazine, Thomas Nast's cartoons had more influence than cartoons "came near having in any [other] country." This one predicts "Boss" Tweed's escape from jail. Four years later Tweed did escape.

didates he favored. Moreover, when election outcomes seemed doubtful, the ballot boxes were stuffed with votes in favor of Tweed's candidates. That is, Tammany supporters voted several times, using different names and addresses each time.

How did Tweed use his power? He gave city jobs to many of his friends. He demanded kickbacks from people who wanted city jobs. He demanded bribes from companies that wanted to provide city services. A courthouse, started in 1868, was to cost $250,000. Three years later, still uncompleted, it had cost $8 million. In three years Tweed and his crooked ring stole an estimated $20 million from New York City. It is estimated that between 1868 and 1871 "Boss" Tweed's ring and his business friends cost the city close to $100 million.

Reasons for corruption. Why was public morality at such a low level in the years following the Civil War?

The war itself was partly responsible. In the crisis of wartime, the all-important consideration is to get things done quickly. Cost is secondary to what is considered national survival, and money flows freely into war industries. During the war years, with business booming, unscrupulous business interests and legislators had a rare opportunity to engage in dishonest practices. These practices were continued in the postwar years.

A related and equally significant explanation of the postwar graft was the rapid growth of large-scale industry, about which you will read in Chapter 22. In earlier times, when factories and businesses were small, their owners were well known in their own communities. If their practices were dishonest, they were likely to lose their neighbors' good will.

The new large corporations were impersonal. The people who controlled them were hardly known even by many of their own stockholders. Within the corporations, it was easier for dishonest individuals to get away with questionable practices.

What evidence in this section supports this conclusion?

2. Why did people blame Grant for the scandals that occurred during his administration?

3. Give examples of graft and corruption on the state and local levels during the postwar years.

4. Why was public corruption so widespread during the postwar years?

2 A start is made toward restoring honesty to government

Newspapers in the late 1860's and the early 1870's were filled with stories and cartoons attacking government graft among federal, state, and local officials. The most famous American cartoonist was Thomas Nast of New York, whose powerful cartoons in *Harper's Weekly* helped to reveal to the public the abuses of "Boss" Tweed and his associates.

These revelations of corruption stirred a widespread demand for reform. No reform movement aroused greater interest than the proposal to appoint persons to government jobs on the basis of merit. Under the spoils system, which Andrew Jackson had helped to extend, government jobs were given to political favorites. Under the proposed merit system, those who received the highest grades in competitive examinations would get the jobs. It would not matter whether they were Republicans or Democrats. All these public jobs in the federal, state, and local governments would be called **civil service** jobs.

Growth of the reform movement. In 1871, in response to the demand for reforms, Congress set up a Civil Service Commission to study the problem and to make recommendations. Although President Grant appointed able men to the commission, he gave it little support. In 1875 the chairman resigned in disgust and the commission was discontinued.

Meanwhile, in 1872, a group of reform-minded Republicans had started the Liberal Republican Party, nominating Horace Greely, the editor of the *New York Tribune*, as their Presidential candidate to run against the regular Republican candidate, President Grant. The Democrats also nominated Greeley, hop-

AMERICA'S MASTER CARTOONIST

One Sunday in the summer of 1871, a bank officer visited a New York cartoonist named Thomas Nast. The visitor was authorized, he said, to offer Nast $100,000 for "art study abroad." Nast—who was just thirty-one and had a growing family—showed some interest, even greed. He pushed the amount to half a million. Suddenly he laughed and said, "Well, I don't think I'll do it. I made up my mind not long ago to put some of these fellows behind bars, *and I'm going to put them there!*"

"These fellows" were the Tweed Ring, and Nast was being offered a bribe to stop attacking them in his drawings. His best-known assault was to come a few months later. In "The Tammany Tiger Let Loose," a snarling beast in a Roman arena is about to devour the "Republic," pictured as a helpless young woman. In the stands sits Tweed as a bloated emperor. "What are you going to do about it?" asks a line under the drawing. New York citizens took such vigorous action that Tweed fled the country. But he could not escape Nast. Several years later, in Spain, he was identified by someone who recognized him from a Nast drawing. Tweed was returned to New York and sent to prison.

Nast did over 3,000 drawings in his twenty-five-year career. He helped modernize the political cartoon by simplifying and sharpening it. He not only popularized the Tammany tiger but also created Santa Claus as we know him, the Democratic donkey, and the Republican elephant. Lincoln called him "our best recruiting sergeant." Always a crusader, Nast summed up his goal in one sentence: "I try to hit the enemy between the eyes and knock him down!"

---

ing by this means to benefit from the split in the Republican Party.

The Liberal Republican platform included a pledge to fight corruption in public life and a specific plank, or section, urging civil service reform. Nevertheless, Grant was reelected President easily.

The defeat at the polls in 1872 was a disheartening blow to the reformers. Within a year, however, they began to gather strength. For one thing, new public scandals drove more Americans into the reform movement. Also, growing dissatisfaction with Grant's Republican administration enabled the Democrats to win control of the House of Representatives in the Congressional elections of 1874.

The election of 1876. The Democrats, heartened by the growing demand for reform, approached the 1876 elections confident of a victory. They chose as their Presidential candidate Governor Samuel J. Tilden of New York. Governor Tilden had won national atten-tion by helping to break up the Tweed Ring in New York. The Democratic platform demanded civil service reform and an end to graft in public life.

The Republicans, who were running scared, nominated a man well known as a reformer, Governor Rutherford B. Hayes of Ohio. Hayes promised to work for civil service reform in the federal government. He also promised to end the troubled period of reconstruction.

Both Tilden and Hayes were wealthy. Both were closely associated with industrialists and business groups. Tilden's one big asset was the fact that he was running against a party that was identified with scandal.

The election gave Tilden 250,000 more popular votes than Hayes received. The first count of the electoral votes also gave Tilden an advantage over Hayes—184 to 165. Most newspapers at first reported Tilden had won.

However, the papers had jumped to the wrong conclusion. Tilden with his 184 electoral votes was one short of the necessary majority.

413

Ordinarily, when no Presidential candidate has a clear majority of the electoral vote, the House of Representatives chooses the President, but this was no ordinary election. Four states—South Carolina, Florida, Louisiana, and Oregon—had each sent in *two* different sets of returns. In all, 20 electoral votes from these four states were claimed by both the Republicans and the Democrats. Tilden needed only one of these disputed votes to win. Hayes, however, needed all 20.

The single disputed vote from Oregon was quickly settled in favor of Hayes. The 19 votes from the three southern states remained a problem. The Republicans claimed all three states for Hayes. The Democrats insisted that since these states were still under reconstruction governments, the will of the majority had not been expressed. For a time the controversy threatened to plunge the nation into violence.

Settling the dispute. Unfortunately, the Constitution provided no clear procedures for solving this situation. According to the Constitution, the votes had to be counted. But by whom? If the Republican-controlled Senate counted the votes, the Senators would throw out the Democratic returns and give the election to Hayes. If the Democratic-controlled House counted the votes, the Representatives would throw out the Republican returns and give the election to Tilden.

In order to break the deadlock, Congress created an Electoral Commission of 15 members. On it were five Senators, five Representatives, and five Supreme Court Justices. By previous arrangement the Senate chose three Republicans and two Democrats. The House chose two Republicans and three Democrats. Four Justices—two Republicans and two Democrats—were to name a fifth member of the commission—an independent voter without ties to either party.

It was generally understood that the independent member of the Electoral Commission would be Justice David Davis. At the last minute, however, Davis resigned from the Supreme Court because of his election to the Senate. His place on the Electoral Commission went to a Republican. It was not surprising, therefore, that when the disputed votes were counted, they went to the Republicans by a straight party vote of eight Republicans as opposed to the seven Democrats on the Electoral Commission.

Thus it was that Hayes, who had received a minority of the popular votes, entered the White House as President. The controversial election of 1876–77 did, however, represent a victory for compromise and for the process of orderly government.

Difficulties for Hayes. President Hayes had four difficult years in the White House. Throughout his administration the Democrats controlled the House and for two years, from 1879 to 1881, the Senate as well. Although the Democrats did not try to upset the decision of the Electoral Commission, they called Hayes "His Fraudulency" and "Old Eight to Seven" to remind him that they questioned his right to the Presidency.

Hayes also faced opposition from his own party. The election of 1876 split the Republicans into two groups—the Stalwarts and the Half-Breeds. The Stalwarts, sometimes called "Old Guard" Republicans, were against reform and reformers. They also opposed the President himself, whom they called "Granny Hayes." The Half-Breeds, led by James G. Blaine of Maine and John Sherman of Ohio, agreed with Hayes that at least some steps toward reform were needed.

To fulfill his promise of ending reconstruction, President Hayes named a former Confederate leader to his cabinet and withdrew the last federal occupation troops from the South. As the remaining reconstruction governments lost power, southern Democrats were free to manage state affairs in their own way. Southern Democrats elected to Congress from the "Solid South" now allied with northern Democrats to break the power of the Radical Republicans, who had controlled Congress during the period of reconstruction.

Hayes's battle for reform. In spite of strong opposition, Hayes was the first President to take serious steps to reform the civil service. He refused to follow the practice of many earlier Presidents of discharging thousands of officeholders and replacing them with political favorites. He also insisted that all persons recommended by members of Congress for jobs should be carefully investigated. He courageously removed a prominent Republican, Chester A. Arthur, from his job as Collector of Customs in New York because of Arthur's questionable political activities. One of his own cabinet members, Carl Schurz, a German-born

Republican, introduced the merit system into the Department of the Interior.

The election of 1880.   Well before the nominating conventions for the 1880 elections, President Hayes announced that he would not run for reelection. The Stalwart wing of the Republican Party, fed up with talk of reform and eager to return to the "good old days," tried to win the nomination for former President Ulysses S. Grant. The Half-Breed wing of the party managed to block this attempt, and the Republican convention finally nominated a war veteran, General James A. Garfield of Ohio. To win the support of the Stalwarts, the convention nominated for Vice-President Chester A. Arthur, a leading Stalwart.

The Democrats also pinned their hopes for the Presidency on a war veteran, General Winfield S. Hancock of Pennsylvania.

During the campaign, neither the Democrats nor the Republicans faced up to basic problems of the new industrial age—labor legislation, regulation of railroads and other big business, the money issue, and an income tax. Thus it was a third party, the Greenback-Labor Party, as you will read, that squarely faced the controversial issues of the time.

Garfield won the election with an electoral vote of 214 to Hancock's 155. However, the popular vote was close—4,449,053 for the Republicans, 4,442,035 for the Democrats.

Civil service reform.   On July 2, 1881, President Garfield was shot by a disappointed—and mentally unbalanced—government job seeker. Garfield died in September.

The President's tragic death shocked the nation into an awareness of the evils of the old spoils system. Chester A. Arthur, the new President, responded to the widespread demand for reform and supported the Pendleton Civil Service Act.

The Pendleton Act, which became law in 1883, set up a commission to give competitive examinations for those seeking government jobs. The first examinations were to include only about 12 percent of federal jobs, but the President was given authority to broaden the list. The Pendleton Act also forbade the party in power to ask for campaign contributions from federal officeholders. President Arthur appointed an able leader for the new commission and extended the list of jobs for which civil service examinations had to be taken.

Thus, after years of agitation, reformers at last managed to write into law the principle that federal jobs below the policy-making level should be filled by merit. A long step had been taken toward making government more honest and efficient.

The election of 1884.   When the election year of 1884 rolled around, Chester A. Arthur made it clear that he wanted to run for the Presidency. However, his Republican Stalwart supporters had lost faith in him because of the reform activities he had supported. Instead of Arthur, the leader of the Half-Breed wing of the Republican Party, James G. Blaine, won the nomination.

Blaine was a handsome, colorful, and persuasive candidate, but during his long political career, he had made many enemies. These

In an attempt to save President Garfield after his assassination, his doctors used a device invented by Alexander Graham Bell. It found the exact location of the bullet near his spine, but blood poisoning set in and eventually killed Garfield.

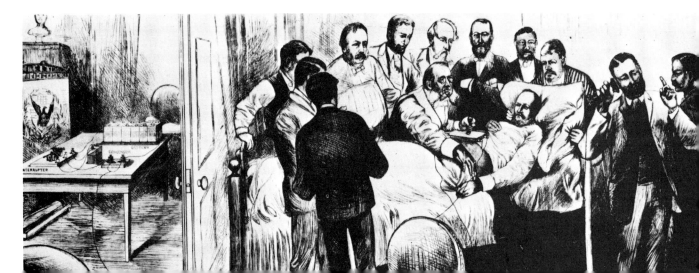

enemies now accused Blaine of having used his political influence to secure favors for big business—at a generous profit for himself. Unhappy with Blaine's nomination, a large group of Republicans, nicknamed "Mugwumps," bolted from the party and chose to support the Democratic candidate.

The Democrats made the most of Blaine's reputation as "a tool of the special interests." They chose a reformer as their Presidential nominee, Grover Cleveland, who had been governor of New York. Cleveland was known to be honest, courageous, independent—and stubborn when fighting for a principle.

In the campaign the big issues of the day were almost forgotten as the politicians heaped abuse upon the rival candidates. Each party raked over the personal life of the opposition candidate.

Throughout the campaign the two candidates, Blaine and Cleveland, ran neck and neck. Then, on the very eve of the election, at a reception given for Blaine by a group of Protestant clergy, a speaker called the Democrats the party of "Rum, Romanism, and Rebellion."

The speaker's use of the word "rum" was a deliberate attempt to smear the Democrats. His use of the word "rebellion" referred to the alliance between northern Democrats and the "Solid South" Democrats. Both references were bad enough, but the speaker's reference to "Romanism"—the Roman Catholic religion—was fatal. It was generally agreed that Blaine's failure to rebuke the speaker for this insult to Roman Catholic voters cost him the election. Grover Cleveland thus won the Presidency, squeaking through with 219 electoral votes to Blaine's 182.

The election of 1884 was the first Presidential victory for the Democrats in 28 years. It was one sign that memories of the Civil War were beginning to fade.

SECTION SURVEY

IDENTIFY: Thomas Nast, civil service, Horace Greeley, Samuel Tilden, Rutherford Hayes, James Blaine, James Garfield, Chester Arthur, "Mugwumps."

1. How is the spoils system different from the merit system of appointing people to government jobs?
2. In what ways was the election of 1876 one of the most unusual in American history?
3. What position did each of the following take concerning reform: (a) Liberal Republicans, (b) Stalwarts, (c) Half-Breeds?
4. (a) Explain the provisions of the Pendleton Act of 1883. (b) Why was it enacted?
5. What factors led to Cleveland's election in 1884?

3 Efforts at political reform move forward

When President Cleveland entered the White House in 1885, the movement for political reform entered a new phase.

Cleveland's firm stand. President Cleveland strongly believed that "a public office is a public trust." He took a firm stand on important issues, even though he knew that his action would antagonize influential members of his own party.

He supported civil service reform by doubling the number of federal jobs on the classified list. He took a step toward conserving the nation's natural resources by recovering vast areas of public land illegally held by railroads, lumber companies, and cattle interests. He signed a bill in 1887 creating a federal Division of Forestry.

One of his most courageous acts was his attempt to block "pension grabs" by veterans of the Union army. For many years the Pension Bureau had been very generous in handing out pensions. Now and then, however, requests for pensions were based on such flimsy grounds that even the bureau rejected them. Often, when this happened, the disappointed pension seeker asked his representative in Congress to get the pension for him by pushing a special bill through Congress. Cleveland vetoed more than 200 of these bills. He thus angered many ex-soldiers, who were united in the politically powerful veterans' organization the Grand Army of the Republic, known as the G.A.R.

Important laws. In addition to Cleveland's personal accomplishments, Congress adopted several important laws during the years from 1885 to 1889.

The Presidential Succession Act of 1886 provided that if both the President and the Vice-President died or were disabled, the cabinet officers would succeed to the Presidency in the order in which their offices had been created.

The Electoral Count Act of 1887 was designed to prevent another disputed election similar to the election of 1876. The act provided that if a state sent in more than one set of electoral returns, Congress had to accept the returns approved by the governor of the state.

In 1887 Congress tried to quiet the clamor of small business people and farmers against unfair business practices by the railroads. It passed the Interstate Commerce Act, about which you will read in Chapter 24. Congress refused, however, to accept President Cleveland's strong recommendation that tariff rates be lowered.

The election of 1888. President Cleveland's reform activities and especially his campaign for lower tariffs antagonized political leaders in his own party. Nevertheless, in 1888 the Democrats nominated him for a second term.

Although Cleveland won nearly 100,000 more popular votes than his opponent, Benjamin Harrison, he lost by an electoral count of 233 to 168. The Republicans won the Presidency and control of both houses of Congress.

Cleveland's policies reversed. Benjamin Harrison was a successful lawyer, a veteran of the Union army, and the grandson of former President William Henry Harrison. He was not, however, a strong President. In his opinion, his duty as Chief Executive was to follow the wishes of the Senators and Representatives, who in turn had the responsibility of carrying out the wishes of the people.

During President Harrison's administration, the Republicans reversed many of President Cleveland's policies. Instead of supporting the civil service system, they replaced Democratic officeholders (except those on the classified list) with Republicans. Congress passed an act that almost doubled the number of pensioners and their dependents. Congress also adopted the highest protective tariff the country had had up to that time, the McKinley Tariff of 1890.

The "Old Guard" Republicans did not have everything their way. In an effort to appeal to farmers, laborers, miners, small business people, and the American public in general, Congress passed two important laws in 1890. The Sherman Silver Purchase Act was in-

According to this cartoon, Uncle Sam had little reason to be pleased with Benjamin Harrison's Presidency. What failings does the cartoonist lay at Harrison's door?

tended to appeal to western mining interests. The act was also meant to increase the amount of money in circulation as a benefit to farmers, wage earners, and small business interests. The Sherman Antitrust Act was intended to protect the public from monopoly practices and other abuses of free enterprise that had arisen with the growth of industry. You will read about these two laws in the next unit.

Growing dissatisfaction. Neither the Sherman Silver Purchase Act nor the Sherman Antitrust Act stopped the growing dissatisfaction with President Harrison's Republican administration. Wage earners had no reason to hope their demands would be met by Republicans. Many farmers, abandoning hope of help from either party, began to join labor organizations in efforts to win control of the government and bring about reforms. Many Americans, struggling to make ends meet at a time of rising prices, blamed their troubles on the Republican-sponsored McKinley Tariff.

Two widely read books expressed the growing dissatisfaction with the concentration of wealth in the hands of a few. Henry George's *Progress and Poverty,* first published in 1879, contrasted the wealth of the privileged few

417

with the poverty of many people. George blamed this inequality on the fact that a few persons had monopoly control over the nation's choicest land sites and other natural resources. George proposed a new system of taxing land. He thought that this system would abolish great fortunes and provide a good standard of living for everyone.

In 1894 the book *Wealth Against Commonwealth* by Henry Demarest Lloyd was published. The author concluded that the giant new corporations and business enterprises were running the new industrial economy for their own gain.

Lloyd's book expressed the deep discontent of millions of Americans. What concerned many Americans was that the new industrialism had created extremes of poverty and wealth. Expanding industries brought vast wealth to a few owners, while the majority of workers lived in poverty. For a solution to this problem, many Americans turned to government—whether controlled by Republicans or Democrats.

By 1892 the demand for government action could not be ignored. Owners of small businesses, wage earners in every section of the country, and especially the western farmers were calling for reform.

The election of 1892. Increasing discontent turned the election of 1892 into a spirited three-way contest. Both the Republicans and the Democrats realized that they had to do something about reform. They were prodded into action by the strength of a new party, the Populist Party, which had been created in 1891. The Populist Party, which you will read about later, was organized by farmers, but it also attracted wage earners and other discontented voters.

The Republicans were on the defensive. President Harrison and the Republican Party received widespread criticism. Nevertheless, the Republicans decided to stand on their record. The party nominated President Harrison for a second term.

The Democrats were eager to take advantage of the demands for reform from both workers and farmers. They nominated Grover Cleveland, who was already known as a champion of honest politics.

The Democrats won, with Cleveland gathering 277 electoral votes to Harrison's 145. The Democrats also won control of Congress, but

the new Populist Party—an out-and-out reform party—made a remarkable showing. Although the Populist candidate, James B. Weaver, collected only 22 electoral votes, his popular vote totaled more than 1 million. The Populist Party also elected three governors and numerous representatives to state legislatures and to Congress.

The Wilson-Gorman Tariff. From the beginning President Cleveland was in trouble. His election had stemmed in part from his promise to lower the McKinley Tariff. A tariff bill that he supported was introduced in the House in December 1893. By the time the bill had gone through the House and Senate, over 600 amendments had been tacked on to it raising tariff rates for particular products.

The Wilson-Gorman bill, as the amended bill was called, did provide overall lower average tariff rates than the McKinley Tariff. However, it was still a high protective tariff, and President Cleveland was furious. He refused to endorse it by signing it, preferring instead to leave it on his desk for ten days. After that time it automatically became law without his signature.

During the tariff debates in the Senate, powerful lobbies, or pressure groups, tried in every way possible to influence the votes of doubtful Senators. Producers of iron, steel, wool, glass, and hundreds of other products demanded tariff protection.

One of the most active lobbies was the American Sugar Refining Company, usually called "the sugar trust."° The original House bill had completely removed the tariff on raw and refined sugar. The sugar trust, determined to get the tariff restored, immediately went to work on the Senate. In the end, the trust won, and the tariff on sugar was restored.

The Wilson-Gorman Tariff cost the Democrats the support of millions of Americans who were convinced that the Democrats had broken their campaign promise to do away with a high protective tariff.

Decision against an income tax. The original tariff bill favored by President Cleveland would have sharply lowered the tariff rates. Expecting a loss in government revenue because of the lower rates, the House added a

°**trust:** a group of companies centrally controlled to regulate production, reduce production costs, and eliminate competition.

418

Panic hit the floor of the New York Stock Exchange as investors raced to sell their stocks in May 1893. Plunging stock prices set off a crippling depression that would last five years and cause hardship for millions across the nation.

clause to the tariff bill providing for a 2 percent tax on all incomes of more than $4,000.

The income tax clause provoked violent debate, but it finally became law. Opponents of the income tax immediately tested the new measure in the courts. In 1895 the Supreme Court declared it unconstitutional. The Supreme Court ruled against the income tax because it was a direct tax not apportioned among the states according to population, as required by the Constitution (page 168).

The Democratic administration could not be held responsible for the Supreme Court's negative decision on the income tax. Nevertheless, millions of Americans considered the Court's decision as merely one more example of how the government favored big business. Thus the Supreme Court's rejection of the income tax helped to fan the flame of protest sweeping the country.

Financial panic. On May 5, 1893, only two months after Cleveland took office, a financial panic began as the value of stocks on the New York Stock Exchange suddenly plunged. As the weeks passed, the situation rapidly became worse. Thousands of businesses failed. Facto-

ries closed their doors. Perhaps as many as 4 million workers were unemployed. The prices of farm produce dropped so low that farmers could not afford the cost of shipping it. By the end of the year, the American nation was in the grip of one of the worst depressions in its history.

SECTION SURVEY

IDENTIFY: "pension grabs," Benjamin Harrison, McKinley Tariff of 1890, Populist Party, Wilson-Gorman Tariff, lobbies, trust, panic of 1893.

1. What did Grover Cleveland mean when he said that "a public office is a public trust"?

2. Explain how each of the following laws helped to prevent a potential national problem: (a) Presidential Succession Act of 1886, (b) Electoral Count Act of 1887.

3. Summarize the main ideas in the writings of Henry Demarest Lloyd and Henry George.

4. How did the issue of tariffs play a part in politics during the 1880's and 1890's?

5. Cartoon Study: Look at the cartoon on page 417. What is the cartoonist's attitude toward Harrison? How does the cartoonist express this attitude?

419

Chapter Survey

Change, unrest, new ways of living, and new problems—these were characteristics of every section of the United States during the years from 1865 to 1900. Many of the new problems that Americans faced were the result of the Civil War, which for four long years had shaken the nation and disrupted long-established ways of living. To an even greater extent, however, the new problems were the result of the transformation of the United States from an agricultural nation into a great industrial power.

Industrialization, already under way before the war, roared ahead during the war years. Northern industry continued to expand after 1865 with ever-increasing speed. Industri-alization was also transforming life in the South. As you will read in the next chapter, it contributed to the conquest of the last frontiers in the West.

The new ways of living brought serious problems as well as excitement and drama. Morality in public life sank to an all-time low as a "get-rich-quick" spirit and greed for power infected millions of Americans. Wealth and power became concentrated in the hands of a relatively few pioneers of the new industrial age. Through their control of the railroads, mines, factories, banks, and giant corporations, the new industrial and financial leaders exerted powerful influence over government at every level. The control exercised by this small group threatened the working of the democratic process.

There is, however, another side of the story. As Americans became increasingly aware of the threat to democracy, they began to take steps to correct the situation. In later chapters you will read how the American people undertook to solve the many problems that were confronting them.

Inquiring into History

1. Explain how the Pendleton Act made a significant contribution to the development of democracy in the United States.
2. During the late 1800's, many workers and farmers felt that the government favored big business and the well-to-do. (a) What events made them feel this way? (b) Do you think they were justified?
3. (a) Compare the views held by Grover Cleveland and Benjamin Harrison on the proper role of the President. (b) In what ways did their views affect their actions as President? Give specific examples to support your answer.
4. Historians have rated American Presidents by the following categories: great, near great, average, below average, and failure. Make a list of the Presidents elected between 1865 and 1896 and evaluate them according to these categories. What factors did you consider in making your judgments?

Relating Past to Present

1. (a) Name examples of graft and corruption in local, state, or federal government in recent years. (b) Compare the methods and motivations of these officials and of corrupt officials in the late 1800's.
2. Does the word "reform" seem to have a different meaning today from the one it had during the 1880's and 1890's? Explain.
3. (a) What groups of people made up the majority of the Republican Party and of the Democratic Party during the period from 1865 to 1897? (b) What major groups make up each party's majority today? Compare and comment.

Developing Social Science Skills

1. Study the cartoon on page 417. (a) Identify the characters shown in the cartoon. (b) What is the point of view of the cartoon? (c) How effective do you think the cartoon is?
2. Compare the Presidential Succession Act of 1967 (Amendment 25, see page 198) with the one enacted in 1886. Why do you think the act of 1967 was necessary?
3. Benjamin Harrison was elected President in 1888 although he received fewer popular votes than his opponent, Grover Cleveland, did. Consult an almanac or other reference books to find out if other candidates have won the Presidency despite receiving fewer popular votes than their opponents.

Chapter 21

Conquering the Last Frontier

1865-1900

Chief Joseph, leader of the Nez Percé Indians, surrendered to his conquerors sorrowfully, but with dignity. "I am tired of fighting," he said. "Our chiefs are killed. . . . It is cold and we have no blankets. The little children are freezing to death. . . . My heart is sick and sad. From where the sun now stands I will fight no more, forever." The year was 1877. The place was the plains of Montana, only a few miles from the Canadian border.

For years beyond memory, the Nez Percés had lived in the region where the present states of Oregon, Washington, and Idaho meet. For half a century, they had dwelt in peace with the whites.

By the mid-1860's, however, it had become clear that the peaceful days were ending. Land-hungry pioneers moving into the Pacific Northwest were looking with greedy eyes at the fertile valleys and hunting grounds of the Nez Percés. In 1877 the federal government ordered the Nez Percés to leave their homeland for a remote region. They started the move, but trouble broke out and a small band of Indians murdered 19 whites.

Certain that the United States Army would punish all of the Nez Percés, Chief Joseph decided to flee to safety and a new homeland in Canada. For two months the band of 200 warriors and 600 women and children outwitted and outfought much larger forces of pursuing troops. Finally, after traveling more than 1,300 miles (2,100 kilometers) through unbelievably rugged terrain, they were surrounded by United States troops and forced to surrender almost within sight of the border.

Thus, in 1877, Chief Joseph faced his conquerors on the last frontier of the West, the Great Plains. This vast area, stretching from the Canadian border to Texas, had belonged to the Indians from earliest times. Now it was being claimed by people from the North and South and from distant Europe. This is the story of the conquest of the Indians. It is also the story of the West itself and of new ways of life on the last frontier.

THE CHAPTER IN OUTLINE

1. The Indians make their last stand on the Great Plains.

2. The government tries to "Americanize" the Indians.

3. Ranchers build a cattle kingdom on the plains.

4. Farmers plow the tough sod of the last frontier.

5. Miners find new treasures in the western mountains.

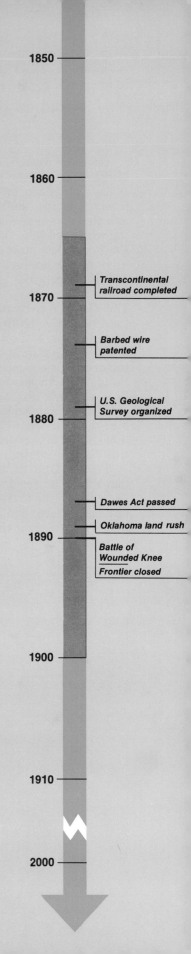

1850

1860

1870 — Transcontinental railroad completed

Barbed wire patented

U.S. Geological Survey organized

1880

Dawes Act passed

Oklahoma land rush

1890 — Battle of Wounded Knee

Frontier closed

1900

1910

2000

1 The Indians make their last stand on the Great Plains

On their western edge, the prairies of the Middle West merge into the Great Plains. Although no sharp line separates the prairies from the plains, the 100th meridian is usually accepted as the dividing line. A traveler heading westward from the 100th meridian toward the Rocky Mountains will notice that the annual rainfall gradually decreases and the grass gets shorter.

The Great American Desert. It was along the line of the 100th meridian that the westward advance of the settlers halted for at least a generation during the early 1800's. The reluctance of the pioneers to settle on the Great Plains arose in part from misinformation. Earlier explorers, accustomed to wooded country with abundant rainfall, had established the idea that the Great Plains were arid and uninhabitable. Maps of the times called the plains the "Great American Desert."

For as long as the whites believed the plains to be barren desert, they were content to leave the region to the Indians. In fact, the federal government had moved many tribes to the plains from east of the Mississippi and promised to keep white settlers out. "A country west of Missouri and Arkansas has been assigned to [the Indians], into which white settlements are not to be pushed," President Andrew Jackson had declared in 1835.

By the 1850's, however, the mistaken notion of the plains as desert was being dispelled. Traders and pioneers who crossed the plains on their way to California and the Pacific Northwest reported that much of the plains country was good for farming and cattle raising. White settlers gradually began to move onto the plains.

Bows and arrows against guns. The Plains Indians were determined to defend their hunting grounds and their way of life. They had learned what later white settlers would have to learn—how to adapt to the plains environment. Herds of wild horses, descendants of those of the Spanish conquistadors, now roamed the plains. The Indians had mastered these horses and had become expert riders. On horseback they could easily hunt the buffalo, or bison, which provided them with food, clothing, and shelter.

The Indians were powerful adversaries. They rode superbly. Before they secured rifles, they fought with spears and with short bows, from which they could drive their arrows with amazing rapidity and penetrating force. To protect themselves they used shields made of

Here artist George Catlin captures a moment in a Plains Indian buffalo hunt. The Indians who hunted with bows and arrows or with spears did not threaten to wipe out the buffalo population, but the white newcomers with rifles did.

buffalo hide. These they coated with glue made from horses' hooves and hardened over the fire to an almost iron-like consistency. A favorite Indian tactic was to gallop around the enemy, hiding behind their horses and shields and deliberately drawing enemy fire. When the enemy's ammunition was exhausted, the Indians darted in to strike with arrows and long spears.

Faced with these weapons and tactics, white intruders at first were at a disadvantage. Their long rifles could be reloaded and fired from the back of a galloping horse only with great difficulty.

The invention of the revolver in the late 1830's ended the Indians' temporary superiority in weapons. The revolver could be reloaded easily at full gallop. Several bullets could be fired in rapid succession without reloading. Armed with this new weapon, settlers in the 1850's could move out onto the plains with more confidence.

A new Indian policy. This new movement of white settlers brought about a change in government policy toward the Indians. In 1849 the Bureau of Indian Affairs became part of the Department of the Interior. The bureau had responsibility for carrying out the federal government's Indian policies. One early policy was **concentration.** This was the attempt to confine the Indian tribes to certain limited areas of the West. In these areas the tribes would be free to carry on their own affairs and continue their lives as hunters. It was hoped the policy would reduce warfare among the tribes and would clear routes for white settlers heading for California and Oregon.

More settlers on the plains. An individual traveling on foot across the Great Plains was in grave danger of dying from thirst, sunstroke, or cold. Thus the early pioneers who crossed the plains depended upon horses and oxen for transportation. A rider on horseback, however, could not transport goods in bulk. To fill this need, caravans of covered wagons set out upon the plains, forming circles around campfires at night for protection against Indian attack. As time passed, stagecoach lines offered a speedier form of transportation.

After the Civil War, the Great Plains attracted increasing numbers of land speculators, ranchers, miners, engineers, and farmers. These newcomers were determined to possess the land and its resources for themselves.

Government policy toward the Indians changed again, now calling for their resettlement on **reservations.** These were sharply defined tracts of land set aside by the government for the Indians. Most reservations were too small to support the hunting way of life. Therefore, the Indians were supposed to get food through government agents on the reservation. Also, the Indians were expected to take up farming, although reservations were usually located on the poorest land.

Railroads cross the plains. The railroads finally conquered the Great Plains for the white settlers. Construction of the first transcontinental railroad began in 1866. Chinese workers were imported to do most of the physical labor on the Central Pacific. Most of the workers on the Union Pacific, building from Omaha, in Nebraska Territory, were recent Irish immigrants. All work was done under the watchful eyes of scouts, who protected the railroad builders from hostile Indians. The Central Pacific and the Union Pacific met in 1869 at Promontory, in what is now Utah. This "wedding of the rails" was an occasion of jubilation. Silk-hatted gentlemen surrounded by grimy workers drove a golden spike to hold the last rails in place while the news was telegraphed to Americans everywhere.

The first transcontinental railroad contributed enormously to the nation's economic growth. It brought the Atlantic and the Pacific seaboards within a week's journey of each other and opened a speedy route to the rich resources of the West, a route followed by northerners and southerners alike.

The railroad also split the vast buffalo herds of the plains. The herds were split again and again as other rail lines were built across the grasslands. Finally the completion of the Northern Pacific Railway in 1883 sealed the fate of the last, northernmost buffalo herd (see map, page 430).

Destruction of the buffalo. The Plains Indians depended mainly on the buffalo for their living. Government agents and army officers, knowing this, sometimes encouraged the destruction of the great herds as a means of keeping the Indians on reservations. Parties of hunters debarked from trains with horses and equipment, killed the buffalo at will, and loaded the hides on trains bound for eastern markets. It has been estimated that between

White Bird, a Cheyenne who had fought against General Custer's troops as a boy, painted this picture of the Battle of Little Bighorn. News of Custer's defeat in the West by Sioux and Cheyenne Indians led by Crazy Horse and Gall reached the East just as the nation began celebrating its 100th birthday on July 4, 1876.

1871 and 1874, hunters killed nearly 3 million buffalo each year. By 1875, buffalo hides were selling from 65 cents to $1.15 apiece. The waste was frightful. Buffalo carcasses were abandoned, and for every hide taken, four were left on the plains.

The disappearance of the buffalo doomed the Plains Indians. The Indians saw the dwindling herds and the increasing number of white settlers. They saw the treaties, by which they agreed to give up land or to move to reservations, broken again and again by whites. They learned that the agents who ran the reservations were often corrupt. The Indians also came to resent the restrictions of the reservations and the attempts by the federal government to change their way of life.

Many Indians decided to resist the whites. They left the reservations and tried to resume their lives as hunters on the plains. This brought another change in government policy toward the Indians, one in which the United States Army played a key role. The army's mis-sion was to keep the Indians on the reservations and to force the return of those who fled.

The Indian wars. Despite their advantages over the Plains Indians, white settlers and the army had to fight long and hard to drive them from their hunting grounds. Between 1865 and 1886, the United States conducted a costly and brutal campaign against the Plains Indians. In all the engagements of this campaign, former soldiers who had fought for the South or the North in the Civil War now fought together against the Indians.

In 1866 Congress decided to recruit four all-black regiments — the 24th and 25th Infantries and the 9th and 10th Cavalries — to fight in the Indian wars. One fifth of the army's soldiers on horseback in the western campaigns were enrolled in the 9th and 10th Cavalries.

During the 30-odd years of the Indian wars, the Indians fought back against white and black military forces in an effort to hold on to their lands and to keep their distinctive ways

424

of life. As in earlier conflicts with settlers, the Indians were not always united in their struggle. Traditional tribal rivalries explain in part why the federal regiments were often able to enlist Indians as highly useful scouts.

Still, Indian resistance was remarkable. The smaller the area into which the Indians were driven, the more desperately they fought back. There was brutality on both sides, and army leaders fought not only with guns but also with broken promises. In 1877, the same year in which Chief Joseph made his heroic attempt to lead his people to freedom in Canada, President Hayes admitted, "Many, if not most, of our Indian wars have their origin in broken promises and acts of injustice on our part."

Custer's last stand. Just the year before, one broken promise had brought disaster. The Sioux had been promised as a permanent home the Black Hills in what are now South Dakota and Wyoming, which they considered sacred. However, after gold was discovered in the Black Hills, the 7th Cavalry, in 1876, was ordered to remove the Indians to a less desirable area. The removal operation was under the command of General George Custer, an experienced Indian fighter. Several years earlier, Custer had attacked a peaceful Indian village on the Washita River in Oklahoma. In the attack unarmed women and children as well as warriors were killed.

In June of 1876, General Custer attacked a large camp of Sioux and Cheyenne near the Little Bighorn River in Montana. The Sioux and Cheyenne warriors had two outstanding leaders. One was Sitting Bull, able, honest, and idealistic. The other was Crazy Horse, uncompromising, reckless, a military genius, and the most honored hero of the Sioux.

In fierce fighting along the Little Bighorn, Custer and his whole detachment of 264 troops were killed and some bodies mutilated. General Custer's last stand provoked long controversy, but none could deny that it was a major humiliation for the United States government. Still, the action at the Little Bighorn for a time marked the end of major fighting on the northern Great Plains. Troops pursued and harried the Sioux and Cheyenne until Crazy Horse and Sitting Bull were defeated and the Indians forced onto reservations.

Resistance ends in the Southwest. To the south and west, meanwhile, the Apaches continued their three centuries of almost uninterrupted war against the whites. First there had been the Spaniards, then the Mexicans, and finally the North Americans. From time to time, bands of Apaches and Comanches led by Cochise, Victorio, Geronimo, and others rode out of their reservations and spread terror along the Mexican–United States border. Finally, in 1886, Geronimo surrendered. With his surrender, organized resistance came to an end on the southern plains and in the rugged mountains of the Southwest.

The end of the fighting. It was on the northern plains, however, that the United States cavalry wrote the final bloody chapter in the long and tragic history of Indian-white warfare.

The events leading up to this final tragedy had their roots in 1889 with a religious revival that swept through the Indian tribes. The revival was celebrated in what the whites called the "Ghost Dance." It was based on the belief that an Indian Messiah was about to appear. With his arrival dead Indians would rise from their graves to join the living, the buffalo would again roam the plains, and the white intruders would vanish from the Indian lands like mist under the morning sun.

The Ghost Dance was not a call to war. It was, on the contrary, the celebration of a vision — the restoration of the old and treasured Indian way of life. As such, it awakened new hope in the hearts of a broken, despairing people. The Ghost Dance cult quickly gained followers, including many Sioux on the northern plains. White miners and settlers, alarmed at what they feared might be another outbreak of warfare, demanded that the army put an end to the activity.

At Wounded Knee in South Dakota in December 1890, a unit of the 7th Cavalry responded to this demand. The cavalry arrested a band of Sioux men, women, and children who were traveling to the Pine Ridge Reservation in search of food and protection. The troops surrounded the Indians and disarmed them. During the process a disturbance broke out, and someone fired a shot. Immediately, without warning, the troops opened fire with rifles and with Gatling guns, the earliest type of machine guns. They poured a deadly hail of lead into the band of unprotected Sioux, killing or mortally wounding 90 men and 200 women and children.

Many Americans expressed their horror at such brutality. Others rejoiced that at last General Custer had been "avenged." As for the Indians, the brutal massacre at Wounded Knee brought an end to all organized armed resistance in the United States.

SECTION SURVEY

IDENTIFY: Great American Desert, Bureau of Indian Affairs, concentration, reservations, transcontinental railroad, Chief Joseph, George Custer, Geronimo, Ghost Dance, Wounded Knee.

1. How did the following contribute to the defeat of the Indians: (a) the revolver, (b) the railroads, (c) the destruction of the buffalo?
2. Describe and explain the purpose behind each of these United States policies toward the Indians: (a) concentration, (b) reservations, (c) military force.
3. Compare the actions of Chief Joseph and Geronimo in response to United States policy toward the Indians.

2 The government tries to "Americanize" the Indians

The Indians, the first Americans, had once claimed all the North American continent as their own. By 1890 their conquerors had stripped them of most of their land and their freedom. They had also confined the Indians to reservations.

The reservations. On the reservations, far removed from their original tribal lands, the Indians confronted the problem of adapting their ways of life to unfamiliar climates and terrains. When they tried to escape, they were pursued, captured punished, and sent back to the reservation. To make matters worse, just when some of the Indians were beginning to adjust to their new environments, the government would move them to different reservations.

Legally, the reservation Indians were **wards** of the government, like minor children without parents. In return for the lands they had given up, they were supposed to receive certain supplies, such as blankets, seed corn, and basic food. These supplies were often poor in quality and quantity and slow in reaching the Indians. Some agents in charge of the reservations were honest, but many agents profited from corrupt deals with traders and with those who provided the supplies. The Indians were commonly treated with contempt or, at best, as children might be treated.

"Americanizing" the Indians. Even with the Indians confined to the reservations, there was still a serious "Indian problem" in the view of most white Americans. Most white Americans believed that it was necessary for the Indians to be "Americanized." This meant that the Indians had to be assimilated into the white

This photograph shows the Pine Ridge Indian Reservation in southwestern South Dakota. It was the final, government-run home of the Sioux, who had tried to stop the spread of settlement onto their lands but had been unable to do so.

These young men were part of an effort in 1900 to "Americanize" the Indians. They attended a school for Indians near Carson City, Nevada. Judging from the photograph, what means were used to "Americanize" them?

American way of life and forced to accept the culture of the dominant majority. To the Indians—reduced in numbers to between 200,000 and 300,000 at that time—this idea meant giving up many of their deeply held values and customs. These included the collective or tribal ownership and use of land; a belief that work was only a means of providing food and shelter, not an end in itself; marriage traditions, including having more than one wife; many religious beliefs; and even clothing styles and adornments. Indian men, for example, resented efforts to make them cut their long, braided hair. Nor did Indian men and boys accept the idea that they were supposed to plant and cultivate the soil; that had always been women's work.

The vast majority of white Americans neither understood nor appreciated the Indian cultures. They were unaware of the importance of these cultures to the Indians' sense of identity and self-respect.

Reform activities. Some Americans, however, were deeply troubled by the long history of the white settlers' injustice to the Indians.

Helen Hunt Jackson, in her book *A Century of Dishonor* (1881), provided documentary evidence of the government's broken promises. The reformers were also deeply disturbed by the corruption, inefficiency, and lack of leadership in the Bureau of Indian Affairs.

Sarah Winnemucca, daughter of a Nevada Paiute chief, played a unique role in urging reform. She was a scout, a guide, an interpreter at army posts, a teacher of Indian children, the widow of one army officer, and the wife of another. In lectures at Boston, San Francisco, and elsewhere, she spoke out against the injustices to her people. She denounced the corruption of agents of the Bureau of Indian Affairs and called for better distribution of lands to Indians. General Oliver Otis Howard, for whom she was a scout and interpreter, declared that she "should have a place beside the name of Pocahontas in the history of our country."

One reform group, the National Indian Defense Organization, argued that the deep-rooted cultures of the Indians could not be rapidly changed without grave consequences. Members of this group argued that the Indians should be allowed to retain their own tradi-

427

tions and customs. Most other reform organizations, however, believed that the Indians could and should be speedily "Americanized." They felt that the Indians must adopt Christianity, white American forms of education, and individual land ownership.

Reformers who urged individual land ownership for the Indians actually strengthened, without intending to, the more selfish interests of land speculators, miners, ranchers, and farmers who were already occupying the unsettled areas of the West. These groups, who wanted the more valuable parts of Indian reservations, supported the reformers' policy of individual Indian ownership. Since individuals could more easily be persuaded or bribed to sell their land, such a policy would open remaining reservation lands to white occupation.

Writing the policy into law. The federal government in the Dawes Act of 1887 made a general policy of what it had been trying to do in a piecemeal fashion. With the Dawes Act, Congress hoped to hasten the time when the Indians living on reservations would be successfully "Americanized."

The Dawes Act provided that each male head of an Indian family could, if he wished, claim 160 acres (64.8 hectares) of reservation land as his own. Bachelors, women, and children were to be entitled to lesser amounts. Legal ownership of the property was to be held in trust by the federal government for 25 years. During this period the Indians could neither sell their land nor use it as security for a mortgage. This restriction was intended to protect the Indians from unscrupulous land speculators. The Burke Act of 1906 modified this provision. It gave the Secretary of the Interior authority to reduce the 25-year trust period in those cases where the Secretary was persuaded that the Indians were capable of handling their own affairs.

The Dawes Act and the Burke Act also provided that Indians who accepted the land and abandoned their tribal way of life were to be given citizenship, including the right to vote. Meanwhile, Congress voted larger but still inadequate funds for the education of Indian children. Regular day schools or boarding schools far from their homes were set up. In these schools the children were taught, often by poorly trained and unsympathetic teachers, to look down on Indian ways of life as inferior and degraded.

Failure of the policy. The new laws persuaded and enabled some Indians to adopt the way of life of the white majority and to become American citizens. Even so, Indians who left the reservations to live in American towns and cities often met with discrimination in jobs and unfair treatment. Most Indians remained on the reservations, clinging as best they could to their tribal customs and living as wards of the federal government. The government policy of encouraging individual land ownership and individual farming among the Indians largely failed when land speculators found loopholes in the Dawes Act. Between 1887 and the 1920's, much of the reservation land was, in one way or another, taken from the Indians. The land that remained was generally eroded and inferior. Moreover, provisions for safeguarding the health of the Indians were neglected. Malnutrition and disease were widespread.

The late 1800's and early 1900's were in many ways the Indians' darkest period. Yet their vitality and spirit were not extinguished. Many continued to insist that they be treated as separate peoples with worthy ways of viewing human relationships, of understanding their environment, and of sensing their place in the universe.

SECTION SURVEY

IDENTIFY: ward of the government, "Americanization," Helen Hunt Jackson, Sarah Winnemucca, Dawes Act of 1887, Burke Act.

1. It has been said that much of United States policy toward Indians during the 1800's consisted of broken promises and acts of injustice. Give examples to support this view.
2. Describe the efforts by reformers to improve conditions for Indians during the late 1800's.
3. (a) What arguments were made for and against "Americanizing" the Indians?

3 **Ranchers build a cattle kingdom on the plains**

Cattle raisers began to move out onto the Great Plains in the 1860's, long before the Indians were conquered. By the 1890's the cattle industry had become big business. Its prod-

This 1898 photograph shows how working cowboys actually looked and dressed. While the horse at right eats from its feedbag, the cowboys pause for a quick meal served from the tailgate of a chuck wagon.

ucts passed from the western ranges through the stockyards, slaughterhouses, and packing plants to become major items of domestic and world trade.

Rise of the Cattle Kingdom. Many of the animals for the cattle industry came from the ranches in southeastern Texas formerly operated by Spaniards and Mexicans. These ranches were occupied by the Texans, who also took over the huge herds of wild cattle, called longhorns, estimated in 1865 to number about 5 million head. The wild herds sprang from the cattle that were lost by the Spaniards and by the American wagon trains crossing the plains in earlier days.

It was no easy task for the first Texans to learn how to handle the cattle, wild or tame. A writer in the 1870's warned that "the wild cattle of Texas, . . . animals miscalled tame, are fifty times more dangerous. . . than the fiercest buffalo."

In learning how to handle cattle, the Texans owed a good deal to Mexican **vaqueros** (vah·KAIR·ohs), or cowboys, and to Indians. Many slaves also learned the dangerous business of handling cattle. After emancipation freed slaves comprised perhaps one third of

those working in cattle raising. With the aid of the horse, the saddle, the rope, and the revolver, white and black cowboys learned how to handle the longhorns on the open grasslands. Mexican Americans, who made up a large part of the cowboy population, continued to play an important role in cattle ranching. It became a profitable occupation and a distinctive way of life.

The long drive. People in the nation's growing cities needed enormous quantities of beef. The problem was to find a means of getting the steers to urban markets. The solution was transportation provided by the railroads, which in the 1860's began to push out upon the Great Plains.

As the steel rails moved westward, enormous herds of steers were driven from Texas north on long drives to towns that grew up along the railroads. By 1870, Kansas cattle towns like Abilene, Ellsworth, and Ellis, all on the Kansas Pacific Railroad, and Dodge City and Wichita on the Atchison, Topeka, and Santa Fe Railway had become roaring, riotous, lawless communities (see map, page 430).

During the early years of the long drives, nearly all the steers driven from Texas were

429

sold in the cattle towns at good prices. In time, however, the number of cattle began to exceed the demand. Texans who arrived in late fall were either unable to sell their steers or had to sell them at a loss.

The open range. At this point, enterprising cattle raisers began to winter their surplus steers on the open range, or unfenced grazing lands, near the cattle towns. After fattening them during the winter, they sold them at high prices in the towns before the new cattle drives from Texas arrived to glut the market.

This was not the first time that cattle had been pastured on the short grass of the Great Plains. Many wagon trains had wintered on

the plains, and the pioneers had discovered that their horses and cattle grew fat on the short and thin, but nutritious, grass. The open-range cattle industry did not develop, however, until the railroads provided access to markets and the Texans provided the cattle.

News that quick money could be made in the open-range cattle business soon reached the eastern seaboard and spread to Europe. The cattle rush that followed was similar to the gold rush that had populated California in 1849–50. Prices for land and steers soared as newcomers on the Great Plains staked out their claims.

People rushed to the cattle country to make their fortunes. They built dugouts, sod huts, or

WESTERN RAILROADS AND CATTLE TRAILS

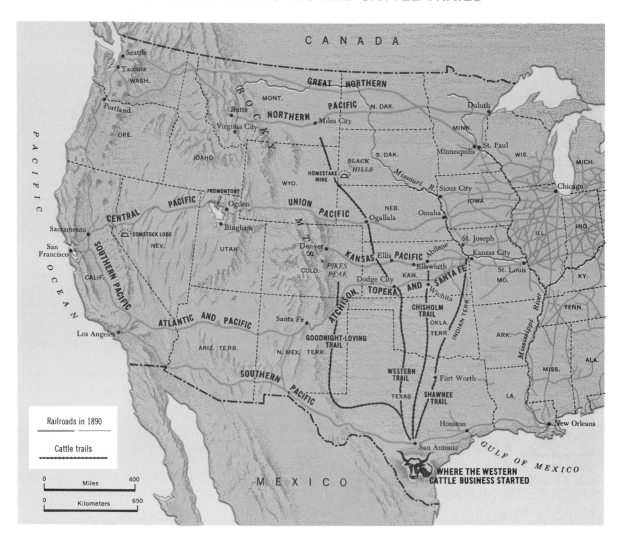

Railroads in 1890

Cattle trails

IT ALL STARTED IN MEXICO

What could be more American than a cowboy? From Paris to Peking, he is for millions *the* symbol of the United States. But the American cowboy—the whole cattle business, in fact—could never have existed without the Mexicans and the Spaniards before them.

First, of course, came the cattle themselves. In the days of the open range, the herds that roamed freely consisted of so-called Texas longhorns. These were descended from long-horned cattle first brought to America by Columbus in 1493.

Next was the horse. The type favored for ranging was descended from the mustang [Spanish *mestengo* (mes·TENG·goh), meaning "belonging to shepherds," and *mostrenco* (mohs·TRENG·coh), meaning "stray beast"]. The mustangs, like the longhorns, were the wild offspring of tame livestock introduced by Spanish settlers.

It was the Mexicans who first put men on horseback to roam the open range, round up wild cattle, and brand them to show ownership.

In fact, the first brand in America was probably the one used by Hernando Cortés. It was called Three Christian Crosses, and that is just what it looked like.

The Mexican cowboy was called a *vaquero* (vah·KAY·roh). In English this became the word "buckaroo," another term for a ranch hand. Almost everything the cowboy did or used on the job had a Spanish-Mexican origin.

When rounding up cattle, he used a rope called a lariat [Spanish *la reata* (LAH ray·AH·tah)] or lasso [Spanish *lazo* (LAH·soh)]. He protected his legs from thorny brush with chaps [Spanish *chaparreras* (chah·pah·RAY·rahs)]. If he got cattle into a *corral* [Spanish for "pen"], there was less danger of a stampede [Spanish *estampida* (ehs·tahm·PEE·dah)]. For fun he might ride bucking *broncos* [Spanish for "wild horses"] in a *rodeo* [Spanish for "cattle ring"]. But the cowboy had to be careful. If he celebrated too noisily, he might end up in the hoosegow [Spanish *juzgado* (hoos·GAH·doh)], or jail.

simple ranch houses and pastured their herds on the open grasslands. Some, though by no means all, did become wealthy.

Until the 1880's the cattle ranchers ruled the Great Plains. This was the period of the long drive, the open range, the roundup, and the picturesque roving cowboy.

End of the open range. The open-range cattle industry ended, however, almost as quickly as

it had started. As the supply of steers rapidly increased, beef prices fell disastrously low. In 1885 a severe drought burned up the grasses on the overstocked range, and cattle starved by the thousands.

Even more disastrous for the cattle ranchers was the development of the sheep industry and farming. To be sure, Mexican Americans had been grazing sheep in New Mexico for a long time. However, the arrival in

431

the 1880's of large numbers of sheepherders and farmers from the older areas of the United States doomed the open range. Sheep cropped the grass so close that little was left for the cattle. Farmers broke up the open range with their farms and barbed-wire fences (page 434). The cattle ranchers fought desperately to keep the range open, but it was a hopeless battle. By the late 1880's, the open, unfenced range was fast becoming a thing of the past.

By the 1890's the western cattle industry centered in the high plains running through eastern Montana, Wyoming, Colorado, the New Mexico Territory, and western Texas. Most ranchers by now owned their grazing land and fenced it in with barbed wire.

Ranches varied in size from about 2,000 to 100,000 acres (about 800 to 40,000 hectares). Western ranches had to be large since each steer required a grazing area of 15 to 75 acres (or about 6 to 30 hectares). The size of the area depended upon the amount of rainfall and the resulting growth of grass.

With the invention of better instruments for drilling into the ground and the improvement of windmills for pumping water, many cattle raisers watered their herds from wells scattered over their ranches. In years of abundant rainfall, cattle ranchers might prosper, since their herds could fatten on the natural grasses. In years of drought, they had to feed their cattle hay or cottonseed cake, a costly practice that could wipe out their profits.

Growth and specialization. The cattle industry tended to become more and more specialized. Many ranchers on the plains began to concentrate on breeding and raising cattle. The steers were then sold to farmers in the rich corn and pasture lands of the prairies. After being fattened for market, the cattle were shipped to nearby stockyards in Omaha, Kansas City, St. Joseph, Sioux City, St. Paul-Minneapolis, and Chicago (see map, page 430). There they were slaughtered and transported in refrigerator cars to eastern cities and sometimes from there to Europe.

Ranchers used the prairies, the semiarid plains, the high plateaus, and the mountain valleys of the West for cattle grazing lands. On these lands they produced a substantial portion of the nation's meat and wool. By the 1890's the western livestock industry had become an organized, specialized business, closely tied to the nation's economic life.

SECTION SURVEY

IDENTIFY: Cattle Kingdom, longhorns, vaqueros, long drive, open range, ranch.

1. What was the relationship between the railroads and the long drive?
2. (a) Why was the open range important to the cattle industry? (b) Why did it disappear?
3. Map Study: Look at the map on page 430. (a) Locate the original cattle-grazing area in Texas. (b) Locate three cattle trails and name them. (c) Why was Kansas City important to the cattle industry? (d) How can you tell that Chicago was an important trading center in 1890?

4 Farmers plow the tough sod of the last frontier

Farm families, single men, and some single women followed the cattle ranchers onto the prairies and plains. From 1870 to 1900, American pioneers settled more land than had all previous generations combined.

In the 263 years from the first tiny settlement at Jamestown in 1607 until 1870, white settlers claimed and occupied nearly 408 million acres (165 million hectares) of what had once been Indian land. This pace was almost leisurely compared to the speed with which later settlers conquered the prairies and the plains. In the 30 years between 1870 and 1900, pioneers settled an additional 430 million acres (174 million hectares). This was an area roughly equal to the combined areas of Norway, Sweden, Denmark, the Netherlands, Belgium, Germany, and France.

What was happening in America at this time to make possible the rapid settlement of the last frontier?

Free land. One attraction of the West was free land. In 1862 Congress enacted the Homestead Act, which granted 160 acres (64.8 hectares) to any individual who wished to settle a farm, or, as it was called, a "homestead."

Farmers as well as land speculators rushed to accept the offer. Thousands were ex-soldiers who sought new homes in the West. Thousands of others came from worn-out farms in the East, particularly from New England, in the hope of finding more fertile land. Still other

In 1888 these settlers in Custer County, Nebraska, used the side of a hill as the basis for their home. The house is part dugout and part sod walls and roof. Here the members of the family proudly pose in front of their home with their possessions — cow, horses, cart, and plow — for a traveling photographer.

thousands came from Europe. In many areas of the Middle West, more than half of the pioneer settlers were immigrants — Germans, Norwegians, Swedes, Danes, Czechs, Finns, and Russians.

Railroads and settlement. Without the railroad, however, the free land in the West, no matter how attractive, would have remained unpopulated. During the 1870's and the 1880's, four great transcontinental railroads crossed the prairies and the plains. These railroads along with their branch lines opened up the western country for settlement.

The rail lines into and through the wild western country were built only at enormous cost. Moreover, the investment was extremely risky. Investors did not know when, if ever, the new railroads would begin to make a profit and reward them for their risks. Thus the government, which was eager to have the railroads built, encouraged the pioneer railroad companies with cash subsidies and grants of land.

At the time the grants were made to the railroads, the land itself was almost worthless. Before the railroad companies could profit from their grants, they had to persuade people to move into the unsettled areas. Because the land was close to the railroads and therefore would be valuable, the railroad companies could hope to sell it, even though free land was available in more remote areas. More important was the fact that once the land was settled, the railroads would gain revenue from passengers and freight. In addition, any land that the railroads could not sell immediately would rise in value as settlers built farms, villages, and towns along the right of way.

With such things in mind, the railroads started extensive advertising campaigns. They sent literature and agents all over the United States and even into Europe. Life on the plains was pictured in glowing colors. As an added lure, prospective purchasers were sometimes

433

offered free railroad transportation to any land they might buy. The transatlantic steamship lines were always eager to obtain passengers and freight. They also began advertising campaigns in Europe.

The problems of houses and fences. Despite such efforts, settlers did not at first pour into the plains. For one thing, many still believed the old myth of the Great American Desert. An even more important factor slowing settlement was the scarcity of wood.

Pioneer families solved the problem of housing, as people have always done, by making use of whatever building material was available. On the plains this was sod. Cut out of the soil, bricklike chunks of sod formed the walls of shelters. With a few precious pieces of wood the settlers framed the roof, finishing it with a layer of sod to keep out wind and rain and snow.

Fencing presented an even more difficult problem. Pioneer families could not farm without fences to protect their crops, and on the plains there was no material for fences. The first pioneers tried everything, even mud

Changing Ways with TECHNOLOGY

DETAIL OF BARBED WIRE

BARBED-WIRE FENCE

On the Great Plains, fences were needed to hold range cattle and keep them off farmland. There were too few trees for stump fences or rail fences (page 60). In 1874 farmers and herders began using barbed wire, which cattle learned to avoid. Fence posts were made from scrap lumber or from the few available trees.

walls, but without success. Ordinary wire strung between a few precious wooden posts was not effective. Cattle could get their heads through the smooth strands of wire and gradually work an opening in the fence.

The problem of fencing was finally solved by Joseph Glidden with his invention of barbed wire. Glidden took out his patent in 1874. Barbed-wire fences proved effective as a barrier to cattle, and within 10 years the open range was criss-crossed by a network of barbed-wire fences.

The problem of water. Scarcity of water, like scarcity of wood, was a problem that pioneer farm families had never had to face in the eastern part of the United States. Eastern farmers took their water from springs bubbling to the surface or from shallow wells. On the Great Plains, where the water was much deeper underground, machinery was needed to drill deeper wells. Once the well shafts had reached the water, the farmers then needed mechanical pumps to draw the water to the surface.

In a search for oil during the 1860's, petroleum companies developed new drilling machinery capable of penetrating farther beneath the surface than ever before. This machinery speedily found its way to the Great Plains. Farmers and ranchers used it to tap water supplies deep underground.

Meanwhile, other inventors were developing windmills capable of operating pumps to draw water to the surface. Daniel Halladay of Connecticut developed the self-governing windmill. This device automatically adjusted itself to wind pressure and thus operated at a uniform speed.

Windmills were first used on the Great Plains to provide water for steam locomotives crossing the plains and for herds of cattle. The windmill really came into its own when farmers began to settle on the semiarid lands. Factories producing windmills were soon doing a thriving business.

Other problems. Railroads, barbed wire, factory-made windmills—all products of the new industrial age—helped farmers conquer the Great Plains. So, too, did the development of dry farming. Dry farming involved deep plowing and careful cultivation to keep the surface of the soil pulverized and thus conserve as much precious moisture as possible.

The pioneer farm families had other prob-

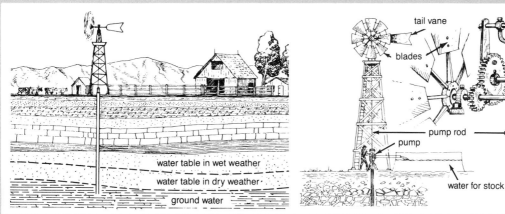

water table in wet weather

water table in dry weather

ground water

tail vane

blades

pump rod

pump

water for stock

WINDMILL FOR WATER

On the Great Plains, the table of ground water was so deep that human strength could not bring the water to the surface. The windmill solved this problem for settlers. The circular motion of the windmill blades was translated by a series of gears into the up-and-down motion of a rod. The rod powered a pump that brought water from the water table to the surface. Here the water flowed into tanks from which livestock could drink.

lems to solve, problems for which inventors, manufacturers, and agricultural experts had no ready answers. For one thing, the cattle ranchers resented the settlers who broke up the open range with their fences. Bitter fights raged in the early days between ranchers and farmers, and many unmarked graves soon dotted the plains. However, it was an unequal struggle, and by sheer force of numbers the farmers eventually won.

Nature also contributed to the settlers' difficulties. Until men and women learned how to deal with the plains environment, life was sometimes extremely harsh. The unrelieved round of daily labor impressed writers who tried to describe the life of the farmers on the Great Plains. O. E. Rölvaag (ROHL·vahg), author of *Giants in the Earth* and *Peder Victorious,* was one such writer. His novels provide a picture of empty plains and lives spent beneath a burning sun, of grasshopper plagues, of drought, of ruined crops, of bitter cold, and of blinding blizzards. Many pioneers gave up the difficult struggle and moved back east, but others remained.

Farm families in the 1880's and 1890's also encountered many new problems created by industrialism. In the new industrial age, as you will read, farmers became increasingly concerned with freight and shipping charges, prices fixed in distant markets, the cost of farm machinery, interest rates on mortgages, and many other factors they could not control.

The Oklahoma Sooners. After the Civil War, many Plains Indians were moved to western portions of Indian Territory. This left a large area of unoccupied land in the central part of present-day Oklahoma. Several treaties had reserved these lands for the Five Civilized tribes—the Cherokees, Creeks, Chicasaws, Choctaws, and Seminoles. When white intruders moved onto this land, federal troops at first drove them off. In 1885, however, the government negotiated with the Creeks and Seminoles to open this part of Indian territory to white settlement.

In March 1889 President Benjamin Harrison issued a proclamation that set in motion a wild rush to the District of Oklahoma. The President announced that free homesteads of 160 acres (64.8 hectares) would be available "at and after the hour of twelve o'clock noon, on the twenty-second day of April." The army immediately set up patrols along the district boundaries to guard against premature entry and waited for the rush to begin.

It was a short wait. By April 22 almost 100,000 land-hungry pioneers—some in wagons, others on horseback—were packed solidly along the boundary line. Exactly at noon the officer in charge fired a shot, and the wild stampede began.

Even the swiftest riders discovered that they were not there soon enough. Many Sooners had evaded the patrols, slipped across the boundary, and staked out claims before the area was officially opened.

Within a few hours of the deadline, every inch of Oklahoma District was occupied. Thousands of disappointed landseekers started back along the roads they had eagerly traveled a short time earlier.

More land was soon available—again at the expense of the Indians. In 1889 land previously reserved for the Sauk, Fox, Potawatomi, Cheyenne, and Arapaho Indians were thrown open to white settlement. In the years that followed, the huge Cherokee Strip and reservations assigned to the Kickapoo, Iowa, Comanche, Apache, and Wichita Indians were also opened to settlement. All told, the Indians lost more than 11 million acres (nearly 4.5 million hectares) of land to white settlers.

The last frontier. The roll call of states entering the Union in the half-century after 1865 is an impressive one. Nebraska entered in 1867; Colorado in 1876; North Dakota, South Dakota, Montana, and Washington all in 1889; Idaho and Wyoming in 1890; Utah in 1896; Oklahoma in 1907; and New Mexico and Arizona in 1912.

In 1890 the Superintendent of the Census Bureau made a significant statement: "Up to and including 1880," he declared, "the country had a frontier of settlement, but at present the unsettled area has been so broken into by isolated bodies of settlement that there can hardly be said to be a frontier line."

SECTION SURVEY

IDENTIFY: sod houses, Joseph Glidden, Daniel Halladay, dry farming, Oklahoma Sooners, the last frontier.

1. How was western settlement speeded by (a) the Homestead Act and (b) the railroads?

2. How did the farmers on the plains solve the problems of housing and fencing?

3. Why was the windmill important to the Great Plains farmers?

4. Picture Study: Look at the picture on page 433. (a) What does it indicate about what life was like for farm families on the plains? (b) How did the natural environment affect farmers' lives?

5 Miners find new treasure in the western mountains

Developments of the new industrial age made it possible for the farmer to conquer the last western frontiers. The West, in turn, helped to speed the Industrial Revolution. From western farms came unending food supplies for the growing city populations. From western mines came an apparently limitless supply of gold and silver to provide capital to build industries. From other western mines came a steadily swelling volume of iron, copper, and other metals.

"Forty-Niners" and "Fifty-Niners." The discovery of gold in California drew fortune hunters by the tens of thousands to the Pacific coast in 1849–50. Some of the "Forty-Niners" made fortunes, but most were disappointed. Refusing to admit defeat, prospectors began to explore the valleys and slopes of the mountainous regions between the Pacific Ocean and the Great Plains. The development of mining communities again put pressure on the government to force Indians onto reservations.

In 1859, prospectors discovered gold near Pikes Peak in the unorganized territory of Colorado. More than 100,000 "Fifty-Niners" rushed to the scene to stake their claims. Caravans of covered wagons lumbered across the plains with the slogan "Pikes Peak or bust" lettered on the white canvas. Some prospectors shouldered packs and crossed the plains on foot. Others pulled handcarts behind them. Perhaps half of the fortune hunters returned the way they had come, with their slogan changed to "Busted, by gosh!" Nevertheless, enough remained to organize the Territory of Colorado in 1861.

Even more valuable than the Colorado deposits were the discoveries of silver in 1859 in

Taylor, Nevada, was one of many mining towns that boomed for a while, then faded away. Here it is in its heyday in 1881. Note the American flag flying at half-mast in honor of the recently assassinated President Garfield.

the western part of the Territory of Utah. Within a decade nearly $150 million worth of silver and gold had been extracted from the famous Comstock Lode in what is now Nevada (see map, page 430). By 1890 the total had reached $340 million. Enough of the early prospectors stayed after the stampede of 1859 to organize the Territory of Nevada, which became a state in 1864.

Gold in the Black Hills. In 1874, as you have read, prospectors found gold in the Black Hills of South Dakota (see map, page 430), and another gold rush followed. This area was Indian territory, the Sioux Reservation, which the federal government was supposed to preserve for the Indians. However, the government made only half-hearted efforts to keep prospectors out of the region. The lure of gold was too strong, and the government soon completely abandoned its efforts to protect the Indians. In 1877 the government opened the entire area to white settlers.

Early mining communities. During and after the Civil War, mining communities sprang up in many areas of the West. Life in these mining camps has been described vividly in *The Luck of Roaring Camp* by Bret Harte and in *Roughing It* by Mark Twain. These and other contemporary accounts present a picture of wild, lawless communities of tents, rough board shacks, and smoke-filled saloons strung along a muddy street.

Each mining camp passed through several stages of development. At first, people made their own laws, relying for safety upon fists or guns to protect themselves and their families. Then some citizens began to organize as private police forces, often called "vigilantes" (vij·ih·LAN·teez), in an effort to maintain order. Soon men and women built schools and churches—crude shacks, but important steps toward civilized living. With the schools and churches came organized local government. Then came the appeal to Congress for recognition as a United States territory. Eventually

437

The lack of women in mining camps did not mean that there could be no dances. "Ladies" at such a dance were often designated by their clothing or by a handkerchief on their sleeves.

the territory would adopt a constitution and be admitted to the Union as a state.

Today the mountain regions, the valleys, and the high plateaus of the West are dotted with abandoned mining communities—ghost towns. The gaping mine shafts and the sagging, windowless cabins stand as mute testimony to the fact that prospectors and miners once pioneered on this vast frontier.

Systematic exploration. The early discoveries of gold and silver acted like magnets, drawing adventuresome prospectors into the unexplored regions of the West. Before long, however, exploration was conducted on a more systematic basis, partly because of federal efforts. Between 1865 and 1879, the federal government sent many expeditions into the mountains, and in 1879 the United States Geological Survey was organized. Private industry also sent out carefully organized expeditions. The picturesque prospector with pack horse and hand tools continued to roam the mountains. Long before the end of the 1800's, however, an increasing number of the mineral deposits were discovered by expeditions equipped with the latest technological devices and knowledge of geology.

The development of the nation's industries brought a growing demand for metals of all kinds. Copper, needed when the electrical industry developed, was found in enormous quantities around Butte, Montana; Bingham, Utah; and in Nevada and Arizona. Lead and zinc were discovered in the same area. These and other metals have helped the United States to become the leading industrial nation in the world.

Mining as big business. Other developments brought about great changes in mining. New methods of extracting the metal from the ore were discovered. Colleges of mining engineering were opened, powerful machinery was invented, great corporations were organized, and armies of skilled technicians and engineers moved into the mining regions. New equipment and the growing knowledge of chemistry and metallurgy enabled companies to work low-grade ores with profit.

By the 1890's mining had become big business. Engineers, equipped with the latest tools of science and technology, were converting the West into a region of enormous value to the industrial development of the nation.

SECTION SURVEY

IDENTIFY: "Pikes Peak or bust," Comstock Lode, Bret Harte, Mark Twain, vigilantes, ghost towns, United States Geological Survey.

1. (a) Who were the "Forty-Niners"? (b) Who were the "Fifty-Niners"? (c) What impact did these people have on settlement of the West?

2. (a) Describe life in the early mining communities. (b) What stages of development did the communities go through?

3. How and why was the individual prospector replaced by organized mining expeditions?

4. What circumstances helped mining to become big business by the 1890's?

438

Chapter Survey

Summary: Tracing the Main Ideas

The conquest of the Plains Indians and the settlement of the land west of the Mississippi River took place, for the most part, during and immediately after the Civil War. Settlers poured into the prairies and plains in great numbers. By the 1890's they had settled so much of the West that the Superintendent of the Census Bureau announced that the frontier no longer existed.

This vast region, almost half of the total area of the present United States, had from time immemorial belonged to the original inhabitants, the Indians. The white government and the onrush of settlers drove the Indians from their lands and forced them to live on reservations. Efforts to "Americanize" the original Americans ended in failure.

The West that the whites had conquered was not one region, but many regions, each basically different from the others. The groups of settlers—cattle ranchers, farmers, and miners—learned to adapt themselves to their environment. They learned to make use of the most easily developed natural resources—the grasslands, the fertile soil, and the precious metals. As the years passed, they learned how to modify the environment and to seek out and develop other resources.

The conquest of the West was, in one sense, merely a prelude to an even larger chapter in American history—the transformation of the nation from a mainly agricultural country to one of the great industrial giants of the modern world. That industrial transformation is the subject of Unit Seven and of later chapters in this book.

Inquiring into History

1. The United States tried to solve the "Indian problem" by eliminating the Indians. Do you agree or disagree with this statement? Give evidence to support your answer.
2. What actions did the federal government take to encourage the settlement and development of the West?
3. (a) Compare the problems that miners, cattle raisers, and farmers faced in settling the land west of the Mississippi River. (b) What solutions did each find for their problems? (c) How effective were these solutions?
4. The last frontier disappeared by 1890. (a) Explain how this occurred. (b) In your opinion, what is the significance of the frontier in American history?
5. (a) What effect did the Industrial Revolution in America have on the development of the American West? (b) What effect did the development of the American West have on the Industrial Revolution in America?

Relating Past to Present

1. (a) Is scarcity of water still a problem in the West? Give evidence to support your answer. (b) How do present methods of water conservation compare with those of the early West?
2. Compare American mining in the late 1800's to mining today in terms of (a) major minerals mined, (b) importance of these minerals to the economy, and (c) mining methods.
3. Do railroads today play the same role in the economy of the West that they did in the late 1800's? Why or why not?

Developing Social Science Skills

1. Study the map on pages 834–35. (a) Locate the Great Plains. (b) Name an important river that crosses the Great Plains. (c) With the help of the map and chart on page 838, determine from what other geographical areas new states entered the Union after the Civil War.
2. Prepare a bulletin board display about the cowboy's life. You might include such items as illustrations of equipment, lyrics from cowboy songs, and copies of paintings by Frederick Remington or Charles Russell.
3. Conduct research and prepare a report on one of the following: dry-farming methods; the role of women in the development of the West; the importance of blacks in western development; the life of Cochise, Black Elk, or Sarah Winnemucca.
4. Look at the pictures and read the captions on pages 434–35. How did the settlers of the Great Plains use technology to help them adapt to local conditions?

Unit Survey

For Further Inquiry

1. (a) Describe Reconstruction, as it was finally carried out under the Radical Republican Congress. (b) Do you think Reconstruction was successful? Explain.
2. Compare the situation of Southern blacks and western Indians from 1865 to 1900. Consider (a) economic status, (b) relations with the federal government, (c) treatment by whites.
3. Did the federal government become more powerful in the years after the Civil War? Give evidence to support your answer.
4. What evidence is there that industrialization was increasingly affecting the nation's development after the Civil War?
5. Trace the relationship between Congress and the President between 1865 and 1900.
6. Did the United States become more or less democratic during the years 1865–1900? Give reasons for your answer.

Projects and Activities

1. Imagine you are a journalist in the South just after the Civil War. Write a feature story describing the conditions that you observe in the cities and the countryside.
2. Write a skit about the impeachment of Andrew Johnson. Perhaps some of your classmates can join you in acting out the skit for the class.
3. On a blank map of the United States, illustrate the major events in U.S.–Indian relations from 1865 to 1900. Include such items as (a) battles, (b) signing of treaties, (c) establishment of reservations.
4. Conduct research and prepare an oral or written report on the roles of women on the "last frontier." Look into their political status, as well as their roles in daily life.
5. Select one event from the timeline here. (a) Form two hypotheses (educated guesses) about consequences that might have followed from the event. For example: 1874 — grasshopper plague. (1) Many farmers soon went bankrupt. (2) The price of bread later went up. (b) Conduct research in order to test your hypotheses against additional information.

Exploring Your Region

1. Find out what life was like in your region at the time when it was part of the frontier. How do your findings compare with the account of the "last frontier" in your textbook?
2. (a) What were the main ways of making a living in your community in 1880? (b) What sort of economic relations did your community have with other areas of the country? (For example, did it send finished products to other areas? or buy food from other areas? or serve as a trading center for several areas?)

Suggested Reading

1. *Dr. George Washington Carver, Scientist,* Shirley Graham. Biography of the son of a slave whose determination enables him to become a distinguished scientist.
2. *Bury My Heart at Wounded Knee,* Dee Brown. A dramatic account of the "last frontier" from the Indian point of view.
3. *History of the Confident Years,* American Heritage. A highly illustrated history of the years from 1865 to 1900.
4. *Giants in the Earth,* Ole Edvart Rölvaag. Moving novel of the difficult life of pioneers in North Dakota.
5. *Duel in the Sun,* Nevin Busch. Excellent novel of the "wild west."

Unit Seven

The Rise of Industrialism

1860's-1890's

Chapter 22

Business Pioneers and the Growth of American Industry

1. Transportation and communications systems bind the nation together.
2. Expanding business creates more products for more people.
3. New forms of business organization appear as industry expands.
4. Business pioneers give new directions to American life.

Chapter 23

The Struggle of American Workers to Organize

1. Industrialism creates new problems for wage earners.
2. Immigration adds strength and variety to American society.
3. Wage earners organize to overcome their grievances.
4. Organized labor faces opposition as it seeks reforms.

Chapter 24

The Revolt of Farmers Against Big Business Practices

1. Farm life remains laborious, but simple.
2. Farmers face complex new problems in the industrial age.
3. Farm organizations join efforts to regulate the railroads.
4. Farm organizations put increasing pressure on government.
5. The farmers fail to win control of the national government.

Chapter 25

New Life Styles in the New Industrial Age

1. Cities grow and change under the impact of industrialism.
2. Education responds to the changing patterns of American life.
3. American writing reflects the new industrial age.
4. Architecture and other fine arts respond to a changing society.
5. New forms of recreation enrich American life.

Chapter 22

Business Pioneers and the Growth of American Industry

Changing Ways of American Life

1860's–1890's

In the 1870's a large majority of Americans lived in the country or in small rural villages and towns. This was the age of dirt roads, of carriages and wagons, and of covered bridges, their wooden sides plastered with circus posters and notices of county fairs. It was the age of oil lamps, woodstoves, the hand pump or the open well, and the Saturday-evening bath in a washtub in the center of the kitchen floor.

This was the age of sewing circles and spelling bees, the one-room schoolhouse, and the country store with its tubs of butter and pickles, its cracker barrel, and its clutter of groceries and clothing and household articles hanging from the ceiling and spilling over the shelves. Symbols of the age were the small family-owned factory and the blacksmith shop at the crossroads with its charcoal fire, its huge bellows, and its burly smith in grimy leather apron shaping and fitting a new set of shoes to a neighbor's horse.

But a new age was coming into being. Symbols of the new age were the rapidly growing cities, large factories with smoke pouring from their towering stacks, long lines of railroad cars rumbling across the countryside, and a growing number of farm machines standing outside barns or operating in the fields. In brief, life in the new industrial age was being transformed in many ways.

This, then, is the story of how America began to change from a rural, agricultural economy to an urban, industrial way of life.

THE CHAPTER IN OUTLINE

1. Transportation and communications systems bind the nation together.

2. Expanding business creates more products for more people.

3. New forms of business organization appear as industry expands.

4. Business pioneers give new directions to American life.

1 Transportation and communications systems bind the nation together

The heart of an industrial society is the city. It is here that most factories and workers are concentrated and that most raw materials are fashioned into finished products. It is also here that most goods and services are bought and sold.

If the city is the heart of an industrial society, the routes of transportation are the veins and arteries. Into the city flow the vital resources gathered from farm and mine and forest and sea. Out of the city flow the unending supplies of manufactured articles. These move day and night over a vast transportation network to every corner of the land and overseas to other lands.

Just as the human body cannot function without heart and veins and arteries, so an industrial economy cannot function without its urban manufacturing centers and an efficient system of transportation and communications.

The growth of cities. During the years between 1865 and 1900, the modern city with its busy railroad yards, its smoking factories, its wage earners, and its office workers took shape. During these years, scores of American cities grew from sprawling towns to huge urban centers. In 1870 about 75 percent of the people lived in the country or in communities of fewer than 2,500 inhabitants. By 1900 only about 60 percent of all Americans lived on farms or in small rural communities. The urban population had skyrocketed. In 1870 only about 10 million of the nation's total population of 40 million were urban dwellers. By 1900 more than 30 million of America's 76 million people lived in urban areas.

By 1899 the population of Chicago had passed the million mark. The city's position as a center of transportation was one reason for its remarkable growth. Every day steam-powered ships moved people and cargo between Chicago and other points along Lake Michigan, including Milwaukee.

Many revolutionary developments aided the growth of cities. Among them were the discovery of new sources of power, the application of hundreds of new inventions and new processes, and the enormous expansion of the nation's transportation and communications network.

The growth of railroads. Between 1870 and 1900, railway mileage in the United States increased from 53,000 miles (85,000 kilometers) to more than 190,000 miles (306,000 kilometers). During these same years, the railroads improved in speed, comfort, and safety. Double sets of tracks replaced single sets, allowing streams of traffic to flow in two directions at once. Iron rails, which had shattered beneath heavy loads, were replaced by steel rails. Bridges of iron and later of steel replaced wooden bridges. Coal, a more efficient fuel, replaced wood in the tenders of locomotives. In 1869 George Westinghouse patented the air brake, a system of power braking more efficient than the old hand brake. George M. Pullman's sleeping cars increased the comfort of passengers, and dining cars and parlor cars also appeared.

The success of the first transcontinental line (page 423) quickly led to the construction of several others. By 1893 a half-dozen major, or trunk, lines crossed the plains and mountains to the Far West. All over the United States feeder, or branch, lines linked the trunk lines with surrounding areas. Soon a network of steel rails served every part of the country.

Financing railroad construction. The construction of railroads, especially of lines reaching into the still unsettled West, was enormously expensive. To encourage the building of new lines, the government provided grants of land and loans of money.

The original land grants set aside large areas of land within which the railroad could claim a specified amount. Until the railroads exercised their claim, none of the land could be sold to the public. Some railroads ran into construction or other difficulties and did not exercise their choice for ten years or more. Others never exercised the right at all, and the government took title to the land. In round figures, the national government turned over 131 million acres (53 million hectares) of land to the railroads. At the time, this land was worth a total of approximately $123 million. The government also made loans of close to $65 million to the railroads.

In return, the land-grant railroads and their competitors carried government troops, military freight, and United States mail for less than the standard rates. In 1945 a Congressional committee reported that the railroads had already "contributed over $900 million in payment of the lands which were transferred to them under the Land Grant Act." In addition, the railroads repaid the original government loans along with an additional $103 million in interest.

Other transportation. While land transportation improved, traffic on the sea lanes and inland waterways also developed. After 1850, sailing ships on the oceans and on the Great Lakes were replaced by steam-driven, steel-hulled freighters and sleek passenger liners. These ocean-going vessels carried millions of emigrants from Europe to the rest of the world, mostly to the United States. They also carried raw materials and manufactured goods to and from the expanding world markets.

Meanwhile, in the growing urban areas, new methods of transportation enabled people to move quickly within the crowded cities. By the late 1800's, electric trolleys were rapidly replacing horse-drawn cars. Steam-driven and, later, electric-powered elevated trains rumbled along above crowded city streets. By the early 1900's, subway trains carried passengers below the streets of New York and Boston.

As steel-framed skyscrapers climbed higher into the air, elevators, powered first by steam and then by electricity, carried passengers and freight from story to story. Without the elevator skyscrapers could not have been used.

From telegraph to telephone. Equally important developments came in the field of communications. Until the 1870's the telegraph had been the most significant advance in communication since the invention of printing from movable type. From the 1870's on, however, major new inventions appeared one after the other.

The telegraph had been first successfully developed in the United States by Samuel F. B. Morse and in England by Charles Wheatstone during the late 1830's and the early 1840's — just as the new steam railroads began to appear. The telegraph moved across the country with the railroads. Indeed, without a telegraph

Before Christopher Sholes developed the typewriter, business correspondence had to be handcopied. As women learned how to operate the new machine, increasing numbers of them entered the nation's labor force.

system the nation's railroads could not have operated safely.

In 1866, about 25 years after Morse's invention, Cyrus W. Field succeeded in laying a transatlantic telegraph cable. During the next few years, additional underwater cables connected North America with other continents. Americans now had almost instantaneous communication with the rest of the world.

In 1876 Alexander Graham Bell, a teacher of the deaf in Boston, applied for a patent on a telephone he had invented. Bell's telephone quickly captured the public's imagination, and in 1885 the American Telephone and Telegraph Company was organized to put the new invention into widespread use.

Other inventions. The telegraph, the underwater cable, and the telephone were landmarks in the history of communications, but other important inventions and developments also reshaped American life. In the 1860's Christopher Sholes of Wisconsin developed the typewriter, which later became an essential part of all business operations. An improved postal system, without which modern business could not function, was also developed.

New machines for making cheap paper from wood pulp and for printing newspapers, books, and magazines also contributed to more effective communication. There was also the camera, which later provided new forms of recreation as well as new techniques for industry and research.

By 1900, improvements in transportation and communications were binding all parts of the United States into a single complex economic unit. The National Banking Act of 1863 had established a sound, uniform currency for the entire country. Specialized business enterprises, both agricultural and industrial, sprang up in all parts of the land, each playing its part in the ever-expanding, interlocking economic system.

445

IDENTIFY: urban center, George M. Pullman, trunk lines, telegraph, Cyrus W. Field, Alexander Graham Bell.

1. Explain this statement: If the city is the heart of an industrial society, the routes of transportation are the veins and arteries.
2. (a) Why did the federal government help finance the building of the railroads? (b) What methods did it use? (c) How did the railroads repay the government for federal aid granted them?
3. Timeline Study: (a) Prepare a timeline of the major inventions mentioned on pages 444–45. Include at least one invention that depended for its development on an earlier invention.

2 Expanding business creates more products for more people

The industrialization of the United States was the result of many different developments in many different fields. These developments, taking place more or less at the same time, combined to transform the older ways of life. They included new sources of energy, new machines, new and bigger industries, and new methods of distributing and selling products and services.

New sources of energy. In the late 1700's, people learned how to convert the energy of wood and coal into steam and to use the steam as a source of power in tasks that had been done for centuries by human, animal, or water power. For more than a hundred years, the steam engine remained the most important "mechanical slave" ever developed up to that time. Then, in the late 1800's, two new sources of power—oil and electricity—were harnessed.

From earliest times people had known about the dark, thick substance that oozed from the earth in certain places and that is now called "petroleum," or "oil." In the early 1850's, kerosene, an efficient and inexpensive fuel for lamps, was first refined from petroleum. The growing demand for kerosene prompted Edwin L. Drake, a retired railroad conductor, to try to drill an oil well near Titusville, Pennsylvania, in 1859. While he was drilling, people thought he was crazy. When the oil began to flow, how-

ever, people quickly began sinking wells of their own.

Kerosene rapidly replaced whale oil as an efficient fuel for lamps. In every American city, peddlers carted kerosene through the streets, selling it from door to door. As the years passed, oil was also increasingly used as a lubricant for the nation's many new machines.

The development of the internal combustion engine, which burned gasoline or diesel fuel—both refined from oil—finally turned oil into one of the nation's major sources of power. In Chapter 27 you will read how oil as a source of power had a revolutionary affect on American life.

Power from electricity. Electricity, like oil, was known long before it was put to practical use. The work of two Italians, Galvani and Volta, led in the late 1700's and early 1800's to the invention of the storage battery. The storage battery supplied small amounts of electric current at low voltages and greatly aided those who were experimenting with the uses of electricity. The discoveries of the principles governing the electric motor and the dynamo had even greater effects. Although many persons contributed to these discoveries, a major share of the credit belongs to England's Michael Faraday and America's Joseph Henry.

Thousands of Americans first learned about the dynamo at the Centennial Exhibition at Philadelphia in 1876, where they saw one in operation converting mechanical energy into electrical energy. In 1882 Thomas Edison built in New York City the first large central power plant in the United States for generating electricity. Edison drove his dynamos with steam engines. Other steam-powered electric generating plants soon appeared in other cities. Another giant stride forward came in 1895 with the opening at Niagara Falls of the first large hydroelectric plant for producing electricity from water power. In spite of these developments, by 1900 only about 2 percent of America's manufacturing industries were powered by electricity.

Steel for new industries. Behind the story of new sources of power lies still another story—the discovery of new ways of producing steel. Steel, a mixture of iron, carbon, and other elements, was not a new material. People had made it for centuries and fashioned it into weapons, tools, and utensils. Until the mid-

1800's no one knew how to produce steel cheaply and in large quantities.

The United States had an abundance of the raw materials vital to the new industrial age — iron ore and coal. Immense deposits of iron ore lay near the western shores of Lake Superior. Nearly one half of the world's known coal deposits were waiting to be tapped.

In the 1850's Henry Bessemer in England and William Kelly in the United States independently discovered a new process for making large quantities of steel cheaply by burning out impurities in molten iron with a blast of air. During the next few years, even more effective processes were developed.

The annual production of steel in the United States soared. In 1870, for example, the United States produced only about 68,000 tons (about 62,000 metric tons) of steel. By 1918 production had increased to 44 million tons (40 million metric tons).

The growth of mass production. Much of the growing steel production at this time went into the construction of railroads, bridges, heavy machinery, factories, mills, and other industrial enterprises. American businesses were laying the foundations of an industrial system that eventually would make the United States the most productive country in the world. The system would also provide Americans with the highest national standard of living in history.

As businesses expanded and factories grew larger, their owners and managers developed more and more efficient methods of production. During the first half of the 1800's, Eli Whitney and others had developed interchangeable parts. This development in turn called for a **division of labor.** For instance, a shoemaker no longer made an entire shoe. Instead, in large shoe factories, one worker might run a machine that cut only heels. Another worker might run a machine that shaped soles. All the different parts were then brought together at a central location and assembled by other workers into a shoe. In this way, vast quantities of shoes could be made quickly and cheaply. This division of labor was soon adopted by most American industries. It made possible the **mass production** of products of every kind.

New ways of selling products. The small general store as well as the small family-owned factory became less important in

After 1859 the sound of an oil gusher was welcome to most Americans (though not to the young girl here). Such wells soon made the United States a major oil producer, adding greatly to its industrial growth.

America during the late 1800's. New types of stores arose to handle the ever-growing quantities of products from the nation's factories.

The **specialty store** concentrated upon a single line of goods — hardware, clothing, groceries, shoes, and so forth.

The **department store** combined many specialty stores under one roof. John C. Wanamaker opened one of the first department stores in the United States in Philadelphia in 1876. Marshall Field opened another in Chicago in 1881. Other department stores soon opened in other cities.

Chain stores—stores with branches in many cities—also began to appear. Pioneers in this field of selling were the Great Atlantic and Pacific Tea Company (A & P), founded in 1859, and the chain of stores started by Frank Woolworth in 1879. Chain stores, like department stores, bought goods in large quantities at low prices. They then passed on these low prices to their customers. Since women were commonly paid less than men, managers gladly hired women as clerks.

Large-scale professional advertising began to appear in the 1880's. Such advertising introduced new products, promoted mass purchasing, and helped create large national markets for the streams of new manufactured products that were now available.

Specialty stores, department stores, and chain stores were all part of the urban scene. In 1872, however, Aaron Montgomery Ward started in Chicago a mail-order business aimed at the rural market. A few years later, the Sears, Roebuck mail-order business was started. Montgomery Ward and Sears, Roebuck used the same business methods. Customers placed orders and paid for them by mail; their goods were shipped to them by mail or railway express. Catalogs from these two mail-order houses became prized possessions in rural households and in the bunkhouses and camps of cattle ranchers and sheepherders. They helped to bring the outside world to isolated farms and speeded the transformation of farm life.

SECTION SURVEY

IDENTIFY: Edwin L. Drake, Michael Faraday, Joseph Henry, Thomas Edison, Bessemer process, division of labor, mass production, Marshall Field, chain store.

1. In what ways did the revolution in power affect (a) workers and (b) manufacturers?
2. How did each of the following developments help transform the lives of average Americans in the late 1800's: (a) availability of kerosene, (b) cheap steel, (c) mass production?
3. What basic premise or idea did the following people have regarding the selling of goods: (a) Frank Woolworth, (b) John Wanamaker, (c) Montgomery Ward?

CHANGING WAYS WITH TECHNOLOGY

LANTERN

shade

chimney

flame regulator

reservoir and wick

TABLE LAMPS

KEROSENE LIGHTING

The wick was lit after it had absorbed kerosene from the reservoir. The glass chimney had to be cleaned frequently because soot from the flame accumulated inside.

3 New forms of business organization appear as industry expands

Most of America's factories and stores in the 1860's and 1870's were of the type known as **individual proprietorships**—small enterprises owned by individuals or families. The individual or the family members who owned a small factory knew all the workers, often by their first names. Most wage earners in the 1860's lived in small towns, worked in small factories, and often took part in community activities with their employers.

During the next 30 years, much of this small-town, personal relationship disappeared. It was crowded out by the huge industrial plant located in or on the outskirts of a large city and employing hundreds, even thousands, of wage earners, who were often strangers to one another and even more remote from the owners.

Partnerships. As businesses grew in size, the owners had to find ways of sharing expanding costs and responsibilities. The **partnership** as a form of business organization became more and more common.

A partnership of two or more persons offers greater capital and skill than a single person can usually provide, but partnerships do have one major weakness. Each partner is completely liable, or responsible, for anything that happens to the business.

Corporations. As industries grew another form of organization, the **corporation,** became more common. It gradually replaced individual proprietorship and partnerships as the leading form of business organization.

To start a corporation, three or more persons apply to a state legislature for a **charter,** or license, to start a specific business en-terprise. This charter allows persons to organize a corpo shares of **stock,** or certificates raise the capital needed to ca terprise. The **stockholders** or those who invest money in tl may periodically receive **dividends,** that is, a share of the corporation's profits. Legally, a corporation is regarded as an individual – an "artificial person" entirely separate from its owners. It possesses certain rights, such as the right to make contracts, to buy and sell property, and to sue and be sued in court.

The corporation has important advantages over the individual proprietorship and the partnership. First, the corporation can draw upon very large supplies of capital because it can sell shares of stock to many people. Second, the charter gives the corporation perpetual life; that is, the corporation is not ended by the death or resignation of one or several of its owners. Third, stockholders can sell all or part of their stock whenever they choose. Finally,

Massachusetts had served as the cradle of the American Industrial Revolution. The state maintained its leading position in manufacturing during the late 1800's. The huge factory complex shown in this picture is the Assabet Manufacturing Company, located in Maynard, Massachusetts.

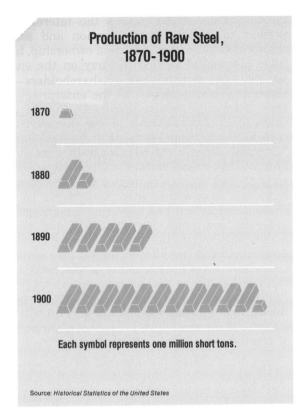

Production of Raw Steel, 1870-1900

1870

1880

1890

1900

Each symbol represents one million short tons.

Source: *Historical Statistics of the United States*

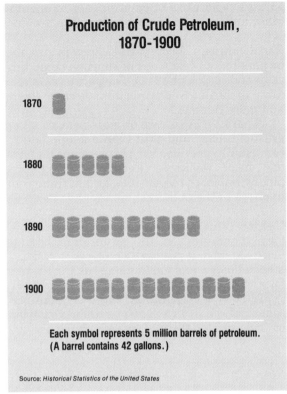

Production of Crude Petroleum, 1870-1900

1870

1880

1890

1900

Each symbol represents 5 million barrels of petroleum.
(A barrel contains 42 gallons.)

Source: *Historical Statistics of the United States*

investors have only limited liability. That is, if the corporation fails, they lose only the money they have invested in its stocks; they cannot be made to pay any debts owed by the bankrupt corporation.

During the first half of the 1800's, only a few large American industries were organized as corporations, and these were usually owned by only a handful of persons. By the 1860's, however, business owners needed increasing amounts of capital to build, equip, and operate the new enterprises that were exploiting the vast resources of America's forests, soils, mines, and waters. Because corporations could gather large amounts of capital, they became very common after 1860.

Business consolidation. During the latter half of the 1800's, there was also a growing trend toward business combination, or consolidation. Corporations in the same type of business would frequently join together to create large combinations.

Economists have pointed out many advantages in these combinations. Several corporations, when banded together, could save some of the costs of production and distribution. They could eliminate competing salespeople and advertising. They could purchase larger quantities of raw materials at lower prices and make better use of byproducts. They could arrange better bargains with banks, transportation companies, and workers. In short, through consolidation, businesses could substitute cooperation for competition and thus reduce waste, costs, and risky losses.

These large enterprises sometimes presented dangers to important principles of freedom in the American economic system. Through consolidation a group of corporations might gain monopoly control over a particular field of business. Monopoly control could lead to restraint of trade. That is, it could reduce competition, which lies at the heart of a free enterprise economy.

For example, a business combination might have so much power that it could undercut prices until its competitors failed. Then the combination could raise prices to make up its losses. Or if a consolidated enterprise gained monopoly control of an entire business field, it could charge excessive prices for its products or services. In such cases, consumers lost the right to shop around for the best bargains. These and other economic practices stemming from monopoly created problems for everyone.

Corporation pools.   One of the earliest ways in which corporations combined was by organizing **pools.** To form a pool, several corporations simply agreed to divide all their business opportunities among themselves. For example, several railroads serving the same city might agree on what percentage of local business each would handle. Or they might agree to charge uniform freight rates so that none would gain a price advantage. Or a group of manufacturing corporations might agree to divide the country into several market areas, each reserved for the sales force of one of the corporations in the pool and off limits to all the others.

Unlike the corporation, which operated under a legal charter, a pooling agreement had no legal standing. For that reason, courts refused to judge cases in which a member of a pool violated such an agreement with the other members. However, in 1887, pools were declared illegal in interstate commerce and practically disappeared.

Powerful trusts.   Meanwhile, other business owners developed a second form of business consolidation, called the **trust.** Business owners who wanted to organize a trust first had to reach an agreement with the major stockholders in the several corporations involved. The promise of greater profits from a larger organization was often all that was needed to persuade stockholders to enter a trust.

Under the trust agreement, the promoters of the trust, called the "trustees," gained control of the stock in all the corporations and thus of the corporation themselves. In exchange, the trustees gave the stockholders of the corporations trust certificates on which dividends were paid out of the profits of the trust.

With control of the stock in their hands, the trustees could run several corporations as a single giant business enterprise. If the trustees could get control of enough corporations, they could secure monopoly control of an entire business. They could then control prices. They could, for example, lower prices temporarily in one area to drive a competitor out of business, while raising prices everywhere else.

During the 1870's and the 1880's, giant trusts swallowed up corporations in many of the nation's largest industries, including oil, steel, sugar refining, and whisky distilling. When a trust did get control of enough corporations to secure a monopoly and end competition, it often raised prices on the products it controlled. The consumers and smaller competing businesses complained bitterly as the trusts closed in on them.

Magazines and newspapers of the time were filled with articles, letters, and editorials pointing out the evils of the "all-powerful monopolies" and pleading with the government to step in and restore freedom of enterprise. However, local, state, and federal governments had passed no laws that said trusts and monopolies were illegal, although under the **common law,°** which courts might or might not enforce, "conspiracies in restraint of trade" were forbidden.

The Sherman Antitrust Act.   Finally, in 1890, during the administration of President Benjamin Harrison, Congress passed the Sherman Antitrust Act. The public assumed that the act was intended to restore a larger measure of free competition by breaking up giant "trusts"—a term that had come to mean any monopoly or near-monopoly of an industry. This also seemed to be what Congress intended, for Section 1 of the act declared, "Every contract, combination in the form of trust or otherwise, or conspiracy, in restraint of trade or commerce among the several states or with foreign nations is hereby declared to be illegal." The act further stated that individuals and corporations found guilty of violating the law would be liable to legal penalties.

Actually, few Americans, including lawyers and members of Congress, understood what the new law did and did not prohibit. The act failed to define such words as "trust," "combination," "conspiracy," and "monopoly." Because of such loose wording, the Sherman Antitrust Act was difficult to enforce. The government lost seven out of the first eight cases that it brought against giant business combinations, or trusts.

In 1895 the Supreme Court handed down a decision in the case of *U.S. v. E. C. Knight Company* that made the antitrust law almost meaningless. The Court ruled that the company, which had control of 98 percent of the sugar-refining business, was not guilty of violating the antitrust law because its control of the

°**common law:** a system of law based upon custom, tradition, and precedents established by courts of law.

refining process alone did not involve restraint of interstate trade. A monopoly itself was not illegal, the Court stated. It became illegal only when it served to restrain interstate trade.

This and other decisions by the Supreme Court convinced businesses that they were free to consolidate. Thus the movement to form business consolidations actually speeded up in the years after the Sherman Antitrust Act was passed. Some historians see in this development evidence that the act was not really a reform measure. Such historians instead regard the act as an effort by big business to combat the growth of organized labor.

Despite its glaring weakness, the Sherman Antitrust Act was an attempt by the federal government to make rules for the conduct of big business. It established an important precedent for later and more effective laws.

Holding companies. After 1890 some of the nation's business leaders abandoned the trust for another form of business consolidation — the **holding company.** To form a holding company, it was necessary to get a charter from one of the states. The directors of the holding company then issued stock in the holding company itself. With the money raised by selling this stock, the directors bought controlling shares of stock in two or more corporations that were actually engaged in producing goods or services, such as manufacturing companies or transportation companies. The holding company did not itself produce either goods or services, but the company did control all the corporations whose stock it held.

After the 1890's the holding company became very popular. It was legal. It was responsible for its actions because, unlike the trust, it operated under a charter that could be revoked if the terms were violated.

Other ways to consolidate. Another form of consolidation was an **interlocking directorate.** In an interlocking directorate, some or all of the directors of one company served as directors of several other companies. Thus they could develop a uniform policy for the entire industry.

There were, of course, other ways to establish a uniform policy. Directors of different companies could simply meet and make secret agreements on prices and other matters.

Business leaders who tried to establish uniform policies for an entire industry — either through interlocking directorates or through secret understandings — were subject to prosecution under the Sherman Antitrust Act. However, it was difficult to prove that a monopoly existed. It was especially difficult when the monopoly had been created by means of interlocking directorates and secret agreements.

SECTION SURVEY

IDENTIFY: partnership, corporation, stock, dividends, business consolidation, monopoly.

1. What advantages does the corporation have over the partnership as a method of business organization?
2. (a) Summarize the provisions of the Sherman Antitrust Act of 1890. (b) Why was this law difficult to enforce?
3. How did the Supreme Court decisions in the late 1800's aid big business?
4. Chart Study: Make a chart entitled "Forms of Business Consolidation" with four columns headed Pools, Trusts, Holding Companies, and Interlocking Directorates. Below each heading (a) define this form of business consolidation, (b) give reasons for its creation, (c) name objections to it, and (d) name methods used to control its abuses.

4 **Business pioneers give new directions to American life**

Those who presided over the new world of throbbing machines, noisy factories, and crowded cities were the business leaders and the financiers. Their influence was reflected in local, state, and national politics.

Influence of business leaders. Between 1789 and 1860, thirteen Presidents had been elected — seven from the South, six from the North. Between 1860 and 1900, each of the seven Presidents elected was from the industrial regions of the Northeast or from the Middle West. On nearly all essential issues, moreover, the major differences between the Republicans and Democrats diminished during these years.

The business leaders of this period were not all of a single type. They varied greatly in personalities, abilities, and methods of doing business. They were pioneers, with the virtues as well as the shortcomings of pioneers. Some were rough, some were refined. All were eager to seize the unlimited opportunities of the new industrial world emerging around them. Some were fabulously successful. Others, the small business owners, never amassed fortunes or won great power. All of them—big-business leaders and small-business owners alike—shared the ideal of self-reliant individualism. This ideal was also shared by the few women who were permitted to take an active part in business. Among these women were Nettie Fowler McCormick in farm machinery, Lydia Pinkham in patent medicines, and Kate Gleason in machine tools.

Cornelius Vanderbilt. "Commodore" Cornelius Vanderbilt was born in 1794, when George Washington was President of the United States. By 1865 Vanderbilt, who had started life as a poor boy, had accumulated great wealth and owned a fleet of steamships worth $10 million. When he died in 1877 at age 82, he was worth $105 million.

Even in his seventies, "Commodore" Vanderbilt was an energetic man with a defiant bearing. He could hardly write, his spelling was impossible, and his temper earned him many enemies. He seemed to act on impulse, following his own hunches. He even consulted astrologers or fortunetellers about how to manage his business affairs.

What did Vanderbilt contribute to American life? For one thing, he consolidated the railroad companies that provided service between New York and Chicago. Before he took control of the different lines, passengers and freight had to be transferred 17 times between the two cities during a 50-hour trip. When he had completed the consolidation, one train made the entire trip in about 24 hours. He replaced iron rails and wooden bridges with steel rails and steel bridges. He built double tracks to make two-way traffic safe and speedy. He constructed new locomotives and terminals. Achievements such as these helped to make possible the rapid development of America's industrial economy.

Andrew Carnegie. Andrew Carnegie was another fabulous business leader during the early decades of industrialism. Born in 1835 in Scotland, Carnegie came to America at age 12 and

Cornelius Vanderbilt began work at age 16 by founding his own business. With money borrowed from his parents, he bought a boat and used it to ferry passengers and freight across New York Harbor.

Andrew Carnegie's philanthropy in his later years grew out of his personal philosophy, expressed in 1889: "The man who dies . . . rich dies disgraced."

453

MORE LUCK THAN PLUCK

"My brave boy, I owe you a debt I can never repay. But for your timely service I should now be plunged into an anguish which I cannot think of without a shudder."

Our hero was ready enough to speak on most occasions, but always felt awkward when he was praised.

"It wasn't any trouble," he said, modestly. "I can swim like a top."

"Our hero" was Ragged Dick, a New York City shoeshine boy. Saving the life of little Johnny Rockwell, who had carelessly fallen off a ferry boat, earned him not only the gratitude of the boy's father but also a job in Mr. Rockwell's business. From there, clearly, Ragged Dick would have smooth sailing on his way to fame and fortune.

Ragged Dick, published in 1868, was the eighth book written by Horatio Alger. It was the one that launched Alger on his own road to fame and fortune. The former Unitarian minister was to write over 100 novels. Almost all of them stuck to a very simple formula: poor boy works hard and makes good. The titles of Alger's books highlight this formula: *Fame and Fortune, Luck and Pluck, Strive and Succeed, Do and Dare.*

Few of Alger's thousands of readers read his books for their uplifting message. Few could have found much value in his wooden prose ("swim like a *top*"?). His world was a fantasy world. Although his heroes worked hard, they succeeded mainly through strokes of luck, which made for more interesting reading. Melodramatic events were common, as in Ragged Dick's act of heroism. What Alger did was write old-fashioned adventure stories in seemingly realistic settings. And Alger, like one of his characters, had his own stroke of luck. He combined these adventure stories with his formula at a time when the self-made millionaire had become a key figure in the American dream.

settled with his parents in Allegheny, now a part of Pittsburgh. At 14 he was working 12 hours a day as a bobbin boy in a cotton mill for $1.20 a week. He studied hard and at 16 was a telegraph clerk earning about $4.00 a week—a fair salary in those days. At 17 Carnegie became private secretary to the president of the Pennsylvania Railroad.

In 1850 Carnegie bought an oil well, and he made money in the new oil industry, but he soon turned to the steel industry. In it he spent the rest of his business life.

Carnegie frankly admitted that he knew nothing about steel manufacturing. His success lay in his ability as a seller and promoter. He knew how to gather around him people who were specialists. He was a relentless driver, never satisfied with himself or with others. One day he received a telegram from one of his plant superintendents: "We broke all records for making steel last week." Carnegie sent back another telegram: "Congratulations. Why not do it every week?"

Carnegie, however, also recognized the achievements of others. People he liked rose rapidly up the ladder to financial success. Charles M. Schwab, for instance, entered one of Carnegie's plants as a stake driver at a dollar a day. He became president of the Carnegie Steel Company at age 34. Schwab's share of profits in 1896 was $1.3 million. Similar stories are told of Carnegie's friendship for Henry Phipps, Henry C. Frick, and others.

By 1900 Andrew Carnegie, who began as a poor immigrant boy, was said to be the second richest man in the world. He owned all the types of property and equipment necessary for the mass production of steel, including deposits of iron ore, limestone, and coal; ships and railways to carry the raw material to smelters and mills; and huge steel plants from which the finished products poured forth.

Carnegie sold his steel property in 1901 for nearly $500 million. This tremendous financial deal was negotiated by J. P. Morgan, the most famous investment banker of the time. Out of the negotiations, in which 11 steel companies were merged, was born the mighty United States Steel Corporation, then the largest corporation in the world. Many economic historians have regarded this event as a critical point in the development of American capitalism. It marked a shift from **industrial capitalism,** in which corporations were controlled by their industrial owners, to **finance capitalism,** in which whole industries were dominated by bankers.

Carnegie retired in 1901. He spent much of the rest of his life giving away his money for education and other causes. "I started life as a poor man," he once said, "and I wish to end it that way." Before his death he had disposed of more than $350 million. Many public libraries stand today as monuments to Carnegie's generosity. Foundations created by his money still support causes such as education, world peace, and medical research.

John D. Rockefeller. Even richer than Carnegie was John D. Rockefeller, born in 1839, who during his lifetime accumulated the world's greatest fortune. One of five children, Rockefeller left high school after one year to work as a clerk for about $3 a week. In 1858, at age 19, he went into the wholesale food business. The Civil War brought large profits to the new company, and Rockefeller promptly invested his money in oil refineries. From this point on, oil became his major interest. He pioneered in developing the trust as a form of big business organization. Although he was ruthless in forcing his competitors to choose between joining him or going down to ruin, Rockefeller is given major credit for introducing order and efficiency into the highly chaotic and wasteful oil industry.

By 1900, Rockefeller's interests had broadened. He owned controlling stock in the gigantic Standard Oil Company, in railway lines, in steamship lines, in iron ore deposits in Colorado and in the Lake Superior region, in steel mills, and in many other enterprises. When the United States Steel Corporation was being organized by J. P. Morgan, Rockefeller sold to the newly formed corporation his iron ore deposits and Great Lakes steamers, receiving $80 million for the iron ore deposits alone.

Like Carnegie, Rockefeller later gave away many millions, and the foundations created with his money today continue to foster research and promote the welfare of the American people.

Pioneers of industrialism. These were only a few of the many pioneers of the new industrial society. Like other pioneers—cattle raisers, prospectors, frontier farmers, and wage earners—they helped to develop the resources of a new land. They were endowed with great energy and rare ability. They were gamblers, willing to take chances in the hope of gain. They were highly competitive people in a highly competitive society at a time when few laws had been passed to bring order into the mad rush of business enterprise. They were absorbed in the excitement of building a new industrial world, of creating huge fortunes, of securing power.

These business leaders have often been condemned as "robber barons" for their selfishness and ruthless business methods, for exploiting their workers and forcing their rivals out of business. At the same time, their critics have acknowledged that they also benefited the nation. They were responsible for building new industries, introducing efficient organization, and providing opportunities that enabled many people to invest their savings profitably in the new industries springing up all over the nation. However they are viewed today, these business leaders played an important part in an important period of the nation's development. They helped to give new directions to American life.

IDENTIFY: Nettie Fowler McCormick, J. P. Morgan, industrial capitalism, finance capitalism, Standard Oil Company.

1. (a) In what ways could Vanderbilt, Carnegie, and Rockefeller be considered "pioneers of industrial society"? (b) In what ways could they be considered "robber barons"?

2. What important contributions did the business pioneers of the late 1800's make to American economic life?

3. Find evidence to support the following statement: The most successful business leaders of the late 1800's generally believed in the ideal of self-reliant individualism.

Chapter Survey

Summary: Tracing the Main Ideas

During the years between 1865 and 1900, the United States grew rapidly. By the opening years of the 1900's, the United States had become the leading industrial nation in the world. Smoking factory chimneys, rumbling machinery, and long trains of freight cars pulling into and out of congested urban centers were symbols of the industrial world.

In the Northeast and Middle West and to a lesser extent elsewhere in the nation, industrialism was transforming the lives of the people. Raw materials from America's vast reservoir of natural resources poured into the mills and factories. Finished products in ever-growing quantities flowed from the factories into the marketplace and people's home's.

Mass production led to specialization. Financiers raised the capital to build the railroads and the factories. Manufacturers developed more efficient methods of producing goods. Merchants developed new methods of advertising and selling. Many workers— clerks, stenographers, managers, factory workers, and others—staffed the new industrial plants. New methods of business organization were developed and employed. Great corporations and combinations of corporations were increasingly replacing the individual or family-owned enterprises that had been the most common form of business organization.

Throughout America a new spirit of fierce competition drove people at a faster and faster pace. It was an exciting and a productive period in the nation's history, but some of the changes created problems for many people. Much of the nation's history since 1865 is concerned with the efforts of Americans to adjust their ways of life to the new forces of growing industrialism.

Inquiring into History

1. How were industrialization, improvements in transportation, and the growth of cities in America interrelated?
2. How did the abundance of natural resources and the development of advanced technology in America help contribute to its rapid growth as an industrial power?
3. (a) List the discoveries or inventions between 1865 and 1900 that you think did the most to encourage America's industrial growth. (b) How did each affect the growth of industry? (c) Were any of them interdependent?
4. (a) How do you suppose J. P. Morgan felt about the passage of the Sherman Antitrust Act? (b) What arguments might he have made to support his position?

Relating Past to Present

1. Read about one of the following inventions or innovations of the 1800's and trace its development to its present-day counterparts: telephone receiver/transmitter, typewriter, skyscraper, camera, dynamo.
2. Are today's objections to business monopolies the same as the ones raised during the period covered in this chapter? Explain.

3. Is it likely that a person today could rise "from rags to riches" as Vanderbilt or Carnegie did in their time?
4. (a) Should industries in the United States bear responsibility for what happens to the environment as a result of their activities? Why or why not? (b) How do the environmental efforts of government, business, and private groups today compare with those of the late 1800's?
5. Use reference books to find out the annual sales and total assets of the largest American corporations in 1900. (a) Are these corporations among the largest today? Why or why not? (b) Compare the 1900 figures with those of the largest corporations today, taking inflation into account. To what extent has big business gotten bigger in this century?

Developing Social Science Skills

1. Look at the graphs on page 450. What can you conclude from the information in the graphs about the rate of industrial growth in the United States after the Civil War?
2. Study the pictures in this chapter. (a) What evidence do they provide about industrialization? (b) Do any aspects of life under industrialization seem to be missing? (c) If so, how might you find out about these aspects of American life?

456

Chapter **23**

The Struggle of American Workers to Organize

On April 14, 1865, when President Lincoln was shot in Ford's Theater in the nation's capital, the United States was still chiefly an agricultural country. By 1900 it had experienced a period of unprecedented industrial development and become the leading industrial and manufacturing nation in the world.

America's amazing industrial growth was possible because of a number of factors. Improvements in the transportation system allowed raw materials and finished products to reach their destination quickly and cheaply. The development of power-driven machines and the construction of giant factories and other industrial plants greatly expanded production. The organization of business into larger corporations and the cooperation of government added to the efficiency of industrialization. Finally, the machines in the new industrial plants were operated by rapidly growing numbers of workers.

The new industrial workers—women and children as well as men—came from America's farms and rural areas. They also came from Europe in the hundreds of thousands every year, a mighty flood of immigration.

Both the older Americans and the newcomers entered a new world when they moved into America's growing industrial communities. In the early days of power-driven machines and mass production, they were as much pioneers as those who had earlier pushed America's frontiers westward to the Pacific. Like pioneers in every age, wage earners in the late 1800's faced complex problems.

1860's–1890's

THE CHAPTER IN OUTLINE

1. Industrialism creates new problems for wage earners.

2. Immigration adds strength and variety to American society.

3. Wage earners organize to overcome their grievances.

4. Organized labor faces opposition as it seeks reforms.

1 Industrialism creates new problems for wage earners

The industrial developments that transformed the United States between 1865 and 1900 created new problems as well as new opportunities for wage earners. Like all other Americans, wage earners had to adapt themselves to a rapidly changing industrial society.

New owner-worker relations. For one thing, large corporations hiring thousands of workers changed the old-time relations between owners and employees. In earlier days when factories were small, the owner knew the workers and sometimes took a personal interest in their welfare. In the huge factories, however, workers seldom saw the owners, most of whom were stockholders living in widely separated parts of the country.

Nor did many owners know at first hand what working conditions were like in their factories and mines. They bought shares of stock as an investment and hired managers to run the plants. As the factories grew larger, the workers, as individuals, became less important. If a worker objected to the way a factory was run, he or she could easily be replaced.

Workers in so-called "company towns" faced the greatest disadvantages. There were mining districts in Pennsylvania and West Virginia and textile-mill regions in the South where companies owned entire towns—all the houses, stores, and other buildings. The companies employed the teachers and the doctors. The local magistrates and the police owed their jobs to the company. In these towns workers did not dare to protest the rent they paid for their company-owned houses or the prices they paid in the company-owned store. Frequently, the workers received part of their wages not in cash but in credit at the company store.

Individual workers in the new industrial society could not hope to improve their working conditions. Nor could they reasonably hope to become an owner beyond, perhaps, buying a few shares of stock. To be sure, some workers

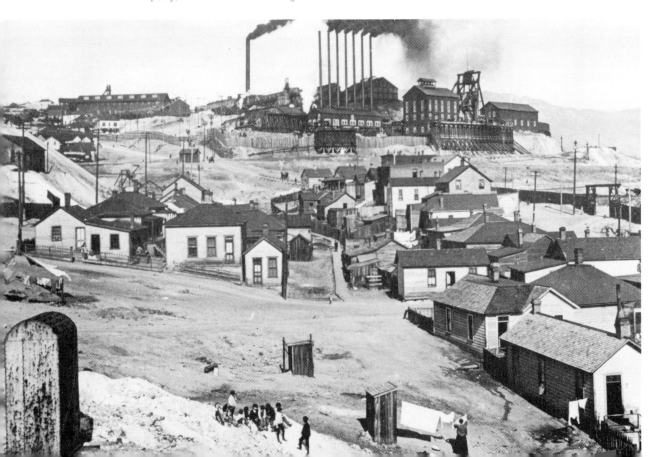

One byproduct of industrialism was the "company town." The one shown here is Butte, Montana, in 1890. It grew up around the Anaconda Copper Mining Company, which was then mining "the richest hill on earth."

did become supervisors and managers, and a few rose to positions of wealth and power. In general, though, as factories grew larger and more impersonal, it became harder for individual workers or groups of workers to bargain with employers over their wages and their working conditions.

Effects of mechanization.   The use of power-driven machines in factories also created new problems for wage earners. Factory work became increasingly specialized and increasingly monotonous. Often machines were geared to high rates of output, and workers ended the day exhausted. Moreover, the new machinery often produced much more with fewer workers. Thus the installation of new machines could cause **technological unemployment** by throwing workers out of jobs. Sometimes new and different jobs were created because workers were needed to build and repair the machines. Also, the higher output of the machines increased the nationwide production of goods and thereby created new jobs of many kinds. However, displaced workers often found it difficult to learn new skills and get new jobs.

Machines were also physically dangerous. Until about 1910 little was done to safeguard workers from accidents. When an accident occurred, the worker was usually blamed. If disabled, he or she received no compensation to pay the costs of doctors and hospitalization. When a worker was killed, the worker's family was usually left without an income, for employers did not insure the lives of workers.

Industrial hazards were a major problem. Between 1900 and 1910, for example, 3 percent of all employed workers in the United States were killed or injured annually in industrial accidents. In 1911 a fire in the unsafe Triangle Building in New York City brought death to 146 women textile workers. In a strike just the year before, the women had protested against their unsafe working conditions.

Effects of the railroads.   Before the nationwide network of railroads was built, American manufacturers usually sold their products only in nearby markets. With the railroad network, however, a manufacturer could hope to sell products anywhere in the country, provided the manufacturer's prices were as low as those elsewhere.

This creation of a competitive national market for goods also created a competitive na-

tional market for labor. For example, if cotton goods were being made cheaper in southern mills because of lower wages, then New England manufacturers of cotton goods were inclined to lower wages to compete with the lower-priced output of the southern mills.

Business cycles and the frontier.   Like other citizens, workers were greatly influenced by what economists call the **business cycle.** This was the expansion of business and industry during periods of prosperity and their contraction during periods of depression. Workers lived in constant dread of being laid off or having their wages sharply reduced whenever business conditions took a downturn. Even when business was good, unemployment per-

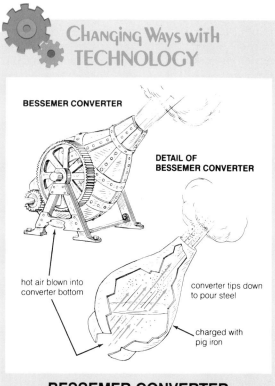

CHANGING WAYS WITH TECHNOLOGY

BESSEMER CONVERTER

DETAIL OF BESSEMER CONVERTER

hot air blown into converter bottom

converter tips down to pour steel

charged with pig iron

BESSEMER CONVERTER

Pig iron created in blast furnaces (page 100) still contained impurities that had to be removed to produce steel. The Bessemer converter, developed in the 1850's, forced a blast of hot air through molten pig iron. Oxygen in the air combined with the impurities and they were burned out. A substance was added to remove excess oxygen and otherwise strengthen the mixture. The molten steel was then poured out and shaped.

sisted and brought misery to many industrial workers.

Between 1870 and 1900, hundreds of thousands of jobless persons searched for work. In 1889, a fairly typical year, about 19 percent of the workers in manufacturing and transportation were jobless.

As long as the frontier remained open, farmers on worn-out eastern land could choose between migration to the frontier or migration to the city. Many chose to continue farming and moved west. After about 1900, however, eastern farm families had fewer and fewer opportunities to find good, cheap western land. They turned in larger numbers to the cities for work, swelling the work force of the cities and driving down industrial wages.

Low wages and long hours. During the last quarter of the 1800's, many wage earners complained bitterly about their low wages. Unskilled male workers might earn no more than $10 a week. Skilled male workers — those whose jobs required a certain amount of training and education — might earn no more than $20 a week. In both skilled and unskilled jobs, the wage scale for women workers was even lower. In 1903, for example, a woman might receive $2.16 for a 62-hour workweek in a cap factory. Still, industrial expansion brought higher **real wages**° to workers as a whole. Nevertheless, large numbers of workers, like many farmers, believed that they were not receiving a fair share of the profits from the country's industrial growth.

Wages tended to be low for several reasons: the increasing power of employers over employees, the competitive national labor market, depressions, and the flood of immigrant workers into the labor market.

Wage earners also complained about their long working hours. After 1865 an 11-hour day was common in American industry. Yet even in the 1880's, many textile workers worked from 12 to 14 hours daily, and the 12-hour day was common in the steel industry.

It was indeed a new and rapidly changing world with which the American wage earner wrestled in the late 1800's. The problems of wage earners were complex, and the workers, the owners of the industries, and Americans in general lacked ready answers.

°**real wages:** wages measured in terms of actual purchasing power, or what the money will buy.

IDENTIFY: "company town," technological unemployment, Triangle Building fire, business cycle.

1. How did the move toward huge, corporation-owned factories change relations between owners and workers?
2. Discuss the problems faced by workers as a result of increasing mechanization.
3. How did each of the following affect workers: (a) railroads, (b) the business cycle, (c) the end of the frontier?
4. Picture Study: Look at the photograph on page 458. Do you find any evidence to show that industrialization could bring problems as well as benefits?

2 Immigration adds strength and variety to American society

Immigrants played an essential part in the industrial development of the United States between 1865 and 1900. Immigrants came seeking jobs and new opportunities. In trying to find places for themselves in their new homeland and in the industrial age, the immigrants were often greeted with suspicion.

The immigrants. Part of the difficulty was the overwhelming number of immigrants who poured into the country. From 1870 to 1899, more than 11 million women, men, and children entered the United States.

The changing character of immigration as well as the swelling tide alarmed many Americans. Until the early 1880's, most immigrants came from northwestern Europe — Great Britain, Ireland, Scandinavia, Germany, and the Netherlands. After 1890 an increasingly large number came from southern and eastern Europe — Russia (including Poland), Greece, Austria-Hungary, and Italy. The languages, customs, and ways of living of these immigrants were quite different from those of immigrants from northwestern Europe.

Effects of immigration on labor. The immigrants had an enormous influence on American life. Although some settled on farms, the great majority moved to the densely crowded slum areas of the cities. Here tenement owners

In 1869 Joseph Becker painted this picture of cheering Chinese "gandy dancers," or railroad workers. Gandy dancers took their name from the Gandy Manufacturing Company, which made tools used in railroad construction. Chinese immigrants supplied much of the labor that built the western railroads.

profited in higher rents from the competition for housing between native-born Americans and newcomers from Europe.

Most immediate of all, however, was the immigrants' effect upon established workers. Immigrants competed for jobs, thereby lowering wages. To be sure, immigrants helped to stimulate the economy by creating new demands for factory and farm products. Most wage earners, however, were more disturbed by the job competition of the immigrants than they were impressed with the stimulating effects of immigration.

Tensions on the Pacific Coast. Chinese workers on the Pacific Coast, particularly in California, were early victims of the rising distrust of all immigrants. By the terms of the Burlingame Treaty of 1868, Chinese people had the right to immigrate to the United States. For some years Chinese laborers had been welcome additions to the labor supply. They had been forced to accept the hardest and least desirable jobs for very low wages. They were the backbone of the construction gangs that built the western section of the first trans-

continental railroad. By the 1870's nearly 75,000 Chinese workers had settled in California, where they made up about 20 percent of the labor force.

Then in 1873 a depression hit the country. As unemployment mounted, California workers worried that the Chinese would take their jobs at low wages. Fear and insecurity were intensified because the Chinese, for reasons not always of their own choosing, lived entirely to themselves. Thus they did not have an opportunity to learn and adapt to the ways of living accepted by most Californians.

Restricting Chinese immigration. Ill feeling was fanned into violence by crowds of unemployed California workers who gathered on street corners and sand lots. The "sand lotters" soon attacked the Chinese, killing some and burning the property of others.

In cooperation with distressed farmers, California workers were able to influence the writing of a new state constitution in 1879. California's new constitution discriminated against the Chinese by prohibiting them from owning property or working at certain jobs.

461

The opponents of Chinese immigration also succeeded in getting Congress to pass an exclusion bill in 1879. This bill prohibited all but a few Chinese from settling in the United States in any year. Because this bill violated the Burlingame Treaty of 1868, President Hayes vetoed it. Under pressure, however, the Chinese government agreed not to object if the United States regulated immigration. In 1882 Congress enacted a new Chinese Exclusion Act, which, with several extensions, continued in effect until World War II. The Chinese Exclusion Act forbade the immigration of Chinese laborers and denied American citizenship to Chinese born in China. Only students and a few other groups of Chinese could enter the United States.

Other restrictions. The Chinese Exclusion Act of 1882 was the first of a long series of restrictions on immigration, enacted mainly because of pressure from worker groups. The second was the repeal in 1885 of the Contract Labor Law.

The Contract Labor Law had been adopted by Congress in 1864, when booming wartime industries desperately needed workers. This law permitted American employers to recruit laborers in Europe. Under the law it was legal for employers to have workers abroad sign contracts agreeing to come to the United States to work for a specified employer for specified wages for a specified time. It was illegal for the workers to leave their jobs while the contract was in force. American workers objected to the law because (1) it came dangerously close to setting up a slave-labor system and (2) it subjected American workers to the unfair competition of cheap foreign labor.

After the repeal of the Contract Labor Law, American wage earners pressured Congress for other restrictive measures. One bill that kept coming up for 30 years would have forbidden entry to any immigrant who could not read and write. Congress actually did pass this law on several occasions, but each time the President then in office vetoed the bill. In 1917, however, Congress passed a "literacy test" bill over President Woodrow Wilson's veto, and the door to immigration was shut a little further.

The role of immigrants. Except for the Chinese Exclusion Act, the restrictions placed on immigration from 1865 to 1900 were relatively minor. Without the more than 11 million im-

migrants who poured into the United States between 1870 and 1900, profits to owners of industry would have been much smaller. As it was, employers could keep wages of immigrants lower than those of established Americans. Without immigrants America's industrial progress also would have been much slower. Immigrant muscles and brains helped to transform the United States from a predominantly agricultural country into a giant industrial power.

SECTION SURVEY

IDENTIFY: immigrants, slums, "sand lotters," "literacy test" bill.

1. How did the composition of the immigrant population change after 1880?
2. Discuss three ways in which immigration affected American workers.
3. Why did Congress pass the Chinese Exclusion Act of 1882?
4. (a) Explain the provisions of the Contract Labor Law of 1864. (b) Why was it repealed?
5. Give evidence to support this statement: Immigrant muscles and brains helped to transform the United States.

3 Wage earners organize to overcome their grievances

Faced with numerous problems brought on by the new industrial age, wage earners, like farmers, looked for solutions to their problems through organization.

The National Labor Union. Labor organizations were not new. During the war years 1861–65, however, as industry boomed and the cost of living soared, the labor movement gained new momentum.

In 1866 the National Labor Union was launched under the leadership of William Sylvis, an experienced and able organizer of iron molders. In 1868 the National Labor Union helped push through Congress a law setting an 8-hour workday for laborers and mechanics employed by or in behalf of the federal government. After unsuccessfully supporting a third-party movement in the election of 1872, this union faded away.

By 1890, when Thomas Anshutz painted this scene of steelworkers taking a lunch break, the United States had become the world's leading steel manufacturer.

The Knights of Labor. Far more important than the National Labor Union was the Knights of Labor, founded in 1869 in Philadelphia by Uriah S. Stephens, a tailor. The Knights of Labor tried to unite all American workers into one great union—foreign-born and native-born, blacks and whites, skilled and unskilled, women and men. Several women headed local units or "assemblies" and a few became national leaders. The Knights aimed "to secure to the toilers a proper share of the wealth that they create; more of the leisure that rightfully belongs to them." Among other things, they favored an 8-hour workday.

The Knights of Labor also tried to organize and run cooperative stores and manufacturing plants, as some farmers already had done. They hoped to save for themselves the profits that normally went to manufacturers and distributors and at the same time to produce lower-priced goods. However, most of their cooperative enterprises failed, largely because they did not have enough money to buy good machinery and to hire qualified managers.

In some of their efforts the Knights of Labor were more successful. They were influential, for example, in causing Congress to pass the Chinese Exclusion Act in 1882 and to repeal the Contract Labor Law in 1885.

The Knights of Labor officially frowned on strikes, preferring to settle disputes between management and laborers through industrial **arbitration.**° However, a successful railroad strike in 1885 did much to boost the group's membership. For the first time in American labor history, railroad operators met strike leaders on equal terms and agreed to labor's

°**arbitration:** the judging of a dispute between two sides by an impartial person whose decision they agree in advance to accept.

463

chief demands. When the railroad strike occurred, the Knights numbered about 500,000 members. By 1886 their membership had reached 700,000. This growth also owed much to the idealism and enthusiasm of Terence V. Powderly, who succeeded Uriah S. Stephens as leader of the Knights of Labor.

The Haymarket Affair. On May 4, 1886, while the Knights were at the peak of their power, a large group of workers gathered in Haymarket Square in Chicago. They were there to protest an attack on strikers on May 3 in which one striker had been killed and a number of others wounded.

The meeting was orderly and the crowd was just beginning to leave when nearly 200 police officers appeared. Suddenly, without warning, a bomb burst in the midst of the police. Seven people were killed and many others wounded.

No one ever identified the bomb thrower. Nevertheless, eight "radicals," who on earlier occasions had advocated violence, were arrested. Seven were sentenced to death, the eighth to 15 years in prison.

No evidence was ever produced to indicate that organized labor was responsible for the Haymarket Affair. Yet no other event during the 1880's did more to turn public opinion against organized labor.

Decline of the Knights of Labor. The Knights, as the leading labor organization, suffered most of all. The decline of the organization was almost as rapid as its rise. From 1886 to 1888, its membership dropped from the high of 700,000 to only 260,000, and by 1890 only about 100,000 members were enrolled.

There were several reasons for this decline in membership. For one thing, the Knights lost an important railroad strike in 1886. This strike angered the public because of violence accompanying it and because of shortages of food and coal resulting from it. In the second place, the Knights included too many opposing groups to develop real strength. Skilled workers especially disliked the Knights' policy of taking in unskilled workers, with whom they felt they had little in common.

Finally, Terence V. Powderly's aims came to be too general to satisfy numerous workers. Many wage earners were now convinced that a strong labor movement had to avoid political crusades and concentrate on improving conditions for specific groups of workers.

Other organizations rose to take the place of the Knights. Some, like the American Railway Union and the United Mine Workers, had specialized goals. The most important labor organization was the American Federation of Labor (A. F. of L.).

The A. F. of L. Started in 1881 under another name and reorganized in 1886, the A. F. of L. quickly replaced the Knights of Labor as the leading American labor organization.

Unlike the Knights of Labor, the A. F. of L. was a federation of separate national **craft unions.** Each craft union represented a group of skilled workers in a separate trade, or craft, such as carpentry, welding, or typography. The A. F. of L. sought to organize all skilled workers by their craft rather than by the industry in which they worked. However, the A. F. of L. did include a few **industrial unions** that tried to organize all workers, unskilled as well as skilled, in a single industry.

Each A. F. of L. union was free to bargain collectively for all its members, to call strikes, and to manage its own affairs. The A. F. of L. also differed from the Knights of Labor in keeping itself aloof from general reform movements and from independent or third-party political activities. The A. F. of L. was an economic organization of workers emphasizing craft unionism — "pure and simple unionism."

The A. F. of L. program called for an 8-hour workday and a 6-day workweek. It backed legislation protecting workers on dangerous jobs and compensating them and their families in case of injury or death. It also demanded higher wages and better working conditions. The A. F. of L. threw its weight in political contests to whichever party or candidate came closest to representing its aims.

The A. F. of L. accepted the capitalist free-enterprise system. Its leaders in general discouraged strikes and favored bargaining with management. The A. F. of L. did insist, however, on controlling the skilled labor market, on getting a larger share of the output of industry through higher wages and shorter hours, and on improving labor conditions.

With the exception of a single year, the president of the A. F. of L. from 1886 to 1924 was its principal founder, Samuel Gompers. Under Gompers's leadership the A. F. of L. grew rapidly. In 1890 it had only 100,000 members, but by 1900 membership had climbed to 500,000.

1. Why did some American workers decide to organize unions during the mid-1800's?

2. Describe the (a) purpose, (b) successes, and (c) reasons for the decline of the Knights of Labor.

3. How did the American Federation of Labor differ from the Knights of Labor?

4. (a) What is the difference between a craft union and an industrial union? (b) Give examples of each today.

4 Organized labor faces opposition as it seeks reforms

When American workers began to organize during the late 1880's, they encountered many obstacles. The workers' attempts to form unions and to seek recognition of their unions' right to bargain for them met strong and widespread opposition.

Public opposition. During the late 1880's, Americans in general as well as the government usually supported employers in conflicts between employers and unions or between employers and workers striking for union recognition. This opposition to unions is not hard to understand. Most Americans had grown up in the older, rural America. Individual workers then had more control over their fates than they now had in the giant corporations. Most Americans also believed that employers had the right to hire and fire as they pleased.

Many Americans resented union demands for the **closed shop.** The businesses that had such agreements with a union could hire only union members. Employers resented this restriction on what they considered their right to hire anyone they pleased. Many workers also resented these closed-shop agreements, which forced them to join a union whether they wanted to or not.

Moreover, many Americans believed that most workers were quite content with their lot. The fact that as late as 1914 only about one worker out of ten belonged to a labor organiza-

tion seemed to support this belief. Many Americans held that the best workers could still rise to become managers and even owners. Most Americans blamed the entire labor problem as well as industrial conflict itself on "power-hungry" labor leaders interested in their own personal advancement.

Immigrants and labor unions. Many union leaders were of foreign birth. In several labor organizations, especially in the textile and coal-mining industries, immigrant workers were a source of strength. Immigrant workers took leading parts in the strikes of New York garment workers as well as in the textile workers' strike in Lawrence, Massachusetts.

However, a great many immigrants opposed labor unions. Coming from rural backgrounds in Europe, most immigrants had no previous experience with labor organizations. Bewildered by their new environment, they often did not feel a need to join with native-born American workers in an effort to promote common interests.

Many immigrants had left Europe partly to be as free as possible from all sorts of restrictions. Thus they did not like labor unions, with their dues, their rules, and their insistence that no one work for less than a certain wage. Many immigrants felt that however bad working conditions in the United States might be, they were better than working conditions back in Europe.

Most immigrants, also, were unskilled workers. Thus the A. F. of L. made little or no effort to admit them to the craft unions. Finally, there was widespread prejudice among native-born American workers toward immigrant workers. This prejudice deepened when foreign-born workers were recruited by business managers to break strikes.

Women and unions. Many unions did not admit women to membership, but in a few craft unions women played important roles. Most notable was the International Ladies Garment Workers Union, in which Rose Schneiderman and Leona O'Reilly were leaders. The A. F. of L. expressed interest in organizing women but did not vigorously pursue this aim.

In 1903 the National Women's Trade Union League was founded, largely by middle-class women. It assisted women workers in several ways, especially by providing financial support during strikes. The league stressed voting rights for women as a means for advancing their economic equality and promoted minimum, or "living," wages for women.

Blacks and unions. Because of the racial prejudice of many white workers, blacks were excluded from most labor organizations. A notable exception was the Knights of Labor, which enrolled black workers without discrimination, at least until the organization's later years.

At first the leaders of the A. F. of L. favored including skilled black workers in their craft unions. They believed that if this were not done, black workers might undermine the purposes of the federation by accepting lower wages. When the machinists' union and others refused to admit blacks, Samuel Gompers, by then the dominant power in the A. F. of L., backed down. He insisted that union constitutions should not specifically exclude black members but admitted that in practice the unions might do so. The United Mine Workers and a few other A. F. of L. unions admitted black members on equal terms with white members. Most of the other unions insisted, however, that any black workers admitted to A. F. of L. membership had to be organized in separate unions.

Most northern blacks were unskilled workers. Thus after the decline of the Knights of Labor, the A. F. of L. policy of organizing only skilled workers in effect excluded black wage earners from northern labor organizations. In the South, where there were many skilled black workers, the labor market in the skilled trades was controlled by all-white A. F. of L. unions. As a result, many skilled southern black workers were forced to take jobs as unskilled laborers.

By 1902 in both the North and the South, 43 national labor unions had not a single black member, and 27 others had only a handful. Gompers argued that blacks had only themselves to blame for their exclusion because few were skilled workers and fewer still were willing to accept the self-discipline and cooperation necessary in trade unionism. Booker T. Washington, however, declared that the union movement itself was holding back the economic progress of black workers by refusing to admit them as apprentices and by making no effort to organize them.

The virtual exclusion of blacks from the American labor movement closed off to the great mass of black Americans an important opportunity to be included in the mainstream of American life. It also weakened the effectiveness of the labor movement itself.

Division in the ranks of labor. The mechanization of industrial plants also weakened the power of wage earners to unite. When factories were small, skilled workers could see that the work of unskilled workers, however minor, was an essential part of the production process. When factories grew large and workers became strangers, skilled workers came to look down on unskilled workers.

Thus the wage earners themselves divided into two groups: (1) a small number of skilled workers who gained more and more bargaining power with employers, and (2) a large number of unskilled, unorganized laborers whose voices and interests counted for very little.

Industry against the unions. With most Americans generally distrustful of unions, huge industrial enterprises did not find it difficult to influence public opinion and government in their own favor. They hired lawyers to fight their battles in the courts. They spent money on advertising and publicity to win public sympathy. They paid skillful lobbyists to get favorable laws passed or to defeat bills that employers did not like. Some corporations contributed to the political party they thought most likely to win an election, hoping to secure government favors.

To discourage workers from joining unions, employers also developed more direct methods. For example, employers' associations, made up of several manufacturers, compiled **black lists.** These were lists of workers considered as undesirable—sometimes because the workers were incompetent, sometimes because they were labor organizers, sometimes merely because they belonged to a union. A black list was circulated throughout an entire industry all over the country. Any person whose name appeared on a black list was barred from getting a job in that industry, at least under her or his own name.

Many employers also required workers applying for a job to sign a written agreement not to join a union. The workers called these agreements **yellow-dog contracts.** A worker who violated such a contract was fired.

Employers used still other methods to prevent workers from organizing. Sometimes pri-

The cartoonist who drew this picture in 1883 obviously saw the battle between management and labor as a very uneven one. What advantages does the cartoonist think that one side enjoyed over the other in the struggle?

vate detectives, posing as workers, joined unions and reported strike plans and names of union leaders to employers. Sometimes when strikes broke out, employers actually paid agents to commit acts of violence, which were then blamed on labor. At other times, the workers themselves resorted to violence. In either case, such violence gave employers a good excuse for calling in the local police, the state militia, or even federal troops to restore order and break the strike.

Sometimes employers fought strikes with another weapon—the **lockout.** They closed their plants, thus locking out the workers. Then they brought in **strikebreakers**— nonunion workers hired to do the work of those on strike—and the plant was reopened despite the angry strikers picketing outside its gates. At other times, owners simply locked their plants and waited until the hungry, impoverished strikers were willing to return to work on any terms.

Government support of industry. With public opinion on their side, employers counted on government aid in conflicts with workers. Despite some exceptions they generally got such aid.

In most serious labor disputes, governors sent the state militia to the scene, which was to the employers' advantage. Whenever they sent the militia, the governors argued that the troops were needed to protect property, prevent violence, and maintain order. Since the governors were sworn to uphold law and order, this seemed reasonable. On the other hand, the arrival of the state militia often made it impossible for the workers to continue to strike.

In the last quarter of the 1800's, the Presidents of the United States in general followed the example of the state governors in ordering troops to a scene of trouble. Thus during a series of railroad strikes in Pennsylvania and Maryland in 1877, when state troops could not restore order, President Hayes sent federal

467

A PETITION WITH BOOTS ON

Jacob Coxey was a model citizen, a successful, hard-working quarry owner from Massillon, Ohio. But beneath his quiet exterior beat the heart of a reformer. The depression of 1893 had thrown thousands out of work, and Coxey thought the government should do something about it.

Early in 1894 Coxey—together with a colorful Populist orator named Carl Browne—decided to make Congress aware of the problems of the down-and-out. "Browne," he exclaimed, "we will send a petition to Washington with boots on!"

Coxey had a sympathetic Congressman introduce bills based on his ideas. These provided for government sponsorship of vast road-building projects, which would furnish work for the unemployed. While the bills were in Congress, Coxey organized his march on Washington. Circulars proclaimed: "We want no thieves or anarchists to join us. We want patriots, not bummers." Only about a hundred men marched out of Massillon on that Easter Day, but additional recruits joined up as the group traveled eastward to Washington. By the time Coxey's "army" reached the nation's capital, at the end of April, it numbered about 500.

A big crowd lined Pennsylvania Avenue when Coxey's "army" trooped toward the Capitol on May 1. Coxey's daughter Mamie rode on horseback as the goddess of peace, dressed in white and carrying a tiny parasol. At the Capitol, however, hundreds of police kept the marchers back and prevented Coxey from speaking. Coxey and Browne were arrested—for walking on the grass. A few days later they were sentenced to twenty days in jail and fined $5 apiece.

Coxey's "army" seemed to be good for nothing but chuckles. But Coxey had the last laugh. In 1944, at the age of 90, he at last got to make his speech on the Capitol steps. By that time Congress had enacted the kinds of laws that Jacob Coxey had first called for fifty years earlier.

soldiers to keep the trains running. The strikes collapsed.

Federal troops also stepped in near Chicago in 1894 when a strike was called against the Pullman Palace Car Company by the American Railway Union led by Eugene V. Debs. The strike was supported by railway workers around Chicago and elsewhere, who refused to handle trains that included Pullman cars. When Governor Altgeld of Illinois refused to call out the state militia or ask for federal help, President Cleveland sent federal troops anyway. Cleveland declared that such action was justified in order to guarantee mail delivery, although mail trains were in fact running and the mails were being delivered. Organized labor resented such use of federal troops.

The courts support industry. In the late 1800's, the courts generally sided with management. For example, during the Pullman strike the railroad owners asked a federal court in Chicago to issue an **injunction,** or court order, forbidding Debs and other labor leaders to continue the strike. The court issued the injunction. It claimed that the strikers had entered into "a conspiracy in restraint of trade" and were therefore violating the Sherman Antitrust Act of 1890, which declared such conspiracies illegal.

Debs defied the court order. He was promptly arrested and sentenced to six months in jail for refusing to obey the injunction. Labor denounced this conviction as "government by injunction," but the Supreme Court upheld the ruling. Debs was jailed, and the Pullman strike was broken.

After 1895, employers often secured injunctions to prevent or break up strikes. Labor leaders complained bitterly, but their only possible relief was (1) that the Supreme Court would reverse its decision in the Debs case, or (2) that Congress would modify the Sherman Antitrust Act so that it could not be used against labor unions.

Radical movements. After the Haymarket Affair of 1886, many Americans began to identify the labor movement with radicalism. However, most Americans in the 1880's and 1890's did not distinguish among the goals and methods of the three major radical movements —**anarchism, communism,** and **socialism.**

The anarchists believed that people could work and live happily together in voluntary associations if they could be freed from the restraints of government. They believed that their ideal society could be won only by the violent overthrow of the government and of capitalism—the economic system under which industry is owned and controlled by private individuals. Although the anarchists were few in number, their reputation for violence deeply alarmed the nation.

The best-known anarchist was Emma Goldman, an immigrant from Russia. Though feared and hated generally by the middle class and disliked by many workers, Goldman was appreciated in radical circles. She was a tough, fighting champion of working people, of free speech, and of complete freedom for women. Emma Goldman was also an uncompromising foe of militarism and the use of police force in what she regarded as the exploitation of ordinary people.

The followers of Karl Marx believed that wage earners would always be exploited under capitalism. They argued that capitalism had to be replaced by an economic system in which the workers could own and control the means of production.

In time, the followers of Marx developed into two separate groups. One group, known as Communists, insisted that the only way to build the new society of workers envisioned by Marx was by means of revolution and the violent seizure of power.

The other group, known as socialists, generally did not advocate revolution. The socialists believed that the workers, organized in unions committed to socialism and in a political party, could vote themselves into power and by democratic means could reconstruct the economic and social foundations of society. Socialist leaders included Daniel De Leon, Morris Hillquit, Kate Richards O'Hare, Eugene V. Debs, and Victor Berger.

The influence of the radical movements upon American labor organizations was never as strong as it became in some parts of Europe. Union members by and large continued to support Republicans, Democrats, or third-party candidates and policies according to the union members' personal judgment of issues and of their own best interests.

Influence of organized labor. In the face of strong opposition from management, government, and the middle class, organized labor made solid gains. For example, in 1896 there were 5,462 strikes. Of these, 3,913 achieved full or partial success for the workers. In 1903 there were 12,660 strikes that succeeded in whole or in part.

Despite setbacks, organized labor continued to fight for its aims and for public recognition and support. By the early 1900's, the lot of American workers was beginning to improve.

SECTION SURVEY

IDENTIFY: closed shop, National Women's Trade Union League, Pullman strike, anarchism, capitalism, Eugene V. Debs, Emma Goldman, communism, socialism.

1. Why did public opinion in the late 1800's usually support employers rather than workers?

2. Why did many immigrants oppose the labor movement?

3. (a) Why were black workers excluded from the labor movement? (b) What have been the long-term effects of this discrimination?

4. How were women workers treated by the labor movement?

5. How did employers use each of the following against organized labor: (a) publicity, (b) lobbyists, (c) political contributions, (d) black lists, (e) yellow-dog contracts, (f) lockouts, (g) strikebreakers?

Chapter Survey

Summary: Tracing the Main Ideas

The rapid development of large-scale industry between 1865 and 1900 created new problems for wage earners. They attempted to solve these problems by organizing labor unions. Through the labor movement, Samuel Gompers and other labor leaders outlined and pushed for a program of democracy that differed in many respects from the traditional ideas of democracy.

Democracy in the earlier days was largely based on the ability of the individual to help himself or herself. The growth of great corporations made it increasingly difficult for the individual worker to meet and solve his or her own problems. As a result, some workers organized unions through which they could act as a united group. They began to demand government protection in the form of laws providing maximum hours of work, minimum wages, and accident compensation.

By 1900, labor organizations were beginning to exert considerable influence upon government at both the state and the federal level. They were supporting those candidates in the major political parties who were most friendly to the progress of the workers. They were also insisting that it was their democratic right to organize, to bargain as a group, and to strike if necessary to protect their rights. Several bitter strikes had already occurred.

In their demands and in their actions, wage earners were reacting to the new industrial society that was transforming the United States. Like all other Americans, they were seeking to adjust to the industrial age.

Inquiring into History

1. In human terms, what did the United States lose in becoming an industrialized nation? What advantages did it gain?
2. The majority of immigrants coming to the United States during the late 1800's were between the ages of 14 and 45. Why do you think this was the case? How might this fact have been significant for the nation's economy?
3. In the period 1870–1900, what were the major grievances of working people against (a) employers, (b) state governments, and (c) the federal government?
4. In what ways were the radical movements and the labor movement connected during the late 1800's?
5. Give evidence to support the claim that both federal and state governments generally sided with industry and against labor in disputes during the late 1800's.

Relating Past to Present

1. How does the power that labor unions held during the period 1865–1900 compare to the power that they hold today? Use specific examples to support your answer.
2. Compare the demands that labor unions make today with the demands they made during the late 1800's.

3. In general, how did the courts treat labor unions in the late 1800's? Do the courts treat them differently today?
4. Using *Statistical Abstract of the United States* and *Historical Statistics of the United States,* compare the wage rates for and hours worked by American workers in the late 1800's and today. What does this information indicate about the standard of living of working Americans in the two periods?

Developing Social Science Skills

1. Study the graph of immigration on page 842. (a) During which decade did total immigration first reach 1 million? 2.5 million? (b) During which decade between 1860 and 1900 did the most immigrants come to the United States? About how many came? (c) Why do you suppose immigration might have dropped in the following decade?
2. Interview a member or leader of a labor union. Before beginning the interview, be sure to prepare your questions carefully. You might ask questions about union activities and goals, union accomplishments, and worker-employer relations.
3. Conduct research and prepare an oral report or bulletin board display on one of these people: Samuel Gompers, Eugene V. Debs, Emma Goldman, Rose Schneiderman, John Peter Altgeld, Daniel De Leon, George Pullman.

Chapter 24

The Revolt of Farmers Against Big Business Practices

After the Civil War, American farmers stood on the threshold of the industrial age. Yet neither the farmers nor the great majority of other Americans were aware of the sweeping developments that were about to transform life in America, in Western Europe, and eventually throughout the world.

By 1870 the symbols of the new industrial age were beginning to appear and to affect farmers' lives. Steel rails stretched across the prairies and through remote mountain valleys, opening up new farmland to settlement and bringing older farmland in closer touch with the cities. Farm machines had begun to appear on some of the nation's more prosperous farms, enabling the farmer to produce more goods with less labor. The rapidly growing industrial cities were opening up ever-larger markets for farm products. These and other related developments made the farmer an increasingly important part of the new industrial economy.

In the 1870's farm families had every reason to assume that better times lay ahead for the nation's rural population. Better times would eventually come, but not in the 1880's and 1890's. During this period American farmers instead were forced to confront a number of serious new problems.

THE CHAPTER IN OUTLINE

1. Farm life remains laborious, but simple.

2. Farmers face complex new problems in the industrial age.

3. Farm organizations join efforts to regulate the railroads.

4. Farm organizations put increasing pressure on government.

5. The farmers fail to win control of the national government.

Changing Ways of American Life

1860's–1890's

1 Farm life remains laborious, but simple

Every ten years, as required in the Constitution, a federal census has been taken all across America. Occupations, income, and other information have been recorded and published by the government. The returns from the 1870 census showed that the nation's urban population was growing more rapidly than the rural population. In 1860 about 80 percent of all Americans lived in rural areas. By 1870 only about 75 percent lived on farms or in small towns and villages. Even so, the United States was still for the most part a farming country.

The 2.7 million farms that the census takers visited in 1870 varied greatly. Some were large, others small. Some farmers were prosperous; others just managed to earn a living. Regardless of their size or their degree of prosperity, the American farms of 1870 shared certain characteristics.

The day of hand tools. Manual labor and a few simple hand tools characterized work on most farms in 1870. It is easier, perhaps, to visualize life on the typical farm of 1870 by starting with things that the farm family did not yet have.

No farmers, for instance, had gasoline-driven machines or machines powered by electricity. Farmers pumped water by hand, lifted it in buckets from open wells, or, if they were fortunate, ran a pipe from a hilltop spring and allowed the water to flow to the barn and the farmhouse. There were no electric or gas stoves. Farm women usually cooked on iron, wood-burning stoves; only a few had the new kerosene stoves. There were no gas or electric lights; for lighting, farmers used smoky kero-

Winslow Homer's painting "Crack the Whip" captures an everyday scene of American rural life in the 1870's. Recess has released some of the students from their "little red schoolhouse," and they use their free time to play a game.

sene lamps and lanterns. There was no central heating; there were only stoves and, in the milder South, open fireplaces. In 1870 there was no free delivery of mail. Also there were no mail-order catalogs from which farm families could order their ready-made clothing, tools, or equipment.

On some of the nation's large and more prosperous farms, machines were becoming increasingly important. Steel plows were in general use. More horse-drawn corn planters, mowers, hayrakes, and reapers as well as steam-powered threshers were being manufactured in American factories and put to work in the fields.

In 1870 the average farmers depended almost entirely upon hand tools—axes, saws, spades, pitchforks, sickles, scythes, and rakes. For power they relied mainly on their muscles and on horses, mules, or oxen. There was nothing new in this situation. The lives of many American farmers in 1870 were not essentially different from the lives of American farmers in, say, 1770 or 1820.

The self-reliant farm family. Farming was not an easy way of life. The family rose at daybreak—or even earlier in winter—to milk the cows, bring in firewood, feed the pigs and chickens, and fill the water trough for the livestock. When night fell—and long after dark in winter—the family was still busy with its unending chores.

This hard life had its compensations. The family was its own boss. The land and the labor of the farmer, his wife, and their children provided most of their food, clothing, and shelter. A self-reliant farm family developed a spirit of independence that few wage earners could hope to enjoy.

Not all American farmers in 1870 shared this feeling of independence. Nearly one fourth of the families living on farms at this time did not own the land they worked. They either rented farms as tenants or operated them as sharecroppers. Sharecropping, as you have read, was especially common among black farmers in the South.

Social life. Except for farmers who lived close to a growing city or a large town, opportunities for social activities in 1870 were limited. Most farm families had only three centers of social activity—the nearest town, the church, and the school.

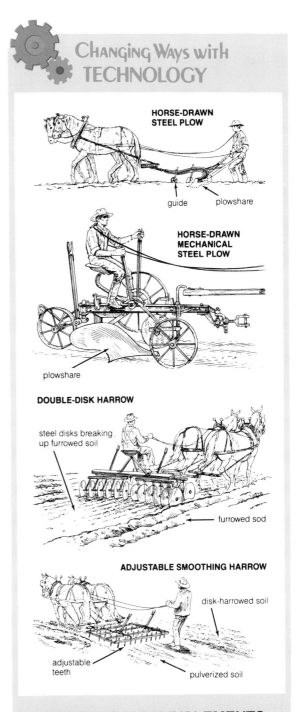

CHANGING WAYS WITH TECHNOLOGY

HORSE-DRAWN STEEL PLOW

guide   plowshare

HORSE-DRAWN MECHANICAL STEEL PLOW

plowshare

DOUBLE-DISK HARROW

steel disks breaking up furrowed soil

furrowed sod

ADJUSTABLE SMOOTHING HARROW

disk-harrowed soil

adjustable teeth

pulverized soil

IMPROVED FARM IMPLEMENTS

The development of steel plowshares aided in turning over the tough sod of the prairie. Mechanical plows transferred much of the labor of plowing to a machine. The pulverizing of the soil, earlier done by hoes and rakes (see page 37), was now performed by harrows. They were fast, thorough, and labor-saving.

473

THE COUNTRY STORE

Farmers and small-town Americans of the late 1800's could not have survived without the country store. In many communities it was the only place within walking or buggy distance where people could buy the necessities of life.

Food, of course, was basic, and much of it was sold in bulk. Ranged along the walls were barrels of flour and sugar, tubs of butter, baskets of eggs, huge blocks of cheese, bins of crackers, and slabs of bacon. Pickle vats, coffee grinders, and jars of spices gave off their distinctive smells.

For men there was chewing tobacco, cut to order. Women could buy family clothing from boots to bonnets or sew it, choosing from a big selection of fabrics, thread, and other supplies. Children were tempted by penny cards, arranged in rows in showcases or jumbled in jars.

The country store's wide range of household goods included crockery, cooking utensils, strong yellow laundry soap, stove polish, lamps, and the kerosene to fill them. Farmers could find seed, hay rakes, milking pails, and axes. Patent medicines promised to ease every ache and pain.

The country store (or general store, as it was often called) was more than a place to buy things. Often it housed the local post office. Above all, it was a sort of community center, where people met to talk and exchange news. In winter the locals gathered around the stove to discuss politics and swap stories all day long. "I am a storekeeper," wrote one merchant in an ad, "and am excessively annoyed by a set of troublesome animals, called Loungers, who are in the daily habit of calling at my store, and there sitting hour after hour." The owner may have felt better after letting off steam in print—but it is doubtful that he ever got rid of his "Loungers."

The Saturday drive to town in a wagon or buggy was a big weekly event. Even a 10-mile (16-kilometer) trip meant about four hours on the road. As for the "town," it might be nothing more than a country store at the crossroads, with a blacksmith shop on the opposite corner. On the other hand, it might be a sizable village or even a county seat with a courthouse, a railroad station, several stores, a bank, a doctor's office, a lawyer's office, and a cluster of houses.

These Saturday trips combined business with pleasure. While the farm women shopped and while the farmers arranged for the sale of their cash crops or settled accounts at the bank or the store, the children played with their friends. The shopping and the business gave families an opportunity to chat with neighbors, to catch up on the latest news, and perhaps to watch some horse trading in front of the blacksmith shop.

The Sunday trip to church was another bright spot in the week. The entire family, freshly scrubbed and dressed in their best clothes, drove to church in the wagon or buggy. There they worshiped, sang hymns, listened to the sermon, and afterward gathered in front of the church for leisurely talk before driving home once again.

The local school. On weekdays the children attended a one-room elementary school. To reach it, some of the boys and girls walked several miles along the country roads. School terms were short, for the children had to help with spring planting and fall harvesting. The teacher, usually a young woman, taught all grades. The emphasis in 1870, as in earlier times, was on "readin', 'ritin', and 'rithmetic." During the school term, the teacher often lived in the homes of the pupils, staying a month in one home, then a month in another, and so on throughout the term.

The school was also a community center. Graduation day was a big occasion, and now and then there were spelling bees and other events in which parents as well as their children could take part.

Loneliness of farm life. For most farm families, however, farming in 1870 was a hard, lonely way of life. It was especially hard and lonely on the prairies and plains.

Hamlin Garland, who spent his boyhood on farms in Wisconsin, Iowa, and the Dakotas, pictured in his writing the dreary loneliness in isolated farming communities. In his famous collection of tales, *Main-Traveled Roads,* Garland wrote:

"The main-traveled road in the West (as everywhere) is hot and dusty in summer, and desolate and drear with mud in fall and spring, and in winter the winds sweep the snow across it; but it does sometimes cross a rich meadow where the songs of the larks and bobolinks and blackbirds are tangled. . . .

"Mainly it is long and wearyful, and has a dull little town at one end and a home of toil at the other. Like the main-traveled road of life, it is traversed by many classes of people, but the poor and the weary predominate."

Immigrant farmers from Europe, who by 1870 were moving out onto the western prairies and plains, faced special difficulties. These immigrant pioneers had to adjust not only to a strange physical environment but also to a strange and bewildering social environment. Churches were different; schools were different; life in nearly every way was different from what they had known in the Old World. At first neither they nor their American-born neighbors understood each other's language and customs.

Hardest of all, perhaps, were the lives of black settlers who ventured onto the prairies and plains. One great exodus of about 15,000 blacks from the southern states arrived in Kansas in 1879, where they hoped to start new lives free from discrimination. These black newcomers—penniless, weary, and often ill from their long journey—took up homesteads in the unfamiliar lands. To buy a calf, a pig, a few chickens, or a plow, the men worked for wages on nearby farms, on railroads, or in mines. Despite these hardships, many of the black settlers managed to carve out homes for their families in Kansas. Smaller groups of blacks settled in other parts of the West. Most of them endured some form of discrimination from their white neighbors.

New problems. Most American farmers of the 1870's were not unhappy with their lot. They expected to work hard, and they expected to live more or less apart from their neighbors. The hardships that troubled them most were new ones growing out of the new industrial economy that was bringing changes to every part of American life.

SECTION SURVEY

1. In what ways was the life of farm families in 1870 quite similar to farm life in 1770 or 1820?

2. (a) List three adjectives that describe farm life in 1870. (b) Explain why you selected each adjective. (c) Do any of the adjectives seem to be negative? Are any of them positive? Explain.

3. Why was the Saturday drive to town such an important part of farm life?

4. (a) Compare the reasons for the movement of blacks to Kansas in 1879 to the reasons for the immigration of Europeans to America. (b) Compare the problems these blacks may have faced adjusting to their new homes to the problems the immigrants faced.

2 Farmers face complex new problems in the industrial age

For American farmers in general, the last 25 or 30 years of the 1800's brought new problems. Not all farm families were equally affected by these problems, but most of the nation's farmers found themselves in serious trouble. What were some of the new problems that farm families faced?

Overproduction and falling prices. The fundamental causes of agricultural discontent—overproduction and falling prices—were rarely understood by farmers.

From 1865 to about 1900, farmers produced more food than people could afford to buy. This increase of food in the American markets was the result of (1) the rapid opening of new farmland on the prairies and plains and (2) the development of new farm machinery and improved methods of farming.

Why did American farmers not sell their surplus products to other countries? They did, but competing agricultural countries such as Russia, Canada, Argentina, and Australia were also seeking customers and often had the same products that American farmers wanted to export. Thus there was an increased amount of certain kinds of food on the world market as well as in the United States.

In an open-market economy, whenever the supply of any commodity is greater than the demand for that commodity, prices fall. Starting in the 1930's, the federal government tried to support farm prices in the United States, but in the late 1800's, only a few farmers even suggested such a possibility. Thus farm prices kept falling.

Wheat, which had sold for $2.50 a bushel (35.2 liters) in 1868, dropped to about 78 cents a bushel in the late 1880's. Because of high transportation costs and other factors, however, the farmers actually often got only 30 cents a bushel. Corn fell to 15 cents a bushel and, being cheaper than coal, was often used for fuel. Cotton, which in the late 1860's had sold for 65 cents a pound (.45 kilogram),

This cartoon depicts the farmer of the late 1800's as a thin, tattered figure in contrast to the well-fed, well-dressed industrialists who were helped by tariffs passed by Congress and President McKinley (shown dressed as the waiter).

dropped to 5 cents a pound in 1895. Thus growers of these important staple crops were often farming at a loss.

High farm costs. To add to their difficulties, farm families had to pay high prices for their shoes, clothing, kerosene, furniture, farm machinery, household equipment, and other goods. In many instances, prices were high because cheaply made European goods had been kept out of American markets by the high tariffs put on imports to protect American manufacturers. In some instances, prices were high because they had been artificially raised by monopolies.

To make matters worse, farm families almost always owed money. Many had borrowed money in the form of mortgages to pay for their land, homes, and barns. They had added to this burden of debt by borrowing money to pay for fences, livestock, seed, and machinery. As prices for farm products fell, the farmers could not pay their debts. To head off disaster, they increased their mortgages by borrowing more money, thus adding to their debt.

The 1880's were often called "the decade of mortgages." Of the total number of farms in the country, 43 percent were mortgaged. In Kansas the number reached 60 percent. Of course, these mortgages often were necessary. By means of mortgages, families with little or no money could borrow the capital they needed to buy a farm, purchase farm machinery, or make improvements on existing farms. It was not so much mortgages themselves but rather the hard times and the high interest rates that troubled the farmers.

During the late 1800's, interest rates on western farm loans ran from 8 to 20 percent. These rates were higher than interest rates charged to industrial and commercial enterprises. Bankers and other money lenders justified the higher rates on farm loans on the ground that farming was a riskier business than industry or commerce. In addition to the high rates, money brokers charged a commission for arranging farm loans. In several farm states, loan brokers starting with nothing became millionaires within a few years.

The problem of money. The farmers blamed their troubles on the shortage of money, which was only part of the problem, but an important part. To understand the farmers' point of view, it is necessary to see how money affected their everyday lives.

The first thing to remember is that money is a **medium of exchange** – that is, something of value given in exchange for goods or services. Its value is determined by the goods or services it will buy. A flour miller might say, "One dollar will buy one bushel of wheat." A farmer might say, "One bushel of wheat will buy one dollar." The miller and the farmer are saying the same thing; both of them are stating the value of a dollar *and* the value of a bushel of wheat.

The second thing to remember is that there are two ways to change the value of a dollar *and* the value of a bushel of wheat. All other things being equal, if you *increase the amount of wheat* – for example, double it – then "one dollar will buy two bushels of wheat" or "two bushels of wheat will buy one dollar." If you *decrease the number of dollars in circulation* – say, by one half – you can accomplish the same result. For example, one half as many dollars will now buy just as much wheat. That is, "50 cents will buy one bushel of wheat" and "one dollar will buy two bushels of wheat," or again, "two bushels of wheat will buy one dollar." In practice, the problem of money value is not this simple, but the illustration may help to clarify the problem of western farmers.

Falling farm prices. Between 1870 and 1900, the price, or value, of farm products fell lower and lower. In other words, the value of money rose higher and higher. Consider a specific example. In 1868 Olaf Erickson sold 1,000 bushels (35,238 liters) of wheat at $2.50 a bushel. In 1868, then, his wheat brought him $2,500. Since his interest payments amounted to $250 that year, Olaf could pay this interest with the income from 100 bushels (3,524 liters) of wheat, or one tenth of his income. Each year from 1868 on, Olaf continued to grow and sell 1,000 bushels of wheat. But by 1890 wheat was bringing only 75 cents a bushel. Olaf's income in 1890, therefore, was only $750. Since his interest payments still amounted to $250, he now had to pay his debt with the income from 334 bushels (11,769 liters) of wheat, or one third of his total income.

As far as Olaf could tell, he had done nothing to cause this. Yet his income had dropped from $2,500 to $750 a year. Something was wrong. Olaf and his family were working as hard and raising as much wheat as ever.

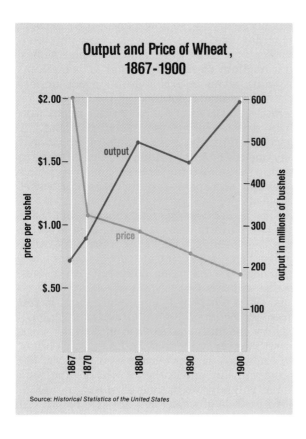

Output and Price of Wheat, 1867-1900

output

price

Source: *Historical Statistics of the United States*

Clearly, Olaf reasoned, the *value of money* had changed. Money was harder to get; money was scarce or "tight." It had gone up in value. That was why, Olaf thought, the same amount of wheat brought him fewer dollars each year.

Olaf forgot that there were many more farmers in 1890, both in the United States and in other countries, than there had been in 1868. These farmers were producing far more wheat than they had produced in 1868.

Although Olaf did not understand the whole problem, he did have his finger upon one key to his difficulties. The supply of money in the United States was not expanding rapidly enough during the late 1800's to meet the needs of the new industrial economy. The answer, as Olaf saw it, was simple enough: Let the government increase the amount of money in circulation. This would "cheapen" the dollar and raise the price of farm products. Olaf could then pay his debts and buy the goods that his family needed.

The distributors. Farmers also blamed many of their difficulties on the distributors who bought from the farmers and sold to whole-salers and retailers. The services performed by these brokers, produce buyers, grain-elevator operators, and stockyard owners were important in the distribution of farm products. However, the farmers believed that the distributors were taking too large a share of the wealth produced on farms and ranches.

Many distributors no doubt did take advantage of the farmers. Farmers, having little cash and credit and needing money to pay their debts, had to sell their goods at harvest time even if prices were low. The distributors, backed by considerable capital, could afford to store what they bought from the farmers until prices went up. Of course, prices did not always go up, and distributors were sometimes ruined when prices fell.

The railroads. Farmers, especially on the prairies and plains, reserved their chief hatred, however, for the railroads. Like other Americans, including small business owners, farmers had at first welcomed the railroad with enthusiasm. They believed that it would open distant markets to them and increase the value of their farmland by bringing more farmers into the community. Farmers who could afford to do so often bought a few shares of railroad stock. The governments of small farming communities often invested money in railroad stocks and bonds in return for the railroad's promise to build a branch line to the community.

Unfortunately, events did not always turn out as the farmers expected. In the first place, the railroad stock that farmers owned represented only a small part of all the stock sold. Therefore the farmers had little voice in determining railroad policies.

In the second place, the farmers expected that competition among the railroads would keep freight rates low. In this hope they were also disappointed. For example, competing railroads bid against each other for long-haul shipments between two distant cities served by two or more lines, sometimes cutting their rates so low that they operated at actual losses. They made up these losses, however, by charging much higher rates for short-haul shipments to those communities that were served by only one railroad.

Farmers and other small shippers protested, of course, against this so-called "long-haul, short-haul abuse" on the part of the railroads. However, it was very difficult for them to do anything about the situation.

Many of the hardships that farmers faced in the late 1800's were new, strange, and complicated. Most farmers did not at first understand the complexities of overproduction, falling prices, "tight money," high interest rates, distributors, and high shipping costs. Like all other Americans, the farmers had to grope their way into the industrial age.

SECTION SURVEY

IDENTIFY: medium of exchange, "tight money," long-haul shipments, short-haul shipments.

1. What were the farmers' grievances against (a) the distributors and (b) the railroads?

2. How were the new problems that farmers faced in the late 1800's related to industrialization?

3. Graph Study: Look at the graph on page 478. How does it illustrate a major problem American farmers faced in the period following the Civil War?

3 **Farm organizations join efforts to regulate the railroads**

The farmers soon learned that only through cooperative action could they hope to share the advantages that were emerging from the new industrial economy.

The Grange. The first national farm organization, started in 1867, was called the Grange, or the Patrons of Husbandry. Its founder, Oliver Hudson Kelley, wanted to establish a national organization with a local chapter in every farm community. Farm families could meet in these chapters for recreation and to learn better ways of farming.

At first Kelley fought an uphill battle in organizing the Grange. By 1872, however, farm prices were falling rapidly, and the farmers, bewildered and disturbed, joined the Grange in growing numbers. By 1875 some 1.5 million farmers, most of them in the Middle West, were Grange members.

Farmers' cooperatives. Kelley had started the Grange primarily to combat social isolation and lack of educational opportunity. The farmers who joined in the 1870's, however, were more interested in solving economic problems and carrying out their slogans — "Cooperation" and "Down with monopoly."

Working together in the Grange and in other local farm organizations, many farmers set up cooperative associations, usually called **cooperatives.** Cooperatives owned and managed by the farmers themselves could bypass distributors. The cooperative could (1) sell the produce of a group of farmers directly to big-city markets and (2) buy farm machines, clothing, and household goods in large quantities at wholesale prices. Before long, farmers set up not only cooperative stores but also cooperative grain storage elevators, creameries, and even factories to manufacture their own farm machines and equipment.

Some of these early cooperative ventures were successful. However, most of them failed, partly because farmers often lacked business experience, partly because farmers did not have enough capital to compete successfully with established businesses. Despite failures the farmers did not give up, for they still had the possibility of political action.

Opposing unfair railroad practices. As early as 1870, farmers, the owners of small businesses, and lawyers persuaded the Illinois state legislature to investigate unfair practices by the railroads. In 1871 the Illinois legislature created a commission to fix maximum freight rates and made it illegal for a railroad to charge differential freight rates. The legislatures of Minnesota and Iowa passed similar laws, as did the legislature of Wisconsin, where the Grangers were the chief backers of railroad regulation.

The railroads opposed these laws and sometimes refused to obey them. In 1876 and 1877, the Supreme Court heard a series of cases known as the "Granger cases," of which the most far-reaching was *Munn v. Illinois.* The Court ruled that state legislatures had the right to regulate businesses that affected the public, including grain elevators and railroads.

Unfortunately for the farmers, the railroads either evaded the laws or exerted enough pressure on the legislators to get the laws repealed. The most serious blow for the farmers, however, came in 1886, when the Supreme Court qualified its decision in the "Granger cases." It now ruled that state legis-

This 1876 poster for the Grange, or the Patrons of Husbandry, reflects the central position that the farmers believed they held in the nation's work and life.

latures had no power to regulate traffic that moved across state boundaries. The Court held that only the federal government could regulate the interstate activities of railroads.

The Interstate Commerce Act. The 1886 Supreme Court decision led Congress to pass the Interstate Commerce Act of 1887 to correct a number of the railroads' practices.

Pooling arrangements by the railroads were one of the practices opposed by farmers, many business people, and the public. Several railroads operating in the same area and across state borders would join to form a pool. All members of the pool then agreed not to compete, but instead to charge certain agreed-

upon rates. As a result, farmers and others using the railroads often had to pay exorbitant rates.

Another practice the public wanted corrected was the granting of special favors. In order to get business, competing railroads often gave large corporations especially low rates. Sometimes, instead of actually lowering the rates, the railroads agreed to grant **rebates,** that is, to refund part of the shipping charges.

Farmers, small businesses, and the public also complained, as you know, that railroads sometimes charged more for a short haul than for a long haul. It sometimes cost more to send goods a few miles than to send the same goods from, say, Chicago to New York.

SOURCES

MUNN v.
ILLINOIS
(1877)

Property does become clothed with a public interest when used in a manner to make it of public consequence, and affect the community at large. When, therefore, one devotes his property to a use in which the public has an interest, he, in effect, grants to the public an interest in that use, and must submit to be controlled by the public for the common good, to the extent of the interest he has thus created. He may withdraw his grant by discontinuing the use; but, so long as he maintains the use, he must submit to the control. . . .

Provisions of the act. The Interstate Commerce Act applied to all railroads passing through more than one state. The act made it illegal for such railroads to (1) make pooling arrangements, (2) give special favors in the form of lower rates or rebates, (3) charge more for a short haul than for a long haul over the same line, or (4) charge unjust or unreasonable rates. The act also required the railroads to print and display their rates and to give a minimum of ten days' public notice before they changed those rates.

Finally, the Interstate Commerce Act created an Interstate Commerce Commission (ICC) of five members appointed by the President and confirmed by the Senate. The commission had authority to (1) investigate complaints against the railroads, (2) summon witnesses, (3) examine a railroad's accounts and correspondence, and (4) require railroads to file annual reports about their operations and finances and to adopt a uniform system of accounting.

The commission, however, had no real authority to fix rates and to enforce its orders. If a railroad refused to accept the commission's proposals, the commission had to appeal to the courts for an order compelling the railroads to obey. In some instances, the courts refused to grant the commission's requests for such orders. In other instances, the courts reversed the commission's decision.

Despite its limitations, the Interstate Commerce Act was the first important attempt by the federal government to regulate transportation and to create a federal regulatory commission. Because the act set a precedent for more sweeping measures later adopted by Congress, it marked a turning point in the history of the relations between the federal government and business.

SECTION SURVEY

IDENTIFY: the Grange, Oliver Kelley, cooperatives, *Munn v. Illinois,* rebates.

1. (a) What were the goals of the Grange? (b) How successful was the Grange in achieving these goals?
2. (a) What were the provisions of the Interstate Commerce Act of 1887? (b) What were its limitations? (c) Why was the act significant?
3. What role did the Supreme Court play in the effort to regulate the railroads?

4 Farm organizations put increasing pressure on government

While struggling with railroad legislation, farmers also turned to a more serious problem — falling prices for farm produce. Ignoring the facts of overproduction and competition from farmers overseas, they blamed low farm prices solely on the scarcity of money.

Politics and paper money. The farmers' analysis of their problem was partly right, for during the late 1860's and the 1870's, money was becoming increasingly scarce. In 1865, for example, the amount of currency, or money of all kinds, in circulation in the United States averaged $31.18 per person. By 1878 the average had dropped to $17.08.

Faced with growing hardship, farmers demanded that the government increase the supply of currency in circulation. When neither the Republicans nor the Democrats promised to help them, farmers began to join the Greenback-Labor Party, commonly called the Greenback Party.

The Greenback Party took its name from the paper money known as "greenbacks," which had been issued by the government during the Civil War. After the war the government began to withdraw the greenbacks from circulation. Farmers and other "cheap money" advocates protested. They wanted *more,* not fewer, greenbacks in circulation.

The "cheap money" people did not get what they wanted. Instead, Congress adopted the Resumption Act in 1875. This act ordered the Secretary of the Treasury to redeem *in gold* all greenbacks presented to the Treasury on or after January 1, 1879. As a result of this compromise, by January 1, 1879, greenbacks were worth their full, or face, value in gold. Under these circumstances, owners of greenbacks did not bother to redeem them. Congress decided to allow 346 million greenbacks to remain in circulation as part of United States currency.

In 1875, dismayed by Congress's decision to redeem the greenbacks in gold, the "cheap money" advocates decided to take their case to the people at the polls. Although the newly organized Greenback Party did not win a significant number of votes in the 1876 election,

This is obviously the work of a cartoonist who had little respect for those who favored greenbacks. What devices does he use to make fun of these people? What kind of people does he show them to be?

the Greenbackers continued their battle for "cheap money."

The silver issue. Rutherford B. Hayes, who became President in 1877, successfully opposed the pressure of the Greenbackers to get more paper money into circulation. However, he was unable to block another move by the "cheap money" people to increase the volume of currency in the economy.

Back in 1834 the government had adopted a law providing for the coinage of both gold and silver, at a ratio of about 16 to 1. That is, the government offered to buy 16 ounces (453.6 grams) of silver for the same price it paid for one ounce (28.3 grams) of gold. At the time, silver was relatively scarce, and silver producers could sell 16 ounces of silver to private buyers for *more than* one ounce of gold. As a result, they did not take silver to the United States Mint to be coined into silver dollars.

In the 1870's, however, this situation changed. With the discovery of huge silver deposits in parts of Colorado and Nevada, the supply of silver increased tremendously. The value of silver **bullion,** or uncoined metal,

began to fall. In 1874, for the first time in more than 30 years, 16 ounces of silver bullion were sold on the open market for *less than* one ounce of gold.

Faced with falling prices, silver producers remembered the government's offer to buy silver at the ratio of 16 to 1. They now tried to sell their silver bullion to the Treasury Department but discovered that in 1873 Congress had passed a law removing silver dollars from the list of standard coins. Furious at the loss of a profitable market for their bullion, silver producers denounced Congress for what they called the "Crime of '73."

The "Crime of '73" became a rallying cry for those who demanded that the government buy silver. This demand came mostly from westerners, but it was also supported by other Americans, including farmers, who wanted more currency in circulation.

The Bland-Allison Act. In 1877 Representative Richard P. Bland of Missouri introduced a bill calling for free and unlimited coinage of silver dollars at a ratio of 16 silver dollars to 1 gold dollar. When this bill reached the Senate, it was modified by Senator William B. Allison of Iowa to become the Bland-Allison bill.

The Bland-Allison bill authorized the Treasury Department to buy and to mint not less than $2 million and not more than $4 million worth of silver each month. President Hayes vetoed the bill, but Congress passed it over his veto in 1878. The new law was a partial victory for the silver interests, the Greenbackers, and other "cheap money" people.

Failure of the Greenbackers. The Greenback Party reached its greatest power in 1878, when it polled 1 million votes and elected members to Congress. This was a shock to the two major parties, but the triumph was short-lived. Two years later the Greenback Presidential candidate, General J. B. Weaver, received only 300,000 votes.

Although it failed to achieve its goal, the Greenback movement, like the Grange movement, taught the farmers several valuable lessons. The farmers learned from their experience with the Grange that they could, if united, gain influence in state legislatures. They learned from the Greenback movement that their influence might be felt even in Congress. Above all, they learned that the secret of power lay in organization.

Farmers' alliances. Even before the Greenback Party began to break up, farmers were forming organizations called "alliances." During the early 1880's, the different state alliances in the North and Northwest set up a loose federation called the Northern, or Northwestern, Farmers' Alliance. The southern groups joined in a much more tightly knit organization known as the Southern Alliance.

Like the Grange, the alliances experimented with cooperative buying and selling organizations. They were prepared to take action to protect the farmers from the exploitation they were subjected to by manufacturers, railroads, and distributors.

Hard times in the late 1880's transformed the alliances into influential political organizations. By 1890, for example, the Southern Alliance had 3 million white members, while 1 million southern black farmers were enrolled in an affiliated Colored Alliance. A proposal to merge the Southern Alliance and the Northwestern Farmers' Alliance failed, however, because southerners insisted upon separate white and black lodges in the merged alliance. The Northern alliance leaders refused to accept this arrangement.

Desperate conditions. Starting in 1886, a 10-year series of droughts on the Great Plains turned farmland into arid desert. Driven to desperation, thousands of farmers finally gave up and moved back east. Others remained and continued to fight the land and those they held responsible for much of their trouble—the owners of railroads and factories, the directors of banks and insurance companies that held farm mortgages, and the distributors who bought and sold farm produce. The farmers also continued their pressure, along with other "cheap money" interests, to get the government to put more money into circulation.

Sherman Silver Purchase Act. In 1889 and 1890, six new states entered the Union—North Dakota, South Dakota, Montana, Washington, Idaho, and Wyoming. These states, all in the West, greatly increased the political strength of the farmers and the silver-mining interests in Congress. Members of Congress representing farming and silver-mining areas agreed to make a deal with the Republicans, who wanted to increase tariff rates. They agreed to vote for the McKinley Tariff Act if the high-tariff members voted for a "cheap money" bill.

As a result of this deal, the Sherman Silver Purchase Act became law in 1890. This act required the United States Treasury to purchase 4.5 million ounces (127.6 million grams) of silver each month at the market price and to pay for this silver with paper money that could be redeemed in gold or silver.

Silver miners hoped that the law would raise the price of silver, and farmers hoped that, by increasing the supply of money, it would raise the prices of farm produce. These expectations were not realized. The purchased silver was not coined, and the money in circulation did not greatly increase.

New farm leaders. Leaders of the Farmers' Alliances who supported the Sherman Silver Purchase Act and other legislation favorable to farmers became national figures. Among them was Ignatius Donnelly of Minnesota, a spellbinder on the platform and a pamphleteer with a biting literary style. In Kansas there was "Sockless Jerry" Simpson, who denounced the rich eastern monopolists. Kansas produced two other influential leaders—Mary Elizabeth Lease, a colorful and dynamic orator, and Annie Diggs, an editor and an effective behind-the-scenes political worker. One of the most effective of the speakers and writers was Sara Elizabeth Emery of Michigan. Her widely read book *Seven Financial Conspiracies*, which was published in 1888, called on farmers and workers to unite and break the "conspiratorial money power."

In the South a new group of political leaders representing the poorer farmers arose to challenge the leaders of the Democratic Party. Among them were Governor James Hogg of Texas, Tom Watson of Georgia, and "Pitchfork Ben" Tillman of South Carolina.

Thanks to such leaders, the voices of farmers would be heard more clearly in the nation. The needs and concerns of the farmers that these leaders addressed would become increasingly important in national politics.

SECTION SURVEY

IDENTIFY. Greenback Party, "cheap money," "Crime of '73," Farmers' Alliances, Sherman Silver Purchase Act of 1890, Sara Elizabeth Emery.

1. (a) What were the goals of the Greenback Party? (b) How successful was it in achieving these goals?

2. Explain how the Bland-Allison Act was a partial victory for "cheap money" advocates.

3. (a) What factors led to the passage of the Sherman Silver Purchase Act? (b) What were its provisions? (c) What did the act's supporters hope it would accomplish?

5 The farmers fail to win control of the national government

By 1890, American farmers were facing a major question: Should they form a third party? This was the question that farmers discussed in schoolhouses and Grange halls in the summer of that year. Many northern farmers favored a third party. Because of a split in southern Democratic ranks, most southern farmers opposed it.

The Populist Party. The Congressional elections in the fall of 1890 drew farm men and women into what seemed to be a fiery crusade. Speakers such as Mary Elizabeth Lease bluntly stated the farmers' grievances. In a powerful speech, she proclaimed, "Wall Street° owns the country. It is no longer a government of the people, by the people, and for the people, but a government of Wall Street, by Wall Street, and for Wall Street. The great common people of this country are slaves, and monopoly is the master. The West and South are bound and prostrate before the manufacturing East. . . . We want money, land, and transportation. . . . The people are at bay. Let the bloodhounds of money who have dogged us thus far beware."

Fired by this new militant spirit, Republican and Democratic farmers decided in 1891 to forget their political differences and form a third party. A meeting made up chiefly of Farmers' Alliance leaders from the West and Middle West launched the People's Party, or the Populist Party, at Cincinnati, Ohio, in 1891. In Omaha, Nebraska, the following year, the Populists drew up a platform and nominated James B. Weaver of Iowa for President of the United States.

°**Wall Street:** a street in New York City's financial district, the nation's principal financial center; often used as a symbol of large banking and business interests.

The Populist platform. On July 4, 1892, the Populists adopted their platform, demanding far-reaching reforms. In part, it stated, "We meet in the midst of a nation brought to the verge of moral, political, and material ruin. . . . The people are demoralized. . . . We have witnessed for more than a quarter of a century the struggles of the two great political parties for power and plunder, while grievous wrongs have been inflicted upon the suffering people. We charge that the controlling influences dominating both these parties have permitted the existing dreadful conditions to develop without serious effort to prevent or restrain them. Neither do they now promise us any substantial reform."

The Populist platform then listed the specific demands of the farmers: (1) an increase in the currency, to be secured by the "free and unlimited coinage of silver at a ratio of 16 to 1"; (2) government ownership of railroads, telegraphs, and telephones; (3) the return to the government of all land held by railroads and other corporations in excess of their needs; (4) a graduated income tax, requiring people with higher incomes to pay a proportionally higher tax; (5) a system of national warehouses where farm produce could be stored until market conditions improved, with the government providing loans on each deposit by a farmer; (6) democratic political reforms, including the direct election of United States Senators and the adoption of the secret ballot, the initiative, and the referendum.

The Populist Party had some support from industrial wage earners. Its platform demanded shorter working hours and restrictions on immigration, which many workers held responsible for unemployment and low wages.

The election of 1892. In the campaign of 1892, great crowds of farmers in the Middle West gathered at outdoor meetings and picnics to listen to eloquent Populist speakers. Weaver, the Populist Presidential candidate, traveled widely and spoke to enthusiastic audiences in the Middle West.

In the South, however, the story was different because of the racial situation. Conservative Democrats and Populists alike were willing to let black southerners vote—but only if it seemed certain that they could control the black vote. Populist leaders, however, urged poor farmers, white and black, to vote together against their "exploiters," the well-to-do planters and business people of the Democratic Party. This angered many white southerners, rich and poor alike, who feared that the Populist bid for black support might endanger white supremacy. Populist speakers in the South were greeted with howls and jeers.

The Populist bid for southern black votes was not very successful. The Populists did not attempt to build a strong or lasting alliance between poor white and black southerners. They did not work for federal supervision of elections, which would have guaranteed the right of black southerners to vote. Nor did the Populists support other efforts of southern blacks to overcome their grievances. Thus Populist candidates in the election of 1892 were generally defeated in the South.

President Benjamin Harrison, running for reelection on the Republican ticket, was defeated by the Democratic candidate, Grover Cleveland. The Democratic victory was a sweeping one, but the Populists made an impressive showing in the nation, despite their weakness in the South. They polled more than 1 million popular votes, won 22 electoral votes for their Presidential candidate, and gained seats in state legislatures and in Congress. Democrats and Republicans alike realized that the Populist movement was much more than the protest of a few discontented Americans.

Depression and discontent. For the two older political parties, however, the Populist movement was only the beginning of their difficulties. In 1893 the country sank into a serious economic depression. Farm prices plunged. Factories closed, and thousands of unemployed workers walked the streets trying to find jobs.

President Cleveland blamed the crisis on the Sherman Silver Purchase Act of 1890. He believed that it was not "tight money" that had led to the depression but rather uncertainty over the value of money. Cleveland insisted that the only way to end the depression was to accept gold as the single standard of value for the nation's currency. This was an oversimplified explanation, for the depression was worldwide, but there was some truth in the President's view.

Farmers and wage earners, on the other hand, blamed the depression on "tight money." They felt that the Sherman Silver Purchase Act had not gone far enough. They demanded that the government increase the amount of

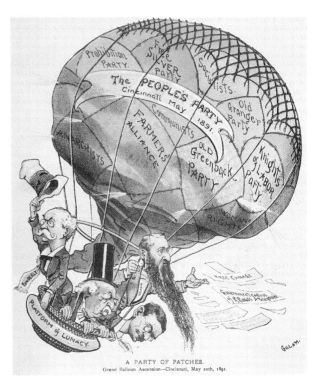

A PARTY OF PATCHES.
Grand Balloon Ascension—Cincinnati, May 20th, 1891.

Here the Populist Party is likened to a balloon made up of a crazy quilt of special-interest groups. Those riding about in the balloon are the groups' leaders.

currency in circulation by the "free and unlimited coinage of silver at a ratio of 16 to 1." They believed that the resulting increase in "cheap money" would end the depression.

Shrinking gold reserves. By 1893, however, the policy of **bimetallism** had become a matter of deep concern for the Treasury Department. This policy meant that two metals, gold and silver, furnished the security for all the nation's currency. The value of silver had fallen until the actual silver in a silver dollar was worth only 60 cents. Since silver as well as gold provided the backing, or security, for the nation's currency, more Americans began to grow uneasy about this situation. As a result, many people began to exchange their silver bank notes for gold coins rather than for silver coins. By March 1893 the gold reserves had shrunk to only a little more than $100 million.

The shrinkage in gold reserves created a serious government crisis. If the gold reserves completely disappeared, the government would not be able to keep its promise to exchange gold coins for paper money. It would, instead, have

In 1892 a Republican and a Democrat in Chicago bet on an election. The one whose candidate lost would have to pull a wagon through the streets of the city carrying the one whose candidate won. Joseph Kir painted the triumphant Democrat and the "workhorse" Republican in his picture "The Last Bet."

to pay with silver. Since by midsummer of 1893 the value of a silver dollar had fallen to 49 cents, prices would soar and the nation would head toward economic disaster.

Stopping the run on gold. President Cleveland called a special session of Congress to repeal the Sherman Silver Purchase Act. Representatives of silver mines, farmers, and "cheap money" people in general refused to consider repeal. By late fall, however, the administration finally had enough votes to push the repeal bill through Congress.

Repeal of the Sherman Silver Purchase Act stopped the flow of silver into the Treasury, but gold reserves continued to shrink. There were still many millions of silver bank notes in circulation, and the Treasury kept on redeeming them in gold. By 1895 the gold reserves had dropped to only $41 million. It seemed to be only a question of time before the United States would go off the gold standard—that is, would stop redeeming its paper currency with gold—and runaway inflation would start.

At this critical point, President Cleveland accepted the offer of a group of bankers headed by J. P. Morgan to lend gold to the government in return for government bonds as security. The arrangement worked. With leading bankers behind the government, confidence returned and the run on the gold reserves ended. Many Americans, those with "sound money" views, felt that President Cleveland and the bankers had acted wisely and had saved the nation from disaster. "Cheap money" Americans were furious and pointed out that the bankers had charged a generous commission for their services. They insisted that the President had made a deal with Wall Street.

Choosing candidates. By the time of the Presidential election of 1896, both major parties were split between the "sound money," gold-standard people and the "cheap money," silver people.

The Republicans chose as their Presidential candidate William McKinley of Ohio. Although McKinley tried to straddle the money

486

issue, he came to be regarded as the leader of those people who favored the gold standard.

The Democratic convention opened with a bitter struggle between the "sound money" wing of the party and the "silver" wing. The "sound money" delegates were soon howled down, and "cheap money" delegates adopted a platform demanding "free and unlimited coinage of both gold and silver." The battle lines were drawn, with the Republicans on the "sound money" side and the majority of Democrats on the "cheap money" side. But the Democratic delegates had not yet selected a Presidential candidate.

William Jennings Bryan. The field was wide open when a handsome young lawyer stepped forward to address the convention. Only 36 years old, William Jennings Bryan of Nebraska had served in the House of Representatives for four years. This was his only political experience in the national capital. Nevertheless, his striking appearance and his compelling speech captured the attention of his audience.

"You come to us and tell us that the great cities are in favor of the gold standard," Bryan cried. "We reply that the great cities rest upon our broad and fertile prairies. Burn down your cities and leave our farms, and your cities will spring up again as if by magic; but destroy our farms and the grass will grow in the streets of every city in the country. . . .

"Having behind us the producing masses of this nation and the world, supported by the commercial interests, the laboring interests, and the toilers everywhere, we will answer their demand for a gold standard by saying to them, 'You shall not press down upon the brow of labor this crown of thorns, you shall not crucify mankind upon a cross of gold!'"

With the closing words of Bryan's "Cross of Gold" speech, wild tumult broke out at the convention. Here was the Democratic candidate!

The Democratic nomination of Bryan and the adoption of a platform demanding free and unlimited coinage of silver left the Populists in an awkward position. The Democrats had stolen their thunder. When they met in convention, the Populists decided to support Bryan as their Presidential candidate. To preserve their party identity, they nominated Tom Watson of Georgia for the Vice-Presidency rather than Arthur Sewall of Maine, who was the Democratic nominee.

Bryan's crusade. Bryan turned the election campaign into a crusade. In 14 exhausting weeks, during which he traveled vast distances by railroad, Bryan made 600 speeches to 5 million people in 27 states. Bryan's speeches succeeded in rousing his supporters to frenzies of enthusiasm.

The "sound money" people threw all their energy and resources into defeating Bryan. Under the leadership of Mark Hanna of Ohio, McKinley's campaign manager and a wealthy business leader, the Republicans raised at least $3.5 million to offset Bryan's $300,000 campaign fund. Some of this campaign fund was used to bring trainloads of people to McKinley's hometown to hear him read disarming speeches from his front porch. Nearly every influential newspaper in the country backed the Republicans. Many factories paid their workers on the Saturday before election with the warning that they would have no jobs if Bryan won the election.

McKinley's victory. Bryan lost with 176 electoral votes to McKinley's 271. The popular vote was much closer—7 million for the Republicans, 6.5 million for the Democrats. Although the country had decided in favor of the gold standard, the farmers and other "cheap money" advocates had come close to winning the Presidency and control of Congress.

Defeat in the 1896 election and the arrival of better times for the farmers ended the power of the Populist Party. As you will read, however, during the early 1900's, a new third party, the Progressive Party, as well as progressive Democrats and Republicans won many of the same reforms that the Populists had demanded.

SECTION SURVEY

IDENTIFY: Mary Elizabeth Lease, James Weaver, bimetallism, gold standard, William McKinley, William Jennings Bryan, "Cross of Gold" speech, Mark Hanna.

1. Explain how the Populist Party planks listed on page 484 would have helped farmers in 1892.
2. In the political struggle in the South, black southerners were caught in the middle. Comment.
3. How did the "tight money" and "cheap money" people each explain the cause of the depression of 1893?

Chapter Survey

Summary: Tracing the Main Ideas

Increasing industrialization created many new problems after 1870 for farmers as well as for all other Americans. Most farmers lost the individual freedom they had possessed when they produced a good part of what they needed on their own land. Overproduction brought falling prices and growing distress. Increasingly, farmers became dependent upon forces that they could not control. They depended upon the railroads that carried their goods to market and upon prices fixed in distant markets. They were also affected by tariffs that sometimes raised the cost of manufactured goods and by the supply of money made available by the federal government.

Faced with these new problems, farmers organized new political parties and increased their role in the old parties in an effort to influence state and federal governments. They hoped to secure laws that would regulate the railroads, the industries, and the other parts of the economic system and thus make life easier for farm people.

Industrialism brought benefits as well as problems. Power-driven machines made life immeasurably easier. Increased production enabled farmers to feed themselves and their fellow citizens far better than people had ever been fed before. Developments in transportation and communications broke down the isolation of farm life and brought farm families into touch with the life of the world beyond the borders of the farm.

It was as difficult for farmers as it was for all other Americans to adjust to the new industrial age. The problems were all too real. By the 1900's, however, farmers began to understand that Americans were becoming more and more interdependent. The farmers began to see that their best hope of realizing the bright promise of the new age was in learning to work together.

Inquiring into History

1. How did industrialization both benefit and hurt farmers during the late 1800's?
2. (a) Why did farmers favor "cheap money" (greenbacks) and free and unlimited coinage of silver? (b) To what extent were farmers successful in obtaining these things?
3. Explain why you would have felt as you did about "cheap money" vs. "sound money" if you had been (a) a debtor farmer, (b) a retired person living on a fixed income, or (c) a banker.
4. Give examples to support this statement: During the late 1800's, farmers learned that one way to gain power was through organization.

Relating Past to Present

1. How does the relationship between government and farmers today compare with their relationship during the late 1800's?
2. Find examples of recent third parties. How did their goals, methods, and results compare to those of the Populists?

Developing Social Science Skills

1. Choose an election discussed in this chapter. Design and prepare campaign posters—one for each major candidate in that election. Be prepared to explain why each poster would be effective in convincing people to vote for the candidate.
2. Imagine that you live on a farm in Kansas in 1880. Prepare a series of journal entries describing some typical activities, such as (a) a trip to town, (b) a day at school, (c) a meeting of the local chapter of the Grange.
3. Make a chart or graph presenting the following information: In 1820, one farm worker produced encough food to feed 4.5 people. In 1890 a farm worker produced enough for 6.5 people; in 1900, enough for 7 people; in 1950 for 16 people; in 1960 for 27 people; and in 1970 for 47 people. Then answer these questions: (a) Why do you think farm production per worker increased between 1820 and 1890? (b) Why can the farmers of the United States today feed the nation's large population even though there are fewer of them than there were in 1900?

AN AMERICAN ALBUM
THEN AND NOW

Industry

In 1876, to mark the nation's 100th birthday, Philadelphia held a huge Centennial Exposition. It housed thousands of exhibits from around the world and drew millions of visitors.

The big attraction was Machinery Hall, where America's new industrial processes were displayed. The wonder of the Hall was the giant 1,600-horsepower Corliss steam engine. The Corliss engine also stood as a symbol of the nation's growing industrial might. More than any other exhibit, it showed that America had taken its place among nations as an industrial giant.

Steelmaking was important to America's industrialization, but in the 1800's it was backbreaking and dangerous work.

The Corliss engine.

The Industrial Revolution had far-reaching consequences and radically changed American life. It was the result of many events and trends that had their origins in Europe and colonial America.

Though originally a land of farmers, from its beginnings the nation was involved in commerce. The early colonists exported many of America's resources to Europe as well as some manufactured goods.

As industrialization increased, Americans made use of the nation's resources right in their own factories. Many people then left farms to become part of the growing urban work force. This industrialization was a slow process and progressed at different rates in different parts of the country.

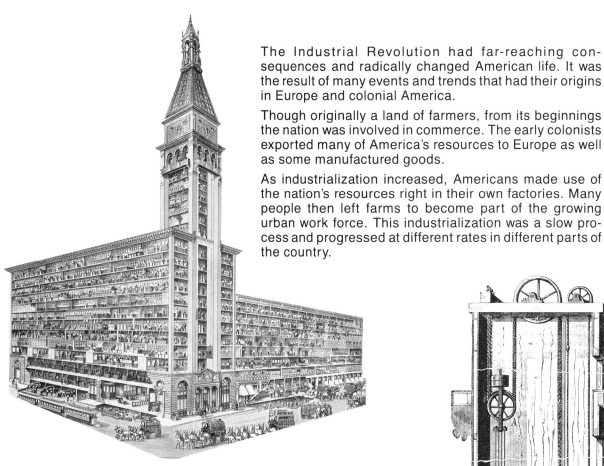

As new products poured out of the nation's factories, new means of selling them were required. The mail-order house of the late 1800's filled an important need.

The Industrial Revolution in America started in New England's textile mills.

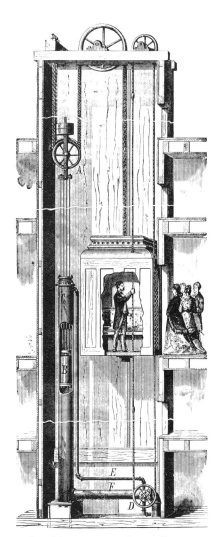

Steel beams were the stuff that made tall buildings possible; elevators, first common in the early 1800's, made them practical.

490

The ingenuity of American inventors such as Thomas Edison was a major factor in the nation's successful industrialization.

In time the new industrial technology moved into the countryside, as this portable steam engine and sawmill demonstrate.

Without its working people, America could never have become an industrialized nation. Many immigrants as well as women and children provided the human power industry needed.

The new technology is at work here. Computers run this steel mill.

"Think big but build small" was a lesson America learned from its space engineers. Soon microelectronics were adapted to many industries.

To some people the mid-1900's marked the beginning of a second industrial revolution. This new era was one of electronics and space-age technology. Computers, microcircuits, satellites, and synthetics were some of the tools of this new age.

The effects of industrialization in the 1800's were highly visible. Huge machines, towering smokestacks, and miles of highways and railroad tracks altered the American landscape. The effects of the new technology were less visible. One would have to look inside the home, the factory, and the laboratory to see how the new technology was changing life.

The Industrial Revolution helped to reshape the nation's landscape.

Chapter 25

New Life Styles in the New Industrial Age

"We cannot all live in cities," Horace Greeley once remarked, "yet nearly all seem determined to do so." Greeley, the famous newspaper editor, was speaking of a change in the way Americans lived. From 1865 to 1900, people were moving away from the rural areas and into the great urban centers, a trend known as "urbanization."

What was the compelling attraction of the growing cities? The answer was "opportunity"—opportunity for adventure, opportunity to win fame and fortune. The city offered jobs in offices and factories, work in the building trades, employment for both skilled and unskilled workers, the chance to carve out a successful career in any of hundreds of enterprises. Many people, especially young people, were eager to share in the excitement of the new industrial age. They found the many attractions of urban life irresistible.

For a number of years, ways of life in the city and the countryside drew far apart, and terms like "city slicker" and "country hick" were often heard. As the years passed, however, the differences between life in rural and in urban areas became less marked.

THE CHAPTER IN OUTLINE

1. Cities grow and change under the impact of industrialism.

2. Education responds to the changing patterns of American life.

3. American writing reflects the new industrial age.

4. Architecture and other fine arts respond to a changing society.

5. New forms of recreation enrich American life.

Changing Ways of American Life

1860's–1890's

1 Cities grow and change under the impact of industrialism

The city had many faces. It was stores and banks and offices, museums and libraries and theaters, churches and schools. It was freight yards—and, in seaports, waterfronts—ringed by factories, warehouses, stockyards, and wholesale markets. It was drab tenement buildings crowded along narrow, dirty streets and alleys littered with rubbish. It was row after row of houses arranged, in newer cities, in a neat pattern of blocks or squares. It was pretentious mansions, the costly show places of the self-appointed leaders of "society." Mainly the city was people—rich people, people with modest incomes, poor people. All were affected by the new industrial way of life in the United States.

Concentration of wealth. In this new industrial age, wealth was concentrated in the hands of relatively few people. To be sure, some Americans had always been rich while others had been poor. However, the gap between the richest and the poorest had never been as great as it was in the late 1800's.

Many of the new millionaires built huge mansions filled with expensive and gaudy furnishings. They bought race horses, yachts, and summer estates. They traveled abroad. Sometimes they gave parties costing tens of thousands of dollars.

As time went on, however, the newly rich, and especially their college-educated children, smoothed off the rougher edges. Many business leaders accepted the responsibility for using their money to improve their communities. They gave money to build and support churches, colleges, art galleries, and libraries.

For example, during his lifetime Andrew Carnegie gave $60 million to help towns and cities establish free public libraries. Men of enormous wealth, such as Ezra Cornell, Leland Stanford, John D. Rockefeller, Sr., Jonas Clark, Matthew Vassar, and Cornelius Vanderbilt, founded or gave endowments to colleges and universities. J. P. Morgan, Henry C. Frick, Andrew W. Mellon, and dozens of others built up costly and valuable art collections, many of which were in time opened to the public. Others, including women, gave financial support to American symphony orchestras, social welfare, and the arts.

In 1892 Theodore Groll painted this busy scene of Indianapolis, Indiana, at dusk. He shows the hurly-burly and the general lack of organization that marked so many of the nation's fast-growing urban areas of the time.

The middle-income group. Lower down on the economic ladder were the professional people, the smaller business people, the clerks, the managers, and the more successful skilled workers. These people raised their standard of living and enjoyed "modern conveniences," such as gas and electric lighting, modern plumbing, and new household appliances. They went to the theater, used libraries, and bought magazines and books. Many of them sent their children not only through high school but also to college.

Women in religion and welfare. In activities such as religion and social welfare, several women achieved international reputations. Mary Baker Eddy founded Christian Science and contributed to its growth with her inspirational leadership and administrative ability. Other women were active in church missionary work abroad, establishing training schools, colleges, and hospitals in Turkey, Japan, India, and other countries. A number of Catholic women founded religious orders. The most famous was Mother Francis Xavier Cabrini. After emigrating from Italy in 1889, she established hospitals, orphanages, and schools in the Italian-American communities of New York, Chicago, and other cities. Mother Cabrini was the first American citizen to become a saint in the Roman Catholic Church.

The tireless and competent Clara Barton, after her contributions to nursing in the Civil War, established the American Red Cross. Despite opposition and indifference, she broadened its purposes to include not only aid to soldiers in wartime but also help to civilians in such disasters as floods, earthquakes, major fires, and epidemics.

Opportunities for women. New coeducational universities in the Middle West and the West and such women's colleges as Mount Holyoke, Wellesley, Vassar, and Smith in the East meant that more young women could obtain an education equal to that once enjoyed only by young men. Many people at first doubted that girls had the physical and mental ability to do college work, but the experiment proved successful. Women college graduates became increasingly active in civic affairs. Some became business executives, and others entered the professions. By 1900 there were 1,000 women lawyers, 3,000 women ministers, and 7,500 women doctors in the United States.

Maria Mitchell, an astronomer on the faculty of Vassar College, had discovered a comet that was named for her.

Non-college women who wanted careers or who were compelled by circumstances to work outside the home found new opportunities in business. The development of the typewriter meant more jobs as stenographers in offices, banks, and industrial plants. Tradition and prejudice, however, blocked opportunities to most of these women to advance into management positions.

A great many women of the white middle class joined the women's clubs that rapidly multiplied after the Civil War. These clubs at first concentrated mainly on discussions of literary and cultural topics. By 1900 they were also fighting for an end to political corruption,

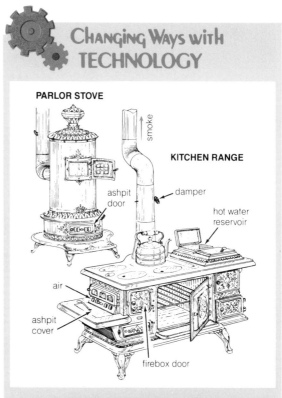

Changing Ways with TECHNOLOGY

PARLOR STOVE

KITCHEN RANGE

HEATING AND COOKING

The parlor stove for heating and the kitchen range for cooking and heating were commonly used until the development of central heating, the gas range, and the electric range. Coal or wood was burned and ashes had to be removed frequently.

As a wealthy young woman, Jane Addams had complained, "I am filled with shame that with all my apparent leisure, I do nothing at all." But over the next 46 years, her efforts at Hull House aided thousands of the needy.

for better health and recreational conditions, and for women's suffrage.

Black women also established clubs, which concentrated on social welfare. Active in this movement were Josephine Ruffin and Mary Church Terrell, who also were leaders in the founding of the National Federation of Afro-American Women and the National Association of Colored Women.

Toward women's suffrage. After the Civil War, you recall, women did not receive voting rights and other rights under the Fourteenth and Fifteenth Amendments. Differences over the stand to be taken on this issue split the women's rights movement. Elizabeth Cady Stanton and Susan B. Anthony refused to support the amendments. In 1869 they organized the National Woman Suffrage Association, which excluded men from membership. The Association adopted as its goal a women's suffrage amendment to the Constitution. Lucy Stone, her husband Henry Blackwell, Mary A. Livermore, and Julia Ward Howe launched the more conservative American Woman Suffrage Association. It worked for woman suffrage amendments to state constitutions. In 1890, after many years of rivalry, the two organizations merged as the National American Woman Suffrage Association.

Veterans of the women's rights movement were reinforced by younger leaders. Abigail Duniway of Oregon, a strong opponent of women's legal disabilities, became an effective speaker and lobbyist. Anna Howard Shaw, a graduate of Boston University in both theology and medicine, was a forceful speaker and untiring campaigner. Carrie Chapman Catt of Iowa, a pacifist as well as a women's-rights advocate, proved herself a brilliant orator and skilled administrator.

Despite the efforts of such leaders, progress toward women's suffrage was slow. The women suffragists were ridiculed and denounced by many women as well as men, by professional politicians, and by some religious groups. They also were opposed by the liquor industry, which feared that voting women might succeed in outlawing the manufacture and sale of alcoholic drinks.

Although by 1900 only a few western states had given women the right to vote, in the next 15 years the number grew. Meanwhile, in states that gave them limited suffrage, women took part increasingly in school-board elections and local politics.

Jane Addams. Jane Addams (1860–1935) was one of America's most influential women—a social reformer, humanitarian, and crusader for peace. Horrified by the suffering she saw in sprawling city slums, Addams decided to dedicate her life to helping the poor. In 1889 she opened Hull House in the slums of Chicago. She provided kindergartens for the children of working mothers, classes in child care, and recreational facilities for youth and adults. She also insisted on the collection of garbage from slum streets and fought incompetent and corrupt politicians and city officials.

For a time many business and political leaders opposed her as a dangerous meddler. Eventually, however, even her most bitter critics admitted that she was performing a great service. Social workers from all parts of the United States and from foreign countries visited Hull House. They then returned to their own communities to apply the new ideas that they had learned.

Jane Addams also helped secure child-labor laws and funds for public parks. In 1931 she received the Nobel Peace Prize for her active work in the cause of world peace. Her most enduring memorial was the growing recognition by people in all walks of life that they shared a responsibility for helping to reduce poverty.

The lower-income groups. On the lower rungs of the economic ladder in American life were the very poor people, including large numbers of immigrants and almost all Mexican Americans, Indians, and blacks. These lower-income groups enjoyed only a few of the advantages of the new urban culture. They could not afford to send their children to school beyond the elementary grades. In fact, children from poor families often had to take jobs in factories even before they finished elementary school. Nor could most of the poorer people afford to go to doctors or hospitals when they were sick.

Yet improvements in urban living affected at least a few of the poor. In the late 1880's, high-minded men and women founded social "settlement houses" similar to Chicago's Hull House in some of the worst slum areas of the major cities. These centers for recreation, education, and decent living gave hope to many immigrant youths and lightened the hardship of many elderly men and women. In addition, the Salvation Army, a religious group founded in England, provided food and shelter to many of the most poverty-stricken urban citizens. By 1900 some cities were building a few playgrounds in the poorest areas.

Opportunities to climb the economic ladder did exist, even for the poor. These opportunities far surpassed those in the Old World. They drew immigrants to the American cities in an ever-swelling volume. Finally, these opportunities encouraged many poorer people to struggle for an education and to rise above the environment into which they had been born.

SECTION SURVEY

IDENTIFY: Mary Baker Eddy, Mother Cabrini, Clara Barton, Maria Mitchell, women's clubs, Mary Church Terrell, National American Woman Suffrage Association, Jane Addams, settlement house, Salvation Army.

1. Explain what is meant by this statement: The city had many faces.

2. (a) What social-class divisions existed in the United States by 1890? (b) To what extent could a person move from one social class to another?

3. What is the relationship between the nation's industrialization and the women's rights movement?

4. Picture Study: Look at the painting on page 494. What evidence can you find in it of new inventions that were transforming American life?

2 Education responds to the changing patterns of American life

Like almost every other aspect of American life, education was transformed by the rising force of industrialism.

In 1870 about 7 million children were enrolled in American schools, most of them in the lower grades. Only 30 years later, in 1900, the number had more than doubled. During this same period, the number of high schools multiplied 10 times. This growth reflected not only the increasing throngs of children in America's cities but also the increasing wealth that could be taxed to support education.

From old ways to new. The character of the schools—including courses of study and methods of teaching—was also changing.

Pupils in the earlier rural classrooms were all too familiar with the sharp sting of the hickory stick, wielded by teachers on the theory "Spare the rod and spoil the child." Children learned reading, writing, and arithmetic and memorized a few more or less related facts about geography and history. The few students who went to high school or to a private academy spent much time learning Latin, Greek, and mathematics. Most educators believed that these subjects provided mental training and therefore fully equipped students for later life.

Some reformers began to demand a new program of education better suited to the industrial age. A few educational pioneers, such as Colonel Francis W. Parker of Chicago, stressed the idea that education is not just the memorization of facts but also the broadening of a child's experience. Education, Parker insisted, must prepare children to live in an ex-

Before 1860 women were admitted into only a few colleges. But by 1901, 128 women's colleges had been founded, other colleges had admitted women, and women made up one fourth of all undergraduates.

panding and complex world of science and industry.

John Dewey also stressed the idea that education is not something apart from the rest of life but an essential part of life itself. By the 1890's Dewey's experimental school in Chicago was attracting attention for its program of "learning by doing" and for its emphasis upon making children physically sound, intellectually competent, and socially well-adjusted. Ella Flagg Young, the head of the Chicago school system, worked closely with both Parker and Dewey. This able educator was the first woman to serve as head of a major school system in the nation.

Most schools, it is true, continued along more traditional lines. Nevertheless, Parker, Dewey, and other pioneers proved to have a great influence on the course of American education.

Influences of industrialism. The needs of the new industrial society were also reflected in the schools. By 1900, educational programs included the natural sciences and such "practical" and "useful" subjects as industrial designing, business arithmetic, bookkeeping, typing, stenography, shopwork, home economics, and manual arts. Superintendents and principals also became more businesslike in emphasizing efficiency and organization.

Colleges and universities. The colleges and universities also responded to the needs of the new age. New technical schools, such as the Columbia University School of Mines, the Massachusetts Institute of Technology, and the Case School of Applied Science, turned out more and more graduates prepared to take important jobs in railroad building, in mining, and in other engineering projects. The state universities and land-grant colleges emphasized practical training for a variety of fields.

Even the older colleges, which emphasized the classics, often added more scientific and "practical" subjects to their traditional courses of study. Under the influence of leaders like Charles W. Eliot of Harvard and Andrew D. White of Cornell, the colleges modified the old, rigid curriculum in which students studied mainly Latin, Greek, and mathematics.

Colleges and universities also enriched their educational programs by adding courses in the social sciences and modern languages as well as in the natural sciences. It was no longer possible for every student to take all the subjects in the curriculum. To meet individual needs, the elective system was introduced.

At the same time, marked progress was made in the professional studies of medicine and law. This was especially important, for people living in cities increasingly needed the services of good lawyers and doctors.

In these and many other ways, education responded to the changing patterns of everyday life after 1865.

SECTION SURVEY

IDENTIFY: Colonel Francis W. Parker, John Dewey, Ella Flagg Young, elective system.

1. What changes were made in the courses of study in public schools to meet the needs of the new industrial society?

2. Describe the ways in which colleges and universities responded to the needs of the new age.

3. Does education today reflect any of the ideas favored by Parker and Dewey? Explain.

3 American writing reflects the new industrial age

Newspapers, magazines, and novels also revealed the influence of the new urban industrial way of life. Most obvious was an enormous increase in circulation of printed material.

Newspapers and magazines. Between 1870 and 1900, the number of daily newspapers in the country increased from 600 to nearly 2,500. Their circulation multiplied six times—a jump far greater than the growth in population. This huge expansion reflected gains in the reading ability of many Americans and a growing interest in the events of the world beyond the local community.

Several mechanical inventions enabled publishers to print more newspapers, magazines, and books at lower costs. Most important of these inventions were the typewriter, improved printing presses, and the linotype, a fast and efficient typesetting machine.

Mass circulation was also stimulated by the rapidly developing art of advertising. Businesses were ready to advertise, but only in newspapers and magazines that reached large audiences. The desire to secure advertising stimulated publishers to print more and more "popular" articles written in a catchy style to attract the largest possible numbers of readers.

"Titans of the press." Three of the outstanding leaders of the new trend in journalism were Charles A. Dana, Joseph Pulitzer, and William Randolph Hearst.

Dana, publisher of the New York *Sun,* dug up sensational news and gave it prominent space on the front pages of his paper. Pulitzer, publisher of the New York *World,* followed much the same technique. His paper appealed to the general reader because of its human-interest stories and many articles on the scandalous activities of the rich and the tragedies of the poor. Stories by Elizabeth Seaman, who defied the prejudice against women reporters, were especially popular. Under the name Nelly Bly, she reported what she found when she worked in a factory, entered a mental institution by pretending to be insane, or got herself jailed. Pulitzer also developed the comic strip, the sports page, and a section with columnists, puzzles, and advice to readers.

Hearst, Pulitzer's chief rival, outdid Pulitzer at his own game. Hearst bought the New York *Journal* in 1895 and raised its circulation beyond that of any other paper. By denouncing the irresponsibility and selfishness of some of the well-to-do, Hearst appealed to the masses of people. His special success rested on his ability to hire gifted feature writers, able sports reporters, and popular comic artists. He also was able to get the most sensational news before anyone else and to play it up for all it was worth—frequently far more than it was worth.

Journalism as big business. Well before 1900 journalism adopted the methods of other big business enterprises. Leading publishers bought up small papers and organized great newspaper chains. Large chains could use the same feature articles, the same comic strips, and even the same editorials. This was especially true as the different parts of the nation and the world became increasingly interdependent and public interest reached out beyond the local community to national and world affairs. The newspaper chains also subscribed to great news-reporting services, or syndicates, such as the Associated Press (AP) and the United Press (UP), which collected news items from every corner of the earth. Even the newspapers that remained independent were influenced by the trend toward standardized practices in journalism.

By 1900 there also were numerous foreign-language newspapers for immigrants and about 150 newspapers for black Americans. Although these publications had limited resources, they served important functions. They gave their readers a sense of identity with other people of the same national origin or racial background. Most of these newspapers also were uncompromising in their opposition to discrimination.

Mass-circulation magazines. Like the newspapers, magazines adapted themselves to the changing times. Some of the older magazines, such as the *Atlantic Monthly, Harper's,* and *Scribner's,* continued to appeal to the better educated. Even before the Civil War, however, a new type of low-priced, popular magazine had appeared, which contained material aimed at mass circulation among "average" readers. The *Ladies' Home Journal,* established in 1883, was one of the most successful, providing reading material that interested millions of

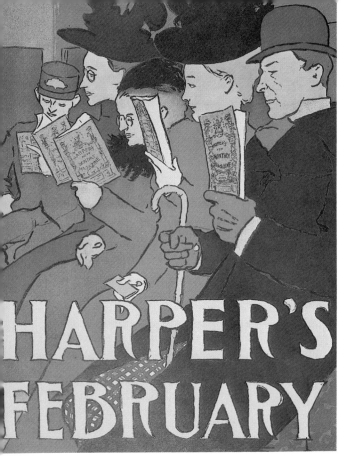

Started as a weekly in 1850, *Harper's* magazine remained popular into the 1900's. It published political cartoons, drawings of major events, and works of important writers, including Charles Dickens.

women. It further built up its circulation by setting its price at 10 cents. Under the editorship of a Dutch immigrant, Edward Bok, the *Ladies' Home Journal* sponsored many crusades to raise standards of living and improve community life.

Literature about urban life. American literature, too, reflected the growing influence of urban industrialism. The success stories for boys that Horatio Alger, Jr., and W. T. Adams (under the name of Oliver Optic) turned out by the dozens were extremely popular. These stories in a sense glorified an urban society in which a hard-working boy from humble beginnings could climb to the top by sheer pluck — and luck.

William Sydney Porter (O. Henry) struck a very different note with short stories that presented realistic pictures of American life, both urban and rural. Different again were the novels of Edith Wharton, which focused on the conflicts between the newly rich and older well-to-do families of New York in the 1880's. Henry James's novels explored the tensions felt by the members of America's leisure class who chose to live in the sophisticated urban centers of Europe.

One of the best-known novels of the period was *The Gilded Age,* written by Samuel L. Clemens (Mark Twain) and Charles Dudley Warner. In a humorous but biting manner, the writers described the corrupt activities of politicians and land speculators in the nation's capital. Edward Bellamy's *Looking Backward: 2000–1887* contrasted an ugly urban America with an imaginary socialist America of the future. In Bellamy's future America, poverty and corruption have been eliminated and people live cooperatively in freedom and dignity. Among the ablest writers of his time was William Dean Howells. In *A Hazard of New Fortunes* and other realistic stories, he provided a faithful picture of middle-class life, chiefly in urban America.

Notable exceptions. There were, of course, many authors whose writing was not influenced by the changing ways of life. Emily Dickinson, for example, created short, thought-provoking poems that have since been recognized as gems of beauty and originality.

The growing reading public also enjoyed highly romantic and sentimental novels as well as colorful Wild West adventure stories that enterprising publishers put out in paper covers for only 10 cents. Many of these famous "dime novels" had the unfortunate side effect of reinforcing the stereotypes of Mexicans and Indians as villains.

Local-color writers. Some writers reacted against the more or less standardized ways of city life. They concentrated upon describing those regions of the United States that still largely followed the older, rural ways of living. One of these local-color writers, Edward Eggleston, touched a "folksy" note in describing life in rural Indiana in his book *The Hoosier Schoolmaster.*

The greatest of the local-color writers was Samuel L. Clemens (Mark Twain), the first important writer from west of the Atlantic seaboard states. His *Life on the Mississippi* dramatized the crude, vigorous, racy aspects of the American steamboat era. *The Adventures of Tom Sawyer* and *The Adventures of Huckleberry Finn* were landmarks in the represen-

500

tation of the adolescent American boy. At the same time, these books satirized the middle-class values and racial prejudices of a rural community in Missouri. Twain's *Roughing It* vividly portrayed the raw life of western mining camps.

The colorful and heroic verses of Joaquin (hwah·KEEN) Miller and the realistic stories of mining camps written by Bret Harte brought the Far West into the nation's literature. Helen Hunt Jackson also did much to increase the awareness of the Far West with her stories of Spanish missions and of Indian life in old California. Hamlin Garland, in *Main-Traveled Roads* and other books, wrote of the harsh conditions endured by many of the pioneers on the northern prairies.

The South, too, had its share of local-color writers. George Washington Cable, Kate Chopin, and Grace King presented life among the French-speaking Creoles of Louisiana. Thomas Nelson Page popularized a romantic image of master-slave relations on Virginia plantations before the Civil War. Joel Chandler Harris of Georgia won fame for his "Uncle Remus" tales, based on stories brought from Africa by slaves.

The writings of black authors also partly reflected the influence of the local-color school of writing. Local color distinguished *My Southern Home,* the last book of the pioneer black novelist William Wells Brown. Another important black writer, Paul L. Dunbar, was hailed as the first black American writer "to feel the Negro life esthetically and express it lyrically." Some of the novels and tales of Charles W. Chesnutt, a black writer of North Carolina, also reflected the local-color school of writing.

New England, like other regions, excited the imaginations of local-color authors, among them Mary E. Wilkins Freeman and Sarah Orne Jewett. These writers pictured the changes in rural life in New England as young people abandoned the rocky, unproductive family farms to seek their fortunes in the growing cities.

SECTION SURVEY

IDENTIFY: journalism, Elizabeth Seaman, Horatio Alger, Edith Wharton, Emily Dickinson, dime novels, local color, Mark Twain, William Wells Brown, Paul L. Dunbar, Sarah Orne Jewett.

1. What factors made possible the mass circulation of newspapers and magazines?

2. How did each of these people contribute to journalism: (a) Dana, (b) Pulitzer, (c) Hearst?

3. (a) Give evidence to show that newspaper publishing became big business. (b) How might this have affected the reading public?

4. Explain how some novels of the late 1800's reflected the growing influence of urban industrialism in American life.

---

4 Architecture and other fine arts respond to a changing society

Architecture and art, no less than journalism and literature, revealed the influence of urban life and the growth of industry in the years after 1865.

Decline and revival. For a number of years after the Civil War, American architecture reached what many have regarded as a low level. During the 1870's and 1880's, many successful business leaders and financiers poured fortunes into huge, gaudy mansions. These overdone showplaces as well as many equally tasteless public buildings and smaller houses were a far cry from the beautiful structures that Americans had designed and built along simple, classical lines during the late 1700's and the early 1800's.

Toward the end of the 1800's, however, a number of architects, notably Henry Hobson Richardson and Richard Morris Hunt, began to design more pleasing, practical houses and public buildings in a more dignified and restrained style.

The World's Columbian Exposition, or World's Fair, held in Chicago in 1893, helped to quicken public interest in good architecture. Many of the buildings that housed the exhibits were designed in the simple classical style. Thousands of visitors carried back to their home communities memories of beautiful structures with noble pillars and clean, direct lines that they had seen.

New trends in architecture. One structure at the Chicago World's Fair, the Transportation Building, heralded a new day in architecture. Its architect, Louis H. Sullivan, taught that "form follows function," meaning that the best-

The 21-story Flatiron Building, New York City's first skyscraper, was completed in 1903. It still stands as a landmark in the series of developments that helped make modern American cities possible.

designed building is one that has a style and uses materials perfectly suited to the purposes of the building. Gradually this idea was adopted by more and more architects, among them Frank Lloyd Wright. Wright started to practice his profession in Chicago in 1893 and became one of the world's foremost architects.

The availability of such new building materials as steel, concrete, and plate glass plus the necessities of urban life did much to stimulate a new type of business structure.

Skyscrapers. As city business districts became more crowded and as real-estate values soared, architects tried to solve the problem by building upward. How could they erect taller buildings? Ingenious architects constructed huge steel frames and filled the spaces with stone, brick, concrete, and glass. The Home Insurance Building, built in Chicago in 1884, set the example for these towering structures.

During the next few years, in both Chicago and New York, builders found ways to erect taller and taller skyscrapers.

The new towering buildings turned the narrow streets below into dark, gloomy canyons. To solve this problem, New York City adopted an ordinance requiring architects to set back the higher stories of all tall buildings so that more light would reach the streets. This ordinance accomplished its purpose. It also relieved the rectangular lines of the box-like skyscraper and accounted for the magically beautiful character of the New York skyline. Like many other activities of American life, architecture revealed more and more the influence of new times and new ways of living.

Painting and sculpture. The new industrial age had less influence on painters and sculptors than it did on architects. Between 1865 and 1900, the most important development in the fine arts was the increasing skill of American artists who had studied in European art centers. The improving standards in American art also rested in part on the ability and the willingness of wealthy Americans to collect masterpieces, to establish art schools, and to buy the works of American artists.

The themes that painters and sculptors chose often seemed to have little to do with the growing urban industrial society. Gifted sculptors created great statues of Lincoln and other national heroes. One outstanding creation was the Adams Monument in Rock Creek Cemetery in Washington, D.C., made by Augustus Saint-Gaudens (saint·GAW·dunz). This brooding, hooded figure, sometimes referred to as "The Peace of God," suggests the mystery of life and death.

A number of painters did equally outstanding work. George Inness captured on canvas the beauties of woodland scenes. Winslow Homer's brilliantly colored seascapes suggested the strength and primitive force of the sea. Mary Cassatt, influenced by the new French impressionist style and by Japanese art, painted portraits of women and children notable for lively charm and for exquisite tone and color.

The work of a number of artists, however, did reveal the influence of industrial and urban America. Thomas Eakins, for example, painted famous and wealthy Americans with such frank realism that they would not buy his works. Eakins, however, refused to change his style for the sake of immediate popularity and profit and continued to paint life as he saw it. In a painting designed to reveal the surgeon's scientific skill, *The Surgical Clinic of Professor Gross,* Eakins suggested very concretely the new scientific trend of the age.

SECTION SURVEY

IDENTIFY: architecture, Frank Lloyd Wright, Augustus Saint-Gaudens, Winslow Homer, Mary Cassatt, Thomas Eakins.

1. How did architecture in the late 1800's (a) meet the requirements of the urban industrial age and (b) take advantage of the new materials made available by the age?
2. What did Louis Sullivan mean by the statement that in architecture "form follows function"?
3. Describe the themes that inspired the noted American sculptors and painters of this period.

5 New forms of recreation enrich American life

Recreation, like all other aspects of everyday living, was transformed by the new urban industrial age. The well-to-do, having time and money, enjoyed such new and at first exclusive sports as tennis and golf. Gradually, however, the middle-income groups also began to enjoy such forms of recreation.

New types of recreation. For many thousands of American children and their parents in the late 1800's, one of the most memorable events of the year was the arrival of the circus. P. T. Barnum's tent circus, which he started in Brooklyn in 1871, was called "the greatest show on earth."

Equally awaited was the arrival of the Chautauqua (shuh·TAW·kwuh). The Chautauqua movement was an educational enterprise started in 1874 on the shores of Chautauqua Lake in upper New York State. Each year thousands of Americans from all over the United States traveled to Chautauqua Lake to enjoy a summer vacation and to benefit intellectually and spiritually from the lectures and sermons provided for them. Study groups using Chautauqua publications were organized in many towns and villages. As the years passed, the program at Chautauqua Lake became increasingly varied. Illustrated travel talks, stage presentations, and humorous acts were added to the more serious lectures and religious services. Other enterprising leaders also organized traveling tent programs similar to those earlier developed at Chautauqua Lake. By the early 1900's, the traveling Chautauquas were bringing a glimpse of the outside world into many rural communities.

The theater gained in popularity during the 1800's, particularly for middle-income groups. At its best the theater offered admirable plays performed by great actors, American and foreign-born. Some of the most appealing programs, however, were the melodramas that reminded city dwellers of their own rural background. Such plays as *Way Down East* and *The Old Homestead* attracted large audiences. There was also an equally popular series of melodramas on significant urban themes, such as *Bertha, the Sewing-Machine Girl.* Vaudeville shows, providing a variety of singing, dancing, and gymnastic acts, also attracted large audiences.

By 1900, amusement parks were attracting crowds of city people and making fortunes for their owners. In many cases trolley-car companies built amusement parks just outside the city, thereby reaping profits from the parks as well as from trolley fares.

Physical exercise and sports. During the last quarter of the 1800's, an increasing number of middle-class city dwellers became aware of the need for physical exercise, especially for youth. One answer was gymnasiums, which appeared in growing numbers in cities and towns as well as in schools and colleges.

In these years the bicycle changed from a clumsy, high-wheeled, dangerous contraption into something like the machine we know today. As a result, bicycling became a popular fad as well as a means of getting to and from work for many people.

These same years also saw the rapid development of three major spectator sports—baseball, football, and basketball.

Baseball in various forms had been played long before the first professional team, the Cincinnati Red Stockings, was formed in 1869. Seven years later, in 1876, the National League was organized. In 1900 the American League was formed. Well before 1900, urban

THE NATIONAL SPORT

King George III played a version of it as a boy. So did Washington's troops at Valley Forge. Even then the game, known as "rounders" or "base ball," was old. Some say it started in English villages in the 1500's, with players using milking stools as bases. (Baseball was *not* invented in 1839 by Abner Doubleday, though his claims were taken seriously at one time.)

Alexander Cartwright standardized rules and the diamond in 1845. The first recorded game played according to his rules took place the following year at Hoboken, New Jersey; the

New Yorks defeated the Knickerbockers 23 to 1 in 4 innings. In those days the first team to get 21 aces (runs) won the game. Players still wore ordinary clothing, only the catcher used a glove, and umpires sometimes carried umbrellas to ward off sun and rain.

After the Civil War, baseball became truly the national sport. Then the rules became much like today's. The first professional teams appeared, and national leagues were formed.

Baseball as played in the early 1900's would be easily understood today, yet there were a good many differences. No blacks played in the major leagues. Players traveled by train, so schedules were less crowded and the season averaged around 140 games. There were no night games. A day game that went extra innings and had to be called on account of darkness was usually played out the next day.

Players wore bulky uniforms and, batting without protective helmets, were often "beaned" by pitched balls. Teams had fewer pitchers and they pitched more games. Even the ball was different, less lively than today's and likely to be used for an entire game. As a result, long balls and home runs were not common. But when bat and ball did connect, the crowd roared and baseball excitement filled the air.

dwellers in growing numbers were crowding into the ballparks to watch what would in time become one of America's favorite spectator sports.

Football, which evolved from the English game of rugby, also became increasingly popular. The first intercollegiate football contest, played between Rutgers and Princeton in 1869, had 25 players on each side. Within a few years, intercollegiate contests were being held in the West as well as in the East. Played mostly by college men, football in the early days was a rough-and-tumble game. It was so rough, in fact, that some people protested against its "brutality" and demanded its abolition. As the years passed, however, new rules of play were developed, and the game became better organized.

Basketball, which also became a typically American sport, was first played in 1892 by students at the Y.M.C.A. college in Springfield, Massachusetts. Its inventor, Dr. James Naismith, then an instructor in physical education, created the game to provide the same

opportunities for recreation in the winter that baseball provided in the summer and football in the fall. Within just a few years, Naismith's game of basketball was being played all over the country.

The older rural forms of recreation— picnics, amateur baseball, horseshoe pitching—continued to enjoy popularity. Increasingly, however, the ways in which the people of the United States relaxed and amused themselves were being transformed in the new industrial age.

SECTION SURVEY

IDENTIFY: P. T. Barnum, Dr. James Naismith.

1. (a) What was the Chautauqua movement? (b) Why was it important to rural dwellers?

2. How did city dwellers satisfy their growing interest in physical fitness?

3. What three major spectator sports developed in the late 1800's?

Chapter Survey

Summary: Tracing the Main Ideas

Growing numbers of people poured into the great urban centers during the late 1800's. Each year the cities exerted a more and more powerful influence upon all aspects of American life, including education, journalism, literature, architecture, art, and recreation.

What had made the cities such a powerful influence?

In trying to answer this question we must remember that the cities were the centers of industry. Thus we find ourselves going back to the factories and mass production. And when we look at the factories, with their mass production, we find that they depended upon power-driven machines. And when we look at the power-driven machines—and the almost countless number of inventions and discoveries that made the new machines possible—we find ourselves face to face with science and technology—that is, with the application of science to industry. Or to put it in other terms, we come face to face with scientists, engineers, manufacturers, and business leaders. Without science and technology, there would have been no thriving factories and no large industrial cities.

The world of the late 1800's was changing with bewildering speed. New leaders were appearing, and new ways of living and working were transforming American society. The American people, rich and poor, city dwellers and country folk—had to adjust their lives to the new conditions.

The new age was full of promise for a richer and fuller life for all people everywhere, but before the promise could be realized, many problems still had to be solved. You will read about some of these problems and the ways in which the American people tried to solve them in the following chapters.

Inquiring into History

1. How did industrialization and urbanization affect (a) education, (b) architecture, (c) art, and (d) journalism?
2. How might American democracy have been affected by (a) the increase in educational opportunity and (b) the mass circulation of newspapers and magazines?
3. Explain how each of the following terms reflects the changing ways of American life during the late 1800's: (a) concentration of wealth, (b) settlement house, (c) elective system, (d) skyscrapers.
4. What might be the relationship between functionalism in architecture and an industrialized society?

Relating Past to Present

1. Does education today reflect the needs of our society? Explain.
2. Compare skyscrapers built in the late 1890's with those built recently in terms of (a) size, (b) cost, (c) structure and design, (d) materials used. What can you conclude from these differences?
3. Do you think that baseball and other sports have been affected by industrialization? Explain.

4. Do you think the federal government should be involved in the support of the arts? Why or why not?
5. Do newspapers today use any of the techniques practiced by Dana, Pulitzer, and Hearst? Why or why not?

Developing Social Science Skills

1. Examine the pictures on pages 498 and 502. How do they help to show the changes taking place during the late 1800's?
2. From primary and secondary sources, find out more about the women's rights movement between 1860 and 1900. (a) Who were the leaders? (b) What gains were made by women in these years? (c) What obstacles still existed? (d) What methods were most effective in promoting women's rights?
3. Read all or part of one of the novels discussed in Section 3. (a) Does the subject of the novel relate to industrialization or urban life? (b) Does the novel seem to express an opinion about the vast changes taking place in society at that time? Explain. (c) How does the novel's description of life in the late 1800's compare to the description presented in your textbook? How can you account for the similarities or differences?

Unit Survey

For Further Inquiry

1. After 1865 in what ways did the government encourage business and industry?
2. How important was each of these in bringing about industrialization in the United States: (a) individual business people, (b) discoveries and inventions, (c) abundant natural resources?
3. Why was city life so attractive to many people during the late 1800's?
4. What effects did large-scale immigration have on American society (a) during the late 1800's, (b) in the long run?
5. Compare the situation of farmers and industrial workers in the late 1800's in terms of (a) grievances, (b) methods of seeking improvement in their situation, (c) relationship with government.

Projects and Activities

1. (a) What is the theme of the timeline above? (b) Does that theme represent a significant aspect of life from the 1860's to the 1890's? Why or why not? (c) From the timeline choose one example of popular culture and one of high culture. Explain how you made your choices.
2. America has been described as a nation of immigrants. Look into your own family background to discover where your relatives or ancestors were born and why they came to the United States. You might also prepare a family tree.
3. Present a report on the problems and contributions of one of the immigrant groups in the United States.
4. Prepare a line or bar graph showing the growth of (a) coal production, (b) iron production, (c) oil production, or (d) railroad lines between 1860 and 1900. Beneath the graph, write a paragraph explaining what is shown on the graph and why it is important.
5. Imagine that you were preparing a museum exhibit on paintings of the industrial age. It will consist of five paintings of your choice. Select the paintings and write the catalogue for viewers of the exhibit. The catalogue should give facts about, as well as your comments on, each painting in the exhibit.

Exploring Your Region

1. Find out about the natural resources in your state—especially minerals or energy sources—that have contributed to the industrial growth of your region or the nation.
2. Prepare a bulletin board display about a city in your region that became important during the industrial age. The display can include pictures, charts, or short descriptions of the important historical facts in the development of the city.

Suggested Reading

1. *The Promised Land,* Mary Antin. Autobiography of a young Jewish immigrant and her struggle to rise above her difficult life in the Boston slums.
2. *Jane Addams: Pioneer for Social Justice,* Cornelia Meigs. Story of Jane Addams's career as a reformer and founder of Hull House.
3. *Altgeld's America: The Lincoln Ideal Versus Changing Realities,* Ray Ginger. A history of the vast changes taking place in the late 1800's as America was transformed from a rural to an urban, industrial nation.
4. *Everyday Life in the Age of Enterprise, 1865–1900,* Robert H. Walker. The story of popular culture and social life in the late 1800's.
5. *The Wind Blows Free,* Loula Grace Erdman. A novel of pioneers in the Texas Panhandle.
6. *The Age of Innocence,* Edith Wharton. A classic novel of high society in New York in the 1870's.

Unit Eight

The Arrival of Reform

1897-1920

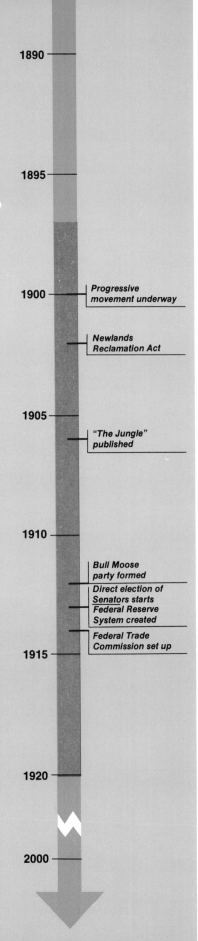

1890

1895

1900 — Progressive
movement underway

Newlands
Reclamation Act

1905

"The Jungle"
published

1910

Bull Moose
party formed

Direct election of
Senators starts

Federal Reserve
System created

Federal Trade
Commission set up

1915

1920

2000

Chapter 26

Reforms Under the "Square Deal" and the "New Freedom"

1897-1920

The election of William McKinley as President in 1896 marked the end of the Populist Party. Many Americans feared that it also marked the end of the reform movement. Within six years, however, a new reform movement, the progressive movement, would sweep the country. Three Presidents would contribute to this movement in different ways.

From 1901 to 1909, Teddy Roosevelt, colorful and dynamic, promised to give Americans a "Square Deal." On the whole, Roosevelt did much to fulfill this promise. From 1909 to 1913, William Howard Taft, a huge man, highly intelligent and thoroughly competent, advanced the reform movement. Taft, however, lacked Teddy's ability to capture the public's imagination. From 1913 to 1921, Woodrow Wilson, a scholar and idealist, promised Americans a "New Freedom" and took important steps toward this goal.

Each of these Presidents grappled with the same basic problem faced by earlier reformers—how to preserve and strengthen democracy in the industrial age.

THE CHAPTER IN OUTLINE

1. The progressives open the door to reforms in America.

2. The progressives promote more democratic forms of government.

3. Theodore Roosevelt promises Americans a "Square Deal."

4. Roosevelt acts to conserve America's natural resources.

5. The progressive movement gains and loses under Taft.

6. Wilson's "New Freedom" expands opportunities for Americans.

508

1 The progressives open the door to reforms in America

In 1897 McKinley and the conservative Republicans seemed to have a clear road before them. Having just defeated William Jennings Bryan in his bid for the White House, Republicans in Congress now passed the Dingley Tariff of 1897, which raised average tariff rates to a new high of 57 percent. In the meantime, the depression of 1893–96 gave way to prosperity. New corporations sprang up, and older corporations merged to form giant trusts and industrial concerns.

Surrounded by prosperity, many Americans in the late 1890's had forgotten the demands of the Populists and other reform groups. Yet by 1900 a new reform impulse known as the progressive movement was underway. This movement adopted and eventually achieved many of the goals of the Populists.

Aims of the progressives. The progressive movement cut across party lines. It included people from the Democratic Party as well as discontented Republicans. Leaders of the progressive movement had specific aims. (1) They wanted to restore control of the government to the rank and file of people. (2) They wanted to correct the abuses and injustices that had crept into American life in the age of urban industrialism. (3) They wanted to restore greater equality of economic opportunity by drawing up new rules for the conduct of business and the great private banks, or "money trust."

The progressives were optimists. They believed that these reforms would create a more prosperous and a more democratic country.

Robert M. La Follette. Robert M. "Fighting Bob" La Follette of Wisconsin was one of the outstanding leaders of the progressive movement. La Follette fought his way upward in local and state politics. He won victories over the Republican political machine that dominated Wisconsin. In doing so, he won a reputation for fearless honesty. An excellent speaker, he sought support from the farmers and working people and won the governorship of Wisconsin in 1900.

As governor, La Follette helped to break the power of the political machine that had been running the state. He persuaded legislators to levy heavier taxes on the railroads and on the newer **public utilities** – the gas, electric, and streetcar companies. He persuaded the legislators to create commissions to regulate these companies. He also started a movement for the conservation of Wisconsin's forests and water-power sites. Many of these sites had come under the control of big industrial corporations.

In the days before radio and television, campaigning for office meant that the candidates had to appear in person to spread their message. In his painting "Electioneering," artist E. I. Henry portrays one such appearance.

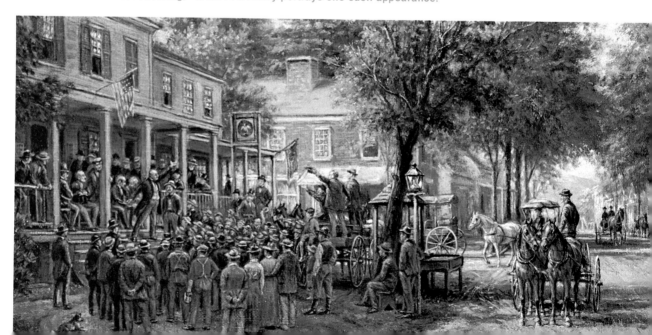

Under the leadership of Frances Willard, the Women's Christian Temperance Union had become a worldwide organization to be reckoned with by the mid-1880's. In addition to supporting the prohibition of alcohol, the W.C.T.U. called for a ban on all harmful drugs.

The La Follette administration promoted good government in Wisconsin by using university scholars to help legislators find needed facts and draft laws that the courts could not easily set aside. He also appointed scholars to serve on the new state regulatory commissions. The "Wisconsin Idea," as the movement started by La Follette was called, soon attracted nationwide attention.

Encouraged by La Follette's example, other public officials attacked corrupt government and powerful corporations. Joseph W. Folk became governor of Missouri in 1906 largely as a result of his success in prosecuting a ring of corrupt politicians in St. Louis. Charles Evans Hughes became governor of New York in 1907 chiefly because of his success in uncovering questionable business practices of certain insurance companies. Hiram Johnson became governor of California in 1910 after fighting the political bosses and powerful railroads that had great influence in the state.

Women reformers. Even though most women still lacked the vote, some of them took part in reforms whose purpose was to influence public opinion and government. The National Consumers League, in which Florence Kelley was a leader, brought unfavorable publicity to stores and companies that paid women less than men for equal work and that maintained unhealthful working conditions. The league urged the public to boycott consumer goods produced by child labor and by women who were unfairly treated. With the cooperation of the National Child Labor Committee, the league also secured legislation in the interests of women and children.

The Women's Christian Temperance Union (W.C.T.U.), founded in 1879, carried on a widespread campaign against the manufacture, sale, and consumption of alcoholic beverages. The W.C.T.U. stressed the physical, psychological, and social dangers of alcohol. It emphasized the threat posed by alcoholics to the wellbeing of their families. Frances Willard, president of the W.C.T.U. for 20 years, persuaded the organization to support women's suffrage as a means to achieve prohibition. The W.C.T.U. used education to achieve its goals. It did not approve of the tactics of Carrie Nation of Kansas, who invaded saloons with a hatchet to smash mirrors and bottles.

Many women also took part in the work of the Anti-Saloon League, which supported political candidates who pledged opposition to the liquor interests and opposed those who did not.

The muckrakers. The progressive movement also included many social workers, scholars, journalists, preachers, and novelists. Theodore Roosevelt applied the name **muckrakers** to the writers who exposed the evils and corruption in politics and the business world. Although Roosevelt used the term in an unfavorable sense, the writers accepted it with pride, and it came into popular use.

The muckraking movement is usually dated from an article, "Tweed Days in St. Louis," written by Lincoln Steffens and Claude H. Wetmore for the October 1902 issue of *McClure's Magazine.* The following month *McClure's* began to publish Ida M. Tarbell's critical *History of the Standard Oil Company.* Many other magazines also began publishing attacks on abuses in American life.

Muckraking novelists included Upton Sinclair, whose sensational novel *The Jungle* exposed unsanitary practices in the meat-packing industry. The book, incidentally, turned many of his readers into vegetarians. Frank Norris's novel *The Octopus* exposed the railroads' control over the political and economic life of the farmers. Jack London in *The War of the Classes, The Iron Heel,* and *Revolution* warned of a revolution that could wipe out private capitalism.

A few of the muckrakers called attention to the plight of American blacks. The most impressive work was *Following the Color Line* by Ray Stannard Baker, a series of magazine articles published as a book in 1908. This was a competent and honest report of segregation in the South and of racial discrimination in the North. As such, it put the problem of white-black relations in a nationwide context.

The root of the problem. The muckrakers brought to light many abuses in American life. Lincoln Steffens, however, pinpointed the basic problem in a series of articles later published as a book entitled *The Shame of the Cities.* Years later, in his *Autobiography,* Steffens summarized his conclusions. The basic problem facing Americans was not the development of industrialism or of business, large or small. The source of the evil was "privilege"—the demand for special privileges from government. This had to be controlled, according to Steffens, or abuses and corruption were sure to be the results.

SECTION SURVEY

IDENTIFY: Dingley Tariff of 1897, progressive movement, Robert La Follette, Charles Evans Hughes, Hiram Johnson, National Consumers League, Women's Christian Temperance Union, Lincoln Steffens, Ida Tarbell, *The Jungle, Following the Color Line.*

1. (a) In what ways did La Follette reform government in Wisconsin? (b) To what degree did his reforms reflect the goals of the progressive movement listed on page 509?

2. Describe the reform activities promoted by (a) Florence Kelley and (b) Frances Willard.

3. (a) Name three muckrakers and explain why they can be described as muckrakers. (b) What do their muckraking activities have in common?

4. What did Lincoln Steffens mean when he identified the basic problem and greatest evil in American life as "privilege"?

2 The progressives promote more democratic forms of government

Millions of Americans in the early 1900's shared the view that special privileges handed out by government were the source of corruption in public life. They also agreed that one way to combat the evils of special privileges was to restore the control of government to the people.

The Australian ballot. A major step toward more democratic government was the adoption of the **Australian ballot,** or secret vote. Until about 1890 each political party printed its own ballots in a distinctive color. Thus when a person cast a ballot—in open view of anybody who cared to watch—it was easy to determine how the person had voted. The secret ballot, developed in Australia and adopted in the United States, eliminated this open voting. Ballots listing the names of all candidates on a single sheet of paper were printed at public expense. The voters could then mark and cast their ballots in secrecy.

The initiative, referendum, and recall. In trying to secure a more democratic government, the progressives supported the use of the initiative, referendum, and recall. All of these reform measures had been advocated by the Populists in the 1890's.

The **initiative** enables voters in a state to initiate, or introduce, legislation at any time. Suppose, for instance, that a group of citizens wanted to increase the amount of state money spent for public schools. They would draw up a bill and attach to it a petition containing the signatures of a certain percentage of the voters in the state (usually from 5 to 15 percent, depending upon state law). When the petition was presented to the state legislature, the representatives were required by law to debate the bill openly.

The **referendum** was a companion to the initiative. By securing a specified number of signatures to a petition, voters could compel the legislature to place a bill before *all* the state's voters for approval or disapproval.

The **recall** enabled voters to remove an elected government official before the official's

These women and their offspring were just a few of the 15,000 supporters of women's suffrage who marched down New York's Fifth Avenue in May 1912. They were eight years from reaching their goal.

term expired. When a specified number of voters, usually 25 percent, presented a petition, a special election had to be held. In this election all of the voters would have the opportunity to vote for or against allowing the official to continue in office.

South Dakota, in 1898, was the first state to adopt the initiative and the referendum. Eventually 20 states adopted initiative and referendum procedures. A total of 12 states adopted the recall.

The direct primary. In trying to make government more responsive to the people's wishes, the progressives also advocated the **direct primary.**

Traditionally, all candidates for government office were nominated in political conventions. These were easily controlled by professional politicians. The direct primary remedied this situation by providing "a nominating election" well in advance of the regular election. Individuals who wanted to run for office would first get a specified number of signatures on a petition. Then they could have their names printed on the primary ballot of any one of the political parties. On the day of the primary election, the registered voters of each party then marked their ballots for the candidate of their choice. First adopted by Wisconsin in 1900, the direct primary soon spread to almost every state.

Women's suffrage. Although the progressives did little if anything to secure the vote for blacks, many promoted woman suffrage. By 1900 four states—Wyoming, Utah, Colorado, and Idaho—had granted full voting rights to women. Vigorous campaigns by woman suffragists between 1910 and 1914 led seven other states, all west of the Mississippi, to give women the right to vote.

Throughout the early 1900's, strong opposition existed even within progressive circles to a Constitutional amendment granting women the vote. Woodrow Wilson, the progressive Democrat who was elected President in 1912, opposed such an amendment on the ground that states alone had the power to fix suffrage requirements. In response, a group of militants led by the courageous and persistent Alice Paul, organized a demonstration against Wilson on his inauguration day that ended in a near riot. Other demonstrations bordered on violence when opposition to them mounted. Activist leaders were jailed and fined. Meantime the militants increased pressure on Congress.

Despite conservative disapproval of militant tactics, the vigorous participation of women in the war effort in World War I broke down much opposition. Finally, in 1920, with the ratification of the Nineteenth Amendment by the states, the right of women to vote throughout the United States was written into the Constitution.

512

Direct election of Senators. Another reform advocated by the progressives was the direct election of United States Senators. According to the Constitution, Senators were chosen by state legislatures. During the early 1900's, however, progressives in the House of Representatives urged the adoption of an amendment that would allow the people to vote directly for Senators. The Senate, which was often criticized as a "rich man's club" and which included many politicians who owed their jobs to political bosses and political machines, blocked this amendment.

In the end, however, the rising power of the progressives proved too much for the machine politicians. In 1913, in the Seventeenth Amendment, the right to choose Senators was given to the voters at large.

Reform of city government. While winning victories at the state and federal level, the progressives were also trying to reform corrupt city governments. Most municipal governments consisted of a mayor and a large city council, elected by the voters and given complete responsibility for running city affairs. Under this system a well-organized political machine, using corrupt election procedures, could easily win control of city governments.

Galveston, Texas, led the way to a new type of government in 1900 after a hurricane and tidal wave killed one sixth of the city's people and destroyed a third of its property. To meet the emergency, Galveston gave a commission of five persons extraordinary power to run the city. The **commission** form of government soon spread to other cities. By 1912 more than 200 American communities had adopted it. Supporters argued that it was simpler, more efficient, and less expensive than older types of city government.

In 1908 Staunton, Virginia, developed the **city manager** form of government. The city manager, an expert in municipal administration without political connections, is appointed by an elected city council or board of commissioners to run the city as efficiently as possible. City manager government soon spread to many cities.

The progressives were, indeed, a powerful force in American life in the early 1900's. In addition to bringing about these changes in government, they also sought to bring about changes in the relations between business and government.

SECTION SURVEY

IDENTIFY: Australian ballot, initiative, referendum, recall, direct primary, Seventeenth Amendment, city manager form of government.

1. How did the use of the Australian ballot help prevent abuses in elections?
2. How successful were women suffragists in reaching their goal during the progressive era?
3. How did the change in the method of electing Senators make the American political system more democratic?
4. It has been said that progressives sought to make America more democratic. Use specific examples to support or refute this statement.

3 Theodore Roosevelt promises Americans a "Square Deal"

President McKinley and the Republicans entered the elections of 1900 confident of victory. The Democrats, who had again nominated William Jennings Bryan, tried to make free silver a major campaign issue, but Americans in general, including most farmers, were enjoying prosperity. They returned President McKinley to the White House with an electoral vote of 292 to 155.

Six months after his second inauguration, on September 6, 1901, McKinley was shot by a half-crazed assassin. He died a few days later and, to the dismay of conservative Republicans, Vice-President Theodore Roosevelt became the nation's Chief Executive.

Roosevelt's background. Theodore Roosevelt was born in 1858 into a well-to-do New York family. He studied at Harvard, where he acquired a taste for history and politics. After graduation he served a two-year term, from 1882 to 1884, in the New York state legislature. For part of the next two years, he lived on a cattle ranch in Dakota Territory. Returning home in 1886, he unsuccessfully ran for mayor of New York City, then devoted the following three years to the study and writing of history.

During the next few years, Roosevelt served on the federal Civil Service Commission, as president of the New York City Police Commission, and as Assistant Secretary of the Navy.

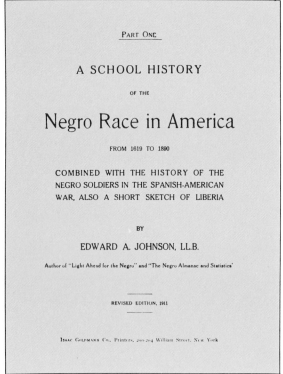

PART ONE

A SCHOOL HISTORY

OF THE

Negro Race in America

FROM 1619 TO 1890

COMBINED WITH THE HISTORY OF THE
NEGRO SOLDIERS IN THE SPANISH-AMERICAN
WAR, ALSO A SHORT SKETCH OF LIBERIA

BY

EDWARD A. JOHNSON, LL.B.

Author of "Light Ahead for the Negro" and "The Negro Almanac and Statistics"

REVISED EDITION, 1911

Isaac Goldmann Co., Printers, 200-204 William Street, New York

Edward A. Johnson, a black textbook author, is shown here with a page from his *School History of the Negro Race in America,* an important study in the growing literature on black Americans.

When war with Spain broke out in 1898, he resigned his Navy post to organize, with Leonard Wood, a volunteer cavalry regiment known as the "Rough Riders." After the war he became the Republican governor of New York. In that post his independent actions so alarmed the Republican political bosses that in 1900 they decided to get him out of active politics by "kicking him upstairs" into the Vice-Presidency.

This was the man who at age 42 became the youngest President the United States had ever had — and, as the conservative Republicans had correctly feared, one of the most independent.

Roosevelt was a good politician, ready to compromise when necessary. He did not start the progressive movement. Nor did he go as far as many progressives felt he could and should go, but he gave the progressive movement dramatic national leadership. His general popularity, his enthusiasm, his ability as a speaker, and his position enabled him to promote a number of reforms. One notable exception was government policy toward Indians, whose needs and rights were largely ignored.

Settling a coal strike. Less than a year after succeeding McKinley as President, Roosevelt took bold action in a struggle involving organized labor. In the spring of 1902, a strike broke out in Pennsylvania in the coal mines owned largely by railroad companies serving the region. The miners worked long hours, lived in company towns, and bought from company stores. Because of low wages, they found it hard to make ends meet. Organized as part of the United Mine Workers union, they had asked for a 9-hour day, a 20-percent wage increase, improved working conditions, and recognition of their right to bargain as a union. The mineowners refused to negotiate with the union, whereupon the miners went on strike.

By autumn the country faced a coalless winter with factories closed and homes without heat. The mineowners demanded that the President send federal troops into the area to break the strike. Roosevelt refused. Instead, he summoned representatives of the owners and of the union to meet at the White House.

At the meeting the mineowners refused to listen to a proposal for impartial arbitration. Furious at this lack of cooperation, Roosevelt let it be known that he might send the army to take over the mines in the name of the government. Faced with this prospect, the mineowners agreed to accept the decision of a board of arbitration.

After four months of study, the board gave the miners a 9-hour day and a 10-percent wage increase. However, the board did not grant the miners the right to negotiate as a union.

Although the miners won only part of their demands, the case was a landmark in the history of organized labor. For the first time, the federal government had stepped into a labor controversy to protect the interests of all concerned—wage earners, owners, and the public.

The Danbury Hatters' case. Organized labor was not pleased, however, with the outcome of another labor dispute. In 1902 the hatters' union started a nationwide effort to boycott, or to halt the purchase of, the hats produced by a manufacturer in Danbury, Connecticut. The hat company claimed that the boycott restrained trade and was therefore illegal under the Sherman Antitrust Act. After a long delay, the Supreme Court decided in favor of the hat manufacturer in 1908. As a result, the members of the hatters' union were held liable for three times the damages that the hat manufacturer had suffered.

Theodore Roosevelt was in no way responsible for the Supreme Court ruling. Nevertheless, organized labor, thoroughly alarmed at the outcome of the Danbury Hatters' case, held the government responsible for failing to draft laws that provided reasonable protection for labor unions.

Roosevelt and blacks. Some progressives fought the exploitation of black workers, established settlement houses for blacks, and organized national societies to protect the legal rights of black citizens. However, the progressives on the whole neglected the plight of black Americans. Many progressive leaders, to be sure, spoke out against racial injustice, but most of them believed that this problem could, at that time, be dealt with realistically only at state and local levels.

Theodore Roosevelt, too, did little to help the blacks. He did become involved in southern politics, where questions of segregation and black leadership were important issues. Thus, against the opposition of segregated southern Republican organizations, Roosevelt sometimes supported the claims of black politicians to federal office and to participation as delegates at Republican national conventions.

In such matters Roosevelt often used Booker T. Washington as his adviser. Once, after a conference with Washington, Roosevelt invited the black leader to lunch with him at the White House. When the episode became known, a storm of criticism swept the South. Roosevelt did not repeat the invitation.

In general, Roosevelt's neglect of blacks reflected the attitudes and prejudices of most white Americans, including most of the progressives, during these years.

Roosevelt as "trust buster." Under pressure from both reformers and business leaders, the federal government during Roosevelt's administration took steps toward regulating business practices in the interest of the public welfare. Before this time, as you recall, the federal government, with few exceptions, had not become greatly involved in business affairs.

Early in his first term, Roosevelt directed his Attorney General to bring suit under the Sherman Antitrust Act against the Northern Securities Company. This was a holding company that controlled the three leading

SOURCES

THEODORE
ROOSEVELT'S
"NEW
NATIONALISM"
SPEECH
(1910)

Our country—this great republic—means nothing unless it means the triumph of a real democracy, the triumph of popular government, and, in the long run, of an economic system under which each man shall be guaranteed the opportunity to show the best that there is in him. . . .

I stand for the square deal. But when I say that I am for the square deal, I mean not merely that I stand for fair play under the present rules of the game, but that I stand for having those rules changed so as to work for a more substantial equality of opportunity and of reward for equally good service. . . .

Americans had long worried about the influence of trusts, as this 1880's cartoon, "Bosses of the Senate," shows. What symbols does the artist Joseph J. Keppler use to demonstrate how powerful these trusts had become?

railroads serving the country between Lake Michigan and the Pacific Northwest. "We do not wish to destroy corporations," Roosevelt announced, "but we do wish to make them subserve the public good." In 1904 the Supreme Court held that the Northern Securities Company did restrain trade and was illegal under the Sherman Antitrust Act.

Early in 1903, while the Northern Securities Company case was still pending in the courts, Congress passed the Expedition Act to speed up antitrust cases by giving them a priority over the other cases in federal courts. Another measure created the Department of Commerce and Labor, with a Secretary in the President's cabinet. The new department included a Bureau of Corporations authorized to investigate and report on corporate activities.

The election of 1904. Roosevelt's progressive ideas antagonized many Republican politi-

cal leaders. When election year 1904 rolled around, the Republican political leaders would have abandoned him in favor of a more conservative candidate had they dared. However, by this time Teddy Roosevelt enjoyed widespread popularity. No other Republican candidate had a chance of taking the nomination from him.

During the campaign, Roosevelt had announced that he was "unhampered by any pledge, promise, or understanding of any kind, save my promise, made openly to the American people, that so far as my power lies I shall see to it that every man has a square deal, no less and no more." This promise carried weight because Roosevelt had convinced voters that he meant what he said.

Roosevelt went on to win a resounding victory at the polls—336 electoral votes to 140 for his Democratic opponent, Judge Alton B. Parker of New York.

Renewed efforts at regulation. After 1904, encouraged by the Supreme Court decision in the Northern Securities Company case and by his reelection, Roosevelt started action against a number of other trusts. Altogether, 44 suits against trusts were started during his administration.

Even when the Supreme Court ordered a trust to dissolve, the business executives who had controlled the various corporations in the trust often continued to meet informally and share in the decisions of the separate corporations. By secret arrangements of this kind—often called "communities of interest"—the corporations continued to do informally what they had previously done as a trust. The advantages of large-scale operations for consumers and sometimes for the corporations were very great. Moreover, big business was so tied together that any attempt to break up a monopoly was like trying to unscramble the eggs in an omelet. The trend of the times was toward larger and larger business combinations. Neither Roosevelt nor anyone else could reverse this trend.

"Good" and "bad" combinations. Before leaving office in 1909, Roosevelt concluded that the problem of trusts was not simply one of size. What really mattered was whether a business combination, regardless of size, was "good" or "bad" for the public as a whole. He asked Congress to pass laws defining "good" and "bad" practices, but Congress refused.

In 1911, two years after Roosevelt left office, the Supreme Court adopted his point of view. The Court ruled that the Sherman Antitrust Act's prohibition of "all combinations in restraint of trade" should mean "all *unreasonable* combinations." The Supreme Court from then on decided whether a large business combination was "reasonable" or "unreasonable" by looking not merely at its size but also at its effect upon the public.

Important railroad legislation. The Roosevelt administration had more success in regulating railroads than in breaking up trusts. On the President's recommendations, Congress adopted two laws that put teeth into the Interstate Commerce Act of 1887 and strengthened the Interstate Commerce Commission.

The Elkins Act of 1903 made it illegal for a shipper to accept a rebate, just as the Interstate Commerce Act had made it illegal for

Cartoonist Clifford Berryman pokes fun at the idea of "good" and "bad" trusts. Bear-hunter "Teddy" has slain the "bad trusts." How does the cartoonist picture him dealing with the "good" ones?

railroads to give one. Many railroads approved of this act, for it freed them from giving special privileges to large shippers.

The Hepburn Act of 1906 gave the Interstate Commerce Commission authority (1) to regulate express and sleeping-car companies, oil pipelines, bridges, railroad terminals, and ferries doing business across state lines; (2) to fix "just and reasonable" rates, subject to approval by the federal courts; (3) to restrict the granting of free passes; and (4) to require that railroads use uniform methods of accounting.

Laws protecting public health. President Roosevelt also gave leadership to a movement to protect public health.

Government chemists had long known that the products of some distilleries, drug companies, and meat-packing plants were endangering public health. Patent medicines often contained harmful habit-forming drugs or ingredients that could not possibly relieve any

517

ailments. Many canned foods were spoiled or were treated with poisonous preservatives. As Upton Sinclair had pointed out in his book *The Jungle,* meats in the packing houses were often from diseased animals.

Against the powerful opposition of the meat-packing interests, Roosevelt and the progressives in Congress secured passage in 1906 of the Meat Inspection Act. The act required government approval of all meat shipped from one state to another. Also under pressure from reform groups, including a women's letter-writing campaign, Congress passed the Pure Food and Drug Act of 1906. The act forbade the manufacture, sale, or transportation of impure food and patent medicines containing harmful ingredients. It also required patent-medicine containers to carry labels listing their exact contents. Five years later, in 1911, Congress supplemented this law by making it illegal to use false or misleading labels.

These acts helped to strengthen the developing theory that the federal government was responsible for protecting the public welfare.

SECTION SURVEY

IDENTIFY: Danbury Hatters' case, Northern Securities Company case, Department of Commerce and Labor, "Square Deal," Elkins Act of 1903, Hepburn Act of 1906, Pure Food and Drug Act of 1906.

1. (a) Why was organized labor pleased with Roosevelt's handling of the 1902 coal strike? (b) Was this a clear-cut victory for labor? Explain.
2. How did Roosevelt's attitude toward black Americans reflect the attitudes and prejudices of most white Americans of the time?
3. Roosevelt claimed to be a "trust buster." Do the facts support his claim? Why or why not?

4 Roosevelt acts to conserve America's natural resources

"The first work I took up when I became President," Roosevelt wrote in his *Autobiography,* "was the work of reclamation." This job of reclaiming and conserving the nation's natural resources proved to be one of his greatest contributions.

Wasted natural resources. Before Theodore Roosevelt became President, almost nothing had been done to safeguard the nation's resources. Indeed, Americans had always used their natural resources without regard for the future. Pioneer farmers had cut and burned their way westward, transforming forest land into farm land. The federal and state governments had carelessly encouraged waste, especially during the latter half of the 1800's. They handed over to private individuals and to corporations priceless natural resources—agricultural and grazing lands, forest regions, mineral deposits, oil fields, and water-power sites.

By 1900 only 200 million acres (81 million hectares) of the nation's original 800 million acres (324 million hectares) of virgin forest were still standing. Four fifths of this timber was privately owned. The executives who ran the nation's corporations cared no more about waste than the pioneer settlers had. Lumber companies destroyed forests without regard for wildlife, flood control, fire protection, replanting, or the preservation of young trees. Cattle raisers and sheepherders overgrazed semiarid lands, stripping them of their protective covering of grass. Often they helped turn these lands into dust bowls.

Coal companies worked only the richest and most accessible veins, leaving the bulk of the coal buried in abandoned mines. Oil companies allowed natural gas to escape unused into the air. The growing cities polluted rivers and streams with sewage and industrial wastes, destroying fish and creating a menace to public health. The American people were simply unused to thinking that their natural resources were exhaustible.

Early conservation efforts. By the late 1800's, a rapidly growing population was making heavier and heavier demands upon the nation's resources. The growing industries were devouring raw materials in ever larger quantities. A few thoughtful Americans realized that the nation's resources could not last forever.

As early as 1873, the American Association for the Advancement of Science had demanded some action to prevent the waste of natural resources. Because of these efforts and the efforts of other farsighted people, Congress in 1887 established the Forest Bureau in the Department of Agriculture. In 1891 Congress authorized the President to withdraw timberlands from public sale. Acting under this law, President Harrison set aside a national forest reserve of 17 million acres (7 million hectares), and Presidents Cleveland and McKinley more than doubled this area.

A small beginning toward the conservation of natural resources had been made. However, the public had not yet learned to think of the need for conservation as a serious national problem.

Roosevelt's leadership.   President Roosevelt awakened public interest to the need for conservation, aroused Congress to action, and managed to get the federal and state governments to adopt new policies. In 1901 he warned Americans that "the forest and water problems are perhaps the most vital internal problems of the United States." In a special message to Congress, he reminded the legislators that "the mineral wealth of this country, the coal, iron, oil, gas, and the like, does not reproduce itself. . . . If we waste our resources today," he went on to say "our descendants will feel that exhaustion a generation or two before they otherwise would."

Roosevelt was never content with mere talk. During his administration he withdrew from public sale 150 million acres (60.7 million hectares) of forest land—an area much larger than France. He also withdrew millions of acres of coal and phosphate lands and potential water-power sites. In response to his urging, Congress created wildlife sanctuaries and national parks. In these activities, Roosevelt met opposition from private interests.

The Newlands Reclamation Act.   One of the most important acts of his administration, however, received considerable support, especially from western members of Congress. Early in his Presidency, Roosevelt supported the Newlands Reclamation Act. This act provided that money from the sale of public lands in 16 western states and territories was to be used to build irrigation projects that would reclaim wasteland—that is, make it suitable for farming. Money from the sale of water to the farmers who settled on the reclaimed land was to go into a fund used to finance other irrigation projects.

Reclamation work started at once. Within four years 28 different irrigation projects were under way. By 1911 the Shoshone (shoh·SHOH·nee) Dam in Wyoming and the Roosevelt Dam in Arizona were in operation. Water from the enormous reservoir created by the Roosevelt Dam flowed through irrigation canals and ditches to transform 200,000 acres (80,940 hectares) of desert into rich farmland. As other projects were completed, additional thousands of acres of wasteland were brought under cultivation.

Paintings like Thomas Moran's "The Grand Canyon of the Yellowstone" helped acquaint Americans with the land's beauty and the need for national parks. Congress established Yellowstone National Park in 1872.

In 1903 Theodore Roosevelt (third from left) spent several days at Yosemite Park in California discussing conservation with the great naturalist John Muir (far right) and other concerned men of the day.

The White House Conference. In 1907 Roosevelt created the Inland Waterways Commission. After studying nearly every aspect of the conservation program, the commission urged the President to hold a national conference to publicize the need for conservation.

This meeting, the White House Conservation Conference of 1908, was a great success. One result was the appointment of a 50-member National Conservation Commission made up of nearly equal numbers of scientists, business executives, and political leaders. This commission went to work at once on a study of the country's mineral, water, forest, and soil resources. Another important outgrowth of the White House Conference was the appointment of state conservation agencies in 41 of the states by governors who were convinced of the need for them.

Thus Theodore Roosevelt helped to arouse public opinion to the need for conservation. Equally important, he established the foundations of a solid conservation program that would have far-reaching effects.

IDENTIFY: conservation, reclamation, natural resources.

1. What actions did Theodore Roosevelt take to arouse the nation to the need for conservation?
2. What was the significance of the Newlands Reclamation Act of 1902?
3. Why did some people oppose the idea of conserving natural resources?
4. In what ways did Roosevelt establish the foundations of a solid conservation program?

5 The progressive movement gains and loses under Taft

Despite a financial panic and depression in 1907, President Roosevelt's popularity with the public was at its peak in 1908. It was clear that the Republican nomination for another term was his for the asking, but Roosevelt stood by an earlier announcement that he would not run again.

The election of 1908. At the Republican convention in Chicago, Roosevelt supported his close friend and associate William Howard Taft of Ohio, who won the nomination on the first ballot. The Republican platform called for strengthening the Interstate Commerce Act of 1887 and the Sherman Antitrust Act of 1890, for conserving the nation's resources, developing an improved highway system, and revising the tariff.

The Democrats again chose William Jennings Bryan as their Presidential candidate. The Democratic platform condemned the Republican Party as the party of "privileges and private monopolies." It called for a lower tariff, new antitrust laws, a federal income tax, and restrictions on the use of court injunctions in labor disputes.

One unusual feature of the election campaign was the action taken by the American Federation of Labor. In 1908 the A. F. of L. abandoned its traditional policy of supporting friends of organized labor in both political parties and came out for Bryan and the entire Democratic ticket.

Despite the support of organized labor, the Democrats lost by a considerable margin, with Taft receiving 321 electoral votes to Bryan's

162. The Republicans also retained control of both houses of Congress.

Reforms under Taft. William Howard Taft, a Cincinnati lawyer and judge, had served the Roosevelt administration in the Philippines and in the War Department. Taft was a cautious man. His training as a lawyer and his temperament led him to stress the legalistic restrictions on his Presidential power. As one commentator put it, the change from Roosevelt to Taft was like changing from an automobile to a horse-drawn carriage. Despite his conservative nature, however, Taft recognized the force of the progressive movement and supported a number of important reforms.

Taft's administration chalked up an impressive list of accomplishments that progressives had favored. Taft's Attorney General started 90 antitrust suits against big corporations compared with 44 suits started under President Roosevelt. Following Taft's recommendation, Congress strengthened the Interstate Commerce Act by passing the Mann-Elkins Act of 1910. This new legislation placed telephone, telegraph, cable, and wireless companies under the jurisdiction of the Interstate Commerce Commission. Congress also created a new department with cabinet rank—the Department of Labor. In response to the growing attack upon the use of child labor, Congress established a Children's Bureau in the Department of Labor. It also established an 8-hour day for all workers on projects contracted for by the federal government.

The Taft administration also took steps to create a healthier political climate. President Taft himself added a considerable number of federal jobs to the civil service list. Congress adopted the Publicity Act requiring political parties to make public sources and sums of money spent in political campaigns.

Taft's administration was partly responsible for the adoption of a constitutional amendment to make possible a federal income tax. The Sixteenth Amendment, which had been proposed in 1909, was ratified in 1913.

Progressive opposition. In spite of these reforms, President Taft began to lose the support of the progressives in the Republican Party. As a result, he relied more and more on conservatives in the party.

The split between President Taft and the progressives appeared as early as April 1909, when Congress adopted the Payne-Aldrich Tariff. The progressives had worked for lower tariff rates, and at first Taft had supported their position. Then he switched to the high-tariff point of view and swung his influence behind the Payne-Aldrich measure. In the new act, some reductions were in fact made, but rates on many thousands of items were actually increased.

In the midst of the tariff battle, Taft was also violently attacked for his stand on conservation. Indeed, some of his most bitter critics charged that he had undermined Roosevelt's conservation program. Although this was an unfair charge, it is true that the conservation movement suffered a setback during the opening months of Taft's administration.

Taft's Secretary of the Interior, Richard A. Ballinger, was a cautious lawyer. Ballinger concluded that the President's authority to withdraw land from sale extended only to timber land. He therefore restored to public sale valuable water-power sites that President Roosevelt had previously withdrawn. Gifford Pinchot, head of the Forest Service under both Roosevelt and Taft, promptly protested. Taft sided with Pinchot, and the lands in question were returned to the forest reserve. However, Pinchot, an ardent conservationist, was convinced that Ballinger favored private interests and was opposed to the conservation program.

Pinchot's fears were strengthened when Ballinger allowed extensive coal lands and timberland in Alaska to pass into private hands. This action aroused a storm of controversy throughout the country. In the midst of the storm, Taft removed Pinchot from office.

Although Ballinger resigned in 1911 and the new Secretary of the Interior restored the Alaskan lands to the federal forest reserve, the damage had been done. Taft's stand on the Ballinger controversy cost the Republicans many votes in the Congressional elections of 1910. For the first time in 16 years, the Republicans lost control of the House of Representatives.

Actually, Taft did a great deal to advance the conservation program. With authorization from Congress, he withdrew almost 59 million acres (24 million hectares) of coal lands from public sale. He also signed the Appalachian Forest Reserve Act, which added large tracts of land in the southern Appalachians and in the White Mountains of New Hampshire to the federal reserves.

Roosevelt's spirited campaign captured the imaginations of cartoonists as far away as Germany. "I'm feeling like a bull moose," Roosevelt told a reporter, and thus was he depicted.

A victory for progressives. Early in 1910 the progressives of the Republican Party launched an attack upon the Speaker of the House. Since 1903 Speaker Joseph "Uncle Joe" Cannon of Illinois had been one of the most powerful officers in the government. As Speaker, he appointed all House committees and selected their leaders. He appointed himself head of the powerful Committee on Rules, which determined the order of business in the House. In this capacity, he could prevent any bill to which he objected from reaching the floor of the House for debate. Moreover, as presiding officer of the House he could determine who should speak during debate by recognizing or refusing to recognize anyone he pleased. As a result of these powers, "Uncle Joe" ruled the House with an iron hand.

The progressives charged that Cannon, a conservative, had used his great power to block progressive legislation. They planned to put an end to Cannon's control. In March 1910 Representative George W. Norris of Nebraska proposed an amendment to the House rules. He moved that in the future the Committee on Rules be elected by the members of the House and that the Speaker be excluded from membership on the Rules Committee.

Speaker Cannon, with solid support from the conservatives, fought desperately to maintain his power. After heated debate, about 40 progressive Republicans voted with the Democrats in favor of Norris's motion and stripped the Speaker of his traditional powers over the Committee on Rules. A year later the House deprived the Speaker of the power to appoint members of the remaining committees. The Speaker remained an extremely influential figure, but the Speaker's power was diminished.

Split in the Republican Party. By 1912 the Republican Party was split wide open, with the "old guard" on one side and the progressives on the other. Theodore Roosevelt, by now dissatisfied with Taft's leadership, decided to run again for the Presidency. To do so, Roosevelt had to brush aside the obvious candidate of the progressive forces, Robert M. La Follette of Wisconsin. Roosevelt also had to line up enough delegates to the nominating convention to insure his own nomination.

President Taft held the advantage that a President always has at a political convention. The Roosevelt supporters claimed that many of their delegates to the convention were refused seats by the Taft forces. Not surprisingly, the convention named Taft as its candidate. Angered by this, Roosevelt's supporters called another convention, which nominated him for the Presidency. Thus a new third party was launched—the Progressive Party, sometimes called the "Bull Moose" Party.°

The Bull-Moose Republicans with Teddy Roosevelt at their head adopted a platform calling for numerous reforms. The platform favored legislation in the interest of labor and advocated tariff reform. It endorsed the initiative, referendum, and recall, and it declared that it stood for government control over unfair business practices. In a spirited campaign, Roosevelt popularized his "New Nationalism" program. "New Nationalism," to Roosevelt, meant extending the powers of the federal government to make it an effective instrument in the battle for progressive measures and social reform.

°The party adopted as its emblem the powerful bull moose as a tribute to Roosevelt, who often used the term to describe a person's strength and vigor.

Wilson as the Democratic candidate. The Democrats were confident that the split in the Republican Party would insure their own victory. Their platform called for tariff reduction, banking reform, laws favoring workers and farmers, and the enforcement of stronger antitrust laws. As their candidate they chose Governor Woodrow Wilson of New Jersey.

Wilson, the son of a Presbyterian minister, had been president of Princeton University before he became governor of New Jersey in 1910. As governor, he fought the political machine bosses of his party, showing remarkable independence. He also took the lead in pushing through the legislature laws designed to reform the weak corporation laws of the state. As he showed more and more interest in other progressive measures, Wilson became the logical choice of the progressives in the Democratic Party.

An idealist and a man of convictions, Wilson was determined, courageous, and independent. He sensed the popular discontent in the country. His neatly turned phrases about establishing a "New Freedom" for ordinary Americans greatly appealed to those who were convinced that special privilege menaced the welfare of the nation.

The election of 1912. Still another party was involved in the election of 1912. The Social Democratic Party or Socialist Party had been organized in 1901. It had shown increasing strength in cities. In 1912, for example, 79 Socialist mayors were elected in 24 states. The Socialist Party candidate for President in 1912 was Eugene V. Debs.

The election proved to be a clear-cut victory for the progressives, a defeat for the conservatives. Wilson received 435 electoral votes and Roosevelt 88, whereas Taft received only 8.

Debs won no electoral votes but received almost a million popular votes.

Despite his overwhelming electoral vote, Wilson was a "minority" President. He received only 6 million popular votes out of a total of more than 15 million. Nevertheless, he could count upon widespread public support for his progressive "New Freedom" program.

SECTION SURVEY

IDENTIFY: Mann-Elkins Act of 1910, Publicity Act, Sixteenth Amendment, Gifford Pinchot, Joseph Cannon, "New Nationalism."

1. (a) Why did Taft's opponents consider him to be against conservation? (b) Do the facts support this charge against him? Explain.
2. (a) What were the reasons for the revolt against "Uncle Joe" Cannon? (b) What were the results?
3. Why did Roosevelt form the Bull Moose Party?
4. Chart Study: Make a chart comparing the parties, candidates, platforms, and results of the elections of 1908 and 1912.

6 Wilson's "New Freedom" expands opportunities for Americans

With his "New Freedom" program, President Wilson hoped to restore the equality of opportunity that many Americans enjoyed when the frontier was still open to settlers. He believed that this equality had been largely destroyed by the closing of the frontier, by great corporations, and by the often corrupt alliance of government and business.

SOURCES

WILSON'S "NEW FREEDOM" SPEECH (1912)

I take my stand absolutely, where every progressive ought to take his stand, on the proposition that private monopoly is indefensible and intolerable. And there I will fight my battle.

. . . I am for big business, and I am against trusts. Any man who can survive by his brains, any man who can put the others out of the business by making the thing cheaper to the consumer at the same time that he is increasing its intrinsic value and quality, I take off my hat to, and I say: "You are the man who can build up the United States, and I wish there were more of you." . . .

President Wilson at once recommended to Congress a positive program to promote the public welfare. Opposed by pressure groups and lobbies representing special business interests, Wilson used all his skills as a speaker to win popular support for his program.

Tariff reform. Like most Democrats, Wilson believed that high protective tariffs benefited the trusts by excluding from the country products that foreign manufacturers could make and market more cheaply. It was also true, of course, that tariffs protected jobs and helped workers maintain higher wages than foreign workers received.

To check the trend toward monopoly and reduce the cost of living, the Wilson administration pushed through Congress the Underwood Tariff Act of 1913. This act did not establish **free trade,**° but it reduced tariffs more than any tariff act had in the previous 50 years. It lowered duties on almost a thousand items, including cotton and woolen goods, iron, steel, coal, wood, agricultural tools, and many agricultural products. The average of all duties was reduced from 41 to 29 percent. The Underwood Tariff Act also included a section providing for an income tax. The new law provided for a graduated tax ranging from 1 to 6 percent on incomes over $3,000 per year.

The Underwood Tariff was passed against strong opposition, but it did answer the widespread cry for tariff reform. Moreover, its income tax provision laid down the principle that those with more income had to bear a heavier share of the expenses of government. This rule is sometimes called the "ability-to-pay" principle of taxation.

°**free trade:** the exchange of goods between countries unhampered by regulations or protective tariffs aimed to keep out foreign goods.

The Federal Reserve System. The second important achievement of Wilson's "New Freedom" program was in the field of money and banking. Almost everyone was dissatisfied with the existing banking system, but people disagreed on how to reform it.

In general, the more conservative business groups wanted greater private control over the existing banking system. They argued that this control would enable the stronger banks to help the less-favored banks in times of financial crisis.

On the other side were the Bryan Democrats and the progressive Republicans. They believed that the existing banking system was already dominated by the "money trust"—the great private investment banking firms like J. Pierpont Morgan and Company, which often controlled big business consolidations. The reformers wanted the government, not private bankers, to control the banking system. This control, they argued, would enable the government to regulate the amount of currency in circulation and thus help to stabilize prices.

The Federal Reserve Act of 1913 was a compromise between these two sides. It provided for the establishment of 12 Federal Reserve districts, each with a Federal Reserve Bank. The operations of these district banks were to be supervised and coordinated by a Federal Reserve Board in Washington, D.C. All national banks were to be members of a Federal Reserve Bank. All state banks that met certain requirements were invited to join.

The Federal Reserve Banks were strictly "bankers' banks." They provided services only for member banks, not for business concerns or private citizens. In times of crisis, when weak banks were on the point of failing, the Federal Reserve Banks could transfer money reserves and thus help prevent failure and the loss of people's savings.

SOURCES

WILSON ON AMERICAN IDEALS (1914)

My dream is that, as the years go on and the world knows more and more of America, it will also drink at these fountains of youth and renewal; that it also will turn to America for those moral inspirations which lie at the basis of all freedom; that the world will never fear America, unless it feels that it is engaged in some enterprise which is inconsistent with the rights of humanity; and that America will come into the full light of the day when all shall know that she puts human rights above all other rights and that her flag is the flag not only of America, but of humanity.

The Federal Reserve System also made it possible to put more money into circulation or to withdraw some from circulation according to the needs of the time. It thus provided a more elastic currency by controlling the amount of lending that member banks could do.

Antitrust laws strengthened. The third major achievement of Wilson's "New Freedom" program was its effort to strengthen the antitrust laws. The Clayton Antitrust Act of 1914 helped to put teeth in the older Sherman Antitrust Act.

The Clayton Act was aimed at business practices that until then had not been illegal. (1) It prohibited business organizations from selling at lower prices to certain favored purchasers *if* such price discrimination helped to create a monopoly. (2) It prohibited "tying contracts" — that is, contracts requiring a purchaser to agree not to buy or sell the products of a competitor. (3) It declared interlocking directorates illegal in companies with capital investments of $1 million or more. (4) It prohibited corporations from acquiring the stock of another company *if* the purchase tended to create a monopoly.

The Clayton Act also attempted to protect farmers and wage earners. The Sherman Antitrust Act of 1890 had been used on a number of occasions against labor unions. The Clayton Act, on the other hand, declared that labor unions and farm organizations had a legal right to exist. It said that they could not "be held or construed to be illegal combinations or conspiracies in restraint of trade, under the antitrust laws."

The Clayton Act also prohibited the granting of an injunction in a labor dispute *unless* the court decided that an injunction was necessary "to prevent irreparable injury to property." This act also declared that strikes, peaceful picketing, and boycotts were legal under federal jurisdiction.

Organized labor hailed the Clayton Act as a great victory. However, as you will read, the courts interpreted the act in such a way that the injunction continued to be used as a weapon against strikes.

The Federal Trade Commission. The Federal Trade Commission, created by Congress in 1914, was also part of President Wilson's "New Freedom" program. The commission was authorized to advise and regulate industries

Woodrow Wilson, shown here on a 1912 election campaign poster, believed that the duty of Progressivism was, "to cleanse, to reconsider, to restore . . . every process of our common life."

engaged in interstate and foreign trade. The commission was to be a bipartisan body of five members.

The commission was authorized to (1) require annual and special reports from corporations, (2) investigate the business activities of persons and most corporations, (3) publish reports on its findings, and (4) order corporations to stop unfair methods of competition. Among the unfair practices investigated by the commission were mislabeling, adulteration of products, and false claims to patents. If a corporation refused to obey an order to "cease and desist" from such practices, the commission could ask the courts to enforce its ruling. The law protected the corporation by providing that it could appeal to the courts if it considered the "cease-and-desist" order to be unfair.

The Federal Trade Commission was intended to prevent the growth of monopolies and to help bring about a better understanding between big business and the government.

Other "New Freedom" measures. The tariff, money and banking, regulation of trusts — these were the major problems tackled by Congress during Wilson's first administration. Much more reform legislation might have been adopted if the outbreak of World War I in

525

Europe in the summer of 1914 had not interfered. Even so, Congress found time to pass several other important measures.

In 1914 Congress adopted the Smith-Lever Act. Among other things, the act provided federal funds for rural education. The educational programs were to be carried on by the Department of Agriculture in cooperation with the land-grant colleges. Federal grants of money were to be matched by similar grants from the states receiving this aid. Three years later, in 1917, just before the United States entered World War I, Congress adopted the Smith-Hughes Act. This additional measure provided federal funds for vocational education in both rural and urban areas of the country.

The Federal Farm Loan Act of 1916 made it easier for farmers to borrow money. This act divided the country into 12 agricultural districts. It established a Farm Loan Bank for each district where farmers could get mortgages at rates lower than those available at regular banks.

Blacks and the "New Freedom". During the election campaign of 1912, Woodrow Wilson promised an officer of the National Association for the Advancement of Colored People (NAACP) that if elected he would promote the interests of black Americans in every way possible. Such was not the case, however. As President, Wilson seemed to agree with most white Americans that segregation was in the best interests of black as well as white Americans.

During Wilson's administration, white employees and black employees in government offices in Washington, D.C., were segregated. Many black office workers were dismissed in southern cities. A black journalist bitterly remarked that Wilson had given black Americans no part in the "New Freedom."

The election of 1916. By 1916 President Wilson had established himself as a vigorous leader. The delegates to the Democratic convention pointed with pride to his solid list of achievements and enthusiastically renominated him for a second term.

The Republicans chose Supreme Court Justice Charles Evans Hughes, former governor of New York, as their candidate. The Progressive Party nominated Theodore Roosevelt. However, Roosevelt was unwilling to split the Republican vote again, refused the nomination, and supported Hughes. The Progressive Party,

deprived of Roosevelt, decided not to nominate another candidate. As a result the Republicans, once more united, entered the campaign hopeful of victory.

The campaign of 1916 centered not only upon Wilson's record of domestic issues but also upon America's relation to the war that had broken out in Europe in 1914. Hughes toured the country, criticizing the Democrats for the Underwood Tariff and for their handling of foreign affairs. Wilson, on the other hand, contented himself with delivering speeches from the front porch of his summer home in New Jersey. Speakers for the Democratic Party adopted the slogan "He kept us out of war."

The election itself turned out to be one of the closest in American history. The final electoral vote was 277 for Wilson, 254 for Hughes. California proved to be the decisive state—the Democrats won in California by a margin of only 3,773 popular votes! Despite the closeness of the vote, Wilson had won against a united Republican Party, as had not been true in the election of 1912. Even more reassuring, he had collected nearly 600,000 more popular votes than Hughes.

Woodrow Wilson seemed to feel that his first term in office had accomplished his goals, though many progressives believed much remained to be done. In any event, it was not "New Freedom" measures that occupied the President during his second administration. Within a month of Wilson's second inauguration on March 4, 1917, the United States entered World War I.

SECTION SURVEY

IDENTIFY: "New Freedom," Underwood Tariff, free trade, elastic currency, "ability-to-pay" principle of taxation, Smith-Lever Act, Federal Farm Loan Act.

1. For what reason did Wilson start the "New Freedom" program?

2. (a) Describe the Federal Reserve System. (b) In what ways was it a compromise between the views of the conservatives and those of the progressives?

3. (a) How did the Clayton Antitrust Act of 1914 put teeth in the older Sherman Antitrust Act? (b) Why did organized labor praise the Clayton Act?

4. What was the function of the Federal Trade Commission?

Chapter Survey

Summary: Tracing the Main Ideas

The victory of the Republicans in the election of 1896 broke the strength of the Populist movement. With the triumph of the Republicans and with the return of prosperity, many people concluded that the reform movement had lost its force.

However, the reform movement was not dead. On the contrary, in the early 1900's it gained new life in the progressive movement. Guided by the progressives, including President Theodore Roosevelt, the relationship of government and business began to change. In earlier times, the government's role had been, in general, that of a referee who stood on the sidelines and stepped in only when it seemed that one of the players had disobeyed the rules. Now, in the twentieth century, the government was beginning to take a more active part, to accept more responsibility for regulating the activities of business in the interest of the public welfare. Both Republicans and Democrats were responsible for this changing view of the role of government in the new industrial age.

The reforms started under President Roosevelt were continued by President Taft and, to an even greater degree, during the Democratic administration of President Wilson. As you will read, the efforts were interrupted by the outbreak of World War I in 1914.

Inquiring into History

1. The basic issue with which Presidents Roosevelt, Taft, and Wilson had to deal was the role of government in the new industrial age. Explain.
2. Compare Roosevelt's "Square Deal" and Wilson's "New Freedom" in terms of (a) goals, (b) legislative accomplishments, and (c) long-range effects.
3. Present evidence to support or refute this statement: Despite his apparent weakness, President Taft was actually a more effective progressive President than Roosevelt.
4. To what extent did black Americans benefit from the progressive movement? Explain.
5. Did the ideals of progressivism agree with the ideals expressed in the Declaration of Independence and the preamble to the Constitution? Explain.
6. How might you have voted in the election of 1912 if you had been (a) a farmer, (b) a banker, (c) an Italian immigrant, and (d) a factory worker? Give reasons for your answers.

Relating Past to Present

1. Which critics in our society today might qualify for the title "muckraker"? Why?
2. (a) What are some of the reforms that are currently being proposed by the national government to help remedy problems of our society? (b) How do the problems and proposed solutions compare with those of the progressive era?

3. Pioneers, governments, corporations, and Americans in general have been responsible for the waste of America's natural resources and the pollution of its environment. Comment on this statement. Was it true in the early 1900's? Is it true today?

Developing Social Science Skills

1. Make a chart with these four headings: Social Reforms, Educational Reforms, Political Reforms, Economic Reforms. Fill in the chart by listing in the appropriate columns the reforms brought about during the progressive era (1895–1917). Then answer these questions: (a) Who benefited the most from each reform? (b) Did anyone get hurt by any of the reforms? (c) Which of these reforms do you consider the most important? Why?
2. Select a controversial issue of the progressive years and draw two political cartoons—one presenting each side of the issue. Give each cartoon a title that helps make clear the point of view presented in the cartoon.
3. Americans tend to elect Presidents who reflect the spirit of the times. Gather evidence to support or refute this hypothesis, using Theodore Roosevelt, William Howard Taft, or Woodrow Wilson as an example. Can you think of earlier Presidents who reflected the spirit of their times? Explain. Can this be said of any of our most recent presidents? Explain.

Changing Ways of American Life

1900–1920

Chapter 27

"The Big Change" in American Ways of Life

As the United States approached the middle of the twentieth century, Frederick Lewis Allen wrote a book reviewing and interpreting 50 years of American history. He called this book *The Big Change* and gave it the subtitle *America Transforms Itself, 1900-1950.*

The transformation, as Allen saw it, was "in the character and quality of American life by reason of what might be called the democratization of our economic system, or the adjustment of capitalism to democratic ends." It was, he went on to say, "the way in which an incredible expansion of industrial and business activity, combined with a varied series of political, social, and economic forces, has altered the American standard of living and with it the average American's way of thinking and his status as a citizen."

During the years from 1900 to 1920, the United States was in full process of passing from a predominantly rural economy to a predominantly industrial economy. A growing number of Americans, including business owners and managers, became increasingly aware of the need to modify some of the attitudes and practices carried over from the early days of the Industrial Revolution. In 1920 there were still many large and difficult problems that remained unsolved. But "the big change" was already beginning to have an important influence on the direction of American life.

THE CHAPTER IN OUTLINE

1. New inventions and new ideas revolutionize American industry.

2. The lives of farmers improve in the early 1900's.

3. Conditions improve for industrial workers in the United States.

1 New inventions and new ideas revolutionize American industry

In 1900 America was still in the horse-and-buggy age, but that age would not last much longer. Great changes were already transforming the country, but even greater changes were to come.

Signs of change. In 1900, Americans still rode in horse-drawn streetcars. Hitching posts and watering troughs were common sights. Livery stables and blacksmith shops were centers of activity in every town. When night fell, the lamplighter turned on the gas lamps that still lighted the streets in most American cities and towns.

It is easier, perhaps, to picture the America of 1900 by listing the things that people did not have and did not know. There were no rock groups, no supermarkets, no income taxes. No one had heard of vitamins or antibiotics. Women could vote in only four states—Wyoming, Colorado, Utah, and Idaho. Motion pictures, radios, television, and airplanes did not exist. In those days automobiles were still curiosities, and people often called them "horseless carriages."

Yet, in 1900, Americans had already entered a new way of life. By 1900, railroad builders had laid down 192,566 miles (309,896 kilometers) of track. All the great trunk lines had been built across the continent. Day and night, long lines of freight cars rumbled across the country loaded with products of America's farmland, mines, mills, and factories. New railroad lines were still being built. By 1920 railroad mileage reached its high mark of 260,000 miles (418,500 kilometers) of track.

The horse-and-buggy age was fast drawing to an end when artist William Sonntag painted "The Bowery at Night," a picture of New York City. Soon automobiles would join elevated trains and trolleys in motorizing transportation.

Automobiles and highways. While this network of steel rails expanded, inventors in Europe and America were experimenting with a new source of power. This was the internal combustion engine, in which fuel, usually gasoline, was converted into a vapor and exploded within the engine walls. Among the American experimenters were Charles E. Duryea, George B. Selden, Elwood Haynes, Alexander Winton, and Henry Ford. These inventors and others developed the gasoline engine.

By 1900, "horseless carriages" were appearing on the roads. At first the automobile was an expensive toy for wealthy people. Mass production soon lowered costs, however, bringing the automobile within reach of people with modest incomes. Whereas in 1900 there were only 8,000 automobiles in the United States, by 1920 there were 8 million passenger cars and 1 million trucks.

Development of the automobile depended, of course, upon other inventions and developments. One was the discovery by Charles Goodyear of the process for vulcanizing, or hardening, rubber, for which he obtained his first patent in 1844. Other inventions led to improvements in refining petroleum into gasoline and in developing batteries, generators, and other electrical devices.

The development of the automobile also depended upon — and helped to stimulate — the construction of paved roads. In 1904 nearly all rural roads were little better than dirt lanes, although some were surfaced with gravel, clay, or crushed oyster shells. By 1924, however, 472,000 miles (760,000 kilometers) of rural highways had paved surfaces. By 1924, older roads were being widened, graded, and paved at the rate of about 40,000 miles (64,000 kilometers) a year, at an annual cost of approximately $1 billion.

The airplane. By 1900, Europeans and Americans, among them Samuel P. Langley, were experimenting with another new method of transportation — powered flight. Orville and Wilbur Wright, on December 17, 1903, became the first to put such a machine into the air. Their first flight went only about 120 feet (37 meters) and did not attract much attention. Within a few years, however, the first crude flying machines were being replaced by more effective planes, and air pioneers were making longer and longer flights. In 1919 a Navy seaplane crossed the Atlantic by way of the Azores. That same year two Englishmen, John Alcock and A. W. Brown, flew nonstop from Newfoundland to Ireland.

Developments in communications. Equally revolutionary were developments in communications. People were barely getting used to the idea of the telephone when in 1895, an Italian inventor, Guglielmo (goo·LYEL·moh) Marconi, first demonstrated wireless telegraphy. Eight years later, from a station at Cape Cod, Massachusetts, he transmitted a message across the ocean to England and received a reply.

One of the most significant inventions in the field of communications was the three-element vacuum tube, invented by Lee De Forest in 1906. This invention made it possible to amplify even weak electrical impulses, or signals. Within a few years, wireless equipment had been installed on all large vessels. Wireless messages in the dots and dashes of Morse code were being sent over land and sea by powerful transmitters. Meanwhile, scientists and engineers were experimenting with transmitting the spoken word through the air. However, commercial radio broadcasting did not become a reality until the 1920's.

The motion picture. Several inventors, American, British, and French, contributed to the development of the motion picture. In 1895 two Americans, Thomas Armat and Woodville Latham, successfully used their projector in public showings.

In the early days, films ran only a few minutes. Then, in 1903, a pioneer "picture story" called *The Great Train Robbery* demonstrated the possibilities of the motion picture. Soon directors and producers were proving to ever larger audiences that the motion picture could do a great deal that was impossible on the stage. One early director, D. W. Griffith, won fame in 1914 for his film *The Birth of a Nation.* Night after night people crowded into the early movie theaters to watch such popular stars as Mary Pickford, Douglas Fairbanks, and Charlie Chaplin.

New methods of production. The new world that was coming into being in the early 1900's depended upon new power sources — oil and electricity. Between 1900 and 1920, oil production in the United States jumped from 63 million to about 443 million barrels a year. By 1914 nearly one third of the nation's factory machines were driven by electricity, and the use of electric power was rapidly increasing. High-voltage transmission lines carried the pulsing energy of dynamos—steam-driven or water-driven—to widely scattered cities. Smaller transmission lines carried electricity to towns and villages throughout the country and even to some isolated farms.

Productivity of America's factories was greatly increased not only by new sources of power but also by the **assembly line.** On an assembly line, workers stood at stations beside a slowly moving track, or conveyor belt. At each station, workers added a new part to the product on the track. Finally, a steady succession of finished products came off the end of the assembly line. Improved in the early 1900's by Henry Ford for use in the manufacture of automobiles, the assembly line soon became an essential part of America's developing industrial economy.

Increasing efficiency. The use of **efficiency engineering** also increased the productivity of factories. Frederick W. Taylor was a major contributor to this idea. Taylor wanted greater efficiency from machines and from the workers operating the machines. To get it, he developed "time-and-motion" studies of plant operation. Using a stop watch, Taylor timed the workers operating machines and counted the number of motions each worker made to complete a particular operation. Then he worked out ways to reduce the number of movements of the workers' hands and feet. Sometimes workers were trained to use their hands and feet more effectively. Sometimes the machine was redesigned and its controls placed in more convenient locations.

Taylor's methods made great economies possible in every stage of mass production. Each process in the mechanized industrial plant was simplified and speeded up along the assembly line. Each worker performed a highly specialized task, working with the least possible effort to produce the maximum output. However, some workers complained that such methods made them, more than ever, like parts in a great machine.

The "Ford idea." Henry Ford had made a major contribution to American industry in developing the assembly line. Even more important was his new and revolutionary theory of increasing employee wages.

THE PIERCE-ARROW CAR

Our idea is that the car should go "there and back" in the shortest possible time, with the least trouble to both owner and driver, with the greatest comfort to the owner in transit, at the least expense, weight of car and equipment considered, and without interruption of the trip by reason of or the fault of the car, and that it should do this not only now and then, but always. That is the service that the Pierce-Arrow Car is planned to perform.

The Pierce-Arrow Motor Car Company, Buffalo, N. Y.

The Pierce Arrow was for years the height of luxury in American cars. This advertisement refers to "both owner and driver," letting the reader know that this car demanded a chauffeur.

On January 5, 1914, Ford announced that he was nearly doubling the wages of the workers in his plants. Beginning immediately, he said, his 13,000 employees would receive a minimum wage of $5 for an 8-hour day. This announcement swept almost all other news off the front pages of America's newspapers. The New York *Herald* called it "an epoch in the world's industrial history."

Why was Ford's action considered so important? In taking this step, Ford had recognized an important fact about the American economic system. Rising wages gave American workers greater purchasing power to buy more and more of the products of America's expanding industry.

Ford was both warmly applauded and sharply criticized for his action. However, the criticism did not prevent the "Ford idea" from spreading to other industries. As the years passed, more people came to understand that mass production and mass purchasing power are interdependent. This understanding was an essential part of what Frederick Lewis Allen called "the big change" transforming America in the opening years of the twentieth century.

SECTION SURVEY

IDENTIFY: Charles Goodyear, Samuel Langley, Wright brothers, Guglielmo Marconi, *The Great Train Robbery*, assembly line, Frederick Taylor.

1. How did mass production of the automobile help to transform American life?
2. Why was the three-element vacuum tube an important invention?
3. (a) What is the purpose of efficiency engineering? (b) Give some examples of how it works. (c) What are its advantages? Its disadvantages?
4. (a) What was the "Ford idea"? (b) Why was it important to the American economy?

2 The lives of farmers improve in the early 1900's

By the early 1900's, the farmer had become an important part of the nation's industrial economy. To be sure, on thousands of small farms tucked away in mountain valleys and in other remote areas, farm families lived much as farmers had lived 100 years earlier. These more or less self-sufficient farms were exceptions. Most of the nation's farm produce was raised by farmers who, whether they liked it or not, had in many respects become owners of a business.

Growing demand for farm products. One factor that helped turn farms into businesses was the startling growth of America's city pop-

Even though tractors could outproduce horse-drawn machines, some farmers resisted buying them in the early 1900's. How does this advertisement for a tractor reflect that fact and how does it try to counteract it?

Have you placed a Sentimental Value on your Horses out of proportion to the work they are able to perform?

BAILOR MOTOR CULTIVATORS

ulation. Between 1900 and 1920, the urban population increased by about 24 million. Urban dwellers increased from about 40 percent of the total population to more than 50 percent. The swelling urban population was made up in part of farm youths leaving home to seek their fortunes in the cities. It was made up in much larger part of the more than 14 million immigrants who poured into the United States between 1900 and 1920. Regardless of the source, however, the growing urban population meant more mouths to feed and a growing demand for farm products. The commercial farmers struggled to meet this demand.

Commercial farms. Some farmers specialized in one, two, or three crops, or in raising dairy cattle or other livestock. Such **commercial farmers** needed money, or capital, to buy machinery and to hire labor. They had to keep careful accounts and to pay careful attention to market conditions. They were, in brief, one part of an abstract thing known as the "nation's economy." When the economy prospered, farmers likewise could hope to prosper. When the economy went into a depression, farmers were certain to suffer accordingly.

The rapidly growing demand for farm products enabled farmers to receive higher prices. Between 1900 and 1920, farm prices increased threefold. In the same period, the average value of farmland quadrupled. As prosperity spread, more and more farmers began to buy agricultural machinery.

Farmers had been using labor-saving machinery long before the turn of the century. Not until after 1900, however, did the shift from hand tools to power-driven machines begin to transform the farming industry. According to census records, in 1870 the total value of all farm implements and machinery in the United States amounted to $271 million. By 1900 the figure had risen to $750 million, by 1920 to $3.6 billion. One revealing measure of the machine age was the use of tractors. In 1910 there were only 1,000 tractors on American farms; by 1920 there were 246,000.

Gasoline and electricity revolutionized rural as well as urban life in the early 1900's. Power-driven machinery—pumps, plows, seeders, harvesters, milking machines, trucks, and tractors—eased the farmers' burden of labor, enabling them to produce far more products with much less toil. However, human sweat and muscle were still necessary on the commercial farms. The need for farm laborers to work on the commercial farms was met in part by an increase in immigration from Mexico and the Philippines, and, for a short time, from Japan.

Growth of scientific agriculture. Scientific knowledge as well as power-driven machinery helped to revolutionize farming. Chemists discovered new fertilizers and better methods of cultivation to stop soil exhaustion and replenish worn-out land. Biologists improved the life span and the productivity of livestock, plants, grains, and fruits. Bacteriologists discovered ways to check blights and diseases in both plants and animals. Scientists also developed new grains and fruits resistant to disease and better adapted to varying climatic conditions.

Federal aid to farmers. Much of the new research and experimentation was carried on by the Department of Agriculture and by the land-grant colleges that were created by the Morrill Act of 1862.

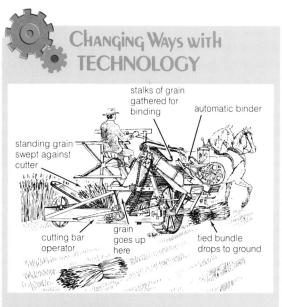

CHANGING WAYS WITH TECHNOLOGY

REAPER-BINDER

The McCormick reaper developed in the 1830's cut the grain stalks and left them to be raked up by hand and tied in bundles. Many improvements led around 1880 to the reaper-binder above, which cut the grain stalks and tied them in bundles automatically.

In later years the federal government greatly expanded this program of aid to farmers. The Hatch Act of 1887, for example, provided money for agricultural experiment stations and farms in each state. The Smith-Lever Act of 1914 provided additional money for the employment of "county extension agents" who carried "practical information on subjects relating to agriculture and home economics" to the farmers of each county. The Smith-Hughes Act of 1917 provided money for the support of vocational education in public schools, including education in agriculture, industries, trade, home economics, and teacher training.

Changing ways of living. The new industrial age altered the everyday lives of farm families, too. By 1920 loneliness and social isolation were becoming memories to many of the nation's farmers. The slender threads of telephone wires were spinning a net of communications across the countryside. The automobile—notably Henry Ford's "Tin Lizzie"—was bringing the farm closer to the town and the city. Once a five-mile (eight-kilometer) drive to town had meant a one- or two-hour trip behind "Old Dobbin." By 1920 the same trip could be made in the family car in half an hour or less. This meant more trips to town, often for an evening at the movies.

With increased prosperity, farm families could provide better education for their children. The one-room school continued to dominate the rural educational scene, but more and more farm children came from miles around to enjoy the advantages of "consolidated schools," which served several towns or school districts. Many children were able to continue their education at the state university. For farm children, no less than for their parents, life "down on the farm" in the early 1900's was far more comfortable and interesting that it had ever been before.

SECTION SURVEY

IDENTIFY: self-sufficient farming, commercial farmers, "consolidated schools."

1. How did each of the following affect and change farm life in the years from 1900 to 1920: (a) urbanization, (b) mechanization, (c) scientific agriculture, (d) federal aid?
2. How did the social life of farm families change as a result of mechanization?
3. Why do you think it was necessary for farmers to receive federal aid during this period?
4. Picture Study: Study the advertisement on page 532. (a) What older product is the advertised product intended to replace? (b) What might be the advantages of this new product over the one it is replacing? (c) How does the ad try to persuade farmers to buy this product? (d) What other changes might the use of this new product bring to the lives of farmers?

3 Conditions improve for industrial workers in the United States

Conditions for the industrial worker as well as for the farmer improved considerably during the early 1900's. First, as you have read, wage earners benefited from the fast-increasing productivity of America's economic system. Second, through organization, wage earners were beginning to exert real influence on state legislatures and on Congress. Third, many Americans were beginning to realize that industrialization had raised serious problems that had to be solved if democracy itself was to survive. Fourth, through articles in popular magazines and in the daily newspapers, the general public was becoming increasingly aware of the wage earners' grievances.

Early social legislation. To improve the conditions of wage earners, legislators began to pass **social legislation,** as these laws were often referred to. These laws mainly were passed by the northern and western states. The South, with its newer industrial development, did little during this period to promote the welfare of workers through state laws.

In general, the first state laws improved working conditions and limited hours of work. As early as 1879, a Massachusetts law prohibited women and children from working more than 60 hours a week. Oregon enacted a similar law in 1903, and other states followed suit. Meanwhile, New York State passed a series of laws protecting workers as well as consumers.

The recognition that certain types of work involved special risk led Utah in 1896 to pass a law limiting the workday of miners to eight hours. In 1902 Maryland passed the first law to compensate workers for on-the-job accidents.

Working conditions like this in a Louisiana oyster-shucking plant were not uncommon in the early 1900's. Photos exposing the plight of child laborers did much to stir public sympathy and get protective laws passed.

This law was declared unconstitutional, but New York passed a successful compensation law in 1910, as did Wisconsin in 1911.

In 1912 Massachusetts set a precedent by passing the first minimum-wage law. The Massachusetts law established a minimum-wage rate—employers could not ask a wage earner to work below this rate.

Supreme Court objections. These early laws represented a new approach to the problems of wage earners in the emerging industrial society. Much of this early social legislation was declared unconstitutional by the Supreme Court. The Court ruled that limiting owners' control over their businesses deprived the owners of part of their property without the "due process of law" guaranteed in the Fifth and Fourteenth Amendments.

The Supreme Court also held that social legislation violated people's rights to enter into any contract they wished. According to the Court, when workers accepted employment and an employer agreed to pay them, a contract had been made even though the terms were not written down. Following this freedom-of-contract line of reasoning, the Supreme Court declared unconstitutional in 1905 a New York law that had fixed a maximum workday of 10 hours for bakers.

Changing Court attitudes. Many people argued that it was unrealistic to assume that the individual worker could actually bargain with a corporation that employed thousands of people. They insisted that in reality the Supreme Court was depriving all workers of freedom to bargain with their employers.

Supreme Court justices gradually changed their attitude toward social legislation. Like other citizens, they were influenced by the progressive temper of the times. The justices found other clauses in the Constitution that enabled states to limit people's right to do as they pleased with their property. The Court increasingly held that the Constitution had reserved to each state the power to enact laws necessary to protect the health and well-being of all of its citizens. On these grounds the Supreme Court upheld an Oregon law that provided a 10-hour day for women. This set a precedent for the Court's approval of other social legislation.

Federal labor laws. The states rather than the federal government enacted most of the early social legislation. However, the state laws were ignored, and certain states, especially in the South, lagged behind others. This situation prompted organized labor to seek relief through federal laws.

535

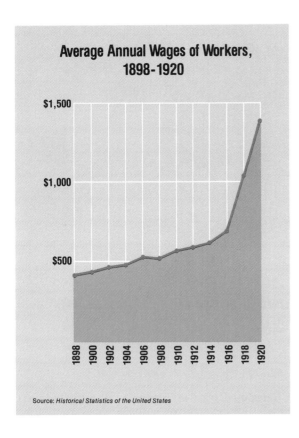

Average Annual Wages of Workers, 1898-1920

$1,500

$1,000

$500

1898 1900 1902 1904 1906 1908 1910 1912 1914 1916 1918 1920

Source: *Historical Statistics of the United States*

Except for its constitutional power "to promote the general welfare" and "to regulate interstate commerce," the federal government had little power to control labor relations. To be sure, the federal government did have the power to control working conditions for its own employees. In 1868, you recall, Congress established an 8-hour day for laborers and mechanics employed by or on behalf of the United States government. In 1892 all federal-government employees were given an 8-hour day.

Later, in 1906, acting under its power "to regulate interstate commerce," Congress passed an Employers' Liability Act. This act protected railroad workers from bearing all the costs of accidents that occurred on the job. Although this law was ruled unconstitutional, later legislation met the Court's objections.

In 1916, when the railroad workers' unions threatened to strike for an 8-hour day, Congress passed the Adamson Act. This act gave railroad workers the same pay for an 8-hour day that they had been getting for a 10-hour day.

During President Wilson's administration, Congress also granted labor's request that it be exempt from the charge of conspiring "to restrain trade." As you have read, the Clayton Antitrust Act of 1914 helped to modify some of the clauses in the Sherman Antitrust Act of 1890 to which labor had objected.

The IWW. Despite the progress in social legislation, many workers still felt the need to organize to win better working conditions. One union that appeared in the early 1900's was the Industrial Workers of the World (IWW). The IWW was set up as a radical union of skilled and unskilled workers. It demanded the overthrow of the capitalist system by general strikes, boycotts, and sabotage.

The IWW, or "Wobblies" as they were known, won some strikes in western mining and labor camps and in the textile mills of Lawrence, Massachusetts. It lost a textile strike in Paterson, New Jersey. Weakened in the years after by its reputation for violence and by federal prosecution, the IWW after 1918 ceased to be a challenge to more conservative trade unions.

Advances for organized labor. By the time World War I broke out in Europe in 1914, labor still had many grievances, and it was still far from its goals. Trade-union activities and political methods for achieving the goals had met only partial success. Nevertheless, organized labor could look back upon a number of reforms gained through 50 years of struggle. Perhaps most important, organized labor enjoyed a small but growing measure of public support.

SECTION SURVEY

IDENTIFY: social legislation, minimum wage, freedom of contract, Employers' Liability Act, IWW.

1. (a) Describe the various kinds of social legislation passed by the states to aid workers. (b) On what grounds did the Supreme Court declare this early social legislation unconstitutional?

2. (a) Why was it that for many years the federal government did not enact social legislation? (b) Why did it later begin to do so?

3. (a) Why did the IWW become less important after 1918? (b) What did its decline mean for the labor movement?

4. Graph Study: Look at the graph on page 536. Does the evidence it gives indicate that conditions for workers were getting better or worse in the early 1900's? Explain.

Chapter Survey

Summary: Tracing the Main Ideas

During the years between 1900 and 1920, the United States completed the process of passing from a mainly agricultural economy to a mainly industrial economy. By 1920 the United States had become the most productive industrial nation on the face of the earth.

In 1900, Americans were still living in the horse-and-buggy age. It was, however, a dying age. Old ways were rapidly giving way to new. People living during the years between 1900 and 1920 saw the emergence of automobiles, airplanes, radios, motion pictures, assembly lines. These and many other developments greatly transformed the ways Americans were living.

The nation's rapidly increasing productivity and its steadily rising standard of living were only the most obvious signs of the new America. Less obvious, but equally important, were the changes that were beginning to take place in the thinking of great numbers of Americans.

More and more people were altering some of the attitudes and practices that they had carried over from the early days of the Industrial Revolution. More and more people were realizing that organized labor had an important role to play in the new industrial economy. Slowly but surely, Americans were taking the first halting steps toward what Frederick Lewis Allen called "the adujstment of capitalism to democratic ends."

In 1920 the American people still had a long, hard road to travel. Although they had no way of knowing it, the road along which they were moving would bring them by mid-century to the highest standard of living the world had ever seen.

Inquiring into History

1. Did industrialization strengthen the belief that America was the land of opportunity? Explain your answer.
2. In what ways did the revolution in communication help initiate reform movements and contribute to the growth of political democracy?
3. By having a national, rather than a local, transportation system, farmers had wider markets as well as more competition. How might this have affected their economic freedom?
4. In 1900 the United States was rapidly passing from a rural to an industrial economy. (a) What were some of the important changes taking place as a result of this revolution in American industry? (b) Why might it have been difficult for people to adjust to these changes?

Relating Past to Present

1. Compare the attitude of the federal government today toward social legislation with its attitude during the early 1900's. Give specific examples to support your answer.
2. (a) Which of the developments in transportation and communication that began in the early 1900's are still important in American life today? (b) How have they been improved or modified in more recent years? (c) Has any of them been completely replaced?
3. Are we still making what Frederick Lewis Allen called "the adjustment of capitalism to democratic ends"? Explain.

Developing Social Science Skills

1. Study the charts on pages 842 and 845. (a) What was the total population in 1900? In 1920? (b) Does immigration seem to have been an important cause of this population growth? Refer back to the chapter text. (c) Did most Americans live in urban or in rural areas in 1900? In 1920? (d) What factors may have accounted for the change?
2. The photograph on page 535 provides evidence about the life of some children during the early 1900's. Conduct research on other aspects of youth in America at that time, such as recreation, education, city life, country life, attitudes toward youth, and family life.
3. Study a Sears Roebuck or a Montgomery Ward catalog published around the turn of the century. What evidence do the ads provide about American life of the period? Name some things that have greatly changed since that time. Name some that have remained much the same.

Unit Survey

For Further Inquiry

1. (a) Make a list of characteristics that you think are necessary for a good President. (b) According to your list, which was the best President—Roosevelt, Taft, or Wilson? Support your answer with evidence.

2. Thomas Jefferson and Andrew Jackson both believed with Thoreau that "that government is best which governs least." Do you think this viewpoint became less practical by the 1900's? Explain your answer by referring to specific events.

3. (a) To what extent did the United States become more democratic during the Progressive era? (b) To what extent was it still undemocratic?

4. (a) Why was there a need for conservation of natural resources during the late 1800's and early 1900's? (b) What was done to make people aware of the problem? (c) Why might some people have opposed conservation?

5. How did industrialization affect (a) the make-up and location of America's population, (b) the daily lives of Americans, (c) differences among the regions of the nation?

Projects and Activities

1. Study the timeline here, which names some of the vast changes taking place in the United States during the early 1900's. (a) Which changes might especially affect the lives of women? (b) Which changes would have had an impact on the nation's health? (c) Which changes in these years would tend to make the nation seem smaller?

2. Interview an officer of a local bank to learn about the workings of the Federal Reserve System. Prepare a diagram or chart to illustrate how the system operates.

3. Read an article or book by a muckraker, such as Ida Tarbell's *History of the Standard Oil Company* or Lincoln Steffen's *The Shame of the Cities.* (a) Write a paragraph summarizing the main point of the book or article. (b) What arguments does the author use to prove the main point? (c) Do you find the book or article persuasive? Why or why not?

4. Select an election discussed in Unit 8. Draw a map illustrating the results of the election. (You could use colors or other symbols to represent the states won by each candidate.)

Exploring Your Region

1. At your local library or newspaper office, locate copies of a local newspaper printed in 1900. Compare the prices of food and clothing in the advertisements with current prices. Then consult an almanac to find out the average family income in the United States in 1900 and the average family income today. Was it easier or more difficult to support a family in 1900?

2. Prepare a report on a national park located in your region. (a) Why was it founded? Under what circumstances? (b) How large is it? (c) What are its main features? If possible, include a map and pictures in your report.

Suggested Readings

1. *Up From Slavery,* Booker T. Washington. Autobiography of an ex-slave who became one of the foremost black leaders in America.

2. *The Age of Reform: From Bryan to F.D.R.,* Richard Hofstadter. A classic history of reform.

3. *How the Other Half Lives,* Jacob Riis. Written in 1890, this book is a famous exposé of slum conditions.

4. *The Jungle,* Upton Sinclair. The novel of conditions in the meat-packing industry that had a great impact on President Roosevelt.

5. *The Great American Novel,* Clyde B. Davis. A novel set in the Progressive era.

Unit Nine

Becoming a World Power

1898-1920

1865

U.S. purchases
Alaska

1875

1885

1895

Spanish-American
War

U.S. acquires
overseas lands

Open Door Policy
in effect

1900 — Boxer Rebellion

Filipinos lose war
for independence

1905 — Treaty of Portsmouth

1910

1915

2000

Chapter 28

American Expansion Overseas

1898-1914

From 1823 until the 1890's, Americans devoted most of their energy to the settlement and development of the continental United States. To be sure, Americans traveled to Europe and Europeans traveled to America. There was also vigorous trade between the two continents. However, it was the conquest of the West and, after 1865, the development of industry that occupied the American people.

By the 1890's, however, a revolution was taking place in American opinion. With the Middle West becoming a major industrial area, more Americans became interested in securing overseas markets where they could sell the surplus products of farms and factories. Some Americans even became interested in acquiring or controlling lands beyond the nation's continental boundaries.

In this chapter you will learn how Americans acquired a new interest in world affairs. You will learn, too, how they emerged from a brief war with Spain in 1898 in possession of the Philippine Islands and other islands in the Pacific Ocean. You will learn how this growing Pacific empire created new problems for the United States. You will also discover how it forced America's leaders to develop new policies for dealing with the nations of East Asia.

THE CHAPTER IN OUTLINE

1. American interest in expansion abroad increases.

2. The war with Spain turns the United States into a colonial power.

3. The United States takes over the Philippines, Hawaii, and Samoa.

4. The United States plays a larger role in East Asia.

1 American interest in expansion abroad increases

Great Britain, France, the Netherlands, Spain, Portugal—these were the old colonial powers. Back in the 1500's and 1600's, they had started their policies of **imperialism**—of establishing colonies and building empires for economic gain, prestige, and missionary purposes. Now, in the mid-1800's, these imperial powers owned and controlled a large portion of the world, but huge areas of it still remained unclaimed.

The new imperialism. During the latter half of the 1800's, there was a mad rush to gain ownership or control of the remaining uncolonized lands. Nations previously little interested in expansion joined the race—among them Belgium, Germany, Italy, Japan, and Russia. Within a few years, the rival colonial powers seized control over almost all of Africa and sliced off large portions of China and other areas in East Asia. By the early 1900's, most of the underdeveloped regions of the world had been divided among the rival colonial empires.

The Industrial Revolution was largely responsible for the mounting interest in colonies. Factories needed raw materials in ever-growing quantities. Manufacturers, to keep their factories operating, had to find new markets for their finished products. Improvements in transportation, especially in the steamship, enabled businesses to buy and sell in a truly worldwide market. As trade increased and profits accumulated, business executives and bankers looked overseas for opportunities to invest savings.

It is not surprising that Great Britain, the world's leading industrial power before 1900, built the largest empire. Right behind Great Britain were France, Belgium, the Netherlands, and Germany. Industrialization in each of these countries was in full swing by the late 1800's.

There were still other reasons for the growth of worldwide imperialism in the late 1800's and the early 1900's. One was the invention of new instruments of warfare, notably repeating rifles and machine guns. By 1900 these new weapons were becoming standard army equipment. With them small bands of professional soldiers could conquer and control people in underdeveloped regions who did not have similar weapons.

Another reason for the growth of imperialism was the attitude of people in the colonial powers. There were objectors in every country, but, in general, ordinary people were as eager for empire as were leaders of government and business. English factory workers, French shopkeepers, German farmers—these and other solid citizens of the colonial powers were all proud of their country's empire. With this support the governments of the colonial powers were able to spend the huge sums of money needed for armies to occupy the colonial territories and for navies to guard the sea lanes to and from the colonies.

A changing American attitude. Americans, with some exceptions, had never been interested in acquiring colonies. Indeed, Americans had cast off their own colonial status in the American Revolution. Thus American sympathies were with colonial peoples, not with the colonizing powers.

America's lack of interest in acquiring colonies is easy to understand. For 300 years the undeveloped American West was, in a sense, an American colony. Even as late as 1867, when Secretary of State Seward bought Alaska from Russia for just over $7 million, Americans referred to Alaska as "Seward's folly" and "Seward's icebox." It was not until 30 years later, in 1897, when gold was discovered in Alaska, that Americans began to realize what a great bargain they had made.

During the late 1800's, the United States became the world's leading exporter of agricultural products. By 1890, however, it was feeling the competition of such agricultural nations as Canada and Argentina. American growers and processors of grain, livestock, and cotton as well as the manufacturers of agricultural machinery were eager to sell their products abroad. It was not surprising, therefore, that America's agricultural interests in general supported government efforts to open up new markets overseas.

Although by 1890 the United States was rapidly becoming one of the world's leading industrial nations, there was a big difference between American and European businesses. European nations lacked sufficient raw materials and markets at home. They needed firm control of new sources of raw materials and new

During the Alaskan gold rush, every day hundreds of gold seekers landed in Alaska. The gold hunters lined up, with packs of supplies on their backs, to make the difficult climb through the pass leading to the gold fields.

markets. American businesses, operating in a young and only partly developed country, were not under the same pressure. The country as a whole, and especially the great American West, still offered large supplies of vital raw materials. There were almost limitless opportunities for the sale of manufactured goods and the investment of surplus money within the United States.

However, some American business leaders realized that this situation would not last forever. For this reason, by 1890 American business and agricultural interests were increasingly pleased to have the United States seek overseas for economic opportunities, if not for actual colonies.

American expansionists. Until 1898, at least, American interest in colonies was stimulated not so much by the leaders of big business as by preachers, scholars, politicians, and military leaders.

One advocate of American expansion was Josiah Strong, a Congregational minister and social reformer. His widely read book *Our Country,* written in 1885, argued that the American branch of the "Anglo-Saxon race"

was destined to extend its "civilizing" influence in Latin America, Asia, and Africa.

An even more influential book was written by Captain Alfred Mahan in 1890 under the title *The Influence of Sea Power upon History, 1660-1783.* Mahan's book attempted to show that the world's greatest nations had risen largely because of their sea power and that greatness depended upon sea power. Therefore, he argued, the United States had to strengthen its navy and also had to secure colonies overseas.

Mahan claimed that colonies were needed as naval bases and as refueling stations, or "coaling stations." He also pointed out that colonies would provide raw materials and markets. Colonies would thereby strengthen the industrial organization on which a modern sea power is forced to rely.

Strengthening the navy. Even before Mahan's book appeared, Congress had taken steps to strengthen the navy. These steps were needed. In 1880, for example, the United States had fewer than 100 "seagoing vessels." Many were "seagoing" in name only, with rusty boilers and rotted planking.

The situation began to change in 1882, however, when Congress authorized the construction of "two steam-cruising vessels of war." Three years later the Navy Department created the Naval War College at Newport, Rhode Island. About this time the Bethlehem Steel Corporation began to manufacture armor plate—tough steel sheets to protect the hulls and superstructures of warships. By 1895 the "White Squadron," sometimes called the "Great White Fleet," was under construction.

Ready for a new role. By 1895 some American business leaders were beginning to worry that their European competitors might gain control of the markets of underdeveloped areas. The nation's industrial system was rapidly becoming one of the most productive in the world. A new navy, small but modern and efficient, was ready for action. For these reasons and others, many Americans felt that the United States was destined to play a leading role in world affairs.

SECTION SURVEY

IDENTIFY: imperialism, Josiah Strong, Alfred Mahan.

1. How did the Industrial Revolution contribute to the mounting interest in acquiring colonies among the newly industrialized nations?
2. How did the transportation revolution encourage the search for colonies?
3. Why was the United States at first not interested in acquiring colonies?
4. Explain how each of the following affected American interest in colonies: (a) closing of the frontier, (b) industrial development, (c) growing power in world affairs.

2 The war with Spain turns the United States into a colonial power

The war with Spain, which lasted only a few weeks in the spring and summer of 1898, marked a turning point in American history. Before the war, the only lands the United States owned beyond its immediate boundaries were Alaska and the Midway Islands. The United States had acquired the Midway Islands in the central Pacific in 1867. Within a few years after the war ended, however, the American flag flew over several islands in the Pacific. The United States was now deeply involved in East Asia, and American influence was strongly felt in the lands bordering the Caribbean Sea.

Trouble in Cuba. Cuba and Puerto Rico, both in the Caribbean, were the last remnants of Spain's once mighty empire in the New World. Spaniards had once called Cuba "the Ever Faithful Isle." In 1868, however, when a violent revolution broke out, the Cubans proved to be something less than faithful to their Spanish rulers. It took Spain ten years to crush this uprising. Spain did so only with a promise of long-awaited reforms, but discontent continued to smolder.

The trouble was that most Cubans worked at starvation wages for extremely wealthy landowners. To make matters worse, the Spanish government's policies, directed from Madrid, managed to anger the wealthier Cuban landowners as well as the landless workers.

Spanish misrule and an economic crisis finally plunged Cuba into another revolution. The United States was partly responsible for the economic crisis. In 1890, you recall, Congress adopted the McKinley Tariff Act. This act allowed Cuban sugar, the major crop of the island, to enter the United States free of duty. As a result, trade between the United States and Cuba prospered, reaching a total of more than $100 million a year. However, in 1894 the United States adopted the Wilson-Gorman Tariff Act. This act placed a 40-percent duty on all raw sugar imported into the United States. When the 1894 tariff went into effect, sugar piled up in Cuban warehouses, plantations closed, and thousands of Cubans lost their jobs.

Revolution in Cuba. Angered by the economic crisis and by Spain's failure to provide the long-promised reforms, the Cubans again revolted in 1895. Bands of revolutionists roamed through the countryside, killing, burning, and plundering.

The Spaniards, led by General Valeriano Weyler, nicknamed "The Butcher," responded savagely. General Weyler ordered all people living in territory controlled by the revolutionists into concentration camps run by the

Spaniards. Spanish soldiers then marched through the abandoned countryside, destroying buildings and putting to death all persons found in the area without permission. What the revolutionists had not destroyed during earlier raids, the Spaniards did. Large areas of Cuba were reduced to utter ruin. Starvation and disease plagued the land.

Growing American sympathy. Legally, the revolution in Cuba was no concern of the United States. Spain was a sovereign, independent nation, free to do as it pleased with its own colonies. This was freely admitted by the American government, which officially adopted a policy of neutrality.

However, the effects of the revolution were not confined to Cuba. The revolutionists themselves did everything possible to win American sympathy and support. They waged a vigorous propaganda campaign in America. José Martí, one of Hispanic America's greatest prose writers, aroused sympathy for Cuba by his persuasive articles. The revolutionists also bought quantities of American arms and ammunition, which they smuggled into Cuba.

The revolution also affected some American pocketbooks. Before the uprising began, Americans had invested more than $50 million in Cuban plantations, transportation projects, and businesses. These investments were in danger. Moreover, trade between Cuba and the United States was crippled by the revolution.

As months passed, more and more Americans expressed their sympathy for the revolutionists. They recalled their own struggle for freedom during the American Revolution.

American newspapers helped to inflame public opinion. Two New York papers— William Randolph Hearst's New York *Journal* and Joseph Pulitzer's New York *World*—were especially active in supporting the revolutionists. These publishers quickly discovered that sales skyrocketed when they printed sensational stories and pictures of the Spanish atrocities in Cuba.

Newspapers in other towns and cities quickly copied the financially successful methods of Hearst and Pulitzer. Before long, many Americans, feeding on the sensational stories and pictures, clamored for intervention. By 1898 even the more conservative newspapers, including weekly religious journals, insisted that the United States had the moral responsibility of restoring order in Cuba.

McKinley's attempts to avoid war. When President William McKinley was inaugurated on March 4, 1897, he strongly opposed war. The United States was just emerging from the depression that had started in 1893. The President, many of his advisers, and business leaders in general feared that war, or even the threat of war, would throw the country back into a depression. For nearly a year, the President held to an official policy of neutrality, but early in 1898 several events forced his hand.

On February 9, 1898, American newspapers headlined a letter written by the Spanish minister to the United States. In the letter, Dupuy De Lôme (LOH·may) described President McKinley as "weak and a bidder for the admiration of the crowd" and as a "would-be politician." The Spanish minister had written the letter to a friend in Havana. It was not meant for publication. Indeed, it had been stolen from the mails and sold to the press, but the harm was done. Unthinking Americans concluded that the uncomplimentary remark reflected the attitude of all Spaniards.

On February 16, Americans read even more startling news in their papers. The night before, the United States battleship *Maine*, which had been sent to Cuba in January to protect American lives and property, had sunk in Havana harbor with the loss of more than 250 American lives. Its captain stated that there had been an explosion of unknown origin and urged that "public opinion should be suspended until further report." In Havana flags flew at half-mast, theaters and places of business were closed, and expressions of sympathy were sent to Washington. All of this was brushed aside by the public. People jumped to the conclusion that the Spaniards had destroyed the ship. "Remember the *Maine!*" quickly became a national slogan.

Despite these incidents, President McKinley refused to declare war. Assistant Secretary of the Navy Theodore Roosevelt declared that the President "has no more backbone than a chocolate éclair." However, McKinley still hoped for a peaceable solution.

Spanish concessions. Late in March, with the President's approval, the Department of State sent an **ultimatum°** to Spain. In the ul-

°**ultimatum:** in diplomatic language, a final statement of terms whose rejection may lead to the breaking off of diplomatic relations or to war.

timatum the United States demanded that Spain (1) immediately cease all fighting and grant an armistice to the revolutionists, (2) negotiate with the Cubans for self-government or independence, and (3) abolish the concentration camps.

On April 9 the Spanish government accepted the ultimatum. The Spaniards hedged on the issue of independence, but the American minister in Madrid felt that with patience independence for Cuba could be achieved. In cabling the good news to President McKinley, he added, "I hope that nothing will now be done to humiliate Spain."

War declared. Despite the Spanish concession, on April 11, 1898, President McKinley asked Congress to intervene in Cuba. It seemed that the war spirit had proved too strong for the President to resist.

On April 19 Congress by large majorities voted to use the land and naval forces of the United States to secure full independence for Cuba. Congress also adopted the Teller Resolution. This resolution stated that the United States claimed no "sovereignty, jurisdiction, or control" over Cuba. The United States wanted only to **pacify**, or bring peace to, the beseiged Caribbean island. The resolution promised that once Cuba was free the United States would "leave the government and control of the island to its people."

Victory in the Pacific. Curiously enough, American fighting in the "war for Cuban liberty" started not in Cuba but in the Pacific. For weeks before Congress declared war, Theodore Roosevelt, the Assistant Secretary of the Navy, had been preparing for any developments. Roosevelt had sent orders to Commodore George Dewey, in command of a fleet anchored at Hong Kong, to prepare for action. When Dewey learned that war had been declared, he promptly headed for the Philippine Islands, the center of Spanish power in the Pacific.

On the night of April 30, 1898, Dewey's six ships slipped past the fortress of Corregidor and into the harbor of Manila, capital of the Philippines (see map, this page). At daybreak on May 1, the American warships opened fire. Their guns outranged those of the Spanish vessels, and by noon the one-sided battle was over. The Spaniards lost nearly 170 men and all their vessels. The Americans lost one man—who died of heatstroke.

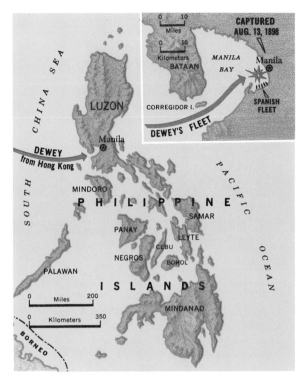

SPANISH-AMERICAN WAR: 1
(Philippine Islands)

Although Commodore Dewey controlled Manila harbor, he did not have a large enough force to land and seize the city. While he waited for a landing force to arrive from the United States, he sent arms and ammunition to a band of Filipinos led by Emilio Aguinaldo (ah·gwee·NAHL·doh). The Filipinos, eager to throw off Spanish rule and win their independence, prepared to attack Manila.

Two months passed. Then, early in August, American transports arrived with a strong landing party. The Spanish position was hopeless. Cut off by Dewey's warships, surrounded by Filipino revolutionists, and faced with an attack by an American army, Manila surrendered on August 13, 1898.

Victory in the Caribbean. Meanwhile, on April 29, Spain's Atlantic fleet under Admiral Cervera (sair·VAIR·ah) had sailed westward from the Cape Verde Islands for Cuba. The Spaniards slipped into the harbor at Santiago, Cuba, for refueling. Here they were bottled up by an American squadron commanded by Admiral William T. Sampson and Commodore W. S. Schley.

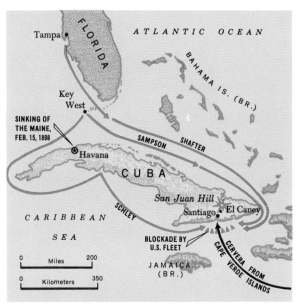

SPANISH-AMERICAN WAR: 2
(Cuba)

On Sunday morning, July 3, 1898, Cervera's fleet made a dash for the open sea, but the American ships were waiting. As the Spanish fleet raced out of the harbor and steamed along the coast, it was met by murderous fire (see map, this page). Within four hours the battle was over. Not a single Spanish vessel managed·to escape.

Fighting in Cuba. In contrast to the United States Navy, which moved swiftly and efficiently, the War Department was quite unprepared. When the war began, the regular army numbered fewer than 30,000 officers and troops, including four regiments of black soldiers. It was scattered in small contingents all across the country.

More than 200,000 Americans immediately volunteered for war service, including four more units of black soldiers. The volunteers also included Theodore Roosevelt. Roosevelt resigned as Assistant Secretary of the Navy to lead a volunteer regiment of cavalry known as the "Rough Riders."

The first American troops to arrive in Cuba were improperly trained and equipped. The food was poor, and the army was without adequate hospital and sanitary facilities. Hundreds of American soldiers died needlessly from dysentery, typhoid, malaria, and yellow fever. The American Red Cross, under the personal direction of Clara Barton, provided such aid as it could.

On June 24 the two armies clashed. Slowly, fighting hard, the Americans under General William Shafter pushed the Spaniards back through the fortified village of El Caney and across San Juan Hill (see map, this page). By July 2, American forces had advanced to within a short distance of Santiago. It was this fact that led Admiral Cervera to make his desperate attempt to escape with the Spanish fleet. The destruction of the Spanish navy was the final blow. The Spanish commander at Santiago surrendered his forces on July 17, just 15 days after Cervera's defeat.

Black soldiers, who had not been allowed to mix with white troops on the ships carrying them to Cuba, fought well in several engagements. Frank Knox, later to be Secretary of the Navy, wrote home that he had never seen "braver men anywhere." He added, "Some of those who rushed up the hill will live in my memory forever."

Many Cuban patriots also fought and gave their lives for the freedom of their country. Among them was Cuba's great leader, José Martí, who was one of the first to die in the Battle of Dos Rios.

Meanwhile another American army, under General Nelson A. Miles, landed on the Spanish island of Puerto Rico, east of Cuba. The Americans encountered almost no opposition and by the end of July were in control of the island.

The rewards of victory. The United States entered the war claiming that it was fighting merely to free the oppressed Cubans. It ended the war with an empire on its hands.

American and Spanish commissioners met in Paris in October 1898 to negotiate a peace treaty. By the terms of the treaty, Spain surrendered all claim to Cuba. In addition, Spain ceded to the United States the following territories: Puerto Rico; the Pacific island of Guam; and the Philippines—in exchange for which the United States agreed to pay Spain $20 million. The United States also acquired Wake Island in the Pacific. American armed forces had landed on Wake on July 4, 1898. Congress later annexed Wake.

The Cuban and Puerto Rican people did not share fully in the fruits of victory. As you will read, their hopes and expectations of freedom and independence were only partly realized.

On July 2, 1898, the American Rough Riders, Roosevelt's volunteer regiment, captured this fort in Cuba, only to be trapped there later. This lithograph shows their rescue by black troops of the 24th and 25th United States Infantry Regiments.

Until 1898, except for the Midway Islands, the United States owned no overseas possessions. When the Senate ratified the peace treaty, however, the United States became a colonial power.

The expansionists—followers of Alfred Mahan, Theodore Roosevelt, and others—were delighted. Many other Americans were deeply troubled. Was it wise and proper, they asked, for the United States to join the European powers in the race for empire?

SECTION SURVEY

IDENTIFY: José Martí, William Randolph Hearst, Joseph Pulitzer, ultimatum, Teller Resolution, Commodore Dewey, Emilio Aguinaldo, Admiral Cervera, "Rough Riders."

1. (a) What were the causes of the Cuban revolt against Spain? (b) Why did this revolt affect the United States?

2. How did each of the following help bring about the war with Spain: (a) sensational press coverage, (b) the De Lôme letter, (c) destruction of the *Maine,* (d) American investments and trade with Cuba?

3. Where did the war over Cuban independence actually begin? Why?

4. The war with Spain marked a turning point in American history. Explain.

5. Map Study: Study the map on page 545. (a) What does the blue arrow indicate? (b) What bodies of water are shown on the map? (c) On the large map, locate the area illustrated by the inset map. (d) When did Dewey capture Manila? Did he have any opposition? How can you tell from the map?

3 The United States takes over the Philippines, Hawaii, and Samoa

The Philippine Islands presented Americans with a difficult problem: Should the United States set the islands free, just as it intended to set Cuba free? Or should it force the Filipinos to accept American rule?

American dilemma. President McKinley wrestled with this problem. Finally he decided to establish American rule in the Philippine Islands. As he later explained, the United States could not return the Philippines to Spain, for "that would be cowardly and dishonorable." It could not give them to France, Germany, or Great Britain, for "that would be bad business and discreditable." It could not turn them over to the Filipinos, for they were "unfit

547

for self-government." McKinley concluded, "There is nothing left for us to do but to take them all, and to educate the Filipinos, and uplift and civilize and Christianize them."

President McKinley's motives were better than his knowledge of the facts. His reference to "Christianizing" the Filipinos ignored the fact that many had long since been converted to Catholicism. A major exception was the Moros, a group of people who were Muslims.

Divided public opinion. Many Americans agreed with McKinley that it was America's duty to "educate" and "uplift and civilize and Christianize" the Filipinos. Others hoped to profit economically by following the path of world empire. Still others believed that America needed the islands as naval and military bases.

Opponents of imperialism viewed the decision with serious misgivings. They argued that in taking the Philippines the United States was violating its own Declaration of Independence and the principle that people had the right to live under a government of their own choice. "It will be only the old tale of a free people seduced by false ambitions and running headlong after riches and luxuries and military glory," warned Carl Schurz, a prominent Republican. A few opponents, including some blacks, argued that imperialism was based in part on the false assumption of white racial superiority. They argued that American expansion abroad could only work to the disadvantage of blacks seeking to improve their lives in the United States.

Conquest and early rule. The conquest of the Philippines turned out to be more difficult than the defeat of Spain. The Filipinos, led by Emilio Aguinaldo, fought as fiercely against American rule as they had against Spanish rule. For three years 70,000 American troops fought in the islands at a cost of $175 million and with a casualty list as high as that of the war with Spain. By 1902, however, the American forces were finally victorious.

Despite this unhappy beginning, the United States tried to live up to McKinley's promise "not to exploit, but to develop; to civilize, to educate, to train in the science of self-government." In the Philippine Government Act of 1902, Congress set up a government for the islands. The act provided for an appointed governor, a small elected assembly, and an appointed upper house. The United States Congress could veto all legislation. The plan did not go into effect until 1907. Meanwhile, William Howard Taft, the first governor, ruled wisely. He cooperated closely with the Filipinos and included many Filipinos in the new government.

Many Americans did not take the Filipino fight for independence seriously. What was the cartoonist's view? How are the Filipinos represented here? The United States? What is Uncle Sam holding? What does he intend to do?

Filipino dissatisfaction. Many Filipinos wanted full self-government—nothing less. Their dissatisfaction became apparent in 1907 when the elected lower house met for the first time. Three quarters of the representatives were pledged to work for independence. Their hopes rose in 1913 when Woodrow Wilson became President of the United States. Leading Democrats had opposed the conquest of the Philippines, and the Democratic Party had pledged itself to grant independence at the earliest possible date.

These hopes, however, were soon dashed. The Jones Act of 1916 did give the Filipinos the right to elect the members of both houses of the legislature. However, Congress did not grant independence but merely promised it "as soon as a stable government can be established."

Meanwhile conditions in the islands improved. Highways, railroads, and telegraph and telephone lines were built. Education reduced illiteracy from 85 percent in 1898 to 37 percent in 1921. Disease was greatly reduced and Filipino health steadily improved. Exports and imports swelled in volume as American tariffs on products from the Philippines were reduced and finally removed. Most important of all, the United States eventually kept its promise to set the islands free.

Early relations with Hawaii. Before 1865 about the only relations that the United States had with the Hawaiian Islands were through traders and missionaries. After 1865, American businesses began to develop the resources of Hawaii—chiefly sugar cane and pineapples. In 1875 Hawaii signed a treaty with the United States. In return for the right to sell sugar in the United States without payment of any duty, the Hawaiians promised not to sell or lease territory to any foreign power. In 1887, when this treaty was renewed, the United States leased Pearl Harbor as a naval base.

Native Hawaiians became increasingly alarmed as the wealth and power of the islands passed into foreign hands. Finally, led by Queen Liliuokalani (leh·LEE·woh·kah LAH·nee), they announced their intentions to end foreign influence.

Revolution and annexation. The American businesses in Hawaii, aided by influential Hawaiians, met this challenge by starting a revolution on January 16, 1893. The American minister to Hawaii quickly intervened. Claim-

Queen Liliuokalani, the last monarch of Hawaii, wanted to reduce the influence of American business groups and missionaries over the affairs of the native Hawaiians but she lost her throne in attempting to do so.

ing that he was acting only to protect American lives and property, he requested the aid of marines conveniently at hand on a nearby warship. The Hawaiian soldiers, concluding that the marines had come to help the revolutionists, refused to fight. The new government, controlled by the foreign business interests and the missionaries, asked to be annexed to the United States. The American minister promptly raised the Stars and Stripes, and on February 1, 1893, marines began to patrol the islands.

When news of these events reached the United States, furious protests poured into Congress. Many Americans did not want island territory. They were indignant at the manner in which American marines had been used in Hawaii. They were also afraid that overseas expansion would lead to heavy military expenditures.

President Cleveland sent a commission to Hawaii to investigate. The commission ordered the American flag hauled down and heard evidence from both sides. The commission found that the revolution had been started largely by

549

American business groups, aided by the American minister and the marines, and that the Hawaiians had no desire to be annexed.

After studying the report, Cleveland concluded that Queen Liliuokalani should be returned to her throne. To do this would require the exercise of American force against the new government. By now Congress was fed up with the whole affair, and in 1894 it adopted a resolution refusing to interfere further in Hawaii.

Then came the war with Spain, which generated a new spirit in America. The question of Hawaii once again was brought up on the floor of Congress. This time, in 1898, by an overwhelming vote the islands were annexed to the United States and given territorial status.

American control of Samoa. As in Hawaii, American interests in the Samoan Islands were of long standing. In 1878 the United States secured from a Samoan chief the right to use the harbor of Pago Pago (PAHN·goh PAHN·goh) on the island of Tutuila (too·too·EE·lah) as a naval base. The Samoans granted similar privileges to Germany and Great Britain.

The three countries—Great Britain, Germany, and the United States—then scrambled to control the islands. At one point, in 1889, a naval clash among the three powers was narrowly avoided, largely because a typhoon blew the rival squadrons out to sea.

Finally, in 1899, the British withdrew and the islands were divided between Germany and the United States. Germany later lost control of its share of the islands when it was defeated in World War I. Tutuila, with its excellent harbor of Pago Pago, remained in the hands of the United States and became a major naval base in the Pacific.

SECTION SURVEY

IDENTIFY: William Howard Taft, Jones Act, Queen Liliuokalani.

1. Do you agree with the anti-imperialists who argued that the United States violated the Declaration of Independence when it took the Philippines? Why or why not?
2. How did the United States acquire Hawaii?
3. The scramble for the Samoan Islands demonstrated the rivalry among nations to acquire colonies. Explain.

4 The United States plays a larger role in East Asia

In 1900 United States territory in the Pacific included Hawaii, Midway, Guam, Wake, the Philippine Islands, and part of Samoa. With this new territory the American people assumed heavy responsibilities. These new responsibilities, plus events taking place in East Asia, led to a change in the United States' relations with China.

Early relations with China. America's interest in China began in the 1780's with profitable trade between the two countries. By the early 1800's, the China trade had become a flourishing business. Ships from Philadelphia, New York, and New England ports made the long, hazardous voyage around South America and up the West Coast to the Pacific Northwest. There they traded with the Indians, exchanging blankets, axes, guns, and other goods for furs. When they had a full cargo of furs, they sailed for China. There they traded the furs for tea, silk, porcelain, jade, and other valuable goods. Many merchants and shipowners in the United States as well as in Great Britain and other European countries made fortunes from the China trade.

As time passed, China's rulers grew disturbed at the influence of foreigners on their country. When China placed restrictions on British traders, however, Great Britain waged a successful war (1839–42) and forced the Chinese to open certain "treaty ports" to British trade.

Americans demanded and secured similar trading privileges. The American envoy to China, Caleb Cushing, negotiated a treaty that gave the United States all the trading privileges granted by China to other nations. In addition the treaty gave Americans the right of **extraterritoriality**. This meant that Americans in China who were charged with violations of Chinese laws had the right to be tried in American courts in China. Other foreign nations also secured similar privileges.

Crisis in China. These concessions from China encouraged foreign traders to settle there. As time passed, outsiders, including missionaries from the United States and other countries, exercised growing influence. Many

American troops move through rubble at the gate to the city of Tientsin after joining with other foreign troops to successfully put down the Boxer Rebellion and free the 300 hostages who had been trapped inside the foreign compound there.

of China's leaders strongly opposed this interference but were powerless to prevent it.

Among all the imperialistic powers interested in East Asia, the United States seemed least eager to grab Chinese territory. As a result, relations between the two countries remained friendly throughout the 1800's.

In the 1890's, however, a major crisis developed. Japan entered the race for colonies with an attack upon China in the Sino-Japanese War of 1894–95. In this war Japan won the large island of Formosa, territory on the Shantung Peninsula, and control of Korea (see map, page 696).

While China was helpless as a result of the Japanese attack, Germany, Russia, Great Britain, and France rushed in to seize their share of the booty. It appeared for the time that China would soon share the fate of Africa, which the European powers had already carved up and divided.

The Open Door Policy. The crisis in China posed a problem for the United States. Americans did not want Chinese territory. On the other hand, Americans did not intend to be squeezed out of the growing trade in Chinese markets by the other nations.

John Hay, who became Secretary of State in 1898, had a solution for the problem. He sent a note to all the powers concerned seeking two assurances. Hay asked (1) that they would keep open all "treaty ports" and (2) that they

would guarantee to all nations engaged in trade with China equal railroad, harbor, and tariff rates. In short, Hay asked for an Open Door Policy. Such a policy would insure American businesses the opportunity to compete on equal terms with other traders in China. Although the response to his note was not encouraging, Hay announced on March 20, 1900, that the Open Door Policy was in effect.

The Boxer Rebellion. Understandably, the Chinese resented the efforts by Japan, Russia, and western powers to control their country. On the rising tide of resentment, the Chinese launched a movement to drive all "foreign devils" from their country. The movement was led by a Chinese secret society that westerners called "the Boxers."°

In the spring of 1900, the Boxers suddenly attacked. They killed about 300 foreigners in north China. Then they surrounded the foreign area in Tientsin (TIN·TSIN) and the foreign legations in Peking, where men and women from many nations gathered for protection.

The foreign powers promptly rushed troops to relieve the besieged people. The force included 2,500 American troops from the Philippines as well as military units from Japan and several European nations. By August 14 the

°the Boxers: the Chinese name for this society literally meant "righteous harmonious band." Westerners wrongly translated the Chinese name to "righteous harmonious *fists*" and hence called the society "the Boxers."

A MEETING OF EAST AND WEST

"It is finally finished. The great agony is over! . . . The egg has hatched its chicken." What the American officer meant, he continued, was that "the Treaty between Japan and the United States was signed today." It was March 31, 1854, but the negotiations had begun several months earlier.

Commodore Matthew Perry had first anchored his small fleet in Yedo (Tokyo) Bay the previous July. The Japanese had never seen steamships before. One onlooker wrote admiringly of what he called a "fire wheel ship that runs as quick as a dragon in swimming." Perry delivered his proposals to government officials and promised to return the following year.

In February 1854, when the Americans steamed back, negotiations were stepped up, with formal processions, booming guns, and exchanges of gifts. For the emperor the Americans had brought a telescope, cases of firearms, clocks, and a barrel of whiskey. The

Japanese presented their guests with fine silks, brocades, and lacquerware. There was entertainment, too: a minstrel show for the Japanese, a wrestling exhibition for the Americans. What made the biggest impression was a quarter-size steam locomotive—made to order in Philadelphia—with a tender and coach, set up to run on a 350-foot (160-meter) track. Japanese officials lined up eagerly for the privilege of riding atop the train as it scooted around in a circle.

However, it was not the gifts or the entertainment that "hatched" the treaty. Nor was it the magnificent banquet on board Perry's flagship, where one Japanese guest got so carried away that he threw his arms around the dignified commodore. It was Perry's ships and their bristling cannon. "We are without a navy and our coasts are undefended," said an official Japanese decree. Japan could do little but agree to increased trade—and plan to build its own "fire wheel ships."

force had relieved the foreigners in Tientsin and Peking, but not before 65 of the besieged had been killed.

The Boxer Rebellion provided an excellent excuse to seize additional Chinese territory, but John Hay took a firm stand in opposition. On July 3, even while the expeditionary force was fighting its way inland to Peking, he announced that the United States wanted to "preserve Chinese territorial and administrative entity . . . and safeguard for the world the principle of equal and impartial trade with all parts of the Chinese Empire."

Largely because of American influence, China did not lose any territory as a result of the Boxer Rebellion. China did, however, have to pay the foreign powers $333 million as compensation for loss, damage, and injury. The

American share amounted to about $24 million. Half of this sum the United States government turned over to American citizens to compensate them for losses of personal property in China. The American government returned the rest of the money to China.

Grateful for this American action, the Chinese government used the money to send Chinese students to the United States. This fund enabled thousands of China's ablest youth to study in American colleges and universities. These students helped to build closer understanding between the two countries.

The Open Door Policy in China had other far-reaching results. It immediately involved the United States in the affairs of Russia and Japan, both of whom were expanding their influence in East Asia.

The opening of Japan. Before 1853 the Japanese had lived in almost complete isolation from the rest of the world. Japan's rulers forbade foreigners to enter Japan. Only the Dutch had won the right to carry on a limited amount of trade through one small Japanese port. In 1853, however, Japan's isolation was shattered when Commodore Matthew C. Perry arrived in Japanese waters with a squadron of American naval vessels. Perry demanded an audience with the Japanese rulers.

The presents that the Americans and Japanese exchanged during a conference in 1854 symbolized the difference between the two countries. The United States received gifts of silk, brocades, lacquerware, and other fine handmade articles. The Japanese received tokens of the new industrial world—a telegraph set, guns, and model railroad trains.

As a result of this conference and a later one, the United States and Japan signed the Treaty of Kanagawa. With this treaty both countries expressed a desire for peace, friendship, and developing trade. Japan also agreed to open two ports to United States trading vessels. Later, Japan opened other ports.

Japan's search for empire. Few events in modern history have had such far-reaching effects as the opening of Japanese ports. Two major developments followed at once. First, American and other traders started a lively commerce with Japan that grew to large proportions in the 1900's. Second, Japanese leaders were convinced that they should adopt the industrial techniques of the western nations.

By the late 1800's, Japan was a transformed country. However, the "new" Japan faced new problems. Knowledge of science, medicine, and sanitation had reduced the death rate, and the lower death rate meant a larger population. This created difficulties, for Japan was small, without enough farmland to feed its people adequately. The Japanese also needed raw materials for their new factories and markets for their products.

Faced with these problems, Japan started upon a program of imperialism similar to that being followed by other industrial nations. Japan needed colonies to secure food for its surplus population and to provide raw materials and markets for its growing industries. Thus Japan entered the race for empire and became one of the contestants in the struggle for control of East Asia.

As you have seen, Japan started its career as an imperial power with an attack upon China in the Sino-Japanese War of 1894–95. Ten years later Japan plunged into another war, this time with Russia.

The United States in the Pacific. Although the Russo-Japanese War of 1904–05 took place nearly half a world away from the United States, Americans were immediately concerned. Their new commitments in the Pacific had given Americans a direct interest in the affairs of East Asia. The war between Russia and Japan, fought on Chinese soil and in Pacific waters, threatened to interfere with American trading and missionary interests in China. It also threatened to weaken, if not destroy, the Open Door Policy.

Acting on his own authority, President Theodore Roosevelt warned Germany and France that if they aided Russia the United States would side with Japan. With Roosevelt acting as mediator, representatives from Russia and Japan met at Portsmouth, New Hampshire, during the summer of 1905. There they worked out terms for settling the conflict. In 1906 Roosevelt received the Nobel Peace Prize for his efforts.

The Treaty of Portsmouth transferred Russia's interest in Korea and Manchuria to Japan. It also gave Japan the southern half of Sakhalin Island (see map, page 696).

Roosevelt was delighted with the results of his efforts to end the Russo-Japanese War. The Treaty of Portsmouth left the Open Door Policy intact. It maintained for a time the balance of power in East Asia. None of the colonial powers, including Japan and Russia, had a dominant position in China. The doors of China remained open to American business and trade.

SECTION SURVEY

IDENTIFY: extraterritoriality, John Hay, Commodore Perry, Treaty of Portsmouth.

1. (a) Describe the circumstances that led to the Open Door Policy. (b) What were the provisions of this policy?

2. (a) What was the Boxer Rebellion? (b) How did it end? (c) What were its effects on United States–China relations?

3. (a) Why did Japan become imperialistic? (b) Why were Americans concerned about growing Japanese imperialism?

Chapter Survey

Summary: Tracing the Main Ideas

During the latter half of the 1800's, the major colonial powers of Europe engaged in a lively race for empire. The United States, however, was not especially interested in entering the race. To be sure, in 1867–68 Secretary of State Seward persuaded Congress to annex the Midway Islands and to purchase Alaska, but Congress did so reluctantly. Americans on the whole were indifferent.

Toward the end of the 1800's, American sentiment began to change. It was the Spanish-American War that finally started the United States down the road of colonialism.

The war with Spain in 1898 began in protest against Spanish policy in Cuba. It ended with a treaty in which Spain agreed to give up its claim to Cuba and in which the United States gained the Philippine Islands as well as Guam and Puerto Rico. In addition to the Philippines and Guam, the United States acquired other territories in the Pacific area. Hawaii was annexed in 1898 and a portion of Samoa was acquired in 1899. To protect its growing interests in the Pacific, the United States insisted upon an equal opportunity to share in the business and trade of East Asia. This Open Door Policy involved Americans in the troubled affairs of East Asia and committed the United States to a role of power politics in the Pacific.

America's interest in colonies was not confined to the Pacific area. As you will read in the next chapter, the Caribbean offered even larger and more inviting opportunities for the development of American interests.

Inquiring into History

1. Why did the foreign policy of the United States change from one of isolationism to one of expansionism?
2. What arguments did the expansionists use to defend their position?
3. Was there a contradiction in the United States' favoring the Open Door Policy for China and the policy of the Monroe Doctrine for the Western Hemisphere? Explain.
4. Some anti-imperialists argued that American imperialist policy worked to the disadvantage of black Americans at home. (a) How might this have been true? (b) Do you agree or disagree with their argument? Why? (c) What was the position of black Americans at home in the 1890's? (See page 404–07.)
5. Why do you suppose the industrial nations were able to dominate the nonindustrialized areas of the world?
6. Recall American attitudes toward mercantilism before the American Revolution. What was our attitude toward our "mother country," Great Britain? Do you think you can generalize and say that most colonies feel this way about their mother country? Explain.
7. The consequences of moving into East Asia were to have a lasting effect on the nation's foreign affairs and domestic conditions. Explain.

Relating Past to Present

1. Is the United States involved overseas today for the same reasons it was involved during the period covered in this chapter? Explain.
2. Compare the role of the press today with that of the sensational press of the late 1890's.

Developing Social Science Skills

1. Examine the picture on page 551. (a) What details has the artist emphasized? (b) Do you think that the Japanese artist has painted American troops as they actually appeared? (c) What do you think influenced the artist to paint the picture in this particular way?
2. Study the world map on pages 856–57. (a) Indicate the territory held by the United States in 1900. (b) Locate the trade route often used by traders in the mid-1800's to get from the eastern United States to China. (c) What does the map suggest about the problems for the United States of governing territories such as the Philippines?

Chapter 29

American Expansion in the Caribbean

1898–1914

On December 10, 1898, the Spaniards signed the Treaty of Paris that formally brought the Spanish-American War to an end. For both the United States and Spain, the end of the war was a turning point.

By the terms of the treaty, Spain agreed (1) to leave Cuba, (2) to cede Puerto Rico and Guam to the United States, and (3) to cede the Philippine Islands to the United States in exchange for a payment of $20,000,000

The signing of the Treaty of Paris was a sad day for the Spanish nation. The Spaniards had reason for their sorrow. The war that they had fought and lost struck the final blow to the once mighty Spanish empire.

It was also a disappointing day for the Cubans who had hoped that peace would bring the freedom for which they had struggled and for those Puerto Ricans who had also hoped for freedom and independence.

For the American people, however, the war marked a crucial step forward on the path of empire and world power. After 1898, as you know, the United States rapidly became a major power in the Pacific and in East Asia. Between 1898 and 1914, as you will read in this chapter, it also gained power in the Caribbean and the rest of Latin America. This course of events turned the Caribbean Sea into what was sometimes called "an American lake."

THE CHAPTER IN OUTLINE

1. Americans begin to build an empire in the Caribbean.

2. The United States modifies and strengthens the Monroe Doctrine.

3. Conflict breaks out between the United States and Mexico.

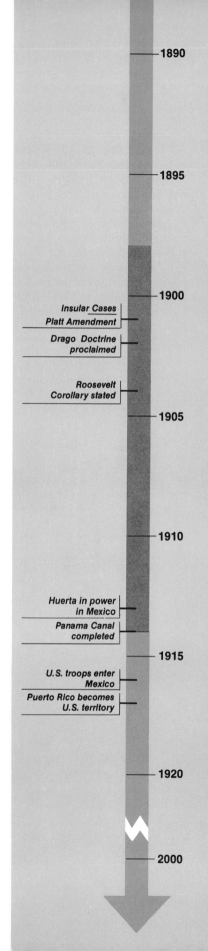

1890

1895

1900

Insular Cases
Platt Amendment

Drago Doctrine
proclaimed

Roosevelt
Corollary stated

1905

1910

Huerta in power
in Mexico

Panama Canal
completed

1915

U.S. troops enter
Mexico

Puerto Rico becomes
U.S. territory

1920

2000

1 Americans begin to build an empire in the Caribbean

Less than 20 years after the 1898 war with Spain, the American flag was flying not only over Puerto Rico but also over the Panama Canal Zone and the Virgin Islands. American advisers were helping to govern small countries in and around the Caribbean. In short, the United States had developed a revised foreign policy for the Western Hemisphere.

The new overseas possessions caused the American government to face several important questions: How would the United States respond to the desires of Cubans and Puerto Ricans for total independence? Were the people who lived in the newly acquired territories entitled to all the rights guaranteed by the Constitution to citizens of the United States? As the question was often stated, "Does the Constitution follow the flag?"

The Insular Cases. In the Insular Cases of 1901, the Supreme Court settled the issue of constitutional rights. It ruled that there were two kinds of possessions—incorporated and unincorporated. The incorporated possessions—Hawaii and Alaska—were destined for statehood. The citizens of these possessions were therefore entitled to all the constitutional rights guaranteed to United States citizens. The unincorporated possessions—Puerto Rico, the Philippines, Samoa, and others—were not destined for statehood. The people of these

In this 1904 cartoon President Theodore Roosevelt is depicted as a police officer. Do you think this view is a flattering or a critical one? Why?

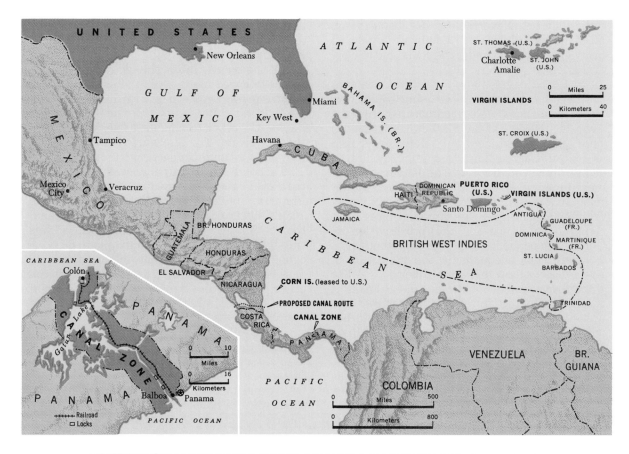

UNITED STATES EXPANSION IN THE CARIBBEAN, 1898–1917

areas were *not,* therefore, entitled to all constitutional guarantees. The people of the unincorporated possessions could not, however, be deprived of the fundamental rights of life, liberty, or property without the due process of law.

The Insular Cases and several similar Supreme Court decisions between 1901 and 1922 helped to develop an American colonial policy. However, it was Congress that passed the laws ruling America's growing colonial empire.

A government for Puerto Rico. In 1900, Congress passed the Foraker Act, which provided a new government for Puerto Rico. It would consist of a governor and an executive council appointed by the President of the United States and a lower house elected by the Puerto Ricans.

Discontented Puerto Ricans demanded a larger voice in their own government. In 1917, shortly after the Filipinos won a similar victory in the Jones Act of 1916, the United States adopted a second Jones Act. This act made Puerto Rico a United States territory and made the Puerto Ricans American citizens. In addition Puerto Ricans were also granted the right to elect members of both houses of their legislature.

In 1950 Congress gave Puerto Ricans the power to write their own constitution. In 1952, after the constitution had been ratified by popular vote, Puerto Rico became a self-governing commonwealth. It makes its own laws and controls its own finances. The United States, however, provides for the island's defense and includes Puerto Rico within its tariff system. It places no restrictions on immigration from Puerto Rico to the United States.

Strings on Cuban independence. Although Cuba was never considered an American colony, American influence over Cuban affairs remained strong after the war. The Teller Resolution, which Congress adopted in 1898, had pledged that the Cubans would be given their independence. Nevertheless, for three years after the war, Cuba was ruled by an American army of occupation under the command of General Leonard Wood.

In 1901 Congress finally turned Cuba over to the Cuban people, but with four conditions. These conditions were incorporated into the Army Act of 1901 as the Platt Amendment. (1) The Cuban government must never enter into any foreign agreements that might endanger Cuban independence. (2) The Cuban government must never incur debts that it could not repay in a reasonable time. (3) The Cuban government must give the United States "the right to intervene for the preservation of Cuban independence [and] the maintenance of a government adequate for the protection of life, property, and individual liberty." (4) The Cuban government must place naval bases at the disposal of the United States. Congress also announced that the United States would not withdraw its military forces until the Platt Amendment had been written into the new Cuban constitution.

This was not the "independence" Cubans had expected, yet they had to agree to American demands. Therefore, they accepted the Platt Amendment, and in 1902 the American forces were withdrawn.

An American protectorate. Actually, Cuba became a **protectorate** of the United States. That is, the United States, a strong nation, tried to supervise Cuba, a weaker nation, by keeping partial control over Cuban affairs. Cubans, who had fought for independence, resented this relationship.

Between 1906 and 1920, American troops landed in Cuba three times to maintain order and to protect American business and property. Moreover, American diplomatic pressure frequently forced the Cubans to accept policies favored by the United States. In 1934, as you will see, Congress abolished the Platt Amendment, thus ending America's role as "protector" of Cuba.

Growing interest in a canal. In 1898, when the Spanish-American War began, the U.S. battleship *Oregon* was in California waters. It immediately started to sail around South America in an effort to join the Atlantic fleet. Public imagination was stirred, and for six weeks daily reports of the ship's progress appeared in every newspaper. The *Oregon*'s lengthy voyage convinced many Americans that a canal between the Atlantic and the Pacific was needed.

In the years after the war, the United States followed along a path of empire. As the empire grew, people began to insist that the United States needed two navies—one in the Pacific, the other to safeguard the Atlantic and the Caribbean. The alternative to a two-ocean navy was a canal connecting the two oceans.

The best site for a canal was that narrow part of Colombia known as the Isthmus of Panama. Indeed, a French company in the 1880's had tried but had failed to build a canal there. Another possible canal route was through Nicaragua (see map, page 557). A canal in either place would enable a fleet to pass easily and quickly from one ocean to the other. It would also be of enormous commercial value to the United States as well as to the merchant fleets of the world.

The United States had considered building a canal through the Isthmus of Panama for many years. As early as 1850, the United States and Great Britain had agreed on terms for a canal in the Clayton-Bulwer Treaty. If a canal were built, both nations would together control it and guarantee that it be unfortified and open to all other nations, even in wartime.

By 1898, however, Americans had concluded that the canal was so vital to their national interests that the United States had to have exclusive control over it. In 1901 Great Britain agreed to give up all rights to share in the building and control of the canal. The United States was now free to build and operate the canal, but it was understood that the canal would be open to all nations, even in time of war.

Negotiations with Colombia. The next step was to secure a right of way either through Nicaragua or across the Isthmus of Panama. The United States decided in favor of the route across Panama, which was then a province of Colombia. Secretary of State John Hay immediately opened negotiations with the Colombian government, and a treaty was soon ready for ratification. In return for a 99-year lease to a 16-mile (26-kilometer) strip of land across Panama, the United States agreed to pay Colombia $10 million and a yearly rental of $250,000.

At this point Colombia's legislators adjourned without taking action, hoping to win

THE CONQUEST OF YELLOW FEVER

Walter Reed checked the time. It was 11:50 on the night of December 31, 1900. At his desk in an American army barracks in northern Cuba, he turned back to the letter he was writing his wife in the United States.

"Only ten minutes of the old century remain," he wrote. "The prayer that has been mine for twenty years, that I might be permitted in some way or at some time to do something to alleviate human suffering has been granted. A thousand Happy New Years!"

Reed was truly benefiting humankind, for he led a team that was conquering yellow fever. This tropical disease had killed countless victims over the centuries, but no one knew what caused it or how to prevent it.

In 1900 yellow fever broke out among American troops stationed in Havana. The United States government promptly sent a team of physicians headed by Reed to investigate. Its other members were James Carroll, Jesse W. Lazear, and Aristides Agramonte. Earlier investigators—including Dr. Carlos Finlay of Cuba—had already suggested that the disease was transmitted by a certain mosquito. The Reed commission decided that experimenting with human subjects was the only way to test this theory. Beginning in June 1900, Carroll, Lazear, and several other volunteers allowed themselves to be bitten by infected mosquitoes. Lazear died, but the others survived.

This courageous experiment proved at last what before had only been suspected. Armed with this knowledge, William C. Gorgas, chief surgeon of the American forces in Cuba, took steps to clean up mosquito-breeding areas in Cuba. Later he continued his work in Central America, making it possible for the United States to build the Panama Canal.

---

better terms. Many Americans, including President Theodore Roosevelt, were furious because Colombia's delay blocked the entire canal project.

Revolution in Panama. Fortunately for the United States, many leaders in the province of Panama also were angry at Colombia's delay. These leaders had dreamed of a canal that would place Panama at a crossroads of world commerce. Moreover, for years the people of Panama had resented control by Colombia. Columbia's delay was the last straw.

In Panama a group secretly organized a revolution. They were encouraged by representatives of the French company that had earlier tried to build a canal and now wanted to recover as much as possible of its investment.

One Panamanian leader secretly traveled to Washington and asked the American government for assistance. Although open aid was refused, the Panamanian left Washington convinced that the United States would not interfere once the revolution began.

According to rumors, the revolution was to begin on November 4, 1903. On November 2 an American gunboat, the *Nashville,* arrived at Colón (see inset map, page 557). Hardly had it landed when a Colombian ship arrived with Colombian soldiers. The Colombian generals commanding the expedition immediately proceeded to the city of Panama, leaving orders for the troops to follow. Shortly after they reached Panama, however, the Colombian generals were seized and jailed. The arrest of the Colombian generals was a signal for the outbreak of the revolution, and the city of Panama quickly fell under the control of the revolutionists.

Meanwhile, during a dispute that broke out in Colón, Colombian soldiers and naval officers threatened to kill every American in the city. At this point United States marines landed. Colombian authorities demanded to know what right the Americans had to interfere. The

The building of the Panama Canal was an enormous undertaking. In this photograph the 70-foot (21-meter) deep Miraflores Lower Locks stand near completion.

Americans said that in a treaty between the United States and Colombia signed in 1846 the United States had guaranteed free passage through the isthmus. The United States government also added that no Colombian troops would be permitted to land within 50 miles (80 kilometers) of Panama.

Right of way through Panama. Largely because of American aid, the revolution in Panama was a success. On November 4, 1903, the new government took control in Panama, and two days later the United States recognized Panama's independence. On November 13 the United States formally received the First Panamanian minister to Washington, Bunau-Varilla (boo·NOH vah·REE·yah). On November 18, only two weeks after the revolution broke out, Panama granted the United States the right of way across the isthmus for the canal.

In the Hay–Bunau-Varilla Treaty, Panama gave the United States a perpetual lease to a 10-mile (16-kilometer) strip of land between the Atlantic and the Pacific Oceans. In return for this land, the United States agreed to pay Panama $10 million outright and a yearly rental of $250,000.

Did the United States help to start the revolution in Panama? President Theodore Roosevelt once boasted, "I took Panama." At other times, he denied that the United States had in any way helped to carry out the revolution. One fact is certain—the revolution worked to the advantage of the United States—and Roosevelt made the most of the situation.

Colombia was furious, of course, and the affair added to the fear and distrust of the "Yankee" that was already strong in Latin America. In 1921 the United States tried to pacify Colombia by giving it $25 million as partial compensation for the loss of Panama.

Building the canal. Meanwhile, work on the canal progressed under the supervision of the United States Army Corps of Engineers. One of the first and most difficult tasks was to conquer malaria, yellow fever, and other tropical diseases. Until these diseases were brought under control, workers from the United States found it almost impossible to live in the Canal Zone.

Dr. Walter Reed and his colleagues working in Cuba discovered that yellow fever was transmitted by a certain mosquito, the *Stegomyia.* Using this and other medical dis-

560

coveries, Dr. William C. Gorgas, the surgeon in charge of the American health program in Panama, was able to turn a deadly tropical jungle into a relatively healthful region.

By 1914 the canal was completed (see inset map, page 557) at the cost of approximately $400 million. Its completion was a major triumph of engineering and a personal triumph for the engineer in charge, Colonel George W. Goethals (GOH·thulz). The first traffic moved through the canal just as World War I broke out in Europe. Since then the canal has added immeasurably to the naval strength of the United States. Its value in peacetime for trade has been almost incalculable.

SECTION SURVEY

IDENTIFY: Insular Cases, protectorate, Hay–Bunau-Varilla Treaty, Walter Reed, George Goethals.

1. How did the Supreme Court answer the question, "Does the Constitution follow the flag"?
2. What provisions did Congress make for the government of Puerto Rico?
3. Why can it be said that the Platt Amendment made Cuba an American protectorate?
4. Why was the United States interested in a canal through Central America?
5. American policies in Latin America contributed to the growing distrust of the "Yankee" there. Explain.
6. Map Study: Refer to the map on page 557 to explain why the Caribbean Sea was once called "an American lake."

2 The United States modifies and strengthens the Monroe Doctrine

During the early 1900's, as you have read, the United States on a number of occasions intervened in the internal affairs of the smaller countries in the Caribbean area. How did the United States justify such interference?

Reasons for interference. Intervention was necessary, Americans argued, to maintain law and order in countries bordering on the United States. In the first place, the United States government had a duty to protect the lives and properties of its own citizens living in other countries. Second, the United States was determined as a matter of self-interest and self-defense to prevent European nations from intervening in the political affairs of the Western Hemisphere. There would be less chance for such intervention if law and order prevailed. Third, the United States was concerned about the defense of the canal it was then building across the Isthmus of Panama.

The Monroe Doctrine of 1823. Americans developed the argument of self-defense into a well-defined foreign policy. As you recall, the original Monroe Doctrine of 1823 warned the European powers (1) not to attempt any further colonization in the Americas and (2) not to interfere with independent nations in the Western Hemisphere.

When this warning was issued and for many years after, the United States did not have the naval strength to enforce it. However, as long as American and British interests did not clash in Latin America, the British Navy could be counted on to support Monroe's words. Moreover, the Latin American countries themselves made several efforts to cooperate in the organization of their own defense. In fact, Mexico, Argentina, and Chile did successfully resist European attempts to interfere.

The first test. The first major test of the Monroe Doctrine came during the 1860's, when Emperor Napoleon III of France tried to establish a French-dominated empire in Mexico. Napoleon III, together with Great Britain and Spain, sent an expedition to Mexico, supposedly to force Mexico to repay its debts. After Mexico repaid its debts, Great Britain and Spain withdrew, but Napoleon III refused to pull out his troops. Instead, aided by Mexicans who opposed the President, Benito Juárez (HWAH·res), the French troops installed Maximilian of Austria as emperor of Mexico. President Juárez fled to El Paso del Norte near the United States border.

The United States immediately protested that French occupation of Mexico was a clear violation of the Monroe Doctrine. However, the United States was fighting the Civil War and until 1865 was unable to take firm action. Then, with the war ended, the United States prepared to send an American army to the Mexican border—farther, if necessary.

The American army was not needed. Napoleon, faced with the danger of war in Europe and convinced that he could not hold Mexico, withdrew his forces. Juárez and his followers destroyed Maximilian's army and executed Maximilian in 1867.

Thus ended a difficult situation. However, the American government had shown its firm resolve to resist European interference in Latin America.

A second test. A second major test of the Monroe Doctrine came in 1895. The immediate issue was a boundary dispute between Venezuela and British Guiana (see map, page 557).

Great Britain had acquired British Guiana in 1814. Time and again Great Britain had pushed the western boundary of British Guiana onto territory claimed by Venezuela. Finally, in 1882, Venezuela had had enough. It demanded that Great Britain submit the controversy to **arbitration,** meaning that the British would have to agree in advance to accept the decision of a neutral party.

The British refused, and in 1895 Venezuela asked the United States to intervene. President Cleveland decided to act. In an extremely strong message, Secretary of State Richard Olney warned Great Britain that the United States would not tolerate any further interference with Venezuela and demanded an immediate settlement of the problem by arbitration.

Great Britain angrily rejected Olney's demands. In the first place, the British retorted, the Monroe Doctrine had not been violated. Second, the Monroe Doctrine was not a recognized part of international law. Third, the United States had no business interfering.

President Cleveland refused to accept this explanation. When the British refusal to arbitrate reached him, he appointed an American commission to investigate the controversy and reach a decision. This was a direct challenge to British imperial power.

Realizing that war between Great Britain and the United States was a real possibility, responsible leaders in both countries urged moderation. Partly because of their efforts and partly because of British difficulties in South Africa at the time, the British government suddenly reversed its position. It agreed to arbitrate the boundary dispute and even offered to help the American commission's investigation.

The Monroe Doctrine had been successfully upheld. On this occasion the United States could claim that it had used its foreign policy to protect a weak nation against a great power. Even more important, perhaps, was the fact that the British, desiring American friendship, now in effect recognized that the United States had special interests in the Caribbean area.

A third test. In 1902, seven years later, Venezuela found itself unable to repay debts owed to Great Britain, Germany, and Italy. After their demands for repayment produced no results, the three countries took joint action. They withdrew their diplomatic representatives, blockaded the Venezuelan coast, and seized several small gunboats.

At this point President Theodore Roosevelt warned the European powers that any attempt to seize territory in the Western Hemisphere would violate the Monroe Doctrine. Then he urged the countries involved to submit the dispute to arbitration. They did, and the matter was settled.

The Drago Doctrine. By the early 1900's, growing numbers of Americans were investing money in the Caribbean countries and other parts of Latin America. Latin-American leaders watched with concern the growth of American investments and the growing influence of the United States. In 1902 one of these leaders, Luis M. Drago, Argentine Minister of Foreign Affairs, expressed this concern in a policy for Latin America that came to be known as the Drago Doctrine.

Drago rejected the claim that any European nation had the right to use force to collect debts from a Latin-American nation. He argued that when individuals or nations lent money, they did so at their own risk.

Nearly all of Latin America's leaders as well as many United States citizens agreed with Drago. However, in 1904 President Roosevelt announced a policy that exempted the United States from the principle that foreign debts concerned only the debtor country and foreign investors.

The Roosevelt Corollary. The Dominican Republic was the reason for Roosevelt's announcement (see map, page 557). It owed long-overdue debts to several European countries as well as to American investors. When the European countries threatened to use armed force to collect the money, President Roosevelt at once intervened.

562

This cartoon refers to the Venezuelan crisis of 1902. "That's a live wire, gentlemen" says Uncle Sam. Whom is he warning? What is the live wire that he is pointing to? What does he imply would happen if they step on the live wire?

Roosevelt announced in 1904 that if it became necessary for any nation to interfere in the affairs of a Latin-American country, the United States had to carry out the task, not a European government.

The policy announced in 1904 came to be known as the Roosevelt Corollary to the Monroe Doctrine. With this policy the United States assumed the role of "international police officer" in the Western Hemisphere. On several occasions during the next two decades, the United States used the Roosevelt Corollary to justify its intervention in the affairs of several Latin-American nations.

There were, of course, two ways of looking at the Roosevelt Corollary. From the United States' point of view, the North Americans were protecting their weaker neighbors from European intervention. On the other hand, Latin Americans were well aware that the policy could be used against them and that it was basically an insult to their national pride.

Dominican Republic as protectorate. The United States first exercised its "international police power" by intervening in the affairs of the Dominican Republic. As part of an agreement with the Dominican government in 1905, President Roosevelt promised to guarantee the Republic's **territorial integrity.** That is, he promised to use American armed forces, if necessary, to prevent any European country from seizing Dominican territory. In exchange for this guarantee, the Dominican government agreed to allow an American agent to collect its customs duties. In addition it agreed to turn over 45 percent of the duties to the Dominican government and to use the rest of the money to pay foreign creditors.

Although customs duties doubled under American supervision and the financial position of the Dominican Republic improved, the Dominican people resented United States control. Finally, in 1916, during President Wilson's administration, the Dominican government announced it intended to end the protectorate.

The United States answered this challenge by landing marines and suspending the Dominican legislature. For eight years, until

The American flag flies high as the United States takes formal possession of the Virgin Islands from Denmark in 1917. For the next 14 years, this territory would be governed under the supervision of the U.S. Department of the Navy.

1924, the Dominican Republic was ruled by a Dominican military dictatorship under the American government. The United States withdrew its military forces in 1924 but did not end its role of "protector" until 1940.

Protectorate in Haiti. The same general methods used to secure control of the Dominican Republic were applied to Haiti (see map, page 557) in 1914. During Wilson's administration revolutions shook the debt-ridden Haitian republic, and the United States landed marines there.

The Haitians were then asked to ratify a treaty prepared by the United States Department of State. This treaty gave the United States the right to (1) supervise Haiti's finances, (2) intervene to maintain order, and (3) control the Haitian police force. After considerable American pressure, Haiti ratified the treaty, which went into effect early in 1916.

Neither the treaty nor the continued presence of American troops restored order completely. During the next four or five years, nearly 2,000 Haitians were killed in riots and other outbreaks of violence.

Nevertheless, some improvements did come to Haiti during the years of United States control. Some Americans, however, agreed with those Haitians who argued that better sanitation, health, and education and increased prosperity were not worth the loss of freedom.

Interference in Central America. Twice between 1900 and 1920, American military forces were used in Nicaragua and Honduras to gain a large measure of control over these republics. In addition, the United States had great influence over the governments of Colombia, Costa Rica, and Guatemala (see map, page 557). This influence was secured by a policy labeled **dollar diplomacy** by its critics.

Under the so-called dollar diplomacy, American bankers, sometimes by invitation of the Department of State, lent money to Caribbean governments. When the debtors failed to repay their debts or the interest on their loans, the United States government intervened to protect American investments. This intervention took various forms, including the landing of marines, the supervision of elections, and support to the political group that favored the United States.

The Virgin Islands. Back in 1868 Secretary of State Seward had tried to get Congress to buy three of the Virgin Islands (see map, page 557) from Denmark. Congress had refused; it refused again in 1902.

In 1917, however, with World War I raging in Europe, the United States feared that Germany might secure control of these strategic bases. It renewed the offer to buy the islands, and this time negotiations were completed. With the payment of $25 million to Denmark, the islands became outposts of America's Caribbean empire.

As the map on page 557 shows, the Virgin Islands lie at the eastern edge of the West Indies. United States naval bases on the islands, in Puerto Rico, and at Guantánamo Bay in Cuba help to guarantee American control over the Caribbean Sea and the approaches to the Panama Canal.

SECTION SURVEY

IDENTIFY: Napoleon III, Benito Juárez, arbitration, Richard Olney, Drago Doctrine, territorial integrity, dollar diplomacy.

1. (a) How did the United States justify its intervention in Latin-American affairs? (b) Do you agree that this intervention was justified? Why or why not?
2. (a) What were the provisions of the original Monroe Doctrine of 1823? (b) Describe two occasions on which the Monroe Doctrine was tested and upheld.
3. (a) In what way did the Roosevelt Corollary modify the original Monroe Doctrine? (b) Give examples of cases in which the Roosevelt Corollary was applied.
4. Cartoon Study: (a) What is the subject of the cartoon on page 563? (b) What attitude does the cartoonist seem to have toward this situation? How can you tell?

3 Conflict breaks out between the United States and Mexico

From the early 1800's and particularly after the Mexican-American War in 1848, the United States and Mexico had been uneasy, if not hostile, neighbors.

Unreconciled . differences. Relations between the two countries had been troubled by repeated acts of violence, some major, others minor. The Mexican people could not forget that through the Mexican-American War they had lost one third of their country to their powerful northern neighbor.

Moreover, in the years following the war, the borderlands between Mexico and the United States remained a source of tension. During the 1870's and 1880's, American troops often pursued bands of Indians across the border into Mexican territory. There were long-standing disputes involving the water rights to the Rio Grande and the Colorado River. Banditry, smuggling, and cattle rustling were common along the border. Underlying all of these conflicts was the deep-seated and mutually-shared prejudice of Anglo-Americans and Mexican Americans in the borderlands.

It was American investments south of the Rio Grande that eventually involved the United States in outright conflict with Mexico. By the time Woodrow Wilson became President in 1913, American citizens had invested nearly $1 billion in Mexican oil wells, mines, railroads, and ranches. Most of Mexico's trade was with the United States.

Dictatorship and revolution. Mexico was closely tied to the United States, and Mexico's President, Porfirio Diaz, was largely responsible for this. Diaz, although called "President," was actually a dictator. With the exception of three years from 1881 to 1884, he had ruled Mexico since 1877. During his long rule, he had brought peace and order to Mexico and had helped to develop the country's resources.

To develop Mexico's resources, Diaz had encouraged foreign investors to finance and operate mines, factories, and other industries by offering them special privileges. With this encouragement, foreign capital, much of it

This painting, "Impassioned Democracy," is part of a giant mural that decorates Mexico's Palacio Nacional. The mural was done by artist Diego Rivera in the 1930's as a visual record of Mexico's leading historical figures and issues.

from American investors, had poured into Mexico. Thus foreign investors and the privileged friends of dictator Diaz enjoyed most of the benefits of Mexico's developing economy.

In 1910 the Mexicans staged a successful revolution and restored constitutional government to their country. Diaz resigned and left for Europe. Francisco Madero then became President, but only for a short time. Early in 1913 Madero was assassinated by Victoriano Huerta (HWAIR·tah), who then seized control of the government.

Huerta had many enemies, including friends of the late President Madero. His enemies also included many Mexicans who demanded drastic social and economic reform. The struggle against Huerta, led by Venus-

tiano Carranza, plunged Mexico more deeply into bitter fighting and bloodshed.

Wilson's "watchful waiting." Many Americans were deeply troubled by this situation. Many were dismayed because Huerta had risen to power as the result of a cold-blooded murder. Others with investments in Mexico were disturbed by attacks on their property. President Wilson was urged to send military forces into Mexico to protect American investments and to restore law and order.

The President chose instead to follow a policy that he hoped would preserve the independence of the Mexican people. He outlined his policy in a speech shortly after his election. "The United States will never again seek one additional foot of territory by conquest," he declared. "We have seen material interests threaten constitutional freedom in the United States," he went on to say. "Therefore we will now know how to sympathize with those in the rest of America who have to contend with such powers, not only within their borders but from outside their borders also." He then urged the Latin-American countries to settle the Mexican problem in their own way.

Although some European countries promptly recognized the Huerta government, Wilson refused to do so. He was convinced that the Mexicans themselves would soon get rid of Huerta. Meanwhile, the United States would follow a policy of "watchful waiting."

Wilson's refusal to intervene pleased most Latin Americans. However, many Americans criticized the President as they saw American lives and property destroyed in Mexico.

American intervention. As the months passed, even President Wilson began to lose patience. Hundreds of small revolutionary groups roamed Mexico, but they were not organized and Huerta remained in power. American citizens in Mexico were killed, and there were rumors that Huerta might try to confiscate, or seize, American property.

The final crisis came in April 1914, when a Mexican official arrested several American sailors near Tampico, Mexico, which was under martial law. The sailors were soon released, but Huerta refused to apologize for the incident. To make matters worse, a German ship arrived at Veracruz with machine guns and other military supplies for Huerta. President Wilson then ordered United States marines to occupy Veracruz. This action united Mexican public opinion against the United States.

The ABC mediation. At this critical stage, Argentina, Brazil, and Chile—sometimes called the "ABC powers"—invited President Wilson to send representatives to meet with Mexican leaders and those of other nations to try to reach a solution. Wilson accepted the invitation, and the conference was held at Niagara Falls, Canada. Among its other recommendations, the conference urged Huerta to retire. Huerta did retire, faced with the fact that his forces were being beaten by those of his rival, Carranza.

Carranza then established himself in power in Mexico, and American forces withdrew from Veracruz. In 1915 Carranza guaranteed that Mexico would respect foreign lives and property, and the United States recognized him as leader of the Mexican government.

American troops in Mexico. Carranza's reforms divided his followers, who began to quarrel among themselves. One of those who turned against Carranza was Francisco "Pancho" Villa (VEE·yah). Villa was angry at the United States for helping Carranza. Hoping to force American troops to intervene in Mexico, Villa and his followers in 1916 seized 18 Americans in northern Mexico and put them to death. Later, Villa crossed the border and raided Columbus, New Mexico, killing 17 Americans.

President Wilson announced he would send an expedition into Mexico to capture Villa "dead or alive." Carranza reluctantly agreed, and General John J. Pershing led some 5,000 troops across the border. The deeper Pershing pushed into Mexican territory, the more hostile the Mexicans became. For a time the threat of war hung over both countries. Finally, in January 1917, American troops withdrew from Mexico without having captured the elusive Villa.

Mexican immigration. One major result of the years of unrest in Mexico was the increased immigration of Mexicans into the United States. Many came as political exiles. Others came to escape from the uncertainties of life in a country torn by revolution. Still others came, as millions of immigrants from other countries had come, in search of a better life in a more prosperous country.

SECTION SURVEY

IDENTIFY: Porfirio Diaz, Victoriano Huerta, ABC powers, Venustiano Carranza, "Pancho" Villa, John Pershing.

1. Give examples to show how the economic interests of the United States and Mexico were closely interwoven.

2. What differences and events contributed to the growing hostilities with Mexico?

3. (a) Describe the circumstances that led to Wilson's policy of "watchful waiting." (b) Explain the policy. (c) Why did Wilson abandon "watchful waiting"?

4. How did the ABC powers help solve the conflict between the United States and Mexico?

Chapter Survey

Summary: Tracing the Main Ideas

The Spanish-American War of 1898 marked a turning point in America's position in the world. After the war the United States embarked upon a program of imperialism similar in many ways to that being followed by the powers of the Western world, as well as Japan.

The influence of the United States was particularly strong in the countries bordering the Caribbean Sea. The Panama Canal provided a connecting link between the various parts of America's rapidly growing empire. To protect that vital artery of trade, the United States took steps to bring other Caribbean countries under its influence. Each new step the United States government took, each new commitment it assumed, led to still further steps and still further commitments.

The United States had long before expressed its special interest in the Caribbean and the rest of Latin America by issuing the Monroe Doctrine. In 1904 the United States added the Roosevelt Corollary to the Monroe Doctrine.

The corollary stated that the United States could intervene in the domestic affairs of Latin American countries, including Mexico. The United States justified this intervention on the ground that it was acting as the friendly police officer for the Western Hemisphere. To Latin-Americans in general, however, the United States appeared instead more like a bully.

In the next chapter, you will see why and how the United States was drawn into World War I and how the nation emerged from that conflict as a great world power.

Inquiring into History

1. (a) How would you justify Theodore Roosevelt's policies in the Caribbean? (b) How would you criticize them?
2. It has been said that the Monroe Doctrine protected Latin America from Europe but not from the United States. Do you agree or disagree? Explain the reasons for your answer.
3. Theodore Roosevelt once boasted: "I took Panama." (a) What did he mean? (b) What does this say about the power of the Presidency? (c) What amends did the United States make to Colombia?
4. The Panama Canal created new commitments for the United States. Explain.
5. What is your opinion of dollar diplomacy? Explain.
6. President Roosevelt stated as his foreign policy, "Speak softly and carry a big stick, and you will go far." (a) What did Roosevelt mean by this statement? (b) Give examples to show that Roosevelt acted on this policy.

Relating Past to Present

1. Do you think Puerto Rico has benefited from its relationship with the United States? Explain.
2. In the 1970's Panama and the United States signed a treaty giving Panama greater influence and control over the Panama Canal. (a) What were the provisions of that treaty? (b) Do you think the United States should have agreed to such a treaty? Why or why not?

Developing Social Science Skills

1. Examine the cartoon on page 556. (a) Explain the subject of the cartoon. (b) What point of view is presented in the cartoon? (c) How effective is the cartoon in presenting its point of view? Explain.
2. Make a timeline for a bulletin-board display for the years 1898 to 1914. (The timeline on page 555 will help you get started.) Use pictures or drawings to show the major events in America's new role as a world power.

Chapter 30

America's Involvement in World War I

1914–1920

On the morning of July 28, 1914, Americans opened their newspapers with shocked surprise. In screaming headlines the New York *Tribune* reported, "AUSTRIA DECLARES WAR, RUSHES VAST ARMY INTO SERBIA; RUSSIA MASSES 80,000 MEN ON BORDER." Other papers carried the same news.

In general, the reaction of the American public was one of both stunned disbelief and withdrawal. For many years and particularly during the early 1900's, governments and individuals had devoted much time and effort to develop international understanding and to promote peace. Now, in the summer of 1914, all of these efforts had suddenly gone up in flames. Well, if the Europeans chose to be so reckless, let them reap the consequences. The American people wanted no part of this European madness.

As the months passed, however, it became clear that the United States as a major power could not remain neutral. Step by step, the nation moved closer to involvement and in the spring of 1917 finally entered the war on the side of the Allies.

The conflict that started in 1914 was the world's first total war. Few people on the face of the earth remained unaffected. Before it ended four years later, 30 nations on six continents would be involved. More than 8 million fighting men would be killed and an equal number of civilians would lose their lives.

THE CHAPTER IN OUTLINE

1. Peace-keeping efforts fail and World War I breaks out.

2. The United States attempts to remain neutral.

3. The United States declares war and mobilizes its strength.

4. American troops and ideals help the Allies win the war.

5. The United States refuses to join the League of Nations.

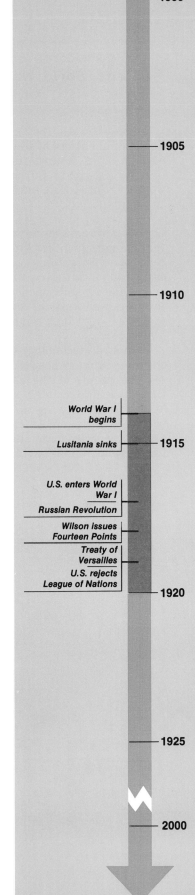

- 1900
- 1905
- 1910
- World War I begins
- Lusitania sinks — 1915
- U.S. enters World War I
- Russian Revolution
- Wilson issues Fourteen Points
- Treaty of Versailles
- U.S. rejects League of Nations — 1920
- 1925
- 2000

1 Peace-keeping efforts fail and World War I breaks out

During the late 1800's and the early 1900's, the leading nations of the world had taken important steps toward international cooperation. By 1914 many Europeans and Americans were convinced that major wars would never again occur.

Growing interdependence. For nearly 100 years, a movement for international peace had been steadily gaining strength. During the early 1900's, antiwar societies in both Europe and America published pamphlets insisting that war was wasteful and failed to solve any problems—and that even the victors paid too high a price.

Industrial technology was rapidly breaking down the barriers of space and time and bringing the people of the earth closer together. Railway trains rumbled across national boundaries. Passenger ships and freighters steamed back and forth across the oceans. The telegraph, the telephone, and underwater cables linked people in all parts of the world.

The number, variety, and importance of activities that people of different nations could and did carry on together increased greatly. Many businesses now bought and sold in worldwide markets and built industries in different countries. Humanitarian associations, including the Red Cross, organized on an international basis. Professional groups—scientists, engineers, doctors, and scholars—formed international societies and pooled their knowledge for the benefit of all peoples.

Governments as well as individual citizens also engaged in a growing number of activities requiring international cooperation. By 1914 at least 30 international agencies of government were dealing with problems shared by many nations. Among them were transportation, communication, disease and sanitation, weights and measures, postal regulations, and maritime rules.

The Pan-American Union. Meanwhile the governments of the leading nations of the world had been making new efforts to prevent war. On several occasions during the late 1800's and the early 1900's, delegates from many different nations met to discuss the issues of war and peace. In 1889–90, delegates from the Latin-American countries and the

During the early 1900's members of the Women's Peace Party used fans to symbolize their hopes—that Americans would keep cool and not allow troubles elsewhere in the world to inflame them into going to war.

United States met in Washington, D.C., and organized the International Union of American Republics. The union aimed to abolish war and to substitute for it arbitration between the American republics.

In 1910 the name of the International Union of American Republics was changed to the Pan-American Union. Under that name it held periodic meetings to discuss common problems. (Later, in 1948, the members of the Pan-American Union created the Organization of American States, known as the O.A.S.)

In the early 1900's, United States expansion and interference in the Caribbean area angered many Latin Americans and thus weakened the influence of the Pan-American Union. Nevertheless, throughout the Americas the Pan-American Union was the symbol of hope for a new, more peaceful world.

The Hague Conference. Millions of people in both Europe and the Americas had also taken hope from two conferences held in Europe.

The First Hague Conference, called by the tsar of Russia, met at The Hague in the Netherlands in 1899. Twenty-six nations sent delegates. The delegates strongly urged nations to try to settle disputes through mediation or arbitration. In cases involving mediation, two or more nations engaged in a dispute would ask a disinterested third party or nation to recommend a solution. In cases involving arbitration, two or more nations engaged in a dispute would agree in advance to accept the decision of a neutral party. To encourage arbitration, the First Hague Conference organized the Permanent Court of Arbitration with headquarters at The Hague. The conference also tried to lessen the horrors of warfare by outlawing certain weapons and by drawing up rules for the conduct of war.

The Second Hague Conference, called by the tsar of Russia and President Theodore Roosevelt, met at The Hague in 1907. This time 44 nations sent delegates. The conference drafted additional rules for the conduct of war and adopted the Drago Doctrine. As you remember, this doctrine stated that no nation should use force to collect debts "unless the debtor country refused arbitration, or having accepted arbitration, failed to submit to the award."

The first two Hague Conferences encouraged those who were working to promote peace. A third conference was being planned when war broke out in Europe.

Other efforts to promote peace. Although President Roosevelt believed that some wars were necessary, he played a leading role in the peace movement. He was responsible for the 1905 peace conference at Portsmouth, New Hampshire. There Japan and Russia reached an agreement ending the Russo-Japanese War. President Roosevelt and his successor, President Taft, also played active parts in other international negotiations.

President Wilson, who took office in 1913, was an even stronger champion of international understanding. He supported his Secretary of State, William Jennings Bryan, who negotiated antiwar treaties with 21 nations in 1913 and 1914. These treaties declared that every dispute had to be submitted to a joint commission for investigation and recommendation. The nations signing the treaties promised not to go to war until the commissions had made their reports.

By 1914 such efforts had built what seemed to be a solid and enduring structure of peace. Why, then, did war break out?

The spark that led to war. In spite of the many efforts made to preserve peace in the early 1900's, the European nations during these years were standing on a powder keg. When a spark was struck to the powder, the hopes and plans for peace of peoples everywhere exploded.

The spark was struck in the Balkan Peninsula of Europe (see map, page 572) in the early summer of 1914. There Serbian nationalists had pledged to free all Slavs° living under the rule of the Austro-Hungarian empire. The Serbian nationalists assassinated the Archduke Franz Ferdinand, heir to the throne of Austria-Hungary, and his wife Sophie as they rode through the streets of Sarajevo (SAH·rah·yeh·voh), the capital of the province of Bosnia. Bosnia had only recently become part of the Austro-Hungarian empire.

The Serbian conspirators were caught and brought to trial, but Franz Joseph, emperor of Austria-Hungary, and his advisers decided to use this opportunity to destroy Serbia's power completely. Thus Austria-Hungary made certain harsh demands against Serbia, which Serbia refused to meet.

°**Slavs:** a people widely spread over central, eastern, and southeastern Europe whose languages come from the same basic root. The Slavs under Austro-Hungarian rule were called South Slavs.

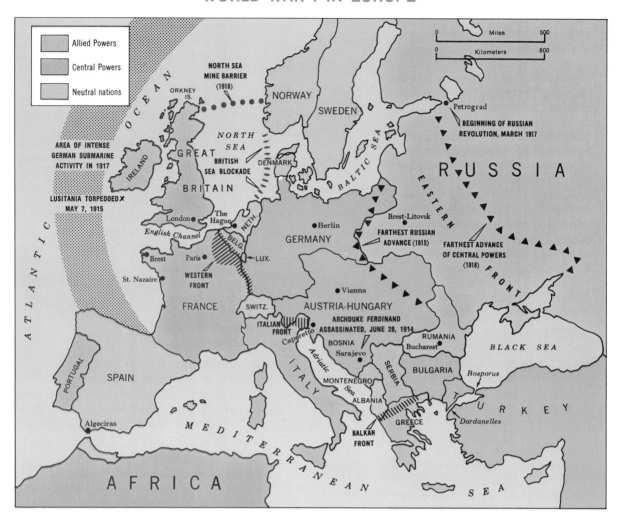

As tension grew, European diplomats struggled to solve the differences between Austria-Hungary and Serbia. The efforts failed and, with the support of Germany, its main ally, Austria-Hungary declared war on Serbia on July 28, 1914.

The movement of Austrian armies across the border into Serbia triggered a chain reaction. Within a week Austria-Hungary and Germany were at war with Russia, France, and Great Britain. Before the conflict ended, it had engulfed 30 nations on six continents. The nations siding with Austria-Hungary and Germany were known as the Central Powers. Those allying themselves with Russia, France, and Great Britain were referred to as the Allied Powers, or simply as the Allies.

Did the tragic incident at Sarajevo really start World War I? Yes and no. It was the immediate cause, the spark that touched off the explosion. However, there were deep, underlying causes that help to explain why the war came and spread so rapidly and widely.

Nationalism as a cause. An intense spirit of nationalism was one of the underlying sources of tension. The term **nationalism** often refers to the strong feeling people have for their own country. It may also refer to the desire of people ruled by others to throw off this foreign rule and create their own nation.

It was the desire to free certain Slavs from Austro-Hungarian rule that led the Serbian conspirators to assassinate the heir to the throne of Austria-Hungary. Austria-Hungary declared war on Serbia in order to crush this rising spirit of nationalism among the Slavic people. This spirit of nationalism was not confined to the Balkan Peninsula. In almost every country of Europe as well as in the colonies overseas, people ruled by other nations longed for independence.

Imperialism as a cause. Another source of tension was imperialism—the struggle for colonies. As you recall, during the late 1800's and the early 1900's the major powers of the world were engaged in a race for empire. By 1914, so far as colonies were concerned, the nations of Europe could be grouped into two classes: the "have" nations and the "have-not" nations.

Great Britain and France, each with huge colonial empires, were among the "have" powers. Although Russia owned no colonies, it possessed immense areas of underdeveloped land and thus was also a "have" nation.

Germany, on the other hand, was a "have-not" nation. It owned colonies in Africa and in the Pacific, but its colonial empire was relatively small, and Germany wanted additional territory. Italy was in a similar situation. One of the reasons that finally brought Italy into the war on the Allied side was a promise of colonies when the war ended.

International rivalries. Rivalry among nations was not, however, confined to the race for colonies. Austria-Hungary attacked Serbia partly to strengthen its hold on the Slavic peoples and partly to increase its influence in the Balkan Peninsula. Russia, on the other hand, came to Serbia's aid to prevent Austria-Hungary from increasing its influence.

France supported Russia not only because it was Russia's ally but also because it wanted to recover Alsace-Lorraine, a former French area that the Germans had conquered in 1871. Italy desired nearby territories within the Austro-Hungarian empire. Every Balkan country looked greedily at territory belonging to its neighbors. Russia longed for ice-free harbors in the Baltic Sea and for an outlet through the Dardanelles and the Bosporus into the Mediterranean Sea. Germany, the major Baltic Sea power, and Turkey, which controlled the Dardanelles, feared and distrusted Russia.

Systems of alliance. The mounting tensions with their accompanying plots and intrigues led to an armaments race, or race for military power. Long before 1914 the relative sizes of their navies and armies occupied a major part of the attention of all of the governments in Europe.

Besides building up their military forces, European nations tried to gain security with the **balance-of-power system.** This meant that every nation tried to increase its own strength by securing as many allies as possible. Thus Germany, Austria-Hungary, and Italy joined in what became known as the Triple Alliance. To maintain a balance of power, Great Britain, France, and Russia joined in what became known as the Triple Entente (ahn·TAHNT). Both of these rival alliances had been completed by 1907.

Austria's declaration of war on Serbia set the whole system of alliances into motion. Of all the nations, only Italy failed to live up to its treaty obligations, which pledged Italy to support Austria-Hungary and Germany. Waiting to see which side would promise the most, Italy did not enter the war until 1915, and then it fought on the Allied side.

Peace or war? During the early 1900's, as you may recall, strong forces pulled peoples and nations in two directions at the same time. With one hand, governments tried to strengthen the bonds between nations and build a solid structure of peace. With the other hand, governments plotted and schemed against one another and desperately planned for war or for the protection of their national interests in case war broke out.

SECTION SURVEY

IDENTIFY: interdependence, mediation, Slavs, Central Powers, Allied Powers, nationalism, imperialism, balance-of-power system, Triple Alliance, Triple Entente.

1. What was the purpose of the Pan-American Union?

2. Why did the first two Hague Conferences greatly encourage those who were working to promote peace among nations?

3. Why is the incident at Sarajevo considered the spark that set off World War I?

4. How did the following factors help cause World War I and encourage its rapid spread: (a) nationalism, (b) imperialism, (c) international rivalries, (d) the balance-of-power system?

573

2 The United States attempts to remain neutral

America's first reaction to the outbreak of war in Europe, as you have read, was one of shocked surprise and withdrawal. The war seemed unreal, a nightmare that surely would not last long.

American neutrality. Nevertheless, the war was all too real, and President Wilson urged the American people to be "neutral in fact as well as in name" and "impartial in thought as well as in action." From the beginning, however, Americans were torn between the desire to avoid war and their sympathy for one side or the other.

Millions of recently naturalized Americans had friends and relatives in Europe. Men and women of German origin—or of Austrian or Turkish origin—wanted the Central Powers to

win. Most Americans, however, were sympathetic to the Allied Powers. The ties of language, similar democratic governments, and deep-rooted traditions bound Americans to Great Britain. The ties with France were also strong. After all, the French back in 1778 had come to the aid of Americans fighting for their independence. As World War I went on, this sympathy for the Allies led thousands of young Americans to enlist in the British, Canadian, and French armed forces. A special unit of volunteer American fliers, called the Lafayette Escadrille, was created as part of the new French flying force.

Although in 1914 American sympathies were divided, most Americans supported the President's policy of neutrality and prayed for an early end to the war.

The German plan of attack. The Central Powers, under the leadership of the German High Command, had every intention of ending the war quickly. They wanted to conquer France before the Russians could fully mobilize. With France at their mercy, they could then turn against Russia.

Long before the war the French, fearful of German attack, had built strong fortifications along the entire Franco-German frontier. However, the French had not fortified the border between France and Belgium. The French counted on an international agreement, which the Germans had signed, that in the event of war Belgium would be respected as a neutral nation.

The German Chancellor, however, declared that the international agreement respecting Belgium's neutrality was merely "a scrap of paper." The German High Command launched an attack against neutral Belgium and Luxembourg, intending to reach the borders of France in six days. As shown on the map on page 575, seven powerful German armies were to strike in a great wheeling action at northern France.

Failure of the plan. The German plan failed, largely because Belgium resisted. Because of gallant resistance by the small Belgian army, the Germans took 18 days to cross Belgium, not the six called for in the German timetable. This delay gave General Joffre, commander of the French armies, time to rush troops to the Belgian border. In addition it gave the British time to transport an army of about 90,000 to northern France.

In 1914 heavy bombing nearly leveled the city of Reims in northeastern France. The bombing also destroyed the interior of the historic Reims Cathedral, including its irreplaceable stained glass windows.

The French and the British arrived too late to save Belgium. Nor were they able to stop the Germans at the Belgian frontier. Crushed by the superior might of the Germans, the French and British retreated to the Marne River, where General Joffre hastily prepared his main defense.

Fighting against seemingly hopeless odds, the French and British stopped the Germans early in September 1914 at the Marne River in the First Battle of the Marne. The Germans then fell back to the Aisne (AYN) River, where they dug a line of trenches and checked an Allied counteroffensive.

The First Battle of the Marne was one of the decisive battles of the war. If the Germans had won, they might have crushed all remaining French and British resistance in a few weeks.

Stalemate on the Western Front. By 1915 the war in Western Europe had reached a stalemate. Both sides were dug in along a 600-mile (965-kilometer) line reaching from the Swiss border to the English Channel. During the next three years, both the Germans and the Allies, with only a thin strip of land called "no man's land" separating their trenches, fought desperately along the Western Front. Neither side was able to break through the enemy line or to end the trench warfare. Thousands died in this bloody struggle, but until the spring of 1918 neither side made a significant gain.

There were other fronts—and on all of them troops were fighting and dying. The Central Powers and Russia were locked in combat along the entire Eastern Front. Turkish troops defended a precarious line that reached southward through Palestine as far as Medina, in Arabia, against the British and French and their allies. The fighting forces of Austria-Hungary and Italy faced each other in the area of their common boundary north of the Adriatic Sea (see map, page 572).

The British blockade. The prospect of a long war was bad news indeed for Americans who hoped to remain neutral. It meant, among other things, that warfare on the high seas would grow fiercer as Great Britain and Germany tried to prevent supplies from the United States and other neutral countries from reaching the other side.

The British fleet controlled the seas, at least during the opening months of the war. It blockaded the German coast (see map, page

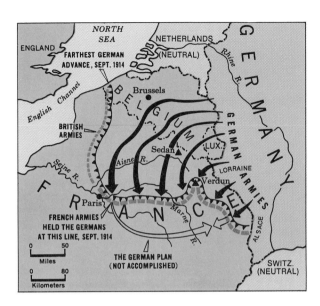

WESTERN FRONT: 1914–1917

572) and laid explosive mines in the North Sea. To the angry astonishment of Americans, the British navy also blockaded neutral countries, such as Norway, Sweden, Denmark, and the Netherlands, through which American goods flowed into Germany. American anger increased when the British began to examine American mail bound for Europe and ordered all neutral ships to stop at British ports, where their cargoes were searched. The United States protested that Great Britain's actions were illegal. Such actions violated the rights of neutrals to travel the high seas, provided they were not carrying war materials.

Submarine warfare. American anger at Great Britain subsided, however, in the face of German submarine warfare. According to international law, naval vessels of countries at war had the right to stop and search a neutral ship for weapons, munitions, and other materials useful in war, known as **contraband.** The naval vessel had the right to seize a neutral ship carrying contraband and take it into port as a prize of war. If it were impossible to take the neutral vessel into port, the warship was required to take its passengers and crew to a safe place before sinking the prize.

Submarines were not armed to defend themselves against enemy warships while on the surface. Thus they could not take seized vessels into port. Nor could submarines take the passengers and crew of a large vessel on board. Least of all could they surface and search neutral ships, for the moment they rose to the surface they were "sitting ducks" for even one well-aimed shot from a naval gun. Submarines were designed to lurk in the ocean depths, to strike suddenly without warning at an enemy ship, and to slip away quickly before a counterattack.

The German surface fleet, although powerful, was still no match for the British navy. The Germans, therefore, had concentrated on building submarines, called U-boats. Early in the war, the Germans notified President Wilson that they intended to turn their subma-

Notices like this one appeared in American newspapers, warning citizens of the dangers of sailing on British ships. Many Americans resented the threat that submarine warfare posed to freedom of travel.

NOTICE!

TRAVELLERS intending to embark on the Atlantic voyage are reminded that a state of war exists between Germany and her allies and Great Britain and her allies; that the zone of war includes the waters adjacent to the British Isles; that, in accordance with formal notice given by the Imperial German Government, vessels flying the flag of Great Britain, or of any of her allies, are liable to destruction in those waters and that travellers sailing in the war zone on ships of Great Britain or her allies do so at their own risk.

IMPERIAL GERMAN EMBASSY

WASHINGTON, D. C., APRIL 22, 1915.

rines loose in the Atlantic. President Wilson promptly replied that the United States would hold Germany responsible for any acts that endangered American property and lives on the high seas.

The *Lusitania*. The Germans were convinced that their submarine blockade would ruin Great Britain. They therefore ignored President Wilson's warning and ordered their U-boats to patrol the Atlantic shipping lanes. On March 28, 1915, a British steamer was torpedoed and sunk near Ireland, carrying to their deaths more than 100 persons, including an American.

This and other incidents led to the sinking of the British liner *Lusitania* off the southern coast of Ireland on May 7, 1915, with the loss of 1,198 lives, including 128 Americans. Since the *Lusitania* was carrying war materials bound for England, the Germans believed that their action was justified.

In three strongly worded messages to the German government in Berlin, the American State Department protested against the sinking of the *Lusitania*. The messages warned that any repetition of such action would have serious consequences. American anger at the *Lusitania* affair was still at the boiling point when on August 9, 1915, another U-boat sank the *Arabic*, a British liner, with the loss of two American lives.

Alarmed at the American reaction, Germany on September 1 gave a written promise that in the future "liners will not be sunk by our submarines without warning . . . provided that the liners do not try to escape or offer resistance." Americans had to be content with this promise.

The sinking of the *Lusitania* marked a turning point in American feeling about the war. Increasing numbers of Americans began to realize that the conflict in Europe was not far off but close at hand. They began to understand that neutrality might become impossible. Nevertheless, in 1915 most still hoped that the United States could avoid war.

More sinkings, more promises. In March 1916 the Germans broke their promise and attacked a French passenger vessel, the *Sussex*. Lives were lost and several Americans were injured. President Wilson threatened to break off diplomatic relations with Germany unless it agreed to abandon submarine warfare.

576

In what became known as the "*Sussex* pledge," Germany renewed its earlier promise not to sink liners without warning and without providing for the safety of the passengers. However, the Germans added an important reservation. They would keep the promise on condition that the United States would persuade the Allies to modify the food blockade of Germany, which, according to Berlin, was inflicting hunger and even starvation on the German people. The United States replied that the British blockade had nothing to do with German violation of American neutral rights on the high seas.

A rising war spirit. American opinion was divided over Wilson's efforts to enforce neutrality. Some people, including former President Theodore Roosevelt, felt that the United States was not firm enough. Others believed that the American government was unwisely going too far in its threatening demands on Berlin. Secretary of State Bryan, for example, resigned during the *Lusitania* crisis. In Bryan's opinion, the United States should forbid American citizens to travel on British and French ships. Bryan also believed that Congress should stop Americans from selling war materials to nations at war.

President Wilson refused to follow the advice of those who shared Bryan's views. Instead, Wilson supported a program for strengthening the army and navy. The National Defense Act, passed in June 1916, increased America's regular army from 106,000 to 175,000 soldiers and provided for officers' training camps. A three-year naval program was started in 1916. In 1916 the government also created the Council of National Defense and the United States Shipping Board. These agencies planned the mobilization of the country's resources in case of war and began a huge shipbuilding program.

The war preparations did not mean that either Wilson or the public had abandoned all hope of remaining neutral. Indeed, many Americans voted for the reelection of Wilson in November 1916 on the ground that "he kept us out of war."

Six months later, under the leadership of President Wilson and Congress, the American people entered the conflict, millions of them with considerable enthusiasm. What happened to lead the administration to abandon neutrality and take this step?

SECTION SURVEY

IDENTIFY: trench warfare, contraband, U-boats, *Lusitania,* "*Sussex* pledge."

1. President Wilson stated that the United States had to be "neutral in fact as well as in name" and "impartial in thought as well as in action." Why did many Americans find it difficult to maintain such impartiality?

2. America's neutral rights were violated by both Great Britain and Germany. Explain.

3. Map Study: Study the maps on pages 572 and 575. (a) Locate the area in the first map that is shown enlarged in the second map. (b) Which map would be more useful in gaining an overall impression of the war? In gaining information on military strategies? In naming the countries on each side? Explain your answers.

3 The United States declares war and mobilizes its strength

During the winter of 1916–17, all American hope of remaining neutral finally vanished. The German leaders themselves were largely responsible for this development.

Diplomatic relations broken. On February 1, 1917, Germany decided to renew unrestricted submarine warfare, thus going back on the "*Sussex* pledge." A German proposal to permit only one American passenger ship to sail to England each week added insult to injury.

The German High Command made this decision fully aware that it would almost certainly bring the United States into the war. The High Command took the calculated risk that submarines could destroy Great Britain's power and will to fight before the United States could provide effective help.

Wilson met the new challenge promptly. On February 3 he broke off diplomatic relations with the German government.

Moving toward war. On February 24, British naval intelligence agents revealed a German message they had intercepted and decoded. The message had been sent from Germany by Foreign Secretary Arthur Zimmerman to the German minister in Mexico. It contained instructions about what to do in case war broke out between Germany and the United States. In this event, the German minister was to offer Mexico an alliance with Germany. With German support Mexico was to attack the United States and "reconquer the lost territory in New Mexico, Texas, and Arizona." When Wilson released the Zimmermann note to the Associated Press on March 1, Americans were shocked and angry.

On March 12 President Wilson, through the State Department, announced that all American merchant vessels sailing through war zones would be armed for defense against German submarines. The public received this announcement with mixed reactions but in general approved.

Still other and deeper forces moved American sympathies toward the Allies and toward war with Germany. For one thing, American ties with Great Britain and France were traditionally closer than those with Germany. Not least important, American shipments of munitions to the Allied Powers had risen from $6 million in 1914 to nearly $500 million in 1916. By April 1917, American bankers had loaned about $2 billion to the Allies. Naturally, these American investors wanted an Allied victory. However, historians have found no evidence to show that economic interests consciously influenced Wilson's conduct in the critical weeks before the United States entered the war.

The President's "War Message." As the weeks passed, President Wilson reluctantly concluded that America's entrance into the war was inevitable. Supported by his entire cabinet, the President called for a special session of Congress. On April 2, 1917, a solemn and hushed group of Senators, Representatives, and distinguished guests gathered to hear President Wilson present his impassioned "War Message."

The President condemned Germany's submarine warfare as "the wanton and wholesale destruction of the lives of noncombatants, men, women, and children, engaged in pursuits which have always, even in the darkest periods of modern history, been deemed innocent and legitimate. Property can be paid for; the lives of peaceful and innocent people cannot be. . . . The challenge is to all mankind," the President declared. "The wrongs against which we now array ourselves are no common wrongs; they cut to the very roots of human life."

Wilson was too great an idealist to rest his case upon the evils of unrestricted submarine warfare alone. He also summoned the American people to rise in a crusade for a better world: "We are glad to fight thus for the ultimate peace of the world and for the liberation of its peoples, the German peoples included: for the rights of nations great and small and the privilege of men everywhere to choose their way of life and of obedience. The world must be made safe for democracy. Its peace must be planted upon the tested foundations of political liberty. We have no selfish ends to serve. We desire no conquest, no dominion. We seek no indemnities for ourselves."

Congress promptly declared war. The Senate approved a war declaration on April 4, the House on April 6, 1917. America's entry into the conflict had an immediate effect upon other neutral countries. Between April 1917 and July 1918, a number of Latin-American states declared war. Most of the other American countries, although unwilling to enter the war, severed diplomatic relations with Germany.

Raising an army. As soon as war was declared, the United States began to mobilize its work force, its industries, and its natural resources. On May 18 Congress adopted the Selective Service Act, which required the registration of all men between the ages of 21 and 30. The act was amended on August 31, 1918, to include all men between 18 and 45. During the war more than 24 million Americans were registered by their local draft boards, and 2.8 million of this group were drafted into the army. Before the war ended, more than 4.7 million Americans served in the armed forces.

About 371,000 black Americans served in World War I, but, as in earlier wars, they often met prejudice and discrimination. They were restricted to separate units, recreation centers, and living accommodations. Most of the 200,000 black troops sent to Europe served in noncombatant battalions, though many of them requested combat duty. All of the 10,000 blacks who served in the navy were assigned to noncombat duties.

As the war progressed, the bravery and courage of black units under fire were plain to see. The first Allied unit to drive through to the River Rhine was the 369th, a black regiment attached to the Ninety-third Division. For outstanding courage in battle, Henry Johnson and Needham Roberts of the 369th became the first black Americans to be awarded the *Croix de Guerre,* or Cross of War, a coveted French military honor.

Financing the war. To finance the war, Congress decided to raise approximately two thirds by borrowing, the remaining one third by taxing current income. The government borrowed money by selling war bonds. Through four Liberty Loan Drives and a Victory Loan Drive, the government borrowed more than $21 billion. The government also boosted income-tax rates and levied excise taxes on railroad tickets, telegraph and telephone messages, alcoholic beverages, tobacco, and certain amusements.

Mobilizing industry. Materials were as important as workers and money. The big problem was to stimulate production and prevent waste. To achieve this goal, Congress gave President Wilson sweeping wartime powers.

The President was authorized to set prices on many commodities, including such essentials as food and fuels. He was also authorized to regulate, or even to take possession of, factories, mines, meat-packing houses, food-processing plants, and all transportation and communication facilities. The President exercised these vast powers through a number of wartime agencies, or boards.

The War Industries Board, established in 1917, became the virtual dictator of manufacturing. It developed new industries needed in the war effort. It regulated business to eliminate waste and nonessential goods. Before the war's end, the War Industries Board was engaged in regulating the production of some 30,000 commodities.

Other federal agencies also took an active part in planning the war program. The War Finance Corporation loaned public funds to businesses needing aid in manufacturing war materials. The Emergency Fleet Corporation built ships faster than German submarines could destroy them. The Railroad Administration took over the operation of the railroads, reorganized the lines, and controlled rates and wages. The Fuel Administration stimulated a larger output of coal and oil and encouraged economies in their use.

Mobilizing labor. The successful mobilization of industry depended, of course, upon the full cooperation of labor. In an effort to deal

JOIN THE ARMY AIR SERVICE BE AN AMERICAN EAGLE! CONSULT YOUR LOCAL DRAFT BOARD. READ THE ILLUSTRATED BOOKLET AT ANY RECRUITING OFFICE, OR WRITE TO THE CHIEF SIGNAL OFFICER OF THE ARMY, WASHINGTON, D.C.

When the United States entered the war, the Army Air Service had only 130 pilots and only 53 serviceable planes. Dramatic posters like the one shown above helped to attract recruits and build up the service.

with labor disputes, President Wilson in April 1918 appointed the National War Labor Board. This board was authorized to arbitrate disputes between workers and employers. In June, Wilson appointed the War Labor Policies Board. This board could establish general policies affecting wages, hours, and working conditions. These measures and the cooperation of organized labor reduced labor disputes to a minimum during the war years.

As war-related industries expanded and more and more men entered the armed forces, women helped ease the labor shortages. They worked in shops, factories, the construction industry, and in steel mills. Some became conductors on trolley cars and engineers on trains.

Conserving food. The problem of food was equally critical. Late in 1917 Congress adopted and submitted to the states an amendment to

Colleges, schools, the press, churches, fraternal lodges, women's and civic groups all cooperated with the government's campaign "to sell the war to the American people." The poster shown here illustrates some of the roles occupied by women during World War I.

the Constitution prohibiting the manufacture, sale, or transportation of alcoholic liquors. The amendment was passed, in part, to help conserve grain, which is used in making alcohol. This Eighteenth Amendment was ratified by the necessary three fourths of the states in 1919 and went into effect on January 16, 1920.

The government also made other moves to guarantee food for the American people and their allies. Herbert Hoover, who had successfully managed food relief in war-stricken Belgium, was placed in charge of the Food Administration. Hoover brought about a vast expansion of agriculture and reduced the hoarding and waste of food. He encouraged people to plant "victory gardens" and urged them to observe "wheatless" and "meatless" days. The sale of sugar and other commodities was limited. All this took place without rationing. In-

stead the Food Administration, with the crucial help of women's groups, used persuasion to get people to cooperate.

Public opinion and dissent. The government also undertook to gain the cooperation of all Americans in the war effort. The Committee on Public Information circulated millions of leaflets describing in glowing language America's official war aims and denouncing the German government. Colleges, schools, the press, churches, fraternal lodges, women's organizations, and civic groups all cooperated with the government's campaign "to sell the war to the American people." In all sorts of public gatherings, well-known people gave brief speeches publicizing the nation's war aims and philosophy.

From the beginning most Americans enthusiastically supported the war. There were, however, some dissenters, who, in greater or lesser measure, were not in sympathy with the government's war effort.

To deal with those people, Congress in June 1917 adopted the Espionage Act. This act was aimed at treasonable and disloyal activities. In May 1918 Congress strengthened the Espionage Act by an amendment, often called the Sedition Act. This act provided penalties of up to $10,000 in fines and 20 years' imprisonment, or both, for anyone found guilty of interfering with the sale of war bonds, attempting to curtail production, or using "disloyal, profane, scurrilous, or abusive language" about the American form of government or about any of its agencies.

Under these laws, the Department of Justice arrested at least 1,597 persons. Of these, 41 received prison sentences of from 10 to 20 years. In addition, newspapers and periodicals found guilty of criticizing the government's conduct of the war were deprived of their mailing privileges.

Many loyal Americans, themselves thoroughly in sympathy with the war effort, objected to the Espionage Act and Sedition Act. They held that the constitutional rights of citizens should not be interfered with, even in wartime.

For the most part, however, Americans did not need arguments or laws to secure their loyalty. Americans entered the war on a great wave of enthusiasm. They were convinced, as Wilson had put it, that this was indeed a crusade "to make the world safe for democracy."

IDENTIFY: Zimmermann note, unrestricted submarine warfare, Selective Service Act, Henry Johnson, Espionage Act.

1. In his "War Message," President Wilson asked Congress to declare war on Germany. (a) What reasons did he give? (b) Why did he view the war as a crusade?

2. How did the United States mobilize (a) workers, (b) industries, (c) natural resources, and (d) public opinion?

3. In the crusade "to make the world safe for democracy," black members of the American armed forces often faced discrimination. Comment on this contradiction.

4. Picture Study: Examine the poster on page 580. (a) What roles does it show for women? (b) Were any of these roles new for women? (c) What effects do you think World War I may have had on the movement for women's rights?

4 American troops and ideals help the Allies win the war

America's declaration of war came none too soon. In the spring of 1917, the Allies were facing a grim situation, and by the end of the year their position was desperate.

The military situation in 1917. By early 1917 the Allies, who had suffered enormous losses, were war-weary and discouraged. In March they were further disturbed by news that the tsar of Russia had been deposed and a new revolutionary government established. America's entry into the conflict in April was one of the few bright spots in a year during which Allied fortunes sank lower and lower.

In the fall Germany threw a number of crack divisions into the Austrian campaign, and on October 24 the Austrians and Germans crashed through the Italian lines at Caporetto (see map, page 572). French and British troops, rushed from the Western Front, helped to stop the rout and saved Italy from collapse.

Most serious of all, however, was the news from Russia. On November 7 the Bolsheviks, a party of radical Communists, seized power. A month later the Bolsheviks signed an armistice with Germany. Almost three months later, in March 1918, they concluded the peace treaty of Brest-Litovsk (BREST lih·TOFSK). Meanwhile Rumania, unable to stand alone against the Central Powers in eastern Europe, in 1918 signed a peace treaty at Bucharest.

Thus, by the end of 1917, the Germans were free to concentrate most of their forces on the Western Front. General Ludendorff, commander of the German armies, prepared for an offensive intended to end the war before American troops could play an important role.

American naval forces. Meanwhile the United States Navy, which had been rapidly building its strength since 1916, went into action. Before the war ended, the United States had established 45 naval bases, which were located as far north as Murmansk, in Russia, and as far south as Greece.

In cooperation with the British Navy, American naval forces patrolled the North Sea and effectively bottled up the German fleet. They also laid most of a 230-mile (370-kilometer) barrier of mines that stretched across the North Sea from Norway to the Orkney Islands (see map, page 572). This barrier greatly increased the hazards for German submarines seeking to reach the open waters of the Atlantic Ocean or to return to their bases in Germany.

Meanwhile other naval vessels helped to convoy merchant ships and troop transports through the submarine-infested waters of the Atlantic Ocean. The convoy system was so effective that 2 million American soldiers or more were transported across the Atlantic with the loss of only a few hundred lives. It was a remarkable tribute to naval efficiency and a severe blow to the Germans.

The A.E.F. in France. While the United States Navy was busy on the high seas, American land forces were being organized. President Wilson appointed General John J. Pershing as Commander of the American Expeditionary Forces (the A.E.F.). Pershing had served in Cuba, in the Philippines, and as commander of the expedition sent into Mexico to capture Pancho Villa.

Pershing landed in France early in June 1917. By the end of June, the first regiments of the First Division arrived. On July 4 several thousand "Yanks" marched through Paris amid the heartfelt cheers of the French people.

American troops arrived in ever-swelling numbers. By the fall of 1918, more than 2 million had landed in France. To supply and maintain this huge army, the Americans built huge docks and railroads as well as networks of telephone and telegraph lines in Europe. They landed 17,000 freight cars and more than 40,000 trucks. The Americans also built training camps, hospitals, storage houses, and ammunition dumps.

Germany's last bid for victory. On March 21, 1918, the Western Front exploded into violent action once more. The Germans, reinforced by seasoned troops released from the Russian front, launched a powerful campaign, or "peace offensive," to end the war. At the end of two weeks, the Germans had gained a large area of land and inflicted 160,000 casualties. By the end of May, they were at the River Marne, only 37 miles (59 kilometers) from Paris.

Pershing's original plans had called for a period of training behind the lines before his troops went into action. He had also insisted that American troops fight as a separate army under their own top command. However, in the spring of 1918, he consented to putting every available soldier into the lines immediately. French, British, and American troops fought together under a unified Allied command directed by the French military leader Marshal Foch (FOSH).

Under the command of General John J. Pershing, the American Expeditionary Force distinguished itself during the allied victory drive. Here, in July 1918, American troops perform bravely at the front near Méry, to the east of Paris.

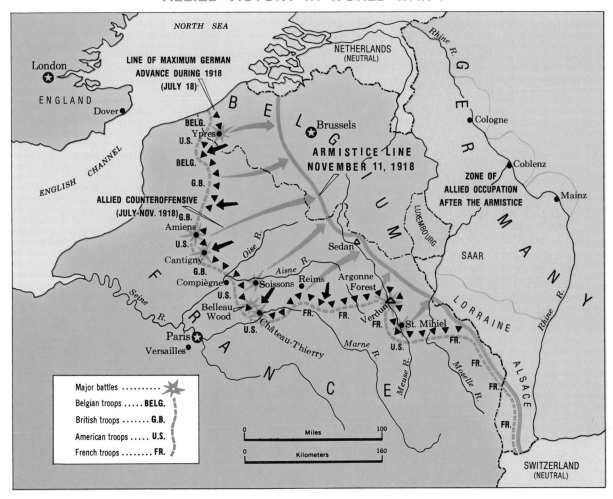

Stopping the German advance. Fighting desperately, French, British, Belgian, and American troops finally stopped the Germans. On May 28 the First Division of the United States Army took Cantigny (kahn·teen·YEE). Three days later the Third Division, in a last ditch defense of Paris, only 40 miles (64 kilometers) away, helped the French hold the Germans at Château-Thierry (shah·TOH teh·REE). At Belleau (BEL·loh) Wood the Second Division, strengthened by the 4th Marine Brigade, held back the Germans in six days of fighting (see map, this page).

Then, on July 15, the Germans threw everything they could into one final, ferocious assault around Reims (REEMZ). In this action, the beginning of the Second Battle of the Marne, the Allied lines held. On July 18 Marshal Foch ordered a counterattack spearheaded by the First and Second American Divisions and the First French Morocco Division. The Germans began to fall back. The tide at last had turned.

The Allied victory drive. The Allies now took the initiative. In July Foch launched a terrific offensive along the entire length of the line. The Germans were driven back.

The Americans fought as a separate army under General Pershing's command. The American troops, 500,000 strong and supported by French troops and British planes, launched a powerful attack on the area around St. Mihiel (SAN mee·YEL) in September 1918. After three days of savage fighting, this key section of the southern front was safely under American control.

Then, against heavy artillery and machine-gun fire, the Americans drove toward Sedan, the highly fortified position that the Germans had held since 1914. For 47 days the United States troops pushed toward their objective. The fighting in this tremendous Meuse-Argonne (MYOOZ ahr·GUN) offensive involved 1.2 million combatants. The Americans suffered 120,000 casualties, but they pushed the German line back and captured 28,000 prisoners and large supplies of war materials.

Important though they were, the American victories were only part of the offensive against the crumbling German lines. Belgians, British, and French, confident of victory, were fighting fiercely against the enemy.

Under such hammer blows, the German morale began to sag, and Germany's allies lost heart. In September the Turkish armies in Palestine and Arabia suffered crushing blows, and Bulgaria surrendered unconditionally. On November 3 the crews of the German ships at Kiel, a German naval base, mutinied rather than go to sea. Army units also mutinied, and riots broke out in a number of German cities. On November 3 Austria signed an armistice with the Italians.

Convinced at last that the war was lost, Kaiser Wilhelm II, ruler of Germany, fled to the Netherlands, leaving the country in the hands of revolutionists. Germany finally signed an armistice with the Allies on November 11, 1918.

The armistice terms. The armistice was signed in a railroad car in the forest of Compiègne (kon·PYEN·yuh) in France on the eleventh hour of the eleventh day of the eleventh month of 1918. The Germans signed grimly, for the terms were severe.

The Germans agreed to evacuate France, Belgium, Luxembourg, and Alsace-Lorraine without delay. They agreed to surrender to the Allies an enormous amount of war materials, including most of Germany's naval vessels, and to return prisoners, money, and all valuables which they had taken from the occupied countries. They agreed to renounce the Treaty of Brest-Litovsk with Russia and the Treaty of Bucharest with Rumania.

In addition, the Allies reserved the right to occupy all German territory west of the Rhine as well as a strip of territory about 18 miles (29 kilometers) wide along the east bank of the Rhine (see map, page 583).

Wilson's Fourteen Points. An American expression of idealism as well as American fighting strength played a large part in breaking the Central Powers' will to fight. As you recall, in November 1917 the Bolsheviks seized control of Russia and shortly thereafter signed a peace treaty with Germany. At this time the Bolsheviks published a number of secret treaties that the Allies had drawn up at the beginning of the war. These secret treaties outlined in great detail how the Allies planned to divide the spoils of war if they defeated the Central Powers.

President Wilson chose this opportunity to lay before the world what he firmly believed was "the only possible program for world peace." Wilson's program, which he presented to Congress on January 8, 1918, included fourteen points, or principles.

The first group of points aimed to end the causes of modern war, as Wilson understood these causes. Specifically, he called for open, instead of secret, diplomacy; for freedom of the seas instead of their control by the strong naval powers; for removal of tariffs and other economic barriers between nations; for reduction of land weapons; and for temporary international control of colonies in place of the existing imperialism.

President Wilson also called for the liberation of peoples whose lands had long been ruled by Russia, Austria-Hungary, Germany, and Turkey. Among these peoples were the Poles, Czechs, Slovaks, and South Slavs. Wilson's proposal also included the people living in the German-held region of Alsace-Lorraine. These and other groups were to have the right of self-determination. That is, they were to decide for themselves the country in which they wished to live.

The Fourteenth Point was the heart of President Wilson's program. In it Wilson urged the creation of a "general association of nations" to give "mutual guarantees of political independence and territorial integrity to great and small states alike."

Influence of Wilson's program. The Fourteen Points and statements explaining them were printed during the war in the languages of the peoples of central Europe. They were dropped by plane into the heart of enemy country. All this publicity encouraged the Slavic peoples within Germany and Austria-Hungary to boycott the war efforts of their rulers and to speed up their own liberation. Even the German people read the Fourteen Points and found in them hope for a just and lasting peace rather than a continued regime of absolute rule and militarism.

As defeat pressed closer upon them, the German and Austrian peoples saw in the Fourteen Points an escape from the harsh penalties that the Allies would otherwise impose upon them. Thus when the great German military offensives failed in the summer of 1918, and when President Wilson made it clear that he would not negotiate with any German authority that was not representative of the people, the people of Germany and Austria-Hungary took steps to overthrow their rulers.

SECTION SURVEY

IDENTIFY: Bolsheviks, convoy, General Pershing, Marshal Foch, armistice, Fourteen Points, self-determination.

1. What contributions did the United States Navy make to winning the war?

2. Who considered the armistice terms of 1918 severe? Why?

3. (a) How did Wilson's Fourteen Points help win the war? (b) Why was the Fourteenth Point the heart of Wilson's program?

4. Map Study: Examine the map on page 583. (a) What do the black triangles represent? The green solid line? The green arrows? (b) Name and locate three major battles. (c) What is the approximate distance from the capital of France to the capital of Belgium?

5 The United States refuses to join the League of Nations

On November 11, 1918, almost everyone in America took the day off from work. Factories, offices, stores, and schools closed their doors. Americans, old and young, poured into the streets of every city and town and village across the land to celebrate the armistice that ended World War I. In a joyful statement to the press, President Wilson announced, "Everything for which America fought has been accomplished." So it seemed to him, and so it

seemed to Americans in general on November 11, 1918.

Three weeks later, on December 4, 1918, the army transport *George Washington* steamed out of New York harbor for Europe. Its most distinguished passenger was President Woodrow Wilson, bound for the peace conference at Paris.

Wilson hoped to persuade the other representatives at the conference to adopt the Fourteen Points that he had earlier outlined as "the only possible program for world peace."

The "Big Four." The peace conference, which opened on January 18, 1919, had much of the tension of a melodrama. The stage, however, was the world. The principal characters were the chief officials of the four leading powers—Great Britain, France, Italy, and the United States. The outcome of the drama would affect millions of people.

Wilson arrived at the conference after a triumphal journey through Great Britain, Italy, and France. Masses of people had turned out to greet the man who symbolized their hope for a better world. Encouraged by this reception, Wilson felt that he could use his great popularity to bring about a just peace based on his Fourteen Points. However, the three other leading delegates at Paris, supported by powerful interests in their homelands, had very different aims.

David Lloyd George, the British Prime Minister, had just won a general election by using such slogans as "Hang the Kaiser" and "Make Germany Pay." He had no intention of becoming unpopular with the British voters by showing generosity toward the Germans. He had no wish to give up England's naval supremacy and accept Wilson's idea of "freedom of the seas."

The "Tiger" of French politics, Premier Georges Clemenceau (ZHORZH klay·mahn·SOH), believed that the only way to defend France was to crush Germany. Italy's Vittorio Orlando wanted to acquire territory that had been secretly promised to Italy when it joined the Allies in 1915.

Secret treaties. The united opposition of Lloyd George, Clemenceau, and Orlando was not the only problem President Wilson faced. There was also the problem of secret treaties. In 1917 the Russian Bolsheviks published secret treaties that the Allies had made before

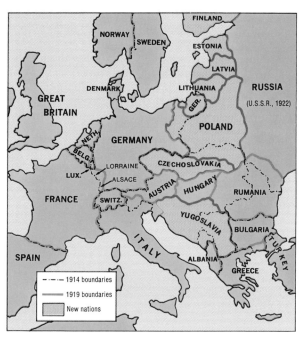

the United States entered the war. The new Communist rulers of Russia hoped to discredit the Allies by exposing these treaties as "imperialist diplomacy."

Under these treaties the Allies agreed to divide the spoils of victory. Great Britain was to take over Germany's colonies, except for certain territories in the Pacific Ocean that were to go to Japan. (Japan had declared war on Germany in 1914.) France, Russia, Serbia, and Italy were to enlarge their national boundaries at the expense of Germany and Austria-Hungary. Finally, Germany was to make huge payments, called **reparations,** to the Allies to compensate for damages resulting from the war. These secret treaties contradicted several of Wilson's Fourteen Points, such as open diplomacy, national self-determination, and the end of colonialism.

Wilson's dilemma. Faced with these secret treaties and with the opposition of Lloyd George, Clemenceau, and Orlando, Wilson could either compromise or walk out of the Paris Peace Conference. Indeed, at one point he almost did walk out, but he realized that such a step might be regarded as a confession of failure. He was also afraid that communism might

spread from Russia into central Europe if a peace treaty were delayed and conditions remained unstable. His strongest reason for staying, however, was his faith in a League of Nations. Such a League, he was convinced, would in time remedy any injustices that the peace treaty might contain.

The Treaty of Versailles. The final peace treaty, called the Treaty of Versailles, was completed and signed late in June 1919. The treaty showed the results of bargaining between Wilson on one side and Lloyd George, Clemenceau, and Orlando on the other.

The Treaty of Versailles and related treaties made important changes in the map of the world. Germany's colonies were given to the Allied victors, but under a **mandate system.** This system required the new owners to account for their colonial administration to the League of Nations.

Certain border areas of pre-war Germany were lopped off. One important area, Alsace-Lorraine, was returned to France. Other areas were included in a new country, Czechoslovakia, and in a recreated Poland. To satisfy the nationalist desires of various peoples in eastern Europe, several other independent states

586

were created. These included Finland, Estonia, Latvia, Lithuania, and Yugoslavia. Certain border changes were made for Italy, Greece, Rumania, and Belgium (see maps, page 586).

Under the Treaty of Versailles, the German government had to accept full responsibility for starting the war and had to agree to remain disarmed. Germany also agreed to pay large reparations for war damage.

Wilson realized that vengeance and greed were weak foundations for a lasting peace, and he successfully opposed some of the more unreasonable Allied demands. Moreover, he had the great personal satisfaction of seeing the Covenant of the League of Nations written into the Treaty of Versailles.

The League of Nations. The League of Nations, with headquarters at Geneva, Switzerland, provided international machinery to make war less likely. The machinery consisted of (1) a permanent Secretariat, or administrative and secretarial staff; (2) an Assembly, in which each member nation had one vote; and (3) a Council, the all-important executive body. The Council had five permanent members—the five great powers of France, Great Britain, Italy, Japan, and the United States. Other nations were also represented by means of rotating membership. Germany and the Soviet Union (Russia) were excluded from League membership. Closely related to the League were the Permanent Court of International Justice and other agencies. They dealt with such issues as reducing armaments and improving conditions of health and labor throughout the world.

The League Covenant did not outlaw war. However, each League member agreed, before going to war, to make every effort to solve its difficulties in a friendly way and even then to wait during a "cooling off" period before striking a blow. If any member failed to do this, the other members might then decide, through the Council, to apply economic sanctions. This meant that they would refuse to trade with the offender. Moreover, the Council might go further and recommend the use of force against the aggressor nation. To forestall efforts to change the new map of the world by force, each League member was to guarantee the territorial integrity and political independence of every other member.

Weaknesses of the League. The League of Nations had several serious weaknesses. For

Representatives from 27 Allied Powers met in the mirrored Palace of Versailles, just outside Paris, to draw up the 1919 peace treaty. Woodrow Wilson, Georges Clemenceau, and David Lloyd George appear in the center of this painting.

one thing, taking action against an aggressor was almost impossible for several reasons. First, the term "aggressor" was not clearly defined. Second, the Council could only recommend that nations take action, but could not force them to act. Third, any Council member could block the wishes of the other members, because all important Council decisions had to be unanimous.

Another basic weakness of the League was its guarantee of existing political boundaries. When the map of Europe was redrawn, some peoples found that they were now part of a different nation—one that they did not want to belong to. These peoples had no way to secure further changes in their national boundaries.

A third weakness was the League's failure to provide adequate machinery for recommending solutions to economic problems that might lead to war. Trade rivalries, tariff barriers, and imperialism still existed, yet the League could not do much more than study such problems. Another weakness was exclusion of the Soviet Union and Germany from membership. Finally, the League was unable to tackle the problem of reducing armaments.

Despite its shortcomings, the League of Nations was a promising beginning in the difficult task of creating a new world order, dedicated to international peace and justice. In the 1930's about 60 nations belonged to the League. The League was bringing an important new ingredient into international affairs —the organized moral judgment of a majority of the nations of the world.

The Senate rejects the League. Early in July 1919, President Wilson returned from Paris to ask the Senate to approve the Treaty of Versailles and thus bring the United States into the League. The Senate shattered his hopes by rejecting the treaty. Senator Henry Cabot Lodge of Massachusetts, head of the Committee on Foreign Relations, and other Republican Senators opposed the League.

Many Americans thought that the Treaty of Versailles was unjust. They were unwilling to have the United States join a League that pledged its members to carry out the provisions of the treaty. Many Americans pointed with alarm to the article of the Covenant that pledged each member to guarantee the existing political boundaries of the other members. Americans argued that such a pledge might involve the United States in war.

Despite the opposition to the League of Nations, the Senate might have voted for it if Wilson had been willing to accept amendments proposed by Senator Lodge and his supporters. These amendments were designed to safeguard American interests and to prevent the United States from being drawn into European wars. Wilson believed, however, that these amendments would so weaken the League that it would become ineffective. He refused to compromise.

To win public support, Wilson traveled across the country making speeches in defense of the League. Finally, exhausted by the long strain, in the fall of 1919 he collapsed and for seven months lived in seclusion. His one remaining hope was that the public would support his cause by electing a Democratic President in the 1920 election. As you will read, the Republican landslide of that year and the election of President Harding seemed to indicate that Americans wanted to forget the League and world problems in general. They ignored Wilson when he warned, "Arrangements of the present peace cannot stand a generation unless they are guaranteed by the united forces of the civilized world."

The rise of Japanese, Italian, and German expansionism in the 1930's proved the accuracy of Woodrow Wilson's prophecy. For by that time, as you will read, the League of Nations had become too weak to prevent the outbreak of another world war.

SECTION SURVEY

IDENTIFY: "Big Four," reparations, Treaty of Versailles, mandate system, economic sanctions, Henry Cabot Lodge.

1. Compare the views of Wilson, Lloyd George, Clemenceau, and Orlando concerning the treaty of peace.

2. (a) Describe the structure of the League of Nations. (b) What machinery did the League set up for the prevention of war?

3. Describe some of the major weaknesses of the League.

4. (a) List two arguments presented by people who opposed the League. (b) What evidence is there that Americans generally agreed with these arguments?

5. Map Study: Using the maps on page 586, identify four ways in which the Treaty of Versailles changed the map of the world.

Chapter Survey

Summary: Tracing the Main Ideas

The outbreak of World War I in the summer of 1914 came as a blow to millions of Americans and other peoples throughout the world. During the opening years of the 1900's, great strides had been made toward international cooperation. Suddenly, in 1914, all hopes for peace were shattered under the blows of fierce national rivalries.

Despite America's desire to remain neutral, it became increasingly clear that the United States as a major power would not remain apart in a conflict involving the other great powers. Step by step the United States moved toward war and, in 1917, entered the conflict.

The war had far-reaching consequences for the American people. As "total" war it involved directly and deeply every man, woman, and child in the country and every part of life. It created a vast government bureaucracy to manage and control agriculture, labor, transportation, and the naval and military effort. Education, religion, and recreation were mobilized for the task of winning the war. The government directed and to a large extent controlled public opinion. Constitutional guarantees of freedom of speech and of the press were sometimes ruthlessly disregarded by the government in the name of "national security" and "Americanism."

In the United States and in other countries, war-weary people hailed the armistice of November 11, 1918, as a turning point in history. Hundreds of millions of people looked to the United States for leadership in the effort "to make the world safe for democracy." President Wilson reminded Americans that they had a major responsibility in the building of a lasting structure of peace. His advice went unheeded, however, and the United States turned its back on the League of Nations. During the 1920's and 1930's, the United States and the rest of the world disregarded the lessons of World War I. This neglect would lead, in 20 years, to the even more terrible bloodbath of World War II.

Inquiring into History

1. Why did the United States enter World War I?
2. What part did American troops play in the victory of the Allies?
3. The end of World War I brought with it a spirit of high idealism and hope to people throughout the world. Explain.
4. (a) How were the factors that led to World War I —nationalism, imperialism, international rivalries, and the balance-of-power system— related? (b) Did the Treaty of Versailles diminish any of these factors as a future cause of war? Explain.
5. (a) How was the League of Nations supposed to protect world peace? (b) Why did the United States not join the League?

Relating Past to Present

1. (a) Why are civil liberties often restricted during a period of crisis? (b) Have there been any recent instances of such restrictions?
2. Do other nations still look to the United States for leadership in the difficult task of building a peaceful world? Explain.

Developing Social Science Skills

1. Read excerpts from *Good-Bye to All That* by Robert Graves or *All Quiet on the Western Front* by Erich Maria Remarque, describing the fighting in World War I. (a) What does the author's attitude toward war seem to be? (b) How does the excerpt compare with your ideas about war? (c) What effects does fighting a war seem to have on individuals?
2. One method used by the government to encourage support of the war was the displaying of patriotic posters, such as the one shown on page 579. Create one or more posters that would have aroused Americans to serve their nation during the war either in the armed services or on the home front.
3. Create a cartoon depicting Wilson's failure to sell the League of Nations to the American people.

Unit Survey

other events on the timeline and add an event either before or after each one that will create a "cause-and-effect" relationship.

Tracing the Main Events: Trade Around the World

1899 Open Door Policy established.

1901 U.S. exports worth $1.6 billion; imports worth $.9 billion.

1909 Policy of "Dollar Diplomacy" begins.
Payne-Aldrich Tariff lowers tariffs to about .38 percent.

1911 Canada rejects U.S. proposal for reciprocal lowering of tariffs.

1913 Underwood-Simmons Tariff Act lowers duties to about .30 percent.

1914 Panama Canal opens.
Britain seizes U.S. food being shipped to neutral north European countries.
U.S. exports worth $2.5 billion; imports worth $2 billion.

1915 U.S. denounces German interference with shipping rights.

1917 U.S. arms all merchant ships traveling in war zone.
U.S. enters World War I.
Trading with the Enemy Act bans trade with enemy nations.

For Further Inquiry

1. In acquiring overseas possessions, the United States was carrying on its tradition of "manifest destiny." Do you agree or disagree? Why?

2. How did Theodore Roosevelt interpret the power of the President in the area of foreign policy? Give evidence to support your answer.

3. How might you have felt about the control of Puerto Rico by the United States if you had been (a) an American farmer, (b) a citizen of Nicaragua, (c) a British merchant?

4. (a) Describe Wilson's 14 Points. (b) What was the reaction of Europe's leaders to them? (c) What factors might account for their reactions?

5. (a) Describe the United States' relations with Asia in the years 1898 to 1920. (b) Do they seem to be consistent with United States foreign policy in other parts of the world? Explain.

Activities and Projects

1. Study the timeline above. (a) Give two examples of "cause-and-effect" relationships shown on the timeline. Explain your examples. (b) Choose two

2. Read *All Quiet on the Western Front,* the well-known novel of the First World War. (a) What seems to be the author's attitude toward war? How can you tell? (b) How reliable is this novel as a source of information about World War I? Explain. (c) In what way is a novel a valuable source of information about an event or period in history?

3. Select one event in United States relationships with Latin America from 1898 to 1920. Write an account of the event as it might appear in a Latin American textbook for high school students.

4. Conduct research on one of these topics: (a) the role of blacks during World War I, (b) the role of women during World War I, (c) songs of World War I, (d) George Creel and the Committee of Public Information, (e) military technology of World War I.

5. Draw a map showing battles and other events of World War I that will illustrate why the war could be called a *world* war.

Exploring Your Region

1. Contact the local chapter of the Veterans of Foreign Wars or other veterans organization. Arrange to interview one or more veterans of World War I. Be sure to prepare your questions in advance. Perhaps the veteran would agree to let you tape the interview for presentation to your class.

2. Investigate the specific provisions of the Underwood-Simmons Tariff and find out about the economy of your region around 1913. How might the tarrif have affected your region?

Suggested Reading

1. *Trail Blazer: Negro Nurse in the Red Cross,* Jean Pitrone. Story of a determined woman who became the first black nurse in the American Red Cross.

2. *The Making of a World Power,* Paul Angle, ed. Using many primary sources, this book tells the exciting story of the development of the United States into a world power.

3. *The Guns of August,* Barbara Tuchman. An award-winning history of the early days of World War I that reads like a novel.

4. *One of Ours,* Willa Cather. A novel of a young Nebraska man and how his life was transformed by World War I.

5. *They Came to Cordura,* Glencon Swarthout. A novel of the American expedition against Pancho Villa.

Unit Ten

The "Golden Twenties" and the New Deal

1920 - 1941

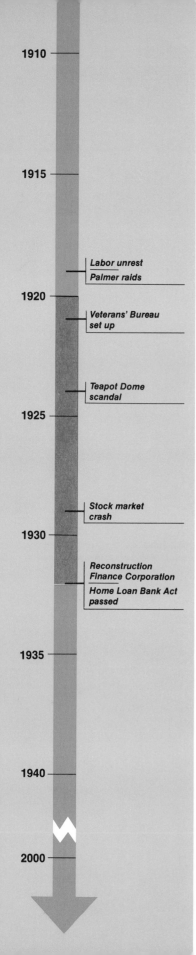

1910

1915

Labor unrest
Palmer raids

1920

*Veterans' Bureau
set up*

*Teapot Dome
scandal*

1925

*Stock market
crash*

1930

*Reconstruction
Finance Corporation*
*Home Loan Bank Act
passed*

1935

1940

2000

Chapter 31

A Decade of Prosperity Ends in a Crash

1920–1932

The signing of the armistice on November 11, 1918, brought an end to World War I. It also marked the high point in Wilson's Presidential career. Democracy had triumphed. To many Americans, Wilson's vision of an orderly and peaceful world seemed about to become a reality.

The President's triumph was to be short-lived. During the next two years, he bore the heavy burden of frustration, shattered dreams, and broken health. Even before the armistice, in the Congressional elections on November 5, 1918, American voters revealed their dissatisfaction with Wilson's leadership by returning Republican majorities to both the House and the Senate. Two years later, in the elections of 1920, the voters of the country turned their backs completely on Wilson and the Democratic Party. They selected instead a Republican President, Warren G. Harding, to lead the nation.

During the 1920's three Republican Presidents—Harding, Calvin Coolidge, and Herbert Hoover—presided over a country that, on the whole, enjoyed a period of unparalleled prosperity. To be sure, there were hard times for many. Farmers suffered from higher operating costs and lower prices for their goods. Minorities still did not receive equal opportunities. Nevertheless, the nation's growing wealth was widely shared. By 1928, real wages were one third higher than they had been in 1914. Two out of three households owned automobiles.

But this era of the "Golden Twenties" ended with a stunning economic collapse. It was followed by the most shattering depression in American history.

THE CHAPTER IN OUTLINE

1. The Democrats lose popularity and face growing unrest.

2. Republicans assume responsibility for governing the country.

3. The Great Depression shatters the prosperity of the 1920's.

1 The Democrats lose popularity and face growing unrest

Before America's entry into the war, President Wilson had concentrated on his program of domestic reform. As you have read, his first administration, from 1913 to 1917, reduced tariffs, strengthened the antitrust laws, and established the Federal Reserve System. In these and other ways, Wilson tried to restore competition in American business and to protect consumers.

Even before the war, however, Wilson felt that the "New Freedom" program had largely achieved its goals. After the war he became deeply involved in organizing world peace. As a result, he had little time left for domestic affairs. Such problems included a postwar business slump, a decline in farm prices, and widespread unemployment.

Losing support at home. The American people, however, were tired of international issues. They were more interested in domestic affairs than in a peace treaty or a League of Nations. The Congressional elections of 1918, held just before the armistice, showed this. President Wilson appealed to the voters for a Democratic Congress. Instead, the voters elected a Republican majority in both the House and Senate.

When Wilson returned from the Versailles Conference in the summer of 1919, he found many Senators critical of the Covenant, or constitution, of the League of Nations. However, the President refused to compromise on the covenant's basic points and instead tried to win the public to his point of view.

Late in the summer of 1919, after three weeks of a grueling nationwide speaking tour, Wilson suffered a stroke. It left him partially paralyzed, and he remained an invalid until his death in 1924.

The postwar depression. Wilson's illness came at a time when the country was suffering from a severe postwar depression. With the signing of the armistice, the government began to cancel its wartime contracts. Wartime industries suddenly faced the problem of converting to peacetime production. New machinery had to be installed and new customers found. During the conversion, factories closed down or operated with greatly reduced labor forces.

Farmers also suffered during the transition from war to peace. As European farmland returned to normal production, the American farmers' wartime markets in Europe disappeared. Farm prices, which had soared during the war, dropped as competition increased. Wheat, for example, which had sold for as high as $2.26 a bushel (35.2 liters), dropped to less than $1 a bushel in 1922. Almost half a million American farmers, unable to pay their debts, lost their farms during this troubled period.

Wage earners also suffered. Many who had worked in government wartime agencies lost their jobs when the war ended. Hundreds of thousands of wage earners were thrown out of work when factories closed down or cut back operations. And the nation's war heroes were not spared. Many of the 4.5 million returning veterans could not find work.

As the depression deepened, as wages fell, and as more people lost their jobs, discontent swelled. To make things worse, the high cost of living rose even higher. In 1919 it climbed 77 percent above prewar levels. In 1920 it rose an additional 28 percent. Under such conditions, many workers resorted to strikes. During 1919 more than 4 million workers were at one time or another out on strike. Three strikes were especially serious.

The Boston police strike. On September 9 the Boston police force went on strike for higher wages and improved conditions, leaving the city without police protection. When rioting and looting broke out, the state guard was called in. The police force, realizing that the strike was lost, announced that they would return to their posts.

At this point, however, the Boston police commissioner refused to allow them to return to their jobs. He announced that he intended to hire a new police force. Governor Calvin Coolidge supported the commissioner. "There is no right," Coolidge flatly stated, "to strike against the public safety by anybody, anywhere, any time." Coolidge's statement was widely applauded. It brought him to public attention and helped him win the Republican Vice-Presidential nomination in 1920.

The coal strike. Less than two months after this police strike, on November 1, 1919, the United Mine Workers (U.M.W.) went out on strike. Led by their colorful and combative president John L. Lewis, they demanded higher wages and a shorter workweek. On November 9 United States Attorney General A. Mitchell Palmer secured an injunction ordering the officers of the U.M.W. to stop all activities tending to encourage the strikers.

However, the coal miners refused to return to work. Finally, on President Wilson's suggestion, the problem was submitted to a board of arbitration. The board gave the miners a 27-percent wage increase, but refused to consider a reduction in the weekly hours of work.

The steel strike. Discontent in the steel industry led to a strike involving more than 300,000 workers. The steelworkers had long been dissatisfied with their working conditions. In some plants they worked as long as 12 hours a day, 7 days a week. Moreover, they had not been able to form a union to bargain for them. During the summer of 1919, however, an A. F. of L. committee launched a vigorous organizing campaign in the steel towns. The strike started on September 22, 1919, after management refused to recognize the committee's right to speak for all steelworkers.

As the weeks passed, violence erupted around some of the steel mills. At Gary, Indiana, martial law was declared, and federal troops moved in to keep order. Finally, with public opinion running against the steelworkers, the strikers returned to their jobs in January 1920. Three years later, however, the steel companies agreed to the steelworkers' demand for an 8-hour day.

Labor's declining strength. The postwar depression did not last long. By early 1920 American export trade was soaring as orders for goods poured in from the war-devastated countries. The value of American exports rose to three times the 1913 level.

As economic conditions improved and jobs became more plentiful, many workers lost interest in unions. Membership in the A. F. of L., which had reached a peak of more than 4 million early in 1920, began to decline.

There were, of course, other reasons for the decline of the labor movement. The failure of the steel strike and of other strikes during 1919 discouraged workers. The use of the injunction, as in the strike of the United Mine Workers, was another discouraging factor. Also, Supreme Court decisions broadened the base for use of the injunction, restricted labor organizing activities, and ruled that legislation intended to improve working conditions was unconstitutional. Industrial management, moreover, launched a widely publicized campaign against the "union shop." In it labor unions were identified with socialism and communism. A "Red scare" that swept the country in 1919–20 caused many Americans, including many workers, to turn against organized labor.

Artist Ben Shahn was one who felt that Sacco and Vanzetti, two anarchists, were unjustly convicted of murder in 1921 because of their beliefs. His painting shows Sacco and Vanzetti after the execution with the judge and two of the trial's key witnesses.

The "Red scare." During the postwar years, federal and state governments conducted a vigorous drive against anarchists, Communists, and socialists. The Espionage Act, passed in wartime to punish treasonable or disloyal activities, remained in effect after the war. Under this law revolutionists and suspected revolutionists were arrested and fined. Some who were aliens were deported to the countries from which they had come.

One important reason for the postwar concern with radicals was the Russian Bolshevik Revolution of 1917. This event frightened many Americans who feared that radicals in the United States might try to follow the Bolshevik example. Rumors of revolutionary plots circulated widely from 1917 through 1920.

There was more than rumor to arouse alarm, even though radical leaders disapproved of acts of irresponsible violence. During the spring and summer of 1919, more than 30 bombs were discovered by postal authorities in packages addressed to prominent citizens. In New York City on September 16, 1920, a bomb exploded in crowded Wall Street at noontime, killing 38 persons and injuring hundreds.

Meanwhile, in the fall of 1919, Attorney General Palmer instructed agents in the Department of Justice to arrest radicals throughout the country. Among those arrested were several hundred aliens who were deported.

Many Americans, both Democrats and Republicans, criticized this drive against radicals, pointing out that many of the raids were conducted without search warrants. They argued that Attorney General Palmer's actions sometimes ignored the constitutional rights of free citizens.

The critics also directed their fire against state governments. During this postwar period, about one third of the states had passed laws to punish advocates of revolutionary change. By 1920 many Americans who had no sympathy with radicals were growing alarmed at the widespread violation of civil liberties. Leaders from both major political parties agreed with President Wilson that Americans could not solve their problems by trying to suppress unpopular political views.

SECTION SURVEY

IDENTIFY: John L. Lewis, Bolshevik Revolution.

1. (a) Describe the causes and nature of the depression that followed World War I. (b) How was the depression related to the many strikes that occurred in 1919?

2. During the Boston police strike, Governor Coolidge made this statement: "There is no right to strike against the public safety by anybody, anywhere, any time." (a) What did he mean? (b) Do you agree with his viewpoint? Why or why not?

3. Why did labor unions decline in the early 1920's?

4. (a) What conditions produced the "Red scare"? (b) Explain the arguments for and against the drive against radicals.

2 Republicans assume responsibility for governing the country

In the Presidential election of 1920, the country's unsettled condition gave the Republican candidate, Senator Warren G. Harding of Ohio, a clear advantage over his Democratic opponent, Governor James M. Cox of Ohio. Many voters blamed the administration in office for the troubled times, including the race riots and other minority problems. The Republicans' plea for a return to "normalcy" had great appeal. Many Americans were tired of Europe and its wars and tired of Wilson's attempts to "make the world safe for democracy." Business people were worried about the 1919 depression. Workers and farmers suffered from unemployment and falling prices.

The election of 1920. Warren G. Harding, the Republican candidate, was a genial Ohio newspaper owner who had climbed to the top of the political ladder in his own state. He had served as a United States Senator. Handsome and distinguished, with a warm, easygoing manner—much too easygoing, as it turned out—he had many friends in every walk of life.

Harding won the election with approximately 16 million votes to Cox's 9 million. The electoral vote was even more sweeping, giving Harding 404 to Cox's 127. Eugene V. Debs, the Socialist candidate, who was in prison for violating the Espionage Act, received nearly 1 million votes.

Farm relief and financial reform. Harding did not take over an easy job when he entered the White House. Late in 1920 a second postwar depression had hit the country. Farmers,

FLYING THE MAIL

Somebody plastered a postage stamp on actor Douglas Fairbanks's forehead before settling him on top of several bags of mail in the small plane. It was October 1918, and his flight from Washington, D.C., to New York was part of a publicity campaign to sell war bonds. After the flight Fairbanks scribbled his thanks to the pilot: "Handled with care—arrived right side up. Great trip."

Regular airmail service was just five months old. At this time the single route was between the nation's capital and its largest city. In 1921 a transcontinental route was tested, with a first flight that took over 33 hours. Gradually other routes were added until an airmail network crisscrossed the country.

Flying the mail in the 1920's was a serious business. Pilots rarely had companions, let alone famous ones. During the first few years, planes carrying mail flew only by day. In 1924, around-the-clock flights were started, with flashing beacons spaced every 25 miles (40 kilometers) to guide planes through the darkness. Even so, night flying was hazardous, for storms obscured beacons and landing fields were poorly lit.

The pilots who flew the mail in those early days needed nerves of iron. One of the best of them, Charles Lindbergh, had to abandon his plane and parachute to safety on four separate occasions in 1926. In a newspaper article of the time, the writer may have over-emphasized the romance, but certainly not the danger, of flying the mail:

Adventure rides with the United States mails today just as it did many years ago, when it went astride a wiry pony. Death lurks nearby just as it did when robbers and . . . Indians infested the lonely roads of the frontier. The means of transporting the mails have changed, but not the chances.

---

wage earners, business leaders, and the public in general were clamoring for government action and for President Harding's promised return to "normalcy."

Responding to widespread demands for help, Congress adopted the Emergency Tariff on May 27, 1921. This measure raised rates on some farm products but failed to raise farm prices generally. Congress also adopted the Budget and Accounting Act. This law was designed to reduce excessive spending and waste in government and to provide a more efficient method of handling government expenditures. It also created a Bureau of the Budget in the Treasury Department, with a director appointed by the President.

Up to this time, Congress had made annual appropriations on a piecemeal basis. No great concern was given to balancing the budget. Under the new system, all government agencies and departments had to submit annual requests for funds to the Director of the Budget. The director then drew up a detailed budget. Estimated income and expenditures for the coming **fiscal year**° were listed on this budget. The President submitted the budget to Congress. Congress could then raise or lower the estimates, if it so desired.

°**fiscal year:** the 12-month period considered as a year for general accounting and budgeting purposes. The fiscal year of the United States government begins on July 1.

Charles G. Dawes, the first Director of the Budget, was an extremely capable administrator. Under his leadership and that of the Secretary of the Treasury, Andrew W. Mellon, the government used surplus revenues to reduce the national debt. At the end of World War I, the debt totaled more than $25 billion. During the 1920's it was cut by about one third.

Some critics held that Mellon's financial measures reduced the taxes of the wealthy and placed too heavy a burden on the average wage earner, while checking a needed expansion of social services for the poor. However, most Americans approved of economy in government spending and of the reduction of the national debt.

War veterans. Congress also tackled the problem of the war veterans. Many war veterans as well as many other Americans felt that the government should provide "adjusted compensation" for veterans. These people pointed out that during the war members of the armed forces had risked their lives for low pay while workers at home earned high wartime wages in more or less safe jobs.

In 1921 Congress created the Veterans' Bureau. Harding then appointed Charles R. Forbes as its first director. The Veterans' Bureau handled veterans' claims for compensation and hospitalization, provided medical care for sick veterans, and administered the veterans' insurance program.

The Veterans' Bureau was only a partial answer to the demands of veterans. The American Legion, the Veterans of Foreign Wars, and other veterans' organizations continued to press for adjusted compensation. Congress responded in 1922 with a bonus bill. Harding vetoed the bill because it did not include any provision for raising the money to be spent.

The Fordney-McCumber Tariff. In 1922 Harding signed the Fordney-McCumber Act into law. The new tariff wiped out the reductions made in the Underwood Tariff of 1913 and set considerably higher rates on hundreds of manufactured products. It also continued the limited protection for farmers provided by the Emergency Tariff of 1921.

The Fordney-McCumber Tariff also authorized the President, under certain circumstances, to raise or lower any tariff rate by as much as 50 percent. As it turned out, most of the adjustments made were upward.

Public scandals. Despite some solid accomplishments, the Harding administration left a long, sorry record of corruption. Harding was not himself involved in the corruption. His mistake was in appointing certain undeserving men to office. His cabinet did contain such able and respected men as Charles Evans Hughes, the Secretary of State; Andrew W. Mellon, who headed the Treasury Department; and Herbert Hoover, the Secretary of Commerce. However, Harding's administration also contained dishonest politicians who disgraced his administration.

Self-seeking politicians known as the "Ohio Gang" placed one of their members, Harry M. Daugherty, in the cabinet as Attorney General. Daugherty used his position to protect persons who violated the Prohibition amendment. Another Harding official, Thomas W. Miller, defrauded the government in the sale of alien properties—that is, foreign-owned properties that were seized by the American government during World War I. Charles R. Forbes, the head of the Veterans' Bureau, could not satisfactorily account for $200 million spent by his organization.

The most famous scandal took its name from the naval oil reserve lands at Teapot

This cartoon shows the Senate washing out the "dirty linen" of the Harding administration. Several of President Harding's prominent political appointees were involved in the political scandals.

"The chief business of the American people is business," President Calvin Coolidge stated in 1925. Coolidge firmly believed that government should leave business to itself, without additional legal controls.

Dome in Wyoming. Secretary of the Interior Albert B. Fall persuaded the Secretary of the Navy, Edwin C. Denby, to transfer the Teapot Dome reserve and another oil reserve at Elk Hills, California, to Fall's jurisdiction. In return for bribes, Fall leased the oil reserves to private oil speculators.

Some hint of this corruption reached Harding early in 1923. However, the scandals did not become public until later, when Fall, Forbes, and Miller were prosecuted and imprisoned. Meanwhile, Harding's health broke under the strain, and he died in the summer of 1923 of a heart attack.

On Harding's death, Calvin Coolidge, the Vice-President, became President. Coolidge, a man of unquestioned honesty, helped to restore public confidence in the Republican Party.

The election of 1924. In the decade following their defeat in 1920, the Democrats gener-

ally failed to work out a clear-cut program to challenge the Republicans. They turned away from the spirit of reform that had marked Wilson's first administration. More and more the Democrats accepted the same conservative principles followed by the Republicans. As the years passed, it became difficult to distinguish between the two parties.

Only once during the 1920's did the Republican program face any serious opposition. Curiously enough, the opposition came in part from within Republican ranks.

The revolt broke out in 1924 when the Republicans nominated the staunchly conservative Calvin Coolidge for the Presidency. Coolidge believed that government should encourage, but not regulate, business. He also disapproved of special legislation to help workers or farmers.

Resisting these conservative policies, a group of progressive Republicans broke away and formed a new Progressive Party. They nominated Senator Robert M. La Follette of Wisconsin as their standard bearer. The Progressive Party received the backing of farmers, organized labor, and the socialists. The party called for federal credit and other assistance for farmers, and social legislation and additional laws to protect the rights of labor. In addition it advocated government ownership of railroads and water-power resources.

La Follette received almost 5 million votes, the largest number any third party had ever mustered. La Follette died shortly after the campaign, however, and the Progressive Party lost its strength and faded into insignificance.

The Democrats in 1924 nominated John W. Davis, a conservative corporation lawyer. During his campaign Davis concentrated on the scandals of the Harding era. The Republicans met this challenge by claiming credit for the prevailing prosperity, and this claim proved effective. Despite the Progressive revolt, which split the Republicans into two factions, Coolidge won the election by a landslide. He piled up 382 electoral votes to 136 for Davis and just 13 for La Follette.

Thrift in government. In a period of extravagance and "big money," Coolidge became a symbol of the thrifty, old-fashioned, simple country American. He emphasized thrift in government.

In 1924 Congress passed a bonus bill that provided adjusted compensation for all veterans except those with ranks above captain. The payments were not to be given in cash but in the form of a paid-up 20-year life insurance policy. Veterans who held the policy for 20 years would receive full compensation. In the name of economy, Coolidge vetoed the bonus bill, but Congress passed this bill over his veto.

Coolidge also vetoed a bill to stabilize farm prices by allowing the government to buy up farm surpluses and sell them abroad.

In other matters, too, Congress and the President disagreed, but the President remained popular. "Keep Cool with Coolidge" was a slogan of the day. He probably could have been re-elected in 1928, but a year before the election he announced that he did not choose to run.

The election of 1928. The Republicans then nominated Herbert C. Hoover of California. Hoover was a successful mining engineer with a notable record as administrator of food relief in Europe during and after the war and as Secretary of Commerce after 1921.

The Democrats nominated New York's governor Alfred E. Smith. Smith advocated a federal farm-relief program and also urged stricter regulation of public utilities. These planks in the Democratic platform had strong appeal for many Americans. However, Smith had political handicaps that cost him support within his own party. He was opposed to Prohibition, he was a Roman Catholic, and he had ties with the Tammany political machine in New York City. All these things made him unpopular with large groups of voters, especially in the South and West.

Hoover received 444 electoral votes to Smith's 87. Smith lost his own state of New York. In addition he lost several traditionally Democratic states in the South that for the first time since the Civil War gave their votes to a Republican.

Herbert C. Hoover President Hoover expressed his political beliefs in the phrase "rugged individualism." His general point of view was very close to Harding's idea of "normalcy" and to Coolidge's belief that government should encourage business but not give special assistance to individuals. Hoover, however, displayed greater imagination than his Republican predecessors. He believed that experts in fields other than government could make important contributions to government.

He also believed that the government should take some part in planning for the social and economic development of the nation.

When Hoover took office, he looked forward to a long period of increasing prosperity. He believed that Americans now expected more than the necessities of life. "The slogan of progress," he declared, "is changing from the full dinner pail to the full garage." For about six months, booming business and heavy consumer buying seemed to bear out Hoover's optimistic prediction.

SECTION SURVEY

IDENTIFY: return to "normalcy," "Ohio Gang," Teapot Dome scandal, Robert La Follette, Alfred E. Smith, "rugged individualism."

1. How did Coolidge's election to the Presidency in 1924 reflect the temper of the times?
2. Despite some solid accomplishments, the Harding administration left a long, sorry record of corruption. Explain.
3. Compare the elections of 1924 and 1928 in terms of (a) parties, (b) candidates, (c) issues, and (d) results.
4. Cartoon Study: Look closely at the cartoon on page 597. (a) What do the elephant and donkey represent? (b) In a sentence or two, explain the meaning of the cartoon.

3 The Great Depression shatters the prosperity of the 1920's

Flourishing business conditions and a rising standard of living contributed to the political success of the Republican Party during the 1920's. Between 1922 and 1929, jobs were plentiful. Americans on the whole were better fed, clothed, and housed than ever before.

"Easy money." During the prosperity of the so-called "Golden Twenties," many Americans made and spent money with ease. Millions of workers received relatively high wages and many businesses earned large profits. An ever-growing number of stockholders received substantial dividends.

As Americans bought more and more consumer goods, the retail trade recorded ever-increasing sales. Some of the business profits supported expansion and new product research. Some paid for workers' recreational facilities, some for company programs providing insurance and pensions for employees. Large sums flowed into medical research, education, and the welfare of the poor.

As surplus income piled higher and higher, more and more Americans were tempted to invest their savings or their profits in the stock market, hoping for big returns.

Not all Americans shared in the prosperity of the "Golden Twenties." This was notably true of Indians, Spanish-speaking Americans, and most blacks. Many workers lost their jobs when new machines were installed in factories. Some, such as blacksmiths and harness makers, whose skills were no longer needed, found it difficult to adapt to the monotonous work on assembly lines. Furthermore, some industries —such as coal, textiles, and leather—never fully recovered from the postwar slump of the early 1920's.

Falling farm income.   Finally, many farmers did not share in the general prosperity. One of their problems was a shrinking market for farm products. After 1918, as you recall, American farmers lost many of their wartime European markets. Moreover, during the 1920's Congress passed laws that almost ended immigration into the United States. As a result of these laws, American farmers lost a traditional source of new customers. Although the markets were shrinking, farm production—aided by new machines and techniques—rose by more than 20 percent between 1919 and 1929.

With fewer people able or willing to buy food and with more food available, farm prices dropped. While the farm prices were falling, the prices of industrial goods that the farmers needed rose higher and higher. Many farmers found it increasingly hard to meet their mortgage payments or the payments on their farm machines. Thus during the industrial prosperity of the 1920's, many farmers sank deeper and deeper into debt, and many lost their farms. The situation of sharecroppers and tenants, white and black alike, was even worse than that of the small farmers.

Effort to aid farmers.   By the end of the 1920's, the nation's farm economy had deteriorated to the point that the government could no longer afford to ignore it. President Hoover gave his support to the Agricultural Marketing Act, which was adopted in the summer of 1929. This act created a Federal Farm Board with power to lend up to $500 million to cooperative farm groups to help them store crops during years when a surplus of farm products brought falling prices. The theory was that the farmers could sell their stored products later when prices went back up. Unfortunately, surpluses continued year after year and prices continued to fall. In the end the Farm Board used up its financial resources without bolstering farm income.

Prosperity ends in the crash.   In spite of the failing agricultural economy, few Americans other than the farmers and those at the bottom of the economic ladder were concerned about the nation's economic health. Most Americans believed, with Herbert Hoover, that "we in America are nearer to the final triumph over poverty than ever before in the history of any land." Given this widely shared belief, the depression that started late in 1929 came as a stunning blow to most Americans.

SOURCES

HERBERT HOOVER'S "RUGGED INDIVIDUALISM" SPEECH (1928)

During one hundred and fifty years we have built up a form of self-government and a social system which is peculiarly our own. It differs essentially from all others in the world. It is the American system. It is just as definite and positive a political and social system as has ever been developed on earth. It is founded upon a particular conception of self-government in which decentralized local responsibility is the very base. Further than this, it is founded upon the conception that only through ordered liberty, freedom, and equal opportunity to the individual will his initiative and enterprise spur on the march of progress. And in our insistence upon equality of opportunity has our system advanced beyond all the world. . . .

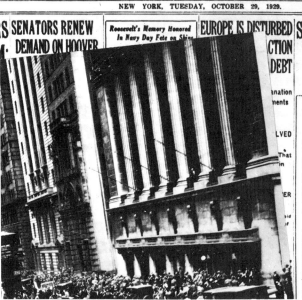

Copyright, 1929, by The New York Times Company.

NEW YORK, TUESDAY, OCTOBER 29, 1929.

TWO CENTS

S SENATORS RENEW DEMAND ON HOOVER

Roosevelt's Memory Honored In Navy Day Fete on Ships

EUROPE IS DISTURBED

STOCK PRICES SLUMP $14,000,000,000 IN NATION-WIDE STAMPEDE TO UNLOAD; BANKERS TO SUPPORT MARKET TODAY

Sixteen Leading Issues Down $2,893,520,108; Tel. & Tel. and Steel Among Heaviest Losers

A shrinkage of $2,893,520,108 in the open market value of the shares of sixteen representative companies resulted from yesterday's sweeping decline on the New York Stock Exchange.

American Telephone and Telegraph was the heaviest loser, $448,905,162 having been lopped off of its total value. United States Steel common, traditional bellwether of the stock market, made its greatest nose-dive in recent years by falling from a high of 202½ to a low of 185. In a feeble last-minute rally it snapped back to 186, at which it closed, showing a net loss of 17½ points. This represented for the 8,151,055 shares of common stock outstanding a total loss in value of $142,293,446.

In the following table are shown the day's net depreciation in the outstanding shares of the sixteen companies referred to:

Issues.	Shares Listed.	Losses in Points.	Depreciation
American Radiator	10,096,289	10⅝	$104,748,907
American Tel. & Tel.	13,203,083	34	448,905,162
Commonwealth & Southern	30,764,468	3¼	96,138,962
Columbia Gas & Electric	8,477,307	22	186,500,754
Consolidated Gas	11,431,188	20	229,023,760
DuPont E. I.	10,322,481	16⅜	169,080,625
Eastman Kodak	2,229,703	41⅛	93,368,813
General Electric	7,211,484	47⅝	342,345,490
General Motors	43,500,000	6½	293,625,000
International Nickel	13,777,408	7⅞	108,487,088
New York Central	4,637,088	22⅝	104,914,071
Standard Oil of New Jersey	24,843,643	8	198,749,144
Union Carbide & Carbon	8,730,172	20	174,603,440

PREMIER ISSUES HARD HIT

Unexpected Torrent of Liquidation Again Rocks Markets.

DAY'S SALES 9,212,800

Nearly 3,000,000 Shares Are Traded In Final Hour—The Tickers Lag 167 Minutes.

NEW RALLY SOON BROKEN

Selling by Europeans and "Mob Psychology" Big Factors in Second Big Break.

Newspapers across the country chronicled the stock market crash of 1929. The superimposed picture shows the sad crowds that clustered around the Stock Exchange, vainly hoping to salvage some of their investments.

For years the prices of stocks had been moving upward. After Hoover's election in November 1928, moreover, a frenzy of speculation gripped the country. Convinced that they were entering "four more years of prosperity," investors bought feverishly. Despite repeated warnings that stock prices were too high, Americans, rich and middle class alike, invested in stocks, often on credit. During most of 1929, stock prices soared to ever higher levels.

The stock market crash. Then the bubble burst. On October 24, 1929, a panic of selling hit the New York Stock Exchange as frantic orders to sell stock came pouring in. The causes of this panic were chiefly overproduction and overspeculation. More goods had been produced than could be profitably sold. A great many stocks were either worthless or wildly inflated. That is, either the businesses behind such stocks existed on paper only, or the actual value of the stocks was far less than their market value.

Overproduction and overspeculation had caught up with the American people. The inflated prices of stocks tumbled downward. On October 29, prices sank to a shattering new low when over 16 million shares of stock were dumped on the market. By mid-November the average value of leading stocks had been cut in half, and stockholders had lost $30 billion. With this crash of the stock market, the Great Depression started.

At first business and government leaders tried to reassure the American people. "Business is fundamentally sound," announced Secretary of the Treasury Mellon. Such words, no matter how reassuring, could not stem the tide of economic disaster sweeping the country.

The Great Depression. Before 1929 ended, banks all over the nation were closing their doors. Businesses everywhere cut back production, and many concerns, finding themselves without customers, were forced out of business. Factories and mines were shut down. Empty railroad cars piled up on the sidings. By 1930 between 6 and 7 million Americans were un-

601

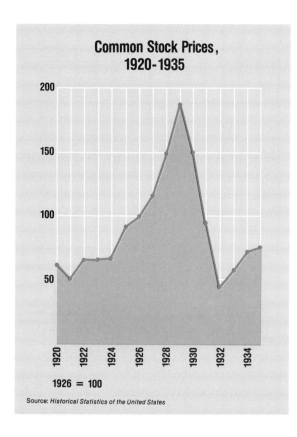

Common Stock Prices, 1920-1935

200

150

100

50

1920 1922 1924 1926 1928 1930 1932 1934

1926 = 100

Source: *Historical Statistics of the United States*

employed. The result was a chain reaction. Unemployment meant fewer customers; a decrease in customers caused further cutbacks in production; these cutbacks, in turn, resulted in more unemployment. By 1932 nearly 12 million Americans were out of work.

The depression struck at all classes. Many well-to-do Americans helplessly watched their fortunes, invested in stocks or businesses, disappear. The industrial workers and the farmers suffered most. Most wage earners had no savings to tide them over a period of unemployment. In every city thousands of unfortunate men and women stood in lines to get free meals of bread and soup. Families forced out of their homes moved to makeshift huts that they built on unused land at the edges of the city. Such huts were often made of scrap lumber, packing boxes, and corrugated iron.

For the farmers the depression came as a final blow. Between 1929 and 1932, farm prices fell lower and lower, and more and more farmers lost their farms to their creditors. In some midwestern states, desperate farmers used force to prevent sheriffs from foreclosing mortgages on their farms.

Many thousands of jobless people from cities and farms wandered over the land seeking jobs at any wages, hitchhiking or riding in freight trains and sleeping on park benches. Never had America known such widespread suffering.

Causes of the depression. There is no simple way to explain the Great Depression. President Hoover insisted that the major cause was the worldwide economic disorder that followed World War I. Many economists agreed. They pointed to the vast destruction of property during the war and the worldwide dislocation of trade during and after the war.

Other economists argued that America's high tariff policies helped to stifle world trade and hurt American business. High tariffs, they claimed, prevented other countries from selling their goods in the United States. This in turn prevented them from securing the dollars that they needed to buy American products.

Still other economists blamed the depression on the excessive borrowing of money—for stocks, for comforts purchased on the installment plan, or for the expansion of businesses. These critics also claimed that the federal government failed to control bank loans and to protect the public against the sale of stocks that had no value.

Some economists have argued that depressions are an inevitable part of the American economic system. According to this view, business expands during periods of prosperity in order to obtain the largest possible profits. When factories produce more goods than consumers can buy, the factories have to cut down on production, at least until their surpluses are consumed. For this reason, these economists have argued, prosperity and depression are inevitable parts of the business cycle.

Finally, some economists have traced the Great Depression to uneven distribution of income. These economists have argued that if farmers had received better prices for their products and if workers had received higher wages, the American people would have been able to buy a larger proportion of the surplus goods. Had this happened, these economists claim, the factories would have kept busy and the depression could have been avoided.

Hoover and the depression. The depression confronted the Hoover administration with two emergencies. First, there was the widespread misery of people without jobs or farms, without money to buy enough food or clothing, and increasingly without hope. Some Americans urged the federal government to extend direct relief to those in need. Hoover, however, believed that direct aid was a responsibility of local communities. Direct federal relief, he said, would create a vast, inefficient bureaucracy and undermine the self-respect of the persons receiving it. Unfortunately, local communities did not have the resources to cope with the ever-rising tide of human misery.

To the second emergency, the collapse of business and agriculture, Hoover responded more actively. He instructed the Farm Board to buy up agricultural surpluses in an effort to raise falling farm prices. With the support of Congress, he started several public works programs, among them Boulder Dam (later called Hoover Dam) on the Colorado River. These projects were intended to stimulate business and provide employment for jobless workers.

Also at Hoover's urging, Congress created the Reconstruction Finance Corporation (RFC) in February 1932. The RFC could lend large sums of money to banks, life insurance companies, railroads, farm mortgage associations, and other enterprises. Hoover hoped that federal loans would strengthen these key businesses and thus provide jobs for millions of workers. Although the RFC advanced nearly $2 billion in loans to American business before the end of the Hoover administration, the depression grew worse.

In response to a recommendation by Hoover, Congress also passed the Home Loan Bank Act in July 1932. This act created a series of special banks designed to provide financial assistance to savings banks, building and loan associations, and insurance companies—all of which lent money on mortgages. By providing financial aid to such institutions, Hoover hoped to reduce foreclosures on homes and farms as well as to stimulate the construction of residential buildings.

In adopting these measures, the President and Congress were accepting, for the first time, the idea that the government had to assume certain responsibilities when the nation's economy suffered a serious setback. Unfortunately, the measures adopted did not stop the downward trend.

The election campaign of 1932. In the summer of 1932, the Republicans renominated

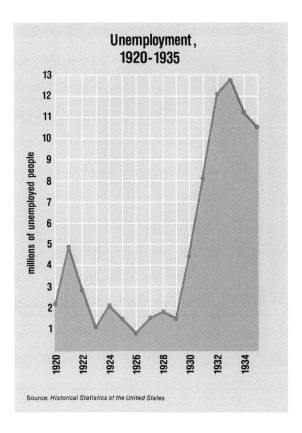

Herbert Hoover for President. As their candidate the Democrats chose Franklin Delano Roosevelt of New York.

Roosevelt had extensive political experience. He had served as a state senator in New York and as Assistant Secretary of the Navy. In 1920 he had been the Democratic nominee for Vice-President. In 1921 Roosevelt had been stricken with polio. Paralyzed from the waist down, he fought back to regain partial use of his legs. Roosevelt then regained the attention of the nation while serving as governor of New York.

There was really only one important issue in the campaign—the depression. Hoover continued to blame the depression on international conditions. He declared that his policies were beginning to bring recovery and that Roosevelt's would destroy the American system.

Both of these claims were rejected by Roosevelt. He maintained that Republican policies, not international conditions, were to blame for the depression. He argued that the federal government should help provide direct relief to the needy and direct aid to farmers. He called for a

Auto license tags like this one aimed to show the stand that the 1932 Democratic candidates, Franklin Delano Roosevelt and John Nance Garner, took favoring repeal of the Eighteenth Amendment that banned the sale of alcohol.

broad program of public works. He also demanded that safeguards be set up to prevent wild speculation and fraudulent issues of stock. To accomplish this he proposed laws to protect the bank depositor, the purchaser of stocks, and the homeowner. Referring to the unemployed workers, the desperate farmers, and others, Roosevelt stated that these "forgotten" Americans "at the bottom of the economic pyramid" had to have a "new deal."

Roosevelt's victory. Roosevelt and his running mate, John Nance Garner of Texas, won a sweeping victory in 1932, with Roosevelt winning 23 million popular votes to Hoover's 16 million. Roosevelt carried 42 states and piled up 472 electoral votes to Hoover's 59.

Moreover, the Democrats secured decisive majorities in both houses of Congress. These Democratic victories meant that Roosevelt's programs would have strong support in Congress.

A majority of voters throughout the 1920's had given the Republicans credit for the prosperity of those years. Now a great many Americans seemed to be saying that the Republicans would have to take the blame for the depression. Many of those who voted for the Democrats were really voting against Hoover rather than for Roosevelt. Many more saw in Roose-

velt the kind of dynamic personality that they believed was needed to lead the country out of its troubles.

Roosevelt had promised the American people a "new deal." During the four months between Election Day and Inauguration Day—March 4, 1933—workers, farmers, and even many business leaders waited hopefully to see how the new President would carry out his campaign pledge.

SECTION SURVEY

IDENTIFY: stock market crash, depression, RFC, Home Loan Bank Act, Franklin D. Roosevelt.

1. How do economists explain the major causes of the Great Depression?

2. (a) What measures did Hoover take to combat the depression? (b) How did these measures reflect his philosophy of government and the role it should take in economic affairs?

3. According to the 1920 census, more Americans were living in cities than on farms. How does this fact relate to the hardships experienced by the "little people" with the coming of the depression?

4. Graph Study: Look at the graphs on pages 602 and 603. How do they illustrate the events that are described in this section?

Chapter Survey

Summary: Tracing the Main Ideas

The joyous celebrations of victory that followed the signing of the armistice on November 11, 1918, soon came to an end. In 1919 and 1920, the United States was troubled by two short but severe postwar depressions, plus serious labor unrest and feverish concern over what was termed a "radical" threat to the country. During this period America's minorities suffered from renewed prejudice and discrimination.

By 1921, however, Americans were beginning to enjoy a decade of unparalleled prosperity. During the "Golden Twenties," as the decade was called, business activity reached an all-time high and relatively few Americans were unemployed.

Here and there warning voices called attention to the difficulties faced by large numbers of farmers and to other weaknesses of the economic system. For the most part, however, Americans were willing to believe that prosperity had come to stay.

Then, toward the end of 1929, the great industrial machine that the United States had built up began to grind to a halt. At first people refused to believe that the situation was serious. However, as the months passed, increasing numbers of businesses failed. Millions of Americans lost their jobs, farms, homes, and their life's savings. It became clear that the nation was confronted with a crisis of major proportions.

What was wrong?

Americans did not agree on all the answers to this very important question. They did agree that something had to be done to save the country from complete economic collapse.

In such an atmosphere, the election campaign of 1932 was fought. With the victory of Franklin Delano Roosevelt and the Democratic Party, Congress began a series of experiments that together came to be referred to as the "New Deal."

Inquiring into History

1. Why were Americans more interested in domestic affairs than in international relations in the year 1920?
2. Was the "Red scare" the first experience of this kind in American history? Explain.
3. During the Boston police strike, Governor Coolidge made the following statement: "There is no right to strike against the public safety by anybody, anywhere, any time." What did he mean? Do you agree or disagree with this viewpoint? Why?
4. The Fordney-McCumber Tariff of 1922 established high tariff rates. (a) How did this tariff affect foreign countries? (b) How did it affect American industries? (c) How did it affect American farmers?
5. When the cost of living goes up, how does it affect (a) buying power and (b) people living on fixed incomes?
6. Speaking in the 1920's, Herbert Hoover said, "We in America are nearer to the final triumph over poverty than ever before in the history of any land." (a) What facts supported his opinion? (b) Why were some Americans critical of his view?
7. Why was the Republican Party so successful in electing its candidates during the 1920's?

Relating Past to Present

1. Is it fair to blame or praise a President or a political party for (a) a war, (b) a depression, or (c) prosperity? Explain.
2. Compare the position of farmers in the 1920's with that of farmers today. Consider such factors as (a) the number of farmers, (b) the percentage of farmers in the population, (c) farm income, and (d) government farm programs.

Developing Social Science Skills

1. Find out more about the Sacco-Vanzetti trial which finally led to the execution of the two anarchists. (a) Where did they live? (b) What were their backgrounds? (c) Their beliefs? (d) Why did some people think they were innocent? (e) What do you think?
2. Interview one or more people who lived during the 1920's and 1930's to learn their impressions of each decade. Be sure to prepare your questions in advance of the interview. You might ask the following questions: (a) In what ways did your life change after the depression began? (b) Where did you live? (c) How did you spend each day? (d) What did you think should be done to end the depression?

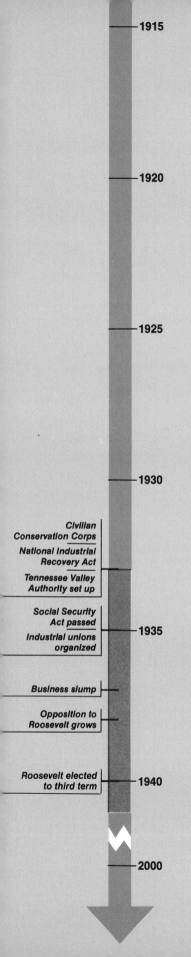

— 1915

— 1920

— 1925

— 1930

Civilian
Conservation Corps

National Industrial
Recovery Act

Tennessee Valley
Authority set up

Social Security
Act passed

Industrial unions
organized

— 1935

Business slump

Opposition to
Roosevelt grows

Roosevelt elected
to third term

— 1940

— 2000

Chapter 32

The Great Depression and the New Deal

1933–1941

President Franklin Delano Roosevelt took office on March 4, 1933, at the height of the Great Depression. He began his administration with a ringing call to the American people to face the future with courage and faith. "The only thing we have to fear is fear itself," he confidently stated. His calm words helped to lift the nation from its despair and to rally the people behind the new administration.

The President outlined his New Deal program in a crisp, dramatic Inaugural Address. He then presented his proposals, with recommendations for immediate action, to a special session of Congress. He had called for this session himself upon taking office.

The New Deal had three general aims—relief, recovery, and reform. Because the American people were clamoring for action, the three aims were often mixed together as objectives of a single act of Congress. Sometimes measures adopted to realize one of the aims interfered with other measures designed to achieve the other aims.

The New Deal was interrupted by America's entry into World War II. But for eight years, from 1933 to 1941, a seemingly endless series of New Deal measures poured out of Washington. Each measure was meant in some way to contribute to the restoration of the nation's social, economic, and political health.

THE CHAPTER IN OUTLINE

1. New Deal measures provide relief and speed recovery.

2. Recovery measures stimulate agriculture and industry.

3. The New Deal carries out reform measures.

4. Opposition increases toward New Deal policies and programs.

5. New Deal reforms continue despite growing criticism.

6. The New Deal's great experiment comes to an end.

1 New Deal measures provide relief and speed recovery

By 1933 the American people had endured two full years of the depression. Each year, each month, each week, the situation had become increasingly desperate.

"I am afraid," Charles M. Schwab, chairman of the Bethlehem Steel Corporation said. "Every man is afraid."

These were true words. Rich and poor alike, Americans lived in growing fear. Despair was widespread throughout the nation. "We are at the end of our rope," retiring President Hoover declared on his last day in office. "There is nothing more we can do."

Restoring confidence. Fortunately, the incoming President, Franklin D. Roosevelt, did not share this fear. In his Inaugural Address, he challenged Americans to rise above their fear. Speaking in a strong, calm, confident voice, he promised "action, and action now."

Roosevelt's confidence was contagious. He had been in the White House only two months when Will Rogers, one of America's most popu-lar humorists, expressed the feeling generally held throughout the nation. "The whole country is with him, just so he does something," Rogers declared. "If he burned down the Capitol, we would cheer and say, 'Well, we at least got a fire started anyhow.'"

President Roosevelt did indeed "get a fire started." On March 5, 1933, his first full day in the White House, he rolled his wheelchair into the Oval Office and began the "New Deal" for "the forgotten man." One of his first acts was to call a special session of Congress. During the next hundred days, he sent fifteen messages to the Congress, which responded by adopting fifteen major relief and recovery measures.

Restoring the banking system. On March 4, when Roosevelt took office, the nation's economic system was paralyzed. For months people had been selling stocks and rushing to the banks to withdraw their money before the banks failed. Throughout the country people were hiding their money in mattresses, under carpets, and in other places they considered safe. As a result of this run on the banks, many banks failed. Others closed their doors in an effort to avoid failure. With so many banks closed, the everyday business life of the nation ground to a halt. People could not pay their

In 1933, throngs of depositors like these in Ohio gathered to learn the fate of their savings. Many banks had failed. Others closed to avoid failure. Eventually the government stepped in and took action to protect the depositors.

SOURCES _____

bills by checks. There was not enough currency in circulation to meet the everyday needs of even a depressed economy.

On March 5 President Roosevelt issued a proclamation closing every bank in the nation for an indefinite period. The newly convened Congress then rushed through emergency banking laws forbidding any bank to reopen until it could prove its ability to carry on business without endangering its customers' deposits. Most banks were able to satisfy the financial authorities in the Treasury Department and quickly reopened.

In order to make sure people would never again lose their bank savings, Congress in June created the Federal Deposit Insurance Corporation (FDIC). The FDIC insured individual bank deposits up to $2,500. (The

amount insured by the FDIC has been increased through the years to the present figure of $100,000.)

Cheaper dollars. Congress also authorized the Secretary of the Treasury to call in all gold coins and gold certificates then in circulation. With this action Congress abandoned the gold standard, which in the past had meant that all paper currency was redeemable in gold. In so doing Congress devalued the dollar. The administration hoped that cheaper dollars would help the farmers by forcing agricultural prices upward. In this respect, however, the measure was a disappointment.

Pump priming. In its efforts to revive the nation's economy, the New Deal followed a procedure called "pump priming." When the pump in a well does not draw water, it is sometimes necessary to prime the pump by pouring a little water down the well shaft. This water seals the crack around a washer in the shaft and thus helps to create a vacuum into which the well water rises so that it can be pumped up.

Roosevelt's administration planned to pump money into the nation's economy through federal loans and spending. The hope was that such action would stimulate the flow of more money.

One of the major pump-priming agencies was the Reconstruction Finance Corporation. The RFC had been started in Hoover's administration (see page 603). Under Roosevelt it continued to pour huge sums into the nation's economy. It did this in the form of loans totaling $11 billion to railroads, banks, insurance firms, and industrial enterprises. Much of this money was quickly repaid.

Direct relief for the unemployed. In addition to emergency measures to reopen the banks and to get more money into circulation, the New Deal provided direct relief to jobless, hungry Americans.

By 1933 nearly 14 million men and women were out of work. In response, the Roosevelt administration immediately launched what seemed at the time to be a colossal program of direct relief. In two years federal agencies distributed $3 billion to the states. Local authorities were allowed to use the money as they chose — to provide direct relief or jobs. At one time nearly 8 million families were on direct relief. However, few Americans liked this

CRITIC WITH A LASSO

He would amble out on stage wearing cowboy gear, a loose cowlick of hair falling over his forehead. He might do a few simple rope tricks with the lariat he always carried. But the important part of any appearance by Will Rogers was the talk—his dry, humorous comments on current events. He spoke sense so appealingly— not only on the stage but also on the radio and in a weekly newspaper column—that he once received 22 votes for President at a Democratic convention.

Will Rogers, born in Oklahoma in 1879 (he was part Cherokee), tackled almost any subject in the news. About taxation he said, "Income tax has made more liars out of the American people than golf has." On automobiles: "Ah, for the good old days, when you lived until you died and not until you were just run over." On men and women: "You know, women always could endure more than men. Not only physically, but mentally—did you ever get a peek at some of the husbands?"

It was politics that brought out the best, and sharpest, in the homespun humorist. "This President business," he wrote, "is a pretty thankless job. Washington, or Lincoln either, didn't get a statue until everybody was sure they was dead." Congress came in for a big share of ridicule: "All I can say about the United States Senate is that it opens with a prayer and closes with an investigation." And again: "America has the best politicians money can buy."

Few people ever took offense at Rogers's gibes. There was no malice behind them. He is probably best remembered for something he said about himself: "I joked about every prominent man of my time, but I never met a man I didn't like."

kind of help. What the unemployed wanted were jobs, and plans were made to replace direct relief with programs to provide work.

Work relief. The federal government attacked this problem in several ways. For instance, during 1933–34 it paid nearly $1 billion in wages to men and women on relief lists who were given jobs on "make-work" projects. Many of these projects—raking leaves and picking up litter in parks—had relatively little value. Critics of the New Deal called this kind of work "boondoggling."

President Roosevelt and other New Dealers knew that federal charity and "make-work" projects were at best necessary evils. What Americans needed and what the New Dealers wanted to provide was socially useful work. To this end, a new agency, the Works Progress Administration (WPA) was created in 1935, with Harry L. Hopkins as its head. The WPA cooperated with state and local governments, which shared in both the cost and the administration of the work relief program.

The WPA helped people in many different ways. By 1936 more than 6,000 schoolhouses had been constructed or repaired; new sewage plants had been built in 5,000 communities; about 128,000 miles (206,000 kilometers) of secondary roads had been constructed or improved. Many other public improvements had been made as well. Unemployed actors, musicians, and writers enriched American life by providing plays, concerts, guidebooks, and other forms of recreation. At the peak of its activity, in March 1936, nearly 4 million Americans were working for the WPA.

Work for youth. Perhaps the greatest tragedy of the depression was its effect upon millions of young Americans. Many were forced to leave school or college because they lacked food and clothing or were homeless. Those who graduated during the depression years faced unemployment. Thousands of jobless young Americans roamed across the nation in search of work.

Two agencies were created to bring immediate work relief to the nation's youths. In 1933 the Civilian Conservation Corps (CCC) was organized. At times as many as 500,000 young men between 18 and 25 were enrolled in the CCC. Nearly all of them were unmarried; most came from poverty-stricken families. These youths lived in work camps scattered across the land in which they received food, clothing, and shelter. They were also paid wages, which they were expected to share with their families. In the CCC they had opportunities for recreation and education.

The young Americans in the CCC did socially useful work. They built fire trails in the forests, cleared swamps, planted trees, built small dams for flood control, cleared land for public parks, and in other ways helped to conserve the nation's natural resources.

A second New Deal work relief measure aided young people who were still in school. The National Youth Administration (NYA), created in 1935, distributed federal money to needy students willing to work. These students were paid regular wages for performing useful tasks in and around their school. During its first year, the NYA gave jobs to more than 400,000 students.

The New Deal youth programs saved hundreds of thousands of youths from idleness, helped them to maintain their self-respect, and enabled many to get an education. It also kept many young Americans out of the overcrowded job market in business and industry.

Evaluating the relief program. The New Deal relief projects aroused much criticism. It is true that many mistakes were made; there was bad management; there was waste.

Some New Dealers admitted the truth of these criticisms. They explained, however, that there had been no successful past examples to follow in the gigantic tasks they had undertaken. They also pointed out that they had been handicapped by lack of trained personnel to carry out some of their programs.

Despite admitted weaknesses in the work relief program, New Dealers claimed that it had justified itself. Work provided by the federal government, they insisted, had saved millions of Americans from hunger and allowed them to retain some measure of self-respect.

SECTION SURVEY

IDENTIFY: New Deal, pump priming, direct relief, work relief, WPA, CCC, NYA.

1. What immediate problems faced Roosevelt when he took office in 1933?

2. How did the New Deal respect the rights of states in distributing funds for relief purposes?

3. Why can it be said that the greatest tragedy of the depression was its effect on millions of young people?

4. (a) What criticisms were leveled against the New Deal relief program? (b) How did the New Dealers answer these criticisms? (c) In your opinion were the New Deal measures well conceived? Explain.

 Recovery measures stimulate agriculture and industry

The New Deal measures to provide direct relief and work relief were intended to meet the urgent needs of millions of suffering Americans. At the same time, the New Deal administration launched a recovery program designed to restore the nation's economic health.

Saving the farmers' homes. When Roosevelt became President, two out of every five American farms were mortgaged. Moreover, farmers all over the country faced mounting debts—back taxes, interest payments, and payments on the principal of their loans. Unable to pay their debts, many farmers lost their farms to banks, insurance companies, and private mortgage holders. Some farm families then rented as tenants the land they had once owned. Others were left homeless and jobless.

To relieve this situation, the federal government made available a huge sum of money that farmers could borrow at low interest rates. Some farmers borrowed to buy seed, fertilizer, and equipment necessary to continue operations. Others borrowed to buy back their farms or to pay their taxes.

Still others borrowed money from the government to refinance loans that they could not afford to repay at the time. Under the new government program, a farmer could borrow $5,000 from the Federal Land Banks to pay off the debt to a mortgage holder. The new loan

Poor farming methods and recurring drought turned much of the Middle West into a "Dust Bowl" during the 1930's. The Farm Security Administration (FSA) sent photographers to record the plight of farmers in the stricken area.

from the government could run as long as 50 years, with interest at 2 1/4 percent.

This liberal system of federal credit enabled hundreds of thousands of farm families to protect their land and homes. The farm credit programs were administered by the Farm Credit Administration (FCA), created in 1933.

Higher income for farmers. The New Dealers also tried to increase the farmers' income. The basic plan for farm recovery was simple. The first step was to raise the prices of farm products.

The government set out to increase farm prices by using the principle of supply and demand. Consider the example of a grocery store that has bought more oranges than it can sell. The surplus oranges are about to rot. What does the store do? It reduces the price of the oranges. Next time, of course, the store will order fewer oranges, hoping that by reducing the supply it can sell all the oranges at a good price. This is essentially the policy that the New Deal applied to farm goods in the Agricultural Adjustment Act of 1933.

Limiting farm production. The government reduced the supply of farm products by several

methods. Under the Agricultural Adjustment Administration (AAA), farmers were urged to sign agreements not to use one quarter to one half of their land. The government then paid farmers a certain sum of money for each acre that they took out of production. The money for these subsidies, or benefit payments, came from taxes on the food processors—the meat packers, canners, flour millers, and others who prepared or processed farm products.

Under this program large amounts of farmland were taken out of production. In 1933 a million cotton planters plowed under cotton. They did not plant about 10 million acres (405,000 hectares) that they ordinarily would have planted. As a result the 1933 cotton crop was reduced by about 4 million bales and the price of cotton almost doubled. Meanwhile the cotton planters received almost $200 million in federal subsidies. Producers of wheat, corn, hogs, rice, tobacco, dairy products, cattle, rye, barley, peanuts, flax, grain, sorghum, and sugar signed similar agreements to limit their production.

Evaluating the farm program. New Dealers were pleased with their agricultural recovery program. They pointed out that the prices of

611

farm products had risen and farmers were earning more money. They also pointed out that farmers were now spending more money and thus helping to get industry rolling again. These favorable results, the New Dealers said, were the outcome of sound federal planning.

However, there was also severe criticism of the New Deal farm program. Critics pointed out that the money for subsidies came from taxes on the food processors. These taxes were passed along to consumers in the form of higher prices. Thus money was being taken from consumers and given to the farmers. While farmers were getting more money, city dwellers were experiencing a decline in purchasing power.

Also, the owners of large farms benefited far more from the program than did the owners of small farms. Poorer farmers felt that the benefit payments that finally filtered down to them were inadequate for their needs.

Many critics felt that the program resulted in red tape, confusion, and inefficiency. They believed that it concentrated too much power in too many government agencies.

Finally, millions of Americans condemned a program that deliberately decreased food supplies when hunger was widespread.

The AAA declared unconstitutional. The Supreme Court brought the Agricultural Adjustment Act of 1933 to an end. In a 1936 decision in the case of *United States v. Butler,* the Court stated that Congress had no constitutional right to regulate agricultural production. The Court ruled that this power belonged to the states and that the federal government had no authority to interfere.

Construction of public works. New Deal programs also attempted to revive the building industry. The New Dealers recognized that the building industry is one of the keys to a nation's economic health. The industry uses large quantities of materials from many sources. As a result, when construction work is going on, workers are busy in forests, mines, and factories throughout the country.

The building program of the New Deal started in June 1933. At that time, the Public Works Administration (PWA) began to contract with private firms for the construction of public works, such as bridges, government buildings, power plants, conservation projects, and dams. The federal government also en-

couraged states and municipalities to carry on their own building programs, offering them loans and gifts.

By the summer of 1936, public works projects included about 70 municipal power plants, several hundred schools and hospitals, nearly 1,500 waterworks, and many federal, state, county, and municipal buildings.

Repair and building of homes. The New Dealers also sought to revive the building industry by stimulating the construction of homes. Like so many New Deal measures, this program was double-barreled; it had as a second goal the relief of homeowners.

When President Roosevelt took office, an average of 1,000 American homes were being foreclosed and sold at public auction every day. In June 1933 Congress tried to end this situation by creating the Home Owner's Loan Corporation (HOLC). With money borrowed at low interest rates from this government agency, many homeowners could pay off their old mortgages. At the same time, they arranged with the HOLC to pay off their new mortgages over a long period with much smaller monthly payments. Between 1933 and 1936, the homes of more than 1 million American families were thus saved.

To provide further aid to the owners of homes and businesses and the building industry, the Federal Housing Administration (FHA) was established in 1934. The FHA encouraged banks to lend money to individuals for repairing and building homes and business properties. It did this by insuring the banks against losses on such loans. Yet so desperate was the financial position of most Americans that relatively few people were able to take advantage of the FHA loans.

A federal housing program to provide homes for the very poor was no more successful. Although the PWA lent and gave money to some 27 cities for clearing slums and building low-cost apartment houses, the results were disappointing. For one thing, rents for the finished apartments were usually more than poor families could afford.

Aid to transportation. No less important than the building industry to a nation's economic life is its transportation system. The depression hit the railroads a stunning blow. Between 1929 and 1933, almost one third of all the railroad companies in the United States went bankrupt. Others were saved from complete collapse only by loans from the RFC.

To recover lost business, some western railroads lowered their passenger rates from 3.2 cents to 2 cents per mile. The experiment proved so successful that the Interstate Commerce Commission ordered all lines to adopt the same rate. Government loans also enabled the railroads to install modern equipment, such as diesel engines and streamlined trains.

All of these measures helped the railroads. However, at the same time, the government also spent huge sums of money to improve the nation's highways and waterways, thereby giving a boost to the railroads' competitors.

The NIRA. All these New Deal recovery measures were more or less indirect methods of reviving the nation's industrial machine. With the National Industrial Recovery Act (NIRA), the New Deal tackled the problem head on.

The NIRA went into effect in June 1933 as a two-year emergency measure. It was intended to aid industry, consumers, and labor. Under the act employers would cooperate in stabilizing prices, finding employment for jobless workers, and raising wages. Cooperation was to replace competition as one of the major driving forces of American industry. Antitrust legislation, such as the Sherman and Clayton antitrust acts, was disregarded.

The NIRA provided that each industry should, with the aid of the National Recovery Administration (NRA), adopt a "code of fair practices." Once these codes had been approved by the President, they became binding upon the entire industry.

Some 95 percent of American industries adopted fair-practices codes within a few months. In general, the codes limited production and provided for the common control of prices and sales practices. Most codes also outlawed child labor and required that adults not work more than 40 hours a week and that wages not be less than $12 to $15 a week.

Perhaps the most important—and certainly the most controversial—provisions in the NIRA were contained in the famous Section 7a. This section guaranteed workers the right to bargain collectively with their employers.

Criticisms of the NIRA. Critics of the NIRA were many and outspoken. Owners of small businesses charged that the NRA codes of fair practices had mostly been made by and for large corporations. They insisted that the minimum-wage provisions in the codes favored the highly mechanized factories that could afford to pay higher wages. Other critics charged that it was difficult to enforce the codes. Also, the courts usually refused to enforce the fair-practices provisions of the codes. Finally, while the NRA was supposed to aid recovery by increasing the purchasing power of consumers, many manufacturers defeated this purpose by raising prices to cover increases in wages.

The main objection to the NIRA for many businesses was that it stimulated unionization and collective bargaining. Moreover, certain provisions in Section 7a of the act were not clear. For instance, did company unions, under the influence of managers and owners, have the right to engage in collective bargaining? Labor said that company unions could not honestly represent the workers and should be outlawed. Management disagreed.

The National Labor Board. To settle the confused points of the law, Congress established an agency that later became the National Labor Relations Board (NLRB). The board could conduct elections in plants and determine which labor organization had the right to bargain for all the workers in that particular plant. It also served as a board of arbitration to settle labor disputes.

The board was unpopular with business managers and owners. They claimed that it usually settled disputes in favor of labor. As a result, business began to oppose the entire NRA program. When management refused to grant union demands, a wave of strikes broke out. Despite these problems the National Labor Board, before the summer of 1935, settled more than four fifths of the 3,755 disputes referred to it and avoided nearly 500 strikes.

The NIRA declared unconstitutional. In May 1935, in the case of *Schechter v. United States*, the Supreme Court declared the NIRA unconstitutional. The Court held that in giving the federal government the right to regulate interstate commerce, the Constitution did not give the government the power to regulate every aspect of business.

The Wagner Act. One important idea in the NIRA was quickly reborn. In 1935 Congress passed the famous National Labor Relations Act. This measure was often called the Wagner

Act after one of its sponsors, Senator Robert F. Wagner of New York.

The Wagner Act, like the equally well-known Section 7a of the NIRA, guaranteed to labor the right to organize, to bargain collectively with employers for better wages and working conditions, and to engage in "concerted activities . . . for other mutual aid." The Wagner Act condemned as unfair to labor such practices as discriminating against or discharging a worker for belonging to a union. It also declared that the majority of the workers in any plant or industry could select representatives to bargain with management.

Under the Wagner Act, the organization of labor proceeded rapidly. While the Wagner Act was in a sense a reform measure, it was also intended to promote industrial recovery. It aimed to do this by guaranteeing to organized labor a better chance of raising workers' wages and thus increasing their purchasing power. No single measure of the New Deal aroused more controversy than the Wagner Act.

SECTION SURVEY

IDENTIFY: AAA, subsidy, bureaucratic, *United States v. Butler,* HOLC, Section 7a, NLRB, *Schechter v. United States,* Wagner Act.

1. (a) Explain the basic New Deal plan to aid farmers. (b) What were the major arguments for and against the New Deal farm recovery program?
2. Why did the Supreme Court declare the Agricultural Adjustment Act of 1933 unconstitutional?
3. What steps were taken during the New Deal to help the transportation industry?
4. (a) What was the aim of the NIRA? (b) How was the aim to be carried out?
5. Why did the Supreme Court declare the NIRA unconstitutional?

3 The New Deal carries out reform measures

Although relief and recovery measures were urgently needed in the early 1930's, only fundamental reforms could protect the nation against another depression. Such reforms became increasingly important goals of the New Deal in 1935 and thereafter.

Protection for investors. New Deal reforms strengthened banks in several ways. For example, the power of the Federal Reserve System was increased by placing commercial and savings banks under its supervision. The Federal Reserve Board was given additional power to regulate credit as a check upon reckless speculation.

Another series of laws was designed to protect the public against worthless stocks. Any bank, brokerage house, or salesperson that failed to give full and honest information about the true value of stocks and bonds offered for sale was subject to a severe penalty. In 1934 the Securities and Exchange Commission (SEC) was created to administer these laws and to regulate the stock exchanges.

Social security for the people. One key reform measure of the New Deal, the Social Security Act of 1935, tackled the problem of individual security. The act had three major goals.

First, it provided unemployment insurance for individuals who lost their jobs. The money to be used for this purpose was raised by a payroll tax on businesses employing more than eight workers.

A second goal of the Social Security Act was to provide old-age pensions ranging from $10 to $85 a month for persons over 65. The money for this purpose was raised by a payroll tax on employers and a social security tax on the wages of employees.

A third goal of the Social Security Act was to help the handicapped—the blind, the aged, the disabled—as well as dependent children. Federal pensions up to $20 a month were available for needy persons over 65, provided that the states paid an equal amount. Federal funds were also available for those states that sought to protect the welfare of the handicapped.

President Roosevelt called the Social Security Act "a cornerstone in a structure which is being built." It was admittedly only a beginning, for it did not include all workers. Nevertheless, by 1937 nearly 21 million workers were entitled to unemployment benefits, and 36 million retired workers to old-age pensions.

Electricity for homes. Another reform movement sought to bring electricity to more Americans. Despite widespread development of electric power up to the 1930's, only one third of America's homes had electricity. In rural areas only 15 out of every 100 houses were wired.

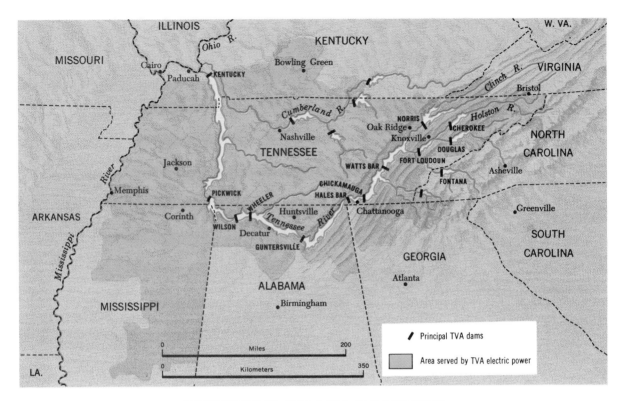

TENNESSEE VALLEY AUTHORITY

To solve this problem, the President in 1935 created the Rural Electrification Administration (REA). The REA had the responsibility of developing a program for generating and distributing electricity to isolated rural areas.

Regulating utility companies. In 1935 also, Congress passed the Public Utility Holding Company Act, also called the Wheeler-Rayburn Act. This measure gave the Federal Power Commission authority to regulate the interstate production, transmission, and sale of electricity. It gave the Federal Trade Commission similar authority over gas. It gave the Securities and Exchange Commission authority to regulate the financial practices of public utility holding companies.

By regulating the financial operations of the public utility holding companies, the New Deal hoped to end a trend toward monopoly in public utilities. The measure was designed to prevent any holding company from controlling more than a "single integrated public utility system" operating in a single area of the country. Under the law utility companies were

forbidden to engage in any business other than the production and distribution of gas or electric power. They were also forbidden to issue new stocks and bonds without the approval of the Securities and Exchange Commission.

Finally, in a "death-sentence" clause, the Public Utility Holding Company Act gave the public utility holding companies five years to readjust their financial affairs. At the end of five years, any company that could not prove that it was actually distributing gas or electricity in a given area would be dissolved.

The TVA. With the creation of the Tennessee Valley Authority (TVA), Congress in 1933 launched the United States upon an experiment that had no parallel in American history. The scene of this monumental experiment included parts of seven states in the region drained by the Tennessee River and its tributaries (see map, this page).

The TVA moved into this region with a plan for the unified development of all its resources. The plan was to improve economic and social conditions for the benefit of the people who

615

lived in the valley. It would also benefit all Americans by setting a standard of cost for producing and distributing electric power.

Over the next ten years, the TVA constructed 21 large dams on the Tennessee River and its major tributaries and thousands of smaller dams on creeks and brooks. Power plants were erected to convert the "white coal" of the river into vast quantities of electricity. Whereas in 1935 only 1 in every 100 homes in Mississippi had electricity, by 1945 about 20 homes out of 100 were wired. The per capita consumption of electric power in the TVA region was 50 percent higher than the average per capita consumption for the entire United States. Moreover, rates for electric power had been cut by about one third.

The TVA dams were also planned as part of a program to control floods, to prevent soil erosion, and to restore the fertility of the land. Under the TVA fertilizer plants were opened, river and road transportation improved, and public parks, schools, and hospitals were con-

structed. Vast changes have come to the region because of TVA programs.

Criticisms of the TVA. There is another side to the TVA story. Privately owned power companies, representing a $12 billion industry, bitterly fought the TVA. They declared that the TVA was an unnecessary intervention by the federal government into the affairs of private industry. They insisted that the lower TVA rates for electric power were not the result of more efficient production. If the TVA paid taxes as all private industries did, critics insisted, the power agency would have to charge much more for its electricity.

Advocates of the TVA believed that its rates should be used as a standard to govern the rates charged by private power producers. The private power companies insisted that the TVA was an unfair standard, and the less expensive electricity it generated was a gift from the taxpayers of the entire nation to the people of one region.

This 1933 painting shows the earliest of the TVA projects—the construction of the Norris Dam near Knoxville. The dam was named for Senator George W. Norris of Nebraska, who was an early and outspoken supporter of the TVA.

1. What were the three main purposes of the Social Security Act of 1935?

2. (a) What was the purpose of the Tennessee Valley Authority? (b) Although the TVA was located in a single region, how might it be seen as a benefit to the whole nation?

3. (a) What arguments have been used against the TVA? (b) Do you think these are valid arguments? Explain.

4 Opposition increases toward New Deal policies and programs

By 1936 the United States had made considerable progress in its battle against the depression. National income had risen sharply since 1932, having jumped from a low of less than $47 billion to almost $70 billion. Industrial production was double that of 1932.

However, the depression was far from conquered. In 1936 as many as 3.5 million people were still working on relief projects. Nine million men and women were still unemployed. Many factories and mines were still closed or were working at far less than full capacity.

Such was the situation when in 1936 the voters entered another Presidential election year. Should Roosevelt be reelected? Should the New Deal be continued? These were the big questions facing the voters.

Roosevelt's supporters. In June 1936 the Democrats enthusiastically renominated Roosevelt for a second term. Their platform strongly endorsed the New Deal.

Lined up behind the President were not only most Democrats but also countless rank-and-file Republicans. Most of the progressive Republican leaders who had supported him in 1932 continued to do so. Labor was overwhelmingly for the President, as were many farmers who remembered the New Deal benefits they had recently received. Many of those who had received federal relief money also supported Roosevelt. And finally, black voters in the North almost solidly rejected their traditional

Republican ties and supported the party that, in some measure, had responded to their needs and grievances.

Roosevelt's critics. The President and the New Deal also had many critics, including a number of influential Democrats. Roosevelt's Republican critics included most big business leaders, many small business people who had suffered under the NRA, bankers, private power companies, newspapers, and many professional people. Some critics objected to Eleanor Roosevelt's efforts on behalf of black Americans.

Opponents of President Roosevelt sometimes claimed that he was undermining the Constitution. They pointed out that the Supreme Court had declared unconstitutional seven out of nine important New Deal measures. They insisted that the American way of life—individualism, free enterprise, and private property—was being abandoned for socialism and government control. Roosevelt's critics denied that the New Deal had restored prosperity. They pointed to the nation's continued unemployment. They stressed the fact that the administration had piled up a huge national debt of over $33 billion and had failed to balance the budget.

Republican promises. The Republicans in 1936 nominated friendly, thrifty Alfred M. Landon, Governor of Kansas, for President. Landon was a liberal Republican. Although he was in the oil business, he had the support of many farmers who trusted his judgment. Moreover, in a period when most states and the federal government had piled up huge debts, Governor Landon had balanced the Kansas budget.

The Republican platform promised to continue most New Deal measures, which, they claimed, they could carry out more effectively and economically than the Democrats. The Republicans also promised to balance the budget and to restore to the states certain powers that the federal government had seized to carry out the New Deal program. Thus the Republicans adopted what had traditionally been the Democratic states' rights position.

Roosevelt's victory. The election campaign was filled with angry charges and countercharges. More than 45 million Americans voted, reflecting keen popular interest. Roosevelt swept the country with an electoral

This 1934 cover of the magazine *Vanity Fair* reflected the thinking of those Americans who believed that Roosevelt had assumed too much power in the first year of his Presidency. Many of them were worried that Roosevelt would soon ride the nation into the ground.

vote of 523 to 8. Roosevelt's popular vote was also impressive—27,476,673 to Landon's 16,679,583. Moreover, the Democrats won or kept control of all but six governorships and maintained their leadership of both houses of Congress. Not since the reelection of President Monroe in 1820 had a Presidential candidate won such strong backing.

Roosevelt and the Supreme Court. Early in his second term, Roosevelt opened an attack on the Supreme Court. Roosevelt was upset because the Court had set aside as unconstitutional seven important New Deal laws. He was also disturbed because the Court had declared unconstitutional a New York State measure providing minimum wages for women and children. Moreover, the federal courts had used the injunction to block federal agencies from carrying out New Deal measures.

Roosevelt declared that all too often certain Supreme Court justices thought in terms of the "horse-and-buggy" era. "A dead hand was being laid upon this whole program of prog-

ress," the President later declared. It was, he said, the hand of the Supreme Court.

President Roosevelt asked Congress for power to appoint an extra justice to the Supreme Court for each existing justice who did not retire upon reaching age 70. At the time, six of the nine justices were 70 or older. Roosevelt's proposal, therefore, would have enabled him to appoint six new justices more favorable to the New Deal.

Changes in the Supreme Court. Although the President fought vigorously for his "reform" proposal, he lost. Members of Congress in his own party refused to support him, and public opinion ran against him. In general, people did not want to tamper with the delicate balance of legislative, executive, and judicial powers written into the Constitution.

Although Roosevelt lost the battle for Court "reform," he gained most of the things he wanted. The Court began to approve important New Deal measures. The National Labor Relations Act and the Social Security Act were tested and found constitutional. Moreover, the Court approved an act passed by the state of Washington establishing minimum pay for women and children. This act was almost identical to the New York State law that the Court had earlier declared unconstitutional.

Had the Court suddenly realized that it might be well to approve certain popular legislation to prevent a drastic reform of the Court itself? Many Americans believed this to be true. In any case, Roosevelt was able to replace, because of death or retirement, all but two of the original justices with members who appeared to be more sympathetic to New Deal legislation.

Business slump in 1937–38. Early in 1937, while the issue of the Supreme Court was being argued across the land, the nation's industrial machinery once again slowed down. By the autumn of 1937, factories were closing and unemployment was rising.

The Democrats spoke of what was taking place as a **recession,** that is, a business slump less severe than a depression. The Republicans, on the other hand, called it the "Roosevelt depression." Roosevelt's opponents blamed the Democrats and the New Deal for the present business slump in just the same way that the Democrats in 1931 had blamed the Republicans for the Great Depression.

Politics aside, there was fairly widespread agreement on the major cause of the slump. Instead of balancing the budget as he had promised to do back in 1932, Roosevelt had piled up the largest national debt in history. The Republicans had made the most of this fact in the 1936 election campaign. However, many Democrats and friends of the New Deal had also become increasingly uneasy about the mounting debt.

Mindful of the growing criticism, by 1936 Roosevelt had begun to cut spending for relief and public works. Unfortunately, private industry was not yet strong enough to give jobs to the men and women who were dropped from relief projects because of the cutbacks. Once again, therefore, the nation's economic system started on a downward spiral.

New pump priming. Fortunately, measures adopted to fight the Great Depression acted as brakes against the 1937–38 recession. More than 2 million wage earners in 25 states, protected by the Social Security Act, began to collect unemployment insurance. The new banking laws protected the savings of depositors. Many government agencies were ready to lend money to business and to construct public works, thus creating new jobs.

Roosevelt and Congress began once again to prime the economic pump by increasing government lending and spending. The Reconstruction Finance Corporation again came to the rescue of businesses in trouble. The WPA doubled the number of workers on its payroll from 1.5 million to 3 million.

By the end of 1938, the nation's economic machinery was once again picking up speed. The Democrats were quick to claim another victory for the New Deal. The Republicans, on the other hand, insisted again that recovery had come in spite of the New Deal. Many Americans, Democrats and Republicans alike, continued to express alarm at the ever-growing national debt.

SECTION SURVEY

IDENTIFY: Alfred M. Landon, recession.

1. (a) On what major issues did the election of 1936 focus? (b) What positions did each party take on these issues?

2. (a) Why did Roosevelt try to reform the Supreme Court? (b) Why did his plan fail? (c) What position would you have taken on the issue? Give arguments to support your opinion.

3. How did the measures adopted to fight the Great Depression act as brakes against the recession of 1937–38?

---

5 New Deal reforms continue despite growing criticism

During the 1936 election campaign, President Roosevelt had promised that, if reelected, he would continue the New Deal. Neither the business recession of 1937–38 nor the mounting criticism of his policies prevented Roosevelt from continuing his program.

The A. F. of L. and the CIO. As you may remember, the Wagner Act of 1935 guaranteed to workers the right of collective bargaining and forbade employers to discriminate against organized labor. Under the protection of this law, the American Federation of Labor began to organize unskilled workers in the mass production industries—steel, automobiles, aluminum, aircraft, utilities. However, the A. F. of L. did not move rapidly enough to please many labor leaders.

Growing impatience with the A. F. of L. led John L. Lewis, powerful head of the United Mine Workers, and a group of like-minded labor leaders to organize in 1935 the Committee for Industrial Organization (CIO). The CIO immediately launched a drive to organize workers in the automobile, steel, rubber, oil, radio, and other industries into industrial unions. The new industrial unions included all workers, skilled and unskilled, in an industry. The United Automobile Workers (UAW), for example, represented all workers in automotive plants. In earlier times workers in the automobile industry had negotiated contracts through many separate unions—electrical, welding, metalworking, and the like. Now they negotiated as a single powerful organization. The CIO also encouraged the inclusion of black workers in the new industrial unions.

Disturbed by the growing influence of the CIO, the leaders of the A. F. of L. ordered it to disband. When CIO leaders refused to obey this order, the A. F. of L. expelled them. However, the CIO continued to operate, and in May 1938

Here, auto workers in a General Motors factory stage a sit-down strike in 1936. It was through this 44 day sit-down strike at Flint, Michigan, that the GM workers won the right to be represented by the United Auto Workers.

it reorganized as a separate body, the Congress of Industrial Organizations (still called CIO), with John L. Lewis as its first president. By 1940 the CIO could boast of having 3.6 million members, roughly equal to the membership of the older A. F. of L.

The sit-down strike. Meanwhile, forceful organizing campaigns by both the A. F. of L. and the CIO resulted in a wave of strikes.

In November 1936 several hundred workers in the General Motors plant at Flint, Michigan, staged a **sit-down strike.** Instead of leaving the plant and organizing picket lines, the striking workers simply sat down at their machines and refused to work. They then announced that they would not leave until management granted their demands.

The sit-down strike, which made it impossible for management to bring in strikebreakers, proved extremely effective. Within a few months, this relatively new labor weapon spread to many other plants, involving more than half a million workers. All of the leading automobile manufacturers except Ford now

recognized the United Automobile Workers, the powerful new CIO union, as the bargaining agent for the automobile industry. The United States Steel Corporation, long a foe of labor unions, finally accepted the CIO steelworkers' union as the bargaining agent of the steelworkers. The CIO also organized the workers in many other industries.

In 1939 the Supreme Court ruled that sit-down strikes were illegal. Nevertheless the CIO—as well as the A. F. of L.—continued to forge ahead. In general, the Wagner Act of 1935, with its guarantee of collective bargaining, had given organized labor its great opportunity for growth.

Jurisdictional strikes. Much of the labor unrest of the late 1930's sprang from bitter rivalry between the A. F. of L. and the CIO. Disputes arose over which had **jurisdiction,** or the right, to enroll a particular group of workers. Sometimes these disputes led to jurisdictional strikes. In such cases management found it hard to know which side to recognize or to bargain with, and the government stepped in to settle the issue. The great wave of strikes that reached its peak in 1937 and 1938 diminished in the following years as both labor and management reluctantly came to accept government intervention.

Fair Labor Standards Act. The New Deal labor program did not merely encourage and support organized workers. It also aimed at reforming labor conditions in the United States. To this end, President Roosevelt in 1937 proposed the Fair Labor Standards Act, sometimes called the Wages and Hours Law. This law provided a minimum wage scale and a maximum workweek for many workers.

Strong opposition quickly developed to the Fair Labor Standards Act. Many employers claimed that it encouraged unneeded and unwise government interference and control over industry. However, the law went into effect in October 1938.

The Fair Labor Standards Act provided that a legal maximum workweek of 44 hours in 1938 be decreased to 40 hours by 1940, with time-and-a-half pay for overtime. It also provided that minimum wages of 25 cents an hour in 1938 be increased to 40 cents an hour by 1945. It prohibited the employment of children under 16 in industries producing goods for interstate commerce. The Department of Labor was responsible for enforcing the act.

Although the Fair Labor Standards Act affected only workers employed in interstate industries, by 1940 about 13 million men and women were benefiting from the law. Roosevelt hailed the new law as being, after the Social Security Act, "the most farsighted program for the benefit of workers ever adopted in this or in any other country."

Important though the Fair Labor Standards Act was, it did not insure freedom from racial discrimination in employment. In 1941 A. Philip Randolph, a powerful and militant black labor leader, threatened to march on the national capital with 10,000 blacks to demand equal employment opportunities. Responding to this pressure, Roosevelt established the Fair Employment Practices Committee (FEPC). The FEPC worked to counteract racial discrimination in industries that had contracts with the federal government.

Helping the farmers. Other far-reaching New Deal measures were meant to improve the economic position of the nation's farmers. In 1936, when the Supreme Court ruled against the Agricultural Adjustment Act of 1933, Congress passed another law.

The Soil Conservation and Domestic Allotment Act of 1936 set up a soil conservation program. Farmers who took part in the program leased part of their lands to the government. Under the supervision of state farm agencies, the farmers worked to restore the fertility of the leased land by practicing conservation measures, by using fertilizers, and by sowing soil-restoring plants, such as clover. In return, the farmers received a certain sum of money for every acre they withdrew from production.

By this means the government hoped to develop nationwide knowledge of sound conservation practices. Equally important, by limiting production the government hoped to raise the prices of farm products.

The Bankhead-Jones Act. With the Bankhead-Jones Farm Tenant Act of 1937, the New Deal undertook to help tenant farmers, sharecroppers, and migratory farm workers, who moved from place to place in search of jobs. The new law created the Farm Security Administration (FSA) to lend money at low interest to tenant farmers, sharecroppers, and farm laborers wishing to buy farms. Those who received the loans had 40 years to repay.

Agricultural Adjustment Act of 1938. The heart of the New Deal agricultural reform program was the second Agricultural Adjustment Act, passed in 1938. This act contained a number of important provisions:

(1) It provided payments to farmers in proportion to the number of acres that they withdrew from production and planted in soil-conserving crops.

(2) The government was authorized to decide the amount of various staple crops that could be marketed each year. With the approval of two thirds of the producers of these commodities in each locality, the government then assigned a certain allotment to each farmer. Farmers who exceeded this allotment had to pay a fine when they sold such crops during a time of surplus.

(3) When harvests were large, the surpluses were stored by the government for later use in lean years. However, farmers did not lose their income from the surplus crops. The government gave them commodity loans on all stored crops.

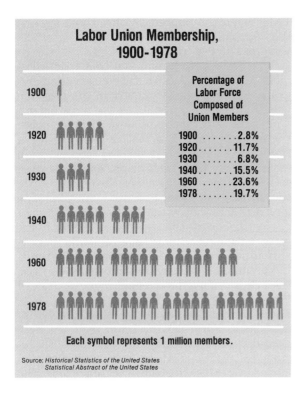

Labor Union Membership, 1900-1978

	Percentage of Labor Force Composed of Union Members
1900	1900 .... 2.8%
1920	1920 .... 11.7%
1930	1930 .... 6.8%
1940	1940 .... 15.5%
1960	1960 .... 23.6%
1978	1978 .... 19.7%

Each symbol represents 1 million members.

Source: *Historical Statistics of the United States
Statistical Abstract of the United States*

The amount of these loans was fixed at slightly below **parity**. Parity was a figure based on average prices of each of the commodities for the base period from August 1909 to July 1914, a relatively prosperous period for farmers. When the market price of a commodity rose to the parity level, farmers were to sell their stored crops and repay the loans. If the market price remained below parity, the farmers kept the money and the government kept their crops. By this method the government hoped to keep the price of agricultural products at a steady level and benefit both farmers and consumers.

(4) The act also authorized the government to insure wheat crops against drought, flood, hail, and plant diseases.

Evaluating the farm program. In 1932, in the depths of the Great Depression, farm income had sunk to less than $5 billion. By 1938 it had risen to more than $8 billion. By 1940 it totaled more than $9 billion.

Critics reminded the country that the increased income came from higher prices paid by consumers and from subsidies paid by the government—with taxpayers' money. These critics charged that money had been "taken from Peter to pay Paul."

Critics, including many farmers, also resented increasing government controls over farm production. They feared that subsidies would destroy farmers' independence. Moreover, critics charged that the government's price support program was causing America's agricultural products to lose out in the highly competitive foreign markets.

Such criticisms ended, at least temporarily, in 1941 when the United States was plunged into World War II. Then, as New Deal supporters were quick to point out, the country owed much to the farm legislation of the 1930's. This legislation had improved the economic condition of many Americans, had increased the fertility of millions of acres of land, and had enabled the United States to feed a large portion of the war-devastated world.

Housing for low-income groups. During his second term, Roosevelt also continued his efforts to ease the housing problem. The National Housing Act of 1937, usually called the Wagner-Steagall Act, had two aims: (1) to stimulate business by government spending for the construction of houses and (2) to "remedy the unsafe and unsatisfactory housing conditions and the acute shortage of decent, safe, and sanitary dwellings for families of low income in rural and urban communities."

The National Housing Act created the United States Housing Authority (USHA), which began an ambitious program of housing construction. By 1941 the USHA had lent $750 million for the construction of more than 160,000 housing units.

Other New Deal reforms. In 1938 Congress passed the Food, Drug, and Cosmetic Act, which replaced the earlier Pure Food and Drug Act of 1906. The 1938 act required adequate testing of new drugs before they were offered for sale. It also required manufacturers to list the exact ingredients of their products on their labels. In addition, the Wheeler-Lea Act, also passed in 1938, prohibited manufacturers from making false or misleading claims about their products in their advertising.

In 1939 Congress tackled the problem of improper political practices. The Hatch Act placed restrictions upon federal officeholders below the policy-making level in the executive branch of the government. Such officeholders were prohibited (1) from taking an active part in political campaigns, (2) from soliciting or accepting political contributions from workers on relief, and (3) from using their official positions to try to influence Presidential or Congressional elections. In 1940 the Hatch Act was amended to include state and local government employees whose pay came completely or partially from federal funds. The 1940 amendment also limited the amount of money a political party could spend in any one year. A maximum of $3 million was established. The amount any individual could contribute was $5,000 a year. This legislation was not effective because both parties soon found ways legally to avoid these limits.

SECTION SURVEY

IDENTIFY: John L. Lewis, CIO, industrial union, sit-down strike, jurisdictional strike, minimum wage, A. Philip Randolph, FEPC, parity, Hatch Act.

1. (a) Why was the CIO organized? (b) How did it differ from the A. F. of L.?
2. (a) How did the Fair Labor Standards Act benefit workers in the United States? (b) Why did some people oppose it?
3. What measures were taken from 1936 to 1938 to help improve the economic conditions of farmers?
4. Graph Study: Look at the graph on page 622. According to the graph, during what period did labor unions achieve their greatest growth?

6 The New Deal's great experiment comes to an end

By the middle of his second term, President Roosevelt's influence was beginning to decline. In 1937, as you have read, he had suffered a major defeat when he failed to push through Congress his bill for reorganizing the Supreme Court. In the Congressional elections of 1938, he suffered an even more serious defeat.

Congressional elections of 1938. As the elections approached, Roosevelt decided to liberalize the Democratic Party. Singling out those conservative Democrats who had voted

against his reform program, he urged voters to defeat them at the polls.

Roosevelt's effort to liberalize the Democratic Party failed. With only one exception, all the members of Congress whom Roosevelt had opposed were reelected. Moreover, the voters chose a great many new Democratic members who were foes of the New Deal. Adding to Roosevelt's dismay, the Republicans won additional seats in Congress. Nevertheless, the Democrats continued to hold a sizable majority in both the House and the Senate.

New Deal activities suspended. President Roosevelt, a shrewd politician, was quick to see the meaning of the 1938 elections. Realizing that public opinion was turning against him, he began to suspend earlier New Deal activities. By 1939 Congress was cutting appropriations for many New Deal agencies.

As a result of the threatening world situation, the PWA and the WPA shifted their attention from public works to projects involving national defense, such as the building of airports and military highways. Other New Deal agencies, such as the Civilian Conservation Corps and the National Youth Administration, ended operations when Congress cut off further appropriations. Although the TVA weathered attacks both in and out of Congress, the President's recommendation for similar projects in six other areas of the country received little support.

The driving impulse of the New Deal had spent itself. Those who maintained that the reform objectives of the New Deal were still far from being realized faced stiffer opposition and growing public indifference.

Opposition to New Deal finances. Much of the opposition to the New Deal came from people who believed that Roosevelt's financial policies were undermining the nation's economic system. In general, three different methods were used for financing New Deal relief, recovery, and reform programs.

One method was inflation. Although Congress authorized President Roosevelt to print paper money, he never did so. He did, however, take the nation off the gold standard. This cheapened the value of the dollar.

A second method was **deficit spending**. This meant that the government spent more than it received in taxes, leaving the budget unbalanced, or showing a deficit. In the 1930's the

As opposition to President Roosevelt's policies grew, he frequently took to the radio airwaves to defend them. The highly persuasive "fireside chats" often won support for his programs and reassured the nation.

national debt increased from about $16 billion to more than $40 billion. Men and women in both parties, but business leaders in particular, lost confidence in an administration that piled up a larger and larger national debt.

The third method by which the New Deal had financed the operation of new programs was by raising taxes. Despite strong opposition, Congress passed the Revenue Act of 1935, often called the Wealth Tax Act. With this measure Congress increased the income tax for individuals and large corporations and levied taxes on gifts and estates. In spite of these measures, the new revenue did not balance the budget, and the national debt continued to grow.

In the Revenue Act of 1936, Congress laid a steeply graduated tax on those corporate profits that were not distributed to stockholders. Business bitterly complained that the new tax would discourage business expansion and prevent the accumulation of surpluses for use in depression years.

In 1938, however, as a result of growing opposition to the New Deal, Congress began to reverse the taxation policy of earlier years. The Revenue Act of 1938 sharply reduced corporation taxes. In 1939 Congress abolished the tax on undistributed profits. At the same time, it raised the corporation income tax to a maximum of 19 percent. In addition, for the first time in history, Congress required employees of cities and states to pay taxes to the federal government.

A third term. Despite the fact that his influence was weakening, and despite the fact that the two-term tradition for Presidents was widely accepted as part of the unwritten Constitution, Roosevelt decided to run for a third term. The President did not at first announce his decision to the public, although he hinted that the critical world situation might compel him to be a candidate. However, behind the scenes he arranged matters so that it would have been almost impossible for any Democrat to run against Roosevelt without obtaining his consent.

The Democratic convention chose Roosevelt on the first ballot at Chicago in July 1940. It also, without general enthusiasm, accepted Henry A. Wallace of Iowa as his running mate. Wallace, a former Republican, had been Roosevelt's Secretary of Agriculture.

The Democratic platform promised to extend social security, to stress the low-cost housing program, and to advance government ownership of public utilities. The platform also promised to keep the United States out of the war that had broken out in Europe and to send no American armies abroad unless the nation were attacked.

Wendell Willkie. The Republicans chose as their candidate Wendell L. Willkie of New York, a powerful Wall Street lawyer with Democratic leanings and a long progressive record. Willkie favored many of the principles of the New Deal. On the other hand, he felt that the New Deal was extravagant. He also believed it had been administered in such a way as to endanger individualism, free enterprise, and democracy. Warmhearted and engaging, Willkie developed a strong following and became a formidable candidate.

The Republican platform condemned the New Deal for its "shifting, contradictory, and overlapping administrations and policies." It promised to revise the tax system to stimulate private enterprise and to promote prosperity. It also promised to keep the major New Deal reforms but to administer the laws governing these reforms with greater efficiency and less waste. The Republicans also demanded a constitutional amendment that would limit Presidents to a maximum of two terms in office. Like the Democrats, the Republicans promised to keep America out of war unless the nation were attacked.

The campaign of 1940. The threat of a second World War hung over the election campaign of 1940. Indeed, in the fall of 1940, while the American people were preparing to vote in the Presidential election, Great Britain was fighting desperately for survival.

Both Roosevelt and Willkie advocated a strong program of national defense. Both urged all aid to Great Britain short of war. In general, there was no important difference in their attitudes toward the terrible conflict that was raging abroad.

On domestic issues, however, they differed sharply. Willkie attacked Roosevelt for irresponsibility and Roosevelt attacked Willkie for "unwitting falsifications of fact." Willkie traveled thousands of miles through 34 states in a whirlwind campaign. Roosevelt limited himself to a few speeches.

Roosevelt won a sweeping victory in an election in which more Americans voted than in any previous contest in American history. But the returns clearly showed that the President had lost some of his earlier popularity. Roosevelt's 60 percent popular majority in the election of 1936 was reduced to just under 55 percent. In round numbers this meant that 27 million Americans voted for Roosevelt, and 22 million for Willkie. The popular vote was therefore much closer than indicated by the electoral vote of 449 for Roosevelt and 82 for Willkie. Although the Democrats retained control of Congress, the Republicans increased their strength in both Congress and the state legislatures.

During Roosevelt's third term, the New Deal domestic programs received less attention as foreign problems and war itself absorbed American energies. Thus a great period of reform in American history came to an end.

In August 1940, Wendell Willkie returned in triumph to his hometown of Elwood, Indiana, on his way to accept the Presidential nomination of the Republican Party. The wealthy New York lawyer was personable and charming and a strong candidate.

Whether this suspension of reform activities was the result of war or whether the reform impulse had spent itself remains unanswered.

SECTION SURVEY

IDENTIFY: deficit spending, national debt, Henry Wallace, Wendell Willkie.

1. (a) Describe the three methods used by New Dealers to raise money. (b) Why were these methods criticized?

2. Present evidence to support the view that Roosevelt's influence was decreasing by 1940.

3. In what ways did Roosevelt and Willkie disagree on domestic issues?

4. Do you think the fact that Roosevelt was running for a third term as President had any influence on the way people voted? Explain.

625

Chapter Survey

Summary: Tracing the Main Ideas

When Franklin D. Roosevelt became President of the United States in 1933, the nation was in the depths of the worst depression it had ever experienced. President Roosevelt, a person of great energy and overwhelming enthusiasm, inspired the people with his own confidence and faith in the future.

Surrounding himself with men and women who for the most part shared his views about the nation's problems, Roosevelt immediately opened a three-pronged attack upon the depression. In a series of relief measures, Congress, led by the administration, provided food, clothing, and shelter for the millions of unemployed and needy Americans. In a second series of recovery measures, Congress attempted to revive the nation's agriculture and industry and place the economy on a solid foundation. In a third series of reform measures, Congress developed a program designed to protect future generations from such a catastrophe.

By 1936 the New Deal program faced a large and growing body of opposition, some from within the Democratic Party itself. Many critics felt that the government was interfering too much with the free enterprise system and, in so doing, was threatening individualism and democracy.

By the end of 1938, the opposition had become so strong that President Roosevelt decided to postpone other far-reaching reforms that he had been considering. Indeed, during 1939, 1940, and 1941, the administration suspended the activities of several of the agencies created by the New Deal.

Another reason for the President's decision to postpone the reform program was his growing concern over the outbreak of war in East Asia and in Europe.

Inquiring into History

1. (a) Why was the New Deal controversial? (b) What were the major arguments in favor of the New Deal? (c) What were the major arguments against it?
2. Summarize the various ways in which the New Deal tried to help (a) the consumer, (b) low-income families on farms and in cities, (c) young people, (d) the aged, and (e) workers.
3. (a) Why did Roosevelt say that certain members of the Supreme Court thought in terms of the "horse-and-buggy" era? (b) How did he propose to remedy this situation? (c) How would his proposal have affected the balance of powers among the branches of the federal government?

Relating Past to Present

1. Which federal programs begun during the New Deal are still in operation today?
2. (a) How has history proved right the criticisms leveled against the New Deal? (b) How has history proved right the praise given to the New Deal?
3. Using the New Deal as a basis for comparison, how do you think the United States would react to such a severe economic crisis today?

Developing Social Science Skills

1. Read Herbert Hoover's "rugged individualism" speech of 1928 and Franklin D. Roosevelt's First Inaugural Address of 1933. (a) What is each President's view of the role of the federal government? (b) Based on these views, can you explain why each attempted to handle the depression in the way he did?
2. Draw a political cartoon that might have appeared in a newspaper during the Presidential election campaign of 1932, 1936, or 1940. Be sure that the cartoon clearly presents a point of view about a key issue or candidate of the campaign.
3. Read the novel *The Grapes of Wrath* by John Steinbeck or other novels set during the depression. (a) What problems brought on by the Great Depression did the characters face? (b) How did they try to solve these problems? (c) How does your impression of the Great Depression gained from the novel compare with that gained from your textbook? (d) How do you account for these similarities or differences?
4. Study the map on page 615. (a) Name five of the major dams in the TVA region. (b) Which states were included in the TVA region? (c) Why might the president of a privately owned power company in Alabama have opposed the TVA?
5. Write a caption story for the photograph on page 611. Make sure you describe the events that led to this view of devastating loss.

Sports

Joe Louis, 12 years world heavyweight boxing champion.

Helen Wills Moody, 7 times U. S. women's singles tennis champion.

Babe Ruth, 11 years home run king of the American League.

Bobby Jones, 5 times U. S. amateur golf champion.

Jesse Owens, 3 Olympic gold medals in 1936.

The 1920's and 1930's were filled with great highs and lows, but one thing remained constant—America's love of sports and sports heroes. Sporting events offered people a chance to escape from their problems and lifted their spirits.

Of Babe Ruth, a fellow baseball player once said, "There was nobody like him...He was a god." Certainly the great slugger was no god, but to many Americans he and the other greats pictured here seemed almost superhuman.

The Puritans did not approve of sports, but that did little to keep America from becoming a nation of sports fans.

On these pages are just a few of the activities that have appealed to Americans from colonial days to the present. Individual tests of strength, courage, and endurance, simple team games, and highly organized ones have all been part of America's love of sports.

Lawn tennis was first played in America in 1874.

On the frontier, turkey shoots were popular and skills sharp.

Horse racing was the nation's first organized sport.

Long before the first settlers arrived, American Indians were playing lacrosse.

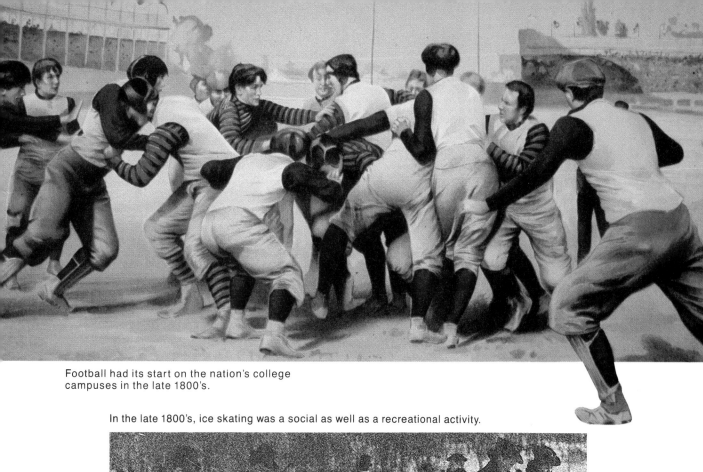

Football had its start on the nation's college campuses in the late 1800's.

In the late 1800's, ice skating was a social as well as a recreational activity.

Baseball began as a game called rounders in the early 1800's.

The heart pounds. The knees wobble. Sweat pours down the face. But the runner "never felt better." The runner has just finished 345th out of the 3,000 who entered this marathon.

This runner is not a star of the sports world, but simply one of millions of Americans trying to keep fit. Medical evidence has shown the links between exercise and good health. Americans have responded by lacing up running shoes, swinging tennis rackets, and pressing barbells. Spectator sports have long been big business in America. Today participant sports are, too.

For some, running was not only a way to keep fit, but a way to experience nature.

Thousands trained long hours in order to participate in the New York City marathon.

Chapter 33

From the "Jazz Age" Through the Great Depression

Writers and historians have pinned many different labels on the decade of the 1920's. Among these labels are the "Golden Twenties," the "Roaring Twenties," the "Age of Disillusionment," the "Decade of Wonderful Nonsense," the "Jazz Age," and the "Ballyhoo Years."

These labels suggest the character of the 1920's. These years were marked by widespread prosperity, by a sharp increase in the productivity of American industry, by disillusionment with the outcome of World War I, by an emphasis on the material aspects of life, and by the desire to get rich quick and to have a good time.

The decade of the 1930's was a very different story. The labels for the 1920's become a mockery when applied to the grim years of the Great Depression. The 1930's opened with the collapse of the nation's economy. Many banks failed and people throughout the nation lost the savings of a lifetime. Millions of Americans lost their jobs. Millions were homeless and hungry. Despair was widespread in the nation.

By the mid-1930's, however, hope was beginning to replace despair. Inspired by President Franklin D. Roosevelt and the New Deal, Americans in growing numbers faced the future with renewed faith and confidence.

Even so, progress was limited, and millions of men and women were still looking for work. Moreover, as the 1930's drew to a close, growing problems in Europe and Asia cast longer and darker shadows across the land.

1920's–1930's

THE CHAPTER IN OUTLINE

1. Machines continue to transform countryside, town, and city.

2. Industrialization speeds up changes in American society.

3. The depression drastically alters people's lives.

4. America's minorities struggle against hard times and discrimination.

5. Literature and the arts reflect changing ways and times.

1 Machines continue to transform countryside, town, and city

By 1920 the power-driven machine had become one of the dominant symbols of America. There were machines in factories, on farms, and in the home—and still the number and variety of machines kept multiplying. These machines helped transform America from a mainly rural to a mainly urban nation.

They also affected the daily lives of all Americans both in the city and on the farm.

Energy and efficiency. American industry in the 1920's could draw on vast reserves of energy to power its machines. There were enormous deposits of coal, huge underground pockets of oil and natural gas, water-power sites, and the know-how to generate large amounts of electrical power.

Use of the "new" sources of power, oil and electricity, soared during the 1920's. Between 1920 and 1930, petroleum production doubled. In the same years, production of electricity

In his 1928 painting "Boomtown," Thomas Hart Benton presented a view of America's spreading industrialization. Cars and the oil production on which they depend explain the boom experienced in this Western town.

went from 50 billion kilowatt-hours annually to 114 billion.

Manufacturers and engineers tackled the problem of using this abundance of energy most efficiently. Older machines were improved, and new machines were developed for factory, farm, and home. However, it was the organization of machines on a conveyor-belt assembly line that provided one of the striking characteristics of the American economy during the 1920's.

As you have read, mass production was an essential element of American industry long before the 1920's. Manufacturers had been using standardized interchangeable parts ever since Eli Whitney and European inventors had developed them more than a century earlier. The conveyor belt greatly increased the efficiency of the manufacturing process. First used on a large scale in automobile production by Henry Ford in 1914, the assembly line was soon adopted by other industries.

Efforts to increase efficiency were applied to workers as well as to machines. During the 1920's "time-and-motion" studies of machines and their operators were generally undertaken before a new machine or process was installed in an industrial plant.

Business executives also applied this efficiency engineering, or scientific management, to business planning and bookkeeping. This new approach to industrial efficiency was called "cost accounting." Cost accountants found out the cost of every item of machinery, materials, and labor that went into the total cost of producing or selling a product. They were then in a position to show business concerns how to cut costs and at the same time gain greater production at lower prices.

Bigger and bigger industries. Mass production could be carried on only by large, highly organized industrial concerns. During the "Golden Twenties," there was plenty of surplus capital to finance industrial development. As a result, older industries grew by leaps and bounds, while new industries climbed into the ranks of the giants.

Most of the growth of industry was the result of mergers—that is, the combining of two or more independent companies into one larger company. Between 1919 and 1929, for example, more than 1,000 mergers took place in manufacturing and mining. By 1930 only 200 corporations owned nearly half of the country's corporate wealth and one fifth of the total national wealth.

The attitude of government also encouraged the growth of large-scale industry. In the 1920's the government did not make any great effort to enforce the Sherman and the Clayton Antitrust Acts. Business and government were more interested in industrial efficiency than in industrial competition.

Advertising and marketing. Marketing techniques also became more effective during the 1920's. Advertising firms studied public psychology to discover how to appeal to consumers most effectively. Advertising firms also encouraged Americans to abandon the deeply rooted American ideal of thrift. In an age of abundance, they said, continued prosperity depended upon spending, not saving.

Mail-order houses, department stores, and chain stores continued to grow in number and size. The companies that had pioneered new methods of marketing during the late 1800's— Montgomery Ward, the Great Atlantic and Pacific Tea Company, F. W. Woolworth, Marshall Field, and Sears, Roebuck—were still among the leaders in their fields. These companies and many new ones were getting a big portion of the nation's retail business.

Two new developments that would contribute to a future revolution in the packaging of goods emerged in the 1920's. In 1923 Clarence Birdseye developed a method of quick-freezing for preserving perishable foods. In the same year, the Du Pont company bought the American patent rights to cellophane, a transparent wrapping material. By the late 1920's, frozen foods were being sold in stores, and cellophane was attracting attention.

The "automobile revolution." Even more important to the story of America's economic expansion in the 1920's was the development of the automobile. In 1920 about 8 million passenger cars and about 1 million trucks were registered in the United States. By 1930 about 23 million cars—an average of one car for every six citizens—and 3.5 million trucks were traveling the nation's roads.

This "automobile revolution" had far-reaching consequences. By 1930, cars, trucks, and buses had almost completely replaced horse-drawn vehicles. Even railroads and trolley cars were beginning to suffer from the competition of the gasoline-driven vehicles.

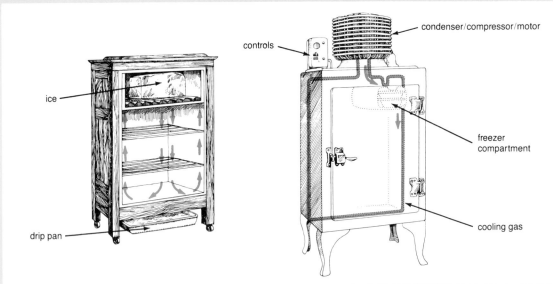

ICEBOX AND ELECTRIC REFRIGERATOR

In an icebox warm air rises. At the top it melts some ice, which absorbs the air's heat. The chilled air falls and more rises to be cooled. As the air circulates, it refrigerates the contents of the icebox. The melting ice drips into a pan and is replaced periodically.

In an electric refrigerator, a refrigerant, such as ammonia, is changed back and forth from a liquid to a gas by a compressor. When depressurized, the liquid refrigerant evaporates and absorbs heat. The gas then flows to a condenser where it is repressurized and reliquefied.

By the end of the 1920's, the automobile industry had become the nation's biggest business, with an annual product valued at $3.5 billion in 1929. This new industrial giant used huge quantities of steel, glass, rubber, and other materials in manufacturing automobiles. It also created a rising demand for materials to build paved roads, garages, and service stations. It is estimated that 5 million persons, or one of every nine American workers, were employed in the automobile industry or a related business by 1930.

New industries. Many other new industries emerged during the 1920's. The increasing availability of electricity stimulated production of many labor-saving devicies for the homemaker. Among them were refrigerators, vacuum cleaners, toasters, electric fans, and electric stoves.

The chemical industry became one of America's most rapidly growing enterprises in the 1920's. By 1929 several American chemical companies were larger than any European competitors. In 1930 Du Pont, the giant among chemical companies, was producing 1,100 different products in 80 different factories in the United States. Among the products pouring out of the chemical plants were rayon, synthetic resins, and a growing variety of plastics.

Despite all the benefits, there was a negative side to the nation's rapid industrialization. Chemicals, gasoline, and other technical innovations began to pollute America's rivers and lakes—and even the air. In the cities, traffic and air pollution became problems. In the 1920's, however, few Americans paid much attention to these disadvantages. Most were content to enjoy the advantages of the machine age's quickening tempo.

Workers' gains and losses. The nation's growing industrialization greatly affected the lives of wage earners. The ever more rapid development of power-driven machines continued to free workers from backbreaking toil. Increases in productivity brought generally higher wages and an improved standard of living for the workers.

Wage earners at times benefited from the "time-and-motion" studies. Such studies could discover ways of lessening fatigue and eliminating accidents on the job. These studies showed that workers were happier and produced more when employers showed an interest in them. Applying this lesson, some employers introduced profit sharing and retirement plans and provided cafeterias, game rooms, and ballparks for employees.

Although employers as a whole showed increasing interest in working conditions, they opposed labor unions even more vigorously than before the war. A growing number of corporations in the 1920's started company unions. These were unions organized by the employers or their representatives rather than by the workers. Company unions as well as the higher standard of living contributed to the decline in strength of organized labor during the 1920's.

Urbanization. The growing industrialization also affected where Americans lived. It encouraged the movement of people from the countryside to cities and industrial centers. This is the process known as **urbanization.**

According to the 1920 census, the population of the United States was almost 106 million. For the first time in American history, those living in cities and towns outnumbered farm and country dwellers. The urban population then totaled 54 million, the rural population 51 million. By 1930 almost 69 million people lived in urban areas; the rural population, on the other hand, had reached only about 54 million. Moreover, a large percentage of the rural population lived in small towns and villages, not on farms.

Towns and cities were undergoing spectacular growth. Between 1920 and 1930, the rapidly growing population pushed 25 of America's older cities above the 100,000 figure. By 1930 as many as 93 cities had populations of 100,000 or more. Some of these urban areas more than doubled their population during this decade.

Changes in urban life. The very appearance of urban centers began to change. Huge new apartment houses appeared on what had been vacant lots or the sites of one-family houses. New skyscrapers pierced the skyline as builders tried to provide office space for the cities' growing industries. On the darker side, crowded housing conditions spurred the growth of slums in many cities.

Streets built in earlier times for horse-drawn vehicles and for a more leisurely way of life became increasingly crowded and noisy as automobiles and trucks multiplied. During the 1920's a new method of transportation, the bus, began to compete with the older electric trolleys. Although not a single bus was registered in the United States in 1920, about 40,500 were registered by 1930.

Perhaps most spectacular of all was the development of suburban areas. Streetcar lines and paved roads pushed out from the cities into the surrounding countryside. Farms in outlying areas were divided into building lots, and row after row of houses appeared in developments with such fanciful names as "Sunset Acres," "Grand View," and "American Venice."

Changes on the farms. By the 1920's developments in technology were breaking down the isolation and loneliness of farm life. Paved roads were reaching deeper into the countryside. Telephone and electric wires stretched along roads and across fields to farmhouses. Radio sets, a product of the 1920's, brought music, news, and entertainment into remote areas. Henry Ford's "Tin Lizzies" were parked beside barns and houses.

Machines also helped to ease farmers' burdens. Where electricity was available, it was used for lighting, for pumping water, and for refrigeration. Milking machines could now be found on many dairy farms. Trucks, tractors, and power-driven farm implements were being used by growing numbers of farmers. At the same time, more efficient farming methods and better plants and breeds of livestock were increasing farm productivity.

Farm problems. Increased productivity also created problems. A surplus of farm products drove farm prices downward. To be sure, not all farmers were hit equally hard by rising surpluses and falling prices. Dairy and truck farmers profited from the shift in American eating habits away from cereals toward more milk, butter, vegetables, and fruit. The citrus-fruit industries of California, Texas, and Florida experienced spectacular development. Tobacco growers also enjoyed a seller's market as cigarette smoking became more popular. The large, mechanized farms continued to prosper, mainly because they could afford the best equipment and could market their products most economically.

While the large, mechanized farms prospered, many of the small, family-owned farms were hard-hit. Handicapped by lack of money to buy expensive equipment, the farmers found it increasingly difficult to make a living.

These economic problems, coupled with the lure of the cities, led to a drop in farm population. Between 1920 and 1930, the number of people actually living on farms decreased from 31.6 million to 30.4 million. Young people in growing numbers were leaving farms to seek new opportunities in the booming cities.

SECTION SURVEY

IDENTIFY: assembly line, mass production, cost accounting, merger, Clarence Birdseye, cellophane, company union, urbanization.

1. Would it be correct to say that the machine and the word "efficiency" characterized America in the 1920's? Explain your answer.
2. (a) What was the "automobile revolution"? (b) In what ways did the automobile change life in the cities? In the country?
3. How were the lives of workers affected by (a) power-driven machines, (b) "time-and-motion" studies, and (c) company unions?
4. Graph Study: Reread this section, making note of all the population statistics given. Then make a line or bar graph showing the urban population, rural population, and total population from 1920 to 1930.

2 Industrialization speeds up changes in American society

The urbanization and industrialization of the 1920's altered the structure of American society. They led to changes in how people lived, learned, and amused themselves.

Growth of school enrollment. After World War I, it became increasingly clear that Americans needed a far more extensive education than that which had once been considered adequate. This fact, linked with the growth in urban population and improvements in transportation, led to an increased enrollment in the nation's schools.

In 1900 total high school enrollment had been under 700,000. By 1920, it had risen to about 2.5 million. The enrollment soared to 4.8 million by 1930 and continued to increase even during the heart of the depression.

The colleges showed similar gains. By the end of the 1930's, nearly 1.5 million students, or one out of every six or seven of college age, were enrolled in colleges and universities.

Minority groups made significant, though limited, gains in education. For example, a growing number of blacks in the North and South received a high school education, and more attended colleges and universities. By 1930 about 15,000 black Americans held academic degrees. Yet many blacks as well as Indians and Spanish-speaking Americans found that even an adequate elementary education was impossible to obtain. Because of prejudice and neglect, the doors of opportunity all too often remained closed to them.

Changes in the schools. To meet the needs of the enormously increased student body, American states and communities had to spend huge sums for new school buildings, textbooks, equipment, and teachers' salaries. The wealth created by the growing industrialization provided taxes that paid for these changes.

Some of the larger cities began to build high schools for as many as 5,000 to 10,000 students. In rural areas cars and buses permitted students from widely scattered areas to attend centrally located consolidated schools.

America's schools had to make other changes as well. Industrial society, with its emphasis upon highly specialized skills, called for men and women trained in mathematics, engineering, science, and the skilled trades. To meet the new needs, educators enlarged the curriculum to include more work in vocational training, home economics, commercial courses, health, physical education, foreign languages, and civic education. Special trade schools, technical schools, and commercial schools were built throughout the country in an effort to keep up with the machine age.

By the 1930's great strides were also being made in adult education. Radio stations began to give reports and commentaries on the news of the day. By 1936 at least 350 forums provided the chance to hear discussions of public issues. At the same time, vocational training for adults was also becoming more common.

Toward more effective education. During these years students of education were reaching new conclusions about how people actually learn and about the process of education. Educators, following the lead of psychologists William James and G. Stanley Hall, were proving that a child's mind can be molded—within limits. Other scholars, among them John Dewey, continued to teach that life itself is an education. They felt that the way to produce effective citizens is to give boys and girls actual experience in democratic living. Still other scholars, led by psychologists such as Edward L. Thorndike, worked out tests useful in measuring intelligence and evaluating the educational process.

New opportunities for women. During the 1920's the role of women underwent changes as striking as those in education. These changes brought new freedom and opportunity to women in American society.

An important step toward this new freedom was the adoption of the Nineteenth Amendment in 1920. This amendment gave women the right to vote in national elections. This right was a landmark in the struggle to win equality with men. The new League of Women Voters and other groups encouraged women to take an active part in political life.

Industrialization brought other changes in women's roles. The rapidly multiplying machines in mills, plants, and factories created new jobs on assembly lines for women. This was especially true in the textile and tobacco factories springing up in the South. Moreover, women were finding increasing opportunities to work as sales clerks, office workers, stenographers, and secretaries.

Equally important, the burden of housework was eased by new labor-saving devices— washing machines, irons, new types of stoves, vacuum cleaners, and refrigerators. Ready-made clothing and inexpensive sewing machines also relieved women of much of their labor. Packaged foods and canned goods helped to lighten the task of preparing family meals.

Middle-class women now had more time to read, to attend art exhibits, to hear lectures. Others now had time to work for civic improvements, to take part in political affairs, and to influence public opinion through such organizations as the League of Women Voters. Still others took active parts in parent-teacher associations. Never before had so many women found time and opportunity to develop interests outside the home.

The "new woman." The changing status and roles of women brought various expressions of a new sense of freedom. The "new woman," often a career woman, was more or less independent economically. She openly challenged what Charlotte Perkins Gilman, a leader of the new feminism, called "this man-made world." The new woman rejected the traditional female roles and refused to believe in the superior competence of men. She also denounced the different standards that were imposed on women in economic, sexual, and social relationships.

This defiance of conventional conduct among women was, in part, symbolized by the flappers. These young women, wearing above-the-knee dresses, bobbed hair, and lipstick, shocked older Americans as well as many people their own age. They took advantage of the freedom and mobility of the automobile, discussed sex openly and frankly, and smoked cigarettes. Flappers also defied the national Prohibition law by drinking in illegal bars called "speakeasies."

To some militant feminists, such indications of social freedom and equality did not go far enough. The Woman's Party challenged remaining legal discriminations against women. It demanded full equality in politics, business, the professions, sports, and the arts. In particular, the Woman's Party set as its goal an equal rights amendment to the Constitution of the United States that would outlaw all discrimination based on sex.

Influence of the automobile. Other changes in American society were a result of the nation's increasing prosperity.

By the 1920's the automobile was no longer the exclusive possession of the well-to-do. When working-class families were interviewed in a typical midwestern city in 1923, nearly half of them owned cars. The automobile was a major source of American recreation, as entire

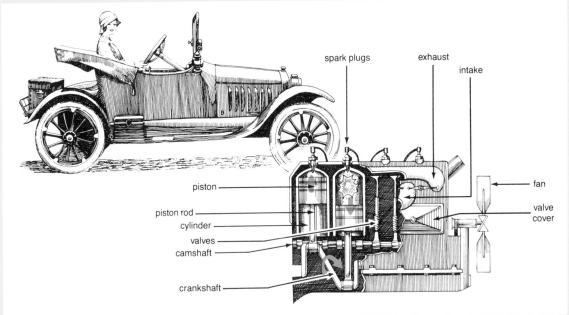

INTERNAL COMBUSTION ENGINE

The internal combustion engine of an automobile changes up-and-down motion into rotary motion to turn the wheels. The intake valve admits a mixture of fuel and air into each cylinder, where a piston moves up and down. The piston rises and compresses the mixture and a spark plug ignites it. This ignition pushes the piston down and causes it to turn a crankshaft, which brings rotary motion to the wheels. The crankshaft also returns the piston to the top of the cylinder. Now an exhaust valve opens, and the piston pushes out the waste products of the ignition. After the piston falls again, it is ready to repeat the cycle. The ignitions in the cylinders are staggered by the timing of the spark plugs and by the design of the crankshaft so that the power that is generated can be spread out most evenly.

families piled into the car for an evening's ride or a weekend trip.

Although the automobile made travel comfortable and private, it also created new problems. Traffic accidents and deaths kept rising. Young people asserted their independence by driving off in the family car, free from parental supervision. Many Americans believed that the automobile was disrupting the family and destroying the nation's moral code.

The automobile also increased the difficulties of law enforcement by providing a convenient means of escape. It played a major role in the breakdown of Prohibition by providing a means for transporting illegal liquor.

Prohibition problems. In January 1919 the Eighteenth Amendment was ratified (see pages 579–80). This amendment gave the federal government power to prohibit "the manufacture, sale, or transportation of intoxicating liquors."

In October 1919 Congress passed the Prohibition Enforcement Act, usually called the Volstead Act, over President Wilson's veto. This act defined as "intoxicating liquor" any beverage containing more than one half of one percent of alcohol, thereby making even beer and wine illegal.

The Prohibition experiment created serious problems in American life. Long coastlines in

638

the east and west and unguarded frontiers to the north and south made it impossible to stop the flow of illegal liquor into the country.

Bootlegging became big business controlled by criminal elements in the large cities. The gangster Al Capone, who ruled Chicago's underworld, commanded a small army of gangsters equipped with revolvers, sawed-off shotguns, and submachine guns. Gang wars and other violence became common in many American cities during the "Roaring Twenties." Moreover, the gangs branched out to seize control of gambling establishments and dance halls. By the end of the decade, they had begun to develop the so-called "rackets." The racketeers collected "protection" money from businesses, threatening violence if their victims failed to pay.

The people themselves were partly to blame for this widespread violation of the law. Many Americans who were otherwise law-abiding refused to take Prohibition seriously. Finally, in 1933, the Prohibition era ended with the adoption of the Twenty-first Amendment, which repealed the Eighteenth Amendment. It returned the power to control the sale of intoxicating drinks to the states themselves.

Radio. Meanwhile another new development—radio—was helping to transform the lives of millions of Americans, both young and old alike.

KDKA, the first commercial broadcasting station, began to operate in Pittsburgh on November 2, 1920. Radio immediately became a craze. By 1929, sales of radio sets and parts amounted to almost $400 million. More than 600 broadcasting stations had been licensed, and one third of all American homes owned radio receivers.

Radio brought an enormous variety of information and entertainment directly to American families in their homes. The most popular programs featured "crooners," jazz musicians, comedians, sports announcers, and newscasters. However, many Americans felt that radio was not fulfilling its great promise as an instrument of education and culture. They criticized the dominant role of advertisers, who paid the broadcasting companies and entertainers and often determined what programs would be presented.

Despite the trivial content of many programs, however, radio served the nation in a variety of ways. By providing common experi-

Thousands of law officers like this one in Philadelphia tried to stop the flow of illegal liquor and beer during Prohibition in the 1920's. But as fast as government officials destroyed a supply of liquor, more was produced to replace it.

ences for all Americans, it increased the feeling of national unity. Radio also helped to overcome the isolation of rural life. It encouraged popular interest in current events, including sports, and offered useful information on health, home economics, and farming techniques. It made serious music available to more Americans than ever before. Finally, radio provided greater safety for airplanes and ships.

Sports. During the 1920's public interest in sports grew markedly. Baseball remained the most popular professional game, with between 9 and 10 million people attending major league games annually. Babe Ruth, who replaced Ty Cobb as the idol of fans, in 1927 astounded the baseball world with a record 60 home runs.

College football drew some 30 million spectators in the same year. Red Grange, a halfback for the University of Illinois, became a national hero. Jim Thorpe, with a Sauk, Fox, Potawatomi, and Irish heritage, also became a national hero. After playing football at Carlisle, an Indian college in Pennsylvania, he won medals in several events at the Olympic Games in Stockholm, Sweden, in 1912. Later, as an outstanding player in big league baseball and professional football, Thorpe was acclaimed as "the outstanding athlete of the half century." In boxing, fans in 1927 spent over $2.6 million to see the famous Dempsey-Tunney match. Amateur as well as professional interest also increased in such sports as golf, tennis, swimming, skating, and bowling.

Feats and fads. Americans in the 1920's were unusually responsive to new fads and fashions and dramatic public events. This period has been called the "Jazz Age" with some justice, for the rhythmic music of jazz was perhaps the most consistently popular of the new fashions. Other fads shifted rapidly from year to year: from the Chinese-originated game of mah-jongg, to crossword puzzles, to dances like the Charleston, to eccentric activities like flagpole sitting.

Some of the nation's enthusiasm was directed to individual accomplishments. The first glorified hero of the time was Charles A. Lindbergh, who in May 1927 made the first nonstop flight from New York to Paris in his plane *The Spirit of St. Louis*. Another fearless voyager was Commander (later Admiral) Richard E. Byrd. Byrd made the first flights to both

the North and the South Pole. Other Americans who followed the example of Lindbergh and Byrd proved that the postwar period was an age of daring and feats as well as fads.

SECTION SURVEY

IDENTIFY: John Dewey, Edward Thorndike, Nineteenth Amendment, Charlotte Perkins Gilman, flappers, Woman's Party, Babe Ruth, Red Grange, Jim Thorpe, Charles A. Lindbergh, Richard E. Byrd.

1. (a) Why did school enrollment increase during the 1920's? (b) How did school curriculums change?

2. (a) How did women's lives begin to change during the 1920's? (b) What was the "new woman"?

3. What problems arose as a result of Prohibition?

3 The depression drastically alters people's lives

It can't be true! That was the initial reaction of Americans everywhere to the collapse of the nation's economy.

Unhappily, it was true. In a few short months during the winter of 1929–30, the prosperity and promise of the "Golden Twenties" had been replaced by unemployment, poverty, despair, and desperation.

What was it like? By 1932 industrial output had been reduced to half the 1929 figure. Wages had been cut by 60 percent, and one fourth of the nation's work force was jobless. The best estimates place the number of unemployed at 13 to 15 million.

A white-collar worker opened his pay envelope. It contained a pink slip informing him that his services were no longer needed. He had worked for the same company, one of the nation's largest corporations, for 40 years. He was 56 years old. He joined the millions of other jobless men and women.

No one really knew the number of people looking for work, and those seeking work were the breadwinners. Some 30 million others depended on them for food, clothing, and shelter.

These were the statistics. They translated into hunger, into the sad eyes of starving chil-

Much art in the 1930's depicted the plight of the down-and-out. In his painting titled "How Long Since You Wrote to Mother?" Raphael Soyer captured the loneliness of hungry men who came to missions for bread and coffee.

dren, into long lines of haggard men and women waiting for handouts of thin soup and dry bread provided by private and public charities. The men and women in the bread lines came from all walks of life and all social classes. There were former middle-income people and people from poor backgrounds. There were wage earners, business executives, and professional people. Hunger played no favorites.

Hunger was everywhere. "We saw a crowd of some 50 men fighting over a barrel of garbage which had been set outside the back door of a restaurant," one observer reported. This was not an isolated incident. Across the country men and women followed garbage trucks to the city dumps. Four hospitals in New York City reported 95 deaths from starvation in 1931. How many went unreported was never known.

Death came from self-inflicted causes as well. The Metropolitan Life Insurance Company reported that 20,000 Americans committed suicide in 1931.

Uprooted people. More than a million men and some women, many of them teen-agers, roamed the country looking for work. They rode the freight trains, thumbed rides on the roads, and did odd jobs where they could find them. They begged or stole food and slept wherever they could find shelter, on park benches or in shantytowns.

Every city had its shantytowns. Homeless people built them on vacant lots or on the city dumps out of packing boxes and scrap metal. "Hoovervilles" they were sometimes called, mocking the Hoover administration's failure to provide direct relief. There were also "Hoover blankets"—old newspaper used for warmth on park benches.

Many city people moved into the country hoping to find shelter and to raise their own food. Many farmers moved into the cities hoping to find work. People who had lost their homes or could no longer afford to pay rent moved in with relatives or friends. It was common to find several families crowded together in four or five rooms.

Rebellion on the farm. By 1932, farmers in some areas of the country were burning their corn to keep warm. Others armed with clubs, pitchforks, and shotguns confronted sheriffs who were trying to deliver foreclosure notices.

641

Other farmers, also armed, formed roadblocks and forced trucks loaded with milk to dump it on the road. With milk selling at 10 cents a quart in the stores, dairy farmers could not afford to operate. "They say blockading the highway's illegal," an Iowa farmer said. "Seems to me there was a Tea Party in Boston that was illegal, too."

The "Bonus Army." Farmers were not the only demonstrators. The "Bonus Army," 17,000 strong, arrived in Washington, D.C., in June 1932. They were veterans of World War I and they called themselves the "Bonus Expeditionary Force." Many arrived with their families. They traveled in freight cars, trucks, and wagons and on foot. They were in Washington to plead for a war bonus owed them. The money was not due until 1945, but they wanted it in advance.

They were allowed to live in empty government buildings and to camp on a swampy area across the Potomac River. The army provided them with tents, cots, field kitchens, and food. When the Senate refused to grant the bonus payment, most of them gave up and returned home with money provided by the government.

Some 2,000 of the veterans, many of whom had no place to go, decided to stay. They were ordered to leave. In a clash with the police, several veterans and police officers were killed. Army troops then moved in with machine guns, tanks, and tear gas. The troops drove the veterans from the buildings and broke up their encampment across the river, burning the shacks as they did so.

Slowing population growth. By the mid-1930's the New Deal had relieved much of the worst suffering and had restored a measure of hope. Nevertheless, grinding poverty continued to crush the dreams of millions of men, women, and children across the country. "I see one third of the nation ill-housed, ill-clad, ill-nourished," President Roosevelt said in 1937.

The Statue of Liberty still stood in New York harbor to welcome the poor, the homeless, the oppressed from other countries. However, the United States was no longer the "land of promise." Immigration had almost ceased. During the 1930's more people left America than entered it.

The number of marriages and the number of births also slowed. Many young people could not afford to marry and start families. In the decade of the 1930's, the population increased only about half as much as it had during the prosperous years of the 1920's.

More subdued living. Many of the rich and the well-to-do continued to live much as they had during the 1920's. For most Americans, however, even those who managed to hold onto their jobs, everyday life was much more subdued than it had been during the years of the "Golden Twenties."

Fewer people bought houses, household appliances, and new clothes. The sale of newspapers and magazines declined. At the same time, however, people read more, borrowing books from the public libraries.

People also tried to make things last. They kept their automobiles longer. This was possible, in part, because the number of service stations and repair shops doubled during the depression years.

Recreational activities reflected the slower pace of everyday life in the depression years. Not surprisingly, free recreation received the most attention. Hobbies, such as stamp collecting, became increasingly popular. So, too, did games that could be played at home, including cards, particularly bridge.

The radio. Radio, already popular in the 1920's, was the most common and the most influential form of entertainment in the 1930's. E. B. White, one of the keenest observers of the American scene, commented on the impact of the radio on rural folk. When they speak of "The Radio," White wrote, they have in mind "a pervading and somewhat godlike presence which has come into their lives and homes."

The growing popularity and influence of the radio, not only in rural areas but throughout the nation, was understandable. It provided something for just about everyone — news; music, including symphonies and operas; quiz programs and comedians; soap operas; church services; and adventure stories. All of these entered American homes through the mere turning of a dial.

President Roosevelt understood how effective radio could be in reaching people and broadcast a series of "Fireside Chats." These brought the people close to their government and added comfort and hope to the lives of millions. The "Fireside Chats" also helped Roosevelt gain and hold his popularity and win four successive Presidential elections!

1. How did some farmers react to the depression?
2. (a) What was the "Bonus Army"? (b) Was its stay in Washington, D.C., successful? Explain.
3. What effects did the depression have on population growth in the United States? Why?
4. Picture Study: Study the pictures in this section. Based on them, write a description of life during the depression.

4 America's minorities struggle against hard times and discrimination

The 1920's and 1930's were difficult times for America's minorities. They did not share equally in the growing prosperity of the "Golden Twenties." Later, when the depression of the 1930's hit, the minorities bore the heaviest burden.

Black migration to the North. Before World War I, many black families had moved from the South to the growing northern industrial centers. There they had hoped to escape poverty and discrimination and to find jobs, housing, and better education for their children.

World War I, with its heavy demand for industrial workers, had increased this migration. During the war about half a million southern blacks had found jobs in such places as the coal mines of West Virginia and Illinois, the steel mills of Pittsburgh, and the automobile factories of Detroit.

The movement into urban areas continued after the war. Between 1910 and 1930, the black population of the northern states rose from a little over 1 million to nearly 2.5 million. In the same years, the number of black wage earners in American industries nearly doubled, rising from about 600,000 to nearly 1 million.

Black families did not find in the North all the opportunities they sought. Blacks got the hardest jobs and the lowest pay. Northern white wage earners sometimes staged protest strikes against the hiring of blacks. Housing shortages, brought on by wartime building re-

strictions, also led to tensions when blacks tried to move into white neighborhoods in search of places to live.

Disappointed hopes. World War I, the war "to make the world safe for democracy," had naturally aroused the hopes of black Americans. Black soldiers returning from Europe, where they had been treated as equals, looked forward to new and greater freedom at home. They were angry and disappointed to find conditions in America little changed.

They were especially discouraged to find a new Ku Klux Klan operating in the North as well as in the South. The new Klan harassed Jews, Catholics, foreign-born citizens, and anyone else it chose to call "dangerous" and "un-American." However, blacks were the special object of Klan violence.

There were other reasons for black bitterness as well. In 1919–20 the nation's economy went into a postwar depression. This heightened the competition for jobs between blacks and whites and led to increased racial tension.

The riots of 1919. The rising tensions burst out in violence during the summer of 1919. Riots in more than 20 cities, northern and southern, brought death and injury to hundreds of men and women and destroyed thousands of tenements in city slum areas.

The riots generally began when blacks fought back against some especially discriminatory act. Frightened whites, convinced that black Americans were trying to threaten them and gain control, responded with more violence. Police forces, ill-equipped to deal with riots, usually sided with whites, causing blacks to take even more desperate actions.

The riots solved no problems. Nor did they spur local or national officials to try to remedy even the more obvious causes of the trouble. As a result, black Americans were now more ready to follow leaders who insisted that blacks had a lawful right to defend themselves when the law itself failed to do so.

Black pride. In the 1920's many blacks felt a growing sense of racial identity and pride along with an increasing interest in their African backgrounds. These feelings were strongly expressed by Marcus Garvey, a black immigrant from Jamaica in the West Indies.

Garvey became convinced that blacks could never win true freedom and equality in the

Black migration from the rural South to the urban North began during the first World War. The movement continued through the 1920's and the 1930's. Here black artist Jacob Lawrence depicts this trend in "The Migration of the Negro."

United States. He popularized among black city slum dwellers a form of black nationalism that emphasized a "back-to-Africa" movement. He eloquently described the achievements of black Africans and urged his listeners to return "home," where they might enjoy opportunities they could never find in white-dominated America.

None of Marcus Garvey's half-million black followers ever moved to Africa as he suggested. Nonetheless, Garvey's program did help to awaken in many blacks a new sense of racial pride.

Most black leaders of the 1920's opposed Garvey's movement as unrealistic and escapist. They insisted that blacks, having long been Americans, could and had to win the rights and opportunities that other Americans enjoyed. However, these leaders also encouraged American blacks to become interested in the achievements and hopes of black people in Africa and other parts of the world. Racial solidarity, they urged, should replace the narrow outlook that separated black Americans from blacks in other lands and that divided black Americans into different economic and social groups.

The "new Negro." Growing black pride was also stimulated by new achievements in arts and literature. One work that encouraged the rise of younger black leaders was *The New Negro* by Alain Locke, a professor at Howard University. This important book both reflected and encouraged the changes taking place in black communities.

The new black leaders insisted that the "new Negro" had to be proud of the black heritage. They insisted that black Americans stop being defensive and apologetic to white Americans. The "new Negro" had to realize that self-assertiveness, not accommodation, was the only effective way to gain full equality.

As part of this assertion of identity, many blacks came to believe that it was necessary to develop a separate black economy within the American economy. Businesses owned and operated by blacks would serve the black communities. The profits from these businesses would flow to blacks and further stimulate financial independence.

By 1929, blacks ran some 25,700 stores. Many factories, banks, and insurance companies were owned and operated by blacks as well.

Gains in civil rights. The growing sense of pride and self-assertiveness led blacks in both the North and the South to make headway in their struggle for equal justice under the law. Black leaders denounced lynching, white terrorism, and discrimination in housing and in the courts. In these areas the efforts of the NAACP to bring lawsuits designed to bring about the enforcement of equal rights for blacks began to show important progress.

The major political parties did little to further the struggles of blacks in the 1920's. The Republican Party was trying to build strong political organizations in the South. As a result, the Republican administrations hesitated to meet the demands of southern blacks for federal protection of their voting rights or for a fair share of federally appointed jobs. Nevertheless, Oscar de Priest of Chicago ran as a Republican and in 1928 became the first black elected to Congress in 28 years.

The Democratic Party held power in the South and continued efforts to exclude black voters. In spite of this, Democrats in northern cities began to seek black support, and blacks slowly began to join the Democratic Party.

Blacks and the depression. For blacks the coming of the depression was a catastrophe. Many businesses and banks owned by blacks went bankrupt. Black workers lived with the bleak knowledge that they were "the first fired and the last hired." During the worst years of the depression, an estimated two thirds of the blacks in American industry lost their jobs.

The New Deal provided black Americans with relief and employment in the Works Progress Administration, the Civilian Conservation Corps, and the National Youth Administration. By 1936, one sixth of those on relief were blacks. One black newspaper writer explained the meaning of one New Deal program to blacks: "The really important thing about the WPA is that it is a guarantee of a living wage." Blacks also had a share of new low-cost housing, and black farmers and sharecroppers received benefits from New Deal agricultural agencies. However, blacks suffered some degree of discrimination in almost all New Deal programs. A smaller percentage of blacks were employed in the work programs, and the housing and agricultural programs were particularly unfair to blacks.

Nevertheless, blacks did receive more aid under the New Deal than they had under Hoover's administration. In addition, at the urging of Eleanor Roosevelt, the President's wife, blacks were appointed to important federal positions. Among them were Mary McLeod Bethune, Ralph Bunche, and Robert C. Weaver. These and other leaders made up an informal group of advisers often called the "black cabinet."

Such New Deal actions revolutionized the voting habits of black Americans. By 1936, black voters were shifting to the Democratic Party. By the end of the decade, the Democrats had firmly secured the black vote.

The depression and the new opportunities provided by the New Deal increased the determination of blacks to win their legal and constitutional rights. In many northern cities, black leaders organized "don't-buy-where-you-can't-work" campaigns. In the rural areas, tenant farmers, black and white, often joined together against wealthy landlords. The National Negro Congress united black and interracial organizations from all across the nation in the struggle for black rights.

Despite these advances and the progress stimulated by New Deal programs, much remained to be done. For the vast majority of blacks, the elimination of prejudice and full acceptance into the mainstream of American life remained an unfulfilled dream.

Indian policy. Other racial and ethnic problems in the nation were becoming critical in the 1920's. The policy of "Americanizing" the Indians under the Dawes Act (page 428) had failed. Individual farm ownership was contrary to Indian traditions. Many tribes had never engaged in farming. Indians who did try to learn modern methods of farming often had to struggle with worn-out, nonfertile land. As for education, the government-sponsored boarding schools and day schools deprived Indian children of their tribal identity but gave them no identity that they could find meaningful.

In 1924 the Indian population as a whole received United States citizenship, partly in recognition of the young Indian men who had fought in World War I. Citizenship did not lessen the harsh fact that Indian poverty was greater than that of any other group in the United States. The discovery of oil on some Indian lands brought unexpected wealth to a few Indians, but for most life was grim. Still, earlier predictions that the Indians were a vanishing race proved incorrect. The Indian population increased from about 243,000 in 1863 to about 350,000 in 1924.

Indians and the New Deal. In 1928 a report by the Institute for Government Research described the destructive conditions on Indian reservations. The report and other criticisms led Congress in 1934 to pass the Howard-Wheeler Act, or the Indian Reorganization Act.

The new law halted the breaking up of reservations by granting lands to individual Indians. It tried to restore to tribal ownership parts of reservations that had not yet become individual homesteads. The act also emphasized local control. It permitted tribes to choose whether or not they wished to practice local self-government. It allowed them to strengthen community life by reestablishing traditional beliefs, customs, and crafts. Under the act, Indians were allowed to engage in any business of their choice, to make contracts, and to sue or be sued in court.

The Howard-Wheeler Act also tried to teach Indians to use their land more effectively. Soil-conservation practices and improved methods of raising and marketing crops and livestock were taught. The new educational program included adults and children and made the school a center of community life.

Many problems remained in spite of the change in policy. Some tribes that had been more or less successfully "Americanized" disliked the new policy. They believed it would keep them inferior in American society. Efforts to improve unused Indian lands met with little success. Thus although the new policy brought greater freedom and recognition to the Indians, its aim of raising Indian standards of living was not realized.

Mexican Americans. As you may recall, many former citizens of Mexico became citizens of the United States at the close of the Mexican War in 1848. In the 1890's increasing numbers of Mexicans migrated into the United States looking for jobs. The need for labor during World War I and the desire of many Mexicans to escape the troubled economic and political conditions in Mexico increased the flow across the border. During the 1920's about half a million new Mexican immigrants arrived.

Most of these immigrants were poor families from rural areas. They were forced to work for low wages as migrant laborers in agriculture, in mining, and in railroad construction throughout the Southwest and, increasingly, the Middle West. They entered the United States speaking a different language and practicing different customs. For the most part poor and ill-educated, they met with prejudice and discrimination in jobs, housing, and schools.

Established labor groups resented them because they lowered wage scales by accepting, out of necessity, almost any rate of pay. White resentment also grew because these new immigrants could cross and recross the border as economic conditions in Mexico improved or worsened.

Despite these burdens, Mexican Americans took an increasingly active part in the organized labor movement. They shared each other's problems and developed a sense of cooperation through *mutalistas,* or self-aid societies. Particularly in New Mexico, they made their influence felt politically.

The United States and Mexico jointly developed a program to deal with immigration from Mexico. The Expatriation Program, as it was called, was designed to persuade Mexican immigrants to return to their own country. From the Mexican point of view, the purpose of the program was to revitalize the Mexican economy by making use of the skills the Mexicans had learned while in the United States. Some 500,000 men and women did return to Mexico. Only too often, however, they were disappointed with their decision. Conditions in their native land were bleak and they were ready, whatever the obstacles, to try once again to improve their lives in the United States.

The depression added to the burdens of the Mexican Americans. Jobs in agriculture and on railroads became scarce. Increasingly, the Mexican Americans moved from rural areas into the cities, where there was at least some hope, however slim, of finding work. At least in the cities, if jobs were not available, New Deal relief programs were.

SECTION SURVEY

IDENTIFY: Marcus Garvey, *The New Negro,* Oscar de Priest, "black cabinet," National Negro Congress, Indian Reorganization Act, *mutalistas,* Expatriation Program.

1. What factors helped cause the race riots of 1919?

2. (a) What does the term "new Negro" mean? (b) How did growing black pride affect business? How did it affect politics?

646

3. Why did blacks increasingly vote for candidates from the Democratic Party?

4. (a) What was American policy toward Indians during the 1920's? (b) How successful was it?

5. What was the situation of Mexican Americans during the 1920's and 1930's?

5 Literature and the arts reflect changing ways and times

During the 1920's and 1930's, writers and artists struggled to deal with new issues raised by changes in American society. At times, the struggle was with changing standards and values brought on by prosperity during the 1920's and depression during the 1930's. At other times, the struggle was to find new forms of expression that seemed appropriate to the machine age in America.

Concern for a vanishing past. Although American literature in many ways reflected the changing ways of life, one group of writers revealed their concern for a rapidly vanishing past. Edith Wharton and Ellen Glasgow contrasted the order and stability of bygone New York and Virginia with the restless materialism of the newly rich in a new age. In her writings Willa Cather recaptured the vitality and heroism of pioneer life in Nebraska and compared it to the empty lives of those whose major goal was material success.

Reactions to life in the 1920's. Many writers, however, focused directly on the conflicts and confusions of the emerging industrial world. T. S. Eliot in his poem *The Waste Land* (1922) pictured society in the machine age as grim, barren, standardized, cheap, and vulgar.

Several writers revealed the tragedy of equating success with money and the things money could buy. Theodore Dreiser's *An American Tragedy* (1925) unraveled the sordid story of a youth who deliberately let his girlfriend drown in order to pursue what in the end proved to be a futile goal. F. Scott Fitzgerald in his first novel, *This Side of Paradise* (1920), vividly pictured the confusion of the college "jazz set," bored with the futility of fast living and hard drinking. Later, in *The Great Gatsby*

(1925), Fitzgerald portrayed the emptiness of life devoted primarily to a frenzied struggle to make money. Sinclair Lewis wrote a number of books highlighting the deadening conformity and hypocrisy of middle-class life in America, among them *Main Street* (1920), *Babbitt* (1922), and *Elmer Gantry* (1927). In 1930 he received the Nobel Prize in literature, the first American writer to be so honored.

Literature of the 1930's. Several writers reacted forcefully to the crushing impact of the depression. The most gripping picture of those years was John Steinbeck's novel *The Grapes of Wrath* (1939). The story follows the sad fortunes of a poor but self-respecting Oklahoma family. Driven from their home in the dust bowl, they sought survival in California. Unhappily, life in California proved lonely and harsh. Sad though the story is, it ends on a glimmer of hope for the homeless, downtrodden wanderers.

Sinclair Lewis viewed the depression from a different angle. In a sobering novel, *It Can't Happen Here* (1935), Lewis contended that American society in the 1930's was ripe soil from which a dictatorship might arise.

Ernest Hemingway was another writer who came to grips with basic issues confronting America and the world. In *A Farewell to Arms* (1929), he stripped the romance and glamor from World War I. In *For Whom the Bell Tolls* (1939), he presented a graphic picture of the violence and brutality of the Spanish Civil War and in so doing provided a preview of World War II.

The Harlem Renaissance. Black writers and artists, inspired by the image of the "new Negro," produced important works that led to a cultural renaissance or rebirth. Their works aroused the interest of many white Americans while strengthening the growing pride of black Americans. This cultural rebirth of the 1920's centered in New York City's black community of Harlem. It has been called the "Harlem Renaissance," but its rich expressions were not confined to Harlem.

These new cultural contributions were marked by originality, freshness of style, and vigor. Jazz music, with its exciting and spontaneous rhythms, and the blues, reflecting the joy, laughter, sadness, and pain of black Americans, found outstanding composers and performers in the 1920's and 1930's. Among these

Edward Hopper, 1887-1967. "Early Sunday Morning." Oil on canvas. 1930. 35 x 60. Collection of Whitney Museum of American Art, New York.

One of the great painters who captured the look of America in the 1920's and 1930's was Edward Hopper. There is a quality of starkness and loneliness that can be found in many of his scenes such as this one, "Early Sunday Morning."

were W. C. Handy, Jelly Roll Morton, Louis Armstrong, and Duke Ellington. Black spirituals became part of the repertory of Marian Anderson, who in the 1920's was just beginning her career as one of the world's greatest singers of classical as well as folk music. Also during the 1920's, Paul Robeson began his brilliant career as an actor, concert singer, and civil rights activist.

The literature of the Harlem Renaissance reflected the racial pride of the "new Negro." Langston Hughes, Claude McKay, and Countee Cullen wrote verse marked by haunting bitterness and defiance but also by joy and hope. This many-sided emotional richness among black writers was exemplified by Jean Toomer's *Cane.* This work portrayed black environments in the rural South, in Washington, D. C., and in New York City. It starkly revealed its characters' intense emotions while also portraying their beauty and dignity.

Among the black writers of the 1930's, Richard Wright was a towering figure. In the four short novels that make up *Uncle Tom's Children* (1938), he explored Southern racial

problems. His most famous novel, *Native Son,* is a harsh picture of life in the slums of Chicago. His autobiography, *Black Boy,* is a powerful portrayal of his family's experiences during his childhood years.

Journalism. Newspapers and magazines also reflected the influence of the machine age. By the 1920's journalism had become big business. *Reader's Digest,* started in 1922 by Dewitt Wallace, won nationwide circulation with its collection of condensed articles from other journals. *Time,* the brainchild of Henry R. Luce, was widely read for its concise reporting of current events. The enormous success of *Time* led to the founding of competitors, chief among them *Newsweek,* started in 1933 during the depth of the depression. Luce, who had made a fortune out of *Time,* bought the humorous magazine *Life* in 1936. He transformed it into the first American publication devoted to photojournalism, in which articles are developed largely through the use of photographs. It, too, soon attracted competitors, the most successful of which was *Look.*

648

Meanwhile, many of the individually owned newspapers were being bought by large newspaper chains. Chain newspapers ran the same syndicated columns and editorials, the same comics, sports news, and advertisements. They subscribed to the same news services—the Associated Press, the United Press, and the International News Service. Like the magazines, the newspapers reflected the problems of industrial America.

Painting and design. In painting and design, Americans were more and more influenced by such European artists as Cézanne, Manet, Monet, Degas, Matisse, and Picasso. Some modernists boldly experimented with geometric designs that often resembled machines in their emphasis on hard angles, masses, and abstract form. Many American artists continued to paint the more conventional themes, but they painted them in new ways. Others tried to reveal the meaning of the machine age in their paintings of factories, warehouses, slums, railroads, and other scenes of urban life.

New art forms. The machine age also opened up entirely new forms of art. In the hands of artists, the camera captured the spirit and meaning of the new age. New methods of art reproduction enabled people to own inexpensive yet excellent copies of the world's outstanding works of art. When these reproduction techniques were adopted by the mass-circulation magazines, millions of Americans were able to see the work of the world's greatest photographers, illustrators, and artists.

Aided by commercial artists and industrial designers, manufacturers began to produce telephones, furniture, fabrics, clothing, typewriters, glassware, refrigerators, stoves, automobiles, and many other articles that showed that machines and machine products might be beautiful in design and structure.

The movies. Motion pictures, the movies, were one new product of the machine age. They were a fascinating combination of new technology, big business, and art.

The movies rapidly became an important part of American life. In the 1920's huge and lavish motion picture palaces were built in large cities throughout the country. By the end of the decade, the motion picture industry had become the fourth largest one in the nation. Even during the hard times of the depression, movies remained popular. In 1938, movie audiences numbered more than 80 million a week. In that same year, more than 500 American movies were produced.

The movies both reflected and shaped American society. Traditional values—the home, hard work, thrift—were usually upheld in movie stories. However, the movies often popularized less traditional values. The world of the "jazz set" and the flappers, when portrayed on the screen, looked glamorous. People began to copy the styles and manners of the movies.

Artistically, movies made great advances. Storytelling in the silent films of the 1920's was much more polished and sophisticated than in most prewar films. Directors also explored more demanding themes. Erich von Stroheim's *Greed* described with great power how greed for money warped the character and finally destroyed the lives of a working-class couple. Robert Flaherty's *Nanook of the North,* a documentary, captured the grandeur of nature and the difficulty of life in the Arctic. Great comics like Charlie Chaplin and Buster Keaton left audiences rocking with laughter—and furthered the art of silent-movie making.

In 1927 Warner Brothers released the first successful "talkie," *The Jazz Singer.* For a time, as moviemakers adapted to using sound, motion pictures became more stiff and stagy. Soon, however, sound techniques were mastered, and movies became more exciting and popular than ever.

In the 1930's Fred Astaire and Ginger Rogers sang and danced through a series of films that took people's minds off the problems of the depression. Directors like Howard Hawks, in *His Girl Friday,* and Frank Capra, in *Meet John Doe* and *Mr. Smith Goes to Washington,* studied manners and morals in contemporary society. John Ford, in *Stagecoach, Young Mr. Lincoln,* and *The Grapes of Wrath,* produced works that questioned and celebrated American history.

Architecture. Inspired by such outstanding architects as Louis Sullivan and Frank Lloyd Wright, other architects began to promote the idea that a building ought to use the materials and follow the forms most suitable to the purposes for which it was to be used.

For many people the skyscraper became a symbol of the influence of the machine upon architecture. Built of steel, glass, and concrete, it towered into the sky in order to use as little

INVASION FROM MARS

At eight o'clock on the evening of October 30, 1938, millions of radio listeners throughout the country heard the following announcement: "The Columbia Broadcasting System and its affiliated stations present Orson Welles and the Mercury Theater of the Air in *The War of the Worlds* by H. G. Wells."

There was a brief pause, followed by a weather report. Then an announcer declared that the program would be continued from a New York hotel. A jazz band came on the air. Suddenly the music stopped. An announcer, his voice tense and anxious, broke in to declare that a professor had just observed a series of explosions on Mars. Other announcements followed in rapid order. A meteor had landed near Princeton, New Jersey. Fifteen hundred people had been killed. No, it wasn't a meteor. It was a spaceship from Mars. Martian creatures were emerging from the ship. The creatures were armed with powerful death rays. They had come to wage war against the people living on earth.

An untold number of listeners were seized with panic. Some fell to their knees and began to pray. Others gathered their families, rushed from their homes, and fled on foot or by car into the night.

Yet it was only a radio play. CBS stated this fact clearly four different times during the hour-long program. Numerous explanations were advanced for the outburst of mass hysteria. But one thing was clear—the extraordinary power of broadcasting.

---

expensive ground space as possible. Upper stories were set back to prevent the streets from being darkened. In the emphasis upon clear-cut vertical lines and the massing of windows, the skyscraper was an excellent example of how purpose and materials dictated design.

Music and dancing. Music, too, showed the influence of the industrial age. Many people believed that jazz expressed the rhythms and the accelerated speed and energy of the machine. Music also became increasingly available through the radio, the phonograph, and musical instruments manufactured at lower and lower costs. Moreover, wealth created by the new industrial age supported symphony orchestras and opera companies.

Social dancing was transformed by jazz, while the dance as an art form was revolutionized by Isadora Duncan, Ruth St. Denis, Katherine Dunham, Ted Shawn, and Martha Graham. These dancers emphasized free and expressive movements in contrast to the traditional, formal patterns of the ballet.

SECTION SURVEY

IDENTIFY: Edith Wharton, Ellen Glasgow, Willa Cather, *The Waste Land, An American Tragedy,* F. Scott Fitzgerald, Sinclair Lewis, *The Grapes of Wrath,* Ernest Hemingway, Harlem Renaissance, *Cane,* Richard Wright, chain newspapers, Charlie Chaplin, *The Jazz Singer,* Frank Lloyd Wright, Isadora Duncan.

1. How did some writers show their disillusionment with the America of the 1920's?

2. How did the movies both reflect and shape American society?

3. How did the skyscraper symbolize the influence upon architecture of (a) land values and (b) industrialization?

650

Chapter Survey

Summary: Tracing the Main Ideas

During the 1920's the process of industrialization rapidly gathered momentum. Machines replaced or lightened human labor on the farm, in the factory, and in America's homes. The developing technology created a higher standard of living. At the same time, it began to give new directions to people's goals and to transform their daily lives.

Many critics of American life claimed that modern technology was standardizing life. These critics were disturbed that the machine, which had given people such immense power, was being used largely to make money and to provide more or less meaningless recreation.

Other students of American society defended the new technology. They pointed to the obvious fact that it relieved people of backbreaking toil and that it made possible more leisure, more consumer goods, more comforts, and more time for education and for pleasure. All of these advantages, they argued, provided a greater measure of freedom for the individual American.

As the 1920's drew to a close, however, the arguments over the advantages and disadvantages of modern technology were suddenly buried beneath the crushing impact of the Great Depression. For three desperate years, life for many Americans, and especially for the minorities, became a grim struggle for survival. The New Deal, born with the inauguration of President Franklin D. Roosevelt in March 1933, brought new hope to suffering Americans. In the following years, it brought growing relief from the heaviest burdens of unemployment and poverty.

The decades of the 1920's and the 1930's—the one characterized by widespread prosperity, the other by poverty and unemployment—left distinctive marks upon the American scene. Every aspect of life—including education, literature, and the arts—was influenced by the changing ways and times.

Inquiring into History

1. How did industrialization affect the lives of people (a) on farms and (b) in cities? Does industrialization always mean progress? Explain.
2. (a) How did the radio, movies, and newspaper chains contribute to conformity? (b) How did they contribute to individualism?
3. What are the relationships between industrialization and the role of women?
4. During the 1920's many black Americans left the South to go North. Did the northern cities turn out to be an escape to freedom? Explain.
5. (a) In what ways were the situations of blacks, Indians, and Mexicans similar during the 1920's and 1930's? (b) How were they different?

Relating Past to Present

1. Do you think television today has more, the same, or less effect on society than radio did in the 1920's? Explain.
2. Was poverty in the Great Depression different from poverty that exists today? If so, how?
3. What similarities can you cite between the woman's movement of the 1920's and the woman's movement of today? Explain.
4. During the depression, people were making special efforts to make their dollars stretch and such things as automobiles last. Do you think people have reasons to be doing the same sorts of things today? Explain.

Developing Social Science Skills

1. Read some of the poetry written by a poet of the Harlem Renaissance, such as Countee Cullen, Claude McKay, or Langston Hughes. (a) What do the poems tell you about the lives and concerns of black Americans in the 1920's? (b) What are the poet's attitudes about American society and values?
2. Assume that you lived during the Great Depression and your family left its home to seek jobs and a better life in another part of the country. Write a letter to a friend describing your experiences on the road and in your new home.

Unit Survey

For Further Inquiry

1. Explain how each of the following demonstrates a rejection of Progressivism and the ideals of the New Freedom: (a) President Harding's campaign slogan of "a return to normalcy," (b) President Coolidge's statement, "The business of America is business." (c) President Hoover's belief in "the American system of rugged individualism."
2. (a) Make a list of five words or phrases that describe American life during the 1920's. (b) Explain each of your choices.
3. (a) Why did the Great Depression happen? (b) Could such an economic collapse ever happen again? Why or why not?
4. Do you think the New Deal changed the basic character of the federal government? Why or why not?
5. Would either Hamilton or Jefferson have approved of the New Deal? Give evidence to support your answer.
6. (a) How did the depression affect the lives of America's minorities? (b) Why did it affect them that way?

Projects and Activities

1. Study the timeline here. (a) According to the timeline, was the situation of workers improving? How can you tell? (b) How were conditions for farmers? For Indians and blacks? (c) Does the information on the timeline seem to conform to the information in Unit 10? Which is more useful as a source of information about economic trends during the 1920's and 1930? Why?
2. Research the history of the Ku Klux Klan. How did the various stages of its history reflect the times?
3. Prepare a bulletin board display entitled, "Heroes of the Golden Twenties." Include in the display pictures, short biographies, or newspaper headlines to feature people such as Charles Lindbergh, Babe Ruth, Gertrude Ederle, and Bill Tilden.
4. Prepare a series of political cartoons on the New Deal. Be sure to keep the cartoons simple and to make clear the point of view expressed in each one.
5. Make a bar or line graph on one aspect of the 1920's and 1930's, such as (a) government spending, (b) average family income, (c) cost of living, (d) number of bank failures.

Exploring Your Region

1. In your community, try to locate buildings, roads, or bridges that were built during the New Deal. Find out the circumstances under which they were built. Prepare a map of your community that indicates their location.
2. Make a list of items in your home or school that were not yet invented or in use during the 1920's and 1930's. Describe what daily life would have been like without those items.

Suggested Readings

1. *Winged Legend: The Story of Amelia Earhart,* John Burke. Biography of America's outstanding woman aviator, whose plane disappeared over the Pacific in 1937.
2. *Black Boy,* Richard Wright. The story of the early life of a major American writer.
3. *The Great Depression,* David Shannon. Eyewitness accounts of life during the depression, including discussion of farming, relief, and education.
4. *Only Yesterday,* Frederick Lewis Allen. A popular history that documents the fads and fashions of the 1920's.
5. *Babbitt,* Sinclair Lewis. A satirical novel of middle-class life in the 1920's.

Unit Eleven

From Isolation Through World War II

1920 - 1945

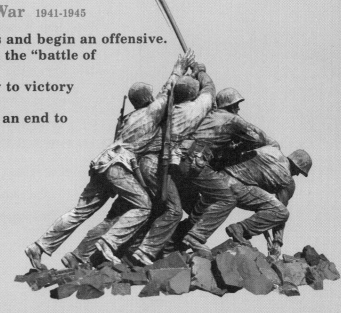

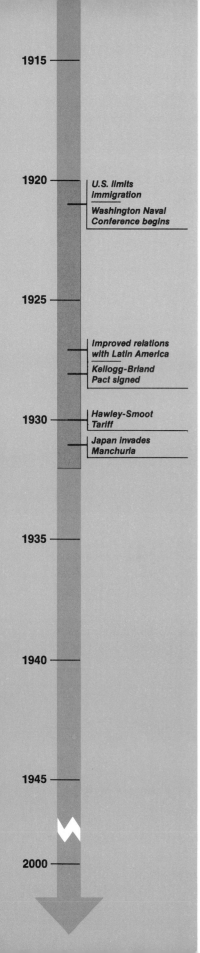

1915 —

1920 —
U.S. limits
immigration

Washington Naval
Conference begins

1925 —

Improved relations
with Latin America

Kellogg-Briand
Pact signed

1930 —
Hawley-Smoot
Tariff

Japan invades
Manchuria

1935 —

1940 —

1945 —

2000 —

Chapter 34

The United States Moves Toward Isolation

1920-1932

During the 1920's and 1930's, Americans had faced rapidly changing conditions at home. The economy had moved from a postwar depression to a boom to almost complete collapse in the Great Depression.

Relations with foreign nations went through equally complex changes during these years. The end of World War I in 1918 had released emotions long held in check. Millions of people on every continent mourned for loved ones killed in the war. Mixed with the sorrow, however, was wild joy that the war to end all wars was over. Millions of people offered prayers of thanksgiving and prayers for the fulfillment of President Wilson's vision of a world rebuilt on a foundation of lasting peace.

Wilson realized, as millions of Americans did not, that it is easier to win a victory on a battlefield than it is to build a lasting peace. He warned Americans that great problems remained to be solved and he challenged them to take up the responsibility of world leadership.

Unhappily, Wilson's plea went unheeded, and the idealism that marked the end of the war soon faded. Americans were tired of wartime restrictions and eager to return to the everyday business of living. Also, as the European Allies with whom the United States had fought began to quarrel over the spoils of war, Americans became increasingly disillusioned.

President Wilson struggled to keep his vision before the American people. However, during the 1920's, the American people rejected his policies, both domestic and foreign. They refused to join the League of Nations, and, in the following years, they turned their backs on Europe and on the chance to take on the challenge of world leadership.

THE CHAPTER IN OUTLINE

1. America closes its doors to Europe's people and goods.

2. The United States moves toward the Good Neighbor Policy.

3. Americans cooperate with other nations in efforts to prevent war.

654

1 America closes its doors to Europe's people and goods

After World War I, the United States in some ways drew back from involvement in world affairs. America refused, for example, to join the League of Nations in part to avoid becoming entangled again in Europe's troubles and quarrels.

The United States also tried, with considerable success, to keep out the people and products of Europe and Asia. The immigration and tariff laws passed during this period were the most restrictive in American history.

Closing the doors. During the 1920's the United States reversed one of its oldest traditions by almost completely halting immigration. Earlier, it is true, laws and international agreements had excluded the Chinese, the Japanese, and most other Asians. Despite these exceptions, few Americans had questioned the historic role of the United States as a place of refuge and of opportunity for immigrants. Indeed, during the decade before World War I,

more Europeans settled in the United States than in any previous decade.

Why did a nation of immigrants and descendants of immigrants suddenly close its doors? One reason was the anti-European feeling that swept over America after the war. However, certain Americans had reasons of their own.

Organized labor, for example, argued that new immigrants were willing to work for lower wages than American workers and thus pulled down the standard of living. Industrialists had formerly favored immigration as a source of cheap, unskilled labor. By 1920, with the railroads built and basic industries such as steel well developed, they no longer needed masses of unskilled workers. Finally, many established Americans felt that the newer immigrants, mainly from eastern and southern Europe, did not easily become "Americanized."

The immigration laws. Congress passed three laws in the 1920's that progressively restricted immigration from Europe. The Emergency Quota Act of 1921 introduced a **quota system.** This limited the number of Europeans and others who could be admitted to 3 percent of the total number of persons of their nationality

Ill-will toward the growing numbers of immigrants coming to the United States began long before the 1920's, as this 1891 cartoon shows. What is the cartoonist's opinion of the immigrants of the time? What evidence can you find of it?

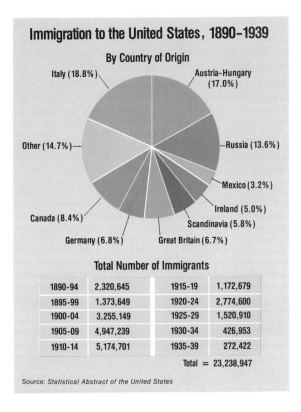

Immigration to the United States, 1890–1939

By Country of Origin

Italy (18.8%)
Austria-Hungary (17.0%)
Other (14.7%)
Russia (13.6%)
Mexico (3.2%)
Ireland (5.0%)
Canada (8.4%)
Scandinavia (5.8%)
Germany (6.8%)
Great Britain (6.7%)

Total Number of Immigrants

1890-94	2,320,645	1915-19	1,172,679
1895-99	1,373,649	1920-24	2,774,600
1900-04	3,255,149	1925-29	1,520,910
1905-09	4,947,239	1930-34	426,953
1910-14	5,174,701	1935-39	272,422
		Total =	23,238,947

Source: *Statistical Abstract of the United States*

residing in the United States in the year 1910. The act also set a total yearly limit of about 350,000 immigrants.

In 1924 an even more restrictive law reduced the yearly quota from 3 to 2 percent. It also changed the base year from 1910 to 1890. This change discriminated against Italians, Austrians, Russians, and other eastern and southern Europeans who had immigrated to America mainly after 1890.

Finally, the National Origins Act of 1929 shifted the base year of immigration to 1920. However, it counterbalanced this more liberal provision by reducing the yearly limit on immigrants to 150,000.

The new immigration policies aroused a great deal of bitterness, especially among eastern and southern Europeans. The Japanese were also aroused because the immigration act of 1924 ended the Gentlemen's Agreement of 1907. Japan had faithfully observed the agreement and resented the policies which closed the doors to Japanese immigrants.

The war of tariffs.   While closing its doors to immigrants, the United States also raised tariff barriers to keep out foreign products. In fact,

the ink was hardly dry on the peace treaties before the nations of the world were engaged in another war — a trade war fought with tariffs. As you have read, the Fordney-McCumber Tariff of 1922 increased import duties on hundreds of items.

In 1930 Congress passed the Hawley-Smoot Tariff Act, providing for the highest tariff in American history. President Hoover felt that some of the rates were too high. He also pondered a petition signed by 1,000 leading economists who argued that such high tariffs would raise prices, create hardships for American consumers, and seriously interfere with world trade. Nevertheless, believing that protective tariffs encouraged business prosperity, Hoover signed the bill.

America's high-tariff policy proved a cruel blow to many countries in Latin America and in Europe. When America's high tariffs deprived these countries of their best markets in the United States, their economic strength declined. Factories closed, people were thrown out of work, and the surplus of farm products mounted steadily.

Some countries struck back by raising their own tariff barriers against American goods. Thus the high tariffs that Congress hoped would aid American industry in the end deprived many American businesses and farms of the foreign markets they badly needed.

War debts and high tariffs.   America's high-tariff policy created still another problem. How could European countries pay their war debts to the United States if they could not sell their goods in this country?

The war had changed America's relation to Europe from debtor to creditor. Before the war American business leaders had borrowed money from Europeans to finance new industries. During the period before the United States entered the war in 1917, however, Europeans began to sell their American stocks and bonds to buy war goods. As the war progressed, the American government also loaned huge sums to the warring countries. As a result, by 1918 nearly all the European countries owed money to the United States. The total amounted to about $10 billion.

The American government reduced the interest rates on the loans. It also arranged for the debtor nations to repay the money over a long period of time. Despite the generous terms, the bankrupt European countries emerged from the war not knowing how they could repay their debts.

President Wilson reminded Congress of one possible solution to Europe's problems. He declared that if the United States wished Europe to repay its debts, Americans had to buy European products. However, this became impossible when the United States adopted a high-tariff policy.

War debts and reparations. The only other solution open to the European Allies was to collect war damages, or **reparations,** from Germany. They could then use this money to repay their war debts to the United States. In 1921 a Reparations Commission fixed the total of German reparations at $33 billion. Germany, however, was in the midst of a severe economic crisis and completely unable to pay such a huge sum. In an effort to secure the money, Germany borrowed from bankers in the United States and Europe.

There was a limit to the amount that the German government could borrow, and, as the years passed, the reparations had to be reduced. In spite of this relief, however, Germany's economic situation grew steadily worse. By 1930 the Germans could make no further payments.

A legacy of bitterness. Faced with this situation, the debtor countries notified the United States that they could no longer meet their payments on the war debts. They argued that they had contributed far more to victory in blood and sacrifice than had America. It would be only fair of the United States, they said, to cancel all war debts.

The American government refused to admit such a claim. It insisted that the war debts to the United States and German reparation payments to the Allies were two entirely separate matters. Americans pointed out that some of the loans—perhaps as much as a third of the total—had, in fact, been made after the armistice. Americans also reminded the European countries that they were not too poor to spend large sums for armaments.

In 1931 the debtors, with the exception of Finland, refused to make even a token payment. President Hoover then declared a year's halt, or **moratorium,** on the payment of war debts and reparations. However, Germany did not make any more payments, and the whole question was left unsolved.

In the end, most of the war debts and most of Germany's reparations remained unpaid. Nevertheless, America's unsuccessful attempt to collect the war debts increased Europe's resentment against the United States. Also, the European victors' unsuccessful attempt to collect reparations from Germany created a feeling of bitterness among the German people. This bitterness, as you will see, contributed to the rise of Adolf Hitler in the early 1930's.

SECTION SURVEY

IDENTIFY: quota system, Hawley-Smoot Tariff, reparations, moratorium.

1. List four reasons why various Americans favored restricting immigration after World War I.
2. (a) What reasons did the European Allies give for stopping payments on their war debts? (b) How did Americans answer these arguments?
3. In what ways did America's high-tariff policies backfire?
4. Graph Study: Look at the graph on page 656. According to the graph, from what countries did the largest percentage of immigrants come?

2 The United States moves toward the Good Neighbor Policy

During the early 1900's, you may recall, Presidents Theodore Roosevelt, William Howard Taft, and Woodrow Wilson had all intervened in Latin-American affairs. They had claimed that intervention was necessary (1) to safeguard the Panama Canal, (2) to prevent European countries from extending their influence in the Caribbean, and (3) to protect American citizens and property.

This Caribbean policy was continued by Presidents Harding and Coolidge. Critics of the policy—and there were many on both sides of the border—referred to it as "dollar diplomacy." Many Latin Americans called it "Yankee imperialism."

Investments and intervention. The prosperity of the "Golden Twenties" provided many Americans with money to invest. The underdeveloped countries of Latin America offered

657

President Coolidge (center) came to Cuba in 1928 to open the seventh Pan-American Conference there. He hoped his trip would show that the United States wanted to work together with Latin America.

many inviting opportunities for investment. American dollars financed the building of factories, railroads, mines, and ranches in the lands to the south. Whereas in 1913 United States investments in Latin America totaled $1.3 billion, by 1928 these investments totaled more than $5 billion.

American interest in Latin America grew in proportion to the amount of American money invested there. President Coolidge frankly declared that the United States government would protect the property and lives of American citizens wherever they went.

During these years many Latin-American countries were undergoing social and economic revolutions. Frequently two groups in a country struggled to gain control. Each group claimed that it alone represented the people and was the legal government. When this happened, the United States tended to recognize the group most friendly to American interests.

In some instances, the United States played an active role in the struggle for power. On oc-

casion it forbade the sale of arms to the group it disliked and armed the group it supported. Worst of all from the Latin-American point of view, the United States sometimes sent armed forces to protect American lives and property.

Relations with Nicaragua. American policy toward Nicaragua offers an example of the kind of intervention that Latin Americans fiercely resented. The United States was particularly interested in Nicaragua because of large American investments there. Moreover, Nicaragua was close to the vital Panama Canal. Finally, there was the prospect that a new canal might eventually be built through Nicaragua itself. President Taft had sent marines into the country during an internal conflict to protect American investments and the nearby Panama Canal. President Coolidge withdrew the marines in 1925 but sent them back in 1926 when new disturbances broke out.

This policy was unpopular throughout Latin America. It was also unpopular with many Americans who claimed that the United States was really making war. President Coolidge denied this and spoke of the American occupation as a police duty. However, criticism was so strong that the administration took measures to solve the problem by more peaceful means.

In 1927 President Coolidge withdrew most of the marines, leaving only enough to protect American property if violence again broke out. This relieved some of the tension, but the Nicaraguans demanded the withdrawal of *all* marines and the end of American interference. In 1933 President Hoover finally withdrew all United States troops.

Relations with Mexico. Relations with Mexico also reflected the determination of the United States to protect American interests south of the Rio Grande. During Wilson's administration a sweeping social revolution in Mexico had raised new problems in the uneasy relations between the two countries. American lives and property suffered in the upheaval. Far more threatening to Americans who had invested in Mexican property was a new policy established in the Mexican constitution of 1917.

Article 27 of the Mexican constitution declared that "only Mexicans . . . have the right to acquire ownership [of, or] . . . to develop, mines, waters, or mineral fuels in the Republic of Mexico. The nation may grant the same right to foreigners, provided that they agree to be considered Mexicans in respect of such property, and accordingly not to involve the protection of their government in respect of the same." This article also canceled concessions made to foreigners by earlier governments. Foreign investors were quick to protest.

During 1917 and 1918, the United States was too involved in the European war to take any action in regard to Mexico. Moreover, not all of the provisions of the constitution were at once applied. However, after the armistice in 1918, oil investors and other American owners of property in Mexico clamored for intervention. These business interests were joined by many American Catholics who were disturbed by anti-Catholic provisions in the Mexican constitution and the anticlerical policies of the Mexican government. The situation grew worse when the Mexicans supported the anti-American faction in Nicaragua. By 1927, American-Mexican relations were close to the breaking point.

In 1927 the United States began slowly to modify its policy. President Coolidge took the first step by sending Dwight W. Morrow, a successful banker, as ambassador to Mexico. Instead of threatening Mexico with United States power, Morrow tried to understand the Mexican point of view. His sincerity, intelligence, and charm quickly won him many friends in Mexico. The skillful work of Morrow and other American "ambassadors of good will" repaired much of the damage done in the past. The Mexicans agreed to recognize American titles to subsoil minerals, such as petroleum, that had been in effect before the constitution of 1917.

New relations with Latin America. The Morrow mission marked a turning point in American relations with Mexico and with other Latin-American countries. From 1927 on, both Coolidge and his successor, Herbert Hoover, worked hard to develop friendlier relations with the Caribbean republics and with the South American nations. Coolidge went to Havana, Cuba, in 1928 and personally opened a Pan-American Conference. Hoover toured South America in the months before his inauguration.

Latin Americans were pleased by the friendly attention of an American President and a President-elect. They were also pleased

when the United States stopped using the 1904 Roosevelt Corollary to the Monroe Doctrine. The Corollary stated that the United States had the right to act as police officer of the Western Hemisphere.

In 1930 the State Department declared that the Monroe Doctrine would no longer be used to justify United States intervention in Latin-American domestic affairs.

Thus by the early 1930's, relations with Latin America had been considerably improved. The governments of these nations now encouraged American investments and gave those investments greater protection than in the past.

SECTION SURVEY

IDENTIFY: "Yankee imperialism," police duty, Dwight W. Morrow.

1. Why did United States Caribbean policy during the early 1900's arouse resentment in Latin America and criticism in the United States?

2. Why did many Latin Americans resent United States policy toward Nicaragua?

3. What were the reasons for American hostility toward Mexico from 1917 to 1927?

4. What steps did the United States take from 1927 to 1930 to improve its relations with Latin America?

---

3 Americans cooperate with other nations in efforts to prevent war

While the United States was improving relations with Latin America, it also took steps to move toward international cooperation.

America and the League of Nations. As time passed, American experts in international law, public health, and finance became important advisers in activities of the League of Nations. During Harding's administration the United States began to send observers to Switzerland to take unofficial parts in League committee work dealing with epidemics, slavery, and the narcotics trade. By 1924, American delegates were attending League conferences.

The League of Nations held its first informal meeting in Geneva, Switzerland, in 1920. No official American delegates attended the League's meetings at the start, though some Americans later served the League as advisers.

Both Harding and Coolidge recommended that the United States join the Permanent Court of International Justice, popularly known as the World Court, created in 1920 to arbitrate international disputes. However, the Senate, guarding its right to make treaties and influenced by Americans who feared "entangling alliances," agreed to join only on its own terms. The nations already belonging to the World Court refused to accept the Senate's terms, and the matter was dropped.

The armaments race. The government was more successful in its efforts to stop the naval armaments race in which it was engaged with Great Britain and Japan. Relations with Japan were particularly strained after World War I. Americans resented the Japanese occupation of the Shantung Peninsula in China. This occupation, begun in 1914, violated America's Open Door Policy, which was designed to keep China's territory intact and to prevent any single power from dominating China. Americans were concerned because Japan was allied with Great Britain.

As a result of the tension created by this situation, each of the three powers was rapidly building up its naval strength. Many people in all three countries feared that the naval armaments race might lead to war.

The Washington Conference. Against this disturbing background, nine powers with interests in Asia met in the American capital during 1921 and 1922. Secretary of State Charles Evans Hughes opened the Washington Naval Conference by boldly proposing a 10-year naval holiday during which no new warships were to be built. He suggested that the United States, Great Britain, and Japan each scrap enough of its own warships to bring the naval strength of the three great sea powers into a ratio of 5:5:3. These limitations applied only to capital ships, that is, to battleships and heavy cruisers. According to this plan, Great Britain and the United States would be equal in naval strength while Japan would have three fifths as much tonnage as each of the other two countries. France and Italy were to have fleets of equal size, with a ratio of 1.75 to the other powers.

At first, Japan refused to accept the plan. Finally, eager to make economies at home, the Japanese accepted the proposal on the condition that Great Britain and the United States would not further fortify any Pacific colonies, except Hawaii. These agreements were included in what came to be called the Five-Power Treaty.

Other agreements. The Five-Power Treaty was only one of the agreements reached at the conference. Among others were the Four-Power Pact and the Nine-Power Treaty.

In the Four-Power Pact, Japan, Great Britain, France, and the United States agreed to respect one another's rights in the Pacific. The four nations also agreed to consult with one another in the event of any act of aggression in the Pacific area.

In the Nine-Power Treaty, the nations represented at the Washington Conference guaranteed the territorial integrity of China. They promised to uphold the Open Door Policy by promoting trade and relations "between China and the other powers upon the basis of equality of opportunity."

Events in Asia following the Washington Conference seemed to justify the belief that a major step toward peace had been taken. Japan withdrew, at least partially, from the Shantung Peninsula. Japan also withdrew troops that had occupied parts of Siberia during the Russian Revolution. At a London Naval Conference in 1930, Japan agreed to extend the naval holiday. This agreement marked the high point of Japanese cooperation with the Western powers.

The attempt to outlaw war. The United States also tried to prevent war by what has been called a policy of "wishful thinking." In 1928 Secretary of State Frank B. Kellogg joined with the French foreign minister, Aristide Briand (ah·rees·TEED bree·AHN), in asking all nations to sign a pledge outlawing war "as an instrument of foreign policy." The signers were also to agree to settle all disputes by peaceful methods.

Eventually 62 nations accepted the document. However, the Kellogg-Briand Pact, or the Pact of Paris as it was called, proved to be little more than a statement of good intentions. In signing, each nation added its own reservations. Not one was willing to outlaw war waged in self-defense. Since nearly every nation going to war justifies its actions by pleading self-defense, this reservation destroyed the pact's effectiveness.

Finally, the document said nothing about enforcement. Those who signed it were not even bound to consult with one another in case some government acted aggressively.

The crumbling peace structure. The opening act in the tragedy that later engulfed the entire world began in 1931. Without warning, the Japanese army rolled across the frontiers of Manchuria (see map, page 673). China, large but helpless, could do little to defend its great northern province. Within a few months, the Japanese had torn the province away from the Chinese. A Japanese program to sweep

"foreign" influence out of the Far East and to build an Asia for Asians had begun.

Japan's aggression violated the Covenant of the League of Nations. It was an outright challenge to the Open Door Policy of the United States. Japan was bluntly reminded of these facts by Secretary of State Henry L. Stimson. In a formal note issued in 1932, Stimson protested Japan's flagrant violation of the Nine-Power Treaty and of the Kellogg-Briand Pact, both of which Japan had signed. President Hoover and Congress, however, were unwilling to use force or even economic sanctions to enforce the Stimson declaration.

Meanwhile, the League of Nations met to consider what action, if any, should be taken. President Hoover sent an American representative to this meeting. The League sent a commission to Manchuria to investigate, but beyond a statement of its agreement with Stimson's declaration, the League failed to act. Confident that the nations of the world would not act together to preserve peace, Japan withdrew from the League of Nations. It then made preparations to invade and conquer China and Southeast Asia.

The structure of peace had begun to crumble. As you will see, Fascist Italy and, after 1933, the rising Nazi regime in Germany realized that they too could safely embark upon programs of aggression. The peace structure was not firm enough to stand a heavy blow. The world powers, which by collective action might have reinforced the crumbling structure of world peace, were unwilling and unable to act together.

SECTION SURVEY

IDENTIFY: World Court, armaments race, Charles Evans Hughes, naval holiday, Frank B. Kellogg, Henry L. Stimson.

1. What conditions led to the Washington Naval Conference of 1921–22?

2. (a) What were the major provisions of the Five-Power Treaty? (b) What was the reason for the Four-Power Pact?

3. Why was the Nine-Power Treaty significant for (a) China, (b) the United States, and (c) Japan?

4. Why was the Kellogg-Briand Pact of 1928 little more than a statement of good intentions?

5. (a) How did the United States react to the Japanese invasion of Manchuria? (b) What was the reaction of the League of Nations? Why?

Chapter Survey

Summary: Tracing the Main Ideas

During the 1920's the American people as a whole rejected President Wilson's call to assume world leadership. To be sure, during the immediate postwar years, the United States did help Europe by supplying food, clothing, medical supplies, and huge loans of money. During the 1920's the United States worked closely with the League of Nations in efforts to reduce international friction and took steps to establish better relations with Latin America.

Nevertheless, the United States' refusal to join the League of Nations, its harsher immigration policies, and its higher tariff barriers did not win friends for America.

By 1932 the faith and good will that had been so widespread throughout the world in 1918 were rapidly evaporating. In place of the prosperity of the 1920's, the world was faced with a deepening economic depression. In place of faith and good will, the world was confronted by intense international rivalry and a growing feeling of suspicion and distrust. Japan had already begun its program of aggression, the Italians were threatening their neighbors, and the Nazi movement was gathering strength in Germany. The structure of peace was breaking into fragments.

Inquiring into History

1. During the years after World War I, the United States shut its doors to many immigrants and placed high tariffs on foreign goods. How are these two actions related?
2. What efforts toward world peace did the United States make during the 1920's?
3. What actions taken by nations during the 1920's caused resentments that might later flare into war?
4. The Kellogg-Briand Pact did not survive the challenges posed by the Japanese invasion of Manchuria. Why?
5. How would you characterize American attitudes toward (a) Europe, (b) Latin America, and (c) Asia during the 1920's? How do you account for those attitudes?

Relating Past to Present

1. Does the United States follow one or several policies in dealing with the nations of the world today? Explain.
2. How do United States relations with Latin American nations today compare with those of the 1920's?
3. In the period just studied, world peace was crumbling in part because the world powers could not act collectively to counteract aggression. Can you think of any events in recent years that might have destroyed world peace if left unchecked? How was peace maintained?

Developing Social Science Skills

1. Using the graph on immigration on page 842, (a) compare immigration to the United States from 1901–11 with immigration from 1921–30. (b) How do you explain this radical change? (c) What effect did it have on the makeup of our population? (d) What other effects may it have had on the nation? (Consider the contributions that immigrants have made to the United States throughout its history.)
2. Conduct research and prepare a report on United States relations with one Latin American country from around 1900 to 1930. Try to find material that gives the points of view of *both* nations.
3. Examine the cartoon on page 655. (a) Where does the scene take place? How can you tell? (b) Who are the hoards of people beneath the platform? (c) How would you describe them? (d) What evils does the cartoonist hold these people responsible for? How do you know? (e) How does Uncle Sam feel about these people? How can you tell?
4. Create a cartoon that exhibits a point of view opposite to the one put forth in the cartoon on page 655.

Chapter 35

Moving from Isolationism into War

1932–1941

In 1933, when Franklin Delano Roosevelt became President for the first time, it was clear that few Presidents had entered office under more unfavorable circumstances.

The Great Depression, the worst depression the country had ever experienced, was becoming worse week by week, not only in the United States but throughout the world.

Equally disturbing was the growth of warlike dictatorships in Asia and Europe. Americans were deeply troubled because the Japanese war machine had already rolled across the borders of Manchuria and, as you have read, seized that province from the defenseless Chinese.

However, there was no way for President-elect Roosevelt or anyone else to foresee that in 1933 Hitler would win control of Germany. No one could foresee that by 1936 a powerful German army would move into the Rhineland, violating the Versailles Treaty. Nor could anyone then know that by 1940 Hitler's Nazis, Mussolini's Fascists, and the Japanese warlords would have plunged the world into the most devastating conflict in its entire history.

During the 1930's the United States took an increasingly active interest in foreign affairs. It recognized the Soviet Union. It made provisions to grant independence to the Filipinos. It expanded the Good Neighbor Policy. Although the United States tried to remain neutral in a war-torn world, by the end of 1941 the American people found themselves playing a leading role in the struggle against the dictatorships.

THE CHAPTER IN OUTLINE

1. The United States broadens its relations with other countries.
2. Americans try to follow a policy of isolationism.
3. The nation finds isolationism difficult to maintain.
4. The United States becomes involved in World War II.

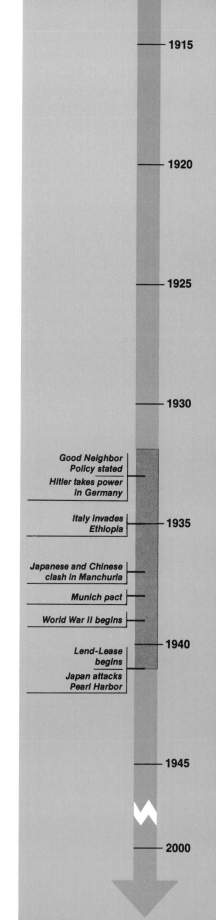

1915

1920

1925

1930

Good Neighbor Policy stated
Hitler takes power in Germany

Italy invades Ethiopia — 1935

Japanese and Chinese clash in Manchuria

Munich pact

World War II begins

1940

Lend-Lease begins

Japan attacks Pearl Harbor

1945

2000

1 The United States broadens its relations with other countries

American foreign policy in the 1930's was influenced by two basic considerations: (1) the Great Depression at home and abroad and (2) the rise of dictatorships in Europe and Asia.

The Soviet Union. In 1933, during the first year of the New Deal administration, the United States recognized the Soviet Union. Those favoring this move argued that it was only realistic to recognize a regime that had been in power for 16 years. They pointed out that an increased flow of trade between the two countries would be helpful to the United States. Finally, they insisted that the two countries shared a concern about the threat of Japanese aggression.

In reply to these arguments, the opponents of recognition pointed out that the Communists made no secret of their goal of world conquest. This objection was met when the Soviet Union promised to stop all propaganda activities in the United States. As it turned out, this promise was not kept. Moreover, recognition of the Soviet Union did not greatly increase trade between the two countries.

Toward Philippine independence. In the Jones Act of 1916, as you may recall, the United States promised to give the Filipinos their independence. During the 1920's this action was postponed on the ground that the Filipinos were not yet ready for independence. In 1933, however, late in Hoover's administration, Congress passed an independence act for the Philippines over the President's veto.

The Philippine legislature rejected this measure. Many Filipinos feared that one of the act's provisions, giving the United States the right to keep military and naval bases, would enable Americans to continue their control in the Philippines anyway. Other Filipinos argued that once they were free, the United States would then raise its tariff barriers against Philippine products.

Trying to overcome these fears, Congress in 1934 passed the Tydings-McDuffie Act. This measure was more acceptable to the Filipinos. It provided for the establishment of a Philippine Commonwealth and outlined a gradual 10-year tariff increase on Philippine goods imported into the United States. This would give the Filipinos an opportunity to adjust to an independent economy.

Ten years after the establishment of a commonwealth—on July 4, 1946, as it turned out—the Philippines were to become entirely independent. The United States would retain its naval bases in the area, however.

The Good Neighbor Policy. During the 1930's the United States also redoubled earlier efforts to improve relations with Latin America. The policy started by Coolidge and Hoover was expanded by Roosevelt.

Self-interest as well as a genuine desire for friendship motivated the Good Neighbor Policy. During the 1920's many Americans began to realize that the United States could not afford to continue antagonizing its Latin-American neighbors. When the Great Depression came, this realization hardened into firm conviction. The United States needed Latin-American trade. The rise of dictatorships in both Europe and Asia further strengthened the conviction among Americans that the United States had to establish friendlier relations with Latin America.

SOURCES

PROCLAMATION OF PHILIPPINE INDEPENDENCE (1946)

Whereas it has been the repeated declaration of the . . . government of the United States of America that full independence would be granted the Philippines as soon as the people of the Philippines were prepared to assume this obligation; and

Whereas the people of the Philippines have clearly demonstrated their capacity for self-government; . . .

Now, therefore, I, Harry S. Truman, . . . do hereby recognize the independence of the Philippines as a separate and self-governing nation. . . .

In 1933 President Roosevelt declared, "In the field of foreign policy, I would dedicate this nation to the policy of the good neighbor — the neighbor who resolutely respects himself and, because he does so, respects the rights of others." Later that year, in a conference held in Montevideo, Uruguay, the United States joined the other American countries in a pledge not to interfere in the affairs of their neighbors. "No state," the pledge declared, "has the right to intervene in the internal or external affairs of another state."

The Montevideo Pact marked a turning point in United States relations with Latin America. As President Roosevelt put it, "The definite policy of the United States from now on is one opposed to armed intervention."

The policy in action. Nor were these mere words. In 1934 the United States canceled the Platt Amendment, under which it had claimed the right to intervene in Cuban affairs. That same year the remainder of American troops were finally withdrawn from Haiti. In 1936 the United States gave up its right to intervene in Panama's affairs. Also the United States gradually ended its control over the customhouses of the Dominican Republic — a control exercised since 1905.

The Good Neighbor Policy was put to a severe test in 1938. In that year President Lázaro Cárdenas (LAH·sah·roh KAHR·day·nahs) of Mexico confiscated the properties of all foreign oil companies. Foreign investors, including Americans, protested and demanded action from their governments. President Roosevelt refused to intervene on behalf of American investors. Instead, he urged the American oil companies to negotiate directly with Mexico. As a result of these negotiations, the Mexican government agreed to pay a small part of what the American companies had claimed.

President Franklin Roosevelt's Good Neighbor Policy inspired this song, set to a Latin-American beat. The writers wanted to promote a spirit of friendliness throughout the nations of the Americas.

International trade agreements. The United States also tried to promote an international revival of trade. The Roosevelt administration offered to negotiate with any country special trade agreements that would provide for lowering tariffs.

In the Trade Agreements Act of 1934, Congress authorized the President to raise or lower existing tariffs by as much as 50 percent without Senate approval. As a result, the Roo-

SOURCES

ABROGATION OF THE PLATT AMENDMENT (1934)

Article I. The Treaty of Relations which was concluded between the two contracting parties on May 22, 1903, shall cease to be in force, and is abrogated, from the date on which the present treaty goes into effect.

Article II. All the acts effected in Cuba by the United States of America during its military occupation of the island, up to May 20, 1902, the date on which the Republic of Cuba was established, have been ratified and held as valid; and all rights legally acquired by virtue of those acts shall be maintained and protected. . . .

sevelt administration could bargain, or reciprocate, with other countries at its discretion. A nation that lowered its tariffs on United States goods would, in turn, receive more favorable tariffs on the goods that it sent to the United States. By 1940 Secretary of State Cordell Hull had signed 22 such reciprocal trade agreements.

Equally important was the provision of the Trade Agreements Act known as the "most-favored nation" clause. This clause offered any country the opportunity to be treated as well as the nation seemingly "most favored" in any tariff agreement. This act therefore helped to end tariff discriminations against the United States. The Trade Agreements Act also stimulated American business by improving trade relations with other nations.

New tariff agreements worked out with Canada and Great Britain under the Trade Agreements Act were especially important. They led to a great increase of trade between these countries and the United States. They also provided an economic foundation for the political cooperation that became so important in World War II.

SECTION SURVEY

IDENTIFY: dictatorship, Good Neighbor Policy, Montevideo Pact, Lázaro Cárdenas, reciprocal trade agreements, Cordell Hull, "most-favored nation" clause.

1. What were the arguments for and against recognition of the Soviet Union in 1933?
2. (a) What conditions led to the passage of the Tydings-McDuffie Act? (b) What was the major provision of the act?
3. (a) What were the conditions that prompted the Good Neighbor Policy? (b) Give examples of the United States following this policy.

2 **Americans try to follow a policy of isolationism**

In the early 1930's, the threat of war loomed larger and larger. In Asia and Europe, the militaristic leaders of Japan, Italy, and Germany started building up their armies and weapons arsenals. Their leaders seemed determined to prepare for aggression.

The rise of dictatorships. As the years passed, the Roosevelt administration had to deal with a growing number of **totalitarian°** rulers. In 1922 Benito Mussolini seized power in Italy as the leader of **Fascism.** Fascism was a system of government concentrating all political, economic, and cultural power in the state. It was dedicated to aggressive expansionism. Mussolini, a swaggering, domineering ruler, dreamed of controlling the Mediterranean and the Middle East.

The Japanese warlords who seized control of Japan in the late 1920's also had dreams of expansion and military glory. Their seizure of Manchuria in 1931 was only one step in a program designed to win complete control of East Asia and the Pacific.

Adolf Hitler, the Austrian-born, Jew-hating fanatic who climbed to power in Germany in 1933, was a ruthless dictator who also longed for conquest. Josef Stalin, who in the 1920's succeeded N. Lenin as the leader of the Soviet Union openly intended to spread communism throughout the entire world.

There were other dictators, including General Francisco Franco, who came to power in Spain in 1939 after a bloody civil war. However, the dictatorships of Japan, Italy, and Germany proved to be the most aggressive.

Hitler, Mussolini, and the Japanese warlords expressed their contempt for democracy. It was, in Mussolini's words, "a rotting corpse" that had to be replaced by "efficient" government and a "superior" way of life.

All of the dictatorships scorned the democratic rights of free speech and a free press. In totalitarian systems individuals existed to serve the state and had no rights except those that the state chose to give them.

All of the dictatorships glorified force. Compelling the people to work for "bullets rather than butter," they converted their industries to war production. Their major efforts were devoted to building powerful military machines.

Mounting tension. By the mid-1930's the dictators were ready to move. In 1935 Mussolini's blackshirted Fascists attacked the African nation of Ethiopia (see map, pages 672–73). They used bombers and poison gas against a practically defenseless people.

°**totalitarian:** This term refers to a dictatorship that exercises total control over a nation and suppresses individual freedom.

In 1934 and 1935, the Japanese broke the pledges made at the Washington Naval Conferences of 1921–22 and in later treaties. They began a rapid build-up of their navy.

Then in March 1936, German troops moved into the Rhineland (see map, page 670), clearly violating the Treaty of Versailles. In July civil war broke out in Spain. In October Germany and Italy signed a military alliance and began to call themselves the **Axis**° Powers. In November 1936 Germany, Italy, and Japan joined in an Anti-Comintern† Pact, thus hiding their aggressive designs under the pretense of resisting communism.

On July 7, 1937, Japanese and Chinese troops clashed on the Chinese-Manchurian border. This border incident developed into a full-scale war. In time, historians referred to it as the start of World War II in East Asia.

Roots of isolationism. Despite the growing threat to peace, most Americans remained determined not to become involved in war. They believed that the United States could and should isolate itself from other people's wars. Why did Americans feel this way?

In the first place, most Americans were disillusioned about the results of World War I. The war had not brought peace, disarmament, and democracy across the earth. Instead, it had been followed by constant quarreling among the European powers, by tariff wars, and by failures to reduce armaments.

Most important, the League of Nations had not become an effective instrument for peace. American isolationists refused to believe that the League might have been more successful had the United States joined. They argued that the League's weakness was the best possible evidence that the United States had been wise *not* to join. This widespread disillusionment became increasingly intense when the League failed to check the aggressions of Italy, Germany, and Japan in 1935–37.

American disillusionment about the war grew more intense in 1934 when the Senate started to investigate war profits. Figures re-

"Worker," this German election poster of 1932 urges, "Elect the Front-line Soldier, Hitler!" The Nazis won a majority of seats in the German Parliament and Hitler became the nation's supreme ruler.

leased by the Senate suggested that many American bankers and munitions makers had reaped rich profits from World War I. Many people concluded that America's loans to the Allies were largely responsible for drawing the nation into war. This conclusion has since been rejected by most historians. In the 1930's, however, it fed the spirit of disillusionment.

Disillusionment about World War I was not the only basis for American isolationism. Most Americans believed that the Atlantic and Pacific oceans would protect the United States from attack even if the dictators succeeded in crushing all opposition in Europe and Asia. Many also argued that the improved relations with Latin America gave the nation another safeguard against attack.

°**Axis:** a name made up by Mussolini, who said that the line from Rome to Berlin formed the "axis" on which the world would turn thereafter. Eventually Japan was included among the Axis Powers. The nations who fought the Axis Powers were known as the Allies.

†**Comintern:** an international organization, dominated by the Russian Communist Party, whose aim was to spread communism throughout the world.

Most Americans disapproved of acts of aggression by the Axis Powers. Even so, many were firm isolationists and joined groups that supported a policy of neutrality for the United States, as this poster shows.

The isolationists were strengthened by two other groups. Many Americans believed that the government's first responsibility was to combat the depression. Many others, deeply convinced pacifists, believed that all wars were unjustifiable and that the United States had to avoid being drawn into another conflict. Pacifism was strong, especially among young people, in both the United States and Great Britain during the 1930's.

Isolationism in practice. In 1934, American isolationists won a victory when Congress passed the Johnson Debt Default Act. This act forbade the American government and private citizens to lend money to any country that had **defaulted,** or failed to repay, its war debts.

The Johnson Debt Default Act underscored Americans' annoyance at the failure of all European nations except Finland to repay their war debts. Americans were especially annoyed because some of the defaulting nations were pouring money into weapons. Americans did not intend to provide them any more money for weapons or to risk becoming involved in another war because of entangling investments.

Between 1935 and 1937, the isolationists won other victories in a series of neutrality acts passed by Congress. These acts, which reflected widespread public sentiment against war, were prompted by Mussolini's attack upon Ethiopia, by the civil war in Spain, and by the aggressive actions of Germany and Japan.

In general, the neutrality laws did three things. (1) They prohibited the shipment of munitions to **belligerents,** or warring nations. (2) They authorized the President to list commodities other than munitions that could be sold to belligerents only on a "cash-and-carry" basis. (3) They made it unlawful for Americans to travel on the vessels of belligerent nations.

The neutrality laws were intended to keep Americans out of war and to prevent the involvement of American citizens in such disasters as the sinking of the *Lusitania* in 1915. With these laws the United States abandoned its long-established doctrine of freedom of the seas and withdrew the traditional rights of citizens to travel where and how they wished.

Dissatisfaction with neutrality. Isolationism by no means represented the thinking of all Americans. Many Americans were dismayed by totalitarian governments and their abandonment of individual rights that earlier generations had fought so hard to establish.

Still other Americans regretted that the neutrality laws made it difficult for the United States to help the victims of aggression. In their view, if the United States allowed aggressors to crush weaker neighbors, the United States might one day find itself surrounded by powerful enemies.

Finally, many citizens argued that the United States had a moral duty to aid the victims of unprovoked aggression. This attitude cut across party lines. There were internationalists as well as isolationists in both the Democratic and Republican parties.

Changes in policy. Between 1933 and 1937, President Roosevelt did not take a firm stand on America's responsibility in a troubled world. At times he sided with the isolationists, at other times with the internationalists.

By 1937, however, Roosevelt had become more deeply impressed with the seriousness of the world situation. He felt that the United States should take a positive stand against aggression. In a speech on October 5, 1937, the President said, "If we are to have a world in which we can breathe freely and live in amity without fear—the peace-loving nations must make a concerted effort to uphold laws and principles on which alone peace can rest secure. . . .

"When an epidemic of physical disease starts to spread, the community approves and joins in a quarantine of the patients in order to protect the health of the community against the spread of the disease."

Continuing isolationism. In the "quarantine" speech, Roosevelt expressed views that most Americans were not yet ready to accept. Proof of this came with the *Panay* incident. On December 12, 1937, Japanese planes bombed and strafed a United States gunboat, the *Panay,* and three American oil tankers on the Yangtze River in China (see map, pages 696–97). Several Americans were killed and many were wounded in the incident.

Secretary of State Hull immediately sent a sharp note to the Japanese government. He demanded full apologies, compensation, and a promise that no such incident would recur. The Japanese agreed to all of Hull's demands.

During this incident, the American public revealed how strongly it favored keeping out of war. A public opinion poll taken at the time showed that 54 percent of all Americans felt that the United States should completely withdraw from China.

By the end of 1937, the tide of aggression was rising rapidly in Asia as well as in Europe. Many Americans, including President Roosevelt, were becoming increasingly alarmed. Nevertheless, most Americans clung strongly to the belief that the United States could remain isolated.

SECTION SURVEY

IDENTIFY: totalitarianism, Benito Mussolini, Adolf Hitler, Josef Stalin, Francisco Franco, Axis Powers, isolationism, pacifists, belligerents, "quarantine" speech, *Panay* incident.

1. What were the philosophies of the totalitarian dictators in terms of (a) the role of the individual and the role of government and (b) the role of their nation in the world.

2. What were the roots of the widespread isolationism of the 1920's and early 1930's?

3. (a) What were the neutrality acts of 1935–37? (b) Why were they passed? (c) Why opposed?

4. What were the major events from 1935 to 1937 that threatened peace?

3 The nation finds isolationism difficult to maintain

By 1938 the dictators were becoming more ruthless. During 1938 and 1939, headlines of new aggressions and new crises often crowded other news off the front pages of America's newspapers.

The spread of warfare. In 1938, Japanese forces were attacking along the length of the Chinese coast and pushing inland up the river valleys. Meanwhile, in Europe the Spanish Civil War was bringing misery to hundreds of thousands of other people.

Spain had become an international battleground. Hitler and Mussolini were helping Franco. This provided them the opportunity to test their latest military equipment and to give picked "volunteers" actual battle experience. Soviet "volunteers" were fighting against Franco and his Nazi and Fascist allies. Among Franco's foes in the "International Brigade" were volunteers from many other countries, including the United States.

The United States reacted to this threat to world peace by joining France and Great Britain in a program of nonintervention. With President Roosevelt's approval, Congress in January 1937 barred all shipments of war materials to either side in the civil war in Spain.

New aggressions—and Munich. Another crisis developed when, on March 11, 1938, Hitler's powerful army moved into Austria (see map, page 670). Two days later Hitler announced the union of Austria and Germany.

With Austria under his control, Hitler turned greedy eyes toward western Czechoslovakia. This area, known as the Sudetenland (soo·DAY·tuhn·land), contained a large proportion of German-speaking people. Hitler demanded that Czechoslovakia turn over the region to Germany. Czechoslovakia, with one of the best-trained armies in Europe and with the sympathy of other democratic nations overwhelmingly on its side, refused to bow to Hitler's demands.

Tension was at the breaking point when Hitler and Mussolini met with the prime ministers of Great Britain and France at Munich.

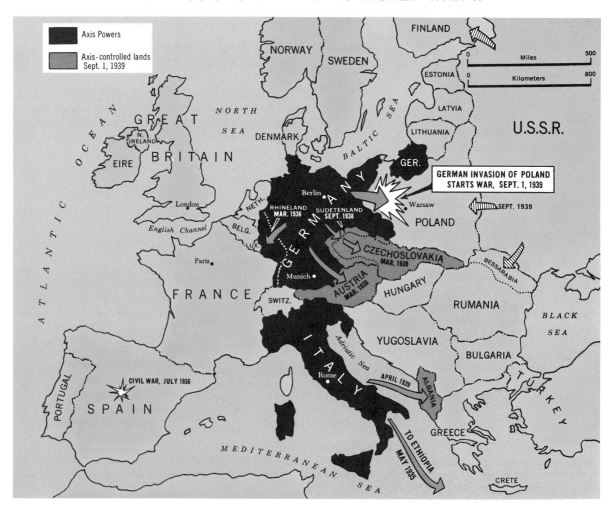

There on September 30, 1938, the four leaders signed a pact that gave Hitler almost all he demanded. The Czechs, forsaken by their friends, had no choice but to turn over most of the disputed region to Germany.

Neville Chamberlain, Prime Minister of Great Britain, returned to England blindly confident. He expressed the certainty that the Munich agreement had ended the threat of aggression in Europe. "I believe," he said, "it is peace for our tiem."

Other leaders did not share Chamberlain's confidence. They believed that his policy of appeasement would only lead Hitler to make further demands. Throughout Europe nation after nation tooled up to rearm themselves with greater speed.

Growing American concern. President Roosevelt viewed the events of 1938 with deepening concern. As early as January 28, in a special message to Congress, he coupled a promise to work for peace with a warning that it was time for the United States to build up its defenses. Congress increased appropriations for the armed forces and, in May, authorized more than $1 billion for a "two-ocean navy."

Roosevelt privately referred to the aggressions of Japan, Italy, and Germany as "armed banditry." Officially, however, the President sent personal notes to foreign rulers, including Hitler and Mussolini, urging them to settle their differences by negotiation and international cooperation. Since the United States was openly committed to a hands-off, isolationist policy, no one paid much attention to the President's words of caution.

Defending the Western Hemisphere. As the Czech crisis worsened, Roosevelt did make one commitment. In August 1938, in a speech to Canadians, he extended the protection of the Monroe Doctrine to Canada. He promised that "the people of the United States will not stand idly by if domination of Canadian soil is threatened by any other Empire."

Roosevelt's promise to Canada was only one of several steps the United States was taking to develop a defense policy for the nations of North and South America. Earlier, at the Buenos Aires Conference of 1936, the United States and the 20 other members of the Pan-American Union had agreed to regard a threat to any American country as a threat to the security of all. The 21 members also agreed to consult together if such a threat developed.

In December 1938, with the clouds of war rapidly gathering, the Pan-American Union met again in Lima, Peru. The delegates repeated their pledge to oppose foreign intervention in the Western Hemisphere.

Roosevelt's promise to Canada and the Declaration of Lima demonstrated that the Monroe Doctrine had become a multilateral, or many-sided, policy rather than a unilateral, or one-sided, policy. By 1938 it was clear, as Roosevelt said, that "national defense has now become a problem of continental defense."

New crises lead to World War II. On January 4, 1939, in his annual message to Congress, President Roosevelt warned that the world situation had become extremely grave. He urged greatly increased appropriations for the armed services. He also urged Congress to reconsider the neutrality legislation adopted during 1935–37.

The President's worst fears were soon confirmed. On March 15, 1939, Hitler's armies moved into the rest of Czechoslovakia. On April 7 Mussolini's troops invaded Albania (see map, page 670).

Awakening at long last to their common peril, Great Britain and France decided to stand firm. They announced that an attack upon Poland would mean war.

Great Britain and France also tried to get the Soviet Union to join with them in resisting, by force if necessary, any further aggression by either Hitler or Mussolini. It was with shock, therefore, that the domocratic nations learned on August 23, 1939, that the Soviet Union had just signed a nonagression pact with ots warring neighbor, Germany.

Seemingly freed by the Soviet pact from the danger of a two-front war, Hitler struck swiftly. On September 1, without warning, German bombers and powerful armored divisions crossed the border into Poland (see map page 670). On September 3, 1939, Great Britain and France declared war on Germany.

While Great Britain and France were busy mobilizing their armies, Soviet troops invaded Poland from the east. By the end of September, all organized Polish resistance had been crushed, and Germany and the Soviet Union divided Poland between them.

SOURCES

FRANKLIN D. ROOSEVELT'S "FOUR FREEDOMS" SPEECH (1941)

In the future days, which we seek to make secure, we look forward to a world founded upon four essential human freedoms.

The first is freedom of speech and expression—everywhere in the world.

The second is freedom of every person to worship God in his own way—everywhere in the world.

The third is freedom from want—which, translated into world terms, means economic understanding which will secure to every nation a healthy peacetime life for its inhabitants—everywhere in the world.

The fourth is freedom from fear—which, translated into world terms, means a worldwide reduction of armaments to such a point and in such a thorough fashion that no nation will be in a position to commit an act of physical aggression against any neighbor—anywhere in the world. . . .

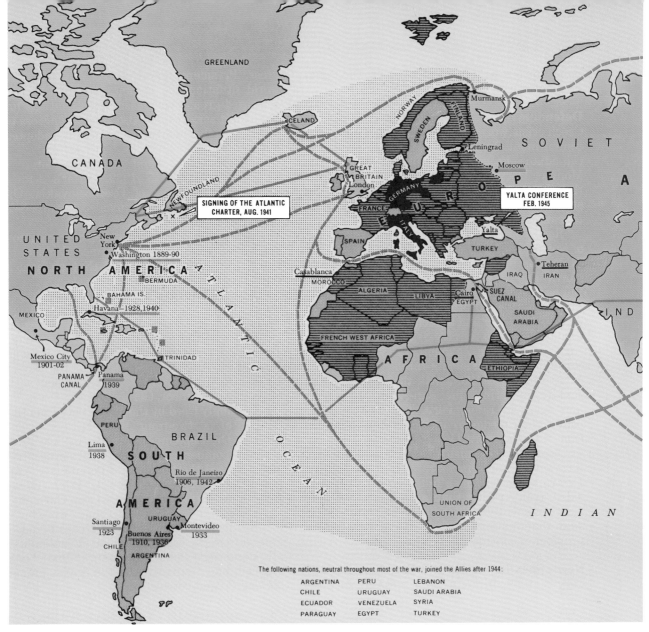

ARGENTINA	PERU	LEBANON
CHILE	URUGUAY	SAUDI ARABIA
ECUADOR	VENEZUELA	SYRIA
PARAGUAY	EGYPT	TURKEY

THE WORLD AT WAR: SEPTEMBER 1939 — AUGUST 1945

The Soviets then demanded and won the right to establish military and naval bases in Estonia, Latvia, and Lithuania, all independent republics at the time. (See map, page 670.) The Soviet Union also demanded the right to establish military bases on Finnish soil. Finland, too, was an independent republic. On November 30, after Finland refused to grant Soviet demands, the U.S.S.R. attacked its small neighbor. The Soviet government claimed that its actions were necessary to protect the Russian homeland from invasion.

Thus World War II started and began to spread across Europe.

SECTION SURVEY

IDENTIFY: Neville Chamberlain, Munich agreement, appeasement, Declaration of Lima, multilateral, unilateral, nonaggression pact.

1. How did the Spanish Civil War become an international event as well as an internal conflict?

2. (a) How did Neville Chamberlain view the Munich agreement? (b) Why did others have a different view?

3. (a) What actions did the United States take to prepare for the defense of North America? (b) How did these actions broaden the Monroe Doctrine?

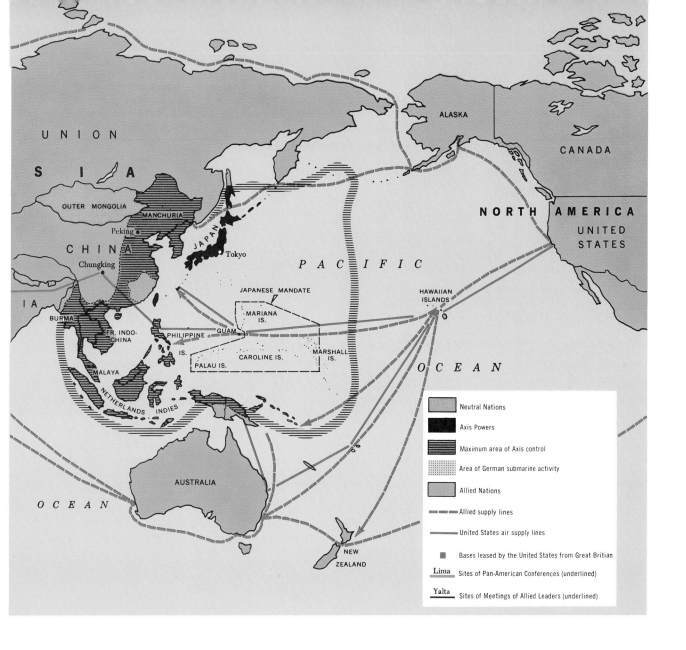

The legend on the map reads:

Neutral Nations
Axis Powers
Maximum area of Axis control
Area of German submarine activity
Allied Nations
Allied supply lines
United States air supply lines
Bases leased by the United States from Great Britian
Lima — Sites of Pan-American Conferences (underlined)
Yalta — Sites of Meetings of Allied Leaders (underlined)

4 The United States becomes involved in World War II

Although in 1939 Americans were overwhelmingly in favor of the Allies, they were determined to stay out of war. President Roosevelt voiced a widely shared feeling in a "fireside chat" over radio on September 3. He firmly announced, "As long as it remains in my power to prevent, there will be no blackout of peace in the United States."

Neutrality laws amended. On September 21, 1939, however, Roosevelt again urged Congress to amend the Neutrality Act of 1937. "I regret that Congress passed the Act. I regret equally that I signed the Act," he declared. Roosevelt pointed out that the existing embargo on the export of munitions actually favored Germany. If it were not for the embargo, Great Britain and France could use their control of the seas to secure from the United States the arms that they desperately needed. Adolf Hitler, did not need military equipment, for he had been preparing Nazi Germany for war for many years.

THE WAR AGAINST
THE JEWS

Our town is burning, brothers, burning. . . .
Don't look on with folded arms
While the fire spreads!

These lines from a Yiddish song describe the fate of thousands of Jewish communities in Europe after the Nazis rose to power in the 1930's. The fire in the song did spread, and millions died before it was put out.

From the beginning, Hitler based much of his Nazi message on anti-Semitism—the hatred of Jews—which had had a long history in Europe. Jews were blamed for every misfortune the Germans faced, especially their economic troubles after World War I. In 1933 the Nazis began a systematic program to settle the "Jewish problem" in Germany. Jews were deprived of their citizenship, forbidden to use public facilities, and gradually driven out of almost every type of work.

Thousands of Jews left Germany, some for other nations of Europe and some for the United States. (The best-known American immigrant was physicist Albert Einstein.) However, escape soon became almost impossible. One factor was the war itself. After it began in the fall of 1939, movement was extremely difficult. At the same time, Hitler's war against the Jews was extended to all the territories occupied by the Germans. Another factor was the reluctance of Allied nations to accept refugees. The United States held strictly to its immigration quotas and took in only about 100,000. England accepted 80,000, and Latin America only about half that number.

Some 8 million Jews were trapped in Europe —from Russia in the east to France in the west, from Norway in the north to Greece in the south. First they were isolated in ghettos or sent to concentration camps as forced laborers. In 1942 began what the Nazis called the "final solution"—extermination. (Actually, thousands of Jews had already died.) At special camps, such as Auschwitz and Treblinka in Poland, hundreds of thousands were mercilessly gassed and cremated.

Six million Jews died in what has come to be remembered as the Holocaust. (Another 6 million—gypsies, political prisoners, and prisoners of war—also perished in the camps.) Before they died, many of these victims of Nazi brutality sang this song:

Our brothers across the ocean
Cannot feel our bitter pain. . . .
Rivers of tears will flow,
When they will find some day
The biggest grave in the world
In Treblinka, in Treblinka.

After a six-week debate, Congress finally agreed on a compromise proposal. The new law abolished the arms embargo and allowed any country to buy weapons or munitions from the United States, provided that the goods were transported to that country on foreign ships. This new neutrality law, which went into effect on November 4, 1939, greatly helped the Allied nations resisting Hitler.

Declaration of Panama. While Congress debated the problem of neutrality, the delegates to the Pan-American Union issued a declaration. It warned all belligerent war vessels to stay out of a "safety zone" around the Americas roughly 300 to 1,000 miles (480 to 1,600 kilo-

meters) wide. Germany, Great Britain, and France challenged this declaration. They claimed that no nation or group of nations had the right to close any part of the high seas to their ships. The declaration was nevertheless an important indication of cooperation among the nations of the Western Hemisphere.

The fall of France. While Hitler carried on his **blitzkrieg**, or "lightning war," against Poland in 1939, the French mobilized. They prepared for an attack against the Maginot (mah·zhee·NOH) Line—the chain of forts along the eastern frontier. But Hitler did not attack. People joked about the "phony war," calling it a "sitzkrieg," or sitting war.

674

Great Britain and France declared war on Germany after Hitler invaded Poland in 1939. Here, German soldiers fire at snipers in the Polish capital of Warsaw. Scenes like this became common all across Europe in the next five years.

On April 9, 1940, the joking ceased as Hitler demonstrated the true meaning of "blitzkrieg." In the following weeks, his powerful armored divisions, supported by fighter planes and bombers, rapidly overran Denmark, Norway, the Netherlands, Belgium, Luxembourg, and northern France (see map, pages 684–85). On May 26 the British began a heroic evacuation of their troops from the beaches of Dunkirk, a seaport in northern France. Although the British were forced to leave much of their equipment, they succeeded in saving most of the troops. On June 10 Italy, sensing that France was doomed, declared war on France and Great Britain.

Hitler's blitzkrieg did not halt until June 22, 1940, when France signed an armistice with Germany. In London the French National Committee pledged continued resistance by the Free French under General Charles de Gaulle. The French nationalists began to rally parts of the French colonial empire against the Nazis. Meanwhile, Marshal Pétain (pay·TAN) became the leader of a German-controlled French government. Headquarters for the occupation government was at Vichy (vee·SHEE) in central France (see map, pages 684–85).

The Battle of Britain. With the fall of France, Great Britain stood alone and almost defenseless. On May 10, 1940, Winston Churchill replaced Neville Chamberlain as Prime Minister of Great Britain. With a rare gift for leadership, Churchill rallied the British people, strengthening their hopes and their will to fight. Churchill promised that the British would never surrender. If by chance Great Britain itself were to fall, he declared, "then our Empire beyond the seas, armed and guarded by the British fleet, would carry on the struggle until, in God's good time, the New World, with all its power and might, steps forth to the rescue and liberation of the Old."

By the end of June, with France under Nazi control, Churchill prepared his people for the coming Battle of Britain. "Hitler knows that he will have to break us in this island or lose the war," Churchill said. "If we can stand up to him, all Europe may be free and the life of the world may move forward into broad, sunlit uplands. But if we fail, then the whole world, including the United States, including all that we have known and cared for, will sink into the abyss of a new Dark Age. . . . Let us therefore brace ourselves to our duties, and so bear our-

"We shall defend our island, whatever the cost may be . . . ; we shall never surrender." This was Prime Minister Winston Churchill's pledge to the people of Great Britain. Here, in 1940, Churchill gives his famous "V for victory" sign.

selves that, if the British Empire and its Commonwealth last for a thousand years, men will still say, 'This was their finest hour.' "

The supreme test for the British came in the late summer of 1940. In August Hitler unleashed his fighters and bombers against Great Britain. The Royal Navy fought back furiously. The Royal Air Force, though almost hopelessly outnumbered, flew day and night, sometimes shooting down as many as 100 Nazi bombers in a single 24-hour period. In October, advised by his military chiefs that an attempt to invade Great Britain would be suicidal, Hitler postponed his invasion plan.

"Never in the field of human conflict," Churchill declared "was so much owed by so many to so few." The proud leader was referring, of course, to the Royal Air Force.

American defense measures. During the summer and fall of 1940, the United States was strengthening its own defenses.

Many Americans feared the possibility of subversive activities. To guard against such activities, Congress passed the Alien Registration Act, commonly known as the Smith Act. This law reinforced legislation controlling aliens and made it illegal for any person in the United States to advocate the overthrow of the government by force or violence or to belong to an organization that advocated the violent overthrow of the government.

In July Secretary of State Hull and the foreign ministers of the other American nations gathered in Havana, Cuba. They drew up plans for preventing Germany from seizing the Western Hemisphere colonies of the countries it had conquered. The Act of Havana stated that the moment any colony was in danger, the American republics, acting singly or collectively, would take control of the colony. From then until the end of the war, the colony would be governed by a group of trustees from the American republics.

Two weeks later President Roosevelt met with Prime Minister Mackenzie King of Canada. At this meeting the two leaders created a Permanent Joint Board of Defense to plan for the "defense of the north half of the Western Hemisphere."

In 1940 Congress furiously debated the pros and cons of the first peacetime draft in American history. The Burke-Wadsworth Act was finally passed and signed by President Roosevelt on September 16, 1940. The law required all men between 21 and 35 to register for the draft. It also made them liable for one year of military training.

Roosevelt's Lend-Lease proposal. By the end of 1940, American supplies were flowing to Great Britain and America's defense program was gathering momentum. Still, Roosevelt was worried that the British could not afford much longer to pay cash for needed war materials. In his annual message to Congress, Roosevelt declared, "Our country is going to be what our people have proclaimed it to be—the arsenal of democracy." Roosevelt proposed that the United States increase greatly its production of military equipment so that it could lend or lease to the British and to the other Allies any materials needed to carry on the fight.

Roosevelt's Lend-Lease proposal provoked a storm of controversy. Many people agreed with the President that the Lend-Lease proposal offered the best hope of avoiding full-fledged participation in the war. Others, including the isolationists, were sure that Lend-Lease would involve America in a shooting war.

Congress finally passed the Lend-Lease Act in March 1941. It appropriated an initial sum of $7 billion for ships, planes, tanks, and anything else that the Allies needed. When on June 22, 1941, Hitler's armies invaded the Soviet Union despite the German-Russian nonaggression pact, the United States made Lend-Lease materials available to the U.S.S.R.

The Battle of the Atlantic. The Lend-Lease arrangement inevitably drew the United States closer to war. By the spring of 1941, German and Italian submarines were turning the North Atlantic into a graveyard of ships. In April American naval vessels began to trail enemy submarines, radioing their location to British warships. In July American troops occupied Iceland (see map, pages 672–73) to prevent its occupation by Germany.

In September Roosevelt issued "shoot-on-sight" orders to American warships operating in the "safety zone" established back in 1939. American warships also began to accompany and protect, or **convoy**, merchant vessels as far as Iceland. In November Congress voted to allow American merchant vessels to enter combat areas. Roosevelt armed the merchant vessels and provided them with gun crews.

The Atlantic Charter. In 1941 the United States was moving rapidly toward undeclared war with Germany. That August, Roosevelt and Churchill met to discuss the larger issues involved in the conflict. At this meeting the two leaders drew up a broad statement of war aims that came to be called the Atlantic Charter.

Like Woodrow Wilson's Fourteen Points, the Atlantic Charter listed a number of common principles for building a lasting peace and a better world. In the Atlantic Charter, Roosevelt and Churchill pledged themselves to work for a world free of aggression, a world in which every nation, large or small, would have the right to adopt its own form of government. Once the aggressors were crushed, the Charter declared, all nations had to work together to free all people everywhere from the burden of fear and want.

Growing threat from Japan. While war raged in Europe, Japan was adding to its conquests in the Far East. In July 1941, Japanese troops occupied French Indochina (see map, pages 696–97). Thoroughly alarmed, President Roosevelt immediately froze all Japanese assets in the United States. He also placed an embargo on the shipment of gasoline, machine tools, scrap iron, and steel to Japan. Japan promptly retaliated by freezing all American assets in areas under its control. As a result, trade between the United States and Japan practically ended. Then in August the United States sent a Lend-Lease mission to China.

The Japanese were convinced that American resistance was stiffening. They began to make plans for an attack upon the United States. Even as its war leaders made the final preparations, however, the Japanese government sent a "peace" mission to Washington. On November 20, 1941, this mission demanded that the United States (1) unfreeze Japanese assets, (2) supply Japan with as much gasoline as it needed, and (3) cease all aid to China. The

The Japanese bombed the base at Pearl Harbor on the morning of December 7, 1941. The attack ended America's long period of isolationism and thrust the surprised nation headlong into the war that now spanned the entire globe.

United States refused to meet these demands but offered several counterproposals.

Pearl Harbor and war. On Sunday, December 7, 1941, the Japanese mission announced that further negotiations were useless. The Japanese said that the United States had failed "to display in the slightest degree a spirit of conciliation."

That morning, even before Japan's reply had been delivered to the American government, Japanese planes attacked without warning the United States fleet anchored in the huge American naval and air base at Pearl Harbor, in Hawaii (see map, pages 696–97). The Americans lost almost all of their planes and eight battleships and suffered the partial destruction of several other naval units. More than 2,000 soldiers, sailors, and civilians were killed, and almost 2,000 more were wounded. The same day the Japanese also attacked Wake, Midway, Guam, the Philippine Islands, and other American bases.

Shocked and angered, Americans almost unanimously supported President Roosevelt the next day when he asked Congress for a declaration of war against Japan. The Senate declared war unanimously, the House with only one dissenting vote. Great Britain and the governments-in-exile that had fled their countries when Hitler conquered them also immediately declared war against Japan. Three days later, on December 11, Germany and Italy declared that a state of war with the United States existed, whereupon Congress declared war upon those two countries.

SECTION SURVEY

IDENTIFY: Declaration of Panama, blitzkrieg, Charles de Gaulle, Marshal Pétain, Winston Churchill, Smith Act, Act of Havana, "arsenal of democracy," Lend-Lease, convoy, Atlantic Charter, Pearl Harbor.

1. How did the United States' arms embargo aid the aggressor nations?
2. What actions did the United States take to prepare for the possibility of war?
3. Trace the events that led to the Japanese attack on Pearl Harbor.
4. Map Study: Study the map on pages 672–73. (a) Locate the Axis Powers. (b) Where did Churchill and Roosevelt meet to sign the Atlantic Charter? (c) Trace the area protected by the Declaration of Panama.

678

Chapter Survey

During the 1930's the curtain began to rise upon one of the greatest tragedies of the modern world. The tragedy started with the Great Depression, which plunged millions of people all over the world into unemployment, confusion, and unrest. Then, in the middle 1930's, the armies of Japan, Italy, and Germany began to march across the troubled face of the earth, leaving death and destruction behind them. Before 1941 drew to a close, most of the nations of the world were involved in the most terrible conflict in human history.

The overwhelming majority of the American people were at first determined to remain out of the war. They supported Congress when it enacted neutrality legislation in 1935, 1936, and 1937. However, as the dictators crushed their weaker neighbors, Americans realized that the democratic way of life and the fate of free people everywhere were in danger. More and more, the Americans saw that by helping other nations to resist aggression, the United States would strengthen democracy and protect itself.

By 1939, when World War II broke out in Europe, the United States had begun to reverse its policy of isolationism. During the next two years, neutrality was abandoned as the United States became "the arsenal of democracy." American ships carried cargoes of war materials to Great Britain, the Soviet Union, and China. America's navy, air force, and army were strengthened with feverish speed. Then, on December 7, 1941, the Japanese struck at Pearl Harbor. The curtain had finally risen. The United States was at war.

Inquiring into History

1. How was the Great Depression related to the rise of dictatorships during the 1930's?
2. How were nationalism, imperialism, and belief in racial superiority related to the causes of World War II?
3. In 1938 the Latin-American nations became partners with the United States in enforcing the Monroe Doctrine. (a) Explain. (b) What steps led to this partnership?
4. Munich has become a symbol of the policy of appeasement. (a) What does this statement mean? (b) How did appeasement help lead to World War II?
5. (a) Why did many Americans believe in isolationism during the 1930's? (b) Why did that attitude start to change by the late 1930's?

Relating Past to Present

1. Do you think America's dealings with other nations today have been affected in any way by what was learned from the events leading to World War II? Explain.

2. Why might it be necessary to recognize a country's government, even if the United States does not approve of that government's policies?

Developing Social Science Skills

1. Draw a timeline for the years 1931 to 1939. (a) Below the line list the international events that led to World War II. (b) Above the line list United States actions or foreign policy decisions. (c) Find examples of actions on the top part of the timeline that led to actions on the bottom part.
2. Read the source on page 671. (a) What were the Four Freedoms? (b) Why might Roosevelt have given this speech? (c) To whom might he have been speaking? Explain.
3. (a) List the events that finally led to the outbreak of World War II. (b) On the map on page 670, locate the nations affected by these events. (c) Which nations were under Axis control by September 1, 1939? (d) Study the map on pages 672–73. What other European nations eventually came under Axis control? (e) Compare the map to a world atlas. What Mediterranean Islands were part of the Axis alliance? Can you say why?

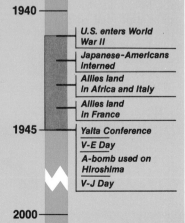

1915 ——

1920 ——

1925 ——

1930 ——

1935 ——

1940 ——

U.S. enters World War II

Japanese-Americans Interned

Allies land In Africa and Italy

Allies land In France

1945 ——

Yalta Conference

V-E Day

A-bomb used on Hiroshima

V-J Day

2000 ——

Chapter 36

Americans in the Second World War

1941–1945

World War II had been under way a little more than two years when on December 7, 1941, Japan's savage blow at Pearl Harbor plunged America into the conflict.

America's enemies had the great advantage of what military leaders call "interior lines of supply and communication." Germany, Italy, and Japan were so situated geographically that the supply lines from their farms and factories to the fighting fronts were relatively short.

The United States and its allies, on the other hand, had to establish and protect supply lines that often stretched thousands of miles across sea and land to fighting forces in far-off areas of the earth.

America's enemies had an even greater advantage. They had been preparing for war for many years. During these years they had raised and trained huge armies and converted their factories to the production of war materials. They had built up vast supplies of rifles, machine guns, tanks, planes, and other instruments of modern warfare.

The United States, on the other hand, had not really begun to prepare for war until the summer of 1940. Even then preparations had been limited. Indeed, it was America's lack of preparation that led Hitler, Mussolini, and the Japanese war leaders to believe that they could win the war before the United States could mobilize its enormous resources.

Faced by such overwhelming odds, the American people grimly entered the conflict.

THE CHAPTER IN OUTLINE

1. The Allies overcome early disasters and begin an offensive.

2. Americans accept controls and win the "battle of production."

3. The Allies gradually fight their way to victory in Europe.

4. Allied victories in the Pacific bring an end to World War II.

The Allies overcome early disasters and begin an offensive

Throughout most of 1942, while Americans were desparately trying to convert to a war-time economy, the United States and its allies suffered a series of almost unrelieved disasters in every theater of the war.

Disaster in the Pacific. The scene at Pearl Harbor on the evening of December 7, 1941, was one of nearly total destruction. America's offensive power in the Pacific had been wiped out by the Japanese surprise attack.

The Japanese soon struck again in the Pacific. By the end of December, Japan had seized the American islands of Guam and Wake and captured the British colony of Hong Kong. They had also launched attacks upon Thailand, British Malaya, and the American-controlled Philippine and Midway islands (see map, pages 696–97).

The new year brought a mounting fury of destruction. Japanese conquests covered a widening area of the Pacific and Far East (see map, pages 696–97). On January 2, 1942, Japanese troops poured into Manila, capital of the Philippines. On January 11 the Japanese invaded Borneo and Celebes (SEL·eh·beez) in the Netherlands Indies. On February 15 the advancing tide of Japanese troops overran the British naval base at Singapore. Later in the month, in the Battle of the Java Sea, a Japanese naval force delivered a crushing blow to a fleet of American, British, Dutch, and Australian warships.

By the end of March, the Japanese had conquered most of the Netherlands Indies with its rich supplies of oil, tin, rubber, quinine, and other vital war materials. They had also seized Rangoon, Burma, and were driving British, Indian, and Chinese troops out of Burma.

In the Philippines, a small force of Americans and Filipinos under General Douglas MacArthur continued their heroic but hopeless resistance against the Japanese. In January 1942 Manila surrendered, and MacArthur's forces retired to the Bataan Peninsula. In March MacArthur himself was ordered to Australia to take command of the Allied forces in the South Pacific. Fighting against over-whelming odds, the hungry, sick, exhausted survivors on Bataan were captured on April 9. On May 6 the outnumbered and starving troops on the fortress of Corregidor guarding Manila Bay surrendered. The Japanese also cut the Burma Road, destroying the last land route to China (see map, pages 696–97).

Thus by the end of May 1942, less than six months after their attack on Pearl Harbor, the Japanese had overcome almost all opposition. They were poised to strike west at India, south at Australia, and east through Hawaii at the Pacific coast of the United States.

American gains in the Pacific. Despite some opposition at home, the United States accepted the British argument that the defeat of Hitler in Europe had to be the first Allied objective. However, the war in the Pacific proved to be more than a mere holding operation.

Japan suffered its first serious reverse early in May 1942. Carrier-based planes from a British-American naval force caught a Japanese fleet moving southward in the Coral Sea, off the northeastern coast of Australia. The planes sank or severely damaged more than 30 Japanese warships.

Japanese forces received another setback early in June 1942 when they launched a two-pronged seaborne attack on the Aleutian Islands and Hawaii. The ultimate Japanese objective was an invasion of the United States. American forces stopped the northern campaign, but only after Japanese troops had occupied the Aleutian islands of Attu and Kiska (see map, pages 696–97). American naval forces were able to block the southern campaign by defeating the Japanese in a major battle off the island of Midway.

Turning the tide in the Pacific. There are several reasons why the United States began to stem the Japanese tide. First, early in 1942 the United States and Great Britain had pooled their resources to create a unified Pacific command. Second, the American people were beginning to win the important "battle of production" at home. The products of the nation's farms and factories were pouring into Pacific supply depots and forward bases. Finally, time had been gained by the courageous resistance of Americans and Filipinos on Bataan and Corregidor.

On August 7, 1942, the United States undertook its first major offensive action when marines stormed ashore at Guadalcanal in the Solomon Islands (see map, pages 696–97). For four desperate months, American marines and army troops clung to a toehold around Guadalcanal's airport. They repelled savage attacks from the air, from the sea, and from the surrounding jungle.

In November the Japanese made a desperate effort to regain their former bases in the Solomons, which they needed to carry out their planned invasion of Australia. Admiral William F. Halsey intercepted the huge Japanese fleet and in a furious battle on November 12–15 completely routed the Japanese. The island of Guadalcanal was at last secure. The tide of battle in the Pacific had turned in the Allies' favor.

Disaster in Europe. The situation in the Atlantic and in Europe during most of 1942 was grave. German and Italian submarines in the Atlantic sank ships more rapidly than the United States and Great Britain could build new ones. Great Britain, now an isolated fortress in the Atlantic, could not hold out much longer unless reinforcements arrived and unless the devastating Nazi bombings were stopped.

On the continent of Europe, the tide of Axis conquest was rolling with terrifying speed. Yugoslavia fell to the Axis powers. The Greeks had been reduced to near starvation. The Soviet Union had lost its rich grainfields in the Ukraine region, and many Soviet industrial centers had been ruined. Part of the destruction was done by the Soviet people themselves. As they retreated before the Germans, they applied a "scorched-earth" policy to their land, destroying everything that they could not carry with them.

Despite Soviet resistance, the Nazi divisions rolled on in the summer offensive of 1942. The Germans overran the oil fields of the Caucasus and rumbled into the outskirts of Stalingrad on the Volga River (see map, pages 684–85). Beyond lay the Ural Mountains, where the Soviet people were feverishly building new industries to help in the war effort.

An American naval officer painted this picture of U. S. marines as they spearheaded the invasion of the Pacific island of Bougainville in 1943. By capturing this Japanese stronghold in the Solomons, the marines gave the Allies yet another stepping-stone on the path that would lead to Japan.

The Allies were able to turn the tables on the Axis forces in part because of the injection of U. S. manpower and materials into the war effort. Here, guarded by U. S. warships, a huge convoy moves toward an Allied battlefront.

In the Mediterranean the Axis forces were triumphant everywhere. German and Italian aircraft with bases in Italy, Greece, the Greek island of Crete, and North Africa all but forced British naval craft out of the Mediterranean. They thus denied the British the use of the Suez Canal route to the Indian Ocean. Great Britain was compelled to send its ships thousands of miles around Africa to reach Egypt, the Middle East, and India. By the autumn of 1942, the German *Afrika Korps* under General Erwin Rommel had advanced to the frontiers of Egypt. There the well-trained corps stood poised for a final thrust at the Suez Canal and the oil fields of the Middle East.

Allied victories. November 1942 marked a turning point of the war. In the Pacific, as you have read, the three-day naval battle of Guadalcanal started the Allies on their long drive toward Tokyo. In North Africa British General Bernard L. Montgomery caught Rommel by surprise late in October at El Alamein in Egypt and drove him back across the desert into Libya toward eventual defeat.

On November 8 a mighty invasion fleet led by General Dwight D. Eisenhower landed thousands of British, Canadian, and American troops on the northern coast of Africa (see map, pages 684–85). On November 19 the Soviet troops began to encircle the German forces at Stalingrad. Within several weeks the Soviet troops overwhelmed the Germans at Stalingrad and forced them to surrender.

"This is not the end," Winston Churchill said in November 1942. "It is not even the beginning of the end. But it is, perhaps, the end of the beginning." Subsequent events justified Churchill's reassuring words. Before 1942 was over, the Allies held the initiative in Europe, as in the Pacific.

Wartime cooperation. How had the Allies been able to survive the earlier disasters? Why were they able in November 1942 to begin to seize the initiative? One answer is that the tremendous combination of America's human resources and war materials was beginning to have its effect. Another answer is that in their struggle the Allies were working as a team.

On January 1, 1942, the 26 Allied nations, calling themselves the **United Nations°**, issued a joint declaration. The countries (1) promised full cooperation in the war effort, (2) agreed not to make a separate peace, and (3) endorsed the war aims outlined in the Atlantic Charter by Churchill and Roosevelt (page 677).

Early in 1941, as you recall, even before the United States had entered the war, Congress laid the basis for cooperation among the Allies with the Lend-Lease program (page 677). After the attack on Pearl Harbor, the aid program went into high gear. The United States shipped immense quantities of war materials across the submarine-infested sea routes to its allies in the Pacific and to Great Britain, the U.S.S.R., and the British armies in Egypt and the Middle East. Before the war ended, Lend-Lease aid reached more than $50 billion. Of this total 69 percent went to Great Britain, about 25 percent to the U.S.S.R., and small quantities to other Allies.

Text continues on page 686.

°**United Nations:** The wartime Allies called themselves the United Nations. When in 1945 they formed a permanent organization, they continued to use this same name for that organization.

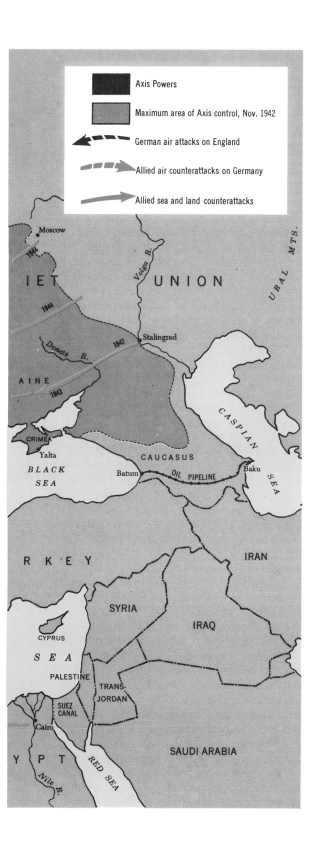

WORLD WAR II IN EUROPE

Dark days for the Allies

1939

SEPT.–OCT. German invasion and conquest of Poland.

1940

APR.–JUNE German invasion of Denmark, Norway, Luxembourg, Belgium, Netherlands, France.

MAY British evacuation from Dunkirk.

JUNE–JULY Fall of France; establishment of Vichy government.

AUG.–OCT. Battle of Britain (German air attacks).

OCT. Axis aggressions in Balkans.

NOV.– British offensive in Mediterranean and
FEB. 1941 North Africa.

1941

FEB.–MAY Battle of the Atlantic begins.

MAR.–APR. Axis counteroffensive in North Africa.

APR.–JUNE German invasion of Greece, Yugoslavia, Crete.

JUNE German invasion of U.S.S.R. begins.

Allied gains: the tide turns

1942

MAY–AUG. Allied air attacks on Germany begin.

OCT.–NOV. Allied counteroffensive in North Africa begins.

NOV.– Russian counteroffensives in U.S.S.R.;
MAR. 1943 German surrender of Stalingrad.

1943

MAY Allied victory in North Africa; end of African campaign.

JULY–AUG. Allied invasion of Sicily.

JULY– Russians drive Germans back in U.S.S.R.
JAN. 1944 and enter Poland.

SEPT. Allies begin Italian campaigns.

SEPT. 8 Italy surrenders.

1944

JUNE 6 Allied invasion along Normandy coast (Operation Overlord).

AUG. Allied forces land in southern France.

AUG. 25 Allies liberate Paris.

SEPT. Allies liberate Belgium, Luxembourg.

SEPT. Battle for Germany begins.

SEPT.–DEC. Russians conquer Yugoslavia and Hungary.

DEC. Battle of the Bulge (last German counteroffensive).

Allied victory in Germany

1945

FEB.–APR. Allied invasion of Germany.

MAY 7 Germany surrenders.

MAY 8 V-E Day (end of war in Europe).

Lend-Lease was not a one-way arrangement. During the war the United States received in exchange goods and services valued at nearly $8 billion, most of which came from Great Britain. For example, when the American air forces began to arrive in England, the British provided bases, housing, and equipment. The Lend-Lease program was an outstanding example of Allied cooperation.

Cooperative planning. Joint planning of strategy was an even more decisive Allied effort. Shortly after the attack on Pearl Harbor, Prime Minister Churchill and a group of military, naval, and technical aides met in Washington, D.C., with General George C. Marshall, Chief of Staff of the Army, and the commanders of America's air, land, and sea forces. This meeting was the first of a series held by the Allied military leaders.

These conferences required a tremendous spirit of give-and-take. Final decisions were not always popular with all concerned. For example, the Soviets, hard-pressed in the summer of 1942, urged their Allies to relieve the pressure on the Soviet Union in Eastern Europe by opening a second front in Western Europe. Roosevelt and American military leaders finally agreed with Churchill that the Allies were not sufficiently prepared to do this. They decided instead to land troops in North Africa, where they could strike at southern Europe. Despite such differences among the Allies, the high degree of cooperation achieved was indispensable to the final victory.

SECTION SURVEY

IDENTIFY: Douglas MacArthur, William Halsey, "scorched-earth" policy, *Afrika Korps*, Erwin Rommel, Bernard Montgomery, Dwight D. Eisenhower, United Nations.

1. November 1942 marked a turning point of the war. Why?

2. How did the Lend-Lease program help both the United States and its allies?

3. (a) Why was Allied cooperation so important in winning the war? (b) In what specific ways did the Allies cooperate?

4. Map Study: Study the map on pages 684–85. (a) Locate the Axis countries. (b) In November 1942, which countries were under Axis control? (c) How does the map illustrate the fact that 1941 to mid-1942 were dark days for the Allies?

2 Americans accept controls and win the "battle of production"

The Allied victories were won on the farms and in the factories of the Allied nations as well as on the fighting fronts. By the end of 1942, the United States in particular had made itself "the arsenal of democracy."

Hitler's errors. When Hitler declared war upon the United States, he had already made two grave mistakes. First, he had failed to conquer Great Britain. He might have done this if he had launched an invasion immediately after the British armies lost most of their equipment at Dunkirk. Second, his surprise attack upon the U.S.S.R. in June 1941 and his failure to take Moscow led to the disaster of his troops at Stalingrad.

On December 11, 1941, Hitler made a third major mistake by declaring war upon the United States. He failed to realize how swiftly the American people could convert their peacetime industries to war production.

America's soaring production. One of the amazing demonstrations of America's productivity took place on the nation's farms. Despite the fact that 2 million agricultural workers served in the armed forces, farmers managed to raise record-breaking crops. They raised enough food to supply the American people as well as their Allies.

The output of America's mines and factories was equally impressive. For example, between July 1940 and July 1945, United States manufacturing plants produced 296,601 military planes, including about 97,000 bombers; 86,388 tanks; 88,077 scout cars and carriers; 16,438 armored cars; 2.4 million trucks; 991,299 light vehicles, such as jeeps; 123,707 tractors; 17.4 million rifles and side arms; 2.7 million machine guns; 315,000 pieces of artillery; and 41.4 billion rounds of ammunition.

In addition, America's shipbuilders created the greatest navy and merchant marine the world had ever seen. By 1943 five ocean-going vessels were being launched every 24 hours.

All in all, production during the war years was 75 percent greater than in peacetime. According to Donald M. Nelson, first chief of the

WOMEN IN THE COCKPIT

One afternoon at an Air Force base in Florida, a fighter pilot awaited his new plane, due to be ferried in from the factory. There was a heavy overcast.

Then we heard it. The apron sort of filled up with guys who wouldn't admit they were worried, of course. But they did want to see what was coming in through this stuff. Sure enough, a *Thunderbolt* broke out at about 500 feet, made a smooth turn to the end of the runway and rolled to as pretty a stop . . . as I ever saw. . . . I ran up to the wing and out stepped the teeny-weeniest little girl I ever saw in my life. . . . She had kind of a tired grin. "Your plane, captain?"

The "girl" (in the 1940's women were commonly called "girls" until they were elderly) was a member of the Women's Airforce Service Pilots, or WASP. She and others like her were constantly proving to astonished men that airplane controls responded as well to a woman's touch as to a man's.

The WASP, organized in 1942 by racing flier Jacqueline Cochran, trained about a thousand women. Their purpose was to free men for combat duty. A major WASP task was ferrying planes from factories to military bases. Its pilots also made weather flights and towed targets for aerial gunnery training.

In spite of their qualifications and excellent safety record, women in the WASP fought an uphill battle. They were never paid as much as men doing the same work and were never incorporated into the Air Force. By the end of 1944, when the shortage of male trainees had ended, the WASP was disbanded. Its members had made an important wartime contribution, however. They had also proved decisively, in the words of one woman flier, that "all a good airplane needs to fly it is a good pilot."

War Production Board, created in January 1942, "American industry turned out more goods for war than we ever produced for our peacetime needs—yet had enough power left over to keep civilian standards of living astonishingly high."

Financing the war. Where did the money come from to finance the war? A little more than one third came from taxes, which were raised to the highest level in American history. The government borrowed the remainder, chiefly by selling huge issues of bonds. Because of this borrowing, the national debt shot upward from about $49 billion in 1941 to nearly $259 billion by the spring of 1945.

The dollar cost of the war was staggering. By 1945, military expenditures totaled $400 billion. This was twice the sum that the federal government had spent for all of its activities, including all wars, between 1789 and 1940!

Government agencies. In its efforts to organize the war effort and to mobilize the nation's resources, the federal government created a complex network of agencies.

At the top there was a policy-making board called the Office of War Mobilization (OWM). Its job was to unify the activities of the many war agencies.

Just below the OWM was the War Production Board (WPB). This board affected the daily lives of nearly every man, woman, and child in the United States. The WPB controlled the allocations of raw materials to industrial plants. It searched the country for scrap iron and the nation's kitchens for fats, tin, and aluminum. It directed the conversion of factories from peacetime to wartime production and stimulated the construction of new plants.

In addition, the WPB restricted the production of all consumer goods that required materials necessary to the war effort. It rationed

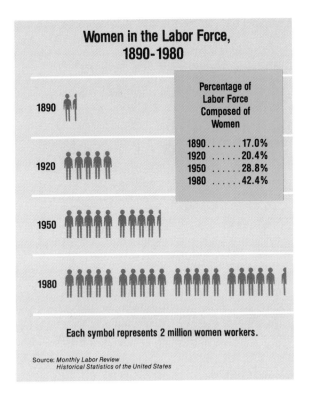

Women in the Labor Force, 1890-1980

Percentage of Labor Force Composed of Women
1890 . . . . .17.0%
1920 . . . . . . .20.4%
1950 . . . . . . .28.8%
1980 . . . . . . .42.4%

Each symbol represents 2 million women workers.

Source: *Monthly Labor Review*
Historical Statistics of the United States

gasoline to conserve oil and rubber. It even controlled clothing styles to save wool, cotton, rayon, and other vital materials.

To prevent transportation shortages and bottlenecks, the federal government also created the War Shipping Administration and the Office of Defense Transportation. These agencies supervised the railroads, express services, and shipping. The result was that supplies and troops moved efficiently over land and sea.

Mobilizing human resources. The Office of War Information bolstered the morale of the armed forces and of civilians by publicizing the achievements of war production. It also gained support for Allied war aims by broadcasting them in dozens of languages to people all over the world.

The War Manpower Commission (WMC) discouraged men and women from working in nonessential occupations. By 1945 it had channeled nearly 30 million wage earners into the war production effort, including 12 million black American workers and 50,000 Indian workers. By 1943 the labor force included 2 million women working in war plants, replac-

ing men who had left to serve in the nation's armed services.

The WMC also operated the Selective Service System. By the end of the war, the Selective Service had drafted nearly 10 million out of the more than 15 million Americans who served in the armed forces. Included were more than 350,000 Mexican Americans and 1 million black Americans, among them both volunteers and draftees. Despite black protests, official military policy required blacks to serve in segregated units, as in previous wars. In 1944–45, however, some white and black troops in Europe were integrated to meet an emergency situation.

Also included in the armed forces were about 25,000 Indian volunteers. Among tribes with warrior traditions, the rate of enlistment was high. In general, the Indian volunteers enjoyed the respect of their white and black fellow soldiers. Indian soldiers who returned to the reservations after the war took back with them new ideas to their families and their tribal communities.

For the first time the American armed forces, which had previously used women only as nurses, accepted women in uniform to replace men in noncombatant jobs. More than 250,000 women entered the army (as Wacs), the Coast Guard (as Spars), the Navy (as Waves), and the Marine Corps. As full-fledged military personnel, women worked as machinists, storekeepers, office workers, radio operators, and drivers of jeeps and trucks. The performance of women in the armed forces and in the nation's war plants did much to break down prejudices about what women could and could not do.

Government price control. One of the ways in which the government most closely regulated the lives of civilians was through price controls. In World War I, the shortage of consumer goods and the increased purchasing power of industrial and agricultural workers had driven prices skyward. This brought on inflation and caused suffering, especially among the poor.

The government was determined to prevent inflation in World War II. As a first step, the government raised income taxes. This drained off dollars that would otherwise have been spent on goods in the stores. As a second step, the government encouraged Americans to buy war bonds, arguing that such purchases were both a patriotic duty and a sound investment. However, these measures alone could not prevent inflation.

In 1942, following the example of European governments, Congress created the Office of Price Administration (OPA). The OPA established ceilings, or top limits, on prices and set up a **rationing** system. The OPA issued ration books containing coupons that purchasers had to use in addition to money to buy gasoline, fuel, shoes, coffee, sugar, fats and oils, meat, butter, and canned goods. The OPA also established rent controls.

Despite these efforts, the prices of consumer goods rose, especially food prices. By 1944 the cost of living had risen 30 percent above 1941 prewar levels. Some Americans violated the price control and rationing system by paying exorbitant prices to obtain more than their share of rationed products. Most Americans, however, accepted price controls and rationing as wartime necessities.

Control of wages and profits. Shortly after the attack on Pearl Harbor, the leaders of organized labor promised President Roosevelt that American workers would not strike during the war. At the same time, they insisted that the government had to ensure that workers would be fairly treated. By the spring of 1942, however, the cost of living had risen, and workers were becoming restless.

In July 1942 the National War Labor Board (NWLB) tried to work out a compromise. It granted a 15-percent wage increase to meet the rises in living costs. Several months later Congress and President Roosevelt authorized the NWLB to freeze the wages and salaries of all workers at the newly established levels.

For a time there was relatively little trouble. However, as prices continued to rise, labor again became restless, and here and there strikes broke out. In such instances the government usually stepped in and for the most part settled the disputes quickly.

The government also tried to regulate profits—mainly by means of taxation. Personal income taxes were greatly increased for people in the higher income brackets. The most drastic means of controlling profits was the excess profits tax, levied in 1940. This tax obliged corporations to pay to the government as much as 90 percent of all excess profits. Americans did not like government controls. Nevertheless, they accepted them with the understanding that they would be removed when the emergency was over.

The Japanese Americans. The upheaval in everyday life resulting from these controls and from the whole vast war effort revealed the extraordinary willingness of the American people to make sacrifices for the national emergency. Despite discomforts and sacrifices,

Hastily built tarpaper barracks were the new homes for Japanese Americans in 1942 when they were forced to leave their former homes and relocate in detention camps. This camp was set up in the desert near Manzanar, California.

the people maintained a remarkably high level of morale.

Americans also suffered deep anxieties and fears. However, these fears did not lead to the widespread repressions of minority groups that occurred in World War I. The tragic exception to this overall tolerance was the forced relocation of some 100,000 Americans of Japanese birth or parentage.

After the Japanese attack on Pearl Harbor, many Americans were genuinely fearful of a Japanese attack on the United States. This fear was soon turned against the **Nisei**—native-born Americans whose ancestors came from Japan. As a result, most Japanese Americans—the great majority of whom lived in California—were forced to leave their homes and were taken to detention camps in other states, where they were imprisoned until the end of the war. Most of the Nisei lost their homes and businesses. Yet there had never been any real proof that these Japanese Americans had been disloyal. Indeed, nearly all of the Nisei remained loyal, patriotic American citizens despite their harsh, unfair treatment. Many of those allowed to serve in the armed forces distinguished themselves for bravery.

After the war Americans regretted their unjustified actions against the Nisei. In 1945 the Nisei were permitted to leave the detention camps and settle wherever they wished. In 1948 Congress passed an act to help the Nisei recover a part of their losses.

Minorities in wartime. American minorities contributed not only to the fighting but to efforts on the home front as well. In 1941 President Roosevelt directed that a Fair Employment Practices Committee be set up to end discriminatory hiring policies in defense industries. As a result, the doors of the defense industries opened to minority workers.

Less was accomplished, however, in promoting equal housing opportunities in the overcrowded cities. Discrimination on the part of white Americans led to outbursts of violence and even riots in several cities. In Detroit in 1943, for example, federal troops restored order after 25 blacks and 9 whites died in a riot.

In 1942 the United States and Mexico signed a treaty. Under its terms thousands of Mexicans known as *braceros* entered the United States on a temporary basis as farm workers. Their efforts helped keep vital food production high during the war.

Prejudice and discrimination against Mexican Americans in jobs, housing, and recreation facilities also aroused bitter resentment. This resentment, reaching a boiling point in Los Angeles in 1943, erupted in a riot between servicemen and Mexican Americans.

Aware of their contributions to the war effort, blacks and other minorities became increasingly restless. As they listened to patriotic speeches about freedom for all, they became more determined to make these ideals meaningful for themselves.

SECTION SURVEY

IDENTIFY: OWM, WPB, WMC, Selective Service System, price controls, rationing, Nisei.

1. (a) Why did the federal government establish controls and regulations over many aspects of American life during the war? (b) What were some of these controls? (c) How did they affect individuals?

2. How did the following contribute to the war effort: (a) unions, (b) women, (c) minorities.

3. Graph Study: Examine the graph on page 688. (a) About how many women were in the labor force in 1920? in 1950? (b) What percentage of the labor force were women in 1920? in 1950? (c) What may have contributed to the changes?

3 The Allies gradually fight their way to victory in Europe

In the summer of 1942, as the tide of war was turning in favor of the Allies, President Roosevelt and Prime Minister Churchill decided to strike at what Churchill called the "soft underbelly" of the Axis.

Victory in North Africa. The opening blow, as you recall, fell late in October 1942, when the British broke through Rommel's lines at El Alamein and began to drive the Germans back into Libya. Meanwhile, on November 8, a force of 500 troop transports and 350 warships under General Eisenhower's command landed thousands of Allied troops in French Morocco and Algeria. The African offensive was the greatest combination of land, sea, and air forces brought together up to that time.

The loss of French areas in North Africa was a serious blow to the Germans. Although they continued to fight with great skill, their efforts were hopeless. Allied planes and ships cut their supply lines from Italy. General Montgomery's British Eighth Army drove steadily westward, while American forces moved eastward. Outnumbered and caught between the jaws of two enemy forces in Tunisia (see map, pages 684–85), the Germans and Italians surrendered early in May 1943.

In the victory in North Africa, the Allies captured more than 250,000 Axis troops. Far more important, the Allied nations now had control of the Mediterranean, their warships protected by planes based at airfields along the North African coast. The Allies could ship supplies to India through the Suez Canal and to the Soviet Union by way of Iran.

Invasion of Italy. From their newly won North African bases, the Allies subjected Sicily and Italy to merciless bombing. Then, early in July 1943, British, Canadian, and American troops landed in Sicily. The Sicilians offered little resistance, and the crack German troops were greatly outnumbered by the invaders, who swiftly overran the island.

Americans and other Allied peoples were thrilled at the rapid conquest of Sicily and by other good news during the summer of 1943. Late in July the Italians ended Mussolini's dictatorial rule and organized a new government. Before dawn on September 3, the British Eighth Army landed on the southern coast of the Italian mainland. On September 8 the Italian government surrendered unconditionally, and the following day an Allied invasion force landed at Salerno.

Despite these great successes the campaign for Italy was one of the longest and most difficult of the war. German troops were rushed in to fill the gaps left by the Italians. Difficult mountain terrain and bad weather helped the Germans. On October 1 Naples fell to an American army under General Mark W. Clark, but for several months the Allies were unable to advance beyond Cassino (see map, page 684). In an effort to outflank the German lines, Allied troops landed on the Anzio beaches southeast of Rome on January 22, 1944, but the Nazis fought desperately and held them off. It was not until June 4, 1944, that the Allied armies entered Rome.

From Rome they moved north. Progress was slow, and every inch of soil was won at great cost by the Allies—Americans, British, Canadians, Indians, New Zealanders, South

General Dwight D. Eisenhower visited the battle-weary American soldiers along the front lines five months after the invasion of France on D-Day in 1944. In another month, the Germans would stage their last offensive against the Allies.

Africans, French, Moroccans, Algerians, Senegalese, Poles, Greeks, Arabs, Brazilians, and a Jewish brigade from Palestine.

Importance of the Italian campaign. The victories of 1943–44 in Italy were immensely important. Through them the Allies strengthened their control of the Mediterranean. The loss of Italy deprived Germany of desperately needed troops. Moreover, from Italian bases Allied fliers were able to bomb southern Germany and the German-held Balkans, including the rich oil fields in Rumania.

Finally, in their efforts to check the Allies in North Africa and Italy, the Germans had been forced to withdraw troops from the Soviet front. This had helped the Soviet Union to regain great stretches of valuable farmland in the Ukraine. Despite the Italian campaign, however, the Nazis continued to concentrate most of their military forces against the Soviet Union, and the Soviets continued to call for a second front in Western Europe.

Victory in the Atlantic. The victories in Italy were possible only because the Allies had won control of the Atlantic Ocean. During the early months of the war, German submarines waged a mighty battle against ships carrying supplies to Europe. The Allies suffered staggering losses of ships, vital war materials, and lives.

Gradually, however, the Allies gained the upper hand. Radar and other devices for detecting planes and submarines were developed. New warships, including small aircraft carriers, were built by American and British shipyards. In 1942 the Axis sank 585 Allied and neutral vessels in the Atlantic. In 1943 the Axis sank only 110 ships. By the end of 1943, the Battle of the Atlantic was won.

Over the sea lanes, great convoys carried urgently needed military supplies to the Mediterranean war fronts and to Great Britain, which by 1943 had been converted into a vast base for the invasion of Western Europe.

Victory in the air. While the Allied navies were winning the Battle of the Atlantic, Allied planes began their offensive against Germany and German-occupied Europe. By early 1943 the Anglo-American air assault had become a major factor in the struggle. During the last year of the war, fleets of as many as 2,000 heavy bombers were dropping tons of bombs on a single target area.

The constant blows against German transportation centers, industrial plants, and military installations weakened German morale. The Allied air raids brought relief to Great Britain, which had suffered tremendous damage from German air attacks. They also helped Soviet armies who were seeking to drive the Nazis from Soviet soil.

Liberation of Western Europe. The terrific air assault on Germany was part of a larger strategy—the invasion and conquest of Germany. By June 1944 General Eisenhower, who had been named Supreme Commander of the Allied invasion armies in Western Europe, was satisfied that it was time to launch the attack.

Operation Overlord, as the invasion was called, began before dawn on the morning of June 6, 1944 (D-Day). More than 11,000 planes roared into the air. Some dropped airborne troops at key points a few miles inland from the German-occupied French coast. Others bombed roads, bridges, railway junctions, and German troop concentrations. Still others formed a mighty umbrella under which a huge invasion fleet of nearly 4,000 troop transports, landing craft, and warships moved across the English Channel to the Normandy beaches (see map, pages 684–85).

The Germans had worked for years to make these beaches unconquerable. Heavy artillery and machine guns were located in reinforced concrete pillboxes. Barbed wire and tank traps lined the shores. Other tangles of barbed wire were strung on steel and concrete piles and sunk just below the water's surface for hundreds of feet offshore.

Despite the years of preparation, the Germans were powerless to stop the invasion. The Nazis resisted fiercely, but they were outplanned, outnumbered, and outfought. Allied tank forces ripped through the German defenses and fanned out behind the lines. Aided by the French resistance, or underground movement, they quickly overran the countryside. On August 25, 1944, Paris fell. By this time the Allies had landed more than 2 million troops and millions of tons of munitions and supplies.

Meanwhile, early in August, the United States Seventh Army landed on the southern coast of France. It pushed rapidly up the Rhone Valley to join the Allied troops pouring in from Normandy. Within six months after D-Day, France had been liberated and the Allies had swept into the outer defenses of Germany's

Even in time of war there is a place for humor. Here, in caricature, an Iranian artist shows the Allied leaders hunting down Mussolini, Hitler, and Hirohito. Can you find President Roosevelt? Whom is he spearing?

famous Siegfried Line (see map, page 694). Here the attack at last ground to a halt. The Allied armies paused while new ports were opened, supplies were brought up, and military units were regrouped.

The election of 1944. The preparations for the final drive into Germany did not interfere with the regular November elections in the United States. The Republican candidate for the Presidency was Thomas E. Dewey, governor of New York. He had attracted national attention when, as a district attorney, he had successfully prosecuted racketeers in New York. The Republicans considered Dewey a strong candidate. However, the war was going well, and the Democrats argued that it would be unwise to replace experienced leaders. The argument proved convincing. Roosevelt, running for a fourth term, won with an electoral vote of 432 to Dewey's 99. The new Vice-President was Harry S. Truman of Missouri.

Germany's last counterattack. While the Allies were regrouping and the Americans were electing a President, the Germans were preparing a counterattack. On December 16 some 24 German divisions struck at a weakly held point in the Allied lines. German armored forces broke through, creating a dangerous bulge in the Allied lines. Christmas 1944 found the Allies fighting desperately in the Battle of the Bulge (see map, page 694), trying to prevent the Germans from plunging onward to the sea. Reinforcements were rushed up. The German divisions were shattered and thrown back behind the Siegfried Line.

Their defeat cost the Germans dearly in troops and equipment. Even more important, as General Eisenhower pointed out, was "the widespread disillusionment within the German army and Germany itself."

Invasion of Germany. By February 1945, Allied preparations had been completed for the invasion of Germany. The air forces continued to blast industrial areas, military bases, and transportation lines. Then, in March, the Allies crossed the Rhine, encircled Nazi troop concentrations, and plunged toward the heart of Germany (see map 694).

Meanwhile, the Soviets had been driving the Germans out of the Ukraine. They had conquered Nazi-held Rumania and Hungary and were closing in upon the Nazis from the south and east. Churchill had grown concerned over the Soviet Union's postwar intentions. He was alarmed at the deep penetration of the Soviet armies into Europe and argued that the Allies should race the Soviets to Berlin and Prague. This vital political problem might have been decided by the leaders of the Allied governments including, of course, President Roosevelt. Instead, the civilian leaders left the

693

ALLIED VICTORY IN EUROPE

decision to General Eisenhower. He, as Supreme Commander, concluded that his first objective should be the immediate and total destruction of the German armies. It would be "militarily unsound," he declared, to depart from this objective for political considerations. As a result of this decision, American forces under Eisenhower's command advanced only as far as the Elbe River (see map, this page). There on April 25 they joined the Soviet forces at Torgau.

Victory in Germany. Events that ended the war in Europe then followed in rapid order. On May 1 Hitler reportedly took his own life in the burning ruins of Berlin. On May 2 the Soviet troops hammered their way into the last Nazi strongholds of the city, and nearly 1 million German soldiers in Italy and Austria surrendered. Germany was in chaos. Within a week the Nazi forces in the Netherlands, Denmark, and Germany stopped fighting. Early on the morning of May 8, the German High Command surrendered unconditionally. Thus May 8, 1945 (V-E Day), marked the formal end of the war in Europe.

In Churchill's words, the victory over Germany was "the signal for the greatest outburst of joy in the history of mankind." As for himself, he wrote, his joy was tempered by "an aching heart and a mind oppressed by forebodings." He was weighed down by the awful tragedy of the war and concerned over the postwar intentions of the U.S.S.R.

Revelations of Nazi horrors. The first outbursts of joy at the end of the war in Europe were soon dulled by shocking news coming out of Germany. During the war the few refugees that managed to escape Nazi control had brought reports of terrible persecution and massacres of Jews. When the Allied armies entered and occupied the conquered country, the full extent of Nazi horrors came to light.

The world now heard in detail the blood-curdling crimes the Nazis had committed in their concentration camps. In one of the most terrible displays of brutality in human history, the Nazis had created these camps, or "death factories," to destroy their "political enemies" and to exterminate the entire Jewish population (see page 674).

The horrified world labeled this program of extermination the **Holocaust.** In it nearly 12 million men, women, and children, about half of them Jews, had been slaughtered after suffering indescribable anxieties, agonies, indignities, and tortures.

Roosevelt's death. President Roosevelt did not live to see the end of the war or to share in the world's horror over the Nazi atrocities. Worn out by his vast responsibilities, he died suddenly on April 12, 1945, in the "Little White House" at Warm Springs, Georgia. People all over the world were stunned at the news of his death. For three days American radio stations canceled programs to devote time to his memory. Vice-President Harry S. Truman, who now became President, declared, "His fellow countrymen will sorely miss his fortitude and faith and courage in the time to come. The peoples of the earth who love the ways of freedom and hope will mourn for him."

SECTION SURVEY

IDENTIFY: Operation Overlord, D-Day, Siegfried Line, Battle of the Bulge, V-E Day, concentration camps, Holocaust.

1. Why was the Allies' Italian campaign important?

2. (a) Why was it vital for the Allies to win the Battle of the Atlantic? (b) Why were they able to defeat the Germans in this battle?

3. Describe the events of 1945 that led to the fall of Germany and to the end of the war in Europe.

4 Allied victories in the Pacific bring an end to World War II

President Roosevelt's death in April 1945 came only a month before the Allied victory in Europe and only four months before the defeat of the Japanese ended World War II.

By 1943, you recall, the United States and its Allies were taking the offensive in the Pacific. The overall strategy, directed by Admiral Chester W. Nimitz, had three parts. (1) Air, land, and naval forces would strike westward at the Japanese-held islands in the Central Pacific. (2) A fleet under Admiral Halsey would drive the Japanese from the Solomon Islands. (3) General MacArthur would advance with troops along the New Guinea coast and on to the Philippine Islands. The ultimate objective was Japan.

Early victories. During 1943, American, Australian, and New Zealand troops pushed forward through the steaming jungles and across the vast stretches of the Central and South Pacific. The struggle was grim, for the Japanese clung to every foot of land. Few prisoners were taken.

Driving the Japanese from their threatening position before Port Moresby, which defended Australia, American and Australian troops fought their way up the New Guinea coast. Before the end of 1943, much of New Guinea had been recovered. American and New Zealand forces also won victories in the Solomon Islands.

Meanwhile, in the Central Pacific, Admiral Nimitz's powerful fleet moved into the Gilbert Islands, and American marines seized Tarawa and Makin (see map, page 696). Far to the north, Japan's troops were dislodged from the Aleutian strongholds of Attu and Kiska. The threat to Alaska was now ended.

Despite these successes, won at extreme cost in lives after ferocious fighting, the major Japanese positions remained untouched.

Island hopping. By 1944 a growing volume of troops and supplies was arriving in the Pacific. Powerful new warships and aircraft carriers, grouped into swift task forces, swept through the outer screen of protecting islands blasting Japanese installations and shipping routes. Carrier planes were raining explosives on the Japanese-held islands prior to invasion.

Suddenly, on January 31, 1944, the Allies struck again, this time against the Marshall Islands (see map, page 696). Three days later they seized Kwajalein (KWOJ·ah·lin), one of the keys to Japanese control of the Marshalls. Kwajalein was the first Japanese possession occupied by the Allies. Three weeks later Eniwetok (en·ih·WEE·tok) was stormed successfully. From these two bases, strong fleets of B-24 bombers began to blast Truk, a major stronghold in the Carolines and key to Japanese control of the Southwest and Central Pacific. Meanwhile General MacArthur, continuing his advance up the New Guinea coast, seized Hollandia. By July all of New Guinea was in his hands, with only bypassed pockets of Japanese troops left to surrender or to starve.

A month earlier, in June 1944, task-force raids and swift strikes by carrier-based planes pinned down Japanese air and naval forces and hammered the defenses of Saipan and Guam in the Mariana Islands (see map, page 696). Then, under cover of intense air and naval bombardment, landing craft swept in upon the beaches. From fleets near the Philippines, the Japanese sent out swarms of planes, only to lose more than 400 in a few hours. The following day hundreds of American planes roared from the decks of carriers to strike a severe blow at the retreating Japanese fleet.

Though shocked and saddened by the appalling loss of life, the American people were thrilled at the victories on Guam and Saipan. They had long dreaded the thought of a slow, bloody, island-by-island advance to Japan. Now Americans realized that the nation's tremendous sea and air power enabled it to seize key positions in the Pacific, leaving Japanese forces isolated and helpless on numerous islands far behind the line of battle.

Victory in the Philippines. Probably the most gratifying news from the Pacific in 1944 was the reconquest of the Philippines. In October vast naval forces moved up from the New Guinea–Solomons theater of war and in from

Text continues on page 698.

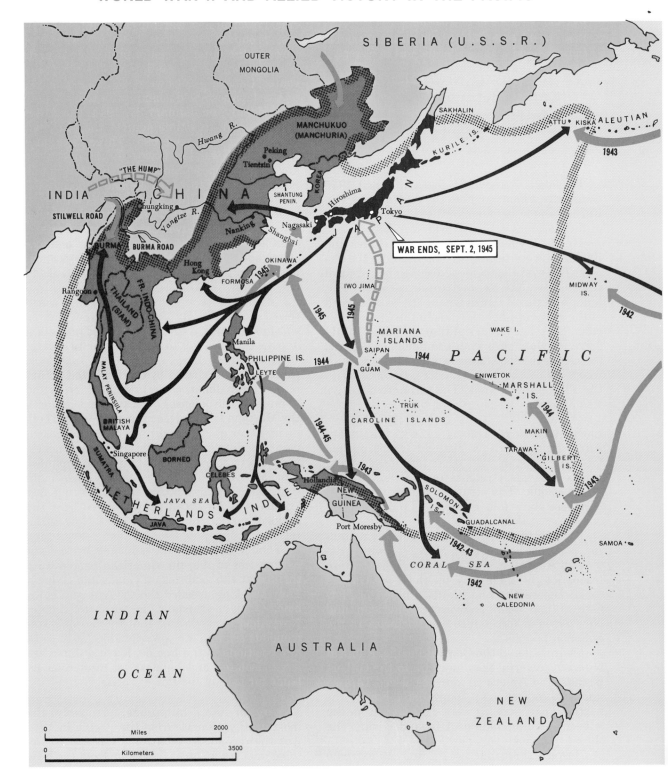

SIBERIA (U.S.S.R.)

OUTER MONGOLIA

SAKHALIN

ALEUTIAN
ATTU • KISKA
1943

MANCHUKUO (MANCHURIA)

KURILE IS.

"THE HUMP"

Peking
Tientsin

KOREA

Hwang R.

INDIA CHINA

Chungking

SHANTUNG PENIN.

Hiroshima

J A P A N

Tokyo

MIDWAY IS.

1942

STILWELL ROAD

Yangtze R.

Nanking

Shanghai

Nagasaki

WAR ENDS, SEPT. 2, 1945

BURMA BURMA ROAD

Hong Kong

OKINAWA

1945

FORMOSA

1945

IWO JIMA

1945

Rangoon

THAILAND (SIAM)

FR. INDO-CHINA

MARIANA ISLANDS

WAKE I.

P A C I F I C

Manila

SAIPAN

1944

PHILIPPINE IS.

1944

GUAM

ENIWETOK

MARSHALL IS.

1944

MALAY PENINSULA

LEYTE

BRITISH MALAYA

TRUK

MAKIN

CAROLINE ISLANDS

Singapore

BORNEO

TARAWA

GILBERT IS.

SUMATRA

CELEBES

1944-45

1943

N E T H E R L A N D S   I N D I E S

JAVA SEA

Hollandia

NEW GUINEA

SOLOMON IS.

1943

JAVA

Port Moresby

GUADALCANAL

1942-43

SAMOA

INDIAN

CORAL SEA

1942

NEW CALEDONIA

OCEAN

AUSTRALIA

NEW ZEALAND

0   Miles   2000

0   Kilometers   3500

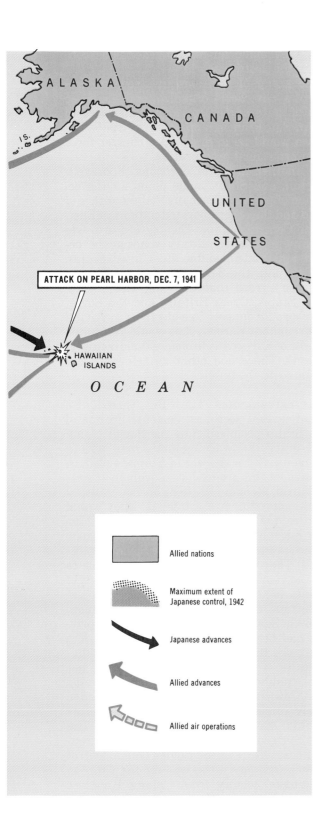

Dark days for the Allies

1941

JULY	Japanese invasion of French Indo-China.
DEC. 7	Japanese attack Pearl Harbor.
DEC. 8–11	United States declares war against the Axis.
DEC.	Japanese invasion of Thailand and Br. Malaya; capture of Wake, Guam, Hong Kong; invasion of Philippines, Midway.

1942

JAN.	Fall of Manila.
JAN.–MAY	Japanese occupy Netherlands Indies and Burma.
FEB.	Singapore surrenders to Japanese.
FEB.–MAR.	Battle of the Java Sea.
APR.–MAY	Fall of Bataan and Corregidor.
MAY	Battle of the Coral Sea.
JUNE	Battle of Midway.
JUNE	Japanese occupy Attu and Kiska in Aleutians.

Allied gains: the tide turns

AUG.	U.S. marines land on Guadalcanal.
NOV.	Allied victory in naval battle of Guadalcanal.

1943

JAN.–SEPT.	Allied gains in New Guinea.
MAR.–AUG.	Allies force Japanese from Aleutians.
JUNE–DEC.	Allied offensive in South Pacific: Solomon Is.
NOV.–FEB. 1944	Allied offensive in Central Pacific: Gilbert Is., Marshall Is., Kwajalein, Eniwetok.

1944

APR.–JULY	Allies seize Hollandia and regain New Guinea.
JUNE–AUG.	Allies capture Saipan and Guam in Mariana Is.
OCT.	Allied campaign to reconquer Philippines begins.

1945

FEB.	Allies liberate Manila; end of Philippines campaign.
FEB.–MAR.	U.S. marines conquer Iwo Jima.
APR.–JUNE	U.S. marines conquer Okinawa.
MAY–AUG.	Allied air offensive against Japanese home islands.

Allied victory in the Pacific

AUG. 6	Atomic bomb dropped on Hiroshima.
AUG. 9	Atomic bomb dropped on Nagasaki.
AUG. 10	Japan surrenders.
AUG. 14	V-J Day (end of war in Pacific).
SEPT. 2	Japan signs formal surrender on U.S.S. *Missouri*.

697

Saipan and Guam. The converging forces poured upon the beaches of Leyte (LAY·teh) in the central Philippines (see map, page 696) and eventually captured the island. Meanwhile, in the Battle of Leyte Gulf, American naval forces shattered Japan's remaining sea power.

Overcoming bitter land resistance, the conquering troops then spread over the Philippines. Early in February 1945, Manila fell to the Americans. "I shall return," MacArthur had promised when, following orders, he had left Corregidor in 1942. "I'm a little late, but we finally came," he said in Manila in 1945 as the American and Filipino flags were raised above the city.

The Yalta Conference. Long before the Allied victories in 1945, leaders of the great powers had met at a series of conferences to develop a common strategy and to form plans for a lasting peace. Early in February 1945, President Roosevelt, Prime Minister Churchill, and Premier Stalin met at Yalta in the southern part of the Soviet Union (see map, page 000). There they made far-reaching decisions concerning the postwar world.

One group of decisions involved the creation of a new world organization. The three heads of state agreed to call a conference to meet in San Francisco on April 25, 1945. The purpose would be to draw up a charter for a new international organization.

In another group of decisions, Roosevelt, Churchill, and Stalin made plans for the occupation of postwar Germany and the future of Poland and the other liberated nations in Eastern and Central Europe. They agreed to divide Germany into four military zones to be occupied and controlled by the United States, Great Britain, the Soviet Union, and France. They also agreed that the "Big Three"—the United States, Great Britain, and the Soviet Union—would support free elections in Poland and throughout Europe. This would guarantee the right of Europeans to choose their own governments. These and other agreements were announced to the public.

Secret agreements. The "Big Three" also reached several secret agreements. In one of these, Stalin promised that the Soviet Union would enter the war against Japan within three months after the war in Europe ended. In exchange for this promise, Roosevelt and Churchill, upon recommendation of top military leaders, agreed to two points. (1) They would recognize the Mongolian People's Republic, which had once been part of China but now claimed its independence under Soviet protection. (2) They would allow the Soviet Union to have the Kurile Islands, the southern half of Sakhalin Island, an occupation zone in Korea, and certain rights in Manchuria (see map, page 696). Several of these territories and privileges had been held by Russia before it lost them in the Russo-Japanese War of 1904–05.

Details of the Yalta Conference did not become public until long after Roosevelt's death. Down through the years, critics have severely condemned Roosevelt for what they called his "surrender" to Soviet demands. The critics charged that as a result of his "surrender," Roosevelt gave the Soviet Union control of Manchuria, paved the way for the Chinese Communists' victory over Chiang Kai-shek (CHAHNG KI·SHEK), the Chinese Nationalist leader, and opened the door to Communist aggression in Korea. They also held him responsible for the Soviet occupation of East Berlin and East Germany and the creation of Communist governments in Eastern Europe. These governments were created without the free elections that Stalin had promised.

Roosevelt's defenders have replied to these charges by reminding the critics of the military situation at the time of the Yalta Conference. Soviet armies had already conquered most of Eastern Europe, including Poland. American troops, on the other hand, had not yet crossed the Rhine and were still fighting the Japanese in the Philippines. Moreover, Allied military leaders had warned that the invasion of Japan, scheduled for the spring of 1946, might cost the United States as many as 1 million troops.

Also, Roosevelt's defenders insisted, Stalin had given Churchill and Roosevelt reason to believe that the Soviet Union would cooperate in building a new world organization designed to establish the foundations of a lasting peace. As Churchill himself later wrote, "Our hopeful assumptions were soon to be falsified. Still, they were the only ones possible at the time."

The road to victory. On February 19, 1945, a week after the Yalta Conference ended, United States marines landed on the beaches of Iwo Jima (EE·woh JEE·mah). Nearly 20,000 American marines were killed or wounded in the successful effort to gain control of this barren volcanic island, only 750 miles (1,200 kilometers) from Tokyo (see map, page 696). Among the marines who helped raise a flag of victory over Iwo Jima was Ira Hayes, an Indian. Hayes later received the Congressional Medal of Honor as an outstanding hero of World War II.

A few weeks later, the largest landing force in Pacific history invaded Okinawa (oh·kih·NAH·wah), a Japanese island some 300 miles (480 kilometers) from the Japanese homeland. Despite bitter Japanese resistance, Okinawa fell in June 1945.

Japan's air and sea power were broken, but Japan still had many well-trained and well-equipped divisions of soldiers. It still controlled large areas of China, although badly needed American supplies were being flown across the eastern Himalayas and transported by trucks over the newly opened Stilwell Road (see map, page 696) to embattled Chinese troops. These supplies were only a fraction of what China needed, and Chinese troops were in no position to undertake a major offensive. Moreover, the inner defenses on the Japanese homeland were strong. On the other hand, Japan was blockaded, and, after the war in Europe ended in the spring of 1945, the full weight of the Allies was available for the final struggle in the Pacific.

Day by day the American task forces grew bolder. They drove the remaining Japanese ships from the seas and shelled shore installations on the Japanese mainland. Day by day huge fleets of bombers, now within easier striking distance of Japan, dropped fire bombs and high explosives in devastating raids on the Japanese home islands. By the early summer of 1945, the blockade and the relentless bombings were destroying Japan's power to resist.

The end of World War II. With Roosevelt's death in April 1945, the responsibility for making decisions to bring about the defeat of Japan fell upon his successor, President Truman. In July Truman met with Stalin and Clement Attlee, the new British Prime Minister, at Potsdam, Germany. At this meeting the three

This statue of the raising of the flag at Iwo Jima can be seen in Washington, D. C. It commemorates the heroism of American marines in the Pacific.

This scene of destruction is Hiroshima, Japan, after it was hit by an atomic bomb dropped by an American bomber. Nearly 100,000 of the city's people were killed by the bomb which actually fell a mile from this site.

Allied leaders discussed plans for the control and occupation of Germany. They also issued an ultimatum to Japan, calling for its unconditional surrender. Japan rejected the ultimatum on July 29.

On August 6, 1945, at 8:15 A.M., a single American bomber flew high over the Japanese city of Hiroshima. No alarm was sounded. Then suddenly the city disintegrated in a single searing atomic blast. Nearly 100,000 of the 245,000 men, women, and children in Hiroshima were killed instantly or died soon after. A new force had been added to warfare, a force that would enormously complicate the postwar world.

In authorizing the atomic bombing of Hiroshima, President Truman knew that he had made an extremely grave decision. He had given the order only after days of conferring with his key military and political advisers. His decision was made to force Japan to surrender immediately and thus to save the lives of hundreds of thousands of American troops. Despite the devastation of Hiroshima, the Japanese failed to surrender.

On August 8 the Soviet Union declared war on Japan. On August 9 the United States drop-ped a second atomic bomb. This one destroyed the city of Nagasaki. On August 10 the Japanese government finally asked for peace.

On August 14, 1945 (V-J Day), President Truman announced by radio that Japan had accepted the Allied peace terms. The formal surrender was signed on September 2, 1945. World War II had come to an end.

SECTION SURVEY

IDENTIFY: Chester Nimitz, Ira Hayes, Harry S. Truman, Potsdam Ultimatum, Hiroshima.

1. What was the Allied strategy for winning the war in the Pacific?

2. (a) Summarize the agreements reached at the Yalta Conference of 1945. (b) Explain the arguments made by some Americans for and against these agreements.

3. (a) Why did the Japanese finally surrender? (b) Was the dropping of the atomic bomb necessary to end the war? Explain.

4. Map Study: Examine the map on pages 696–97. (a) Trace the area of maximum Japanese control during the war. (b) With the help of the map, explain the island-hopping strategy.

Chapter Survey

Summary: Tracing the Main Ideas

The cost of World War II in human lives, money, and property was enormous. In the United States alone, the federal government spent more money than it had during the entire period from 1789 to 1940, including the cost of all earlier wars. Billions of dollars of property went up in smoke and flames. Parts of many of the world's major cities were reduced to rubble.

The loss of human life was staggering. According to General Marshall's final report, 201,367 Americans had been killed by the end of June 1945. About 600,000 had been wounded, and 57,000 were missing. Other nations lost much more heavily. It has been estimated that more than 3,000,000 Germans, more than 3,000,000 Russians, more than 1,500,000 Japanese, and more than 375,000 British troops were killed in battle. Civilian deaths resulting from bombs, starvation, disease, and concentration camps ran into countless millions. The exact number can never be known, for vast numbers of people simply disappeared. Many more millions of people were uprooted and left homeless as death and destruction raged across the face of the earth.

These were only some of the immediate and terrible effects of the most devastating war the world had ever seen.

Inquiring into History

1. What were the most important reasons for the Allied victory in Europe?
2. What role did science and technology play in winning the war?
3. What role did air power play in both the European and Pacific theaters of the war?
4. United States action against the Nisei was justified because the constitutional rights of all citizens are suspended in wartime. Do you agree or disagree? Why?
5. At certain times in a country's history, the power of a single personality becomes an extremely important force. Apply this idea to (a) Churchill in Great Britain, (b) Hitler in Germany, or (c) Roosevelt in the United States.

Relating Past to Present

1. Despite their deeply rooted belief in individualism and free enterprise, Americans accepted many new governmental controls during World War II. (a) Why? (b) Are there any circumstances under which Americans might accept such controls today?
2. The atomic bomb was used to end World War II. Are nuclear weapons an important part of America's defenses today?
3. If a war involving as many nations as World War II were fought today, what do you think its outcome would be?

Developing Social Science Skills

1. Use primary and secondary sources to find out more of the role of women during World War II. (a) Why did women enter the work force? (b) For the most part, what kinds of jobs did they work at? (c) What happened to these jobs at the end of the war? (d) What effects do you think the war had on the role of women in American society? Explain.
2. Study the maps on pages 684–85 and 694. (a) Trace the area on the map on pages 684–85 that corresponds to the area on the map on page 694. (b) Which map provides more information? (c) How do the purposes of the two maps differ? (d) How did the area of Axis control change from 1942 to 1945?
3. Use the *Reader's Guide to Periodical Literature* to locate articles written during the war years and post-war years about the Holocaust. (a) How much did the American people know about the Holocaust before the war's end? Explain. (b) What did the American people learn about the Holocaust after the war? How did they react?

Unit Survey

For Further Inquiry

1. In what ways did the "peace" ending World War I lead to World War II?
2. (a) What is isolationism? (b) Why was the United States basically isolationist after World War I? (c) In what ways was the United States *not* isolationist in that period?
3. During the 1930's, some nations resorted to dictatorship governments in order to resolve problems caused by the worldwide depression. (a) How might a dictatorship be able to solve such problems? (b) Why do you think the United States did not become a dictatorship during this period?
4. World War II was as much a battle of the scientists and engineers as a battle of the footsoldiers. Explain.
5. Review America's attempts to remain neutral before the War of 1812, World War I, and World War II. (a) What were the similarities and differences? (b) Why did each of these attempts fail?

Projects and Activities

1. Study the timeline here. (a) Which items concern an achievement or contribution of a minority person or group? (b) Which items concern Americans' reactions to minorities? (c) Which items concern government actions toward minorities? (d) Based on the timeline, write a short paragraph describing the status of minorities in America from around 1920 to 1945.
2. Examine the map on pages 696–97. (a) By what routes did the Allies try to attack Japanese areas from bases in India? (b) Locate examples of the "island-hopping" strategy. (c) Trace the boundaries of maximum Japanese control in 1942. Calculate the area (in square miles or square kilometers) of maximum Japanese control.
3. Investigate the Supreme Court cases, such as *Korematsu v. U.S.*, that arose from the internment of Japanese-Americans. (a) What were the major questions raised by the cases? (b) How did the Court resolve the questions?
4. Make a tape recording (from records or your own performing) of songs that were popular during World War II. You might include both patriotic and "pop" songs.

Exploring Your Region

1. Interview relatives or acquaintances who lived in your area during World War II. Ask them to comment on aspects of the war effort that directly affected their lives. You might ask them about such subjects as food and gas rationing, civil defense activities, changes in local factory output or employment.
2. Take a tour of local World War II memorials. Find out about ways in which the war dead are honored during the year.

Suggested Readings

1. *Pacific War Diary, 1942-1945,* James J. Fahey. The secret diary of an American sailor who fought in the Pacific during World War II.
2. *Diary of a Young Girl,* Anne Frank. A vivid account of a young Jewish girl and her family as they hide from the Nazis.
3. *Negro Medal of Honor Men,* Irvin H. Lee. Story of the heroic deeds of black soldiers in America's wars.
4. *No Time for Glory, Stories of World War II,* Phyllis Fenner, ed. Ten exciting short stories of World War II.
5. *Von Ryan's Express,* David Westheimer. An action-packed novel of British and American prisoners of war who make a daring escape in the last days of World War II.

Unit Twelve

Reshaping the Postwar World

1945-1960

Timeline

- **1935**
- **1940**
- **1945** — United Nations charter drafted
- Marshall Plan proposed
- Berlin airlift
- Communists win Chinese civil war
- **1950** — Korean War begins
- French defeated in Vietnam
- **1955**
- Suez crisis
- Sputnik launched
- **1960**
- **1965**
- **2000**

Chapter 37

Assuming the Responsibilities of World Leadership

1945–1960

The end of World War II in 1945 brought rejoicing in all the victorious countries. But the joy and gaiety were restrained. The dominant feeling was one of immense relief.

The mood of the American people was summed up by the reporter who wrote that "everybody talked of the 'end of the war,' not of 'victory.'"

It was all so different from the aftermath of World War I. In 1918, Americans had been content to let the world take care of itself. In 1945 they felt they knew better.

Senator Arthur H. Vandenberg of Michigan, who in the 1930's had been one of the leading isolationists in Congress, spoke for millions of Americans when he was in London in 1944 during a German rocket attack. "How can there be immunity or isolation," he asked, "when man can devise weapons like that?"

Later, in the Senate, Senator Vandenberg renounced his isolationism. He came out in favor of American cooperation in building a new world order. "I want a new dignity and a new authority for international law," he announced. "I think American self-interest requires it."

In 1945 the American people were rapidly becoming aware that, like it or not, the United States was destined to play a new role in the world. However, not even the most farsighted among them realized the heavy burden of responsibility they would carry in the troubled years ahead.

THE CHAPTER IN OUTLINE

1. The United States helps to organize the United Nations.
2. The United States and the U.S.S.R. engage in a "cold war."
3. Growing nationalism and Communist aggression lead to a "hot war" in Asia.
4. The United States continues to meet the challenges of communism.

704

1 The United States helps to organize the United Nations

Even before World War II ended, many world leaders were considering ways to build an enduring peace. American officials were among the leaders in this effort.

During the war the Allies—or United Nations, as they called themselves—promised to join together to defeat Italy, Germany, and Japan (page 683). Allied leaders—among them Roosevelt, Churchill, and Stalin—agreed to convert the wartime alliance into a permanent organization for peace.

Many Americans pledged to support such an international organization of nations. Democrats and Republicans alike agreed to back a program of international cooperation.

Planning the United Nations. Delegates from the United States, Great Britain, the U.S.S.R., and China met in 1944 at Dumbarton Oaks, an estate in Washington, D.C. There they began planning for a postwar United Nations organization. On most of the questions concerning procedure, the delegates quickly reached agreement. Some problems, however, were more difficult to solve.

What, for instance, should they do about the U.S.S.R.'s demand that it be represented in the United Nations not by one delegation but by 16—one for each of the 16 Soviet republics? What should they do about the Security Council, the body that was charged with keeping peace in the world?

At Yalta in February 1945 (page 698), Roosevelt, Churchill, and Stalin reached agreement on several issues that had deadlocked the Dumbarton Oaks Conference. They agreed that two of the Soviet Union's 16 republics would be admitted to the United Nations as though they were independent nations. The leaders also worked out a compromise on voting procedure in the Security Council. Finally, they agreed to call a conference in San Francisco on April 25, 1945, to draw up the official Charter of the United Nations.

Delegates from 50 nations, representing three fourths of the peoples of the earth, took part in the San Francisco Conference. Despite their differences, the delegates all worked for one objective—to form a world peace organization. In just eight weeks, the Dumbarton Oaks and the Yalta proposals were reshaped into the

The United Nations' General Assembly serves as a forum for discussion of world problems and is often referred to as the "town meeting of the world." Membership in the Assembly consists of all members of the United Nations.

United Nations Charter. On October 24 – now celebrated as United Nations Day – the United Nations (UN) came into official existence.

Purposes and organization. The purposes of the UN are clearly stated in the Preamble to the Charter. "We the peoples of the United Nations, determined to save succeeding generations from the scourge of war, . . . to promote social progress and better standards of life in larger freedom, . . . have resolved to combine our efforts to accomplish these aims."

In general, the UN seeks to maintain peace, to provide security, to promote justice, to increase the general welfare, and to establish human rights. Six major organs and many related agencies were created to carry out the work of the UN.

(1) The Security Council was to be the police authority of the world, charged with preventing war. It was to consist of 11 members.° Five of these, the so-called "Big Five" powers – the United States, China, France, the Soviet Union, and Great Britain – were to hold permanent seats. The six nonpermanent members were to be elected for two-year terms. The Security Council was to have at its command an international military force to check aggression. On matters of peace and security, any one of the five permanent members could prevent action by its negative vote, or veto.

(2) The General Assembly was to be the "town meeting" of the world, in which all UN members were to be equally represented. It was to make recommendations for the peaceful settlement of disputes. It was to elect all the nonpermanent members of the Security Council and members of other agencies.

(3) The Economic and Social Council, composed of 18 members (now 57), was to study world economic, social, cultural, and health problems. It was to make recommendations on these problems to the General Assembly or to individual member countries.

(4) The International Court of Justice, modeled after the World Court, was to decide legal questions referred to it by disputing nations. It was to give advisory opinions when asked to do so, but it could not enforce its decisions.

(5) The Secretariat was to handle the administrative work of the UN.

°It later was increased to 15 members – five permanent members plus ten nonpermanent members.

(6) The Trusteeship Council was to look after the welfare of peoples living in colonial areas of the world.

Early years of the UN. Early critics of the UN insisted that it was doomed to fail because the member nations had not given up any of their national sovereignty. Other people, however, shared the opinion expressed by President Truman in 1945. "This charter," he stated, "points down the only road to enduring peace. There is no other."

As crises broke out in many parts of the world, Truman's statement took on new meaning. By 1948 the world situation had become so tense that Trygve Lie (TRIG·vuh LEE), the first Secretary-General of the UN, issued a warning. "The trouble," he declared, "lies in the intense conflict over the settlement of the last war . . . between the two most powerful single nations in the world today – the United States and the Soviet Union."

SECTION SURVEY

IDENTIFY: Dumbarton Oaks Conference, San Francisco Conference, "Big Five," Trygve Lie.

1. (a) What problems were left unsolved at the Dumbarton Oaks Conference? (b) How were these issues resolved later at Yalta?
2. What are the purposes of the United Nations?
3. What are the major functions of the Security Council and the General Assembly?

2 The United States and the U.S.S.R. engage in a "cold war"

At the end of World War II, millions of people throughout the world suffered from lack of food, clothing, shelter, and medical care. The United States responded generously to this desperate worldwide need for help.

America's new role. The United States played an active role in creating three important UN agencies: (1) the United Nations Relief and Rehabilitation Administration (UNRRA), (2) the International Bank for Reconstruction and Development, and (3) the International Monetary Fund. These agencies supplied food, clothing, shelter, and medical care to millions of people in war-damaged nations and provided money to rebuild ruined industries. A large part of the money for these activities came from the United States.

After the war ended, American dollars and supplies flowed directly to the war-devastated areas. Major contributions came from private American organizations—churches, schools, fraternal societies, and civic groups. An even larger contribution came from the United States government in the form of supplies, equipment, loans, and the assistance of specialists and experts.

Expanding Soviet influence. America's new role of world leadership brought it into conflict with the Soviet Union, which also emerged from the war as a major power. The postwar policies of the Soviet Union in some ways continued the expansionist policies of tsarist Russia. However, the U.S.S.R. now regarded itself as the leader of a Communist revolution destined to replace the "capitalist" and "imperialist" world—a world in which the United States was the principal power.

Even before World War II ended, the Soviets had begun to move aggressively against their weaker neighbors. In 1940 Latvia, Lithuania, and Estonia—countries to which the Russians had some historical claims—were incorporated into the Soviet Union. As a result of World War II, the U.S.S.R. also acquired large parts of Poland and Rumania. Through Communist governments that they helped to set up, the Soviets by 1948 had gained control of the "free" governments of Poland, Rumania, Hungary, Czechoslovakia, and the eastern part of Germany. Moreover, Soviet influence reached beyond Eastern Europe into the Mediterranean area. Moscow-trained Communists were especially active in Greece and Italy.

The U.S.S.R. was deeply entrenched in East Asia, as well as in Europe. As a result of the Yalta agreements and because of its last-minute entry into the war against Japan, the Soviet Union gained control of large areas that had been Chinese and Japanese territory.

Mounting tensions. The Communist leaders defended their actions on grounds of self-defense. They pointed out that in 1918–19 during the Bolshevik Revolution, the Allies, including American troops, had occupied north-ern Russia and Russian Siberia. Believing that war between communism and capitalism was inevitable, they feared that the United States would lead the capitalist nations in a new attack against the U.S.S.R. They reminded the world that the Nazi invasion of their country had cost them 21 million lives and the destruction of hundreds of their towns and cities. In view of these facts, the Soviets insisted on maintaining powerful military forces and on controlling bordering areas from which new attacks might be launched.

The United States objected bitterly to the Soviet Union's domination of its weaker neighbors. The United States, which had demobilized most of its own troops, resented the Soviet policy of maintaining huge military forces. Moreover, Americans loathed the ruthless methods used by the Soviet Union to crush all opposition. Most Americans regarded the Soviet Union as the world's newest aggressor.

As friction increased, the Soviet press and radio, rigidly controlled by the government, became increasingly anti-American. The Soviet government refused to join the United Nations Educational, Scientific, and Cultural Organization (UNESCO), which had been established to promote understanding among the peoples of the world. It permitted only a very few Americans to visit the U.S.S.R. or its satellite nations—those nations dominated by the U.S.S.R.

Deadlock over atomic energy. Inability to reach agreement on international control of the atomic bomb greatly added to the mounting tension between the United States and the U.S.S.R. Early in 1946, acting on American initiative, the UN created an International Atomic Energy Commission. At the Commission's first meeting, the United States representative, Bernard M. Baruch (buh·ROOK), presented America's proposal for international control.

Baruch proposed that complete control of atomic energy be turned over to an international agency responsible to the UN. This agency would have full authority to enter any country to inspect atomic energy installations. The United States—at that time the only nation that had atomic bombs—was ready, Baruch announced, to give up its secrets to the new world authority. However, he warned, the United States would not reveal any secrets until the UN provided for "immediate, swift, and sure punishment for those who violate the agreements that are reached by the nations." Baruch insisted that each of the "Big Five" on the Security Council give up its right to the veto on all matters involving atomic energy.

When the United States proposal reached the Security Council, the Soviet Union killed it by a veto. The Soviet Union then offered its own proposal. It opposed any system of international inspection and control. Instead, it insisted that the United States destroy its atomic bombs, that the UN declare atomic warfare illegal, and that all nations promise not to manufacture atomic bombs. However, the Soviet Union flatly refused to give up its veto right in the Security Council. This meant that if any nation, including the U.S.S.R., violated its promise not to make atomic bombs, the Soviet Union or any other permanent Security Council member could block all UN action by a single veto.

The Truman Doctrine. Wary of Communist aggression, the United States formulated a policy of containment. This policy aimed to contain, or restrict, Soviet expansion and to check the spread of communism. The new policy was first applied to Greece and Turkey.

In 1947, Greek Communists supported by the Soviets were about to seize control of the conservative Greek government. At the same time, the Soviet Union was trying to force Turkey to give up control of the Dardanelles, the strait between European and Asiatic Turkey. Soviet control of Greece and the Dardanelles would enable the U.S.S.R. to dominate the northeastern Mediterranean and the Suez Canal.

This situation prompted President Truman in 1947 to announce the Truman Doctrine. This doctrine stated that the United States had to "help free people to maintain their free institutions and their national integrity." He then asked Congress for authority to help the Greeks and Turks strengthen their armed forces to check the spread of communism. Congress responded with an initial appropriation of $400 million. In 1948 the United States also established and later increased its naval forces in the eastern Mediterranean.

The Marshall Plan. Aid to Greece and Turkey, however, was not enough to prevent the spread of communism. All of war-torn Europe was in economic difficulty. Throughout Europe Communists were winning converts among hungry, disillusioned people.

Early in June 1947, Secretary of State George C. Marshall suggested a solution to Europe's economic problems. The "Marshall Plan," as this program came to be called, proposed to help European countries to get their farms, factories, and transportation systems operating efficiently again. The United States would provide money, plus supplies and ma-

World War II left many European cities in utter ruin. With their economies, like their cities, in desperate need of restoration, many European nations looked to the United States for help. The Marshall Plan was part of America's response.

chinery, to any nation that would take part in the program. The Soviet Union and its satellites were included in the offer.

The Marshall Plan provoked heated Congressional debate. Those who favored the proposal insisted that the best way to block communism and strengthen America's own economic system was to restore Europe's economic health. Opponents of the program declared that the United States could not afford to "carry Europe on its back." In the spring of 1948, however, Congress approved the Marshall Plan, officially known as the European Recovery Program.

The Soviet Union and its satellites denounced the plan as "Yankee imperialism." Nevertheless, the Marshall Plan was an outstanding success. Slowly but steadily Europe began to recover from the war.

The Berlin airlift. Meanwhile tension had mounted in Germany. In 1945 the great powers had agreed to a joint occupation of Germany. Great Britain, France, and the United States occupied western and southern Germany, and the Soviet Union occupied eastern Germany. Berlin, within the Soviet-controlled zone, was also divided into four sections, each controlled by one of the four powers.

On June 24, 1948, the Soviets suddenly blocked all roads, canals, and railways connecting Berlin and the Western Zone of Germany. By this move they apparently hoped to force the three Western powers out of Berlin.

The British-American answer to the Soviet challenge was the Berlin airlift. Starting in the summer of 1948 and continuing for more than a year, British and American planes transported over 2 million tons of food and supplies to Berlin. This crisis in relations between the East and the West was finally resolved in 1949 with the aid of the UN.

NATO. The Soviet blockade of Berlin and communist efforts to wreck the Marshall Plan aroused growing alarm in Western Europe. In April 1949 nine Western European nations° joined the United States, Canada, and Iceland in an alliance known as the North Atlantic Treaty Organization (NATO).

In the Atlantic Pact—the treaty proposing the NATO alliance—each member nation

°Great Britain, France, Belgium, the Netherlands, Luxembourg, Italy, Denmark, Norway, and Porgugal. West Germany, Turkey, and Greece joined later.

SOURCES

THE MARSHALL PLAN (1947)

It is logical that the United States should do whatever it is able to do to assist in the return of normal economic health in the world, without which there can be no political stability and no assured peace.

Our policy is directed not against any country or doctrine but against hunger, poverty, desperation, and chaos. Its purpose should be the revival of a working economy in the world so as to permit the emergence of political and social conditions in which free institutions can exist. . . .

Any government that is willing to assist in the task of recovery will find full cooperation, I am sure, on the part of the United States government. Any government which maneuvers to block the recovery of other countries cannot expect help from us. Furthermore, governments, political parties, or groups which seek to perpetuate human misery in order to profit therefrom, politically or otherwise, will encounter the opposition of the United States. . . .

agreed that "an armed attack against one or more of them in Europe or North America shall be considered an attack against them all." They also agreed to resist such an attack with armed force, if necessary.

Since the Atlantic Pact was a treaty, it had to be approved by the United States Senate. Senate debate focused on whether or not the Atlantic Pact would compel the United States to go to war to assist a member nation without an act of Congress. This, you may remember, was the main issue that had kept the United States out of the League of Nations in 1919. However, in July 1949 the Senate did ratify the agreement. Eventually General Eisenhower was named Supreme Commander of the NATO forces.

Thus by the end of 1949 an American policy of containment had taken shape, at least in regard to Europe. NATO strengthened the military defenses of Western Europe. The Marshall Plan strengthened the economy of Western Europe, thus reducing the discontent that so often helped the spread of communism.

Meanwhile, however, trouble was brewing in the Middle East and in Asia.

1. (a) Why did the Soviet Union try to expand its influence during the postwar period? (b) How did the Soviets justify their actions?

2. (a) Compare the Soviet and the American plans for control of atomic energy. (b) Why did efforts at control end in deadlock?

3. How did each of the following help to contain communism: (a) the Truman Doctrine, (b) the Marshall Plan, (c) the Berlin airlift, (d) NATO?

3 Growing nationalism and Communist aggression lead to a "hot war" in Asia

Postwar troubles were not confined to Europe. During President Truman's administration, growing tensions threatened peace in the Middle East and Asia.

Middle East tensions. Iran soon became a trouble spot. During World War II, both American and Soviet troops were stationed in Iran. After the war the United States pulled out its troops. However, the Soviets were eager to control the oil-rich land adjoining their border to the south and did not remove their troops. Tension mounted. Finally, after the UN intervened in 1946, the Soviets withdrew their military forces from Iran.

Meanwhile trouble broke out in Palestine, at the eastern end of the Mediterranean Sea. Since World War I, Great Britain had ruled Palestine under a mandate from the League of Nations. On May 14, 1948, Great Britain voluntarily gave up this mandate. The Jews in Palestine then proclaimed the independence of the new state of Israel.

This action angered Arabs and plunged Israel into war with the neighboring Arab countries of Egypt, Transjordan (later renamed Jordan), Lebanon, Syria, Iraq, and Saudi Arabia. The UN at once took steps to end the fighting. Finally a UN mission under the leadership of a black American, Dr. Ralph J. Bunche, managed to get both sides to agree to an armistice. As a result of his peace making efforts, Dr. Bunche received the Nobel Peace Prize.

Communist victory in China. While an uneasy peace was being restored in the Middle East, Chinese Communists were rapidly winning control of China. The struggle for control of China had begun long before World War II.

In 1927, four years before the Japanese moved into Manchuria, Chiang Kai-shek, leader of the Chinese Nationalist forces, opened war on the Chinese Communists. For a time China was torn by civil conflict. But after Japan attacked China, both of the opposing Chinese factions fought against the Japanese. During World War II, the United States encouraged such cooperation. Chinese troops heroically resisted the invading armies of Japan. In 1945, in recognition of these valiant efforts, China was admitted to the United Nations as one of the "Big Five."

With the end of World War II, the struggle between Chiang's Nationalist forces and the Chinese Communists once again erupted. The Soviet Union gave limited support to the Chinese Communists, led by Mao Tse-tung (MAU TSAY-TOONG). The United States at first provided military assistance to Chiang's Nationalists, but the Nationalists were weakened by internal conflicts and corruption. As the outlook for Nationalist victory grew dim, the United States withdrew its support. By 1949 the Communists had conquered most of China. Chiang and the Nationalist government, together with a small army, retreated to the island of Formosa, or Taiwan.

The United States continued to recognize the Nationalists as the legal government of China. Also, the Nationalists continued to represent China in the UN Security Council.°

The division of Korea. Meanwhile trouble was brewing in Korea. Between 1910 and 1945, the Koreans had been ruled by Japan. During the closing days of World War II, however, Soviet and American troops swept the Japanese out of Korea. After the war General Douglas MacArthur was appointed Supreme Commander of the Allied Powers and placed in charge of the occupation forces in Japan.° His responsibilities also included the southern portion of Korea.

°During the occupation period, relations between Japan and the Western powers were restored to a friendly basis. In 1951 Japan received independence in a treaty signed at San Francisco.

°The People's Republic of China replaced Nationalist China in the Security Council in 1972.

At the end of the war, a line drawn across the Korean peninsula at the 38th parallel (see map, page 712) separated American occupation forces in the south from Soviet occupation forces in the north. Americans and most other concerned peoples considered this a temporary arrangement.

Despite UN efforts to unite the country, Korea remained divided, and Soviet and American troops were not withdrawn. Then in 1948 North Korea and South Korea set up separate governments, each claiming authority to rule the entire country. The North Korean government, controlled by Communists and supported by the Soviets, called itself the "People's Republic of Korea." The South Korean government, of which Syngman Rhee (SING·man REE) had been chosen president in an election sponsored by the UN, called itself the "Republic of Korea." The United States and 30 UN members (but not the Soviet Union) recognized the Republic of Korea as the country's lawful government.

Finally the United States and the Soviet Union withdrew their troops. Each left behind a Korean army it had helped to train. These two Korean armies now faced each other across the 38th parallel.

The Korean challenge. On June 25, 1950, the North Korean army suddenly launched a full-scale invasion of South Korea. In an emergency session, the UN Security Council adopted a resolution ordering an immediate cease-fire. Had the Soviet delegate been present, he would undoubtedly have vetoed this action. However, the Soviet government was boycotting the Security Council because of its refusal to admit Communist China to the United Nations.

Meanwhile President Truman was busy conferring with the heads of the State and Defense departments. On June 27, 1950, the President pledged American aid to South Korea. That same evening the Security Council adopted a second resolution. It termed North Korea an "aggressor" and called on UN members to furnish all possible assistance to the South Koreans.

War in Korea. The UN itself had no troops to throw into action. Soviet vetoes in the Security Council had blocked every effort to create a UN military force. Although 19 UN members finally contributed assistance, the major burden

Ralph Bunche (right) took the job of peacemaker in Palestine with the knowledge that a predecessor had been assassinated for his efforts. Bunche received the Nobel Peace Prize for his work.

of defending South Korea against the North fell upon the United States.

In response to the UN's call, President Truman ordered the United States Seventh Fleet into action. It was charged with preventing any attack upon Formosa and blockading the Korean coast. Truman also ordered United States air and ground forces into Korea.

For a time it looked as though the North Koreans would overrun all of Korea. The South Koreans were hopelessly outnumbered. Neither they nor the first American troops rushed to the scene could stand up against the heavily armored, Soviet-made tanks of the North Korean army. By early August the South Korean and UN troops under General MacArthur were desperately defending a small area around Pusan in southeast Korea (see map, page 712).

Then the tide suddenly turned. On September 15, 1950, MacArthur staged a seaborne attack against Inchon and then swept eastward, recapturing Seoul (SOHL), the capital of South Korea. At the same time, a strongly reinforced UN army, now well equipped and powerfully supported from the air, attacked from southeastern Korea. The North Korean

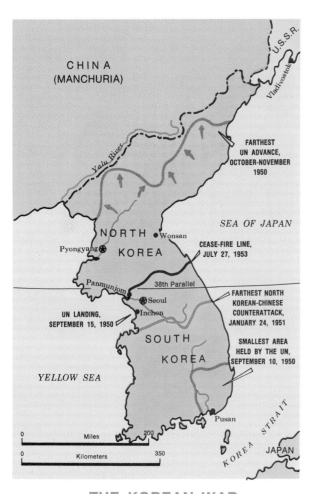

THE KOREAN WAR

Map labels:
CHINA (MANCHURIA)
U.S.S.R.
Vladivostok
Yalu River
FARTHEST UN ADVANCE, OCTOBER-NOVEMBER 1950
NORTH KOREA
Wonsan
SEA OF JAPAN
Pyongyang
CEASE-FIRE LINE, JULY 27, 1953
Panmunjom
38th Parallel
Seoul
Inchon
UN LANDING, SEPTEMBER 15, 1950
FARTHEST NORTH KOREAN-CHINESE COUNTERATTACK, JANUARY 24, 1951
SOUTH KOREA
SMALLEST AREA HELD BY THE UN, SEPTEMBER 10, 1950
YELLOW SEA
Pusan
KOREA STRAIT
JAPAN
Miles 0 200
Kilometers 0 350

forces, caught in a huge trap, began to break up. Thousands surrendered. The rest fled northward across the 38th parallel. MacArthur's troops followed in hot pursuit. By November the UN forces were at the Yalu River, the boundary between North Korea and Communist China.

Then suddenly the tide turned again. Late in November hundreds of thousands of Chinese Communist "volunteers" swarmed across the Yalu River to reinforce the North Korean troops. The UN troops, their lines extended, were outnumbered in many cases by hundreds to one. Finally, after weeks of desperate fighting, MacArthur's forces managed to set up their defense line near the 38th parallel.

The Great Debate. The entry of Chinese Communist troops completely changed the na-

ture of the war. President Truman faced new, serious questions. Should he heed MacArthur's request and allow him to blockade the China coast and bomb the Chinese mainland? Should he also help Chiang Kai-shek's Nationalist forces to launch an invasion of China?

MacArthur's proposal provoked heated debate. His supporters argued that quick, decisive action would bring a speedy end to the Korean conflict. Those who disagreed argued that an attack upon Communist China might cause the U.S.S.R. to support its Communist ally openly. This would certainly start another world war.

MacArthur's opponents also pointed to another danger. If the United States committed its military forces to a major war in Asia, the Soviet Union would be free to do as it pleased in Europe.

Stalemate in Korea. By January 1951 President Truman had reached his decision. He ordered General MacArthur to establish the strongest possible defense line near the 38th parallel. However, he forbade blockading the China coast, bombing China, and using Chiang's troops to invade China. The war in Korea was to remain strictly a "police action" to protect South Korea. In 1951, therefore, the Korean War reached a stalemate.

MacArthur refused to accept Truman's decision as final and tried to appeal to Congress over the President's authority. In April 1951 President Truman removed MacArthur from his post. "I could do nothing else and still be President," Truman explained. General Matthew B. Ridgway replaced MacArthur as Commander of the UN forces.

American policy and Point Four. During 1951 and 1952, the United States continued the rapid buildup of its land, sea, and air forces. This military buildup was only part of America's response to the challenge of communism around the world. With economic aid and technical assistance, the United States helped less fortunate areas of the world to raise their standards of living. The Marshall Plan was intended primarily for Europe. A new plan, the Point Four program, was intended to help developing areas anywhere in the world. The Point Four program consisted of bringing many scattered activities for providing scientific and industrial aid into a carefully planned, coordinated program.

"In war there is no substitute for victory," said General Douglas MacArthur (seated next to driver), commander of UN forces in Korea. Here, seeking victory, he inspects troop positions along the front lines early in the war.

The Point Four program got off to a slow start. The Korean War, however, convinced even the most hesitant Americans that the world was facing a grave crisis. By 1952 most Americans believed that United States policy should include provisions for foreign aid and the strengthening of military defenses throughout the non-Communist world.

SECTION SURVEY

IDENTIFY: Ralph Bunche, Chiang Kai-shek, Mao Tse-tung, Taiwan, Douglas MacArthur, 38th parallel, Syngman Rhee, "police action," Point Four program.

1. Describe the postwar events that created tension in the Middle East.
2. (a) How did China come to have two governments by 1949? (b) What was the American position concerning China?
3. (a) What were the causes of the Korean conflict? (b) What issues provoked the Great Debate during that conflict?
4. Map Study: Examine the map on page 712. (a) Locate the line of farthest North Korean advance. (b) Describe the events of the war from September to November 1950. (c) What geographic advantage did China have when it sought to aid North Korea that the United States did not have?

4 The United States continues to meet the challenges of communism

Dwight D. Eisenhower was elected President in November 1952. When he took office, he and his Secretary of State, John Foster Dulles, continued the bipartisan foreign policy that had been followed since America's entry into World War II.

Ending the Korean War. During the 1952 election campaign, Eisenhower had promised to do everything within his power to end the Korean War. In December 1952 he visited the battle area for talks with political and military leaders. Peace talks were being carried on at this time in Panmunjom (PAN·MUHN·JUM) in Korea (see map, page 712). Finally, on July 27, 1953, North Korea and the UN signed an armistice agreement. This agreement recognized the division of Korea into two countries—North Korea and the Republic of South Korea.

In a formal treaty, the United States promised to defend South Korea against any future attack. The United States also undertook to

713

French troops look out glumly from their trenches at Dienbienphu, Vietnam, in May 1954. The French were unable to hold this key fortress and eventually faced defeat by Vietminh forces led by Ho Chi Minh after years of war.

help the South Koreans improve their economic and social conditions.

The Korean War had lasted three years and cost 33,629 American lives (and an estimated 1.5 million Communist casualties). The war had been unpopular at home. It did not change the dictatorship that ruled South Korea. It did, however, increase the prestige of the United Nations. It also showed that the prompt use of force could, at least in some cases, check Communist aggression.

Developments in Indochina. Only a few months after the Korean armistice, world peace was threatened by another crisis in East Asia. Ever since the end of World War II, Indochina, a French colony, had been torn by armed conflict. A group of revolutionary nationalists, the Vietminh (VYET·MEEN), who were mainly Communists, had been fighting to win control of the entire country from the French and their anti-Communist Vietnamese allies. When it became clear that Communist China was actively aiding the Vietminh, the United States during President Truman's administration began to send military equipment and economic help to the Vietnamese and French armies.

Early in 1954 the Vietminh, supported by the Chinese, launched a powerful drive against the French and their Vietnamese supporters. In May 1954 the key French fortress of Dienbienphu (dyen·byen·FOO) (see map, page 783) fell to the Vietminh.

In July 1954 a conference was held in Geneva, Switzerland, to discuss the fate of Indochina. Although the United States had helped finance the French cost of the war, it preferred to play the role of observer at Geneva. The delegates from France, Indochina, Communist China, the Soviet Union, and Great Britain recognized the independence of Cambodia, Laos, and Vietnam. The area of Vietnam to the north of the 17th parallel became the Communist state of Vietminh, later North Vietnam; the portion of Vietnam to the south of that line became South Vietnam (see map, page 783).

Changes in American foreign policy. Under President Eisenhower and Secretary of State Dulles, American foreign policy underwent several changes. Dulles announced a firmer American policy toward the Communist world. Instead of containment, Dulles spoke of a "rollback" of the Soviets in Eastern Europe.

714

Dulles also developed a policy that some people called **brinksmanship.** Dulles believed that the Communists only understood force. Therefore, he felt that in order to maintain peace the United States had to be ready to go to the brink of war. "The ability to get to the verge of war without getting into war is the necessary art," Dulles claimed.

Such a policy was increasingly frightening in the mid-1950's. By that time, both the Soviet Union and the United States had developed hydrogen bombs. These weapons were vastly more powerful than the atomic bombs dropped at the end of World War II.

Soon the United States and the Soviet Union were engaged in an arms race. Each side built up a stockpile of nuclear weapons. The reason for stockpiling was to threaten the other side. Each side was demonstrating its willingness to destroy the other if attacked. This policy was known as **massive retaliation.**

The United States also continued its efforts to strengthen Western Europe. In October 1954 the United States and its European allies agreed to give the Federal Republic of Germany (West Germany) full sovereign powers. They also agreed to admit West Germany to NATO and to allow it to build an army of 500,000 troops to serve under the NATO command. The United States, Great Britain, and France also agreed to regard an attack upon West Germany as an attack upon themselves.

Changes in Communist policy. In February 1956 startling news came out of the So-viet Union. Communist Party leader Nikita Khrushchev publicly attacked his predecessor, Josef Stalin, calling him a cruel tyrant. Stalin had died in 1953.

What was behind this attack? Was Khrushchev about to adopt a friendlier attitude toward the "free world"? Was he about to loosen the U.S.S.R.'s tight grip on its satellites in Eastern Europe? Would he be willing to end the arms race? Hope began to stir, and in the satellite countries people began to demand greater freedom from Soviet control.

In October 1956 the leaders of the Communist Party in Poland elected the Polish nationalist Wladyslaw Gomulka (VLAH·dee·slaf goh·MUL·kah) as first secretary of the party. Although a long-time Communist, Gomulka promised the Poles freedom of speech, press, and religion. Encouraged by Gomulka's stand, Poles staged anti-Soviet demonstrations in the streets. On several occasions they exchanged shots with Soviet troops.

The Polish revolt attracted worldwide attention. What would Khrushchev do? Instead of crushing the revolt, Khruschev surprised the world and granted concessions. He withdrew some Soviet troops from Poland and granted some freedom to the Poles.

Revolt in Hungary. Inspired by the example of the Poles, the Hungarians also rebelled against the Soviets. On October 23, 1956, Hungarian students and workers rioted in the streets of Budapest, demanding greater freedom.

Hungarian freedom fighters rebelled against the Soviets in October 1956. At first they appeared victorious and pushed the Soviets out of Budapest. However, Soviet troops later returned to ruthlessly crush all Hungarian resistance.

The next morning Soviet tanks, guns, and armored cars, supported by jet planes, moved into Budapest. Violent fighting broke out as units of the Hungarian army joined the "freedom fighters." After four days of fighting, the U.S.S.R. agreed to pull its troops out.

Even while the Hungarians were celebrating, Soviet forces began a massive attack upon Budapest. "All Budapest is under fire," the Budapest radio reported. "The Russian gangsters betrayed us."

Within a few days, the Hungarian fight for freedom came to a tragic end. With all organized resistance ruthlessly crushed, a new Hungarian government, a puppet of the U.S.S.R., began to round up the rebels and imprison them or deport them to the Soviet Union. Refugees by the thousands fled across the frontier into Austria.

Egypt and the Suez Canal. In the same week that the Hungarians rebelled, another crisis developed, this time over the Suez Canal in Egypt. For a few tense days, the world hovered on the brink of another war.

The Suez Canal, connecting the Mediterranean and the Red seas, ran entirely through Egyptian territory. Owned and operated by an international company, the canal was open on equal terms to ships of all nations. By arrangement with Egypt, British troops were stationed at the Canal Zone to safeguard it and protect British interests.

After World War II, the Egyptians became increasingly dissatisfied with British military occupation of the Canal Zone. Finally, in June 1956 the last British troops withdrew.

In the meantime, in 1954, Colonel Gamal Abdel Nasser led a successful revolution and became President of the Republic of Egypt. Nasser was determined to modernize the country and extend Egyptian influence throughout the Middle East. One of Nasser's major plans involved building a large irrigation dam and electric generating plant at Aswan on the Nile River. Furious when the Soviets, Americans, and British failed to finance the project, Nasser announced that Egypt was going to seize the canal and operate it.° The Western powers tried in vain to persuade Nasser to agree to international control by the 18 nations that regularly used the canal. Great

°In 1959 the Soviet Union agreed to provide money and engineers to build the dam. Construction began in 1960 and was completed in 1969.

Britain and France in particular saw Nasser's nationalization of the Suez Canal as a threat to the free flow of oil from the Middle East to Western Europe.

The Suez crisis. On October 29, 1956, the Israeli army moved rapidly westward through the Sinai Peninsula toward the Suez Canal. The Israeli government announced that its troops had invaded Egyptian territory to forestall a planned attack upon Israel by Egypt.

On October 30 the British and French issued a 12-hour ultimatum. They demanded that Egypt and Israel cease fighting and allow French and British troops temporarily to occupy key points in the Canal Zone. When Egypt refused, the British and French bombed Egyptian airfields and moved troops into the northern part of the Canal Zone.

In response the Soviet Union denounced Israel, France, and Great Britain as aggressors. It threatened to intervene with force if the three nations did not immediately withdraw.

The United States now found itself in an embarrassing position. Great Britain and France, its allies in NATO, had ignored both Washington and the UN. They had created a situation that could easily lead to a general war. Moreover, the United States was unwilling to permit the Soviet Union to claim that it was the only champion of Egypt and other small nations against "Western imperialism." Reluctantly the United States voted in favor of a UN General Assembly resolution calling for an immediate cease-fire and the withdrawal of British, French, and Israeli troops. Great Britain, France, and Israel accepted these terms.

The Eisenhower Doctrine. One result of the Suez crisis was that the United States adopted what came to be known as the Eisenhower Doctrine. In January 1957 President Eisenhower asked Congress to authorize him to use military force if this were requested by any Middle Eastern nation to check Communist aggression. He also asked Congress to set aside $200 million to help those Middle Eastern countries that desired such aid from the United States. Congress granted both requests. The United States thus indicated its intention of checking Communist influence in the Middle East.

The Eisenhower Doctrine was soon tested. Early in 1958 Egypt and Syria, linked in a temporary union, urged the other Arab nations to join them in opposing Western influence.

During the next few months, the Arab world was torn by intrigue. Rebellion broke out against the pro-Western government in Lebanon. In Iraq army officers killed the pro-Western leaders and seized control of the government. The leaders of Lebanon and Jordan, now convinced that their pro-Western governments would soon be overthrown, too, appealed to the United States and Great Britain for help. President Eisenhower immediately sent American marines to Lebanon. At the same time, Great Britain flew paratroopers into Jordan.

For several weeks American and British forces remained ready for any emergency. Late in September, after the Secretary-General of the UN reported that the situation was improving, Great Britain and the United States withdrew their troops.

The race into space. The crisis in the Middle East was not the major development of 1957–58. The most startling news, which broke on October 4, 1957, was compressed into a single word: *Sputnik.* The Russians had succeeded in orbiting an artificial satellite around the earth.

The American public, long convinced that no nation was superior to the United States in science and technology, was shocked. Recognizing the Soviet feat, President Eisenhower assured the American people that the United States had its own rocket and missile program. On January 31, 1958, the United States launched a small satellite, Explorer I, into orbit, and the space race was under way.

Rockets powerful enough to carry satellites into space could also be used to launch atomic and hydrogen bombs. By 1960 both the Soviet Union and the United States were building stockpiles of intercontinental ballistic missiles (ICBM's). Each of the missiles was equipped with a nuclear warhead. Push-button war that could destroy millions of lives in an instant had become a dreadful possibility.

Tension over Berlin. Meanwhile, in November 1958, the Soviet Premier issued an ultimatum on Berlin. Khrushchev gave the Western powers six months to agree to withdraw from Berlin and make it a free, demilitarized city. If the Western powers did not agree, the Soviet Union would turn over to Communist East Germany complete control of all lines of communication to West Berlin. If the Western powers then tried to gain access to West Berlin without the permission of the East German government, the Soviet Union would help the East Germans to meet force with force. The United States, Great Britain, and France replied by repeating firmly that they would remain in West Berlin.

During 1959, however, the situation began to improve. The Soviet Union met with the Western leaders in a "Big Four" foreign ministers' conference. Although the conference failed to reach any important agreements, it did open the door to further negotiations.

Premier Khrushchev himself seemed to be opening the door a bit wider when, in September, he visited the United States. At the end of his visit, he and Eisenhower issued a joint declaration, stating that the most serious issue facing the world was disarmament. They also agreed that the problem of Berlin and "all outstanding international questions should be settled, not by the application of force, but by peaceful means through negotiation."

SOURCES _____

DWIGHT D. EISENHOWER'S DISARMAMENT PROPOSALS (1955)

I should address myself for a moment principally to the delegates from the Soviet Union, because our two great countries admittedly possess new and terrible weapons in quantities which do give rise in other parts of the world, or reciprocally, to the fear and danger of surprise attack.

I propose, therefore, that we take a practical step, that we begin an arrangement very quickly; as between ourselves—immediately. These steps would include:

To give each other a complete blueprint of our military establishments . . .

Next, to provide within our countries facilities for aerial photography to the other country. . . .

FROM FICTION TO FACT

In Jules Verne's science fiction classic, *Twenty Thousand Leagues Under the Sea,* Captain Nemo performed an incredible feat. Submerging his electric-powered submarine, the *Nautilus,* under the Antarctic Ocean, he crossed the South Pole. It was a fascinating adventure story for readers of 1869, and later—but, of course, it was fiction.

At least it was fiction until 1958. In that year an American submarine actually made the first transpolar voyage, through the Arctic at the North Pole. This modern-day *Nautilus* (named after Verne's creation) was also the first nuclear-powered submarine. Since it was not dependent on oxygen, it could stay submerged much longer than previous underwater craft.

Preparations for the pioneering voyage of the *Nautilus* were highly secret. (The wife of its commanding officer, William Anderson, thought he was in Panama.) On August 1 the submarine, with 116 crewmen and scientific observers aboard, submerged off Point Barrow, Alaska. It carried ten special sonar instruments for ice detection, as well as a closed-circuit television system. The ship traveled through a series of underwater valleys, skirting vast blocks of ice that looked "like clouds going by extremely rapidly."

On Sunday, August 3, the *Nautilus* reported that its position was "latitude 90, longitude indeterminate"—in other words, the North Pole. The depth of the sea floor was 13,410 feet (4,087 meters), almost 2,000 feet (656 meters) lower than previous estimates.

The *Nautilus* continued its voyage, resurfacing on August 5 near the island of Spitsbergen. Commander Anderson was immediately flown to Washington, D.C., to receive the Legion of Merit from President Eisenhower. When questioned by reporters, he admitted that he could have made the crossing "in a much more relaxed fashion." But, he grinned, "we were in a hurry."

Encouraged by Khrushchev's apparent willingness to negotiate, the Western powers agreed to meet with the Soviet Premier at a summit conference.

Summit conference abandoned. The summit conference was never held. Early in May 1960, shortly before the conference was scheduled to open in Paris, Premier Khrushchev charged the United States with "aggression." He announced that on May 1 the Soviets had detected and shot down a United States plane flying over Sovet territory.

American officials at first insisted that the U-2, as the plane was called, was engaged in weather research and had strayed off its course. Later the United States admitted that the U-2 had been engaged in aerial reconnaissance over the U.S.S.R.

Premier Khrushchev was furious. He refused to take part in the summit conference unless Eisenhower agreed to stop all such future flights over his country, apologize for past acts of "aggression," and punish those responsible for the flights.

Hoping that the meeting could still be held, President Eisenhower announced that the U-2 flights had been stopped and would not be resumed. He refused, however, to apologize. Khrushchev, refusing to accept anything less than an apology, left for home. Plans for the conference had to be abandoned.

During the remaining months of his second term, President Eisenhower continued to seek ways of reducing world tensions. His efforts were fruitless. Khrushchev refused to budge.

SECTION SURVEY

IDENTIFY: Dwight David Eisenhower, John Foster Dulles, brinksmanship, arms race, Nikita Khrushchev, Gamal Abdel Nasser, nationalization, Aswan Dam, Sputnik, ICBM.

1. How did each of the following reveal the continuing challenge of communism: (a) developments in Indochina, (b) revolt in Hungary, (c) tension over Berlin?

2. (a) What were the causes and results of the Suez crisis in 1956? (b) Explain the position taken by the United States.

3. (a) What was the Eisenhower Doctrine? (b) How was it tested by events in the Middle East?

4. Why was the summit conference scheduled for May 1960 not held?

Chapter Survey

Summary: Tracing the Main Ideas

World War II transformed America's relations with the rest of the world. Any hopes that the United States could return to a position of isolationism vanished in the smoke and flames of the conflict. As the richest and most powerful nation on earth, the United States had to accept the responsibilities of world leadership. During the postwar years, these responsibilities proved far heavier than anyone could have foreseen as the war ended in 1945.

The immediate problem was the worldwide challenge of communism. During the Truman administration, the United States developed a foreign policy that sought to contain the Soviet Union and to check the spread of communism. The United States offered military aid to friendly as well as to uncommitted nations. It also formed collective defense arrangements, notably the North Atlantic Treaty Organization, with other nations. By such means the United States tried to build a shield of military might around the non-Communist world.

The United States also sought in a number of ways to remove the threat of war and to strengthen the foundations of peace. Under Democratic and Republican Presidents alike, the United States continued to support the United Nations, to work for disarmament, and to help less fortunate countries achieve a richer and more rewarding way of life. The United States developed the Marshall Plan and other programs of economic and technical assistance. Through such programs the United States brought new hope, first to the war-ravaged countries of Europe, later to the emerging nations of the underdeveloped world.

During the 1950's both Democratic and Republican administrations followed these two basic policies—one seeking to maintain the military defenses of the non-communist world, the other to strengthen its economic foundations. America's leaders continued to insist that through firm resolve and through cooperation with allies, the United States would in time help people everywhere to realize the age-old dream of peace and freedom.

Inquiring into History

1. (a) In what ways is the United Nations a world government? (b) In what ways is it not?
2. In 1948 a world leader said, "The trouble lies in the intense conflict . . . between the two most powerful single nations in the world today—the United States and the Soviet Union." Give evidence to support this statement.
3. Was the Korean War a victory for the United States and the United Nations? Why or why not?
4. (a) How successful was the Marshall Plan? (b) What was its basic philosophy? Explain.
5. How effective were the actions taken by the United States during the years 1945–60 in meeting the challenge of communism?
6. The Eisenhower Doctrine was really an extension of the containment policy first developed during the Truman administration. Discuss.

Relating Past to Present

1. What do you think would be gained if the United Nations were given additional powers in order to protect world peace? What might be lost?

2. (a) How do the major areas of concern in foreign policy in the 1950's compare with those of today? (b) How does present United States policy toward these areas compare with policy in the 1950's?

Developing Social Science Skills

1. Study the primary source reading on page 709. (a) According to this document, what was the purpose of the Marshall Plan? (b) Which countries could expect to benefit from the plan? (c) What other kinds of primary sources might you investigate to learn more about the Marshall Plan? (d) What would be the advantages to a researcher of each of those sources?
2. Make a map of the world that (a) indicates the areas of influence of the United States and the Soviet Union in 1960 or that (b) illustrates the events in one world area where tension arose between the two powers during the 1950's. Be sure to include a legend on your map.
3. The U-2 incident raised important questions about the rights of one nation to spy on another. Is there evidence that such activities are going on today? Explain. How do you feel about the issue?

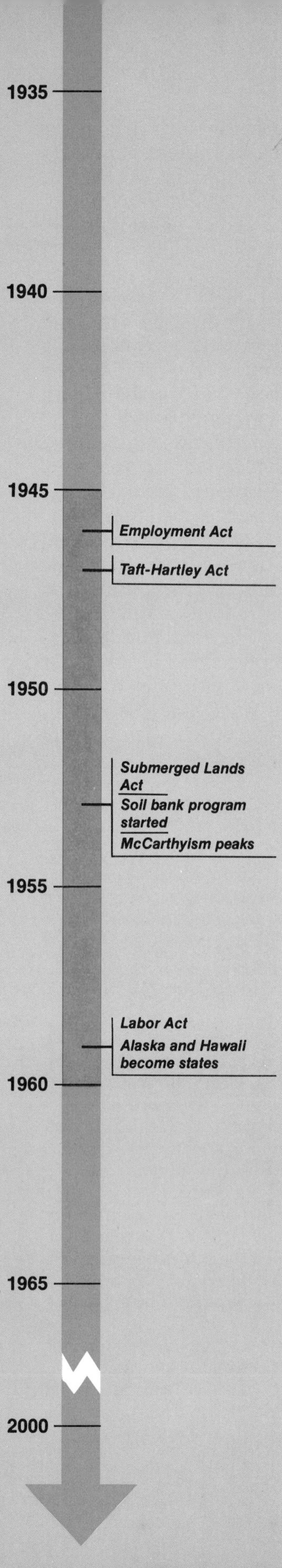

Timeline (left margin):

- 1935
- 1940
- 1945
  - Employment Act
  - Taft-Hartley Act
- 1950
  - Submerged Lands Act
  - Soil bank program started
  - McCarthyism peaks
- 1955
  - Labor Act
  - Alaska and Hawaii become states
- 1960
- 1965
- 2000

Chapter 38

Returning to Peace and Prosperity

1945–1960

International problems after World War II, as you have seen, were complex. Problems at home were equally involved. The nation had faced a decade of depression and almost five years of bitter warfare. Now Americans were eager to return to the business of daily life.

The problems of leading the nation through this period fell to Harry S. Truman, who had become President upon Roosevelt's death in April 1945. The new leader was almost 61 years old, gray-haired, plain, and folksy, with a winning grin and a liking for people. Born and raised on a Missouri farm, Truman had served overseas in World War I. After a successful career in local politics, he had been elected to the United States Senate. In the Senate he had supported New Deal programs and had attracted attention as head of a committee that investigated the national defense program. In 1945, after having served only a few months as Vice-President, he was suddenly elevated to the highest office in the land.

This was the new President who would have to handle the problems and challenges of the postwar period. The task he faced was enormous. Truman expressed it simply when he learned that he had become President: "I felt like the moon, the stars, and all the planets had fallen on me." Both Truman and his successor, Dwight D. Eisenhower, would struggle to deal with the huge burden of guiding the nation toward peace and prosperity.

THE CHAPTER IN OUTLINE

1. President Truman promotes a Fair Deal program.

2. President Eisenhower encourages Modern Republicanism.

3. The nation admits two states and prospers during Eisenhower's Presidency.

1 President Truman promotes a Fair Deal program

After World War II ended, the American people were concerned with two major efforts at home. (1) They wanted to transform the economy from wartime production to prosperous peacetime purposes. (2) Most Americans also wanted to resume and extend the social programs of the New Deal, many of which had been suspended during World War II.

Return of the armed forces. After Japan surrendered in August 1945, Americans were eager to return to peacetime conditions. They wanted their sons and daughters, brothers and sisters, husbands and friends, home again. Most of the men and women in the armed forces were just as eager to return to their homes in the states.

The nation's military leaders, involved in the postwar occupation of defeated enemy nations, reluctantly gave in to public pressure. Within two years after the war ended, the army, the navy, and the air force had sharply reduced their strength.

After World War II, the government did far more to help veterans return to civilian life than had ever been done before. Government help came through the Servicemen's Readjustment Act of 1944. This "GI Bill of Rights," as it was called, provided for (1) government loans to help veterans set up businesses or farms, (2) government loans to buy homes, (3) pensions and hospital care, and (4) educational opportunities. Under the GI Bill, hundreds of thousands of veterans received money for tuition, books, and part of their living expenses while they attended school or college.

The Employment Act of 1946. The federal government also, for the first time, assumed responsibility for maintaining a high level of employment. Although the Employment Act of 1946 did not guarantee "full employment," it did commit the federal government to maintain a strong economy and high employment through federal spending. The act's effectiveness was marred by the decision of Congress, against Truman's wishes, to abolish the Fair Employment Practices Committee. During the war this committee had helped to enlarge job and other opportunities for blacks and other minorities.

On their way home after serving in World War II, these soldiers look forward to starting their lives anew. Many of these returning veterans would use the G.I. Bill to help them go to college, buy homes, and begin businesses of their own.

Other postwar legislation. In August 1946 President Truman signed the Atomic Energy Act. This act established a government monopoly over the production of all fissionable materials. It placed the control of nuclear research and production in a newly created Atomic Energy Commission (AEC).

The National Security Act of 1947 centralized the responsibility for military research and planning. It created a new executive department, the Department of Defense, headed by a civilian Secretary of Defense. The act provided the new Secretary with three assistants, the Secretaries of the Army, Navy, and Air Force. The act also created the Central Intelligence Agency (CIA) to gather intelligence data abroad.

In 1947 Congress also proposed the Twenty-second Amendment (page 196), which became part of the Constitution in 1951. This amendment limited a President's length of service to two terms. The Twenty-second Amendment reflected the widely shared opinion that executive power might get out of hand if a President were not limited to eight years in office.

Postwar inflation. Some Americans had feared a postwar recession in the economy as industry shifted from wartime to peacetime production. However, there was no serious unemployment as veterans returned to civilian life. Most Americans—with important exceptions—had jobs and enjoyed a high degree of prosperity.

Prosperity did bring its own problems, including inflation. For more than a year after the war ended, President Truman kept wartime price controls (page 688). However, demands for ending these controls grew stronger. When Republicans, who opposed controls, gained a majority in Congress in 1946, Truman ended all controls on prices and wages, though not on rents.

Prices at once started to rise. High wartime wages, saved during the war years when most consumer goods had been scarce, had created an enormous reserve of purchasing power. With money to spend and an ever-increasing demand for goods of all kinds, American consumers created a seller's market for American business.

President Truman retained rent controls because of a severe housing shortage that would have caused rents to skyrocket. Few houses had been built during the Great De-

pression and almost none during the war, even though the population was increasing. Truman tried to provide government subsidies for new housing but failed. By 1947, however, the housing industry was moving into high gear. The housing situation, while still serious, began to improve.

Labor unrest. Rising prices led to demands for higher wages. In many cases industry met the demands—but raised prices to cover the increased costs of production. The rise in prices, in turn, spurred labor to demand even higher wages. Thus inflation continued its upward spiral, with workers blaming industry, industry blaming workers, and consumers caught in the middle.

Labor unrest led to strikes. In 1946 almost 4.6 million workers went out on strike at one time or another. Two of the most serious strikes involved the railroads and the coal-mining industry. President Truman, who was generally sympathetic to organized labor, ended the railroad strike by threatening to draft the strikers into the army. The federal government also ended the coal miners' strike by seizing the mines and issuing an injunction ordering the miners to return to work.

The Taft-Hartley Act. The postwar labor unrest and strikes led to public demand for stronger federal controls over organized labor. When the Republicans won control of Congress in 1946, they felt that their victory in part reflected a rising demand for new labor legislation. In June 1947 Congress passed the Labor-Management Relations Act, better known as the Taft-Hartley Act. President Truman vetoed the act, which he called "a clear threat to the successful working of our democratic society." Nevertheless, Congress passed the Taft-Hartley Act over his veto.

In general, the new law aimed to reduce the power that organized labor had won during the New Deal. The Taft-Hartley Act restricted the contributions of unions to political campaigns. It permitted management to seek injunctions to end strikes and to sue union officials for violations of contracts or for engaging in certain strikes. The law forbade closed-shop agreements requiring workers to belong to a union before they could be hired. It also gave the President power to require an 80-day cooling-off period when a strike threatened to affect the national health and safety. The law also required employers and union leaders to sign non-Communist oaths of allegiance.

Another provision of the Taft-Hartley Act allowed states to ban union-shop agreements within their borders. Such union-shop agreements require workers to join a union within a specified period after they are hired. By 1950, twelve states had passed legislation, known as **right-to-work laws,** barring such agreements.

The Taft-Hartley Act proved highly controversial. Supporters argued that it merely corrected the unfair advantages granted to labor in the Wagner Act of 1935 (page 613). Organized labor, on the other hand, protested that the new law deprived workers of many benefits won over a long period.

Gains for organized labor. During the postwar years, however, organized labor did make notable gains. Workers in general won substantial wage increases.

One labor agreement set an important precedent. In 1948, General Motors and the United Automobile Workers (UAW) signed a contract with an escalator clause. This clause tied wage increases to the cost of living. Other unions soon adopted similar contracts. Some union contracts linked pay increases to formulas based on increases in the cost of living as well as rising productivity. Union contracts often included welfare provisions, among them pro-visions for retirement pensions and health insurance.

The election of 1948. By 1948 the nation was enjoying a high level of prosperity. Under such favorable conditions, the Democrats met to choose their Presidential candidate.

The Democratic convention nominated President Truman on the first ballot. Largely at Truman's insistence and that of Mayor Hubert H. Humphrey of Minneapolis, the delegates included a strong civil rights plank, or section, in their platform. This plank urged Congress to guarantee the right of every adult (1) to vote and take part in politics, (2) to have an equal opportunity to work at any job for which he or she was qualitifed, (3) to receive personal security, and (4) to enjoy equal treatment in the armed services. The Democratic platform also favored repeal of the Taft-Hartley Act, federal support of housing, education and farm income, and broader social security benefits.

The Democratic platform split the party. Southern delegates vigorously opposed the civil rights plank. A number of southern Democrats formed a separate States' Rights Party and nominated Governor J. Strom Thurmond of South Carolina for President.

Former Vice-President Henry A. Wallace also left the Democrats to head a new third

In the 1948 campaign, Harry S. Truman promised, "there will be a Democrat in the White House—and you're looking at him." Few believed him, including this newspaper, which headlined his defeat before the returns were in.

party. Wallace's Progressive Party attacked Truman's foreign policy for being too anti-Communist. The Party warned that Truman's policies might lead to war with the Soviet Union. The Progressive Party also sought the support of labor and liberals by promising to renew and extend many New Deal measures.

With the Democrats divided, public opinion polls and most newspapers predicted that the Republican candidate, Governor Thomas Dewey of New York, would win. But President Truman launched a shrewd election campaign. He asked a special session of the Republican-controlled Congress to live up to its 1946 campaign promises and do something to halt rising prices and solve the housing crisis. When Congress adjourned without acting on these measures, Truman toured the country and denounced the legislators for failing to meet their responsibilities.

The election result was an astonishing victory for President Truman. He polled 49.4 percent of the popular vote to Dewey's 45 percent. Truman won 303 electoral votes, Dewey 189, and Thurmond 39. Wallace won no electoral votes at all. The Democrats also regained control of Congress and won many important state and city elections.

The Fair Deal. Heartened by his victory, President Truman decided to launch a broad program of reform. He urged Congress to adopt a Fair Deal program and extend some of the New Deal reforms. Many observers doubted that the President could win support for his program from the various groups in his own party. Time after time during Truman's second term, many southern and some northern Democrats did join the Republicans to block Fair Deal measures.

President Truman did, however, have some success with the Fair Deal program. Between 1949 and 1952, Congress did the following: (1) It extended social security benefits to include 10 million more persons. (2) The minimum wage for workers in interstate industries was raised from 40 to 75 cents an hour. (3) Congress authorized the federal government to clear slums and to build 810,000 low-income housing units over a six-year period. (4) Rent controls were continued to 1951. (5) A new Agricultural Act established farm price supports at 90 percent of parity through 1950 and thereafter on a sliding scale of 75 to 90 percent. (6) More federal employees were brought under civil ser-

vice. (7) The work of the Reclamation Bureau in flood control, hydroelectric plants, and irrigation projects was expanded.

On the other hand, President Truman failed to persuade Congress to repeal the Taft-Hartley Act, to broaden support for education, to enact health insurance, and to secure all of the civil rights proposals he favored.

Concern over internal security. In 1947 President Truman asked the Federal Bureau of Investigation (FBI) and the Civil Service Commission to investigate the loyalty of all federal employees. By the end of 1951, more than 3 million employees had been investigated and cleared, 2,000 had resigned, and 212 had been fired as "security risks."

Meanwhile, in 1948 the FBI and the Department of Justice began an intensive investigation of Communist activity in the United States. Before the year ended, 11 Communist leaders had been indicted, tried, and sentenced to prison.

Finally, Congress passed the Internal Security Act of 1950. This law required all Communist organizations in the United States to file their membership lists as well as statements of their financial operations with the Attorney General's office.

In its deepening concern over internal security, Congress was reacting not only to the possibility of Communist subversion at home but also to the increasingly serious international situation. Both of these issues weakened the efforts to promote the Fair Deal program. Both also played major roles in the Presidential election of 1952.

SECTION SURVEY

IDENTIFY: GI Bill, Twenty-second Amendment, right-to-work laws, Hubert H. Humphrey, Strom Thurmond, Henry Wallace, Internal Security Act of 1950.

1. (a) Why was the Taft-Hartley Act passed? (b) What were its provisions?

2. (a) What were the provisions of the civil rights plank of 1948? (b) Why did these provisions cause controversy?

3. Describe some important achievements of Truman's Fair Deal program.

4. Chart Study: Make a chart comparing the parties, candidates, issues, and results of the election of 1948.

2 President Eisenhower encourages Modern Republicanism

In the 1952 Presidential campaign, the Republicans adopted the slogan "It's time for a change." However, they did not agree among themselves as to the nature of the change they wanted. Like the Democrats, they split into a conservative wing and a liberal wing.

The election of 1952. Confident of a Republican victory, each wing of the Republican Party fought vigorously to control the nominating convention. The conservatives failed to gain the nomination for their candidate, Senator Robert A. Taft of Ohio. The liberals won, nominating General Dwight D. Eisenhower for the Presidency and Richard M. Nixon of California for the Vice-Presidency.

In 1952 President Truman chose not to run for reelection. Consequently the democrats then entered their 1952 nominating convention as a divided party. In general, conservative Democrats had little liking for the New Deal and the Fair Deal. Moreover, southern Democrats differed sharply with many of their colleagues on the issue of civil rights. Faced with this party split, the Democrats finally chose Governor Adlai E. Stevenson of Illinois for their Presidential candidate and Senator John Sparkman of Alabama as their Vice-Presidential nominee.

Both parties waged hard-fought campaigns. The Republicans charged the Democrats with "political corruption" and promised to "clean up the mess in Washington." The Republicans condemned their opponents for steadily enlarging the powers of the federal government over the states. Further, Eisenhower charged the Truman administration with "bungling" in the Korean War.

Stevenson was an effective campaigner. He defended the Fair Deal and the foreign policies of the Truman administration. He insisted that there was no easy road to the "peace, prosperity, and progress" that the Republicans were promising the voters.

On November 4, 1952, voters in record numbers cast their ballots. Eisenhower won 57 percent of the popular vote and an overwhelm-

"I like Ike!" people chanted wherever Dwight D. Eisenhower appeared. When Eisenhower returned from service in Europe, he was one of the most popular persons in America — a fact that led to his landslide election as President.

TRIUMPH OVER A CRIPPLER

In 1921 Franklin D. Roosevelt—then a promising politician of 39—was vacationing at his family's summer home. Suddenly he was hit by a high fever, the onset of polio. When he recovered, his legs were paralyzed; never again could he walk without braces and canes. Roosevelt's election later to the Presidency was a vivid reminder for other polio sufferers that their lives might still be fulfilling. Still, the question remained: What could be done to control the spread of the disease?

Almost every year throughout the 1900's brought a worse epidemic. Most of the victims were children. (For this reason polio was often called infantile paralysis.) In the worst year of all, 1952, almost 58,000 Americans were struck. Of these over 20,000 were paralyzed and more than 3,000 died.

Medical experts knew that polio was caused by a virus. Yet much experimentation was needed before an effective vaccine could be produced. Beginning in 1939, a team of researchers led by a young doctor named Jonas Salk searched for such a vaccine. In 1953, having inoculated some 7,500 children (as well as himself and his family) with good results, Salk announced his findings publicly.

The following year over 1.8 million children took part in a testing program remarkable for its scope. Results were announced at Ann Arbor, Michigan, on April 12, 1955—a day chosen by chance but marking the tenth anniversary of the death of Franklin D. Roosevelt. Over 500 guests heard a report of the trials: the vaccine was 60 to 90 percent effective. Then Salk was introduced, and the room exploded with television lights, flashbulbs, and shouts of "It's here!" and "It's safe!"

Never again would polio attack with its earlier force. Soon doctors were also administering an oral vaccine pioneered by Dr. Albert Sabin. By the mid-1960's there were scarcely a hundred cases of polio in the entire United States.

---

ing majority of 442 to 89 in the electoral count. To the dismay of the Democrats, he carried even the traditionally Democratic states of Virginia, Tennessee, Florida, and Texas. Nevertheless, the Republicans won control of Congress by only bare majorities in both houses.

Eisenhower's background. Dwight D. Eisenhower, the newly elected President, had been born in Texas in 1890 and raised in Kansas. An average student and a good athlete, he entered West Point in 1911. After graduation he served in the army at posts in Texas, Kansas, France, and the Philippines.

As World War II drew nearer, Eisenhower's abilities as a planner and organizer attracted attention. He advanced rapidly in rank and was finally named Supreme Commander of the Allied Forces in Europe.

By the end of the war, Eisenhower was one of the country's most popular heroes. Both the

Democrats and the Republicans urged him to accept nomination for the Presidency in 1948, although his political preferences were not known. Despite the pressure, Eisenhower at that time refused to get involved in politics. He left the Army to become President of Columbia University in 1948. In 1950, he returned to military service as the military commander of the NATO forces. Eisenhower held this position until he decided to run for the Republican nomination in 1952.

Eisenhower's administration. Eisenhower's style of Presidential leadership was a sharp change from the styles of Roosevelt and Truman. They had been active, vigorous leaders who had pressed Congress to pass their programs. Eisenhower believed that a President should not do too much leading. Instead, he felt that Congress should shape its own programs and that the President should carry them out. In carrying out these programs, Eisenhower expected his Cabinet members and his various appointees to handle the daily business of government. Only the most difficult problems were to be referred to him.

Economy in government and a balanced budget were "the first order of business" in Eisenhower's administration. Appropriations for defense and foreign aid were reduced significantly in spite of arguments from some Democrats that the administration was weakening national security. In 1956, for the first time in eight years, the government ended its fiscal year with a surplus.

Despite concern for a balanced budget, the Eisenhower administration did not attempt to repeal the basic social and economic legislation of the New Deal–Fair Deal era. President Eisenhower was personally in sympathy with much of this legislation. He supported a moderate extension of some of the New Deal- Fair Deal programs. This middle-of-the-road policy in domestic affairs — together with support for the United Nations, military aid for American allies, and economic and military help for underdeveloped countries — came to be called "Modern Republicanism."

Social legislation. Early in April 1953, President Eisenhower signed a joint resolution of Congress, transforming the Federal Security Agency into the Department of Health, Education, and Welfare (HEW). Oveta Culp Hobby, who had commanded the Women's Army Corps, became HEW's first Secretary. In January 1954, in his State of the Union message, Eisenhower urged Congress to expand the social security program and consider ways of providing additional federal aid for housing, education, and health.

Congress responded by extending social security to an additional 10.5 million persons and by increasing benefits. By 1955 about 90 percent of the nation's workers were covered by social security.

Congress also set aside additional money for the construction of hospitals and for medical research. In 1955 it authorized $500 million for slum clearance and urban redevelopment.

However, Congress refused to appropriate money to build schools and raise teachers' salaries. Many members of both political parties feared that federal support of education might lead to federal control. In 1958, however, after the Russians had successfully launched several earth satellites, Congress adopted legislation providing loans for able students, chiefly for students of science.

The farm problem. While dealing successfully with a number of domestic problems, the Eisenhower administration grappled with others for which there appeared to be no ready solutions. One such problem was the state of the nation's farms.

During the Eisenhower years, surplus crops from the nation's farms continued to be a problem. In an effort to discourage farmers from overproducing, Congress in 1954 replaced its fixed price support system with a flexible one.

Between 1952 and 1956, farm income dropped 26 percent. There were a number of reasons for this situation, including the loss of foreign markets and growing competition from farmers in other countries. Basically, however, the problem was an old one—overproduction in relation to the nation's needs. Since the early 1930's, farm productivity had almost doubled, largely because of advances in technology.

From 1942 to 1954, the government tried to guarantee farmers a fixed price support of 90 percent of parity. When prices dropped below this 90-percent level, the government bought surplus crops at the fixed price. Under this policy, grain elevators, warehouses, and storage facilities were overflowing. Storage charges alone were costing the government nearly a million dollars a day. Surpluses continued to pile up, and prices continued to fall.

In an effort to prevent these huge surpluses, Secretary of Agriculture Ezra Taft Benson persuaded the Eisenhower administration to end fixed price supports. In their place Congress adopted a flexible scale of price supports. This new policy aimed at discouraging farmers from growing crops that were flooding the market.

In 1956 the government made a major change in the farm program. The "soil bank program," as it was called, was designed to encourage the use of more land for providing forage, for growing trees, and for creating reservoirs. Farmers were to be paid for withdrawing land from commercial cultivation. By the end of 1958, the soil bank had paid $1.6 billion to farmers for withdrawing land previously used for growing crops.

Encouraging private business. The Eisenhower administration generally tried to reduce government interference with the states and with private business. For many years there had been controversy over the ownership of oil fields lying off the coasts of Florida, Louisiana, Texas, and California. Who owned these oil fields, the federal government or the states? With the approval of the Eisenhower administration, Congress settled this offshore oil controversy with the Submerged Lands Act of 1953, which gave the states control of the underwater oil deposits.

The Tennessee Valley Authority also became an issue in 1954 when the Atomic Energy Commission required additional electricity. Opposing a TVA proposal to build steam plants

Senator Joseph McCarthy (center) aired charges of communism against the U.S. Army during the 1954 Senate hearings. As millions of Americans watched the proceedings broadcast live on television, McCarthy's popularity plummeted.

to generate electricity for the AEC, the administration awarded the contract to a group of private utility companies. However, the contract aroused such a storm of controversy that it was canceled.

The Eisenhower administration made other efforts to encourage private enterprise. (1) Shortly after taking office, the President abandoned the wage and price controls imposed during the Korean War. (2) Former President Hoover agreed to head a new commission to recommend ways of securing greater efficiency in government and removing government competition with private business. (3) In 1954 Congress amended the Atomic Energy Act, giving private industry a larger opportunity to develop atomic energy for peaceful uses. (4) The federal government reduced or completely ended its participation in business activities. Among the activities curtailed were the manufacture of synthetic rubber, the operation of railroads, ships, and hotels, and the production of motion pictures.

Internal security. President Eisenhower faced the continuing problem of internal security during his administration. As you have read in Chapter 37, concern over the spread of communism became widespread after World War II. Revelations that American atomic secrets had been passed on to the Soviet Union, the victory of the Communists in China, and the outbreak of the war in Korea increased this concern.

During the Truman administration, Senator Joseph McCarthy of Wisconsin began to charge high government officials of sympathy with communism. In 1951 he even attacked General George C. Marshall, accusing him of conspiracy against the government. By the time Eisenhower became President, McCarthy, as head of a Senate subcommittee, was investigating the State Department and other government agencies. In his relentless hunt for Communists, he was joined by large numbers of private citizens. Actors, writers, educators, and other individuals and organizations were investigated and accused of communism or sympathy toward it.

Many Americans praised McCarthy for his patriotic zeal. Others criticized him for recklessness and disregard of constitutional rights. By the end of 1953, a national poll indicated that Americans who supported his activities outnumbered his critics by almost two to one.

The Senator was at the peak of his power and influence when he began to look for spies and Communists in the Army. The Army counterattacked with the revelation that McCarthy had attempted to use his influence to get the Army to give preferential treatment to one of the young men on his staff. McCarthy, claiming that the Army was trying to blackmail him in an effort to stop his investigation, demanded a public hearing.

The hearing, begun in April 1954 in full view of television cameras, continued into June. Huge numbers of Americans, sometimes numbering 20 million, watched the event daily on their television screens. Before it was over, Senator McCarthy was a discredited man. He had destroyed himself by his sarcasm, his endless interruptions, and his reckless and unsupported accusations. By the end of the year, the Senate had effectively finished McCarthy's career by voting to censure him. The vote was 67 to 21.

SECTION SURVEY

IDENTIFY: Adlai Stevenson, Oveta Culp Hobby, soil bank, Joseph McCarthy, censure.

1. What did Eisenhower think was the proper role of the President?
2. What was meant by Modern Republicanism?
3. In what ways did the Eisenhower administration encourage private enterprise?
4. (a) What problem faced farmers during the 1950's? (b) What attempts were made to solve this problem?

3 The nation admits two states and prospers during Eisenhower's Presidency

Toward the end of his first term, Eisenhower's popularity as President seemed undiminished. However, this popularity did not carry over to the Republican Party as a whole. In the 1954 Congressional elections, the Republicans had lost control of Congress. As the months passed, it became increasingly clear that Republican chances for victory in the 1956 elections depended upon Eisenhower's willingness to run for a second term.

The election of 1956. In September 1955 the nation was shocked to learn that President Eisenhower had suffered a heart attack. Even after his recovery was certain, the public wondered whether he would run for reelection. Eisenhower himself answered that question in February 1956 with the declaration that he was willing to be a candidate.

Both of the major parties held nominating conventions in August. The Republicans enthusiastically renominated Eisenhower and Nixon. The Democrats renominated Adlai Stevenson and chose as his running mate Senator Estes Kefauver of Tennessee.

In the campaign the Republicans reminded voters that the country was enjoying the highest standard of living in American history. The Democrats blamed the Republicans for the continuing high cost of living and for falling farm prices. They also charged that the Republicans had failed to develop an effective foreign policy.

In his bid for the Democratic nomination, Adlai Stevenson got a royal welcome. He was a popular candidate. However, he was unsuccessful in his attempt to unseat the even more popular Eisenhower from the Presidency.

Eisenhower's popularity returned him to the White House with a popular vote of more than 35 million to Stevenson's nearly 26 million and an electoral vote of 457 to 73. Nevertheless, the voters returned a Democratic majority to Congress, increasing the lead that the Democratic Party had won in 1954.

In the 1958 Congressional elections, the Democrats won by a landslide, piling up large majorities in both houses. Thus, for his last six years in office, Eisenhower had to work with a Congress controlled by the Democrats.

The Labor Act of 1959. During Eisenhower's second term, there were problems with organized labor. In 1957–58 a Congressional committee headed by Senator John L. McClellan revealed corrupt leadership in certain unions, notably in the powerful Teamsters Union. Several labor officials were brought into court and given jail sentences. The leaders of the AFL-CIO insisted that the corrupt practices were confined to only a small segment of organized labor. They took steps, however, to put their own house in order.

In the meantime, Congress adopted the Labor-Management Reporting and Disclosure Act of 1959. This law contained a number of important and far-reaching provisions: (1) It prohibited Communists or persons convicted of felonies within the five previous years from serving as officials or employees of labor unions. (2) It prohibited **secondary boycotts°** and the picketing of parties other than those directly involved in the strike. (3) It required labor unions to file with the Secretary of Labor annual reports giving complete information about their financial activities and other matters. (4) It required employers to report any loans or payments made to unions as well as any payments made to labor relations consultants. (5) It required national labor organizations to hold elections at least every five years. (6) It provided a bill of rights guaranteeing members of labor unions the right to attend meetings, nominate candidates for office, and vote in elections using secret ballots.

The new labor legislation went into effect in September of that year. In the meantime, President Eisenhower and Congress had been facing another difficult problem of labor-management relations.

°**secondary boycott:** the support of a boycott by other unions and other parties not directly involved in the dispute.

730

One of the outstanding events of the Eisenhower years was the opening of the St. Lawrence Seaway which made it possible for oceangoing ships to sail from the Atlantic to American and Canadian ports along the Great Lakes.

The steel strike of 1959. In 1959 the contract between the steel industry and the United Steel Workers of America came up for renegotiation. The workers asked for a wage increase and other benefits. They claimed that the steel industry could afford to meet these requests without raising the price of steel. The industry refused to discuss a wage increase unless the union would agree to changes in work rules.

In July the union called a strike involving 500,000 steelworkers and plants that produced 85 percent of the nation's steel. Negotiations dragged on for week after week. Finally, President Eisenhower, using powers granted him in the Taft-Hartley Act, asked for an 80-day anti-strike injunction. The injunction went into effect in November, and the workers returned to their jobs.

The injunction did not, of course, settle any of the issues. It was not until January 1960 that the union and the industry reached an agreement providing for step-by-step wage increases over a period of 30 months. In the dispute over work rules, the union maintained the right to place its own workers.

Gains for organized labor. During Eisenhower's administration organized labor won several notable advances. Congress raised the hourly minimum wage under the Fair Labor Standards Act from 75 cents to $1. In June 1955 the Ford Motor Company and the General Motors Corporation signed contracts that moved the United Automobile Workers toward a guaranteed annual wage. The new contracts provided, among other things, for the companies to pay unemployment benefits to the workers.

During the 1950's a growing number of unions set up welfare funds to aid unemployed, disabled, and retired workers. Some of the unions used surplus capital to buy stocks, bonds, and real estate.

In 1955 the A. F. of L. and the CIO voted to combine. The new organization, called the AFL-CIO, with George Meany as president and Walter Reuther as vice-president, had 15 million members.

Alaska and Hawaii. In 1959, during President Eisenhower's second term, Alaska and Hawaii were admitted as the 49th and 50th

731

states of the Union. They were the first states that did not share a common border with any of the other states. Alaska, now the largest state in the Union, adjoins northwestern Canada, far to the north of the state of Washington. Hawaii, a group of islands in the Pacific Ocean, is located about 2,400 miles (3,860 kilometers) west of California.

Alaska, as you have read, was purchased from Russia in 1867 by Secretary of State William Seward at a time when several nations were competing for its fur trade. So little was known then of its riches that for years Americans called Alaska "Seward's Folly." In the 1900's, however, Alaska became an important American source of timber and fish and of gold and other minerals. Later, in the early 1970's, a massive pipeline was built to transport enormous supplies of crude oil from the far north to the southern shore of Alaska for shipment in tankers.

Alaska's population today exceeds 300,000. About one fifth are native Americans—Eskimos of the north, Aleuts of the southwest and the Aleutian Islands, and various Indian tribes, mainly from along the southeastern coast of the state. Adult members of these minority groups became American citizens when Alaska became a state.

The first known inhabitants of the Hawaiian Islands were Polynesians. They were expert seafarers who probably sailed there in ocean-going canoes from other Pacific islands hundreds of years ago. Beginning in the late 1700's, European and American ships stopped in the islands for fresh water and food. American missionaries arrived in the 1820's. In the late 1800's, American planters, as you may recall, developed prosperous sugar and pineapple plantations and gained control of the islands. The United States annexed the islands in 1898, and Hawaii became a territory.

Many immigrants from Japan and other parts of East Asia came to the Hawaiian Islands to work on the plantations. They remained to become farmers, factory and service workers, and business people. Out of a population of more than 800,000, about 60 percent are of Japanese, Chinese, Filipino, Korean, or Polynesian ancestry or of mixed ethnic descent.

In 1959 the citizens of Anchorage, Alaska, celebrated their new statehood. Some of them added a 49th star to the American flag, which would soon be redesigned. Alaska adopted as its state motto "North to the Future."

Riding through the streets of Waikiki in an open car seemed a good way for Hawaiians to celebrate admission to statehood in their tropical climate in 1959. The headline of the newspaper proclaims the happy long-awaited event.

Continuing prosperity. By 1960, Americans still faced stubborn domestic and international problems. Nevertheless, they continued to enjoy a rising standard of living. To be sure, during the 1950's economic progress had been slowed down twice by recessions—the first in 1953–54, the second in 1957–58. The 1957–58 recession was the more severe of the two. Unemployment climbed to more than 5.5 million, the stock market slumped, and many Americans feared the country was entering another depression. However, by 1959 unemployed workers were returning to their jobs. The stock market had reached record high levels, business was booming, and a spirit of optimism prevailed throughout the land.

In 1950 the **gross national product°** (GNP) had been 264.7 billion dollars. By 1960 it had risen to about 510 billion dollars. Never before in the nation's history had so many Americans

°**gross national product (GNP):** the total money value of all goods and services produced in the nation.

enjoyed such prosperity. The enjoyment of "Eisenhower prosperity" was tempered, however, by the continuing need to struggle with communism and the growing tensions throughout the world.

SECTION SURVEY

IDENTIFY: AFL-CIO, George Meany, Walter Reuther, GNP.

1. (a) Why was the Labor-Management Reporting and Disclosure Act of 1959 passed? (b) What were its provisions?

2. (a) Why was Alaska called "Seward's Folly" during the 1800's? (b) Why would it be unlikely to be called a "folly" today?

3. Map Study: Turn to the map on pages 840–41 and answer these questions: (a) If it is 1:00 A.M. in Denver, Colorado, what time is it in Fairbanks, Alaska? (b) What is the capital of Hawaii? (c) How far is it from Ketchikan, Alaska, to Barrow, Alaska?

Chapter Survey

Summary: Tracing the Main Ideas

In 1945 the immediate problem facing the nation was that of converting from a wartime to a peacetime economy. During the postwar years, Americans met this problem squarely, made the necessary adjustments, and entered the 1950's on a wave of unprecedented prosperity. Harry S. Truman, a devoted follower of President Roosevelt, had some success in continuing the New Deal reforms with his Fair Deal program. Nevertheless, the Republican party made political gains.

With the election of Dwight D. Eisenhower in 1952, twenty years of government by the Democrats came to an end. President Eisenhower promised to reform the federal government by reducing spending, taxes, and regulations. He also wanted to transfer many federal programs to the state and local governments. The Republicans discovered that this was easier said than done. In 1960, when the Eisenhower administration drew to a close, the size of the federal bureaucracy remained about the same as it had been in 1952.

For a few years in the early 1950's, the search for Communists in government and in private life had seriously crippled the everyday life of the nation. Even so, the majority of Americans enjoyed eight years of relative calm and prosperity during the Eisenhower administration. There were, however, serious domestic problems calling for solutions. As you will see in the next chapter, important steps were made toward these solutions. Also, multiplying troubles in Africa, the Middle East, and Asia demanded attention.

Inquiring into History

1. Describe America's demobilization and conversion to peacetime after World War II. What problems did the nation face? What steps did it take to solve them?
2. From 1954 to 1960, the government operated with a Republican President and a Congress controlled by Democrats. (a) What does this tell you about the state of national politics at this time? (b) Why might this split in control of the Congress make it difficult for the Federal government to get things done?
3. Describe the tension between internal security and constitutional rights that arose during the 1950's.
4. Compare the Presidencies of Truman and Eisenhower in terms of (a) their attitudes toward the job, (b) the support they received from the American people, and (c) their accomplishments while they held office.

Relating Past to Present

1. In what ways have the states of Alaska and Hawaii contributed to the well-being of the nation as a whole?

2. (a) How does the situation of farmers today compare to their situation during the 1950's? (b) How does the government's relationship to farmers today compare to that of the 1950's?
3. President Eisenhower wanted to reduce the size of the Federal bureaucracy, but he failed to do so. Have any Presidents in recent years expressed the same wish? Have they succeeded or failed?

Developing Social Science Skills

1. Draw a political cartoon that might have appeared in a newspaper during the Truman or Eisenhower administration. Make sure that the cartoon presents a point of view about an event or person of the time.
2. Interview someone who was an adult during the 1950's. Ask him or her to share impressions of the political events of those years. (a) How does the information gathered from the interview compare to the information in your textbook? (b) What are the advantages of such an interview for learning about the events of an era? What might be the disadvantages of an interview as a source of information? (c) What other sources of information might be used for learning about the political events of a historical period?

AN AMERICAN ALBUM
THEN AND NOW
Communications

The few bits of metal, wire, and wood hardly looked impressive yet they revolutionized communication and altered American life forever.

Until the mid-1800's, long-distance communication had depended on transportation. Letters, news, and messages of all types had to be carried to distant places by horse, boat, or train. Then in 1844 that unimpressive-looking device, Samuel Morse's telegraph, changed all that. The telegraph allowed messages to be sent in an instant over wires to distant points.

Today news is beamed around the world. Invisible signals are relayed across continents or bounced off satellites that orbit the earth. A television news bulletin that is broadcast from Illinois might be seen instantly in Australia.

The early telegraph recording instruments were simple devices.

By contrast, a modern television studio employs complex technology.

Early humans communicated by word of mouth, gestures, and simple signals. In time people developed ways of communicating with pictures, for example, the Indian painting shown here. After centuries this led to written language. Movable type and the printing press made possible the wider distribution of the written word in books and newspapers.

Beginning in the mid-1800's, advances in communication came more quickly. The first transatlantic cable for the telegraph was laid in 1858. Less than 20 years later, Alexander Graham Bell invented the telephone. The wireless telegraph appeared 20 years after that. One by one new devices for communications were invented, binding Americans together and linking them with people across the seas.

Before humans developed a written language, many important events were recorded in pictures.

Advertising was an important means of communication in the early days of the nation as it is today.

The printing press, first used in the 1400's, made newspapers possible.

For its brief life, 1860 to 1861, the pony express was the fastest means of transcontinental communication.

In the 1920's listening to the radio required the use of earphones.

Photography, developed in the mid-1800's, was an important communications development.

From its beginnings, the railroad became an important means of carrying mail.

Bell's telephone did much to link people together.

Americans live today in a world where instant communication is a way of life. Telephones keep us in touch with our friends. Television and radio give us up-to-the-minute news. Home computers provide the latest stock-market prices and weather reports.

With 1,800 daily newspapers, 16,500 magazines, 7,500 radio stations, 900 television stations, and thousands of computers, the United States has the largest communications system in the world. New technological developments will put increasing amounts of information at our fingertips, changing the ways we live, work, and play.

The importance of the printed word in communications is demonstrated by the collection of newspapers and magazines at this newsstand.

Modern communications systems allow signals to be relayed instantly by satellite to stations all around the globe.

Microcircuits and computers have opened up new possibilities for the development of communications systems.

Chapter 39

Entering an Age of Rapid Growth and Change

Change and *growth* are the words that best describe American society in the years following World War II. To be sure, change has been a central feature of American life from the day the first European settlers landed on the shores of the New World. Through the course of the three and a half centuries that followed, Americans had lived with change as they conquered the continent. They had lived with change as they built it into one of the world's most prosperous nations.

But the new and startling fact in the postwar years was the *increasingly rapid rate* of change that Americans were experiencing. Never before in human history had so much change been compressed into such a brief span of time. One observer, writing in the early 1960's, declared that the changes in these years were "so wide-sweeping that they are taking us from one epoch of human history into another."

During the 1940's, however, not even the most far-sighted observers could foresee the amazing developments that would, in the years immediately ahead, profoundly alter older ways of living in the United States and throughout the world. In 1945 the opportunities and challenges of the new age had not yet been fully revealed.

By 1960 Americans had profited from the opportunities and had accepted the challenges of this new age. The United States was the richest, most productive nation in the world. This wealth was not shared equally among the citizens of the nation. Minorities still bore the burdens of poverty and prejudice. But they had taken major steps toward achieving full equality.

THE CHAPTER IN OUTLINE

1. Science and technology make revolutionary advances.
2. The nation builds an economy of abundance.
3. Most Americans enjoy the advantages of a booming economy.
4. Poverty in a land of abundance haunts the nation's minorities.

Changing Ways of American Life

1945–1960

1 Science and technology make revolutionary advances

Before World War II, major advances had been made in science in both Europe and America. Breakthroughs had been made by scientists working by themselves or with a few colleagues in the laboratories of prominent universities or private industry. During and after the war, however, scientific research and development became increasingly a carefully organized team effort.

The successful completion of the Manhattan Project, which led to the development of an atomic bomb in 1945, was not the end of atomic testing. Bigger, more powerful weapons were designed and built. This atomic device was exploded in the Nevada desert in 1951.

Organizing human intelligence. The distinguished scholar Alfred North Whitehead observed that when human beings began to organize research, they invented "the art of inventing." This "invention," he concluded, was one of humanity's greatest achievements. The first dramatic demonstration of what scientists and engineers could accomplish by such large-scale cooperation had occurred during World War II.

Late in 1939 the federal government committed its first funds for the exploration of atomic energy. This exploration soon became an all-out, top-secret effort to develop an atomic bomb for the United States. Thousands of the nation's leading scientists, engineers, and construction workers devoted their time and talents to what came to be called the Manhattan Project.

Never before had so much money ($2 billion), so much intelligence, and so much effort been channeled into a single undertaking. The atomic bombs that leveled Hiroshima and Nagasaki in August 1945 provided evidence, terrible though it was in this case, of the effectiveness of organized research. This effectiveness was to be demonstrated again during the 1960's with another massive project. This was the Apollo program—the successful effort conducted over nearly 10 years to land American astronauts on the moon.

The growth of organized research. The successes of wartime efforts like the Manhattan Project and the development of radar prompted government and private industry in the postwar years to devote more and more money to scientific research and development. In 1930 only $166 million was spent for this purpose. By 1960 the total had risen to more than $12 billion, approximately two thirds of which came from the federal government. However, most of the work itself was carried on in the laboratories of private industry, universities, and independent research institutes.

As a result of organized scientific activity, knowledge began to accumulate at a staggering rate. People began to speak of the "knowledge explosion." The amount of information available to the human race, it was estimated, was doubling every 10 years. Even more significant, each advance opened up new horizons for science and made possible further progress in technology. As you will see, new industries were created and thousands of new products became available. Most important, scientists made fantastic progress in understanding the basic forces of nature.

Each fresh discovery also created new problems. With the invention of the art of inventing, changes were occurring so rapidly that the world could never be the same again.

International scientific research. As the years passed, international scientific research came to be carried on by teams of scientists from many countries. For example, during the period from July 1, 1957, to December 31, 1958 — known as the International Geophysical Year — scientists of 66 nations worked together. They conducted worldwide studies of gravity, geomagnetism, meteorology, oceanography, solar activity, cosmic rays, and other fundamental subjects.

In 1959 the United States and 11 other nations, including the Soviet Union, signed a treaty governing the use of Antarctica. They agreed not to exercise any territorial claim over the vast, ice-covered continent. They also set the continent aside as a scientific preserve open to the scientists of all nations.

Looking ahead, in 1967 a similar treaty relating to outer space was signed by 62 countries. The treaty (1) prohibits the orbiting of nuclear weapons and (2) prohibits any nation from claiming sovereignty over the moon or any planet. President Johnson called the treaty "the first firm step toward keeping outer space free forever from the implements of war."

The computer revolution. The electronic computer was one of the most significant postwar products of the technological revolution. The first modern computers were developed shortly after World War II. By 1960 there were about 5,000 computers in use in the United States. Nevertheless, what was to become a computerized society was still in its infancy. Eventually, thousands of computers would be installed in laboratories, business offices, government agencies, hospitals, schools, banks, scores of other organizations, and increasingly in private homes.

In a fraction of a second, computers can perform calculations that even the most efficient individual could not complete in a lifetime. Computers available by the 1960's could perform in one second 357,000 additions or subtractions or 178,000 multiplications or 102,000 divisions. They were being used in laboratories to provide instant analysis of complex tech-

LOOK   JOHN DEMPSEY

"Merfson, I'm afraid I have some rather unpleasant news for you."

Automation was a topic of great interest and concern to many Americans in the 1950's. It was a source of hope to some, a source of worry to others. In this drawing, cartoonist John Dempsey presents a lighter view of one of the problems produced by automation.

nical problems that could not be studied in any other way. They were being used in businesses and banks for accounting, bookkeeping, and billing. They were being used by governments to check income tax returns and to record data on births, marriages, public health, car registrations, and criminal records. They were being used in industry to forecast economic trends and control assembly lines in automated factories.

In brief, machines were doing much of certain kinds of mental work once performed by men and women. In fact, any data that could be measured or counted could be handled more efficiently by computers than by human beings.

Business and industry automate. Other equipment performed still other operations far more swiftly and efficiently than individuals could hope to do. For example, the Bell Telephone Company reported that if it had not installed automatic switchboards, by 1962 a work force equal to the total of all the women in the nation between the ages of 18 and 30 would have been required to handle the 90 billion telephone calls made in the United States in that year alone.

Changing Ways with TECHNOLOGY

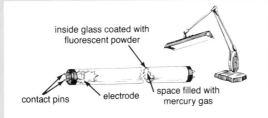

inside glass coated with fluorescent powder

contact pins electrode space filled with mercury gas

FLUORESCENT LAMPS

Fluorescent lamps were introduced at the New York World's Fair of 1939–40. They use about one fifth of the electricity of an incandescent light bulb to produce the same amount of light. When an electric current is applied to the electrodes, an arc is created between them. The arc causes mercury gas in the tube to give off invisible, ultraviolet light. A coating on the inside of the glass absorbs the ultraviolet light and gives off visible light.

The automated machines used in many industries performed a whole series of operations. Some adjusted themselves to correct their own errors. Automated factories could turn raw materials into finished products with only a handful of technicians on the job to plan and control the process.

Americans watched the rapid increase in automation with mixed feelings. Some hailed it as a triumph of human ingenuity that would lead the nation to higher and ever higher standards of living. Others shared the deep concern of Walter Reuther, president of the United Automobile Workers, who was worried about jobs. He toured a plant in which automatic machines had reduced the number of workers from 800 to 15. Reuther agreed that the plant was indeed efficient. "But," he pointedly asked, "are these machines going to buy cars?"

The leaders of organized labor were not opposed to automation as such. Instead they criticized "irresponsibly introduced" automatic machines that could "result in unprecedented unemployment." They made it clear that they expected wage earners to receive a fair share of the prosperity that would come from increasingly efficient production.

SECTION SURVEY

IDENTIFY: Manhattan Project, "knowledge explosion," International Geophysical Year, automation.

1. Why can it be said that the organizing of research is one of humanity's greatest achievements? Do you agree? Why or why not?

2. In what ways have the United States and other nations cooperated in scientific research since World War II?

3. How have automation and computers affected business? Give some examples.

4. Cartoon Study: Examine the cartoon on page 741. (a) What is the unpleasant news for Mertson? (b) How can you tell? (c) What is the attitude of the cartoonist?

2 The nation builds an economy of abundance

The most obvious impact of the revolution in science and technology was upon the nation's economy. After World War II ended, the United States entered a period of unprecedented prosperity. This prosperity was built on what economists called "an economy of abundance." This term applied to an economic system that was capable of producing more goods and services than Americans as a whole could consume.

Growing productivity. In the 1950's a group of distinguished economists stated that "America today has the strongest, most productive economic system in human history.... The United States, with little more than 6 percent of the world's population and less than 7 percent of the land area, now produces and consumes well over one third of the world's goods and services and turns out nearly one half of the world's factory-produced goods."

During the 75 years preceding World War II, the United States had doubled its output of goods about once every 24 years. After World War II, the rate of growth climbed sharply. If it continued, the United States would double its production every 18 years.

The roots of prosperity. There were many reasons for America's remarkable economic growth. Among them were an abundance of natural resources, an excellent transportation system, and great numbers of skilled workers. Growth was spurred, too, by steadily improving labor-management relations, highly organized and efficiently managed industries, efficient methods of distribution, and an economic system that rewarded both individual effort and teamwork. The role of advertising in stimulating the desire of consumers for more goods and services also played a part in economic growth.

Above all, advances in science and technology sent the economy spiraling upward. Power-driven machinery and increasingly complex equipment were now common in nearly every field of human activity. They were found on farms and in mines, in factories and laboratories, in offices and homes. Out of America's industrial plants using new machines and new processes poured an endless variety of products in ever-increasing quantities.

American farm production was also setting new records. Advances in agricultural science and technology, in farm management, and in marketing helped make Americans on the whole among the best-fed people in the world. Each year the nation's farms produced huge amounts of food to feed Americans and to export to other nations.

New and expanding industries. New industries joined older ones in providing products, services, and opportunities for more and more Americans.

The aircraft industry, still in its infancy in the 1920's, grew in the years following World War II to a multibillion-dollar enterprise. Commercial airlines directly employed thousands of men and women. Many other thousands of workers were employed in the plants producing aircraft for the airlines and for private individuals, business firms, and the armed services.

The electronics industry had been small in the early 1920's. It boomed during World War II with the production of radio transmitters, radar, and other military equipment. During the postwar years, it grew still more rapidly with the production of television sets, computers, automation controls, radios, phonographs, and countless complex items for homes and businesses. In the late 1950's, the electronics industry received another big boost. It joined with the aircraft industry and hundreds of other enterprises in an entirely new undertaking—the space program.

Another completely new industry, atomic energy, also expanded greatly during the postwar years. Although military uses continued to dominate, peaceful applications of atomic energy were growing more numerous. For example, the first commercial nuclear-powered plant for generating electricity began operations near Pittsburgh in 1957. By 1960 three more plants were operating, and several others were nearing completion. Moreover, radioisotopes produced by nuclear reactors were being used for research in many fields, including

America's space program was, literally, getting off the ground in 1958 when this U.S. Army Jupiter-C Explorer II rocket was launched. Though it was a sign of things to come, few people then could have predicted the sweeping extent of today's space achievements.

medicine, where they were also used in the treatment of patients. By 1960 the United States and the world had crossed the threshold of the nuclear age. As you will read, the new age presented problems as well as promise.

While new industries grew, older industries modernized their plants and expanded their operations by mergers and by continuing to develop new products. Among the postwar industrial giants were the steel, automotive, petroleum, chemical, pharmaceutical, and business-machine industries. The giant of industrial giants was the American Telephone and Telegraph Company, which was the largest corporation in the world.

The revolution in transportation. The nation's advance into an economy of abundance would not have been possible without revolutionary developments in transportation.

In 1945, commercial airlines were still operating out of small airports. They carried only about 3 million passengers annually, most of them in two-engine, propeller-driven planes that could hold only 20 to 40 passengers. By the 1960's they operated out of huge, sometimes overcrowded airports. They used jet aircraft and carried more than 60 million passengers annually as well as ever-growing amounts of freight.

Speed as well as size and versatility became a major factor in aircraft design during the postwar years. By the late 1950's, jet aircraft had been designed for use on commercial air routes that could fly at 600 miles (965 kilometers) an hour, close to the speed of sound.

During the postwar years, traffic problems on the nation's streets and highways became an engineer's nightmare. Between 1945 and 1960, the number of automobiles, buses, and trucks more than doubled, from 31 million to nearly 74 million. The Federal Aid Highway Act, adopted by Congress in 1956, provided for the construction of 42,500 new miles (68,400 kilometers) of superhighways. Almost as soon as the act was passed, traffic experts began to talk of the need for an even more ambitious highway construction program.

As the number of cars on American roads quadrupled, the federal government started a $75-billion interstate highway program to accommodate them. Cloverleaf designs like this soon appeared across the landscape.

The railroads, once the main carriers of the nation's passengers and freight, did not share in the transportation boom. Although they still carried more than half the nation's freight, the railroads met stiff competition from the trucking industry. Moreover, they lost most of their passenger business to private automobiles, buses, and planes.

Some daily trains carrying workers to and from their city jobs were still crowded, but with few exceptions even the commuter railroads operated at a loss. Rising taxes and increasing operating costs added to the gloomy picture. Railroad managers argued that if commuter services were to continue in full force, federal, state, and local governments would have to subsidize train service. During the 1950's their pleas for help fell for the most part on deaf ears. By 1960 many railroads were in bankruptcy or nearing it.

However, the railroads were one of relatively few victims of the economic revolution that was transforming the nation. The American economy as a whole had never been more prosperous.

SECTION SURVEY

IDENTIFY: economy of abundance, Federal Aid Highway Act.

1. What were the causes of America's dramatic economic growth after World War II?
2. What new industries developed rapidly after World War II?
3. What was the connection between the transportation revolution and (a) the airline industry, (b) the trucking industry, and (c) the railroads?

3 Most Americans enjoy the advantages of a booming economy

The rapidly rising standard of living in the late 1940's and the 1950's sprang from phenomenal advances in almost every field of science and technology. There were, however, other contributing factors. For one thing, during the depression and the war—a period of more than 15 years—millions of Americans had not been able to buy the things they wanted and, in many cases, badly needed. Equally important, there was a postwar population explosion, called by some the "baby boom." It created millions of new citizens who required food, clothing, housing, education, and entertainment.

The population explosion. During the war and the prosperous postwar years, young people married earlier and had larger families. The resulting growth in population was spectacular. Where during the depression years of the 1930's the population increased by only 9 million, during the 1940's it rose by 19 million. In the 1950's it exploded with an increase of 28 million. In that single ten-year period, the increase was about equal to the total population of the country on the eve of the Civil War.

The nation's growing prosperity also attracted immigrants. Between 1951 and 1960, more than 2.5 million men and women arrived to swell the nation's population.

America's population was not only growing. It was also moving in a great human tide across the face of the land. Two major migrations of people—one into the central cities, the other out of them—were producing dramatic changes in American life.

Changes in the central cities. The migration into the central cities consisted for the most part of impoverished men, women, and children from the rural areas. Many of these came from the South and from Appalachia, the area around the Appalachian Mountains in the eastern United States. Growing numbers also poured into the cities from Puerto Rico and Mexico and increasingly as the years passed from other Spanish-speaking countries.

The hearts of the cities—the business and financial centers—were being completely rebuilt. Urban renewal programs were started during Truman's administration and continued under President Eisenhower. Under such programs older sections of cities were torn down. Old, decaying structures were replaced by new housing and buildings. In city after city, blocks of gleaming new office buildings and apartment houses towered as visible symbols of the nation's wealth and vitality.

At times, however, urban renewal programs destroyed good, low-cost housing. Such programs could disrupt established neighborhoods and force low-income families into poorer housing. At times the wealth and vital-

745

During the 1950's, a great building boom enabled millions of Americans to become homeowners for the first time. Giant residential developments like this one in California spread across former farmlands, turning them into suburbs.

ity of the business centers of cities stood in grim contrast to the decay in many surrounding residential areas. As you will see in Chapter 42, even while the nation as a whole was enjoying the economic boom of the postwar years, the central cities and the millions of newcomers to the cities faced increasingly critical problems.

The expanding suburbs. In the meantime, many young married couples were moving out of the cities to seek better living conditions for raising families. This movement strengthened the trend toward more widespread ownership of homes. By 1960 more than 60 percent of all American homes were occupied by people who owned them. One of America's oldest dreams was being realized.

All over the nation, families who could afford to do so were moving out of the older cities into the suburbs. The countryside around the cities was being leveled by bulldozers at a rate, according to one estimate, of some 3,000 acres (1,200 hectares) every day. Huge suburban housing developments were springing up almost overnight. Department stores and banks were opening branches in the new suburban shopping centers. Many industries were also following the people out of the central cities. The new suburban communities had to create new schools, police departments, fire departments, water and sewage systems, churches, libraries, hospitals, parks, and scores of other public services almost from scratch. These expanding metropolitan areas were being tied together by the ever growing network of highways and superhighways.

Rural America was rapidly being replaced by a new and very different way of life. By 1960 almost 85 percent of the total increase in population was taking place around urban centers. These changes were creating new problems.

As the suburbs spread in an unplanned sprawl, the housing developments, shopping centers, highways, and roads ate up irreplaceable farmland at an alarming rate. The lack of planning contributed to the deterioration of the environment and of the quality of life itself.

The building boom. The changes in American life were also creating new opportunities. The movement into the suburbs stimulated a building boom. New jobs were available for millions of workers in housing, lumbering, and related industries. During the war years, almost no new houses had been built. After the war the pent-up demand for much-needed housing suddenly exploded.

Between 1950 and 1960, nearly a million new houses and apartments went up each year. In several of these years, the number even passed the million mark. The housing boom was accompanied by a similar boom in the construction of schools, hospitals, offices, factories, and government buildings. The need for highways to connect the suburbs with the central cities further stimulated the building boom.

More goods for more people. With jobs available and money to spend, Americans went on a buying spree. During the 1950's they bought nearly 50 million new automobiles. By 1960 about three fourths of all American families owned at least one car, and one out of every seven was a two-car family.

The sales of household appliances and other products also soared as the nation's young families furnished their new homes and older families began to enjoy the fruits of prosperity. Washing machines, dishwashers, toasters, vacuum cleaners, refrigerators, freezers, radios, and—newest of all—television sets poured from the factories into America's homes.

Television, invented and developed before World War II, appeared on the market in the late 1940's. By 1950 some 3 million Americans owned sets. By 1960 the number had risen to 50 million. More homes had television sets than had running water or indoor toilets.

A changing labor force. The labor force that produced these goods and services was different from that of only a generation earlier. It contained a much larger proportion of women. In 1940 one out of every four employed workers had been a woman. By 1960 the proportion had risen to one out of three.

The rapid rise in the number of women workers was the result of several developments. In the first place, the demand for workers during World War II broke down prejudices and gave women a chance to show that they could do as well as men in many different jobs. Even more significant, the rapidly expanding economy in the postwar years created thousands of new jobs. Many of these new jobs called for brainpower and manual dexterity

rather than sheer muscle. Moreover, the growing use of labor-saving appliances freed women from many of the burdens of housework.

Another striking change in the labor force was the growth in the number of white-collar workers—teachers, lawyers, doctors, computer operators, clerks, office workers, and so on. In 1956, for the first time, men and women in white-collar occupations, including the rapidly growing service industries, outnumbered blue-collar workers. By 1960 almost one in every seven Americans worked for the local, state, or federal government.

Leisure time. Shorter workweeks and paid vacations gave most Americans more leisure time than they had even dreamed of a generation before. Between 1940 and 1960, the average workweek dropped from 44 to 40 hours. In some of the skilled trades it was down to 35 hours. During this same period, the average paid vacation increased from one to two weeks.

With more free time and more money, Americans piled into their cars for vacations in the mountains, in the country, or at the seashore. Motels, fast-food chains, and service stations multiplied along the highways. Golf courses were crowded. Sailboats and power launches appeared in growing numbers on lakes and small harbors along all of the nation's coastline.

At home the major source of entertainment was the television set. In the average home, according to one estimate, the TV was turned on at least five hours every day. More than any other single development, television began to weaken regional differences and to shape a uniform culture for the entire country.

Television did not, however, devour all of America's newly-acquired leisure time. The sale of books, magazines, records, and tapes soared into the millions during the years following the war.

Need for better education. The changes transforming American life in the postwar years placed a heavy burden on the nation's educational system. The growth of population was in itself a problem. Between 1950 and the early 1960's, the number of students enrolled in America's schools and colleges increased from about 31 million to more than 50 million. This flood of students severely taxed the already overcrowded classrooms. And even larger numbers were certain to follow in the immediate future.

The number of students was not the only problem facing the schools. When the Soviet Union launched Sputnik in 1957, American confidence was shaken. Was the Soviet success due to a better educational system?

Critics in increasing numbers began to question the quality of American education. They charged that school standards were far too low. Schools, they said, were failing to prepare students for life in the rapidly changing postwar world. Such critics called for more demanding courses in mathematics, the sciences, English, and foreign languages.

In response to such criticism, Congress passed the National Defense Education Act in 1958. The act granted federal money to schools and colleges for teaching science and foreign languages. It also provided funds for loans to college students.

An uncommitted generation. Another issue troubled many older Americans. This was the indifference of young people as a whole to many of the traditional values of American life. The young men and women coming of age in the late 1940's and the 1950's were sometimes labeled as "the uncommitted generation." Their goals in life appeared to be a good job, a house in the suburbs, and a retirement program that would provide them with security in their old age. They were, it seemed, unconcerned about politics and reluctant to be bothered about the larger issues confronting the nation and the world.

This tendency to conform, to avoid controversy, was not confined to youth. It was widely shared among all age groups, women and men alike. During the 1950's America seemed on the verge of becoming a homogenized society. One historian referred to the decade of the 1950's as "the years of repose."

Books of the period. A number of the more serious books mirrored the attitudes and the problems of the times. Two of the best-selling books dealing with the war years were James Jones's *From Here to Eternity* and Norman Mailer's *The Naked and the Dead.* Among the

As television technology grew more sophisticated, a new teaching tool entered the classroom — educational television. Broadcast by the new network NET (National Educational Television), these televised classes had mixed success.

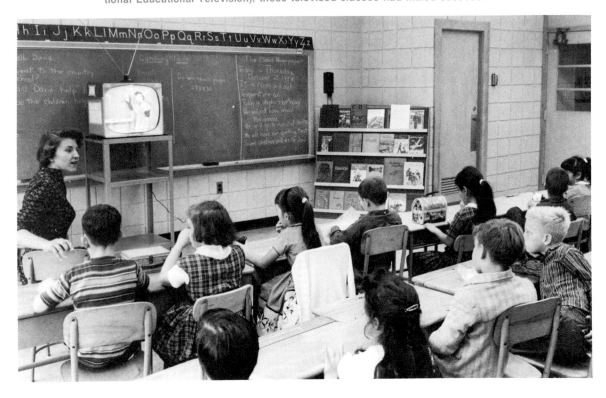

novels reflecting the deadening effect of conformity were Sloan Wilson's *The Man in the Gray Flannel Suit* and W. H. Whyte, Jr.'s, *The Organization Man.* J. D. Salinger's widely read *The Catcher in the Rye* vividly captured the life of an adolescent boy coming of age in the postwar years. Ralph Ellison's novel *Invisible Man* dealt with the attempt by a black to find his place in a hostile white society.

One of the most influential books of the 1950's was *The Affluent Society* by the Harvard economist, John Kenneth Galbraith. Galbraith reminded privileged Americans that in their pursuit of personal wealth they were neglecting the nation's poor, permitting the cities to decay, and causing the environment to deteriorate alarmingly.

SECTION SURVEY

IDENTIFY: "baby boom," urban renewal, suburb, National Defense Education Act of 1958, John Kenneth Galbraith.

1. During the 1950's America's population was moving in a great human tide across the face of the land. Explain this statement in terms of (a) the growth of central cities and (b) the growth of suburbs.

2. How were the following related to one another: (a) increased leisure time, (b) the two-car family, (c) the rising popularity of television?

3. Why were more women entering the labor force in the 1950's?

4. Graph Study: In 1930 the population of the United States was about 120 million. Make a chart or graph reflecting population growth in the years that followed: 1930's—increase of 9 million people; 1940's—increase of 19 million; 1950's—increase of 28 million. Why was the increase so great during the 1950's?

4 Poverty in a land of abundance haunts the nation's minorities

Millions of Americans did not share in the prosperity of the postwar years. The poor came from all races and all national backgrounds. They lived in rural areas and in the cities. However, it was the nation's minorities— particularly Indians, Hispanic Americans, and blacks—that bore the heaviest burdens of poverty. In their struggle to overcome prejudice and discrimination, America's minorities battled for freedom, justice, and dignity as well as for a share of the nation's material goods.

The first Americans. In this struggle no minority in the country faced more obstacles than the American Indians. In addition to discrimination, severe unemployment, and widespread poverty, the Indians have had to cope with numerous federal regulations and controls. Their problems have been compounded by shifting federal policies and programs.

The efforts to overcome these handicaps have been carried on by Indians from all walks of life—doctors, lawyers, scientists, writers, teachers, singers, athletes, and others. Theirs has been a long, difficult, and at times disheartening struggle.

Failure of the Reorganization Act. As you have read (pages 645–46), Congress had reversed a long-standing policy when it adopted the Indian Reorganization Act in 1934. This act was intended to encourage Indians to practice self-government and to strengthen tribal customs and tribal life. The promises of the act were seldom fulfilled. Some tribes that had already managed fairly well in adapting to the white culture rejected the new policy. They claimed that it would keep them in an inferior status in relation to the white majority.

Also, many of the 25,000 young Indians who had served in the armed forces during World War II were reluctant to return to tribal ways of life. These Indian veterans felt that the country for which they had fought and for which many had died owed them the full rights and opportunities of American citizenship. They believed that the complete recognition of these rights was more important than preserving tribal ways of life.

The termination policy. During the 1950's the federal government once again adopted a new Indian policy. In this policy it reversed much of the 1934 program and established entirely new goals. One of the new goals was known as "termination."

The termination program was intended to end all federal ties with the Indians. Responsibility was to be transferred to those states with large Indian populations. Acting under this policy, the government terminated federal ser-

Puerto Ricans were often at the bottom of the economic ladder, but many nevertheless had a fierce pride in their cultural heritage. This pride is evident here in their annual parade up Fifth Avenue in New York City.

policy of importing contract labor was continued after the war. From the Mexican point of view, it provided work for otherwise unemployed workers. It also provided relief through the money sent home by the *braceros* to impoverished Mexican families. However, opposition to the program was building up on both sides of the border. The Catholic Church opposed it on the ground that it broke up families. The Mexican government began to object because the Mexican economy was expanding and labor was needed in Mexico itself. The program also met growing opposition from organized labor in the United States. The newly-formed farm labor unions pointed out that it was competitively unfair to American workers.

Before the program was abandoned in 1962, more than 4.5 million Mexican workers had been imported as contract laborers into the United States. This number does not include the unknown number of illegal migrants, or undocumented immigrants.

Spanish-speaking immigrants. The *braceros* who came as farm laborers were required to return to Mexico after their contracts ended. During the 1950's, however, more than 360,000 Mexican immigrants entered the United States to become American citizens. They were joined by another 450,000 Spanish-speaking immigrants from countries in Central and South America and the West Indies. These newcomers came from all walks of life. A large percentage were highly educated professionals and white-collar workers.

Puerto Ricans. By the 1950's Puerto Ricans made up one of the largest Spanish-speaking groups in the United States. Unlike other immigrants, who had to be naturalized to become American citizens, Puerto Ricans were American citizens at birth. As you recall, Puerto Rico became an unincorporated territory of the United States in 1898 and then, after 1932, a commonwealth. Since 1898, Puerto Ricans have been legally entitled to the rights and privileges of American citizenship.

Even before the depression of the 1930's brought severe hardships to their island, many Puerto Ricans had migrated to New York City in search of jobs. During and after the depression, they came in ever-increasing numbers. Between 1945 and 1960, migration to the United States varied between 30,000 and 45,000 annually.

vices for a number of tribes, including the Menominees of Wisconsin and the Klamaths of Oregon. The policy was a disaster for the Indians because states were unwilling or unable to provide needed services.

The second goal of the new Indian policy was to assimilate the Indians into the majority culture. This called for relocating as many Indians as possible in cities. The Bureau of Indian Affairs attracted thousands of Indians to cities with promises of job training and job placement. In many cases these promises were not kept. Some Indians managed to overcome great odds and achieve success. Many others, facing discrimination and without the support of tribal life, lived in loneliness and poverty in the cities, which remained for them a strange environment. Some, embittered by the experience, returned to the reservations. For most Indians, relocation, like termination, proved to be a failure.

Immigration from Mexico. People from Mexico also faced hardships during the postwar years. As you have read (page 690), the *bracero* program encouraged the entry of Mexican farm workers during World War II. The

Puerto Ricans who moved to New York City, Newark, Chicago, and other northern cities faced many problems. Most came from rural villages. They lacked the skills necessary to compete for jobs in a highly complex urban environment. Many had only a limited knowledge of the English language, which handicapped them both in the labor market and in the schools. Perhaps most serious, they were victims of prejudice and discrimination.

Because of these handicaps, most of the newcomers were able to get only unskilled jobs that paid the lowest wages. Puerto Rican families were crowded into such tenement districts as Spanish Harlem in New York City.

In some ways the experience of Puerto Ricans in the United States resembled that of earlier immigrants. As you will see (pages 806-07), many gradually moved up the economic ladder and found places in small businesses, semi-skilled trades, the professions, and the arts. In the 1950's, however, progress of this kind remained beyond the grasp of most Puerto Ricans.

A major victory for black Americans. Black Americans returning from World War II, like other minority veterans, often faced bitter disappointments. In spite of their war service, they continued to be treated in many ways as second-class citizens. To be sure, by the 1940's blacks had won substantial successes in every field of activity—science, medicine, the professions, business, music and art, entertainment, and sports. At best, however, only a very small minority of American blacks had achieved such success. For most blacks, the doors of opportunity remained closed or at best only slightly open.

During the years after the war, the movement to end discrimination in government, business, education, and sports speeded up. President Truman urged Congress to adopt legislation strengthening civil rights laws and their enforcement. When Congress failed to act, Truman used his executive powers to order an end to segregation in the armed forces and in the government.

The Supreme Court rules. The most important development, however, was the Supreme Court decision of 1954 during Eisenhower's administration. In *Brown v. Board of Education of Topeka,* the Court reverse the 58-year-old *Plessy v. Ferguson* ruling (see page 406) that

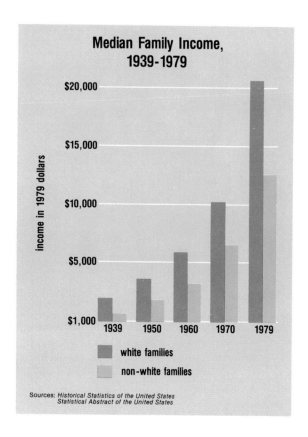

Median Family Income, 1939-1979

income in 1979 dollars

- white families
- non-white families

Sources: *Historical Statistics of the United States*
Statistical Abstract of the United States

"separate but equal" facilities were constitutional. The Court unanimously ruled that state or local laws requiring black citizens to send their children to separate schools violated the Fourteenth Amendment.

Several months after the 1954 decision, the Supreme Court required local school authorities to work out plans for gradually ending segregation in public school systems. The Supreme Court also instructed federal district courts to require local school authorities to "make a prompt and reasonable start toward full compliance" and to move "with all deliberate speed in carrying out the law."

Direct action. Encouraged by the Supreme Court ruling, civil rights supporters redoubled their efforts to break down discrimination. Dissatisfied with the slow response in a number of states to the Supreme Court's rulings, blacks turned to direct action.

Early in December 1955 Rosa Parks, a 40-year-old seamstress in Montgomery, Alabama, took a courageous step. Her action led to a nationwide protest movement. On her way home from work, Rosa Parks boarded a bus and took

A little over a year after Rosa Parks was arrested, she again boarded a bus in Montgomery, Alabama. This time, though, she was no longer expected to sit at the back. The successful boycott had enabled her to sit anywhere she chose.

a seat in the front section reserved for whites. The driver ordered her to move to the back. She refused and was arrested.

The next day, led by a 26-year-old minister, Martin Luther King, Jr., 50,000 blacks joined in a boycott of Montgomery's bus system. It was a peaceful protest, and it worked. When the bus system began to drift toward bankruptcy, King and other black leaders were arrested. Finally, almost a year after Rosa Parks's initial action, the Supreme Court declared that the Alabama segregation law was unconstitutional.

Inspired by the victory in Alabama, Martin Luther King called a conference of southern black leaders. Early in 1957 these leaders organized the Southern Christian Leadership Conference (SCLC). The organization announced to the nation that it intended to attack discrimination everywhere in the country by nonviolent means.

Congress finally acts. Efforts by both whites and blacks to avoid violence were only partially successful. Attempts to integrate schools as the Supreme Court had directed in 1954 led to violence in a number of communities. In 1957 President Eisenhower sent federal troops to Little Rock, Arkansas, to maintain order

when several black students tried to enter the all-white high school.

Responding to the growing unrest and violence, Congress in 1957 adopted a Civil Rights Act designed to secure voting rights for black citizens. This was the first civil rights act since Reconstruction.

During the 1960's and the 1970's, the struggle by blacks and other minorities for freedom and justice became increasingly intense. You will read about this struggle and the government's response in Chapter 42.

SECTION SURVEY

IDENTIFY: termination, relocation, undocumented immigrants, Rosa Parks, Montgomery bus boycott, SCLC.

1. (a) Why did the Indian Reorganization Act fail? (b) What new Indian policy was set up in the 1950's? (c) How successful was the new policy?

2. (a) Identify several groups of Spanish-speaking Americans. (b) How are their backgrounds different from one another? (c) How has their treatment in the United States been similar?

3. Why is each important to the black civil rights movement: (a) *Brown* v. *Board of Education of Topeka,* (b) Eisenhower's action in Little Rock, Arkansas, in 1957, (c) Civil Rights Act of 1957?

Chapter Survey

Summary: Tracing the Main Ideas

During the years following World War II, the United States entered a period of rapid growth and spectacular change. Revolutionary developments in science and technology brought the nation to a position of unprecedented wealth and power.

Who in 1945 could have predicted the amazing developments that took place during the 1950's? Between 1945 and the early 1960's, an almost limitless variety of new products and services became available to a growing number of Americans. Young married couples could buy a new home for a down payment of only a few hundred dollars and have 30 years in which to pay the balance. Millions of cars rolled off the assembly lines. Labor-saving equipment for homes and farms poured out of the nation's factories in an unending stream. Medical science produced thousands of new medical products, including the priceless gift of anti-polio vaccine. Never before in history had so many people enjoyed so much prosperity.

There was, unhappily, a major flaw in the emerging economy of abundance. Millions of people shared only slightly, if at all, in the nation's new prosperity. Poverty in a land of abundance continued to haunt large numbers among the nation's minorities.

Inquiring Into History

1. (a) Why were the young people of the 1950's called the "uncommitted generation"? (b) Do you think it is appropriate to label the people of an era in this way? Why or why not?
2. Why has it become more and more important since World War II for American citizens to be educated?
3. What was the effect of the transformation of the United States from a rural to an industrial society on (a) workers, (b) black Americans, (c) Indians, and (d) young people?
4. (a) Explain why "change" and "growth" are good words to use in describing American society in the years after World War II. (b) What other words would be appropriate to describe those years? Explain.

Relating Past to Present

1. List some of the ways in which computers affect your daily life. Do you consider your contact with computer technology to be positive or negative? Explain.
2. What are some problems and some advantages of living in today's urban society? What were some problems and advantages of living in the rural society of the 1800's?

3. If the young people of the 1950's were called the "uncommitted generation," what might be a good term for the present generation? Explain.
4. Rosa Parks began her protest in Alabama alone. Can you think of more recent examples of people who on their own have taken courageous social action?

Developing Social Science Skills

1. Gather examples of pictures and drawings of American Indians from magazines and newspapers, package labels, book jackets, and other sources. (a) Do you consider the images presented of Indians to be positive or negative? (b) How might such images affect other people's attitudes toward Indians? (c) What sorts of images might Indians hope to see presented by the media?
2. Play a record of popular songs from the 1950's. (a) What is the subject of each song? (b) What do the songs tell you about the lives and concerns of young Americans in the 1950's? (c) How do the popular songs of the 1950's compare with those of today?
3. Visit your local library or historical society. Obtain maps of your community from 1950 and today. How has the map of the community changed over the years? Can any changes be traced to events discussed in this chapter?

Unit Survey

For Further Inquiry

1. Give evidence to support or refute this statement: After World War II, America's foreign policy goals were to maintain the military defenses of the non-communist world and to strengthen its economic foundations.
2. (a) What was the Cold War? (b) In what ways was it a domestic as well as a foreign war?
3. Compare the administrations of Truman and Eisenhower in terms of (a) goals, (b) domestic achievements, (c) foreign achievements, (d) weaknesses.
4. Looking back, who might consider the 1950's the "good old days" or "happy days"? Who might not consider them to have been so good and happy? Explain.
5. Compare the situation of blacks, Hispanic Americans, and Indians during the 1950's.

Activities and Projects

1. Study the timeline above, on science and technology from 1945 to 1960. (a) Which events directly improved the quality of life for Americans? Explain. (b) Do advances in science and technology always improve people's lives? Give examples from the timeline to support your answer.
2. Prepare a map of the world in 1960 that focuses on a theme of your choice, such as communist and non-communist countries, members of the United Nations, "hot spots" of the world, or colonial and colonized countries. Be sure to give the map a title and to include a legend.
3. Imagine that you were a newspaper reporter for TASS, the official Soviet news agency. Write an article on one confrontation between the United States and the U.S.S.R. or on the general topic of the Cold War.
4. Watch a movie of the 1950's, such as "The Wild One" or "Rebel Without a Cause." Write a short report discussing how or if the movie reflects the spirit of the 1950's.
5. Prepare a pictorial timeline showing advances in transportation from 1900 to 1960. If possible, also include short quotations showing how people reacted to each innovation when it was introduced.

Exploring Your Region

1. Find out about one or more Indian tribes living in your region. In particular, try to discover how the tribe was affected by policies of the federal government, such as reorganization and termination.
2. Interview your principal or a teacher in your school who taught there during the 1950's. Try to find out how school curriculum and procedures were affected by such world events as the launching of Sputnik and the McCarthy hearings.

Suggested Reading

1. *Plain Speaking: An Oral Biography of Harry S. Truman,* Merle Miller. A candid look at Truman, the man and the President; written in lively style with many anecdotes.
2. *The Other America: Poverty in the United States,* Michael Harrington. The influential book that alerted affluent Americans to the plight of the poor.
3. *Realities of American Foreign Policy,* George Kennan. A noted diplomat explores the nature and goals of American foreign policy in the years after World War II.
4. *Seven Days in May,* Fletcher Knebel. A suspense-filled novel of intrigue at the highest levels of government.
5. *The Bridges at Toko-ri,* James Michener. An exciting Korean War novel.

Unit Thirteen

Into a New Era

1960-1980's

Chapter 40
Developments on the Domestic Front 1960-1980's

1. President Kennedy calls the nation to a "New Frontier."
2. Johnson urges Americans to build the "Great Society."
3. Nixon promises "to bring America together."
4. The Watergate scandals force Nixon to resign.
5. President Ford completes Nixon's second term.
6. Presidents Carter and Reagan face critical domestic problems.

Chapter 41
Reexamining the Nation's Role in World Affairs 1960-1980's

1. The United States assumes global responsibilities.
2. The United States becomes deeply involved in Vietnam.
3. World tensions are relaxed during the Nixon and Ford administrations.
4. World tensions build up during Carter and Reagan's administrations.

Chapter 42
Reaching for Greater Freedom and Justice

1. New patterns of population growth and distribution alter ways of life.
2. Black Americans demand equal rights and opportunities.
3. Hispanics share the struggle for freedom and justice.
4. Indians refuse to accept the role of "vanishing Americans."
5. Women redouble efforts to win equal rights and opportunities.

Chapter 43
Into the Future

1. Americans begin to reexamine their goals.
2. The American economy remains a source of continuing concern.
3. The United States attempts to resolve its energy crisis.
4. Americans share a growing awareness of environmental issues.

Chapter 40

Developments on the Domestic Front

1960-1980's

"Things are in the saddle, and ride mankind."

The words are those of Ralph Waldo Emerson, a keen observer of the human scene, who lived in Massachusetts more than a century ago. His observation could be accurately applied to the United States and the rest of the world during the years from 1960 through the 1980's.

During those years six different Presidents occupied the White House. They watched over the fortunes of the United States during one of the most turbulent periods in the nation's history. In these same years, the nation celebrated one of its proudest achievements when the first Americans landed on the moon. In these same years, many of the nation's cities, troubled by poverty and decay, exploded in riots. In this period the American economy at first prospered but later slumped sharply.

To what extent did these Presidents lead the nation and shape the course of events? To what extent were they themselves shaped and driven by forces beyond their control? Did they make policies, or were the policies forced upon them by events over which they had little if any control?

Such questions resist easy answers. Nevertheless, the questions themselves, even without answers, may help to illuminate the lives and the fates of the Presidents — Kennedy, Johnson, Nixon, Ford, Carter, and Reagan — who served the nation during those troubled years.

THE CHAPTER IN OUTLINE

1. Kennedy calls the nation to a "New Frontier."
2. Johnson urges Americans to build the "Great Society."
3. Nixon promises "to bring America together."
4. The Watergate scandals force Nixon to resign.
5. President Ford completes Nixon's second term.
6. Presidents Carter and Reagan face critical domestic problems.

Kennedy calls the nation to a "New Frontier"

The nation's unresolved problems at home and abroad were brought strongly to the attention of American voters in the Presidential campaign and election of 1960.

The election of 1960. Both the Republicans and Democrats nominated young, energetic candidates for the Presidency. The Republican nominee, Richard M. Nixon of California, had served in both houses of Congress. Since 1953 he had been Vice-President under Eisenhower. The Democratic nominee, John F. Kennedy of Massachusetts, had also served in both houses of Congress.

During the election campaign, the Presidential candidates faced each other in a series of television debates. Key issues were the nation's defenses and the economy, which had been in a recession since 1958. Kennedy called for a "supreme national effort" to reverse what he called the downward trend of the nation's fortunes at home and abroad. He promised, if elected, "to get America moving again" by leading the nation to a "New Frontier."

Nixon insisted that the United States was stronger in relation to the Communist world than ever. He charged Kennedy with favoring "wild experimentation." Nixon promised, if elected, to build a more secure nation on the foundations of Eisenhower's policies.

Voters turned out in record numbers in the November election. Out of about 68 million votes cast, Kennedy squeezed through by a slim margin of 118,000 votes. In the electoral college, however, Kennedy won 303 electoral votes to Nixon's 219. Lyndon B. Johnson of Texas, who had been Democratic leader in the Senate since 1954, was elected Vice-President.

At 43 Kennedy was the first Roman Catholic and the youngest man ever elected President. He was acutely aware of the problems he faced. Barely half of the voters had shown a willingness to follow the new administration toward a New Frontier. Moreover, conservative Democrats in Congress, mostly from the

At his inauguration as President, John F. Kennedy stirred the nation when he said, "Let the word go forth from this time and place, to friend and foe alike, that the torch has been passed to a new generation of Americans. . . ."

South, had in the past voted with conservative Republicans to defeat measures similar to those Kennedy now wanted.

Economic problems. Once in office, Kennedy prepared to attack the related problems of unemployment and sluggish economic growth. The immediate problem was unemployment. In January 1961 more than 5 million Americans—nearly 8 percent of the total labor force—were unemployed. The unemployment rate among black Americans was double the rate for the nation as a whole.

The problem of unemployment had its roots in the nation's rapidly changing economic life. Some economists stressed that the American economy was not growing as rapidly as it should. Industries were not modernizing or building new factories as rapidly as many of them had done in the past.

Coupled with slow economic growth was the problem of automation, or the use of machines to do the work formerly done by men and women. Also, the increasingly complex American economy called for new skills on the part of workers. As a result, there were far fewer opportunities for the untrained and the poorly educated.

Encouraging employment and housing. In line with Kennedy's proposals, Congress took steps to increase spending power and retrain workers. Minimum wages were raised to $1.25 an hour, and 4 million more workers were included under wage-hour protection. The Area Redevelopment Act of 1961 authorized the federal government to make loans and grants to stimulate business and retrain workers in depressed areas. Congress also set aside $900 million for building public works in areas where more than 6 percent of the labor force was unemployed. In 1962, it passed the Manpower Development and Training Act providing for a three-year worker retraining program. Yet even with these and other measures, unemployment remained a major problem.

The Housing Act of 1961 tried to strengthen the nation's economic and social fabric. This act provided long-term loans at low interest rates to stimulate the construction of moderate-income housing. It included funds to provide hospitals and housing for the elderly. The largest authorization was for urban renewal, including the planning and improvement of mass transportation facilities. Congress also voted nearly $1.5 billion to aid in the construction of buildings for medical and dental schools and to assist colleges in building classrooms, libraries, and laboratories.

The Trade Expansion Act. In 1962 Congress took a major step to stimulate America's foreign trade. This step was prompted in part by the creation of the Common Market, a large trading area composed of six European nations. To improve trade among themselves, the Common Market nations gradually lowered the tariffs that had limited trade. By 1962 the Common Market nations were enjoying increasing prosperity. Recognizing that the Common Market could greatly affect the United States, Congress passed the Trade Expansion Act of 1962.

This act allowed the President, over a five-year period, to cut tariff rates 50 percent below the 1962 level or raise them 50 percent above the 1934 level. The President could also remove *all* tariffs on products for which the

SOURCES

We dare not forget today that we are the heirs of that first revolution. Let the word go forth from this time and place, to friend and foe alike, that the torch has been passed to a new generation of Americans—born in this century, tempered by war, disciplined by a hard and bitter peace, proud of our ancient heritage—and unwilling to witness or permit the slow undoing of those human rights to which this nation has always been committed, and to which we are committed today at home and around the world.

Let every nation know, whether it wishes us well or ill, that we shall pay any price, bear any burden, meet any hardship, support any friend, oppose any foe to assure the survival and the success of liberty. . . .

United States and the Common Market countries together accounted for 80 percent of all world trade.

The act contained an "escape clause" that allowed the President to retain or reimpose tariffs to protect industries hurt by tariff reduction. Endangered industries and workers in them could also receive loans and other government aid.

Congress passed several measures designed to aid the nation's farmers. These acts at best had limited success. By the end of 1963, the nation's farmers continued to struggle with surplus products and declining incomes.

The space program. In April 1961 the Soviet Union, which had launched the first satellite, made another advance into space. It sent the first astronaut, Yuri Gagarin, into orbit around the earth.

A month later Alan Shepard became the first American to make a rocket flight. Nevertheless Shepard did not orbit the earth as the Soviet had. Not until February 1962 was an American, Lieutenant Colonel John Glenn, launched into orbit.

President Kennedy, meanwhile, had become concerned that the United States might lose the race into space to the Soviets. He committed the United States to a program to make the United States first in space exploration. The United States, he declared, would land a man on the moon by 1970.

The space program also proved to be a source of new jobs for American workers. Soon some 9,000 firms were participating in the research and development of space-related products. By 1964 more than 30,000 scientists and specialists were working for the National Aeronautics and Space Administration (NASA), the agency in charge of the program. Estimates of the total number of Americans engaged in some phase of the space program ranged from 3 to 5 million. Moreover, by 1964 the program had created some 3,200 different products, many of which found their way into daily use.

The space program and the other parts of Kennedy's economic program seemed to be successful. By late 1961 the economy had begun to pull out of the recession. It then entered a time of growth that would last until 1970.

Changes in suffrage. During the Kennedy administration, several major changes took place in voting rights. The Twenty-third Amendment to the Constitution, adopted in 1961 (see page 197), enabled residents of the District of Columbia to vote in Presidential elections. The Twenty-fourth Amendment, adopted in 1964 (see page 197), forbade the poll tax as a requirement for voting in federal elections. Poll taxes had been used in many areas to prevent poor blacks from voting.

Other citizens fought for fairer representation in national, state, and local legislatures. Election districts in many states had remained unchanged for many years. However, the population in these states had generally shifted from rural to urban and suburban areas. This meant that rural districts were often over-represented in the legislatures.

Between 1962 and 1964, the Supreme Court handed down several decisions relating to representation. The most far-reaching was the Court's "one person, one vote" ruling. According to this decision, election districts for state legislatures as well as for the House of Representatives must be as nearly equal in population as practicable. The Supreme Court thus set in motion a political revolution intended to make each citizen's vote have approximately equal value. This was meant to provide genuine representative government at both state and federal levels.

Unfinished business. During his time in office, Kennedy took important steps to insure equal justice for blacks (see Chapter 42). In June 1963, for example, Kennedy sent a civil rights bill to Congress. Despite his support, the chances of the bill's passage were uncertain. Kennedy also had plans for mass transit, medical care, and aid-to-education programs. By late 1963 he had not been able to get any of these programs through Congress.

Kennedy was reluctant to put too much pressure on Congress to pass these bills. The next year, 1964, was an election year. Kennedy, who had won so narrowly in 1960, knew he would need broad political support if he wished to be reelected.

One area of the nation where Kennedy's political support seemed weakest was the South. To build up enthusiasm for himself and his programs, Kennedy planned a trip to Texas in November 1963.

At 12:30 in the afternoon on Friday, November 22, 1963, while riding in a motorcade through Dallas, Texas, President Kennedy was killed by an assassin. Vice-President Johnson, who also was in the motorcade, immediately drove under close guard to the Presidential plane. There, in the cabin of the plane at 2:38 P.M., Lyndon B. Johnson was sworn in as the thirty-sixth President of the United States.

The tragic weekend. Americans reacted to the tragic news with shocked disbelief, then with deeply felt anger and grief. For three days, while the body of John F. Kennedy lay in state in the Capitol, radio and television stations suspended regular programming. All but the most essential businesses closed their doors. Messages of sorrow and sympathy poured in from all over the world. The leaders of many nations flew to Washington to pay their respects to the late President.

In the meantime, within an hour and a half of the fatal shooting, the Dallas police had seized a suspect, Lee Harvey Oswald. Oswald was placed under heavy guard in a Dallas jail. Two days later, while being moved from one jail to another, he was shot and killed in full view of millions of Americans who were watching the event on television. His murderer, Jack Ruby, pushed through a group of police officers to shoot Oswald at close range.

Americans were deeply troubled by this new act of brutality. With Oswald gone, grave questions remained unanswered. Was Lee Harvey Oswald truly the assassin? If so, had he acted alone? Or was he part of a conspiracy to assassinate President Kennedy? Was Jack Ruby part of that conspiracy, and did he kill Oswald to keep him from talking?

The Warren Commission. To answer these questions and to put an end to wild rumors and speculation, President Johnson appointed a commission to investigate the case. The commission was headed by Earl Warren, Chief Justice of the Supreme Court.

In September 1964 the Warren Commission released its report. After carefully examining the available evidence and the testimony of 532 witnesses, the commission unanimously concluded that (1) Lee Harvey Oswald had assassinated President Kennedy, (2) he had acted alone, (3) Jack Ruby also had acted alone, and (4) there was no evidence of a conspiracy.

The report did not, however, end the questions and speculations. Critics continued to question the procedures used by the commission as well as its conclusions. In 1979, a committee of the House of Representatives conducted its own investigation of the assassination. It heard from witnesses whom the Warren Commission had not called. It found experts who used new methods to study tapes made at the time of the shooting. Using these methods the committee found evidence that more than one gun had been fired at Kennedy. However, the committee could not say who had fired the other gun or guns, or who else might have been involved in a conspiracy.

SECTION SURVEY

IDENTIFY: New Frontier, automation, Common Market, John Glenn, NASA, Lee Harvey Oswald, Warren Commission.

1. What were the parties, candidates, issues, and results of the election of 1960?
2. (a) What actions did the Kennedy administration take in the areas of unemployment, housing, and foreign trade? (b) How effective were these actions?
3. Why did Kennedy believe it was important for the United States to land a man on the moon by 1970?
4. What was the significance for democratic government of the (a) Twenty-third Amendment, (b) Twenty-fourth Amendment, and (c) "one person, one vote" ruling?

2 Johnson urges Americans to build the "Great Society"

Five days after the assassination of President Kennedy, Lyndon B. Johnson, in his first Presidential address to Congress, dedicated himself to the "ideas and the ideals" that John F. Kennedy had "so nobly represented." President Johnson gave top priority to three items —a civil rights law, a tax cut, and an "unconditional war on poverty." Speaking quietly but firmly, he declared, "All this and more can and must be done." Thus the new President invited Americans to build what he would later call the "Great Society."

Johnson had served long years in both the House and the Senate. He knew the lawmakers well and how they thought and worked. Most important, he understood how to get legislation through Congress.

An impressive record. Congress responded to President Johnson's leadership. Before adjourning in October 1964, Congress chalked up one of the most impressive legislative records in the nation's history. Most far-reaching was the Civil Rights Act of 1964 (see Chapter 42), but there were other important measures.

The Revenue Act of 1964 cut personal and corporate income taxes by $11.5 billion. By leaving more money in the hands of consumers and businesses, the new law greatly stimulated the economy.

The Economic Opportunity Act of 1964 marked an important attempt to "break the cycle of poverty." It created an Office of Economic Opportunity (OEO) and authorized $1 billion to begin the war against poverty. The new agency was to work with state and local governments to increase employment and expand training programs, especially for the nation's needy young people.

Congress also passed several other measures. For example, it authorized $375 million to help cities improve urban and commuter transit facilities. It also established a system to preserve federally owned wilderness areas. However, several measures strongly supported by President Johnson were still being considered when Congress adjourned to begin the 1964 election campaign.

The election of 1964. The Republicans nominated Barry M. Goldwater, a conservative Senator from Arizona, for the Presidency and Representative William E. Miller of New York as his running mate. The Democrats nominated Lyndon B. Johnson and his choice for Vice-President, Senator Hubert H. Humphrey of Minnesota.

From the start of the race, both parties were divided. Goldwater was a firm conservative. He favored a sharply limited role for the federal government. Many moderate Republicans refused to support him. The Republicans also lost the support of most black voters. Goldwater was one of only six Republican Senators who had voted against the Civil Rights Act of 1964.

The Democrats, too, lost many loyal voters. Many white southern Democrats felt that President Johnson, a Texan, had betrayed them by leading the battle for the Civil Rights Act. They supported Goldwater because of his vote against the act and his support of states' rights.

In November nearly 70 million voters turned out. They elected President Johnson by an overwhelming electoral vote of 486 to 52. The popular vote was 42 million to 26 million. The Democrats also won substantial victories in state and local elections and in Congress.

Toward the "Great Society." Encouraged by his sweeping victory, President Johnson challenged Americans to join him in building the "Great Society." He argued that Americans, now more prosperous than ever, could help build a new world, not just a new nation. Americans had three major tasks: "To keep our economy growing. To open for all Americans the opportunities now enjoyed by most Americans. To improve the quality of life for all."

By the time Congress adjourned in the fall of 1965, it had adopted laws dealing with all of the President's major recommendations. In one of the most far-reaching laws, the legislators provided a comprehensive program of aid to education (see Chapter 43). Congress also established Medicare, a national program of health insurance for persons over 65. Medicare provided basic health coverage, with social security paying the larger part of the costs of hospital treatment or home nursing care, the patient paying the rest. Medicare also included

After July 1, 1965, millions of the nation's senior citizens became eligible for Medicare. This program helped them to pay for the ever-increasing cost of their hospital, doctor, and other medical bills.

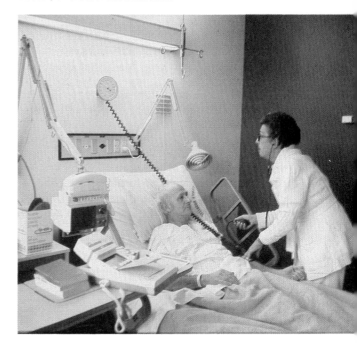

Shanks in The Buffalo Evening News
"Hope I know where we're goin'."

More than any President in modern history, Lyndon Johnson had control of Congress. To what does the cartoonist compare Johnson's persuasiveness? How is Congress portrayed? Is this a flattering view?

voluntary supplementary coverage, enabling individuals covered by social security to buy low-cost health insurance to cover doctors' bills and other health services. The Medicare bill also provided for federal grants to states that wished to start health care programs for the needy. Such care was known as Medicaid.

Responding to President Johnson's urging, Congress reduced federal excise taxes on automobiles, television sets, and other consumer items. The cut in excise taxes was designed to encourage Americans to buy more goods. This in turn would stimulate production and reduce unemployment.

In still other efforts to raise the standard of living of impoverished Americans, the legislators adopted several measures. Congress increased to $1.5 billion the funds for the Office of Economic Opportunity's anti-poverty program. Congress also voted $1 billion to help develop the depressed economy of the 11-state Appalachian region. In addition, Congress authorized $7.5 billion to improve the nation's housing. Much of this money was intended to help those who lived in low-income areas.

Loss of momentum. As it turned out, 1965 marked the peak of Johnson's program and

his popularity. Continued racial unrest in the nation damaged Democratic programs. Also, more people began to question increasing federal spending and government involvement in their daily lives. Most important, by 1966 the war in Vietnam, as you will read in Chapter 41, was absorbing more and more of the nation's resources and the administration's time and energy. As the war intensified, the President became the target of increasing criticism from Congress, from newspapers, and even from the pulpits of churches. Antiwar demonstrations disrupted the President's speeches at public ceremonies. Gradually, Johnson became more cut off from the American people. He was less able to get Congress to carry out his programs.

McCarthy's challenge. Eugene J. McCarthy, Democratic Senator from Minnesota, first revealed the extent of the dissatisfaction with Johnson. In November 1967 Senator McCarthy declared that he intended to campaign for the Presidency against Johnson. His purpose was to give voters a chance to show that they opposed the administration's Vietnam policy.

In the nation's first 1968 Presidential primary, held in New Hampshire in March, McCarthy made a surprisingly strong showing. In part his success was due to the thousands of young volunteers from all over the country who poured into the state to work for him. They campaigned hard for McCarthy because he inspired them with hopeful idealism.

Political developments. The New Hampshire primary triggered a series of political developments. A few days after the primary, Senator Robert F. Kennedy of New York announced that he, too, would seek the Democratic nomination for President. Senator Kennedy, a brother of the late President Kennedy, was an outspoken critic of President Johnson's Vietnam policy.

A second political development, one that stunned the nation, was President Johnson's declaration in March that he would not run for reelection. As Johnson later explained, he hoped that removing himself from the Presidential race would end the growing division among the American people over his conduct of the Vietnam War. Even some of Johnson's political enemies praised his decision.

President Johnson's withdrawal opened the door to the candidacy of Vice-President Hubert

Humphrey. He soon joined Senators McCarthy and Kennedy in the heated race for the Democratic nomination.

Two assassinations. Early in April 1968, the nation mourned the death of the great civil rights leader Martin Luther King, Jr. (see Chapter 42). In June the nation again grieved, this time for Senator Robert F. Kennedy, killed by an assassin's bullet just after he had won a close victory over Senator McCarthy in the California primary.

The assassinations of President John F. Kennedy, Martin Luther King, Jr., and Robert F. Kennedy led many people at home and abroad to wonder if violence was an ingrained part of American society. What, people asked, was happening to the nation? There was no easy answer, but President Johnson did appoint a commission to study the question of violence. Also, Congress, over strong opposition, passed a gun-control law, although critics called the new law a "halfway measure."

The end of a dream. Back in 1963 President Johnson had dedicated himself to building a Great Society—free from poverty, discrimination, and injustice. During his first two years in office, he made substantial progress toward that goal. Then, as the Vietnam War began to absorb the administration's attention, domestic programs suffered. Thus, Lyndon Johnson's dream of a Great Society became marred by the war abroad and by continuing unrest and violence at home.

SECTION SURVEY

IDENTIFY: Great Society, war on poverty, Barry Goldwater, Medicare, Medicaid, Eugene McCarthy, Robert Kennedy.

1. President Johnson believed that two goals of the United States were "to open for all Americans the opportunities now enjoyed by most Americans" and "to improve the quality of life for all." What legislation did he promote to achieve each of these goals?
2. With reference to the election of 1964, discuss (a) the candidates and parties and (b) the results for the parties and the nation.
3. In 1967 Eugene McCarthy triggered a series of political developments. What were they?
4. What did President Johnson hope to accomplish by refusing to run for reelection in 1967?

3 Nixon promises "to bring America together"

It was a restless, disturbed nation that in August 1968 watched the Presidential nominating conventions on television.

Choosing candidates. The Republicans, meeting first, gathered at Miami Beach. Richard M. Nixon, who represented the middle ground as well as the "establishment" of the Republican Party, was nominated on the first ballot. He chose Spiro T. Agnew, Governor of Maryland, as his running mate.

The Democratic convention, held later in Chicago, proved to be one of the most tumultuous in the nation's history. To Americans watching on television, the convention hall was a disorderly arena. There McCarthy and Kennedy supporters contended against "establishment" Democrats represented by Hubert H. Humphrey.

The bitter fight in the convention hall was reflected in the city's streets. Thousands of young people had gathered in Chicago to demonstrate against the Vietnam War and for candidates favoring peace. Claiming that the demonstrations had gotten out of hand, the Chicago police moved in. The violent confrontations that followed, resulting in numerous injuries, were also witnessed by millions of television viewers.

In the convention hall, the "establishment" won. Humphrey was picked on the first ballot and chose Senator Edmund S. Muskie of Maine as his Vice-Presidential candidate.

The campaign of 1968. The three main issues of the campaign were violence and disorder, Vietnam, and racial strife. Public opinion polls showed that seven out of every ten Americans were convinced that "law and order had broken down in the country." Two out of every three felt that the war in Vietnam was being badly managed. The overwhelming majority of white citizens believed that the civil rights struggle was going "too fast." An equally large majority of black citizens were convinced that the movement was "not going fast enough."

During the campaign neither Nixon nor Humphrey aroused great enthusiasm among voters. The emergence of a third-party can-

Here, during the 1968 Democratic convention in Chicago, National Guardsmen surround the hotel where party leaders were meeting. The troops had been ordered to keep demonstrators away from the hotel.

didate, George C. Wallace of Alabama, founder of the American Independent Party, further complicated matters.

George C. Wallace. From the beginning, third-party candidate Wallace hammered at the issue of law and order. Wallace also expressed opposition to existing welfare programs, forced busing of school children, and the federal enforcement of integration. He pledged, if elected, to repeal open housing legislation, to give the police greater power to deal with demonstrations and civil disorders, and to restore to the states and local communities control over welfare programs and the schools. As to Vietnam, he promised to end the war by negotiation, if possible, but to achieve a military victory if negotiations failed.

Richard M. Nixon. Nixon stressed the nation's need for new leadership. He declared that the Democrats had brought the United States close to disaster and that it was "time for a change." Like Wallace, he promised to restore law and order but added the word "justice" to his pledge.

Nixon insisted that the Democratic programs of massive federal spending to combat poverty had failed. He promised to review the entire welfare program and to turn over to private businesses the primary responsibility for retraining unemployed workers and rebuilding the cities.

Nixon also promised the nation that he would "bring an honorable end to the war" in Vietnam. He did not say how he would end the war, explaining that he did not wish to upset the delicate peace talks then going on in Paris.

Nixon was more specific, however, in his ideas about military policy and national defense. He favored a buildup of nuclear capability to insure that the United States held superiority over all potential enemies. His recommendations included the development of an anti-ballistic missile system (ABM).

Hubert H. Humphrey. During most of the campaign, Humphrey found himself in difficulty. His party was badly divided. Millions of people associated the violence in Chicago with the Democrats.

Humphrey was convinced that force, no matter how strongly applied, would not end the unrest and violence afflicting the nation. "We can only cut crime," he declared, "by getting at its causes: slums, unemployment, run-down schools and houses. This is where crime begins and that is where it must end." He cautioned that the attack against crime "must not jeopardize hard-won liberties of our citizens."

To meet the crippling problems of poverty and of urban decay, Humphrey called for "a Marshall Plan for the cities based upon self-help, local initiative, coordinated planning, and private capital."

Vietnam caused Humphrey the most trouble. At the start of his campaign, he lost much support by defending the unpopular administration policy. However, at the end of September he called for a halt to the bombing of North Vietnam, and his chances began to improve. They improved still further when, less than a week before the election, President Johnson announced that he had ordered a halt to all bombing north of the DMZ (Demilitarized Zone) that divided Vietnam, offering hope for an earlier end to the war.

The election results. The 1968 Presidential election was indeed a close one. Out of more than 71 million popular votes cast, Nixon's margin of victory over Humphrey was only 260,000 votes. The electoral vote of 302 for Nixon, 191 for Humphrey, and 45 for Wallace did not, however, reflect this closeness. The Democrats kept control of Congress.

Keenly aware of his narrow victory, President-elect Nixon pledged that his "great objective" would be to unite the country. Convinced that the "silent majority" of the American people stood midway between extreme conservatism and extreme liberalism, Nixon sought to hold to a "center" line.

To the moon. President Nixon was inaugurated on January 20, 1969. Just six months later, on July 20, 1969, American astronauts landed on the moon. The promise that President Kennedy had made back in 1961 to land a man on the moon before the end of the decade had been kept.

The costs were high. Three astronauts had died in a sudden flash fire. About $24 billion had been spent on the moon shot. Some critics argued that such money could have been better spent on solving problems at home.

Nevertheless, Americans stayed near television sets or radios for news when Neil Armstrong, Michael Collins, and Edwin E. Aldrin, Jr., lifted off in Apollo 11 for the moon. Millions of Americans watched in fascination four days later when the lunar lander named *Eagle* settled down on the moon's surface. Many felt a great pride when Armstrong stepped out of the spacecraft and onto the moon saying, "That's one small step for a man, one giant leap for mankind."

Difficulties with Congress. The Nixon administration, handicapped by a Democratic majority in Congress, had more trouble implementing its policies. In an effort to commit the Supreme Court to his own view of a strict interpretation of the Constitution, the President filled the vacancy created by Earl Warren's retirement by appointing Warren E. Burger as Chief Justice. However, Nixon was unable to secure Senate approval for two other nominees to fill a Supreme Court vacancy. Finally, the Senate approved Nixon's choice of Harry Blackmun, a respected moderate judge.

Differences between the administration and Congress also led to other compromises and stalemates. The President insisted on cutting down federal spending, contending that such spending was excessive and that many pro-

President Richard Nixon tried to get many programs passed into law, but Congress, with its Democratic majority, often foiled his efforts. According to this cartoon, what were some of the programs?

grams were unwise and poorly administered. But critics in Congress insisted that cuts in spending for social welfare, education, and other domestic programs were not justified. They also objected to the administration's reluctance to make substantial cuts in the military budget.

Difficulties at home. Nixon had inherited the Vietnam War from President Johnson. He also inherited the anger of antiwar protesters. Huge demonstrations were held in Washington, New York, and other cities calling for an end to the war. Nixon had announced that he had a plan to end the war, but for many of the demonstrators he was not moving fast enough.

Then in May 1970, the nation learned that President Nixon had ordered the invasion of Cambodia. Antiwar activists were outraged by this action. A wave of new protests swept across the nation.

At Kent State University, the protest turned violent. The National Guard was called out. On May 4, trying to break up a gathering of students, the Guard opened fire. Four students were killed.

765

A STEP, A GIANT LEAP

Down a ladder swung a heavy-booted foot. Over 500 million people, watching on television, saw it step out onto a powdery surface. Then they heard the voice of astronaut Neil Armstrong as he surveyed the gray and cratered landscape before him: "That's one small step for a man, one giant leap for mankind." It was Sunday, July 20, 1969, and the first humans had reached the moon.

The official name of this flight, Apollo 11, indicated that it was one of a series. The earliest Apollo missions had taken place in 1967, but the Apollo program had begun in 1961. At that time President Kennedy had committed the nation to a moon landing within ten years.

Early Apollo trials had tested the equipment in unmanned flight. Later ones carried fliers into earth and then lunar orbits. Apollo 7 (October 1968) was the first to broadcast live TV coverage from the cockpit. On Apollo 8 (December 1968), astronauts traveled faster than any humans up to that time. On Christmas Eve they read from the book of Genesis as they orbited the moon.

Apollo 11's Armstrong and Edwin Aldrin had landed on the moon in a small module called *Eagle*. It had separated from the command spacecraft, *Columbia*, which remained in orbit — commanded by Michael Collins — while the moon exploration took place. In two busy hours, the men installed scientific instruments, collected 50 pounds (22.7 kilograms) of moon rocks, and snapped hundreds of photographs. They also set up a metal flag and left a plaque, which read as follows:

HERE MEN FROM THE PLANET EARTH
FIRST SET FOOT UPON THE MOON
JULY 1969 A.D.
WE CAME IN PEACE FOR ALL MANKIND

Then *Eagle* lifted off, leaving behind footprints that might well last forever on the moon's airless surface.

The nation was shocked and sobered. Nixon's campaign promise to "bring America together" now seemed to ring hollow. The war in Vietnam still appeared to be tearing America apart.

Inflation and the energy crisis. Among the other serious problems facing President Nixon when he took office was inflation. The rising rate of inflation was partly a result of vast spending for the Vietnam War. It was also a result of basic problems in the American economy and society, and partly a result of international events. As you will read, Nixon's attempts to handle inflation met with mixed success.

The skyrocketing cost of oil was a major contributor to inflation in the United States and throughout the world. The major oil-exporting nations had in 1960 formed the Organization of Petroleum Exporting Countries (OPEC). OPEC wanted to get higher prices for its oil from importing countries. Then, in the fall of 1973, the Arab oil-producing nations sharply increased the price of oil, and in the midst of a new Arab-Israeli war, the Arab nations cut off all shipments to the United States and other industrial nations that had been supporting Israel. A few months later, the Arabs lifted their embargo, but OPEC kept oil prices high.

High oil prices and the embargo caused critical problems for Western Europe and Japan, which depended almost entirely on Arab oil. The United States, which depended upon Arab oil for only about 6 percent of its total requirements, also faced a serious situation.

For several years there had been a growing scarcity of energy in the United States. The 6-percent cutoff of oil coupled with soaring prices brought a serious "energy crisis" during the winter of 1973–74. The cost of gasoline, heating oil, and electricity rose drastically. In some parts of the country, shortages caused real hardships. As a result, Nixon announced a program to make the United States independent of all foreign countries for its energy requirements by the early 1980's.

Other important developments. In March 1971 Congress adopted the Twenty-sixth Amendment (page 199) lowering the voting age to 18 in both federal and state elections. When the amendment was ratified by the required 38 states three months later, the Census Bureau estimated that 25 million additional young people were now eligible to vote in the next Presidential election.

Shortly before the end of President Nixon's first term, he signed a $30.2 billion revenue-sharing bill. This act channeled federal revenue to states and local communities for various public programs. Nixon regarded this "new federalism" as an essential part of his program for decentralizing the power of the national government.

SECTION SURVEY

IDENTIFY: Spiro Agnew, George Wallace, Neil Armstrong, Warren Burger, inflation, wage and price controls, "energy crisis," Twenty-sixth Amendment, revenue sharing.

1. (a) What were the basic issues of the 1968 Presidential election? (b) What position did each candidate take on these issues?
2. (a) How did the Nixon administration try to control inflation? (b) How effective were its efforts?
3. (a) What was the "new federalism"? (b) What actions did Nixon take to promote the "new federalism"?
4. Cartoon Study: Examine the political cartoon on page 765. Then write a short paragraph explaining its meaning.

4 The Watergate scandals force Nixon to resign

Nixon's second term in office began with the triumph of a sweeping reelection victory. It ended two and a half years later with a disgraced administration and with the President's resignation.

The election of 1972. At their 1972 convention, the Republicans again nominated Richard M. Nixon and Spiro T. Agnew. The Democrats nominated Senator George M. McGovern of South Dakota, a liberal, as their Presidential candidate. Governor George C. Wallace of Alabama, an early contender for the Democratic nomination, had been wounded by a would-be assassin and did not take an active part in the 1972 campaign.

The Democratic convention included among its delegates an unusually large number of black Americans, young people, other minorities, and women. Older party regulars believed that the newcomers were moving the Democrats too far to the left, beyond the majority views of the nation. They bitterly opposed McGovern's nomination.

From the start McGovern was in trouble. He chose Senator Thomas Eagleton of Missouri as his running mate. Then it was revealed that Eagleton had at one time been hospitalized for emotional illness. McGovern first announced his continued support of Eagleton. Then he changed his mind and asked Eagleton to step down. The Democratic National Committee then chose Sargent Shriver, former head of the Peace Corps, to replace Eagleton.

The incident called McGovern's judgment into question and cost him votes. In addition, many traditional Democratic voters opposed him, and others were lukewarm toward his candidacy. Nevertheless, McGovern campaigned tirelessly. He hit hard at inflation, corruption, what he called the Nixon administration's "indifference" to civil rights, and above all against United States participation in the Vietnam War.

Nixon was confident of victory. He could count on most of the 12 million to 15 million votes that might have gone to Governor Wallace if he had run. Moreover, Nixon's achievements in foreign affairs were widely praised by Democrats and Republicans alike. He had sharply reduced America's military role in South Vietnam and had improved relations with both Communist China and the Soviet Union. President Nixon also encouraged his supporters to spend heavily on whatever steps they thought were necessary to insure his reelection.

Nixon won one of the greatest victories in American history, winning about 47 million votes to McGovern's 29 million. The electoral vote was 521 to 17. Nixon's victory was largely personal, and Republicans failed to make significant gains in the House and Senate, which were controlled by the Democrats.

Nixon's social policies. President Nixon saw his landslide victory as a mandate, or command by the voters, to carry out his foreign policies and his domestic policies. These domestic policies called for a reduced role for the federal government.

Nixon believed that the expansion of federally funded social programs had worsened the conditions they were supposed to correct. He opposed large federal spending for job training for the handicapped, special education for the disadvantaged, and the use of school buses to speed up racial integration. He called for a halt to federal support for low-cost housing and urban renewal on grounds that neither had succeeded. He criticized publicly financed day care support for children of working mothers. He urged tighter controls over expenditures for Medicare and Medicaid, declaring his preference for private health insurance plans.

In January 1973 Nixon called for cutbacks or terminations in more than 100 federal programs in the next budget. To get his program through, he relied partly upon his Republican followers in Congress but also upon continuing support from conservative Democrats, chiefly from southern states.

Executive power. Although Nixon in general favored a reduced role for the federal government, his powers as President had grown. Ever since the 1930's, foreign and domestic problems had encouraged, if not required, increased executive power. During this time Congress had allowed a growth in power under both Democratic and Republican Presidents.

However, in Nixon's second term, critics began to worry about his use of executive power. At times Nixon seemed to believe that he as President was, or should be, above criticism or restraint. He had turned over much of the authority of Cabinet officers, where appointment required Senate approval, to his personally appointed White House staff. Nixon also held back vital information from Congress and the public. Members of the administration, especially Vice-President Agnew, attacked newspaper and television reporting as irresponsible and unfair. These events and others fed a growing uneasiness that Nixon's use of the Presidency threatened the constitutional balance of powers.

The Watergate affair. The threat to the balance of powers became clearer as a series of scandals emerged during Nixon's second term. The disastrous Watergate affair, as the scandals were called, began in June 1972 with an attempted burglary of the Democratic National Committee offices in Washington's Watergate Apartments complex. Five men were caught in the building. At first they gave false names, but they were soon correctly identified. The trail then led to the organization for which they had been working, the Committee to Reelect the President.

The White House tried to dismiss the episode as a "third-rate burglary," but news reporters refused to believe this. As the months passed, news reports began to unravel a tangled web of criminal activities that appeared to reach into the highest offices in the land. As a result, by 1973 both the legislative and the judicial branches of government had become actively involved in the Watergate investigations. A special Senate committee, chaired by Senator Sam Ervin of North Carolina, held televised hearings during the spring and summer of 1973. The Attorney General appointed a Special Prosecutor, who organized a staff and began to sift the evidence. A grand jury sitting in a federal district court headed by Judge John Sirica began to gather evidence and prepare indictments.

The resignation of Agnew. Meanwhile, the Justice Department had been investigating the financial affairs of Vice-President Agnew. By the fall of 1973, government investigators were prepared to indict Agnew for crimes, including bribery and extortion, committed while he was Governor of Maryland and Vice-President of the United States.

For a time Agnew angrily proclaimed his innocence of the alleged wrongdoings. However, in the late fall he decided to throw himself on the mercy of the court and plea-bargain for a light sentence.

Agnew's part of the bargain included his immediate resignation as Vice-President and a *nolo contendere* ("no contest") plea to a single count of tax evasion ($29,500 of undeclared income in 1967). In return, the Court agreed not to sentence Agnew to jail for the tax evasion and not to prosecute him for other criminal activities he allegedly committed.

The extremely lenient sentence—a $10,000 fine and unsupervised probation for three years—was widely criticized. Nevertheless, Attorney General Elliot Richardson defended it on grounds that a long trial "would have been likely to inflict upon the nation serious and permanent scars."

In accordance with the Twenty-fifth Amendment to the Constitution, President Nixon nominated a new Vice-President. He chose Gerald Ford, the Republican leader of the House of Representatives. The Senate confirmed the nomination.

Mounting evidence. Meanwhile, the Watergate investigations continued. The grand jury charged that members of the administration, if not the President himself, had approved the Watergate burglary and had then attempted to cover up the administration's part in the affair. The grand jury also charged that members of the administration, if not the President himself, had approved of the illegal entry into the offices of a psychiatrist. This break-in was undertaken in an effort to secure damaging personal evidence against one of the psychiatrist's patients, Daniel Ellsberg. Ellsberg had earlier released classified material relating to the government's plans and actions during the Vietnam War.

Investigators also uncovered evidence of the illegal use by the administration of wiretapping and bugging. There was also a plan to set up a secret White House group known as the "plumbers" authorized to break federal laws in the name of "national security." Investigators also claimed that the White House had tried to involve the CIA and the FBI in some of its illegal activities. They further claimed that during the 1972 election campaign huge sums of money had been collected from corporations with the understanding that the administration would do special favors for such contributors. As the months passed, additional evidence of wrongdoing steadily accumulated. Numerous officials of the White House staff were indicted. Some pleaded guilty and went to jail. Others went to trial; most of them were convicted and sentenced.

The White House tapes. From the beginning President Nixon protested that he was innocent of any wrongdoing. However, White House lawyer John W. Dean, who had already confessed to his own participation in the scandals, challenged him. Although the growing volume of evidence seemed to support Dean, it was his word against the word of the President. The issue remained unresolved.

In July 1973, however, the Senate committee investigating Watergate suddenly learned that for the past two years Nixon had been secretly taping everything said in his offices and over most of his White House telephones. This evidence could prove or disprove the President's claim of innocence of the charge of obstructing justice.

The Senate Watergate Committee and the Special Prosecutor immediately issued subpoenas. They requested President Nixon to turn over those tapes that contained discussions relating to the Watergate affair and the alleged cover-up. Nixon refused to surrender them on grounds of "executive privilege" and "national security."

The courts then ruled that the President had to release those portions of the relevant tapes that did not relate to national security. After considerable delay Nixon released some, but not all, of the tapes. A growing conviction that he was withholding damaging evidence became even more widespread when it was discovered that important parts of certain tapes had been erased. Finally, in August 1974, the Supreme Court ordered Nixon to release the requested tapes.

The Supreme Court ruling was the final blow to the President's efforts to conceal his part in the illegal White House activities during his administration. The tapes Nixon reluctantly turned over to the Special Prosecutor revealed that his repeated claims of innocence had been false. From the beginning he had been involved in efforts to cover up the Watergate affair.

Nixon's resignation. The revelation of Nixon's betrayal of the public's trust came as the House of Representatives was preparing to vote on the issue of Presidential impeachment. After a three-month investigation, the House Judiciary Committee had approved three Articles of Impeachment.

The three articles that the Judiciary Committee sent to the House charged the President with violating his oath of office by (1) obstruction of justice, (2) abuse of power, and (3) willful disobedience of subpoenas issued by the House of Representatives.

Faced with probable impeachment by the House and conviction by the Senate, President Nixon chose to resign. He submitted his resignation on August 8, 1974. He denied any guilt, however, and admitted only to having made

Just about two years to the day after Nixon had accepted the renomination of his party, he announced his resignation from the Presidency. Standing by Nixon in this photograph are his daughter and son-in-law.

some "mistakes" and to having lost his "power base" in Congress.

Nixon was the first President in the nation's history to resign from office. His departure brought an end to a grave constitutional crisis that had threatened to weaken, if not destroy, the democratic process. At issue had been the preservation of the system of checks and balances, the principle of the separation of powers, and the rule of law itself.

SECTION SURVEY

IDENTIFY: George McGovern, Senate Watergate Committee, Judge John Sirica, Gerald Ford, Articles of Impeachment.

1. (a) Why did Nixon win the 1972 election by a landslide? (b) Why was it called a "personal" victory?
2. (a) What was the "Watergate affair"? (b) What role did Congress have in investigating the affair? (c) What part did news reporters play? (d) What role did the courts have?
3. What were the events that led to President Nixon's resignation?
4. Why did some people think that Nixon's administration posed a threat to the principle of the separation of powers?

5 President Ford completes Nixon's second term

On August 9 the Vice-President, Gerald Ford, was sworn in as the 38th President of the United States. Following the procedure set forth in the Twenty-fifth Amendment, he nominated Governor Nelson A. Rockefeller of New York for Vice-President and Congress confirmed the nomination. Thus, for the first time since the Constitution was adopted, both the President and the Vice-President held their high offices by appointment, rather than through election by the voters.

Gerald Ford. Gerald Ford was an unpretentious man gifted with the common touch. Before Nixon appointed him to the Vice-Presidency he had represented his home state of Michigan in Congress for a quarter of a century. As leader of the Republicans in the House, Ford had won the respect of his colleagues in both political parties. He was liked and trusted for his honesty and his open, unassuming manner. "I am a Ford, not a Lincoln," he declared upon becoming Vice-President. In 1974 when he was sworn in as the nation's Chief Executive, he won respect for his candid assessment of his position. "I am acutely aware," he said, "that you have not elected me as your President by your ballots."

The Nixon pardon. A month after he took office, Ford lost much of the early confidence he had won. At that time he granted Nixon an unconditional pardon for all the federal crimes he "committed or may have committed or taken part in" while serving as President. Nixon accepted the pardon, which legally was an admission of guilt.

Ford's critics charged that by granting the pardon he had prevented the American people from ever learning the full truth about the Nixon administration. The critics pointed to the double standard of justice that gave Nixon a full pardon while his fellow conspirators were punished for following their leader's wishes. Some of the critics questioned whether the pardon had not been agreed upon in advance in exchange for Nixon's resignation.

President Ford insisted that these charges were not true. He defended the pardon on the ground that a public trial would have only prolonged the bitterness and the division produced by Watergate. He had acted, he said, because he wanted to heal the nation's wounds.

Ford's amnesty program. A week after he broke the news of the Nixon pardon, Ford dropped another bombshell with the announcement of an amnesty for the Vietnam draft evaders and military deserters. This, too, became a highly controversial issue and further lessened the President's initial popularity.

During the Vietnam War, thousands of young men had crossed the border into Canada or had gone to European countries to escape the draft. A smaller but still substantial number already in the armed services had deserted and fled the country. Both groups felt that the war was morally wrong and that for this reason they could not, in conscience, support it.

Ford declared that he could not condone the draft evasion and desertion. However, he added, it is time to "heal the scars of divisiveness." He then offered a conditional pardon. Those who wanted it would have to reaffirm their allegiance to the United States and agree to spend up to two years of alternative service working for the public. This service might be in hospitals, rehabilitation centers, conservation efforts, or similar activities.

Only a handful of the more than 200,000 resisters and deserters accepted the President's offer. They compared the conditional pardon they were offered with the full pardon granted Nixon. In their view, President Ford measured mercy and justice by a double standard.

Presidential leadership. In spite of his long and close ties with Congress, Ford found himself in repeated conflicts with it during the two years of his administration. In the Congressional elections of 1974, held only three months after Ford became President, the Democrats in both houses were able to greatly increase their already large majorities. Ford, a moderate conservative Republican, could not accept many Democratic proposals for social welfare programs.

Since Republicans in Congress could not defeat the bills, Ford used his Presidential veto to kill them. During his term in office, he vetoed more bills than any President had ever vetoed in such a short time. In most cases, Congress was unable to pass the bills over Ford's veto.

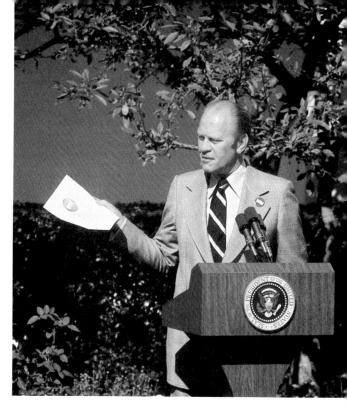

In an effort to beat inflation, President Gerald Ford announced his WIN program—*Whip Inflation Now.* Ford's program urged Americans to counteract rising costs by voluntarily curbing wage and price demands.

Economic problems. President Ford's frequent use of the veto was the result in part of his attempt to combat the problem of inflation. He had inherited this problem from Nixon, just as Nixon had inherited it from the years of the Vietnam War.

Ford, like Nixon, was convinced that excessive government spending was a major cause of the worst inflation the country had experienced since 1947. In 1973 inflation was driving up the cost of living at an annual rate of 9 percent. During 1974 the rate soared above 12 percent. People living on fixed incomes, principally the nation's elderly, were hardest hit.

Ford attempted to reduce federal spending and slow down the economy, but these efforts led to a sharp business slump. To add to the confusion, Ford and Congress disagreed over the best way to handle the still soaring cost of oil and gasoline and the threatening shortage of energy.

The election of 1976. With the election of 1976 approaching, Ford announced that he intended to run for the office that he had been occupying by appointment. His critics, including members of his own party, faulted him for lack of vigorous leadership. His supporters, although not all were enthusiastic about his candidacy, pointed out that he had helped to restore confidence in the Presidency.

Ford won a narrow victory at the nominating convention over Ronald Reagan of California, who represented the conservative wing of the Republican Party. The convention balanced the ticket with the choice of a Reagan conservative, Robert Dole of Kansas, as the Vice-Presidential candidate.

The Democratic convention again had a large representation of young delegates, women, blacks, and liberals. It chose Jimmy Carter of Georgia on the first ballot with Senator Walter F. Mondale of Minnesota as his running mate.

Carter had been almost unknown on the national stage when he first began to run for the nomination. His spectacular campaign in the state primaries attracted wide attention and led to his nomination.

Carter had attended Annapolis. After a successful career as a naval officer, he had returned to his home state of Georgia. There he had built up the family peanut business and later served as governor of the state.

The key issues in the election campaign were inflation and unemployment. Although Carter and Ford met in televised debates, the first since the Kennedy-Nixon debates of 1960, neither candidate aroused much enthusiasm. As a result, right up to election day a large number of voters had not decided for whom to cast their ballots. Political pollsters said the election was "too close to call."

Jimmy Carter won, but by the narrowest of margins—297 electoral votes to Ford's 241. The Democrats once again swept the Congressional contests.

SECTION SURVEY

IDENTIFY: Nelson Rockefeller, amnesty, stagflation, Jimmy Carter.

1. (a) Why did President Ford pardon Richard Nixon? (b) Why did some people criticize the pardon?
2. (a) How did President Ford attempt to fight inflation? (b) What were the results?
3. (a) Describe the events that led up to the nominations of Gerald Ford and Jimmy Carter for President in 1976. (b) Why was the general election too close to call?

6 Presidents Carter and Reagan face critical domestic problems

On January 20, 1977, Jimmy Carter was sworn in as the 39th President of the United States. Following the inaugural ceremony, he and his wife, Rosalynn, walked down Pennsylvania Avenue to the White House.

During the campaign Carter had promised, if elected, to stay in close touch with the American people. The walk—rather than the usual ride in a large limousine surrounded by Secret Service men—was a symbol of his intention to keep the promise.

Beginning "an open administration." The next day, as one of his first Presidential acts, Carter granted an unconditional pardon to the draft evaders of the Vietnam War. The pardon, which President Ford had refused to grant, did not include deserters, whose cases were to be treated individually.

In his first report to the nation, President Carter pledged, among other things, that government regulations would be written in "plain English." He said he would hold "town hall meetings" to keep in touch with the people. He also planned "call-in" sessions on the radio and TV networks to answer questions. He held the first of these "call-in" sessions early in March, and for two hours took phone calls directly from the people. A few days later, he made a trip to New England where he attended an old-fashioned New England town meeting and answered questions directed to him from the audience.

Before long, however, President Carter discovered that his executive duties left him little time for direct communication with even a sampling of ordinary citizens. Problems both at home and abroad confined him closer and closer to the White House. Within a few months, critics were complaining that he was too heavily preoccupied with foreign affairs. They claimed that he was neglecting the increasingly serious domestic problems, particularly unemployment, inflation, and energy.

Combating unemployment. Through the fall and winter of 1976–77, the nation seemed to be slowly but steadily recovering from the recession of 1972–75. Unemployment remained high, however, especially among blacks and Hispanics in the cities. For the country as a whole it averaged about 7 percent. This meant that approximately 7 million men and women were out of work.

Shortly after Carter took office, he sent Congress a plan designed to stimulate the economy and provide jobs. The plan called for a $50 rebate on 1976 taxes for every American citizen. It also called for tax cuts to encourage business to increase capital investments, which in turn would open new employment opportunities. Congress adopted the plan but, with Carter's approval, eliminated the rebates.

The efforts to reduce unemployment met only limited success. In the fall of 1978, almost two years after Carter became President, more than 6 million Americans remained jobless. Congress tried again to remedy the situation with a tax cut. The bill called for $18.7 billion of tax relief, mainly for upper-middle-class and wealthy Americans. Senator Edward M. Kennedy, speaking for large numbers of critics, urged the President to veto the bill. He claimed that it "unfairly ignored the needs of the average taxpayer for tax relief." Despite the widespread protests, Carter signed the bill.

At the same time, Congress adopted and the President approved the Humphrey-Hawkins "full employment" bill. The bill set as a national goal the reducing of unemployment to 4 percent by 1983. It also set as a goal the reducing of inflation to 3 percent by 1983 and to zero by 1988. The law did not say how the President and Congress would achieve these goals. It did, however, state that any programs used to combat inflation must not be permitted to interfere with efforts to reduce unemployment.

Other economic issues. During 1977 and 1978, while the Carter administration was struggling to combat unemployment, the cost of living rose sharply. By the fall of 1978, it was growing at the rate of 10 percent a year. Carter then tried to fight inflation with a voluntary system of wage and price controls.

The President's anti-inflation program was received with mixed reactions. Business, in general, favored it. Organized labor protested that it was unfair. Why, labor asked, had the President failed to include guidelines for interest rates, dividends, and profits?

President Carter also tried to raise the shrunken value of the dollar in the interna-

Following his inauguration in January 1977, President Jimmy Carter broke tradition and walked back to the White House from the Capitol Building, a surprise to the cheering crowds thronging Pennsylvania Avenue.

tional markets. At the same time, he attempted to reduce the nation's unfavorable balance of trade. This imbalance was especially marked in regard to Japan. The Japanese were successfully competing in the American market with automobiles, electronic equipment, agricultural and industrial machinery, and other products. The value of Japanese imports into the United States now far outweighed American sales to Japan.

Finally, in a further effort to control inflation, the President proposed to reduce federal spending. His "lean budget" reduced expenditures for social services while increasing military spending by 3 percent. It was severely criticized by farmers, minorities, and liberals in general.

The anti-inflationary measures also had an undesirable side effect. They increased unemployment. By the summer of 1980, America was moving deeper and deeper into a recession. With the Presidential elections approaching in the fall, this was worrisome news indeed for Jimmy Carter.

The energy problem. The energy problem remained the most urgent of all the long-term domestic problems facing the nation. Energy costs also contributed greatly to the soaring rate of inflation.

Four months after he took office, Carter sent his energy program to Congress. It emphasized the need for conservation. Speaking over the television networks, the President warned of a possible "national catastrophe" unless Congress and the people as a whole united behind the conservation effort.

Carter's program was called a "carrot-and-stick" approach. It mixed incentives to conserve energy with penalties to discourage wasteful practices. It proposed to increase the cost of domestically produced oil and gas by gradually deregulating prices of these fuels. The plan called for Presidential authority to impose additional taxes on gasoline to discourage its use. It stressed the development of other sources of energy, especially coal, nuclear power, and solar energy.

Not until the fall of 1978 did Congress pass an energy bill. The bill was a much watered-down version of Carter's original proposal. It provided some new taxes and tax credits and did begin to deregulate fuel prices. Congress also set aside $54 billion for highway improvement and the development of mass transit systems.

In the meantime Congress had created the Department of Energy (DOE). The DOE was given the major responsibility for improving older energy systems and developing alternative energy sources.

An energy crisis. Events overseas contributed to energy problems in the United States. A revolution in Iran (see page 794) stopped oil shipments from that country. This disturbed the flow of oil to nations around the world.

Americans felt the impact by the spring of 1979. Gas shipments to filling stations were reduced or cut off. Many stations cut back their business hours or closed altogether. Lines of cars waiting for gas soon jammed city streets. Waits of an hour or more were common. Several states adopted systems to restrict the days on which gas could be bought. To add to the crisis, oil exporting nations soon raised their oil prices, which sent the cost of gas and oil products soaring.

By the summer of 1979, Americans had cut back somewhat on their use of gas. The gas shortage eased, but the danger of another crisis

Signs of the worsening energy situation in the late 1970's were the seemingly endless lines of cars stretching from gas stations along jammed city streets in some parts of the nation. People often waited an hour or more to get gas.

still existed. In July Carter set forth another energy plan, calling for a massive program to develop synthetic fuels. The long-range goal of the plan was to cut importation of oil in half.

Obstacles to Carter's success. By the summer of 1980, a public opinion poll revealed that only 21 percent of the American people approved of President Carter's performance in office. This was the lowest figure for a President since the 1930's, when the poll was first taken. It was even lower than the figure for President Nixon at the height of the Watergate affair. Why was Carter's rating so low?

Part of the answer lay in Carter's inexperience. When running for office he had stressed his independence from Washington's political establishment. This helped him in the campaign but hurt him in office. He often had trouble enlisting support for his programs, even among members of his own party.

Part of the problem was the programs themselves. They were hard to define. He proclaimed his first energy program as "the moral equivalent of war" but failed to press Congress to pass the bill. He seemed changeable, almost fickle at times. In 1979 he changed five of his Cabinet members, among them the Secretary of HEW, whom he had just praised for doing an excellent job.

Part of the trouble lay in the nature of the problems Carter faced. Energy, inflation, unemployment, foreign affairs — they were all complicated. They had no easy solutions, and at times it seemed that Carter offered no solutions at all.

Choosing candidates. The campaign for the Presidential nominations in 1980 was a long one. Critics, in fact, began to ask whether the United States needed a system as lengthy, costly, and complex to nominate candidates.

Ronald Reagan was again a leading contender for the Republican nomination. He held off challenges from a variety of opponents and easily won the nomination at Detroit. He picked George Bush, one of those former opponents, as his running mate.

Jimmy Carter wanted to run for reelection. Usually a President in office has little trouble in securing his party's nomination. By early 1980, however, Carter's popularity was low. Many Democrats feared that if Carter ran again it would mean defeat for the Democratic Party in November. Senator Edward Kennedy

of Massachusetts challenged Carter for the nomination. As the incumbent, Carter had the edge and in the end won renomination from his party. Walter Mondale again was the candidate for Vice-President.

Many people were unhappy with the choice between Carter and Reagan. Representative John Anderson of Illinois recognized this dissatisfaction. Originally, he had tried for the Republican nomination but had lost to Reagan. Now he decided to run as an independent candidate who would appeal to such people.

The election of 1980. The election campaign of 1980 was hard fought. Reagan warned of the nation's military weakness. He also stressed Carter's failure to solve the nation's economic problems. He reminded voters of the ever-rising rates of inflation and unemployment and spoke of the current recession as the "Carter depression." If elected, Reagan promised, he would cut spending in government, cut taxes, and stimulate business.

Carter tried to remind people of his foreign policy achievements. For the first time since Herbert Hoover was President, he claimed, no American soldier had died in battle. He spoke of improved relations with China and the Egyptian-Israeli peace treaty. Carter pointed out the number of times in the past when Reagan had favored military intervention. Carter reminded voters that in a nuclear age a President had to show restraint.

Once again political pollsters said the election was too close to call. Thus, for many, the morning after election day was a surprise. Reagan had won a sweeping victory with 42,797,153 popular votes compared with Carter's 34,434,100. The electoral vote was 489 to 49. Anderson received no electoral votes.

Analyzing the results. More surprising than the size of Reagan's victory was the outcome in Congressional races. The Republicans won control of the Senate for the first time since 1952. The Democrats kept control of the House, but Republicans made gains there as well.

Many people asked if the Republican victory represented a new movement in politics. Were Americans becoming more conservative? Were they tired of massive federal programs that raised their taxes and complicated their lives as Reagan charged? Or had they simply rejected Carter for failing to handle the large problems adequately?

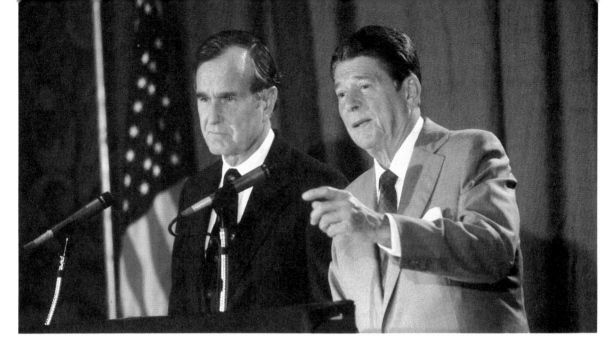

Ronald Reagan and George Bush proved to be a formidable team for the Republican Party. They won the 1980 election by a wide margin, foiling the bid by Democrats Jimmy Carter and Walter Mondale for reelection.

The Republicans take control. President Reagan entered office with widespread support from the public. His warm, winning, relaxed good nature and his reputation for managing personal differences added a nice touch to the "honeymoon" initially enjoyed by new administrations.

Reagan's popularity, high from the beginning, soared to new heights when, 70 days after he became President, he survived an assassination attempt. His courage and grace when he was shot, seriously wounded, and hospitalized won him the sympathy, good will, and respect of the American people.

Reagan's economic program. Reagan outlined his economic program during the election campaign. Once in office, he began immediately to try to win support for it and move it through Congress.

The first priority was victory over inflation. In order to win this victory, the government would have to balance the budget—that is, to reduce expenditures to match the amount of money available from taxes. The Republicans proposed to balance the federal budget by cutting government spending and by reducing taxes at the same time.

The Reagan program aroused a storm of controversy. Many critics charged that the proposed tax cuts favored the wealthy and corporations. They also claimed that spending cuts would damage programs that aided the needy, protected the environment, and supported public education. Critics also insisted that tax cuts could not be combined with the huge military spending Reagan was calling for. They warned that such a policy would only increase inflation.

In the face of such criticism, Reagan argued strongly for his economic program and won much public support. Plans for cuts in both taxes and federal spending were passed by Congress.

Yet even before his program took effect, Reagan called for additional spending cuts to balance the budget. For example, he proposed disbanding the Departments of Energy and of Education. How well the program would work, even with more cuts, remained to be seen.

SECTION SURVEY

IDENTIFY: Humphrey-Hawkins bill, fixed income, energy conservation, Department of Energy, Edward Kennedy, John Anderson.

1. What programs did President Carter support to (a) fight unemployment, (b) reduce inflation, and (c) solve the energy problem? How effective were his efforts in these areas?

2. What factors contributed to President Carter's unpopularity as President?

3. Describe the (a) candidates, (b) issues, and (c) results of the election of 1980.

Chapter Survey

Summary: Tracing the Main Ideas

John F. Kennedy's prediction in 1960 that the United States was entering one of the most critical periods in its history proved all too true. Between 1960 and 1980, the American people had to contend with the problems of unemployment, inflation, and the worldwide threat of a shortage of energy. As you will read later (see Chapter 42), the government and the American people also had to face the crisis confronting the nation's cities, a crisis closely related to the demands by the nation's minorities for freedom and justice.

The Presidents you have read about in this chapter also faced serious difficulties abroad. Warm relations with old allies cooled and old enemies became new friends. New nations began to play an increasingly important part in world affairs. The United States' foreign policies, of which you will read in Chapter 41, influenced and interacted with its domestic policies. Indeed, at times it was difficult to untangle the two.

Inquiring into History

1. Compare the goals and accomplishments of the New Frontier and the Great Society.
2. Make a list of the major legislation passed during the administrations of Presidents Kennedy, Johnson, Nixon, Ford, and Carter. (a) Which Presidents were most successful in getting legislation passed? Why? (b) Which Presidents were generally considered effective? How do their reputations compare with their legislative records?
3. It has been said that the United States has become more democratic in recent years. Do you agree or disagree? Give specific examples to support your answer.
4. List the key issues in the Presidential elections since 1960. (a) In which campaigns were the issues similar? (b) Why do you think these issues kept reappearing?

Relating Past to Present

1. In recent years television has become an important force in American politics. How does television affect elections during the campaigns and on election day?

2. Do you think Congress or the President should have the leading role in shaping government policies? Use examples from the Presidential administrations described in this chapter to support your opinion.
3. How did Reagan's plans for fighting inflation compare to Carter's plans? Carter was unsuccessful in his attempt to deal with the problem. Based on your knowledge of Reagan's administration, do you think he was more or less successful? Explain.

Developing Social Science Skills

1. Make line graphs to illustrate the ups and downs of inflation and unemployment since 1960. (Use a source such as *Statistical Abstract of the United States* to find the statistics.) Where the graph shows years of extreme highs or lows, explain why these extremes occurred.
2. Select one of the Presidential administrations discussed in this chapter. For display on the bulletin board, prepare an illustrated time line of the major events of the administration. Use pictures from magazines, newspaper clippings, political cartoons, or your own drawings to illustrate the time line.

Timeline

1955

1960

Cuban missile crisis

Gulf of Tonkin Resolution

1965

Arab-Israeli war

1970

Nixon visits China

Détente with Soviet Union begins

Cease-fire in Vietnam War

1975

Camp David accords signed

Iran seizes American hostages

1980

Hostages freed

1985

2000

Chapter 41

Reexamining the Nation's Role in World Affairs

1960-1980's

From the 1960's through the 1980's, Americans faced a complex, troubling domestic scene. First President Kennedy and later Presidents Johnson, Nixon, Ford, Carter, and Reagan all tried to cope with these domestic problems. Often, however, their attention was held by events overseas.

The United States had taken on the responsibilities of world leadership. Americans were now learning that such responsibility could be a heavy burden and could have serious effects on their lives at home. Worldwide problems—pollution of the environment, nuclear disarmament, feeding of the rapidly growing population—demanded attention. Trying to solve such problems required international cooperation, a sense of national purpose, and large sums of money.

America's growing involvement in Vietnam was of deepest concern because it affected all the other problems. This involvement in Southeast Asia would prove enormously costly in lives and resources. It would also deeply trouble large numbers of Americans and continue to haunt the nation long after the last Americans had left Vietnam.

In one sense, Vietnam was part of a larger issue confronting Americans: Had the United States assumed more responsibilities around the world than it could possibly meet, even with all its wealth and power?

These were among the issues troubling Americans during the 1960's and 1970's and as the United States entered the third century of its history.

THE CHAPTER IN OUTLINE

1. The United States assumes global responsibilities.

2. The United States becomes deeply involved in Vietnam.

3. World tensions are relaxed during the Nixon and Ford administrations.

4. World tensions build up during the Carter and Reagan administrations.

1 The United States assumes global responsibilities

During the 1960's and 1970's, the dangers of nuclear war and Communist aggression continued to haunt Americans. At the same time, new global developments thrust increasingly heavy demands upon the American people and their leaders.

A changing world. One major development was the growing competition American business faced from Japan, the Soviet Union, and the Common Market countries of Western Europe. These nations, with modern, efficient industrial plants and equipment, had become serious competitors of the United States for world markets.

Another revolutionary development was the entry of a large number of new nations into the world community. By 1979 UN membership had grown to 151 nations. The new member nations represented more than 1 billion people. Most of these new nations had emerged from former colonies in the nonindustrial areas of Asia and Africa.

Shifting relationships. A third major development was the changing balance of world power. After World War II the Communist nations, led by the Soviet Union, had been aligned on one side, the United States and its allies on the other. During the 1960's this alignment began to crumble.

The newly independent nations of Asia and Africa were reluctant to tie themselves to either the Soviet Union or the United States. These nations, together with developing countries in Latin America, made up what came to be called the **Third World.** These Third World nations became increasingly important in world affairs.

Meanwhile the solid front of communism was breaking up as Communist China opposed the Soviet Union's leadership of world communism. By 1964 the leaders of the Soviet Union and Communist China were openly attacking each other's policies. By the late 1960's, the split between the two most powerful Communist countries was complete.

The solid front among anti-Communist nations was also becoming strained. President

In 1966 President Charles de Gaulle of France pulled his country out of the NATO alliance. What attitude does de Gaulle demonstrate in this cartoon? Do you think the cartoonist approves of de Gaulle's action?

Charles de Gaulle of France began to challenge America's leadership role. He hoped to establish France at the head of a group of nations with power and influence equal to that of the United States and the Soviet Union. In 1966 de Gaulle showed that the solid front had cracked by pulling France out of the NATO alliance.

By the 1960's all of the powerful nations—both Communist and non-Communist—were competing for the markets as well as the political support of the Third World nations. Thus many of the world crises facing the United States grew out of the problems of Africa, Latin America, and Asia.

Kennedy's foreign policy. In this rapidly changing world, President Kennedy and, later, President Johnson generally followed the basic foreign policy developed under Truman and Eisenhower. However, there were new steps in foreign policy during the early 1960's. The Trade Expansion Act of 1962 was passed to increase world trade as well as to meet the

779

growing competition of the Common Market countries. Kennedy and Johnson also sponsored programs to strengthen international cultural relations by sending outstanding American musicians, theater groups, writers, and artists to visit friendly, neutral, and Communist countries.

The Peace Corps. The most imaginative new program was the Peace Corps. This was a government-supported organization of Americans who volunteered to live among the people of underdeveloped lands and to help them with day-to-day problems. In September 1961 the first American volunteers arrived in the African nation of Ghana to serve as teachers.

From the beginning the Peace Corps was a notable success. By 1970, Americans, mostly young men and women, were serving overseas in 59 different countries. The Peace Corps symbolized America's desire to provide humane assistance as well as economic and military leadership in the non-Communist world.

Trouble in Africa. President Kennedy had to deal with the problems of America's relations with the emerging African nations. The most serious crisis developed in the Congo (now the Republic of Zaïre).

The Congo, a former Belgian colony, became independent in June 1960. Many rival groups—among them pro-Communist and pro-Western groups—battled for control of the government. The problem grew worse when the mineral-rich Katanga province seceded from the newly formed nation.

In response to an appeal by the Congo government, the UN sent troops from African and Asian nations to police the troubled country.

The UN force prevented a full-scale civil war, but it was not at first able to end the bloodshed. A new crisis developed in 1961 when Patrice Lumumba, leader of the pro-Communist faction, was assassinated. Soviet Premier Khrushchev demanded withdrawal of all UN troops and threatened to intervene. President Kennedy warned that the United States would defend the UN operation.

With firm American backing, the UN continued its difficult peacemaking operation in the Congo. By 1965 the fighting ended and Katanga province rejoined the nation. By the late 1960's, most scars of the civil war seemed healed. The Congo (Zaïre) became one of the most prosperous African nations.

Cuba and the Bay of Pigs. President Kennedy faced a very serious problem in Cuba. Early in 1959, guerrilla forces led by Fidel Castro overthrew the government of Cuban dictator Fulgencio Batista (bah·TEES·tah). At first the United States welcomed Castro's rise to power. However, American sympathy rapidly faded when Castro began to act like a ruthless dictator. He put to death hundreds of political enemies, jailed thousands, and took control of foreign-owned property. In addition, he lashed out against "Yankees" and accepted a Soviet offer of military aid if the United States interfered in Cuba.

By the summer of 1960, the United States had placed an embargo on the purchase of Cuban sugar. It had also urged the Organization of American States (O.A.S.) to condemn Cuba's actions.

Kennedy had inherited a plan developed under Eisenhower to overthrow the Castro government. During 1960 a force of anti-Castro Cubans had been trained in Central America with the active support of the United States Central Intelligence Agency (CIA). The plan called for this force to invade Cuba. According to the plan, the Cuban underground would rise, join the invaders, and overthrow the Castro government. President Kennedy decided to allow the plan to be carried out.

On April 17, 1961, the invasion force landed on the beaches of the Bahía de Cochinos, or the Bay of Pigs. The invasion was a total failure. The Cuban underground never joined the battle. Most of the invading "Freedom Fighters" were killed or captured. In reply to a storm of criticism, President Kennedy admitted that the invasion attempt had been a mistake and assumed full responsibility for it.

The Alliance for Progress. To deal with the Communist presence in Cuba, Kennedy proposed a program called the Alliance for Progress. The United States and 19 Latin-American countries (all but Cuba) had joined the Alliance by 1961.

The Alliance members agreed to a 10-year program to improve social and economic conditions in Latin America. Finances for the program were to come from private and government sources in Latin America and the United States plus Japan, Western Europe, and international agencies such as the World Bank.

During the first four years, the United States contributed $4.5 billion to the program,

MISSILE ERECTOR

CABLE

MISSILE SHELTER TENT

TRACKED PRIME MOVERS

OXIDIZER TANK TRAILERS

FUEL TANK TRAILERS

Photographs like this, taken on October 23, 1962, by an American U-2 spy plane, supplied President Kennedy with evidence of a Soviet-constructed missile launch base in Cuba. Such evidence triggered the Cuban missile crisis.

the Latin-American countries $22 billion. Some progress was made, but the results were disappointing. Much of the money was used to help business interests and military forces in Latin America rather than the masses of poor people. Congress, increasingly impatient, began to reduce the budgets for the Alliance.

The missile crisis. Meanwhile, relations with Cuba worsened. The United States cut off all trade with Cuba. The O.A.S. did not go that far, but it did vote Cuba out of the organization in 1962. Castro announced his commitment to communism, and the Soviet Union stepped up shipments of military equipment to Cuba. This led to a frightening crisis in the fall of 1962.

In mid-October American intelligence sources reported that the Soviet Union was equipping Cuba with long-range jet bombers and offensive missiles that could deliver nuclear bombs to most of the eastern United States. On October 22 President Kennedy ordered the Navy to establish a blockade — or "quarantine" — against any further shipment of offensive weapons to Cuba. He also demanded that the Soviet Union immediately dismantle the Cuban missile bases and withdraw Soviet missiles and bombers from Cuba.

The world waited tensely for Khrushchev's reaction. Faced with the choice between nu-

clear war or meeting Kennedy's demands, Khrushchev backed down. During the next few weeks, the Soviets began to dismantle the missile bases and remove the missiles and bombers. Nonetheless, a Communist nation supported by the Soviet Union was now established only 90 miles (144 kilometers) from the United States.

The Dominican issue. Another Latin-American crisis arose in the spring of 1965. A revolution plunged the Dominican Republic into chaos. Calling the situation "grave," President Johnson ordered 400 marines into the Dominican capital, Santo Domingo. His aim was to protect the lives of Americans there. This was the first time since 1926 that the marines had been ordered into a Latin-American country. During the next two weeks, 22,000 additional American troops landed, and 10,000 more stood by in navy vessels offshore.

President Johnson justified his action on the grounds that it was necessary to prevent a possible Communist takeover and to enable the people to hold free elections. He made it clear that the American forces would be withdrawn as soon as the O.A.S. took responsibility for maintaining order.

Representatives of the O.A.S. accepted the responsibility. By midsummer a small force of

781

troops from four Latin-American nations had arrived in Santo Domingo. Some of the United States troops were then withdrawn. In late August both sides accepted a provisional president who governed until elections were held in June 1966.

Crisis in Berlin. In Europe, too, Kennedy faced a challenge from the Soviet Union. In 1961 Soviet Premier Khrushchev renewed his threat to end the Western nations' rights of free access to West Berlin. Kennedy warned in turn that the United States would not abandon West Berlin.

In August 1961 the East German government began to erect a wall along the line between East and West Berlin. The Berlin Wall cut off the escape of East Germans into West Germany. It became a grim symbol of the conflicts between the Communist and anti-Communist nations of Europe.

The nuclear test ban. In August 1961 Premier Khrushchev also announced that the Soviet Union intended to resume nuclear testing. This news shocked people everywhere, for in 1958 the nuclear powers — the United States, Great Britain, and the Soviet Union — had agreed to suspend all testing for three years. The three-year period had not yet expired. President Kennedy warned that if the Soviets carried out their plans, the United States would be forced in the interests of its own defense to resume nuclear testing.

Nevertheless, the Soviets began a series of nuclear tests in the fall of 1961. The following spring, after the Soviet Union had turned down repeated pleas for a fully effective test ban and a general arms reduction, the United States began its own tests.

The first breaks in the long deadlock came in 1963. In June Moscow and Washington agreed on a "hot line" to provide direct teletype communications between the two capitals to help prevent nuclear war by accident.

In July American, British, and Soviet representatives agreed to ban nuclear tests in the atmosphere, under water, and in space. Underground testing would continue. The United States Senate ratified the agreement, and it went into effect in October 1963.

Communist China. The United States met its most difficult problems in Asia. There Communist China continued to threaten trouble in much of Asia. In 1959 the Chinese Communists took over Tibet. In 1962, following a border dispute, they launched a large-scale attack on India. In response to appeals from the Indian government, the United States and Great Britain airlifted military supplies to the hard-pressed Indian troops. Then China announced a cease-fire and called for negotiations. India, shocked by what it considered unprovoked aggression, began to build up its defenses.

Conflict in Southeast Asia. In addition to China, the new countries of Southeast Asia — Laos, Cambodia, and North and South Vietnam became major crisis areas during the troubled 1960's.

The tiny kingdom of Laos was divided into three political factions — pro-Western, Communist, and neutral. In an effort to secure a strong pro-Western government, the United States poured millions of dollars into Laos. This effort failed. Finally, in 1962, after lengthy negotiations the Laotian factions agreed to a neutral government in Laos.

The United States also gave considerable military and economic aid to Cambodia in an effort to secure a pro-Western government. As in Laos, however, the policy failed. In 1963 Cambodia asked the United States to withdraw its military and technical personnel. You will read about increasing American involvement in Cambodia and in South Vietnam in the following section.

SECTION SURVEY

IDENTIFY: Third World, Trade Expansion Act of 1962, Peace Corps, Congo crisis, Premier Khrushchev, Fidel Castro, Bay of Pigs invasion, quarantine, Berlin Wall, "hot line."

1. (a) How did relationships among Communist nations change during the 1960's? (b) How did relationships among non-Communist nations change? (c) How did the rise of the Third World affect the foreign policy of both the United States and the Soviet Union?

2. The Cuban missile crisis brought the world to the brink of nuclear war in 1962. Explain.

3. Review United States relations with Latin America in (a) the Alliance for Progress and (b) the Dominican crisis.

4. (a) What was United States policy toward Asia in the early 1960's? (b) How successful was that policy?

2 The United States becomes deeply involved in Vietnam

The most serious problem that the United States faced between 1960 and 1980 was a war in South Vietnam. This war had a great impact on the image of America around the world. It also influenced the way Americans perceived their own country and its role in the world.

Background to war. As you have read (page 714), when France pulled out of Vietnam in the 1950's, an international agreement divided that country into two parts. Elections that would have reunited the country, scheduled for 1956, were never held. Instead Vietnam continued to exist as two nations. North Vietnam, with its capital at Hanoi, was under a Communist government headed by Ho Chi Minh. South Vietnam, with its capital at Saigon, was a republic whose president was Ngo Dinh Diem (NOH DIN DYEM). Diem's government had strong backing from the United States.

Although the promised elections were not held, many Vietnamese still wanted a united country. Vietnamese guerrillas, backed by North Vietnam, fought to overthrow Diem's regime and unite the countries. In 1960 the guerrillas took the name of the National Liberation Front (NLF). Their opponents referred to them as the Viet Cong (Vietnamese Communists).

American involvement. The United States was deeply concerned over events in South Vietnam. Not long before, Communists had taken over China and had barely been beaten back in Korea. Now a Communist movement was gaining strength in South Vietnam.

President Eisenhower warned of the danger of a "domino" effect in Southeast Asia. He meant that if the government of one nation there fell to the Communists, then the government of the neighboring nation would topple in turn. According to this view, all of Southeast Asia might end up in Communist hands if one nation fell. To prevent the fall of South Vietnam to the Communists, millions of dollars in military aid and 800 United States military advisers were sent to South Vietnam during Eisenhower's administration.

THE CONFLICT IN VIETNAM

Eisenhower's belief in a "domino effect" was shared by President Kennedy. Kennedy declared that United States foreign policy depended "in considerable measure upon a strong and free Vietnamese nation."

The formation of the NLF in 1960 was followed by increased guerrilla activity. In response, Kennedy increased the amount of military aid and the number of advisers to the threatened Diem regime.

The fall of Diem. However, Diem's administration was corrupt, and he became increasingly unpopular in South Vietnam. He harshly repressed Buddhists and political opponents. Also, his failure to control the NLF angered South Vietnamese military leaders. Kennedy pressured Diem to make reforms, but Diem failed to do so.

783

"Ike made a promise," President Lyndon Johnson often said, "and I have to keep it." Here, on a trip to South Vietnam, he visits some of the hundreds of thousands of American troops sent to that nation to try to keep the promise.

Finally, the United States government learned that South Vietnamese military leaders were planning to seize power from Diem. Kennedy made no effort to stop them or to inform Diem. In 1963, the military took over, and Diem was assassinated.

The new government fared no better than Diem's in the struggle against the NLF. The United States nevertheless remained committed to South Vietnam. After Kennedy's death, President Johnson stated, "I am not going to be the President who saw Vietnam go the way China went." He expanded American aid programs. By late 1964 there were 23,000 American advisers in South Vietnam.

The Gulf of Tonkin Resolution. On August 4, 1964, President Johnson appeared on television with shocking news. He announced that two American destroyers had been attacked by North Vietnamese torpedo boats in the Gulf of Tonkin (see map, page 783). The President stated that he had therefore ordered American planes to bomb North Vietnamese torpedo bases and oil refineries. He also asked Congress to grant him authority to take action against North Vietnam.

The President did not tell the nation that the American ships had been assisting South Vietnamese gunboats that were making raids on North Vietnam's coast. He also did not inform the nation that there was some doubt whether there had been any attack on the American ships at all.

Three days later Congress granted the President's request. It adopted what became known as the Gulf of Tonkin Resolution. This gave the President power "to take all necessary measures to repel any armed attack against the forces of the United States and to prevent further aggression."

The House voted unanimously for the measure. The Senate passed it by a vote of 88 to 2. Senator Wayne Morse of Oregon, who voted against it, warned that "we are in effect giving the President warmaking powers in the absence of a declaration of war. I believe that to be a historic mistake."

A turning point. As late as October 1964, President Johnson still stated that he did not intend to commit American troops to a war in Asia. "We are not," he declared, "about to send American boys nine or ten thousand miles away from home to do what Asian boys ought to be doing for themselves." Nevertheless, the Gulf of Tonkin Resolution changed the situation in South Vietnam and marked a turning point in United States participation there.

Viet Cong attacks in South Vietnam continued, and American responses grew stronger. In February 1965 President Johnson ordered American planes to bomb targets in North Vietnam. The bombing of North Vietnam would continue, with occasional pauses, until March 1968.

President Johnson ordered more United States ground forces to South Vietnam as well. In March 1965 the first marines landed there. By early 1966 there were 190,000 United States troops in South Vietnam. By mid-1966 the number was 265,000. By the end of 1967 it had risen to 500,000.

A widening war. As American aid increased, North Vietnam increased its support of the Viet Cong. Supplies flowed from North to South Vietnam over a network of routes that became known as the Ho Chi Minh Trail. As the war went on, troops from North Vietnam also moved south along the trail to join the Viet Cong in the fighting.

The United States tried in several ways to end the fighting. President Johnson halted bombing raids for brief periods. He also offered $1 billion in economic aid to Southeast Asia. Nevertheless, the North Vietnamese continued to insist that the United States had to get out of Vietnam before peace talks could begin. This the United States refused to do.

Differing strategies. Unlike the Communists, the Americans and the South Vietnamese relied heavily on air power in fighting the war. The Air Force poured bombs, napalm, rockets, and machine-gun fire on Viet Cong villages, hideouts, and supply routes in South Vietnam. In North Vietnam air raids were aimed at supply depots, industrial plants, and strategic roads and bridges. By the end of 1968, Americans had dropped more bombs on North Vietnam than they had used during all of World War II.

With support from the air, South Vietnamese and American ground forces carried out "search-and-destroy" missions against the Viet Cong. In areas they could not hold or defend, they moved the people to refugee centers and burned the villages.

The Viet Cong and the North Vietnamese, who lacked extensive air power, usually avoided large-scale fighting. Instead they used guerrilla tactics and terrorism. They planted bombs in a country marketplace or on a street in a busy city. They tortured or assassinated unfriendly village leaders. They practiced "hit-and-run" warfare, striking swiftly, then melting back into the jungle.

Effects of the war. The war had a shattering impact on all participants. In South Vietnam, a country about the size of the state of Washington, more than 1.6 million troops were fighting by 1968.° By that time American casualties totaled more than 27,000 killed and 92,000 seriously wounded.

Vietnamese civilians bore the heaviest burden of suffering. Though air strikes were aimed at military targets, civilians were often the victims. By the end of 1967, civilian casualties were totaling between 100,000 and 150,000 a year. By 1968 at least 2 million of the 16 million people of South Vietnam were displaced and had become refugees.

Elections in South Vietnam. The United States knew that the people of South Vietnam would have to have faith in their government if the war was to be won. For this to happen, the Vietnamese people would have to believe that their government was genuinely concerned about their welfare.

Unfortunately graft and corruption had continued under the rule of the military leaders who overthrew Diem. The United States urged these leaders to end corruption and move toward a more democratic form of government.

South Vietnam held elections in the fall of 1967. Defying the Viet Cong, who tried to sabotage the elections, an estimated 51 percent of those eligible voted. The South Vietnamese elected General Nguyen Van Thieu (nuh·WIN van TYOO) as President.

Some American observers saw the election as a positive step toward a stable, democratic South Vietnamese government. At the same time, American military leaders were issuing optimistic reports on the progress of the fight-

°By the end of 1968, troops in the war numbered as follows: on the allied side about 750,000 South Vietnamese, 540,000 Americans, 45,000 South Koreans, and 15,000 Australians, New Zealanders, Thais, and Filipinos. There were an estimated 300,000 Viet Cong and North Vietnamese regulars.

SOURCES

THE GULF OF TONKIN RESOLUTION (1964)

Whereas naval units of the Communist regime in Vietnam, in violation of the principles of the Charter of the United Nations and of international law, have deliberately and repeatedly attacked United States naval vessels lawfully present in international waters, and have thereby created a serious threat to international peace; and

Whereas these attacks are part of a deliberate and systematic campaign of aggression that the Communist regime in North Vietnam has been waging against its neighbors and the nations joined with them in the collective defense of their freedom; . . . Now therefore, be it

Resolved by the Senate and House of Representatives of the United States of America in Congress assembled, That the Congress approves and supports the determination of the President, as Commander in Chief, to take all necessary measures to repel any armed attack against the forces of the United States and to prevent further aggression.

ing. The war, they claimed, would be over soon. Victory was in sight.

The Tet offensive. In February 1968 came startling evidence that victory was not near. The Viet Cong and the North Vietnamese launched surprise attacks all across South Vietnam during Tet, the lunar New Year holidays. They seized partial control of or terrorized 26 of the provisional capitals of South Vietnam.

The South Vietnamese and Americans soon beat back this Tet offensive. Nevertheless, the cost of victory was high. Large sections of several cities were blasted into rubble. Thousands of soldiers and civilians were killed. Also, the Viet Cong gained firm control of large areas of the countryside.

Aftereffects of Tet. The Tet offensive dealt a staggering blow to predictions that the enemy was being defeated. It also demonstrated that the "other war" — the effort of the Saigon government to win the loyalty of the Vietnamese people — was still far from won.

At the end of March 1968, with the Tet offensive still a raw memory, President Johnson declared that the United States would limit its bombing to invasion routes and to the area immediately north of the Demilitarized Zone (DMZ). This was a supposedly neutral strip of land separating North and South Vietnam.

The Hanoi government responded to Johnson's steps with the long-awaited offer to begin peace talks. In May 1968 the United States and North Vietnam began these talks in Paris.

Criticism of the war. The Tet offensive contributed to the mounting criticism of the war in the United States. By the fall of 1968, the Vietnam conflict had become the second longest war in American history and the third largest in terms of lives lost and money spent. Only the Revolutionary War had lasted longer, and only World War I and World War II had cost more in money, resources, and lives.

Growing numbers of Americans were convinced that the Vietnam War was a grave mistake. They felt that the conflict was basically a civil war in which the United States should have no part. Moreover, they added, the United States was destroying South Vietnam in the process of "saving it" from communism. These critics urged an immediate end to the bombing and a rapid end to the war.

A constitutional question. Congress criticized the war as well. In March 1968 the Senate Foreign Relations Committee held a televised hearing on the conduct of the war.

At the heart of Congress's concern was an issue of constitutional powers. The Constitution makes the President the commander in chief of the nation's armed forces. It also gives him extensive powers over the conduct of foreign affairs. Nevertheless, the Constitution reserves to Congress the power to declare war. Now in Vietnam the United States was engaged in an undeclared war over which Congress had little control.

Most Americans agreed that at times the President had to make major decisions without waiting for Congress to act. Did this mean, however, that in matters of war and peace the role of Congress was no longer relevant? No one, it seemed, had a conclusive answer.

The costs of commitment. Members of Congress and many Americans were also concerned with the larger issue of American foreign policy in general. The American commitment to stop the spread of communism had become enormous. By 1969 the United States was providing some form of aid to 70 nations. It had formal commitments to defend 42 nations against any form of aggression, Communist or otherwise. To back up these commitments, the United States had 3.5 million men and women in the armed forces. Another 1.2 million civilian employees supported these troops. As of January 1968, total military expenses amounted to $87.6 billion a year, or a total expenditure of $439 for each American.

Critics pointed out that Congress voted only $24 billion for human needs—health, education, and welfare—in that same year. They claimed that the war and huge foreign commitments drained resources that could be spent on problems at home.

Critics also claimed that military expenses were contributing to inflation at home. This would raise prices and make it more difficult to sell American products abroad. Thus even the economy would be damaged.

President Johnson's decision. Such criticisms of the war continued to mount. Debate over the course of the war spilled out onto the streets. Huge demonstrations were held to protest the war. At times, prowar and antiwar demonstrators clashed. Many people feared that the country was being torn apart.

President Johnson was eligible to run for reelection in 1968. Nevertheless, growing criticism of the war and strengthening political opposition meant his victory would be doubtful. In March 1968, when he announced the bombing limits, he also announced that he would not seek reelection.

SECTION SURVEY

IDENTIFY: Ho Chi Minh, Ngo Dinh Diem, NLF, Viet Cong, "domino effect," Gulf of Tonkin Resolution, Ho Chi Minh Trail, "search-and-destroy" missions, General Thieu, DMZ.

1. Trace the steps of American involvement in South Vietnam starting in 1962.

2. (a) What was the Tet offensive? (b) What were some of its consequences?

3. What were some of the arguments presented by opponents of the Vietnam War?

4. Source Study: According to the Source on page 786, why was the United States justified in taking action in South Vietnam?

3 World tensions are relaxed during the Nixon and Ford administrations

The war in Vietnam remained the most serious problem confronting the nation when Richard M. Nixon became its next President in January 1969.

Nixon's plan for Vietnam. During the election campaign, Nixon had declared that if elected he would "bring an honorable end to the war." Nixon's plan called for the gradual withdrawal of American troops as soon as the South Vietnamese showed that they were able to defend themselves. The plan also replaced the "search-and-destroy" policy with a "protective-reaction" policy. Under this new policy, American troops would engage the enemy only when attacked or threatened by attack. Nixon hoped that the new tactics would both reduce American casualties and help quiet the fierce opposition to the war.

The invasion of Cambodia. The Nixon plan disappointed those Americans who wanted a quick end to the nation's military involvement in Vietnam. They were further disheartened in the spring of 1970 by Nixon's startling announcement that South Vietnamese and American troops were crossing the border into "neutral" Cambodia. The objective of the invasion, Nixon said, was to destroy North Vietnamese and Viet Cong supply centers and camps along the eastern border of Cambodia. As soon as these centers from which the Viet Cong had been launching their attacks against South Vietnam had been wiped out, the troops would be withdrawn. Nixon promised that all American forces would be out of Cambodia by the end of June.

President Nixon kept his promise. In the meantime, however, the American invasion of Cambodia had triggered widespread antiwar demonstrations in the United States. Further, it intensified a long-standing conflict between Communist and non-Communist forces in the Southeast Asian nation.

The cease-fire agreement. The "protective-reaction" policy and the withdrawal of some American ground troops from South Vietnam during Nixon's first term in office did reduce American casualties. However, there was no reduction in the fury of the air war. American air power destroyed large areas in South Vietnam that were controlled by the Viet Cong and the North Vietnamese. American planes also mined the harbors of North Vietnam and rained bombs upon North Vietnamese supply routes and ammunition centers in Laos and Cambodia.

Meanwhile the negotiations in Paris continued. Nixon's foreign policy adviser, Henry Kissinger, patiently tried to break the deadlock. Just before the Presidential election of 1972, Kissinger announced that "peace is at hand," but the welcomed announcement was premature. The United States continued military operations for two months, including massive bombing of Hanoi during December. Early in January 1973, a cease-fire agreement finally was reached.

There were three key terms in the agreement. (1) The continued presence of North Vietnamese military forces in South Vietnam was tacitly agreed to. (2) South Vietnam was assured that it was to have a government of its own choosing. (3) The United States guaranteed continued economic and military aid to South Vietnam. President Nixon then withdrew the remaining American troops from South Vietnam. As a result of continuing pressure, most American prisoners of war were later released by North Vietnam.

The costs of war. American participation in this longest and most unpopular war in the nation's history had been enormously costly. By the spring of 1973, when the last troops left Vietnam, direct expenditures totaled $137 billion. Some 45,729 Americans had been killed in action and more than 300,000 wounded. As for the people of Southeast Asia, estimates put South Vietnamese deaths at 160,903 and those of the Viet Cong and North Vietnamese at 922,295. In addition, more than 6 million refugees were uprooted and made homeless. Large areas of Vietnam, Laos, and Cambodia had been devastated.

The Vietnam War left feelings of anger and division in American society. The sharp disagreement over what to do about thousands of American draft resisters and deserters who had fled to Canada, Sweden, and elsewhere was but one example of this lingering bitterness (see Chapter 40).

Most Americans agreed that there had to be "no more Vietnams." One element that had contributed to involvement in Vietnam was the President's war-making power (see page 784). Once the war in Vietnam had started, Congress could at any time have ended America's involvement by cutting off funds for further military operations. However, Congress was reluctant to take this step while American troops were actually fighting in the conflict.

After the war's end, Congress tried to deal with this issue. In November 1973, Congress passed the War Powers Act over Nixon's veto. The act provided that no President could send American troops into combat for a period longer than 60 days unless Congress approved. The law also provided that Congress could, by a joint resolution, order the immediate removal of troops from an area of combat.

Later events in Southeast Asia. The peace in Southeast Asia did not last long. Communist forces there took the offensive in 1973 and 1974. In Cambodia, during 1974 and 1975, Communist troops captured much of the country and surrounded the capital of Phnom Penh. In April 1975 the remaining Americans were evacuated by helicopters and the Communist armies took control of Cambodia.

Meanwhile in South Vietnam, resistance to the Communists also was crumbling. By March 1975, South Vietnamese troops were in retreat before the advancing North Vietnamese and Viet Cong. In a last desperate effort to prevent a complete collapse of South Vietnam, President Ford asked Congress to vote $722 million in emergency military aid. Congress, certain that the South Vietnamese cause was hopeless and fearing a renewal of America's involvement, refused to support him.

By the end of April, Saigon was surrounded. American helicopters and ships lying off the coast withdrew the remaining Americans as well as 100,000 South Vietnamese. The Vietnamese refugees, for the most part destitute, were temporarily housed on American military bases until they could be relocated in the United States. Thus, with the Communist takeover of South Vietnam, three decades of fighting in Vietnam came to an end.

Nixon's foreign policies. Apart from the unpopular Vietnam War, Nixon's foreign policies won widespread approval. His success in improving relations with Communist China and the Soviet Union was impressive.

Nixon, like other recent Presidents, insisted upon maintaining a military force strong enough to meet any challenge to the nation's interests and security. He demonstrated his opposition to communism by insisting upon the continued exclusion of Cuba from the O.A.S. This opposition was also apparent in his approval of the secret use of funds by the CIA to try to prevent a Socialist-Communist election victory in Chile. The CIA later made it difficult for the Marxist government elected by those parties to govern. Like earlier Presidents, Nixon largely ignored the denial of human rights in anti-Communist countries that received American military and economic assistance in exchange for military bases. These countries included Spain, Greece, South Korea, South Vietnam, and Iran.

Nixon's foreign policy stressed skillful, realistic, and flexible diplomacy that would recognize changing conditions in the world. Nixon's chief adviser on foreign policy was Henry Kissinger. Kissinger was a refugee from Nazi Germany who had become a professor of political science at Harvard University.

Without conferring much with the Department of State, Nixon and Kissinger planned the broad outlines of American foreign policy. Their "personal diplomacy" involved an unprecedented number of conferences with leaders in other countries. President Nixon himself traveled to Western Europe, the Soviet Union, China, Canada, Iceland, and the Middle East for talks with other heads of state. Shortly after his reelection in 1972, he appointed Kissinger Secretary of State.

A new policy toward China. In one of his most dramatic moves, Nixon visited the People's Republic of China in February 1972. With this visit, the door that had been shut and barred between the two countries for more than 20 years began to swing open. Each government promised not to seek dominance in the Asian Pacific region, to cooperate in preventing other powers from doing so, and to avoid international war. Both governments agreed to develop trade, improve cultural and scientific relations, and work to restore full diplomatic relations. As for the major obstacle to improved relations, President Nixon promised eventual withdrawal of United States military forces from Taiwan and Indochina. In what was regarded as proof of America's desire to cooperate, the Nixon administration used its influence to support China's ally, Pakistan, when war broke out between Pakistan and India over the independence of East Pakistan (renamed Bangladesh).

Détente with the Soviet Union. In May 1972, three months after Nixon had visited Peking, he met for talks with Soviet leaders in Moscow. Nixon and Communist Party Secretary Leonid Brezhnev (BRESH·nev) agreed to cooperate in efforts to improve trade and to tackle world problems involving space, health, and the environment.

Early in 1972 the world was surprised to learn that a secret arrangement had been made for President Nixon to visit China. Just months earlier, the idea of an American President strolling in Peking would have been unthinkable.

THE MIDDLE EAST

Nixon and Brezhnev also signed two documents intended to limit nuclear armaments. These documents were based upon earlier negotiations known as the Strategic Arms Limitation Talks (SALT). One of the documents, an executive agreement, froze offensive missiles at near existing levels for a five-year period. The other document, a treaty requiring Senate approval, limited each nation to two antiballistic missile sites in its territory. It also placed a limit on the size of American and Soviet land-based and submarine-based missile forces. The Senate ratified this treaty in August 1973. Throughout the world, people hoped that the United States and the Soviet Union were moving away from the confrontations of the Cold War. The two countries seemed to be entering a period of **détente,** or the gradual relaxation and reduction of tensions between them.

Arab-Israeli conflict. One area of the globe that posed a threat to détente was the Middle East. As you have read, the Middle East had long been an area of international tension. After the Suez crisis, the bitter quarrel between Israel and the Arab nations continued.

Another crisis came in 1967 when Israelis believed that the Arab nations were massing large military forces to destroy Israel. In June 1967, powerful Israeli forces struck at Egypt, Jordan, and Syria, defeating them in a war lasting only six days. After the war Israel kept large areas of land that had belonged to these three Arab states.

The Arab nations were bitter at their defeat and doubly determined to destroy Israel. They began sending trained guerrillas into Israel. The Israelis continued to strike back.

For many years the Soviet Union sent aid of various kinds, including military aid, to the Arab nations but not to Israel. The United States tried to help the Arab nations overcome their poverty, and it gave military aid to those nations resisting communism. It also gave military aid to Israel.

The Yom Kippur War. Another Arab-Israeli war erupted in October 1973. The war provided a major test of détente and of Secretary Kissinger's skill as a diplomat. Egypt and Syria, seeking to recover territories lost in the 1967 war, suddenly launched an attack upon Israel. The Israelis at that time were observing Yom Kippur, a day holy to Jews. They were caught by surprise and suffered heavy casualties.

By the second week of the war, however, Israeli troops were driving back Syrian tanks in the north and had crossed the Suez Canal in the south. Soon Israeli forces were within 60 miles (96 kilometers) of Cairo.

In the meantime the United Nations had called for a cease-fire, but the fighting continued. The Egyptians, faced with almost cer-

790

tain defeat, called upon the Soviet Union for help. The Soviets, angered by American failure to get Israel to accept the cease-fire, now threatened to send their own troops to help end the fighting. President Nixon immediately ordered a "precautionary alert" for all American forces around the world. A major military confrontation between the Soviet Union and the United States now seemed possible.

Fortunately, the two great powers persuaded the Arabs and the Israelis to accept the cease-fire and to prepare for negotiations. Détente had survived its first critical trial.

However, many Israelis were bitter at being forced to end the fighting just as a final victory was within their grasp. Also, the Arabs were angered by American support of the Israelis. Several Arab nations cut off all shipments of oil to the United States and other countries that were friendly to Israel. Although the immediate crisis was over, the cease-fire had brought only an uneasy peace.

President Ford's foreign policy. On August 9, 1974, Gerald R. Ford replaced Nixon as President. One of his first acts was to ask Henry Kissinger to continue to serve as Secretary of State. This move indicated that Ford intended to follow the basic foreign policy developed during the Nixon administration.

Congress, in which Ford had served for a quarter of a century, was prepared to accept the President's leadership. However, early in 1975, when Ford urged Congress to provide $222 million in military aid to Cambodia, Congress refused. Congress made it clear that it was determined to close the door on further military adventures by the United States.

A few months later, however, Congress joined in the praise of Ford's action in the *Mayaguez* incident. In May, the *Mayaguez,* an unarmed American cargo ship, was seized by Cambodian Communists. Ford promptly sent air, sea, and ground forces to free the vessel and its crew of 39 men. In the action 15 American servicemen were killed, 50 wounded, and 3 missing. The President was sharply criticized for what many considered an unnecessary and ill-timed venture. Others applauded him for acting decisively.

Changes in détente. When Ford became President, he had taken over negotiations on a trade agreement between the United States and the Soviet Union. Senator Henry Jackson of Washington was one of many critics of the proposed agreement. Jackson insisted that trade between the two nations should not be freer until the Soviet Union relaxed its restrictions on the emigration of its citizens, including political dissenters and Jews who wanted to move to Israel.

In the fall of 1974, the Soviet Union apparently accepted the "Jackson amendment." They agreed at that time to increase the number of exit visas for Jewish citizens. A few months later, however, the Soviets rejected the trade agreement. Moscow declared that it could not allow the United States to interfere with Soviet emigration policy.

The Soviet rejection was a setback for the policy of détente. As you will see, during the Carter administration this rift in the policy became noticeably wider.

SECTION SURVEY

IDENTIFY: "protective reaction" policy, Henry Kissinger, cease-fire, refugee, War Powers Act of 1973, Phnom Penh, "personal diplomacy," Leonid Brezhnev, SALT, détente, Yom Kippur War, *Mayaguez* incident, Senator Henry Jackson.

1. (a) How did the United States wind down its involvement in the Vietnam War? (b) What were the terms of the 1973 cease-fire?
2. How was the conflict between North and South Vietnam finally resolved?
3. Describe President Nixon's policy of détente toward China and the Soviet Union.
4. How did President Ford's foreign policy compare with Nixon's?

4 World tensions build up during the Carter and Reagan administrations

The period of détente between the United States and the Soviet Union promoted by President Nixon and encouraged by President Ford did not last long after 1976. By 1980 tensions were approaching the breaking point.

President Carter's goals. Several months after his inauguration in January 1977, President Carter outlined the goals of his administration in a speech delivered at Notre Dame University. "We are now free," he declared, "of that inordinate fear of communism which once led us to embrace any dictator who joined in that fear. We fought fire with fire, never thinking that fire is better fought with water."

Carter then went on to express the hope that the great powers would resolve not to try to impose their social systems on other countries. During his administration, he said, he intended to work to improve America's relations with its allies, to advance human rights everywhere in the world, and to make genuine progress in arms control.

Carter's inexperience hindered his efforts to carry out this program. In addition, he at times had to resolve the conflicting views of the men and women he had chosen to advise him on foreign affairs. His Secretary of State, Cyrus R. Vance, was an experienced diplomat who preferred to handle problems through patient negotiations. Vance often clashed with the President's tough-minded National Security Adviser, Zbigniew Brzezinski (zuh·BIG·nee·ehv bruh·ZHIN·skee), a Columbia University professor of political science. Brzezinski was more inclined to take a hard line, particularly on issues involving the Soviet Union.

The Panama Canal treaties. The first major test of the President's program developed over the Panama Canal treaties. As soon as the treaties were ratified, Panama would begin to exercise almost total control over the operation of the canal itself. By the year 2000, Panama would gain complete control of the canal.

The treaties caused a storm of controversy in Congress and throughout the country. Critics argued that the United States was surrendering national property and endangering the nation's security. Supporters, including the President, insisted that the United States had never possessed sovereignty over the Canal Zone. They also pointed out that the terms of the treaties prevented any hostile country from ever securing control.

After an extended and often bitter debate, the Senate finally ratified the treaties by a close vote in the spring of 1978.

The issue of human rights. In August 1975 the leaders of 33 European nations plus the United States and Canada had gathered in Helsinki, Finland. There the leaders signed a statement outlining the basic goals of "peace,

security, justice, and cooperation." High on the list of commitments was the pledge to support "human rights."

Carter, as President, also placed the issue of human rights high on the list of priorities for his administration. Nevertheless, Carter's commitment to freedom and justice for all people everywhere met with mixed reactions both at home and abroad.

Not surprisingly, strong opposition came from countries ruled by military dictatorships. Many leaders from such countries often ignored the rights of their subjects. At the same time, however, many diplomats both in the United States and among its allies felt that by insisting upon worldwide observance of human rights the President was interfering in the domestic affairs of other countries. These critics reminded Carter that the United States would resent any effort by other nations to interfere in America's domestic affairs. They argued that the President's emphasis upon this issue did not help to relax international tensions or to promote world peace.

Africa. African affairs were another source of trouble for Carter. The huge continent had vast natural resources, a population of nearly half a billion, and a growing number of newly independent states. As a result, it was the scene of competition between the United States and the Soviet Union. Both powers as well as the other industrial nations attempted to establish their influence and their social and political systems in the African nations.

In 1975, during President Ford's administration, Portugal had withdrawn from Angola, and this last remaining colony in Africa won its independence. Angola was then torn by a civil war. Cuban troops trained and equipped by the Soviets soon moved in to support the Communist-inspired leaders.

Henry Kissinger, then Ford's Secretary of State, warned that the United States could not remain indifferent to Soviet interference in Africa. Yet Americans were reluctant to become involved in another Vietnam-type military venture. Thus, there was little the United States could do. As it developed, the Soviet success in Angola led to similar Cuban-Soviet intervention in other African countries, notably Ethiopia.

During Carter's administration the United States tried to counteract Communist intervention in Africa. The United States encouraged the African states to deal with their own problems and to solve them in their own way. Andrew Young, a black civil rights activist who had supported Carter's election campaign, served the President as Ambassador to the United Nations. Ambassador Young was an outspoken critic of white imperialism in Africa. He sharply criticized the Union of South Africa's racial policies and practices. He also strongly supported black majority rule in Rhodesia (now Zimbabwe).

Young's interest in and concern for Africa and the developing countries made him an influential figure in the United Nations. His followers were dismayed, therefore, when in August 1979 he resigned his post as Ambassador. Young's unauthorized meeting with a representative of the Palestine Liberation Organization (PLO) embarrassed the administration and forced him to submit his resignation. President Carter accepted the resignation with "deep regret."

The Middle East. The troubled Middle East provided the President with a major foreign policy achievement. The renewal of war between Egypt and Israel was a danger when Carter became President. The first really hopeful development came at the end of 1977 when President Sadat of Egypt accepted Premier Begin's invitation to visit Israel. A few weeks later, Begin returned the visit and the door was opened to the first peace negotiations since the Arab-Israeli War of 1973. During the next nine months, Secretary of State Vance worked with the Egyptians and the Israelis in an effort to hammer out an agreement. These discussions ended in a stalemate.

At this point, President Carter invited Begin and Sadat to meet with him in Washington and they accepted. At the end of 13 days of secret discussions at Camp David, the President's mountain retreat in nearby Maryland, they reached a tentative framework for a peace settlement.

In April 1979, gathered on the White House lawn, the three men signed a formal peace treaty. The treaty ended 30 years of war between Egypt and Israel. After the signing, in an emotion-filled moment, the three embraced. Each of them quoted the prophet Isaiah: "And they shall beat their swords into plowshares and their spears into pruning hooks."

Working out the details of the treaty proved a harder task. What should be done with the

This was the happy moment for which the Camp David meetings on Middle East peace were aiming—the signing of a framework for peace by Carter (center), Begin (right), and Sadat (left) at the White House.

lands Israel had occupied during the wars? How should Palestinian demands for a homeland on the Israeli-controlled West Bank of the Jordan River and on the Gaza Strip be handled? Israel did, among other things, return the Sinai to Egypt. Nevertheless, little progress was made on the remaining problems. The possibility of renewed war in the Middle East remained a constant threat.

President Carter's personal efforts to solve the Arab-Israeli conflict did not meet with unqualified approval. The Arabs were furious at what they called Sadat's "betrayal." Also they criticized Carter for bringing Egypt and Israel together into even an uncertain relationship. But many American critics felt that the President had tilted his influence toward the Egyptian-Palestinian side in order to maintain the good will of the Arab oil-exporting nations, particularly Saudi Arabia.

Iran. For many years Iran, across the Persian Gulf from Saudi Arabia's rich oil fields, had been a key to United States defense arrangements in the Middle East. Back in 1953 the United States had helped overthrow what it considered a pro-Communist government in Iran. With American backing the Shah Mohammed Reza Pahlevi had been restored to his throne. During the 1970's the Shah received about $8 billion worth of American military equipment. The Shah harshly repressed political opponents. His secret police, some of whom had been trained by Americans, were accused of torturing and murdering such opponents.

Anger against the Shah flared up in a revolution in 1979, and the Shah fled the country. His government was overthrown by a militant religious leader, the Ayatollah Khomeini (AH·yah·tol·ah HOH·may·nee) and his followers. The new leaders blamed the United States for the sufferings the Iranian people had endured under the Shah. They bitterly resented President Carter's decision to admit the Shah into the United States for medical reasons at the very time the Iranian leaders were demanding his return for trial.

American hostages in Iran. In an attempt to force the United States to return the Shah to Iran, on November 4, 1979, a group of Iranian militants seized 53 American diplomatic and consular personnel. The militants held their captives as hostages in the American Embassy and in the Foreign Office in Teheran.

President Carter reacted by freezing some $8 billion of Iranian assets held by the United States and warned Iran of possible boycotts. He urged America's allies to add their pressure in defense of international law.

After almost six months, the Iranian leaders had either refused or were unable to secure the release of the hostages. President Carter then ordered a daring military rescue mission. The mission ended in disaster due to mechanical failures in the desert some 200 miles (320 kilometers) from Teheran. Eight American marines and airmen lost their lives and several others were seriously wounded in the flaming crash of a helicopter and a transport plane.

Reaction to the rescue mission. President Carter was both praised and blamed for undertaking such a desperate rescue mission. His supporters applauded him for acting decisively and, in so doing, for upholding national honor. His critics included many of America's allies and his own Secretary of State, Cyrus R. Vance. Vance strongly opposed the use of military force as a solution to the problem. On this matter, he disagreed with National Security Adviser Brzezinski. As a result, Vance offered his resignation and Carter accepted it.

The hostages remained in Iran, and it seemed that little progress was being made toward their release. American naval and air forces in the Indian Ocean and the Persian Gulf area continued the buildup in strength that had been started several months earlier.

The situation grew still more dangerous when a border dispute led to war between Iran and Iraq in September. Iran accused the United States of pushing Iraq to go to war to punish Iran for holding the hostages.

Finally, the Algerian government helped to negotiate an agreement between Iran and the United States. On January 21, 1981, just as Ronald Reagan took his oath as President, the hostages were freed. After 444 days of captivity, they returned to the United States as heroes.

The Carter Doctrine. Early in January 1980, the Soviets invaded Afghanistan, a Muslim country on the eastern border of Iran. They intended to replace the existing pro-Communist head of government with another leader whom the Soviets considered more receptive to Soviet influence. As the map shows (page 790), Soviet troops in Afghanistan were close to the Persian Gulf, the lifeline to vital oil supplies.

President Carter labeled the Soviet move a serious threat to world peace. He then warned the Soviet Union to withdraw from Afghanistan. When the Soviets showed no intention of withdrawing, the United States made several countermoves. Carter ordered a cut in sales of electronic equipment and grain to the Soviet Union. The United States withdrew from the 1980 summer Olympics in Moscow, and urged other countries to follow suit. Congress made it clear that a key arms limitation treaty between the Soviet Union and the United States would be postponed indefinitely. Its failure would mean that a new arms race costing both countries vast sums was almost certain.

Finally, the President announced what was called the "Carter Doctrine." He declared that any use of military force by the Soviet Union in the Persian Gulf would be met with a major military response by the United States. The United States thus seemed to be stating that its national interest included the defense not only of Japan and Western Europe, but also of the Middle East and the Persian Gulf.

Reagan's foreign policy takes shape. By the time President Reagan took office, détente was, at best, in a shaky condition. The world faced the possibility of returning to another dangerous period of Cold War.

After 444 long days of captivity, Americans held hostage in Iran were at last freed. Here, in February 1981 at a ceremony held at the White House, President Ronald Reagan welcomes them home to their grateful and happy nation.

Reagan soon made it clear that he would oppose Soviet expansion everywhere, even at the risk of confrontation. Reagan continued the buildup of America's military presence in the Persian Gulf and the Indian Ocean. He warned the Soviets that military intervention by them in Poland would have the gravest consequences. On the other hand, Reagan removed the embargo on agricultural exports to the Soviet Union that Carter had ordered.

Reagan's Secretary of State, Alexander Haig, pointed out that the lifting of the grain embargo did not mean a softening of the administration's position toward the Soviets. Haig warned that there could be no talk of arms limitation until the Soviets abandoned their aggressive meddling in other countries.

In the case of El Salvador, the administration moved from warnings to action. This tiny Central American country was torn by civil war. Guerrilla fighters, supported by some intellectuals and peasants, battled to dispossess the ruling classes and to redistribute the land and other resources. Some of the arms for the guerrillas came from the Soviet Union and Cuba. The Reagan administration countered by increasing its military aid to the government of El Salvador and by sending advisers to assist the troops. Critics feared that the United States was becoming involved in another war like that in Vietnam. Reagan denied this possibility and insisted that the United States could not allow Communist actions to go unchallenged.

Reagan's first budget was evidence of his determination to defend American interests with force if necessary. Military spending, already on the rise before Carter left office, jumped sharply upward. Proposed military expenditures over five years, according to Reagan's plan, would reach $1.3 trillion. The Reagan administration also urged its NATO allies and Japan to increase their military spending.

Under President Reagan's leadership, the United States seemed prepared to challenge Soviet expansion anywhere in the world. That was the message spelled out in the buildup of the nation's military strength. Thus the prospect for a renewal of détente seemed dim.

SECTION SURVEY

IDENTIFY: Cyrus Vance, Zbigniew Brzezinski, Angola civil war, Andrew Young, President Sadat, Premier Begin, Shah Mohammed Reza Pahlevi, Ayatollah Khomeini, Carter Doctrine.

1. What were President Carter's foreign policy goals?

2. (a) What were the terms of the Panama Canal treaties? (b) Why did they cause controversy?

3. (a) How did President Carter move Israel and Egypt closer to peace? (b) What problems remained?

4. Describe the events that led to the taking of American hostages in Iran in 1979.

5. (a) Why did President Carter consider the Soviet invasion of Afghanistan to be a serious threat to world peace? (b) How did he respond?

Chapter Survey

Summary: Tracing the Main Ideas

When John F. Kennedy became President in January 1961, the United States and the Soviet Union were locked in the Cold War. During the next two years, the situation rapidly worsened. The Soviet attempt to install long-range missiles in Cuba brought the two great powers to the brink of a nuclear war. Fortunately, reason prevailed, and the Soviet Union withdrew the offensive weapons.

Under President Johnson the United States became involved in what turned out to be the longest and most costly war in the nation's history. The Vietnam conflict was costly in lives, in money and resources, and in its divisive effect upon the American people.

During the Nixon-Ford years, the United States withdrew from Vietnam, reopened its ties with China, and began to establish improved relations with the Soviet Union. Détente with the Soviet Union offered visions of improved international relations and even a lasting peace.

During President Carter's term, however, the period of détente seemed to draw to a close.

There were a few heartening developments in America's foreign affairs during the Carter years. The highlight was the peace treaty between Egypt and Israel negotiated with Carter's personal help. However, by 1980 no decisions had been reached on the basic issues dividing the Arabs and the Israelis, and the treaty itself hung in the balance.

A more immediate threat to peace was the revolution in Iran and the Soviet invasion of Afghanistan. These events transformed the oil-rich Persian Gulf into a tinderbox. Détente appeared to be a thing of the past. With the buildup of both Soviet and American military forces in the Middle East, world tensions again approached the breaking point.

Inquiring into History

1. (a) What was the policy of détente worked out by Nixon and Kissinger? (b) What major changes among Communist nations made this new policy possible? (c) How did the Arab-Israeli War of 1973 test the policy of détente?
2. (a) Why did the United States commit itself to opposing Communist expansion in Southeast Asia? (b) Describe the actions taken by the Kennedy, Johnson, and Nixon administrations with regard to the conflict in Vietnam.
3. Describe the impact of the Vietnam War on (a) Vietnam and (b) the United States.
4. How did competition between the United States and the Soviet Union affect events in (a) Africa and (b) the Middle East during the 1960's and 1970's?

Relating Past to Present

1. (a) What are the goals of American foreign policy today? (b) Of the Presidents' foreign policies discussed in this chapter, which was most similar to today's policy? Which was most different?
2. (a) What are the trouble spots in the world today? (b) How are the events occurring there today influenced by the events that occurred during the 1960's and 1970's?

Developing Social Science Skills

1. Study the excerpt from the Gulf of Tonkin Resolution on page 786. (a) What power does it give to the President? (b) According to the document, what events led Congress to pass the Resolution? (c) How could this Resolution be used later to justify sending American troops to Vietnam?
2. Write one of the newspaper accounts described here: (a) a Palestinian account of the Camp David meeting among Sadat, Begin, and Carter, (b) a Panamanian account of the Panama Canal treaties, (c) a Congolese account of the Congo crisis in 1960–61.
3. Examine the map on page 790. (a) Parts of what three continents are shown? (b) Locate the Persian Gulf and Suez Canal. (c) Using the map, explain the Carter Doctrine and its importance. (d) Why can the Middle East be called the "crossroads of the world"?

Chapter 42

Reaching for Greater Freedom and Justice

Give me your tired, your poor,
Your huddled masses yearning to breathe free.

These words, engraved on the pedestal of the Statue of Liberty, are those of Emma Lazarus. The words are hers, but the vision they reveal grew out of the thirteen original British colonies along the Atlantic seaboard.

From colonial days to the present, more than 50 million immigrants have come to America. They have come seeking larger opportunities than they could have hoped for in the lands of their birth. The great majority of those who came during the past century entered through New York harbor. Their first glimpse of the New World was the Statue of Liberty, the symbol of freedom and justice.

However, in recent years the ports of entry for the immigrants and the countries of their origin have changed dramatically. Many of the newcomers entered through Florida or crossed the border from Mexico or passed through the ports along the Pacific coast. Today men, women, and children from Asia, Mexico, Central and South America, and the West Indies far outnumber immigrants from Europe.

These were not the only ones "yearning to breathe free." The nation's minorities, including blacks and Indians, had long carried a burden of prejudice and discrimination. Now they were demanding that the vision of freedom and justice be fulfilled. They were demanding that the United States truly become a nation of equal opportunity for all.

Thus the nation entered a time of unprecedented upheaval. The land itself—the farms, the suburbs, the cities—was transformed. Even the values the American people lived by were tried and tested and sometimes reshaped.

Changing Ways of American Life

1960's–1980's

THE CHAPTER IN OUTLINE

1. New patterns of population growth and distribution alter ways of life.
2. Black Americans demand equal rights and opportunities.
3. Hispanics share the struggle for freedom and justice.
4. Indians refuse to accept the role of "vanishing Americans."
5. Women redouble efforts to win equal rights and opportunities.

New patterns of population growth and distribution alter ways of life

During the years after 1960, America's population continued to grow and shift. The movement from rural to urban areas continued. This, in time, led to a severe crisis for American cities.

Growth of population. By 1980 there were 43 million more people living in the United States than there had been in 1960. The increase in that 20-year period alone—from 179 million in 1960 to more than 226 million in 1980—almost equaled the total population of the country a century earlier.

One reason for this growth was the remarkable advances made by medical science. Antibiotics and many other drugs created in the postwar years made important contributions. So, too, did new methods and improved instruments for diagnosis and treatment. As a

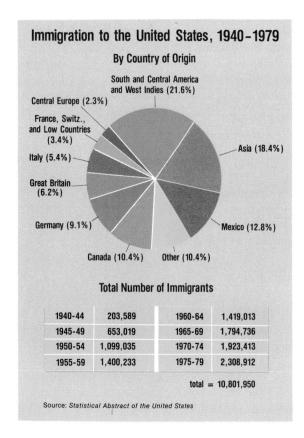

Immigration to the United States, 1940–1979

By Country of Origin

Central Europe (2.3%)
France, Switz., and Low Countries (3.4%)
Italy (5.4%)
Great Britain (6.2%)
Germany (9.1%)
Canada (10.4%)
Other (10.4%)
Mexico (12.8%)
Asia (18.4%)
South and Central America and West Indies (21.6%)

Total Number of Immigrants

1940-44	203,589	1960-64	1,419,013
1945-49	653,019	1965-69	1,794,736
1950-54	1,099,035	1970-74	1,923,413
1955-59	1,400,233	1975-79	2,308,912

total = 10,801,950

Source: *Statistical Abstract of the United States*

result, doctors were able to reduce the nation's death rate, especially among children, and to prolong life.

In the years following World War II, the birth rate soared to an average level of 3.5 births per woman. By the 1970's, however, the birth rate was slowing down. In December 1972 the Census Bureau reported that it had dropped to about 2 births per woman. This is the level of Zero Population Growth (ZPG). This birth rate replaces the existing population but does not increase it.

The birth rate reached its lowest point in the nation's history in 1976. Although it rose slightly during the remaining years of the 1970's, it seemed having two children was the popular goal for many American families.

The redistribution of people. The growing mobility of Americans also had far-reaching effects, particularly after 1960. Americans were increasingly able and willing to move from place to place. In earlier times many people had lived their whole lives in the areas in which they were born. However, by the 1960's and 1970's, this pattern was changing. One out of every five Americans was moving to a new residence each year.

These population movements affected different sections of the country in different ways. The West and the South, particularly the Sunbelt areas, became the fastest-growing sections of the nation. In 1964 California passed New York to become the most populous state. During the 1970's about 40 percent of the nation's total population growth occurred in the Sunbelt states of Florida, Texas, and California.

Meanwhile, the states of the Northeast were losing population in relation to the rest of the country. By 1980 the high cost of home heating during the cold winters was convincing more and more people to move to the warmer Southern states.

Change in rural population. Another dramatic change in American life was the sharp decline in farm population. Between 1940 and 1980, the number of people living on farms dropped from more than 30 million to around 6 million. In some years more than 1 million men and women left the farms to seek better opportunities elsewhere.

Despite the shrinking farm population, America was producing more food and other farm products than ever before. By the 1970's

THE TALL SHIPS

"All you look at for three weeks is the water and your crewmates. When we see land, we shout and jump. I think I lost my girlfriend because I go to sea so often. Are there girls in New York?"

The 20-year-old naval cadet may not have found a romantic replacement in New York, but he undoubtedly received a warm welcome. He was one of the crew on the German training vessel *Gorch Fock,* one of the tall ships that sailed up the Hudson River on July 4, 1976. The stunning naval parade of which it was a part was the highlight of New York City's observance of the bicentennial of the United States.

The waters were full of ships that day. Along the shores were anchored 53 warships, representing 22 nations. Between their ranks cruised some 200 sailing vessels of Operation Sail (Opsail for short). Its stars were the 16 tall ships — square-riggers with a mast height of more than 127 feet (38.7 meters). There are only 20 of these left in active service, and they had come from all over the world: the *Amerigo Vespucci* from Italy, the *Nippon Maru* from Japan, the *Dar Pomoza* from Poland, the *Sagres II* from Portugal, and the *Kruzenshtern* from Russia. They were led up the Hudson by the United States square-rigger *Eagle* and escorted by spouting fireboats. Other notable ships in the waters that day were a Chinese junk, a replica of a Viking boat, and the English schooner *Sir Winston Churchill,* with an all-woman crew, as well as over 10,000 small private craft.

Some 6 million people watched the naval parade that day. The gesture of international good will lifted the spirits of all who saw it. But the day was more. It was a visible bridge between the present and the past. It reminded those who saw it that, for all the striking changes of the past 200 years, the United States as a nation still endured.

each farm worker was producing enough food for more than 50 people. American farms were producing more than enough food to feed Americans. Huge surpluses for hungry people overseas were also available. From the 1960's to the 1980's, farm products were a substantial part of the nation's total exports.

Efficient, large-scale corporation farms and spectacular developments in agricultural science and technology made such productivity possible. Better strains of plants, greater use of fertilizer, and improved breeds of livestock were just a few major developments. They combined to raise the average yield of some farm crops by as much as 50 percent. At the same time, worker productivity increased twice as fast on the farm as in industry.

Although the farm population was shrinking, the 1980 census revealed a surprising fact. For the first time since the 1820 census, rural areas and their small towns were growing faster than metropolitan areas. Between 1970 and 1980, nonmetropolitan areas grew by 15.4 percent. Metropolitan areas grew only by 9.1 percent.

Technological advances now allowed many businesses to move out of urban centers. Improved transportation and communication systems meant that rural areas were no longer as isolated as they once had been. Also the rural areas, at least for the time being, did not suffer from many of the problems that troubled the nation's older urban areas.

Urban areas. Many of those who left farms moved to urban areas. These urban areas included central cities and the suburbs around them. These cities and their suburbs were

No sign was needed here. The ruined building says it all. Buildings like this were on the increase as the middle class fled the cities, leaving them to the urban poor, minorities, and new immigrants.

closely related. Originally the cities were the work-places and the suburbs were the living areas. Gradually such a clear distinction faded. The real boundaries between the cities and the suburbs became harder to draw.

These city-suburbs combinations were given the name of Standard Metropolitan Statistical Areas (SMSA's). By 1980 there were over 280 SMSA's in the nation. Over 72 percent of the nation's population lived in such areas.

New immigrants. These SMSA's received a swelling tide of men and women from other lands. During the 1960's and 1970's, immigration increased sharply. Patterns of immigration also changed dramatically.

The Immigration and Nationality Act of 1965 abolished the old national origins acts of the 1920's (see page 656). It also changed the ethnic character of the nation's population. The new law provided for the annual admission of 120,000 immigrants from the Western Hemisphere and 170,000 from all other nations. No more than 20,000 could come from any single country. Preference was to be given to members of families of American citizens and to those men and women with specialized training and skills.

One result of the law was a sharp increase in the number of Asians and Hispanics entering the country. By the mid-1970's more than 300,000 were arriving each year. In 1977, for example, some 150,000 Asiatics and more than 200,000 Hispanics entered.

Most of the newcomers, although by no means all, were poor. Most settled in the cities. There they moved into the homes and apartments left by the white middle class who had moved to the suburbs or back to rural areas. As immigrants and minorities moved into the cities, increasing numbers of whites moved out. This "white flight" contributed greatly to the decay of the cities.

The urban crisis. In the 1960's and 1970's, conditions in America's cities became desperate. Urban renewal programs had helped rebuild the business and financial areas of many cities. However, the older residential areas had often become heavily overcrowded. Many had deteriorated into slums. Property owners, discouraged by the flight of the middle class to the suburbs, refused to spend money to repair their buildings. The core areas of the cities were so badly run down that they needed to be entirely rebuilt. This would take years and require the investment of billions of dollars.

Meanwhile, people living in the slums needed more and better services—health, education, sanitation, recreation, and police and fire protection. They also needed jobs and job-training programs. However, the cities did not have the finances to do the work that had to be done. The people most able to pay the taxes needed to support such programs were leaving. Those least able to pay and most in need were becoming more numerous. City after city faced the prospect of bankruptcy.

"Social dynamite." The urban crisis was in fact a national crisis. In 1961 James B. Conant of Harvard issued a report titled *Slums and Suburbs* that attracted nationwide attention. The report pointed out the alarming contrast between the poverty of life in the decaying cores of the cities and the growing wealth of the suburbs.

Nevertheless, during the next two decades, conditions grew steadily worse. "We are allowing social dynamite to accumulate in our large cities," Conant warned.

1. What were two major changes in the United States population between 1960 and 1980?
2. How was each of these areas affected by population movements between 1960 and 1980: (a) Southwest, (b) Northeast, (c) rural areas, (d) suburbs?
3. What factors contributed to the urban crisis of the 1960's and 1970's?
4. Graph Study: Study the graph on page 798. From what nation did most immigrants come in 1949? in 1979?

2 Black Americans demand equal rights and opportunities

The "social dynamite" that Conant had warned about exploded in city after city during the 1960's. Meanwhile, black Americans had grown frustrated with their slow progress toward full equality of opportunity. They became increasingly insistent upon "freedom now."

The civil rights movement. During the 1950's blacks at long last began to receive support from both the Supreme Court and Congress. As you have read (page 751), in 1954 the Supreme Court ruled that state and local laws requiring blacks to send their children to separate school systems violated the Fourteenth Amendment. Three years later Congress adopted the Civil Rights Act of 1957. This law, strengthened by a related act in 1960, authorized the Department of Justice to sue local officials who tried to prevent blacks from voting.

These developments were immensely encouraging. More immediately important, however, was action taken by the blacks themselves. Under leaders such as the Reverend Martin Luther King, Jr., they began to use nonviolent methods, such as boycotts and peaceful demonstrations, to win their rights.

The civil rights movement that got under way in the late 1950's and early 1960's was a heroic struggle led and sustained by blacks. However, it also drew the active support of whites—particularly ministers, rabbis, nuns, priests, lawyers, writers, and students. The mass media also helped to stir the conscience of white America by bringing the details of the struggle into millions of homes.

Direct action. The movement developed a number of tactics to speed the integration of all public facilities. In addition to the boycott, which had been effective in Montgomery, Alabama (see page 752), the sit-in became a useful device. In February 1960 four black students in Greensboro, North Carolina, refused to leave a "whites-only" lunch counter at a department store until they were served. Day after day they returned. Meanwhile demonstrations in their support were staged across the nation. In July the Greensboro lunch counter was finally integrated. Similar sit-ins spread rapidly over the South to press for the integration of movie theaters, libraries, parks, and other public gathering places.

"Freedom rides" and "freedom marches" by whites and blacks also dramatized the struggle for civil rights. In 1963 A. Philip Randolph, a veteran black trade union leader, organized a march on Washington. More than 250,000 men, women, and youths gathered in the nation's capital to support passage of a civil rights bill. The highlight of the event was Martin Luther King's speech "I have a dream."

Other demonstrations followed, including the 1965 march for voting rights by more than 3,000 blacks and whites from Selma to Montgomery, Alabama. Thousands of walkers, blacks and whites, were led by Martin Luther King and protected by the National Guard along the 54-mile (86-kilometer) route.

Achievements. Congress responded to the protest movement with the Civil Rights Act of 1964 and the Voting Rights Act of 1965. The 1964 measure outlawed racial discrimination in employment and in public accommodations. The 1965 act authorized federal supervision of registration in districts where fewer than half of those of voting age were registered.

By the mid-1960's race barriers had been largely broken down in hotels and restaurants, in buses and trains and airlines, and in other public places. Impressive gains had also been made in voter registration. In 1965, for example, only 6 percent of the black citizens of Mississippi were registered to vote. By 1967 more than 33 percent had been registered.

In March 1965, Reverend Martin Luther King, Jr. (center) led a march from Selma, Alabama, to the state capital at Montgomery to demand voting rights for blacks. Such marches effectively demonstrated to the American people the need for federal civil rights legislation.

The gains in school desegregation in the South were slower. By 1967 token desegregation was a fact throughout the South. Nevertheless, only 16 percent of black southern students attended integrated schools.

In the fall of 1969, the Supreme Court, in its toughest ruling to date, ordered an end to all racially segregated school systems "at once." By the early 1970's, many southern school districts were integrated, and the movement continued throughout the decade.

By the 1970's, in fact, school segregation was more widespread in northern cities than in the South. The courts then began to rule against this **de facto segregation°** in the northern schools. Often they ordered the busing of students from one school to another to achieve a desired balance of races. Opposition to such busing was often fierce. Demonstrations, at times violent, erupted over busing in Boston, Chicago, and other cities.

A shifting emphasis. In spite of the gains, by the mid-1960's many blacks were frustrated. Essential though civil rights were, they did not

°**de facto segregation:** segregation that exists not by law, but because of neighborhood residence patterns.

provide adequate housing either in rural areas or in overcrowded city slums. They did not provide the training or education that allowed disadvantaged people to build a better way of life. It was also becoming clear that integrated schools were not necessarily better schools in terms of the quality of education they provided.

By the mid-1960's the goals of the movement had shifted from civil rights to economic and social issues—jobs, housing, and discrimination by businesses and by organized labor in hiring practices. But as the war in Vietnam absorbed more and more of the nation's resources, black Americans felt that their problems were being neglected. Their goal of equal opportunity seemed as remote as ever.

Violence in the inner city. The depth of black frustration was starkly revealed in riots that broke out in the community of Watts in Los Angeles, California, in the summer of 1965. The National Guard was finally called in to restore order. In the riots 4,000 persons were arrested, hundreds were injured, 34 were killed, and the damage from burning and looting totaled $35 million.

This urban violence shocked the nation. It especially alarmed those Americans, black and white alike, who had believed that the civil rights movement was making progress and that race relations were improving. Any lingering optimism in that regard was swept away during the next two years when rioting broke out in cities across the nation. Among the hardest hit were Detroit, Cleveland, Newark, Baltimore, and the nation's capital, Washington, D.C.

Many Americans, black as well as white, blamed the violence on a group of new militant black leaders, but this was by no means the whole truth. The rate of unemployment among black workers the country over was double that of white workers. Among black teenagers in the inner cities the jobless rate was much higher. As the riots demonstrated, poverty from which there seems to be no escape is a fertile breeding ground for violence.

New leaders and "black power." One of the best known of the new black leaders was Elijah Muhammad, who headed the Black Muslims, the largest and economically most powerful black group. Another was Malcolm X, formerly a Muslim minister, who preached that the black and white races could exist only if they were completely separated from each other. Before his death, however, Malcolm X gave up his rigid racist position, referring to it as "sickness and madness." In 1965 he was assassinated by black radicals he had antagonized.

Among the other new leaders were Floyd McKissick and Stokely Carmichael, who had been active in militant civil rights organizations. Also included were the founders of the Black Panther Party—Huey P. Newton, Bobby Seale, and Eldridge Cleaver. The Black Panthers advocated immediate confrontation with "the white power structure" and the use of force, if necessary, to protect black Americans against aggressive "white racism."

Black extremists demanded "black power." In economics, black power seemed to mean the growth of independent black businesses. In education it meant local community control of largely black schools. In politics it meant the growth of political power either by the formation of a black political party or by control of politics in black neighborhoods through bloc voting. Socially it meant black self-reliance, self-respect, and racial pride.

Moderate black leaders shared many of the objectives of the black power movement, but they rejected its tactics. Among these leaders were Roy Wilkins of the NAACP and Dr. Martin Luther King, Jr., head of the Southern Christian Leadership Conference (SCLC). King, the most influential of the black leaders and a devoted advocate of nonviolence, denounced the appeal to black racism and the threatened use of force. Those who rejected integration and called for a separation of the races, he believed, did a cruel disservice to black people.

Signs of progress. By the mid-1960's the black power movement was making gains. Politically these gains were revealed in the election of black Americans to public office—for example, Edward W. Brooke of Massachusetts to the United States Senate; Carl B. Stokes and Richard Hatcher as mayors of Cleveland, Ohio, and Gary, Indiana, respectively; Julian Bond to the Georgia legislature. In addition, the Supreme Court also had its first black member, Justice Thurgood Marshall.

In the spring of 1968, Congress adopted a new civil rights act. The new act extended federal protection to civil rights workers and also included a guarantee of open housing. The open-housing provision barred discrimination in the sale or rental of all housing with the exception of owner-occupied homes sold directly by the owner.

The Kerner Commission. In the summer of 1967, President Johnson appointed a National Advisory Commission on Civil Disorders headed by Governor Kerner of Illinois to investigate inner city riots and violence. The Kerner Commission's report in 1968 was the most thorough federal study of the race problem.

The report acknowledged that gains had been made in civil rights laws and desegregation. However, it warned that little or nothing had been accomplished in those basic areas that mattered most to a majority of America's black people—housing, jobs, and economic security, educational opportunities, and living conditions in the inner cities. "Our nation," the Kerner Commission reported, "is moving toward two societies, one black, one white—separate and unequal."

SOURCES

MARTIN LUTHER KING, JR.'S "I HAVE A DREAM" SPEECH (1963)

I say to you today, my friends, that in spite of the difficulties and frustrations of the moment I still have a dream. It is a dream deeply rooted in the American dream.

I have a dream that one day this nation will rise up and live out the true meaning of its creed: "We hold these truths to be self-evident; that all men are created equal."

I have a dream that one day on the red hills of Georgia the sons of former slaves and the sons of former slaveowners will be able to sit down together at the table of brotherhood. . . .

I have a dream that my four little children will one day live in a nation where they will not be judged by the color of their skin but by the content of their character.

I have a dream today. . . .

The commission warned of continued disorder and the destruction of democratic values unless improvements were made at once in those basic areas. This could be done, it said, only by "commitment to national action—compassionate, massive, and sustained."

The death of Martin Luther King, Jr. The assassination of Martin Luther King, Jr., Nobel Peace Prize winner and most respected of black leaders, on April 4, 1968, fell with stunning force on all Americans, white and black alike. Dr. King was in Memphis, Tennessee, to lead a nonviolent demonstration when he was killed by an assassin's bullets. In the last speech he made before his death, Dr. King said, "It is no longer a question of violence or nonviolence. It is nonviolence or nonexistence."

Dr. King's death was a grim reminder of the importance of the Kerner Commission's warnings. While the nation mourned the loss of a leader who had devoted his life to a nonviolent solution of the race issue, riots broke out in various cities across the country. Chicago and Washington were the worst hit.

Political advances. The massive effort called for by the Kerner report did not develop. Yet neither its worst predictions nor the revolution threatened by radical black nationalists had taken place either.

In 1975 the Civil Rights Commission reported that many black citizens, as well as members of other minorities, were still prevented from voting by various unfair means. Even so, black citizens were making important political gains. By the end of the 1970's, 4,503 black Americans were serving in elected public offices. This number was only 10 percent of all such offices, but it was an improvement over earlier years. By 1980 there were 17 black members of the House of Representatives. There were black mayors in such cities as Los Angeles, Atlanta, Detroit, Gary, Newark, and Washington, D.C.

Andrew Young, a civil rights leader, served during part of Carter's administration as the outspoken United States Ambassador to the United Nations. Carter also appointed the first black woman to a Cabinet post. This was Patricia Harris, Secretary of Housing and Urban Development and, later, Secretary of Health, Education, and Welfare.

New black leaders were gaining greater political power. They were learning how to get out the black vote, an important factor in the election of President Carter in 1976. They were forming political alliances and making effective use of lobbying tactics.

An uncertain outlook. The Equal Rights Commission brought lawsuits against corporations and labor unions to end unfair employment practices. In a number of schools and businesses, **affirmative action** programs were begun. This meant that blacks and members of other minorities were at times given preference when applying to schools or for jobs. They were given preference even when their qualifications were no better than those of other applicants. The idea behind such programs was to make up for past discrimination, which had left blacks and minorities at a disadvantage. Nevertheless, many Americans objected. Such programs, they said, did not represent the ideal of "equal justice for all." They were instead, critics claimed, reverse discrimination.

The number of blacks attaining middle-income status also was growing, at least until the recession of the mid-1970's. Nevertheless, the rate of unemployment among black workers continued to be far greater than among whites. In the mid-1970's the median income for white families was $14,000, for black families only $9,000. Moreover, 30 percent of blacks lived below the poverty line, in stark contrast to 10 percent of whites.

In summary, black Americans had made gains on all fronts, but the longest and hardest road still lay ahead. Martin Luther King, Jr., had dreamed of a nation in which men and women and children of every race and creed would be united in peace and justice. Whether and when this dream would be realized remained an open question as the nation moved into its third century.

SECTION SURVEY

IDENTIFY: Martin Luther King, Jr., sit-in, A. Philip Randolph, de facto segregation, Elijah Muhammad, Malcolm X, Black Panther Party, black power, Thurgood Marshall, Andrew Young, affirmative action.

1. What were some actions taken by Congress and the Supreme Court since 1954 to guarantee the civil rights of all Americans?

2. What types of actions did civil rights groups take during the 1960's and 1970's in their effort to end

discrimination and increase opportunities for blacks?

3. In view of the many gains made by blacks by the mid-1960's, why were so many still frustrated?

4. What is the relationship (a) between poverty and violence and (b) between neighborhood housing patterns and school segregation?

5. (a) What is the purpose of affirmative action programs? (b) Why do some people oppose them?

3 Hispanics share the struggle for freedom and justice

The discrimination suffered by blacks was also experienced in varying degrees by other ethnic groups. The Hispanics, some 15 million according to one 1980 estimate, were second only to blacks in terms of numbers. There are some estimates that they will overtake the blacks and become the nation's largest minority during the 1980's.

The Hispanics. The Hispanics are people from a number of different Spanish-speaking countries and their offspring. They include large numbers of Mexicans, Puerto Ricans, Cubans, Filipinos, Dominicans, and recent immigrants from other South American countries and the West Indies. All of these people share a common Spanish-influenced heritage. In addition to the Spanish language and Spanish cultural traits, they often share the ties of the Roman Catholic religion.

Despite their common heritage, the Hispanics are a varied group. These immigrants represent a wide range of jobs, from farm workers to lawyers. In fact, more than 30 percent of the immigrants from South America have been highly educated professionals and white-collar workers. The most numerous of the Hispanics are the Mexican Americans. Among them are the descendants of Mexicans living in California, New Mexico, Arizona, and Texas when these lands belonged to Mexico. These people often call themselves Hispanos.

Migrant farm workers. Most of the recent Hispanic immigrants, including the undocumented or illegal migrants, came from poor rural areas to seek a better life in the United States. The great majority worked for the large commercial farms. Most were illiterate, at least in English, and insecure in their jobs. As migrant workers these men, women, and children labored for low pay in lettuce and asparagus fields, citrus groves, and apple orchards. They moved as the crops matured to Oregon, Washington, Nebraska, and the Great Lake states, living in substandard shacks or mobile trailers. They received little benefit from the social legislation that was intended to protect workers. "We were jailed, beaten, even killed," wrote the historian Dr. Julian Navo.

From the early 1900's on, some efforts had been made to organize the migrant workers. These early efforts met only limited success. In the 1960's, however, Cesar Chavez made headway in organizing the workers in the California vineyards and lettuce fields. Sympathetic priests, civic groups, and idealistic students aided in his efforts. In 1965 he launched a strike that led to a nationwide boycott of produce not bearing the label of the United Farm Workers. In 1970, the strikers finally won. Although the gulf between Mexican Americans and other farm workers was still wide, it had begun to narrow.

Mexican Americans have had success in winning political power, especially in the southwestern states. Henry Cisneros, who is pictured here, was elected mayor of San Antonio, the third largest city in Texas.

Mexican Americans in cities. In time, large Mexican-American communities or *barrios* grew up in such cities as El Paso, Los Angeles, Denver, Seattle, Minneapolis, and Chicago. The residents of the *barrios* met with prejudice and discrimination in employment, in courts of law, in relations with the police, and in schools where English was often an unknown language to them.

Despite obstacles, an increasing number of Mexican Americans went to high school and college, acquiring vocational and professional skills. Loyal to family and to their Mexican-American culture, the city dwellers contributed to the economic development of the country as well as to the arts. During the Vietnam War, the death rate for Mexican-American servicemen was higher than that for any other group. This was due largely to the fact that many fought in high-risk branches of the service, such as the Marines.

The Chicano movement. Inspired in part by the struggles of blacks for their rights, Mexican Americans in the 1960's took increasing pride in their Hispanic background. They, too, struggled to win their civil rights. They also fought to overcome the prejudice that many "Anglos," as they called other Americans, held against them.

Referring to themselves as "Chicanos," leaders of the movement used boycotts, sit-ins, demonstrations, political organizations, and the courts to secure their rights. In New Mexico, Reies López Tijerina formed an organization to regain land that, he claimed, Anglos had taken illegally. In Denver, the boxer, newspaper editor, and poet Rodolfo "Corky" Gonzales won recognition for his work in the Democratic Party. He organized demonstrations and became one of the leaders of the Chicano movement. In Los Angeles Vilma Martinez, like a growing number of Mexican-American women, took an active part in defending the rights of her people.

Many new militant organizations sprang up. One of them, *La Raza Unida,* sought to register Mexican Americans and to see that they voted. Youth organizations also demanded Mexican-American studies and the use of Spanish in high schools and colleges.

Mexican-American studies soon were recognized in many schools and colleges. Able Mexican-American historians, social scientists, and humanists were professors at leading universities. *El Grito del Norte* and other newspapers and periodicals were further evidence of the vitality of the Chicano movement.

The Puerto Ricans. Puerto Ricans made up the second largest Spanish-speaking group in the United States. As you recall, Puerto Rico has long had a special commonwealth relationship with the United States. The inhabitants of the island are legally American citizens. Many Puerto Ricans have left their homeland in search of jobs in the United States. By 1975 more than 5 million Puerto Ricans, including mainland-born descendants, were living in the United States.

The Puerto Ricans were concentrated in New York. There, by the mid-1970's, they made up 10 percent of the city's population. Large numbers also lived in Newark, Philadelphia, Cleveland, Chicago, Boston, and other cities. In these urban areas they faced problems of unemployment, poor housing, prejudice, and discrimination.

The lives of young Puerto Ricans were especially difficult. Making up 33 percent of New York's school population, they were handicapped because they did not speak English. The dropout rate was very high. Street gangs, friction with the police, and high unemployment added to their problems. Yet many realized that education was a road to a better life. Evidence of this was the fact that in 1975 more than 17,000 young Puerto Ricans were enrolled in colleges and universities.

Despite difficulties and discrimination, many Puerto Ricans moved up the economic ladder. Some found places in small businesses, in semi-skilled trades, and in offices. By the late 1970's, about 10 percent of employed Puerto Rican males held professional or technical jobs. More and more were able to leave the crowded slums for better living conditions in the cities or in the suburbs. In the field of the arts, entertainment, and sports, José Feliciano, Rita Moreno, and Roberto Clemente became well known.

Puerto Ricans realized that political methods could improve their position and as a result they set up political organizations. Other politicians soon became aware of their bloc-voting power. In 1970 Herman Badillo of New York City became the first Puerto Rican member of Congress.

Many Puerto Ricans, on the other hand, rejected the "establishment." They emphasized forceful demands and revolutionary tactics to win greater opportunity. Frustration and pride led some to support Puerto Rican independence. Nevertheless, in a number of elections Puerto Ricans have rejected both statehood and independence, preferring instead to remain a commonwealth.

The Cubans. In 1959, as you have read (page 780), Fidel Castro overthrew the government of the reactionary dictator, Fulgencio Batista. When it soon became clear that Castro wished to create a Communist state, refugees began to escape to the United States. Many crossed the 90-mile stretch of water in small fishing boats. From 1961 to 1970, more than 208,000 arrived. During the 1970's the number landing on these shores each year increased steadily. In 1977 alone more than 66,000 entered the United States. Most of them settled in the Miami area.

In an effort to relieve the strain on the city, county, and state, the federal government set up the Cuban Refugee Program. With an annual budget of $40 million, it provided welfare assistance, health services, and vocational training. The refugees, largely middle class, used their assets, skills, and initiative to set up businesses and other enterprises. As a result of their efforts, they soon became an important part of the Miami area's economy.

Efforts by the refugee program to promote settlement in other parts of the country were effective. By the mid-1970's half of the Cubans were living in New York, Chicago, Los Angeles, and other cities. In 1979 the Census Bureau estimated that the Cuban population in the United States had reached 700,000.

Then, in the spring of 1980, a flood of refugees began to pour into Florida. The "Freedom Flotilla," an improvised fleet of privately owned boats, ferried them from Cuba to southern Florida. It was a dangerous, haphazard operation. Some of the boats, estimated to number more than 2,000, were capable of carrying only five or ten people.

At first President Carter welcomed the refugees with "open heart and open arms," but he soon was forced to change his position. By the end of May, more than 60,000 refugees had entered and several thousand more were arriving each day. Increasing numbers of American citizens objected to the arrival of the Cubans. They claimed that the nation was in a recession and that unemployment was high. They feared that the newcomers would take already scarce jobs.

Each year, uncounted thousands of aliens pour into the United States, some legally and some illegally. These newcomers were among the more than 100,000 Cubans who sailed here from their homeland in 1980.

Opposition to the uncontrolled flood of people approached the stage of violence. Finally the Carter administration announced that the "Freedom Flotilla" would be shut down. By that time, more than 125,000 Cubans had entered the United States.

SECTION SURVEY

IDENTIFY: Hispanos, migrant farm workers, Cesar Chavez, *barrio,* "Anglos," Chicanos, Rodolfo "Corky" Gonzales, Vilma Martinez, Herman Badillo, "Freedom Flotilla."

1. (a) What cultural characteristics do most Hispanics share? (b) From what nations do they come?

2. (a) In general, how have Mexican Americans been treated by other Americans? (b) What actions have members of the Chicano movement taken? (c) How successful has the Chicano movement been?

3. Compare the situation of Puerto Ricans with that of Mexican Americans in terms of (a) problems and (b) attempts to solve the problems.

4. (a) Why have many Cubans come to the United States since 1959? (b) How has the Cuban Refugee Program tried to help them adjust to their new life?

807

Indians refuse to accept the role of "vanishing Americans"

From the day the Europeans first invaded their land, the American Indians were forced to battle for sheer survival. A century ago they made their last desperate stand against the United States Army on the Great Plains. By 1892 the wars were over and the Indians had been subdued. Events would demonstrate that they had not been defeated.

Years of frustration. For the next 75 years, government policies toward the Indians changed repeatedly. In some cases they even reversed themselves. Such policy shifts left the Indians confused and frustrated. They also helped to keep the Indians the poorest of the poor among the nation's minorities.

Yet the American Indians refused to fulfill some earlier predictions and vanish. Against great odds they not only survived but also increased in numbers. According to the Bureau of the Census, in 1970 there were about 800,000 Indians living in the United States. More than 350,000 of these are in urban centers, the rest in rural areas.

Growing awareness. In the 1950's the government had adopted a policy designed to "terminate" its responsibilities to the Indians and to relocate them in cities. The policy, as you have read, proved to be a disaster.

Following the example of the blacks, Indian activists in the 1960's began to form organizations to promote Indian interests. They fought to overcome the damage caused by such policies as termination.

One of the oldest of the organizations was the National Congress of American Indians (NCAI). Founded during World War II, the NCAI became increasingly active during the 1960's. Other organizations, among them the National Indian Youth Council and the Native American Movement, joined in the battle for Indian rights.

Books, several written by Indians, attracted public attention to the problems of the Native Americans. The books and the publicity they received helped to stir the consciences of growing numbers of American citizens.

The New Indians by Saul Steiner alerted readers to a new "uprising" led by Indian intellectuals who wanted to develop "red power." In 1969 Vine Deloria, Jr., a Standing Rock Sioux and a former director of NCAI, published one of the most influential books, *Custer Died for Your Sins.* In it Deloria outlined the tragic history of broken white promises, set forth the goals Indians were struggling to achieve, and provided a glimpse of what white Americans could learn from the First Americans. A year later Deloria continued his indictment of white America and his plea for understanding with another book, *We Talk, You Listen.* The following year Dee Brown's *Bury My Heart at Wounded Knee* appeared and became one of the most widely read of the recent books.

People began to pay attention to Indian problems. President Johnson was one of them. In 1968 he asked for, and Congress passed, a program of more than $500 million in aid to the Indians.

Violence. The growing awareness of Indian problems was quickened by militant Indian action. One group of Indians took over Alcatraz Island, a former Federal prison in California, to dramatize their demands.

The American Indian Movement (AIM) was launched by young urban Indian leaders in the late 1960's. In the fall of 1972, some 500 members of AIM banded together, calling themselves "The Trail of Broken Treaties." They marched on Washington, D.C., occupied the Bureau of Indian Affairs, and did some $2 million in damage. They finally received official promises that the government would pay attention to their complaints.

In February 1973, members of AIM seized the trading post and church at the Sioux Pine Reservation in Wounded Knee, South Dakota. This was the village where in 1890 United States cavalry units had brutally massacred more than 200 Indians. For 71 days heavily armed Indians and United States marshals grimly confronted each other over the barricades that separated them. In the end, after the government promised to consider their demands, the Indians surrendered.

The end of termination. Meanwhile the federal government had once again reversed itself. In 1970 President Nixon asked Congress to repeal the termination policy of 1953. He then announced a policy of "self-determination without termination." From now on, Nixon declared, the Indians would be encouraged to develop their own tribal life on their reservations. In supporting them the government would provide assistance for housing, vocational training, and economic development.

Although Indians welcomed the new policy, they could not forget the repeated reversals in the past. They continued to fear that termination would be renewed.

As it turned out, Congress failed to pass the necessary laws to make the proposed policy effective. Moreover, the tactics employed by AIM angered the Nixon administration. As a result the reform movement begun by the federal government was only partially carried out. However, the federal government did lay to rest the policy of termination.

Moving forward. Although AIM's violent tactics lost some support for the Indians, other Indian leaders continued to move toward their goal of running their own lives in their own way. These leaders increasingly relied on educational activities and on court action to gain their ends.

The Indians made gradual progress. By 1975, for the first time in history, Indian men and women made up a majority of the employees of the Bureau of Indian Affairs. At the same time, more and more schools and colleges had developed programs of Indian studies that informed students of the Indians' part in the nation's life.

The Indians won other victories as well. For example, the Indians of the Taos Pueblo in New Mexico recovered 48,000 acres (19,400 hectares) of land, including the sacred Blue Lake, that had been made part of a national park. Indians in Maine, who claimed that more than half of the state had been illegally taken from them, took their case to the courts. Congress awarded them $81.5 million and the right to purchase up to 300,000 acres (120,000 hectares) of land.

The Indian today. Today, as in the past, generalizations about the Native Americans must be made carefully. The Indians of the United States are now divided into more than 450 tribes or communities and speak more than 100 different languages. Although most continue to battle poverty, many have become well-to-do and some have become wealthy. Many are highly educated and highly skilled.

Here, in northern New Mexico, is the Blue Lake, for centuries held sacred by the Indians of the Taos Pueblo. The lake had been made part of a national park in the 1970's, but finally, the federal government returned Blue Lake to its traditional Indian owners.

There are Indian doctors, lawyers, scientists, and engineers. A large number have become completely "Americanized." However, many refuse to abandon traditional ways and continue to live apart from the mainstream of American culture.

For the most part, the First Americans remain intensely proud of their heritage. They believe that they have contributed richly to American life. They also believe that they have much more to contribute—if America will pause long enough to listen.

SECTION SURVEY

IDENTIFY: NCAI, Vine Deloria, Jr., AIM.

1. (a) What methods have Indians used to dramatize their needs and problems? (b) Which have been most effective? Explain.

2. (a) What was President Nixon's Indian policy? (b) How effective was it?

3. Describe the progress made by Indians in recent years.

Women redouble efforts to win equal rights and opportunities

American women make up nearly 53 percent of the population. They are the largest group struggling against discrimination. During the 1960's the struggle came to be known as women's liberation or the women's rights movement and gathered strength.

Reasons for early successes. In part the movement gained strength because of the growing number of American women who were now employed. By the mid-1970's women made up about 50 percent of the nation's labor force. Their average wages, however, were only 60 percent of those paid to men doing comparable work. Even more revealing, only a small percentage of women held higher-paying and more responsible positions. Among the directors of large corporations, for example, only 3 percent were women.

Another factor in the rise of the women's rights movement was the civil rights movement. Many women had been actively involved in the civil rights movement and had gained ability and confidence for their own struggle.

Their struggle was also aided by a clause in the Civil Rights Act of 1964. This clause outlawed discrimination based on sex in employment. Using this clause, women battled to secure equal treatment in business, education, and the other professions.

Growing numbers of women agreed with movement leaders that sex discrimination kept many women from realizing their full potential. According to public opinion polls, a majority of American women did not feel that taking care of a home and raising children were restrictive or frustrating roles. By the mid-1970's, however, a majority of American women did approve of equal opportunities for their sex in all areas of life.

Women's rights organizations. One of the first and most prominent groups within the women's rights movement was the National Organization for Women (NOW). NOW and other feminist groups shared a number of goals. They demanded equal treatment of women in educational programs, including faculty appointments in universities. They worked for publicly financed day-care centers for children. They attempted to get state laws forbidding abortion repealed. They strongly opposed the treatment of women as sex objects. Some of the groups also insisted that men should share in the tasks of homemaking and childrearing.

The ERA. Most of the women's rights organizations pressed for a Constitutional amendment to guarantee women equal rights. By 1978 the Equal Rights Amendment (ERA) that had been passed by Congress in 1972 had been ratified by 35 of the required 38 states. By 1980, however, no additional states had ratified the amendment.

Why had the ERA become stalled?

Many American women believed that the ERA would deprive them of more than it gave them. They feared it might make them subject to the military draft or end alimony payments to women or put an end to laws protecting women in the workplace. More deeply, many of these women believed that such an amendment would help to destroy the traditional bonds of the family.

These women organized their own countermovement. They put pressure on state legislatures and succeeded in preventing ratification in key states. By the early 1980's, passage of the ERA seemed doubtful.

New freedoms for women. Despite the stalling of the ERA, steps were being made toward meeting some goals of the women's rights movement. Legal suits were filed against businesses, colleges, and other institutions. Such suits charged the institutions with sex discrimination in hiring, pay, and promotion practices.

Women also entered careers in fields formerly dominated by men. Women enlisted in the armed forces in growing numbers. Women became police officers and ministers. They won new recognition in sports such as tennis and golf. As a result of such changes, there were fewer strict barriers between men and women in dress and social customs.

In 1973 the Supreme Court ruled that women had the right to have abortions before the sixth month of pregnancy. This controversial decision clashed with existing laws in most of the states. The states then began to change their laws to conform to the Court's ruling. At the same time, anti-abortion groups chal-

In the fall of 1981, Sandra Day O'Connor of Arizona was sworn in as a Justice of the United States Supreme Court. She is seen in this photograph with the other members of the Court. Chief Justice Warren Burger is the fourth from the left.

lenged the right of the Court to make such a decision. They demanded a Constitutional amendment banning abortions.

Political gains. In political affairs women were still underrepresented. However, change was in the air.

Several women in Congress became nationally known. Among them were Bella Abzug, Shirley Chisholm, Barbara Jordan, Elizabeth Holtzman, and Nancy Kassebaum. Of the 52 women who ran for Congress in the 1980 race, 19 were elected.

Women scored impressive gains in state and local politics as well. Approximately 500 women served in state legislatures. Many more took active roles in local party politics. In Connecticut, Ella Grasso served as an extremely popular governor until she resigned because of poor health in 1980. In San Jose, California, Janet Hayes became the first woman mayor of a large American city. Jane N. Byrne was later elected mayor of Chicago.

Other women in government included Carla Hills, Secretary of Housing and Urban Development under President Ford. President Carter appointed two women, Juanita Kreps and Patricia Harris, to his Cabinet. The most widely noted appointment, however, was that of Sandra O'Connor, who was named by President Reagan to a seat on the Supreme Court.

The balance sheet. By the 1980's, despite some growing resistance, the women's rights movement was advancing toward many of its goals. The effects of the movement seemed likely to be far-reaching. Even the women who defended traditional roles and actively opposed the movement did so using political methods and styles that seemed far from traditional.

SECTION SURVEY

IDENTIFY: NOW, Equal Rights Amendment, Shirley Chisholm, Nancy Kassebaum, Ella Grasso.

1. What are some of the goals of the women's rights movement?
2. Why did the women's rights movement gain strength by the mid-1970's?
3. Why did some people object to the women's rights movement?

Chapter Survey

Summary: Tracing the Main Ideas

More than two hundred years ago, the American nation was founded on the principle that "all men are created equal." By the 1980's the promise of 1776 remained only partially fulfilled.

Even so, during the years after World War II, and particularly during the past two decades, the movement toward freedom and justice for all Americans has made steady progress.

Despite progress, problems still remained. The cities, in which so many of the poor and the minorities were concentrated, continued to decay. Also, from the mid-1970's on, the nation's economic health was poor. Soaring prices and scarce jobs damaged the chances of many minority members to better their lives.

In spite of these obstacles, however, blacks, Hispanics, Indians, and the largest group of all, women, were demanding and winning a share of "the American dream." They had moved a great deal closer to full equality. A great distance remained to be traveled.

Inquiring into History

1. Describe the major changes that have occurred in the population of the United States in the years since 1960.
2. (a) How are the problems of Hispanics, blacks, and Indians similar? (b) How are they different? (c) Compare the recent progress made by each group.
3. Today women make up more than 50 percent of the population of the United States. Nevertheless, they are often considered a minority. Why do you think this is so?
4. Equal rights movements often suffer from conflicts between their moderates and militants. (a) What sorts of tactics might be favored by moderates? By militants? (b) How did such conflicts affect the black civil rights movement? (c) How did similar conflicts affect the movement for Indian rights?

Relating Past to Present

1. During the 1800's many Americans considered the United States to be a "melting pot" of many peoples. How would you describe the United States today? Explain.

2. Though there has been a steady decline in the farm population since 1940, many young people today look at farming as an enviable occupation. How do you explain this interest? Why do you suppose even the most interested find it difficult to take up farming?
3. What is the present federal policy toward (a) urban problems, (b) affirmative action, and (c) school desegregation? How does it compare with the policies discussed in this chapter?

Developing Social Science Skills

1. Examine the chart on page 843, showing the national background of immigrants. Design and draw a world map that illustrates the immigration of the people from these countries to the United States.
2. (a) Use the *Reader's Guide to Periodical Literature* to locate articles supporting and opposing the Equal Rights Amendment. Make a list of the most compelling arguments on both sides of the issue. (b) Based on your research, take a stand on the ERA and defend your position in a paper or a speech.
3. Create a cartoon comparing the equal rights movement to the civil rights movement.

Chapter **43**

Into the Future

On January 21, 1981 Ronald Reagan was sworn in as the fortieth President of the United States. His Inaugural Address that day was solemn. In the years after World War II, the nation had reached a level of wealth, productivity, and power never before approached in history. By 1981, however, formidable problems had emerged. Inflation, unemployment, and a deepening recession seemed to defy solutions. Continued poverty in a land of abundance troubled many Americans. A growing loss of confidence in the government cast a darkening shadow over the democratic process. Schools and colleges, faced with rising costs and falling enrollments, began to rethink their purposes and their programs. Shortages and soaring prices convinced many Americans that they could not continue to depend upon oil as a major source of energy.

By 1981 it had become clear that Americans could no longer take for granted the prosperity so many of them had enjoyed for so many years. As never before in the nation's history, men and women in every walk of life faced the urgent need to reexamine the nation's goals as well as their own personal objectives.

In his Inaugural Address, Reagan recognized this need. He called for a "new beginning" and an "era of national renewal." He said, "The crisis we are facing . . . does require . . . our best effort, and our willingness to believe in our capacity, to perform great deeds; to believe that together with God's help we can and will resolve the problems which now confront us."

Changing Ways of American Life

1960's–1980's

THE CHAPTER IN OUTLINE

1. Americans begin to reexamine their goals.

2. The American economy remains a source of continuing concern.

3. The United States attempts to resolve its energy crisis.

4. Americans share a growing awareness of environmental issues.

1 Americans begin to reexamine their goals

Change is by definition an unsettling experience. As the dictionary reminds us, "to change" is "to alter, to become different." Increasingly during the years after World War II, change uprooted traditional values, beliefs, and behavior of Americans and people everywhere on the planet.

Change and its effects. It was not just change, as such, that was so unsettling. Throughout human history people have been compelled to adapt to changing ways and times. The disturbing difference in the second half of the twentieth century was the increasingly swift rate of change.

The rate of change was particularly rapid in the areas of science and technology. According to one estimate, 90 percent of all the scientists who have ever lived were alive and active in the 1970's. This intense scientific activity throughout the world brought new discoveries, new ideas, new processes, and new inventions in an ever-growing volume.

Nothing in the universe was too small to escape the attention of science; nothing was too immense or too remote in time or place. Scientists explored particles of the atom and stars so distant that their light has taken more than 10 billion years to reach earth. Every field of science was probed, and the answers to questions merely prompted scientists to raise still more questions.

Research produced a vast tidal wave of new developments. Many such developments had unexpected and unplanned effects on daily life. People everywhere were finding it more and more difficult to adapt their personal lives and their institutions—religious, educational, social, economic, political—to the demands of changing ways and times.

Space exploration. Many of the things accomplished by science would have been dismissed a generation ago as wild imaginings. The world was startled when in 1957 the Soviet Union launched the first artificial satellite, Sputnik. Yet by 1969 two American astronauts, Neil Armstrong and Edwin E. Aldrin, had landed on the moon. By 1981 American scientists were testing the *Columbia,* a reus-

able space shuttle, with the aim of starting regular manned flights.

Today hundreds of satellites orbit the earth. They serve numerous purposes. Some relay television, radio, and telephone messages across continents and the seas. Some survey military activities, search the earth for oil and other resources, and provide data on the weather. Others enable ships at sea to determine their exact location within a matter of seconds. Still other space craft have explored the solar system, reaching out as far as Jupiter and Saturn and sending scientific data and photographs back to earth.

Other scientific advances. The exploration of outer space was parallelled by equally dramatic discoveries on earth. Medical science made major advances in the cure and control of disease. New materials and techniques enabled medical researchers to produce such products as artificial skin and mechanical hearts. Insecticides, pesticides, herbicides, and thousands of drugs, many of them unknown in the natural world, were created and produced in chemical laboratories.

In biological laboratories scientists experimented with such basic life characteristics as the nature of cells. This experimentation involved splicing together genes from different organisms to form what is known as recombinant DNA. Researchers hoped that the new or different forms of life created in the process would have some practical value—either medical, scientific, or industrial.

Many scientists and nonscientists insisted that this type of experimentation was dangerous and should be abandoned. Others would permit it to continue only under the most rigid supervision. In June 1980, however, the Supreme Court ruled that scientists could patent such new forms of life. In this particular case, patent rights were issued to the "inventor" of a newly developed strain of bacteria that would eat crude oil.

Another major scientific breakthrough was the development in the 1960's of ways to generate, amplify, and control beams of pure, or "coherent," light. Lasers, as they are called, were used to perform surgical operations, including delicate operations on the eye. Far more powerful lasers were being developed by the military as anti-tank and anti-satellite weapons. Laser technology also made it possible to transmit telephone messages through glass fibers,

"We are really in the space business to stay," said Robert Crippen after he and John Young took the *Columbia* on its near-perfect first flight. He was voicing the hope that space shuttle flight would soon become a common occurrence.

rather than through copper wires. These were only a few of the rapidly developing uses of laser technology.

The emerging computerized world. The computer was the key to the new world that was emerging out of the amazing advances in science and technology. Scientists continued to refine and improve computer designs and functions. By 1980 a tiny silicon chip no larger than a small coin could outperform the earliest room-sized computers. The largest computers could perform up to 800 million calculations a second and store as many as four million words. All of the stored data was instantly retrievable and could be communicated at the speed of light to any designated location on the earth.

Advances in design allowed computers to be used in more and more areas. Computers guided robot welders on automobile assembly lines. In hospitals computers were linked to X-ray machines. These CAT scanners, as they were called, provided detailed cross-sectional views of vital organs. Small-sized computers were increasingly found in people's homes, aiding them with bank accounts and budgets or entertaining them with electronic games.

Computer scientists agreed that the computer was still in its infant stage of development. No one doubted that these "thinking machines" would continue to increase the efficiency of the human mind. Yet the spread of computers created new problems. Advances in computer technology meant the loss of jobs for some people. Also the spreading use of computers meant that more information about individuals was being collected in computer memories. The individual's right to privacy could be threatened if unauthorized people gained access to such information. How computers would be used in the future depended, finally, upon the values that men and women held and chose to guide their lives.

A revolution in values. A revolution in manners, morals, and values, as well as in science, also characterized the 1960's and 1970's. This development was not confined to the United States. The experience was shared to a greater or lesser degree by all of the world's industrialized nations and even by some of the developing nations. Nor was this revolution limited to the young, although they often led the way.

The development got under way in the United States in the opening years of the 1960's. Inspired by the relatively young President Kennedy, young people increasingly committed themselves to causes. Some joined organizations like the Peace Corps. Others became active in the civil rights movement.

The high hopes that blossomed in these years withered after the assassination of President Kennedy and America's growing involvement in the war in Vietnam. Many young people became angry, resentful, and frustrated over Vietnam and over continuing poverty and discrimination in their own country. Some of these young people, unable or unwilling to find their place in society, rejected the beliefs and practices of the older generation. As a visible sign of their independence, they adopted dress, hair styles, and ways of living that set them apart from the "establishment." Some of them "dropped out" from the traditional world and joined communes. Others experimented with drugs. Still others turned to political activism and attempted to revamp or overthrow the established order by means of organized protest, political action, and, at times, violence.

During the 1970's the earlier, more violent aspects of the rebellion died down. For one thing, the large majority of America's youth did not drop out or fight against the "system." Instead, they continued their education and their search for ways to earn a living. Moreover, some changes had been made in the "system." For example, young people had been granted a more important role in society. The Voting Rights Act of 1970 and the Twenty-sixth Amendment in 1971 extended to 18-year-olds the right to vote.

In still other ways the "revolution" left its mark on American society. Older Americans were also affected by the changes it brought with it. Divorce rates climbed. Growing numbers of single-parent families took their place alongside the traditional family group—father, mother, and children. Some workers, unhappy with what they saw as the pressures and demands of the traditional business world, sought out less financially rewarding but more personally satisfying jobs. Subjects rarely if ever discussed in private social gatherings as recently as the 1960's were now frankly considered in books, family magazines, motion pictures, and television programs.

There were changes on the political scene as well. Although they had only recently won the right to vote, increasing numbers of young men and women failed to register and exercise that right. The majority of those who did indicate an interest in the political process listed themselves as independents. This movement away from the Democratic and the Republican parties was not limited to young people. It was a growing trend among all age groups. By 1980 there was widespread concern throughout the country that the nation's traditional two-party system was in trouble.

Demand for a return to "basics." By the late 1970's, however, signs of a strong reaction to the turmoil of the earlier years was apparent. Parents called for increased discipline and a "return to basics" in the schools. Other Americans felt that traditional goals and purposes were in danger of being lost. Groups such as the Moral Majority pressed for a return to what they insisted were the traditional values in all aspects of American life. Many observers felt that the strong Republican showing in the 1980 elections offered firm evidence that the nation had entered a more conservative time in its history.

New demands on education. Fast-moving developments created both problems and opportunities for the educational system. During the 1960's one of the more serious problems was overcrowding as the children born during the years of the postwar "baby boom" reached school and college age. Reversing traditional policy, Congress came to the aid of the hard-pressed educational system with federal financial assistance.

During the 1970's, however, even with this federal support, the nation's educational institutions suffered an increasingly serious financial crisis. Although enrollments had begun to decline, expenses skyrocketed, partly because of inflation.

Public schools faced additional problems. Although school enrollments on the whole declined, inner city schools often remained overcrowded. Racial tensions and lack of discipline in some public schools led many parents to enter their children in private schools instead.

These crises came at a time when the schools and colleges were confronted with the heaviest responsibility they had ever been expected to carry. Overriding all other issues was the basic question: What kind of education should American schools provide to prepare their students for life in a complex, rapidly changing world?

The evidence was overwhelming that poorly educated, poorly trained men and women had little hope of earning an adequate living in an increasingly complex society. Far more serious from society's point of view was the fact that inadequately educated citizens could not help to solve critical problems facing the nation and the world.

Strong efforts to improve the quality of education began in the late 1950's with improvements in the teaching of mathematics, physics, chemistry, biology, and other natural sciences. By the mid-1960's these efforts had broadened to include the humanities and the social sciences. Grants from the federal government and from private foundations helped to fund projects to improve both the curriculum and methods of learning. These projects were developed and tried out in research centers and in hundreds of schools.

Efforts were also made to improve the quality of education for disadvantaged students. The Head Start program sponsored by the federal government tried to provide pre-school children with rewarding learning experiences.

These and other developments, including the use of closed circuit television, computer terminals, and other kinds of technology in the classrooms, represented an effort to improve the quality of American education. In 1979 Congress undertook to strengthen this effort by creating a separate Department of Education.°

Foreign aid and defense. By 1980 the issue of assistance to the developing nations had become urgent. For one thing, the world's food supply and distribution of it had not kept pace with its exploding population. By 1980 this had passed the 4.5 billion mark. Moreover, many new nations had been created. The United Nations included 151 members, three fourths of them developing countries.

Compounding the problem was the fact that the gap between the rich, industrialized coun-

°The former Department of Health, Education, and Welfare (HEW) then became the Department of Health and Human Services.

tries and the poor, developing nations was becoming steadily wider and deeper. By 1980 the problem of providing food and other necessities for hundreds of millions of men, women, and children in the poorer nations had reached crisis proportions.

It was plain that the rich, industrial nations would have to play an important part in solving the problems of poverty and hunger in the world. Self-interest, as well as America's cherished belief in human dignity and equality of opportunity, seemed to place a special responsibility on the United States. But by the late 1970's the United States was experiencing serious needs among its own people. How much foreign aid could it afford to give?

At the same time that Americans were deciding how much aid to give other nations, they were trying to determine how much to spend to protect themselves from other nations. In other words, how much of the nation's wealth should be spent on its defense?

During the war in Vietnam in the 1960's, defense spending had represented almost 45 percent of the federal budget. After that the percentage dropped steadily to a low of about 25 percent under President Carter.

President Reagan feared that such cutbacks in spending had given the Soviet Union the chance to gain military superiority. Soviet military spending, he asserted, had greatly increased while America's military budgets had been cut. The only way to counter the growing Soviet threat was with a massive buildup of American arms.

Thus Reagan proposed a program of military spending that would cost $1.3 trillion over a five-year period. Defense spending would climb to over 30 percent of the federal budget. Critics were quick to contrast the Reagan administration's 1980 budget recommendation of $151.5 billion for national defense with the $9.6 billion allocated for foreign aid. Critics also pointed out that most of the money budgeted in recent years for foreign aid was for military assistance, not for the relief of poverty and suffering in the developing countries.

Reexamining government's role. One of the major questions that Americans would have to answer concerned the role of the federal government in their lives.

As you have read, some founders of the nation were concerned that the federal government not have too much power. During the early

1800's debates on how powers should be divided between federal and state governments were common. The Civil War seemed to settle the question, firmly establishing that the federal government had supreme authority.

Nevertheless, the federal government remained reluctant to assert authority in matters of daily life and business. For example, the first federal regulatory agency was not formed until 1887. Also, until the 1930's the federal government took no major role in trying to end the economic depressions into which the country plunged from time to time.

The Great Depression that started in 1929 led to a larger role for the federal government as state and local governments were powerless to relieve the widespread suffering. President Franklin Roosevelt's programs, such as Social Security, brought the federal government into daily life in an unprecedented way.

World War II and America's new role as world leader also encouraged the growth of the federal government. By the 1960's federal programs under Kennedy's New Frontier and Johnson's Great Society were enormous. Presidents Nixon and Ford promised to reduce the size and role of the federal government. In spite of their promises, public employment and federal spending increased.

More and more people began to question the role that the federal government was playing. Disenchantment with the federal government was heightened by the Watergate scandals and rising inflation and unemployment rates.

During the election campaign of 1980 Ronald Reagan asked for the chance to reduce federal involvement in some aspects of people's lives. In his Inaugural Address he cautioned, "In this present crisis, government is not the solution to our problem; government is the problem." In his first messages to Congress, President Reagan called for sharply reduced federal programs in social welfare, education, research, and support of the arts. His calls received much early popular and Congressional support.

Nevertheless, how much the federal government's role could be reduced remained in question. The extent to which the federal government was involved in daily life was not always apparent. For example by 1980, government payments to individuals made up 28 percent of total personal income in the nation. Cutting back on this involvement would mean sacrifice and hardship for many citizens.

SECTION SURVEY

IDENTIFY: lasers, Head Start program, Twenty-sixth Amendment, Moral Majority.

1. Describe some ways in which scientific research and technology have changed the daily lives of Americans.

2. (a) What problems did the educational system face during the 1960's and 1970's? (b) Describe some of the efforts to solve these problems.

3. What did President Reagan mean when he said, "In this present crisis, government is not the solution to our problem; government is the problem"?

2 The American economy remains a source of continuing concern

When President Reagan in his Inaugural Address said "in this crisis . . . government is the problem," the crisis he spoke of was an economic one and had been building throughout the 1970's. In the 1980 Presidential campaign, the economy was the key issue.

The problem of inflation. The most troubling issue was the most obvious one — inflation. Inflation can be simply described as a significant rise in the cost of materials for agricultural and industrial production, labor, consumer goods, services, and credit. It can also be thought of as an overabundance of money in relation to the goods and services that money can buy.

When such a situation exists, prices rise. In 1971 a gallon of gas cost about 37¢; by 1981 it cost about $1.27. In 1971 a rib roast sold for $1.18 a pound; by 1981 it was $3.69 a pound.

Inflation, which was an international problem, was only part of the economic trouble. On many fronts — productivity, growth, investment — America seemed to slip as world leader.

Many economists traced the serious problems with the economy back to the mid-1960's. At that time, inflation was less than 2 percent a year, and the economy seemed healthy. However, the United States was growing more deeply involved in the Vietnam War. The federal government spent heavily for this war without increasing taxes. Money was pumped into the economy and the federal debt rose.

Signs of a troubled economy are unemployment lines like these. During the 1960's unemployment only once dropped to 5 percent. During the 1970's it never dropped below 5.8 percent, reaching a high of 8.5 percent in 1975.

At the same time that President Johnson was waging the war in Vietnam, he declared a war on poverty in the United States. This war on poverty also pumped money into the economy and increased the national debt.

Attempts to curb inflation. President Johnson at last called for a tax increase to cut the growing deficit and cool down the economy. The tax increase did not take effect until 1969, when Richard Nixon took office.

By then inflation was increasing at the rate of 4.7 percent a year. Americans were demanding that the President take action to halt it.

At first, President Nixon tried two methods of controlling inflation. He cut federal spending for education, welfare, housing, urban renewal, and anti-pollution measures, reducing the budget by several billion dollars.

Nixon also encouraged the Federal Reserve Board and the nation's banks to increase interest rates sharply. The "tight money" policy, as it was called, was intended to make borrowing more expensive. This in turn would cut into the overabundance of money that allowed Americans to bid up the prices of goods and services.

Despite these measures, inflation continued at an alarming rate. Finally, in August 1971,

Nixon announced a new economic program. Its main feature was a 90-day freeze on wages, prices, and rents. A Cost of Living Council was set up to develop guidelines for wages, prices, and profits after the freeze ended. Although both business and labor were unhappy with parts of the program, the rate of inflation did slow a little.

Encouraged by this development, Nixon eased the controls in January 1973, claiming that inflation was moderating and the economy was beginning to slow down. With restraints removed, prices began to soar. Nixon again applied partial controls, which he removed in 1974. Once more inflation shot up, and this time the rate was increased by new OPEC (see page 766) demands for higher oil prices.

Inflation and stagflation. When President Ford took office, the annual rate of inflation was 12 percent. Ford, like Nixon, was convinced that excessive government spending was a major cause of inflation. Ford tried to reduce government spending and slow down the economy. By 1975 the rate of inflation had dropped to 7 percent.

Ford's efforts, though, had unfortunate results. They brought about a nationwide slump

819

in business, or recession, the worst since before World War II. During the winter of 1974–75, the nation's industrial output dropped, and millions of people lost their jobs. By the summer of 1975, more than 8 million men and women were unemployed.

A new word, **stagflation,** was used to describe the puzzling combination of a stagnant economy and a high rate of inflation. Traditional measures for aiding the economy were not effective with stagflation. Cuts in spending by the government to reduce inflation produced longer unemployment lines. Increased government spending and tax cuts did help to stimulate employment, but they also increased inflation.

The recession did, finally, slow inflation. When President Carter took office in 1977, the inflation rate was 4.8 percent. However, the rate of unemployment remained high, about 7 percent. Carter tried to reduce this unemployment by putting more money into the economy. Federal spending was increased and federal taxes were cut. Such policies led to another rise in the inflation rate, and by late 1978 it had risen to 10 percent.

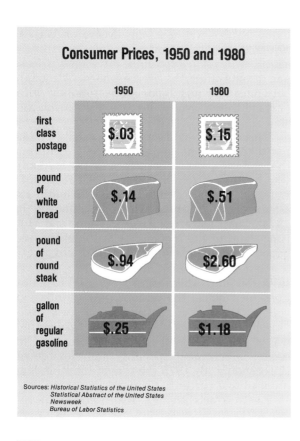

Consumer Prices, 1950 and 1980

	1950	1980
first class postage	$.03	$.15
pound of white bread	$.14	$.51
pound of round steak	$.94	$2.60
gallon of regular gasoline	$.25	$1.18

Sources: Historical Statistics of the United States
Statistical Abstract of the United States
Newsweek
Bureau of Labor Statistics

To combat inflation, Carter called for a program of voluntary wage and price controls. If workers accepted federal guidelines, they would limit wage increases to a maximum of 7 percent, including fringe benefits. Business, for its part, would voluntarily limit price increases to a maximum of 5 percent.

Stronger measures, higher inflation. Carter's voluntary controls did not halt the rising cost of living. The increase was speeded along by OPEC's sharp boosts in the price of oil. By the spring of 1980, the rate of inflation was more than 18 percent a year. The value of the dollar was shrinking. In 1980 it took nearly $5 to buy what $1 had bought in 1940.

The nation's economy was in serious trouble, and the Carter administration redoubled its efforts to find a cure. The Federal Reserve Board tightened credit. Leading commercial banks raised the prime rate of interest on money borrowed to over 20 percent. Carter now also tried to cut federal spending. The anti-inflationary measures had the undesirable side effect of increasing unemployment. America was moving into another recession.

By 1980 the inflation crisis had become serious indeed. In the early years of the inflationary boom, incomes had kept ahead of costs. For example, from 1967 to 1973 the average real income of Americans, adjusting for inflation, rose 17.5 percent. But from 1974 to 1978 it rose only 5.5 percent. Starting in 1979 real income actually declined.

One economist put it this way: "The two-earner family has about peaked, average real weekly earnings are falling, and now you are going to have to put teenagers to work just to keep income stable."

The impact of the economic problems can be expressed another way. In 1972 the United States had the highest standard of living in the world. By 1980, it had slipped to fifth place.

With less real income, Americans were less ready to make major purchases, especially when they faced high interest rates on borrowed money as well. Thus industries vital to the nation's economy, such as the automobile and the housing industries, suffered. Because the inflation rate was usually higher than the rate of interest banks paid on savings accounts, people were also less willing or able to save.

Inflation and business. Inflation ate away at the welfare of businesses as well as that of

At this American plant, automobiles move along a robot welding assembly line. Investment in such equipment was necessary to insure that the American automobile industry remained competitive with those of other nations.

individuals. You have seen that people's unwillingness to make large purchases cut into business sales. Additionally, a reduced rate of savings meant that there was less money available to invest in business.

Inflation also made business less willing to make necessary commitments in costly new equipment. Without such new equipment, the productivity of some of the nation's key industries declined.

The results were striking. In the 1960's the rate of the nation's economic growth averaged 4.1 percent a year. In the 1970's it was only 2.9 percent. Likewise, the output of goods and services per worker, which had been growing at 1.9 percent a year from 1968 to 1973, dropped to .7 percent a year from 1973 to 1979.

World competition. The economic picture looked gloomier still when America's economic performance was compared with that of rival industrial nations. Japan and West Germany, in particular, made amazing economic strides. They invested heavily in new and efficient technology and were able to seize a sizable share of markets in other countries and even in the United States.

In 1962, United States-made aircraft commanded over 70 percent of worldwide sales. By 1979, the figure had shrunk to 58 percent. In this country, the records of automobile sales showed how the United States was losing ground to foreign competition. In 1960, almost 96 percent of all cars sold in this country were American-made. Twenty years later only 79 percent were produced here.

Reagan's program. These, then, were some of the challenges that Ronald Reagan faced when he took office in 1981. Constructing a strong new economic program was his first order of business.

Reagan's first priority was victory over inflation. In order to win this victory, the government would have to balance the budget—that is, reduce expenditures to match the amount of money available from taxes.

The Reagan administration called for a two-pronged attack on the problem. One prong was a sharp reduction in federal spending except for defense. The idea was to reduce expenses by cutting back on some programs, dropping others, and eliminating wasteful practices.

The second prong was a tax cut. This called for across-the-board reductions in personal and corporate taxes. Reagan hoped that these reductions would encourage people and businesses to save and invest. It was assumed that this would lead to the modernization of old plants and the construction of new ones.

This investment would help to revitalize the economy. Revitalization would mean more goods and services, stabilized prices, and more jobs. With more workers on the job and more taxpayers, the government would be able to balance the budget.

That was the broad outline of President Reagan's plan. He and his staff then began to work with Senators and Representatives and soon got the program through Congress.

Reagan had stated, during his Inaugural Address, that he intended to "put America back to work." How well his plan would accomplish this goal remained to be seen.

SECTION SURVEY

IDENTIFY: inflation, Cost of Living Council, stagflation.

1. How can government actions affect the rate of inflation?
2. How did world competition affect the United States economy?
3. Describe President Reagan's program for improving the nation's economy.
4. Chart Study: Look at the chart on page 820. How much did the price of each item rise? What was the percentage of increase for each item?

3 The United States attempts to resolve its energy crisis

Energy topped the list of critical resources. Without it American productivity would be drastically reduced. Sources of energy provided essential power for American farming, lumbering, mining, manufacturing, transportation, communications, heating, cooking, lighting, air-conditioning, and countless other tasks. Americans and people in other industrial countries lived in a world dominated by machines dependent on energy resources.

Dependence upon fossil fuels. The fossil fuels—coal, oil (petroleum), and natural gas—made up 95 percent of the energy resources in the United States in 1980 and a slightly larger percentage for the world as a whole. The world's dependence upon fossil fuels was, however, relatively new.

It was with the Industrial Revolution, hardly more than 200 years ago, that the change came. Only then did people begin to make heavy use of the fuels that had been buried in the earth for millions of years.

During the past 50 years, the industrial nations consumed an alarmingly high percentage of all the fossil fuels that existed on the planet. The United States was the world's largest producer, importer, and consumer of energy resources, mainly oil. The energy required to power America's machines and to heat and cool homes and other buildings doubled between 1950 and 1970 and was expected to double again by the mid-1980's.

The end of an era. By the 1980's, however, it was becoming increasingly clear to the United States and the other industrialized countries that they could not continue much longer to depend upon oil as their principal source of energy. Known reserves of the most widely used fossil fuels—oil and gas—were dwindling steadily. The cost of discovering and developing new sources of these fuels was rising rapidly. In the United States by 1980 domestic deposits of oil supplied only about half of the nation's energy needs.

Twice in the 1970's, the American people were shocked into the awareness that their standard of living and even the security of the nation itself depended upon decisions made in and by other countries. For a nation accustomed to think of itself as a world leader, the discovery was immensely disturbing.

The first shock came in 1973. At that time foreign oil producers formed a cartel, or pool, designed to eliminate competition among themselves and to control the price of oil on the world market. Within a few months, OPEC had increased the price of oil from $4 to $11 a barrel. Even more disturbing, OPEC, which was angered by American support of Israel, temporarily halted all shipments of oil to the United States.

The second shock came in 1978–79 when Iran, which supplied 10 percent of the world's petroleum, was torn by revolution. All shipments of oil from the Iranian oil fields to the United States were cut off.

In the meantime, during the 1970's OPEC had been steadily raising prices. By 1980 the OPEC countries were demanding $28 to $40 a barrel, the price was still rising, and no top limit was in sight.

The era of cheap oil, and therefore of cheap energy, had come to an end. Alternative sources would have to be found. The nation's prosperity and independence in coming years depended upon the success of the search for these alternatives.

Natural gas and coal. For the short term, natural gas, which in 1980 was supplying about one third of United States energy, would continue to be available. However gas, like oil, was becoming increasingly expensive. It, too, was limited in amount. In time gas reserves, too, would be exhausted.

The expanded use of coal, which during the 1970's provided about 18 percent of the energy consumed in the United States, seemed at first glance to provide a more realistic alternative to oil. It was estimated that the world's coal reserves, of which 20 percent are in the United States, were large enough to meet the projected world energy demands for the next 200 to 300 years. Coal was also a potential source for so-called synthetic fuels. These were fuels that could be processed from coal. They included both liquid fuel and gas.

There were, however, serious questions as to the wisdom of depending upon coal as a major source of energy. In the past the mining of coal was enormously costly in terms of human life. Deep mining has been the world's most hazardous occupation. Miners lived with the everpresent danger of accidents and the possibility of suffering from black lung disease. Surface or strip mining was less costly in terms of human life and health. However, such mining could damage the environment.

Increased use of coal as a fuel also presented grave hazards to the environment. The effect of burning coal upon the world's climate was becoming a matter of increasing concern. "Acid rain" produced by chemicals released into the air by burning coal killed all the fish in many lakes and threatened both forests and farmlands.

Advances in technology helped to ease some of these problems. Nevertheless, much more research and planning are still needed.

Nuclear energy. Another energy option included a formidable challenge. This was the continuing development of nuclear power.

After World War II nuclear fission, the splitting of atoms, seemed to promise a safe, cheap, clean, and unlimited source of power. The failure of nuclear fission reactors to meet this early promise was not due entirely to technical problems, although these have been, and continue to be, very difficult and complex. The failure was due in part to the warnings of environmentalists and nuclear scientists, who insisted upon increasingly strict safety precautions. As nuclear knowledge has accumulated, a growing awareness has developed of the terrifying risks posed by this immensely complex technology.

These risks were clearly demonstrated in the spring of 1979 in what was generally acknowledged to be the nation's most serious nuclear accident. The accident occurred when the cooling system failed in a reactor at the

In March 1979 atomic energy experts raced to the Three Mile Island nuclear power plant. The plant's cooling system had malfunctioned, threatening a dangerous core meltdown. A disaster was averted, but clean-up costs were in the billions.

SOLAR-HEATED HOUSE

Solar collectors fitted with absorber plates are positioned on the roof to receive maximum sunlight. The plates heat air which is circulated through the collectors. The heated air is blown by a fan through ducts to the basement. There it heats storage rocks, which, in turn, heat a water system. Another fan circulates heat from the storage rocks throughout the house.

Three Mile Island power plant on the Susquehanna River near Harrisburg, Pennsylvania.

The core of the reactor, where radioactive materials produce the heat used to generate power, was damaged. For a time it seemed that a complete core "meltdown," which would release deadly radiation into the air, was possible. While scientists and engineers struggled to cool the reactor, plans were made to evacuate people within the surrounding area. Fortunately, the reactor was finally brought under control before a meltdown occurred.

The near-disaster heightened world-wide concern over the safety — and cost — of nuclear power. A year and a half after the accident, the power company reported that the cleanup work would cost an estimated $2.8 billion. The damaged reactor could not be back in operation before 1985, if then. Meanwhile, in other countries as well as in the United States, nuclear authorities began to develop stricter regulations for the design, location, and operation of power plants.

The problem of nuclear accidents was only one of the questions that troubled many scientists. How, they asked, is it possible with our present limited knowledge to determine what impact such nuclear installations might have upon human beings and all other forms of life? How could an absolutely foolproof method be developed to seal, transport, and store the deadly wastes produced by nuclear reactors?

The nuclear outlook. Energy from nuclear fission clearly presented serious problems. Nevertheless, many scientists and engineers believed that generating plants using nuclear materials could be reasonably safe sources of energy. Painstaking efforts were carried on throughout the world to control the hazards of nuclear energy. By 1980 more than 20 nations were operating nuclear generating facilities.

The United States had 72 plants in operation in 26 different states, and 90 construction permits had been granted for additional plants.

Scientists were also probing a potentially safer source of nuclear energy than the present process of splitting the atom. In 1980 the House of Representatives voted overwhelmingly to commit $20 billion over the next 20 years in an all-out effort to harness nuclear fusion. This is the process that feeds the fires of the sun. Up to now, scientists have been able to use it only to provide the awesome destructive power of the hydrogen bomb. If fusion could be tamed and controlled, it would provide the world with a virtually unlimited source of energy. Moreover, unlike nuclear fission with its deadly waste products, the principal by-product of fusion is non-radioactive helium.

Energy alternatives. There were, of course, other energy alternatives. One was the increased use of power generated by falling water—hydroelectricity. There were, however, limits to the amount of energy that could be secured from this source. Also, construction of the necessary dams would mean the flooding of valuable timber areas and irreplaceable farmland.

Another energy option was the development of geothermal energy, or power generated from hot gases and steam in the depths of the earth. Several such plants were operating in Europe and the United States. Any substantial increase in the use of geothermal energy would depend on further research and development.

One other potential source of energy was the ebb and flow of the ocean tides. The La Rance Tidal Project, located near St. Malo, France, had been harnessing this tidal energy successfully since 1968. It was the largest such project in the world. However, other countries, including China and the Soviet Union, also operated tidal generating plants. In 1980 Canada, determined to harness the tides in the Bay of Fundy, started construction of what would be the world's largest tidal plant.

The most promising possible energy source was the sun—the original source of all energy, past, present, and future. Solar energy is inexhaustible. Scientists estimated that all of the United States' energy requirements for an entire year could be met by the amount of solar energy that falls on the surface of Lake Erie in a single day!

Efforts to harness solar energy were increasingly successful in recent years. For example, solar batteries were developed to supply electricity to spacecraft. They were at first used in situations where only small amounts of electricity were needed and the high cost was not a problem. Moreover, current research was rapidly reducing the cost of solar batteries, and the prospects for the future seemed highly promising.

In the meantime, researchers in many countries were developing practical solar energy devices to provide hot water, to heat homes, and to supply energy for other uses. In 1975 President Ford signed into law the Solar Heating and Cooling Act to encourage the development of such devices in the United States over the next five years. The Carter administration offered tax incentives to encourage the adoption of other energy conservation measures.

America's energy future. A group of distinguished scholars brought out one of the most comprehensive studies of America's energy future in 1979. The report, *Energy Future,* concluded that none of the present conventional sources of energy—oil, natural gas, coal, and nuclear—would be likely to supply significantly more energy in the future than they were supplying in 1979.

The report contended that America's future depended upon the development of "unconventional" sources of energy—solar and conservation. Conservation includes the increasingly efficient use of conventional sources of energy. The report found that conservation could supply as much as 40 percent of the nation's energy needs during the 1980's. Solar energy, given substantial government support, could by the year 2000 supply some 20 percent of America's energy requirements.

Changes in government policy. The federal government was criticized for failing to act decisively on the energy problem. In the late 1970's it finally began to move.

In 1977 Congress made a modest beginning with the creation of a new Cabinet-level Department of Energy (DOE). One of the major functions of the new department was to conduct research and help coordinate efforts to develop solar energy and other alternative energy sources.

In 1978 President Carter, acting in spite of

strong public opposition, announced that he was going to remove controls regulating the price of domestic oil. The price of American-produced oil and gasoline immediately began to rise to the levels charged by the OPEC countries. Consumers reacted to the higher prices by reducing their consumption of gasoline and oil. This is what the President had hoped would happen when he announced deregulation. At the same time, however, the profits of the oil companies began to climb to record highs.

The following year President Carter presented a comprehensive energy program to Congress and to the American people. He proposed limiting oil imports to the 1977 levels, providing more aid for mass transit systems, and developing energy conservation measures. The heart of his program was a plan for encouraging private industry to develop synthetic fuels and the use of solar energy. The President believed that the entire cost could be covered by a tax on what he termed the "excess" profits of oil companies.

The Reagan administration brought a different approach to the energy problem. President Reagan favored some of Carter's moves. For example, he speeded up deregulation of domestic oil prices. Reagan argued that higher prices for domestic oil would encourage oil companies to search for and develop America's resources. This would, he believed, help free the nation of dependence on foreign oil.

In other areas Reagan's policies differed from Carter's. During his election campaign Reagan spoke of eliminating the Department of Energy. Although he took no immediate steps to do so, he did play down the importance of that department. Also, Reagan was not deeply committed to synthetic fuels projects. He favored heavy cuts in federal support for such projects.

Thus, by the early 1980's, several important changes had taken place in the nation's views on energy. American citizens, stung by higher prices and shortages, did take steps to conserve. Use of gasoline, for example, fell sharply. Owners of homes and businesses added insulation to their buildings and turned down heat in winter and cut back on air-conditioning in summer. Energy companies also made serious efforts to find new fuel sources. How long it would take for the nation to achieve energy independence remained a question.

Windmills have long been features of the American landscape (see page 448). Today scientists are studying the possibility of using windmills to generate electricity. This giant device was built by NASA.

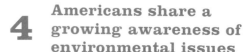

SECTION SURVEY

IDENTIFY: fossil fuels, cartel, OPEC, strip mining, acid rain, hydroelectricity, geothermal energy, conservation.

1. Why was it necessary for Americans to find alternatives to oil as an energy source?
2. (a) Name some of the alternative energy sources being used in the United States today. (b) What are the advantages and disadvantages of each?
3. Compare and contrast the energy programs of Presidents Carter and Reagan.

4 Americans share a growing awareness of environmental issues

The energy crisis of the 1970's was part of a broader problem. Learning to manage energy resources was just a step toward learning to manage the overall environment.

Geothermal power stations, like this one in California, produce energy while doing little harm to the environment. The station draws on the natural heat of the earth in the form of hot water or hot gases and converts it into electricity.

The impacts on the environment. By the 1960's and 1970's it was becoming ever more clear that serious damage was being done to the most essential of all the natural resources — air, water, and the earth itself.

Clean air in many cities had been replaced by smog. Some 200 million tons of pollutants poured into the air each year from motor vehicles, industries, homes, and power plants. Human and industrial wastes pouring into the nation's rivers had turned many into virtual sewers. Growing shortages of fresh water in many areas of the country led to strict regulations and sometimes to rationing.

The earth, as well as the air and the water, was deteriorating. Fertile land was being bulldozed to build highways, shopping malls, and housing developments. Irreplaceable farmland was vanishing at an estimated rate of 10,000 acres (4,000 hectares) every day.

The problem of wastes. The wastes produced by our industrial society created problems for every form of life on the planet. Urban areas alone generated hundreds of thousands of tons of garbage and solid waste every day. Hazardous wastes from chemical plants, nuclear reactors, and other industries polluted the air and accumulated in thousands of dumps across the countryside.

Finding proper ways to dispose of all the wastes, both liquid and solid, was difficult. Much of it could be burned. However, burning introduced pollutants into the air, and some burning wastes released poisonous fumes.

Burial was another widely used method of disposal. Some wastes decomposed safely or remained harmless underground. Other buried wastes could become deadly threats to the environment. This fact was driven home to the nation in a number of incidents. One of the worst disasters came to light in Niagara Falls, New York, in 1978.

There homes had been constructed near a ditch known as Love Canal. The chemical company that owned the ditch dumped steel drums of chemical wastes into it. The company covered the wastes and turned the land over to the city for use as a school and playground.

In time the steel drums rusted and deadly chemicals leaked out. They bubbled to the surface in foul-smelling pools and oozed into the basements of nearby homes. Residents complained of strange skin rashes and breathing

827

problems. A higher than normal percentage of them suffered cancer. Likewise, an abnormal number of children were born with birth defects.

Finally in 1978 President Carter declared a state of emergency in the area. The state government in the end agreed to evacuate about 800 families and to purchase their homes.

Managing resources. Many concerned citizens worried not just about pollutants added to the environment but also about resources removed from it. Oil shortages during the 1970's made clear that one day fuel might run out. Suddenly Americans began to realize that other vital resources might also be limited.

Much of the astonishing productivity of the United States has come from resources within its own borders. At the beginning of the 1900's, the United States produced about 15 percent more raw materials than it consumed. By 1940, however, American industry consumed more raw materials than the nation produced. Since then the gap has widened significantly.

During the past 25 years the United States has become increasingly dependent upon the rest of the world for a large part of the materials it needs to maintain its industrial productivity. Since 1954 the American people have used more minerals than the rest of the world has used since the beginning of human history! In the mid-1960's the United States contained only 6 percent of the world's population. Yet it was consuming more than 50 percent of the world's output of oil and nearly 90 percent of the total output of natural gas. It also consumed vast quantities of iron ore to produce half the world's supply of steel.

Some resources, such as lumber, are renewable. Others, such as metals, can be recycled. Still others, such as fossil fuels, can be used once—and then they are gone forever. Very few—solar energy is one—are inexhaustible.

The slow awakening. By the mid-1960's one historian reminded Americans that "less than a century divides the era when America was looked upon as a Garden of Eden or savage wilderness. Frankly, no people have ever so quickly subdued their natural environment." Usually Americans accomplished this with little concern for the laws of nature or for the consequences of violating these laws.

To be sure, as early as the 1890's the federal government had begun to reflect the concern of a few Americans about the need to conserve the nation's resources (see page 518). However, the early conservation movement, important though it was, had limited goals. The first conservationists were mainly concerned with regulating the use of particular resources—forests, wildlife, minerals, and the soil. A half century later, by the 1950's, more and more people were beginning to understand that the earth itself—including all its resources and all forms of life—was being endangered by the waste and misuse of resources.

Major credit for arousing public concern probably belonged as much to Rachel Carson as to any other single person. In her bestselling book *Silent Spring,* published in 1962, she warned that "along with the possibility of the extinction of mankind by nuclear war, the central problem of our age has . . . become the contamination of man's total environment." This warning received nation-wide attention and influenced the thinking of government officials and private citizens alike. During the next few years growing numbers of ecologists, biologists, and other scientists expressed alarm over the reckless misuse of the environment.

Government action. The Kennedy and Johnson administrations responded to these warnings with new programs to safeguard the environment. In addition, state and local governments stepped up their environmental efforts. In 1970, during Nixon's first term, Congress created the Environmental Protection Agency.

By the mid-1970's an impressive body of federal, state, and local laws had been enacted. Laws regulated the use of pesticides, insecticides, and other potentially dangerous sprays. Species of wildlife threatened with extinction had been protected. Automobile manufacturers had to provide pollution control devices on exhausts of cars, trucks, and buses. Clean-air standards had been established for factories, office buildings, and apartment houses. New waste disposal and sewage treatment plants were being built to prevent further pollution of the land and water and to clean up the rivers and lakes.

Efforts had also been made to restore the natural beauty of the countryside by regulating unsightly junkyards and dumps. Federal and state governments set aside more land to preserve as wilderness or parks for future generations. Considerable progress had been made

PEDAL POWER

The young Californian stood on the coast of southern England and gazed toward France across the English Channel. "It just seemed to go on and on," he recalled later. "I concluded that everybody here was right—we were crazy." Even so, Bryan Allen and his companions went ahead with their plans. Their goal was to fly across the Channel using only human muscle power—that is, Allen's pedaling. Their reward, if successful, would be a prize of £100,000 (about $220,000) offered by a British industrialist. There would also be the satisfaction of having achieved both an air record and an ecological breakthrough.

Allen, who had been training by bicycling for months, was now ready. So was the plane, the *Gossamer Albatross,* designed by Paul Mac-Cready. Built of the lightest carbon-filament tubing sheathed in translucent plastic, the fragile craft weighed just 75 pounds (34 kilograms). Inside the tiny cockpit was Allen's bicycle-like apparatus, its pedals connected to a propeller. He hoped to make the flight in a little under two hours.

Allen took off early on the morning of June 12, 1979. "What audacity," he thought, "to challenge the elements in such a machine." The flight was not an easy one. Air currents sometimes forced the *Gossamer Albatross* down to less than a foot above the choppy waves of the Channel. Allen's radio failed and his water supply also gave out. Head winds cut into his speed, while leg cramps caused him terrible pain.

Then the coast of France came into sight! Allen regained hope, running on reserves he never knew he had. After almost three hours in the air, the exhausted pilot landed among 300 welcomers. Engineer MacCready summed it up: "It's a specialized thing . . . but it certainly does alter one's perspective of what man is capable of, both in design and actual powering of things."

in the management and conservation of America's forests, soil, and water. Only a small beginning had been made in conserving and recycling natural resources.

Economy and environment. In spite of the complexity of environmental problems mentioned above, not all Americans felt that increased action by the federal government was necessary. As economic conditions in the nation worsened in the late 1970's, many people called for the government to ease environmental regulations.

These critics argued that meeting strict clean air and clean water requirements costs billions of dollars. Foreign businesses that did not have to meet these standards were able to produce goods more cheaply and thus gain a larger share of the world market. Also, critics charged, federal regulations were often unclear and contradictory. These critics wanted the cost of such regulations to be weighed against the benefits they produced. Only if the benefits exceeded the costs would the regulations be enforced.

Many Americans also believed that restrictions on the use of federal lands should be relaxed. They felt that since the nation's industries desperately needed mineral resources, it made good sense to search for them on federal lands.

President Reagan agreed with many of these points. He proposed cutting back and simplifying environmental regulations. He also encouraged the search for mineral resources on federal lands. One of the first acts of his Secretary of the Interior, James Watt, was to propose opening sections of the sea floor off California to oil exploration. Environmentalists argued that the risk of oil spills on these sites posed a grave threat to a particularly scenic area of the California coast.

A global matter. Whatever actions the United States took regarding the environment would have consequences far beyond its borders. The same was true for any actions taken by other nations.

Worldwide developments have brought increasing pressure upon the natural environ-

Wrangell, Alaska, is located in an area of great beauty and rich natural resources. The citizens of Wrangell, like other American citizens, will face important decisions in the years to come about how to manage those resources while maintaining the natural environment.

ment. First, world population has been doubling nearly every 35 years. Just to maintain people's standards of living at their present level would require, during the next generation, the production of twice as much food, clothing, shelter, and industrialized goods. The demand upon increasingly scarce raw materials, many of them irreplaceable, will be enormous. Yet such a great increase in production would do nothing to improve the living conditions of most of a projected world population of more than 6 billion men, women, and children by the year 2000.

A question of responsibility. The United States is one of the world's richest nations. It produces more than 25 percent of all the grain grown on the face of the earth. It also has the largest pool of scientists, engineers, and management experts of any industrial nation. With so much wealth and so much talent, the United States cannot avoid sharing the responsibilities of world leadership.

During the twentieth century Americans have been foremost in the movement into the scientific-technological world. Because they have often led the way, Americans have been among the first to meet the consequences of the reckless use of land and resources.

Urgent though the challenges are, the American people had reason to move into the future with confidence. The same scientific genius and engineering talents that unknowingly created many of the as yet unsolved problems remain available to solve them.

In 1976 Americans had celebrated their nation's 200th birthday. They looked back with pride upon all those years of growth. For generation after generation, Americans had repeatedly demonstrated an amazing ability to adjust to changing ways and changing times. Americans in the 1980's were, for the most part, certain that in future years they would meet and overcome new problems and challenges. They recognized that, more than ever before, the power to shape the future lay in their hands.

SECTION SURVEY

IDENTIFY: smog, Love Canal, Rachel Carson, James Watt.

1. By the mid-1970's, what steps had the federal government taken to try to protect the environment?

2. In what ways is the United States dependent on other nations in order to maintain its industrial productivity?

3. Why have some people called for easing environmental regulations?

4. Is environmental pollution simply an American problem? Explain.

Chapter Survey

Summary: Tracing the Main Ideas

Through the centuries the nation has grown from a rural society of small villages and towns to an urban society of large cities and suburbs. The economy of the United States has developed from a simple one based on self-sufficient farming to an infinitely more complex one based on the technology of an industrial society. The nation has emerged from relative isolation to a role of world leadership.

As the nation moved into the third century of its existence, a new generation of Americans faced new problems, new challenges, and new opportunities. The federal government and its budgets had grown greatly since the 1930's, and many citizens were asking if such growth was necessary and helpful. The American economy, a marvel to people the world over, seemed to falter in the face of continuing problems with inflation and increasing international competition. The American land, with its beauty and its wealth of natural resources, needed thoughtful care and management to insure that its treasures would be passed on to future generations.

The American people have solved many immense problems during the course of their nation's history. They need only the will and the commitment to meet the new challenges of the future.

Inquiring Into History

1. How have computers changed Americans' way of life?
2. Describe the economic problems facing the United States when Ronald Reagan became President.
3. Can the United States try to solve its economic problems without regard for the economic situation in the rest of the world? Why or why not?
4. (a) What are some causes of the environmental problems that the United States faces today? (b) How are Americans trying to solve these problems?

Relating Past to Present

1. "Human history becomes more and more a race between education and catastrophe." How does this statement apply to the world today?
2. Pollution of the land and water and misuse of resources began with the first European settlements in America. Explain.

Developing Social Science Skills

1. Read the financial section of a daily newspaper for a week or more. (a) What factors do economists seem to consider in judging the state of the economy? (b) What connections seem to exist between the value of the dollar and the price of gold? between interest rates and stock market averages? (c) What actions for solving economic problems does the newspaper seem to favor?
2. Draw a series of political cartoons about issues discussed in Chapter 43. Be sure your cartoon clearly presents a point of view about the issue.
3. List the advantages and disadvantages of using each of the following as a major source of energy: oil, natural gas, coal, nuclear, solar. Then rank them according to your findings.

Unit Survey

For Further Inquiry

1. Why might conflicts arise between the two goals of protecting the environment and decreasing United States dependence on foreign oil?

2. Do you think that during the 1960's and 1970's the United States assumed more responsibility around the world than it could meet? Give evidence to support your answer.

3. (a) What is the Third World? (b) How did its emergence affect the relationships between the United States and the Soviet Union?

4. Consider the New Deal, the Fair Deal, the New Frontier, and the Great Society. (a) How were they similar? (b) How were they different?

5. Make a chart comparing blacks, Hispanics, Indians, and women in terms of (a) problems, (b) goals, (c) methods used to achieve goals, (d) degree of success.

6. Of the six Presidents since 1960, which do you think was the best? Be sure to explain the standards by which you made your judgment.

Projects and Activities

1. (a) Based on the timeline here, what evidence is there that United States foreign policy has stayed basically the same since 1960? (b) What evidence is there that American foreign policy has changed in significant ways since 1960? (c) Make a timeline of domestic events since 1960. Do there seem to be any connections between foreign and domestic affairs? Explain.

2. Study the map and charts on page 855 concerning America's world trade. (a) In which area of the world are America's major trading partners? (b) Does the United States import more than it exports? How can you tell? (c) Does the United States export more raw materials or manufactured goods?

3. Listen to a record of speeches by Dr. Martin Luther King, Jr. (a) Summarize briefly the main point of each speech. (b) Do you find the speeches persuasive? Why or why not?

4. Draw political cartoons that might have appeared during the administration of one of the Presidents discussed in Unit 13. Be sure to make clear the point of view of each cartoon.

Exploring Your Region

1. What is being done in your area about the energy crisis? (For example, is there increased availability of gasohol? More solar energy in use? More incentives to install insulation in houses?)

2. Prepare a map of all or part of your municipality, divided into its voting precincts. Indicate how each precinct voted in the Presidential election of 1980. Try to find out why the voting results were the way they were. (You might look into the number of voters registered in each party in each precinct or the ethnic or economic breakdown of the population in each precinct.)

Suggested Readings

1. *Promises to Keep,* Chester Bowles. Autobiography of a man who served in diplomatic and other posts under six American Presidents.

2. *The Mexican American People: The Nation's Second Largest Minority,* Leo Grebler, Joan W. Moore, and Ralph C. Guzmán, et al. Thorough study of Mexican Americans in the Southwest.

3. *Silent Spring,* Rachel Carson. An influential and moving warning about pesticides.

4. *Roots,* Alex Haley. Story of the author's search for his own past—from Africa in the 1700's to the American South today.

5. *When the Legends Die,* Hal Borland. A novel of Tom Black Bull, a young Indian man, who tries to "find himself" after leaving the reservation.

Historical
Atlas

of the
United States

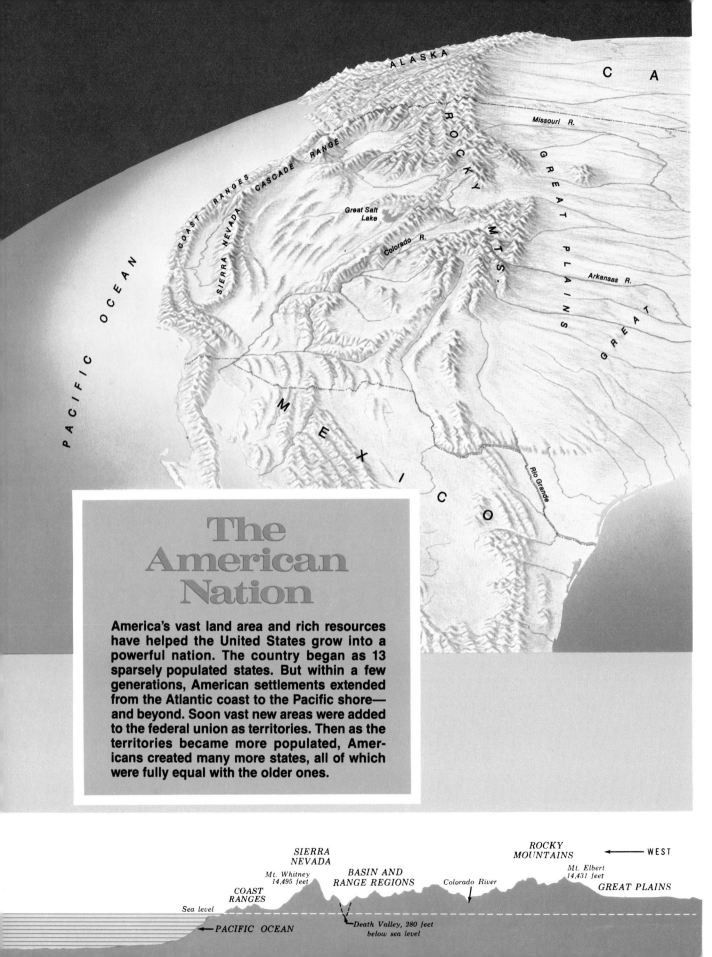

The American Nation

America's vast land area and rich resources have helped the United States grow into a powerful nation. The country began as 13 sparsely populated states. But within a few generations, American settlements extended from the Atlantic coast to the Pacific shore—and beyond. Soon vast new areas were added to the federal union as territories. Then as the territories became more populated, Americans created many more states, all of which were fully equal with the older ones.

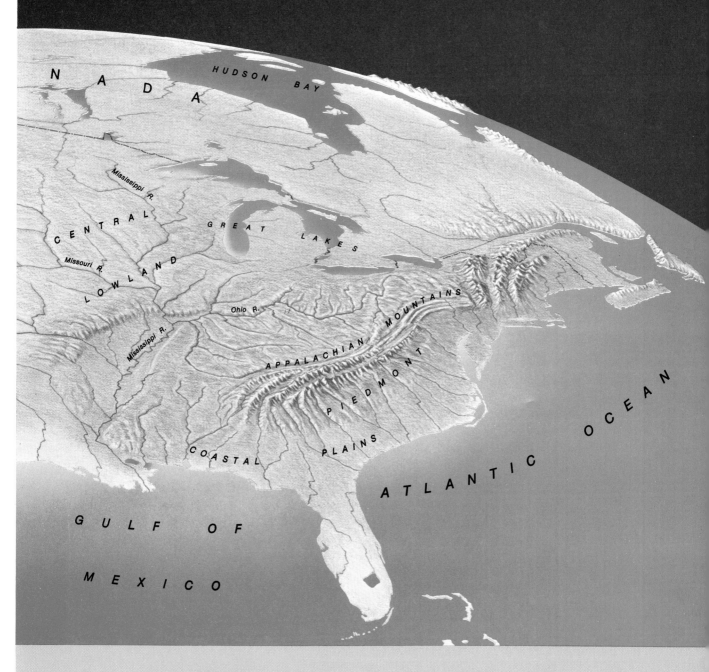

Above is a revealing view of the United States from far above the earth's surface—a view of the country's varied natural features as an astronaut might see them if there were no clouds to hinder observation. The elevation profile below has never been seen by astronauts or anyone else, for this drawing depicts how the country would look if a deep trench were cut from one end of the United States to the other. It reveals a side view of the natural features of the land. See if you can locate the same mountain ranges, plains, and river valleys depicted on both the map and the elevation profile.

EAST ⟶

CENTRAL   LOWLAND

APPALACHIAN
HIGHLANDS

PRAIRIES   OZARK MTS.   ⌐Mississippi River

Mt. Mitchell
6,684 feet

COASTAL
PLAIN

Sea level

ATLANTIC OCEAN ⟶

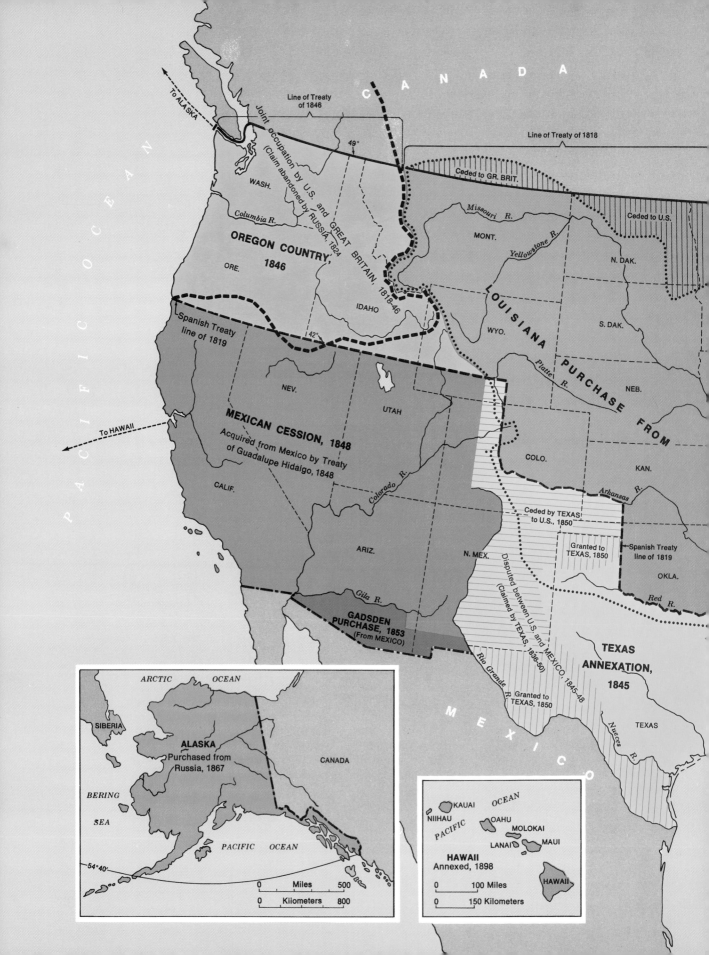

CANADA

To ALASKA

Line of Treaty of 1846

Line of Treaty of 1818

Joint occupation by U.S. and GREAT BRITAIN (Claim abandoned by RUSSIA, 1824)

49°

Ceded to GR. BRIT.

Ceded to U.S.

PACIFIC OCEAN

WASH.

Columbia R.

Missouri R.

MONT.

Yellowstone R.

N. DAK.

OREGON COUNTRY, 1846

ORE.

IDAHO

18-46

WYO.

S. DAK.

LOUISIANA PURCHASE FROM

Spanish Treaty line of 1819

42°

NEV.

UTAH

Platte R.

NEB.

To HAWAII

MEXICAN CESSION, 1848

Acquired from Mexico by Treaty of Guadalupe Hidalgo, 1848

COLO.

KAN.

Ceded by TEXAS to U.S., 1850

Arkansas R.

CALIF.

Colorado R.

Granted to TEXAS, 1850

Spanish Treaty line of 1819

ARIZ.

N. MEX.

OKLA.

Gila R.

Red R.

GADSDEN PURCHASE, 1853
(From MEXICO)

Disputed between U.S. and MEXICO, 1845-48 (Claimed by TEXAS, 1836-50)

Rio Grande R.

Granted to TEXAS, 1850

TEXAS ANNEXATION, 1845

MEXICO

Nueces R.

TEXAS

ARCTIC OCEAN

SIBERIA

ALASKA
Purchased from Russia, 1867

CANADA

BERING SEA

PACIFIC OCEAN

54°40'

0   Miles   500

0   Kilometers   800

OCEAN

KAUAI

NIIHAU

OAHU

MOLOKAI

PACIFIC

LANAI

MAUI

HAWAII
Annexed, 1898

HAWAII

0   100 Miles

0   150 Kilometers

Territorial Growth of the United States

Line of Webster-Ashburton Treaty, 1842

Line of Treaty of Paris, 1783

Line of Webster-Ashburton Treaty, 1842

C A N A D A

Lake of the Woods

Ceded to U.S.

Ceded to U.S.

St. Lawrence R.

ME.

Lake Superior

VT.

N.H.

MINN.

Lake Michigan

Lake Huron

MICH.

WIS.

Mississippi R.

N.Y.

MASS.

Lake Ontario

CONN.

R.I.

IOWA

ILL.

THE UNITED STATES IN 1783

Acquired during the Revolutionary War and by Treaty of Paris, 1783

PA.

N.J.

IND.

OHIO

MD.

DEL.

Ohio R.

W. VA.

VA.

FRANCE, 1803

MO.

KY.

THE ORIGINAL THIRTEEN STATES

N.C.

TENN.

ARK.

Mississippi R.

ATLANTIC OCEAN

MISS.

ALA.

GA.

S.C.

Disputed between U.S. and SPAIN, 1783-95

LA.

Sabine R.

1810

1813

FLA.

WEST FLORIDA

EAST FLORIDA, 1819

CEDED BY SPAIN, 1819

Claimed by SPAIN until 1819

GULF OF MEXICO

	Disputed with Great Britain
	Disputed with Spain
	Disputed with Mexico
·········	Natural boundary of Louisiana
▬ ▬ ▬	Natural boundary of Oregon Country
⌒	Boundary adjustments with Great Britain
– – –	Present-day state boundaries

0 — Miles — 500

0 — Kilometers — 800

C U B A

837

The federal government and the many state and local governments were small at first. But as the country's population and needs grew, so did the number of government employees. Federal, state, and local governments needed more employees and more money to meet their responsibilities in areas such as public welfare, education, and defense. To pay for the increased expenditures, governments increased taxes and added some new ones, such as income taxes and taxes for the social security fund. In recent years there have been many demands to reduce government taxes. There also have been demands for limiting government spending in many areas. You can become more informed about the issues raised in these demands by studying the graphs on the accompanying pages.

The Growth of the Federal Union

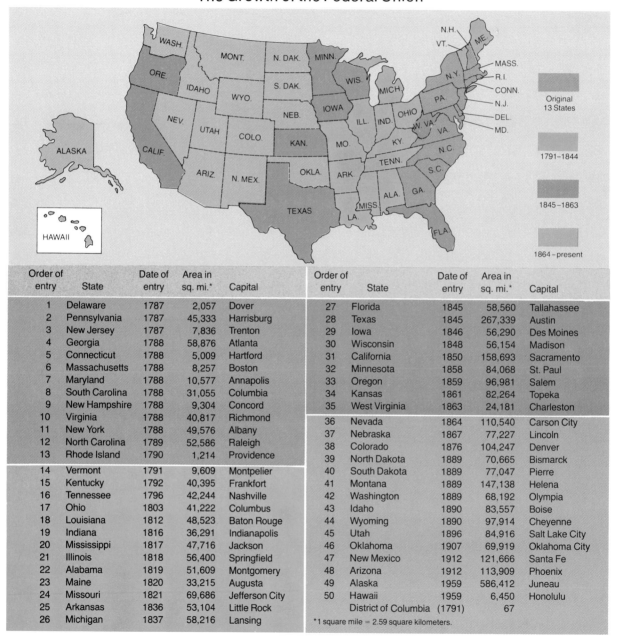

Order of entry	State	Date of entry	Area in sq. mi.*	Capital	Order of entry	State	Date of entry	Area in sq. mi.*	Capital
1	Delaware	1787	2,057	Dover	27	Florida	1845	58,560	Tallahassee
2	Pennsylvania	1787	45,333	Harrisburg	28	Texas	1845	267,339	Austin
3	New Jersey	1787	7,836	Trenton	29	Iowa	1846	56,290	Des Moines
4	Georgia	1788	58,876	Atlanta	30	Wisconsin	1848	56,154	Madison
5	Connecticut	1788	5,009	Hartford	31	California	1850	158,693	Sacramento
6	Massachusetts	1788	8,257	Boston	32	Minnesota	1858	84,068	St. Paul
7	Maryland	1788	10,577	Annapolis	33	Oregon	1859	96,981	Salem
8	South Carolina	1788	31,055	Columbia	34	Kansas	1861	82,264	Topeka
9	New Hampshire	1788	9,304	Concord	35	West Virginia	1863	24,181	Charleston
10	Virginia	1788	40,817	Richmond	36	Nevada	1864	110,540	Carson City
11	New York	1788	49,576	Albany	37	Nebraska	1867	77,227	Lincoln
12	North Carolina	1789	52,586	Raleigh	38	Colorado	1876	104,247	Denver
13	Rhode Island	1790	1,214	Providence	39	North Dakota	1889	70,665	Bismarck
14	Vermont	1791	9,609	Montpelier	40	South Dakota	1889	77,047	Pierre
15	Kentucky	1792	40,395	Frankfort	41	Montana	1889	147,138	Helena
16	Tennessee	1796	42,244	Nashville	42	Washington	1889	68,192	Olympia
17	Ohio	1803	41,222	Columbus	43	Idaho	1890	83,557	Boise
18	Louisiana	1812	48,523	Baton Rouge	44	Wyoming	1890	97,914	Cheyenne
19	Indiana	1816	36,291	Indianapolis	45	Utah	1896	84,916	Salt Lake City
20	Mississippi	1817	47,716	Jackson	46	Oklahoma	1907	69,919	Oklahoma City
21	Illinois	1818	56,400	Springfield	47	New Mexico	1912	121,666	Santa Fe
22	Alabama	1819	51,609	Montgomery	48	Arizona	1912	113,909	Phoenix
23	Maine	1820	33,215	Augusta	49	Alaska	1959	586,412	Juneau
24	Missouri	1821	69,686	Jefferson City	50	Hawaii	1959	6,450	Honolulu
25	Arkansas	1836	53,104	Little Rock		District of Columbia	(1791)	67	
26	Michigan	1837	58,216	Lansing		*1 square mile = 2.59 square kilometers.			

Federal Receipts

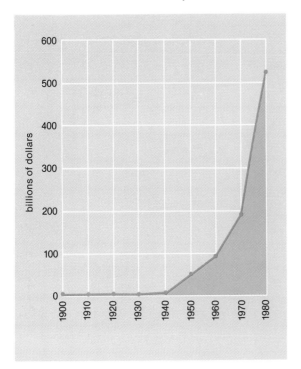

Federal Outlays

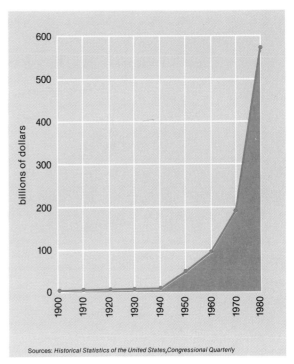

Sources: *Historical Statistics of the United States, Congressional Quarterly*

Distribution of Outlays

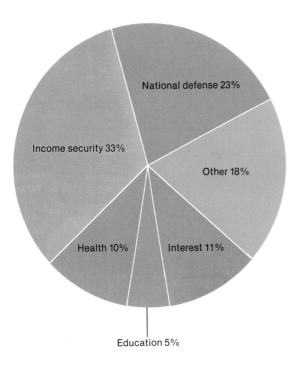

National defense 23%

Income security 33%

Other 18%

Health 10%

Interest 11%

Education 5%

Source: *The United States Budget in Brief*, 1980 data

Number of Government Employees

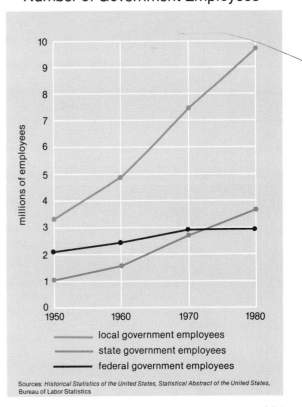

local government employees

state government employees

federal government employees

Sources: *Historical Statistics of the United States, Statistical Abstract of the United States,*
Bureau of Labor Statistics

States and Cities of the United States

ONTARIO

QUEBEC

CENTRAL TIME

EASTERN TIME

CANADA

NEW BRUNSWICK

NOVA SCOTIA

Caribou

MAINE

Bangor

Augusta ⊛

Lewiston

Hibbing

Lake Superior

Duluth

Sault Ste. Marie

Burlington

Montpelier

N.H.

Portland

MINNESOTA

Superior

Lake Huron

VT.

Concord ⊛

Manchester

St. Paul ⊛

WISCONSIN

NEW YORK

Boston ⊛

Minneapolis

Eau Claire

Green Bay

M
I
C
H
I
G
A
N

Syracuse

Utica

Troy

MASS.

Worcester

Rochester

Oshkosh

Lake Ontario

Schenectady

Albany ⊛

Hartford ⊛

CONN.

Providence ⊛

R.I.

Mason City

Madison ⊛

Lake Michigan

Milwaukee

Grand Rapids

Flint

Buffalo

Rochester

IOWA

Dubuque

Racine

Lansing ⊛

Detroit

Binghamton

Scranton

Newark

New York

Sioux City

Cedar Rapids

Rockford

Chicago

Kalamazoo

Lake Erie

Cleveland

Erie

PENNSYLVANIA

Trenton ⊛

Davenport

Rock Island

Gary

South Bend

Toledo

Warren

Youngstown

Philadelphia

Camden

N.J.

Des Moines ⊛

Fort Wayne

OHIO

Akron

Canton

Harrisburg ⊛

York

DE.

Peoria

Dayton

Columbus ⊛

Pittsburgh

Wheeling

Baltimore

Dover ⊛

ILLINOIS

INDIANA

Indianapolis ⊛

Cincinnati

W. VA.

Washington

Annapolis ⊛

MD.

St. Joseph

Hannibal

Springfield ⊛

Charleston ⊛

VIRGINIA

ansas City

Kansas City

St. Louis

East St. Louis

Evansville

Covington

Frankfort ⊛

Lexington

Huntington

Richmond ⊛

Topeka

Louisville

Jefferson City ⊛

MISSOURI

Cairo

KENTUCKY

Roanoke

Norfolk

Cape Girardeau

Paducah

Owensboro

Springfield

Middlesboro

Oak Ridge

Knoxville

Greensboro

Raleigh ⊛

Tulsa

Jonesboro

Nashville ⊛

TENNESSEE

Asheville

NORTH CAROLINA

ee

Jackson

Charlotte

Wilmington

Fort Smith

Memphis

Chattanooga

Greenville

SOUTH

Hot Springs

Little Rock ⊛

Huntsville

Columbia ⊛

Pine Bluff

Birmingham

Atlanta ⊛

CAROLINA

ARKANSAS

MISSISSIPPI

Charleston

rant

El Dorado

Columbus

ALABAMA

GEORGIA

Macon

Tyler

Shreveport

Jackson ⊛

Meridian

Columbus

Savannah

LOUISIANA

Montgomery ⊛

Albany

Alexandria

Natchez

Valdosta

Beaumont

Lake Charles

Mobile

Pensacola

Tallahassee ⊛

Jacksonville

Houston

Baton Rouge ⊛

Biloxi

New Orleans

Gainesville

FLORIDA

Galveston

Orlando

Tampa

GULF OF MEXICO

St. Petersburg

West Palm Beach

Ft. Myers

Boca Raton

Ft. Lauderdale

Miami

Key West

C U B A

ATLANTIC OCEAN

West longitude

North latitude

60°

45°

40°

65°

35°

30°

25°

20°

⊛ State Capital

⊛ United States standard time zones are indicated by clocks (When it is 12:00 noon in Western Alaska, it is 6:00 p.m. along the eastern coast of the United States.)

– – – Boundaries of time zones

0	Miles	500
0	Kilometers	800

95° 90° 85° 80° 75° 70°

841

The American People

The people who settled America came from many lands. Indeed, all Americans were immigrants or the descendants of immigrants. The American Indians, the first Americans, for example, originally were hunting peoples who came to North America from Asia. Today the United States has a diverse population, composed of people with many national and racial backgrounds, religious beliefs, and regional loyalties. The following graphs and charts tell much about these Americans. One graph portrays which decades experienced the largest immigration to this country. Another graph shows which countries were the former homes of large numbers of Americans. The following pages also provide information on how quickly the population of the country grew over the years and how specific regions, states, and cities have participated in this growth. In addition, this section of the Atlas highlights certain trends that concern all Americans. There are graphs which show a rise in average life expectancy, a growth in family income, and an increase in educational enrollment. Graphs and charts, such as these shown here, are valuable reference tools for the study of the history of the United States. They support many of the former themes stated in the text and provide a richer understanding of the American experience.

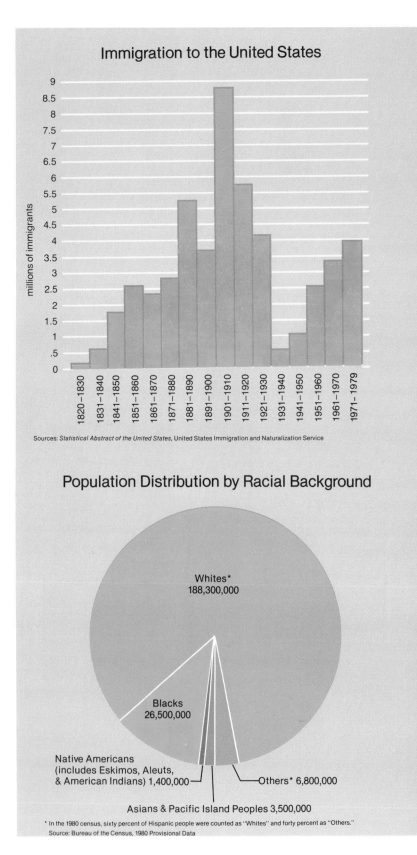

Immigration to the United States

millions of immigrants

Sources: *Statistical Abstract of the United States*, United States Immigration and Naturalization Service

Population Distribution by Racial Background

Whites*
188,300,000

Blacks
26,500,000

Native Americans
(includes Eskimos, Aleuts,
& American Indians) 1,400,000

Others* 6,800,000

Asians & Pacific Island Peoples 3,500,000

* In the 1980 census, sixty percent of Hispanic people were counted as "Whites" and forty percent as "Others."
Source: Bureau of the Census, 1980 Provisional Data

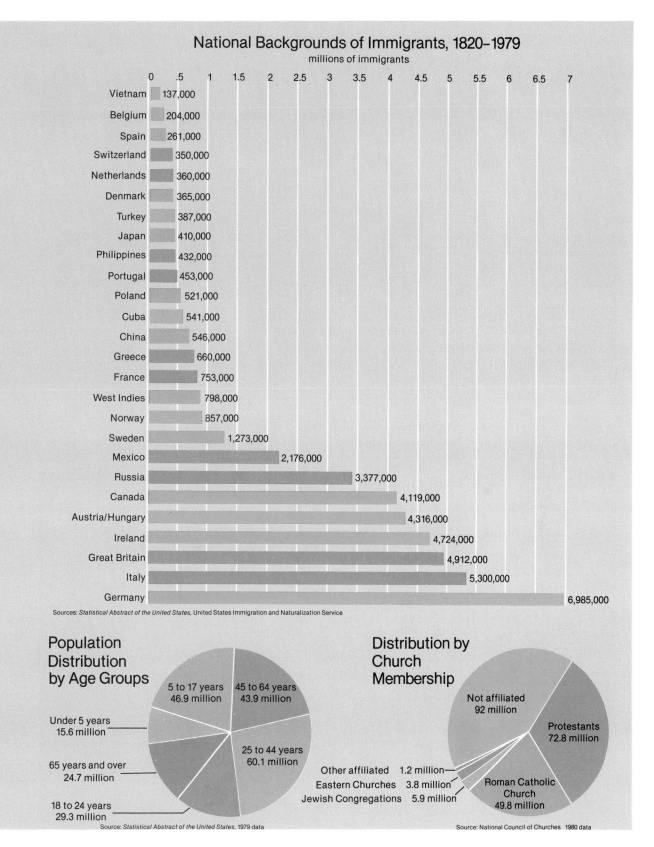

National Backgrounds of Immigrants, 1820–1979

millions of immigrants

Country	Immigrants
Vietnam	137,000
Belgium	204,000
Spain	261,000
Switzerland	350,000
Netherlands	360,000
Denmark	365,000
Turkey	387,000
Japan	410,000
Philippines	432,000
Portugal	453,000
Poland	521,000
Cuba	541,000
China	546,000
Greece	660,000
France	753,000
West Indies	798,000
Norway	857,000
Sweden	1,273,000
Mexico	2,176,000
Russia	3,377,000
Canada	4,119,000
Austria/Hungary	4,316,000
Ireland	4,724,000
Great Britain	4,912,000
Italy	5,300,000
Germany	6,985,000

Sources: *Statistical Abstract of the United States*, United States Immigration and Naturalization Service

Population Distribution by Age Groups

- 5 to 17 years 46.9 million
- 45 to 64 years 43.9 million
- Under 5 years 15.6 million
- 25 to 44 years 60.1 million
- 65 years and over 24.7 million
- 18 to 24 years 29.3 million

Source: *Statistical Abstract of the United States*, 1979 data

Distribution by Church Membership

- Not affiliated 92 million
- Protestants 72.8 million
- Other affiliated 1.2 million
- Eastern Churches 3.8 million
- Jewish Congregations 5.9 million
- Roman Catholic Church 49.8 million

Source: National Council of Churches 1980 data

Settlement of the United States

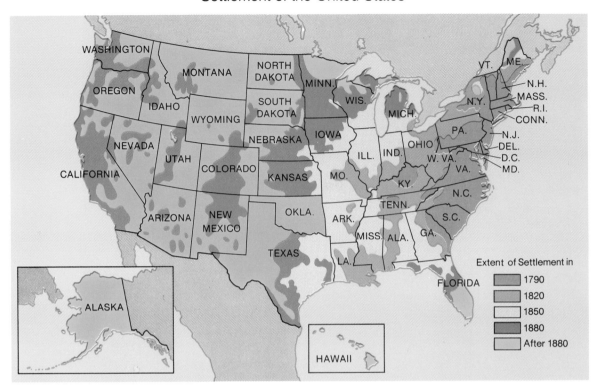

Extent of Settlement in
- 1790
- 1820
- 1850
- 1880
- After 1880

WASHINGTON, MONTANA, NORTH DAKOTA, MINN., VT., ME., N.H., MASS., R.I., CONN., OREGON, IDAHO, WYOMING, SOUTH DAKOTA, WIS., MICH., N.Y., PA., N.J., DEL., D.C., MD., NEVADA, UTAH, NEBRASKA, IOWA, ILL., IND., OHIO, W. VA., VA., CALIFORNIA, COLORADO, KANSAS, MO., KY., N.C., ARIZONA, NEW MEXICO, OKLA., ARK., TENN., S.C., TEXAS, MISS., ALA., GA., LA., FLORIDA

ALASKA

HAWAII

Population Distribution in the United States

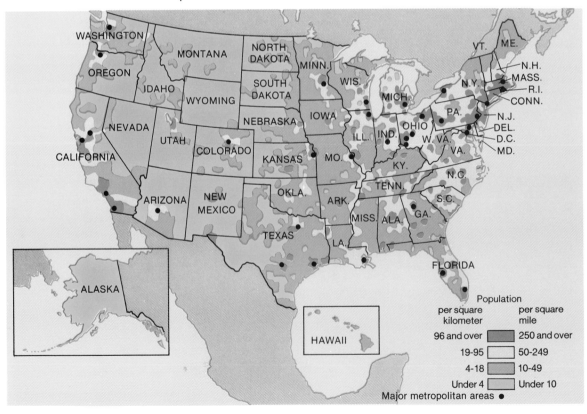

Population
per square kilometer	per square mile
96 and over	250 and over
19-95	50-249
4-18	10-49
Under 4	Under 10

Major metropolitan areas ●

WASHINGTON, MONTANA, NORTH DAKOTA, MINN., VT., ME., N.H., MASS., R.I., CONN., OREGON, IDAHO, WYOMING, SOUTH DAKOTA, WIS., MICH., N.Y., PA., N.J., DEL., D.C., MD., NEVADA, UTAH, NEBRASKA, IOWA, ILL., IND., OHIO, W. VA., VA., CALIFORNIA, COLORADO, KANSAS, MO., KY., N.C., ARIZONA, NEW MEXICO, OKLA., ARK., TENN., S.C., TEXAS, MISS., ALA., GA., LA., FLORIDA

ALASKA

HAWAII

844

Population Growth of States and their Largest Cities

State	Population at first census after entry	State population 1980 (prel.)	Represen- tatives in Congress	Largest city in 1980	City population in 1890	City population in 1930	City population 1980 (prel.)
1 Delaware	59,000	548,000	1	Wilmington	61,431	106,597	70,366
2 Pennsylvania	434,000	11,828,095	23	Philadelphia	1,046,964	1,950,961	1,680,235
3 New Jersey	184,000	7,342,164	14	Newark	181,830	442,337	329,498
4 Georgia	83,000	5,404,384	10	Atlanta	65,533	270,366	422,293
5 Connecticut	238,000	3,096,454	6	Bridgeport	48,866	146,716	142,459
6 Massachusetts	379,000	5,728,288	11	Boston	448,477	781,188	562,582
7 Maryland	320,000	4,198,113	8	Baltimore	434,439	804,874	784,554
8 South Carolina	249,000	3,069,825	6	Columbia	15,353	51,581	97,104
9 New Hampshire	142,000	919,114	2	Manchester	44,126	76,834	90,757
10 Virginia	692,000	5,323,412	10	Norfolk	34,871	129,710	262,803
11 New York	340,000	17,507,541	34	New York	2,507,414	6,930,446	7,015,608
12 North Carolina	394,000	5,847,788	11	Charlotte	11,557	82,675	310,799
13 Rhode Island	69,000	945,835	2	Providence	132,146	252,981	156,519
14 Vermont	154,000	511,299	1	Burlington	14,500	24,789	37,727
15 Kentucky	221,000	3,642,795	7	Louisville	161,129	307,745	298,161
16 Tennessee	106,000	4,545,590	9	Memphis	64,495	253,143	644,838
17 Ohio	231,000	10,772,432	21	Cleveland	261,353	900,429	572,532
18 Louisiana	153,000	4,199,542	8	New Orleans	242,039	458,762	556,913
19 Indiana	147,000	5,461,103	10	Indianapolis	105,436	364,161	695,040
20 Mississippi	75,000	2,511,491	5	Jackson	5,920	48,282	200,338
21 Illinois	55,000	11,355,062	22	Chicago	1,099,850	3,376,438	2,969,570
22 Alabama	128,000	3,870,251	7	Birmingham	26,178	259,678	282,068
23 Maine	298,000	1,123,670	2	Portland	36,425	70,810	61,575
24 Missouri	140,000	4,906,480	9	St. Louis	451,770	821,960	448,640
25 Arkansas	98,000	2,284,037	4	Little Rock	25,874	81,679	153,831
26 Michigan	212,000	9,238,634	18	Detroit	205,876	1,568,662	1,192,222
27 Florida	87,000	9,579,963	19	Jacksonville	17,201	129,549	541,269
28 Texas	213,000	14,173,876	27	Houston	27,557	292,352	1,554,992
29 Iowa	192,000	2,909,463	6	Des Moines	50,093	142,559	190,910
30 Wisconsin	305,000	4,693,941	9	Milwaukee	204,468	578,249	632,989
31 California	93,000	23,545,061	45	Los Angeles	50,395	1,238,048	2,950,010
32 Minnesota	172,000	4,069,356	8	Minneapolis	164,738	464,356	370,091
33 Oregon	52,000	2,618,126	5	Portland	46,385	301,815	364,891
34 Kansas	364,000	2,356,032	5	Wichita	23,853	111,110	279,352
35 West Virginia	442,000	1,930,787	4	Huntington	10,108	75,572	63,626
36 Nevada	42,000	800,312	2	Las Vegas	0	5,165	162,960
37 Nebraska	123,000	1,564,901	3	Omaha	148,514	214,006	312,929
38 Colorado	194,000	2,882,061	6	Denver	106,713	287,861	489,318
39 North Dakota	191,000	652,437	1	Fargo	5,664	28,619	61,281
40 South Dakota	349,000	688,217	1	Sioux Falls	7,205	33,362	81,071
41 Montana	143,000	783,698	2	Billings	836	16,380	68,361
42 Washington	357,000	4,114,738	8	Seattle	42,837	365,583	491,897
43 Idaho	89,000	943,629	2	Boise	2,311	21,544	102,125
44 Wyoming	63,000	468,954	1	Cheyenne	11,690	17,361	47,207
45 Utah	277,000	1,459,010	3	Salt Lake City	44,843	140,267	162,985
46 Oklahoma	1,657,000	3,001,252	6	Oklahoma City	4,151	185,389	401,002
47 New Mexico	360,000	1,295,474	3	Albuquerque	3,785	26,570	382,837
48 Arizona	334,000	2,719,225	5	Phoenix	3,152	48,118	781,443
49 Alaska	229,000	400,142	1	Anchorage	0	2,500	173,992
50 Hawaii	642,000	964,680	2	Honolulu	22,907	138,445	365,114
District of Columbia	8,000 (1800)	635,233	—	Washington, D.C.	188,932	486,869	635,223

Growth of Population in the United States

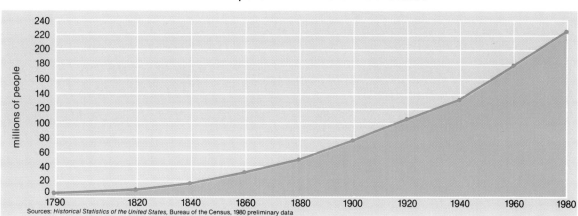

Sources: *Historical Statistics of the United States*, Bureau of the Census, 1980 preliminary data

Population Shifts Among the States

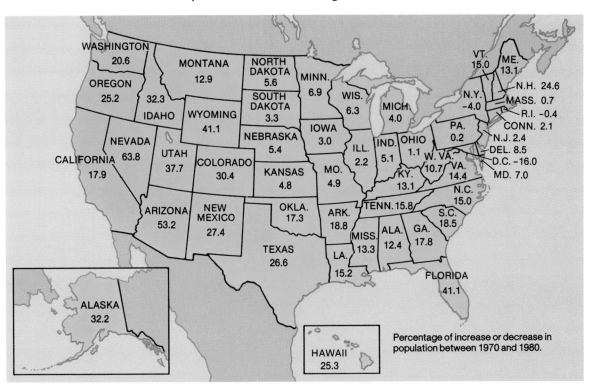

Percentage of increase or decrease in population between 1970 and 1980.

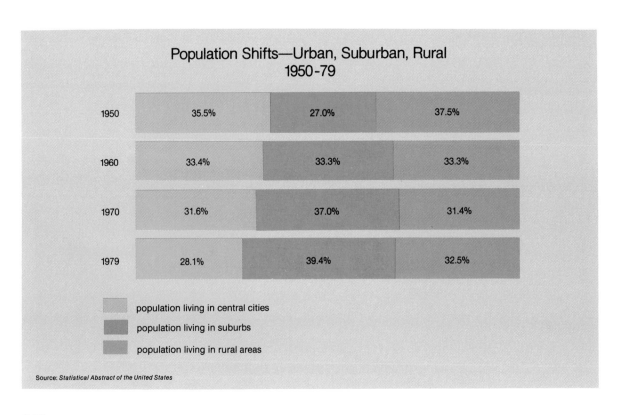

Population Shifts—Urban, Suburban, Rural
1950-79

	population living in central cities	population living in suburbs	population living in rural areas
1950	35.5%	27.0%	37.5%
1960	33.4%	33.3%	33.3%
1970	31.6%	37.0%	31.4%
1979	28.1%	39.4%	32.5%

population living in central cities
population living in suburbs
population living in rural areas

Source: Statistical Abstract of the United States

846

Growth of Family Income

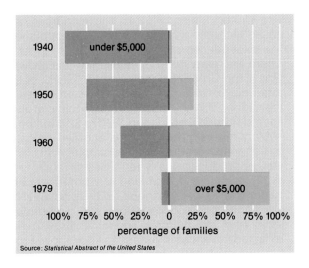

1940 — under $5,000

1950

1960

1979 — over $5,000

100% 75% 50% 25% 0 25% 50% 75% 100%

percentage of families

Source: *Statistical Abstract of the United States*

Average Life Expectancy

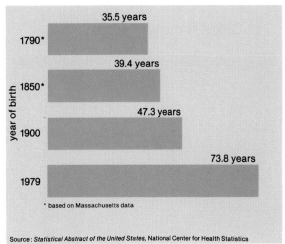

year of birth

1790* — 35.5 years

1850* — 39.4 years

1900 — 47.3 years

1979 — 73.8 years

* based on Massachusetts data

Source: *Statistical Abstract of the United States*, National Center for Health Statistics

High School/College Enrollment

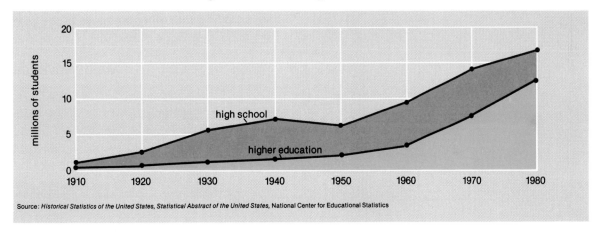

millions of students

20

15

10

5

0

1910 1920 1930 1940 1950 1960 1970 1980

high school

higher education

Source: *Historical Statistics of the United States*, *Statistical Abstract of the United States*, National Center for Educational Statistics

Birth and Death Rates

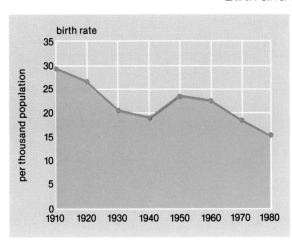

birth rate

per thousand population

35 30 25 20 15 10 5 0

1910 1920 1930 1940 1950 1960 1970 1980

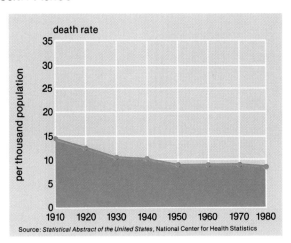

death rate

per thousand population

35 30 25 20 15 10 5 0

1910 1920 1930 1940 1950 1960 1970 1980

Source: *Statistical Abstract of the United States*, National Center for Health Statistics

The American Economy

Gross National Product

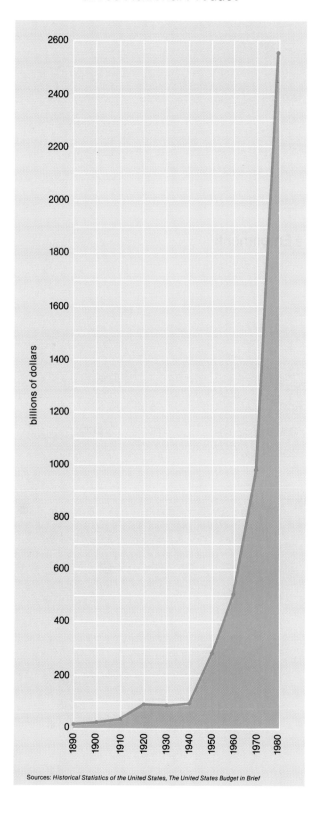

billions of dollars

1890 1900 1910 1920 1930 1940 1950 1960 1970 1980

Sources: *Historical Statistics of the United States, The United States Budget in Brief*

The United States, with its rich resources, advanced technology, and hardworking population, has experienced remarkable economic growth. There are many ways of measuring this growth. One is the Gross National Product (GNP), or the total value of all goods and services produced in the nation. This key measure of economic growth soared from $13.1 billion in 1890 to $2.6 trillion in 1980. Workers' productivity is another indicator of economic progress. For example, each farm worker produced nearly ten times as much food in 1979 as in 1900. The kind of work Americans perform also has changed, with a notable increase in service occupations and government jobs. And the nation's economic growth has reflected advances in American know-how. From the years of hand tools to today's computer-operated machinery, each era has seen major improvements which helped raise Americans' standards of living and improve America's position in trading with other countries of the world.

Major Advances

	1607–1783
POWER	Human muscles Animal muscles Wind and water power
MANUFACTURING MATERIALS	Copper, bronze, iron Wood Clay Plant and animal fibers
FACTORY METHODS	Hand forges and tools Hand-powered equipment
AGRICULTURE	Wooden plows Spades and hoes Axes and other hand tools
TRANSPORTATION	Horses Animal-drawn vehicles Sailing vessels
COMMUNICATION	Hand-operated printing presses Newspapers
MERCHANDISING AND BUSINESS ORGANIZATION	Small shops Peddlers

Average Workweek

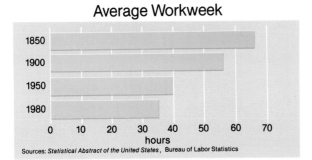

1850	
1900	
1950	
1980	

0 10 20 30 40 50 60 70
hours

Sources: *Statistical Abstract of the United States*, Bureau of Labor Statistics

Output in Manufacturing, 1950–1980

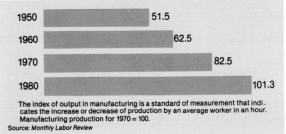

1950	51.5
1960	62.5
1970	82.5
1980	101.3

The index of output in manufacturing is a standard of measurement that indi-cates the increase or decrease of production by an average worker in an hour. Manufacturing production for 1970 = 100.

Source: *Monthly Labor Review*

Changes in Workers' Occupations

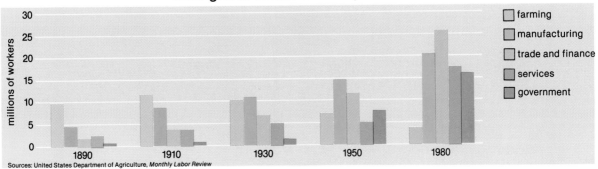

millions of workers

30
25
20
15
10
5
0

1890   1910   1930   1950   1980

Legend:
- farming
- manufacturing
- trade and finance
- services
- government

Sources: United States Department of Agriculture, *Monthly Labor Review*

in American Business and Industry

1783–1850	1850–1900	1900–1920	1920–Present
Steam power	Electric power Internal combustion engines		Atomic energy Solar energy Geothermal energy
Large-scale production of iron	Large-scale production of steel Development of combustion fuels: coal, oil, gas Development of light metals and alloys	Large-scale production of light metals and alloys Development of plastics and synthetics	Large-scale production of plastics and synthetics
Machinery powered by water and steam Interchangeable parts	Mass production, with centralized assembly of interchangeable parts	Conveyor-belt assembly line	Automation Computer-operated machinery
Iron and steel plows Cotton gin Mowing, threshing, and haying machines	McCormick reaper Barbed-wire fencing	Scientific agriculture	Large-scale mechanized agriculture Corporation farms
Canals Clipper ships Development of railroads and steamships	Large-scale steamship and railroad lines City trolleys, elevated trains	Automobiles, trucks, and buses Development of propeller-driven aircraft Subways	Space exploration Monorail trains Supersonic planes
Mechanized printing presses Telegraph Mass-circulation books and magazines	Transatlantic cable Telephones Phonographs Typewriters Cameras	Motion pictures Radios	Television Transistors Magnetic tape Lasers Satellite transmissions
Individual- and family-owned factories and mills General stores	Department stores Chain stores Mail-order houses Growth of corporations Trusts	National advertising Holding companies	Supermarkets Shopping centers Conglomerate corporations Multinational corporations

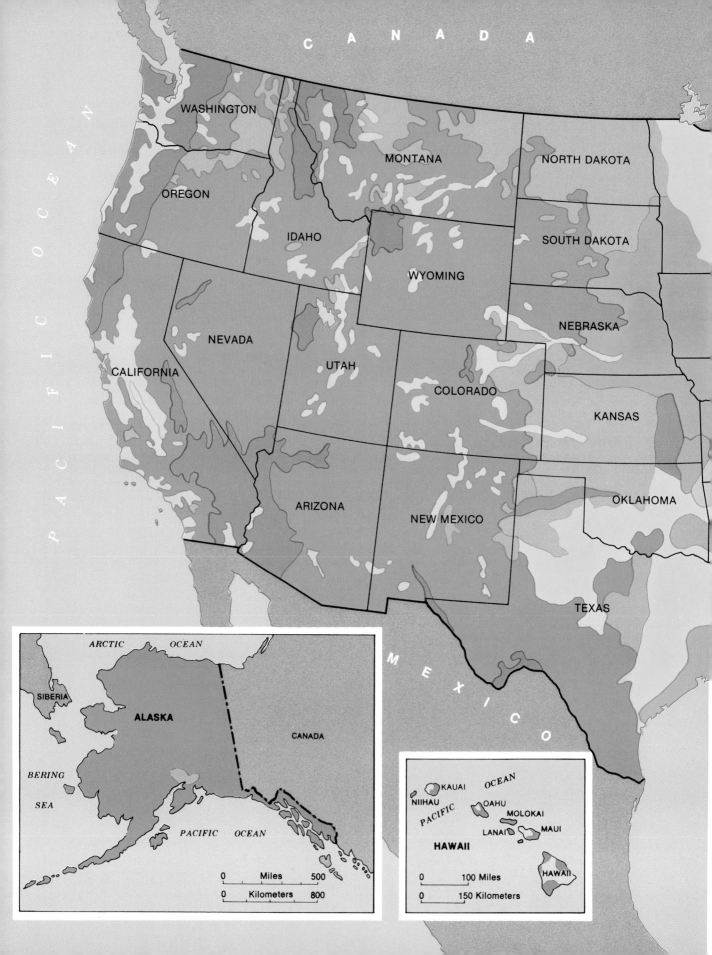

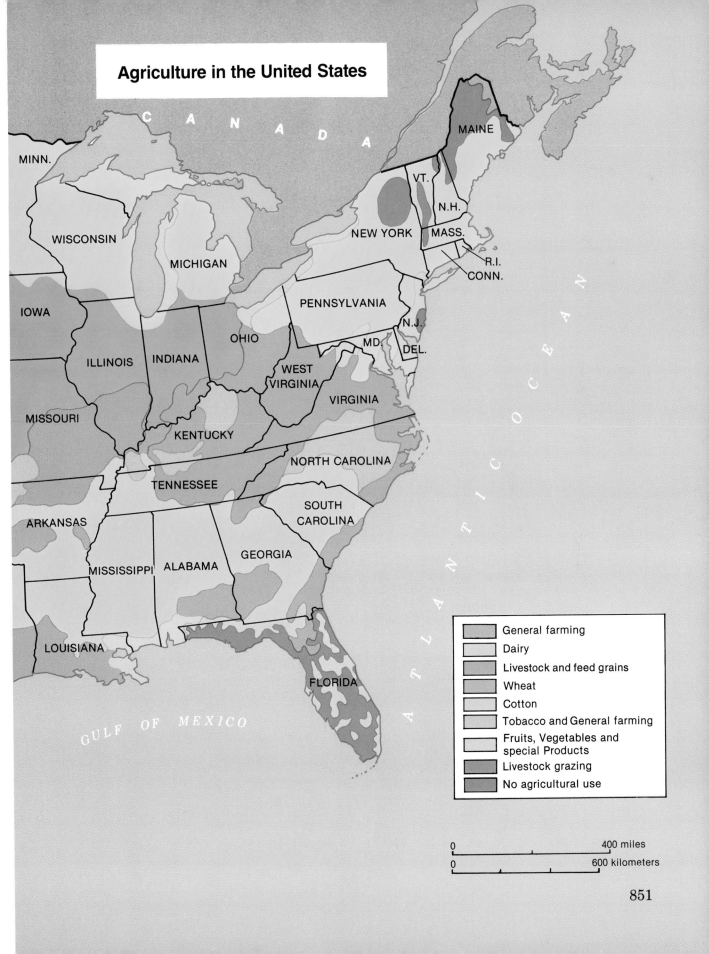

Agriculture in the United States

CANADA

MAINE

MINN.

WISCONSIN

MICHIGAN

VT.

N.H.

NEW YORK

MASS.

R.I.
CONN.

IOWA

OHIO

PENNSYLVANIA

N.J.

ILLINOIS

INDIANA

MD.

DEL.

WEST
VIRGINIA

MISSOURI

KENTUCKY

VIRGINIA

NORTH CAROLINA

TENNESSEE

ARKANSAS

SOUTH
CAROLINA

GEORGIA

MISSISSIPPI

ALABAMA

LOUISIANA

FLORIDA

GULF OF MEXICO

ATLANTIC OCEAN

General farming

Dairy

Livestock and feed grains

Wheat

Cotton

Tobacco and General farming

Fruits, Vegetables and
special Products

Livestock grazing

No agricultural use

| 0 | | 400 miles |
| 0 | | 600 kilometers |

851

Average Size of Farms

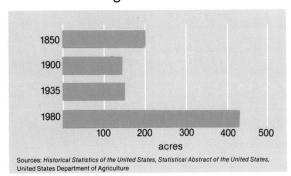

Year	acres
1850	~210
1900	~150
1935	~155
1980	~430

Sources: *Historical Statistics of the United States, Statistical Abstract of the United States,* United States Department of Agriculture

People Fed by One Farm Worker

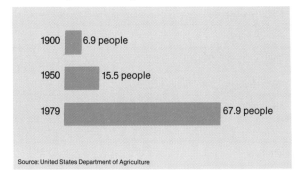

1900	6.9 people
1950	15.5 people
1979	67.9 people

Source: United States Department of Agriculture

Farm Acres Harvested and Farm Production

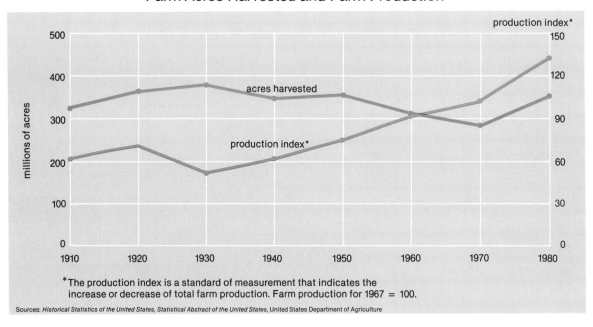

acres harvested

production index*

*The production index is a standard of measurement that indicates the increase or decrease of total farm production. Farm production for 1967 = 100.

Sources: *Historical Statistics of the United States, Statistical Abstract of the United States,* United States Department of Agriculture

America's Exports

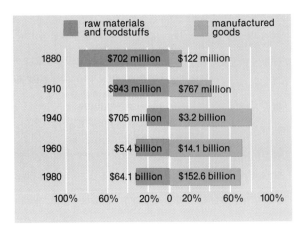

raw materials and foodstuffs | manufactured goods

Year	raw materials and foodstuffs	manufactured goods
1880	$702 million	$122 million
1910	$943 million	$767 million
1940	$705 million	$3.2 billion
1960	$5.4 billion	$14.1 billion
1980	$64.1 billion	$152.6 billion

America's Imports

raw materials and foodstuffs | manufactured goods

Year	raw materials and foodstuffs	manufactured goods
1880	$360 million	$308 million
1910	$905 million	$653 million
1940	$1.6 billion	$968 million
1960	$6.3 billion	$8.8 billion
1980	$109 billion	$132 billion

Sources: *Historical Statistics of the United States, Highlights of United States Export and Import Trade*

The Rise and Fall of U.S. Tariffs

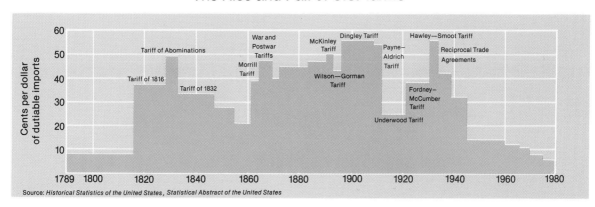

Cents per dollar of dutiable imports

- Tariff of 1816
- Tariff of Abominations
- Tariff of 1832
- Morrill Tariff
- War and Postwar Tariffs
- Wilson—Gorman Tariff
- McKinley Tariff
- Dingley Tariff
- Payne—Aldrich Tariff
- Underwood Tariff
- Fordney—McCumber Tariff
- Hawley—Smoot Tariff
- Reciprocal Trade Agreements

1789 1800 1820 1840 1860 1880 1900 1920 1940 1960 1980

Source: *Historical Statistics of the United States, Statistical Abstract of the United States*

America's World Trade

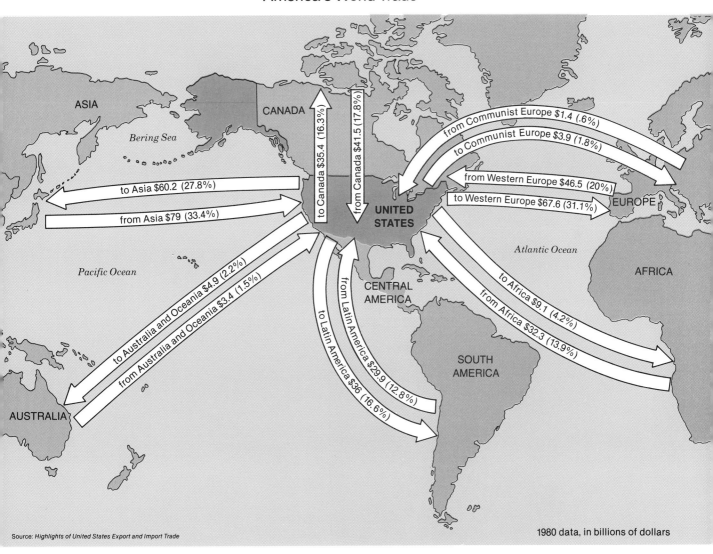

to Canada $35.4 (16.3%)
from Canada $41.5 (17.8%)
from Communist Europe $1.4 (.6%)
to Communist Europe $3.9 (1.8%)
to Asia $60.2 (27.8%)
from Asia $79 (33.4%)
from Western Europe $46.5 (20%)
to Western Europe $67.6 (31.1%)
to Australia and Oceania $4.9 (2.2%)
from Australia and Oceania $3.4 (1.5%)
from Latin America $29.9 (12.8%)
to Latin America $36 (16.6%)
to Africa $9.1 (4.2%)
from Africa $32.3 (13.9%)

Source: *Highlights of United States Export and Import Trade*

1980 data, in billions of dollars

853

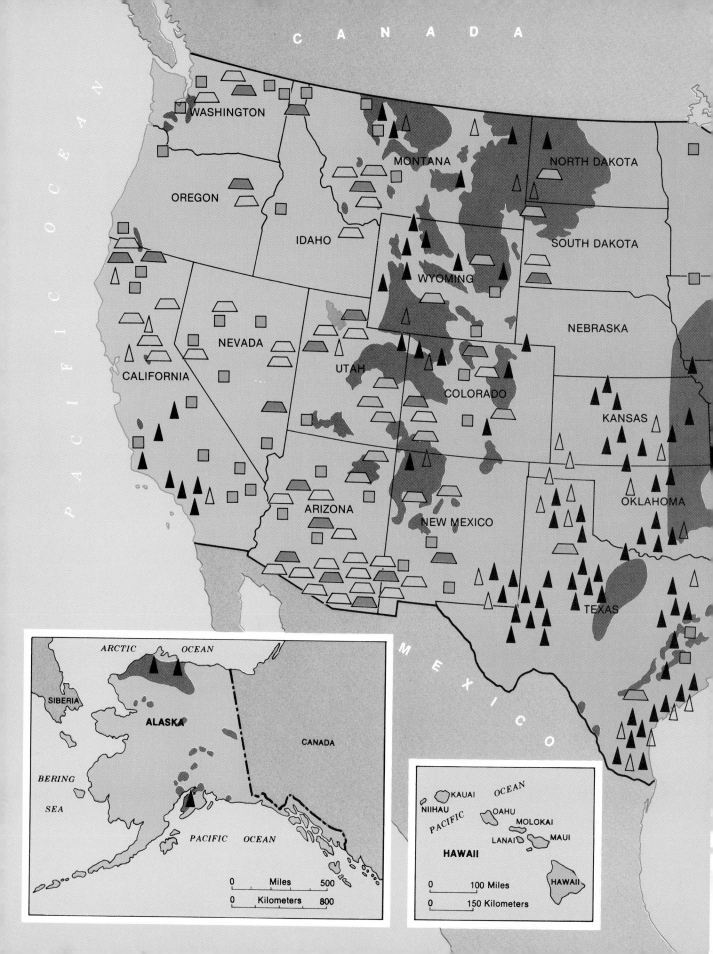

Mineral Resources in the United States

CANADA

MINN.

WISCONSIN

MICHIGAN

IOWA

ILLINOIS

INDIANA

OHIO

MISSOURI

KENTUCKY

TENNESSEE

ARKANSAS

MISSISSIPPI

ALABAMA

GEORGIA

LOUISIANA

FLORIDA

MAINE

VT.

N.H.

NEW YORK

MASS

R.I.

CONN.

PENNSYLVANIA

N.J.

MD.

DEL.

WEST VIRGINIA

VIRGINIA

NORTH CAROLINA

SOUTH CAROLINA

ATLANTIC OCEAN

GULF OF MEXICO

	Legend
	Coal
	Petroleum
	Natural gas
	Silver
	Gold
	Copper
	Iron Ore
	Uranium

0   400 miles
0   600 kilometers

855

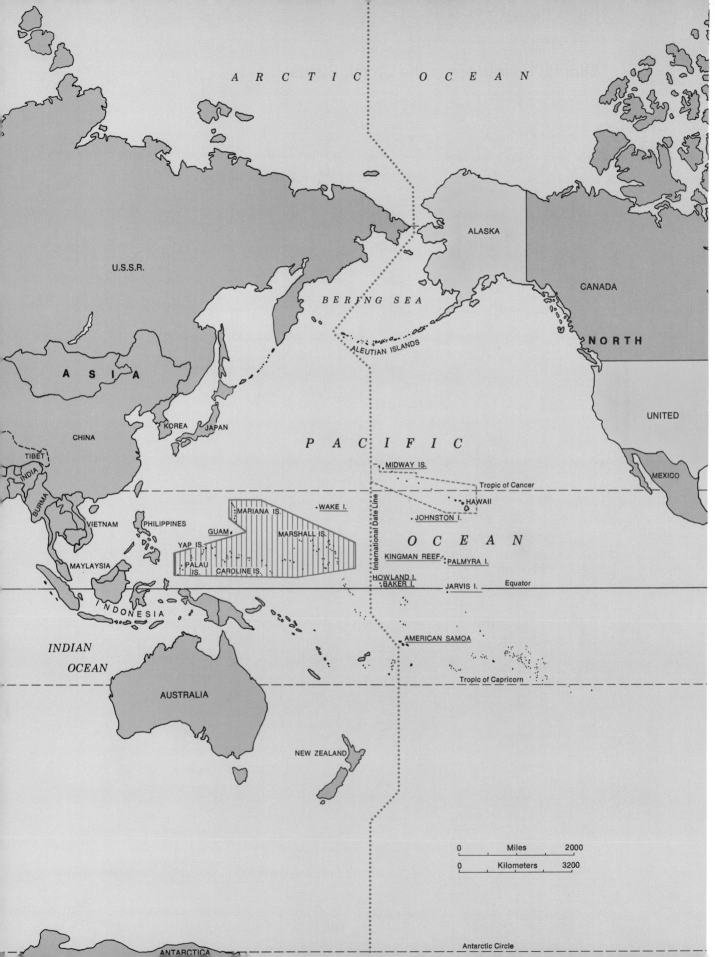

The United States and the World

GREENLAND

Arctic Circle

ICELAND

NORWAY

SWEDEN

FINLAND

ASIA

CANADA

GREAT
BRITAIN

IRELAND

U.S.S.R.

AMERICA

GER.

POLAND

E U R O P E

FRANCE

STATES

PORTUGAL

SPAIN

ITALY

TURKEY

A T L A N T I C

TUNISIA

ISRAEL

SYRIA

IRAQ

IRAN

AFGHANISTAN

PAKISTAN

MOROCCO

ALGERIA

LIBYA

EGYPT

SAUDI
ARABIA

INDIA

CUBA

PUERTO RICO

MAURITANIA

MALI

NIGER

CHAD

VIRGIN IS.

A F R I C A

O C E A N

SUDAN

CENTRAL AMERICA

VENEZUELA

GHANA

NIGERIA

ETHIOPIA

PANAMA
CANAL

COLOMBIA

LIBERIA

SOMALIA

INDIAN

ECUADOR

KENYA

OCEAN

ZAIRE

S O U T H

A M E R I C A

TANZANIA

PERU

BOLIVIA

BRAZIL

ANGOLA

MADAGASCAR

PARAGUAY

CHILE

URUGUAY

ARGENTINA

REPUBLIC OF
SOUTH AFRICA

United States of America

VIRGIN IS.

U.S. possessions and other areas associated
with the U.S. (underlined)

U.N. trusteeship area administered by the U.S.

857

Chronology of Events in American History

1096	Crusades to Holy Land start.
1271–95	Marco Polo's travels in Far East.
1492	Columbus reaches America.
1497–98	John Cabot's explorations.
1498	Vasco da Gama reaches India.
1513	Balboa reaches Pacific Ocean.
1519	Cortés lands in Mexico.
1519–22	Magellan's ships circle earth.
1531–35	Pizarro conquers Incas.
1534	Cartier makes first voyage.
1539–42	De Soto explores Southeast.
1588	English defeat Spanish Armada.
1607	Jamestown is founded.
1609	Hudson explores Hudson River.
1619	First women arrive at Jamestown.
1619	First Africans arrive in Virginia.
1620	Pilgrims reach Cape Cod.
1620	Mayflower Compact.
1624	Virginia becomes royal colony.
1630	Massachusetts Bay Colony founded.
1632	Maryland is chartered.
1636	Roger Williams founds Providence.
1636	Harvard University founded.
1639	Fundamental Orders of Connecticut.
1643	New England Confederation formed.
1647	Massachusetts passes school law.
1649	Maryland Toleration Act.
1651–63	Principal Navigation Acts.
1663	Carolina is chartered.
1664	New Netherland becomes New Jersey and New York.
1673	Exploration by Marquette, Joliet.
1675–76	Bacon's Rebellion.
1679	New Hampshire is chartered.
1681	Pennsylvania is chartered.
1681–82	Exploration by La Salle.
1682	Delaware granted to Penn.
1686	Dominion of New England created.
1693	College of William and Mary founded.
1701	Yale University founded.
1732	Georgia is chartered.
1733	Molasses Act.
1735	Zenger trial.
1750	Iron Act.
1754	French and Indian War starts.
1754	Albany Plan of Union proposed.
1754	Columbia University founded.
1755	Braddock defeated disastrously.
1756	Pitt heads British government.
1759	British capture Quebec.
1763	Treaty of Paris.
1763	Proclamation of 1763.
1764	Sugar Act, Currency Act.

1765	Stamp Act.
1766	Stamp Act repealed.
1767	Townshend Acts.
1770	Boston Massacre.
1772	Committees of Correspondence.
1773	Boston Tea Party.
1774	First Continental Congress.
1775	Fighting at Lexington, Concord.
1775	Second Continental Congress.
1775	Battle of Breed's (Bunker) Hill.
1776	Paine's *Common Sense* appears.
1776	Declaration of Independence.
1776	American victory at Trenton.
1777–78	Howe occupies Philadelphia.
1777	Burgoyne surrenders at Saratoga.
1778	Treaty of alliance with France.
1781	Cornwallis surrenders.
1781	Articles of Confederation go into effect.
1783	Treaty of Paris: United States independence recognized.
1785	Land Ordinance.
1786–87	Shays' Rebellion.
1787	Northwest Ordinance.
1787	Constitution is drafted.

George Washington in Office 1789–1797

1789	Congress creates Departments of State, Treasury, and War.
1789	United States courts are organized.
1790	Assumption Bill is passed.
1791	Bill of Rights is ratified.
1791	Vermont enters Union.
1791	Bank of United States chartered.
1791	Lancaster Turnpike is begun.
1792	Kentucky enters Union.
1793	Proclamation of Neutrality.
1794	"Whiskey Rebellion" is put down.
1794	Jay Treaty.
1795	Pinckney Treaty.
1796	Tennessee enters Union.

John Adams in Office: 1797–1801

1797	XYZ Affair angers Americans.
1798	Navy Department is created.
1798	Eleventh Amendment ratified.
1798	Alien and Sedition Acts.
1798–99	Kentucky and Virginia Resolutions.
1801	Marshall becomes Chief Justice.

Thomas Jefferson in Office: 1801–1809

1803	Ohio enters Union.

1803	*Marbury v. Madison.*
1803	Louisiana Purchase adds vast territory to United States.
1804	Twelfth Amendment ratified.
1804–06	Lewis and Clark expedition.
1805	War with Barbary pirates ends.
1807	Embargo Act.
1809	Non-Intercourse Act.

James Madison in Office: 1809–1817

1811	Indian fight at Tippecanoe.
1811	National Road is begun.
1812	Louisiana enters Union.
1812–14	War of 1812 is fought between United States and Great Britain.
1814	Treaty of Ghent restores peace.
1815	Battle of New Orleans.
1816	Second Bank of United States chartered.
1816	Indiana enters Union.

James Monroe in Office: 1817–1825

1817–25	"Era of Good Feelings."
1817	Mississippi enters Union.
1818	Rush-Bagot Agreement approved.
1818	Illinois enters Union.
1818	Treaty settles Canadian boundary.
1819	*McCulloch v. Maryland.*
1819	*Dartmouth College v. Woodward.*
1819	Alabama enters Union.
1819	Treaty gives Florida to U.S.
1820	Missouri Compromise.
1820	Maine enters Union.
1821	Missouri enters Union.
1821	First public high school opens.
1823	Monroe Doctrine proclaimed.
1824	*Gibbons v. Ogden.*

John Quincy Adams in Office: 1825–1829

1825	Erie Canal opens.
1828	"Tariff of Abominations."
1828	Work begins on Baltimore and Ohio Railroad.

Andrew Jackson in Office: 1829–1837

1830	Webster-Hayne debate.
1831	Slave uprising in Virginia.
1831	First issue of the *Liberator.*
1832	Tariff of 1832.
1832	Ordinance of Nullification.
1832	Jackson vetoes renewal of charter for Bank of United States.
1833	Compromise tariff act.
1836	Texas declares its independence.
1836	Arkansas enters Union.
1837	Michigan enters Union.

Martin Van Buren in Office: 1837–1841

1837	Business panic; depression begins.
1837	Horace Mann starts school reform.
1838	Oberlin admits women.
1841	Jacksonian era ends.

William Henry Harrison in Office: March 4–April 4, 1841

1841	Harrison dies.
1842	Massachusetts recognizes legal right of labor unions to exist.
1842	Webster-Ashburton Treaty.
1845	Florida enters Union.

James K. Polk in Office: 1845–1849

1845	Texas enters Union.
1846	Treaty settles Oregon boundary.
1846	Iowa enters Union.
1846	Congress declares war on Mexico.
1846	Wilmot Proviso is presented.
1847	Mormons settle at Great Salt Lake.
1848	Treaty ends Mexican War; gives U.S. Mexican Cession.
1848	Women's rights convention at Seneca Falls.
1848	Wisconsin enters Union.

Zachary Taylor in Office: 1849–1850

1849	Gold rush to California.
1850	Taylor dies.
1850	Compromise of 1850.
1850	California admitted to Union.
1852	*Uncle Tom's Cabin* is published.

Franklin Pierce in Office: 1853–1857

1853	Gadsden Purchase approved.
1853	Perry arrives in Japan.
1854	Kansas-Nebraska Act.
1854	Republican Party is formed.
1856	Violence breaks out in Kansas.
1857	Dred Scott decision.
1858	Lincoln-Douglas debates.
1858	Minnesota enters Union.
1859	John Brown raids Harpers Ferry.
1859	Oregon enters Union.
1860	South Carolina secedes.
1861	Kansas enters Union.
1861	Confederacy is formed.
1861	Morrill Tariff Act.

Abraham Lincoln in Office: 1861–1865

1861	South fires on Fort Sumter; Civil War (1861–65) begins.
1861	First Battle of Bull Run.
1862	Battle of *Monitor* and *Merrimac.*
1862	Second Battle of Bull Run.
1862	Battle of Antietam.
1862	Emancipation Proclamation.
1862	Union forces reach Vicksburg.
1862	Homestead Act.
1862	Morrill Act for agricultural and industrial education.

1862	Department of Agriculture formed.
1863	Battle of Gettysburg.
1863	Grant takes Vicksburg.
1863	West Virginia enters Union.
1864	Sherman takes Atlanta, Savannah.
1864	Nevada enters Union.
1865	Freedmen's Bureau is created.
1865	Lee surrenders to Grant.
1865	Lincoln is assassinated.

Andrew Johnson in Office: 1865–1869

1865	Johnson recognizes four reconstructed state governments.
1865	Thirteenth Amendment ratified.
1865–86	Conflict between settlers and Indians on the plains.
1866	National Labor Union is formed.
1867	Nebraska enters Union.
1867	U.S. buys Alaska.
1867	Congressional plan of reconstruction is set up.
1867	Grange is organized.
1868	Fourteenth Amendment ratified.
1868	House impeaches Johnson.
1868	Senate acquits Johnson.

Ulysses S. Grant in Office: 1869–1877

1869	First transcontinental railroad completed.
1869	Knights of Labor founded.
1870	Fifteenth Amendment ratified.
1870–71	Force Acts.
1872	Amnesty Act.
1872	Crédit Mobilier scandal.
1873	Nationwide economic depression.
1875	Resumption Act.
1876	Colorado enters Union.
1876	Centennial Exhibition.
1876	Presidential election disputed.
1876–77	"Granger cases" decided.

Rutherford B. Hayes in Office: 1877–1881

1877	Troops withdrawn from South.
1877	Series of railroad strikes.
1878	Bland-Allison Act.
1880–90	New Immigration from eastern and southern Europe.

James A. Garfield in Office: March 4–September 19, 1881

1881	Garfield is assassinated.

Chester A. Arthur in Office: 1881–1885

1882	Chinese Exclusion Act.
1882	Standard Oil Trust organized.
1883	Civil Service Commission set up.

Grover Cleveland in Office: 1885–1889

1886	Presidential Succession Act.
1886	A. F. of L. is organized.
1886	Haymarket Riot.

1887	Interstate Commerce Act.
1887	Hatch Act.
1887	Dawes Act tries to "Americanize" Indians.

Benjamin Harrison in Office: 1889–1893

1889	Washington, Montana, North Dakota, South Dakota enter Union.
1890	Wyoming, Idaho enter Union.
1890	McKinley Tariff.
1890	Sherman Antitrust Act.
1890	Sherman Silver Purchase Act.
1891	Populist Party is organized.
1892	Homestead steel strike.

Grover Cleveland in Office: 1893–1897

1893	Silver Purchase Act is repealed.
1893	World's Fair held in Chicago.
1894	Wilson-Gorman Tariff.
1894	Pullman strike.
1895	Cubans revolt against Spain.
1896	Bryan is free silver candidate.
1896	Utah enters Union.
1896	Gold discovered in Klondike.

William McKinley in Office: 1897–1901

1897	Dingley Tariff.
1898	Spanish-American War.
1898	Treaty of Paris gives U.S. Puerto Rico, Guam, Philippines.
1898	U.S. annexes Hawaiian Islands.
1899	First Hague Conference.
1899–1900	Open Door policy proclaimed.
1900	Boxer Rebellion.
1901	Platt Amendment.
1901	McKinley is assassinated.

Theodore Roosevelt in Office: 1901–1909

1901	Hay-Pauncefote Treaty.
1901–02	Pan-American Conference.
1902	Newlands Reclamation Act.
1902	Drago Doctrine is announced.
1902	American forces withdrawn from Cuba.
1903	Department of Commerce and Labor is created.
1903	Elkins Act.
1903	Wisconsin adopts direct primary.
1903	Canal Zone is acquired by U.S.
1904	Northern Securities Company ruling.
1904	Roosevelt Corollary to Monroe Doctrine.
1905	Treaty of Portsmouth.
1906	Pure Food and Drug Act.
1906	Meat Inspection Act.
1906	Burke Act modifies Dawes Act.
1906	Pan-American Conference.
1907	Oklahoma enters Union.
1907	"Gentlemen's Agreement" with Japan.
1907	Second Hague Conference.
1908	White House Conservation Conference.

| 1908 | Danbury Hatters ruling. |

William H. Taft in Office: 1909–1913

1909	Payne-Aldrich Tariff.
1910	Mann-Elkins Act.
1910	Pan-American Conference.
1911	Transcontinental plane flight.
1912	New Mexico, Arizona enter Union.
1912	Progressive Party is formed.
1912	First state minimum-wage law.
1913	Sixteenth Amendment ratified.

Woodrow Wilson in Office: 1913–1921

1913	Seventeenth Amendment ratified.
1913	Underwood Tariff.
1913	Federal Reserve Act.
1914	World War I starts.
1914	Panama Canal opened to shipping.
1914	FTC is created.
1914	Clayton Antitrust Act.
1916	Jones Act.
1917	Russian Revolution.
1917	U.S. enters World War I.
1917	Smith-Hughes Act.
1917	U.S. buys Virgin Islands.
1918	World War I ends.
1918	Wilson presents Fourteen Points.
1919	Eighteenth Amendment ratified.
1919	"Palmer raids."
1919	Treaty of Versailles (with provision for League of Nations).
1920	Nineteenth Amendment ratified.

Warren G. Harding in Office: 1921–1923

1921	Bureau of the Budget created.
1921	Veterans' Bureau created.
1921–22	Washington Naval Conference.
1921–29	Laws restricting immigration passed.
1922	Mussolini seizes power in Italy.
1922	Fordney-McCumber Tariff.
1923	Harding dies suddenly.

Calvin Coolidge in Office: 1923–1929

1923	Pan-American Conference.
1924	Teapot Dome scandal.
1924	Veterans' bonus bill passed.
1924	All Indians given citizenship.
1927	McNary-Haugen Bill vetoed.
1928	Kellogg-Briand Pact.
1928	Pan-American Conference.

Herbert Hoover in Office: 1929–1933

1929	Stock market crash; start of Great Depression.
1930	Public-works programs started.
1930	Hawley-Smoot Tariff.
1931	Japan invades Manchuria.
1932	RFC is created.
1932	Stimson Doctrine is announced.
1932–33	Federal Reserve powers increased.
1933	Hitler comes to power in Germany.
1933	Twentieth Amendment ratified.

Franklin D. Roosevelt in Office: 1933–1945

1933	CCC is created.
1933	Agricultural Adjustment Act.
1933	Roosevelt declares bank holiday.
1933	NIRA goes into effect.
1933	TVA is created.
1933	U.S. recognizes Soviet Union.
1933	Good Neighbor policy announced.
1933	Twenty-first Amendment ratified.
1934	Roosevelt "devalues" dollar.
1934	SEC is created.
1934	Indian Reorganization Act (Wheeler-Howard Act).
1934	Trade Agreements Act.
1934	Platt Amendment canceled.
1935	WPA is created.
1935	NIRA declared unconstitutional.
1935	National Labor Relations Act.
1935	Social Security Act.
1935–37	Neutrality Acts.
1936	AAA ruled unconstitutional.
1936	Pan-American Conference.
1937	Plan to reorganize Supreme Court.
1937–38	Business slump.
1938	CIO separates from A. F. of L.
1938	Fair Labor Standards Act.
1938	Food, Drug, and Cosmetic Act.
1938	Declaration of Lima.
1939	Germany invades Poland; World War II begins.
1939	Neutrality Act of 1937 amended.
1940	France signs armistice.
1941	"Four Freedoms" speech.
1941	Lend-Lease Act.
1941	Hitler attacks U.S.S.R.
1941	Atlantic Charter states war aims.
1941	Japanese attack Pearl Harbor; U.S. enters World War II.
1942	Corregidor surrenders to Japanese.
1942	Marines invade Guadalcanal.
1942	Allied invasion of North Africa.
1942	OPA is established.
1943	Allied invasion of Italy.
1943	Cairo and Teheran Conferences.
1944	Allies invade Western Europe.
1944	France is liberated.
1945	Yalta Conference.
1945	Roosevelt dies suddenly.

Harry S. Truman in Office: 1945–1953

1945	San Francisco Conference.
1945	War ends in Europe.
1945	Atomic bombs destroy Hiroshima and Nagasaki.
1945	Truman signs UN Charter.
1945	World War II ends.
1946	Philippines become independent.
1946	Wage and price controls ended.
1947	Truman Doctrine is announced.
1947	Marshall Plan is proposed.
1947	Taft-Hartley Act.

1947	Presidential Succession Act.
1948–49	Berlin airlift.
1949	Point Four program is announced.
1949	NATO is formed.
1949	Communists control China.
1950	Internal Security Act.
1950	Korean War starts.
1951	Twenty-second Amendment ratified.
1952	U.S. tests hydrogen bomb.

Dwight D. Eisenhower in Office: 1953–1961

1953	Department of Health, Education, and Welfare created.
1953	States get title to offshore oil.
1953	Korean armistice signed.
1954	Supreme Court rules segregated public schools unconstitutional.
1954	West Germany is admitted to NATO.
1954	Both U.S. and U.S.S.R. have H-bombs.
1955	Summit conference.
1956	Suez crisis.
1957	Civil Rights Commission created.
1957	*Sputnik* in orbit.
1958	First U.S. satellite in orbit.
1958	Congress admits Alaska to the Union.
1958–59	Berlin crisis.
1959	St. Lawrence Seaway is opened.
1959	Congress admits Hawaii to the Union.
1960	Summit Conference called off.

John F. Kennedy in Office: 1961–1963

1961	Peace Corps created.
1961	Alliance for Progress started.
1961	First Soviet cosmonaut orbits earth.
1961	Invasion of Cuba fails.
1961	Berlin wall built.
1962	First American astronaut orbits earth.
1962	U.S. troops sent to South Vietnam.
1962	Trade Expansion Act.
1962	Cuban missile crisis.
1963	Nuclear test-ban treaty.
1963	Kennedy is assassinated.

Lyndon B. Johnson in Office: 1963–1969

1964	Economic Opportunity Act.
1964	Civil Rights Act.
1964	Twenty-fourth Amendment ratified.
1965	Voting Rights Act.
1965	Medicare established.
1965	Escalation in South Vietnam.
1965	Department of Housing and Urban Development created.
1966	National Organization for Women (NOW) is founded.
1966	Department of Transportation created.
1967	Racial disturbances occur in several large cities.
1967	Twenty-fifth Amendment ratified.

| 1968 | Martin Luther King, Jr., is assassinated. |
| 1968 | Vietnam peace talks begin in Paris. |

Richard M. Nixon in Office: 1969–1974

1969	American troop withdrawals from Vietnam begin.
1969	American astronauts land on the moon.
1971	President Nixon visits Communist China and the Soviet Union.
1972	Twenty-seventh Amendment passed by Congress and sent to states for ratification.
1973	Vice-President Agnew resigns.
1973	Vietnam cease-fire.
1974	President Nixon resigns; Gerald Ford becomes President.

Gerald Ford in Office: 1974–1977

1975	Vietnam falls to Communists.
1975	Joint U.S.-Soviet space mission.
1976	The nation celebrates its Bicentennial.
1976	U.S. Viking spacecraft land on Mars.

Jimmy Carter in Office: 1977–1981

1977	Carter announces plan to pardon Vietnam draft evaders.
1977	Department of Energy created.
1978	Panama Canal treaties approved.
1978	Carter proposes voluntary wage and price guidelines.
1978	Carter meets with Begin of Israel and Sadat of Egypt at Camp David for peace talks.
1979	Revolution in Iran; American hostages seized in November.
1979	Accident at Three Mile Island nuclear plant.
1979	Gasoline shortages in U.S.
1979	Soviet Union invades Afghanistan.
1980	"Carter Doctrine" announced.
1980	U.S. cuts off grain shipments to Soviet Union and boycotts Olympics to protest Afghanistan invasion.
1980	U.S. mission to free hostages in Iran fails.
1980	"Freedom flotilla" from Cuba to U.S.

Ronald Reagan in Office: 1981–

1981	Iran releases U.S. hostages.
1981	Reagan survives assassination attempt.
1981	Flight of U.S. space shuttle *Columbia*.
1981	Sandra Day O'Connor becomes first woman appointed to Supreme Court.

Index

Italicized page numbers preceded by *m* or *p* refer to a map (*m*) or picture or feature (*p*) on the page. Italicized page numbers preceded by *c* refer to a chart or graph on the page.

Boldface page numbers are pages on which a definition or explanation is given.

m47, p48; Indochina and, 714, p714, 783; Louisiana purchased from, 222–24, m322; Mexico occupied by, 561–62; under Napoleon, 215, 228, 229; Revolution in (1789), 209; Suez Canal and, 716; in United Nations, 706; U.S. Civil War and, 380; in World War I, 572–75, m572, p574, m575, 581–84, m583, 586, m586; in World War II, 671, 674–75, p675, m684, 692, m694; XYZ Affair and, 214, p215

Franco, Francisco, 666, 669
Franklin, Benjamin: p151; at Constitutional Convention, 151; at Continental Congress, 139; Declaration of Independence and, 118; in France, 126, 133; French and Indian War and, 47; Indians and, 69; newspaper of, 57; as Postmaster General, 51, 52; stove invented by, 59
Franz Ferdinand (archduke, Austria-Hungary), 571
Franz Joseph (emperor, Austria-Hungary), 571
Freedmen's Bureau, 392–94, 397
Freeman, Mary E. Wilkins, 501
Freeport Doctrine, 355
Free-Soil Party, 348
Frémont, John C., 318, m319, 354, 372
French and Indian War (Seven Years' War), 46–49, m47, p48
French National Committee, 675
French Revolution (1789), 209
French West Indies, 209
Frick, Henry C., 454, 494
Frontier, 33, 35; complete settlement of, 436; Confederation government and, 140–43; education on, 83–84; life on, 58–61; whisky produced on, 208
Fuel Administration, 579
Fugitive Slave Laws: Compromise of 1850 and, 349, 350; of 1793, 336; of 1850, 351, 353
Fuller, Margaret, 327, p328
Fulton, Robert, p154, 247, 277
Fundamental Orders of Connecticut, 33, 86
Fur trade, 98, 101; France in, 43–45; in Pacific Northwest, 310, 311, p311

G

Gadsden, James, 319
Gadsden Purchase (1835), 319, m322
Gage, Thomas, 108–09, 112–16
Gagarin, Yuri, 759
Galbraith, John Kenneth, 749
Gallatin, Albert, 226, 244
Galvani, Luigi, 446
Galveston, Texas, 513
Gandhi, Mohandas, 339
Garfield, James A., 415, p415, p437
Garland, Hamlin, 475, 501
Garner, John Nance, 604
Garnet, Henry Highland, 336
Garrison, William Lloyd, 334, 335, 337–38
Garvey, Marcus, 643–44
Gary, Indiana, 594
Gaspee Affair, 106
Gates, Horatio, 125, 127
General Motors, 620, p620, 722, 731
Genêt, Edmond, 209
Geneva, Switzerland: Indochina Peace Conference in (1954), 714; League of Nations in, p660
Geographic Revolution, 12

George III (king, England), 99, 100, 103, 106, p229, p504; Revolutionary War and, 115–16, p117, 118, 131
George, Henry, 417–18
Georgia, m142; Civil War in, 368–69, m369; as colony, 41–42, 105; Constitution ratified by, 156; Indians in, 262; Revolutionary War in, 127, m127; secession of, 357, m357; slavery in, 64
Geothermal energy, 825, p825
German immigrants, 285, 295
Germantown, Battle of, 125, m125
Germany: Berlin crisis (1958) and, 717; Berlin wall in, 782; under Hitler, 666, p667, 668–70; Jews in, p674; Rhineland invaded by, 667; in World War I, 572–78, m572, m575, 581–84, m583; World War I armistice and, 584–88, m586; World War I reparations from, 657; in World War II, p670, 671, m672, 674–77, p675, 680, 682, 683, m684, 690–94, m694; post-World War II, 698, 707, 709, 715
Geronimo, 425
Gettysburg, Battle of, 367, m367
Gettysburg Address, 367
Ghana, p62, 780
Ghent, Treaty of (1814), 235
Ghost Dance, 425
Gibbons v. Ogden (1824), 247
Gilbert, Sir Humphrey, 21
Gilbert Islands, 695, m696
Gilman, Charlotte Perkins, 637
Glasgow, Ellen, 647
Gleason, Kate, 453
Glenn, John, 759
Glidden, Joseph, 434
Glorious Revolution (England), 38
Goethals, George W., 561
Gold: bimetallism policy and, 485–86; discovered in Alaska, 541, p542; discovered in California, 322–23; as election issue in 1896, 487; New Deal and, 608, 623; settlement of West and, 436–48; Spanish conquests and, 18, 20; Spanish conquests and, 15, p16; value of greenbacks in, 481
Goldman, Emma, 469
Goldwater, Barry M., 761
Goliad, Texas, m314, 315
Gompers, Samuel, 464, 466
Gomulka, Wladyslaw, 715
Gonzales, Rodolfo "Corky," 806
Gonzales, Texas, m314, 315
Good Neighbor Policy, 657–59, 664–65, p665
Goodyear, Charles, 530
Gorgas, William C., p559, 561
Gorges, Sir Ferdinando, 34
Gossamer Albatross (human-powered aircraft), p829
Gould, Jay, 411
Government: of Articles of Confederation, 139–48; of charter colonies, 23; civil service reform in, 415–17; of pre-Civil War South, 301; colonial, 86–90, 98–100; compact theory of, 216, 265; under Constitution, 157–59, 166–99; Constitutional Convention and, 152–55; Constitution ratified for, 155–57; corruption in, post-Civil War, 410–13; debate over role of, 817–18; Declaration of Independence on, 118–19; distribution of outlays by, c839; employees in, c839; English Bill of Rights and, 38;

federal, creation of, 203–04; Indian reservations formed by, 426; of Indians, 7, 66–67, 262; of Kansas Territory, 353; labor laws of, 535–36; labor unions and, 467–68; of Mayflower Compact, 29–30; in New England colonies, 31–35; of Oregon country, 312; outlays of, c839; of Philippines, under U.S., 548, 549; progressive reforms of, 511–13; of Puerto Rico, 557; receipts of, c839; of reconstruction states, 390, 392–93, 395, 398–400; religious freedom and, 79, 80, 332; of royal colonies, 24; under Second Continental Congress, 129–30; separation of powers in, 159–60; in Southern Colonies, 40, 41; of Spanish colonies, 19–20; spoils system in, 259; of states, establishment of, 136–38; of territories, 437–38
Government bonds, 205, 377, 687–89
Grand Army of the Republic (GAR), 416
Grange, Red, 640
Grange (farmers' organization), 479–80, p479
Grant, Ulysses S., 415; in Civil War, 365–70; in election of 1868, 396–97, p396; as President, 410–12
Grasso, Ella, 811
Gray, Robert, 310
Great American Desert, 308, 422, 434
Great Atlantic and Pacific Tea Company (A & P), 448
Great Awakening, 80–81
Great Britain: Anglican Church established in, 27; in China, 550; colonies of, 22–24, m24, m29, 30–35, 37–42, m49, 68, 104–10; exploration by, 12, m13; French colonies and, 43, m44, 45–46; in French and Indian War, 46–49, m47, p48; governments of colonies of, 86, 87, 89–90, 98–104; immigration from, 285; imperialism of, 541; Industrial Revolution in, 282; Latin American interests of, 248–50; Middle East and, 710, 716, 717; Oregon claimed by, 310, 312, m322; in Revolutionary War, 113–33, m114; post-Revolutionary U.S. and, 145–47; slavery abolished in, 335; social influence on colonies of, 54, 55; in South America, 558, 561, 562; Spanish Armada defeated by, 21, p21, p22; trade of colonies of, 95–98, m96; United Nations and, 705, 706; U.S. Civil War and, 380; in War of 1812, 230, 232–36, p233; in wars with France, 209–10, 228, 229; at Washington Conference (1921–22), 660; in World War I, 572–77, m572, m575, 581–84, m583, 586, m586; in World War II, 625, 671, 675–78, p675, 682–86, m684, 691, 692
Great Compromise, 152–53
Great Debate (1850), 349–50, p349
Great Depression, 631; Hoover and, 601–04; New Deal programs and, 606–17; role of government and, 818; society during, 640–42, 645
Great Lakes: French exploration of, 43, m44, 45; Rush-Bagot Agreement on, 236
Great Northern Railway, m430
Great Plains, 308, m309; cattle industry in, 428–32, 435; Indians

of, 6–7, 421–26, p422, p426; railroads and cattle trails of, m430; rural life on, in late 1800's, 475; settlement of, 432–36, p433. See also specific states
Great Salt Lake, m309, 321, p321
"Great Society," 760–63
"Great White Fleet," 543
Greece: post-World War I, m586, 587; in World War II, 683, m684; post-World War II, 707, 708
Greeley, Horace, 398, 412–13, 493
Greenback-Labor Party, 415, 481–82, p482
Greene, Nathaneal, 127
Greenland, 12
Green Mountain Boys, 115
Greensboro, North Carolina, 801
Grenville, George, 100, 102
Griffing, Josephine, 392
Griffith, D. W., 530
Grimké, Angelina, 334, 336
Grimké, Sarah, 334
Grist mill, p240
Groll, Theodore, p494
Gross national product, c848
Grundy, Felix, 231
Guadalcanal, 682, m696
Guadalupe Hidalgo, Treaty of (1848), 319–20, 347
Guadeloupe, 49
Guam, 546, 555, 678, 681, 695, m696
Guatemala, m557, 564
Guerrillas, 127
Guilford Court House, Battle of, 127, m127
Guinea, p62
Gulf of Tonkin Resolution (1964), 784–86

H

Habeas corpus, 161, 176
Hague Conferences (1899, 1907), 571
Haig, Alexander, 795
Haiti, 223, 305, m557, 564, 665
Hale, Sarah Josepha, 327
"Half-Breeds," 414, 415
Hall, G. Stanley, 637
Halladay, Daniel, 434
Halleck, Henry W., 365
Halsey, William F., 682, 695
Hamilton, Alexander, p156, 157, 202, 218, 221; at Constitutional Convention, 151; death of, 227; Federalist Party and, 212–13, 243; as Secretary of Treasury, 204–09, 211, 226
Hamilton, Andrew, 85
Hancock, John, 118
Hancock, Winfield S., 415
Handicapped people, 614
Handy, W. C., 648
Hanna, Mark, 487
Hanoi, Vietnam, 783, m783, 788
Harding, Warren G.: in election of 1920, 588, 592, 595; foreign policy of, 657, 659, 660; as President, 596–98, p597
Harlem Renaissance, 647–48
Harper's (magazine), p405, p500
Harpers Ferry, West Virginia, 355–56
Harris, Joel Chandler, 501
Harris, Patricia, 804, 811
Harrison, Benjamin, p417; in election of 1892, 418, 485; as President, 417, 435, 519
Harrison, William Henry: at Battle of Tippecanoe, 231; in election of 1840, 269–70, p269, p270; in War of 1812, m235
Harte, Bret, 437, 501

Acknowledgments

Cover illustration by Sisee Brimberg/Woodfin Camp, Inc. and Bettmann Archive. Title page by Sisee Brimberg. Drawings by Samuel H. Bryant and Manny Haller. Illustration of American bald eagle with banner and shield on *Changing Ways of American Life* chapters by Raul Mina Mora. Maps by Harold K. Faye and Paul Pugliese; charts by Ed Malsberg and Graphic Arts International.

UNIT ONE: p. 1, New York Historical Society; 3, E. Manewal/Shostal Associates; 5, Oronoz, S.A.; 7, Jerry D. Jacka; 9, National Maritime Museum, London; 15, both Oronoz, S.A.; 16, J. Barnell/Shostal Associates; 17, Bradley Smith/Gemini Smith, Inc.; 18, Bradley Smith/Gemini Smith, Inc.; 21, National Maritime Museum, London; 22, Woburn Abbey; 27, John Hancock Mutual Life Insurance Company; 31, Archives of the Commonwealth of Massachusetts; 32, Bettmann Archive; 33, Courtesy of the Essex Institute, Salem, Massachusetts; 35, New York Public Library; 36, New York Public Library; 39, The Thomas Gilcrease Institute of American History and Art, Tulsa, Oklahoma; 41, New York Public Library; 42, Carolina Art Association, Gibbes Art Gallery; 45, National Gallery of Canada, Ottawa; 48, Anne S. K. Brown Military Collection, Brown University; 52, Metropolitan Museum of Art; 53, Courtesy HBJ Library; 54, Museum of Fine Arts, Boston; 57, Historical Society of Pennsylvania; 58, National Museum of American Art, Smithsonian Institution; 62, tl, Granger Collection, tr, Granger Collection; 63, Library of Congress; 64, New York Public Library; 67, National Gallery of Canada, Ottawa; 69, New York Public Library; 71, both, Bettmann Archive; 72, tl, The Brooklyn Museum; all others, Bettmann Archive; 73, t, Kennedy Galleries; b, National Museum of American Art, Smithsonian Institution, Samuel H. Kress Collection; 74 all, Bettmann Archive; 75, t, John Deere; c,b, Bettmann Archive; 76, t, G & W Food Products; c, Shostal Associates; b, Grant Heilman; 78, New York Historical Society; 80, The Edison Institute; 81, New York Public Library; 82, Culver Pictures; 84, Bettmann Archive; 88, Virginia Historical Society; 90, Historical Society of Pennsylvania.

UNIT TWO: p. 93, Valley Forge Historical Society; 95, New York Historical Society; 97, National Maritime Museum, London; 101, John Carter Brown Library, Brown University; 103, Historical Society of Pennsylvania; 105, Museum of Fine Arts, Boston; 106, Bettmann Archive; 107, on loan to the Daughters of the American Revolution Museum, Boston Tea Party Chapter; 109, Museum of the City of New York; 110, The Colonial Williamsburg Foundation; 113, The Concord Antiquarian Society; 117, Collection of Gilbert Darlington, New York; 119, Yale University Art Gallery; 122, Historical Society of Pennsylvania; 124, Valley Forge Historical Society; 126, South Carolina Library, University of South Carolina; 129, Virginia Historical Society; 131, Rhode Island Historical Society; 132, New York Public Library; 136, Massachusetts Historical Society; 138, Metropolitan Museum of Art; 143, Washington University Gallery of Art, St. Louis; 144, Nemo Warr, Detroit Public Library; 146, Historical Society of Pennsylvania; 148, Smithsonian Institution; 151, bl, New York Historical Society, br, Bettmann Archive; 152, tl, Virginia State Library, tr, Independence National Historical Park Collection; 153, Historical Society of Pennsylvania; 154, American Philosophical Society, Philadelphia; 156, Culver Pictures; 158, Fred J. Maroon/Louis Mercier; 162, Virginia Museum of Fine Arts; 163, Bettmann Archive.

UNIT THREE: p. 201, Maryland Historical Society; 203, New York Historical Society; 205, all Larry Stevens; 206, Library of Congress; 208, National Museum of American Art, Smithsonian Institution; 211, Courtesy the Henry Francis du Pont Winterthur Museum; 212, New York Public Library; 213, Historical Society of Pennsylvania; 215, Culver Pictures; 216, National Collection of Fine Arts, Smithsonian Institution; 217, Museum of Art, Rhode Island School of Design; 219, Corcoran Gallery of Art; 222, Chicago Historical Society; 223, New York Historical Society; 225, Oregon State Highway Department; 227, Bettmann Archive; 229, Historical Society of Pennsylvania; 231, Courtesy Field Museum of Natural History, Chicago; 233, Bettmann Archive; 236, National Archives,

Washington, D.C.; 239, Terry McGinnis, Museum of American Folk Art; 242, t, National Portrait Gallery, Smithsonian Institution, b, Corcoran Gallery of Art; 245, Maryland Historical Society; 247, St. Louis Art Museum; 251, New York Public Library; 252, Smithsonian Institution; 253, Courtesy the Henry Francis du Pont Winterthur Museum; 257, t, National Gallery of Art, Washington, D.C., b, George Eastman House; 258, Library of Congress; 261, l, Georgia Historical Society, r, Philadelphia Museum of Art; 262, Woolaroc Museum, Bartlesville, Oklahoma; 265, New York Historical Society; 267, New York Historical Society; 268, Museum of the City of New York; 269, New York Historical Society; 270, New York Historical Society.

UNIT FOUR: p. 273, Chicago Historical Society; 275, Museum of the City of New York; 277, Metropolitan Museum of Art; 283, Massachusetts Historical Society; 284, New York Public Library; 287, Museum of the City of New York; 289, t, Nelson Gallery–Atkins Museum, Kansas City, Missouri, Nelson Fund, b, Historical Picture Service; 290, t, Historical Picture Service, c, Museum of the City of New York, the Harry T. Peters Collection, bl, Bettmann Archive; 290-291, b, Bettmann Archive; 291, tr, ©Tim Kilby/Uniphoto, tl, Bettmann Archive, lc, Historical Picture Service; 292-293 background, ©Diversified Map Corporation, St. Louis, Missouri; 292, t, Bettmann Archive; c, Courtesy, HBJ Library; 292-293, b, all, Historical Picture Service; 293, t, Bettmann Archive, c, Roy H. Blanchard/DPI; 294, tl, Culver Pictures, tr, ©G. Rancinan/Sygma; b, J. Alex Langley/Photo Researchers; 296, Giraudon, ©SPADEM, Paris 1976; 301, Louisiana State Museum; 302, New York Historical Society; 304, Chicago Historical Society; 306, Granger Collection; 310, Butler Institute of American Art, Youngstown, Ohio; 311, The Thomas Gilcrease Institute of American History and Art, Tulsa, Oklahoma; 315, Brass Door Galleries, Houston, Texas; 317, West Point Museum Collection, U.S. Military Academy; 321, From the Permanent Collection of Brigham Young University. Used by permission.; 326, Bettmann Archive; 328, l, Bettmann Archive, c, Culver Pictures, r, Culver Pictures; 329, New York Public Library, Picture Collection; 331, Yale University Art Gallery; 333, Sophia Smith Collection; 334, From the collection of the Charleston Museum; 335, Bettmann Archive; 337, Sophia Smith Collection; 339, New York Public Library.

UNIT FIVE: p. 343, Library of Congress; 345, Library of Congress; 349, Bettmann Archive; 351, Culver Pictures; 358, Museum of the Confederacy; 361, Michigan History Collections, Bentley History Library, University of Michigan; 371, Granger Collection; 373, Library of Congress; 374, Library of Congress; 375, Library of Congress; 377, U.S. Navy; 378, Mariners Museum; 379, Library of Congress; 381, New York Historical Society; 382, Bettmann Archive.

UNIT SIX: p. 385, Bettmann Archive; 387, Library of Congress; 389, Brown University Library; 391, Courtesy, HBJ Library; 395 both, Bettmann Archive; 396, Smithsonian Institution; 398, Library of Congress; 400, Chicago Historical Society; 402, Bettmann Archive; 405, *Harper's Weekly*, March 16, 1867; 406, Library of Congress; 411, Brown Brothers; 413, Brown Brothers; 415, New York Public Library, Frank Leslie's *Illustrated Newspaper*, August 20, 1881; 417, Bettmann Archive; 419, New York Public Library, *Harper's Weekly*, August 12, 1893; 422, National Museum of American Art, Smithsonian Institution; 424, West Point Museum collection, U.S. Military Academy; 426, Bettmann Archive; 427, Nevada State Historical Society; 429, U.S. Department of Agriculture; 431, The Thomas Gilcrease Institute of American History and Art; 433, Nebraska State Historical Society; 437, Nevada State Historical Society; 438, Courtesy of Gene Autry.

UNIT SEVEN: p. 441, Chicago Historical Society; 443, Bettmann Archive; 445, Bettmann Archive; 447, New York Public Library, *Century Magazine,* Vol. XXVI-31; 449, Bettmann Archive; 453, both, Bettmann Archive; 454, Bettmann Archive; 458, Bettmann Archive; 461, Thomas Gilcrease Institute of American History and Art, Tulsa, Oklahoma; 463, Permission of The Fine Arts Museums of San Francisco; 467, Granger Collection; 468, Bettmann Archive; 472, Metropolitan Museum of Art, Gift of Christian A. Zabrisiae; 474, New York State Historical Association; 476, Granger Collection; 480, Bettmann Archive; 482, Granger Collection; 485, Granger Collection; 486, Chicago Historical Society; 489, t, Bettmann Archive, b, Metropolitan Museum of Art, Gift of Lyman G. Bloomingdale, 1901; 490, t, Chicago Historical Society, bl, Barfoot, The Progress of Cotton: #6 Spinning, Yale University Art Gallery, Mabel Brady Garvan Collection, br, Bettmann Archive; 491, t, Courtesy HBJ Library, San Francisco, c, Bettmann Archive, b, Department of the Interior; 492, t, J. Alex Langley/DPI, c, ©Steve Thompson/Uniphoto, b, ©George Hall, Woodfin Camp & Associates; 494, Indianapolis Museum of Art, Gift of A Couple of Old Hoosiers; 496, Culver Pictures; 498, Brown Brothers; 500, Bettmann Archive; 502, Museum of the City of New York; 504, Bettmann Archive.

UNIT EIGHT: p. 507, Kennedy Galleries; 509, Kennedy Galleries; 510, Historical Picture Service; 512, Bettmann Archive; 514, both, Association for the Study of Afro-American Life and History, Inc., Washington, D.C.; 516, Library of Congress; 517, Library of Congress; 519, National Museum of American Art, Smithsonian Institution, Gift of Mrs. Sarah Harrison; 520, Harvard College Library; 522, Historical Picture Service; 525, Bettmann Archive; 529, Museum of the City of New York; 531, Historical Picture Service; 532, Library of Congress; 535, Library of Congress.

UNIT NINE: p. 539, l, Collection of George J. Goodstadt, c, West Point Museum collection, U.S. Military Academy, r, Granger; 542, Library of Congress; 547, Chicago Historical Society; 548, Culver Pictures; 549, Culver Pictures; 551, Brown Brothers; 552, Courtesy, Franklin D. Roosevelt Library; 556, Culver Pictures; 559, Granger Collection; 560, Courtesy, HBJ Library; 563, New York Public Library, *New York Herald,* December 16, 1902; 564, Brown Brothers; 566, M. Farbman, ©TIME, Inc., 1960; 570, Photoworld/FPG; 574, Bettmann Archive; 576, Brown Brothers; 579, Granger Collection; 580, Collection of George J. Goodstadt; 582, Bettmann Archive; 587, Imperial War Museum.

UNIT TEN: p. 591, Department of the Interior; 594, Courtesy, Whitney Museum of American Art; 596, Bettmann Archive; 597, Brown Brothers; 598, The New York Historical Society; 601, Brown Brothers; 604, Courtesy, Franklin D. Roosevelt Library; 607, Brown Brothers; 609, Photoworld/FPG; 611, Bettmann Archive; 617, Photo: E. Irving Blomstrann, New Britain Museum of American Art; 618, Library of Congress; 620, UPI; 624, Brown Brothers; 625, Wide World; 627, all, Bettmann Archive; 628, t, *Harper's Weekly,* October 13, 1883, lc, The Brooklyn Museum, rc, b, Bettmann Archive; 629, t, Bettmann Archive, c, Museum of the City of New York, Byron Collection, b, Richard Pilling /Focus on Sports; 630, t, Russell-Kelly/Focus on Sports, b, Focus on Sports; 632, Memorial Art Gallery of the University of Rochester; 639, Bettmann Archive; 641, Private Collection; 644, Courtesy, The Phillips Collection; 648, Courtesy, Whitney Museum of American Art; 650, Bettmann Archive.

UNIT ELEVEN: p. 653, Charles Phelps Cushing/H. Armstrong Roberts; 655, Granger Collection; 658, Photoworld/FPG; 660, Bettmann Archive; 665, ©Edward B. Marks Music Corporation. Used by permission; 667, Historical Picture Service; 668, Culver Pictures; 674, Bettmann Archive; 675, Wide World; 676, Bettmann Archive; 678, Brown Brothers; 682, Courtesy U.S. Navy; 683, UPI; 687, UPI; 689, Brown Brothers; 691, Bettmann Archive; 693, Courtesy, Franklin D. Roosevelt Library; 699, Charles Phelps Cushing/H. Armstrong Roberts; 700, Brown Brothers.

UNIT TWELVE: p. 703, Grant Heilman; 705, United Nations; 708, UPI; 711, UPI; 713, UPI; 714, French Embassy, Press and Information Division; 715, Wide World; 718, UPI; 721, UPI; 723, UPI; 725, Wayne Miller/Magnum; 726, Bettmann Archive; 727, Pictorial Parade; 728, Wide World; 730, UPI; 731, Erich Hartmann/Magnum; 732, Steve McCutcheon; 733, Wide World; 735, t, Bettmann Archive, b, ©James Foote/Photo Researchers; 736, t, Museum of the American Indian, cl, Historical Picture Service, bl, br, Bettmann Archive; 737, all, Bettmann Archive; 738, t, ©Margot Granitsas/Photo Researchers, bl, ©Larry Mulvehill/Photo Researchers, br, Radio Shack, A Division of Tandy Corporation; 740, Atomic Energy Commission/UPI; 741, Historical Picture Service; 743, UPI; 744, ©1980 George Hall/Woodfin Camp & Associates; 746, Photo Trends; 748, Merrim/Monkmeyer Press Photo; 750, Katrina Thomas/Photo Researchers; 752, UPI.

UNIT THIRTEEN: p. 755, NASA; 757, UPI; 761, Sybil Shackman/Monkmeyer Press Photo; 762, Shanks in *The Buffalo Evening News;* 764, Fred Ward/Black Star; 765, Liederman, *L.I. Press,* N.Y.; 766, NASA; 770, Wally McNamee/Woodfin Camp & Associates; 771, Tiziou/Sygma; 773, M. Naythons/Gamma-Liaison; 774, Andy Leven/Black Star; 776, Rick Friedman/Black Star; 779, Reprinted by permission of the Chicago Tribune–New York News Syndicate, Inc.; 781, Pictorial Parade; 784, Fred Ward/Black Star; 789, Tashi/Black Star; 793, Owen/Black Star; 795, Shelly Katz/Black Star; 799, Wide World; 800, Owen Franken/Sygma; 802, Bob Adel/Magnum; 805, Herman J. Kokojan/Black Star; 807, UPI; 809, ©1970 Dan Budnik/Woodfin Camp & Associates; 811, White House Photo/Black Star; 815, NASA; 819, UPI; 821, Dick Durrance II/ Woodfin Camp & Associates; 823 Skoogsfors/Gamma-Liaison; 826, J.H. Pickerell/Black Star; 827, Tom McHugh/Photo Researchers; 829, UPI; 830, Steve McCutcheon.

A 1
B 2
C 3
D 4
E 5
F 6
G 7
H 8
I 9
J 0